Great Lives from History

The 17th Century

1601 - 1700

The 17th Century

1601 - 1700

Volume 2
Louis XIII-Francisco de Zurbarán
Indexes

Editor
Larissa Juliet Taylor
Colby College

Editor, First Edition
Frank N. Magill

SALEM PRESS
Pasadena, California   Hackensack, New Jersey

Editor in Chief: Dawn P. Dawson

Managing Editor: Christina J. Moose   *Production Editor:* Joyce I. Buchea
Acquisitions Editor: Mark Rehn   *Graphics and Design:* James Hutson
Research Supervisor: Jeffry Jensen   *Editorial Assistant:* Dana Garey
Manuscript Editors: Desiree Dreeuws, Andy Perry   *Layout:* William Zimmerman
Assistant Editor: Andrea E. Miller   *Photo Editor:* Cynthia Beres

Cover photos: Library of Congress
(Pictured left to right, top to bottom: Thomas Hobbes, Molière, Tokugawa Ieyasu, Galileo, Massasoit, Sor Juana Inés de la Cruz, ʿAbbās the Great, Marie de Médicis, Gustavus II Adolphus)

∞ The paper used in these volumes conforms to the American National Standard for Permanence of Paper for Printed Library Materials, Z39.48-1992 (R1997).

Some of the essays in this work originally appeared in the following Salem Press sets: *Dictionary of World Biography* (© 1998-1999, edited by Frank N. Magill) and *Great Lives from History* (© 1987-1995, edited by Frank N. Magill). New material has been added.

Library of Congress Cataloging-in-Publication Data

Great lives from history. The 17th century, 1601-1700 / editor, Larissa Juliet Taylor.
    p. cm.
"Editor, first edition, Frank N. Magill."
Some of the essays in this work originally appeared in other Salem Press publications.
Includes bibliographical references and indexes.
ISBN-10: 1-58765-222-6 (set : alk. paper)
ISBN-10: 1-58765-224-2 (v. 2 : alk. paper)
ISBN-13: 978-1-58765-222-6 (set : alk. paper)
ISBN-13: 978-1-58765-224-0 (v. 2 : alk. paper)
[etc.]
    1. Biography—17th century. I. Title: 17th century, 1601-1700. II. Title: Seventeenth century, 1601-1700.
III. Taylor, Larissa. IV. Magill, Frank Northen, 1907-1997.
CT117.G74 2005
920′.009′032—dc22
                                                                                2005017804

Second Printing

CONTENTS

Key to Pronunciation xli
Complete List of Contents xliii
List of Maps, Tables, and Sidebars xlvii
Maps of the Seventeenth Century li

Louis XIII 551
Louis XIV 554
Marquis de Louvois 558
Richard Lovelace 562
Richard Lower 564
Roger Ludlow 567
Jean-Baptiste Lully 569

Madame de Maintenon 572
Sieur de Maisonneuve 574
François de Malherbe 577
Marcello Malpighi 579
Manasseh ben Israel 582
The Mancini Sisters 585
François Mansart 587
Jules Hardouin-Mansart 590
Maria Celeste 593
Marie de l'Incarnation 595
Marie de Médicis 598
Marie-Thérèse 600
Jacques Marquette 603
Andrew Marvell 605
Mary of Modena 607
Mary II 610
Massasoit 612
Matsuo Bashō 615
Maurice of Nassau 618
Jules Mazarin 620
Ivan Stepanovich Mazepa 624
Cosimo II de' Medici 626
Marin Mersenne 628
Metacom 633
Thomas Middleton 636
John Milton 639
Peter Minuit 643
Molière 646
George Monck 650
Duke of Monmouth 653

Claudio Monteverdi 656
Duchesse de Montpensier 660
Boris Ivanovich Morozov 663
Lodowick Muggleton 665
Murad IV 668
Bartolomé Esteban Murillo 670
Mustafa I 673

Duchess of Newcastle 676
Sir Isaac Newton 679
Nikon 683
Njinga 687
Rebecca Nurse 689

Titus Oates 692
Ogata Kōrin 695
Count-Duke of Olivares 697
Rory O'More 699
Opechancanough 702
Axel Oxenstierna 704

Johann Pachelbel 708
Denis Papin 710
Blaise Pascal 713
William Paterson 716
Paul V 719
Nicolas-Claude Fabri de Peiresc 722
William Penn 724
Samuel Pepys 728
Charles Perrault 731
Sir William Petty 733
Philip III 736
Philip IV 738
Katherine Philips 741
Elena Cornaro Piscopia 743
Pocahontas 745
Nicolas Poussin 749
Powhatan 752
Thomas Pride 756
Samuel von Pufendorf 759
Henry Purcell 763
John Pym 767

Francisco Gómez de Quevedo y Villegas 770

Jean Racine. 773
Pierre Esprit Radisson 777
Marquise de Rambouillet. 779
John Ray 782
Stenka Razin 784
Rembrandt 786
Cardinal de Richelieu 790
Michael Romanov 794
Saint Rose of Lima. 796
Mary White Rowlandson. 798
Peter Paul Rubens 802
Prince Rupert 805
Michiel Adriaanszoon de Ruyter. 807

Santorio Santorio. 810
Thomas Savery 813
Sir George Savile. 815
Wilhelm Schickard 818
Friedrich Hermann Schomberg. 820
Anna Maria van Schurman 823
Heinrich Schütz 825
Madeleine de Scudéry 828
Seki Kōwa 831
Madame de Sévigné 833
Shabbetai Tzevi 835
First Earl of Shaftesbury 838
Shah Jahan 842
James Shirley. 846
Shunzhi. 848
Justine Siegemundin 851
Sigismund III Vasa. 853
Elisabetta Sirani 856
Śivājī 858
John Smith 861
Sophia 865
Sōtatsu 868
Baruch Spinoza. 871
Squanto. 875
Miles Standish 877
Nicolaus Steno 881
First Earl of Strafford. 884
Barbara Strozzi 888
Peter Stuyvesant 890
Sir John Suckling. 893
Duke de Sully 896
Jan Swammerdam 898
Thomas Sydenham 901

Abel Janszoon Tasman 905
Kateri Tekakwitha 908
Tianqi. 911
Tirso de Molina. 913
Tokugawa Ieyasu. 915
Tokugawa Tsunayoshi 919
Evangelista Torricelli. 921
Lennart Torstenson 924
Cyril Tourneur 928
Maarten and Cornelis Tromp. 930
Viscount de Turenne 933

Urban VIII 936
James Ussher 938

Sir Henry Vane the Younger 941
Vasily Shuysky. 943
Sébastien Le Prestre de Vauban 946
Lope de Vega Carpio. 949
Diego Velázquez 953
Jan Vermeer 956
António Vieira 959
Saint Vincent de Paul. 962

Albrecht Wenzel von Wallenstein 966
John Wallis. 969
Wang Fuzhi. 972
Mary Ward 974
John Webster 976
William III 979
Roger Williams. 982
Thomas Willis 985
Gerrard Winstanley. 988
John Winthrop 990
Sir Christopher Wren. 994

Yui Shōsetsu 998

Zheng Chenggong. 1001
Francisco de Zurbarán 1003

Rulers and Dynasties 1009
Chronological List of Entries 1052
Category Index 1059
Geographical Index 1065

Personages Index III
Subject Index XIX

KEY TO PRONUNCIATION

Many of the names of personages covered in *Great Lives from History: The Seventeenth Century, 1601-1700* may be unfamiliar to students and general readers. For these unfamiliar names, guides to pronunciation have been provided upon first mention of the names in the text. These guidelines do not purport to achieve the subtleties of the languages in question but will offer readers a rough equivalent of how English speakers may approximate the proper pronunciation.

Vowel Sounds

Symbol	Spelled (Pronounced)
a	answer (AN-suhr), laugh (laf), sample (SAM-puhl), that (that)
ah	father (FAH-thur), hospital (HAHS-pih-tuhl)
aw	awful (AW-fuhl), caught (kawt)
ay	blaze (blayz), fade (fayd), waiter (WAYT-ur), weigh (way)
eh	bed (behd), head (hehd), said (sehd)
ee	believe (bee-LEEV), cedar (SEE-dur), leader (LEED-ur), liter (LEE-tur)
ew	boot (bewt), lose (lewz)
i	buy (bi), height (hit), lie (li), surprise (sur-PRIZ)
ih	bitter (BIH-tur), pill (pihl)
o	cotton (KO-tuhn), hot (hot)
oh	below (bee-LOH), coat (koht), note (noht), wholesome (HOHL-suhm)
oo	good (good), look (look)
ow	couch (kowch), how (how)
oy	boy (boy), coin (koyn)
uh	about (uh-BOWT), butter (BUH-tuhr), enough (ee-NUHF), other (UH-thur)

Consonant Sounds

Symbol	Spelled (Pronounced)
ch	beach (beech), chimp (chihmp)
g	beg (behg), disguise (dihs-GIZ), get (geht)
j	digit (DIH-juht), edge (ehj), jet (jeht)
k	cat (kat), kitten (KIH-tuhn), hex (hehks)
s	cellar (SEHL-ur), save (sayv), scent (sehnt)
sh	champagne (sham-PAYN), issue (IH-shew), shop (shop)
ur	birth (burth), disturb (dihs-TURB), earth (urth), letter (LEH-tur)
y	useful (YEWS-fuhl), young (yuhng)
z	business (BIHZ-nehs), zest (zehst)
zh	vision (VIH-zhuhn)

COMPLETE LIST OF CONTENTS

VOLUME 1

Publisher's Note ix
Contributors. xiii
Key to Pronunciation. xvii
Complete List of Contents xix
List of Maps, Tables, and Sidebars xxiii
Maps of the Seventeenth Century. xxvii

Abahai. 1
'Abbās the Great 4
John Alden 7
Alexander VII. 9
Alexis 11
Lancelot Andrewes 14
Anne of Austria 18
Angélique Arnauld. 20
Aurangzeb 23
Avvakum Petrovich 26

Nathaniel Bacon. 29
Richard Baxter. 32
Pierre Bayle 36
Johann Joachim Becher 39
Aphra Behn 42
Gian Lorenzo Bernini 45
The Bernoulli Family 48
Thomas Betterton 51
John Biddle 53
Robert Blake. 55
Jakob Böhme 59
Nicolas Boileau-Despréaux 63
Giovanni Alfonso Borelli 65
Francesco Borromini 67
Jacques-Bénigne Bossuet 70
Louyse Bourgeois 73
Saint Marguerite Bourgeoys. 75
Robert Boyle. 78
Mrs. Anne Bracegirdle. 82
William Bradford 84
Anne Bradstreet 88
Margaret Brent. 92
Sir Thomas Browne 94
First Duke of Buckingham. 96
John Bunyan 100
Richard Burbage 104
Thomas Burnet 106
Robert Burton 108

Francesca Caccini 111
Pedro Calderón de la Barca 113
Jacques Callot 116
George Calvert 119
Richard Cameron. 121
Tommaso Campanella 124
Thomas Campion. 127
Canonicus 129
Robert Carr 131
Gian Domenico Cassini 134
Catherine of Braganza 137
Samuel de Champlain 139
Charles I 143
Charles II (of England). 147
Charles II (of Spain) 151
Charles X Gustav. 153
Chen Shu 156
Duchesse de Chevreuse 158
Chongzhen 160
Christina 163
First Earl of Clarendon 166
Claude Lorrain 171
Sir Edward Coke 174
Jean-Baptiste Colbert. 180
The Great Condé 184
Anne Conway 187
Arcangelo Corelli. 190
Pierre Corneille. 193
John Cotton. 196
Abraham Cowley. 199
Richard Crashaw 202
Oliver Cromwell 204
Sor Juana Inés de la Cruz. 208
Cyrano de Bergerac 211

William Dampier. 215
John Davenport. 218
Lady Eleanor Davies 220
Thomas Dekker. 223
René Descartes 226
John Donne. 230
Dorgon 234
Michael Drayton 237
John Dryden 239
Sir Anthony van Dyck 244

John Eliot. 247
Elizabeth of Bohemia 250
Elizabeth Stuart. 253
John Evelyn 256

David and Johannes Fabricius 259
Third Baron Fairfax 261
François de Salignac de La Mothe-Fénelon 265
Ferdinand II 267
Pierre de Fermat 271
Nicholas Ferrar. 274
John Fletcher 277
Robert Fludd 280
George Fox 283
Frederick Henry 286
Frederick William, the Great Elector. 290
Frederick V 293

Girolamo Frescobaldi 295
Galileo 298
Giovanna Garzoni 302
Pierre Gassendi. 304
Artemisia Gentileschi 307
Orlando Gibbons 309
Luis de Góngora y Argote 312
Marie le Jars de Gournay. 314
Baltasar Gracián y Morales 316
James Gregory 319
Francesco Maria Grimaldi 321
Hans Jakob Christoffel von Grimmelshausen . . . 324
Hugo Grotius 326
Guarino Guarini 330
Otto von Guericke 333
Gustavus II Adolphus 336
Madame Guyon 339
Nell Gwyn 342

Matthew Hale. 345
Edmond Halley. 348
Frans Hals 352
William Harvey 355
Piet Hein 359
Jan Baptista van Helmont 361
Henrietta Maria. 364
George Herbert 366
Robert Herrick 368
Johannes and Elisabetha Hevelius 371
Thomas Heywood 373
Hishikawa Moronobu 375
Thomas Hobbes 378

Robert Hooke. 383
Thomas Hooker 386
Jeremiah Horrocks 388
Henry Hudson 390
Anne Hutchinson 394
Christiaan Huygens. 397

Pierre Le Moyne d'Iberville 401
Ihara Saikaku 403
Innocent XI. 405
Izumo no Okuni 408

Jahāngīr. 410
James I 413
James II. 416
Cornelius Otto Jansen 419
Saint Isaac Jogues 423
John of Austria 425
John III Sobieski 427
John IV. 430
Louis Jolliet 433
Inigo Jones 436
Ben Jonson 439

Engelbert Kämpfer 445
Kangxi 448
Merzifonlu Kara Mustafa Paşa. 451
Kâtib Çelebî 454
Johannes Kepler 457
Bohdan Khmelnytsky 461
William Kidd 464
Eusebio Francisco Kino 467
Jan Komenský 469
Kösem Sultan. 472

Jean de La Bruyère 475
Madame de La Fayette 477
Jean de La Fontaine 480
John Lambert 483
François de La Rochefoucauld 487
Sieur de La Salle 490
Georges de La Tour 493
William Laud. 495
François Laval 498
Henry Lawes 502
Charles Le Brun 504
First Duke of Leeds 506
Antoni van Leeuwenhoek 509
Gottfried Wilhelm Leibniz 513
Jacob Leisler 518

Ninon de Lenclos. 520
André Le Nôtre. 523
Leopold I 526
Duke de Lerma 530
Louis Le Vau 532

John Lilburne. 534
Hans Lippershey 537
Liu Yin 540
John Locke 542
Duchesse de Longueville. 548

VOLUME 2

Key to Pronunciation xli
Complete List of Contents xliii
List of Maps, Tables, and Sidebars xlvii
Maps of the Seventeenth Century. li

Louis XIII 551
Louis XIV 554
Marquis de Louvois 558
Richard Lovelace. 562
Richard Lower 564
Roger Ludlow 567
Jean-Baptiste Lully. 569

Madame de Maintenon. 572
Sieur de Maisonneuve 574
François de Malherbe 577
Marcello Malpighi 579
Manasseh ben Israel 582
The Mancini Sisters 585
François Mansart 587
Jules Hardouin-Mansart 590
Maria Celeste. 593
Marie de l'Incarnation 595
Marie de Médicis. 598
Marie-Thérèse 600
Jacques Marquette 603
Andrew Marvell 605
Mary of Modena 607
Mary II 610
Massasoit. 612
Matsuo Bashō 615
Maurice of Nassau 618
Jules Mazarin. 620
Ivan Stepanovich Mazepa 624
Cosimo II de' Medici. 626
Marin Mersenne 628
Metacom 633
Thomas Middleton 636
John Milton. 639
Peter Minuit 643
Molière 646

George Monck 650
Duke of Monmouth. 653
Claudio Monteverdi 656
Duchesse de Montpensier 660
Boris Ivanovich Morozov 663
Lodowick Muggleton. 665
Murad IV 668
Bartolomé Esteban Murillo. 670
Mustafa I 673

Duchess of Newcastle 676
Sir Isaac Newton 679
Nikon. 683
Njinga 687
Rebecca Nurse 689

Titus Oates 692
Ogata Kōrin. 695
Count-Duke of Olivares 697
Rory O'More 699
Opechancanough 702
Axel Oxenstierna. 704

Johann Pachelbel 708
Denis Papin. 710
Blaise Pascal 713
William Paterson 716
Paul V 719
Nicolas-Claude Fabri de Peiresc 722
William Penn 724
Samuel Pepys. 728
Charles Perrault 731
Sir William Petty. 733
Philip III 736
Philip IV 738
Katherine Philips 741
Elena Cornaro Piscopia. 743
Pocahontas 745
Nicolas Poussin. 749
Powhatan 752
Thomas Pride 756

Samuel von Pufendorf 759
Henry Purcell. 763
John Pym 767

Francisco Gómez de Quevedo y Villegas 770

Jean Racine. 773
Pierre Esprit Radisson 777
Marquise de Rambouillet. 779
John Ray 782
Stenka Razin 784
Rembrandt 786
Cardinal de Richelieu 790
Michael Romanov 794
Saint Rose of Lima 796
Mary White Rowlandson 798
Peter Paul Rubens 802
Prince Rupert 805
Michiel Adriaanszoon de Ruyter 807

Santorio Santorio 810
Thomas Savery 813
Sir George Savile 815
Wilhelm Schickard 818
Friedrich Hermann Schomberg 820
Anna Maria van Schurman 823
Heinrich Schütz 825
Madeleine de Scudéry 828
Seki Kōwa 831
Madame de Sévigné 833
Shabbetai Tzevi 835
First Earl of Shaftesbury 838
Shah Jahan 842
James Shirley 846
Shunzhi 848
Justine Siegemundin 851
Sigismund III Vasa 853
Elisabetta Sirani 856
Śivājī 858
John Smith 861
Sophia 865
Sōtatsu 868
Baruch Spinoza 871
Squanto 875
Miles Standish 877
Nicolaus Steno 881
First Earl of Strafford 884
Barbara Strozzi 888
Peter Stuyvesant 890
Sir John Suckling 893
Duke de Sully 896

Jan Swammerdam 898
Thomas Sydenham 901

Abel Janszoon Tasman 905
Kateri Tekakwitha 908
Tianqi 911
Tirso de Molina 913
Tokugawa Ieyasu 915
Tokugawa Tsunayoshi 919
Evangelista Torricelli 921
Lennart Torstenson 924
Cyril Tourneur 928
Maarten and Cornelis Tromp 930
Viscount de Turenne 933

Urban VIII 936
James Ussher 938

Sir Henry Vane the Younger 941
Vasily Shuysky 943
Sébastien Le Prestre de Vauban 946
Lope de Vega Carpio 949
Diego Velázquez 953
Jan Vermeer 956
António Vieira 959
Saint Vincent de Paul 962

Albrecht Wenzel von Wallenstein 966
John Wallis 969
Wang Fuzhi 972
Mary Ward 974
John Webster 976
William III 979
Roger Williams 982
Thomas Willis 985
Gerrard Winstanley 988
John Winthrop 990
Sir Christopher Wren 994

Yui Shōsetsu 998

Zheng Chenggong 1001
Francisco de Zurbarán 1003

Rulers and Dynasties 1009
Chronological List of Entries 1052
Category Index 1059
Geographical Index 1065

Personages Index III
Subject Index XIX

List of Maps, Tables, and Sidebars

Volume 1

Africa in the 17th Century (*map*) . . . . *xxvii*
America in the 17th Century, North (*map*) . . . . *xxxi*
America in the 17th Century, South (*map*) . . . . *xxxii*
Art of Tea, Kämpfer on the (*primary source*) . . . 446
Asia in the 17th Century (*map*). . . . . *xxviii*

Bayle's Major Works (*list of works*). 37
Behn's Major Works (*list of works*) 43
Böhme on the Clash of Opposites
  (*primary source*) 61
Böhme on the Soul After Death
  (*primary source*) 60
Boileau-Despréaux on Cleverness
  (*primary source*) 64
Bradford's Major Works (*list of works*) 86
Bradstreet's "To My Dear and Loving
  Husband" (*primary source*) 88
Bunyan's Major Works (*list of works*) 101

Calderón's Major Works (*list of works*) 114
Campion's Major Works (*list of works*) 128
Christina Questions René Descartes
  (*primary source*) 164
Cleverness, Boileau-Despréaux on
  (*primary source*) 64
Colonization in the 17th Century, European
  (*map*). . . . . *xxx*
Corneille's Major Works (*list of works*) 194
Cruz's Major Works (*list of works*) 209

David and Johannes Fabricius Look at
  the Sun (*primary source*) 260
Death, Böhme on the Soul After
  (*primary source*) 60
Dekker's Major Works (*list of works*) 224
Descartes Thinks, Therefore He Is
  (*primary source*) 228
Descartes's Major Works (*list of works*) 227
Divine Right of Kings, James I on the
  (*primary source*) 414
Donne's Major Works (*list of works*) 231
Dryden's Major Works (*list of works*) 242

Elizabeth of Bohemia in Passionate
  Correspondence with René Descartes
  (*primary source*) 251
Europe in the 17th Century (*map*) . . . . *xxix*
European Colonization in the 17th Century
  (*map*). . . . . *xxx*

Fabricius's Look at the Sun, David and
  Johannes, The 260
Fletcher's Major Works (*list of works*). 278

Galileo on the Pendulum's Motion
  (*primary source*) 299
Grimmelshausen on the Thirty Years' War
  (*primary source*) 324
Grotius's Major Works (*list of works*) 328

Herbert's Major Works (*list of works*) 367
Hobbes on the State of Nature
  (*primary source*) 379
Hobbes's Major Works (*list of works*) 380
Horrocks Views Venus's Transit
  (*primary source*) 389
Hutchinson, The Trial of Anne
  (*primary source*) 395
Huygens Considers Life on Other Planets
  (*primary source*) 398

Ihara Saikaku's Major Works (*list of works*). . . 404

Jahāngīr's Court, Life at (*sidebar*) 411
James I on the Divine Right of Kings
  (*primary source*) 414
Jonson's Major Works (*list of works*) 441

Kämpfer on the Art of Tea (*primary source*) . . . 446
Kings, James I on the Divine Right of
  (*primary source*) 414

La Bruyère's Major Works (*list of works*) 476
La Fayette's Passionate Princess, Madame de
  (*primary source*) 478

La Fontaine's Major Works (*list of works*). 481
La Rochefoucauld's General Maxims
   (*primary source*) 488
Leeuwenhoek Explains the Stuff Between and
   Upon Teeth (*primary source*) 511
Leeuwenhoek Responds to a Misconception
   (*primary source*) 510
Leibniz's Major Works (*list of works*) 514
Leibniz's Method of Reason
   (*primary source*) 515
Life on Other Planets, Huygens Considers
   (*primary source*) 398
Locke's Major Works (*list of works*). 546
Locke's Preface to the *Second Treatise of*
   Government (*primary source*). 544

Maxims, La Rochefoucauld's General
   (*primary source*) 488

Nature, Hobbes on the State of
   (*primary source*) 379
New World, The Pilgrims Arrive in the
   (*primary source*) 85
North America in the 17th Century (*map*). . . . . *xxxi*

Opposites, Böhme on the Clash of
   (*primary source*) 61
Orthodox Church, The Unity of the Russian
   (*sidebar*) 13

Pendulum's Motion, Galileo on
   (*primary source*) 299

Pilgrims Arrive in the New World, The
   (*primary source*) 85
Planets, Huygens Considers Life on Other
   (*primary source*) 398

Reason, Leibniz's Method of
   (*primary source*) 515
Russian Orthodox Church, The Unity of the
   (*sidebar*) 13

Saikaku's Major Works, Ihara (*list of works*) . . . 404
Second Treatise of Government, Locke's
   Preface to the (*primary source*) 544
Soul After Death, Böhme on the
   (*primary source*) 60
South America in the 17th Century (*map*) . . . . *xxxii*
State of Nature, Hobbes on the
   (*primary source*) 379
Sun, David and Johannes Fabricius Look at
   the (*primary source*) 260

Tea, Kämpfer on the Art of (*primary source*) . . . 446
Teeth, Leeuwenhoek Explains the Stuff
   Between and Upon (*primary source*) 511
Thirty Years' War, Grimmelshausen on the
   (*primary source*) 324
"To My Dear and Loving Husband,"
   Bradstreet's (*primary source*) 88
Trial of Anne Hutchinson, The
   (*primary source*) 395

Venus's Transit, Horrocks Views
   (*primary source*) 389

VOLUME 2

Africa in the 17th Century (*map*) . . . . *li*
America in the 17th Century, North (*map*). . . . . . *lv*
America in the 17th Century, South (*map*) . . . . . *lvi*
Asia in the 17th Century (*map*) . . . . *lii*
Attack on Rowlandson's Homestead, The
   (*primary source*) 800

Bankruptcy and Its Aftermath, Rembrandt's
   (*primary source*) 788

Bashō's Major Works, Matsuo
   (*list of works*) 616

Calculator, Schickard's Early
   (*primary source*) 819
Cockfight, Pepys Attends a
   (*primary source*) 729
Colonization in the 17th Century, European
   (*map*) . . . . *liv*

Europe in the 17th Century (*map*). . . . . *liii*

European Colonization in the 17th Century
  (*map*) . . . . *liv*

Evil, and Intelligent Life, Spinoza on the
  Good, (*primary source*) 873

Good, the Evil, and Intelligent Life, Spinoza
  on the (*primary source*) 873

Intelligent Life, Spinoza on the Good, the Evil,
  and (*primary source*) 873

"Little Tom Thumb," Perrault's
  (*primary source*) 732

Louis XIV's Court, Madame de Sévigné's
  Letter on a Tragic Dinner at
  (*primary source*) 834

Marvell's Major Works (*list of works*) 605

Matsuo Bashō's Major Works (*list of works*) . . . 616

Middleton's Major Works (*list of works*) 637

Milton's Major Works (*list of works*) 641

Molière's Major Works (*list of works*). 648

Motion, Newton's Laws of (*primary source*) . . . 680

Newton's Laws of Motion (*primary source*). . . . 680

Newton's Major Works (*list of works*). 681

Nikon, A Contemporary Account of
  (*primary source*) 684

North America in the 17th Century (*map*) . . . . . *lv*

Pascal on Reconciling Reason's Possibilities
  and Limits 714

Pepys Attends a Cockfight (*primary source*) . . . 729

Perrault's "Little Tom Thumb"
  (*primary source*) 732

Pocahontas, Smith's Account of His Rescue
  by (*primary source*) 863

Racine's Major Works (*list of works*) 775

Reason's Possibilities and Limits, Pascal on
  Reconciling (*primary source*). 714

Rembrandt's Bankruptcy and Its Aftermath
  (*primary source*) 788

Rowlandson's Homestead, The Attack on
  (*primary source*) 800

Schickard's Early Calculator
  (*primary source*) 819

Sévigné's Letter on a Tragic Dinner at
  Louis XIV's Court, Madame de
  (*primary source*) 834

Shaftesbury's Major Works (*list of works*). . . . 839

Smith's Account of His Rescue by
  Pocahontas (*primary source*) 863

South America in the 17th Century (*map*). . . . . *lvi*

Spinoza on the Good, the Evil, and Intelligent
  Life (*primary source*) 873

Spinoza's Major Works (*list of works*). 872

Tom Thumb," Perrault's "Little
  (*primary source*) 732

Vega Carpio's Major Works (*list of works*) 951

Webster's Major Works (*list of works*). 977

AFRICA IN THE 17TH CENTURY

Tunis

Mediterranean Sea

Tripoli

Alexandria

Cairo

MOROCCO
Alawi Atlas Mountains

Berbers

S a h a r a   D e s e r t

Cape
Bojador

Cape
Blanco

Nile R.

Arabs

ARABIAN
PENINSULA

Red Sea

Arabs

Tuareg

Arma

GHANA SONGHAI
Soninke Timbuktu

Kumbi Gao
Saleh Jenne

MALI

MOSSI
STATES

Fulani

KANEM-
BORNU

HAUSALAND BORNU

WADAI DARFUR

L. Chad Njimi

ETHIOPIA

Somali

Gorée
SENEGAMBIA

Niger R.

ASANTE
AKAN OYU
STATES *Yoruba* *Ife*
BENIN

Guinea Coast

Elmina
Gold Coast

Slave Coast

Gulf of
Guinea

CONGO
BASIN

Congo R.

*Congo
R.*

Rift
Valley

BUGANDA

L. Victoria

Mogadishu

RWANDA
BURUNDI

Malindi Pate Island
Mombasa
Pemba

*Indian
Ocean*

KONGO KUBA

L. Tanganyika

LUBA

Bantu

Kilwa

Luanda NDONGO
LUNDA

*Atlantic
Ocean*

Benguela

Zambezi R.

MUTAPA Tete
Great Zimbabwe

Mozambique

*MALAGASY
MERINA*

Madagascar

Bantu

Kalahari
Desert

Orange R.

Cape Town

Cape of
Good Hope

■ = European fort/base
Igbo = indigenous peoples
GHANA = civilizations

li

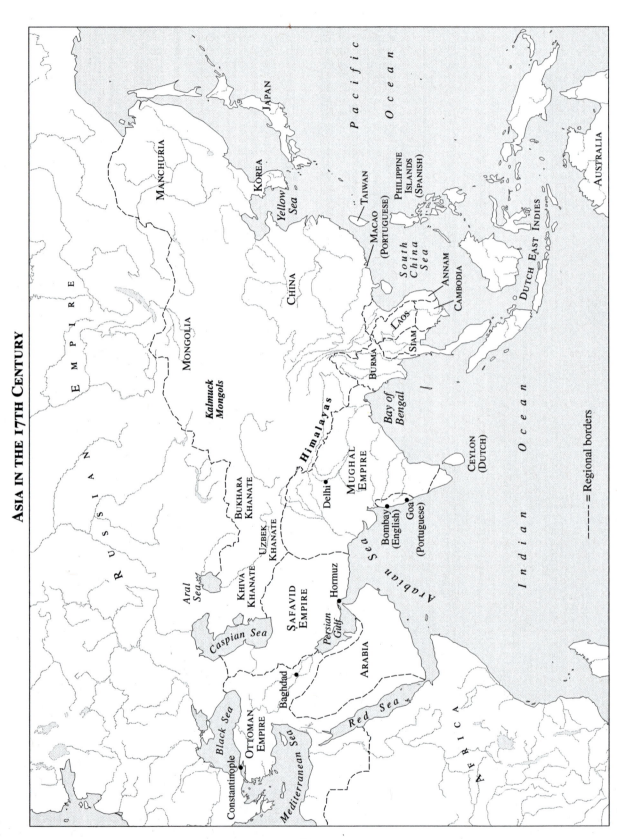

ASIA IN THE 17TH CENTURY

MANCHURIA

JAPAN

KOREA

Yellow Sea

MONGOLIA

Kalmuck Mongols

EMPIRE

RUSSIAN

CHINA

TAIWAN

MACAO (PORTUGUESE)

PHILIPPINE ISLANDS (SPANISH)

Pacific Ocean

South China Sea

ANNAM

CAMBODIA

LAOS

SIAM

BURMA

DUTCH EAST INDIES

AUSTRALIA

Himalayas

BUKHARA KHANATE

UZBEK KHANATE

KHIVA KHANATE

Aral Sea

Bay of Bengal

MUGHAL EMPIRE

Delhi

CEYLON (DUTCH)

Indian Ocean

SAFAVID EMPIRE

Hormuz

Caspian Sea

Bombay (English)

Goa (Portuguese)

Arabian Sea

Persian Gulf

Baghdad

ARABIA

Red Sea

AFRICA

Black Sea

OTTOMAN EMPIRE

Constantinople

Mediterranean Sea

- - - - = Regional borders

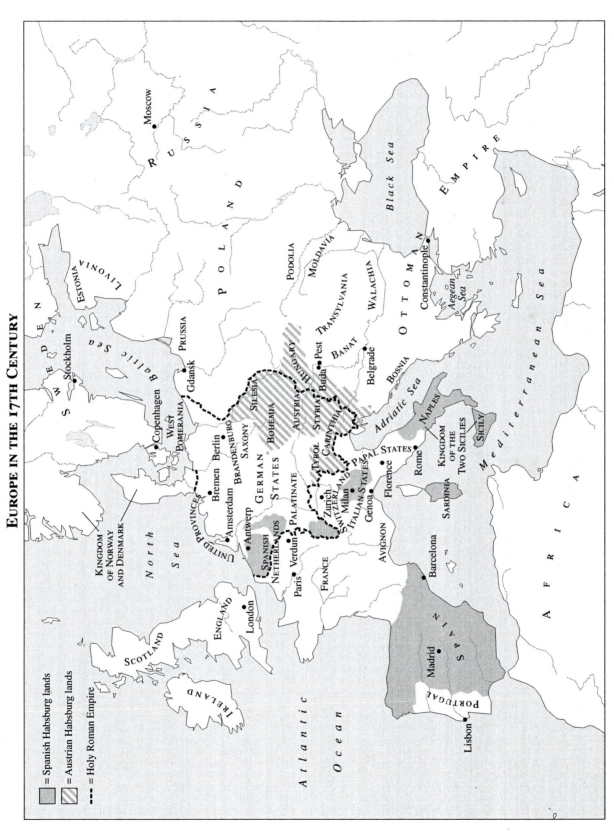

EUROPE IN THE 17TH CENTURY

Legend:
- = Spanish Habsburg lands
- = Austrian Habsburg lands
- = Holy Roman Empire

RUSSIA

Moscow

POLAND

SWEDEN

Stockholm

Baltic Sea

ESTONIA

LIVONIA

PRUSSIA

Gdansk

Copenhagen

KINGDOM OF NORWAY AND DENMARK

WEST POMERANIA

Berlin

Bremen

BRANDENBURG

SAXONY

SILESIA

BOHEMIA

GERMAN STATES

Amsterdam

UNITED PROVINCES

Antwerp

SPANISH NETHERLANDS

Verdun

Paris

FRANCE

PALATINATE

Zurich

SWITZERLAND

TYROL

AUSTRIA

STYRIA

CARINTHIA

HUNGARY

Pest

Buda

BANAT

Belgrade

BOSNIA

TRANSYLVANIA

WALACHIA

MOLDAVIA

PODOLIA

OTTOMAN EMPIRE

Black Sea

Constantinople

Aegean Sea

Adriatic Sea

NAPLES

SICILY

KINGDOM OF THE TWO SICILIES

SARDINIA

PAPAL STATES

Rome

Florence

Genoa

Milan

ITALIAN STATES

AVIGNON

Mediterranean Sea

AFRICA

Barcelona

SPAIN

Madrid

PORTUGAL

Lisbon

North Sea

Atlantic Ocean

ENGLAND

London

SCOTLAND

IRELAND

EUROPEAN COLONIZATION IN THE 17TH CENTURY

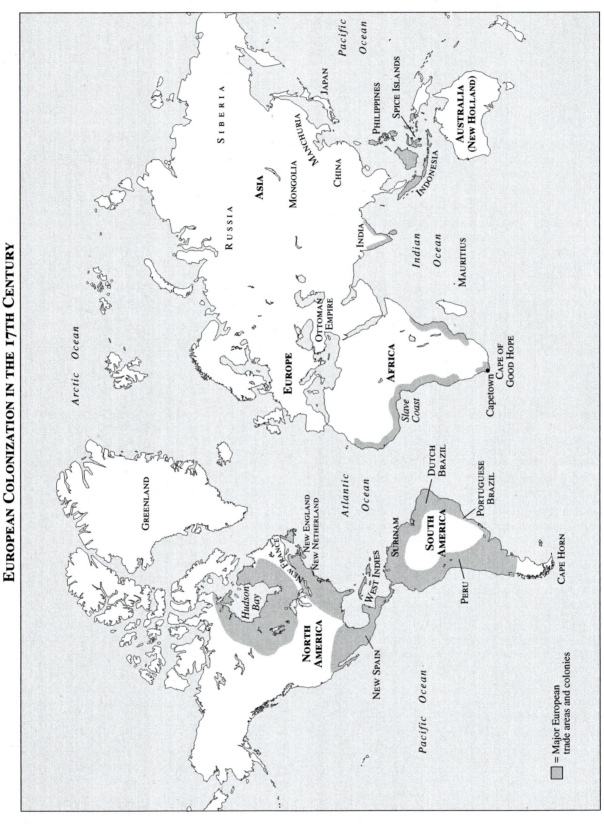

Arctic Ocean

SIBERIA

RUSSIA

ASIA

MONGOLIA

MANCHURIA

JAPAN

CHINA

Pacific Ocean

PHILIPPINES

SPICE ISLANDS

AUSTRALIA (NEW HOLLAND)

INDONESIA

INDIA

Indian Ocean

MAURITIUS

EUROPE

OTTOMAN EMPIRE

AFRICA

Slave Coast

CAPE OF GOOD HOPE

Capetown

GREENLAND

Hudson Bay

NORTH AMERICA

NEW FRANCE

NEW ENGLAND

NEW NETHERLAND

Atlantic Ocean

WEST INDIES

NEW SPAIN

SURINAM

DUTCH BRAZIL

PORTUGUESE BRAZIL

SOUTH AMERICA

PERU

CAPE HORN

Pacific Ocean

☐ = Major European trade areas and colonies

NORTH AMERICA IN THE 17TH CENTURY

Eskimo-Aleut

Athapascan

Arctic
Ocean

GREENLAND

Eskimo-Aleut

Hudson
Bay

NEWFOUNDLAND

Wakashan

James Bay

NEW
BRITAIN

NEW
SOUTH WALES

Salishan

Algonquian

ACADIA

NEW FRANCE

NOVA
SCOTIA

St. Lawrence R.

NEW
ENGLAND

Algonquian

Iroquoian

*Massachusetts
Bay*

Uto-Aztecan

Great Lakes

ALTA
CALIFORNIA

Great
Salt L.

Siouan

Missouri R.

NEW NETHERLAND

Drake's
Bay

Athapascan

VIRGINIA

NEW
MEXICO

Mississippi R.

Atlantic Ocean

Yuman

Rio Grande

Muskogean

CAROLINAS

BAJA CALIFORNIA

Uto-Aztecan

NEW SPAIN

LOUISIANA

FLORIDA

Sea of Cortés

Pacific Ocean

Gulf of
Mexico

Arawakan

Mayan

WEST INDIES

GUATEMALA

Caribbean Sea

Chibchan

Athapascan = Native American language groups and related peoples

lv

SOUTH AMERICA IN THE 17TH CENTURY

VENEZUELA

NEW
GRANADA

GUIANAS

Amazon R.

San
Mateo
Bay

NEW
HOLLAND

Palmares

São Francisco R.

Lima

Cuzco

Salvador

PERU
Incas

PARAGUAY

B R A Z I L

Guaraní

Mato
Grosso

Pacific Ocean

A n d e s

Rio de Janeiro

São Paolo

Buenos Aires

Atlantic

PATAGONIA

Ocean

Cape Horn

The 17th Century

1601 - 1700

LOUIS XIII
King of France (r. 1610-1643)

Louis XIII governed France during an era of conflict and was overshadowed by his father and son. Nevertheless, he increased the power of the Crown with the help of the chief minister Cardinal de Richelieu.

BORN: September 27, 1601; Fontainebleau, France
DIED: May 14, 1643; Saint-Germain-en-Laye, France
ALSO KNOWN AS: Louis the Just
AREAS OF ACHIEVEMENT: Government and politics, military

EARLY LIFE

France entered the seventeenth century with a royal wedding. The groom, Henry of Navarre, came to the throne of France on the death of his cousin, Henry III, after civil war and conversion from his Huguenot faith. The bride was Marie de Médicis, niece of Phillip III of Spain. She brought Catholic stability and the hope of an heir for the new royal house. The newlyweds met in December, 1600, and a healthy son, Louis, was born the next September.

The early childhood of Louis XIII passed in the shelter of the royal nursery. He was attended by his own physician, indulged by an adored nurse, and surrounded by a retinue of servants shared with his siblings and the many royal bastards. Louis was a stubborn child with a violent temper and was often beaten on his father's orders. Henry was an expansive, promiscuous, hot-tempered man, intelligent but manipulative. He alternately ignored and overwhelmed Louis. Henry looked for adult qualities in the small son who both adored and feared him. He openly preferred his older bastards. Louis was a timid child but overcame fears of loud noises and rough weather to develop kingly courage. He also strove to conquer his temper and submit to Henry to win his love. Marie was a shallow, cold woman with little affection to share with her children. She largely ignored Louis during his nursery days.

An intelligent and perceptive child with a retentive memory, Louis learned early lessons in reserve and in secrecy from his courtiers. Rumored to be a simpleton, he later said that he had not been taught to read or write. In fact, he could do both before leaving the nursery in January, 1609. He used rumors of disability as a protective cover, although he resented them. Books did not appeal to him; he preferred military studies and hunting. Louis was surrounded by older men, friends of his father who were skilled in military arts. He excelled in falconry, was fond of dogs and horses, and showed precocious skill with firearms. Scrupulous in Catholic observances, Louis may have lacked deep Christian faith. He was passionately attuned to questions of rank and greatly resented his father's preference for his other children. In his features and physical makeup, Louis was a Habsburg like his mother. He was intelligent like Henry but reserved and suspicious as a result of a childhood spent among manipulative adults.

On May 14, 1610, Henry of Navarre was assassinated. He had been preparing to go to war against Spain. Louis became king, with his mother as regent. At first, Marie retained Henry's counselors, but she changed policies. She humbled France to Spain and Austria and arranged marriages for Louis and for her eldest daughter with the eldest children of the king of Spain. This policy angered many of France's most powerful nobles, who also resented the fact that she never learned to speak French well and surrounded herself with Italians. Her beloved foster sister, Leonora Galigai, and her husband, Concino Concini, were the courtiers most hated by the French. Led by Henry II of Bourbon, third prince of Condé, the nobles rose in a series of revolts against the regent. Condé's first revolt ended in a lucrative agreement that gave large pensions to the rebels and demanded a meeting of the Estates-General, begun in October, 1614.

Louis had reached his official majority by this date, but he was still helpless. He resented the power of the Concinis and their following as well as his mother's extravagance. The Estates-General brought no great reforms but gave the young Bishop of Luçon (later known as Richelieu) the chance to flatter the regent in a closing speech. He became a favorite of the Queen Mother, devoted to her service for years, a role Louis XIII later found hard to forgive. In November of 1615, the royal court celebrated the weddings of Elizabeth of France with the future Philip IV of Spain and of Louis XIII with the young infanta Anne of Austria. Condé led another uprising but was upstaged by the pageant of the royal weddings. Louis's marriage was not happy, owing to court intrigues, and the young couple did not establish regular conjugal relations for three years. Anne suffered a number of miscarriages, and Louis's younger brother Gaston remained the royal heir until the birth of the future Louis XIV in 1638.

Louis began his personal rule in April, 1617, with the murder of Concini and the exile of the regent, soon fol-

Louis XIII. (Library of Congress)

Louis's trust in his queen had been compromised by the extravagant court paid her by George Villiers, duke of Buckingham, the special envoy who arranged the marriage of Charles I of England to Henrietta Maria of France. In 1626, a plot was discovered for the destruction of Richelieu and the removal of Louis in favor of Gaston. Anne's distant implication in the intrigue damaged relations even more. Richelieu was named a cardinal in 1622. By 1624, he joined the Royal Council. He gave Louis absolute fidelity coupled with a visionary focus on French national destiny. Both men shared a taste for military life.

It was almost a relief for Louis when open war broke out with the Huguenots of La Rochelle in 1627. Cardinal de Richelieu prepared to lay siege to the rebellious port city by fortifying islands in the harbor. Buckingham countered in June with a fleet of English ships. Louis and the cardinal joined the French troops in October, and the king himself worked on the construction of a dike across the harbor. Buckingham was forced to retreat in November. Two more English fleets appeared and retreated, and the people of La Rochelle suffered a siege that reduced their number from twenty-five thousand to five thousand. On their surrender in November, 1628, Louis guaranteed their religious freedom and spared the lives of their leaders but razed the city walls.

No sooner was La Rochelle pacified than Louis and Richelieu plunged into another campaign over the succession of Mantua, in Italy. A French nobleman had fallen heir to the city-state, but his inheritance was contested by both Spain and Austria. The French army made a winter crossing of the Alps and enjoyed early successes in Italy, but worries over the continuing religious troubles in France and Louis's health forced a return to France. Louis was to enjoy more victories over his Huguenot subjects, but the stress of war and intrigue made him ill. By the fall of 1630, he lay near death and received last rites. At the same time, the Diet of Ratisbon was meeting in Germany to decide the affairs of the Holy Roman Empire.

As Richelieu grappled with the political maneuvers of the German meeting, which eventually allowed him to defuse the Mantuan situation, Louis was reconciled with his wife and mother. The two queens hated and feared Richelieu and demanded his removal. The situation culminated on November 10, 1630, the Day of the Dupes, when Marie's extravagant behavior completely estranged her from Louis. She was sent into exile, never to return, and died in Cologne in 1642. Richelieu was firmly established and his policies vindicated.

lowed by the trial and execution of Marie's beloved Galigai. He reinstated several of his father's former ministers but continued his mother's pattern of rule by favorites in following the wishes of his hunting companion, Charles d'Albert, duc de Luynes.

LIFE'S WORK
When Louis assumed control of the government, France was surrounded by Habsburg holdings in Austria, Germany, Italy, Spain, and the Netherlands. Europe was a hotbed of religious tension, with conflict between Catholics and Protestants. Henry's Edict of Nantes guaranteed Huguenots religious freedom and possession of certain free cities, but in May, 1621, the La Rochelle Assembly established a Protestant state within France. The free cities were fortified as if in preparation for war. Protestant England and Catholic Spain encouraged the rebels, even though the queens of both countries were sisters of Louis XIII.

Family and political life were mingled and were unlucky for Louis. Although reconciled with his mother after the death of Luynes, Louis suspected her of complicity in plots to replace him with his brother Gaston.

Although often at odds with his wife, Louis was a faithful husband and pursued his conjugal duties on a regular schedule, though with no great enthusiasm. Popular history attributes the birth of their first surviving child, the future Sun King, Louis XIV, to a snowstorm that forced Louis XIII to share the only royal bed in the Louvre in December of 1637. Great joy greeted the birth of a dauphin on September 5, 1638. The succession was secured when a second son was born in 1640.

Plagued by illness and unable to trust Anne of Austria, who was known to have pursued secret correspondence with Spain during wartime, Louis designed limits to be enforced on her regency in the case of his death. Richelieu died, after a long illness, on December 4, 1642. Louis spent the winter of 1642-1643 in preparation for a campaign against the Spanish governor of the Netherlands but fell ill and died on May 14, 1643, just before the great French victory over the Spanish at Rocroi (May 19). Anne immediately had his reservations set aside and entered into an unlimited regency for her four-year-old son.

SIGNIFICANCE

In many ways, Louis XIII was an ordinary man caught in an extraordinary period in history. His father had been able to charm by flamboyant personality. His son enjoyed a long reign marked by personal absolutism. Louis was handicapped by the limits of his personality, his health, and the politics of his time. Intelligent, conscientious, and hardworking, he was lucky in the service of men such as Richelieu. He was able to consolidate and hold power for France and for the monarchy. He bequeathed his son a hunger for military victory and an empty treasury. Yet he reformed and strengthened the French navy and army. Although personally intolerant, he continued to protect Protestant worship after religious wars curtailed Huguenot political powers. The French Academy took wing under him. Despite a tendency toward resentment and suspicion, he gained a reputation for clemency and was known in his time as Louis the Just.

—*Anne W. Sienkewicz*

FURTHER READING

Belloc, Hilaire. *Richelieu*. Garden City, N.Y.: Garden City, 1929. The prolific biographer centers his study on the establishment of French nationalism through the partnership of Richelieu and Louis XIII.

Bergin, Joseph, and Laurence Brockliss, eds. *Richelieu and His Age*. Oxford, England: Clarendon Press, 1992. Collection of essays by eight historians. The authors reject the depiction of Richelieu as an exponent of realpolitik, and maintain he was a devout and politically astute diplomat with a genuine desire to establish a more just and peaceful Europe.

Burckhardt, Carl J. *Richelieu and His Age*. Translated by Edwin Muir and Willa Muir. New York: Harcourt, Brace & World, 1940. This three-volume work has a dual focus: illuminating with a wealth of detail the great cardinal and the king he served. The bibliography is arranged by chapter, and the last volume includes genealogical charts.

Levi, Anthony. *Cardinal Richelieu and the Making of France*. New York: Carroll & Graf, 2000. Levi argues that Richelieu sought to create a French national unity as much through cultural symbolism as through political means.

Marvick, Elizabeth Wirth. *Louis XIII: The Making of a King*. New Haven, Conn.: Yale University Press, 1986. Marvick has produced an unusual book, based on the detailed journal kept by Louis's personal physician. She marshals fascinating and illuminating materials to provide a Freudian perspective of Louis's life and personality.

Moote, A. Lloyd. *Louis III, The Just*. Berkeley: University of California Press, 1989. Insightful and readable biography. Moote describes how Louis was not overshadowed by Richelieu, but was an equal, if not controlling element, in the partnership that enabled France to grow and emerge as a superpower.

Ranum, Orest A. *Richelieu and the Councillors of Louis XIII*. Oxford, England: Clarendon Press, 1963. Ranum studies the interplay of power and personality in the managerial policies of Louis XIII and Richelieu. Includes an appendix of documents and a bibliography.

Tapié, Victor Lucien. *France in the Age of Louis XII and Richelieu*. Edited and translated by D. Lockie. New York: Cambridge University Press, 1984. Translation of a monumental study, recounting the two men's policies and how their actions affected the French people and the nation's culture.

SEE ALSO: Anne of Austria; Charles I; Louis XIV; Cardinal de Richelieu.

RELATED ARTICLES in *Great Events from History: The Seventeenth Century, 1601-1700:* 17th century: Europe Endorses Slavery; 1610-1643: Reign of Louis XIII; 1625: Grotius Establishes the Concept of International Law; 1625-October 28, 1628: Revolt of the Huguenots; November 10, 1630: The Day of Dupes; 1661: Absolute Monarchy Emerges in France.

LOUIS XIV
King of France (r. 1643-1715)

Known as Le Roi de Soleil, the Sun King, Louis XIV led France to the pinnacle of power and prestige in seventeenth century Europe, and more than any other monarch, he embodied the principle of absolutism in royal authority. Dedicated to bringing glory to France, he was the sponsor of what became magnificent cultural achievements but left his country bankrupt and weakened through a series of costly wars.

BORN: September 5, 1638; Château de Saint-Germain, Saint-Germain-en-Laye, France
DIED: September 1, 1715; Versailles, France
ALSO KNOWN AS: Louis the Great; The Sun King
AREA OF ACHIEVEMENT: Government and politics

EARLY LIFE

Louis XIV was born the son of Louis XIII and Anne of Austria. At age four, he succeeded his father to the throne, under the regency of his mother. As a result, much of his character and outlook was shaped in a harrowing environment of court intrigue and conspiracy, as noble factions fought one another for power and influence. Though regarded by French law as a sacred person, he was frequently neglected. Once, he wandered into a pond and nearly drowned. When he was nine, many of the nobility, supported by the Parlement de Paris (a powerful law court), revolted against the prime minister, Cardinal Jules Mazarin. As the symbol of power, Louis was dragged about the country and often simply left in places supposedly safe from the rebels. One evening, some of them burst into his bedroom, and he barely escaped with his life.

After five years of civil war known as the Wars of the Fronde (1648-1653), Mazarin finally quelled the revolt and began rebuilding the central government and administration, as well as training Louis for the role of king. By age fourteen, when Louis reached his legal majority, he had acquired an education in horseback riding, dancing, hunting, and the uses of power. As a king, he would be expected to lead his armies, so he served his apprenticeship in the war that had erupted between France and Spain in 1635. This conflict was part of the Thirty Years' War (1618-1648), in which political leadership in Europe passed from the Habsburg rulers of Spain and the Holy Roman Empire to France.

As Louis matured, he developed an inveterate hatred for anyone who would seek to limit his authority. When Mazarin died in 1661, Louis astonished his royal council

of ministers by announcing that no successor to Mazarin would be appointed—he himself would assume all power and responsibility for ruling the kingdom.

LIFE'S WORK

For the next fifty-four years, Louis dedicated his life to the task of ruling France. No detail of administration escaped his notice, and he tried to control every action of his government, from the system of administration to proper etiquette at court. In fact, he used the ceremony and protocol of the court to help him resolve the greatest long-standing threat to the authority of the French monarchy: the landed nobility.

Since the development of the feudal system in the Middle Ages, French kings had had to contend with the determination of the nobles to rule their territories independently of the Crown. Because the nobility formed the officer corps of the army, medieval French kings had often been at their mercy. An informal alliance between the kings and the rising middle classes, however, had gradually given the monarchy the tax income to create a professional army, and technological changes had made the mounted knight obsolete. This eliminated the feudal justification for the power of the nobility. The nobles were not to be humbled without a fight, and they had frequently revolted against the growing centralization of the royal government. The Fronde was the last of these revolts, proving that the nobility was still a force with which to be reckoned.

Louis accomplished this task by building a magnificent palace, the envy of Europe, at Versailles and luring the nobles to his court with high-sounding but meaningless titles and the opulence of court life. He kept them occupied with a constant round of entertainment, sponsoring playwrights such as Molière and Jean Racine and composers such as Jean-Baptiste Lully and fostering a complex web of competition and intrigue for his favor. The lord who could best master the intricate system of courtesies, ceremonies, and flattery might well be rewarded with a high-sounding but inconsequential position, while the real work of government was performed by Louis himself and a small circle of trusted ministers.

Among these ministers was Jean-Baptiste Colbert, a financial genius who attempted to revolutionize the French economy through the establishment of a mercantilist system. Under Louis's supervision, Colbert sought to make France self-sufficient through the construction of a merchant fleet and a navy to protect it. He awarded monopoly charters to royally subsidized companies to trade with French colonies and implemented a massive program of road, port, and canal construction. At the same time, Louis's minister of war, the marquis de Louvois, modernized the French army by limiting the practice of purchasing officers' commissions, expanding its peacetime base to more than 100,000 men (and more than 400,000 in wartime) and developing an efficient procurement and supply system. Between them, Colbert and Louvois forged the state and the army into an effective instrument of royal policy.

Louis soon put this instrument to use. In 1648, the Treaty of Westphalia had ended the Thirty Years' War and established the "balance of power" as the fundamental principle of international relations within Europe. Even though Louis's Habsburg rivals had seen their fortunes decline in the war, they were still in control of the thrones of Austria, which possessed territories on the eastern border of France, and of Spain, which also ruled the portion of the Netherlands that became Belgium. Thus, Louis was surrounded on three sides by enemies. In 1667, he invaded the Spanish Netherlands, claiming that they were the rightful inheritance of his wife, the daughter of the Habsburg king of Spain. This inaugurated a half century of wars, which eventually gained for France the provinces of Lorraine and the Franche-Comté to the east, and part of Flanders to the north.

Yet these rewards had a terrible price. Not only did Louis expend tremendous sums of money and large numbers of men but also he earned the enmity of nearly every other power in Europe. Then, he created hostility and fear within France itself by revoking the Edict of Nantes, which had guaranteed religious and political rights to the Huguenots, or French Protestants, since 1599. The revocation prompted a wave of persecution, forced conversions to Roman Catholicism, and drove thousands of refugee Huguenots into the arms of Louis's enemies. Since most of the Protestants were hardworking businessmen and skilled artisans, France was thus deprived of a great national resource. Many historians have dated the beginning of the decline of France's industrial development from this time.

In 1688, the English, the Dutch, and the Habsburgs united to break Louis's hegemony over Western Europe in a war that lasted until 1697 and forced Louis to return part of the territories he had won. Finally, in 1700, Charles II, the last Habsburg king of Spain, died, leaving his kingdom to Louis's grandson, Philip of Anjou. Louis had little choice but to accept the inheritance, since declining it would have meant Austrian control of Spain. The Holy Roman Emperor, Leopold I, immediately contested the award and began constructing another coalition against France. In the resulting War of the Spanish Succession, lasting from 1701 to 1714, Louis lost nearly all the territorial gains of previous wars, bankrupted his treasury, and gained only the hatred of his own people.

At the same time, he suffered untold personal grief, as his son, two grandsons, and a great-grandson died within the space of a few months. The new heir to the throne, Louis's sickly great-grandnephew, was only five years old. This nearly guaranteed that a domestic power struggle over the regency would ensue upon Louis's death. Louis attempted to avoid this by drawing up a will that gave the actual power of the regency to the duc de Maine, his son by one of his mistresses. After Louis died, how-

Louis XIV. (Library of Congress)

ever, on September 1, 1715, the Parlement de Paris was convened to nullify the will. In so doing, the *parlement* asserted a new political power: As the body charged with responsibility for registering royal edicts before they became law, the *parlement* now claimed the right to approve or disapprove of edicts before they were registered. Without a strong king to suppress this power, the Parlement de Paris was able to defer royal reforms that might have prevented the French Revolution. Thus, ironically, the king who had brought royal power to its peak may also have been responsible for its ultimate destruction. As Louis's funeral cortege carried his body to the tomb of French kings in the basilica at Saint-Denis, his own people jeered and spat upon him.

SIGNIFICANCE

The reign of Louis XIV lasted seventy-three years, the longest of any known monarch in history. So thoroughly did he stamp his imprint into the consciousness of Europe that historians refer to this period as the Age of Louis XIV. His brilliant court and the unparalleled splendor of Versailles were the envy of and model for all the other crowned heads of Europe, who vainly tried to copy French culture, manners, and power. Louis made French the international language of royalty and diplomacy. On the other hand, those same crowned heads feared Louis's ambition, regarding him as a bloodthirsty tyrant who sought to conquer them all.

Louis embodied both the principle of absolutist monarchy and the myth of the glory of France. In fact, Louis identified so completely with his role as king that it is virtually impossible to discern an individual personality lurking beneath the role. Louis was proud, courageous, highly self-disciplined, intolerant, and passionate in his love for beauty and order; yet all these qualities are reflected in his actions as king, rather than in his personal life. When asked what defined the French state, he is said to have replied, *"L'etat, c'est moi"* (I am the state). This was not an expression of arrogance but of his belief that God had entrusted him with the responsibility for the power and prosperity of France.

As is true for many other of the greatest figures in history, a balance sheet of Louis's reign reveals a roughly equal total of credits and debits. His support of Colbert's program brought France a colonial empire and encouraged industry and internal development, but his view that colonies existed solely as a royal preserve discouraged settlement. As a result, the more populated British colonies easily overwhelmed French North America only fifty years after Louis's death. While the new roads and canals Colbert created reduced internal trade barriers, Louis's persecution of the Huguenots precluded the maximum utilization of France's economic potential. Louis's destruction of the power of the nobles ended much of the anarchy of provincial administration, but it also centralized the government to the extent that it became removed and remote from the people of France and could no longer cope well with local problems. Louis preferred to think in grander terms, and he ignored grievances of the rural peasantry that would eventually fuel the French Revolution and destroy the monarchy. Louvois made the French army the largest, best-trained, and best-equipped in Europe, but Louis wasted it in ill-advised wars; yet, when he died, Louis left France more territorially secure and slightly larger than it had been.

The king's patronage of the arts fostered a renaissance in French music, literature, drama, and painting, and his regal tastes became those of Europe. His palaces, monuments, and court, however, came to be seen as an expensive irrelevance by a peasantry without bread and a middle class without status. These contrasts have made Louis's reign subject to much interpretation and furious debate. None could deny, however, that his impact and influence upon the course of European history was immense.

—Thomas C. Schunk

FURTHER READING

Beik, William. *Louis XIV and Absolutism: A Brief Study with Documents*. Boston: Bedford/St. Martin's, 2000. A collection of newly translated documents, with commentary, demonstrating how Louis became an absolute monarch. The documents examine a range of issues, including the problems of the Fronde, Colbert's understanding of finance, popular rebellion, and royal image-making.

Bernier, Oliver. *Louis XIV: A Royal Life*. Garden City, N.Y.: Doubleday, 1987. Well written and entertaining, this intimate biography cites modern research to suggest that many of the traditional criticisms of Louis are no longer valid.

Cronin, Vincent. *Louis XIV*. London: Collins, 1964. Well written and thoroughly researched, this biography is exceptionally useful for the general reader. Focuses sympathetically on Louis as both individual and monarch.

Dunlop, Ian. *Louis XIV*. New York: St. Martin's Press, 2000. Dunlop presents Louis XIV as his contemporaries saw him—an adored monarch who was the power and glory of France incarnate.

Erlanger, Philippe. *Louis XIV*. Translated by Stephen Cox. New York: Praeger, 1970. Biography with excellent illustrations by a well-known expert on French history. Takes a balanced, if somewhat melancholy, view of Louis's reign.

Levi, Anthony. *Louis XIV*. New York: Carroll & Graf, 2004. Probes Louis's personality, depicting him as a man conflicted by his normal insecurities and his pursuit of grandeur.

Lewis, W. H. *The Splendid Century: Life in the France of Louis XIV*. Prospect Heights, Ill.: Waveland Press, 1997. A classic look, first published in 1953, at French life during Louis's reign. Includes a brief biography of Louis and information on politics, the life of peasants and nobility, religion, the army, medicine, and literature.

Lossky, Andrew. *Louis XIV and the French Monarchy*. New Brunswick, N.J.: Rutgers University Press, 1994. Details Louis's domestic, international, and religious policies to show the evolution of his political ideas over the course of his life. Focuses on Louis's failure to establish Catholic uniformity in France.

Moote, A. Lloyd. *The Revolt of the Judges: The Parlement of Paris and the Fronde, 1643-1652*. Princeton, N.J.: Princeton University Press, 1971. Examines the anarchy and conflict within French society and government early in Louis's life. Essential reading for an understanding of Louis's attempts to centralize authority.

Packard, Laurence Bradford. *The Age of Louis XIV*. New York: Henry Holt, 1929. A classic, brief introduction to the period. Summarizes developments in France and Europe, and includes a thorough, annotated bibliography.

SEE ALSO: Anne of Austria; Nicolas Boileau-Despréaux; Jean-Baptiste Colbert; Louis XIII; Marquis de Louvois; Marie-Thérèse; Jules Mazarin; Viscount de Turenne.

RELATED ARTICLES in *Great Events from History: The Seventeenth Century, 1601-1700:* 1601-1672: Rise of Scientific Societies; 1610-1643: Reign of Louis XIII; June, 1648: Wars of the Fronde Begin; November 7, 1659: Treaty of the Pyrenees; 1661: Absolute Monarchy Emerges in France; 1661-1672: Colbert Develops Mercantilism; March 18, 1662: Public Transportation Begins; 1664: Molière Writes *Tartuffe*; 1665-1681: Construction of the Languedoc Canal; May 24, 1667-May 2, 1668: War of Devolution; January 23, 1668: Triple Alliance Forms; April 6, 1672-August 10, 1678: French-Dutch War; 1673: Renovation of the Louvre; 1673-1678: Test Acts; August 10, 1678-September 26, 1679: Treaties of Nijmegen; December, 1678-March 19, 1687: La Salle's Expeditions; 1682: French Court Moves to Versailles; 1685: Louis XIV Revokes the Edict of Nantes; April 4, 1687, and April 27, 1688: Declaration of Liberty of Conscience; 1688-1702: Reign of William and Mary; November, 1688-February, 1689: The Glorious Revolution; 1689-1694: Famine and Inflation in France; 1689-1697: Wars of the League of Augsburg; September 20, 1697: Treaty of Ryswick; October 11, 1698, and March 25, 1700: First and Second Treaties of Partition; January 26, 1699: Treaty of Karlowitz; May 1, 1699: French Found the Louisiana Colony.

MARQUIS DE LOUVOIS
French administrator

Louvois used his administrative genius and harsh discipline to create and maintain France's first military complex. He established unprecedented civilian control over the military and heavily influenced King Louis XIV's foreign policy.

BORN: January 18, 1639; Paris, France
DIED: July 16, 1691; Versailles, France
ALSO KNOWN AS: François-Michel Le Tellier (given name)
AREAS OF ACHIEVEMENT: Military, diplomacy, government and politics

EARLY LIFE

François-Michel Le Tellier, the marquis de Louvois (mahr-kee deh lewv-wah), was born in Paris. His father, Michel Le Tellier, had a tremendous impact upon his son's life. Yet while the elder Le Tellier was gentle, modest, and intelligent, Louvois, who was equally intelligent, was often brusque, violent, and arrogant. Like his father, however, Louvois hated extravagance and inefficiency. Michel Le Tellier was an excellent administrator and passed his skills on to his son. He also taught his son how to survive and prosper as a minister in the king's council. Le Tellier, well versed in courtly intrigue, taught his son to use flattery and to bow with humble submission. Furthermore, he instructed that no act of servility was too great in satisfying the needs of the monarch.

Le Tellier, as secretary of state for war, perceived himself as rivaled in the eyes of King Louis XIV by one man only: Jean-Baptiste Colbert, the king's minister of finance. Le Tellier passed on this jealousy and animosity to his son. Under Colbert, France's economy and treasury had recovered from severe depression, and France was enjoying great prosperity. Louvois's intent was to rival Colbert for the king's confidence and eventually replace him by bringing him into disgrace. Eventually, Louvois would have more influence over the king than Colbert, but, for most of his life, many of Louvois's actions were motivated by this jealousy.

Louis, who became king of France at age four in 1643, was only a few years younger than Louvois. The two boys went to school at the same time, experienced similar problems of youth, and developed an unusual relationship. The king quickly recognized Louvois's talents; Louvois was energetic, ruthless, persistent, and an administrative genius. Louis knew that he could always depend upon Louvois to finish any project he began. Louis

liked Louvois not only because of his abilities but also because he played to the king's vanity and pettiness.

In 1656, Louvois was guaranteed succession to his father's position, which Le Tellier had held since 1643. For five years, beginning in 1661, Louvois was an assistant in his father's office. In 1666, Louvois was given the title minister of war; however, Le Tellier did not relinquish complete control of the war ministry to his son at this time. Louvois was astute enough to recognize his father's brilliance and to capitalize upon it. He spent the first few decades of his career building upon his father's work. When Le Tellier became chancellor in 1677, Louvois was formally named secretary of state for war and became a member of the king's inner council.

LIFE'S WORK

Louvois knew that through military victory he could ingratiate himself to Louis and possibly undermine Colbert. Thus, in 1667, he devised his first military campaign with the Spanish Netherlands (particularly Flanders) as the target. Louis's wife, a Spanish princess, had renounced her claim to this land in exchange for payment of a dowry when she married Louis. Thus, even though Louis was attracted to the idea, he was hesitant. Quickly, Louvois found several lawyers and theologians who eased the king's conscience by citing the fact that the dowry had never been paid.

The greatest obstacles to Louvois's plans came from the minister of finance and from one of Louis's greatest generals. Colbert, whose economic policies depended upon the continuation of peace, told Louis that France could continue to prosper only if internal and external tranquillity were maintained. At the same time, General Henri de La Tour d'Auvergne, viscount de Turenne, warned that France's neighbors were already envious and that if France attempted any military action against Holland or Germany, it might cause the formation of a league of European nations against France. Louvois realized that Louis was heavily influenced by these two adversaries. Therefore, he played upon the king's intense interest in the military and his need for glory. Louvois brought Louis to one of the various encampments constructed to maintain military habits during peace. Louis, predictably, was totally captivated with the pomp and pageantry and immediately announced his military intentions. Louvois won his first victory over Colbert and Turenne, who now had to support their king's military effort.

Louvois's great administrative talents were demonstrated for the first time during this military campaign. With ease and brilliance, he transported several large forces. He developed an excellent system of storage places to provide food and supplies anywhere on the frontier. Louvois also enlisted Sébastien Le Prestre de Vauban, the chief engineer responsible for constructing fortifications. Louvois was often on the battlefield making certain that all the troops' needs were met.

Thus, his first military action was an easy victory over a veteran army. In less than three months, France controlled a substantial number of fortifications as well as Flanders. Louis returned to Paris victorious and with an appetite for military conquest, which his minister of war would happily try to satisfy.

Even as negotiations for Flanders were being conducted, Louis was looking for yet another conquest. At the suggestion of Louvois, Louis asked his cousin, Louis II de Bourbon, prince de Condé (later known as the Great Condé), to command an army against Franche-Comté. Louvois employed all of his wiles in this war effort and established an ingenious precedent. He began a war of corruption in the area before the advancement of troops. His plan called for secret agents to bribe many of the magistrates. The area would then split into factions, making it easy prey. The plan worked without incident, and Condé led a military force into the region. Louvois preceded him, undermining local control and maintaining the flow of supplies. Within less than three weeks, all of Franche-Comté was invaded. Meanwhile, in 1668, Louvois became the superintendent general of the mail in France, and he organized a "black chamber," which enabled him to observe foreign correspondence. He always informed Louis of any questionable information.

By this time, the Triple Alliance of 1668 (England, Sweden, and the United Provinces) formed and forced Louis into negotiations. Louis was given Franche-Comté as a peace offering and hostilities ended. By the early 1670's, Louis was interested in conquering Holland, and Louvois encouraged him. Louvois began a campaign to develop apathy regarding Holland in France's neighbors. He entered into negotiations with various rulers who granted France two towns on the Dutch frontier as French depots. Thus, he was able to move magazines and military stores far into the territory before hostilities began. He sent agents in disguise to buy supplies and munitions from the Dutch for the French army.

Louvois then recommended invasion. In the beginning of the Franco-Dutch War (1672-1678), Condé and Turenne faced little resistance. As the army advanced, it systematically destroyed fortified cities. Louvois recommended that these cities be spared. Playing on the king's vanity, Louvois suggested that Louis keep the captured cities, thereby increasing his own power and prestige. Again, Louis heeded Louvois's advice. Many of the troops were used as occupation forces, however, and thus fewer could be used on the battlefield.

By 1673, French troops were approaching Amsterdam. The Dutch government sent diplomats to meet with Louvois to discuss terms. When Louvois finally opened negotiations, he treated the envoys rudely and made excessive demands. The Dutch responded with greater resistance. Because the number of battle-ready French troops was now reduced, France was unable to crush the renewed resistance.

Marquis de Louvois. (Library of Congress)

On August 30, 1673, the United Provinces, Spain, the Holy Roman Empire, and Lorraine composed the first important military coalition against Louis XIV. By the end of 1673, the French army experienced severe military reversals. Coalition forces took the offensive. Turenne needed reinforcements, which Louvois refused to send. Louvois, apprehensive about the military reversals, drafted very specific battle plans, which he issued to the generals in the field. Insulted by this interference, Turenne and Condé blamed Louvois for the military failures. Le Tellier heard rumors of the plot to disgrace his son and successfully bribed Condé. When Turenne brought his charges against Louvois, Condé did not support these charges, and they were dropped. Louis forced Louvois and Turenne to reconcile, but the issue was never resolved. By this time, the French treasury was nearly exhausted, and Louvois was losing favor with the king. Louvois regained Louis's respect by uncovering a conspiracy to overthrow the king. Louvois named the conspirators and was instrumental in their arrest.

In 1675, Turenne was killed in battle and Condé retired. The war was not going well for France, but by 1678 Louis and Louvois managed to turn potential defeat into victory. After the fall of Ghent, the Treaty of Nijmegen (1678) was signed against Louvois's recommendation. The next year, French troops advanced toward Strasbourg. On September 30, 1681, the French army and Louvois captured the city in less than twenty-four hours. Again, Louvois had employed intrigue, bribery of local magistrates, and terrorism to facilitate the conquest of a city known for its defensive complement of nine hundred cannons.

By the 1680's, France was torn by religious conflict with the Huguenots. The Catholic church and Louvois urged Louis to take action against them. Louvois saw an opportunity to disgrace Colbert (who had always favored the Huguenots) by Colbert's association with the Reformers. By 1681, the Crown forced Colbert to issue a decree banning the Huguenots from certain business associations and Louvois obtained a decree that stated that all Huguenot children at age seven had to renounce their religion. Children not complying would be arrested and soldiers would be quartered in their parents' homes. Many Huguenot families fled France. As many of the Huguenots were artisans and sailors, the council issued a decree that made it illegal for these professionals to leave France. Many of the Huguenot ministers were persecuted, and places of worship were closed. The Huguenots were stripped of their noble rank, and certain profes-

sions were closed to them. Many of the Huguenot leaders were physically tortured and executed.

After the death of Colbert in 1683, Louvois dominated the royal council. He was named superintendent of buildings, arts, and manufacturing. By 1685, Louvois recommended that stronger measures be taken against the Huguenots. Places of worship were demolished, Huguenots were forced to renounce their religion or die, and the Edict of Nantes (1598), which guaranteed religious toleration, was revoked by the Edict of Fontainebleau. This last act proved disastrous for France, as a mass exodus of Huguenots occurred, and most of the Protestant nations of Europe united against Louis. Once again, the advice of Louvois did not serve the best interests of France.

On July 9, 1686, the Holy Roman Empire, Spain, and Sweden formed the League of Augsburg as a defensive coalition to halt French expansion. In August, 1688, Louis invaded Germany, and in September, he invaded the Palatinate. England joined the coalition (now called the Grand Alliance), and the War of the League of Augsburg (1689-1697) began. In February, 1689, Louvois ordered the complete destruction of the Palatinate to interdict the league's means of supply, to save Lorraine and Alsace, and to prevent the potential invasion of France. The army advanced into the territory, warned the citizens to evacuate, and sacked, ravaged, and burned everything. Europe was shocked at the cruelty, and army officers were ashamed of their own actions. Consequently, they blamed Louvois, who had advised Louis strongly to take such action. Louvois did, however, make provisions for the refugees. They were invited to live in Alsace and Franche-Comté and were exempt from taxation for the next ten years.

By 1689, the treasury was practically empty, and France experienced a number of military defeats that caused Louvois's influence with Louis to diminish. Louvois managed one last great maneuver by capturing two major cities. The coalition was determined, however, and Louis was pessimistic about France's chance for victory. On July 16, 1691, while at a strategy session with the king in Versailles, Louvois collapsed. Within hours, the secretary of state for war was dead. Louvois's son, the marquis de Barbesieux, inherited his father's position, but Louis assumed full responsibility for the war effort.

SIGNIFICANCE

The marquis de Louvois revolutionized the military system in France. He accomplished this feat by the creation, maintenance, training, and disciplining of a large force (more than 100,000 troops) in times of peace, which could be transformed easily into a force more than double its size in times of war. Louvois assembled Europe's first great standing army by actively recruiting troops from other countries such as England, Scotland, Ireland, Germany, Switzerland, and Italy. He devised a method for transporting the large force and organized a system by which he could supply this great army with munitions and other necessary supplies during war. Old fortifications were always well stocked, and new ones were inspected, redesigned, and rebuilt to Louvois's specifications. His knowledge of the army went beyond his desk, as he had been an apprentice to Turenne on the battlefield.

Upon assumption of his position, Louvois gradually began constructing a regular military administration. First, he divided control of the army into four sections: administration, inspection, munitions, and supplies. As there was no regimentation or discipline but much corruption and abuse of privilege, he devised France's first systematic ranking of officers, the order of seniority, which named the king as the highest ranking officer. Louvois also coordinated the various branches of service, grouped regiments into brigades, and gave permanence to companies. He introduced strict discipline by demanding it of the officers as well as of the men, a move that did not make him well liked among the noble officers. He also issued a military uniform, created specific insignia to distinguish units and ranks, and introduced the idea of marching in time. Louvois provided systematic training for artillerymen at schools located in Douai, Metz, and Strasbourg. He also appointed inspectors to maintain the high standards he had set forth. One such man was Inspector-General Jean Martinet, whose model regiment, the "King's Regiment," was known for its rigid militarism, and whose name became synonymous with strict discipline. These innovations and others helped Louis transform France into the leading military nation of Europe in the 1600's.

—Victoria Reynolds

FURTHER READING

James, G. P. R. "Life of François Michel Le Tellier, Marquis de Louvois." In *Lives of Cardinal de Retz, Jean Baptiste Colbert, John de Witt, and the Marquis de Louvois*, Vol. 2. Philadelphia: Carey, Lea and Blanchard, 1837. A two-volume work detailing the lives of several European personalities. Volume 2 contains a chapter on Louvois, which is biased against him, often blaming him for Louis XIV's errors or cruelties.

Levi, Anthony. *Louis XIV*. New York: Carroll & Graf, 2004. This comprehensive biography contains information about Louvois and other military figures during Louis's reign.

Lynn, John A. *Giant of the Grand Siècle: The French Army, 1610-1715*. New York: Cambridge University Press, 1997. A comprehensive overview of army administration and tactics, including information about Louvois and other military officials.

_____. *The Wars of Louis XIV, 1667-1714*. London: Longman, 1999. A history of French military campaigns during the final years of Louis's reign, including information on Louvois's participation in those battles.

Packard, Laurence Bradford. "Louvois and the First Great Standing Army." In *The Age of Louis XIV*. New York: Henry Holt, 1929. Focuses on Louvois's positive contributions to the development of the French army.

Voltaire. *The Age of Louis XIV*. Translated by Martyn P. Pollack with a preface by F. C. Green. London: J. M. Dent & Sons, 1966. Originally published in 1751, this work is sometimes difficult to comprehend, but presents excellent background information about France under Louis. Examines Louvois's military campaigns and his persecution of the Huguenots.

Wolf, John B. "The First World War: Louvois." In *Louis XIV*. New York: W. W. Norton, 1968. Provides excellent background information and objective information about Louvois. Emphasizes the relationship between Louvois and Louis, and Louvois's role in their military exploits.

SEE ALSO: Jean-Baptiste Colbert; The Great Condé; Louis XIV.

RELATED ARTICLES in *Great Events from History: The Seventeenth Century, 1601-1700:* 1617-1693: European Powers Vie for Control of Gorée; 1661: Absolute Monarchy Emerges in France; 1661-1672: Colbert Develops Mercantilism; August 10, 1678-September 26, 1679: Treaties of Nijmegen; 1685: Louis XIV Revokes the Edict of Nantes.

RICHARD LOVELACE
English poet

*Remembered now for only a few lines of verse,
Lovelace was the quintessential English Cavalier poet.
A courtier and soldier under Charles I, his poetry
celebrated love, loyalty to the Crown, and the
companionship of kindred spirits, even as he sacrificed
his estates and suffered imprisonment under the
Parliamentary regime.*

BORN: 1618; Woolwich, Kent, England, or Holland
DIED: 1656 or 1657; London, England
AREA OF ACHIEVEMENT: Literature

EARLY LIFE

Richard Lovelace came from an old Kentish family and
was probably born in Woolwich in Kent, England. He
may, however, have been born in Holland, where his
mother joined his father during a military campaign. His
date of birth is not known more precisely than the year,
1618. Lovelace's father and paternal grandfather, both
named William, were professional soldiers and were
knighted in the course of their military careers. His father
was killed in combat at Grolle, Holland, in 1627. Richard
(the eldest son, then age nine), his four brothers, his three
sisters, and their mother were left in reduced circumstances, which were then relieved by inheritance upon
the death of Richard's grandfather, who had amassed
considerable property.

Lovelace was given the honorary court position of
Gentleman Extraordinary Wayter to the King in 1631.
He is believed to have attended the Charterhouse School
in London from about 1629 until 1634, during three of
which years poet Richard Crashaw was a fellow student.
Lovelace went on to Oxford as a gentleman commoner in
June, 1634. At Oxford, he was, according to Anthony à
Wood in *Athenae Oxoniensis* (1691-1692), "accounted
the most amiable and beautiful person that ever eye beheld, a person also of innate modesty, virtue and courtly
deportment, which made him then, but especially after,
when he retired to the great City much admired and
adored by the female sex."

In his first year at Oxford, Lovelace wrote a comedy,
The Scholar(s) (pr. 1636?), which was performed but
never printed except for the Prologue and Epilogue, both
published later in *Lucasta: Posthume Poems of Richard
Lovelace, Esq.* (1659). In 1636, when King Charles I and
Queen Henrietta Maria visited Oxford, Lovelace was
awarded the degree of master of arts by special request of
one of the queen's ladies. The following year, he went for
some months to Cambridge and then to London and the
royal court.

LIFE'S WORK

In 1639, Lovelace was commissioned an ensign under
George, Lord Goring, the future earl of Norwich. He embarked upon the English expedition to Scotland during
the bloodless First Bishops' War. He served as a captain
in the Second Bishops' War in 1640, during which he
found time to write a tragedy, never performed or published (the theaters shortly being closed), of which only
the name remains: *The Soldier* (wr. 1640). Once the conflict ended, Lovelace being then of age, he settled on his
family estates in Kent. The king, meanwhile, had called
what came to be known as the Long Parliament, in order
to pay war expenses. Parliament, however, began the
process of diminishing royal power, and friction continued in the country at large, including Lovelace's home
county.

When the Kent Assizes (the county assembly) debated a counter-petition to one favoring the king, Lovelace led a group that clapped on their hats in protest and
then seized the document and tore it up. In April, 1642,
he and the other Royalists having prevailed in Kent,
Lovelace and Sir William Boteler led a group to London
to deliver to Parliament the famous Kentish Petition,
which urged policies favoring the king. Lovelace and
Boteler were quickly imprisoned. They were released
seven weeks later on bonds of ten thousand pounds
apiece. Lovelace is thought to have written "To Althea,
from Prison" (pb. 1649) at this time. The often-quoted
line "Stone walls do not a prison make/ Nor iron bars a
cage" would have been drawn from this personal experience.

Lovelace also began heavily subsidizing two of his
brothers and others in support of the Royalist cause. He is
not known himself to have taken up arms in the English
Civil War, perhaps because of the terms of his release
from prison. Instead, he seems to have spent much of the
next several years on the Continent, in Holland and
France. Following the family tradition of soldiering
abroad, Lovelace fought in the French army against the
Spanish and was wounded at the Siege of Dunkirk in late
1646. Returning to England, now-Colonel Lovelace was
able for a while to enjoy the lifestyle of a well-off gentleman and to keep acquaintance with such social figures as

poet Andrew Marvell, courtier Endymion Porter, and painter Peter Lely.

Lovelace's interest in visual art was sufficient that he was admitted to the Painters' Company (guild) in 1647. Then, in 1648, Parliamentary troops searching for his brother Francis raided Lovelace's house in Maidstone, Kent. Lovelace was present and protested and was then imprisoned again, this time for ten months. He spent the time preparing for publication a book of poems, *Lucasta: Epodes, Odes, Sonnets, Songs, &c. to Which Is Added Aramantha, a Pastorall* (1649), which appeared a month after his release, in June, 1649. Shortly thereafter, Lovelace liquidated what remained of his property. Little is known of the rest of his life. Scholars today doubt Anthony à Wood's description of his last years spent in extreme poverty, though his circumstances must have been considerably reduced from what they had once been. He probably died in 1656 or 1657. The posthumous volume of his poems, *Lucasta: Posthume Poems of Richard Lovelace, Esq.*, was published by his brother, Dudley Lovelace, dated 1659.

Though probably known in his own time more for political and military activities, as well as his social standing and personal attractiveness, Lovelace was also recognized by his contemporaries as a poet. He wrote chiefly brief lyrics, a number of which were set to music. Today his fame is as a poet, albeit a minor one in a century renowned for great poetry. Along with others of that cluster of seventeenth century English writers now sometimes called the Cavalier poets, Lovelace celebrated loyalty to the Crown, fellowship with kindred spirits, and love of women. His corpus is small, consisting almost entirely of the two *Lucasta* volumes, which contain just over one hundred poems. By far his best-known works are "To Althea, from Prison" and "To Lucasta, Going to the Wars" (1649). The latter contains the famous declaration, "I could not love thee (Dear) so much,/ Lov'd I not Honour more."

Of his several poems about small creatures, "The Grasshopper" (1649), wherein the insect serves as metaphor for a man in such troubled times as the Civil War, is the best known. Like other contemporaries, Lovelace followed a long tradition of giving the women in his poems classically inspired names. His general popularity with women is attested by Marvell, who speaks of "Lovelace that thaw'd the most congealed breast." Though it seems clear that "Lucasta," whom Lovelace commemorated in twenty-seven poems as well as the title of his collection, was a real woman, her identity is unknown, as Wood's identification is discredited. "Al-

thea," to whom what has always been Lovelace's most popular poem is addressed, also remains unidentified.

SIGNIFICANCE

Only a few brief pieces of Lovelace's poetry are much noted today, but they are known throughout the English-speaking world, even to many persons unaware of the author's identity. The entirety of Lovelace's extant corpus is embodied in the two slim volumes, *Lucasta: Epodes, Odes, Sonnets, Songs, &c. to Which Is Added Aramantha, a Pastorall* and *Lucasta: Posthume Poems of Richard Lovelace, Esq.* Even so, Lovelace's reputation rests upon the thirty-two lines of "To Althea, from Prison" and the twelve lines of "To Lucasta, Going to the Wars." Both embody the loyalty, love, courage, and seemingly effortless beauty and wit that typify the best Cavalier poetry.

—*C. Herbert Gilliland*

FURTHER READING

Bence-Jones, Mark. *The Cavaliers*. London: Constable, 1976. Sketches the English Civil War period, with emphasis on the lives of noteworthy Cavaliers, including a section on Lovelace.

Kelly, Erna. "Small Types of Great Ones." In *The English Civil Wars in the Literary Imagination*, edited by Claude J. Summers and Ted-Larry Pebworth. Columbia: University of Missouri Press, 1999. Analyzes Lovelace's poems on small creatures in the political context of the Civil War period.

Lindsay, Philip. *For King or Parliament*. London: Evans Brothers, 1949. Contains journalistic biographies of Lovelace and three contemporaries, Buckingham, Strafford, and Hampden.

Miner, Earl. *The Cavalier Mode from Jonson to Cotton*. Princeton, N.J.: Princeton University Press, 1971. Analyzes the works of Lovelace and the other Cavalier poets.

Schmidt, Michael. *Lives of the Poets*. New York: Vintage Books, 2000. The chapter titled "An End of Delicacy" smoothly summarizes Lovelace's life and works in their political and literary context.

Weidhorn, Manfred. *Richard Lovelace*. New York: Twayne, 1970. After a biographical chapter, following chapters give the most extended available treatment of the poetry. Selective bibliography very useful.

Wilkinson, C. H., ed. *The Poems of Lovelace*. Oxford, England: Clarendon Press, 1930. The commonly used complete edition. Contains all of Lovelace's works, plus an authoritative biographical sketch and comments on the text. Omits the song settings and some other ancillary material contained in Wilkinson's two-volume 1925 edition.

SEE ALSO: Charles I; Richard Crashaw; Henrietta Maria; Andrew Marvell.

RELATED ARTICLES in *Great Events from History: The Seventeenth Century, 1601-1700:* March-June, 1639: First Bishops' War; November 3, 1640-May 15, 1641: Beginning of England's Long Parliament; 1642-1651: English Civil Wars; September 2, 1642: Closing of the Theaters.

RICHARD LOWER
English physician and physiologist

Lower was one of the first scientists to conduct rigorous studies of injection and blood transfusion and is known for his advances in cardiology, respiratory physiology, neuroanatomy, and medical instrumentation. Working in the tradition of William Harvey and Thomas Willis, he vigorously defended his teacher Willis against all criticism.

BORN: January 29, 1631 (baptized); Tremeer, near Bodmin, Cornwall, England
DIED: January 17, 1691; London, England
AREAS OF ACHIEVEMENT: Medicine, science and technology

EARLY LIFE
Richard Lower was baptized at Saint Tudy's, Cornwall, on January 29, 1631. His parents, Humphry Lower and Margery Billing, were wealthy landowners. As a student from 1643 to 1649 at the prestigious Westminster School in London, Lower earned commendation from the headmaster, Richard Busby. Busby sent Lower on a studentship to his own alma mater, Christ Church College, Oxford University. Lower arrived at Oxford in 1649, matriculated in 1651, and received a B.A. in 1653, an M.A. in 1655, and both a B.Med. and a D.Med. in 1665. In 1666, he married Elizabeth Billing, with whom he had two daughters, Loveday and Philippa.

At Oxford, Lower studied chemistry under Peter Stahl and was the student, assistant, and protégé of Thomas Willis, the leader of the "Oxford physiologists," investigators in the spirit of William Harvey. With Willis, he studied mostly the nervous system. He also worked closely with Robert Boyle on the circulatory and respiratory systems and on various chemical problems in physiology. Lower's other research collaborators at Oxford included Ralph Bathurst, Robert Hooke, John Locke, John Mayow, Thomas Millington, Walter Needham, Sir William Petty, Henry Stubbe, John Wallis, John Ward, and Sir Christopher Wren.

Lower was especially skilled as an anatomist. He and his Oxford colleagues performed thousands of postmortem dissections of humans and vivisections of animals. Historians generally agree that Lower performed most of the dissections upon which Willis based his groundbreaking book, *Cerebri anatome* (1664; *The Anatomy of the Brain,* 1681). This work was the joint project of Lower, Millington, Wren, and Willis, despite the fact that Willis took primary credit for it.

LIFE'S WORK
Lower's contributions to medicine and science can best be understood in terms of his discipleship to Willis. In the mid-seventeenth century, a bifurcation existed between bioscientists who were loyal to Galen and those who were persuaded by Harvey's new physiology, especially his views of circulation. The Oxford physiologists, led by Willis, were all Harveians. In 1665, Edmund Meara, a resolute Galenist, viciously attacked Willis in *Examen diatribae Thomae Willisii de febribus* (1665; an examination of the discourse of Thomas Willis on fevers). Lower reacted quickly and strongly to defend his mentor, putting out his first publication, *Diatribae Thomae Willisii de febribus vindicatio* (1666; a vindication of the discourse of Thomas Willis on fevers), only four months after Meara's book.

Lower's *Diatribae Thomae Willisii de febribus vindicatio* did more than just counterattack Meara. It also endorsed Boyle and Harvey, presented new facts and a specific research agenda for blood physiology, and correctly analyzed recent observations on lung function, heart-lung interaction, arterial and venous blood, and the relation of respiration to blood color. In retrospect, the work demonstrates that Lower was among the first properly to understand the cardiac cycle and pulmonary circulation.

Lower moved to London to establish a private medical practice in 1667, following Willis, who had moved there in 1666. The two continued to work together on several projects, but after moving to London, Lower gradually did less research and more clinical work. In 1675, he was elected a fellow of the Royal College of Physicians and succeeded Willis as physician to the king. His opinions upon the heated debate over whether to allow the Roman Catholic James, duke of York, to remain next in succession to the throne, however, soon created political enemies. Lower favored the 1679 attempt to remove James from the line of succession, earning for himself the label of a Whig. As a result, the status he had inherited from Willis as London's leading physician evaporated as his aristocratic patients abandoned him.

In the 1650's, the Oxford physiologists, especially Willis, Lower, Wren, and Boyle, experimented with using needles and quills as lancets to inject various substances, not including blood, into animals. Boyle and Lower were particularly interested in analyzing three specific results of injection: the effect on the life and health of the animal, the effect on respiration, and any changes in the color and consistency of the blood.

On the strength of articles published in *Philosophical Transactions of the Royal Society* between 1665 and 1667, Lower is generally considered to be the first person to perform successful blood transfusions, although early research in this area predated Lower's work by several generations. From early in the seventeenth century, several surgeons and other medical investigators, mainly on the European continent, had suggested and sometimes tried injecting or transfusing blood to rejuvenate the old, heal the sick, or invigorate the exhausted, either by putting blood from young into old humans or from healthy animals into diseased humans. In 1615, German physician and alchemist Andreas Libavius had specifically advocated transfusion for these purposes. His idea slowly came into practice in the midseventeenth century throughout western Europe, especially after Giovanni Colle performed transfusion experiments in the 1620's. The earliest experiments transfused blood from animal to animal, then from animal to human, and finally from human to human.

Lower improved on these early experiments, refining both the instrumentation and the technique of blood transfusion in the early 1660's. He published the results of his dog-to-dog transfusions in *Philosophical Transactions of the Royal Society* in 1665. Meanwhile, Jean Baptiste Denis in Paris and Giovanni Guglielmo Riva in Rome were doing similar research. Denis performed the first blood transfusion into a human in June, 1667, using the blood of a sheep. The patient barely survived, and the experiment was considered unsuccessful.

Richard Lower. (National Library of Medicine)

In November, 1667, Lower and Edmund King, who had duplicated some of Lower's transfusion results in 1666, successfully performed a sheep-to-human transfusion on Arthur Coga. The plan was that the boisterous Coga would become in temperament more like the lamb, a placid animal, by receiving its blood. Coga did not calm down, but he did not die either and even claimed to feel better. Lower was skeptical about the therapeutic value of just one transfusion and wanted to continue treatments, but Coga refused. Lower's success in transfusion, though limited, earned him election to the Royal Society in 1667. The following year, however, a man named Antoine Mauroy died after Denis transfused him with the blood of a calf. Even though Denis was acquitted of manslaughter in Mauroy's death, the adverse publicity generated by the incident effectively ended transfusion research for the next 150 years. The almost universal failure of these experiments led to prohibitions by British scientists in 1668, the Roman Catholic Church in 1669, and the French government in 1678.

Until 1741, however, revised editions of a standard

surgical textbook by Johannes Scultetus, *Armamentarium chirurgicum* (1655; arsenal of surgery), contained an illustrated chapter on transfusion that described the work of Lower and Denis in detail. Although Scultetus himself probably never tried transfusion and died in 1645, before Lower's first experiments with it, his posthumous editors apparently thought that the technique was important enough for surgeons to learn, despite the bans. Nevertheless, blood transfusion as either serious science or medical therapy was not revived for mainstream medicine until James Blundell invented a practical transfusion apparatus early in the nineteenth century.

SIGNIFICANCE

Lower's contributions to medicine and bioscience consist mostly of minor discoveries and inventions that became the basis of more important discoveries and inventions by later scientists. The new direction that his experiments with subcutaneous and intravenous injections took around 1662 led him to improve the design of syringes and laid the groundwork for the invention of the hypodermic syringe around 1850 by Charles Gabriel Pravaz and Alexander Wood.

Lower's *Tractatus de corde* (1669; *A Treatise on the Heart*, 1932) included the first accurate description of the detailed anatomy of heart muscle, an improvement on Harvey's account of blood circulation, and theories about why arterial blood and exposed blood are red while venous blood is blue. *A Treatise on the Heart* is Lower's greatest work, and made him famous in cardiology. A digressive chapter in it, "Dissertatio de origine catarrhi" ("A Dissertation on the Origin of Catarrh"), demonstrated that mucus drips from inside the nose and not, as

had been traditionally thought, into the nose from the brain.

—Eric v.d. Luft

FURTHER READING

Felts, John H. "Richard Lower: Anatomist and Physiologist." *Annals of Internal Medicine* 132, no. 5 (March 7, 2000): 420-423. A clear and accurate outline of the basic facts of Lower's life and scientific career.

Frank, Robert Gregg. *Harvey and the Oxford Physiologists: A Study of Scientific Ideas.* Berkeley: University of California Press, 1980. This standard work devotes much attention to Lower and places his life's work clearly within its historical context.

Lower, Richard. *A Treatise on the Heart.* Translated by K. J. Franklin. Birmingham, Ala.: Classics of Medicine Library, 1989. A reissue of Franklin's 1932 critical edition of Lower's masterpiece.

Moore, Pete. *Blood and Justice: The Seventeenth-Century Parisian Doctor Who Made Blood Transfusion History.* Hoboken, N.J.: Wiley, 2003. Although its subject is Denis, not Lower, this semifictionalized account of governmental, legal, and religious opposition to blood transfusion in Louis XIV's France provides an interesting interpretation of the early days of blood transfusion in England as well.

SEE ALSO: Robert Boyle; William Harvey; Robert Hooke; John Locke; Sir William Petty; John Wallis; Thomas Willis; Sir Christopher Wren.

RELATED ARTICLE in *Great Events from History: The Seventeenth Century, 1601-1700:* 1601-1672: Rise of Scientific Societies.

ROGER LUDLOW
English-born colonial American statesman

Ludlow drafted the first legal document resembling a constitution in colonial America. Ludlow's Fundamental Orders of Connecticut established the principle of self-government by extending limited control to the populace, a revolutionary idea in keeping with the community-values tradition of the Puritans. The basic model of government contained in the Fundamental Orders is essentially still intact.

BORN: March 7, 1590 (baptized); Dinton, Wiltshire, England
DIED: c. 1666; Dublin, Ireland
AREAS OF ACHIEVEMENT: Law, government and politics

EARLY LIFE

Roger Ludlow was born into an English Puritan family. He attended Oxford University in 1610 and then trained in law at the Inner Temple in 1612. At the age of thirty-two, Ludlow married Mary Coogan, and they had six children over the next twelve years. In the late 1620's, Ludlow worked for the Massachusetts Bay Company in England. At that time, the Crown controlled the judiciary and could replace judges who did not decide cases in accordance with the Crown's legislative or ecclesiastical doctrines. The English subjects, especially the Puritans, became increasingly discontent over arbitrary justice, interminable magisterial appointments of the ruling aristocracy, and the religious struggles between the Anglican Church and the Catholics for power.

The lure of new land, economic prosperity, and the promise of religious freedom prompted Ludlow to sail to the Massachusetts Bay Colony, which had been granted a royal charter to settle the area by Charles I. Ludlow arrived in June, 1630, and served for four years as assistant to the General Court of Massachusetts, as land commissioner, land viewer, and justice of the peace. He became deputy governor of Massachusetts in 1634. The wealthy leaders of the Massachusetts Bay Colony sought to maintain their power by rejecting an electoral process that would allow common citizens into their ranks and by ignoring any limitations on their power that were noted in the charter. Moreover, when the people demanded written codification of their laws, the governor and magistrates refused, claiming that a body of statutes would be inconsistent with the legal system of England, which was based predominantly on common law, and would create great peril for the colony.

When Ludlow's campaign for the Massachusetts governorship failed, he sought new opportunity by joining the founders of Connecticut. The emigrants to Connecticut encountered immediate difficulties, however, when they learned that Robert Rich, second earl of Warwick, had granted the same land to another group of English gentlemen. Ludlow drafted a settlement called the March Commission, which received approval from the Massachusetts General Court in March of 1636. The settlement allowed the emigrants to inhabit Connecticut for a year, from March, 1636, to March, 1637.

LIFE'S WORK

In 1636, Ludlow joined the colonists who had moved to the Conectecotte River (later renamed Connecticut) to establish settlements near present-day Windsor, Connecticut. The colony's representatives asked Ludlow to preside over the General Court for the townships of Windsor, Hartford, and Wethersfield. For many years, Ludlow also served as deputy governor of Connecticut.

Most of the Connecticut Indian tribes were friendly to the colonists, but a surprise raid on Wethersfield by the Pequot Indians in 1636 caused Ludlow to be sent as an adviser to the Connecticut force that engaged the Pequots. The Pequots made a stand at at Sasqua, on July 13, 1637. The settlers defeated the Pequots in the Great Swamp Fight. This victory served to warn the rest of the Indian tribes, as well as the nearby Dutch settlers, that the Puritans could assemble a powerful military force.

In August of 1639, Ludlow and his fellow colonists returned to a place known to the local Indians as Unquowa, near Sasqua. The settlers offered glass beads and wool fabric to the Indians for the purchase of about 12 square miles (31 square kilometers) of land. This area encompassed hundreds of acres of flat fields, so they named it Fairfield. Under Ludlow's leadership, the purchase of the land from the Indians was finalized, and Fairfield was founded, in 1641.

The General Court asked Ludlow to draft orders for the settlers that would establish a representative form of government. Ludlow, the Reverend Thomas Hooker, and Governor John Haynes were prominent in structuring the document. On February 9, 1638, the members of the General Court stepped down from their positions so they could be replaced by a new, democratically elected General Court.

In 1639, with inspiration from Puritan sermons, Ludlow drafted the Fundamental Orders of Connecticut, which was adopted on January 14, 1639, on land still claimed by Charles I, and is often recognized as the first written constitution for the New World. The orders sought to conjoin the townships into one confederation and to maintain the purity of the Gospel of Jesus. This forerunner of American democracy was to be enacted and enforced by governors and magistrates who were always to be members of an approved Christian congregation.

The Fundamental Orders mandated that admitted inhabitants would elect the colony's deputies. The deputies could convene the General Court and elect magistrates to serve on that court. This potential for review encouraged the magistrates to be circumspect in the use of their judicial power, unlike the magistracies in other New England colonies. The governor's powers also were limited, in order to prevent tyrannical rule. Since he was elected, he was subject to the will of the freemen. He himself could not vote (except as a tie-breaker), appoint magistrates, dissolve the General Court, interfere with elections, or serve for more than two years. These limited term appointments forced leaders to relinquish their positions and resume their place in society. Further, the Fundamental Orders did away with titles of nobility, preferential treatment for upper class citizens, primogenitor, and laws that imposed penalties before a trial had taken place.

In 1646, the General Court asked Ludlow to create a code of laws for their commonwealth that would ground the decisions of their magistrates in precedent and authority. This topically alphabetized code became known as the Code of 1650, for the year in which it was adopted by the General Court. It was an extension of the Fundamental Orders. Together, the Fundamental Orders and the Code of 1650 guaranteed people the right to elections, to liberty, to freedom from taxation without representation, and to enumerated privileges and immunities from persecution. Any powers not clearly granted to the state belonged to the people. The Code of 1650 also contained laws that prohibited heresy, idleness, and stubbornness.

Ludlow served as a commissioner of the United Colonies of New England and, from 1651 to 1653, helped draft the New England Confederation for the initial protection of the colonies of New Haven, Connecticut, Massachusetts Bay, and Plymouth. The confederation provided for mutual aid and cooperation in resisting attacks by Indians, hostile countries, or fugitives. No colony was permitted, without the general consent, to engage in war, unless there was a sudden or unavoidable attack.

When the citizens of Fairfield felt threatened by the Dutch, they ignored the confederation and declared war, appointed Ludlow commander, and raised a volunteer army. The General Court of New Haven disagreed with these actions and punished Ludlow's officers for insurrection. Ludlow was angered and humiliated. He refused to remain in their jurisdiction and returned to England in 1654. He later settled in Dublin, Ireland, where he served as a law officer for Oliver Cromwell for the remainder of his professional life. While the exact date of Ludlow's death is unknown, most historians believe he died around 1666. After the Restoration of Charles II, the king ratified the Fundamental Orders of Connecticut in the Charter of 1662. After the American Revolution in 1776, however, all references to royalty were removed from the Charter of 1662. It was readopted as the Constitution of the State of Connecticut.

SIGNIFICANCE

Ludlow was a gifted leader and energetic statesman who provided important public services for colonial Connecticut. Ludlow's legacy was the framing of a legal model for constitutional rights in the New World. While this model initially extended to the inhabitants of wilderness settlements along the Connecticut River, the model represented affected all the constitutions of colonial and post-revolutionary America.

The Fundamental Orders of Connecticut protected the rights of the people by ensuring that legal authority did not become arbitrary and tyrannical. The requirement that aristocratic magistrates be subject to election by secret ballots was revolutionary. Ludlow's essential principles demanded due process of law, equal treatment, and self-government free from any outside power. Many other territories also adopted the Fundamental Orders, which were produced for a Puritan citizenry that refused to allow government to control its faith. The principle of religious freedom put forward by Ludlow acknowledged that God's authority supercedes all liberties and that the community must be guided by the study and application of Christ's Gospel. In the Fundamental Orders, Connecticut leaders rejected the monarchic conception of power that was in practice back in England and taking root in other colonies. Incorporating democracy and equality, Ludlow's Fundamental Orders became, in essence, the first constitution in the New World. The Code of 1650 has served Connecticut to this day.

—John Roger Elliott

FURTHER READING

Adair, John. *Puritans: Religion and Politics in Seventeeth-Century England and America.* Stroud, Gloucestershire, England: Sutton, 1998. Traces the seventeenth century political and religious influence of the Puritans in the New England colonies.

Chartrand, Rene. *Colonial American Troops, 1610-1774.* Oxford, England: Osprey, 2002. Documents the colonists' creation of militias with other colonies and alliances with different tribes in order to protect themselves from Indians.

Cohn, Henry S. "Connecticut Constitutional History, 1636-1776." *Connecticut Bar Journal* 64, no. 5 (October, 1990): 330-334. Cohn, former assistant attorney general for Connecticut, outlines the original government at the founding of Connecticut, along with the factors that led to the drafting of the Fundamental Orders, and examines how the government actually functioned before the American Revolution.

McCook, Philip. "The Fundamental Orders." *Connecticut Bar Journal* 13, no. 1 (January, 1939): 52-65. Speech delivered by Connecticut Supreme Court Judge McCook at the three-hundredth anniversary celebration of the adoption of the Fundamental Orders by the Connecticut colonies.

Taylor, John. *Roger Ludlow: The Colonial Lawmaker.* New York: G. P. Putnam's Sons, 1900. Reprint. Holmes Beach, Fla.: Gaunt, 2004. This biographical book focuses on the challenges and accomplishments of Roger Ludlow.

SEE ALSO: Charles I; Charles II (of England); Oliver Cromwell; Thomas Hooker.

RELATED ARTICLES in *Great Events from History: The Seventeenth Century, 1601-1700:* Fall, 1632-January 5, 1665: Settlement of Connecticut; July 20, 1636-July 28, 1637: Pequot War; September 8, 1643: Confederation of the United Colonies of New England; May, 1659-May, 1660: Restoration of Charles II.

JEAN-BAPTISTE LULLY
French composer

The Italian-born Lully, considered the founder of national French opera, developed, with librettist Philippe Quinault, a new—and controversial—genre of music called tragédie en musique, *or* tragédie lyrique, *about life at court. Also, he set the patterns and guidelines for French Baroque musical style.*

BORN: November 29, 1632; Florence (now in Italy)
DIED: March 22, 1687; Paris, France
ALSO KNOWN AS: Giovanni Battista Lulli (given name)
AREAS OF ACHIEVEMENT: Music, theater

EARLY LIFE

The youngest child of a merchant in Florence, Jean-Baptiste Lully, who was given the name Giovanni Battista Lulli at birth, had an irregular education. He apparently learned to play the violin and guitar, taking music lessons from a local Franciscan friar. What other training he received is unknown, as are any contacts he made.

At age thirteen, Lully was taken into the service of a powerful French noblewoman, the duchesse de Montpensier, Anne-Marie-Louise d'Orléans, a cousin of King Louis XIV and popularly known as La Grande Made-

moiselle. To assist her study of the Italian language, she had her uncle, on a visit to Florence, recruit Lully to tutor her. It is not known how or why Lully was chosen, only that he set out for France in late February, 1646.

Legend says that Lully first worked in the lady's kitchens, but, actually, he was one of La Grande Mademoiselle's salaried *garçons de chambre.* Lully mastered the French language, Gallicized his name to Jean-Baptiste Lully, and learned the ways of the courtier. La Grande Mademoiselle was a devotee of music in particular, and at her court in the Tuileries the young Lully attended performances by the best musicians of the day. He cultivated his contacts while diligently acquiring further instrumental training, thus becoming an outstanding violinist and a competent keyboard player. He also became a skilled dancer and comic actor.

In 1652, at age nineteen, Lully composed a choreographic piece for his patron in which he also danced. His dancing skills had attracted the attention of the young king, himself an ardent terpsichorean (interested in dance). When, in 1652, La Grande Mademoiselle suffered disgrace and exile, the king arranged Lully's transfer to royal employment. Two months later, Lully, then twenty years old, danced in a spectacular court production, together with the king, who was then fourteen years old. The young monarch was so impressed that in less than one month he made Lully composer of instrumental music at his court.

LIFE'S WORK

From the outset, Lully faced rivals and hostile intrigues. His grace, precision, and cleverness as a dancer, however, won the king's personal favor and support. Acquiring his own orchestral ensemble, he first contributed to collaborative court ballets. From 1656 onward, he advanced aggressively, composing his own dance and vocal scores. In 1660, and again in 1663, Lully won attention with his earliest sacred works.

As an Italian by birth, Lully enjoyed the support of the king's chief minister, Cardinal Jules Mazarin (also a French-naturalized Italian), who sought to introduce into French cultural life Italian musical styles, especially opera, an Italian invention and monopoly until then. To this end, Mazarin imported the leading Venetian operatic master, Francesco Cavalli, to compose a lavish opera to celebrate the king's marriage in 1660. The project became mired in delays and was not realized until early 1662, when its foreign character—with long recitatives in Italian—ran counter to French tastes. Mazarin died during this time of delay, on March 9, 1661. That, combined with the Cavalli failure, doomed the efforts of cultural Italianizers at court, to whom Louis was not really sympathetic.

With Mazarin's death, Louis XIV assumed full personal power. One of his first acts was to appoint Lully superintendent of the music of the King's Chamber. The ambitious composer had recognized that his future depended upon shedding Italian associations and fully accepting French identity. In December, 1661, Lully received from the king formal naturalization as a French subject. Soon after (July 16, 1662), Louis appointed Lully master of the royal family's music. Eight days later Lully married the daughter of the distinguished singer and composer Michel Lambert. The contract witnesses included the king, the queen, the Queen Mother, and the chief minister Jean-Baptiste Colbert.

Lully's soaring status in France was matched by a growing reputation abroad. Ever self-serving, Lully cultivated important collaborators, such as Pierre Corneille. In 1664, he launched a partnership with the great comic playwright and actor Molière, resulting in several *comédies-ballets*. Their collaboration produced the immortal *Le Bourgeois gentilhomme* (1670; *The Would-Be Gentleman*, 1675), in which Lully also danced. Their collaboration foundered on financial disputes, however, and ended as Lully plunged into his greatest project.

In 1669, the king had created the Académie d'Opéra, contracted to Pierre Perrin. Lully was very critical of Perrin's efforts, arguing ostentatiously that the French language was unsuitable for opera. However uneven, though, Perrin's experiments in French opera had shown that possibilities existed. When Perrin was beset by financial troubles in early 1672, Lully bought out his rights and then secured a royal grant (March 13, 1672) authorizing the new Académie Royale de Musique (now the Grande Opéra), which replaced the Académie d'Opéra. A series of royal decrees then guaranteed Lully almost total control of musical theater in France. This process reflected the king's determination to centralize control over all areas of French life, notably by creating academies in each sphere of cultural activity. Lully, meanwhile, by this time had the power to stymie and hobble his musical competitors.

Converted to the idea of a distinctly French opera, Lully quickly found a congenial new literary partner—librettist Philippe Quinault, who was to write eleven of the librettos for the sixteen operas that were to become Lully's great achievements. The first of their *tragédies lyriques*, or *tragédies en musique*, as he called them, was *Cadmus et Hermione* (1673). Molière's death enabled Lully to take over Molière's theater: With that, Lully's company became known as the Paris Opéra. *Alceste: Ou, Le triomphe d'Alcide* (1674) provoked such harsh criticism from Lully's enemies that the king had the opera's successors—*Thésée*, *Atys*, and *Isis* (1675-1677)—produced in a royal theater. Suspicions of court satire in the last of these operas brought temporary disgrace to Quinault, obliging Lully to seek new collaborators. He used librettos by Thomas Corneille for his next two operas, *Psyché* and *Bellérophon* (1678-1679), but could resume work with Quinault for six more operas: *Proserpine*, *Persée*, *Phaëton*, *Amadis*, *Roland*, and *Armide* (1680-1686).

The king stood as godfather to Lully's eldest son (1677), and allowed Lully the new title of counsellor to the king, conveying noble status. Nevertheless, strains developed between them: Lully's homosexuality caused the increasingly religious Louis to withdraw favor. The composer found patronage elsewhere, and his last completed opera, the pastorale *Acis et Galaté* (1686), was performed privately outside Paris. Still, despite difficult legal entanglements, Lully ran his enterprises skillfully and accumulated considerable wealth.

Matching the king's religious bent, Lully composed

more sacred music in these last years. It was at a performance of his *Te Deum* in a ceremony in January of 1687 that he injured his foot with a blow of the staff with which he was directing. The wound's infection led to his death two months later.

For all his dancing skill and courtly grace, Lully was often coarse—even violent—in manners and language. While he carefully nurtured his musicians, he often fell into fits of rage and brutality: When one female singer threatened to withdraw from a production because of pregnancy, Lully kicked her in the stomach, forcing her miscarriage and saving his schedule.

SIGNIFICANCE

Lully's style set the obligatory guidelines for French composition during and after his lifetime. In church music, he consolidated the distinction between the *petit motet* (for soloists and instruments) and the *grand motet* (for soloists, chorus, and orchestra), leaving admirable models. He revitalized French dance and ceremonial music, blending an Italian clarity with the French love for ornamentation.

In his operas, Lully developed a pliant vocal line, avoiding the sharp Italian distinction between recitative and aria, while fitting the rhythms and flow of the French language. He set the ABA pattern for the French form of the overture: slow, in dotted rhythm; fast, fugal; and the reprise of the opening. He favored the French love for dance by decreeing the inclusion of danced *divertissements* in opera scores, culminating in a formal chaconne or *passacaille*. The next century of French Baroque music would have been inconceivable without him, while his style and forms were imitated widely abroad, especially in Germany.

—*John W. Barker*

FURTHER READING

Anthony, James R. *French Baroque Music: From Beaujoyeulx to Rameau.* 1974. Rev. ed. New York: Norton, 1978. An authoritative work, placing Lully's music in the larger context of French development.

_____, ed. *French Baroque Masters.* New York: Norton, 1986. Introducing essays about four other composers, Anthony's own useful sketch of Lully, with a full bibliography, is expanded and updated from its original form in *The New Grove Dictionary of Music and Musicians* (1980).

Heyer, J. H., et al., eds. *Jean-Baptiste Lully and the Music of the French Baroque: Essays in Honor of James R. Anthony.* New York: Cambridge University Press, 1989. Important studies of aspects of the composer's career and art by leading specialists.

Isherwood, Robert M. *Music in the Service of the King: France in the Seventeenth Century.* Ithaca, N.Y.: Cornell University Press, 1973. A probing study that relates Lully and his music to patterns of French royal image-building.

Newman, J. E. W. *Jean-Baptiste de Lully and His Tragédies Lyriques.* Ann Arbor: University of Michigan Press, 1979. An important analysis of the composer's chief musical legacy.

Scott, R. H. F. *Jean-Baptiste Lully.* London: Peter Owen, 1973. A brief but still-useful study of the composer's life and work.

Wood, C. *Music and Drama in the Tragédie en Musique, 1673-1715: Jean-Baptiste Lully and His Successors.* New York, 1996. Traces the evolution of the Lulliste tradition in French opera.

SEE ALSO: Francesca Caccini; Jean-Baptiste Colbert; Pierre Corneille; Jean de La Fontaine; Girolamo Frescobaldi; Louis XIV; Jules Mazarin; Molière; Barbara Strozzi.

RELATED ARTICLES in *Great Events from History: The Seventeenth Century, 1601-1700:* c. 1601: Emergence of Baroque Music; February 24, 1607: First Performance of Monteverdi's *La favola d'Orfeo.*

MADAME DE MAINTENON
Queen consort of France and educator

After her secret marriage to King Louis XIV, Maintenon was instrumental in encouraging the growth of his religious fervor and was an early leader in efforts to educate poor noble girls by founding the acclaimed school at Saint-Cyr and by writing about the education of girls.

BORN: November 27, 1635; Nirot, France
DIED: April 15, 1719; Saint-Cyr, France
ALSO KNOWN AS: Françoise d'Aubigné (given name); Françoise Scarron; Marquise de Maintenon
AREAS OF ACHIEVEMENT: Education, women's rights, religion and theology

EARLY LIFE

Françoise d'Aubigné, later known as Madame de Maintenon (mahn-teh-noh), was born in a prison in Nirot, where her father, Constant d'Aubigné, was in custody with Maintenon's mother, Jeanne de Cardilhac. Coming from a prominent family with firm roots in the Huguenot Protestant church, her father was the black sheep of the family, convicted of robbery and counterfeiting money. Although he was a nominal Huguenot, Jeanne was firmly committed to the Catholic Church. Maintenon's grandfather was Huguenot commander and writer Théodore-Agrippa d'Aubigné (1552-1630). Maintenon was baptized according to the rites of her mother's religion, even though she spent some of her early years with Huguenot relatives.

Following Constant's release from prison, he and Jeanne and three children left France for the Caribbean island of Martinique. Unable to support the family, Constant soon returned to France in search of work. Within a few months, however, he died. Jeanne, in desperate conditions, returned to France, abandoned her children to relatives, and then disappeared for unknown reasons. Maintenon at first was placed with a Huguenot aunt on her father's side. Her maternal relatives, however, gained control over the young girl through a court order. They sent her to be educated at an Ursuline convent, where she became firmly grounded in Catholic doctrines. Later in life, she would often refer to her love and admiration for her teachers at the convent.

In 1652, after leaving the convent, Maintenon married Paul Scarron, a popular writer who had a reputation for burlesque poetry. He was forty-two years old and in poor health; she was sixteen. She brought no dowry to the marriage. Despite his heavy debts, her husband had many contacts, and he introduced her to the social and literary elite of Paris. Through these contacts, she came to the attention of Anne of Austria, the mother of King Louis XIV. When Scarron died in 1660, his young widow was left penniless, and she auctioned off the household furniture to pay for her husband's debts. Within a year, however, friends convinced the Queen Mother to award her a modest pension that allowed her to continue participating in Parisian society.

LIFE'S WORK

During the late 1660's, there were rumors that Maintenon had become the mistress of a rich gentleman. Whether or not the rumors were true, in 1670, Maintenon was introduced to the gentleman's cousin (and the king's mistress), Françoise-Athénaïs, Rochechouart de Mortemart (1641-1707), better known as Madame de Montespan. Montespan had been looking for a nurse and governess to take care of her illegitimate child. Maintenon was an ideal choice because she liked working with children, had more education than most women at the time, and was a practicing Catholic—all essential qualifications for the governess of the king's children. Also, Maintenon needed a source of livelihood. During the next four years, Montespan gave birth to four more babies, and they all moved into Maintenon's apartment in the village of Vaugirard.

When Montespan's children were legitimized on December 20, 1673, they moved into chambers at court, taking their governess with them. Two years later, she was awarded the title madame de Maintenon, which was soon elevated to marquise de Maintenon. The title came from the name of the château she had purchased. Happily, she no longer carried the name of a poet of questionable reputation. Her intelligence and nurturing qualities favorably impressed the king, so that he began to have regular conversations with her. Based on a careful examination of her correspondence, historians have concluded that she most likely became his mistress sometime between 1674 and 1681. During these years, Louis was losing interest in Montespan, who was dismissed from her high position at court in 1681.

Maintenon strongly encouraged the king to spend more time with the queen, Marie-Thérèse, who maintained a friendly relationship with her. In 1683, the queen unexpectedly died, possibly from blood poisoning. The king's friends found that Louis was not especially sad, for he was being "consoled" by Maintenon, whom he married in a secret ceremony, possibly in early 1684.

During a marriage that lasted more than thirty years, Maintenon increasingly played an important role in the life of the king, who prized her companionship highly. Most historians think, however, that observers such as Louis de Rouvroy, the duke of Saint-Simon (1675-1755) and a writer on court life, exaggerated her influence over his decisions. During the first half of the marriage, she apparently exercised little influence on the formation of policies. From about 1700, however, the king paid more attention to her opinions on matters of state and sometimes even allowed her to attend cabinet meetings. Even then, however, he often rejected her advice, especially on foreign policy.

Because of Maintenon's religious devotion, it is not surprising that her greatest influence was in religion. She was instrumental in bringing about Louis's religious fervor and had a hand in changing the moral tone of the court. There is no evidence, however, that she was associated with the so-called *devotes*, who were known for their extremism and intolerance. Historians agree that she had no part in the king's decision in 1685 to revoke the Edict of Nantes (1598), which took away the right of

Protestants to practice their religion in France. In contrast to most of her contemporaries, she never spoke favorably of the infamous revocation, even though she did not hesitate to advise her brother about the opportunity to profit from buying the property of desperate Protestants. Although she endorsed the king's anti-Jansenist policies, his efforts against the movement began before his contact with Maintenon.

Maintenon demonstrated a great deal of passion for the education of children. She helped found the Institute of Saint-Louis at Saint-Cyr in 1686. Endowed by the king and its construction directed by François Mansart, the institute eventually lodged 250 daughters of impoverished noblemen. Its fame attracted many visitors. Theologian François de Salignac de La Mothe-Fénelon preached at the institute, and dramatist Jean Racine had some of his plays performed by the students.

Maintenon stayed by the side of the king when he was on his deathbed. The king had said that Maintenon had helped him in everything, especially the saving of his soul. In 1715, two days before Louis's death, Maintenon left Versailles, gave away most of her money to charity, and retired to the Saint-Cyr school. Upon her death, she was buried at the school.

Madame de Maintenon. (Hulton Archive/Getty Images)

SIGNIFICANCE

Madame de Maintenon spent a great deal of time and effort in organizing the rules and curriculum at the Saint-Cyr school. Recognized as one of the first serious efforts to provide an education for poor girls of noble birth, the school would continue to exist until the French Revolution.

Much of Maintenon's massive correspondence, which has been published in French, discusses her educational views and gives advice to both teachers and students. In an educational manifesto, "Maxims to Serve as Examples to the Demoiselles of the Saint-Cyr School," she asserts the values of traditional morality, modesty, obedience, altruism, religious piety, and broad preparation for an unknown future. Despite her strong advocacy of female education, nevertheless, she never challenged the patriarchal assumptions of the age.

—*Thomas Tandy Lewis*

FURTHER READING

Barnard, Howard. *Madame de Maintenon and Saint-Cry.* Hingham, Mass.: Charles River Books, 1977. An interesting study of Maintenon's educational views and the school she founded.

Chandernogon, Françoise. *King's War: Reflections of Françoise d'Aubigné, Marquise de Maintenon, Wife of the King of France.* New York: Harcourt Brace Jovanovich, 1984. A respected novel that, despite some unfounded speculation, still has historical value.

Cruttwell, Maud. *Madame de Maintenon.* London: Dutton, 1930. A standard biography, but not as scholarly as that by Charlotte Haldane.

Durant, Will, and Ariel Durant. *The Age of Louis XIV.* New York: Simon & Schuster, 1963. A good portrait of Maintenon, although modern historians reject the assertion that Maintenon refused to be Louis's mistress.

Gibson, Wendy. *Women in Seventeenth-Century France.* New York: St. Martin's Press, 1989. For background, this book provides a good synthesis about the condition of women in different socioeconomic classes.

Haldane, Charlotte. *Madame de Maintenon: Uncrowned Queen of France.* London: Constable, 1970. The best and most complete biography of Maintenon in the English language.

Levi, Anthony. *Louis XIV.* New York: Carroll & Graf, 2004. An interesting and provocative biography, although Levi's psychological interpretations are often questionable.

Norton, Lucy, ed. *Memoirs Duc de Saint-Simon.* 3 vols. New York: Prion, 2000. An English-language abridgment that includes the interesting observations, rumors, and anecdotes written by a resident at Louis XIV's court.

Rapley, Elizabeth. *The Dévotes: Women and Church in Seventeenth Century France.* Montreal: McGill-Queen's University Press, 1990. Although recognizing the continuation of subordinate status for women, Rapley points to Maintenon as an example of their increasing influence.

Wolf, John B. *Louis XIV.* New York: W. W. Norton, 1968. A lively biography that includes a balanced summary of Maintenon's influence on the king, with abundant documentation of both English and French sources.

SEE ALSO: Anne of Austria; François de Salignac de La Mothe-Fénelon; Louis XIV; François Mansart; Marie-Thérèse; Jean Racine; Anna Maria van Schurman.

RELATED ARTICLES in *Great Events from History: The Seventeenth Century, 1601-1700:* 1682: French Court Moves to Versailles; 1685: Louis XIV Revokes the Edict of Nantes; 1689-1694: Famine and Inflation in France.

SIEUR DE MAISONNEUVE
French-born first governor of Montreal (1642-1665)

A soldier and deeply pious man, Sieur de Maisonneuve was the first governor and administrator of the Isle of Ville-Marie, now Montreal, Canada. Maisonneuve, whose intended goal was to Christianize the indigenous peoples of the area, led the colony for twenty-two years and helped it grow into a larger community of religious inhabitants and traders.

BORN: February 15, 1612 (baptized); Neuville-sur-Vannes, France
DIED: September 9, 1676; Paris, France
ALSO KNOWN AS: Paul de Chomedey (given name)
AREAS OF ACHIEVEMENT: Government and politics, religion and theology

EARLY LIFE
Born in Neuville-sur-Vannes in Champagne to the noble Louis de Chomedey and Marie de Thomelin, Paul de Chomedey, later called Sieur de Maisonneuve (syehr deh mehz-oh-nehv), was baptized on February 15. Two years later, his father bought the seigneury of Maisonneuve. Although little is known of his childhood, some details can be surmised about his education. His father's profession as a magistrate and the family's noble status would have ensured a grounding in the basics needed to follow in the family tradition. His elegant handwriting, literary skills, and able administration of the colony of Montreal suggest an aristocratic education, which would have included religious instruction.

Consistent with his family's social stature, Paul began his military career in 1625 at the age of thirteen. France was embroiled in the Thirty Years' War, and Paul most likely served with the troops in Holland. By the age of nineteen, he was not happy with his advancement in the military, nor did he wish to follow in his father's footsteps. His sister Louise, a member of the Congrégation of Nôtre-Dame at Troyes, who had become an avid reader of the periodical *Jesuit Relations*, encouraged her brother to consider a vocation in the French colonies. During one of his visits to Paris, he visited father Charles Lalement, who supervised Canadian recruitment work in the colonies. Lalement, impressed by Paul's background and interests, approached Jérôme Le Royer de la Dauversière, the wealthy and pious founder of the Society of Gentlemen and Ladies of Nôtre-Dame of Montreal. When they met, Dauversière recognized that Paul de Chomedey was the right man to head the missionary enterprise and appointed him the first governor of Ville-Marie de Montreal. In December, 1640, the Company of New France granted the group the island of Montreal for its mission.

LIFE'S WORK

As Dauversière's "instrument of God," Paul de Chomedey set out from La Rochelle on May 9, 1641, with several companions and a priest. A second ship carried philanthropist Jeanne Mance (1606-1673), who would be the founding mother of the colony and the first nurse in North America. The ships became separated and Mance and her companions arrived in Quebec in August, while the other ship was delayed by storms. Chomedey's ship arrived before September 20, too late in the year to begin the foundation of Ville-Marie. The company had to winter in Quebec. There, the opposition to the new settlement was strong because of a great Iroquois threat and because the governor viewed the proposed new colony as a scattering of needed resources. The governor even offered the Île d'Orléans to dissuade Chomedey from the Montreal project. The latter responded that even if all the trees on the isle of Montreal were to turn into Iroquois, he would still settle there.

On May 17, 1642, Chomedey was given title to the island in the name of the Society. The early settlers built a log palisade to protect their huts, and they cleared enough land for cattle and sheep and some crops. More settlers and provisions arrived in summer. While the colony had a social hierarchy from the beginning, it was possible to become a landowner. Anyone who cleared four arpents of land and agreed to become a permanent settler was given more land, a stipend, and the title of habitant. Habitants were allowed to engage in what would later become the lucrative fur trade.

Floods threatened Ville-Marie during the first winter. While the colonists prayed, Chomedey set up a small cross near the river, asking God to save the colony. In return, he vowed he would carry a cross up Mount Royal, which he did on the Feast of the Epiphany.

Chomedey's vision was to re-create an early apostolic community in Montreal. Chomedey, Mance, Madame de la Peltrie, and the Jesuits worked to construct a fort, hospital, communal house, and church. In spite of the dangers, missionary work began, and the first baptism, of an Algonquian boy, occurred in July, with Chomedey and Mance named godparents. Mance, a laywoman, had such political and financial acumen that she was able to save the colony on several occasions. Recognized from the beginning was her "partnership" with Maisonneuve as a leader of the community.

On March 26, 1644, Chomedey received his official appointment, with full judicial and administrative powers. Almost continuous Iroquois attacks followed, though, which took a great toll during the next twenty-five years. That same year, Chomedey's father died, making Paul heir to the title sieur de Maisonneuve. Called back to France to settle family affairs, he had no sooner returned to New France when he was informed that his brother-in-law had been murdered and his mother was planning a disastrous remarriage. He was forced to return to France.

On his return, some expressed doubts about Maisonneuve's military leadership, because of his attempts to prevent retaliations that could provoke further Iroquois attacks. On March 30, 1644, he led a sortie of thirty Frenchmen against two hundred attackers. Maisonneuve ordered his men to retreat, but he stayed behind. Realizing who he was, the Iroquois left him to be captured by their chief. However, Maisonneuve's gunshot hit the Iroquois leader, helping Maisonneuve escape unscathed. His authority was secure.

Maisonneuve began developing a society that would respond to the unique circumstances of the colony. In charge of political, military, and judicial affairs, he was also given the power to grant land to those willing to settle on the island. Maisonneuve made the first land grants to colonists between 1648 and 1651, all the more necessary in view of the increasing Iroquois menace when few were willing to risk settlement outside the fort. In 1649, the colony seemed on the verge of collapse. Dauversière was seriously ill, but with Mance's fundraising trip to France and some creative bookkeeping, the society was given a reprieve.

Iroquois attacks against French settlers and their Huron allies intensified in the 1650's. Hurons fled to Ville-Marie for refuge, but the decimation of their nation led to direct Iroquois assaults against the French. In 1651, Maisonneuve left for France in the hope of recruiting men to defend the colony. For two years, he received pledges from future colonists and recruited more than one hundred men for his return trip. Also on the ship was Marguerite Bourgeoys, who would become the founder of the Congrégation de Nôtre-Dame and the colony's first schoolteacher. In 1653, Maisonneuve gave Bourgeoys a stone house for her school. By the 1650's, Montreal had expanded from a place resembling a monastery to a village. By 1654, more colonists were willing to assume the risks involved in becoming habitants.

By the 1660's, although the colony had achieved a certain permanence, interference from France and a hostile governor and bishop in Quebec challenged the authority wielded by Maisonneuve. Because of the financial difficulties of the society, seigneurial power was transferred to the Sulpician order, which had been working in Montreal since 1659. Bishop François Laval named a judge, notary, and procurator for the village, effectively undermining the power structure Maisonneuve had been building since 1642. When King Louis XIV sent colonists to New France in 1663, only ten were sent to Montreal.

In the fall of 1665, Maisonneuve was forced back to France by the authorities in Quebec. Although he remained governor until 1668, he would never again set foot in New France. He returned to Paris, where he led a reclusive life. His will, dictated the day before his death on September 9, 1676, left substantial inheritances to Marguerite Bourgeoys and the Congrégation de Nôtre-Dame as well as the Hospitallers of St. Joseph.

SIGNIFICANCE

Paul Chomedey de Maisonneuve, as first governor of the colony of Ville-Marie, developed for Montreal, in the course of twenty-four years, a civil and military government, a hospital, churches, religious houses, a school, a court, and a land registry. He worked together with Jeanne Mance and Marguerite Bourgeoys to raise funds and recruit settlers in spite of the almost constant dangers from the Iroquois, the harsh Canadian winters, and the hostility of the leaders in Quebec. The small outpost of Ville-Marie, which would grow into one of the most important settlements of New France, owed its existence to the bravery, commitment, and determination of Maisonneuve and his colleagues.

—*Larissa Juliet Taylor*

FURTHER READING

Delâge, Denys. *Bitter Feast: Amerindians and Europeans in the American Northeast, 1600-1664.* Vancouver: University of British Columbia Press, 1993. A native perspective on the history of French and Dutch colonization in northeastern North America.

Desrosiers, Léo-Paul. *Paul Chomedey, Sieur de Maisonneuve.* Montreal: FIDES, 1967. The only available scholarly biography of Maisonneuve. In French. Extensive original source quotations.

Eccles, W. J. *The French in North America, 1500-1783.* East Lansing: Michigan State University Press, 1998. A general history of New France, with sections on the foundation of Montreal and Maisonneuve.

Moogk, Peter N. *Le Nouvelle France: The Making of French Canada, a Cultural History.* East Lansing: Michigan State University Press, 2000. Moogk traces the roots of the current conflict between English- and French-speaking Canadians to the political and social developments that occurred in New France in the seventeenth century.

Simpson, Patricia. *Marguerite Bourgeoys and Montreal, 1640-1665.* Montreal: McGill-Queen's University Press, 1997. Simpson provides significant information on Maisonneuve, who worked with Bourgeoys and other female lay and religious persons in the early decades of the colonization of Montreal. Extensive notes and bibliography.

Thwaites, Reuben Gold, ed. *The Jesuit Relations and Allied Documents: Travels and Explorations of the Jesuit Missionaries in New France.* 73 vols. New York: Pageant Books, 1959. One of the most important collections of original sources for the early history of New France.

SEE ALSO: Saint Marguerite Bourgeoys; Samuel de Champlain; Pierre Le Moyne d'Iberville; Saint Isaac Jogues; Louis Jolliet; François Laval; Louis XIV.

RELATED ARTICLES in *Great Events from History: The Seventeenth Century, 1601-1700:* March 15, 1603-December 25, 1635: Champlain's Voyages; Spring, 1604: First European Settlement in North America; 1611-1630's: Jesuits Begin Missionary Activities in New France; April 27, 1627: Company of New France Is Chartered; May, 1642: Founding of Montreal; August, 1658-August 24, 1660: Explorations of Radisson and Chouart des Groseilliers.

FRANÇOIS DE MALHERBE
French poet

Malherbe's neoclassicist literary principles had a decisive impact on seventeenth century literature in France and on the development of an elegant and codified version of the French language. His doctrine on poetic composition argued for form, order, purity, simplicity, clarity, and restraint and against the baroque and mannerist tendencies of his time, establishing a standard for French classical literature.

BORN: 1555; Caen, France
DIED: October 6, 1628; Paris, France
AREA OF ACHIEVEMENT: Literature

EARLY LIFE

François de Malherbe (frahn-swah deh mah-lehrb) was born in 1555 in the region of Normandy. His father was a nobleman, municipal councilman in Caen, and had Protestant leanings. Malherbe was educated mostly in Caen, except for a year spent in Paris and stays at the universities of Basle and Heidelberg (1571-1573). He quickly was introduced to Caen's Reformed circles, especially during his time in boarding school, before his prolonged stay abroad.

Upon his return to Caen, however, he preferred the city's Catholic circles, above all a group that included the eminent literary figures Jean Vauquelin de La Fresnaye and Guy Le Fèvre de La Boderie. Malherbe's first poems date from that period (1575) but were not published until 1872. After this introduction to literary and intellectual life, Malherbe decided to leave his parents' home in 1576 to try to establish himself in Paris.

The next thirty years were marked by his struggles to gain the royal recognition that he thought he deserved, struggles that were exacerbated by constant personal and financial problems. His protector, Henri d'Angoulême, an illegitimate son of King Henry II, was appointed royal governor of Provence in 1577, where Malherbe followed him as his secretary and became a member of the court society of Aix-en-Provence. His marriage to Madeleine de Coriolis (1581) would result in four children, who all died young. D'Angoulême was killed in 1586 in a duel, which left Malherbe without a protector. He soon returned to Caen and tried to regain Henry III's favor by presenting him with his first published poem, *Les Larmes de Saint Pierre* (1587; the tears of Saint Peter), whose baroque style is in stark contradiction to his later teachings.

In 1590, he composed his best-known poem, *Consolation à Monsieur du Périer sur la mort de sa fille* (pb. c. 1600; consolation to Mr. du Périer on the death of his daughter). In 1594, Malherbe was elected municipal magistrate of Caen, but he decided nonetheless to return to Aix in 1595, where he stayed until 1605 (in 1598-1599, he was in Caen).

Near the end of the century, his poetry had gained some public recognition: His writings were included in a number of collections published between 1597 and 1603. Malherbe's reputation as a teacher was also increasing. Playwright and economist Antoine de Montchrestien sought his advice for his tragedy *Sophonisbe*, whose numerous corrections between 1596 and 1601 illustrate Malherbe's fledgling doctrine.

LIFE'S WORK

A turning point in Malherbe's life came in 1605. After being recommended to King Henry IV, he left Aix in the company of the eminent moralist Guillaume du Vair, president of the *parlement* of Provence, and Nicolas-Claude Fabri de Peiresc, one of the era's foremost scholars. Henry IV finally awarded Malherbe the coveted royal appointment, and he held the position of court poet until his death.

Very quickly, Malherbe tried to strengthen his position by discrediting his rival, poet Philippe Desportes, a favorite of King Henry III and his court poet. Malherbe believed that Desportes's "disorderly" baroque poetry was a symbol of an obsolete aesthetics. He annotated a copy of Desportes's poetry with very severe criticism in *Commentaire sur Desportes* (wr. 1605-1606), a project that was not published until the nineteenth century because the critic abandoned it after his rival's death in 1606. Because Malherbe never published a formal treatise laying out his famous doctrine, this text remains its most complete illustration.

As Malherbe became increasingly interested in prose, he would refer to his translation of Livy's twenty-third book as a model for writing in French. Moreover, Vair's 1594 treatise *De l'Éloquence française* contains the nucleus of Malherbe's formal and linguistic demands, which also shows that Malherbe cannot be considered the inventor of a revolutionary set of new rules but rather the most adamant advocate and teacher of guidelines that corresponded to the changing literary tastes of an era still recovering from the turmoil of the French Wars of Religion (1562-1598). Even Desportes had adopted a more sober style of writing toward the end of his life.

Three things set Malherbe apart from his contemporaries: his influential position at court, his sternness, and his pedagogical activities. In Paris, he intensified his mentoring efforts and held nightly meetings in his apartment, where he counseled his disciples on matters of style, versification, and grammar. His most devoted admirers include poet François Maynard, who was Marguerite de Valois's secretary and one of the founding members of the Académie Française (1635), as well as poet Honorat du Bueil, seigneur de Racan. Another follower, Pierre de Deimier, published *Académie de l'art poétique* (1610), which contained the bulk of Malherbe's doctrine.

In essence, Malherbe's doctrine was a reaction against the predominant poetic currents of the second half of the sixteenth century, marked by the poetry of La Pléiade and by baroque and mannerist tendencies in literature. His theory amounted to the purification and simplification of the French language, whose submission to logic and reason would constitute, in his opinion, a major step toward the restoration of order in a country tormented by decades of civil strife.

Malherbe's doctrine prescribed the outright suppression of archaisms, regional expressions, neologisms, involuntary repetitions, and other stylistic devices such as hiatus, inversion, and enjambment. The use of metaphors and images was to be restricted, and the rules of etiquette (*les bienséances*) were to be respected. The exclusive use of simple rhyme schemes and basic vocabulary completed a project whose overarching objective was clarity, expressiveness, and visual and aural beauty. Governed by such principles, poetry would be accessible to everyone. As laudable as this process of democratization of poetry seemed, however, it constituted—by its neglect of the genre's lyrical qualities—in many ways a return to the late medieval concept of poetry as an "art of second rhetoric," utilitarian writing meant to expose and logically develop ideas, a discourse in verse form, so to speak. This strict set of rules stood in stark contrast to Malherbe's personal life: He was nicknamed Father Lust, mostly because of his turbulent love life and the circulation of a number of his obscene poems. Moreover, many admirers of La Pléiade poets, admirers such as, above all, Mathurin Régnier, Desportes's nephew, continued to criticize Malherbe's poetry for its lack of inspiration.

The regency (1610-1614) marked Malherbe's most influential time at court. Marie de Médicis liked his work, and the poet kept flattering her in his official poetry, which resulted in several monetary awards and a raise of his pension. He frequently complained about difficulties collecting his pay, however, which contributed, along with several trials, to his continuing financial difficulties. Such preoccupations might explain his diminished poetic production during the remainder of his career. He returned to religious poetry, celebrated official court events, and resumed his translation projects. His poetry was published mostly in collections, which attested to his unbroken popularity, the most important works being the two-volume *Délices de la poésie française* (1615, 1620), the *Dernier recueil* (1621), and the *Recueil des plus beaux vers* (1627).

The end of Malherbe's life was marked by the problems of his son Marc-Antoine, who had killed a man in a duel in Aix in 1624 and then sought refuge in Normandy. After two years of lobbying, Malherbe obtained an official pardon, but his son was killed the following year (in 1627). Despite his influence at court and a trip to La Rochelle to implore King Louis XIII (he was still appreciated by the king and by Cardinal de Richelieu), Malherbe was unable to obtain the issuance of the death sentence against his son's murderers. Upon his return to Paris, Malherbe became ill and died on October 6, 1628.

SIGNIFICANCE

Malherbe's influence on neoclassicist poetry was tremendous, even though Nicolas Boileau-Despréaux's hyperbolic praise of Malherbe's impact was integral in ensuring this prominent position. Malherbe's rules were generally accepted in a seventeenth century that is still widely considered the peak of France's literary production, especially in the dramatic genre. Malherbe's doctrine also led to a neglect of Renaissance poetry for about two hundred years, until its "rediscovery" by the Romantics.

Even though his poetry had been largely forgotten, contradicting thus his confident self-assessment that whatever he wrote would be eternal, Malherbe's doctrine has proven to be pivotal for the development of French language and letters. Many of its principles remain indispensable for "good" writing.

—*Bernd Renner*

FURTHER READING

Abraham, Claude K. *Enfin Malherbe: The Influence of Malherbe on French Lyric Prosody, 1606-1674.* Lexington: University of Kentucky Press, 1971. This is still the most solid book-length study of Malherbe's life and work in the English language. The author strives to avoid the usual polemical discussion between unconditional admirers and opponents to determine Malherbe's actual influence on French letters.

Randall, Catherine. "Possessed Personae in Early Modern France: Du Bellay, d'Aubigné, and Malherbe." In *Seventeenth Century and Beyond*, Vol. 2 in *Signs of the Early Modern*, edited by David Lee Rubin. Charlottesville, Va.: Rockwood Press, 1997. A refreshing look, from the equally refreshing perspective of the "possessed persona," at Malherbe's work as the endpoint of a literary development rather than its starting point.

Sweetser, Marie-Odile. "The Art of Praise from Malherbe to La Fontaine." In *The Shape of Change*, edited by Anne Birberick and Russell Ganim. Amsterdam: Rodopi, 2002. This book takes up a topic that was predominant in the late medieval *grands rhétoriqueurs* (great rhetoricians) tradition and examines its seventeenth century development.

Winegarten, Renée. *French Lyric Poetry in the Age of Malherbe*. Manchester, England: Manchester University Press, 1954. This thoughtful study examines Malherbe and his work as integral to seventeenth century, French lyric poetry.

SEE ALSO: Nicolas Boileau-Despréaux; Jacques-Bénigne Bossuet; Marie le Jars de Gournay; Madame de La Fayette; Jean de La Fontaine; Louis XIV; Marie de Médicis; Molière; Nicolas-Claude Fabri de Peiresc; Charles Perrault; Jean Racine; Madeleine de Scudéry.

RELATED ARTICLES in *Great Events from History: The Seventeenth Century, 1601-1700:* c. 1601-1620: Emergence of Baroque Art; 1610-1643: Reign of Louis XIII; 1637: Descartes Publishes His *Discourse on Method*.

MARCELLO MALPIGHI
Italian scientist and physician

Malpighi's microscopic anatomy led him to discover the blood capillaries and demonstrate the fine structure of the lungs, thus laying the foundation for knowledge of the physiology of respiration. His other important studies were in embryology, plant anatomy, and invertebrate zoology.

BORN: March 10, 1628; Crevalcore, near Bologna, Papal States (now in Italy)

DIED: November 29, 1694; Rome, Papal States (now in Italy)

AREAS OF ACHIEVEMENT: Science and technology, medicine

EARLY LIFE

Marcello Malpighi (mahr-CHEHL-loh mahl-PEE-gee) was born in 1628, the year that William Harvey's book on the circulation of blood was published. His parents were farmers and financially independent. Not much is known of Malpighi's childhood. As the eldest child in the family, he had the advantages of masters and schools, and he began attending the University of Bologna on January 8, 1646, where he studied Aristotelian philosophy and met Bartolomeo Massari, a professor of anatomy. Massari soon became aware of Malpighi's genius in science, and the latter rose from being a pupil to become an associate and close friend.

In 1649, both of Malpighi's parents and his paternal grandmother died within a few days of each other. Since he was the eldest child, he had to interrupt his studies to settle his father's affairs and look after his brothers and sisters. His uncle, Alessandro Alfiere Malpighi, came to his aid, and he was able to resume his studies. In 1651, Malpighi decided to study medicine and soon became a candidate for doctoral degrees in both medicine and philosophy. On April 26, 1653, both degrees were conferred. He began to practice medicine, and, toward the end of the 1655-1656 academic year, he was also a lecturer in logic at the University of Bologna.

Malpighi's brilliance soon became apparent, but some opposition to his anti-Galenist, proexperimental ideas and his advanced views in medicine delayed his advancement. In 1656, when the Senate of Bologna established a professorship for him, he declined and accepted an appointment to the chair of theoretical medicine at Pisa, where the grand duke of Tuscany, Ferdinand II de' Medici, had instituted a new university on a much more liberal scale. At Pisa, he became acquainted with Giovanni Alfonso Borelli, who was then professor of mathematics with an interest in biology. This association developed into a lifelong, mutually beneficial friendship.

LIFE'S WORK

Malpighi's true scientific career began at Pisa. By 1659, he returned again to Bologna, for his health, where he was appointed an extraordinary lecturer in theoretical

Marcello Malpighi. (National Library of Medicine)

tigated the lungs of frogs, which are more transparent, and demonstrated the capillary circulation as a connecting link between arteries and veins.

In his treatise *De cerebro* (1665; on the brain), Malpighi showed that the white matter of the central nervous system is composed of bundles of fibers, arranged in tracts connecting the brain with the spinal cord. His *De viscerum structura exercitatio anatomica* (1666; on the structure of viscera) contains his basic observations on microscopic mammalian anatomy. He described the histology of the liver and determined that it secreted the bile that passes through a duct to the gall bladder, which simply stores and releases it. In addition, he determined the structure and function of the kidneys.

On February 21, 1667, Malpighi married Francesca Massari, the fifty-seven-year-old sister of his former teacher Massari. In 1667, Malpighi received an invitation from Henry Oldenburg, secretary of the Royal Society in London, to correspond with the society. He gracefully accepted and was honored the following year by being elected a fellow of the society.

Malpighi's publication on the silkworm moth, *De bombyce* (1669), represents the first full account of the anatomy of an insect. With his microscopes and wonderful skill, he was the first to observe the spiracles and the system of air tubes associated with them, the multichambered heart, the ventral nerve cord with its ganglia, and the silk-forming apparatus. He showed that the method of gas exchange was through the system of air tubes or tracheae, communicating with the exterior through the spiracles. He anatomized all phases of the species, and he discovered the system of excretory tubules now known as Malpighian tubules.

In the field of embryology, Malpighi published two pioneer works, *Dissertatio epistolica de formatione pulli in ovo* (1673; on the formation of the chick in the egg) and *De ovo incubato* (1675; both works in English translation in *Marcello Malpighi and the Evolution of Embryology*, 1966). The subject was not quite a new one; Aristotle, Harvey, and others had preceded him. He, however, enjoyed one great advantage over his predecessors; he was able to use a microscope in his studies and proceeded to produce a masterpiece, one of the best studies of the subject ever made.

medicine. He also applied himself assiduously to the investigation of microscopic anatomy. In 1662, upon Borelli's recommendation, he was invited to fill the primary chair in medicine at the University of Messina. Four years later, he returned to Bologna, where a professorship awaited him, to lecture in practical medicine. He held this position with honor for twenty-five years.

Malpighi's greatest contribution to science was his demonstration and description of the capillaries in the lungs. This was the first important discovery made with the aid of the microscope, and it completed Harvey's work on the circulation of blood. These studies were described in two letters to Borelli, who published them as *De pulmonibus observationes anatomicae* (anatomical observations on lungs), in 1661. The lung was thought to be a fleshy organ in which blood and air freely mixed. Working at first on the lungs of dogs, Malpighi determined them to be an aggregate of membranous vesicles (alveoli) opening into the tracheobronchial tree surrounded by a capillary network. Subsequently, he inves-

In addition to the extensive studies of animal anatomy, Malpighi made the structure of the plant the subject of detailed and systematic investigations. In 1675, he published the first part of his *Anatome plantarum* (plant anatomy) and the second part in 1679. This, one of his largest and best monographs, earned for him acclaim, along with Nehemiah Grew, as the founder of the study of plant anatomy. Malpighi used a variety of microscopes and was able to magnify objects up to 143 times. In his investigations of stems, he found tiny ducts that possessed a spiral structure. Because of their resemblance to the tracheae of insects, he incorrectly attributed a respiratory function to them. He discovered stomata on the leaves but was unable to determine their function. In his studies of plant anatomy, Malpighi anticipated, to a certain degree, the cell theory. He described plants as being composed of separate structural units, which he called utricles.

Malpighi devoted special attention to the study of gall formations in several plants. He believed, as did nearly all scientists of his era, that these growths were spontaneous productions. He demonstrated, however, that several galls contained insect larvae. These, in some instances, he traced to an egg and onward to an adult insect. Malpighi's description of the egg-laying apparatus (ovipositor) of the gallflies was so detailed and accurate that it enables modern entomologists to identify the species. His research on plant galls convinced him that they were produced by the action of insects. He also determined that the tubercles on the roots of leguminous plants, which were first described by him, were not caused by insects; he failed, however, to explain their origin.

On February 6, 1684, Malpighi's house caught fire during the night and burned, resulting in the loss of many microscopes, books, research notes, and observations. In subsequent years, he suffered from nephritic and articular pains, and his health continued to decline steadily. In 1691, Malpighi reluctantly accepted an invitation from Pope Innocent XII to become the pope's personal physician in Rome. On October 4 of that year, he left Bologna with his aged wife, a maid, and a servant and moved to Rome. Despite his new position and ill health, he continued his research. On August 11, 1694, his wife and loving companion for twenty-seven years died. Three months later, on November 29, an apoplectic stroke ended Malpighi's life. After his death in Rome, his body was returned to Bologna to be interred with great pomp and ceremony.

SIGNIFICANCE

Malpighi was a physician, an anatomist, an embryologist, a botanist, and a naturalist. He was comparative in his approach and among the first to make use of the microscope. His work on the lungs and the discovery of capillaries explained a major step in the process of respiration. What Harvey had made a logical necessity, Malpighi showed to be a reality. Malpighi made the first microscopic analyses of the structure of the spleen, the kidney, the liver, the tongue, the skin, and the brain. He introduced the use of stains and wax injections in his histological studies. His name has deservedly become an eponym of numerous anatomic structures. His monograph *De bombyce* is an original and important contribution to zoology. Malpighi's study of the embryology of the chick was the best that had yet been made. Although he had no deep interest in causal factors and thus contributed little in this area, his descriptive embryology was masterful. His monograph on plant anatomy was so important for botany that, with the exception of Grew's work, which readily admits Malpighi's priority in several areas, it was not surpassed by a single production during the next 120 years.

Malpighi's career at the University of Bologna is a contrast to that of the scholars who worked at Padua. Bologna was under the jurisdiction of the pope. Literature and ideas were censored, and the Inquisition was ready to investigate serious heresy. The forces of dogmatism were so powerful that anatomical demonstrations and microscopic proof were inadequate to enlighten these opponents of progress. Malpighi, as one who dared to combat the ancient ideas, was confronted with much hostility, yet he triumphed and was recognized as one of the greatest scientists of the seventeenth century.

—*Ralph Troll*

FURTHER READING

Adelmann, Howard B. *Marcello Malpighi and the Evolution of Embryology.* 5 vols. Ithaca, N.Y.: Cornell University Press, 1966. A monumental and definitive work that highlights the major controversies and publications of Malpighi's career and interprets his role in the evolution of embryology.

Cole, F. J. *A History of Comparative Anatomy from Aristotle to the Eighteenth Century.* London: Macmillan, 1949. Reprint. New York: Dover, 1975. An excellent presentation of the works of notable comparative anatomists, including Malpighi.

Foster, Michael. *Lectures on the History of Physiology During the Sixteenth, Seventeenth, and Eighteenth*

Centuries. Cambridge, England: Cambridge University Press, 1901. Nine lectures presenting specific highlights in the history of physiology. Lecture 5 is a superb presentation of Malpighi's life and work, with translations of some of his writings.

Locy, William A. *The Growth of Biology*. New York: Henry Holt, 1925. Contains a well-balanced presentation on Malpighi, with valuable information on his personal qualities, education, university positions, honors received, and research.

Meli, Domenico Bertoloni, ed. *Marcello Malpighi: Anatomist and Physician*. Florence, Italy: L. S. Olschki, 1997. Collection of essays about Malpighi's scientific work, including his use of the microscope and the medical discoveries outlined in his letters to Borelli.

Miall, L. C. *The Early Naturalists, Their Lives and Work, 1530-1789*. London: Macmillan, 1912. Contains biographical information on naturalists of this period, including Malpighi, who is well covered in section 5. Although all of Malpighi's major contributions are described, his work on plant anatomy receives the most extensive coverage.

Nordenskiöld, Erik. *The History of Biology: A Survey*. Translated by Leonard Bucknall Eyre. New York: Tudor, 1928. Still the best one-volume history of the biological sciences, with an emphasis on the philosophical and medical background.

Singer, Charles. *A History of Biology to About the Year 1900*. New York: Abelard-Schuman, 1931. Still one of the best books on the history of biology. A brief but well-balanced account on Malpighi is given in part 2.

Piccolino, Marco. "Marcello Malpighi and the Difficult Birth of Modern Life Sciences." *Endeavour* 23, no. 4 (1999). Focuses on Malpighi's contributions to science, including his pioneering work in microscopic medical anatomy, composition of the human body, and the pathology of diseases.

SEE ALSO: Giovanni Alfonso Borelli; William Harvey; Jan Baptista van Helmont; Robert Hooke; Christiaan Huygens; Antoni van Leeuwenhoek; Santorio Santorio; Nicolaus Steno; Jan Swammerdam.

RELATED ARTICLES in *Great Events from History: The Seventeenth Century, 1601-1700:* 17th century: Advances in Medicine; 1612: Sanctorius Invents the Clinical Thermometer; 1617-1628: Harvey Discovers the Circulation of the Blood; 1660's-1700: First Microscopic Observations; 1672-1684: Leeuwenhoek Discovers Microscopic Life.

MANASSEH BEN ISRAEL
Dutch theologian and scholar

Manasseh ben Israel was instrumental in gaining readmission of the Jews into England, from which they had been expelled in 1290. He was a scholar who wrote theological interpretations of the Bible, and he founded the first Hebrew printing press in the region.

BORN: c. 1604; Island of Madeira, United Provinces (now in the Netherlands)

DIED: November 20, 1657; Middelburg, Zeeland, United Provinces (now in the Netherlands)

ALSO KNOWN AS: Manoel Dias Soeiro (given name)

AREAS OF ACHIEVEMENT: Religion and theology, government and politics, social reform, scholarship, science and technology

EARLY LIFE

The ancestry of Manasseh ben Israel (meh-NAHS-eh behn IHZ-ray-ehl) was Jewish, but for more than a century, his family had lived as Marranos, Jews forcibly converted to Christianity but who secretly maintained a Jewish identity. Manasseh had been baptized as Manoel Dias Soeiro. Manasseh's father, likewise a baptized Marrano, called himself Joseph ben Israel, while Manasseh's mother took the name Rachel. Their children, named for biblical characters, were Esther, Ephraim, and Manasseh. Many of these "secret Jews" had escaped the religious persecution of Spain and Portugal, and immigrated to Amsterdam, where a large Spanish community had developed. It was this climate in which Manasseh was raised.

Jewish education in Amsterdam was noteworthy even by European standards of the time. Manasseh began his study of the Torah at age twelve, and was known as a highly intelligent, if precocious, student. Among his teachers was Isaac Uzziel, formerly the rabbi of Oran, who was a primary rabbi in the Amsterdam community.

Here, Manasseh also was trained in the fluent use of several languages and in the classics. Manasseh's classmates included many who would later become equally prominent in the Jewish community.

By the age of thirteen, Manasseh was invited to become a member of several prominent Yeshivot, academies known for their biblical scholarship. By seventeen, he had written his first book, *Safah berurah* (1621), an unpublished work on grammar. The following year, after the death of Rabbi Uzziel, Manasseh became head of the congregation.

LIFE'S WORK

As head of the congregation Neveh Shalom, Manasseh's duties included serving as an elementary teacher and also teaching the Talmud to fellow scholars. Within two years, he was ordained as a rabbi, probably by his colleague, Saul Levi Mortara. Manasseh's parents lived long enough to witness the honor. During this same period, Manasseh met and married Rachel Abravanel, daughter of a prominent Spanish family that had likewise fled its homeland. Manasseh and Rachel would produce three children, a daughter and two sons.

During this period of significant growth in European Jewry, Manasseh recognized a dependency on foreign printers, principally those in Venice, for the publication of Hebrew texts. In 1626, Manasseh entered a partnership with a Jewish scribe and Gentile craftsperson to prepare the special fonts, and a printing press was placed in his house. It was here that he would eventually publish his works, numbering more than sixty and in several languages. Three Hebrew Bibles were among the printed works. In 1627, the first work Manasseh printed on the press was *Sefer ha-jirah*, a twelfth-thirteenth century work on ethics and ascetics by Rabbi Jonah of Gerona (Jona Gerondi). Manasseh's own first work to be published, *Penei rabbah* (1628), an index to the Midrash Rabbah, was also printed on the new press.

Manasseh addressed many of his writings to a non-Jewish audience specifically, and for a generation, his writings would represent the epitome of Jewish scholarship in their eyes. He spent five years putting together the first section of one of his greatest works, *El conciliador* (1632; *The Conciliator of R. Manasseh ben Israel*, 1842), an attempt to explain a number of biblical passages. The first part was written in both Spanish and Latin, while the remaining three parts appeared only in Spanish (1641-1651).

Several of his philosophical writings, including *De creatione problemata XXX* (1635), *De termino vitae* (1634), and the two-part *De la fragilidad humana* (1642), were soon published. These works, while subtly opposing certain tenets of Christianity, attempted to address aspects of Judaism for a non-Jewish audience.

Manasseh's *Piedra gloriosa, o de la Estatua de Nebuchadnessar* (c. 1655), a commentary on the biblical Book of Daniel, was noteworthy for another reason: its inclusion of four etchings by Rembrandt.

Rembrandt at the time was living in the Jewish quarter of Amsterdam because of financial straits and most likely not because of an affinity with Jews. Rembrandt was interested, however, in depicting prominent Jews for his paintings, and during this thirty-year period, he produced some twenty paintings and etchings. One of these etchings was of Manasseh.

Manasseh ben Israel's role in the readmission of Jews to England could be seen as mutually beneficial. Among the goals of Oliver Cromwell, lord protector of England since 1653, was the expansion of English commerce. He was well aware of the role of Jewish merchants in helping to make several regions and cities on the Continent prosperous, most notably, Amsterdam. The reintroduction of Jewish merchants, including both their capital and their connections, was thought to be vital in the quest to establish a competitive market from London.

At the same time, Manasseh believed that the reintroduction of Jews to England would fulfill the biblical prophecy of the redemption of Israel, a view he described in his treatise *Esperança de Israel* (1650; *The Hope of Israel*, 1650). The thought process was roundabout. In 1641, Antón de Montesinos, a Marrano visitor in South America, reported the presence of Ecuadoran indigenous peoples allegedly descended from the tribes of Reuben and Levi. If this were true, only England would be devoid of Jews. Using the Deuteronomic interpretation that the term "the ends of the Earth" referred to England, Manasseh presented a petition to the English Parliament that readmission of the Jews had messianic implications. Whether for theological or practical reasons, Cromwell recommended the acceptance of Manasseh's petition. The petition, however, was rejected.

In September, 1655, Manasseh appeared before the British Counsel to argue for his petition; it was accepted. In 1657, the first Jewish cemetery and synagogue in four hundred years in England were established. While in England, Manasseh responded to anti-Jewish attacks with his final writing, *Vindiciae judaeorum* (1656; English translation, 1656). That fall, Manasseh returned to the Netherlands, where he soon died.

SIGNIFICANCE

Manasseh ben Israel was one of numerous European scholars of the period whose work emphasized interpretation of Jewish or biblical writings. Most of his writings did not specifically deal with Talmudic interpretations, though he did have training in that area. Rather, he was the first Jewish scholar to provide an outreach to the non-Jewish communities of Spain and Portugal. Much of his later writings were carried out with a specifically Christian audience in mind, and some have named him an "apostle to the Gentiles."

Manasseh was able to bridge the Jewish and Christian communities of Amsterdam, no small achievement given the times. In reality, though, he remained under the suspicion of Christians and Jews; Christians would on occasion disparage his Judaism, while Jews were uneasy with his imparting of Kabbalah to those outside the community.

His friendship with Rembrandt resulted in a famous portrait, while his work with Oliver Cromwell led to the return of Jews to England. The charter of protection granted to Jews in England in 1664 attests to Manasseh ben Israel's influence, even after his death.

—*Richard Adler*

FURTHER READING

Endelman, Todd. *Jews of Modern Britain, 1656-2000*. Berkeley: University of California Press, 2002. The return and resettlement of European Jews to England during the period of Cromwell is the major focus of the beginning portion of this work. While acknowledging a continual presence of Jews throughout the period of expulsion, the author places emphasis on reintegration within English societies in the centuries that followed the return.

Kaplan, Yosef, Henry Mechoulan, and Richard H. Popkin. *Manasseh ben Israel and His World*. Boston: Brill Academic, 1989. A collection of essays on the subject. Discussion of Manasseh's writings in the context of the period's Jewish mysticism and Christian theology.

Roth, Cecil. *A History of the Jews in England*. New York: Oxford University Press, 1964. The Jewish presence in England began with the period of William the Conqueror. The author describes the expulsion of the Jews in 1290, the role of Manasseh in their readmittance some four centuries later, and continues through their legal emancipation in the nineteenth century.

_____. *A Life of Manasseh ben Israel, Rabbi, Printer, and Diplomat*. Philadelphia: Jewish Publication Society, 1934. Remains the classic work on the subject. In addition to biographical information, the author discusses Manasseh in the context of the Christian theology of the period.

Zell, Michael. *Reframing Rembrandt: Jews and the Christian Image in Seventeenth Century Amsterdam*. Berkeley: University of California Press, 2002. Examines the influence of Jewish scholarship on the depiction of biblical themes by artists of the period. Particular emphasis is placed on Manasseh's role on themes depicted by Rembrandt.

SEE ALSO: Oliver Cromwell; Hugo Grotius; Rembrandt; Anna Maria von Schurman; Shabbetai Tzevi.

RELATED ARTICLES in *Great Events from History: The Seventeenth Century, 1601-1700:* 1656-1662: Persecution of Iranian Jews; January, 1665: Shabbetai Tzevi's Messianic Movement Begins.

THE MANCINI SISTERS
Italian noblewomen

The Mancini sisters, whose marriages were carefully arranged by their uncle, France's chief minister Jules Mazarin, played key roles in the social and political dynamics of the royal courts of France and England. Mazarin used his nieces for important political alliances that helped consolidate his power and authority and establish an absolute monarchy in France.

LAURA MANCINI

BORN: 1636; Rome, Papal States (now in Italy)
DIED: February 8, 1657, Paris, France
ALSO KNOWN AS: Laure; Victoria; Duchesse de Mercoeur

OLYMPIA MANCINI

BORN: 1639; Rome, Papal States (now in Italy)
DIED: 1708; Brussels, Spanish Netherlands (now in Belgium)
ALSO KNOWN AS: Olympe; Comtesse de Soissons

MARIE MANCINI

BORN: 1640: Rome, Papal States (now in Italy)
DIED: May 11, 1715: Pisa, Tuscany (now in Italy)
ALSO KNOWN AS: Princess of Colonna

HORTENSE MANCINI

BORN: June 6, 1646; Rome, Papal States (now in Italy)
DIED: July 16, 1699; Chelsea, England
ALSO KNOWN AS: Hortensia; Duchesse de Mazarin

MARIE-ANNE MANCINI

BORN: 1649; Rome, Papal States (now in Italy)
DIED: June 20, 1714; Paris, France
ALSO KNOWN AS: Marianne; Mariana; Duchesse de Bouillon
AREA OF ACHIEVEMENT: Government and politics

EARLY LIVES

When King Louis XIII of France died on May 14, 1643, his five-year-old son Louis XIV became king. Queen Anne of Austria, Louis XIV's mother, became regent, but the person who truly ruled was Cardinal Jules Mazarin, who ran the government until his death in 1661. Mazarin, who had succeeded Cardinal de Richelieu in 1642, was the chief minister of France, the queen's closest adviser, and Louis XIV's mentor.

Mazarin's sister, Girolama Mazarini (1614-1656), had married the Roman nobleman Michele Lorenzo Mancini in 1634. They had five beautiful daughters whom Mazarin would use in political marriages to help consolidate his power and position. The Mancini sisters—Laura, Olympia, Marie, Hortense, and Marie-Anne—were called the Mazarinettes. In 1647, Mazarin began bringing his young nieces from Rome to live in France. First came eleven-year-old Laura and eight-year-old Olympia. The nine-year-old Louis XIV enjoyed their company. The charming sisters also delighted the queen and were popular with the royal court.

There were many suitors for the sisters. In 1649, Laura became engaged to Louis de Bourbon, duke of Vendôme and duke of Mercoeur, and grandson of King Henry IV. When Laura and Louis were married in 1652, she became the duchesse de Mercoeur. Fourteen-year-old Marie and eight-year-old Hortense arrived in France in 1654. Hortense was the cardinal's favorite niece. When she was only ten, Marquis Armand-Charles de La Porte de La Meilleraye asked to marry her, but he rejected the cardinal's counteroffer that he might marry Olympia or Marie. Meanwhile, Louis XIV had become enamored of Olympia. She was his mistress for two years, although both Mazarin and the queen disapproved. Mazarin arranged for Olympia to marry the count of Soissons, Eugène-Maurice de Savoie-Carignan on February 20, 1657. Also in 1657, Louis XIV again fell in love, this time with Marie, who shared her love of books with him. Although never his mistress, Marie was considered his first true love.

LIVES' WORK

There was tragedy in 1657. The oldest Mancini sister, Laura, became paralyzed and died at the age of twenty-one. Her grief-stricken husband entered a monastery and became a cardinal (1667). Of Laura and Louis's two surviving sons, the older son, Louis-Joseph, duke of Vendôme (1654-1712), would become a renowned general and marshal of France.

When Louis XIV became ill and nearly died in 1658, Marie wept constantly at his bedside. After his recovery, Louis asked for permission to marry Marie, but the queen and Mazarin had planned for Louis to marry Marie-Thérèse, the oldest daughter of King Philip IV of Spain.

This matrimonial alliance with Spain occurred on June 9, 1660, concurrent with the Treaty of the Pyrenees (1659). Mazarin sent Marie and Hortense into exile on the Normandy coast. After a farewell meeting, Louis and Marie wrote letters, but she terminated the correspondence in September of 1659.

In 1658, Hortense turned twelve years old, and Mazarin wanted her to marry someone who would abandon his own name and take the Mazarin name, since the cardinal had no heirs. The would-be couple were set to inherit the tremendous Mazarin fortune. The persistent Armand-Charles was agreeable to such terms. However, in 1659, Hortense had a marriage proposal from the exiled Charles II of England. The cardinal rejected Charles's proposal but later offered Hortense when Charles II regained his throne with the Restoration in 1660. Charles II, though, declined this offer.

Mazarin became ill and was dying, so he was quick to arrange a marriage contract between the fifteen-year-old Hortense and the twenty-nine-year-old Armand-Charles; they were married in Paris on March 1, 1661, and became the duke and duchess of Mazarin. In 1666, the couple divorced. In 1675, she settled in London and became a mistress of Charles II, then moved to Chelsea in 1694, lived a life of pleasure-seeking, and died there on July 16, 1699. Hortense and Armand-Charles had one son, but he died without a male heir, so the Mazarin name ultimately became defunct.

Before his death, Mazarin had arranged for Marie to marry Prince Colonna, the grand constable of Naples, and the ceremony took place on April 15, 1661. Marie moved to Rome with Colonna but left her unfaithful husband in 1672 and lived in Spain for two decades until he died. Their three sons then provided an allowance for her, and she died in Pisa in May of 1715.

Olympia and the count de Soissons had three daughters and five sons. The second son, born in 1663, became Prince Eugene, the legendary military hero. Olympia and Marie-Anne were implicated in the so-called Affair of the Poisons, a scandal involving many in King Louis XIV's court. Olympia's husband had died under circumstances that suggested he was poisoned. Allegedly a client of the sorceress Catherine Deshayes, Madame Monvoisin (or La Voisin), Olympia also was suspected of wanting to kill the king's mistress, Françoise-Louise de la Baume Le Blanc de La Vallière (1644-1710). In 1680, Monvoisin was burned as a witch and murderer. Although never formally charged, Olympia had to leave Paris and live the last twenty-eight years of her life in exile. She died in Brussels in 1708.

In 1662, a year after Mazarin died, thirteen-year-old Marie-Anne married Maurice de La Tour, duke of Bouillon, and all four of their sons became soldiers. Marie-Anne had a respected literary salon and was the patron of the celebrated poet Jean De La Fontaine. During the Affairs of the Poisons in 1680, Marie-Anne also was accused of wanting to poison her husband. She was tried and acquitted, but Louis XIV exiled her. She eventually returned to Paris and died there in 1714.

SIGNIFICANCE
The amazing history of the Mancini sisters is an incredible tale of intrigue, power, greed, and love among the nobility and royalty in seventeenth century France and England. The five sisters continue to fascinate historians and readers. Their intricate story combines unrequited love, political marriages, love affairs with kings, military heroes, exiles, and more.

Using his nieces for important political alliances helped Cardinal Mazarin consolidate his power and authority. Mazarin's rule and example enabled Louis XIV to become an absolute monarch after Mazarin's death.

However, the Affairs of the Poisons was a serious scandal for Louis XIV and a significant event in French history. Like the witchcraft trials in Europe and New England during this period, the affair involved accusations, witch-hunts, trials, and executions. Fortune-tellers and sorcerers had become wealthy as they offered their services to the nobility, including members of Louis's court. In addition to Olympia and Marie-Anne, Monvoisin's clientele included the renowned military hero, Marshal Luxembourg, and even Louis's mistress, Madame de Montespan, who had seven children with the king.

The story of the Mancini sisters and their arranged marriages serves as a classic example of the irony of life. In the end, Cardinal Mazarin's name and lineage ended with the death of his favorite niece's son.

—Alice Myers

FURTHER READING
Chapman, Hester W. *Privileged Persons: Four Seventeenth-Century Studies*. New York: Reynal, 1966. The study of Hortense Mancini includes a bibliography of both primary and secondary sources.

Levi, Anthony. *Louis XIV*. New York: Carroll & Graf, 2004. Chapter 5 covers "The Sacre, Marie Mancini and Marriage." Other sections discuss Mazarin, the Poisons Affair, Olympia, and Hortense. Includes illustrations, maps, genealogy, and a chronology.

Mackenzie, Faith. *The Cardinal's Niece: The Story of*

Marie Mancini. New York: Charles Scribner's Sons, 1935. A complete biography of Marie Mancini. Includes a genealogical chart and illustrations.

Mallet-Joris, Francoise. *The Uncompromising Heart: A Life of Marie Mancini, Louis XIV's First Love.* Translated by Patrick O'Brian. New York: Farrar, Straus & Giroux, 1966. This is a long biography based on Marie's own memoirs and letters.

Norton, Lucy. *The Sun King and His Loves.* London: Hamish Hamilton, 1982. Includes the story of Marie Mancini as the king's first love. Illustrated.

Rosvall, Toivo. *The Mazarine Legacy: The Life of Hortense Mancini, Duchess Mazarin.* New York: Viking Press, 1969. This complete biography of Hortense includes accounts of her sisters. Illustrations, a genealogical chart, and bibliography.

Sainte-Beuve, C. A. *Portraits of the Seventeenth Century: Historic and Literary.* New York: Frederick Ungar, 1964. Chapter III is "Cardinal Mazarin and His Nieces." Footnotes and illustrations.

Somerset, Anne. *The Affair of the Poisons.* London: Weidenfeld & Nicholson, 2003. This comprehensive study of the Affair of the Poisons describes Olympia's and Marie-Anne's involvement. Illustrations, extensive notes and bibliography.

Treasure, G. R. R., and Geoffrey Treasure. *Mazarin: The Crisis of Absolutism in France.* New York: Routledge, 1995. This definitive English-language biography of Mazarin has a section about Louis XIV and Marie Mancini. Bibliography and genealogical chart.

Williams, H. Noel. *Five Fair Sisters: An Italian Episode at the Court of Louis XIV.* New York: G. P. Putnam's Sons, 1906. The complete story of the Mancini sisters, with illustrations and footnotes.

SEE ALSO: Anne of Austria; Charles II (of England); Jean de La Fontaine; Louis XIV; Jules Mazarin; Cardinal de Richelieu.

RELATED ARTICLES in *Great Events from History: The Seventeenth Century, 1601-1700:* May 24, 1667-May 2, 1668: War of Devolution; June 2, 1692-May, 1693: Salem Witchcraft Trials.

FRANÇOIS MANSART
French architect

Mansart is generally recognized, along with Louis Le Vau, as one of the two greatest French architects of the seventeenth century and is credited with reviving classicism in French architecture while retaining enough vestiges of the prevailing Gothic to produce buildings that were truly unique.

BORN: January 23, 1598; Paris, France
DIED: September 23, 1666; Paris
ALSO KNOWN AS: François Mansard
AREA OF ACHIEVEMENT: Architecture

EARLY LIFE

In the time of François Mansart (frah-swah mahn-sahrt), individuals who wanted to be architects did not go to school to learn their profession. Rather, they apprenticed to people in the building trades, who were the designers of most new buildings. Mansart was born into a family of carpenters and masons. His father, Absalom Mansart, was the king's carpenter and his mother, Michelle Le Roy, was a sensitive woman of exquisite taste. Mansart began to learn carpentry from his father as soon as he was old enough. When Absalom Mansart died in 1610, the training of his twelve-year-old son fell to the boy's brother-in-law, Germain Gaultier, a sculptor and architect of some repute.

Someone interested in architecture and design could not have been born at a more challenging time. Henry IV, who reigned from 1589 to 1610, sought to enhance the royal revenues by curtailing the extravagant building of palaces that had been going on and by emphasizing building projects that would benefit the people both by employing them in the building trades and by revitalizing Paris.

Henry encouraged members of his court to build country houses, and this encouragement resulted in the emergence of an interesting domestic architecture, designed generally for economy, achieved by a new simplicity of design. On Henry's death, Louis XIII began a thirty-three-year reign that emphasized the building of churches and royal palaces. The Palace of Luxembourg in Paris was completed in 1615, following the design of Salomon de Brosse, with whom François may have served a brief apprenticeship as an adolescent.

Soon Mansart began to work with his mother's brother, Marcel Le Roy, a noted contractor. He presumably worked on site with Le Roy's contracting syndicate when it built a bridge across the River Garonne at Toulouse, and it is thought that Mansart, now around twenty-two, might have designed the bridge's triumphal arch. It is known that, in the same year, his uncle dispatched him to collect some money owed the contracting syndicate by the city of Toulouse.

During his early twenties, Mansart, thin and wiry with sharp features, a long pointed nose, and dark, animated eyes, again represented his uncle's construction syndicate, presenting to the city fathers of Rouen their proposals to build a bridge. Mansart clearly had sufficient aplomb and self-assurance to handle intensive questioning from these burghers, most of them more than twice his age. He obviously controlled enough technical information to explain to them intricate details of the proposed project and to respond effectively to their searching questions. He withstood the most rigorous tests of accountability and was soon widely recognized as someone who understood construction and design well enough to be entrusted with his own commissions.

LIFE'S WORK

Mansart received two of his own commissions around 1623. One was to design the facade of the Church of the Feuillants, later destroyed, in Paris. The other was to remodel the Château de Berny, south of Paris, part of which survives. In that work, he was able to display one of his greatest talents, that of working from the original design of an extant building and, within the structural and physical limitations of that building, to create something unique. Mansart retained the two side pavilions and courtyard of the Château de Berny but added a towering central portion to the plan, linking it with colonnades to the side pavilions and adding a pavilion that contained a remarkably graceful staircase. A portion of one of the side pavilions has survived, but Mansart's plans are preserved in the National Archives in Paris.

In the nearly two decades between 1623 and 1642, Mansart was actively engaged in all sorts of architectural projects, civic, domestic, and ecclesiastical. His Château de Balleroy in Normandy, begun in 1626, survives and reflects the kind of design Mansart favored. Using the native yellow stone of the region as his base, he faced the walls of the château with thin squares of white ashlar, a stone that lends a serenity and dignity to the surface it creates. Like the Château de Berny, Balleroy has a high center structure, in this instance crowned with a cupola. It took more than a decade to complete Balleroy, and by that time Mansart had begun to imbibe the baroque influ-

ence coming to France from Italy, so the central portion of Balleroy and its quadrant colonnades, reminiscent of Berny's, are more ornate.

Mansart provided designs for such ecclesiastical structures in Paris as the high altar in the Church of San Martin des Champs (c. 1625), the Altar of the Virgin in the Cathedral of Nôtre Dame (1628), the Convent of the Visitation (c. 1633), and the Church of the Visitation (c. 1633). During the same period, however, Mansart also engaged in all sorts of secular projects, including such diverse construction or remodeling jobs as the Château de Plessis-Belleville (1628), the Hôtel de l'Aubespine (c. 1630) and the Hôtel de la Vrillière in Paris (c. 1637), an aqueduct for the Château de Limours (1638), and walls around the park of the Château de Chambord (1639). During this period, he was gaining great confidence in his ability to produce fine structures, and he enjoyed a reputation that made him known throughout France. He received more commissions than he could accept.

The self-assurance that had been an asset to Mansart in his twenties was turning into an arrogance that offended many people during this middle period of his life. Jean-Baptiste Colbert, as emissary of Louis XIII, commissioned Mansart to draw plans for an addition to the Louvre. Colbert, knowing that Mansart had a reputation for changing designs and demolishing already completed work to accommodate his changes, stipulated that Mansart could not make changes once his designs were in and construction was begun. Mansart refused the commission, viewing it as an inhibition to his artistic freedom.

Among those willing to tolerate Mansart's arrogance and changeability was René de Longueil, a wealthy merchant, for whom, between 1642 to 1651, Mansart designed and erected the Château de Maisons on the banks of the Seine. This building, which has survived, is one of Mansart's two greatest works, and the only one for which he received full credit. Mansart brilliantly adapted this château to its surroundings. Well into the project, Mansart revised his plans drastically, and all the construction that had been done was torn down so that he could begin again, instituting the new, more imaginative design he had devised. His patron's wealth was sufficient to permit this costly redirection, and apparently de Longueil was willing to bow to Mansart's superior architectural knowledge despite the inordinate cost and unseemly delay it occasioned.

Maisons deviated from Mansart's earlier practice of building a high central portion. The central part of this building and its two wings are of almost equal height except for a small tower and cupola in the central portion. The main building itself is starkly classical, its pilasters unadorned. Two courts in front of the building are surrounded by a dry moat, and a substantial terrace extends to the river front.

The pitch of the roofs and the chimney stacks are adaptations of the Gothic architecture that prevailed in France during the preceding century. The château is known for its gracefully dramatic staircase, a hallmark of Mansart's domestic architecture. As the early Greeks had done in the Parthenon, Mansart used optical illusion and slight distortion to create proportion in the eyes of those who beheld the building from ground level.

Mansart's other truly great project was the palace, convent, and Church of the Val-de-Grâce in Paris, begun in 1644. The work was commissioned by the Queen Mother, Anne of Austria, widow of Louis XIII. Mansart's plans for this vast project were highly elaborate and imaginative. His concern was with the creation of beauty in its purest form. He viewed money merely as a necessary commodity to be provided by his patrons in whatever quantity his extravagant plans demanded.

The Queen Mother was a frugal woman, too timid to lock horns directly with Mansart, who was something of a bully, intolerant of artistic opinions save his own. After putting up with Mansart's antics for more than a year, the Queen Mother in 1646 replaced him quietly with Jacques Lemercier. By this time, the foundation was laid and considerable progress had been made toward completing the church. When Lemercier took over, he scrapped most of Mansart's plans, although the church definitely reflects Mansart's genius. The palace plans were completely redone; Lemercier's palace is a more pedestrian building than the church.

Mansart lived for another twenty years, his fortunes now in decline, largely because of his cantankerous personality. His reputation for artistic excellence remained unsullied, but commissions were scarce. He continued to work on projects, few of them executed, and those few were usually for remodeling jobs or for funerary monuments.

SIGNIFICANCE

Mansart was almost too large for life. He had colossal ideas that captured the imaginations of the rich. When he was able to capture the purses of the rich as well, he could bring these ideas to fruition spectacularly. When he could not do so, he was incapable of compromise and resorted to tactics that made people avoid him. Mansart is often credited with having invented a roof that bears a corruption of his surname, mansard. Actually, this type of roof, common in much modern domestic architecture, existed before Mansart's time. He employed variations of it in some of his châteaus, but he cannot be credited with its invention.

When the famed British architect Christopher Wren visited France in 1665, the year before London's great fire, he visited Mansart and expressed his admiration for and appreciation of Mansart's contributions to classical French architecture. Techniques Mansart used in the Church of the Val-de-Grâce, particularly in the dome, show up in St. Paul's Cathedral in London, for which Wren was chief architect. Mansart's great-nephew, Jules Hardouin-Mansart, adopted Mansart's surname and went on to become a famous architect in the last half of the seventeenth century. His most famous design was the palace at Versailles.

—*R. Baird Shuman*

FURTHER READING

Arts Council of Great Britain. *François Mansart, 1598-1666.* London: Author, 1970. This brief pamphlet offers highlights of Mansart's life and professional career, pictures of some of his buildings, and copies of some of his architectural plans. Allan Braham and Peter Smith contribute biographical notes, and the chronology is useful.

Blunt, Anthony F. *Art and Architecture in France, 1500 to 1700.* Baltimore, Md.: Penguin Books, 1953. Blunt makes pertinent comments about Mansart's contributions to French architecture, identifying him as one of the two greatest French architects of the first half of the seventeenth century. The section on Mansart, although only twenty pages long, is accurate and informative.

_____. *François Mansart and the Origins of French Classical Architecture.* London: Warburg Institute, 1941. The first full treatment of François Mansart in English, the book is rich in information, examining Mansart against the larger backdrop of French classical architecture. Blunt's book remains an authoritative source for the study of Mansart and his work.

Braham, Allan, and Peter Smith. *François Mansart.* London: A. Zwemmer, 1973. Braham and Smith present a full treatment of Mansart, replete with illustrations. A valuable adjunct to Blunt's earlier work, this book fully discusses each of Mansart's major works and provides valuable information about the plans of those buildings that have not survived.

Watterson, Joseph. *Architecture: A Short History.* Rev.

ed. New York: W. W. Norton, 1968. Although Watterson devotes only a few pages to Mansart, his comments are serviceable, offering insights into Mansart's most important buildings. Also provides a social commentary that places Mansart in the political milieu in which he functioned professionally.

SEE ALSO: Anne of Austria; Jean-Baptiste Colbert; Louis XIV; Sir Christopher Wren.
RELATED ARTICLES in *Great Events from History: The Seventeenth Century, 1601-1700:* 1673: Renovation of the Louvre; 1682: French Court Moves to Versailles.

JULES HARDOUIN-MANSART
French architect

Hardouin-Mansart contributed extensively to French architecture and city planning during the reign of Louis XIV, especially in designing and in altering the huge complex of Versailles Palace and its environs. His further legacy included training architects, sculptors, stonecutters, Gobelin tapestry weavers, porcelain specialists, and crystal cutters. From his architectural achievements emerged a more beautiful Paris and Versailles.

BORN: c. April 16, 1646; Paris, France
DIED: May 11, 1708; Marly-le-Roi, France
ALSO KNOWN AS: Jules Hardouin (given name)
AREAS OF ACHIEVEMENT: Architecture, education

EARLY LIFE

Jules Hardouin Mansart (zheuhl ahr-dwah mahn-sahrt), Mansart being the name he took in 1668, was born into a family that produced architects, artisans, and artists for generations. He is often mistaken by the casual reader for his great-uncle François Mansart, a formidable architect whose building designs reflect classicism. Because Jules's early years were spent in François Mansart's household, he was taught architecture by his great-uncle and imbued with his bias. He was also trained in drawing by C. Poerson. François Mansart hosted famous statesmen and architects such as Jean-Baptiste Colbert, a virtual dictator of the arts, as well as an important governmental figure, André Le Nôtre, Louis Le Vau, and Libéral Bruant. Hardouin was thus influenced by such men of distinction.

Hardouin was one of four children—the third child and the second of three sons. His father held the position of first painter in the cabinet of the king. The Mansarts descended from artisans in Italy (the Mensartos), who had gravitated to France at the beginning of the French Renaissance. In 1556 their name appeared as Hardouyn. By the time of François Mansart's death in 1666, Jules (then twenty years old) had been directly influenced in

architecture by his great-uncle, but at the same time he developed his own métier. Hardouin inherited not only his great-uncle's drawings and papers but also his considerable fortune. Among the inherited papers were designs that had been commissioned by the king but not used, although the king technically was still privy to them. Two years later, Hardouin married Anne Bodin; the couple had five children: three girls and two boys. His own sons became the fathers of architects. That year, Hardouin took his great-uncle's surname, Mansart.

Louis XIV, the Sun King, ascended the throne at age four in 1643 and had one of the longest reigns in French history. Mansart's professional life was inextricably associated with this monarch. The king presided over a virtual bureaucratic stronghold in business and also in all the arts. To survive, let alone to prosper, under Louis XIV, an aspirant needed to subscribe at least partly to his vagaries. The king's goal in the arts was to revive classic expression filtered through the French spirit. Scholars are in agreement that during Louis's reign the thrust of the arts was to compete with Periclean Athens and Augustan Rome. The arts did flourish, and dozens of brilliant people emerged in this era—Jean-Baptiste Colbert, Molière, Pierre Corneille, Claude Lorrain, Jean Racine, and Jean-Baptiste Lully, among many others. Mansart joined these luminaries in his eventual appointment as architect in chief to the court; Versailles is invariably linked with the name and the work of this architect.

At age twenty-four, Mansart assisted the work in progress on the Hôtel des Invalides, the modern tomb of Napoleon. By that time, he had already designed a number of buildings and the next year was at work in a limited position at Versailles. Four years later, Colbert, the minister and financier of the court, recognized the talents of Mansart and gave him the opportunity to design the Château de Clagny, in the forest of Saint Germain, belonging to Madame de Montespan, the king's favorite. This celebrated and headstrong beauty of royal blood, who was aggressive and ambitious, convinced the king of the importance of architecture as a metaphor of royal power. It is believed that because of her influence, Louis arranged for royal commissions of extravagant and ornate designs, a practice that continued throughout much of his reign. Mansart's first royal commission to build the Château de Clagny was fortuitous for his career, but his architectural initiative was always to be narrowed by the demands of royal edict. This limitation consigned Mansart to following plans that interfered with a level of his creative development. Colbert continued to be closely affiliated with Mansart; at age twenty-nine, the architect was pressed by Colbert into membership in the Academy of Architecture, a highly conservative group. Soon afterward, Mansart was introduced to the king and given the remarkable commission of designing and building huge additions to Versailles, plans that were often structured by Louis XIV. Mansart was then only thirty years old.

LIFE'S WORK

Mansart is closely associated with the additions to Versailles, both interior and exterior, which became his main preoccupation from 1678 until his death. At his death, he was held to be the undisputed main architect of Louis's kingdom. His impact on the design and execution of Versailles' development is greater than any other architect's work. During his tenure there, significant and stunning designs were executed, including the great forecourt, the Hall of Mirrors, and the horsehoe-shaped stables (for approximately six hundred horses and equipage), which formed part of the entrance design. Numerous additions to the principal facade contributed to the splendor of Versailles: the central block of the garden facade, two sprawling wings that extended the main structure to 1,935 feet, and the Hall of Mirrors (which remains one of the favorite apartments of visitors). Specialists and tourists also delight in the orangerie. Mansart was also involved in the design of the Grand Trianon and the charming *buffet d'eau* fountain, as well as with the Parish Church of Versailles. Although built from his plans, the church was not completed until after Mansart's death.

Mansart, who was inundated with commissions while architect at Versailles, also designed the impressive châteaus at Saint Cyr and Marly-le-Roi. The aqueducts and waterworks of Marly-le-Roi are also the inspiration of Mansart. Paris is studded with his monuments, considered outstanding by architects the world over—the Place des Victoires (where only remnants are visible), the Dome des Invalides, and the Place Vendôme, which re-

mains one of the most impressive squares in all Europe. What is notable about the Place Vendôme is the design, in which the interior angles are limited. The use of space hems in the square without distracting from the central axis. Art critic Anthony Blunt suggested that it is a Baroque concept with details of classicism.

Mansart garnered most of all the possible honors during his mature years. In 1683, he was ennobled; ten years later, he was made comte de Sagonne; and at age fifty-three he was given the post of *superintendant des bâtiments du roi*. Unlike his great-uncle François Mansart, he worked within the limitations of the king's wishes, and he was rewarded with honors and money. By age fifty-nine, he ranked as one of the most influential people in the court and held the post of cabinet minister.

Apart from his work on official monuments, buildings, and Parisian palaces, Mansart also worked on town houses. His designs altered the appearances of town houses to make them seem more informal, light, and cozy. He diversified the shaping of rooms, made frequent use of mirrors, and adopted a lightness and elegance of decorative line. With his design of the Hôtel de Noailles at Saint Germain, he developed a new horizontality. These same effects are noted in the Hôtel de Lorges, the

Jules Hardouin-Mansart. (Library of Congress)

Convent des Recollets, and in his own magnificent *maison* in the rue des Tournelles. The Palais Royale was redesigned, and, in conjunction with A. J. Gabriel, he made additions to the Pont Royal.

Having achieved eminence as a result of his architecture and his influence through the teaching and the training of many artisans, Mansart was the subject of many paintings and sculptures. In one engraving, Mansart is depicted with a strapping physique, his huge, curly periwig framing a large face with a dimpled chin and broad brows, his observant eyes staring with a calm assurance. After his death at age sixty-two, Mansart was interred in his own parish of Saint-Paul, with a Latin epitaph stating that he had influenced architects, sculptors, painters, and ornamentalists.

SIGNIFICANCE

Mansart is not definitely associated with any particular school of architecture. Certainly, he worked in the Palladian school (a revival classic style based on the works of Andrea Palladio). Accomplished at composition, adept at managing proportion and scale, Mansart designed the wondrous Hall of Mirrors at Versailles, the Grand Trianon, and the stables. The Place Vendôme near the Louvre remains the quintessential Parisian square. Typical of Mansart's period is the elevation in his structures, his capacity for good massing (like that of his greatuncle) reflected in the Dome des Invalides, which is freestanding. This monument is notable because of the baroque energy of the lines, which virtually dance to the very top of the dome. Such an effect is characterized by some historians as a main sign of seventeenth century architecture.

Centuries after Mansart's death, much evaluation still needs to be done to determine his architectural niche. Because he was deluged with commissions, both royal and private, he catered to many of the preconceived ideas and styles of his monarch and his patrons. Often he was too pressed to be discriminating, and thus, according to some critics, elements of his work suffer because of an architectural eclecticism. He is denounced for ruining Le Vau's Ionic order on the principal story of Versailles, which looked "mean" when the pattern was repeated over the six hundred yards of the extended front.

Mansart's influence is far-reaching because of his training of architects and allied artisans, his work with city planning, and his reorganization of the Royal Academy. Even Thomas Jefferson's Monticello, some insist, bears the stamp of Mansart's inspiration. Some French writers and historians believe that Mansart has not received the recognition that he deserves; others deem that he has been overpraised. Still, Versailles clearly reflects his influence in the second stage of redesigning and rebuilding, and it is significant, indicating the unlimited resources of the architect. Paris, too, reveals the treasures of Mansart's work in architecture, gardening design, and the arts, a distinct contribution to the enrichment of Western civilization.

—Julia B. Boken

FURTHER READING

Berger, Robert W. *A Royal Passion: Louis XIV as a Patron of Architects*. New York: Cambridge University Press, 1994. Explains how Louis assumed the role of builder prince, commissioning buildings to emulate and surpass the glory of ancient Rome. Surveys the work of Mansart and other architects who designed buildings for the Sun King.

Blunt, Anthony. *Art and Architecture in France, 1500 to 1700*. Baltimore, Md.: Penguin Books, 1953. Gives a succinct yet detailed overview of history, politics, and architecture during the life of Mansart, including the influence of the Cardinal de Richelieu, Cardinal Jules Mazarin, and Colbert. Particular emphasis is placed on the work of Mansart at Versailles and on his other designs in Paris and throughout France.

Braham, Allan, and Peter Smith. *François Mansart*. London: A. Zwemmer, 1973. An exhaustive study of the great-uncle of Mansart. Examines François Mansart's designs of town houses and drawings for the Louvre and his significant influence on his greatnephew.

Cronin, Vincent. *Louis XIV*. London: Collins, 1964. This biography of the Sun King provides a context for the life and work of Mansart. Material on Madame Athénaïs de Montespan and Colbert is informative and amusing.

Kalnein, Wend von. *Architecture in France in the Eighteenth Century*. Translated by David Britt. New Haven, Conn.: Yale University Press, 1995. Two chapters in this book provide information about Mansart's work and influence on eighteenth century architects.

Mitford, Nancy. *The Sun King: Louis XIV at Versailles*. New York: Harper & Row, 1966. A lively, well-illustrated book containing valuable information on Louis and devoting ample attention to the genius and contributions of Mansart. Emphasizes the solid reputation of Mansart, after which he was given the challenge and responsibility of a major overhauling and additional architectural design of Versailles.

Van Derpool, James Grote. *Jules Hardouin-Mansart.* New Haven, Conn.: Connecticut Society of Civil Engineers, 1947. Gives an overview of Mansart, who, Van Derpool says, determined the character of French architecture during Louis XIV's reign. Provides a basic discussion of the techniques of architecture and Mansart's contributions.

SEE ALSO: Claude Lorrain; Jean-Baptiste Colbert; Pierre Corneille; Louis Le Vau; Louis XIV; Jean-Baptiste Lully; Jules Mazarin; Molière; Jean Racine; Cardinal de Richelieu.
RELATED ARTICLE in *Great Events from History: The Seventeenth Century, 1601-1700:* 1682: French Court Moves to Versailles.

MARIA CELESTE
Italian nun

Maria Celeste, daughter of Galileo, lived a life of poverty, prayer, and solitude as a nun and is remembered primarily for her correspondence with her father. More than one hundred of her letters survive, although her father's replies have not. The letters reveal a loving daughter who provided encouragement and assistance to Galileo in areas ranging from domestic affairs to religion and science.

BORN: August 12, 1600; Padua, Republic of Venice (now in Italy)
DIED: April 2, 1634; Arcetri, Republic of Florence (now in Italy)
ALSO KNOWN AS: Virginia Galilei (given name); Maria Celeste Galilei
AREAS OF ACHIEVEMENT: Religion and theology, science and technology

EARLY LIFE

Maria Celeste (seh-LEHST), given the name Virginia at birth, was the first child of Italian physicist and astronomer Galileo. According to the baptismal notice in the parish registry of San Lorenzo in Padua, Virginia, who was named after Galileo's sister, was listed as the daughter of Marina Gamba from Venice, "born of fornication" (out of wedlock), with no mention of her father. When Virginia was born, Marina was twenty-two and Galileo was thirty-six. Galileo never married, but he fathered three children, all born to Marina.

After teaching mathematics for three years at the University of Pisa, Galileo accepted the chair of mathematics at the University of Padua in 1592. His twelve-year relationship with Marina began in Padua, although she lived in Venice where he would visit her by ferry on the weekends. When she became pregnant, he moved her to a small house in Padua, about five minutes walk from his house. Like most professors at the time, he rented out rooms to his students and was expected to remain single.

Two more children followed: Livia in August, 1601, named after another sister of Galileo; and Vincenzio in August, 1606, named after Galileo's father. In 1609, when Virginia was still a child in Padua, her father began his pioneering work with the telescope, including one that he set up in the garden behind his house. There is no evidence of any formal schooling for Virginia, but she probably was tutored by her father and later by his mother.

After his discoveries with the telescope, Galileo was invited to Florence in 1610 as court philosopher and mathematician to the grand duke of Tuscany, Cosimo II de' Medici. His two daughters joined him there, all staying with his mother until a rented house became available. Little Vincenzio remained with his mother, who then married a respectable citizen with Galileo's approval and his continued support for Vincenzio. By 1613, Galileo came under increasing attacks for his support of Copernican theory. About the same time, he received a special dispensation for twelve-year-old Livia and thirteen-year-old Virginia to be admitted into the nearby convent of San Matteo in Arcetri, even though they were still too young to take their vows.

LIFE'S WORK

Following the Rule of Saint Clare, Virginia and Livia had their hair shaven and they donned the dark brown religious habits worn in the Franciscan order. The decision to cloister one's daughters was not unusual in seventeenth century Italy, especially since Galileo knew that their illegitimacy would make it difficult for them to get married. The city of Florence alone had fifty-three convents and some four thousand nuns. The work of a nun was held in high honor and viewed as valuable for leading prayer vigils, much of which was done during the plague, as which was requested by the Florentine magistracy of public health.

Three years later, on the feast day of Saint Francis of Assisi, October 4, 1616, Galileo heard his elder daughter profess her vows at the convent of San Matteo, where she remained for the rest of her life. At this ceremony, Virginia took the name Suor (sister) Maria Celeste, an obvious reference to her father's fascination with the celestial realm of the planets. One year later, after Livia reached her sixteenth year, she took the name Suor Arcangela. As members of the Poor Clares order of the Franciscan nuns, they were committed to lives of seclusion, prayer, and poverty.

In 1617, Galileo moved to a hilltop villa overlooking Florence, with a view of Arcetri to the east, where his daughters were cloistered within the walls of the San Matteo convent. The first of Maria Celeste's surviving letters is dated May 10, 1623, the day after the funeral of Galileo's sister Virginia, offering her condolences and assuring him of her prayers. Over the next ten years, her frequent letters reveal the human dimensions of Galileo's most turbulent years in his struggle with religious authorities. In contrast with his strange, silent second daughter, the letters of Maria Celeste reveal a kindred spirit with Galileo, a confidante reflecting his brilliance, sensibility, and industry. Maria Celeste remained devoted to her father even as he grew older, suffered from increased illness, and faced increased conflict with the Holy Office of the Inquisition.

In the convent, Maria Celeste exercised the gifts that characterized her talented family. She often directed the choir, teaching the novices how to sing Gregorian chant. She was probably apprenticed as an apothecary by the nuns and visiting doctors at the convent's infirmary. In this capacity, she assisted the doctors, produced pills and tonics to remedy diseases, and nursed sick nuns in the infirmary, including her often ill sister Arcangela. She also attended to her father's many ailments, sending him her handmade medicines with ingredients such as dried rhubarb, saffron, aloe, and rose water. She even responded to his domestic needs, washing his collars and caring for his wardrobe. Galileo responded by sending gifts of food and money to the convent, and he even wrote a play for the nuns to use in recreation.

In Maria Celeste's letters (translated in full in *Letters to Father*, 2001), there is little discussion of astronomy or physics, but she does remind Galileo when he forgets to send a telescope he had promised. The letters do reveal her interest in his books and raise questions about his work. In 1629, as Galileo was completing his infamous and controversial book, *Dialogo sopra i due massimi sistemi del mondo, tolemaico e copernicano* (1632; *Dia-*logue Concerning the Two Chief World Systems, Ptolemaic and Copernican*, 1661), she assisted him in copying his draft manuscript in her perfect penmanship, providing corrections and additions in preparation for publication. When the book was soon condemned and banned, she still provided encouragement and support. She never suggests in the letters that her father's science was inappropriate or that his accusers were right. In fact, she encourages him with news that her fellow nuns support her faith in his cause.

In 1631, Maria Celeste learned that a villa adjacent to the convent was for sale and Galileo was able to secure it for the last twelve years of his life, most of it under house arrest. When he was finally summoned to Rome in 1633, Galileo authorized Maria Celeste to assume control of his personal and household affairs. After his condemnation, part of Galileo's punishment was to perform penance by reciting the seven penitential psalms once a week for three years. In August of 1633, Maria Celeste informed him that she was able to substitute herself to do this penance. During this period, she suffered from increasing ill health, but was encouraged by daily visits from her father. After a rapid decline from dysentery, Maria Celeste died on April 2, 1634.

SIGNIFICANCE

The life and letters of Maria Celeste reveal an inspiring example of religious commitment and service by a humble and isolated nun. They illuminate the religious life and the role of convents in seventeenth century Italy, and they show a variety of personal responses to difficult circumstances. The encouragement and assistance provided by Maria Celeste to her father played an important role in his daily life and in his scientific contributions. They demonstrate how religion can inspire science, and how science can inspire religion, regardless of conflicts and contradictions.

The letters also shed new light on the complex personality and work of Galileo. The human side of Galileo is made clear in a new way, including his dedication to his children and his devotion to the Church in spite of conflicting ideas. The letters illuminate one of the most important decades in the history of science, filling in new details in the effort to establish a new view of the universe and the religious struggle that followed.

—*Joseph L. Spradley*

FURTHER READING

Allan-Olney, Mary. *The Private Life of Galileo, Compiled Principally from His Correspondence and That of His Eldest Daughter, Sister Maria Celeste*. London: Macmillan, 1870. This biography of Galileo is based on the first English translations of the letters of Maria Celeste by the author, who provides selected excerpts.

Fermi, Laura, and Gilberto Bernardini. *Galileo and the Scientific Revolution*. New York: Basic Books, 1961. This work contains a short chapter entitled "Father and Daughter," describing the relationship between Maria Celeste and Galileo.

Sobel, Dava. *Galileo's Daughter: A Historical Memoir of Science, Faith, and Love*. New York: Walker, 1999. This bestselling biography of Galileo and Maria Celeste is based on original translations of the letters of Maria Celeste by the author, about two dozen of which are included in this work.

_____, trans. *Letters to Father: Suor Maria Celeste to Galileo (1623-1633)*. New York: Walker, 2001. This book, with a helpful introduction, contains 124 surviving letters of Maria Celeste in both the original Italian and English translation on facing pages. Occasional annotations accompany the translations.

SEE ALSO: Cosimo II de' Medici; Galileo.

RELATED ARTICLES in *Great Events from History: The Seventeenth Century, 1601-1700:* 1610: Galileo Confirms the Heliocentric Model of the Solar System; 1632: Galileo Publishes *Dialogue Concerning the Two Chief World Systems, Ptolemaic and Copernican.*

MARIE DE L'INCARNATION
French mystic and educator

After her conversion at age twenty-one, Marie de l'Incarnation embarked for Canada, where she founded an Ursuline teaching convent. She wrote an autobiography, letters, treatises, and Indian-French dictionaries, all of which contain aspects of social history neglected by her male counterparts. Her stature in the colony was so high that she could negotiate power with Jesuits and bishops and achieve a freedom of activity unknown to most women of the time.

BORN: October 28, 1599; Tours, France
DIED: April 30, 1672; Quebec, New France (now in Canada)
ALSO KNOWN AS: Marie Guyart (given name); Mary of the Incarnation; Marie Guyard
AREAS OF ACHIEVEMENT: Religion and theology, education, women's issues

EARLY LIFE

Marie de l'Incarnation (mah-ree deh lahn-kahr-nah-syohn), the fourth of eight children born to a master baker and his wife, was given the name Marie Guyart at birth. She was educated in a school for artisans' children. Marie experienced her first vision at age seven and asked her parents to allow her to enter the Benedictine order at age fourteen, but her mother felt she was unsuited for the cloister.

At age seventeen, she was married to silk-weaver Claude Martin. The marriage was ill-fated, for Martin was involved in a love affair with another woman. Upon Martin's death two years later, litigation forced his business into bankruptcy. At nineteen, Marie was left penniless with a young son, also named Claude. From a small room atop her father's house, she embroidered to earn money. She refused remarriage, saying later how grateful she had been that she was free, with only God in her heart.

On the Feast of the Incarnation, March 24, 1620, Marie had a life-changing experience. Walking through the streets of Tours, she lost consciousness and experienced a vision of the Precious Blood of Jesus. When she regained consciousness in the convent of the Feuillants, she explained that she had seen herself bathed in the blood of Jesus. She found her first spiritual directors at the convent, who encouraged and guided her in reading works by Saint Teresa of Ávila and Francis de Sales. Her eucharistic devotion was matched only by austerities such as fasting and mortification. In the next decade of her life, Marie received further visions. She traced her mission to Canada to these early revelations.

When, in 1625, her sister and brother-in-law asked for help running their business, Marie became its manager, using talents she had learned earlier. Her practical skills, ranging from bookkeeping to horse grooming to carpentry would later benefit the fledgling Ursuline convent in Quebec.

LIFE'S WORK

In the years following, Marie's piety intensified until, in January of 1631, she joined the Ursuline order of Tours, leaving her eleven-year-old son in her father's care. Adopting the name Marie de l'Incarnation because of her devotion to the Word Incarnate, she served as assistant mistress of novices and later mistress of the boarders. In 1634, she took formal vows in the presence of her still-unforgiving son Claude.

Jesuits were frequent preachers at the convent. Marie learned about the mission in Canada by reading *Jesuit Relations*. In a vision, she saw herself walking in a "strange and difficult land," which both she and her spiritual director recognized as Canada. From 1635, her goal was to teach and evangelize the indigenous peoples of New France. Two years later, she and another Ursuline left for Paris, where preparations for the voyage began. In 1639, Marie made the acquaintance of the noblewoman Madame de la Peltrie, who offered herself as well as her wealth for the mission. In May, 1639, Marie sailed from Dieppe with a group of Jesuit monks and nuns. Not without misgivings, the Jesuit fathers recognized the need both for lay and religious women in the colony, understanding that in the education of girls, more indigenous peoples would be converted to the faith.

The colony in which they landed in August of 1639 contained fewer than three hundred inhabitants. After she disembarked and kissed the earth, Marie and the others were led to the church of Nôtre-Dame de Recouvrance, where a Te Deum of praise was sung. While their convent was being constructed, Marie and the nuns were given tours of Quebec as well as the Jesuits' Algonquian mission upstream at Sillery. Marie described their temporary lodgings as a contrast to the cloister that would soon be imposed: "the house never emptied out." By August 7, their convent, consisting of an attic, two rooms, and a cellar, was completed with the help of the nuns who had fetched stones, pushed wheelbarrows, and laid bricks. Only then was cloister imposed. As the convent's first Mother Superior, Marie used the skills learned early in life for building, hauling lumber, painting, and cooking, as well as taking care of personnel and financial matters. By 1645, the Jesuit Jerôme Lalemant drew up a constitution governing the Ursulines, which allowed them independence of the mother house in Tours and freedom to adapt to local necessities.

Even as they began teaching, other challenges confronted the Ursulines, including epidemics of smallpox, Iroquois attacks, and fire. The great fire that destroyed the Ursuline convent in 1650 provided another opportunity to break free of the constraints placed on sisters in the Old World. Although the house was rebuilt with amazing speed, Marie and the nuns took the opportunity

to tour the Jesuit house, the parish church, and the fortress.

Originally intended for indigenous girls, the convent's instruction in basic Christianity, prayer, devotions, and French language soon were in high demand, and indigenous men also would come to the convent grille for instruction and food. Later, daughters of French settlers would be educated there as well.

Marie began writing to her son Claude soon after her arrival. Claude, who would enter the Benedictine order at Marie's request, served as a conduit for her writings, giving them the weight of religious authority. At his request, Marie wrote her autobiography, hundreds of letters (270 of which are still extant), and some of the *Jesuit Relations*. She also composed catechisms, devotional works, and dictionaries in Algonquian, Huron, and Iroquois, works now lost. Her writings describe aspects of indigenous life thought irrelevant by the Jesuits. Most of the indigenous peoples would return to their native ways, but Marie rejoiced in some shining examples of conversion.

The last two decades of Marie's life in Canada saw the slow growth of the Ursuline mission, which had twenty-three members by her death, including some of the daughters of colonists. Marie also raised funds by writing to devout women in France. While her years in France had conformed to many of the stereotypes expected of religious women during the Catholic Reformation, including obedience, mysticism, mortifications, and ill health, the conditions in New France allowed for a more assertive female spirituality that demanded physical health and active (if cloistered) involvement in colonial affairs. In 1668, she expressed her anger about rumors that her order was useless. She complained that if the Ursulines were "useless" because they received little mention in the *Jesuit Relations*, then so too were the Sulpicians, the Hospital Canonesses, and the Jesuits themselves, all of whom together formed the backbone of the new land. She also took on Bishop François Laval, who tried to change the constitution drawn up earlier by Father Lalement. Realizing that his changes would undermine their authority, Marie wrote to the superior in Tours that they would accept his changes only if forced to. Her will was sufficiently strong, so that in 1662, Laval officially recognized the rule and constitutions of the Ursulines of Quebec.

By her death in 1672, Marie had fulfilled her dreams of a promised land full of possibility, not only for those she helped educate but also for herself and her nuns, who were able to break free of the many restraints imposed on religious women and live an "active" spirituality. In her writings, Marie compared herself to a bird that had learned to fly.

SIGNIFICANCE

As spiritual leader, business manager, teacher, and fundraiser, Marie de l'Incarnation guided the Ursuline community in Quebec in spite of the harsh climate, fire, attacks by indigenous peoples, and official interference. In her authorship of sacred works and dictionaries in Iroquois, Algonquian, and Huron, she taught the indigenous peoples and aided the Jesuits. Increasingly, the Ursulines also taught the daughters of French settlers, some of whom later joined the order.

Marie's autobiography, treatises and letters provide insights into life in early New France that are often missing from the traditional male sources, such as the *Jesuit Relations*. The first Mother Superior of the Ursulines of Quebec, Marie used her authority in a "new world" setting to resist the impositions increasingly placed on female religious in Europe and helped cultivate life in the colony.

—Larissa Juliet Taylor

FURTHER READING

Bruneau, Marie-Florine. *Women Mystics Confront the Modern World: Marie de l'Incarnation, 1599-1672, and Madame Guyon, 1648-1717.* Albany: State University of New York Press, 1998. Studies how Marie manipulated her gendered experiences in ways different from those expected in Catholic Reformation France. Bruneau argues that the mortification, sickness, and mysticism of Marie's French life hindered in Canada, where strength, business acumen, and intelligence were highly valued. Includes notes and a bibliography.

Choquette, Leslie, "Ces Amazones du Grand Dieu: Women and Mission in Seventeenth-Century Canada." *French Historical Studies* 17 (1992): 627-655. Examines how early French religious and lay women fought for the right to teach, catechize, and minister in Canada despite official discouragement. In the process, they created a strong presence in the early years of the colony. Includes notes.

Davis, Natalie Zemon. *Women on the Margins: Three Seventeenth-Century Lives.* Cambridge, Mass.: Harvard University Press, 1995. Davis explores how three women, removed from centers of political power and education, were able to push the boundaries normally imposed on women to reach beyond. Includes extensive notes.

Mahoney, Irene. *Marie of the Incarnation: Selected Writings.* New York: Paulist Press, 1989. An excellent selection of Marie's writings. Includes an extensive bibliography and notes.

Parkman, Francis. *The Jesuits in North America in the Seventeenth Century.* Vol. 2 in *France and England in North America.* Reprint. Lincoln: University of Nebraska Press, 1997. Vividly recounts the efforts of the Jesuits in New France.

Thwaites, Reuben Gold, ed. *The Jesuit Relations and Allied Documents.* 73 vols. Cleveland, Ohio: Burrows Brothers, 1896-1901. The definitive source for documents of the Jesuit missions.

SEE ALSO: Samuel de Champlain; Saint Isaac Jogues; François Laval; Jacques Marquette.

RELATED ARTICLES in *Great Events from History: The Seventeenth Century, 1601-1700:* March 15, 1603-December 25, 1635: Champlain's Voyages; 1611-1630's: Jesuits Begin Missionary Activities in New France; May, 1642: Founding of Montreal; December, 1678-March 19, 1687: La Salle's Expeditions.

MARIE DE MÉDICIS
Queen dowager and regent of France (r. 1610-1617)

Marie de Médicis ruled France as regent for her young son, the future king Louis XIII, during which time she promoted her own pro-Catholic policies and secured alliances with Spain, actions that alienated her son and the French people. In keeping with her Italian Medici family heritage, Marie spent lavishly on artistic and architectural commissions, many of which serve as hallmarks of the baroque style.

BORN: April 26, 1573; Florence (now in Italy)
DIED: July 3, 1642; Cologne (now in Germany)
AREAS OF ACHIEVEMENT: Art, patronage of the arts, government and politics

EARLY LIFE

Marie de Médicis (mah-ree deh-may-dee-sees) was born at the height of the Early Renaissance. As the daughter of Grand Duke Francesco de' Medici of Tuscany and Archduchess Joanna of Austria, the young Marie was raised in the privilege and splendor of the Medici courts. After her mother died in 1578, her father remarried and sent his children to live in the Pitti Palace, apart from himself and his new wife, Bianca Cappello. The deaths of both her brother and a sister, along with the marriage of another sister, left Marie with few companions, so the family brought Leonora Dori, later known as Leonora Galigai, to court as a companion for Marie. In keeping with her social standing, Marie received a good education, especially in fields relating to the arts and classical history.

As for most girls of aristocratic birth, a good marriage was essential. After failed negotiations with several prospective husbands, it was deemed that Marie should marry King Henry IV of France, even though he was still married to his first wife, Marguerite of Valois. Historians speculate that Henry's interest in Marie stemmed more from his desire to relieve his financial indebtedness to the Medici family than from his interest in Marie, who, by most contemporary accounts, was not a great beauty. Henry's marriage to Marguerite was dissolved and Marie was sent to the French court, bringing with her 600,000 crowns as a dowry. Marie and Henry were married in late 1600. Their first child, the future King Louis XIII, was born September 27, 1601, at Fontainebleau. The couple's other surviving children are known to history as Gaston, duke of Orleans; Elizabeth, queen of Spain; Christine, duchess of Savoy; and Henrietta Maria, queen of England. A sixth child, Nicholas, died when he was four.

LIFE'S WORK

The early years of Marie's marriage were devoted to her family, and Marie gave little indication of any political aspirations. As time passed, however, she began to press Henry to pronounce her queen of France officially, a title that had been retained by his first wife as part of their marriage dissolution settlement. Henry forestalled the declaration and some historians speculate that his procrastination came from his fear that, once Marie was declared queen, she would plot to usurp power for herself. As a compromise, Henry declared Marie regent in March, 1610, placing her at the head of a small council of fifteen members.

Marie was still not satisfied, so she continued to pressure the king for a coronation. Henry eventually gave in to Marie's continued insistence and crowned her queen on May 13, 1610. Henry IV was assassinated the following day. Two hours after the king was pronounced dead, Marie's confidant, Nogaret de La Valette, duc d'Épernon, had *parlement* declare Marie regent for her eight-year-old son, Louis XIII. Contemporaries and historians alike have accused Marie of having a hand in Henry's assassination, since Marie's confidant Nogaret was present but did nothing to intervene when the courtier François Ravaillac, a Catholic acquaintance of the queen, stabbed and killed Henry on a Paris street.

Marie wasted no time exerting her newly bestowed authority. She promptly reversed her late husband's popular policies of religious toleration, particularly those policies that favored toleration of the Huguenots (French Protestants), choosing instead to promote her own Catholic beliefs through new domestic religious policies and in alliances with Catholic nations. In an effort to ally with Spain, Marie entered into the Treaty of Fontainebleau (August 22, 1612), which betrothed her young son Louis XIII to the infant Anne of Austria (daughter of Philip III of Spain) and betrothed her even younger daughter, Elizabeth (Isabella), to the infant Philip (the future Philip IV of Spain). Favoring her Italian country folk, Marie appointed Concino Concini, the Florentine husband of her friend and lady-in-waiting, Leonora Galigai, to the posts of marquis d'Ancre and marshall of France. Thereafter, Concini served as Marie's closest adviser.

Marie's pro-Catholic and pro-Spanish policies inflamed both the French aristocrats and the French Protestants. In 1614, in an effort to assuage their mounting anger, Marie convoked the Estates-General, an assembly representing three orders (classes) of French citizens. Without regard to the ongoing proceedings of the Estates-General, Louis XIII was married to Anna on November 28, 1615, with Marie's blessings. The people's discontent turned to hatred and revolts broke out, causing Marie to summon Cardinal de Richelieu to serve as her minister of war in 1616. By her willful disregard of the Estates-General, Marie had lost the opportunity to win the favor of the French people and to secure her regency. This futile meeting of the Estates-General would be the last convening of the popular assembly until the French Revolution and the overthrow of the French monarchy.

In April of 1617, three years into his legal majority, Louis XIII finally asserted his displeasure regarding his mother's destructive policies. Louis ordered the assassination of his mother's Italian adviser, Concini, and the beheading of his mother's dearest friend, Leonora Galigai. On May 2, 1617, in an effort to keep Marie away from the spheres of influence at court, Louis sent his mother into exile at the Château Blois, where she remained for two years. Marie's ambition was not so easily

Nineteenth century engraving of Marie de Médicis. (The Granger Collection, New York)

contained however. On the night of February 21, 1619, Marie escaped from Blois and, along with her younger son, Gaston d'Orléans, launched an aristocratic revolt against her eldest son Louis XIII. Marie's attempted coup was promptly put down by the king's superior forces at Les Ponts-de-Cé in August, 1620.

Despite her actions, and with the somewhat surprising intervention of Richelieu, Marie and Louis were reconciled. Marie was permitted to sit on the Royal Council and to exercise her interest in lavish artistic patronage. During this period, Marie directed the extensive rebuilding of the Luxembourg Palace. To decorate the new palace, in January of 1622, Marie commissioned the famed Flemish artist Peter Paul Rubens to execute two cycles of monumental paintings, one cycle in commemoration of her own life and the other cycle in commemoration of the life of her late husband Henry (the latter cycle was never completed). The project in its entirety is known as *The Apotheosis of Henry IV and the Proclamation of the Regency of Marie de Médicis* (May 14, 1610) and is dated 1622 to 1625. It is best known as the Marie de Médicis cycle.

Marie's jealousy over her son's increasing attachment to Richelieu led her to attempt a second coup, again with the help of her son Gaston d'Orléans, on November 10, 1630. This ill-conceived and ill-executed effort is known to history as the Day of the Dupes for its brief duration—a single day. For this intrigue, Marie was exiled to Compiègne in February, 1631. Marie escaped to Brussels that same year, however, where she remained until 1638, when she sought refuge with King Charles I of England, who was her son-in-law and the husband of her daughter Henrietta Maria. Finding the religious climate in England hostile to Catholics, Marie moved back to the Continent, to Cologne, in 1641, and resided there until her death on July 3, 1642. Marie de Médicis is buried in St. Denis.

SIGNIFICANCE

Marie de Médicis' life is a story of missed opportunities. Placed at the summit of French power, she used her position to squander the wealth of France and to alienate the French people. Marie's flagrant disregard for the Estates-General, which she herself had convened, cemented the foundation of popular resentment of the French monarchy, which eventually led to the French Revolution. Marie de Médicis' positive legacy can be found in her numerous art commissions, the greatest of which is the Marie de Médicis series by Rubens, originally commissioned for her Luxembourg Palace and now on display in the Louvre Museum in Paris.

—*Sonia Sorrell*

FURTHER READING

Cohen, Sarah R. "Rubens's France: Gender and Personification in the Marie de Médicis Cycle." *Art Bulletin* 85, no. 3 (September, 2003): 490-522. Cohen discusses the symbols of royal power represented in Rubens's female allegorical figures in his famed Marie de Médicis panels, now in the Louvre. Includes color and black-and-white photographs.

Crawford, Katherine. *Perilous Performances: Gender and Regency in Early Modern Europe*. Boston: Harvard Historical Studies, 2004. A study of the relationships between female regents and their child kings and the effects of female regency on the public's perception of the loci of royal power. Includes an analysis of Marie de Médicis' regency. Illustrated.

Marvick, Elizabeth Wirth. *Louis XIII: The Making of a King*. New Haven, Conn.: Yale University Press, 1987. A scholarly recounting of the childhood of Louis XIII and the effect that his mother, Marie de Médicis, had on his future development and personality.

Millen, Ronald F., and Robert E. Wolf. *Heroic Deeds and Mystic Figures: A New Reading of Rubens' Life of Maria de Medici*. Princeton, N.J.: Princeton University Press, 1989. Using original sources contemporary to the cycle itself, the authors argue that Marie de Médicis both commissioned the cycle and instructed the artist to include specific symbols as veiled references to the ingratitude and ineptitude of her son Louis XIII.

Tapie, Victor L. *France in the Age of Louis XIII and Richelieu*. Translated by D. M. Lockie. New York: Cambridge University Press, 1984. An excellent history of the period during which France transitioned from a weak kingdom into a great monarchy.

Thuillier, Jacques. *Rubens' Life of Marie de Médicis*. New York: H. N. Abrams, 1967. A lavishly illustrated art book depicting the Marie de Médicis cycle.

SEE ALSO: Anne of Austria; Louyse Bourgeois; Charles I; Henrietta Maria; Louis XIII; François de Malherbe; Cosimo II de' Medici; Cardinal de Richelieu; Peter Paul Rubens.

RELATED ARTICLES in *Great Events from History: The Seventeenth Century, 1601-1700:* c. 1601: Emergence of Baroque Music; c. 1601-1620: Emergence of Baroque Art; February 24, 1607: First Performance of Monteverdi's *La favola d'Orfeo*; 1610-1643: Reign of Louis XIII; 1625-October 28, 1628: Revolt of the Huguenots; November 10, 1630: The Day of Dupes; July 13, 1664: Trappist Order Is Founded; 1685: Louis XIV Revokes the Edict of Nantes.

MARIE-THÉRÈSE
Queen consort of France

Marie-Thérèse of Spain had a great influence on seventeenth century world events, as Spain's inability to pay her large dowry to France led to the downfall of Spain—and the growth of France—as a world power.

BORN: September 10, 1638; El Escorial Palace, Madrid, Spain
DIED: July 30, 1683; Versailles, France
ALSO KNOWN AS: Margaret Theresa; Maria Theresa of Spain; María Teresa de Austria
AREA OF ACHIEVEMENT: Government and politics

EARLY LIFE

Like all royal princesses of her day, the future marriage of Marie-Thérèse (mah-ree-tay-rehz) was of primary concern from the moment of her birth. Although she wielded limited direct power in her lifetime, the daughter of Philip IV of Spain and of Elizabeth (Isabella) of France (1602-1644) was destined to have an influential life. She was raised in the Spanish court of her strict, puritanical father, whom, it was rumored, smiled only three times in his entire life. Indeed, her early childhood lessons included the extremely strict court etiquette of the era and serious Catholic religious instruction, which was to influence her life profoundly.

Although she remained in the background, behind the throne, so to speak, for most of her life, Marie-Thérèse was to play a major role in the seventeenth century political arena. In 1659, her father signed the Treaty of the Pyrenees to end the Thirty Years' War between France and Spain. Part of the treaty arranged marriage between

Marie-Thérèse and her cousin, who was the son of her aunt, Anne of Austria. After lengthy negotiations with the French chief minister, Cardinal Jules Mazarin, Philip of Spain permitted a diplomatic mission to court his daughter on behalf of her future husband, King Louis XIV. The formal proposal occurred in the throne room of the Alhambra.

At the age of twenty-two, the highly virtuous and devout Marie-Thérèse was wed in a diplomatic marriage of convenience in June of 1660. The whole Spanish court, including the Spanish king, accompanied her to the Ile des Faisans (Isle of Pheasants) near the Basque coast to meet her groom, Louis. Her marriage brought peace between Spain and France for the first time in twenty-four years.

LIFE'S WORK

While her early role in life as a princess of the Spanish crown was to marry well, Marie-Thérèse came to fully realize, after fulfilling this duty, that her real life's work as queen consort was to produce as many royal children as possible for France. However, while many men would have found her good nature and her deep sense of religious devotion favorable, Louis, also known as the Sun King (Le Roi de Soleil), favored other women for his sexual pleasures. Louis, who ruled as monarch of France for seventy-two years, came to neglect Marie-Thérèse early on and continued to disregard her throughout their marriage by taking a string of mistresses, primarily Françoise-Louise de la Baume Le Blanc de La Vallière (1644-1710), the love of his life, and Françoise-Athénaïs, Rochechouart de Mortemart (1641-1707), the marquise of Montespan. However, the extremely patient and pious Marie-Thérèse, although severely jealous and deeply in love with her husband, kept her anger to herself and never showed resentment to the king's open infidelities.

After just a year into their marriage, Marie-Thérèse found out that her royal husband was passionately in love with the very docile Vallière, who provided him with four children and who remained his mistress until 1667, when he fell in love with the power-hungry Montespan. Unlike Vallière, Montespan attempted to gain personal power over the king by usurping Queen Marie-Thérèse's

Marie-Thérèse. (Library of Congress)

position at court. Marie-Thérèse had to suffer through the open resentment of Montespan, a woman who had once been her maid of honor and who ultimately became the mother of six of the king's children. However, in time, the queen came to show great kindness toward Montespan when, as a matter of course, the king's reliance on his mistress forced him to pay more loving attention to his wife.

At some unknown point, though, Marie-Thérèse's jealousy and despair led her into the arms of a teenage lover, a slave and jester named Nabo, who was "given" to her as a gift by members of the Spanish court. Also, in 1664, she gave birth to an illegitimate daughter, Louise Marie-Thérèse, who became known as the Black Nun of Moret (1664-1732). The girl was confined from birth and spent most of her life in a Benedictine convent, where she was visited by her mother and other members of the royal court throughout her life. Her father, however, disappeared. This little-known fact of history is highlighted in *Las Meninas*, a 1997 play by Lynn Nottage.

In 1670, Marie-Thérèse found herself in despair as the work of her life—bearing children—became imperiled. She had given birth to five of the king's children (four of whom were dead: three daughters died shortly after birth and her son survived until he was three years old). To her great chagrin, however, her husband's illegitimate children flourished. Only the heir, her son Louis, survived to adulthood.

Although she was to affect world events, indirectly, Marie-Thérèse had no part in political affairs, except in 1672, when she acted as regent during Louis XIV's campaign in Holland. She died suddenly at her palace in Versailles on July 30, 1683, in the arms of Madame de Maintenon, who was to replace her as Louis XIV's wife. Although it was rumored that Marie-Thérèse was poisoned by her doctors, no proof of this has been found. Marie-Thérèse is perhaps most famous for saying, "If they have no bread then let them eat cake!" Even though Marie-Thérèse was the one who voiced this renowned line, its authorship has been passed on to her unfortunate descendant Marie-Antoinette, who was to lose her head to the guillotine (in 1793) during the French Revolution.

SIGNIFICANCE

As queen consort to Louis XIV, Marie-Thérèse wielded minimal direct power, but she was destined to have an influential and significant life. As part of the Treaty of the Pyrenees, Marie-Thérèse was to relinquish any claim to the Spanish throne in return for an enormous dowry. Unfortunately, because of Spain's increasing financial difficulties, the dowry was never paid. The failure to pay the dowry resulted in the War of Devolution, which was fought between France and Spain. Louis XIV claimed that the possession of the Spanish Netherlands would devolve to his wife, Marie-Thérèse, upon the death of her father, Philip IV of Spain.

When the unfit Charles II inherited the Spanish throne, France invaded and conquered the area of what is now Belgium and also seized the Franche-Comté, a Spanish possession that bordered Switzerland. The failure to pay Marie-Thérèse's dowry also played a major factor in the War of the Spanish Succession (1701-1714), which in effect ruined Spain's preeminent power in Europe and greatly heightened the status of France in the

eyes of the world, bringing France to the summit of its power. Until this time, Spain had been the most significant world power, dominating Europe and with an enormous treasure in the Americas.

—*M. Casey Diana*

FURTHER READING

Frey, Linda, and Marsha Frey, eds. *The Treaties of the War of the Spanish Succession*. Westport, Conn.: Greenwood Press, 1995. An excellent reference source with short articles on European rulers and the partition treaties.

Levi, Anthony. *Louis XIV*. New York: Carroll & Graf, 2004. Although this book deals with the king and his court, a large amount of attention is paid to Marie-Thérèse and, in particular, her role as a possible heir to the Spanish throne.

Lewis, W. H. *The Splendid Century: Life in the France of Louis XIV*. Prospect Heights, Ill.: Waveland Press, 1997. Lewis explores the political, economic, and social forces that influenced the lives of Marie-Thérèse and her husband Louis XIV. Originally published in 1953.

Mitford, Nancy. *The Sun King*. New York: Penguin Books, 1995. A large, illustrated volume that covers the daily life of the court and the government during the period of France's greatest power. Makes many references to Marie-Thérèse's life at Versailles.

Montespan, Madame la Marquise de. *Memoirs of Madame de Montespan*. Honolulu: University Press of the Pacific, 2004. A modern translation of a work written by the longest reigning of Louis XIV's mistresses.

SEE ALSO: Anne of Austria; Charles II (of Spain); Louis XIV; Madame de Maintenon; Jules Mazarin; Philip IV.

RELATED ARTICLES in *Great Events from History: The Seventeenth Century, 1601-1700:* 17th century: Europe Endorses Slavery; March 31, 1621-September 17, 1665: Reign of Philip IV; November 7, 1659: Treaty of the Pyrenees; 1661: Absolute Monarchy Emerges in France; May 24, 1667-May 2, 1668: War of Devolution; January 23, 1668: Triple Alliance Forms; October 11, 1698, and March 25, 1700: First and Second Treaties of Partition.

JACQUES MARQUETTE
French-born colonial American explorer, priest, and missionary

Father Marquette, a Jesuit priest, joined French explorer Louis Jolliet in the discovery and exploration of the Mississippi River. His remarkable journal is the only detailed record of that famous journey. After learning several Native American languages, Marquette acted as an interpreter and was instrumental in converting the Native Americans to Roman Catholicism.

BORN: June 1, 1637; Laon, France
DIED: May 18, 1675; near Ludington, Michigan
AREAS OF ACHIEVEMENT: Exploration, diplomacy, religion and theology

EARLY LIFE

Jacques Marquette (zhok mahr-keht) was born into a family in north-central France that was well known for sending its members into civic, military, and religious service. He continued that tradition in 1654, when, at the age of seventeen, he joined the Society of Jesus, better known as the Jesuits. For the next twelve years, Marquette endured the rigorous training required of a Jesuit priest. He was ordained in 1666. Later that year, he was sent to labor in Native American missions in French Canada.

Marquette landed in Quebec, on the Saint Lawrence River, on September 20, 1666. On October 10, he was assigned to the mission at Three Rivers, between Quebec and Montreal, where Gabriel Druilletes was the director. Under Druilletes, Marquette began his study of Native American languages. After eighteen months, he was fluent in six dialects. His linguistic ability was to serve him well during the remaining years of his life.

In 1668, Marquette was sent to his first western mission. For the next eighteen months, he labored as a missionary to the Ottawa tribe at Sault Sainte Marie, between Lake Huron and Lake Superior. From there, he was sent, in September, 1669, to a Huron village at La Pointe, on the southwestern shore of Lake Superior. While at La Pointe, Marquette began to keep a journal. Also at La Pointe, Marquette was visited by members of the Illinois tribe, which lived much farther south. The Illinois described a river that ran through their territory, so mighty that they did not know its destination. From their descriptions, Marquette concluded that the river must flow into the Gulf of California, part of the Pacific Ocean. The Illinois asked Marquette to come and work in their villages. Enticed by the Illinois' description of their river, the young missionary resolved to accept their invitation.

LIFE'S WORK

In 1671, the Huron at La Pointe faced the threat of an attack by the Dakotas (Sioux) from the west. They were forced to abandon their village. Marquette followed the entire tribe to the Straits of Mackinac (Mackinaw), between Lake Huron and Lake Michigan. On the northwest shore of the straits, Marquette founded his own mission, which he named Saint Ignace, but he also began making plans to go to the land of the Illinois and to search for and explore their mighty river.

Father Claude-Jean Allouez, from the Mission of Saint Francis Xavier at Green Bay, on the west side of Lake Michigan, had also heard from the Chippawa tribe about the river they called Messipi, meaning "Father of Waters." Allouez and Father Claude Dablon, a trained geographer, initiated the route that later led to the Mississippi River.

Word about this mighty river soon reached Quebec. Louis de Buade, count of Frontenac and Palluau, came to that city as governor of New France in April, 1672. He soon endorsed Marquette's plan to search for the river. A French native of New France and a friend of Marquette, Louis Jolliet, was soon appointed to be part of the expedition. Jolliet was a fur trader and explorer who had been on several trips into the Great Lakes region. Jolliet left Quebec with orders from Marquette's Jesuit superior, Father Dablon, for Marquette to join Jolliet in a voyage of discovery. Jolliet arrived at St. Ignace in December, 1672, with the much-anticipated news.

On May 17, 1673, Jolliet, Marquette, and five French woodsmen left St. Ignace in two birch bark canoes. Dried corn and smoked buffalo meat comprised the bulk of their food supply. They soon met the Folles-Avoines ("wild oats"), a friendly tribe of Canadian Indians already known to Father Marquette. The Folles-Avoines warned the explorers of danger ahead from hostile tribes, from monsters in the mighty river, and from heat so severe that it would cause death. Grateful for the warning, but not heeding it, the expedition skirted the northern end of Lake Michigan and soon entered Green Bay on the west side. They then pushed up the strong current of the Fox River into Lake Winnebago.

The Mascoutens ("fire nation") tribe, who lived in the Lake Winnebago region, agreed to send two guides along with the explorers to lead them to the great river. On June 10, the expedition began the nearly impossible 2.5-mile (4-kilometer) portage to the Wisconsin River. Marquette gave full credit for the success of this march to the Mascouten guides, who even carried the canoes. At the Wisconsin River, a tributary of the Mississippi, Jolliet and Marquette entered a world about which they knew nothing.

June 17 was to be a climactic day for Marquette's voyage. Exactly one month after leaving St. Ignace, near Prairie du Chien, Wisconsin, the explorers floated into the broad, swift, and peaceful waters of the upper Mississippi River. Marquette vividly described the moment in his journal, and drew a map showing their route and the topography of the land.

Their first human contact along the Mississippi River came on June 25, after the expedition had observed a path coming down to the river from the west. They followed the path to a village of the Illinois on the banks of the Des Moines River, in present-day Iowa. It had been members of this tribe who had first told Marquette about the river that ran through their land. When the explorers left the Illinois after a short rest, the tribe gave them a calumet, a feathered peace pipe, to protect them from hostile tribes to the south.

Resuming their journey, the expedition passed the mouth of the Illinois River from the east, which the Illinois told them would be a shortcut for their return trip. Next they came to the muddy Missouri River from the west, where they the saw the "monsters" about which they had been warned by the Folles-Avoines. They were painted on high rocks above the east bank of the Mississippi. After passing the mouth of the Ohio River from the east, they saw the Arkansas River coming from the west.

At the Arkansas River, Jolliet and Marquette faced their first danger from a Native American tribe. The Quapaw were deterred from massacring the seven men only when the recognized the calumet from the Illinois. From the Quapaw, they learned that the Mississippi River ran south to the Gulf of Mexico rather than west to the Gulf of California. They also learned that farther south they would be in great danger from the Spanish and their Native American allies. Marquette wrote in his journal that, after considering the possibility of losing all that they had accomplished, the expedition members decided to turn around and return to Quebec.

Their return voyage began on July 17. They ascended the Illinois River, portaged to the Chicago River to Lake Michigan, and returned to Saint Francis Xavier Mission on Green Bay in late September. They had traveled twenty-five hundred miles in four months. While Jolliet returned to Quebec with the results of the journey, Marquette remained at Green Bay. He sent his journal back to his superior, Father Dablon.

Kaskaskia, a large village of the Illinois, had asked Father Marquette to return and minister to them. On October 25, 1674, he left Green Bay to fulfill that request, but his health forced him to stop and spend the winter in a small hut, the first known dwelling place to be erected in what is now Chicago. Marquette set out again in March and reached Kaskaskia on April 8, 1675. After converting several thousand natives to the Roman Catholic Church, Marquette felt his strength ebbing away. He left after three weeks, wanting to spend his last earthly days at St. Ignace. On the eastern shore of Lake Michigan, however, he was carried ashore by his two companions. He died there on May 18, at the age of thirty-seven. Two years later, Native Americans took his bones to St. Ignace.

SIGNIFICANCE

Two centuries after his death, the state of Wisconsin placed a statue of Marquette, created by a Native American, in the United States capital in Washington, D.C. In addition to this statue, Marquette's lasting legacy is the journal he kept of his exploration of the Mississippi River. That journal provides detailed descriptions of tribal customs, the flora and fauna, and the future commercial value of the rivers and streams encountered by the expedition. Scientific information in the journal, such as his explanation of lake tides, is still accepted as accurate. Without the information in this journal, later exploration of the area would have been significantly more difficult.

—*Glenn L. Swygart*

FURTHER READING

Kupperman, Karen Ordahl, ed. *America in European Consciousness, 1493-1775*. Chapel Hill: University of North Carolina Press, 1995. The chapter by Luca Codignpla discusses Roman Catholic missions to the native tribes along the Mississippi during the time of Marquette. It does not mention Marquette by name, but it includes the map that Father Dablon made in 1671, very likely used by Jolliet and Marquette on their voyage.

Shea, John Gilmary. *The Discovery and Exploration of the Mississippi*. New York: Redfield, 1852. Includes the original journal of Marquette and the original narratives by Allouez, Dablon, and others. Also provides a facsimile of Marquette's map of the route of the journey and of the Mississippi River as far as Jolliet and Marquette were able to go.

Volo, James, and Dorothy Denneen Volo. *Daily Life on the Old Colonial Frontier*. Westport, Conn.: Greenwood Press, 2002. Discusses the information provided by Marquette on trade with the Native American tribes. Examines how Marquette convinced many of the tribes to trade only with the French and the advantages they would have by doing so. Also covers the establishment of the French fort at Mackinac near Marquette's St. Ignace mission.

SEE ALSO: Samuel de Champlain; Louis Jolliet; Sieur de La Salle; Marie de l'Incarnation.

RELATED ARTICLE in *Great Events from History: The Seventeenth Century, 1601-1700:* Beginning 1673: French Explore the Mississippi Valley.

ANDREW MARVELL
English poet, satirist, and politician

For a century after his death, Marvell was remembered for his long career as a member of Parliament and for his political writings. His considerable talents as a lyric, Metaphysical poet, however, form the basis of his modern reputation, a reputation largely initiated by T. S. Eliot's reevaluation of his work.

BORN: March 31, 1621; Winestead-in-Holderness, Yorkshire, England
DIED: August 16, 1678; London, England
AREAS OF ACHIEVEMENT: Literature, government and politics

EARLY LIFE

Andrew Marvell was born on March 31, 1621, the fourth of five children of the Reverend Andrew Marvell and his wife, Anne Pease. Marvell and his family moved to Hull in 1624, when his father was appointed as lecturer at Holy Trinity Church and was also made master of the Charterhouse School. Marvell most likely attended Hull Grammar School, and in 1633, he entered Cambridge University. He received a B.A. after four years, then began working toward an M.A. However, he left Cambridge in 1641 without completing the master of arts degree.

Although Marvell's father, while at Cambridge, had attended Emmanuel College, a college with strong Puritan connections, Marvell was sent to Trinity College, which was more moderate. Like other students of the time, Marvell would have studied Latin, Greek, and Hebrew, as well as logic, rhetoric, philosophy, and mathematics. His skill with languages is evinced in his professional career. Marvell was already writing poetry at Cambridge, and his first published poetry was a contribution to a university collection, published in 1637, which celebrated the birth of Charles I's daughter, Anne.

It appears that Marvell was recruited briefly by the Jesuits and left the university for a few months, probably in 1638. The attraction did not last and may in some way be connected to the strong anti-Catholic position Marvell held throughout his life. Both of Marvell's parents died while he was at university, his mother in 1638, and his father in an accidental drowning in 1641. It may be that the death of his father precipitated the end of Marvell's formal education.

LIFE'S WORK

Marvell's activities after leaving Cambridge are not certain. It is likely that he spent much of the time from 1641 to 1647 traveling in Europe. It is also possible that he was employed as a tutor during at least some of this time. A 1653 letter by John Milton, unsuccessfully recommending Marvell for a position as assistant Latin secretary, mentions that Marvell had spent time in Holland, France, Italy, and Spain.

In 1650, Marvell became the tutor of Mary Fairfax, the twelve-year-old daughter of the third Baron Fairfax. Fairfax had served in the English Civil War as commander in chief for the Parliamentary forces. Marvell,

MARVELL'S MAJOR WORKS	
1655	*The First Anniversary of the Government Under His Highness the Lord Protector*
1672	*The Rehearsal Transpros'd*
1673	*The Rehearsal Transpros'd: The Second Part*
1676	*Mr. Smirke: Or, The Divine in Mode*
1677	*An Account of the Growth of Popery and Arbitrary Government in England*
1678	*Remarks upon a Late Disingenuous Discourse*
1681	*Miscellaneous Poems*

who up to this point had shown moderate Royalist tendencies, was now aligned with Oliver Cromwell's Puritans. The complexity of Marvell's political views is apparent in his poem, "An Horatian Ode upon Cromwell's Return from Ireland" (wr. 1650; pb. 1681). It is likely, though not certain, that many of Marvell's lyric poems date from his three years at Fairfax's home, Nun Appleton, Yorkshire, including his famous country house poem, "Upon Appleton House, to My Lord Fairfax" (pb. 1681). Other well-known poems, including "To His Coy Mistress" (pb. 1681), "The Nymph Complaining for the Death of Her Faun" (pb. 1681), and the four Mower poems, are usually associated with the early phase of Marvell's life, but they cannot be dated with confidence.

In 1653, Marvell left Nun Appleton and became the tutor of William Dutton, a ward of Cromwell. He continued in this position until 1657, when he was finally appointed assistant Latin secretary, aiding Milton in the translation and writing of diplomatic correspondence. There is evidence that Marvell visited Milton in his home and that their friendship continued after Charles II's Restoration in 1660, when it might have been detrimental to Marvell. Marvell was more than likely one of the men involved in saving Milton from the purges that took place with the Restoration. He paid tribute to Milton's talents in the poem "On Mr. Milton's *Paradise Lost*" (1674), which appeared in the 1674 edition of Milton's poem. Marvell continued to write topical poems, including *The First Anniversary of the Government Under His Highness the Lord Protector* (1655).

Marvell continued in his civil service post until 1659. In the same year, he was elected as member of Parliament representing Hull. He continued to serve as an M.P. until his death in 1678. While Marvell accepted the Restoration of the monarchy in 1660, he sided with those in opposition in Parliament. He was a dedicated M.P., serving on committees, writing frequently to his constituents, and making a name for himself as an honest politician dedicated to constitutional monarchy and religious toleration, marred only by his vehement anti-Catholicism. Marvell even participated in an unsuccessful diplomatic mission to Russia, Sweden, and Denmark.

Far more is known of Marvell's political career than of his private life. He apparently never married. He seems to have had a close relationship with his nephew, William Popple. Some of their correspondence has survived. The income Marvell received as an M.P. was a modest one, and while the evidence has been debated, it seems that Marvell was never financially well off.

During his career as an M.P., Marvell continued to

Andrew Marvell. (Library of Congress)

write, producing satirical, political poems and pamphlets. Some works necessarily appeared anonymously, so ascription of a given poem to Marvell is at times tenuous. He is credited with political poems that satirized the corruption of the court, such as the highly critical "Last Instructions to a Painter" (wr. 1667; pb. 1689). His engagement in the religious controversies of his day is best represented by two satirical works, *The Rehearsal Transpros'd* (1672) and *The Rehearsal Transpros'd: The Second Part* (1673), the first of which appeared anonymously. One of his final works, *An Account of the Growth of Popery and Arbitrary Government in England* (1677), was more serious in tone.

Marvell died in London on August 16, 1678, as a result of fever, perhaps made worse through the medical treatment he received. After Marvell's death, his housekeeper, Mary Palmer, claimed to be his wife, although the claim was not supported and appears to have been part of a complicated financial scheme. Palmer, however, was responsible for the publication of *Miscellaneous Poems* (1681), a volume that preserved nearly all of Marvell's significant poetry.

SIGNIFICANCE

No continuous line can be drawn from the first publication of Marvell's poetry in 1681 to the present. For about two hundred years after Marvell's death, his reputation as a poet was eclipsed by his reputation as a political satirist and politician. From the nineteenth century on, however, attention to Marvell as a lyric poet grew steadily. Interest in his poetry was first expressed by writers such as William Hazlitt, Ralph Waldo Emerson, Edgar Allan Poe, and Alfred, Lord Tennyson, and continued to grow throughout the nineteenth and twentieth centuries. T. S. Eliot's praise of Marvell's poetry brought Marvell even more attention. In fact, Marvell's lyric poetry garnered so much interest that it eclipsed his satirical and prose works. Critics in the later twentieth and early twenty-first centuries accordingly began an effort to bring the latter works back into the light.

—*Christine Cornell*

FURTHER READING

Donno, Elizabeth Story. *Andrew Marvell: The Critical Heritage*. London: Routledge & Kegan Paul, 1978. While not a biography, this book is immensely useful for an assessment of Marvell's early impact. Index.

Kavanagh, Art. "Andrew Marvell 'in Want of Money': The Evidence in *John Farrington v. Mary Marvell*." *Seventeenth Century* 17, no. 2 (Autumn, 2002): 206-212. Brings new evidence to light on the question of Marvell's poverty and concludes that he was in fact poor.

Legouis, Pierre. *Andrew Marvell: Poet, Puritan, Patriot*. Oxford, England: Clarendon Press, 1965. An abridged and updated English version of the 1928 French original. The standard twentieth century biography. Index.

Murray, Nicholas. *World Enough and Time: The Life of Andrew Marvell*. New York: St. Martin's Press, 1999. Careful and well-researched biography. Balances an interest in the poetry with attention to Marvell's political career. Illustrations and index.

Patterson, Annabel. *Marvell: The Writer in Public Life*. Harlow, Essex, England: Longman, 2000. Includes a helpful chapter on Marvell's life. Illustrations, bibliography, and index.

Von Maltzahn, Nicholas. "Andrew Marvell and the Lord Wharton." *Seventeenth Century* 18, no. 2 (Autumn, 2003): 252-265. Interesting for its insights on Marvell's friendship with Philip, fourth Baron Wharton.

Wheeler, Thomas. *Andrew Marvell Revisited*. Twayne's English Authors Series 531. Edited by Arthur Kinney. New York: Twayne, 1996. Chapters on Marvell's life and reputation, as well as studies of his works. Time line, bibliography, and index.

SEE ALSO: Charles I; Charles II (of England); Oliver Cromwell; Third Baron Fairfax; John Milton.

RELATED ARTICLES in *Great Events from History: The Seventeenth Century, 1601-1700:* 1642-1651: English Civil Wars; May, 1659-May, 1660: Restoration of Charles II.

MARY OF MODENA
Queen of England (r. 1685-1688)

Selected by Louis XIV of France as a suitable Catholic bride for the future King James II of England, Mary of Modena provided her husband with support, might have influenced his religious policies, and ultimately provided him with a son and heir, an event that contributed significantly to the Glorious Revolution.

BORN: October 5, 1658; Modena (now in Italy)
DIED: May 7, 1718; Saint-Germain-en-Laye, France
ALSO KNOWN AS: Marie Beatrice Eleanor Anne Margaret Isabella d'Este (given name)
AREA OF ACHIEVEMENT: Government and politics

EARLY LIFE

The daughter of Duke Alphonso IV of Modena and Laura Martinozzi, Mary of Modena (MAW-day-nah) was raised to be a deeply pious Catholic and, until the age of fifteen, was focused upon entering the Visitation order of nuns. It came as a huge shock to her, therefore, when she was suddenly told that she was to marry the widowed James, duke of York, the brother of King Charles II of England and (since Charles had no legitimate children), the heir to the English throne. Mary was beside herself in grief and panic for two days and was only reconciled to the union through the personal intervention of Pope Clement X.

The duke of York, formerly a Protestant Anglican, had converted to the Roman Catholic faith. The pope and the powerful French king Louis XIV therefore saw the death of James's first wife, Anne Hyde, as an opportunity. They hoped that, by marrying the English heir ap-

Detail of Mary of Modena, from a portrait by William Wissing in London's National Portrait Gallery. (Hulton Archive/Getty Images)

parent to a Catholic bride, they could set in motion a chain of events that would lead to the birth of a Catholic heir and the foundation of an English Catholic dynasty, thereby reclaiming England as a Catholic nation.

This strategy represented the only hope for Clement and Louis, because James had already had two daughters with Anne Hyde, Mary and Anne, who were both baptized into the Anglican Protestant Communion at the insistence of their uncle, King Charles. Mary , the elder of the sisters, would marry her cousin, Prince William III of Orange, who was to become stadtholder of the Netherlands and was himself a staunch Dutch Reformed Protestant. Thus, the only way to institute a Catholic line of succession for England would be for James and his next wife to produce a Catholic son, who would take precedence over the elder, Protestant daughters.

King Louis, seeking eligible Catholic princesses for James, settled on Mary of Modena because of reports of her religious zeal and commitment, as well as her beauty. She was described as being dark-haired, dark-eyed, fine-

featured, and of a sweet and gentle disposition. Persuaded finally by the pope that she was duty-bound to go through with the marriage to do what she could to bring England back into the Catholic fold, Mary was wed by proxy to the duke of York on September 30, 1673, in Italy, through the agency of the British envoy, Henry Mordaunt, second earl of Peterborough.

LIFE'S WORK

Mary journeyed to London via Paris and met her husband on November 21; according to one report, she broke down and sobbed uncontrollably. She was only fifteen, and her new husband was forty. Settling in to life at King Charles's rather eccentric court, Duchess Mary was well accepted by the king and by her husband's daughters, and her marriage grew into a lasting and loving relationship (despite the intermittent, casual affairs James engaged in with other women at court, which would sometimes cause Mary to break down emotionally). She generally assumed a very low political profile but, notwithstanding, she was subject to harsh attacks from members of Parliament who believed that she was Louis XIV's agent, sent to influence the court to follow a stronger pro-Catholic agenda. It certainly is true that she remained quite openly steadfast in her faith, and this could not have helped but to have had some effect upon her husband's policy decisions.

Shortly after the arrival of Duchess Mary, some members of Parliament moved to declare the marriage null and void, and during the Exclusion Crisis of the 1670's-1680's, in which attempts were made to bar the duke of York from the line of succession, Madame East (as she was popularly dubbed) shared the same unpopularity as her husband. Accordingly, she accompanied him into exile for three years. The couple experienced great deal of personal tragedy as well: The duke and duchess's first ten children died young: Catherine Laura (January 16-October 3, 1675); Isabel (August 28, 1676-March 2, 1680); Charles (November 7-December 12, 1677); Elizabeth (born & died at unspecified dates in 1678); Charlotte (August 15-October 6, 1682); and five unnamed infants, who were born and died, respectively, in: 1674, 1675, 1681, 1683 and 1684.

In 1681, the political tide began to turn against the pro-exclusionary forces, who by this time had been dubbed the Whigs, and their opponents, the so-called Tories, gained ground. Two years later, the Rye House Plot of 1683, hatched by Whig extremists to assassinate King Charles and his brother James (the latter newly returned from exile), completely discredited the Exclusionist cause. By the time of Charles II's death on February 6, 1685, the duke of York was in such a strong position that there was no immediate opposition when he succeeded to the throne as King James II.

Mary of Modena's life as queen was, if anything, even more challenging than it had been before: Her husband's infidelities continued, and his absolutist and pro-Catholic actions made him increasingly unpopular, even among the loyal Tories. The queen continued to be the object of suspicion, and she was even credited as a major factor in urging increasingly restrictive and discriminatory measures against Protestants. There is, however, little evidence to show how her counsels influenced royal policy.

Nonetheless, opposition to King James was slow in forming; one of the chief factors contributing to the initially weak opposition was the fact that the king himself, who was nearing the age of fifty-five, could not last that much longer and that his daughter Mary and her husband William of Orange were next in line to the throne and would reverse what James was doing. However, on June 10, 1688, Queen Mary gave birth to a healthy, robust male child who was christened into the Catholic faith as James Edward Stuart. This set James's daughter Mary back in the line of succession and seemed to portend a potentially endless line of Catholic Stuart rulers, a prospect that frightened most of the king's Protestant subjects.

Stories circulated that James Edward was not the actual son of King James and Queen Mary but really a local miller's son who had been smuggled into the delivery room in a warming pan. These rumors seem to have been nothing more than desperate propaganda with no basis in fact whatsoever. Nevertheless, an increasingly vehement opposition movement gathered in support of William III and Mary, and in November, 1688, at the urging of both Whigs and Tories, William III's forces landed on the southern English coast near Torbay.

James II's actions when confronted with William's forces and the role that Mary of Modena might have played in what was to be dubbed the Glorious Revolution of 1688 have been the subject of much debate. It seems undeniable that James suffered some sort of breakdown or failure of nerve. Queen Mary and Prince James Edward were obviously too valuable to risk falling into William's hands, and they were sent to France. Later that same day, December 10, 1688, James himself fled Britain and joined his wife and son in exile. Mary of Modena

has been variously depicted either as providing her husband with a source of purpose and sanity or as precipitating, through entreaties and persuasion, his disastrous decision to leave England and thus allow William III and Mary II to usurp his throne.

Whatever was the case, Mary of Modena was supportive of James's attempts to regain the throne through the Siege of Londonderry (1689) and the succeeding War of the Two Kings in Ireland (1689-1691), but it was William and Mary who again prevailed, and the deposed royal family settled into permanent exile in France at Saint-Germain-en-Laye. Their last child, Louisa Maria, was born there on June 28, 1692 (she would only live 19 years, passing away on April 18, 1712, whereas James Edward would survive until 1766).

After 1692 and the dashing of his last hopes at restoration by the naval defeat of the French fleet at La Hogue, James sank into depression and eventually lost his grip on reality. He died almost unnoticed on September 6, 1701. It was Mary of Modena who kept the Jacobite cause alive for the next generation, contributing large subsidies to Jacobite groups in Britain and Ireland, and who encouraged James Edward in his unsuccessful uprising in Scotland in 1715. She died of cancer on May 7, 1718.

SIGNIFICANCE

Scholars disagree over whether Mary of Modena was, in the end, an asset or a liability to her husband and her adopted nation. Lack of documentation makes it hard to determine how profound her influence was. According to some historians, she was a tower of strength whose words and example could bolster her husband's resolve. Her charm, piety, and moral character won continuing, dedicated support for the Jacobite cause on both sides of the English Channel. Others theorize that she made James even more fanatical in his Catholicism than he already was and that her behind-the-scenes prodding and suggestions may have precipitated his downfall by isolating him politically from all except Catholic supporters.

—*Raymond Pierre Hylton*

FURTHER READING

Callow, John. *The Making of King James II: The Formative Years of a Fallen Monarch.* Stroud, Gloucestershire, England: Sutton, 2000. Implies that James's character had been fixed for a long time and that Mary's influence may have been less than consequential.

Coward, Barry. *The Stuart Age: England, 1603-1714.* Harlow, Essex, England: Pearson Education, 2003. Thorough scholarly study of the Stuart monarchs. The author is, in the end, rather dismissive of Queen Mary.

Speck, W. A. *James II.* New York: Longman, 2002. The author concedes the presence and influence of a Catholic element at court led by Mary and Father Edward Petre but does not elaborate on the extent of its impact.

SEE ALSO: Charles II (of England); James II; Louis XIV; Mary II; William III.
RELATED ARTICLES in *Great Events from History: The Seventeenth Century, 1601-1700:* August, 1682-November, 1683: Rye House Plot; 1688-1702: Reign of William and Mary; November, 1688-February, 1689: The Glorious Revolution; April 18-July 31, 1689: Siege of Londonderry.

MARY II
Queen of England (r. 1689-1694)

In the Glorious Revolution of 1688, Mary II usurped the throne of her Catholic father, James II, thereby preserving England's existence as a Protestant nation. She also gained recognition as a highly effective political leader who deeply influenced British domestic policy and as a strong negotiator.

BORN: April 30, 1662; London, England
DIED: December 28, 1694; London
ALSO KNOWN AS: Mary Stuart (given name)
AREA OF ACHIEVEMENT: Government and politics

EARLY LIFE

Mary II was born Mary Stuart on April 30, 1662, at Saint James's Palace, London, England. As the elder daughter of King James II and his first wife, Lady Anne Hyde (1637-1671), Mary Stuart's short life was a difficult one that was, from her birth, filled with conflict. Mary was brought up under the watchful eye of her uncle, Charles II, who, after failing to produce a legitimate heir, saw in young Mary the probable heir to the British throne.

Since the Reformation, Britain had been a Protestant monarchy, and the idea of Mary's father, James, the Catholic duke of York, succeeding his Protestant brother Charles filled much of Parliament with dread. (This faction in Parliament acquired the nickname "Whigs," while supporters of James's right to the throne despite his Catholicism came to be called Tories.) Thus, Mary and her younger sister, Anne (1665-1714), who was eventually to become the last Stuart monarch in 1702, were educated in the faith of their mother, as Protestants. Knowing full well that Mary's husband would very likely rule Britain one day, a great deal of care went into the search for a proper husband for the young Stuart princess, who it seems was in love with the beautiful Frances Apsley.

William, prince of Orange, son of William II, stadtholder of the Netherlands, and Mary Henrietta of England (herself the daughter of Charles I), was brought forth as an appropriate suitor. Upon finding out she was to be married to her asthmatic cousin, however, it is said that Mary wept nonstop. Their betrothal took place in October, 1677, and was quickly followed by their marriage in London on November 4. The couple, who were also first cousins, each being a grandchild of Charles I, lived, unhappy and childless, in the Netherlands, where Mary found herself popular among the Dutch people. In 1685, the Restoration monarch Charles II died, and Mary found herself one step closer to the British throne when her father became king of England. Even this event, however, did not diminish her husband's poor treatment of her.

LIFE'S WORK

Mary saw her father's ascension to the throne upon the death of King Charles as a matter of course. The subsequent birth of a male heir, however, changed everything. Mary's newborn brother, Prince James, son of her father James II and his second wife, the Catholic Queen Mary of Modena, caused great conflict for Mary, who stood to lose her place in the succession. It was a far greater problem, however, to the nation as a whole, which feared that the monarchy would fall back into Catholic hands and that England would once again become a Catholic nation.

King James II, after all, was already a Catholic king in a Protestant country, a king who showed favoritism in promoting Catholics to high office and suspended the legal rights of dissenters. James's reign could be a mere aberration, but if his son were raised Catholic as well, as seemed likely, a permanent Catholic dynasty could result. Thus, whereas before, Parliament had been content to bide its time waiting for the death of the fifty-two-year-old monarch and the subsequent reign of his Protestant daughter, it now became imperative to both the Whigs and the Tories to take steps to ensure the Protestant succession.

Mary acted diligently and brilliantly to prevent her young Catholic brother, James Francis Edward Stuart, from acquiring the throne she had been waiting her whole life to attain. Mary's husband, Prince William of Orange, was invited by seven Whig and Tory leaders to invade England and seize control, in order to protect his wife's claim to the throne, and Mary supported him and her Anglican faith. In November, 1688, William landed at Torbay, Devonshire, England, with a Dutch army. The Catholic king's forces, under John Churchill (1650-1722), later the first duke of Marlborough, deserted him, as did both Mary and his other daughter, Anne. In December of 1688, James escaped to France with his wife and infant son. His flight was looked upon as an abdication of the throne of England.

Thus, Mary was instrumental in bringing about the Glorious Revolution, or the Bloodless Revolution, as it

Mary II. (The Granger Collection, New York)

also came to be known. It was Mary II's claim to the monarchy, not her husband's, that placed them firmly on the British throne as joint monarchs over England, Scotland, and Ireland—the only time this happened in British history. Although Mary was asked to rule as a sole monarch, she refused unless her husband was named king. Thus, in a show of brilliant statesmanship, Mary captured the throne of England along with the military power of Holland to back up her claim. The couple's reign is usually referred to as that of William and Mary.

An efficient and very successful politician, Mary effectively dealt with Parliament and the court when William was occupied in a series of wars against Louis XIV (1638-1715) of France, the Catholic monarch who befriended James II and his infant son. She held down the fort, so to speak, when William was defeated by James's supporters at Killiecrankie in 1689, when he defeated James at the Battle of the Boyne (1690) in Ireland, and while he successfully fought the Wars of the League of Augsburg (1689-1697; also known as the War of the Grand Alliance or, in part, King William's War). Although as a married couple they experienced unhappiness, some would even say misery, as a political couple they were able to put up a united front and gain much glory.

Mary, who had maintained a reputation for piousness and charity throughout her life, died from smallpox on December 28, 1694, at the age of thirty-two, at Kensington Palace, London, and was buried in London at Westminster Abbey. Her husband William, although not nearly as popular while Mary was alive, continued to reign until his death from complications after falling off his horse in 1702, at which point Mary's sister, Anne, ascended the throne.

SIGNIFICANCE

As a Stuart princess, Mary II played a major role in securing Britain as a Protestant country by usurping her father's throne and bringing about the Glorious Revolution. Her decision to replace her father on the throne ushered in the present-day Parliamentary system: Before their coronation in 1689, Mary and her husband accepted and signed the Declaration of Rights, which in effect set out the conditions under which they were granted the throne. This document redefined the relationship between the monarchy and the people, ensuring that the rule of law could not be overwritten on a royal whim. In addition, it provided for the unconditional rule of Parliament and not the monarch. It also assured the succession to the throne. The Glorious Revolution, however, led to the Jacobite Rebellions in which many lost their lives. The Jacobites, supporters of James II and his offspring as the rightfully rulers of Britain, staged two major rebellions in 1715 and 1745 against Protestant Hanoverian rule.

—*M. Casey Diana*

FURTHER READING

Curtis Brown, Beatrice. *Anne Stuart: Queen of England*. New York: Kessinger, 2003. Although this illustrated book deals primarily with Mary's sister Anne, it portrays the personal history of both sisters, particularly Mary's role in the 1688 Glorious Revolution.

Farquher, Michael. *A Treasury of Royal Scandals: The Shocking True Stories of History's Wickedest, Weirdest, Most Wanton Kings, Queens, Tsars, Popes, and Emperors*. New York: Penguin, 2001. Goes into great detail about the renowned Stuarts and discusses Mary's relationship with her husband, William III.

Van der Kiste, John. *William and Mary*. Stroud, Gloucestershire, England: Sutton, 2003. Comprehensive overview of the fascinating lives and turbulent times of William and Mary. Discusses the personal relations between the monarchs, as well as their political legacy.

Wallar, Maureen. *Ungrateful Daughters*. New York: St. Martin's Press, 2003. Renowned historian Maureen Wallar reveals the dark family dynamics, the rages, and the jealousies that resulted in the loss of the crown by James II. While she posits Anne as the far darker, more responsible sister, Wallar divulges much about Mary II, her conflicts and her motivations.

SEE ALSO: Charles I; Charles II (of England); James II; Louis XIV; William III.

RELATED ARTICLES in *Great Events from History: The Seventeenth Century, 1601-1700:* 1688-1702: Reign of William and Mary; November, 1688-February, 1689: The Glorious Revolution; 1689-1697: Wars of the League of Augsburg; February 13, 1689: Declaration of Rights.

MASSASOIT
Wampanoag grand sachem (r. before 1620-1661)

Wampanoag leader Massasoit arranged the first Native American meetings with the Pilgrims. His people assisted the Pilgrims during their first hard winters in the New World, taking part in the first Thanksgiving with them. Massasoit counseled peace, but his son Metacom went to war in the mid-1670's, after his people's land base had been severely depleted.

BORN: c. 1580; near present-day Bristol, Rhode Island
DIED: 1661; near present-day Bristol
ALSO KNOWN AS: Ousamequin; Yellow Feather
AREAS OF ACHIEVEMENT: Government and politics, diplomacy

EARLY LIFE

Because the English encountered Massasoit (mas-uh-SOYT) at middle age, very little reliable published information exists on his early life. Massasoit allied with the Pilgrims out of practical necessity, because many of his people had died in an epidemic shortly before the whites arrived, and he sought to forge an alliance with them against the more numerous Narragansetts. Massasoit, father of Metacom, favored friendly relations with the English colonists when he became the Wampanoags' most

influential leader. Massasoit also became a close friend of the dissident Puritan Roger Williams, providing Williams with life-sustaining lodging during a blizzard that accompanied his flight from Boston to found the new colony of Providence Plantations, now Rhode Island.

Massasoit called on two English-speaking Native Americans, Samoset and Squanto, to communicate with the English immigrants. Samoset (c. 1590-c. 1653), an Abenaki whose name means "he who walks overmuch," made contact with English fishermen near the home of his band, the Pemaquid Abenakis, on Monhegan Island off the coast of Maine. Samoset had had enough contact that, by the time the Pilgrims reached the area in 1620, he was able to greet them in English. On March 21, 1621, Samoset surprised the English immigrants by walking into Plymouth Plantation and announcing a welcome in their language.

Samoset returned to the settlement March 22 in the company of Squanto, who also had learned English. Squanto (also called Tisquantum), had probably been kidnapped from his native land in 1614 by English explorers. They sold him and twenty Pawtuxet companions on the slave market at Malaga, Spain. A Christian friar

Wampanoag leader Massasoit (center). (Library of Congress)

smuggled Squanto to England, where he worked for a rich merchant as he learned the English language. Squanto obtained passage back to America on a trading ship, before the arrival of the Pilgrims, who came ashore in 1620. Like Samoset, Squanto surprised the Pilgrims by greeting them in English. He showed the immigrants how to plant corn in hillocks, using dead herring as fertilizer (the seeds of English wheat, barley, and peas did not grow). Squanto also taught the Pilgrims how to design traps to catch fish, and he acted as a guide and interpreter.

Samoset and Squanto arranged a meeting between the colonists and Massasoit. This meeting was the beginning of Massasoit's long-term friendship with the New England settlers. During the first years of settlement, Samoset "sold" large tracts of land at the Pilgrims' behest. He acknowledged the first such deed in 1625 for twelve thousand acres of Pemaquid territory.

Massasoit was described by William Bradford in 1621 as "lustie . . . in his best years, an able body grave of countenance, spare of speech, strong [and] tall." Williams met Massasoit when the latter was about thirty

years of age and, in Williams's words, became "great friends" with the sachem. Williams also became close to Canonicus, elderly leader of the Narragansetts. With both, Williams traveled in the forest for days at a time.

LIFE'S WORK

By January, 1635, the Puritans' more orthodox magistrates had decided that Roger Williams must be exiled to England, jailed if possible, and silenced. They opposed exiling Williams in the wilderness, fearing that he would begin his own settlement, from which his "infections" would leak back into Puritania. About January 15, 1636, Captain John Underhill was dispatched from Boston to arrest Williams and place him on board ship for England. Arriving at Williams's home, Underhill and his deputies found that he had escaped. No one in the neighborhood would admit to having seen him leave.

Aware of his impending arrest, Williams had set out three days earlier during a blinding blizzard, walking south by west to the lodge of Massasoit, at Mount Hope. Walking eighty to ninety miles during the worst of a New

England winter, Williams suffered immensely, and he most likely would have died without Indian aid. Nearly half a century later, nearing death, Williams wrote: "I bear to this day in my body the effects of that winter's exposure." Near the end of his trek, Williams lodged with Canonicus and his family. He then scouted the land that had been set aside for the new colony.

A statement by Massasoit has served for more than three centuries to illustrate the differences in conception of the earth and property ownership between many Native American and European-derived cultures. In *Brave Are My People* (1993), Frank Waters describes a "purchase" by Miles Standish and two companions of a tract of land fourteen miles square near Bridgewater, for seven coats, eight hoes, nine hatchets, ten yards of cotton cloth, twenty knives, and four moose skins. When native people continued to hunt on the land after it was "purchased" and were arrested by the Pilgrims, Massasoit protested:

> What is this you call property? It cannot be the earth. For the land is our mother, nourishing all her children, bears, birds, fish, and all men. The woods, the streams, everything on it belongs to everybody and is for the use of all. How can one man say it belongs to him only?

While Standish and his companions thought they had carried away an English-style deed, Massasoit argued that their goods had paid only for use of the land in common with everyone.

As he aged, Massasoit became disillusioned with the colonists, as increasing numbers of them pressed his people from their lands. He had fathered three boys and two girls. The two younger men, who would become chiefs of the Wampanoags after Massasoit's death, were named Wamsutta and Metacom by their father, and Alexander and Philip by the English. Alexander succeeded Massasoit as principal chief of the Wampanoags after his father's death, and Philip, later called King Philip by the English and the progenitor of King Philip's War or Metacom's War, assumed the office among a people increasingly angry over English treatment after Alexander's death in 1662.

SIGNIFICANCE

Massasoit is potentially among the most controversial of figures in American history, since the significance of his relationship to the Pilgrims is open to diametrically opposed interpretations. He may be seen as the enlightened soul who made the decision not to allow the first European immigrants to his land to starve to death and who made possible the foundation of the most famous and culturally significant English settlement in the New World. That is, he may be seen as a hero of the story of the prehistory of the United States of America. Alternatively, he may be seen as the naive or myopic leader who allowed the colonial powers of Europe to gain a foothold in New England and to begin the slow but inevitable process of dominating, displacing, and ultimately killing the Native American population—as an inadvertent traitor to his own people.

—Bruce E. Johansen

FURTHER READING

Covey, Cyclone. *The Gentle Radical: A Biography of Roger Williams.* New York: Macmillan, 1966. This biogrpahy of Roger Williams contains information about Williams's associations with Massasoit.

Drake, James David. *King Philip's War: Civil War in New England, 1675-1676.* Amherst: University of Massachusetts Press, 1999. Unlike many authors, who maintain King Philip's War was a battle between two different cultures — one Native American and the other British — Drake argues the conflict was a civil war within a more cohesive New England culture.

Schultz, Eric B., and Michael J. Tougias. *King Philip's War: The History and Legacy of America's Forgotten Conflict.* Woodstock, Vt.: Countryman Press, 1999. An in-depth history of the war as well as a guide to the sites of the raids, ambushes, and battles.

Waters, Frank. *Brave Are My People: Indian Heroes Not Forgotten.* Santa Fe, N.Mex.: Clear Light, 1993. One chapter of this book contains biographical material on Massasoit.

Weeks, Alvin G. *Massasoit of the Wampanoags.* Fall River, Mass.: The Plimpton Press, 1919. Reprint. Scituate, Mass.: Digital Scanning, 2001. Digital Scanning, Inc. has digitized Weeks's book and made it available in a PDF format that can be downloaded from the company's web site, http://www.pdflibrary.com.

SEE ALSO: William Bradford; Canonicus; Metacom; Pocahontas; Powhatan; Squanto; Miles Standish; Roger Williams.

RELATED ARTICLES in *Great Events from History: The Seventeenth Century, 1601-1700:* December 26, 1620: Pilgrims Arrive in North America; March 22, 1622-October, 1646: Powhatan Wars; June 20, 1675: Metacom's War Begins.

MATSUO BASHŌ
Japanese poet

Bashō is considered one of Japan's greatest poets, especially as master of the haiku. While the haiku was already established as a poetic form prior to the Tokugawa era, Bashō is credited with reinvigorating the form at a time when it was in severe decline.

BORN: 1644; Ueno, Iga province, Japan
DIED: October 12, 1694; Ōsaka, Japan
ALSO KNOWN AS: Bashō; Matsuo Munefusa; Matsuo Kinsaku (given name)
AREA OF ACHIEVEMENT: Literature

EARLY LIFE

Matsuo Bashō (maht-soo-oh bah-shoh) was born Matsuo Kinsaku in Ueno, in the province of Iga, near Kyōto, on the island of Honshu in Japan. His father, Matsuo Yozaemon, was a samurai of minor rank and a teacher of calligraphy. His mother was also of samurai stock. He had an elder brother and four sisters. When Bashō was a young boy, he became a page at Ueno Castle and was a companion to the son of the lord of the castle, Tōdō Yoshitada. The two boys had a common interest in poetry, and they no doubt influenced each other. During this time, Bashō assumed a samurai's name, Matsuo Munefusa. This relationship with Lord Yoshitada's son came to an untimely end when the young lord died in 1666. Grief-stricken, Bashō left his service at Ueno Castle and began to devote more of his time and commitment to his poetry. While the later years of his youth are not well documented, it appears that Bashō spent much of his time wandering about Kyōto and studying with masters of literature there. At some time during this period, he abdicated his samurai status.

In his late twenties, probably around 1672, Bashō left the Kyōto area and settled in Edo. Why he moved is not clear, and he apparently had a difficult time getting established. Around 1677, he began to gather around himself a circle of pupils, many of whom would become his disciples and perpetuate his style. During this period, Bashō gained some reputation as a master of haiku, the brief seventeen-syllable verse form for which he is best known. In 1680, he was the recipient of a cottage that had banana trees planted on the land, and soon he was known as the "banana tree man," hence the name change to Bashō. Thought to have been a gift of Sampū, an admirer, the hut was located near the Sumida River in an isolated area. Two years later, the Bashō hut burned, to be replaced the following year. That same year, his mother died in Ueno.

Although some early biographers have suggested that Bashō may have had a mistress and one or more children, such a relationship cannot be clearly documented.

LIFE'S WORK

Bashō's life's work divides itself rather naturally into five stages, beginning with his earliest extant haiku written at age eighteen, in 1662, and lasting about ten years. For some years, his work showed evidence of change and maturity as he sought to master new techniques. In 1684, Bashō became a Buddhist priest and began a series of pilgrimages. His first important journey is recorded in *Nozarashi kikō* (1698; *The Records of a Weather-Exposed Skeleton*, 1959). Most of Bashō's finest haiku are written in his travel journals, and these diaries are themselves of high literary quality. Perhaps the best idea of his physical appearance is to be found in a wooden image, by an unknown carver; Bashō is in the dress of a Zen monk and has a typically Japanese expression of serenity

Matsuo Bashō. (Adapted from a portrait in the Itsuo Museum, Ikeda City, Osaka, reprinted by permission of Branden Press)

MATSUO BASHŌ'S MAJOR WORKS
1687   *Nozarashi kikō* (*The Records of a Weather-Exposed Skeleton*, 1959)
1691   *Sarumino* (*Monkey's Raincoat*, 1973)
1694   *Oku no hosomichi* (*The Narrow Road to the Deep North*, 1933)
1704   *Sarashina kikō* (*A Visit to Sarashina Village*, 1957)
1709   *Oi no kobumi* (*The Records of a Travel-Worn Satchel*, 1966)
n.d.   *Haikai shichibu-shū*

and wisdom. Between the years 1686 and 1691, Bashō was at the peak of his career, producing five poetic diaries containing haiku: *Kashima kikō* (1687; *A Visit to the Kashima Shrine*, 1965), *Sarashina Kikō* (1704; *A Visit to Sarashina Village*, 1957), *Oku no hosomichi* (1694; *The Narrow Road to the Deep North*, 1933), *Saga nikki* (1691; the saga diary), and *Oi no kobumi* (1709; *The Records of a Travel-Worn Satchel*, 1966). In addition, he was overseer for an anthology of haiku poems, *Sarumino* (1691; *Monkey's Raincoat*, 1973).

Prolific output of poetry is not, in itself, a sign of quality; indeed, compared with other haiku poets, Bashō is far from being the most prolific. What was characteristic of the work during this peak period was the distinctive style that Bashō developed. While he would continue to borrow from and allude to classical Chinese literature, as poets before him had done, he would continue to refine techniques that he had established in his earlier writing. In much of the poetry of this period, however, the unique quality of *sabi*, or loneliness, appeared. Always at the heart of this "loneliness" is the recognition of the fragility and transience of some manifestation of life merging into the vastness of nature. As Makoto Ueda has noted, the haiku that use *sabi* by implication, if not more explicitly, center on "the merging of the temporal into the eternal, of the mutable into the indestructible, of the tiny and finite into the vast and infinite, out of which emerges a primeval lonely feeling shared by all things in this world."

Bashō's haiku are inseparable from the frequent journeys that occasioned their composition. In perhaps the most relaxed, even carefree, period of Bashō's life, he traveled to Kashima, a small town some fifty miles to the east of Edo. Bashō's reason for the journey was to view the harvest moon. This journey provided the materials for *A Visit to the Kashima Shrine*. The first half of the journal describes the trip, and the latter half is a collection of poems by Bashō and others from the area of Kashima. This journal has as its primary motif the appre-

ciation of the beauty of nature and the idea that through this appreciation one can have union with poets of the past. Objectivity perhaps best describes Bashō's eight haiku in this volume.

In 1687, Bashō undertook a long journey westward that resulted in *The Records of a Travel-Worn Satchel*. This volume records the first half of the journey that extended into 1688. In this, one of his longer journals, Bashō records his travel from Edo westward to his hometown of Ueno and then to the coastal town of Akashi. The prose style resembles that of the earlier journal *A Visit to the Kashima Shrine* in using restrained language. The distinctive feature of *The Records of a Travel-Worn Satchel* is that in it Bashō makes a theoretical statement as an aesthetic primitivist, an advocate of a "return to nature." In this aspect, it is something of an extension of the earlier Kashima journal. While Bashō retains the modest tone characteristic of his writing, he nevertheless exhibits a clear sense of self-confidence.

During the same year, 1688, Bashō's shortest journal recorded his travel to Sarashina village. The half of the journal devoted to poetry contains eleven haiku by Bashō. Although Bashō had presumably gone through a period of having nothing new to say, he apparently found in the fresh, undeveloped, natural beauty of Sarashina a source for poetry that he had not considered appropriate earlier. The Sarashina journal provides an opportunity to record a new stage in Bashō's development.

Struck with this new dimension of nature, Bashō's next journey was northward, to the least developed area of Japan. This 1694 volume, *The Narrow Road to the Deep North*, is the longest of the journals. What is particularly interesting about the diary is its metaphorical title: It is a record of a spiritual journey as well as a literal one. While it is a journey in quest of the best of nature, it is also a search for what Bashō believes humankind has lost in the contemporary world.

The 1691 journal *Saga nikki* is, in some ways, most like an ordinary diary in that each entry of an approximately two-week visit in Saga is dated. In other ways, it is clearly akin to the other travel journals, especially in the central theme of forgetting one's material poverty and enjoying a serene, leisurely life attuned to nature.

Early in the summer of 1691, at the peak of the Bashō-style haikai, Mukai Kyorai and Nozawa Bonchō, under Bashō's guidance, published an anthology of haikai,

Monkey's Raincoat. The volume is especially significant because it lent credence to the haikai as a serious art form.

In 1692, the third Bashō hut was built, and the next year Bashō closed his gate and did not receive visitors for a time. In the summer of 1694, however, the poet began what was to have been a long journey, although one of his haiku documents his awareness of approaching death. He became increasingly ill, and, in early autumn, surrounded by some of his disciples and relatives, Bashō died in Ōsaka.

SIGNIFICANCE

Matsuo Bashō is without question among the greatest, if not the greatest, of the haikai poets that Japan has produced. Hundreds of years after his death, his reputation remains secure. Many of his pupils perpetuated his style and passed on the tradition to others: In bringing to new life the artificial, steadily dying form of the earlier haikai, he raised the genre to a new height; indeed, he founded a new genre.

Bashō was a master in his use of season words; in his use of associations with historical places or situations, and with historical sources for materials; and in his parody of old poems. Especially noteworthy were his style of expression and his ability to evoke the quality of *sabi.* Bashō also excelled as a critic and is considered a major contributor to Japanese literary aesthetics.

— *Victoria Price*

FURTHER READING

Aitken, Robert. *A Zen Wave: Bashō's Haiku and Zen.* New York: Weatherhill, 1979. A commentary on Bashō's haiku, with comparison of various English translations of a given poem. The introduction provides a concise sketch of Bashō's life and a discussion of the historical development of the haiku.

Hammill, Sam, trans. *The Essential Bashō.* Boston: Shambhala, 1999. Hammill presents Bashō as a poetic and philosophical wanderer engaged in a lifelong process of literary experimentation and discovery. Includes a fascinating overview of Bashō's transformation from a highly derivative stylist to a powerfully original poet.

Henderson, Harold G. *An Introduction to Haiku.* Garden City, N.Y.: Doubleday, 1958. Based on an earlier work, *The Bamboo Broom* (1934). The author makes an excellent translation of about seventy of Bashō's haiku.

Keene, Donald. *World Within Walls: Japanese Literature of the Pre-Modern Era, 1600-1867.* New York: Holt, Rinehart and Winston, 1976. In a chapter devoted to Bashō's haiku, Keene evaluates the poet's reputation in his lifetime and points out how some haiku are based on particular incidents in Bashō's life.

Miner, Earl. "Basho." In *Textual Analysis: Some Readers Reading,* edited by Mary Ann Caws. New York: Modern Language Association of America, 1986. Argues the poet is less well known in the West than he should be. Contrasts the Western concept of mimesis, what is real and what is fiction, with its Eastern counterpart and discusses misunderstandings resulting from the distinction.

Shirane, Harou. *Traces of Dreams: Landscape, Cultural Memory, and the Poetry of Bashō.* Stanford, Calif.: Stanford University Press, 1998. The author depicts Bashō as a cultural conservationist, whose poems draw upon deeply held concepts of nature.

Ueda, Makoto. *Bashō and His Interpreters: Selected Hokku with Commentary.* Stanford, Calif.: Stanford University Press, 1992. Chronologically organized anthology of 255 of Bashō's poems, each accompanied by the original Japanese text (transliterated into Western characters) and literal translations. Also includes commentary by Japanese poets and critics from the late seventeenth to the late twentieth centuries.

_____. *Matsuo Bashō.* New York: Twayne, 1970. Brief biography offering perspective on the development of Bashō's literary career and his major works. Discusses Bashō's *renku* (long collaboratively written poems) and prose works in addition to his haiku.

SEE ALSO: Hishikawa Moronobu; Ihara Saikaku; Ogata Kōrin; Sōtatsu.

RELATED ARTICLES in *Great Events from History: The Seventeenth Century, 1601-1700:* 1680-1709: Reign of Tsunayoshi as Shogun; 1688-1704: Genroku Era.

MAURICE OF NASSAU
Dutch stadtholder (1585-1625), prince of Orange (1618-1625), and military leader

Maurice reorganized the Dutch army and united under his rule most of the area currently known as the Netherlands, and he strengthened the newly independent United Netherlands in the face of its lengthy war with Spain and its ruling Habsburg Dynasty, the leading power of that era.

BORN: November 14, 1567; Dillenburg, Holland, United Provinces (now in the Netherlands)

DIED: April 23, 1625; The Hague, Holland, United Provinces (now in the Netherlands)

ALSO KNOWN AS: Maurits van Nassau; Prince of Orange

AREAS OF ACHIEVEMENT: Government and politics, military, warfare and conquest

EARLY LIFE

Born at Dillenburg Castle, Maurice of Nassau (NAS-aw) was the second son of Prince William of Orange (William the Silent), and Princess Anna of Saxony. Named after his maternal grandfather, Elector Maurice of Saxony, he was raised at Dillenburg by his uncle Jan de Oude (Jan the Old). He studied in Heidelberg with his cousin Willem Lodewijk and later in Leiden with his brother Filips. The states of Holland and Zeeland paid for Maurice's studies because his father had run into financial problems after spending his entire fortune leading the early stages of the Dutch revolt, which began in 1568.

Throughout Maurice's entire life, the Netherlands struggled for independence from the Spanish Habsburgs, who had dominated the Low Countries. He never married, but he did father illegitimate children by Margaretha van Mechelen and Anna van de Kelder.

In January of 1579, a new Spanish governor, Alessandro Farnese, duke of Parma, oversaw the formation of the Union of Arras, a pro-Spanish alliance of the southern provinces of the Netherlands (now called Belgium). Later that same month, Maurice's father united the northern Protestant provinces of Holland, Zeeland, Utrecht, Gelderland, and Groningen in the Union of Utrecht. Joined by the provinces of Overijssel, Drenthe, and Friesland, this union declared its independence from Spain as the United Provinces of the Netherlands (also known as the United Netherlands) in 1581. Roman Catholicism was fully restored in the south during the next decade, while the north became increasingly Calvinist (Protestant).

England, which supported the United Netherlands un-

officially for years, intervened directly in 1585, when Queen Elizabeth I sent Robert Dudley, earl of Leicester, to assist the Dutch with six thousand troops and one thousand horses. England's presence in the conflict, a presence that lasted until 1604, was the main reason why Spanish king Philip II sent his Armada against England in 1588; but the Spanish lost.

LIFE'S WORK

Following his father's assassination in Delft in 1584, Maurice took over as *stadhouder* (stadtholder), though this title was not heritable. From the fifteenth to the eighteenth century, stadtholders were officials who ruled areas of the Low Countries in the name of their landowners. After the Dutch provinces declared their independence, the function of stadtholder effectively became that of provincial ruler. Although each province could assign its own stadtholder, most stadtholders governed several provinces simultaneously.

Maurice's mentor was Landsadvocaat (civil administrator) Johan van Oldenbarnevelt, who had aided Maurice's father in the Dutch Revolt from its beginning. Representing the patrician commercial oligarchies that ruled Holland, Oldenbarnevelt oversaw a spectacular expansion of Dutch commerce and the founding of the Dutch East India Company (in 1602) and, chartered after his death, the Dutch West India Company (1621). He opposed the dictatorial policies of Robert Dudley, first earl of Leicester, who the States-General (Dutch parliament) had chosen as governor-general in 1586. Unified by their commercial ties, the powerful cities of Holland were hotbeds of republicanism. Relatively unimportant until that time, Amsterdam rose dramatically in population and power. Spain's fortunes, in contrast, were declining. Madrid's golden age was drawing to a close. Bankrupt in 1596, the first of many shortfalls, the Spanish treasury had been depleted by costs resulting from the loss of the Armada and French king Henry IV's declaration of war against Spain in 1595.

Meanwhile, Maurice had become stadtholder of Holland and Zeeland in 1585. With Oldenbarnevelt's backing, he was also appointed captain-general of the army and admiral of the United Netherlands in 1588, bypassing Dudley, who returned to England. Also, Maurice was named stadtholder of Gelderland, Overijssel, and Utrecht in 1590 and of Groningen and Drenthe in 1620 following the death of Willem Lodewijk, who had been stadtholder in Groningen, Drenthe, and Friesland. In 1618, Maurice succeeded his elder brother, Philip William, as prince of Orange.

As military leader and one of the best strategists of his age, Maurice reorganized the Dutch army into an effective, modern force. Together with Lodewijk and the great mathematician Simon Stevin, he applied his extensive studies in military history, engineering, mathematics, and astronomy to good effect. Paying special attention to the science of siege warfare, he took the offensive against the Spanish under Farnese and captured key fortress towns: Breda in 1590, Steenwijk in 1592, and St. Geertruidenberg in 1593. His later victories at Turnhout in 1597 and Nieuwpoort in 1600 earned him fame throughout Europe.

Relations between Maurice and Oldenbarnevelt, however, were strained when the impatient, overly optimistic landsadvocaat encouraged the reluctant stadtholder to invade the Spanish Netherlands (now Belgium), vainly believing that the Flemings would join the Dutch in expelling the Spanish. Then, despite Maurice's protests, Oldenbarnevelt signed the Twelve Years' Truce with Spain, which lasted from 1609 to 1621. The two men quarreled over strategy and the funding of the army and navy.

When troubles flared between Gomarists (strict Calvinists) and Remonstrants (reformed Calvinists), the struggle between Oldenbarnevelt and Maurice intensified. Maurice sided with the Gomarists and Oldenbarnevelt with the Remonstrants. Summoned by Maurice, the Synod of Dort (1618) suppressed the Remonstrants. Brooding and sometimes vengeful, Maurice seized greater power, a move that later historians would call a *coup d'état*. Despite numerous pleas for mercy, Oldenbarnevelt was arrested, tried, and decapitated for treason in 1619. This dispute and the public attention it attracted were the most important reasons why the Dutch were distracted from helping the Calvinist cause in the opening phase of the Thirty Years' War (1618-1648).

After the resumption of hostilities with Spain, Maurice's campaigns met with little success. The Spanish, led by Genoese general Ambrosio de Spínola, recaptured Breda in 1625. Embittered by his later defeats and deteriorating health, Maurice died shortly thereafter. He was succeeded as third stadtholder of Holland and heir of the Orange family by his youngest half brother Frederick Henry, whom he had earlier urged to marry to preserve the dynasty. Stadtholdership of Friesland, and then Groningen and Drenthe, passed to Count Ernst Casimir, a cousin of Maurice and Frederick Henry. The line of Nassau-LaLecq, which descended from his illegitimate heirs, became extinct in 1861.

SIGNIFICANCE

Despite the successes of William the Silent and Maurice of Nassau, the House of Orange did not attain much respect among European royalty, as the stadtholdership was not heritable and the Dutch system was a mixture of monarchical and republican elements. Maurice's drive for power only served to heighten this ambiguity. More and more aware of the Orange family's sweeping powers, even in religious matters, the United Netherlands became increasingly republican in sentiment. As long as war with Spain necessitated that Maurice be a warlord, he could rule in unchallenged safety from his palace in The Hague. However, an often rebellious Dutch spirit remained ever present.

Despite his military misfortunes and his debilitating quarrel with Oldenbarnevelt, Maurice of Nassau greatly strengthened the Dutch nation, thereby ensuring its survival in a bloody, destructive era. Indeed, the Netherlands and its far-flung overseas empire grew to the status of a world power. Maurice's scientific approach to military matters influenced generations of Dutch leaders. Spain was further weakened in 1639, when an armada with twenty thousand troops bound for Flanders was destroyed by Dutch admiral Maarten Tromp. The Twelve Years' Truce of 1609 had virtually secured recognition of Dutch independence, finally recognized by Spain on January 30, 1648, in the Treaty of Münster, one of two treaties comprising the Treaty of Westphalia.

—Randall Fegley

FURTHER READING

Blom, J. C. H., and E. Lamberts, eds. *History of the Low Countries*. Translated by James C. Kennedy. New York: Berghahn Books, 1999. An excellent history of Belgium, the Netherlands, and Luxembourg, with much material on Maurice of Nassau and the Dutch Wars of Independence.

Israel, Jonathan. *The Dutch Republic: Its Rise, Greatness, and Fall, 1477-1806*. Oxford, England: Clarendon Press, 1995. A detailed history of the Dutch Republic from the fifteenth century to the early nineteenth century.

Parker, Geoffrey. *The Dutch Revolt*. New York: Penguin Books, 1990. A thorough history of the Dutch Wars of Independence.

_____. *Spain and the Netherlands, 1559-1659*. Short Hills, N.J.: Enslow, 1979. An important interpretive study of the diplomatic relations of Spain and Holland. Deals with such topics as the length of time of the Dutch revolt, the larger world of international politics to which this conflict belonged, and the revolt's economic consequences.

Rowen, Herbert H. *The Princes of Orange: The Stadtholders in the Dutch Republic.* New York: Cambridge University Press, 1988. This book provides biographical information on all stadtholders of the House of Orange, including a history of the house in the context of politics, government, and rulership.

Wedgwood, C. V. *William the Silent, William of Nassau, Prince of Orange, 1533-1584.* London: Jonathan Cape, 1944. An excellent biography of Maurice's father, which contains much on Maurice's early life as well.

SEE ALSO: Charles I; Charles II (of England); Oliver Cromwell; Frederick Henry; Frederick William, the Great Elector; Hugo Grotius; Gustavus II Adolphus; Piet Hein; Friedrich Hermann Schomberg; Maarten and Cornelis Tromp; Lennart Torstenson; Viscount de Turenne.

RELATED ARTICLES in *Great Events from History: The Seventeenth Century, 1601-1700:* 17th century: Age of Mercantilism in Southeast Asia; July 5, 1601-April, 1604: Siege of Oostende; Beginning Spring, 1605: Dutch Dominate Southeast Asian Trade; September, 1608: Invention of the Telescope; 1609: Bank of Amsterdam Invents Checks; 1617-1693: European Powers Vie for Control of Gorée; 1625: Grotius Establishes the Concept of International Law; 1630-1660's: Dutch Wars in Brazil; August 26, 1641-September, 1648: Conquest of Luanda; Spring, 1645-1660: Puritan New Model Army; 1654: Portugal Retakes Control of Brazil; 1670-1699: Rise of the Asante Empire.

JULES MAZARIN
Italian-born French statesman and diplomat

Mazarin played a central role in stabilizing the French monarchy and laying the political foundations for French absolutism in the critical period between 1643 and 1661. Mazarin's patronage of the arts and letters was extravagant, and he exercised profound influence in shaping the foundations of modern French art, music, and drama.

BORN: July 14, 1602; Pescina, Kingdom of Naples (now in Italy)
DIED: March 9, 1661; Vincennes, France
ALSO KNOWN AS: Giulio Mazarini
AREAS OF ACHIEVEMENT: Government and politics, religion and theology, diplomacy, patronage of the arts

EARLY LIFE

Jules Mazarin (jewlz maw-zaw-rahn) was born in the Abruzzi region of central Italy. The oldest son of a minor government official, he received his early education from the Jesuits in Rome. From 1622 to 1624, he studied law at Alcalá in Spain. In 1624, Mazarin became a captain in a papal regiment. In 1626, he took up the position as secretary to G. F. Sacchetti, who received an appointment two years later as papal nuncio to the Spanish viceroy of Milan.

Continuing his service in Milan under Sacchetti's successor, Cardinal Antonio Barberini, Mazarin undertook his first important mission as a diplomat in 1630, when he carried out negotiations with the French minister Cardinal de Richelieu at Lyons. In October, 1630, as the Spanish forces besieging the French at Casale prepared to attack, Mazarin boldly rode through the Spanish lines shouting "Peace!" as though hostilities had been suspended. In the resulting talks, he persuaded the Spanish to call off their attack.

Rewarded for his daring diplomacy with a canonry (a minor ecclesiastical office not requiring holy orders), Mazarin's star was clearly on the rise. From 1632 to 1634, Pope Urban VIII entrusted Mazarin with a series of special diplomatic missions and in 1634 named him special nuncio to France. Once in France, Mazarin took every opportunity to acquaint himself with the workings of the French government, and while he failed to prevent France from declaring war on Spain in 1635, his services were so valued that he was soon acting as France's unofficial ambassador in Rome. Mazarin received France's nomination for the cardinalate in 1636, but the Spanish faction in Rome blocked his hopes for the honor. Officially entering France's service in December, 1639, Mazarin began a career that would bring him to the heights of power and wealth in only a few short years.

Jules Mazarin. (Library of Congress)

LIFE'S WORK

Entering Richelieu's diplomatic entourage, Mazarin immediately became the French plenipotentiary at the peace talks with the Habsburgs. At that point in the Thirty Years' War (1618-1648), neither side saw any advantage to immediate peace and the talks came to nothing. After undertaking several additional diplomatic missions, he was created cardinal in December, 1641. A trusted adviser to Richelieu, Mazarin's scope of political activity expanded when he assisted in dealing with the conspiracy of Cinq-Mars. Strongly recommended to the king, Mazarin joined Louis XIII's council immediately after Richelieu's death in December, 1642. Following the king's own death six months later, Mazarin joined the regency council formed to govern in the name of the five-year-old Louis XIV. Within days, however, the Queen Mother, Anne of Austria, had disbanded the council, claimed the regency for herself, and named Mazarin her principal minister. From that point until Mazarin's death in 1661, Mazarin and Anne of Austria ruled France—in

Louis's name until 1651, when he declared his majority, with the king's authority thereafter.

Historians have devoted much attention to the relationship between Mazarin and Anne of Austria, especially over the question of a secret marriage. Such a liaison was not inconceivable (Mazarin never took the vows of the priesthood) but if known would have proved problematic and extremely damaging. No known documents support the notion of the marriage, but to concentrate exclusively on such legal formalities is to miscast the historical questions concerning their relationship. They never lived as husband and wife, but they shared an intimacy and a convergence of interests so close as to mark their union as extraordinarily personal. Moreover, Mazarin formed an extremely paternalistic bond with Louis, Anne's son. For his part, the young king clearly responded to Mazarin as a son would to a father.

Mazarin became Richelieu's successor as France's principal minister, but his tenure in that position was marked by circumstances dramatically different from those Richelieu had enjoyed. First, he served a regency government that had to defend itself from enemies among the highest nobility, several of whom enjoyed claims to the regency at least as strong as Anne's. Second, Mazarin's Italian birth and speech marked him as a foreigner, and he did nothing to diminish the French tendency toward xenophobia as he brought numerous members of his extended family to France to arrange marriages or place them in political offices. Indeed, Mazarin's nepotism and his persistence in pursuing advantageous marriages for his many nieces became legendary. Third, as the French involvement in the Thirty Years' War deepened and as the fighting dragged on year after year, the people of France became increasingly restive under the extraordinary tax burdens Mazarin and Anne imposed.

Following the first outbreak of opposition among the *parlementaires* (judges and lawyers of the Paris law court) and the Parisian bourgeoisie in mid-1648, Mazarin and Anne pressed the military commanders in the field to provide a quick resolution to the war. The Great Condé, a prince of the blood, provided that victory at Lens in August, 1648, and with Condé's victory all the major belligerents, except France and Spain, arrived at terms in a series of treaties that has come to be known as the Treaty of Westphalia. Although the specifically

French-Spanish conflict dragged on for another ten years, the peace of 1648 marked a reduction in hostilities that allowed Mazarin and Anne to turn their attention to subduing the *parlementaires*. Supported by Condé's troops, Mazarin and Anne instituted a reversal of earlier concessions to the Paris opposition. This move led to the first war of the Fronde (January to March, 1649), a rebellion that pitted the city of Paris against a coalition headed by Mazarin, Anne, and Condé. Quickly victorious in quelling the Fronde of the *parlementaires*, Condé sought higher positions for himself and for his entourage.

Frictions with Anne and Mazarin finally led Condé to declare a second Fronde against them. This second prince's Fronde lasted from January, 1650, until February, 1651, only to be succeeded by the third Fronde (December, 1651, to February, 1653), once again led by Condé. In the second Fronde, the battle was for the regency over Louis XIV, and the basis for that war ended with Louis's premature declaration of his majority in September, 1651. With the third Fronde, Condé had lost any claim to legality for his actions and the fighting ended only with his military defeat and a formal charge of treason against him. From 1653, until the Treaty of the Pyrenees (1659) put an end to war (and gave reinstatement to his title and lands in France), Condé fought in Spain's service.

The three Fronde and Condé's treason pointed up the weakness of the French monarchy. Twice during the Fronde, Mazarin had been forced to flee into exile in the Germanies to escape not only the frondeurs but also the wrath of factions loyal to the monarchy. Following the Fronde, Mazarin devoted all of his energy to rebuilding the monarchy's political foundations. Among his more important acts, the reestablishment of the royal commissioners (intendants) in the provinces and his gathering together of supporting ministers proved to have the most enduring consequences. Later formalized under Louis XIV and his minister Jean-Baptiste Colbert, the system of intendants furnished the basic administrative mechanism for royal government until the Revolution. In that sense, Mazarin's reforms following the Fronde marked the end of the traditional feudal form of the French monarchy. The feudal nobility retained its titles and status, but following the establishment of the intendancies the monarchy moved quickly toward a centralized, bureaucratic administration.

In bringing together his own circle of advisers, Mazarin also selected and trained the ministers who were to dominate the first half of Louis's personal reign: François-Michel Le Tellier, Hugues de Lionne, Colbert, and the ill-fated Nicolas Fouquet. Many have noted the brilliance of these ministers and have credited Mazarin with much of the success of Louis's early personal reign. Such a claim can have only limited value, but it is borne out to some degree through comparisons drawn between the successes of Le Tellier, Lionne, and Colbert and the lackluster performances common among Louis's later ministers. Certainly, Mazarin had a talent for selecting and preparing his favorites for political service.

During his last years, Mazarin was preoccupied with achieving an advantageous peace with Spain and arranging the king's marriage. He succeeded in both these tasks at the same time, making Louis's marriage to King Philip IV's eldest daughter Marie-Thérèse one of the terms included in the Treaty of the Pyrenees. The marriage posed a serious obstacle to the negotiations, since Philip insisted on protecting the Spanish inheritance from the possibility of its falling into Bourbon hands. In what was perhaps his greatest diplomatic victory, Mazarin persuaded Philip to agree to an extraordinarily large dowry (500,000 gold ecus) as the price for Louis's renunciation of all claims to the Spanish crown. Mazarin saw clearly that Spain would never be able to make the payments on this astronomical sum, which was scheduled to be paid in installments. He thus laid the basis for later French claims (and ultimate Bourbon succession) to the Spanish throne.

Throughout his service to France, Mazarin proved himself to be an avid patron of the arts and letters as well. His most noteworthy accomplishments in this regard are found in his devotion to his library and his patronage of the Academy of Painting and Sculpture, which he founded in 1648. After his library had been broken up and sold by his enemies during the Fronde, he patiently reassembled the collection during the late 1650's. Following his death, his library formed the basis for the first of the great royal collections, and his endowments established the College of the Four Nations, an educational institution established for the king's non-French subjects. The Institut de France in Paris was built through money he had bequeathed for its construction, and his library serves as the core of that institution's collections.

Mazarin died of cancer at the château of Vincennes on March 9, 1661. Popular hostility toward the cardinal minister had never abated. He was the continuing target of scurrilous lampoons and pamphlets that came to be known as *mazarinades*. Nevertheless, he enjoyed Louis's steadfast support to the end, and when Mazarin willed all of his earthly goods to the king, Louis returned them as a gift to demonstrate his confidence in the minister. Clearly, Louis held Mazarin in the very highest regard, and it is certain that so long as Mazarin lived, he delayed implementing his plan to take personal responsibility for ruling France. At Mazarin's death, the king did announce that decision, and in that sense Mazarin's passing marked one of the most significant turning points in the history of France.

Significance

Mazarin stands as the pivotal figure between Cardinal de Richelieu's first policies tending toward absolutism and Louis XIV's implementation of a full-scale, centralized monarchy. Acting as regent and principal minister, Mazarin steered the monarchy through the perilous years of Louis's minority and early reign. Certainly, his foreign birth and his style of governing contributed to the antagonisms engendered in the Fronde, but any minister who sought to pursue Richelieu's vision of the state would have faced severe difficulties in the France of the 1640's. Given the circumstances he faced in 1643, Mazarin achieved remarkable successes: He pursued war with France's foreign enemies to successful conclusion; he broke the hold of the high nobility over the throne; he avoided financial collapse; and he exercised a guardianship over the young Louis XIV that must be counted as one of the most successful apprenticeships in statecraft ever achieved.

Perhaps the best measure of his success is simply to compare the political, social, and economic condition of France at the moment of his rise to power (1643) against conditions at his death in 1661. There is no question that Mazarin deserves major credit for laying the foundation for Louis XIV's France.

—*David S. Lux*

Further Reading

Bonney, Richard. *Political Change in France Under Richelieu and Mazarin, 1624-1661*. New York: Oxford University Press, 1978. Bonney, a historian who specializes in early modern French history, provides an overview of the changing political climate under the two powerful ministers.

_____. *Society and Government Under Richelieu and Mazarin, 1624-1661*. New York: St. Martin's Press, 1988. In his second book about Richelieu and Mazarin, Bonney focuses on French society and government during the two men's administrations.

Croxton, Derek. *Peacemaking in Early Modern Europe: Cardinal Mazarin and the Congress of Westphalia,*

1643-1648. Selinsgrove, N.J.: Susquehanna University Press, 1999. Examines France's position during negotiations to end the Thirty Years' War, focusing on Mazarin's role in the negotiations.

Levi, Anthony. *Louis XIV*. New York: Carroll & Graf, 2004. A comprehensive biography of Louis XIV and his reign. Levi speculates that Louis XIV probably was not the son of Louis XIII but of Mazarin, the real power in France during Louis XIV's childhood.

Maland, David. *Culture and Society in Seventeenth-Century France*. New York: Charles Scribner's Sons, 1970. Still the best survey in English treating French high culture and political involvement with patronage. Places Mazarin and his patronage against the larger backdrop of rapid developments in art, drama, and literature.

Ogg, David. *Europe in the Seventeenth Century*. 9th ed. London: A. and C. Black, 1971. Ogg's political survey is excellent for placing Mazarin's ministry in a larger European perspective.

Shennan, J. H. *The Parlement of Paris*. Ithaca, N.Y.: Cornell University Press, 1968. The two chapters on the seventeenth century provide excellent material on the basic constitutional issues facing Richelieu and Mazarin. The material on the period of the Fronde is heavily weighted toward discussion of opposition to Mazarin.

Sturdy, David J. *Richelieu and Mazarin: A Study in Statesmanship*. New York: Palgrave MacMillan, 2004. Concise and comparative analysis of the public and private careers of the two ministers, including an assessment of their historical significance.

Treasure, Geoffrey. *Mazarin: The Crisis of Absolutism in France*. New York: Routledge, 1995. Treasure argues that Mazarin was a remarkable statesman, who helped the French monarchy survive during the Fronde rebellion, provided guidance to a young Louis XIV, and offered diplomatic assistance to end the Thirty Years' and the Franco-Spanish Wars.

Wolf, John B. *Louis XIV*. New York: W. W. Norton, 1968. Particularly valuable for insights into the personal relations between Mazarin, Anne of Austria, and Louis XIV. Wolf's scholarship is authoritative, and the work stands as one of the most widely respected treatments of Louis's reign. The material on Mazarin's policy objectives is particularly insightful.

See also: Anne of Austria; Jean-Baptiste Colbert; The Great Condé; Cornelius Otto Jansen; Duchesse de Longueville; Louis XIII; Louis XIV; The Mancini

Sisters; Axel Oxenstierna; Philip IV; Urban VIII; Saint Vincent de Paul; Viscount de Turenne.

RELATED ARTICLES in *Great Events from History: The Seventeenth Century, 1601-1700:* 1610-1643: Reign of Louis XIII; 1618-1648: Thirty Years' War; November 8, 1620: Battle of White Mountain; November 10, 1630: The Day of Dupes; 1638-1669: Spread of Jansenism; May, 1640-January 23, 1641: Revolt of the Catalans; July, 1643-October 24, 1648: Peace of Westphalia; June, 1648: Wars of the Fronde Begin; November 7, 1659: Treaty of the Pyrenees; 1661: Absolute Monarchy Emerges in France; 1661-1672: Colbert Develops Mercantilism; 1664: Molière Writes *Tartuffe*; May 24, 1667-May 2, 1668: War of Devolution; 1682: French Court Moves to Versailles.

IVAN STEPANOVICH MAZEPA
Ukrainian Cossack hetman (r. 1687-1709)

A prudent and statesmanlike ruler of the Cossacks of the Dnieper, Mazepa sought to work loyally with the Muscovite state, until Czar Peter the Great's exploitation of the Ukraine led him to defect to Charles XII of Sweden, sharing in the latter's 1709 defeat at Poltava.

BORN: March 20, 1639; Mazepyntsi, near Belaya Tserkov, Ukraine

DIED: October 2, 1709; Bendery (now Tighina, Moldova)

AREAS OF ACHIEVEMENT: Government and politics, warfare and conquest

EARLY LIFE

Ivan Stepanovich Mazepa (ih-VAHN styih-PAHN-uhv-yihch muh-ZYAY-puh) was born into a respected gentry (*starshyna*) family of Ukrainian Cossacks. For his class, he was unusually well-educated, being sent first to the Kiev Academy and then to a Jesuit college in Warsaw. Thereafter, he entered the service of the Polish king John II Casimir Vasa (r. 1648-1668) as a gentleman usher, which enabled him to travel to western Europe and acquire a broader outlook than that of the typical Cossack of his time. It was probably during his stay in Poland that there occurred, if indeed it did occur, the episode narrated in George Gordon, Lord Byron's celebrated poem *Mazeppa* (1819).

In 1669, Mazepa returned to the Ukraine and entered the service of the hetman of the Cossacks of the Right Bank of the Dnieper River, Petro Doroshenko, thereby securing a first foothold on the ladder of power. Not long afterward, he fell into the hands of the Left Bank hetman, Ivan Samoilovych. Mazepa's capture might have proved his undoing, but his sophistication and assiduous manners impressed Samoilovych, who promoted him to be his confidante.

Mazepa was one of the most significant figures in a turbulent period in Cossack history. During his lifetime, the Cossack communities of the Ukraine had grudgingly submitted to Muscovite rule. The word "Cossack" drives from the Turkish *qazaq*, meaning "masterless men," and the Cossacks were indeed dissidents, runaway serfs, and criminal outcasts. Devoutly Orthodox, they were bitterly hostile to Catholics, Muslims, and Jews. Most of all, they were rugged lovers of freedom, and they resented even the abstract authority of the Russian czar over them, much less any actual exercise of that authority.

Following the 1648-1654 Cossack revolt of Bohdan Khmelnytsky against Poland, the Cossacks had become signatories to the Treaty of Pereyaslavl (1654), which placed them under Muscovite suzerainty. This treaty resulted in increased interference by Muscovite tax-collectors, law-officers, and garrison-commanders in Cossack affairs. One effect of this situation was to diminish the older egalitarianism of the Cossack social order and to replace it with far more differentiated social hierarchy. A man like Mazepa, therefore, was elevated to the rank of a virtual Cossack nobleman.

LIFE'S WORK

In 1687, events in Russia played into Mazepa's hands. Czarena Sophia, the Russian regent, despatched a military expedition against the Crimean Tatars with her chief minister, Prince Vasily Golitsyn, in command. On the march toward the Crimea, the Russian forces were joined by Hetman Samoilovych and his Cossacks, including Mazepa, who had a considerable personal following. The campaign proved a disaster, not least because of devastating fires lit on the steppes. At first, the Tatars were blamed for the fires, but later the rumor spread that it was Samoilovych, angered by Russia's recent peace with Poland, and fearful that defeat of the Tatars would weaken Cossack bargaining-power, who had had them lit.

The rumors led to Samoilovych being deposed from power. Mazepa was elected hetman in his stead and confirmed by Moscow on July 25, 1687. Prince Golitsyn led a second expedition against the Tatars, in which Mazepa again participated, but it proved similarly disastrous. In September, 1689, Sophia's half-brother, Peter I (later known as Peter the Great), engineered a coup to get rid of her. Thereafter, freed of Sophia's regency, Peter ruled in fact as well as name.

For approximately twenty-one years (1687-1709), the fortunes of Mazepa and those of the Ukraine were synonymous, although his rule was not without controversy. He clearly favored the *starshyna*, the Cossack officer elite, enriching them, as well as himself, with extensive land grants. He was also generous to the Orthodox Church, providing funds for church building and for the maintenance of religious and cultural institutions, such as the Kiev Academy. Also in Kiev, Mazepa was said to have spent seventy-four thousand gold ducats on the bell tower of the Pechersk monastery and between 1690 and 1707 to have made baroque additions to Saint Sophia. His magnificent church of Saint Nicholas in Kiev, built between 1690 and 1693, was destroyed by the Soviets in 1934. These and others structures were built in a style known as Ruthenian, Cossack, or Mazepist Baroque.

The favors that Mazepa lavished on the elite, the clergy, and the small student class were in stark contrast to the heavy weight of his rule upon the peasants and ordinary Cossacks. In 1692, there was even an unsuccessful uprising by a group who aspired to create an independent Ukraine centered on the Zaporozhian Sech (an island on the lower Dnieper River regarded as the birthplace of Ukrainian Cossackdom). In fact, the strength of Mazepa's position during the 1690's was based upon his close working relationship with Czar Peter, who seemed to trust him and to whom Mazepa looked for unfailing support. With the passing of time, however, Peter came to regard Cossack autonomy as a historical anachronism, and he may have grown increasingly suspicious of the wily old hetman. Mazepa, for his part, had little sympathy with Peter's sweeping modernizing goals and their brutal implementation, from which the Ukraine was certainly not spared.

Mazepa's disillusionment with Peter was brought to a head during the early phase of the Great Northern War (1700-1721), in which Russia, in alliance with Denmark and Poland, confronted Charles XII of Sweden. The struggle strained Russia's resources to the uttermost, and Mazepa's Ukraine was called upon to make unprecedented sacrifices in a war against Sweden, a nation with which the Cossacks (traditionally in conflict with Poles, Tatars, and Ottoman Turks) had no quarrel.

The Cossacks were treated as cannon fodder in the war, experiencing losses of 50 percent to 70 percent each year, while from 1705 onward, Russian and German officers were put in command of Cossack units, spreading bitter resentment among the *starshyna*. Meanwhile, Ukrainian peasants and townsmen suffered from the appalling weight of Peter's fiscal exactions and the brutal behavior of Russian garrisons. Mazepa began to doubt the value of Russian overlordship, especially when Sweden threatened to invade the Ukraine and Peter declared that he could spare no troops to help defend it, despite the guarantees of the Treaty of Pereyaslavl.

When, in October, 1708, Charles XII, instead of advancing on Moscow, turned south to seek food and fodder for his army in the agriculturally rich Ukraine, Mazepa, with three thousand Cossacks and his principal supporters among the *starshyna*, defected to the Swedes. Charles promised to protect the Ukraine from the czar and, in an eventual peace treaty, guaranteed its independence, but Charles—superb commander that he was—had nevertheless blundered in his march south. He found himself beset by logistical difficulties, and he could ultimately do nothing for his new Ukrainian allies.

Peter's vengeance came swiftly. On October 31, 1708, Peter's favorite, Prince Aleksander Menshikov, entered Baturyn, Mazepa's capital, and massacred the entire population of six thousand men, women, and children, following the massacre by a reign of terror throughout the Dnieper River's Left Bank directed against supporters or supposed supporters of Mazepa. On November 11, 1708, Mazepa was excommunicated and deposed from the hetmanate. Peter ordered the *starshyna* to elect a new hetman, Ivan Skoropadsky. In May, 1709, Russian forces penetrated to the Zaporozhian Sech and wiped it out. Finally, on June 28, 1709, Charles XII was decisively defeated at the Battle of Poltava, after which the Swedish king, accompanied by Mazepa, fled into Ottoman territory, where Mazepa died at Bendery the following October.

SIGNIFICANCE

Mazepa attained the hetmanate through his martial qualities, political astuteness, and powers of leadership. For over twenty years, his rule over the Ukraine was humane and enlightened, albeit calculating and autocratic. He gained much by winning Peter's confidence, but in the end, he concluded that Moscow's treatment of the Cossacks was unbearably exploitive, and he was beguiled into believing that Charles XII would support an independent Ukraine. It was a gamble that he lost, but, as one scholar has expressed it, "But for the tragedy of Poltava, this gifted and humane ruler might have been termed 'the Great' by East European history, while Peter, for all his modernizing, might in many minds have joined the company and epithet of Ivan IV [the Terrible]." History, however, is written by the victors, and throughout most of the Romanov period, Mazepa was anathemized in the annual state Easter services.

Mazepa's story is a classic case of a traditional ruler pitted against a brutal modernizer. It can also be seen as a case of a still embryonic national identity being forced to give way to one that was more developed. After Poltava, first the Dnieper River region and then the other Cossack communities were brought into subjugation to the expanding Russian state. In historical retrospect, Mazepa became a "non-person," and those Ukrainians who dreamed of political independence were dismissed as Mazepintsy (Mazepists). Today, in an independent Ukraine, cultural tourists are proudly shown the monuments to the first stirrings of Cossack nationalism, in which Mazepa remains a somewhat ambiguous figure.

—*Gavin R. G. Hambly*

FURTHER READING

Arndt, Walter. *Alexander Pushkin: Collective Narrative and Lyrical Poetry.* Ann Arbor, Mich.: Ardis, 1984. Excellent translation and discussion of the epic *Poltava.*

Gajecky, G. *The Cossack Administration of the Hetmanate.* 2 vols. Cambridge, Mass.: Harvard Ukrainian Research Institute, 1978. The definitive study on the subject.

Hughes, Lindsey. *Russia in the Age of Peter the Great.* New Haven, Conn.: Yale University Press, 1998. Excellent introduction to the period.

Longworth, Philip. *The Cossacks.* New York: Holt, Rinehart & Winston, 1970. General introduction to the Cossack phenomenon.

Subtelny, Orest. "Mazepa, Peter I, and the Question of Treason," *Harvard Ukrainian Studies* 2 (1978): 158-183. Discussion of Mazepa's ambiguous relations with the Russian state.

_____. *The Mazepists Ukrainian Separatism in the Eighteenth Century.* Boulder, Colo.: Eastern European Monographs, 1981. Illuminating for Mazepa's separatist legacy.

_____. *Ukraine: A History.* 3d ed. Toronto: University of Toronto Press, 2000. Authoritative overview of Ukrainian history.

SEE ALSO: Merzifonlu Kara Mustafa Paşa; Bohdan Khmelnytsky; Sophia.

RELATED ARTICLES in *Great Events from History: The Seventeenth Century, 1601-1700:* 1632-1667: Polish-Russian Wars for the Ukraine; Summer, 1672-Fall, 1676: Ottoman-Polish Wars; 1677-1681: Ottoman-Muscovite Wars; Beginning 1689: Reforms of Peter the Great.

COSIMO II DE' MEDICI
Grand duke of Tuscany (1609-1621)

Though he was often sick, died young, and was called simply an agreeable nonentity, Cosimo was responsible for continuing his father's economic and political policies as grand duke of Tuscany, expanding the Pitti Palace, and bringing Galileo to Florence as a member of his court.

BORN: May 12, 1590; Florence (now in Italy)
DIED: February 28, 1621; Florence
ALSO KNOWN AS: Cosimo II
AREAS OF ACHIEVEMENT: Patronage of the arts, government and politics

EARLY LIFE

Cosimo II de' Medici (MEHD-ee-chee) was born to Ferdinand, the grand duke of Tuscany, and Christina, the granddaughter of Catherine de' Médicis and the daughter of the duke of Lorraine, Charles II. Cosimo was raised at the glittering Medici court of the Pitti Palace and Medici villas in and around Florence.

At court he learned etiquette and the court arts, such as hunting, dancing, and horsemanship, under the direction of Silvio Piccolomini of Siena. At his mother's insistence, he also was trained in the classics, drawing, German, and Castilian Spanish. She also brought Galileo, already a noted scholar, to the court to tutor him in cosmography, mathematics, and mechanics, a course of study that lasted sporadically from 1605 to 1608. In 1606, Galileo dedicated his treatise on the operations of the geometric and military compass to the young, soon-to-be grand duke.

From an early age Cosimo suffered from the effects of tuberculosis and, after 1614, had serious stomach ailments. These troubles not only affected him physically—he spent a good deal of his adult life in bed—but also made him psychologically more dependent on the women in his life, especially his mother and his wife.

In 1608, he married Maria Magdalena of Austria, sister of the future Holy Roman Emperor Ferdinand II. Unlike many such arrangements, theirs would be an affectionate and loving relationship, one that would produce five sons and three daughters in less than thirteen years. The state wedding was celebrated with an elaborate pageant based on the ancient Greek tale of Jason and the Argonauts. The audience filled bleachers along the riverbank as the spectacle unfolded on floating rafts that stretched from the Ponte Carraia to the Ponte Trinità in the Arno River. It was the first of many such extravagant pageants that would be produced during Cosimo's reign as grand duke, which began with the death of his father Ferdinand in 1609.

LIFE'S WORK

At Cosimo II's accession as fourth grand duke of Tuscany, Florence was thriving and at peace, though international waters were increasingly dangerous and Tuscany's economic base was deteriorating. Only nineteen years old, he decided to retain most of his father's ministers, and he came to rely most heavily on his uncle Giovanni, on Belisario Vinta, and on his mother and wife. It became clear early on that he would leave the traditional family financial concerns to others and spend his time dabbling in the international arena.

With Vinta's advice Cosimo managed to maintain relative neutrality in the hostilities between Spain and France. He successfully mediated a marriage (1615) between King Louis XIII of France and Anne of Austria, a daughter of King Philip II of Spain, and a second match (1621), the future King Philip IV of Spain with Elizabeth (Isabella) of France. He was, however, dragged briefly by an old alliance with Spain into wars in northern Italy over Milan and Mantua.

As his own wedding pageant suggested, Cosimo was interested in maritime matters and expended a great deal of effort in building up the duchy's port of Livorno (Leghorn). He doubled its population and built up the artificial barrier, or mole, that helped create a deep water harbor for international trade. He also was a great patron of the naval Order of San Stefano in its fight against Muslim fleets from Turkey and from Barbary in North Africa. The order's admirals, Iacopo (Jacopo) Inghirami and

Giulio da Montauto, scored many minor victories against fleets of pirates, and also fueled hopes of a major crusade against the Turkish Levant. As part of his effort to forge a grand anti-Turkish alliance, he even hosted the shah of Persia, 'Abbās the Great(1609), who suggested that success might lead to a Tuscan colony in Syria.

Despite the Livorno project and the creation of a canal for the grain trade near Grossetano, Cosimo's development policies were collectively a failure. Industry continued to relocate outside Tuscany, and the once proud banking and financial infrastructure had migrated to northern Europe. He tried establishing an agricultural colony near Florence of some three hundred Moors who had been ejected from Spain, but their lack of experience and discipline led him to uproot the group and send them to the Barbary Coast.

In Florence itself, he reformed the funded debt of Monte di Pietà as well as the rather loosely jointed *consultato*, or Grand Ducal Council, whose powers and membership were strengthened and formalized. Cosimo also saw to the extension of the wings of the Pitti Palace, the family's main residence, and the expansion of the Boboli Garden behind it. The work was designed and overseen by Giulio Parigi, the court architect. Cosimo's only new construction was that of a new villa, Poggio Imperiale. His taste in art was quite narrow and ran to small, technically fine painted works by such artists as Agostino Tasso. He did, however, enjoy visiting artists' workshops, which was odd for a duke but in line with his dilettantish interest in techniques and processes.

The great Italian scientist and mathematician Galileo opened his formal relationship with the young grand duke in 1610 by sending him from Padua a telescope and a copy of his groundbreaking work *Sidereus nuncius* (*The Sidereal Messenger*, 1880), which he dedicated to Cosimo. In this he named the planets of Jupiter he had discovered after the Medici family, ensuring favor at court. Cosimo reciprocated by granting his former tutor a pension and a residence at Arcetri in May of 1610. From that point, Galileo was part of the Medici court, often sparring with the less-enlightened Aristotelians there and at the University of Pisa, at which he held a sinecure. Galileo's official title was chief mathematician of Pisa and philosopher of the grand duke. Cosimo enjoyed intellectual fireworks and even sponsored a significant debate over Copernicanism within court circles. In 1616, however, the Church banned the teaching of Copernican theory, and specifically admonished Galileo, who avoided the subject for the remainder of Cosimo's reign.

Cosimo died of tuberculosis in February of 1621,

leaving an eleven-year-old heir, Ferdinand II, in the hands of Magdalena and the court's ministers.

SIGNIFICANCE

Without a doubt, Cosimo II de' Medici is best known for his relationship with Galileo. In many ways, Cosimo's reign as grand duke of Tuscany was otherwise a nonevent. His accomplishments were few and rather technical: reforms in Florentine and ducal government and the expansion of the port of Livorno and of the Pitti Palace. Galileo's acceptance of Cosimo's patronage gave the great scientist a useful Italian protector, first in Cosimo and then in Cosimo's son Ferdinand II, whom Galileo also tutored. This provided Galileo the free time and resources to further his experiments and observations and advance the scientific understanding of the age.

—*Joseph P. Byrne*

FURTHER READING

Biagioli, Mario. *Galileo Courtier: The Practice of Science in the Culture of Absolutism.* Chicago: University of Chicago Press, 1994. Studies Galileo's fortunes at Cosimo II's court, from 1610 to Cosimo's death in 1621.

Cleugh, James. *The Medici: A Tale of Fifteen Generations.* New York: Dorset Press, 1990. A short discussion of Cosimo and his accomplishments.

Giusti, Annamaria, ed. *Masters of Florence: Glory and Genius at the Court of the Medici.* Memphis, Tenn.: Wonders, 2004. A well-documented exhibition catalog of art and artifacts from Florentine museums. Places the works in the context of Medici rulers, including Cosimo.

Goldberg, Edward L. *Patterns in Later Medici Art Patronage.* Princeton, N.J.: Princeton University Press, 1984. Includes several brief references to Cosimo's artistic interests and patronage.

Hale, John Rigby. *Florence and the Medici.* London: Phoenix, 2001. Discusses Cosimo's contributions to the arts in Florence as part of the pattern of Medici power patronage.

Hibbert, Christopher. *The House of Medici, Its Rise and Fall.* New York: Perennial, 1999. The best short discussion in English on Cosimo and his reign.

Nagler, Alois Maria. *Theatre Festivals and the Medici, 1539-1637.* Translated by G. Hickenhoyer. New Haven, Conn.: Yale University Press, 1964. Discusses the importance of Florentine pageants as models for the development of Stuart masques and early opera.

SEE ALSO: ʿAbbās the Great; Anne of Austria; Francesca Caccini; Ferdinand II; Galileo; Marie Celeste; Marie de Médicis.

RELATED ARTICLES in *Great Events from History: The Seventeenth Century, 1601-1700:* c. 1601: Emergence of Baroque Music; 1610: Galileo Confirms the Heliocentric Model of the Solar System.

MARIN MERSENNE
French scientist and mathematician

Mersenne is best known as the priest-scientist who facilitated the cross-fertilization of the most eminent minds of his time. He is widely commemorated for helping to establish modern science by promoting the new ideas of Nicolaus Copernicus, Galileo, and René Descartes and by attacking what he believed to be the pseudosciences of alchemy, astrology, and natural magic.

BORN: September 8, 1588; La Soultière, France
DIED: September 1, 1648; Paris, France
AREAS OF ACHIEVEMENT: Physics, mathematics, music, philosophy, religion and theology

EARLY LIFE

Marin Mersenne (mah-rahn mehr-sehn) was born in a small town about 120 miles southeast of Paris. His mother and father, both laborers, were devout Catholics, and their son was baptized on the day he was born and received the unusual name Marin because his birth date fell on the feast of the Nativity of Mary. From his earliest years of schooling, Mersenne showed a disposition for piety and study. His parents, despite their modest condition, were able to send him, first, to the Collège de Mans, where he studied Latin, Greek, and grammar, and, later, to the new Jesuit college at La Flèche, where he went through the already famous course of studies of the Society of Jesus, with its emphasis on the humanities, rhetoric, and philosophy. At this school, Mersenne also studied Aristotelian physics, mathematics, and astronomy. The philosophy he learned was Scholasticism. René Descartes was also studying at La

Flèche at this time, but they did not become close friends until 1623.

After finishing his studies at La Flèche in the summer of 1609, Mersenne went to Paris, where he spent two years studying theology. There he came into contact with the Minims, a mendicant order of friars founded in 1435 by Saint Francis of Paola. Their rule, modeled on Saint Francis of Assisi's, emphasized humility, and they were encouraged to regard themselves as the least (*minimi*) of all religious persons. Mersenne, impressed by their piety and asceticism, decided to enter the order. He became a Minim friar in 1611, and after a short novitiate he professed his vows of poverty, chastity, and obedience at the age of twenty-four. He returned to Paris and was ordained soon afterward, celebrating his first mass in 1613.

The provincial of the Minims assigned Mersenne in 1614 to teach philosophy to young friars at the convent at Nevers. During his five years there, he became interested in mathematics and science. Religious reasons were inextricably bound up with the development of this interest, because he saw the contemporary proliferation of the occult arts of alchemy, astrology, and magic as a danger both to science and to religion. Followers of the occult arts were sometimes called naturalists, because they believed that nature had a soul. Modern scholars call them Hermeticists, because their inspiration was Hermes Trismegistus, the legendary author of works on astrology, alchemy, and magic. Mersenne fought this animistic world with every weapon at his disposal, because to him it was false religion and false science. According to Saint Thomas Aquinas and other Catholic theologians, God created a hierarchical world, from angels through human beings to animals, plants, and the inanimate world. Hermeticists attacked this system. For them the world existed on a single level, and therefore religious and natural facts were blended, a pantheistic view that Mersenne found abhorrent. In the Hermeticists' system, the causality that was once assigned to God or spirits became the province of plants, animals, metals, and especially stars. Certain stones could provoke storms, the position of the Sun in the zodiac at a person's birth could determine his or her character and destiny, and the like. Because physical contact was no longer necessary for one thing to have an effect on another, occult influences could be multiplied endlessly.

LIFE'S WORK

By the time he began to teach philosophy at the Priory of the Annunciation in Paris in 1619, Mersenne had taken up his life's task to oppose the superstitions of the

Marin Mersenne. (Library of Congress)

Hermeticists. He lived at the Minim convent near Place Royale, which would remain his home, except for travels to the Netherlands, Spain, Italy, and the south of France, for the rest of his life. A contemporary engraving depicts him in friar's robes, his face lightly bearded, his high forehead capped by a receding hairline, and his widely separated eyes in a gaze both piercing and kindly.

Mersenne's literary career began in the 1620's with the publication of a group of massive polemical works that he directed against the enemies of science and religion—atheists, Deists, skeptics, alchemists, astrologers, and Hermeticists. His first major publication was *Quaestiones celeberrimœ in Genesim* (1623; the most famous questions of Genesis), a formidable folio of nearly two thousand columns. On the surface, this book seemed to be a biblical commentary, but Mersenne had a broader apologetic intent: He wished to defend orthodox theology against the magical interpretations of the world presented by such Hermeticists as Giovanni Pico de la Mirandola, Tommaso Campanella, and especially Robert Fludd, whom he called an evil and heretical magician.

Mersenne continued his attack on these believers in the occult in *L'Impiété des déistes, athées, et libertins de ce temps* (1624; the impiety of modern Deists, atheists, and libertines). His purpose was to defend the teachings of the Catholic Church against those who denied the existence of a loving creator. He was particularly disturbed by Giordano Bruno, whom he called one of the wickedest men whom Earth has ever supported. Mersenne's refutation of Bruno's doctrines of a plurality of worlds, the infinity of the universe, and the universal soul, as well as his defense of the rationality of nature, attracted the attention of Pierre Gassendi, whom he met in 1624 and who became his closest friend.

By 1625, Mersenne's defense of religion increasingly involved a defense of science. This approach characterized *La Vérité des sciences, contre les sceptiques ou Pyrrhoniens* (1625; the truth of the sciences against the skeptics or Pyrrhonists), a long book in the form of a discussion involving an alchemist, a skeptic, and a Christian philosopher. The philosopher argues that a genuine science of nature will develop only after mathematics and experimentation replace the false magical approach of the alchemists, who even propose that the creation of the world can be understood through chemistry. The skeptic tries to convince everyone that nothing is certain. The philosopher, though conceding that some things cannot be known, believes that many things are not in doubt, for example, relationships discovered by the scientists and equations discovered by the mathematicians.

Despite his opposition to the occult sciences, Mersenne was attracted to the modern sciences by their marvelous character. For example, he was more favorably disposed than Gassendi to comets presaging the death of kings. Mersenne could also be gullible, as when he accepted the story of a dog's giving birth to a puppy with a human head. These lapses aside, Mersenne strongly believed that both religion and science had a rational basis but that it was important to keep religious and scientific facts separate. As time went on, however, science, which first had only influenced his religious thought, gradually came to dominate it. An example of this development was his growing acceptance of the Copernican theory that the Sun rather than Earth was at the center of the universe. In 1623, he had opposed the Copernican theory because sufficient evidence was lacking, but by 1624 he was claiming that this theory was irrefutable.

During these years, Mersenne's circle of friends and correspondents was widening. He began to exchange letters with Descartes, who became an important influence on his thought. He also had much to do with advancing Descartes's ideas, particularly after Descartes went to the Netherlands. In the 1620's, Mersenne's correspondence increased to such an extent that he was soon playing the role of communication link to a wide variety of European scientists and philosophers. His friendliness, curiosity, and eclecticism made him the ideal intermediary. His religious house in the Place Royale became a meeting place for such eminent thinkers as Pierre de Fermat, France's foremost mathematician; Girard Desargues, the founder of descriptive geometry; and Gassendi. Because no scientific journals and no international societies existed then, these meetings at Mersenne's residence and his widely circulated letters helped to create a genuine scientific community that would later be formalized in the French Academy of Sciences. Although his intent in his gatherings and correspondence was still basically apologetic, his visitors and correspondents did not have to be Catholic, for it was becoming increasingly clear to him that the cause of science was the cause of God. He even became friendly with Thomas Hobbes at a time when his work was being viciously attacked for its materialism but which Mersenne interpreted as a genuinely new science of humankind.

The decade of the 1630's was important in the evolution of Mersenne's thought. He did significant work in music and mathematics, embraced mechanism (the doctrine that the world can be explained in terms of matter and motion), and came to the defense of Descartes and Galileo, whose works were being attacked by officials of the Catholic Church. In 1634, he published four books on music. His scientific analysis of sound and its effects on the ear and soul began with his demonstration that pitch is proportional to frequency and that the intensity of sound is inversely proportional to the distance from its source. He discovered, in a law that now bears his name, that an increase in mass and a decrease in tension produce lower notes in a string of given length. He went on to discover similar relations for wind and percussion instruments. He offered quantitative explanations for consonance, dissonance, and resonance, and also measured the speed of sound, which he showed to be independent of pitch and loudness, and pioneered the study of the upper and lower limits of audible frequencies.

In his acoustical studies, Mersenne recognized the importance of mathematical and mechanical models. He believed that using mechanical models to imitate the workings of nature could also serve as a weapon against the Hermeticists, because these models revealed that the world was a machine and not an ensouled body. In this way, Mersenne withdrew the soul from the world of the animists and gave it back to the theologians. Mersenne the scientist provided Mersenne the priest with those principles necessary to save the religious values he held most dear. The spread of the mechanical philosophy owed much to Mersenne and Descartes, who relied on Mersenne as a theological consultant.

Despite Galileo's difficulties with the Church, Mersenne came to see his discoveries as superlative illustrations of the rationality of nature governed by mechanical laws. He was largely responsible for making Galileo's work known in France through his translations of Galileo's studies in mechanics into French. Nevertheless, he did not accept Galileo's ideas and experiments uncritically. He commented on the lack of precision in Galileo's experiments using inclined planes to investigate the acceleration of falling objects. His doubts about whether Galileo had actually performed these experiments led him carefully to repeat them. He discovered discrepancies and doubted the relationship between the distance traveled by an object under acceleration and the square of the time that Galileo had discovered.

The Roman Catholic Church's condemnation of Galileo's Copernicanism occurred in 1633, but this did not stop Mersenne from defending Galileo's work. This might seem odd for a person of Mersenne's piety, until one realizes the naïve simplicity with which Mersenne blended his conceptions of faith and science, both of which led to the truth. Nevertheless, the Galileo affair had a profound effect on both Mersenne and Descartes, but whereas Descartes timidly refrained from publishing, Mersenne continued to issue works on Galileo, and in 1634 he even published a summary account of part of Galileo's *Dialogo sopra i due massimi sistemi del mondo, tolemaico e copernicano* (1632; *Dialogue Concerning the Two Chief World Systems, Ptolemaic and Copernican*, 1661). Mersenne agreed with the Church's need to preserve Scripture from error, but he saw no conflict between Scripture, which instructed humans on how to go to Heaven, and science, which showed humans how the heavens moved.

Mersenne's publication of the complete text of *Harmonie universelle* (1636-1637; universal harmony) marked the culmination of his achievements in music and science. This work, greatly valued by modern musicologists, contains a useful summary of Renaissance knowledge about acoustics and detailed information on a host of musical instruments.

During the last years of his life, Mersenne worked on mathematics. His most important studies were in number theory, especially on prime and perfect numbers. In 1644, he proposed a formula for generating primes, and although his formula produces only some of them, it inspired other mathematicians to devise better ways of finding prime numbers.

Mersenne fell seriously ill at the end of August, 1647. He became worse as a result of the ineptitude of a surgeon, who cut an artery in his right arm, allowing gangrene to set in. Despite his crippled arm, on a warm day at the end of July, 1648, he left to visit Descartes in the Netherlands. He arrived ill and tired at a Theatine monastery on the route and was quickly returned to Paris and confined to bed. The doctors eventually diagnosed an abscess on the lungs. The surgeons made an incision that caused him much suffering, without discovering his malady. Understanding that the end was near, Mersenne ordered his affairs: He gave instructions on his unfinished manuscripts, made a general confession, and arranged for an autopsy to discover the cause of his approaching death. On the first day of September, 1648, at three o'clock in the afternoon, Mersenne died in the arms of his friend Gassendi. At the autopsy, the surgeons found that their incision had been made too low. This knowledge was Mersenne's last contribution to science.

SIGNIFICANCE

Despite his vital role in the scientific revolution of the seventeenth century, Mersenne has been largely neglected and misunderstood. In his study of Mersenne and the birth of mechanism, Father Robert Lenoble did much to rescue Mersenne from oblivion for French scholars, but Mersenne is still remembered principally because of his friendship and correspondence with Descartes, Fermat, and other scientists. In the modern view, these friendships, rather than his ideas, constitute his significance. In contrast to this view, Lenoble sees Mersenne as one of the most important figures in the history of modern thought. Mersenne's life, which adventitiously placed him on the watershed between the medieval and modern worlds, allowed him to play a pivotal role in the scientific revolution.

Throughout his career, Mersenne's devotions to religion and to science were in constant interaction. Indeed, his career involved him in several dual roles: priest and scientist, Renaissance man and modern man, naïve believer and skeptic of the occult. Through his vast correspondence and many contacts with the makers of the scientific revolution, Mersenne not only called on specialists in every branch of science to work together but also kept these scientists attuned to religious and moral principles. In this way he did much to foster the new scientific movement and to prevent it from developing initially in an antireligious direction.

Mersenne helped to place science in its modern context. A new type of outlook arose with Mersenne, a science without metaphysics, a science that was verifiable and useful. He was an apostle of this new view, and he had the rare ability to serve the ideas of others. He contributed more than any of his contemporaries to expanding the knowledge of, and interest in, the scientific achievements of his time. Blaise Pascal once said that Mersenne had the very special talent for posing the right questions, and he posed these questions to the right people.

Mersenne believed deeply that false science pulled people away from God whereas true science led people to him. Although his intention was to place religion first in whatever he said and did, he was living in an age that was leaving theology for science, and ironically, in attempting to do the opposite, he encouraged this trend. He fought the Hermeticists, encouraged the mechanists, and was the catalyst for the spread of many important scientific ideas. He did all this for the greater glory of God. From the vantage point of the modern world, one can see that what he actually did was to help separate science from its religious roots.

—*Robert J. Paradowski*

FURTHER READING

Boas, Marie. *The Scientific Renaissance, 1450-1630.* New York: Harper & Row, 1962. Boas presents a valuable summary of a significant period in the evolution of science. She discusses Mersenne's role in organizing scientists through his extensive correspondence.

Chappelle, Vere, ed. *Grotius to Gassendi.* New York: Garland, 1992. Collection of essays about sixteenth and seventeenth century philosophers, including Mersenne.

Dear, Peter Robert. *Mersenne and the Learning of the Schools.* Ithaca, N.Y.: Cornell University Press, 1988. Dear describes how Mersenne developed a mechanistic view of nature, replacing Aristotle's earlier philosophy of the nature of the schools.

Debus, A. G. *Man and Nature in the Renaissance.* New York: Cambridge University Press, 1978. An introduction to science and medicine during the early phase of the scientific revolution, from the mid-fifteenth to the mid-seventeenth century.

Holden, Constance. "Another Mersenne." *Science* 304, no. 5677 (June 11, 2004). On May 28, 2004, about seventy-five thousand math enthusiasts from around the world announced the discovery of a seven-million-digit prime number. Holden discusses the findings of this group, called The Great Internet Mersenne Prime Search, and its attempts to find a ten-million-digit prime number.

Popkin, Richard H. *The History of Scepticism from Erasmus to Descartes.* Assen, the Netherlands: Vangorcum, 1964. Explores the influence of skeptical philosophy on the evolution of modern thought. In several of his works, Mersenne attacked skepticism as the enemy of science and religion, and Popkin makes many references to Mersenne.

Simmons, George Finlay. *Calculus Gems: Brief Lives and Memorable Mathematics.* New York: McGraw-Hill, 1992. This collection of biographies includes a chapter on Mersenne, with a discussion of his theories on prime numbers and cycloids.

Thorndike, Lynn. *The Seventeenth Century.* Vol. 7 in *A History of Magic and Experimental Science.* New York: Columbia University Press, 1958. The chapter on Mersenne and Gassendi contains much of interest about the two priest-scientists. Thorndike is not always accurate, and some of his work has been superseded by later scholarship, but his many translations of original materials scattered throughout his presentation make this a valuable and fascinating compendium.

SEE ALSO: Jakob Böhme; René Descartes; Pierre de Fermat; Galileo.

RELATED ARTICLES in *Great Events from History: The Seventeenth Century, 1601-1700:* 1601-1672: Rise of Scientific Societies; 1610-1643: Reign of Louis XIII; 1651: Hobbes Publishes *Leviathan*; 1673: Huygens Explains the Pendulum.

METACOM
Wampanoag grand sachem (r. 1662-1676)

Famed for organizing the most devastating native resistance war in America's history, Metacom of Pokanoket was the paramount sachem of the Wampanoag people from 1662 to 1676.

BORN: c. 1639; Pokanoket, probably present-day Massachusetts
DIED: August 12, 1676; near present-day Bristol, Rhode Island
ALSO KNOWN AS: King Philip; Philip of Pokanoket; Metacomet
AREAS OF ACHIEVEMENT: Diplomacy, warfare and conquest, government and politics

EARLY LIFE

Born when his father, Massasoit, was already around sixty years old, Metacom (meh-TAHK-uhm) was destined to lead his people at a young age. Native peoples of seventeenth century southern New England such as the Pokanoket formed autonomous bands, living congregated in villages consisting of a cluster of dwellings and a communal field. Their lives were determined by the seasons; they moved to fertile areas near water in preparation for planting season, more sheltered valley areas for winter, and waterways during early spring for the large numbers of migratory birds and fish. Bands of particular areas were associated by ties of kinship, and they acknowledged occasional paramount chiefs, called "sachems" or "sagamores," who functioned in consensus with a spiritual leader and a people's council. These loose aggregations were the so-called tribes with which European colonists had to deal in the seventeenth century; prominent among them were the Wampanoag and the Narragansett.

The Wampanoag peoples are perhaps best known in America for the part they played in keeping the colonists of Plymouth Plantation alive in their first years of settlement. During this period, Metacom's father, Massasoit, was sachem, and the two cultures were mutually beneficial. During the first half century of settlement, in fact, there was no clear frontier line separating the cultures, native village and colonial town intermixing in much of southern New England, each culture influencing and benefiting the other. Native-settler trade flourished, first with corn and then with wampum.

Over time, purists in both cultures were troubled by this relationship. Puritan ministers claimed that colonists were "degenerating" into savage-like behavior. To native leaders, it seemed that native power was diminishing. There were growing numbers of "praying Indians," who were expected to adopt Christianity and to forsake all traditional ways. Also unsettling were the stringent Puritan codes to which all native peoples were forced to adhere and a judicial system that was more and more racist. In addition, native lives increasingly revolved around the colonial trading post, with the people becoming more and more dependent on a system that was, by Metacom's time, beginning to exclude them. With the price of wampum spiraling downward and the appearance of European coinage, it became clear that transatlantic trade would supplant internal.

The only tradable commodity left native peoples was land, a finite resource and one that the two cultures viewed differently. Because of their lack of a conception of private property, for Native Americans the "sale" of land did not involve the relinquishment or conferral of exclusive possession in perpetuity but rather signified the admission of a neighbor or kinsman to the right of participation in the use of the land. Settlers believed in private property. For them, the sale of land meant that the sellers were forever excluded from that land.

LIFE'S WORK

In the seventeenth century (and for many historians today), Metacom symbolized Native American presence and resistance in southern New England, a political and cultural world that was attempting to exclude his people and to push them off their lands. Soon after Massasoit's death in 1661, his oldest son, Wamsutta, now sachem, asked colonists for an English name, the taking of a new name at a new stage in life being an Algonquian tradition, a diplomatic move that earned for him the name Alexander Pokanoket and for his younger brother Metacom the name Philip of Pokanoket. After being sachem for less than a year, Wamsutta was force-marched by Plymouth officials to Duxbury to be questioned about growing rumors that he was plotting war. He died on the return; Metacom believed that he had been poisoned. Soon after Metacom's ascension, he himself was called before colonial representatives. In fact, in the 1660's and 1670's, he was frequently called, the colonial officials usually inflicting a penalty of money, arms, and allegiance in return for the time and expense they had spent on questioning him.

According to colonial propaganda, the period between September, 1671, and summer of 1675 was too quiet: King Philip was planning his war and securing alliances. Clearly, by January, 1675, when John Sassamon, a Christianized native who had informed colonists that Metacom was planning an attack, was found dead, the sachem signified native resistance to the increasingly alarmed settlers. After the Sassamon trial, very probably an unfair one, Plymouth officials sent diplomatic correspondents to Metacom's territory, and both Massachusetts and Rhode Island also planned diplomatic missions; the colonists wanted to pacify Metacom. The sachem accepted Rhode Island's invitation, going to Providence in full regalia with forty of his warriors and counselors and insisting that his voice be heard.

After focusing on his concerns regarding Christian missionary work, Metacom recounted the history of native-colonist relations; he noted that when the settlers were as "a little child," his own father had protected them from other native peoples and taught them how to survive, but that now the settlers had "a 100 times more land" than Metacom's people. At one point, Metacom declared, "I am determined not to live until I have no country." Pertaining to the judicial system, the sachem pointed out that the testimony of twenty native witnesses against the testimony of a colonist was discounted, while the testimony of one native against that of another native was sufficient if it suited colonial interests.

Metacom noted, too, that when he or other sachems sold land, the settlers said the acreage was more than what was agreed upon and that a piece of paper was proof against native word, that the settlers often first plied the native rulers with alcohol and then transacted business, and that straying cattle and horses (a long-standing problem) continued to ruin native crops. In response to Rhode Island's warning that the settlers were too powerful for the native forces, Metacom countered that if that were the case, the settlers should treat the weaker native forces as Massasoit treated the colonists when they were the weaker.

Despite this diplomatic conference, by mid-June there were scattered attacks localized in the Plymouth Colony area. By June 30, colonial forces had swept into Metacom's territory, destroying his village and stores of food. The sachem and his people had already moved into the trackless swamps of Pocasset territory, and the militia, saddled as it was with indecision and intercolonial conflict, failed to pursue. Once they did, Metacom's superior knowledge of the terrain allowed him to go around and even through the hunting parties.

At this point, the sachem physically disappears from contemporary chronicles; the war, however, continued to spread in his name. Because they were afraid that King Philip's diplomatic powers would incite a pan-Indian alliance, the colonial government decided to attack the then-neutral Narragansetts. The resulting Great Swamp Battle of December, 1675, marked the bloodiest moment of the war. Colonists killed six hundred of the swamp fort's inhabitants (half of whom were women and children) and captured three hundred others. In retaliation, Canonchet, sachem of the Narragansetts, joined Metacom's cause.

In January, 1676, Metacom seems to have headed Hfarther north into Mohawk territory on a diplomatic mission in search of more allies. The Mohawk, traditional rivals of the Wampanoag, not only refused but also launched a brutal attack that wiped out most of Metacom's men. On the front, though, what began as a series of disconnected uprisings became a total war. In response, the colonial militia eventually changed its strategy, accepting the advice of men such as Benjamin Church, who recommended heavy reliance on native intelligence and warriors. With the May destruction of the supply base for the western division of the Algonquians, the western battle front closed. On the eastern front, Church was able to get the woman sachem Awashonks of the Sakonnet to promise that "before the corn is ripe" she would hand him the head of Metacom, who at that time was making his way back to Mount Hope in search of food for his people.

On August 1, the sachem's wife and nine-year-old son were captured; they were eventually sold into slavery. At the same time, bands of starving native peoples began surrendering. According to tradition, when one of his own counselors suggested surrender, Metacom killed him. It was Alderman, the brother of that counselor, who led Church's troop (a large proportion of whom were native) in an August 12 ambush, and it was he who fired the shot that killed Metacom. Church ordered the sachem beheaded and quartered (customary European punishment for treason). According to Church, the native warrior who performed the punishment said that the sachem had been "a very great man and had made many a man afraid of him." Back in Plymouth, the quarters were hung in various trees, and Metacom's head, which had carried a thirty-shilling reward, was displayed on a spike for decades. For his part, Alderman received one of the sachem's hands, and with this trophy he enjoyed many free drinks in colonial taverns.

SIGNIFICANCE

Metacom's War was a devastating one. More than half of the colonial settlements were destroyed. Supporting both the war effort and the homeless, colonial treasuries were bankrupt. The British crown, claiming that the colonies could not govern themselves, took away their charters, a situation not to be reversed until the American Revolution in the next century. In proportion to population, this brief war stands as America's most deadly. Of a total population estimated at eighty thousand, nearly nine thousand died during the war; one-third of those were settlers and two-thirds native peoples (more than half of New England's native population). Thousands of native peoples were sold as slaves to the West Indies or were placed on reservations.

There was no written native language, and thus there are no contemporary native accounts of the war. Within eight years after "King Philip's War," however, the colonists had written about two dozen different accounts, and there are hundreds of other public and private relevant colonial manuscripts of the period. To contemporary Puritan chroniclers, the war represented a demonic uprising against God's chosen but wavering people, and they personified that evil in the person of Metacom. Seventeenth century tourists flocked to Plymouth to see the great King Philip's skull bleaching on a pole. Yet King Philip did not act alone, nor could any sachem. His manpower was in no way equal to that of other sachems.

Most historians feel that Metacom's name was invoked in order to personify the deviltry the settlers felt was behind the war and to give the sense of a grand, pan-Indian alliance being orchestrated by one devilish man. Certainly, in the contemporary accounts, Metacom is ubiquitous, even supernatural; he was seen at attacks when it was known he was elsewhere—seen, too, on the battlefield, his skin impervious to the bullets flying his way. As one historian has noted, the colonial militia began chasing Metacom the man; they then chased his spirit. Native peoples clearly knew Metacom's symbolic value, joining colonial forces (and significantly altering the outcome) in the pursuit of King Philip. For seventeenth century colonists and native peoples, Metacom signified native resistance.

—*Anna Dunlap Higgins*

FURTHER READING

Bourne, Russell. *The Red King's Rebellion: Racial Politics in New England, 1675-1678.* New York: Atheneum, 1990. A very readable text with extensive native information and little scholarly citation. An exhaustive chronicle of the causes, events, and results of the war.

Drake, James David. *King Philip's War: Civil War in New England, 1675-1676.* Amherst: University of Massachusetts Press, 1999. Unlike many authors, who maintain King Philip's War was a battle between two different cultures—one Native American and the other British—Drake argues the conflict was a civil war within a more cohesive New England culture.

Josephy, Alvin M., Jr. "The Betrayal of King Philip." In *Patriot Chiefs: A Chronicle of American Indian Resistance.* Rev. ed. New York: Penguin Books, 1993. Josephy devotes a chapter of his book to Metacom's relations with the British colonists.

Lepore, Jill. *The Name of War: King Philip's War and the Origins of American Identity.* New York: Alfred A. Knopf, 1998. A very readable text filled with interesting and pertinent anecdotes and little-known facts. Examines the cultural implications of the ways in which the settlers chronicled the war.

Schultz, Eric B., and Michael J. Tougias. *King Philip's War: The History and Legacy of America's Forgotten Conflict.* Woodstock, Vt.: Countryman Press, 1999. An in-depth history of the war as well as a guide to the sites of the raids, ambushes, and battles.

Slotkin, Richard, and James K. Folsom, eds. *So Dreadfull a Judgment: Puritan Responses to King Philip's War, 1676-77.* Middletown, Conn.: Wesleyan, 1978. Contains many of the most important firsthand accounts of the war, including those of Captain Benjamin Church and the hostage Mary Rowlandson.

SEE ALSO: Canonicus; Massasoit; Pocahontas; Powhatan; Squanto.
RELATED ARTICLES in *Great Events from History: The Seventeenth Century, 1601-1700:* December 26, 1620: Pilgrims Arrive in North America; March 22, 1622-October, 1646: Powhatan Wars; June 20, 1675: Metacom's War Begins.

THOMAS MIDDLETON
English playwright and poet

Middleton composed an extraordinary range of poetry, prose satire, almanacs, pamphlets, masques, civic pageants, comedies, and tragedies. His works expressed a cynical, Calvinistic attitude toward the follies of every social class in Jacobean London. A popular and occasionally controversial writer, he wrote bluntly realistic exposés of religious hypocrisy and passionately questioned contemporary sexual, social, and political conventions.

BORN: April 18, 1580 (baptized); London, England
DIED: July 4, 1627; Newington Butts, Surrey, England
AREAS OF ACHIEVEMENT: Literature, theater

EARLY LIFE

Thomas Middleton was christened on April 18, 1580, at Saint Lawrence in the Old Jewry, in London. His father, William Middleton, a successful London bricklayer and member of the Tilers' and Bricklayers' Company, had married his mother, Anne Snow, daughter of another Londoner, on February 17, 1574. A sister, Avis, was born in 1582. Middleton's father died when he was five, on January 20, 1586, having earned the rank of gentleman and leaving a substantial estate to his widow and children. His mother was remarried, on November 7, 1586, to Thomas Harvey (1559?-1606?), a gentleman and swindler. The marriage quickly became contentious, and until his death around 1606, Harvey embroiled his wife and stepchildren in lawsuits contesting their inheritance.

Middleton himself was named in a lawsuit regarding the family's estate in 1598, and the three successive suits that he faced in 1600 significantly depleted his finances. However, this litigious background did serve to inspire the dominant themes of his mature dramas, as well as his acid perspective about the realities of money, power, women's position in marriage, and the law.

Middleton's first paid work was the poem *The Wisdom of Solomon, Paraphrased* (1597), dedicated to the second earl of Essex. He went on to Oxford in 1598, selling his inheritance in 1600 to pay for his studies. While at Oxford, Middleton wrote two lengthy poems, *Microcynicon: Six Snarling Satires* (1599), an attack on urban corruption, and *The Ghost of Lucrece* (1600), whose violent tone foreshadows his later revenge tragedies. In 1601, Middleton left Oxford to write full-time in London, probably for Philip Henslowe's company, the Admiral's Men.

In 1603, Middleton married Mary Marbecke (1575-1628), daughter of one of the six clerks in the Court of Chancery and sister of one of the actors in the Admiral's Men. Their only child, Edward, was born a year later. Middleton, persistently short on cash throughout his lifetime, composed in several genres during the next few years. He contributed to *The Magnificent Entertainment Given to King James* (1603), a celebration of James I's accession to the throne, and wrote his first extant play, *The Phoenix* (pr. 1604, pb. 1607); two pamphlets, *Father Hubburd's Tales* (1604) and *The Black Book* (1604); and, in collaboration with Thomas Dekker, the comedy *The Honest Whore, Part I* (pr., pb. 1604). From 1603 to 1606, Middleton wrote several comedies for an all-boy acting company, the Children of Saint Paul's, including *The Phoenix*, *Michaelmas Term* (pr. c. 1606, pb. 1607), *A Mad World, My Masters* (pr. c. 1606, pb. 1608), *A Trick to Catch the Old One* (pr. c. 1605-1606, pb. 1608), and *The Puritan Widow* (pr. 1606, pb. 1607).

LIFE'S WORK

Middleton's dramatic genius for appealing to audience tastes was early manifest in the highly successful "citizen comedies" like *Michaelmas Term* and *A Trick to Catch the Old One*, composed for the elite audiences of the children's troupes, as well as for the popular audiences of adult acting companies like the Admiral's Men and the King's Men. This type of comedy portrayed all of the various social classes resident in London, and Middleton's scathing satiric wit and skill for the lascivious found ample targets, whether in the court of the extravagant new king, in the general citizenry's lust for money (especially the legal profession), in the social pretensions of the bourgeoisie and landed gentry, or in the hypocrisy of devout Puritans. Middleton later returned to the cheaters and the gullible sinners of citizen comedy in *A Chaste Maid in Cheapside* (pr. 1611, pb. 1630), considered his finest comedy; *Wit at Several Weapons* (pr. 1613, pb. 1647), his first partnership with William Rowley, sometimes attributed to Francis Beaumont and John Fletcher; and *Anything for a Quiet Life* (pr. c. 1621, pb. 1662), probably a collaboration with John Webster.

Middleton's prodigious output during these years included pamphlets, drama and theatricals for the royal court, and processional celebrations for the city. For King James's pleasure, he produced court masques as well as civic pageants such as *Triumphs of Truth* (pr., pb.

1613) and *Civitas Amor* (pr., pb. 1616). This type of adulatory work continued up to the 1626 processional *The Triumph of Health and Prosperity* (pr., pb. 1626). Middleton's principal work was for the theater, however, and he is one of the few known playwrights to have collaborated with William Shakespeare, in composing *Timon of Athens* (pr. c. 1607-1608); he was later commissioned to revise Shakespeare's *Macbeth* (pr. 1606) and *Measure for Measure* (pr. 1604).

If Shakespeare's gift was his extraordinary grasp of the ambiguity and complexity of human character, Middleton's was his ability to manipulate dramatic effect. He pursued savage parody in comedy and reached to sensationalism in tragedy. His caustic dissection of the underside of human behavior is everywhere evident in the dramas. In the comedies, scarcely any character behaves without guile, from pawnbrokers and impoverished aristocrats to prostitutes and self-proclaimed Puritan worthies. Along with his often merciless ironic tone, moreover, Middleton possessed a committed, albeit pessimistic, moral drive. The biting sarcasm of a comedy like *A Chaste Maid in Cheapside* segued, in his tragedy and tragicomedy, into depictions of most of the seven deadly sins.

Middleton had, early on, dramatized a notorious domestic murder as a tale of villainy and fateful retribution in *A Yorkshire Tragedy* (pr. 1605, pb. 1608), which bears a thematic resemblance to medieval morality plays, with their didactic displays of sin and inevitable punishment. *A Yorkshire Tragedy* was followed by the more character-driven analysis of revenge and its due punishment in Middleton's *The Revenger's Tragedy* (pr. 1606-1607, pb. 1607), which at one time was mistakenly attributed to Cyril Tourneur.

For the dramas of his mature years, some of which were written in collaboration with Thomas Dekker, William Rowley, and John Webster, Middleton retained his piercing judgment and cynical wit, using well-known persons and scandals to comment upon the social issues and political circumstances of the age. The bawdy antics of *The Roaring Girl: Or, Moll Cutpurse* (pr. c. 1610, pb. 1611, written with Dekker), based on the escapades of the androgynous London rebel Mary Frith, showcase that woman's dissent from the misogynistic repression of women's social and sexual freedom.

Indeed, Middleton possessed an exceptional capacity to portray women of depth, who may resist but do not ultimately escape patriarchal control or the dramatist's own censure for acting on their desires. The portraits of Beatrice-Joanna, whose capitulation to lust traps her in the revenge plot of her rapist in *The Changeling* (pr. 1622, pb. 1653, written with Rowley), and Livia, the pandering mother who typifies the political and sexual license of *Women Beware Women* (pr. c. 1621-1627, pb. 1657) demonstrate Middleton's Calvinistic pessimism as well as his sardonic view of behavior at King James's court. The virginity test plot and the murder of the inconvenient husband in *The Changeling* were drawn from the scandal regarding the marriage of Catholic

MIDDLETON'S MAJOR WORKS	
1597	*The Wisdom of Solomon, Paraphrased*
1599	*Micro-cynicon*
1600	*The Ghost of Lucrece*
1603	*The Magnificent Entertainment Given to King James* (with Ben Jonson and Thomas Dekker)
1604	*The Black Book*
1604	*Father Hubburd's Tales* (includes poetry)
1604	*The Honest Whore, Part I* (with Thomas Dekker)
1604	*The Phoenix*
c. 1604-1607	*The Family of Love*
1604-1607	*Your Five Gallants*
c. 1605-1606	*A Trick to Catch the Old One*
c. 1606	*A Mad World, My Masters*
c. 1606	*Michaelmas Term*
1609	*Sir Robert Sherley*
c. 1610	*The Roaring Girl: Or, Moll Cutpurse* (with Dekker)
c. 1610	*The Witch*
1611	*A Chaste Maid in Cheapside*
c. 1613-1627	*No Wit, No Help Like a Woman's*
c. 1615	*More Dissemblers Besides Women*
c. 1615-1617	*A Fair Quarrel* (with William Rowley)
c. 1616	*The Widow* (with Ben Jonson and John Fletcher?)
c. 1616-1620	*The Major of Queenborough*
c. 1618	*The Old Law: Or, A New Way to Please You* (with Rowley and Philip Massinger)
1620	*The World Tossed at Tennis* (with Rowley)
c. 1621	*Anything for a Quiet Life* (with John Webster?)
c. 1621-1627	*Women Beware Women*
1622	*The Changeling* (with Rowley)
1624	*A Game at Chess*

Frances Howard to the king's favorite, the earl of Somerset.

Middleton, in *The Changeling*, may have been aiming insult at the court and at English Catholics, but there is little doubt of his political target in his last, controversial, hit, *A Game at Chess* (pr. 1624, pb. 1625). That tragicomedy represented an attack on the proposed alliance of England and Spain through the marriage of Prince Charles with the Spanish Infanta. It ran for nine consecutive days (an unprecedented success at the time), until it was closed by royal order in response to formal complaints lodged by the Spanish ambassador, Count Gondomar.

In his final years, Middleton continued writing in his capacity as London's first chronologer of city events. Financial difficulties bedeviled Middleton in his last year, 1627, as he was involved in disputes regarding payment for the lord mayor's pageants and his work on the coronation pageant for King Charles I. After his death, he was buried in Newington Butts on July 4, 1627.

SIGNIFICANCE

Just as there is ongoing debate about the extent of Middleton's extraordinary canon, there remains critical disagreement about the nature of Middleton's vision. The latter argument centers on whether Middleton is an ironic realist or a bitterly sectarian moralist. Margot Heinemann ignited the debate about the perspective expressed in Middleton's works in *Puritanism and Theatre: Thomas Middleton and Opposition Drama Under the Early Stuarts* (1980), arguing that Middleton was a fierce Puritan, opposed to the moral excesses of the Jacobean court and the city of London, as well as to King James's policy of absolute royal power. Under later critics, as the study of Middleton burgeoned, the pendulum of cricitical opinion swung midway, and critics, including Gary Taylor, the general editor of the collected works, defined Middleton as an astonishingly prolific writer whose driving moral passion triumphed in theater.

—*M. Sheila McAvey*

FURTHER READING

Bawcutt, N. W. "Was Thomas Middleton a Puritan Dramatist?" *Modern Language Review* 94 (1999): 925-939. Argues against Margot Heinemann's 1980 thesis that Middleton was sympathetic to Puritans, insisting that the reference to Puritan attitudes is distinctly satiric. Discusses Middleton's patrons, pageants, and *A Game at Chess*.

Chakravorty, Swapam. *Society and Politics in the Plays of Thomas Middleton*. Oxford, England: Clarendon Press, 1996. Analyzes several of Middleton's dramas as subversive criticism of the sexual and social restrictions, and the corruption, of Jacobean England.

Heinemann, Margot. *Puritanism and Theatre: Thomas Middleton and Oppositional Drama Under the Early Stuarts*. New York: Cambridge University Press, 1980. Develops the now-challenged thesis that Middleton used the theater to express his Puritan protest to the social, political, and religious milieu of his time.

Jowett, John. "Thomas Middleton." In *A Companion to Renaissance Drama*, edited by Arthur F. Kinney. Oxford, England: Blackwell, 2002. Reviews Middleton's life, canon, satire of court life, and dramatization of the abusive treatment of women in society.

Taylor, Gary, and John Lavagnino, eds. *The Collected Works of Thomas Middleton*. Oxford, England: Clarendon Press, 2002. Reissue of all the works currently attributed to Middleton, arranged in chronological order. Includes essays on Middleton's life and reputation, on London, and on drama of the English Renaissance.

SEE ALSO: Robert Carr; Charles I; Thomas Dekker; John Fletcher; James I; Cyril Tourneur; John Webster.

RELATED ARTICLES in *Great Events from History: The Seventeenth Century, 1601-1700*: c. 1601-1613: Shakespeare Produces His Later Plays; March 24, 1603: James I Becomes King of England.

JOHN MILTON
English poet and writer

An important writer of revolutionary prose during the English Commonwealth, Milton was also England's greatest heroic poet. His Paradise Lost *is among the most widely read depictions of the Fall outside the Bible.*

BORN: December 9, 1608; London, England
DIED: November 8, 1674; London
AREA OF ACHIEVEMENT: Literature

EARLY LIFE

John Milton was born on December 9, 1608, on Bread Street near Saint Paul's Cathedral in London. His father, also named John Milton, had come to London a decade earlier following a conflict over religion with his staunchly Catholic father, Richard Milton. The elder John Milton achieved sufficient success as a scrivener—a combination of legal adviser, notary, and financial broker—to provide well for his wife, Sara Jeffrey Milton, and their children, John, Anne, and Christopher. Their first child had died at birth.

The younger John was provided with a tutor, Thomas Young, a Scottish Presbyterian cleric with whom Milton would correspond for many years and with whom he would find himself allied against the bishops during the early years of the Commonwealth. When Young left London, Milton was enrolled in Saint Paul's School in 1620, and later in Christ's College, Cambridge, in 1625. He placed fourth out of 259 candidates for the bachelor's degree in 1625 and was awarded his M.A. cum laude in 1632. He declined to join the clergy, a career for which his education had prepared him, in part because he was increasingly opposed to the governance and ceremonies of the Anglican Church, as they constrained the liberty of the individual conscience, and in part because he was increasingly committed to the vocation of poetry.

Milton is regarded as the greatest English epic poet and as second only to the greatest dramatic poet, William Shakespeare. England's foremost poets both transformed the literary conventions of the age, and though their lives overlap in time, they differ in many crucial ways. Of Shakespeare little is known, but of Milton little is unknown. Details of his appearance and personality—medium height; auburn hair; delicate, almost feminine features; a cheerful egotism; a ladies' man by the age of sev-

enteen; popular with his schoolmates; and possessed of a scathing wit—and his daily work habits, education, religious and political thought, employment, health, family fortunes, travels, and friendships are all voluminously recorded in his own writing and in letters and biographies written by those who knew him.

Shakespeare's genius seems romantically untutored, whereas Milton's talents were certainly developed through exhaustive study. As a boy, he read by candlelight past midnight, and he continued his devotion to study throughout his life, even after he was totally blind. He had learned Latin and Greek from Young by the age of twelve and added several other languages, including Hebrew and Italian, soon after. He read the church fathers and the Testaments in Latin, Greek, and Hebrew. He read the classical philosophers, historians, and poets. He mastered the trivium of grammar, rhetoric, and logic, and found that analysis, paraphrase, and imitation of classic authors came easily. His academic exercises at Christ's

John Milton. (Library of Congress)

College, delivered in Latin, are models of rhetorical invention. His early education equipped his capacious mind with the best that the classical and the Judeo-Christian traditions could offer.

He continued preparing for his vocation as a poet following his attendance at Christ's College by a period of retirement at his parents' house near London (1632-1638). He wrote few poems, but important ones, including *Comus* (1634), which was printed as *A Masque Presented at Ludlow Castle 1634 on Michaelmas Night* (1637), the pastoral elegy "Lycidas" (1637), and his first eight sonnets, including his apology for his long preparation, "How Soon Hath Time" (1632).

Following his mother's death in 1637, Milton visited the Continent, spending most of his time in Italy, a country that was anathema to English Puritans for its Catholicism but that Milton valued as the seat of learning and civilization. There, he was received by many distinguished artists and patrons and met with a number of famous academies, democratic societies that met regularly to hear and critique scholarly papers and literary works in progress. He met Giovanni Battista Manso, patron of Torquato Tasso, who praised the native fluency of Milton's Italian verses. He also met the aging Galileo, a captive of the Inquisition, who became a symbol in Milton's prose writing of how religious dogmatism could restrain the progress of human knowledge.

Milton also encountered the power and monumental vastness of the Baroque, a style of art fostered by Catholicism, which Milton used particularly in *Paradise Lost* (1667, 1674) to portray the realms of the infernal and divine. Milton also heard Italian music and opera. Milton's father, an amateur composer, had taught him to play the organ and to sing. Music—the music of the spheres, of angels, of humankind, and of all living things—was his preoccupation from first to last. His blindness must have heightened his love of music, which so tuned his ear that auditory images supersede the visual in his poems, and the sound and cadence of his language, so often compared to the grandeur of organ peals and vast choirs, would epitomize the grand heroic style that later writers have imitated and parodied, but not surpassed. The greatest benefit of his Italian journey was his being accepted and praised as an accomplished poet in Italy, a country proud of its vernacular poets, which helped him decide to write his masterpiece in his native tongue, rather than in the international language of Latin.

Milton returned to England earlier than planned, in 1639. King Charles I and Parliament were moving toward civil war, and it seemed to Milton that England was preparing itself to become God's own kingdom on earth and that the new nation would need his as-yet-unwritten historical epic, which he initially conceived as based in English history. First, however, he would contribute to the cause in the way he best could, with his pen. The effort cost him his eyesight, briefly his liberty, and very nearly his life.

LIFE'S WORK

Milton never intended his studies to make him a reclusive scholar. In his tractate *Of Education* (1644), he defines education as "that which fits a man to perform justly, skillfully, and magnanimously all the offices, both private and public, of peace and war." Milton brought his vast learning, his passionate convictions, and often his barbed satire to bear on the most pressing controversies of the Commonwealth, including matters of religious, domestic, political, and individual liberty. He made numerous enemies with his antimonarchic, often heretical stances (which partisan readers have frequently confused with his poetry), but his efforts always bespoke great moral courage. Though disillusioned with the failed promise of the Commonwealth, Milton almost single-handedly tried to prevent the reestablishment of the monarchy by publishing his final book of controversial prose, *The Ready and Easy Way to Establish a Free Commonwealth* (1660), barely a month before King Charles II assumed the throne, when most former Republicans were already in exile or hiding for their lives.

He began this period writing against the ecclesiastical government of the Anglican bishops; five books resulted, of which the most important are *Of Reformation Touching Church Discipline in England* (1641) and *The Reason of Church-Government Urg'd Against Prelaty* (1642). In *The Doctrine and Discipline of Divorce* (1643) and two other tracts, he argued for divorce as a right of incompatible couples to separate and avoid wasting their domestic lives. His finest prose work is *Areopagitica* (1644), an argument addressed to Parliament against the reestablishment of censorship and in favor of free intellectual inquiry and expression. Milton advocated the people's right to call a tyrant to account in *The Tenure of Kings and Magistrates* (1649), contending that the governor rules on behalf of, and with the consent of, the people. He also defended the unpopular execution of King Charles I in *Eikonoklastes* (1649) and *Pro Populo Anglicano Defensio* (1651; the first defense of the English people).

The gifted, supremely articulate Milton accepted an appointment in the new government as secretary of foreign tongues (later Latin secretary) in March, 1649. This, his first real job, entailed handling correspondence with the rulers and diplomats of Europe, an important task in a democratic island near a monarchic continent. He had been tutoring his sister's sons John and Edward Phillips—Edward was his most vivid early biographer—since returning from Italy, and his little academy had grown steadily.

The conflict that split the nation also severed his marriage in 1642 to Mary Powell, the seventeen-year-old daughter of a Royalist family in Oxford, where the king would encamp up the road from Republican London. Mary went to visit her family after two months of marriage and did not return for three years. Hazards of travel during the war, their families' differing politics, and the hostility of Mary's mother toward Milton (to whom her husband was in debt) contributed to her absence. She returned unannounced one evening, Milton forgave her, and the couple lived together until Mary's death on May 5, 1652, three days after the birth of their third daughter, Deborah. The couple had two other daughters, Anne and Mary, and a son, John, who died a month after his mother.

Milton by that year was totally blind, though his eyes appeared unclouded. For ten years he had been troubled by severe headaches and bodily discomfort associated with his failing vision that certainly sharpened his temper and shortened his patience. His work load as Latin secretary was enormous, as was that which he imposed on himself: conducting compendious research for his massive *De doctrina Christiana* (1825), which is the fullest, most systematic statement of his beliefs.

Milton apparently had little time for his daughters. Their recorded disaffection for him has been a chief support for his critics' accusations of misogyny, a charge that has been repeatedly refuted by those who have studied his friendships with women and his loving, admiring portrait of Eve in *Paradise Lost*. He continued to seek domestic happiness. In 1656, he married Katherine Woodcock, who gave birth to their daughter Katherine the next year. The mother never recovered from childbirth and died on February 3, 1658. The child lived only six

MILTON'S MAJOR WORKS	
1634	*Comus* (pb. 1637 as *A Maske Presented at Ludlow Castle*)
1641	*Animadversions upon the Remonstrant's Defence Against Smectymnuus*
1641	*Of Prelatical Episcopacy*
1641	*Of Reformation Touching Church Discipline in England*
1642	*The Reason of Church-Government Urg'd Against Prelaty*
1642	*An Apology Against a Pamphlet . . .*
1643	*The Doctrine and Discipline of Divorce*
1644	*Areopagitica*
1644	*The Judgement of Martin Bucer Concerning Divorce*
1644	*Of Education*
1645	*Colasterion*
1645	*Poems of Mr. John Milton*
1645	*Tetrachordon*
1649	*Eikonoklastes*
1649	*The Tenure of Kings and Magistrates*
1651	*Pro Populo Anglicano Defensio*
1654	*Pro Populo Anglicano Defensio Secunda*
1655	*Pro Se Defensio*
1659	*Considerations Touching the Likeliest Means to Remove Hirelings Out of the Church*
1659	*A Treatise of Civil Power in Ecclesiastical Causes*
1660	*The Readie and Easie Way to Establish a Free Commonwealth*
1667	*Paradise Lost* (revised 1674)
1670	*The History of Britain*
1671	*Paradise Regained*
1671	*Samson Agonistes*
1673	*Of True Religion, Heresy, Schism, and Toleration*

months. Milton married Elizabeth Minshall in 1663, and for twelve years she provided him with the companionship and tranquillity he needed to write his masterpieces.

The collapse of the Commonwealth and the Restoration of monarchy in 1660—the ruin of Milton's hopes, in other words—brought threats against the life of this most vocal Republican, advocate of divorce, and defender of regicide. Milton's stature among the intellectuals of Europe saved his life, and though he was imprisoned briefly and lost most of his estate, Milton was invited by Charles II in 1664, according to Elizabeth Milton, to write for his court. Milton declined out of conscience but also because he was midway through the seven years of composing his epic, which he had postponed for twenty years while preparing his country, without success, to receive it.

Paradise Lost is his great study of the first failure to establish the sovereignty of human reason that explains all subsequent failures. Reason for Milton was the image of God that remains in humankind, and its exercise requires the harmonious operation of all human faculties. Why, Milton asks, with all circumstances apparently favorable, did God allow his Englishmen to fail in their attempt to establish his kingdom in England's green and pleasant land? Furthermore, where might there be found the model of Christian heroism that might yet teach the human race the virtue that eludes it at the very moment it is most needed?

Milton's answer is the motive behind his epic, his Old Testament tragedy *Samson Agonistes* (1671), and his New Testament brief epic *Paradise Regained* (1671). In all three, the argument lies between the bondage of the Law and the liberty of the Gospel—the dilemma of human will suspended between the letter and spirit of God's Word, between conformity and the exercise of divinely creative will—as it was in the controversial prose and in the *De doctrina Christiana*. The ideas that he formulated in the prose he represented in the drama of the poetry.

Milton's central artistic problem was to animate Christian virtue in response to the temptations of evil. To portray virtue as a refusal is to make it a merely paralyzing reaction, as indeed the chaste Lady of *Comus* is fixed in her chair after resisting Comus's seduction. In *Paradise Lost*, he portrays more active virtues in Adam and Eve, the angel Abdiel, and the Son. Samson in *Samson Agonistes* breaks the letter of the Hebrew Law but fulfills its spirit in destroying the temple. By outwitting Satan, the young Jesus in *Paradise Regained*—Milton's favorite among his works—is the most successful exemplar of reason that Milton created.

Milton spent his post-Restoration years composing his final works and receiving numerous admiring visitors from abroad, even as he had once visited Galileo. He died quietly on November 8, 1674, the year he reissued *Paradise Lost* in twelve books. He was buried in the cemetery of the Church of Saint Giles, Cripplegate. In 1790, some young men, drunk after a party, dug up the coffin, and relic-mongers sold bits of his hair, teeth, fingers, ribs, and other bones. Milton believed that poetry still served to tame the wild beast in humankind, as it did in the myth of Orpheus, the first poet, whose body was also torn into pieces and distributed throughout the world. Milton would not have been surprised at the human perversity that desecrated his grave, or that his end, like his artistic life, would so resemble that of Orpheus, or of a saint, which he believed everyone was capable of being.

SIGNIFICANCE

Milton lost nearly every battle he entered with his prose from 1640 to 1660, though the ideas he advanced later prevailed. The limitation of the monarchy, the dethroning of the bishops, the freedom of printing and expression, and the institution of divorce have all come to pass in Great Britain. The guarantees of freedom in the United States Constitution owe more to Milton's *Areopagitica* than to John Locke. Yet Milton is primarily valued not as a political thinker but as a poet. His works have gone through hundreds of editions and been the subject of more commentary than those of anyone else, save Shakespeare. His achievements are monumental; his greatest works mark the culmination of ancient traditions, and it has been claimed that much later literature is a series of footnotes to Milton. His *Paradise Lost* ended the tradition of the classical epic by incarnating the epic virtues in Satan, whose business is death and whose essential form is the serpent. Satan's posturing is ultimately irrelevant except as a parody of the true heroism of human life that is lived by the Adams and Eves of this garden called Earth.

—*Robert Bensen*

FURTHER READING

Barker, Arthur E. *Milton and the Puritan Dilemma*. Toronto: University of Toronto Press, 1942. A brilliant intellectual biography, offering analysis of Milton's circumstances and development of the ideas that transformed his life and poetry.

Brown, Cedric C. *John Milton: A Literary Life*. New York: St. Martin's Press, 1995. An introduction to Milton's career, focusing on his persuasiveness and skill in self-presentation, as well as his literary achievements.

Darbishire, Helen, ed. *The Early Lives of Milton*. New York: Barnes and Noble Books, 1932. Reprint. 1965. Contains early biographies by John Aubrey, John Phillips, Anthony Wood, Edward Phillips, John Toland, and Jonathan Richardson.

Hanford, James H. *John Milton, Englishman*. New York: Crown, 1949. An engaging introduction to Milton's life and work. Provides extensive commentary on the major poems, although Hanford overemphasizes the centrality of the conflict between passion and discipline in Milton's personality and work.

Hill, Christopher. *Milton and the English Revolution*. London: Faber and Faber, 1977. An astute reading of Milton's political thought and how it anticipated later European revolutionary movements. Hill, a noted historian, stresses the modernity of Milton's ideas at the expense of his fundamentally religious grounding.

Levi, Peter. *Eden Renewed: The Public and Private Life of John Milton*. New York: St. Martin's Press, 1997. A popular biography, providing an entertaining account of Milton's life but little analysis of his work.

Lewalski, Barbara Kiefer. *The Life of John Milton: A Critical Biography*. Malden, Mass.: Blackwell, 2000. An extensive 754-page analysis of Milton's life and work, focusing on the development of his ideas and art. Lewalski explains how Milton invented himself as a new type of author, a writer who used the resources of learning and artistry to develop radical politics, poetics, and prophecies.

Masson, David. *The Life of John Milton*. 7 vols. London: Macmillan, 1859-1894. Reprint. Gloucester, Mass.: Peter Smith, 1981. An exhaustive, encyclopedic compendium of records, notes, testimony, and minute detail of Milton's life and concurrent British history. Endlessly interesting to browse through, it supplies copious material on many facets of Milton's life and circumstances.

Milton, John. *Selected Prose*. Edited by C. A. Patrides. London: Penguin Books, 1974. Rev. ed. Columbia: University of Missouri Press, 1985. Contains most of the autobiographical passages from Milton's prose.

Parker, William R. *Milton: A Biography*. 2d. ed. 2 vols. Oxford: Clarendon Press, 1968. Essentially a superb distillate of Masson's massive but unwieldy work. Portrays Milton the man in the midst of his labors and difficulties, taking into account his astonishing intellect and achievement.

Wilson, A. N. *The Life of John Milton*. New York: Oxford University Press, 1983. A highly readable work by a novelist who brings wit and affection to the task of representing Milton as an attractive yet formidable figure.

SEE ALSO: Charles I; Charles II (of England); Galileo; John Locke.

RELATED ARTICLES in *Great Events from History: The Seventeenth Century, 1601-1700:* 1642-1651: English Civil Wars; December 6, 1648-May 19, 1649: Establishment of the English Commonwealth; May, 1659-May, 1660: Restoration of Charles II; 1667: Milton Publishes *Paradise Lost*.

PETER MINUIT
Dutch colonist and administrator

Minuit reorganized the Dutch colony of New Netherland, purchasing Manhattan Island and founding New Amsterdam as its capital. Also, he led the expedition that established a Swedish colony in the New World.

BORN: c. 1580; Wesel, duchy of Clèves (now in Germany)
DIED: June, 1638; Caribbean Sea
ALSO KNOWN AS: Peter Minnewit
AREAS OF ACHIEVEMENT: Government and politics, exploration, diplomacy

EARLY LIFE
The parents of Peter Minuit (mihn-wee) were Walloons, French-speaking Protestants who fled the Spanish Netherlands (from an area now in Belgium) to escape Spanish armies. He grew up in a German area close to the Dutch border, speaking both languages and probably French as well, as Walloons were notorious for their tenacity in retaining their native tongue. His surviving letters are in Dutch, but Minuit preferred the French spelling and pronunciation of his surname.

In 1613, he married the daughter of the burgomaster of Kleve (Clèves). The two moved to the Dutch city of Utrecht in 1615, where Minuit trained as a diamond cutter, a trade he soon abandoned. Later, he returned to Wesel and served as ruling elder of the Walloon Reformed Church.

LIFE'S WORK
In 1624, Minuit arrived in Amsterdam and volunteered to accompany an expedition of the Dutch West India Company to its colony, New Netherland, in North America. Minuit sailed for New Netherland in January, 1635, explored the Hudson and Delaware Rivers, and returned to Holland later that year to report his observations. On May 4, 1626, he was back at the colony, where the colony's council appointed him director general, replacing the previous governor, whose leadership was unsatisfactory.

New Netherland faced a crisis in its relation with the American Indians. The commander of Fort Orange (later called Albany) had unwisely aided the Mahicans in a losing battle with the Mohawks. The Mohawks won the battle, killing the commander and three of his soldiers.

Artist's rendering of Peter Minuit purchasing land from the Indians. (Library of Congress)

Minuit sent an agent north, who succeeded in repairing relations with the Iroquois tribes. He decided to concentrate the colony population for greater safety. The first settlement plan had spread colonists over the three rivers the Dutch claimed, placing families at Fort Orange on the upper Hudson River, at trading posts on the Delaware and Connecticut Rivers, and on Nut (Governor's) Island at the mouth of the Hudson. Minuit reduced Fort Orange to a garrison that would protect fur traders. Posts on the Delaware and Connecticut Rivers were occupied only during the summer fur-trading season. Because Nut Island was too small for Minuit's purposes, he moved the settlers to Manhattan Island (now New York City), founding New Amsterdam, where farmers would be protected by a fort. Following standard Dutch practice, Minuit arranged in mid-May to buy Manhattan Island from the indigenous peoples who lived there for trade goods valued at sixty guilders.

The purchase of Manhattan has given rise to one of the most persistent myths in U.S. history—that Peter Minuit cheated the American Indians by buying the most valu-able tract of land in North America for twenty-four dollars worth of beads and trinkets. Determining the present value of sixty guilders is close to impossible; the twenty-four dollar figure, first suggested in 1846 and repeated since, is as meaningless as the thirty-one billion dollar sum calculated in 1986 (what sixty guilders would amount to if it were kept invested at six percent compound interest from 1626 to 1986). The price Minuit paid did not differ significantly from what the Dutch paid each other for unimproved acreage in the early seventeenth century. Furthermore, the American Indians did not settle for "beads and trinkets." Trade goods regularly accepted by the local population included desirable European textiles and metal objects that they could not produce themselves: heavyweight woolen cloth valued for blankets and clothing, kettles, knives, axes, hatchets, hoes, and drilling awls.

By 1628, New Amsterdam boasted a stone warehouse for the Dutch West India Company's goods, two typical Dutch windmills for grinding grain and sawing lumber, and more than two hundred settlers living in thirty wooden houses clustered around the fort. In 1627, Minuit established friendly relations with Plymouth Colony to the north. The first ordained Dutch Reformed pastor arrived in April, 1628, and appointed Minuit an elder of his newly organized church. In 1630, the pastor became hostile and denounced Minuit as morally corrupt, accusing him of cheating the company.

The directors of the West India Company disagreed about the future of the colony. One faction wanted to encourage settlement using patroonships—large land grants that would be profitable only if the owner imported farmers to plant crops. The other faction wanted to concentrate on the fur trade and send traders and soldiers only to New Netherland. Minuit believed the colony needed more people, so he sided with the pro-patroon faction, which lost the struggle for control of the company. In 1631, the company recalled Minuit and spent several months examining his conduct before discharging him as director general in the summer of 1632.

When Minuit heard that Sweden had become interested in international trade and colonization, he wrote to the Swedish chancellor in June, 1636, proposing that Sweden plant an outpost on the west bank of the Delaware River, across from the Dutch seasonal fur-trading post. Minuit also hoped to encourage agricultural settlement, knowing there were many peasant refugees produced by the ongoing Thirty Years' War who would welcome a chance to start over in the New World.

The Swedes adopted his proposal, and in December of 1637, Minuit led a fleet of two Dutch ships carrying Swedish soldiers. To avoid notice by the Dutch, he sailed up a tributary stream of the Delaware to the site of what is now Wilmington. Minuit erected a fort there to protect the fur traders and farmers he planned to bring to the outpost on the next voyage. In March, 1638, acting in the name of the queen of Sweden, Minuit purchased from the American Indians a tract of land extending some 67 miles along the Delaware River. The life of New Sweden was short, however. After a brief seventeen-year existence, Peter Stuyvesant annexed the colony to New Netherland in 1655.

Leaving a garrison of twenty-four soldiers, Minuit sailed for the Caribbean Sea in June of 1638, hoping to trade for tobacco, a commodity highly desired in Sweden, before heading home. He stopped at the island of St. Christopher, where he and his ship's captain visited a vessel from Rotterdam that was anchored in the harbor. Diarists in New England and London noted in their journals that a record storm hit St. Christopher in the summer of 1638. While Minuit was on board the Rotterdam boat, the hurricane blew it out to sea, and Minuit was never seen again. His own ship received little damage and was able to return to Europe with news of his demise.

SIGNIFICANCE

Historians have repeated the legend that Minuit swindled the American Indians by buying Manhattan Island for a handful of beads and trinkets. This myth is often the only thing people know about him. His successful effort to maintain friendly relations with the Iroquois, however, saved the Albany trading post for the Dutch West India Company; by concentrating the scattered settlers on Manhattan, he provided the Dutch with a secure base for future expansion. Although the British would conquer the colony and end the role of the company and the Dutch government in North America, the Dutch population would remain a significant element in marking the ethnic diversity that began in New Amsterdam, characterized New York City from its start, and ultimately typified the entire nation.

The major cultural impact of New Sweden occurred long after Minuit's death. Finns, encouraged to settle in New Sweden, brought with them a skill particularly adapted to a forest environment—they knew how to build log cabins. Wood was too precious a commodity in deforested Holland and Britain to be used as logs; early colonists from both countries built sawmills in the forests to turn trees into boards. Once the Finns had shown the way, the log cabin was widely copied and became emblematic of the North American frontier.

By setting New Netherland on a firm footing and beginning New Sweden, Peter Minuit helped to form the diverse ethnic and cultural life of what would become the United States.

—*Milton Berman*

FURTHER READING

Burrows, Edwin G., and Mike Wallace. *Gotham: A History of New York City to 1898*. New York: Oxford University Press, 1999. Contains an excellent, illustrated account of the history of New Amsterdam.

Francis, Peter, Jr. "The Beads That Did *Not* Buy Manhattan Island." *New York History* 67 (January, 1986): 4-22. Refutes the myth that Minuit bought Manhattan Island for twenty-four dollars worth of beads.

Hoffecker, Carol E., Richard Waldron, Lorraine E. Williams, and Barbara E. Benson, eds. *New Sweden in America*. Newark: University of Delaware Press, 1995. A collection of articles, several of which discuss Minuit's contributions to the development of the colony.

Shorto, Russell. *The Island at the Center of the World: The Epic Story of Dutch Manhattan and the Forgotten Colony That Shaped America.* New York: Doubleday, 2004. Praises Minuit's leadership of New Amsterdam.

Weslager, C. A. *A Man and His Ship: Peter Minuit and the Kalmar Nyckel.* Wilmington, Del.: Kalmar Nyckel Foundation, 1989. Contains much useful biographical detail, based on extensive consultation of Dutch and Swedish sources.

_____. *The Swedes and Dutch at New Castle.* Wilmington, Del.: Middle Atlantic Press, 1987. This work covers the Dutch-Swedish rivalry for control of the Delaware Valley from 1638 to 1664. Includes an excellent sketch map of the Delaware River area.

SEE ALSO: Christina; Frederick Henry; Jacob Leisler; Axel Oxenstierna; Peter Stuyvesant.

RELATED ARTICLES in *Great Events from History: The Seventeenth Century, 1601-1700:* July, 1625-August, 1664: Founding of New Amsterdam; May 6, 1626: Algonquians "Sell" Manhattan Island; March 22, 1664-July 21, 1667: British Conquest of New Netherland.

MOLIÈRE
French playwright

By grafting character study and social commentary upon traditional farce, Molière became the creator of modern French comedy and continues to be ranked as France's finest comic playwright.

BORN: January 15, 1622 (baptized); Paris, France
DIED: February 17, 1673; Paris
ALSO KNOWN AS: Jean-Baptiste Poquelin (given name)
AREAS OF ACHIEVEMENT: Theater, literature

EARLY LIFE

Molière (mawl-yehr) was given the name Jean-Baptiste Poquelin at birth, and he was the eldest child of Marie Cressé Poquelin and Jean Poquelin. Both came from well-to-do families, prominent for two generations as merchant upholsterers. Jean-Baptiste was followed by five other children, only three of whom survived. When he was ten years of age, his mother died, and his father remarried and moved to a house in the cultural and social center of Paris. Meanwhile, Poquelin was assuring his son's future. He sent Jean-Baptiste to the Jesuit College of Clermont, an excellent school that was attended by students of the most prominent families, and then had him begin the study of law in Orléans. In 1641, Jean-Baptiste became a notary.

In a society whose center was the king, anyone who was ambitious needed court connections. In 1631, Jean Poquelin had purchased from his brother the largely honorary office of valet and upholsterer to the king. Six years later, he had obtained hereditary rights to the position for Jean-Baptiste and had him take the oath of office. Given his family background, his education, his profession, and his future court position, Jean-Baptiste's pathway to prosperity seemed clearly marked.

Jean-Baptiste, however, had fallen under the influence of the actress Madeleine Béjart, and in 1643 he renounced his court position, abandoned his social status, and even risked damnation, according to the clerics of his time, to become an actor. Béjart, her brother Joseph, her sister Geneviève, Jean-Baptiste (now calling himself Molière), and nine other actors formed a theatrical company, rented a theater, and, at the beginning of 1644, began to produce their plays. They were, however, unsuccessful. Their financial condition was so poor that Molière, who had become the manager of the troupe, was twice imprisoned for debt and had to be rescued by his father.

In 1646, Molière and the three Béjarts, along with several other actors, began a tour of the provinces. During the next twelve years, Molière learned his craft as an actor, who before long was regularly cast in leading roles; as a producer and financial manager; and as a writer, who practiced his skill in farcical sketches before proceeding to full-length plays. By 1658, Molière and his troupe of seasoned actors were ready once again to attempt the conquest of Paris. Although his self-discipline, his energy, and his dedication to the theater, Molière was to prove a brilliant leader. Although his hatred of hypocrisy, which he expressed in telling satire, would earn for him enemies, his genius would bring him friends to defend him, not the least his king. While he was uncompromising in principle, Molière was tolerant in practice and equipped with consistent good humor. It was fortunate that Molière possessed such qualities, for there would be adversities during the last fifteen years of his life that must have made him yearn for the carefree, vagabond days in the provinces.

LIFE'S WORK

On October 24, 1658, Molière and his troupe gave the performance that would determine their future. They appeared at the Louvre before the young King Louis XIV, his brother Philippe, or "Monsieur," and the court. Although the king was unenthusiastic about their major play, a tragedy by Pierre Corneille, he enjoyed Molière's farce. As a result, the troupe was granted permission to play at the royal Petit-Bourbon theater, where they shared performance days with the Italian Comedians until the Italians went back to Italy in July, 1659. Because they were under the patronage of Philippe, Molière's troupe was called the *troupe de Monsieur* (Monsieur's troupe).

It is not surprising that the king preferred Molière's comedies to other plays that the company performed. Although they were based on Italian comedies and farces, Molière's plays

Molière. (Library of Congress)

were superior in language, in wit, in the inventiveness of their plots, and, above all, in the realistic depiction of character. Soon the company was reviving Molière's earlier full-length plays, written when he was in the provinces, *L'Étourdi: Ou, Les Contre-temps* (1653; *The Blunderer*, 1678) and *Le Dépit amoureux* (1656; *The Love-Tiff*, 1930). Molière followed them with his first comedy of manners, *Les Précieuses ridicules* (1659; *The Affected Young Ladies*, 1732), which satirizes the affectations of Parisian society. This play was then followed by *Sganarelle: Ou, Le Cocu imaginaire* (1662; *Sganarelle*, 1755), a complicated story of love and misunderstanding, which became one of Louis's favorites.

A contemporary portrait of Molière at breakfast with Louis XIV reveals the strength of character that was one of the playwright's dominant traits. Molière's sharp features, hawklike nose, and firm chin reflect his determination; barely resting on the chair, he is all nervous energy, a creative artist temporarily restrained only by the presence of his monarch.

Unfortunately, the approval of the king and the adulation of the public aroused the jealousy of rival troupes, who intrigued against him and in 1660 succeeded in having his theater torn down without notice, supposedly because it was in the way of a new facade for the Louvre. Unwilling to interfere with the plans formulated by his own officials, Louis instead permitted Molière's actors to use the theater of the Palais Royal. This was to be the home of Molière's company for the rest of his life.

The first play to be produced in the Palais Royal was a failure. The second, *L'École des maris* (1661; *The School for Husbands*, 1732), was very popular. The play is based on the situation in a comedy by Terence, in which two boys receive very different kinds of education. In Molière's play, however, the children are girls. Molière's audience was delighted with the success of the heroine, who foils her severe guardian in his plans to wed her and even tricks him into helping her into the arms of the young man with whom she is in love.

Probably to strengthen his position at court, in 1660, when his brother died, Molière resumed his rights to the court office of his father and later performed the quarterly duty of making the king's bed. In 1661, Molière also produced the first of a number of comic ballets, which was presented at an entertainment in the king's honor. Critics have lamented the fact that thereafter

Molière spent so much of his time on various court entertainments, yet without the king's favor Molière would have been in serious trouble during the years to come.

Although Molière's greatest works were still ahead of him, so were his greatest difficulties. In 1662, when he was forty, Molière married the charming, spoiled actress Armande Béjart, who was the twenty-year-old sister of Molière's friend and mistress Madeleine Béjart. Scholars do not credit the persistent rumor that Armande was really Madeleine's daughter, perhaps by Molière. They do, however, agree that Armande brought Molière more misery than joy. It is obvious that the themes of jealousy and infidelity, so often arising from the marriage of an older man to a young woman, as in *L'École des femmes* (1662; *The School for Wives*, 1732), reflected Molière's own unhappy experience with a girl much like the coquettish Célimène of his *Le Misanthrope* (1666; *The Misanthrope*, 1709).

The more successful Molière became, the more his enemies sought to destroy him. Calling Molière godless, they attempted to suppress *The School for Wives*, the story of a country girl made vulnerable by her own innocence. In 1663, in a series of essays, verses, and plays, Molière and his friends battled against those who traduced the playwright, calling him a cuckold and charging him with incest. In 1664, Molière was forbidden to perform *Tartuffe: Ou, L'Imposteur* (1664; *Tartuffe*, 1732), the story of a pious hypocrite; because of objections from religious fanatics at court, the play was not approved until 1670. Meanwhile, in 1665, pressure on Molière forced the withdrawal of his play *Dom Juan: Ou, Le Festin de Pierre* (1665; *Don Juan*, 1755), which dealt with the legendary seducer.

In 1666, Molière's troupe performed the work that many critics consider his masterpiece, *The Misanthrope*, which, significantly, relates the difficulties encountered by an outspoken, honest person in a dishonest society. The play was only moderately successful. By now, Molière's troubles with his wife had become worse, his father's business was in difficulty, and his own health was declining. Yet he continued to produce plays, including *Le Médecin malgré lui* (1666; *The Doctor in Spite of Himself*, 1672), *Amphitryon* (1668; English translation, 1755), *L'Avare* (1668; *The Miser*, 1672), and *Le Bourgeois Gentilhomme* (1670; *The Would-Be Gentleman*, 1675).

Despite the success of most of his plays, Molière's last years were dark. In 1670, his father died in poverty, and in 1672 a newborn son died. Molière himself was desperately ill and forced to depend on the doctors whom, as his plays indicate, he deeply distrusted. Meanwhile, Molière's enemies triumphed: He lost the right to stage musical entertainments for the king, and finally he was refused permission to stage a play at court. Molière's play *Le Malade imaginaire* (1673; *The Imaginary Invalid*, 1732) was about a healthy man who imagined himself to be ill. On February 17, 1673, Molière, who was playing the title role, became ill onstage. Although he managed to finish the performance, he died later that night. Even then, the clergy were not done with him; they insisted that he should not be buried in consecrated ground. The king intervened, and, during the night of February 21, Molière was quietly interred in the cemetery of Saint-Joseph in his native Paris.

SIGNIFICANCE

Molière is generally said to have created modern French comedy. Examined carefully, Molière's plots are farfetched, with the farcical situations of his dramatic predecessors. Yet he develops them masterfully, piling complication on complica-

---

MOLIÈRE'S MAJOR WORKS

1653	*L'Étourdi: Ou, Les Contre-temps* (*The Blunderer*, 1678)
1656	*Le Dépit amoureux* (adaptation of Niccolò Secchi's *L'Interessé*; *The Love-Tiff*, 1930)
1659	*Les Précieuses ridicules* (*The Affected Young Ladies*, 1732)
1661	*L'École des maris* (*The School for Husbands*, 1732)
1662	*L'École des femmes* (*The School for Wives*, 1732)
1663	*La Critique de "L'École des femmes"* (*The Critique of "The School for Wives,"* 1957)
1663	*L'Impromptu de Versailles* (*The Versailles Impromptu*, 1714)
1664	*Tartuffe: Ou, L'Imposteur* (revised pr. 1667; *Tartuffe*, 1732)
1665	*Dom Juan: Ou, Le Festin de Pierre* (*Don Juan*, 1755)
1665	*L'Amour médecin* (*Love's the Best Doctor*, 1755)
1666	*Le Misanthrope* (*The Misanthrope*, 1709)
1666	*Le Médecin malgré lui* (*The Doctor in Spite of Himself*, 1672)
1668	*Amphitryon* (English translation, 1755)
1668	*L'Avare* (*The Miser*, 1672)
1670	*Le Bourgeois Gentilhomme* (*The Would-Be Gentleman*, 1675)
1671	*Les Fourberies de Scapin* (*The Cheats of Scapin*, 1701)
1672	*Les Femmes savantes* (*The Learned Ladies*, 1693)
1673	*Le Malade imaginaire* (*The Imaginary Invalid*, 1732; also known as *The Hypochondriac*)

tion and reversal on reversal, until, in the denouement, he resolves the difficulties that he has so carefully created. More important was his handling of character. Misers and misanthropes, foolish women and greedy doctors, court flatterers and pious hypocrites were familiar types in earlier plays. Although his comic characters, like those of Ben Jonson in England, were still types, Molière individualized them. In *Tartuffe*, for example, the autocratic father Orgon, who is so easily deceived by the hypocrite, is not only a fool; he is a middle-aged man, married to a young wife, who does not believe that he can control her, his domineering mother, his rebellious children, or even his outspoken maid. Thus, Molière converts a standard character into a realistic and complex person, with whom the audience can sympathize, even while they condemn his folly.

By providing a serious basis for comic drama, the satirical denouncement of hypocrisy, vice, and folly, Molière changed the nature of French comedy. His influence spread through the Continent and across the Channel to England, where the Restoration Wits imitated his plays. In later centuries, his popularity has persisted; his plays are frequently performed throughout the world, and his characters have become immortal.

—*Rosemary M. Canfield Reisman*

FURTHER READING

Chapman, Percy Addison. *The Spirit of Molière: An Interpretation*. Edited by Jean-Albert Bédé. Princeton, N.J.: Princeton University Press, 1940. A portrait of Molière in the context of his times, written by a scholar who knew the period extremely well. Includes analysis of six of the major plays and information on the court and theater in seventeenth century France.

Gossman, Lionel. *Men and Masks: A Study of Molière*. Baltimore: Johns Hopkins University Press, 1963. In seven brilliant essays, five major plays are studied in detail, with particular emphasis on the issue of identity in Molière's characters. The last two chapters survey criticism of Molière in his own period and in subsequent centuries.

Koppisch, Michael S. *Rivalry and the Disruption of Order in Molière's Theater*. Madison, N.J.: Fairleigh Dickinson University Press, 2004. Critical analysis of ten plays in which characters' desire and rivalry endanger the existing order and collapse differences.

McCarthy, Gerry. *The Theatres of Molière*. New York: Routledge, 2002. Explores the practice and method of Molière's play writing and acting.

Mander, Gertrud. *Molière*. Translated by Diana Stone Peters. New York: Frederick Ungar, 1973. Mander's work is organized, thorough, and useful for the general reader. Includes analysis of fourteen plays, a detailed chronology, excerpts from reviews of twentieth century productions, and an extensive bibliography.

Moore, Will G. *Molière: A New Criticism*. Oxford: Clarendon Press, 1949. Moore employs an analytical approach to resolve contradictory interpretations of Molière's plays.

Polsky, Zachary. *The Comic Machine, the Narrative Machine, and the Political Machine in the Works of Molière*. Lewiston, N.Y.: E. Mellen Press, 2000. Examines the general nature of comedy and the specific nature of seventeenth century French comedy to understand how these ideas apply to six of Molière's plays.

Scott, Virgina. *Molière: A Theatrical Life*. New York: Cambridge University Press, 2000. In the first significant English biography written in many years, Scott recounts the incidents of Molière's life and describes his plays within the wider context of French seventeenth century theater.

SEE ALSO: Pierre Corneille; Jean Racine.

RELATED ARTICLES in *Great Events from History: The Seventeenth Century, 1601-1700:* February 24, 1631: Women First Appear on the English Stage; 1664: Molière Writes *Tartuffe*.

GEORGE MONCK
English military commander and politician

A consummate professional soldier, Monck began the English Civil War on the Royalist side, but he later fought for Parliament in Scotland and defended his country at sea against the Dutch. He was also the central figure in the Restoration of Charles II, whom he served in a variety of roles until his death.

BORN: December 6, 1608; Great Potheridge, Devonshire, England
DIED: January 3, 1670; London, England
ALSO KNOWN AS: First duke of Albemarle; earl of Torrington; George Monk
AREAS OF ACHIEVEMENT: Government and politics, military, warfare and conquest

EARLY LIFE

George Monck (MUHNK) was born on December 6, 1608, in Great Potheridge, Devonshire, the fourth child and second son of a squire of modest means. Although the Monck family was an established part of the Devonshire gentry and had connections with a number of prominent west country families, George, as a younger son, would have to make his own way in life. As a youth, he spent time with his grandparents and an Exeter merchant, Sir George Smyth. Smyth was his godfather and saw that Monck received an education at a grammar school in Exeter.

Younger sons in Stuart landed families traditionally sought their fortunes in trade, in the Church, or in military service. One of Monck's brothers, Nicholas, became a clergyman, but George turned to the military at age sixteen and spent virtually his entire life thereafter as a soldier. Given the west country's traditions, particularly since the days of Elizabeth I, Monck's career choice was not unusual.

What was unusual about Monck's life's work were the circumstances of his entry and his degree of success. In 1625, he joined a company commanded by his kinsman Sir Richard Grenville and served in the first duke of Buckingham's ill-fated Cádiz expedition. Monck's decision to volunteer was stimulated by a recent altercation with an undersheriff in Exeter, who had insulted his father. From that rather inauspicious beginning emerged perhaps the most complete and technically competent general to serve during the Civil War and Interregnum.

Buckingham's failure at Cádiz did not sour Monck on military life. Indeed, Monck came to view it as his natural habitat and to find combat exhilarating. When Charles II recalled him from duty with the fleet in the Second Anglo-Dutch War to maintain order in London following the Great Fire in 1666, Monck was reported to have wept with disappointment.

Through the 1620's, Monck continued to serve in Buckingham's other unsuccessful expeditions. By the end of the decade, he turned to service with the Dutch in their ongoing struggle against Spain. His action was quite typical for Englishmen of his day. Most participants in the English Civil War with any prior military experience acquired it in the Low Countries.

Although commonly described as a rather slow and plodding man, Monck had an astute mind and was a careful student of his craft. He was neither particularly glamorous nor blessed with a magnetic personality, yet he was able to attract the loyalty, trust, and respect of the men in his command by his quiet self-confidence and thorough competence. Monck was, to be sure, unpolished by the standards of the wealthier landowners of his time, but he had learned much in the Low Countries and had an exceptional grasp of the art of warfare.

By the eve of the Civil War, Monck was back in Great Britain. He served as a lieutenant colonel against the Scots in the Bishops' Wars and then led an infantry regiment in Ireland. When England divided between king and Parliament, Monck remained in the royal service as part of a force sent from Ireland to England in 1643. Captured by parliamentary forces in early 1644, he was consigned to the Tower of London for two years. During his captivity, two important events that would shape the rest of his life took place. After Charles I's defeat, Monck agreed to change sides and serve Parliament. Before that, however, he became involved with his prison laundress and future wife, Anne Clarges Ratsford.

At the time, Anne was married to a London perfumer. She was from a family of some substance and education and was dissatisfied with her husband. By the time of Monck's release, she was his mistress; they were married in January, 1653, her husband having vanished three years earlier. Although Anne was not popular at court after the Restoration and has been criticized by both her contemporaries and later writers, she was a major source of happiness for Monck and an important part of his life. She was also a none-too-subtle Royalist throughout the Interregnum.

LIFE'S WORK

Service with Parliament's forces ultimately placed Monck in a position to determine England's fate, but in 1646 his new allegiance was simply that of a professional soldier accepting the new de facto civilian authority in his homeland. Monck always stressed the subordination of the military to civil authorities, and after the end of the Civil War he accepted the verdict of the battlefield and served a new master.

Monck was first sent to Ulster as a major general, and he performed well under very difficult circumstances. Despite parliamentary criticism over a militarily necessary armistice with Irish rebels, Oliver Cromwell recognized both his talent and his loyalty and made Monck a part of his 1650 campaign against Scotland. After the English victory at Dunbar, in which Monck personally led his men into the Scottish lines, Cromwell made him commander in chief for Scotland. Monck finished the pacification of that kingdom with ruthless efficiency. Except for one interlude, Monck served in Scotland until 1660.

In 1652, England became involved in a bloody naval war with the Dutch Republic, largely over trade. Along with Robert Blake and Richard Deane, Monck was appointed general at sea. All three men were experienced soldiers and were appointed primarily because of their expertise with artillery. Monck quickly distinguished himself in this unfamiliar environment. Although no seaman, he excelled at both the strategy and the tactics of war at sea, and with Deane he wrought a major change in naval warfare. Monck saw the value of keeping his ships in formation and concentrating on broadside fire to break the enemy. Capturing ships as prizes became a secondary goal. These changes allowed the navy to gain a decided advantage. In the Second Anglo-Dutch War, the Navy forgot these lessons under the duke of York's leadership, much to England's regret.

By the end of 1653, Monck was back in Scotland to crush a rebellion in the Highlands. He governed the kingdom for Cromwell with an effective mix of discipline and kindness. Whatever his future preferences, he was loyal to Cromwell until the lord protector's death, and then Monck served Richard Cromwell loyally. Unfortunately, Richard was unable to replace his father effectively and England soon moved toward political confusion and renewed warfare. By mid-1659 the Rump of the Long Parliament was back in power, the army's officers were maneuvering for advantage, and the threat of risings by both Royalists and religious radicals was very real. Monck watched and waited in Scotland, resisting pressure from the several pro-Royalists in his entourage,

including his wife, and prepared for the uncertain future. He moved to ensure the loyalty of his officers and men through a combination of indoctrination and purges, and he obtained significant financial support from a Scottish assembly to supplement his well-stocked war chest.

After the army, led mainly by Major General John Lambert, expelled the Rump, Monck felt compelled to move. He called for the restoration of parliamentary rule, but he also indicated that the Rump ought to admit the members excluded by Thomas Pride's Purge in 1648 and hold elections to fill vacant seats. Monck carefully articulated his demands in stages to minimize opposition and use the Rump to legitimate his challenge to Lambert and the army. Monck may have had the restoration of the Stuarts as his ultimate goal, but the evidence is largely circumstantial. He was deeply concerned about a religious settlement and feared that the radical sectarians, especially the Quakers, were on the verge of seizing power. Monck favored a broad and tolerant Presbyterian settlement and probably intervened in politics to protect that interest. As events unfolded, however, recalling Charles II took on an increasingly powerful logic.

By December of 1659, Monck and Lambert faced each other across the Scottish border, the former at Coldstream and the latter at Newcastle. Lambert had twice as many troops initially, but Monck's were better trained, were more reliable, and, most important, were receiving regular pay. Monck waited, sure that Lambert could not afford to attack or withdraw. By the end of the year, the political situation in London and the south forced Lambert to withdraw, and at that point his unpaid troops melted away and the road to London was open for Monck.

Monck advanced slowly, gathering petitions for new elections and pledges of support as he went. By early February, when he arrived in London, he was England's indispensable man of the moment. He thwarted one last effort by the Rump to remove him, secured financial backing from the City of London, and convinced the Long Parliament, which now included the secluded members from the 1640's, to dissolve itself after nearly twenty years of rule.

Until late March, Monck hid his plans from his closest associates and the Royalist court. This act probably reflects both his caution and his uncertainty about a return of the Stuarts. Once he determined that the new Convention Parliament and most of the political nation desired a return to monarchy, Monck moved quickly to bring Charles II back to England. Charles's Declaration of Breda, which sought to reassure Englishmen that a restoration would not be vengeful, was based on Monck's advice. When Charles landed at Dover on May 25, 1660, Monck was there to greet him and accompany him to London.

Charles II rewarded Monck with numerous offices, stipends, and titles, the most important of which was the dukedom of Albemarle. Monck's Coldstream Guards regiment was retained to protect the new monarchy, but Monck quickly left the political stage to enjoy his new wealth and position. Charles called on him regularly, particularly when he needed a show of stability, such as during the outbreak of plague in London in 1665 or after the Great Fire the following year. Monck was, however, content to remain in the background. His most notable service came during the Second Anglo-Dutch War. Despite his age, he returned to active sea duty and managed to salvage a draw for England. He died at Whitehall on the tenth anniversary of his departure from Coldstream, a loyal soldier to the end.

SIGNIFICANCE

Monck rose from a modest provincial beginning to a position of wealth, influence, and nobility. Of the principal figures who fought during the English Civil War and Interregnum, he was the most professional in both his background and his attitude. He served his country by serving the government in power at the moment. His changes of sides may be viewed as opportunism, but they also support the view that he was following the nation's interests in order to serve England better. He always managed to hold the loyalty of his men while maintaining firm discipline, often while facing very difficult circumstances. When the crisis with the army leaders came in late 1659, Monck's men stood by him while the popular and flamboyant Lambert saw his forces disintegrate. That in itself is a testimony to Monck's thorough professionalism.

Monck was not an office-politician, as so many of Cromwell's generals were. His one venture into politics was tremendously important, though, because he reestablished stability in the wake of Oliver Cromwell's death and then orchestrated the Restoration of Charles II. This was, for Monck, an aberrant act, one forced on him by necessity and duty. His duty done, he accepted his rewards, which were plentiful, and moved offstage to await further orders from his new superior. Charles II relied on his duke of Albemarle because Monck understood the mind of the political nation and because his loyalty was beyond question. Monck was unquestionably fond of money, but he sold neither his sword nor his soul, and he served his country well.

—*Vinton M. Prince, Jr.*

FURTHER READING

Ashley, Maurice. *Charles II: The Man and the Statesman.* New York: Praeger, 1971. While focusing mainly on Charles, this work provides a good summary of Monck's actions between the battle of Worcester and the Restoration. His career as Albemarle receives little attention here.

_____. *General Monck.* Totowa, N.J.: Rowman and Littlefield, 1977. The only modern study of Monck, this replaces and expands upon Ashley's treatment of Monck in *Cromwell's Generals* (1955). Fair, but favorable and thorough, this is by far the best work on the subject.

Farr, David. *John Lambert: Parliamentary Soldier and Cromwellian Major-General, 1619-1684.* Rochester, N.Y.: Boydell Press, 2003. A recent biography about Monck's opponent in the Scottish wars and in the struggle to control the military.

Hill, Christopher. *The Century of Revolution: 1603-1714.* New York: W. W. Norton, 1966. Reprint. 1982. A survey of the Stuart years organized into both narrative and topical chapters. A good source for Monck's context, although challenging in places.

Hutton, Ronald. *The Restoration: A Political and Religious History of England and Wales, 1658-1667.* New York: Oxford University Press, 1985. The best current account of the Restoration. Views the event in a sufficiently broad time frame to show the complexities and continuities involved. Very good on Monck's role as both military leader and duke.

Jamison, Ted R., Jr. *George Monck and the Restoration: Victor Without Bloodshed.* Fort Worth: Texas Christian University Press, 1975. A step-by-step account of Monck's role from Cromwell's death through the Restoration. Accepts the traditional view of Monck as a secret Royalist and is somewhat short on analysis. Repeatedly confuses John and Robert Lilburne.

Jones, J. R. *Country and Court: England, 1658-1714.* Cambridge, Mass.: Harvard University Press, 1978. Provides a good analysis and narrative of Monck's actions from 1658 to 1660, with some attention to his career as Albemarle. Has several stimulating insights into Monck's character and abilities.

Kenyon, J. P. *Stuart England.* 2d ed. New York: Penguin Books, 1985. A provocative account of the seventeenth century, with many original insights. Puts Monck's times in perspective, but not for the neophyte.

Lee, Maurice, Jr. *The Cabal.* Urbana: University of Illinois Press, 1965. While concerned primarily with events after 1667, this work is useful for Monck's later years and his relationship with the second generation of Charles II's ministers.

Ogg, David. *England in the Reign of Charles II.* 2d ed. 2 vols. Oxford, England: Oxford University Press, 1956. Reprint. Westport, Conn.: Greenwood Press, 1979. Old, Whiggish, but still valuable for its solid narrative of Charles II's times. Volume 1 covers the Monck/Albemarle years.

Powell, J. R. *Robert Blake: General-at-Sea.* New York: Crane-Russak, 1972. Provides a good discussion of Monck's role in the First Anglo-Dutch War, when he was Blake's colleague.

Stoyle, Mark. "The Honour of George Monck." *History Today* 43, no. 8 (August, 1993): 43. Provides newly obtained information about Monck's adolescence, describing how he committed murder to defend his family's reputation. Discusses how the concept of "honour" pervaded upper-class Tudor and Stuart society.

SEE ALSO: Robert Blake; First Duke of Buckingham; Charles I; Charles II (of England); Oliver Cromwell; James II; John Lambert; Thomas Pride.

RELATED ARTICLES in *Great Events from History: The Seventeenth Century, 1601-1700:* November 3, 1640-May 15, 1641: Beginning of England's Long Parliament; 1642-1651: English Civil Wars; December 6, 1648-May 19, 1649: Establishment of the English Commonwealth; May, 1659-May, 1660: Restoration of Charles II; March 4, 1665-July 31, 1667: Second Anglo-Dutch War; September 2-5, 1666: Great Fire of London.

DUKE OF MONMOUTH
English pretender and rebel leader

An illegitimate son of King Charles II, Monmouth became the hope of radical Protestants opposed to the succession of Charles's Catholic brother, James II. The duke's ill-conceived invasion of England failed and led to his execution.

BORN: April 9, 1649; Rotterdam, Holland, United Provinces (now in the Netherlands)

DIED: July 15, 1685; London, England

ALSO KNOWN AS: James Scott (given name)

AREAS OF ACHIEVEMENT: Government and politics, military, warfare and conquest

EARLY LIFE

The early life of James Scott, duke of Monmouth (MAHN-muhth), scarcely foretold his future prominence in Restoration English politics. He was the illegitimate son of Lucy Walter, a young English woman who by 1648 was living in The Hague under the pseudonym of Mrs. Barlow. Initially the mistress of Cavalier Robert Sidney, in the summer of 1648, she began an affair with Charles II, then the exiled prince of Wales. Despite later attempts by Monmouth and his supporters to prove that a clandestine marriage between the pair occurred, no such evidence exists.

Lucy and Charles named their son James in honor of Charles's brother and grandfather. The first decade of young James's life was traumatic and unstable. His parents' liaison apparently ended in 1651 when Charles returned from a vain attempt to regain his crown only to find Lucy living with an Irish nobleman whose daughter she had borne. For the next several years, Charles tried to gain possession of his son. Lucy, in turn, demanded a pension to support her and her son and even began spreading embarrassing rumors that Charles had secretly married her. James's education was severely neglected as his mother drifted from one relationship to the next. Finally, in 1658, Lucy agreed to hand over her son to Charles in return for a generous pension. James never saw his mother again, as she died later the same year.

Charles initially placed his son under the care of Lord Crofts in Paris, with James posing as Crofts's nephew. Dowager Queen Henrietta Maria, living in exile in Paris at the time, took an interest in her grandson, whose prospects dramatically improved in 1660 when his father regained the English throne. When Henrietta returned to England in early 1662, she brought James with her.

The king openly acknowledged James as his illegitimate son and showered him with honors as a sign of his affection. In 1663, Charles created him duke of Monmouth and gave him precedence over all dukes not of the royal blood. The same year, he arranged a lucrative marriage with Anne Scott, countess of Buccleuch, the wealthiest heiress in the realm. Henceforth, he was known as James Scott, duke of Monmouth and Buccleuch. As

Duke of Monmouth. (Library of Congress)

was the case with many arranged marriages, the relationship proved unsatisfactory. The couple had six children, but Monmouth was frequently unfaithful, and the two eventually separated.

LIFE'S WORK

Following his dramatic turn in fortune, the young duke emerged as an increasingly prominent figure at court, honored by his father and increasingly popular with the people. His behavior at court became raucous and irresponsible, and his reputation was somewhat tarnished when he and several other young nobles were implicated in the murder of a watchman in 1670. Later the same year, he engineered an attack on Sir John Coventry, who had dared to attack Charles II's morals in Parliament.

These early stains on Monmouth's character did not prevent his receiving important military commissions from the king. He began his military career at age sixteen, serving with his uncle James, duke of York, aboard the royal flagship and participating in a great sea battle against the Dutch. In 1670, King Charles made Monmouth a privy councillor and appointed him captain general of the army. Twice during the 1670's, the young duke commanded English forces on the Continent, first leading an English contingent aiding Louis XIV in his

war against the Dutch in 1672-1673 and later in 1678 fighting for the Dutch in their struggle against the French. On both occasions, Monmouth fought bravely, increasing his prestige at home. In 1679, Charles entrusted his son with command of the English forces against a Covenanter revolt in Scotland. Monmouth crushed the rebels at the Battle of Bothwell Bridge and enhanced his popularity by his clemency toward the defeated rebels.

Bothwell Bridge marked the apogee of the duke's military career. By this time, he had become involved in what ultimately proved to be the more dangerous business of political intrigue. By the late 1670's, England was embroiled in a serious controversy regarding the succession. Although King Charles fathered some fifteen children by numerous mistresses, his marriage to Catherine of Braganza was barren. The king's legal heir was his brother James, who in the 1670's had publicly embraced Catholicism. The prospect of a Catholic king ruling over a largely Protestant nation alarmed much of the country, and various public and private plots arose to exclude James from the throne.

Anthony Ashley Cooper, first earl of Shaftesbury, and other leading Whig politicians became increasingly attracted to the idea of having Monmouth declared legitimate and thus the heir to the throne. Hailed by his Whig supporters as "the Protestant duke," Monmouth foolishly involved himself in these intrigues. The king twice denied before the Privy Council that he had married Lucy Walter, and in 1679, he deprived his son of his position as captain general of the army and ordered him into exile in Holland. Within months, Monmouth returned to England without permission and unsuccessfully sought an audience with his increasingly estranged father. The angry king stripped Monmouth of his remaining offices and openly declared he would rather see him hanged than become his successor.

Defying his father's orders to leave the kingdom, Monmouth remained in the country and continued to conspire with Whig radicals and to court popularity with the people. Twice during this period, he made elaborate progresses throughout the west of England, where he received much acclaim from the local gentry and peasantry as their potential savior from the dangers of Catholic tyranny. These progresses encouraged Monmouth's ambitions and undoubtedly contributed to his belief that the people of this region would flock to his banner to help him gain the throne.

Throughout 1682 and 1683, Monmouth involved himself in dangerous schemes to raise an insurrection, although it remains unlikely that he sanctioned the Rye House Plot that planned to assassinate the king and the duke of York. Upon receiving his wayward son's confession, King Charles pardoned Monmouth but banished him from court. The disgraced duke left England for a second exile in the Netherlands in 1684. He still hoped for a reconciliation with his father, but in February, 1685, received news that the king had died and been peacefully succeeded by the duke of York as King James II.

With his Catholic uncle now on the throne, Monmouth allowed himself to become involved in a plot with Whig radicals and Scottish dissidents to invade England. The plan involved a dual assault on Britain, with Archibald Campbell, the Scottish earl of Argyll, invading from the north and Monmouth from the south. Argyll's ill-fated invasion of Scotland in May was a fiasco, leading to his capture and execution. Unaware of his fellow conspirator's failure, Monmouth sailed from Amsterdam on May 30 with fewer than one hundred men, landing at the port of Lyme Regis in southwestern England on June 11. The duke's hopes that massive numbers would flock to his cause was unrealistic. No prominent nobles or members of Parliament supported his uprising, and the gentry of the west also were unenthusiastic. His recruits came almost exclusively from the ill-trained peasantry, tradesmen, and Nonconformist Protestants. At their peak, his forces numbered only some six or seven thousand.

On June 20, Monmouth formally proclaimed himself king, but King James had been decisive in his handling of the crisis, securing firm control over London and arresting many of his rebellious nephew's potential supporters. After failing to take the key port of Bristol and with his supporters reduced by desertion to some thirty-five hundred, the increasingly desperate duke on July 6 ordered a daring night attack on royalist forces encamped at Sedgemoor. The assault failed, and the royalists slaughtered nearly a third of the rebels. Monmouth fled before the battle ended, hoping to escape to the Continent. He was captured two days after the battle, disguised as a peasant.

Vainly hoping to save his life, the would-be king wrote his uncle begging for forgiveness and requesting an audience. Arriving in London on July 13, Monmouth received his interview and abjectly begged for mercy, but James remained unmoved, even after the frightened rebel hinted he might consider converting to Catholicism. Two days later, Monmouth was beheaded on Tower Hill, the executioner taking several blows to sever the head from the body of the ill-starred duke.

SIGNIFICANCE

Ultimately, the duke of Monmouth was a vainglorious and ill-educated young man who allowed himself to be manipulated into ambitions that exceeded his reach. Following his tempestuous childhood, he had briefly played a significant role at the ribald court of his indulgent father. With graceful manners and an affable personality, he became a widely popular figure both at court and in the country. Although Monmouth served bravely on several military expeditions, his unrealistic expectations drew him into intrigues with King Charles's enemies. Only a few radical Whigs and Dissenters, fearful of a Catholic sovereign, wanted to see Monmouth as king. He could have served his country better by being satisfied with his dukedom and military career rather than giving way to unrealistic expectations that he could gain the throne.

Monmouth's 1685 invasion was premature, for James had yet to alienate his subjects in any significant respect. The duke's delusions that large numbers of Protestant gentry and nobles would join his rebellion were fatal to his cause. The few thousand artisans and peasants who were willing to fight for "King Monmouth" were hopelessly outmatched by royalist forces.

Monmouth's rebellion did have one important political consequence. A vindictive King James authorized the so-called "Bloody Assizes" to punish those suspected of complicity in the uprising. Hundreds of Monmouth's supporters in the west were executed, and more than a thousand others became virtual slaves in the West Indies. The brutality and unmerciful nature of these trials darkened James's reputation and were the first of many steps that led to his alienation from his subjects and his ultimate deposition from the throne in the Glorious Revolution of 1688.

—*Tom L. Auffenberg*

FURTHER READING

Bevan, Brian. *James, Duke of Monmouth.* London: Robert Hale, 1973. This well-illustrated eighteen-chapter biography contains an especially strong bibliography of primary and secondary sources related to Monmouth.

Clifton, Robin. *The Last Popular Rebellion: The Western Rising of 1685.* London: Maurice Temple Smith, 1984. Two of the monograph's six chapters discuss the duke's life. Most of the book focuses upon the 1685 rebellion and the nature of Monmouth's leadership. Well researched with useful maps.

D'Oyley, Elizabeth. *James, Duke of Monmouth.* Edinburgh, Scotland: J. and J. Gray, 1938. Still considered one of the best biographies. Provides a thorough account of Monmouth's life and times.

Fraser, Antonia. *Royal Charles: Charles II and the Restoration.* New York: Alfred A. Knopf, 1979. This thorough and entertaining study by one of Britain's most famous contemporary biographers provides an excellent overview of the social and political environment that shaped Monmouth's life. Superb bibliography of primary and secondary sources of Restoration history.

Lee, Maurice, Jr. *The Heiresses of Buccleuch: Marriage, Money and Politics in Seventeenth-Century Britain.* East Linton, Scotland: Tuckwell Press, 1996. Contains information on Monmouth's arranged marriage, as well as his life and attempt to seize the British throne.

Little, Bryan. *The Monmouth Episode.* London: Werner Laurie, 1956. A highly readable account of Monmouth's life and the rebellion he led, based on extensive primary sources. Includes numerous illustrations and maps of the 1685 campaign.

McClain, Molly. "The Duke of Beaufort's Defense of Bristol During Monmouth's Rebellion, 1685." *Yale University Library Gazette* 77, no. 3/4 (April, 2003):

177. Explains the factors that contributed to Beaufort's successful defense of Bristol against Monmouth's forces.

Wigfield, W. MacDonald. *The Monmouth Rebellion: A Social History, Including the Complete Text of Wade's Narrative, 1685, and a Guide to the Battlefield of Sedgemoor.* Totowa, N.J.: Barnes & Noble Books, 1980. Provides an adequate introduction to Monmouth's life, but the main focus is the men who fought for him in 1685, the Battle of Sedgemoor, and its consequences. Good bibliography and useful illustrations of the types of weapons used in the 1685 campaign.

SEE ALSO: Catherine of Braganza; Charles II (of England); Henrietta Maria; James II; Louis XIV; First Earl of Shaftesbury.

RELATED ARTICLES in *Great Events from History: The Seventeenth Century, 1601-1700:* 1642-1651: English Civil Wars; August 17-September 25, 1643: Solemn League and Covenant; May, 1659-May, 1660: Restoration of Charles II; April 6, 1672-August 10, 1678: French-Dutch War; August, 1682-November, 1683: Rye House Plot; November, 1688-February, 1689: The Glorious Revolution.

CLAUDIO MONTEVERDI
Italian composer

Monteverdi was the outstanding Italian composer of his age. He made equally significant contributions to the fields of sacred and secular music, especially in the genres of opera and the madrigal, and forged for himself and his successors an expressive musical style by combining the established techniques of his predecessors with the innovations of his contemporaries.

BORN: May 15, 1567; Cremona, duchy of Milan (now in Italy)
DIED: November 29, 1643; Venice (now in Italy)
ALSO KNOWN AS: Claudio Monteverde; Claudio Giovanni Antonio Monteverdi (full name)
AREA OF ACHIEVEMENT: Music

EARLY LIFE

Claudio Giovanni Antonio Monteverdi, better known as Claudio Monteverdi (KLOWD-yoh mohn-tay-VAYR-dee), was the eldest child of Baldassare Monteverdi, a chemist and barber surgeon, and his first wife, Mad-dalena (née Zigani). Claudio and his brother Giuleo Cesare studied music with Marc' Antonio Ingegneri, the *maestro di cappella* of Cremona Cathedral. In 1582, Claudio published a book of three-part motets titled *Sacrae cantiunculae* in Venice, and the next year he published a book of sacred madrigals for four voices in Brescia. These were followed in 1584 by a book of canzonettas for three voices, again published in Venice. As was the custom at the time, many of Monteverdi's early works were modeled on specific pieces by older composers. In addition to his compositional talent, he developed his skills as a string player.

After an interval of three years, Monteverdi published his first book of madrigals in 1587. These works for five voices illustrate the grasp of structural organization and contrapuntal technique that he had acquired from Ingegneri as well as the more modern approaches to text setting of the Ferrarese composer Luzzasco Luzzaschi and the Roman Luca Marenzio.

Monteverdi's second book of five-part madrigals, published in 1590, displays even more clearly the influence of Marenzio. This book also shows the new influence of Giaches de Wert, especially in the setting of amorous but not emotionally charged texts by Torquato Tasso. This book was the last publication in which Monteverdi acknowledged himself to be a pupil of Ingegneri, and he was clearly hoping to follow in the footsteps of other Cremonese composers, such as Benedetto Pallavicino, Giovanni Gastoldi, and Costanza Porta, by seeking work outside his hometown. After an unsuccessful attempt to land a job in Milan in 1589, he soon accepted another as a string player in the musical establishment of the Gonzaga court at Mantua. He was then nearly twenty-five, with five publications to his name and in command of a highly polished compositional technique.

Surviving portraits of the young Monteverdi show a handsome youth of above-average height, with an oval face and penetrating eyes. In most of the portraits of Monteverdi as an older man, his face is lined and somewhat haggard, perhaps a legacy of his ill health in the years following his wife's death. He was clearly embittered by his dealings with the Gonzaga family and was difficult at times, but in his later years he was capable of a certain amount of happiness. His character was essentially serious, and he made few concessions either to his colleagues or to his audiences, but he was a good provider for his family and a generous teacher.

LIFE'S WORK

The Gonzagas were active patrons of the arts and maintained a spirited rivalry with their neighbors the Estes at Ferrara. Peter Paul Rubens, Tasso, and Battista Guarini were all resident at Mantua at different times, and Duke Vincenzo I was responsible for several large-scale performances of the latter's tragicomedy *Il pastor fido* (1590; *The Faithful Shepherd*, 1602). The musical establishment was smaller than that at Ferrara but hardly less distinguished. Under the direction of Wert the *cappella* included the composers Pallavicino, Francesco Rovigo, and Salomone Rossi, while Lodovico Viadana was organist at the cathedral and Giovanni Gastoldi was director of music at the ducal chapel of Santa Barbara. Monteverdi's initial duties included participating in the weekly concerts in the ducal palace, at which the court singers attempted to rival the exploits of the famous "three singing ladies" (*concerto delle donne*) of Ferrara.

Claudio Monteverdi. (Library of Congress)

Almost immediately, Monteverdi published his third book of madrigals, heavily influenced by the essentially serious style of Wert. The book included a number of texts from Tasso's *Gerusalemme liberata* (1581; *Jerusalem Delivered*, 1600), in direct emulation of Wert's Tasso settings of the 1580's, and an even larger number of madrigal texts and excerpts from Guarini's *The Faithful Shepherd*. The collection was popular enough to be reprinted two years later, in 1594. Monteverdi continued to compose madrigals throughout the 1590's but did not publish another collection until 1603.

He traveled with the duke on the duke's military expedition to Austria and Hungary in 1595 and again on a visit to Flanders in 1599, returning from each voyage richer only in experience. He had hoped to succeed Wert when the latter died in 1596 and was disappointed when the post went to Pallavicino. He may have sought employment at Ferrara and was certainly about to dedicate a book of madrigals to Duke Alfonso II d'Este, when that nobleman died in 1597.

On May 20, 1599, Monteverdi married one of the Mantuan court singers, Claudia Cattaneo, who had three children in rapid succession. Only the two sons survived infancy: Francesco, who eventually became a singer in the choir at St. Mark's, Venice, and Massimilione, who became a medical doctor in Cremona. Finally, in 1601, on the death of Pallavicino, Monteverdi was appointed *maestro di cappella* of the Mantuan court, and in April, 1602, he and his family were given Mantuan citizenship.

Monteverdi's madrigals of the 1590's had circulated in manuscript, and several were attacked in print by the theorist Giovanni Maria Artusi in 1600, instigating a controversy that continued for some years. Artusi objected specifically to Monteverdi's use of certain harmonic idioms and of unprepared or unresolved dissonances. Monteverdi defended these devices as being necessary to express the meaning and emotional content of the text rather than merely to reflect the syntax of the poem and graphically to depict certain key words through the use of stylized musical formulas.

In 1603, Monteverdi published his fourth book of madrigals, to be followed the next year by his fifth. These two largely retrospective collections contain some of his most original and emotionally intense music, especially in the settings of epigrammatic texts by Guarini in book 4. The last six madrigals of book 5, however, show an increased interest in formal musical structure, in contrast to direct expression of the emotional content of the text, with the introduction of an obligatory *basso continuo*, or figured bass, in which the figures indicated chords to be played by a keyboard or plucked string instruments. Thus, in a symbolic way, book 5 marks the boundary between Renaissance and Baroque music.

An even more striking and clearly Baroque technique was monody, which permitted the flexible musical declamation of a text by a solo voice to the accompaniment of a *basso continuo*. This technique had been developed at Florence in the late 1590's and led directly to the creation of opera. For a variety of reasons, the Gonzagas had become interested in Florentine activities around 1600, and these latest musical developments were well known at Mantua, at least by report. This knowledge led to the composition and performance in early 1607 of the opera *La favola d'Orfeo*, with music by Monteverdi and a libretto by Alessandro Striggio, the Younger. Both parties were clearly inspired by the Florentine opera *Euridice* of 1600, with music by Italian composer Jacopo Peri and a libretto by Italian poet Ottavio Rinuccini.

La favola d'Orfeo was performed before the Accademia degli Invaghiti in a room in the ducal palace in February, 1607. Although it employed a large orchestra, the vocal and staging requirements were modest by the standards of court operas—presumably because it was not composed to celebrate a state occasion. In the music,

Monteverdi combined the new Florentine monody, in particular Peri's development of theatrical recitative, with various techniques from his own *a cappella* and *continuo* madrigals, with the instrumental forms with which he was familiar, and with his own sense of formal structure, to produce the first full-fledged opera.

La favola d'Orfeo was well received and was repeated at the command of the duke. Although it was published in 1609 and again in 1615, no further performances were forthcoming. Meanwhile, Monteverdi had returned to Cremona to be with his seriously ill wife. She died in September, leaving him desolate. He briefly refused to return to Mantua but changed his mind when another opera was required of him. This opera was *L'Arianna*, with a libretto by Rinuccini, commissioned by Vincenzo to celebrate the wedding of Prince Francesco Gonzaga to Margherita of Savoy in early 1608. Again, the composer was confronted with tragedy, for the young singer Caterina Martinelli, whom he had taught for several years and who had lived in his household almost as an adopted daughter, died of smallpox in March, 1608, while preparing the title role. The opera was postponed while another singer was found and was finally given on May 28 to an enthusiastic reception.

L'Arianna was Monteverdi's most renowned opera, and it was later performed at Naples and, as late as 1640, at Venice. The famous lament, in particular, was widely admired and served as the model for the string of laments written by other composers in the 1620's and 1630's. The lament was printed in several different forms by Monteverdi himself and is the only piece of music to survive from the opera.

After the festivities, to which Monteverdi also contributed a ballet in the French style entitled *Il ballo delle ingrate* (1608) and a prologue to Guarini's pastoral play *L'idropica* (1609), he returned to Cremona in a state of physical collapse and deep depression. He blamed the climate of Mantua for his wife's death and his own ailments, he blamed Mantuan officials for withholding his salary while paying exorbitant sums to visiting musicians such as the Florentine composer Marco da Gagliano, and he requested release from Gonzaga service. In the end, his salary was increased, and he was granted an annual pension, which he had difficulty collecting for the rest of his life.

In 1610, Monteverdi published a collection of church music in a variety of styles and forms, both archaic and modern, generally referred to as the *Vespers of 1610*. Although much of the music may have been intended for use at Mantua, and the motets in particular were clearly designed for virtuoso singers, the publication seems primarily to have been an advertisement of his suitability and availability for a new position involving church music, perhaps at Rome or Venice. He remained at Mantua until (following the death of Vincenzo) he was dismissed by the new duke Francesco in July, 1612, along with a number of Mantuan artists, including his brother Giuleo Cesare. He then returned to Cremona for a year before being appointed to the prestigious and remunerative position of *maestro di cappella* at St. Mark's in Venice on August 19, 1613.

Monteverdi's first task at St. Mark's was to restore the standards of the musical establishment. That involved recruiting and training singers, regularizing the pay structure of the choir and instrumental ensemble, and introducing new music. He must have contributed new works of his own, but few were published. He gradually appointed younger men, many of whom had been his students, to take over some of the responsibilities for the music program; most prominent among these were Francesco Cavalli, Alessandro Grandi, the Elder, and Francesco Rovetta. Monteverdi continued to compose secular works throughout the next two decades. Among the products of this period was his last commission from Mantua, the opera *La finta pazza Licori*, projected for 1627 but never performed. Of Monteverdi's late Mantuan stage works, only the music for the ballet survives.

All musical activity decreased in Venice during the early 1630's as a result of the plague and related financial difficulties, and Monteverdi, who was already in his sixties and preparing to take holy orders, seems to have composed less himself. The opening of the first public opera houses at Venice in 1637, however, prompted him to undertake a final series of stage works. The opera *L'Arianna* was revived in 1640, to be followed the same year by *Il ritorno d'Ulisse in patria*. In 1641, Monteverdi composed a ballet, *La vittoria d'amore*, on commission from the count of Parma for performance at Piacenza. Finally, in 1642, he produced his last opera, *L'incoronazione di Poppea*, which contains music of an astonishing variety (some of which may have been added posthumously by other composers for subsequent performances outside Venice). He died in Venice, after a final visit to Cremona, and is buried in the Church of the Frari.

SIGNIFICANCE

Monteverdi's career demonstrates both his versatility and his adaptability. His first two books of madrigals and first book of canzonets are essentially student works, but

they display his grasp of the musical idioms and techniques of the 1580's. The madrigals of books 3-6 show an increased interest in selecting poetry with serious emotional content and expressing those emotions through a heightened use of dissonance, contrast, and rhetorical declamation. These books mark the zenith of the madrigal as an expressive musical form.

The opera *La favola d'Orfeo* offered Monteverdi the chance to draw upon all the techniques he had mastered in his madrigals and incorporate with them the newer developments of monodic song and recitative developed by the earliest Florentine opera composers. *La favola d'Orfeo* thus stands as Monteverdi's first attempt to consolidate conflicting musical styles into a musical and dramatic whole, and is rightly considered the first great opera.

Monteverdi's enduring works are memorable for their expression of human emotions, depiction of individual characters, and sheer beauty of sound. His first six books of madrigals mark the culmination of a great Italian tradition of secular polyphony. Of his operas, *La favola d'Orfeo* was the first fully formed, *L'Arianna* the most influential, and *L'incoronazione di Poppea* arguably the greatest opera of the seventeenth century. The remarkable variety of styles in the *Vespers of 1610* provides an overview of Italian sacred music at the beginning of the Baroque era as interpreted by the composer who was largely responsible for the introduction of secular style to sacred music. Monteverdi was recognized as a giant by his contemporaries, and, although he had little direct influence on the music of succeeding generations, that status was recognized anew in the twentieth century.

—*Graydon Beeks*

FURTHER READING

Arnold, Denis. *Monteverdi*. Edited by J. A. Westrup. Rev. ed. London: J. M. Dent & Sons, 1975. The standard biography of the composer in English. Contains a summary list of works and a select bibliography.

Arnold, Denis, and Nigel Fortune, eds. *The New Monteverdi Companion*. London: Faber & Faber, 1985. An excellent collection of essays on Monteverdi's musical environment, his compositions, and questions of performance practice. Contains an extensive bibliography.

Fabbri, Paolo. *Monteverdi*. Translated by Tim Carter. New York: Cambridge University Press, 1994. The English translation of Fabbri's comprehensive account of Monteverdi's life and musical compositions.

Monteverdi, Claudio. *The Letters of Claudio Monte-*

verdi. Edited and translated by Denis Stevens. Rev. ed. New York: Oxford University Press, 1995. The authoritative English translation of Monteverdi's extensive correspondence, with detailed annotations by the editor.

Schrade, Leo. *Monteverdi: Creator of Modern Music.* New York: W. W. Norton, 1950. Reprint. New York: Da Capo Press, 1964. A detailed, full-length biography of Monteverdi, the first in English. Contains a select bibliography.

Stevens, Denis. *Monteverdi in Venice.* Madison, N.J.: Fairleigh Dickinson University Press, 2001. An account of Monteverdi's life and work in Venice, where he spent the last thirty years of his life.

_____. *Monteverdi: Sacred, Secular, and Occasional Music.* Rutherford, N.J.: Fairleigh Dickinson University Press, 1978. A brief introduction to Monteverdi's works, treated categorically rather than chronologically. Calls attention to many of the lost works and their place in his output. Contains a select bibliography.

Tomlinson, Gary. *Monteverdi and the End of the Renaissance.* Berkeley: University of California Press, 1987. An insightful discussion of the development of Monteverdi's musical style and his place in Italian cultural and intellectual life of the period. Contains numerous musical examples and an extensive bibliography.

Whenham, John, ed. *Claudio Monteverdi: "Orfeo."* New York: Cambridge University Press, 1986. One of the Cambridge Opera Handbooks, this is a collection of essays on the composition, production, and reception of the opera *La favola d'Orfeo.* Includes a bibliography and a discography.

SEE ALSO: Francesca Caccini; Arcangelo Corelli; Girolamo Frescobaldi; Jean-Baptiste Lully; Heinrich Schütz; Barbara Strozzi.

RELATED ARTICLES in *Great Events from History: The Seventeenth Century, 1601-1700:* c. 1601: Emergence of Baroque Music; February 24, 1607: First Performance of Monteverdi's *La favola d'Orfeo.*

DUCHESSE DE MONTPENSIER
French princess and writer

The duchesse de Montpensier, refused succession to the throne because she was female, would successfully lead troops during the Wars of the Fronde. She wrote about court personalities, produced a satire, insisted on gender equity in relationships of intimacy as well as power, and developed an aversion to marriage, believing it was, in part, a form of slavery. Her memoirs—historical, introspective, and autobiographical—led to the further development of the novel.

BORN: May 29, 1627; Paris, France
DIED: April 5, 1693; Paris
ALSO KNOWN AS: Anne-Marie-Louise d'Orléans (given name); La Grande Mademoiselle
AREAS OF ACHIEVEMENT: Government and politics, literature, women's rights, warfare and conquest

EARLY LIFE

Rarely has a child been born with so much and yet so little. Granddaughter of Henry IV and Marie de Médicis, Anne-Marie-Louise d'Orléans (ohr-lay-ahn), duchesse de Montpensier (deh moh-pahn-syay) was born to Gaston d'Orléans (the despicable brother of King Louis

XIII) and Marie de Bourbon, duchesse de Montpensier. Had Anne-Marie-Louise been male, she would have been next in line of succession after her father, but female succession was prohibited by Salic law.

As an infant, she became the richest woman in France, but only as a result of her mother's early death. She loved her father unconditionally but was shamefully neglected by him, preoccupied as he was with faction fighting and plotting against the king, his brother. Because of Gaston's irresponsible behavior, Cardinal de Richelieu, the king's first minister, took the duchess from him and established her in the Tuileries, where she felt terribly alone, even though she was living in one of the most elaborate royal households. Her education consisted of learning court ceremonial and etiquette, while her schooling was generally neglected.

The duchess's governess, who died when the duchess was fifteen, was replaced by a heavy-handed supervisor who earned the duchess's adolescent rebellions. When Louis XIII died the following year (1643), the queen, Anne of Austria, who was regent to the four-year-old Louis XIV, appointed Cardinal Jules Mazarin rather than Gaston (the duchess's father) as the duchess's confidential adviser. She would come to feel the loss of Anne's affection.

Her youthful political perceptions were determined by her love for her father; only gradually and painfully did she begin to see through him. She also began to realize that her rank made her a political commodity in a very restricted marriage pool: She could marry an emperor, a king, or an archduke.

LIFE'S WORK

During the Wars of the Fronde, the civil wars fought between 1648 and 1653, the duchesse de Montpensier acquired the reputation of an "amazon-duchess." She had led her own troops and captured Orléans in 1651 to the enthusiastic approbation of its citizens. In 1652, she turned the cannon of the Bastille on the royal troops, delivering a victory to the rebellious Frondeurs. Subsequently, Mazarin remarked that Montpensier had "killed" her husband with that Bastille cannon shot; that is, she destroyed any chance of marrying Louis XIV.

Marriage prospects were discussed, however, but nothing materialized. Ferdinand, brother of Anne of Austria and Spanish commander in Flanders, had died. After Montpensier's aunt, the queen of Spain, died in 1643, there had been discussion of marriage with Spanish king Philip IV (his wife, Elizabeth, died in 1644). When the Holy Roman Emperor Ferdinand III was widowed, the duchess was mentioned as a possible empress (a prospect that excited her ambitions), but he married elsewhere, as did his brother, Archduke Leopold. Henrietta Maria, the daughter of King Henry IV and the queen of England, who was in exile in France, tried to arrange a marriage between Montpensier and her son, the future King Charles II, but the duchess was not impressed with Charles.

When Ferdinand III was again widowed, Montpensier's dreams of the imperial title reawakened, but they soon were dashed by news that he had remarried. She was considered a possible wife for Philippe, the duke of Anjou and the king's younger brother, but even though the cousins had great mutual affection all their lives, they were not suited to each other. Philippe would later marry the sister of Charles II. Negotiations on behalf of the duchess by the court seemed halfhearted at best, and she sensed that neither the queen nor Mazarin had her interests at heart.

From 1652 to 1657, Montpensier was exiled from court for her participation in the Fronde, and between 1662 and 1664, she was exiled again, this time for refusing to marry King Afonso VI of Portugal. In exile at her

Duchesse de Montpensier. (Hulton Archive/Getty Images)

estate of Saint Fargeau, where she held her own court, she was prodigiously active. She renovated the château; began writing her memoirs, the *Mémoires de mademoiselle de Montpensier* (pb. 1729); acquired her own printing press and printer; and corresponded with the Great Condé. She also established a theater and engaged in hoydenish games, dancing, hunting, and *fêtes champêtres* (outdoor entertainments). She surrounded herself with distinguished company, including Pierre-Daniel Huet, bishop of Avranches; poet Jean Regnault de Segrais, her secretary and, possibly, her literary collaborator; Madame de Lafayette; and Madame de Sévigné. While at Fontainebleau, she socialized with the colorful Christina, formerly queen of Sweden.

Gaston continued, however, to cause her great unhappiness. When she had come of age and assumed control of her own wealth, she discovered that her father had been siphoning her money for years to cover his gambling debts and to support his new family. This resulted in legal disputes and much heartbreak, with Gaston mercilessly deceiving and threatening her until she acquiesced in his financial demands. Even the third woman of France, without a husband to protect her, was powerless against her unscrupulous father. When she finally agreed to give him the sum he demanded, his response, as Montpensier acidly remarked, would be most affectionate. She was proved correct. By acquiescing, she was reconciled with the court (1657).

She continued her writing projects and, in 1659, began a collection of sketches of court personalities, *Divers portraits* (*The Characters or Pourtaicts of the Present Court of France*, 1668). In the same year, she published her *Histoire de la princesse de Paphlagonie*, a *roman à clef* seen by some at the time to have been a satire of Madeleine de Scudéry's *Artamène: Ou, Le Grand Cyrus* (ten volumes, pb. 1649-1653; *Artamenes: Or, The Grand Cyrus*), a ten-volume novel about Cyrus the Great (of the 500's B.C.E.).

When King Louis XIV was to be married to Marie-Thérèse of Spain (1660) following the Peace of the Pyrenees (1659), Montpensier traveled with the court. When they stopped at Blois, Gaston woke her early in the morning, telling her to take care of her stepfamily, because he was likely to die soon. At Aix-en-Provence, Montpensier was overtaken with intense, inexplicable sadness, only to learn that her father had suffered a stroke and died.

Although an important participant in the royal marriage ceremonies, Montpensier had been developing an aversion to the married state. In correspondence with Françoise Bertaut de Motteville, begun around 1660, the two women discussed female-centered pastoral utopias and a "gynocentric" republic, gender equity in love and relationships of power, and marriage as a form of slavery for women. Four of these letters were published as *Recueil des pieces nouveles et galantes* (1667). At the king's marriage, the duchess was drawn to Antonin-Nompar de Caumont de Lauzun, a commander of a company of royal guards, captain of the dragoons, and eventually personal bodyguard to the king—certainly no match in rank for La Grande Mademoiselle.

Montpensier remained in the Luxembourg Palace when the king moved to Versailles. Her salon there was frequented by Madame de Sévigné, Madame de La Fayette, and François de La Rochefoucauld, among others. In 1669, as part of an engagement party, *Tartuffe: Ou, L'Imposteur* (pr. 1664, pb. 1669; *Tartuffe*, 1732), about a religious hypocrite, was performed there, too, with playwright Molière playing the title role.

Lauzun, however, continued to fascinate the duchess. By 1670, the woman who had once turned the cannon of the Bastille on the king's own army had become as vulnerably obsessive as a love-struck teenager, importuning the king for permission to marry Lauzun. At first, he

agreed to his cousin's pleas, but when he reneged, claiming rumors dangerous to the state, the duchess became profoundly depressed. In 1671, Lauzun was arrested and taken personally by the captain of the musketeers to the remote fortress of Pignerol.

During Lauzun's imprisonment, Montpensier worked with her charity school at Eu, established and oversaw a hospital and seminary for the Sisters of Charity who taught at the school and nursed in the hospital, resumed writing her memoirs, built a new summer house at Choisy, and continued to importune the king for Lauzun's pardon. In return for his release, in 1680, she agreed to hand over properties, including Eu and Dombes, to the young duke of Maine, the son of the king and Madame de Montespan. When Montpensier and Lauzun were finally reunited, he prostrated himself at her feet, claiming to owe her "everything." His actions, though, did not prove his devotion, and his protestations did not make up for his philandering and lies. It was rumored that they were secretly married, but there is no firm evidence to prove this.

One irony of La Grande Mademoiselle's life was that her father disavowed her martial activities, often carried out at his request, and estranged himself from her. The other irony is that while in her writings she wrote in support of friendship as a basis for rational love, in her own life she succumbed to an obsessive and semirequited passion.

SIGNIFICANCE

In Montpensier's *Divers portraits*, innovative character descriptions anticipate psychological explorations. Her memoirs and the Motteville correspondence, exemplary of French seventeenth century equity feminism, illuminate the contrast between assumptions about women's possibilities and the increasing rigidity that Louis's system thereafter imposed upon aristocratic French society. In the memoirs, she constructs a matrix of introspection, history, and autobiography with narrative method that contributes to the development of the novel. It has added to understandings of the *ancien régime* through the reflections of one of its most prominent women, who earned a place in military history as the comrade-in-arms of the Great Condé.

—*Donna Berliner*

FURTHER READING

Montpensier, Anne-Marie-Louise d'Orléans. *Against Marriage: The Correspondence of La Grande Mademoiselle*. Edited and translated by Joan DeJean. Chicago: University of Chicago Press, 2002. A translation of the Montpensier-Motteville correspondence with a valuable introduction and a bibliography.

_____. *Memoirs of La Grande Mademoiselle, Duchesse de Montpensier.* Translated by Grace Hart Seely. New York: Century, 1928. An older translation of Montpensier's memoirs, but still useful and necessary reading.

Pitts, Vincent. *La Grande Mademoiselle at the Court of France, 1627-1693.* Baltimore, Md.: Johns Hopkins University Press, 2000. Pitts includes an extensive bibliography of primary and secondary sources, comprehensive notes, information on Montpensier's writings, and detailed information about her vast fortune.

Sackville-West, Vita. *Daughter of France: The Life of La Grande Mademoiselle.* Garden City, N.Y.: Doubleday, 1959. Sackville-West's sense of the historical moment and her writing style make this an excellent introduction.

Steegmuller, Francis. *The Grande Mademoiselle.* New York: Farrar, Straus and Cudahy, 1956. An entertaining account that focuses on Montpensier's love life.

SEE ALSO: Anne of Austria; Charles II (of England); Christina; The Great Condé; Henrietta Maria; Madame de La Fayette; Leopold I; Louis XIII; Louis XIV; Marie-Thérèse; Jules Mazarin; Molière; Philip IV; Cardinal de Richelieu; François de La Rochefoucauld; Madeleine de Scudéry; Madame de Sévigné.

RELATED ARTICLES in *Great Events from History: The Seventeenth Century, 1601-1700:* June, 1648: Wars of the Fronde Begin; November 7, 1659: Treaty of the Pyrenees; 1661: Absolute Monarchy Emerges in France; August 10, 1678-September 26, 1679: Treaties of Nijmegen; June 30, 1680: Spanish Inquisition Holds a Grandiose *Auto-da-fé*; 1682: French Court Moves to Versailles; 1689-1694: Famine and Inflation in France.

BORIS IVANOVICH MOROZOV
Chief minister of Russia (1645-1648)

Morozov directed the education of the second emperor of the Romanov Dynasty, helped to stabilize the Russian economy, and crafted a significant part of the Russian legal code of 1649, which stabilized Russian society but also established serfdom.

BORN: 1590; place unknown
DIED: November 11, 1661; place unknown
AREAS OF ACHIEVEMENT: Government and politics, law, education

EARLY LIFE

Boris Ivanovich Morozov (bohr-YEES i-VAHN-ehv-yihch MOH-raw-zawf) was born into a prominent Russian family. Like most Russians of the time, Morozov had little formal education. He was, however, a shrewd individual who formed close personal connections to the Romanov family. In early 1633, for example, Morozov accompanied the imperial family on its yearly pilgrimage to the monasteries of Trinity-St. Sergius at Zagorsk.

Because of his frequent association with the Romanovs, Morozov began to play an important role in the life of Alexis, the son of the first emperor of the Romanov Dynasty, Czar Michael Romanov. In late 1633, after the death of Alexis's grandfather, Philaret, Morozov was appointed tutor to the young heir to the throne, who was

then four years old. Morozov taught the boy fencing with toy swords, selected playmates for the child, and appointed teachers.

Despite Morozov's own limited education, he pushed Alexis's schedule far beyond the religious teachings that normally constituted the schooling of a Russian prince in the seventeenth century. Alexis built a small library of works on a variety of secular as well as religious subjects. He also studied military strategy and tactics. Morozov was open to influences from Western Europe and helped to introduce Alexis to Western technology and literature.

After becoming tutor to Alexis, Morozov was raised by Czar Michael to the rank of boyar, or noble. Morozov also became a member of the Duma, or czar's council. This began his rise to power. On July 12, 1645, Michael suffered a sudden fit of illness. He then called the sixteen-year-old Alexis to his bedside and appointed his son as his successor. The dying czar also appointed Morozov as the young man's guardian. With the death of Michael's widow, Eudoxia, one month later, Morozov became the most powerful person in Russia.

LIFE'S WORK

As guardian, Morozov also acted as chief minister, running Russia in the name of the emperor. Immediately after he was crowned, the new czar dismissed his father's chief minister and other major governmental figures. Morozov received the most critical offices in the imperial administration, and he appointed his allies and members of his family to other major positions. Alexis showed up at ceremonies and signed the documents that Morozov and the other ministers placed in front of him.

Alexis's own primary concern was to find a healthy, appropriate wife. This was an important matter of state for a new dynasty in a time of high death rates. A sudden illness, accident, or act of violence could leave the country without a clear ruler, or it could plunge it into conflicts such as those Russia had suffered before Alexis's father came to the throne. Morozov's ambition led him to use Alexis's search for a wife as a way of securing his own connections to the imperial family. The tutor encouraged Alexis to marry Mariya Ilinichna Miloslavskaya (d. 1669) in 1648.

Morozov was eager to obtain wealth as well as political power. Gifts from the young emperor and the use of public resources for private profit enabled him to quickly build a vast fortune. It was recorded that within two years after Alexis came to the throne, Morozov owned numerous estates and peasants in six thousand families who lived on the estates. Though Morozov was self-serving, he also was an able and farsighted administrator. He saw the need to improve Russia's military capability and to achieve financial stability. Russia's military was far behind that of the West, a dangerous situation because the country was continually at war with its Western neighbors. Morozov introduced reforms aimed at modernization. He sent a mission to Holland to hire mercenaries to train Russian soldiers and organize new regiments. He also imported firearms from the West and established a government department to oversee the manufacture of modern weapons in Russia.

Morozov believed that government spending in Russia was too high, so to reduce spending, he lowered the pay of many military officers and state officials. He imposed high taxes, especially on salt, and placed administration in the hands of men who were often corrupt. Outrage at corruption and opposition to the tax on salt, which was necessary to preserve fish and other foods, led to rioting in the summer of 1648. An angry crowd surrounded Morozov's home, where they found his wife. Although they did not harm her, they ripped the jewels and ornaments from her dress and sacked the house.

The mob continued, looting the houses of a number of officials. The soldiers managed the crowd, but many resented the cuts in pay imposed by Morozov. Members of the Duma began to suggest to the czar that he get rid of Morozov and perhaps even hand over some of Morozov's allies to the angry crowd.

The influential citizens of Moscow presented the emperor with a petition. Among other requests, they asked that Morozov be removed from office and sent into exile. Bowing to pressure, the czar ordered that his powerful adviser be taken under guard and conducted to St. Cyril Monastery, about 300 miles north of Moscow. However, Alexis also took care that his old guardian would come to no harm.

The rebellion in Moscow spread to other parts of Russia. As a result of pressures from the rebellion and complaints about the corruption and arbitrariness of his administrators, Alexis called a *zemskii sobor*, or assembly of the land, to draw up a code of law for Russia. The assembly produced the Sobornoye Ulozheniye, or code of law, of 1649. The code gave the country a written system of law, but it also defined legal statuses, in particular the status of serfdom. Serfdom tied peasants to the land, making them slaves of those who owned the land.

After the czar issued the order for the *zemskii sobor*, he wrote the authorities at St. Cyril Monastery and instructed them to allow Morozov to leave for his estate in the province of Tver and to provide an escort to ensure Morozov's safety. The exiled minister spent a brief time in Tver before quietly returning to Moscow. Upon Morozov's exile, Alexis dismissed the leader of the soldiers and replaced him with Ilya Miloslavsky, father-in-law to both Alexis and Morozov. Quietly operating within the newly reorganized government, Morozov helped to write the Ulozheniye, and by some accounts was one of its chief authors.

Morozov never again reached the prominence he had held during the first years of Alexis's rule. Still, he continued to serve the czar. When Alexis rode off in person to make war against Poland and claim Ukraine for Russia in 1654, Morozov rode with him. When Morozov was dying toward the end of 1661, Alexis went to his deathbed and then attended the funeral and ordered masses sung for Morozov's soul.

SIGNIFICANCE

Boris Ivanovich Morozov was ambitious, and he enriched himself and his allies through the Russian government. Nevertheless, he helped to stabilize Russia politically by providing the young Alexis Romanov with a wide and practical education. His work on the code of 1649 helped organize Russian society, although the code also established serfdom in Russia.

Morozov's improvement of the Russian military enabled the country to stand up against Western neighbors that had earlier dominated Russia. By these achievements, Morozov helped to prepare for Russia's rise as a major power under the rule of Alexis's son, Peter the Great.

— *Carl L. Bankston III*

FURTHER READING

Kliuchevsky, V. O. *A Course in Russian History: The Seventeenth Century.* Translated by Natalie Duddington. Armonk, N.Y.: M. E. Sharpe, 1994. A translation of a classic work by one of Russia's most eminent historians. Events of Alexis's reign are dealt with throughout. Chapter 16 looks specifically at Alexis and Morozov's guardianship.

Kotilaine, Jarmo, and Marshall Poe, eds. *Modernizing Muscovy: Reform and Social Change in Seventeenth Century Russia.* New York: Routledge Curzon, 2004. An encyclopedic account of politics and society in Russia during the seventeenth century. Includes useful references in footnotes of each article and an index.

Lincoln, W. Bruce. *The Romanovs: Autocrats of All the Russias.* New York: Dial Press, 1981. A comprehensive history of the entire Romanov Dynasty. The first fourth of the book is devoted to the seventeenth century. Includes an extensive bibliography and an index.

Longworth, Philip. *Alexis: Tsar of All the Russias.* New York: Franklin Watts, 1984. Numerous passages in this work deal with Morozov's life, but the second chapter, "In the Shadow of Morozov," looks specifically at his control of Russia.

SEE ALSO: Alexis; Avvakum Petrovich; Ivan Stepanovich Mazepa; Nikon; Stenka Razin; Michael Romanov; Sophia.

RELATED ARTICLES in *Great Events from History: The Seventeenth Century, 1601-1700:* January 29, 1649: Codification of Russian Serfdom; 1652-1667: Patriarch Nikon's Reforms; July 10, 1655-June 21, 1661: First Northern War; April, 1667-June, 1671: Razin Leads Peasant Uprising in Russia; Beginning 1689: Reforms of Peter the Great.

LODOWICK MUGGLETON
English religious leader and theologian

Claiming exclusive spiritual authority, Muggleton (along with his cousin, John Reeve) cofounded a sect known as the Muggletonians that continued into the twentieth century. He also authored books such as A Divine Looking-Glass *and* The Acts of the Witnesses.

BORN: July, 1609; London, England
DIED: March 14, 1698; London
AREAS OF ACHIEVEMENT: Religion and theology, literature

EARLY LIFE

Born in July of 1609, Lodowick Muggleton (LAH-duh-wihk MUH-gul-tuhn) was the youngest of three children and son of John Muggleton, a Northamptonshire farrier. In June, 1612, when Lodowick was less than three years old, his mother, Mary Muggleton, died, and he was sent to live with a rural family. He returned to London at the age of fifteen, when he was apprenticed to a tailor, John Quick. While employed in London, Lodowick received religious instruction from and sympathized with Puritans, admiring their piety and happiness. Spurred by their teachings, he wanted to obey the commandment of

proper Sabbath observance but could not convince his employer.

Because of his desire to acquire wealth, Muggleton wanted to become a pawnbroker, so he began working at a broker's shop in Houndsditch. Eventually, the broker's wife arranged for his engagement to her daughter, promising money as a wedding gift. Soon after their engagement, however, Muggleton went to work as a journeyman tailor with his Puritan cousin, William Reeve. Muggleton's Puritan associates warned him not to become a pawnbroker, citing scriptural references that forbade usury and extortion, and he struggled with the decision of whether or not he should pursue this chosen vocation. He concluded that although he loved his fiancée, he would rather lose her (and his dream of becoming a wealthy pawnbroker) than lose his soul to eternal damnation.

From the Puritans, Muggleton learned to study the Scriptures and developed his skills in prayer. However, after the English Civil Wars in the 1640's, the Puritans divided into many sects, and Muggleton was uncomfortable worshipping with any of these groups. While battling thoughts of atheism, he eventually gave up on public prayer and sermons, choosing instead to follow his conscience and a code of personal integrity.

LIFE'S WORK

In 1650, Muggleton listened to many prophets and prophetesses on the streets. He and his cousins, William and John Reeve, associated with a radical sect called the Ranters and met John Robins, a man who claimed to be the Almighty God and the resurrected Adam and claimed to be able to raise key biblical figures from the dead. One day in April, 1651, Muggleton received a revelation lasting six hours, which quickened his mental faculties. He heard both internal and external voices, and, after initially suffering with disputations in his mind, he received assurance of eternal life and spiritual enlightenment. As a result, he claimed that all difficult spiritual questions became easy for him to answer. Following this initial revelation, Muggleton resolved not to meddle further with religion. This resolution was satisfying, because, since he did not aspire to be a public figure, he could now return to his temporal pursuits knowing that he was personally secure as one of God's elect.

According to Muggleton, however, he continued to receive divine communication, regularly hearing voices that assisted him in scriptural understanding. Muggleton discussed his revelations with John Reeve, who thereafter visited him frequently from April, 1651, through January, 1652, hoping to have a similar experience himself. Over the course of three days, February 3-5, 1652, Reeve received successive revelations revealing that he was to act as God's messenger and Muggleton was to serve as his mouthpiece, just as Aaron had served Moses. Reeve also announced that he and Muggleton were called to be the Two Witnesses prophesied in Revelations 11:3 to appear and testify before the Second Coming of Christ. Their duties were to proclaim the end of the world, teach the true Christian faith, and deliver blessings upon the elect and curses upon the reprobates.

Muggleton's name appeared as joint author with John Reeve of *A Transcendent Spiritual Treatise* (1652), although it is possible that the book was penned solely by Reeve. This book described the commission of Reeve and Muggleton as the Two Witnesses and declared their doctrines. Consequently, because of their heretical teachings regarding the Trinity, both men were arrested in September, 1653, and imprisoned for six months by Lord Mayor John Fowke of London under the authority of the Blasphemy Act. Nevertheless, these Two Witnesses had excited interest in their work, and their adher-

ents formed a sect that became known as Muggletonians. Laurence Clarkson was included among their small band of disciples, and when Reeve died in 1658, Clarkson unsuccessfully sought to take over leadership from Muggleton.

Reeve and Muggleton taught that all humankind came from one of two seeds: the elect were from the seed of Adam, and the damned were of the seed of Cain. They also declared that God is composed of both spirit and body and is in the form of a man, approximately 6 feet tall. God the Father decided to come to the earth, shed his immortality while in the womb of the Virgin Mary, and became the mortal Jesus. While living on earth, God delegated the stewardship of heaven to Elijah, who spoke from heaven when Jesus was baptized, and to Moses.

Muggleton and his first wife, Sarah (1616-1639), had three daughters, the second of whom died in infancy. After less than four years of marriage, Sarah passed away. Muggleton's second wife, Mary (1626-1647), also bore three children—two sons and a daughter. However, two of them died in infancy, and the third lived less than ten years. Shortly after their third child's death, Mary also passed away. At the age of 53, Muggleton married his third wife, Mary Martin, in 1663. That same year, during one of his missionary journeys, Muggleton was arrested and held in Derby jail for nine days. In 1670, authorities seized and destroyed Muggleton's books in London. Arrested and convicted in 1677 for illegally publishing a heretical book, Muggleton, while pilloried for three consecutive days, was forced to watch his books burn before his eyes and was then imprisoned in Newgate for six months.

This public humiliation most likely finally subdued Muggleton, because the last twenty years of his life were relatively quiet and uneventful; he reportedly refrained from further declarations of damnation upon individuals. Although he did publish two theological tracts in 1680 and 1682, his major literary projects were primarily letters and his own autobiography. Muggleton died at the age of 88 on March 14, 1698.

SIGNIFICANCE

As cofounder of the sect that bore his name, Muggleton, together with his followers, formed part of a radical movement of the mid-seventeenth century that was able to loosen the grip of the ruling elite of England. Their unorthodox ideas about God and religion, especially their anticlerical and predestinarian views, included them in the radical religious tradition. Along with other radical sects such as the Fifth Monarchists, the Muggletonians espoused and promoted millenarian expectations. However, unlike other radical sectarians, Muggleton and Reeve claimed exclusive authority from God, declaring their opponents to be religious counterfeits.

The Muggletonians and the Quakers were the only two sects organized in the late 1640's and early 1650's that survived into the twentieth century. Those who followed Muggleton were typically uneducated, low-income artisans like him. Although not concerned with proselytizing or holding formal meetings or worship services, Muggleton found converts, especially among the Ranters. Followers simply had to believe Muggleton in order to achieve salvation. He advised his followers on domestic issues and found new ways of offering blessings via mail order.

Several of Muggleton's most important works are of somewhat unclear authorship. Although Reeve died in 1658, for example, *A Divine Looking-Glass* (1661) bears his name as well as Muggleton's. Muggleton authored other books, such as *A True Interpretation of the Eleventh Chapter of the Revelations of Saint John* (1662), *The Neck of the Quakers Broken* (1663), and his posthumously published autobiography, *The Acts of the Witnesses* (1699).

—*Christopher E. Garrett*

FURTHER READING

Eichenger, Juleen Audrey. *The Muggletonians: A People Apart.* Unpublished doctoral dissertation. Western Michigan University, 1999. Links Muggletonianism to the medieval heretical tradition and emphasizes its uniqueness from other seventeenth-century dissenting sects.

Hill, Christopher. "John Reeve, Laurence Clarkson, and Lodowick Muggleton." *The Collected Essays of Christopher Hill.* Vol. 2. Amherst: University of Massachusetts Press, 1986. Claims that the Muggletonians are historically significant because they and the Quakers are the only two sects founded in the late 1640's and early 1650's that survived into the twentieth century. Hill argues that all major Muggletonian doctrines originated in the writings of John Reeve and asserts that Reeve deserves to be known as the sect's authentic founder.

Hill, Christopher, Barry Reay, and William Lamont. *The World of the Muggletonians.* London: Temple Smith, 1983. This collection of essays features diverse scholarly perspectives on Muggleton, Reeve, and Clarkson.

Lamont, William. "The Muggletonians, 1652-1979: A 'Vertical' Approach." *Past & Present* 99 (May, 1983): 22-40. Utilizing the Muggletonian archive, this essay presents an alternative way of viewing the history of the movement through the perspective of later Muggletonians.

Reay, Barry G. "Lodowick Muggleton." *Biographical Dictionary of British Radicals in the Seventeenth Century.* Vol. 2. Edited by Richard L. Greaves and Robert Zaller. Brighton, Sussex, England: Harvester Press, 1983. Includes a biographical sketch of Muggleton and lists some of the core tenets of Muggletonians.

_____. "The Muggletonians: A Study in Seventeenth-Century English Sectarianism." *Journal of Religious History* 9 (1976): 32-49. Analyzes the major aspects of Muggletonian doctrine, specifically its organization and structure.

Underwood, T. L., ed. *The Acts of the Witnesses: The Autobiography of Lodowick Muggleton and Other Early Muggletonian Writings.* New York: Oxford University Press, 1999. In addition to Muggleton's autobiography and John Reeve's *A Transcendent Spiritual Treatise*, Underwood provides a concise introductory chapter on the Muggletonian founders.

Whiting, C. E. *Studies in English Puritanism from the Restoration to the Revolution, 1660-1688.* New York: Kelley, 1968. Chapter 6, "The Minor Sects," includes a focused, informative discussion on Muggleton's life, disciples, and enemies.

SEE ALSO: George Fox.

RELATED ARTICLES in *Great Events from History: The Seventeenth Century, 1601-1700:* 1642-1651: English Civil Wars; 1652-1689: Fox Organizes the Quakers.

MURAD IV
Ottoman sultan (r. 1623-1640)

Murad IV, who became Ottoman sultan when he was eleven years old but did not rule independently until ten years later, brought order to his troubled empire, improving its financial footing but repressing the populace and the empire's military.

BORN: July 27, 1612; Constantinople, Ottoman
Empire (now Istanbul, Turkey)
DIED: February 9, 1640; Constantinople
ALSO KNOWN AS: Murad Oglu Ahmed I (full name)
AREAS OF ACHIEVEMENT: Government and politics,
warfare and conquest, military

EARLY LIFE

Murad (muh-RAHD) IV was the son of Ahmed I, seventeenth sultan of the Ottoman Empire, and Kösem Sultan, who was of either Greek or Bosnian lineage. Murad IV became sultan at age eleven, succeeding his uncle, Mustafa I, who had been deposed in 1623 because he was mentally unfit to rule the empire.

Murad ruled his first nine years as sultan through the regency of his mother, who was manipulated by the semiofficial cavalry and the officers of the Janissary corps, the once-elite palace guard that had become increasingly corrupt in the preceding half century, particularly after its celibacy rule was rescinded. After the rule changed, the sons of Janissaries, frequently ill-equipped to serve, followed in their fathers' footsteps by becoming corps members as well.

The groups that influenced Kösem forced the execution of officials they disapproved of. Kösem selected Murad's official advisers (grand viziers) carefully and monitored their activities closely, but her actions were limited by the Janissaries. Wishing to avoid interference from the harem, which had weakened the reign of Murad III (r. 1574-1595), who was raised and educated in the harem, she encouraged her son to engage in homosexuality.

The Ottoman Empire was in disarray during the early years of Murad's rule. In 1623-1624, the Ottomans lost Baghdad to Persia, and the city was occupied by Persian shah ʿAbbās the Great (r. 1587-1629). Revolts against the Ottomans erupted in Lebanon, Anatolia, Yemen, Armenia, Azerbaijan, and the Crimea. Provin-

cial governors ignored mandates from Constantinople and tyrannized the people they ruled. They pocketed substantial revenues they were supposed to send to Constantinople.

In 1625, Cossacks attacked the Black Sea coast, then took the Bosporus. The Janissaries revolted frequently, demanding the money the government owed them, but it lacked the resources to pay. The palace eunuchs in charge of Murad's education engaged in blatant nepotism and bribery. The Ottoman treasury was severely strained during the nine years before Murad grasped power and assumed active command of his empire.

Finally, in 1632, when a major revolt erupted in Constantinople, Murad seized the reins of power that were rightfully his. He escaped his mother's domination and emerged as the leader that the Ottomans sorely needed at this time in their history.

LIFE'S WORK

When Murad IV took over independently as sultan, Germany was warring with its neighbors, Spain had begun to deteriorate following the death of King Philip II, England suffered lurking internal problems regarding its

Murad IV. (Hulton Archive/Getty Images)

constitution, and revolts were racking much of Russia. Given the decadent state of the Ottoman Empire when Murad at last took charge, he needed to spring into immediate action to demonstrate to his subjects that he was unquestionably capable of assuming command.

He used the harshest means of suppression to establish his dominance quickly. He ordered the immediate execution of many of the empire's most important military leaders and replaced them during the next two years with leaders of his own choosing.

Murad left no question as to who was running the empire. He took personal charge of military expeditions into the most rebellious provinces, such as Anatolia and the Balkans, where he confronted and annihilated provincial leaders who had previously neglected their sworn duty to the sultan. In 1635, he evicted the Persians from the Ottoman provinces of Armenia and Azerbaijan. He distributed land but gave it only to those whom he considered his faithful followers, and then only on the condition that they commit themselves to serving the state through military service.

Looking upon coffeehouses and wineshops as places where people gathered and plotted against the government, he ordered their closure and also imposed curfews that forbade people from venturing out of their houses at night. Despite his early exposure to homosexuality and its prevalence throughout his empire, he officially banned it after he came to power. He prohibited the use of alcohol and tobacco even though he was a user (and abuser) of both, and he banned coffee as well.

Murad's executioner was never far from him, carrying instruments of torture and death. The penalty for disobeying Murad's mandates was instant execution without a trial. Even *suspected* disobedience could result in death. Under Murad's regime, "innocent unless proven guilty" was unheard of.

As his rule grew increasingly oppressive, Murad sought to establish his supremacy by executing increasingly large numbers of dissidents, including his own brothers. Writing of Murad IV, a seventeenth century Venetian ambassador to the Ottoman Empire is quoted by historian Andrew Wheatcroft as observing that Murad

> turned all his thoughts to revenge, so completely that, overcome by his seductions, stirred by indignation, and moved by anger, he proved unrivaled in savagery and cruelty. On those days he did not take a human life, he did not feel that he was happy and gave no sign of gladness.

He succeeded in restoring order, but at an enormous cost to his subjects. It is estimated that during the last eight years of his reign, Murad was directly responsible for having more than ten thousand of his own people executed. Sometimes he killed them himself.

The bloodshed for which Murad was responsible outside his immediate domain was still more excessive. Among Murad's major positive accomplishments was his retaking of Baghdad. He marched from Constantinople toward Baghdad for 110 days with an enormous army, picking up additional recruits along the way. Murad's ancestor, Süleyman the Great, had conquered Baghdad and claimed it for his empire in April of 1535, but after that empire deteriorated under the rule of several successive ineffective sultans, Baghdad was retaken by the Persians, led by Shah ʿAbbās.

Like Süleyman before him, Murad led the Persian expedition personally. The Persian military staunchly resisted his initial assault upon Baghdad in November, 1638. Murad set an example for his soldiers by working with them in the trenches and by sleeping in the field beside them. He engaged in single-handed combat with the enemy and, because he was large, fearless, and extremely strong, he defeated anyone with whom he entered into such combat.

Finally, on Christmas Day, 1638, Baghdad fell to the Ottomans. Murad ordered the execution of nearly all the Persians within the garrison defending the city. In a single day, it is said that thirty thousand such combatants were slaughtered at his command. A mere three hundred of the soldiers in the garrison survived Murad's brutal onslaught.

This, however, was not Murad's final atrocity in Baghdad. When a powder magazine exploded accidentally and killed a number of Murad's forces, he retaliated, reportedly, by ordering the executions of thirty thousand more Persians, most of them innocent women and children. It appears that in his effort to establish his supremacy in the eyes of his subjects, Murad practiced a brutality that knew no bounds.

Significance

Murad's rule offers a striking example of how an intelligent, gifted, and dedicated ruler who sets himself up as the all-knowing savior of his people can ultimately destroy the society he is fighting to protect. In many ways, it is fortunate that Murad died when he was twenty-seven, because, although he had managed to rescue the Ottoman Empire from the difficulties facing it when he assumed office, his regime had become so unreasoning and brutal that his terrified and subdued subjects rejoiced at his death, which was brought about, ironically, by cirrhosis of the liver, caused by his excessive drinking.

On his deathbed, Murad ordered the execution of his brother, İbrahim, presumably to assure himself full credit for saving the Ottoman Empire. At this point, Kösem, mother of both Murad and İbrahim, countermanded his order because she realized that if İbrahim did not become sultan, she would lose a great deal of her influence. As she approached the dying Murad, she assured him that İbrahim was dead, even though he was not. Murad smiled grimly and took his last breath, and İbrahim would rule from the moment of Murad's death to 1648.

—*R. Baird Shuman*

FURTHER READING

Barber, Noel. *The Sultans*. New York: Simon and Schuster, 1973. Probably the best examination of how sultans of the Ottoman Empire lived and ruled.

Mansel, Philip. *Constantinople: City of the World's Desire, 1453-1924*. New York: St. Martin's Press, 1996. Mansel explores many aspects of Murad's sultancy and provides useful insights.

Somel, Selcuk Aksin. *Historical Dictionary of the Ottoman Empire*. Lanham, Md.: Scarecrow Press, 2003. An indispensable resource for those interested in the Ottoman Empire.

Wheatcroft, Andrew. *Infidels: A History of the Conflict Between Christendom and Islam*. New York: Random House, 2004. Valuable for its brief citation regarding the Venetian ambassador's opinion of Murad IV.

SEE ALSO: ʿAbbās the Great; Merzifonlu Kara Mustafa Paşa; Kâtib Çelebî; Kösem Sultan; Mustafa I.

RELATED ARTICLES in *Great Events from History: The Seventeenth Century, 1601-1700*: 1602-1639: Ottoman-Ṣafavid Wars; 1603-1617: Reign of Sultan Ahmed I; September, 1605: Egyptians Rebel Against the Ottomans; September, 1606-June, 1609: Great Jelālī Revolts; November 11, 1606: Treaty of Zsitvatorok; 1609-1617: Construction of the Blue Mosque; Beginning c. 1615: Coffee Culture Flourishes; May 19, 1622: Janissary Revolt and Osman II's Assassination; 1623-1640: Murad IV Rules the Ottoman Empire; 1632-c. 1650: Shah Jahan Builds the Taj Mahal; September 2, 1633: Great Fire of Constantinople and Murad's Reforms; 1638: Waning of the *Devshirme* System; August 22, 1645-September, 1669: Turks Conquer Crete; 1656-1676: Ottoman Empire's Brief Recovery; 1658-1707: Reign of Aurangzeb; c. 1666-1676: Founding of the Marāthā Kingdom; 1679-1709: Rājput Rebellion; 1697-1702: Köprülü Reforms of Hüseyin Paşa.

BARTOLOMÉ ESTEBAN MURILLO
Spanish artist

Murillo, a major Spanish artist known for his religious paintings, portraits, and genre scenes, was extremely prolific, producing about five hundred paintings. Although some judge his religious paintings as overly pious and sweet, his artworks were perfectly in tune with the century's taste and demonstrate the strong links between art and social context in early modern Spain.

BORN: January 1, 1618 (baptized); Seville, Spain
DIED: March 28, 1682; Seville
AREA OF ACHIEVEMENT: Art

EARLY LIFE

Bartolomé Esteban Murillo (bahr-toh-loh-MAY ay-STAY-vahn muh-REE-yoh) was born into a well-off family in Seville. His father, Gaspar Esteban, was a barber-surgeon, and his mother, María Pérez, was a housewife. With the deaths of his parents in 1627 and 1628, respectively, Murillo was left an orphan and was raised by his brother-in-law. Murillo's artistic training began shortly thereafter, probably around 1630, when he was about age twelve or thirteen. He studied with Juan del Castillo, an artist little known in modern times but one whose important connections to the Sevillian art scene benefited his talented student.

In 1633, at age fifteen, Murillo planned to travel to the Americas, following other family members who had emigrated there, but he seems never to have made the trip. In 1645, at the age of twenty-eight, he married Beatriz Cabrera y Villalobos, with whom he had eleven children in the twenty years they were married. Beatriz died in 1665. The artist's *Self-Portrait* of 1670, which bears the inscription "for my children" (in Latin), provides a tantalizing glimpse of Murillo's personal life.

LIFE'S WORK

Murillo received his first major commission in 1645, a series of eleven paintings on the lives of Franciscan saints, for the friary of San Francisco in Seville. These early works demonstrate the Baroque realist style current at the time as practiced by such Sevillian artists as Diego Velázquez and Francisco de Zurbarán. His most famous work from his first period (1645-1657) is the *Holy Family of the Little Bird*, painted before 1650. It depicts a scene of Christ's childhood, a favorite theme of the Spanish Baroque. The Madonna, working at her needlework, looks to the main scene of Saint Joseph tending the Christ Child and family dog. The interpretation of the scene, with its emphasis on Saint Joseph, is typically Spanish. The artist's representational strategies (earth tone colors, Tenebrist lighting, carefully described still-life elements, broad drapery, and a strong sculptural sense) attempt to re-create the effects of reality. Hints of Murillo's soon-to-come style change, though, can be detected in the idealization of the figures of Christ and the Madonna.

In the late 1650's, Murillo dramatically transformed his style, demonstrating his knowledge of changing artistic taste in Madrid and other European centers. His new approach can be appreciated in such paintings as *The Immaculate Conception of the Escorial* (c. 1660-1665). The subject represents one of the artist's best-loved themes, a visualization of the doctrine that the Virgin Mary was conceived in the womb of her mother, Saint Anne, without original sin. This belief, which was not officially declared dogma by the Catholic Church until 1854, enjoyed great popularity in seventeenth century Seville.

Murillo's approach to the subject was novel. By reducing the number of iconographic symbols seen in previous artists' renditions of the theme, he focused instead on Mary's chaste beauty as emblematic of her purity. His new, more idealized style perfectly matched his innovative interpretation. The delicate figure of Mary, with eyes raised to heaven, floats in a golden celestial ambient, abstracted from all earthly references. His brushwork has changed dramatically, the thickly applied oil paints typical of Baroque realism replaced by evanescent veils of pigment. As a result, the painted forms seem to dissolve in an all-encompassing vaporous atmosphere. Only the most essential iconographic symbols remain, drawn from the Song of Songs and the Book of Revelation: the rose without thorns; the spotless mirror; the crescent

Bartolomé Esteban Murillo. (Hulton Archive/Getty Images)

moon, an ancient symbol of chastity; and the serpent, symbol of heresy and sin.

The dramatic changes seen in his paintings in his second period (1657-1665) define the High Baroque style in Spanish painting. The shift has been attributed to Murillo's exposure to new artistic influences. In 1655-1656, the artist Francisco Herrera, the Younger, with whom Murillo served as copresident of the Seville Academy, returned to Seville from Madrid, bringing with him knowledge of new High Baroque practices. In 1658, Murillo made a trip to Madrid, where he viewed at first hand the works in the Spanish royal collection, and in particular the paintings of the Flemish Dynamic Baroque artists Sir Anthony van Dyck and Peter Paul Rubens, as well as the paintings of the Venetian school. Their greater idealization, painterliness, and energetic compositions served as sources of inspiration for Murillo's High Baroque manner.

Murillo's stylistic transformation can also be linked to changing political and social conditions in Spain. His move from Baroque realism to a more idealized style also parallels a more general shift in European painting, related to Catholic Church politics. Beginning as early as the 1620's in Italy, artists began to abandon Baroque realism, which was associated with the austerities of the Catholic Reformation. In response to the Church's declaration of triumph against Protestantism, a period known as the Catholic Restoration, artists began producing artworks that were not only didactic but also aesthetic in nature. In addition, extreme economic and social problems in Spain facilitated Murillo's shift to a more pleasing, idealized style. In 1649 and 1650, the bubonic plague struck the city of Seville, killing half of its population within eight weeks. Crop failures followed, leading to increased poverty, starvation, and social unrest. Many have suggested that Murillo changed his style to please his viewers, offering in his pictures a taste of heaven to console them amid hard times.

Murillo's late works demonstrate his continued commitment to graceful idealization and a delicate, pictorial style. His *Our Lady of the Immaculate Conception* of around 1678 is typical. Compared to earlier versions of the theme, the spiral composition is now more dynamic, and the increased numbers of angels inhabiting the picture space add greater complexity. The pictorial effects are even richer and softer, leading some art historians to characterize his last style period, which dates from 1665 to 1682, as his "vaporous style." During his final years, Murillo produced a great number of genre pictures, mainly idealized depictions of beggar children. Although possibly related to similar representations of poverty in picaresque literature, one wonders how patrons reconciled these romanticized views with the reality of homeless children begging for food on the city's streets. Murillo died in 1682 while painting his final work, *The Mystical Marriage of Saint Catherine*, for the Capuchin Church in Cádiz, Spain, after falling from the scaffolding.

SIGNIFICANCE

Murillo was the most important Spanish artist of the second half of the seventeenth century. Responsible for the spread of a new, more idealized style, his prolific output demonstrates that he was attuned to the latest developments in European Baroque art. His works inspired many later imitators in Spain and the Americas, and they influenced such painters as Thomas Gainsborough and Sir

Joshua Reynolds in England and Jean-Baptiste Greuze in France. His pious, sweet religious paintings remain popular to this day, reproduced throughout the world as prayer cards for Catholic devotions.

In addition to being a masterful technician of oil painting technique, he was also a talented draftsman. About one hundred drawings by Murillo are extant, more than any other seventeenth century Spanish artist.

—Charlene Villaseñor Black

FURTHER READING

Bartolomé Esteban Murillo, 1617-1682. London: Royal Academy of Arts, 1982-1983. The catalog of a seminal exhibition that brought Murillo to public attention. The text, in both English and Spanish, includes important essays on the artist's life and works.

Brown, Jonathan. *Painting in Spain, 1500-1700.* Pelican History of Art. New Haven, Conn.: Yale University Press, 1991. This textbook, the best general survey of Spanish painting, includes two chapters that treat Murillo's artworks, situating them within the Sevillian tradition.

Cherry, Peter, and Xanthe Brooke. *Murillo: Scenes of Childhood.* London: Merrell, 2001. An important study of Murillo's genre scenes, most of which depict beggar children, that provides new patronage information. Includes an informative essay on the artistic and historical contexts of these paintings' production.

Stratton-Pruitt, Suzanne L. *Bartolomé Esteban Murillo (1617-1682): Paintings from American Collections.* New York: Harry N. Abrams, 2002. The catalog of an exhibition of the artist's works housed in U.S. collections. Includes several useful essays, including one detailing the artist's life and works, a study of his devotional paintings, and analysis of his technique.

SEE ALSO: Sir Anthony van Dyck; Peter Paul Rubens; Diego Velázquez; Francesco de Zurbarán.

RELATED ARTICLES in *Great Events from History: The Seventeenth Century, 1601-1700:* c. 1601-1620: Emergence of Baroque Art; c. 1601-1682: Spanish Golden Age; 1605 and 1615: Cervantes Publishes *Don Quixote de la Mancha.*

MUSTAFA I
Ottoman sultan (r. 1617-1618, 1622-1623)

Mustafa was mentally ill when he became the fifteenth sultan of the Ottoman Empire. Even though he is little more than a footnote in history, his accession marked the first time in three hundred years that the Ottoman throne did not pass from father to son. His sultancy was almost entirely at the mercy of powerful forces that disrupted the empire.

BORN: 1591; Manisa, Ottoman Empire (now in Turkey)
DIED: January 20, 1639; Constantinople, Ottoman Empire (now Istanbul, Turkey)
AREA OF ACHIEVEMENT: Government and politics

EARLY LIFE

Mustafa I (mew-stah-FAH) was the son of Sultan Mehmed III, who came to the throne in 1595 and ruled until 1603. Mustafa's mother was a slave in Mehmed's harem. His life until his accession to the throne was spent entirely in the imperial harem in Constantinople under his mother's care. Upon the death of Mehmed III, Mustafa's thirteen-year-old brother, Ahmed I (r. 1603-1617), inherited the Ottoman throne.

Ahmed's accession to the throne should have marked the end of young Mustafa's life, as it had been the Ottoman practice since the empire's founding to avoid succession controversies by executing all the living brothers of the new sultan as potential usurpers of the throne. When Mehmed III had acceded to the throne, for example, his deceased father's casket was preceded by nineteen coffins bearing his brothers' bodies. Despite the energetic recommendations of important officials in the Porte (the Ottoman government), however, the new sultan broke with centuries of tradition and chose not to execute his younger brother, Mustafa. This radical alteration in tradition was attributed by some contemporaries to Mustafa's mental illness, which may have already begun to manifest itself in Mustafa, thus rendering him an unlikely threat. Sparing Mustafa's life also has been attributed to concerns that young Ahmed would not produce an heir, which would thus endanger the imperial succession. It is more likely that Ahmed was manipulated into sparing Mustafa through the influence of powerful forces within the harem and by the interference of the empire's highest religious officials, the ulema, who considered the boy a useful tool in their machinations.

Although permitted to live, Mustafa was effectively imprisoned in the harem, perhaps confined to a single room, for the next fourteen years, and he lived under the constant threat of execution. According to a report by a contemporary Venetian ambassador, Ahmed several times contemplated killing his brother, after becoming sultan, and he twice issued the order for him to be strangled. An attack of stomach pains and then a ferocious thunderstorm were interpreted as omens by the young sultan, however, so he rescinded his earlier commands.

LIFE'S WORK

Mustafa's life was extended through an important and unprecedented break with Ottoman tradition, and he came to the throne through another unprecedented act. When Ahmed I died in late 1617 of typhus, he left several young sons, the oldest of whom, Osman, was fourteen. Powerful blocs within the government and the religious institutions took advantage of the fact that Ahmed's grand vizier (minister), who was fighting on the eastern front, had pressed for Mustafa, rather than Osman, to occupy the throne. The blocs argued that Mustafa was the oldest living legitimate heir (a situation without precedent) and that the dead sultan's sons were still too young to rule, this despite the fact that Osman had taken the throne at an even more youthful age. Eventually, this argument prevailed, and Mustafa became the fifteenth sultan of the Ottoman Empire in November of 1617.

Mustafa's rule elicited significant debate, as it marked the first time in three hundred years that the Ottoman throne did not pass from father to son. A controversy was accentuated by what most accounts agree were Mustafa's incapacitating mental infirmities. A contemporary Ottoman historian, İbrahim Peçevi, reported that these concerns were overcome when Mustafa's supporters argued that once his confinement in the harem was ended, his eccentricity would be ameliorated through contact with the broader world. In the records of all these negotiations and debates, Mustafa is conspicuous by his absence; clearly he was a pawn in the fierce, often deadly political infighting of the ruling elite at the Porte and within the harem.

Mustafa's mental problems did not improve, however, and he proved completely incompetent and incapable of ruling. The English ambassador, Sir Thomas Roe, in his *A True and Faithfull Relation . . .* (1622), a lively contemporary account of the events surrounding Mustafa's accession to the throne, reported that Mustafa was "a man esteemed rather holy (that is franticke) than wise, and indeed fitter for a Cell, than a Scepter . . . [he] is esteemed a holy man, that hath visions, and Angel-like speculations, in plaine tearmes, [he is] betweene a mad man and a foole." Mustafa was the first sultan to come to the throne who had no experience or exposure of any sort in government, having spent his entire life in the harem. Barely three months after he took the throne, court figures had spread rumors that Mustafa was insane, and on this pretext he was deposed in favor of Ahmed's son, Osman II (r. 1618-1622). For the first time in Ottoman history, a ruling sultan had been removed from the throne.

Osman's reign was relatively brief; he was dethroned and eventually murdered in 1622 by his own Janissaries because of his attempts to reform many of the entrenched institutions of the empire. The Janissaries and their supporters took advantage of the confused and unique situation of the existence of a living, former sultan in Mustafa to legitimize their removal of Osman from the throne. Because Osman left no living sons, his uncle, Mustafa, was again placed on the throne, though with great reluctance. Accounts report that he was dragged from prison by the same Janissaries who would murder his nephew, and was compelled to accept the throne. Although unusual, Mustafa's two terms as sultan were not without precedent. Indeed, Mehmed II and his father, Murad II, alternated rule in the 1440's.

Mustafa's second imperial reign was almost as short as his first, and despite his being depicted as a saint by supporters, it was even more disastrous, characterized once again by incompetence and inertia. For example, he refused to have a concubine and thereby perpetuate the dynasty. Even more serious, the disruptiveness of the Janisssary corps led to a state of anarchy in the capital and to open rebellion in Anatolia, which in turn produced serious financial challenges to the state. Many provincial governors simply refused to remit taxes to Constantinople, claiming that it was illegal for an insane man to occupy the throne.

Mustafa must not be held responsible alone for this chaotic situation, which occurred during both of his reigns. Various grand viziers and other officials, but especially his mother, effectively ruled in his stead, making all significant decisions. He was at the eye of a long-term political and institutional crisis, which had gradually but severely weakened the sultanate over the previous several decades. Barely sixteen months after being placed on the throne for the second time, in September, 1623,

Mustafa was deposed in favor of his nephew, Murad IV (1623-1640). This turn of events was driven in part by a ruling issued by ulema officials that an insane man could not sit on the throne, but it was driven even more so by the ongoing political battles raging in the Porte, wherein Mustafa was a feeble pawn.

Somewhat surprisingly, perhaps, following his second deposition, Mustafa was permitted to live out the remainder of his years, probably because his mental problems made him appear a minimal threat. He died in 1639 and was honorably buried in the Hagia Sophia mosque.

SIGNIFICANCE

In the final analysis, it seems that Sultan Mustafa I warrants little mention in the sweep of Ottoman history. Severely limited mentally and intellectually, he came to the throne and was removed from it as a pawn in the larger power politics that raged in the Porte during the first decades of the seventeenth century. His reigns were brief and characterized by significant struggle and disruption, and so not surprisingly, little was accomplished under his rule.

The only significant political achievement during Mustafa's reign was the peace treaty signed with Poland in February of 1623, in which he had little direct involvement. His significance is more symbolic, however, as he represents the turmoil and challenges that the Ottoman sultanate faced in these difficult years.

—Eric R. Dursteler

FURTHER READING

McCarthy, Justin. *The Ottoman Turks: An Introductory History to 1923.* New York: Longman, 1997. A sweeping historical overview of Ottoman history from the late thirteenth century to the early twentieth century. Includes discussion of the difficult period in Ottoman history during the time of Mustafa.

Peirce, Leslie P. *The Imperial Harem: Women and Sovereignty in the Ottoman Empire.* New York: Oxford University Press, 1993. An insightful discussion of the role of women in the governance of the Ottoman Empire in the troubled seventeenth century. Mustafa was likely influenced by powerful harem women, as he spent many years in the harem after his life was spared.

Shaw, Stanford J. *History of the Ottoman Empire and Modern Turkey: Empire of the Gazis.* New York: Cambridge University Press, 1976. A general history of the Ottoman Empire in the premodern era, this text contains important contextual and biographical details on Mustafa's life.

Somel, Selcuk Aksin. *Historical Dictionary of the Ottoman Empire*. Lanham, Md.: Scarecrow Press, 2003. An indispensable resource for studies of the Ottoman Empire.

SEE ALSO: Merzifonlu Kara Mustafa Paşa; Kâtib Çelebî; Kösem Sultan; Murad IV.

RELATED ARTICLES in *Great Events from History: The Seventeenth Century, 1601-1700:* 1602-1639: Ottoman-Şafavid Wars; 1603-1617: Reign of Sultan Ahmed I; September, 1605: Egyptians Rebel Against the Ottomans; November 11, 1606: Treaty of Zsitvatorok; 1609-1617: Construction of the Blue Mosque; May 19, 1622: Janissary Revolt and Osman II's Assassination; 1623-1640: Murad IV Rules the Ottoman Empire; 1638: Waning of the *Devshirme* System; 1684-1699: Holy League Ends Ottoman Rule of the Danubian Basin; Beginning 1687: Decline of the Ottoman Empire; 1697-1702: Köprülü Reforms of Hüseyin Paşa; January 26, 1699: Treaty of Karlowitz.

DUCHESS OF NEWCASTLE
English playwright, philosopher, scientist, and woman of letters

Newcastle was the first Englishwoman to seek print publication and to publish prolifically. Her written work, thirteen books in twenty-two editions, encompassed poetry, fiction, philosophy, drama, science, biography, and autobiography.

BORN: 1623; St. Johns Abbey, near Colchester, Essex, England

DIED: December 15, 1673; Welbeck Abbey, near Nottingham, England

ALSO KNOWN AS: Margaret Lucas (given name); Margaret Cavendish

AREAS OF ACHIEVEMENT: Literature, science and technology, philosophy

EARLY LIFE

Margaret Cavendish, later the duchess of Newcastle, was the daughter of Thomas Lucas (c. 1573-1625), a wealthy landowner. Thomas was the son of Sir Thomas Lucas (c. 1531-1611), with whom he is sometimes confused. Although it is often mistakenly said that he was earl of Colchester, Newcastle's father had no title, and he died when the future duchess was still an infant. Her mother was Elizabeth Leighton (d. 1647), daughter of John Leighton, a gentleman of London. After the death of her husband, Elizabeth managed the family estates, largely on her own, and provided Margaret with an example of how a woman might act to protect family interests.

Margaret Lucas had several siblings, including Sir Charles Cavendish (d. 1648), a Royalist hero and martyr (summarily executed after the Battle of Colchester); Catherine Lucas Pye (Margaret's favorite sister); Ann Lucas (to whom she wrote a letter of warning about the dangers of marriage for women); Sir John Lucas (later Lord Lucas of Shenfield); and Sir Thomas Lucas (a soldier). Sir John Denham remarked in a poem that Newcastle's brother John was a serious scholar, and it was in this brother's library that she seems to have spent a good deal of time as a child. She was, she said, educated by a gentlewoman, who was employed for that purpose.

In 1645, while a maid of honor to Queen Henrietta Maria and while living with the exiled English court in Paris, Margaret met her future husband, William Cavendish (1593-1676), marquess and later duke of Newcastle. The two were married in late November or early December of 1645, at which time Margaret became the marchioness of Newcastle. She would become duchess upon her husband's creation as duke in 1665. The wedding

ceremony took place in the private chapel of the English resident at the French court, Sir Richard Browne. The bride and groom eventually settled in Antwerp, in a house once owned by the painter Peter Paul Rubens. They had no offspring, though William was father to children from his first marriage.

The marquess was himself a playwright, as were two of his daughters, Lady Elizabeth Brackley and Jane Cavendish. He is important in his own right, both as a playwright and as a military commander in the English Civil War. Elizabeth and Jane are known today for their play *The Concealed Fancies* (c. 1645). Margaret and her husband were the center of a scientific and belletristic circle that included Thomas Hobbes, whose materialist philosophy was important to the development of the marchioness of Newcastle's thinking.

LIFE'S WORK

In November of 1651, the marchioness of Newcastle traveled to England with the marquess's brother, the scientist Sir Charles Cavendish, hoping to gain something from her husband's sequestered estates by appealing to the Parliamentary Committee for Compounding. During this period, she found a publisher for her *Poems and Fancies* (1653) and gained a reputation for odd or eccentric dress. This first book of poems, printed with Newcastle's name on the title page rather than anonymously, was enormously popular, if subject to ridicule, and she may have realized a profit from its publication. *Poems and Fancies*, which appeared in revised editions in 1664 and 1672, incorporates atomic theory resembling that of the natural philosopher Walter Charleton, as well as containing poems on fairy folk. "Hunting the Hare," found in the volume, has been noted as an early poem dealing with cruelty to animals.

The book of poems was followed by several diverse publications. *The World's Olio* (1655) was a collection of brief observations on a wide variety of topics. It included witty remarks on historical and mythological figures and advice on medical matters. *Philosophicall Fancies* (1653; revised as *Philosophical and Physical Opinions*, 1655) demonstrated Newcastle's new emphasis on materialist and vitalist natural philosophy. *Nature's Pictures* (1656), on the other hand, was a collection of love stories in verse and prose. It considered issues of sex and gender, and the first edition contained the much-studied brief autobiographical essay, "A True

Relation." Newcastle's husband also contributed poetry to the volume. Indeed, his prefaces to her printed work make clear that he approved of her writing and occasionally collaborated with her, a situation that later drew derision from twentieth century author Virginia Woolf.

With the Restoration of King Charles II in 1660, the Newcastles returned to England, first to the London court but soon thereafter to Nottinghamshire. The marchioness next published *Plays* (1662), most of which were probably written while she was in Antwerp. The plays deal with issues of sex and gender and sometimes include women warriors. *Orations of Divers Sorts* (1662, 1668) collects exemplary speeches meant to be delivered at set occasions. In one set of speeches, a group of women debate the place of women in society. *CCXI Sociable Letters* (1664) contains highly readable, mostly fictional letters addressed by one woman to another. It includes interesting anecdotes and commentary on courtship, marriage, infidelity, and divorce.

Newcastle's *Philosophical Letters* (1664) critiques René Descartes, Johannes Baptista van Helmont, Thomas Hobbes, and Henry More. It was her first, but not her last, direct engagement with her fellow philosophers. Her *Observations upon Experimental Philosophy* (1666) represents an attack on Robert Hooke's *Micrographia* (1665). The former text contains *The Description of a New Blazing World*, a much-discussed work of science fiction, notable for its depiction of Cavendish as two separate but interacting characters, an empress and the duchess of Newcastle.

The duchess's tribute to her husband, *The Life of William Cavendish, Duke of Newcastle* (1667), translated as *De vita et rebus gentis Guillielmi Duicis Novo-castrensis* (1668), attracted the opprobrium of the diarist Samuel Pepys, who followed the duchess around Hyde Park in the spring of 1667. Pepys found her physically attractive but felt that her husband should not have encouraged her to write. Also in the spring of 1667, Cavendish visited the Royal Society with a huge entourage. This was the first visit by a woman to that male institution. The following year, she published *Grounds of Natural Philosophy* (1668), a reworking of the second edition of *Philosophical and Physical Opinions* in a more tentative and plainer style, as well as *The Description of a New World, Called the Blazing-World*

(1668)—a separate edition of *A New Blazing World*—and *Plays Never Before Printed* (1668), which continues themes found in her first collection of plays.

SIGNIFICANCE

It is difficult to gauge accurately the literary and scientific importance of the duchess of Newcastle, during her own lifetime. Certainly she was widely known, if often the subject of chuckles. Mary Evelyn, wife to diarist John Evelyn, seems to have disliked and envied her. Newcastle's work, moreover, gained little notice of any kind in the first one hundred years after her death. By the middle of the eighteenth century, however, a shift had taken place: Newcastle came to be seen as a harmless and delightful eccentric who produced charming verse on the subject of moods and fairy folk. George Ballard's *Memoirs of Several Ladies of Great Britain* (1752) popularized selected poems of Newcastle, and anthologists of women's poetry generally followed his lead. Horace Walpole, in *A Catalogue of the Royal and Noble Authors* (1758), treated her literary output with contempt, but

Duchess of Newcastle. (Hulton Archive/Getty Images)

Charles Lamb, in "Mackery End" (1823), became the champion of someone he took to be a wonderfully fanciful poet.

Toward the end of the nineteenth century, Newcastle the poet of fairy folk was supplanted by Newcastle the loyal wife, who suffered with her husband in exile and who recorded his war years in his biography. M. A. Lower and C. H. Firth produced new editions of *The Life of William Cavendish, Duke of Newcastle*, both of which were frequently reprinted. Firth's commentary sought to confirm Newcastle's understanding of the English Civil Wars. Finally, early twentieth century treatments of the novel often noted that studies of character found in *CCXI Sociable Letters* foreshadowed developments in eighteenth century realistic fiction.

Today, Newcastle is studied mainly by three groups of readers: (1) those who have an interest in sex, gender, and politics in seventeenth century England; (2) historians of science; and (3) historians of drama. Many feminists find her writing to be a puzzling mix of protofeminist and traditional positions, but they have become less likely to see her as a bad writer whose bad writing derives from oppression by men. Rather, Newcastle is seen as a good writer who overcame the impediments of patriarchy to produce books that are oblique, ironic, and full of fun. *The Blazing World* is often studied in the college classroom, and *The Convent of Pleasure* (1668) is still performed. Her defense of William Shakespeare, among the first extended treatments of that playwright by any writer, is also gaining recognition.

—James Fitzmaurice

FURTHER READING

Cavendish, Margaret. *Paper Bodies: A Margaret Cavendish Reader*. Edited by Sylvia Bowerbank and Sara Mendelson. Peterborough, Ont.: Broadview Press, 1999. This paperback school edition has scholarly authority and gives a good selection of Cavendish's writing.

Clucas, Stephen, ed. *A Princely Brave Woman: Essays on Margaret Cavendish, Duchess of Newcastle*. Aldershot, Hampshire, England: Ashgate Press, 2003. Clucas's collection covers Cavendish's drama, science writing, life, and positions on the place of women in society.

Cottegnies, Line, and Nancy Weitz, eds. *Authorial Conquests: Essays on Genre in the Writings of Margaret Cavendish*. Madison, N.J.: Fairleigh Dickenson University Press, 2003. This collection asserts that Cavendish, rather than being ignorant of the conventions of genre, cleverly adapted them for her own purposes.

Whitaker, Katie. *Mad Madge: The Extraordinary Life of Margaret, Duchess of Newcastle, the First Woman to Live by Her Pen*. New York: Basic Books, 2002. A thorough, reliable, and well-documented biography.

SEE ALSO: Charles II (of England); René Descartes; John Evelyn; Johannes Baptista van Helmont; Henrietta Maria; Thomas Hobbes; Robert Hooke; Samuel Pepys.

RELATED ARTICLES in *Great Events from History: The Seventeenth Century, 1601-1700:* 1642-1651: English Civil Wars; May, 1659-May, 1660: Restoration of Charles II.

SIR ISAAC NEWTON
English physicist

Newton's theory of gravitation and laws of mechanics described, for the first time, a natural world governed by immutable physical laws. In addition to creating a conceptual framework that underlay the practice of science until the twentieth century, Newton's understanding of the world in terms of natural laws profoundly affected the history of ideas and the practice of philosophy in the modern era.

BORN: December 25, 1642 (new style, January 4, 1643); Woolsthorpe Manor, near Colsterworth, Lincolnshire, England
DIED: March 20, 1727 (new style, March 31, 1727); London, England
AREAS OF ACHIEVEMENT: Physics, science and technology

EARLY LIFE

Sir Isaac Newton was born on Christmas Day, 1642, to a farmer and his wife, at Woolsthorpe Manor, just south of Grantham in Lincolnshire. His father died shortly before Newton's birth, and when his mother remarried three years later and moved away to live with her new husband, Newton remained at Woolsthorpe to be reared by his grandparents.

Newton attended the grammar school in Grantham, and he demonstrated scientific aptitude at an early age, when he began to construct mechanical toys and models. Aside from a brief period when his mother tried to persuade him to follow in his father's footsteps and become a farmer, his education continued (it is said that Newton tended to read books rather than watch sheep, with disastrous results). He was accepted as an undergraduate at Trinity College, Cambridge, in 1661.

Although his mother provided a small allowance, Newton had to wait on tables at college to help finance his studies. Even at that time, his fellow students remarked that he was silent and withdrawn, and indeed, Newton throughout his life was something of a recluse, shunning society. He never married, and some historians believe that Newton had homosexual leanings. Whatever the truth of this speculation, it is certain that he preferred work, study, experimentation, and observation to social activity, sometimes to the detriment of his own health. After retreating to Grantham for a short time while Cambridge was threatened by plague, Newton returned to the university as a don in 1667 with an established reputation for mathematical brilliance.

LIFE'S WORK

It was not long at all before Newton proved his reputation for genius to be well deserved. Shortly after his graduation, Newton developed the differential calculus, a mathematical method for calculating rates of change (such as acceleration) that had long evaded other scholars. As a result, in 1669, he was offered the Lucasian Chair of Mathematics at Cambridge, a position he held until 1701.

Newton's second major contribution of this period was in the field of optics. His experiments with light had led him to build a reflecting telescope, the first one of its kind that actually worked. After further refinements, he presented the device to the Royal Society, where he was asked to present a paper on his theory of light and colors. Shortly afterward, he was made a fellow of this august body, which contained all the prominent intellectuals of the day.

Sir Isaac Newton. (Library of Congress)

Newton's paper offered new insights into the nature of color. While experimenting with prisms, Newton had discovered that white light is a mixture of all the colors of the rainbow and that the prism separates white light into its component parts. Newton's theory was controversial, provoking strong feelings at the Royal Society and initiating a lengthy dispute with Robert Hooke concerning the nature of light. Hooke criticized Newton with such vehemence that Newton presented no more theories on the nature of light until 1704, after Hooke's death.

For a scientist such as Newton, the seventeenth century was an interesting period in which to work. Scientific thought was still dominated by the Aristotelian worldview, which had held sway for more than two thousand years, but cracks in that outlook were beginning to appear. Galileo had shown that the planets traveled around the Sun, which was positioned at the center of the universe, while Johannes Kepler had observed that this motion was regular and elliptical in nature. The task confronting scientists, in keeping with the aim of explaining the universe mathematically from first principles, was to find some logical reason for this phenomenon.

Newton, among others, believed that there had to be a set of universal rules governing motion, equally applicable to planetary and earthbound activity. His researches finally led him to a mathematical proof that all motion is

NEWTON'S LAWS OF MOTION

Sir Isaac Newton's "Axioms, or Laws of Motion," provided at the beginning of the Principia, *defined the nature of the physical universe as understood by Western scientists for more than two hundred years.*

Law 1: Every body perseveres in its state of rest, or of uniform motion in a right line, unless it is compelled to change that state by forces impressed thereon.
Law 2: The alteration of motion is ever proportional to the motive force impressed; and is made in the direction of the right line in which that force is impressed.
Law 3: To every action there is always opposed an equal reaction; or the mutual actions of two bodies upon each other are always equal, and directed to contrary parts.

Source: From *The Mathematical Principles of Natural Philosophy*, by Sir Isaac Newton. Translated by Andrew Motte (London: B. Motte, 1729). http://members.tripod.com/~gravitee/axioms.htm. Accessed February 4, 2005.

regulated by a law of attraction. Specifically, he proved that the force of attraction between two bodies of constant mass varies as the inverse of the square of the distance between those bodies (that is, $F_A = k/D^2$, where F_A is the force of attraction between the bodies, D is the distance between them, and k is a constant). From this beginning, he was able to explain why planets travel in ellipses around the Sun, why Earth's tides move as they do, and why tennis balls, for example, follow the trajectories that they do. The inverse square formula also led Newton toward a notion of gravity that neatly tied his mathematics together. When Newton published this work, it led to another major confrontation with Hooke, who claimed that he had reached the proof of the inverse square law before Newton; the argument between the two was lengthy and acrimonious.

In 1684, Edmond Halley, then a young astronomer, went to Cambridge to visit Newton, who was reputed to be doing work similar to Halley's. Halley found that Newton claimed that he had proved the inverse square law but had temporarily mislaid it. (Throughout his life, Newton worked on scraps of paper, keeping everything from first drafts to final copies, so this assertion has the ring of truth to it.) Halley was astounded: Here was a man who claimed to have solved the problem that was bothering many leading scientists of the day, and he had not yet made it public. When Halley returned, Newton had found the proof, and Halley persuaded him to publish his nine-page demonstration of the law. Still, Halley was not satisfied. Realizing that Newton had more to offer the world, he prodded him into publishing a book of his theories. The result was the famous *Philosophiae Naturalis Principia Mathematica* (1687; *The Mathematical Principles of Natural Philosophy*, 1729, best known as the *Principia*), which was published at Halley's expense. A year later, a second and third volume of the work reached the public.

The *Principia* was a highly technical and mathematical work that many of Newton's contemporaries had difficulty following, but its effect on the scientific community was profound. In it, Newton outlined his three laws of motion. The first states that every body continues in a state of rest or motion until it is acted on by a force. The second law states that the acceleration of a body is proportional to the force applied to it and inversely proportional to its mass. The third law, perhaps the most widely quoted, states that for every action there is an equal and opposite reaction. From these three fundamental laws, Newton went on to construct his theory of gravity—a force that acts at a distance between two or more bodies, causing an attraction between them that is in inverse proportion to the distance between them.

Newton's theories were a major challenge to the dominant worldview, constructing the world, as they did, purely from mechanics. His theories seemed revolutionary and initiated a great debate, which continued for the better part of a century after the *Principia* was published. When they were eventually accepted as a useful description of nature, Newtonian science formed the basis of modern thinking until the twentieth century, when Albert Einstein's theories turned the world upside down again.

Writing the *Principia* dominated Newton's life to such an extent that he became completely obsessed with the project, often forgetting to eat or even to sleep while he continued working. Despite his reclusive tendencies, however, in 1687 Newton entered the public arena. Cambridge University and King James II, a Catholic, were in the midst of a battle over religion. The university had refused to grant a degree to a Benedictine monk, and the officials of the university, including Newton, were summoned to appear before the infamous Judge George Jeffreys to argue their case. Shortly afterward, Newton was elected the member of Parliament for Cambridge. Newton's entrance into politics was less than world-shattering, though; it is said that he spoke only once during his term of office, and that was to ask an usher to open a window.

In 1693, Newton suffered a mental breakdown about which little is known, and he withdrew into his previous solitary state. Two years later, he returned to public office when he was asked to take over the wardenship of the mint. There was to be a major reissue of coinage because of the increasingly pressing problem of clipped gold and silver coins. New coins needed to be minted with milled edges, and several prominent scientists were pressed into service to aid in the process. Newton discovered a hitherto unrecognized penchant for administration and proved himself a highly able bureaucrat, being promoted to master of the Mint in 1699. In 1701, he was reelected to Parliament and continued in the public eye for the remainder of his life.

Until his death in 1727, honors were heaped upon Newton, as befitted the most prominent scientist of his generation. In 1703, he was elected president of the Royal Society and was annually reelected to that post for the next twenty-five years. He moved to London and became more sociable but nevertheless earned a reputation

NEWTON'S MAJOR WORKS
1687   *Philosophiae Naturalis Principia Mathematica* (*The Mathematical Principles of Natural Philosophy*, 1729)
1704   *Opticks*
1707   *Arithmetica Universalis* (*Universal Arithmetick*, 1720)
1711   *Analysis per Quantitatum Series, Fluxiones, ad Differentias: Cum Enumeratione Linearum Tertii Ordinis* (includes *De Analysi per Aquationes Infinitas*; *Fragmenta Epistolarum*; *De Quadratura Curvarum*; *Enumeratio Linearum Tertii Ordinis*; and *Methodus Differentialis*)
1728   *The Chronology of Ancient Kingdoms Amended*
1733   *Observations upon the Prophecies of Daniel and the Apocalypse of St. John*
1736   *The Method of Fluxions and Infinite Series*

for being cantankerous and ill-tempered. In 1704, Newton published *Opticks*, a tract about the theories of light that he had earlier expounded to the Royal Society. It was more accessible than the *Principia* and gained a wider audience. A year later, he was knighted by Queen Anne. Meanwhile, the *Principia* was proving to be a best-seller, as everyone wanted to read the theories that were pushing back the frontiers of contemporary science, and it went through second and third editions during Newton's lifetime.

Newton's work in the last years of his life was mainly religious, apart from another acrimonious dispute with the German philosopher Gottfried Wilhelm Leibniz over who had first invented the differential calculus. Newton spent hours attempting to understand the messages hidden in the Book of Revelation, seeing this task as simply another aspect of the search for truth as revealed in God's works, both written and created. Thus, in the end, Newton proved himself to be a medieval thinker, despite his work laying the foundations of modern scientific thought.

SIGNIFICANCE

Newton made an outstanding contribution to the modernization of the Western scientific worldview. He followed in the footsteps of Nicolaus Copernicus, Galileo, Kepler, and others in asserting that the heavens and earth were a part of one solar system (not separated as they are in Aristotelian philosophy), with the Sun at the center. Newton further developed and refined the method of observation and experiment that had already established itself in the seventeenth century, by carefully checking and rechecking his work and by creating experimental verifications of his various theories. Most important, he demonstrated that a comprehensive mechanical description of the world that explained matter and motion in terms of mathematics was actually possible. With the *Principia*, Newton effectively sounded the death knell of the old description of the universe and laid the basis for a modern approach. His was perhaps the greatest individual contribution to a rich and innovative period of scientific development.

—Sally Hibbin

FURTHER READING

Aughton, Peter. *Newton's Apple: Isaac Newton and the English Scientific Revolution.* London: Weidenfeld & Nicolson, 2003. Describes Newton's life and work as part of the scientific rebirth occurring after the English Civil War.

Brewster, Sir David. *Memoirs of the Life, Writings, and Discoveries of Sir Isaac Newton.* Edinburgh: T. Constable, 1855. Reprint. New York: Johnson Reprint, 1965. Brewster's two-volume biography of Newton was the first attempt at a comprehensive survey of his life, drawing on the multitude of private papers that Newton left behind. It does, however, suffer from nineteenth century prejudice and says little of Newton's religious or alchemical work.

Christianson, Gale E. *In the Presence of the Creator: Isaac Newton and His Times.* New York: Free Press, 1984. This thorough, well-researched, and highly readable biography places Newton's life and works in the context of a momentous shift in humankind's perception of the physical world.

Cohen, I. Bernard, and George E. Smith, eds. *The Cambridge Companion to Newton.* New York: Cambridge University Press, 2002. A collection of essays examining Newton's scientific discoveries, comparing his mathematical theories with those of Leibniz, and analyzing his influence upon eighteenth century Christianity.

Fara, Patricia. *Newton: The Making of a Genius.* New York: Columbia University Press, 2002. A cultural history describing how Newton's scientific discoveries and reputation for genius made him a famous and much admired person in the eighteenth century.

Gleick, James. *Isaac Newton.* New York: Pantheon Books, 2003. A short, popular biography, using Newton's letters and unpublished notebooks to explain how he came upon his discoveries in physics, optics, and calculus.

Koyré, Alexandre. *From the Closed World to the Infinite Universe.* Baltimore, Md.: Johns Hopkins University Press, 1957. Follows developments from Galileo to Newton, showing how medieval notions were transformed into more modern ones in the course of the century.

_____. *Newtonian Studies.* Cambridge, Mass.: Harvard University Press, 1965. A collection of essays written by Koyré over a period of years that explore different aspects of Newton's thought, concentrating on the historical and philosophical.

Manuel, Frank E. *A Portrait of Isaac Newton.* Cambridge, Mass.: Harvard University Press, 1968. Reprint. New York: Da Capo Press, 1990. A modern portrait of the man, his life, and his work, written in the light of study of Newton's papers and of contemporary thinking about the methods of development of science.

Newton, Sir Isaac. *Mathematical Principles of Natural Philosophy and His System of the World: Principia.* 2 vols. Berkeley: University of California Press, 1934. Reprint. 1962. This now-standard version of Newton's major work is based on the translation by Andrew Motte in 1729. It has been revised, with detailed and helpful historical and explanatory appendices by Florian Cajori.

_____. *Opticks.* New York: Dover, 1952. A standard version of Newton's second major work, with an informative preface by I. Bernard Cohen that looks at the material both in the light of modern theories and in the context of Newton's contemporaries. Historical introduction by Sir Edmund Whittaker, and a somewhat poetic foreword by Albert Einstein.

Westfall, Richard S. *Never at Rest: A Biography of Isaac Newton.* New York: Cambridge University Press, 1980. A lively biography that attempts to present Newton's scientific discoveries in the context of his life, presenting him as a living man confronting problems to be solved.

SEE ALSO: Galileo; Edmond Halley; Robert Hooke; James II; Johannes Kepler; Gottfried Wilhelm Leibniz.

RELATED ARTICLES in *Great Events from History: The Seventeenth Century, 1601-1700:* 1601-1672: Rise of Scientific Societies; 1615-1696: Invention and Development of the Calculus; Late December, 1671: Newton Builds His Reflecting Telescope; Summer, 1687: Newton Formulates the Theory of Universal Gravitation.

NIKON

Russian church leader and church reformer

Nikon contributed to the liturgical reforms of the Russian Orthodox Church, the introduction of Western intellectualism in Russia, and the definition of the role of the church in the Russian state. Critics argue that his ultimate downfall came out of his hunger for more power for the patriarch, and the church, over that of the czar, and the state.

BORN: 1605; Veldemanovo, Russia
DIED: August 27, 1681; en route to Moscow, Russia
ALSO KNOWN AS: Nikita Minin
AREAS OF ACHIEVEMENT: Religion and theology, government and politics

EARLY LIFE

Nikon (NYEE-kuhn), the future patriarch of the Russian Orthodox church, was born Nikita Minin in the Nizhni-Novgorod province of northern Russia to landless peasants. Nikon, as he would come to be known, was born during a period in Russian history called the Time of Troubles. This historical era was marked by a succession crisis that resulted when Czar Fyodor I Ivanovich died without an heir. Nikon was educated in a local school until the age of twelve. After this, because of parental abuse, he ran away to the Makariev Monastery.

Nikon's parents persuaded him to leave the monastery and be married. In 1625, at the age of twenty, he became the village priest of Kolychevo. A year later, Nikon assumed control of a parish in the Moscow province, where he remained for the next ten years. He had three sons during this time, none of whom survived. In 1634, Nikon persuaded his wife to enter a Moscow convent, thus clearing the obstacles for Nikon to go to the north and live as a hermit.

For several years, Nikon lived in utter solitude, preparing himself to become a monk. He entered the monastery at Kozheezero, in the Kargopol district in the northern tundra region. Between 1641 and 1646, Nikon was the administrator for the monastery. In 1646, while on monastery business in Moscow, Nikon met Stephen Vonifatiev, the confessor of Czar Alexis. Through Vonifatiev, Nikon, a 6-foot, 6-inch-tall, forty-two-year-old monk from the north, met and awed the seventeen-year-old ruler of Russia with his spiritual bearing. Alexis was so impressed with his newfound friend that he named Nikon to the position of archimandrite (head) of the Novo-Spasski Monastery in Moscow.

Nikon soon became involved with church reform. A group led by Vonifatiev established a printing press in Moscow for the purpose of increasing the number of religious texts available. The aim of the reformers was to increase the level of intellectual life in Russia by raising the literacy level of the clergy. Members of this reform group were first to support and later to disassociate themselves from Nikon's ideas concerning church reform.

LIFE'S WORK

In 1648, serious riots erupted in Moscow. The surface cause of the riots was a higher salt tax, but the root of the popular disturbances was the inefficiency of the state. The modern Russian state was formed in 1613, amid the debris accumulated from years of internal conflict (the Time of Troubles). Alexis inherited the problems of the

Nikon. (Library of Congress)

A CONTEMPORARY ACCOUNT OF NIKON

Dutch merchant Nikolas Witsen visited Russia in 1664-1665 as part of a Dutch mission. He chronicled his observations of Nikon in his diary with words so detailed and intimate that he notes Nikon's "red and pimpled face" and that Nikon "feels flabby" before a thunderstorm.

I decided to undertake a secret trip to New Jerusalem [a monastery]. . . .

The monastery is situated 10 miles from Moscow. At night we heard the terrible howling of wolves; they were very close from [to] us; in the morning we saw foxes and heard singing of many birds. A monastery, which they called Jerusalem, is similar to a Russian fortress. It has 10 or 12 towers and it is situated near the river Istra, which now [with the artificial channel] completely surrounds it. . . .

It is necessary to know, that this Patriarch left his service and Moscow. Now he lives far away from the capital in voluntary exile. . . . But as far as Nikon is a very significant person, the Tsar can not or does not want to punish him and gives him all church incomes.

This man has bad manners, he is precipitate and he is hasty, has use to make ugly gestures. . . . He is strong and high, he has [a] red and pimpled face, he is [about] 64 years old. He loves Spanish wine. By the way he often repeats: "our kind deals." He seldom gets sick, but before a thunder-storm or rain he feels flabby, but in the storm or rain he is better. Since he has left Moscow, 7 or 8 years ago, he never cut or brush his hair. His head is like a medusa, it is shaggy as his beard also.

Source: Quoted by Sergei Lobachev. "Nikon: Patriarch of Moscow and All the Russias," Saint Petersburg University, Russia. http://www.spbumag.nw.ru/Nikon/E-Nicon.htm. Accessed December, 2004.

---

fledgling state: debts from years of warfare, a state without a consistent form of collecting taxes, and rulers who relied on others to make decisions. In 1648, Alexis replaced his boyar adviser with Nikon. This rise in station of a religious man to the position of the czar's adviser initiated the struggle between church and state that dominated Russian history until the rule of Peter the Great.

The metropolitan of the Novgorod Church district died in 1649. Using his power as the secular head of the Russian Orthodox Church, Alexis appointed his friend Nikon to the vacant post. Nikon proved his loyalty to and gratitude for the czar's confidence during an armed uprising in Novgorod in 1650. This revolt was against the power of the czar to absorb Moscow's former great rival, the free city-state of Novgorod, into the ever-expanding Russian state. Nikon, appointed as the czar's overseer in Novgorod, brutally repressed the rebelling Novgorodians in Alexis's name. In 1652, Nikon returned to Moscow after the death of Joseph, the patriarch (spiritual leader) of the Russian Orthodox Church. Alexis begged

Nikon to become Joseph's successor and to help guide the czar in secular decisions. Nikon accepted the patriarchy on condition the czar give him a free hand in the reordering of the Russian Orthodox Church.

As patriarch of the Russian Orthodox Church, Nikon's first reform was to bring uniformity to the worship service. He accomplished this by publishing service books to be used by all the clergy. As patriarch, Nikon controlled the printing press, and through it he was able to direct the mission of the church. The *Kormchaia Kniga* (the pilot book), published in 1650, not only was a polemic against Judaism and other religions deemed to be false but also was a work based on canon law. Nikon used this book as the basis for the Russian Orthodox mission to become the center of all religious life in the East.

During the previous two centuries, since the fall of Constantinople in 1453, the Russian Orthodox Church had remained in an intellectual vacuum from the Western world. Through isolation and ignorance, two centuries of silence had led to many alterations in the way in which Christianity was practiced in Russia. Indeed, the fall of the Byzantine Empire, after the earlier fall of the western Roman Empire, led to the idea that pure Christianity and the legacy of Rome itself continued to survive only in Russia, an idea known as the Third Rome.

In his efforts to purify Russian religious texts, Nikon invited scholars from Kiev to aid him. Unlike Russian religious leaders, the Kievan scholars had been trained in both Latin and Greek, which enabled them to correct the Russian deviations from Western and Greek developments. The Nikonian corrections were intended to standardize the texts and in so doing to eliminate the various heresies being practiced as a result of differing versions of the psalter.

Nikon also reformed church services. He changed not only the form but also the substance of church rituals. He added theatrical dimensions to the worship service with expensive robes for the clergy, a grand processional, and a featured sermon given weekly. The Palm Sunday procession of Christ's entrance into Jerusalem before Easter became an important ritual of the church, with the czar leading a donkey on which the patriarch was seated. This ritual was repeated in towns and villages throughout the empire with the civil leaders in attendance to the spiritual leaders of each community.

Another reform of the church service was a change in making the sign of the cross; it was changed from two fingers to three. Nikon also changed the number of loaves of bread consecrated for communion from seven to five. He altered the common people's traditional perspective on the Holy Trinity: God became the Lord, the name of Jesus was spelled differently from the way it had been spelled in previous texts, and the Holy Spirit was openly discussed instead of implied in the service.

The purpose of all the Nikonian reforms was to increase the power and authority of the patriarch. Indeed, Nikon agreed to become patriarch only after the czar and the boyars had taken an oath of loyalty to him. The oath was traditional in the Orthodox Church and had been handed down to the Russian state as part of their Byzantine heritage, but Nikon took their oath of loyalty much more seriously than prior Russian patriarchs. He thought and acted under the assumption that their oath was indeed made in the original Byzantine context. Nikon had read and understood the ninth century Byzantine document that stated that the patriarch and the emperor were corulers and answerable only to God. The emperor was to be the secular leader and the patriarch the spiritual leader of the state. The patriarch was always to put the salvation of souls first, even if he had to go against the will of the emperor. Nikon thus used his position as patriarch, defined by the ancient Byzantine law, to become coruler with Alexis.

Nikon's downfall was the result not of his reforms in the Russian Orthodox Church but of his attempt to garner more power for the office of the patriarch. During the Polish conflict (1652-1655), the czar went to the front, leaving Nikon as the sole ruler. The patriarch acted as an autocrat, becoming repressive and domineering toward everyone, including the czar's wife, the boyars, and influential monastic leaders. Nikon acted as both czar and patriarch, no longer concerned with the separate spheres of power defined in Byzantine law. He condemned boyars and church leaders alike whenever they opposed his ideas. By 1655, the reformers with whom Nikon had associated in the 1640's disassociated themselves from his policies, which were more radical than they were prepared to support. The czar, growing older, preferred increas-

ingly to rule on his own. A crisis between the two men emerged and sharpened. When Alexis stopped attending church services, Nikon retreated to the Voskresenskii Monastery he had built outside Moscow. He vowed not to set foot in Moscow until the czar declared confidence in him and his reforms. Eight years later, Nikon returned to the nation's capital but not in the glory he dreamed. He was brought before a church council, stripped of his title, and sent to a monastery in the north. In 1681, Nikon died on his way back to Moscow after having received a partial pardon from the czar.

SIGNIFICANCE

Nikon attempted to elevate the office of Russian patriarch to the same height as that held by the Byzantine patriarch in the original Orthodox Church that had converted the Ukraine and Russia after 988. He worked throughout his career as metropolitan and patriarch to duplicate within the Russian state the splendor and pomp of the Byzantine Empire, in which religion and politics were so intimately linked. Nikon believed that Russia was the true inheritor of the glories of Constantinople. All of his programs of reform were aimed at creating a Russian state in which the religious sphere would be equal to the secular sphere in all matters. The conflict that resulted between church and state was ended in 1701, when Peter the Great declared that he was secular head of the church and replaced the office of patriarch with a Holy Synod, a group of officials appointed by the czar to make church decisions.

Although a failure in the realm of politics, Nikon was successful in the area of church reform. The changes he introduced in church texts and worship services were to have lasting importance. In the short run, the Church Council of 1666 found in favor of Nikon's religious reforms, while condemning his political aspirations. It upheld and mandated his religious modifications, which were then given the force of law by the czar. Yet the practice of generations was not so easily discarded. Led by the archpriest Avvakum Petrovich, many devout Russians refused to adopt the revolutionary religious laws. The resulting break is known as the great schism. The dissenters contravened state law and thus rejected not only the authority of the church but also that of the czar. The Russian traditionalists viewed Nikon's reforms as Western impositions—foreign impurities thrust upon the pure faith of Russia. Nikon himself was condemned by them as the Antichrist. Avvakum's supporters, known as the Old Believers, were ruthlessly persecuted as religious heretics and dangerous political subversives.

Nikon's religious reforms thus led to a serious split and to a conflict that provokes discussion in Russian Orthodox circles into the twenty-first century. The political objectives sought by the Russian patriarch between 1652 and 1658, when he was head of the church and coruler with Alexis, resulted in the firm subordination of the church to the state, which characterized relations between the two until the Bolshevik Revolution of 1917.

—Linnea Goodwin Burwood

FURTHER READING

Baron, Samuel H., and Nancy Shields Kollman, eds. *Religion and Culture in Early Modern Russia and Ukraine*. De Kalb: Northern Illinois University Press, 1995. A collection that examines seventeenth century church history; articles created during a workshop about early eastern Slavic culture held at Stanford University in 1993.

Billington, James H. *The Icon and the Axe: An Interpretive History of Russian Culture*. New York: Alfred A. Knopf, 1966. Section 3, "The Century of Schism," is not only a detailed account of Nikon's historical role but also an excellent source for discussion of the religious and social debates of seventeenth century Russian history.

Bushkovitch, Paul. *Religion and Society in Russia: The Sixteenth and Seventeenth Centuries*. New York: Oxford University Press, 1992. Bushkovitch explains the fundamental changes that took place in the Russian Orthodox Church, describing how these changes were influenced by Western European ideas and how they eventually led to Peter the Great's secularization of Russia.

Kluchevsky, V. O. *A History of Russia*. Vol. 3. Translated by C. J. Hogarth. Reprint. New York: Russell & Russell, 1960. The second half of this volume explains Nikon's reforms and the reasons for the great schism. Kluchevsky examines the roots of the notion that Moscow is the inheritor of Byzantium and the in- cipient problems this notion created for the Moscow state.

Luprinin, Nickolas. *Religious Revolt in the Seventeenth Century: The Schism of the Russian Church*. Princeton, N.J.: Kingston Press, 1985. Recounts Nikon's reforms and other events leading to the great schism.

Meyendorff, Paul. *Russia, Ritual, and Reform: The Liturgical Reforms of Nikon in the Seventeenth Century*. Crestwood, N.Y.: St. Vladimir's Seminary Press, 1991. Historical overview of the events and people of the reforms. Meyendorff argues the reforms were initiated not by Nikon but by the czar.

Miliukov, Paul, Charles Seignobos, and L. Eisenmann. *From the Beginnings to the Empire of Peter the Great*. Vol. 1 in *History of Russia*. Translated by Charles Lam Markmann. New York: Funk & Wagnalls, 1968. Essays written before Miliukov became leader of the Cadet Party in 1905. Although Miliukov wrote about Nikon, his work discusses the Nikonian reforms as preparation for the later reforms of Peter the Great.

Vernadsky, George. *The Tsardom of Moscow, 1547-1682*. Vol. 2. New Haven, Conn.: Yale University Press, 1969. An excellent source for Nikon's activities as metropolitan and patriarch, with more information on Nikon's contemporaries than other sources. The conclusions about Nikon's impact on Russian history are tied to Vernadsky's prejudice that Russia was a copy of the Byzantine state.

SEE ALSO: Alexis; Avvakum Petrovich; Boris Morozov; Michael Romanov.

RELATED ARTICLES in *Great Events from History: The Seventeenth Century, 1601-1700:* 1632-1667: Polish-Russian Wars for the Ukraine; January 29, 1649: Codification of Russian Serfdom; 1652-1667: Patriarch Nikon's Reforms; April, 1667-June, 1671: Razin Leads Peasant Uprising in Russia; 1672-c. 1691: Self-Immolation of the Old Believers; Beginning 1689: Reforms of Peter the Great.

NJINGA
Queen of Angola (r. 1624-1663)

Through military force, diplomatic cunning, and political manipulation, Njinga successfully resisted Portuguese occupation of central Angola for more than four decades. The first woman ruler of the Mbundu people, she was queen of Ngongo and Mbanda, historic states of modern Angola, and she has become a symbol of indigenous resistance to colonial and foreign control of Angola's extensive natural resources.

BORN: 1582; Ndongo (now in Angola)
DIED: December 17, 1663; Matamba (now in Angola)
ALSO KNOWN AS: Nzinga; Dona Ana de Sousa; Ana de Souza; Zhinga; N'Zhinga; Jinga; Ngola Ana Nzinga Mbande
AREA OF ACHIEVEMENT: Government and politics

EARLY LIFE

Njinga (n-JIHN-guh) grew up in the royal household of the Mbundu people in what today is northern Angola. ("Njinga" is the current official spelling, in accord with the post-1980 orthographic reform of the Kimbundu language by the Angolan government, of the name previously spelled "Nzinga.") The Mbundu lands stretched from the Atlantic coast in the west to the Kwango River in the eastern highlands and from the Dande River in the north to the Kwanza River in the south. The western part of the region, where Njinga was born, was the kingdom of Ndongo; an eastern section, Mbamba, had been an early homeland of the Mbundu. Njinga's father was Ngola Kiluanji, *ngola* being the word for "king" in Kimbundu, the Mbundus' native language. Ngola Kiluanji ruled the kingdom of Ndongo. Njinga's mother, however, was descended from slaves and therefore had no blood ties to the hierarchy of landed chieftains. When Ngola Kiluanji died in 1617, one of his sons succeeded him as Ngola Mbandi. Mbandi had murdered any males who might compete with him for the succession, including a son of Princess Njinga.

Several years before Njinga's birth, the Portuguese began settling south of the Congo River, first occupying the island of Luanda, off the coast of Ndongo territory, then moving up the fertile Kwanza River Valley, seeking gold and slaves. Slaves were in particular demand to supply labor for Portugal's wealthy sugar plantations in Brazil. The Portuguese established Luanda as a slave post. They traded for captives with the Ngolo king and any local chieftains. Penetrating Mbundu territory with troops and missionaries, they named the region Angola, because its people and territory were viewed as the domain of the *ngola*.

LIFE'S WORK

As the Portuguese advanced into the heart of Ndongo territory, they threatened the royal capital, as well as the Ndongo monopoly on trade and slaving routes across the region. To thwart or manipulate this advance, Njinga arrived in Luanda in 1621, presenting herself to the Portuguese governor as an emissary of her half brother, Ngola Mbandi.

Njinga had seen herself as a rival to succeed Mbandi to the throne, believing she could better exercise power and determine and protect Ndongo's interests. Mbundu tradition, however, prohibited women from ruling the kingdom. To help convince the Portuguese to support her bid for the throne, Njinga was baptized in 1622 and agreed to allow Portuguese missionaries and slavers to enter Ndongo. Taking the Christian name Ana, she assumed the surname of the governor of Luanda, de Sousa. Because Portuguese women bore the title of Dona, Princess Njinga of Ndongo became known as Dona Ana de Sousa. She was not, however, submissive to the Portuguese. At her first interview with the governor, knowing she would not be provided a chair, she had one of her maidservants bend over and sat on her back.

By 1624, Mbandi was dead, mysteriously murdered, and Njinga ruled the kingdom. Officially, she was regent for Mbandi's young son, her nephew, because, as a woman, she was hesitant directly to announce herself as monarch. The Portuguese did not accept Njinga as queen of Ndongo any more than the traditional nobility of her kingdom did. Portugal eventually supported a candidate to the succession whose aristocratic lineage was more acceptable and who could thereby prove more useful and malleable to their colonial interests. Outraged by what she saw as Portugal's betrayal, Njinga renounced her Christianity and, formally asserting herself as queen of Ndongo, assembled a resistance force made up of fugitive Portuguese slaves, marginalized members of the Ndongo court, and mercenary warrior bands.

The mercenaries were known as the Imbangala, refugees from drought and from slave raids in central Africa. They had settled along the southern and eastern frontiers of Mbundu territory and sometimes were also identified with Jaga tribesmen. With these forces in her command, Njinga, sometimes styled the Jaga Queen, withdrew up the Kwanza River Valley. Eventually, she and what remained of her followers settled on a high plain in Mbamba territory, resisting and harassing the Portuguese through guerrilla warfare.

From her remote fortified capital, Njinga established her own base for slave trading. During the 1630's, Njinga, now the ruler of Mbamba, expanded into Portuguese-held Ndongo. Her position was further strengthened in the following decade, when the Dutch occupied Luanda. They supported her resistance to the Portuguese, whom she besieged in the Kwanza Valley, and they were ardent clients for her slave trade, because they needed slaves for their own plantation colonies.

Ever sensitive, however, that being a woman undermined her power, Njinga declared herself to be a man and refused to be addressed as "queen," only as "king." She kept as consorts men who were required to dress as women, and she trained her ladies-in-waiting as warriors. She personally led battles and guerrilla raids against the Portuguese.

However, in 1648, the Portuguese expelled the Dutch and reasserted their authority in Angola. Aware of her vulnerability, Njinga attempted to mollify the Portuguese by returning to Christianity. She signed a treaty with them in 1656 that allowed missionaries and representatives of Portuguese trade and government to reside in her capital. She calculated or hoped that having individual Portuguese citizens in her midst, dependent on her for their lives, might be a final strategy to control or repel Portugal's forces if necessary. Although still vigorous enough in 1658 to once again marry, Njinga died in 1663 at the age of eighty-one.

The exceptional historical record that exists for Njinga is due to documents she left behind and to the missionaries who resided at her court in her final years. They frequently interviewed her and chronicled the events of her reign. At her court, she often dressed in the high fashion of Baroque Europe and employed many seamstresses to outfit her in the latest European style. She used royal jewels, including a semispherical, arched crown similar to that of a European monarch, and spoke and wrote fluent Portuguese.

SIGNIFICANCE

Njinga occupies a unique role in early modern Angolan and sub-Saharan African history. For more than four decades in the mid-seventeenth century, she effectively blocked the intrusion into west central Angola of Portuguese colonists, who were attempting to control the region's slave trade. She sustained this trade herself as an economic and political interest for herself and her supporters and effectively established among the Mbundu the practice of female rulership.

Angolan resistance to Portuguese penetration of the country's interior withered, however, after Njinga's death. Although several queens succeeded Njinga, they were all controlled by Portuguese missionaries and governors, who became the primary beneficiaries of the ever-expanding slave trade.

Njinga is often recognized as a heroine of resistance to colonial repression of native African peoples. Nonetheless, although the historical record demonstrates her astuteness and tenacity, it also reveals the extent to which she profited from and was complicit with the colonial institution of slavery. She represents an historical pattern in which marginalized members of an elite challenge established members for rule: To strengthen that challenge, they may ally themselves with outside forces. When opposed, they maintain a persistent resistance. However, over time, they are compromised and absorbed by a power system they wish not so much to eliminate as to placate, profit from, or dominate.

—Edward A. Riedinger

FURTHER READING

Curto, José C. *Enslaving Spirits: The Portuguese-Brazilian Alcohol Trade at Luanda and Its Hinterland, c. 1550-1830.* Leiden, the Netherlands: Brill, 2004. Analyzes Portuguese economic interests in southwest Africa and commercial and sociopolitical consequences in Mbundu territory.

Miller, Joseph Calder. *Kings and Kinsmen: Early Mbundu States in Angola.* Oxford, England: Clarendon Press, 1976. Examines conditions of stability among Mbundu political entities in the sixteenth and seventeenth centuries as territory was wracked by external invasion and internal divisions.

_____. "Njinga of Matamba in a New Perspective." *Journal of African History* 16, no. 2 (1975): 201-216. Original analysis of the objectives, assumptions, tactics, and effectiveness of Njinga in claiming and occupying the rulership of Ndongo and Mbamba.

Schwarz-Bart, Simone. "Ana de Sousa Nzinga: The Queen Who Resisted the Portuguese Conquest." In *Ancient African Queens.* Vol. 1 in *In Praise of Black Women.* Madison: University of Wisconsin Press, 2001. Reviews the life of Njinga as an early Angolan heroine of anticolonialist resistance.

Skidmore-Hess, Cathy. *Queen Njinga, 1582-1663: Ritual, Power, and Gender in the Life of a Precolonial African Ruler.* Unpublished doctoral dissertation. University of Wisconsin-Madison, 1995. Consolidates and reassesses research of the previous generation of Africanist scholars on Njinga.

Thornton, John K. "Legitimacy and Political Power: Queen Njinga, 1624-1663." *Journal of African History* 32, no. 1 (1991): 25-40. Offers a detailed examination of the constitutional and historical claims of Njinga to rule Ngongo as queen.

SEE ALSO: John IV; Philip IV.
RELATED ARTICLES in *Great Events from History: The Seventeenth Century, 1601-1700:* 1619-c. 1700: The Middle Passage to American Slavery; August 26, 1641-September, 1648: Conquest of Luanda; 1644-1671: Ndongo Wars.

REBECCA NURSE
English-born American colonist

Nurse was tried and executed for the crime of witchcraft at the age of seventy-one. Because she was so obviously innocent and saintly, her hanging came to symbolize the hysteria, intolerance, and injustice of the Salem witchcraft trials.

BORN: February 21, 1621 (baptized); Great Yarmouth, Norfolk, England
DIED: July 19, 1692; Salem Village (now Danvers), Massachusetts
ALSO KNOWN AS: Rebecca Towne (given name)
AREAS OF ACHIEVEMENT: Law, women's rights

EARLY LIFE

Rebecca Nurse was baptized Rebecca Towne on February 21, 1621, in Great Yarmouth, England. Her parents, William Towne and Joanna Blessing, had married on April 20, 1620, in Saint Nicholas Church in Great Yarmouth. Rebecca was the oldest of eight children. Her siblings Mary, John, Susanna, Edmund, and Jacob Towne were all born and baptized in England. In about 1635, the family emigrated to America and settled in Topsfield, Essex County, Massachusetts. By 1639, they had moved to nearby Salem Town, where the two youngest children, Joseph and Sarah, were born. Her sisters Mary and Sarah would also be accused at the Salem witch trials.

Little is known specifically about Rebecca's early life. Her parents are known to have been farmers, and in colonial times, parents generally taught their children the skills they would need as adults. Rebecca and her sisters would have learned how to cook, sew, make soap, make candles, and clean the house. As the oldest child, Rebecca would have cared for the younger children and helped manage the household. Girls received a domestic education to prepare them to be proper wives. Rebecca's brothers would have helped with the farming. Church attendance, Bible study, and prayer would have been regular family activities.

LIFE'S WORK

In 1645, Rebecca Towne married Francis Nurse, who had been born on January 18, 1618, in Great Yarmouth, the same English town Rebecca was from. Francis was a skilled artisan who made trays and other household items. They settled near the North River in Salem and had eight children: John (born c. 1645), Rebecca (born in 1647), Sarah (born in 1648), Samuel (born in 1649), Mary (born in 1655), Elizabeth (born in 1656 or 1657), Francis (born in 1660 or 1661), and Benjamin (born in 1665 or 1666). In 1672, Francis served as the constable of Salem Town. He had a reputation for fair judgment in resolving disputes.

In the 1630's, a group of farmers had established Salem Village, five miles (eight kilometers) from Salem Town. In the 1660's, they petitioned for independence and became a separate parish by 1672. On April 29, 1678, Francis Nurse acquired the valuable Bishop farm in Salem Village. Townsend Bishop had originally received the grant for the 300-acre (121-hectare) farm in 1636. James Allen, who owned the property in 1678, rented it to Nurse, who had the option to purchase the land after twenty years. The Nurse family worked the farm and became prosperous. Of their four daughters, only Sarah remained unmarried. Rebecca married Thomas Preston, Mary married John Tarbell, and Elizabeth married William Russell.

In 1689, the Reverend Samuel Parris became the minister of the Salem Village Church. Nurse retained her membership at the Salem Town church but worshiped at the Salem Village church. During 1690-1691, partisan tensions and conflict mounted between the two churches.

Suddenly, in January, 1692, three young girls had inexplicable fits. In February, the three girls, the Reverend Parris's daughter Elizabeth, Abigail Williams, and Ann Putnam, were examined by William Griggs, the local physician. Griggs concluded that possession by the devil had caused the young girls' ailment. Under pressure to explain, the girls finally accused Sarah Good, Sarah Osburn, and Parris's slave Tituba of being witches who had visited them in spectral form.

On March 1, 1692, as magistrates questioned the accused women at the Meeting House, the young girls had fits again, and the three women were charged with witchcraft and jailed. Soon, more villagers, including adults, claimed to be afflicted, and more people were accused.

On March 13, 1692, Ann Putnam identified Rebecca Nurse as one of her spectral tormentors. On March 19, Abigail Williams accused Nurse as well. On March 23, acting on a complaint by John and Edward Putnam, constables arrested Nurse in her bedroom. There had been numerous land disputes between the Putnams and the Nurses in the past. At the time of her arrest, Nurse was a venerable, seventy-year-old grandmother, respected by her fellow Puritans as a devout and kind person. She was also frail, bedridden, and partially deaf.

The hysteria escalated so rapidly that by May, there were about 150 accused men and women in jail on suspicion of witchcraft. Nurse was forced to submit to a physical examination for a "mark of the devil" on her skin. Although Nurse declared her innocence and the exam was inconclusive, she was tried on June 29, 1692. The jury returned a verdict of not guilty, but the afflicted girls went into violent fits again. When questioned about a comment by another accused woman, Nurse was too deaf to hear the question. She did not answer, so the presiding judge, Chief Justice William Stoughton, asked the jury to reconsider the testimony. The jury then decided on a guilty verdict, and Nurse was sentenced to death.

On July 3, Nurse was excommunicated from her church in Salem Town. Many people became outraged at the court's verdict. On July 4, 1692, thirty-nine prominent community members signed a petition on her behalf. Her family went to Boston and presented the petition to Governor William Phips, who granted a reprieve. However, on July 12, Justice Stoughton signed a warrant for execution. On July 19, 1692, Rebecca Nurse, her sister-in-law Elizabeth Howe, Sarah Wildes, Susannah Martin, and Sarah Good were hanged for witchcraft. Her husband and other family members retrieved her body from the common grave and buried her at their homestead.

Nurse's execution led to the first public protests against the trials and their use of supernatural evidence. In October, Governor Phips disbanded the original witchcraft court and replaced it with the Superior Court of Judicature, which disallowed spectral evidence. Consequently, prisoners awaiting trial were released and those awaiting execution were pardoned. The Salem witch trials had ended, but eighteen people had been executed by hanging, at least five had died in jail, and one had been tortured to death.

In 1711, the government made restitution to the Nurse family for Rebecca's wrongful death. On March 6, 1712, the Salem Town church overturned Nurse's excommunication. In 1885, a monument was erected as a memorial to Nurse.

SIGNIFICANCE

Nurse became the most famous and the most iconic victim of the Salem witch trials. Those tragic trials demonstrated the need for reform in the colonial American legal system. The trials' victims were convicted, imprisoned, and executed based on spectral evidence, hysteria, and hearsay. Contrary to legal practice today, the Salem defendants had no legal counsel, they were not considered innocent until proven guilty, judges were biased, and guilty verdicts were not based on evidence of guilt "beyond a reasonable doubt." The execution of Nurse, the most obviously innocent of those convicted, became the impetus for the end of the trials and the reform of the courts.

Today, 27 acres (11 hectares) of the Nurse property and the saltbox home they lived in have been historically preserved as The Rebecca Nurse Homestead in Danvers, Massachusetts. The property has been used in numerous films, including *Three Sovereigns for Sarah*, a 1985 film about Sarah Cloyce, Rebecca Nurse's sister. Sarah and another sister, Mary Esty, were also accused of witchcraft, but Sarah escaped execution and worked to clear the names of her sisters. Her efforts demonstrated that land disputes and other economic factors were the underlying causes of the Salem witch hysteria. Nurse herself has remained an iconic figure representing the innocence of all those falsely accused in the Salem trials. She has been portrayed sympathetically in such works as Arthur Miller's play *The Crucible* (pr., pb. 1953) and the CBS television miniseries *Salem Witch Trials* (2003).

—*Alice Myers*

FURTHER READING

Hill, Frances. *A Delusion of Satan: The Full Story of the Salem Witch Trials*. New York: Doubleday, 1995. Includes well-researched discussions of Rebecca Nurse throughout the book. Illustrated. Bibliography and chapter notes.

_____. *The Salem Witch Trials Reader*. Cambridge, Mass.: Da Capo Press, 2000. An excellent sourcebook with period works, actual documents from the trial, personal eyewitness accounts, and subsequent fiction and nonfiction works. Bibliography, index.

Hoffer, Peter Charles. *The Salem Witchcraft Trials: A Legal History*. Lawrence: University Press of Kansas, 1997. A scholarly, concise history written for students and the general reader, this volume shows clearly how many modern legal rights did not exist in colonial times. Much of the narrative concerns Rebecca Nurse. Chronology and bibliographic essay.

Norton, Mary Beth. *In the Devil's Snare: The Salem Witchcraft Crisis of 1692*. New York: Alfred A. Knopf, 2002. A scholarly, comprehensive study of the Salem witchcraft trials, with numerous sections on Rebecca Nurse. Extensive notes and appendices.

Roach, Marilynne K. *The Salem Witch Trials: A Day-by-Day Chronicle of a Community Under Siege*. New York: Cooper Square Press, 2002. A detailed day-by-day narrative of events from January 1, 1692, through January 14, 1697. An epilogue discusses the aftermath of the trials through 2001. Extensive chapter notes and bibliography. Illustrated, with drawings, maps, and photos. Appendices and index.

Schuetz, Janice. *The Logic of Women on Trial: Case Studies of Popular American Trials*. Carbondale: Southern Illinois University Press, 1994. Based on trial records and other primary sources, this book examines the significance of gender and social and historical context in the felony trials of nine American women, including Rebecca Nurse. Bibliography.

Tapley, Charles Sutherland. *Rebecca Nurse: Saint but Witch Victim*. Boston: Marshall Jones, 1930. The complete biography of Rebecca Nurse, including chapters on the Nurse homestead, the monument, and her descendants. Illustrated.

SEE ALSO: William Bradford; Anne Bradstreet; Margaret Brent; John Cotton; Anne Hutchinson; John Winthrop.

RELATED ARTICLES in *Great Events from History: The Seventeenth Century, 1601-1700:* May, 1630-1643: Great Puritan Migration; June 2, 1692-May, 1693: Salem Witchcraft Trials.

TITUS OATES
English priest and dissembler

A miscreant throughout his life, Oates fabricated a conspiracy by Catholics to murder King Charles II and replace him on the throne with his Catholic brother, James. False reports of this nonexistent conspiracy, known as the Popish Plot, caused an anti-Catholic frenzy to sweep England.

BORN: September 15, 1649; Oakham, Rutland, England
DIED: July 12 or 13, 1705; London, England
AREA OF ACHIEVEMENT: Government and politics

EARLY LIFE

Born in Oakham, Titus Oates was the son of Samuel Oates, a Baptist preacher who later became an Anglican and served as a rector in Norfolk and as a chaplain in Colonel Thomas Pride's regiment, a position from which he was dismissed in 1654 for seditious activity. The name of Oates's mother is not known, and she had little influence on her husband or her son.

From early in his life, Oates revealed a tendency toward unprincipled behavior. The first school he entered in 1665 expelled him within one year. He eventually passed through Sedlescombe School in Hastings and matriculated at Caius College, Cambridge University. In 1669, he moved to Saint John's College, where his father, now employed by the college, baptized him into the Anglican faith. Oates was such a poor student that his Cambridge tutor once described him as "a great dunce." He left Cambridge without a degree.

Despite his failure as a student and his questionable character, in 1673 Oates became a vicar of Bobbing Church in Kent, and in 1674 he became a curate to his father at All Saints Church in Hastings. Within a year, both father and son were tossed out after committing various slanders. For his lies about parishioners, Oates was sent to jail. While still imprisoned, he was indicted for perjury. He escaped and went to London. Shortly thereafter, he became chaplain on a king's ship but was promptly dismissed for misbehavior. He then became chaplain to the Protestants in the Catholic household of Henry Howard, duke of Norfolk. While in this position, Oates made many Catholic acquaintances and began to regularly appear in Catholic coffeehouses.

In 1676, the virulently anti-Catholic Israel Tonge, rector of Saint Mary's Church in Staining, began to regale Oates about his conviction that Catholics (especially Jesuits) were planning a massacre of Protestants in England. He asked Oates to ingratiate himself with his Catholic connections and then report any subversive activities to the appropriate authorities. Oates willingly assisted, not from any belief that Tonge was right, but because such an escapade suited his love of intrigue and talent for mendacity.

Oates pursued the plan by professing his conversion to Catholicism in 1677. He then entered a Catholic seminary in Valladolid, Spain, only to be thrown out after just five months. Undaunted, he moved on to a Catholic seminary in Saint-Omer, France, from which, after six months, he also was expelled in June, 1678. By this time, he had acquired enough "evidence" of a Catholic conspiracy to feed Tonge's rampant paranoia. They set about, between June and August of 1678, to fabricate the Popish Plot that would guarantee them, especially Oates, infamous immortality.

LIFE'S WORK

Oates's endeavors can scarcely be described as a positive contribution to England's politics and society. The Popish Plot that he helped invent in the summer of 1678 led to a reign of terror against supposed Catholic conspirators that resulted in the execution of thirty-five people. Most of them died as a consequence of testimony given by Oates. Relations between Anglicans and Catholics, already tense and prone to violence in the 1670's, were further poisoned by the hysteria Oates created.

As constructed by Oates and Tonge, the Popish Plot was a scheme to kill Charles II and place his Catholic brother, James, duke of York (later James II), on the English throne. Eventually, as Oates found it necessary to expand the conspiracy from time to time, Charles II's Catholic wife, Catherine, and her physician were implicated. The nature of the "plot" was revealed to the king as he strolled through Saint James's Park by Christopher Kirkby, a Lancashire gentleman who had been given a written account of the "conspiracy" by Oates. To his credit, the king never believed the tale. Later, after he questioned Oates directly, Charles II became convinced the plot was all nonsense.

The first public revelation of the Popish Plot came when Oates and Tonge appeared before a London justice of the peace, Sir Edmund Berry Godfrey, and told their story. Shortly thereafter, Godfrey was found murdered, a sword in his back. The circumstances of his murder were never learned, but Oates seized upon it as proof that the

Catholic conspiracy existed. There followed a chorus of accusations against Catholics that did not abate for two years. It was during this time that many Catholic "suspects" were put to death.

In the autumn of 1678, the House of Commons contributed to the panic by listening to "conclusive evidence" provided by a number of street people primed by Oates. The Commons impeached Catholic peers and strengthened existing anti-Catholic legislation. Members of Parliament were predisposed to believe conspiracy stories after learning, in 1672, of the secret Treaty of Dover that Charles II had signed in 1670 with French king Louis XIV, who was married to Charles's sister, Henrietta. By terms of the agreement, Charles II proclaimed that he was at heart a Catholic and would announce his conversion at an appropriate time. In return, Louis XIV promised to send Charles an annual subsidy. To show his good faith, Charles II, in 1672, suspended all penal laws against Catholics and other non-Anglicans. Raging with anti-French and anti-Catholic sentiment, the Commons passed the Test Act in 1673, which, in effect, prevented any Roman Catholic, including the king's brother, from holding office.

The fact that Charles II had not yet announced his conversion to Catholicism by 1678 seemed, in the parliamentarians' convoluted thinking, circumstantial evidence for Oates's fantastic assertions. It was surmised that Catholics had decided not to wait any longer. When the king realized that members intended to pursue charges against his chief adviser, Thomas Osborne, earl of Danby, and against Queen Catherine, he dissolved Parliament in January, 1679.

The political fallout from Oates's accusations now threatened the succession. The new Parliament elected in February, 1679, imprisoned Danby and introduced an exclusion bill to keep James from the throne. Charles II dissolved this Parliament in the summer of 1679 and sent James into temporary exile for protection. Subsequent Parliaments, in 1680 and 1681, continued to press for the exclusion of James. Various factions supported either Mary, James's Protestant daughter, or James Scott, duke of Monmouth, who was Charles II's illegitimate Protestant son. There was, however, no agreement on which of these two should succeed Charles II.

The most dogged and violent opponent of the succession was Anthony Ashley Cooper, earl of Shaftesbury, who pushed the candidacy of Charles II's illegitimate son. The king preempted this effort by declaring officially that the duke of Monmouth was illegitimate. Aside from Shaftesbury and his followers (by this time known as Whigs), Monmouth's support was so limited that he could not have taken the throne. The last serious attempt to pass an exclusion bill came in the 1681 Parliament. This Parliament, which met in Oxford, revealed severe hatreds and divisions, and it appeared to many that England again was heading for civil war. This fear brought a reaction in favor of Charles II and the duke of York and against those who seemed intent on undermining the Stuart monarchy.

Through most of this time, Oates was perceived as a hero and a celebrity. Tradesmen sold Oates fans, matchbooks, cookies, and hats. It was not until the second half of 1680 that the mania for Oates began to fade. This occurred mostly because the king was still alive and no obvious attempt had been made on his life.

Nineteenth century depiction of Titus Oates in a pillory for falsely accusing James, duke of York, of participating in a plot to assassinate Charles II. (Library of Congress)

When the furor had subsided, Oates was taken to court by the duke of York, and in June, 1684, the duke was awarded a large judgment that Oates could not pay. In 1685, after James had succeeded his brother (who died unexpectedly from a stroke), Oates was convicted of perjury and sent to prison after being flogged. He emerged from prison in 1688 to find himself again something of a hero. Opinion had turned in his favor as a result of James's ill-advised attempt, often violently pursued, to re-Catholicize England. The news, in 1688, that the queen had given birth to a Catholic heir led Parliament to invite Mary, James's Protestant daughter, and her husband, William III, stadtholder of the Netherlands, to come to England and restore the Anglican monarchy. Their successful campaign, aided by the decision of James to abdicate, is known as the Glorious Revolution. After William III and Mary II were established as Crowned Heads, the House of Commons voted to grant Oates an annual pension. Oates did not deserve such a recognition, but anti-Catholic sentiments again were at a fever pitch.

Oates lived out the remainder of his life in relative obscurity but not without controversy. In 1693, he became a Baptist, returning to the original church of his father. His behavior had not improved, and he was expelled by the Baptists in 1701 for spreading blatant lies. He died in London on July 12 or 13, 1705.

SIGNIFICANCE

Through his fabrication of the Popish Plot, Oates preyed upon the dangerous anti-Catholic and antipapal strains so alive in England during the 1670's. Although his cohort, Israel Tonge, may genuinely have believed in the existence of a plot to murder Charles II, Oates did not. He participated in the great lie for the excitement and perhaps for the adulation he knew it would engender. The Popish Plot built on already existing fears, confirming, expanding, and intensifying them. It guaranteed that anti-Catholicism would be the dominant theme in English politics for the remainder of the seventeenth century.

James II's controversial reign seemed to prove to Protestants in England that even if the Popish Plot had never existed, it was reasonable to think that Catholics would stop at nothing to bring England back within the Church of Rome. Although the reign of William and Mary relieved much of the pressure on Catholics, parliamentary leaders were determined to prevent the Crown from ever again falling to a Catholic. The 1701 Act of Settlement provided that future English monarchs must be members of the Church of England. The act also further limited the power of the Crowned Head in relation to Parliament. Oates, sinister reprobate that he was, had made his contribution to this major constitutional development.

—*Ronald K. Huch*

FURTHER READING

Bryant, Arthur. *King Charles II*. London: Longmans, Green, 1931. Reprint. London: House of Stratus, 2001. A pleasant melding of a popular writing style with respectable scholarship. Bryant's work, though dated in some ways, is fundamentally reliable. Discusses Titus Oates in the context of Charles II's reign. Includes notes, bibliography, and index.

Greaves, Richard L. *Secrets of the Kingdom: British Radicals from the Popish Plot to the Revolution of 1688-1689*. Stanford, Calif.: Stanford University Press, 1992. The book, one of three Greaves has written about radicalism in seventeenth-century England, focuses on the events of 1688-1689.

Hibbard, Caroline M. *Charles I and the Popish Plot*. Chapel Hill: University of North Carolina Press, 1983. Based on extensive research of manuscript sources, Hibbard examines what she terms "political antipopery and court Catholicism" in England from 1637 to 1642.

Hill, Christopher. *The Century of Revolution, 1603-1714*. 1961. Reprint. New York: Norton, 1982. An account of tumultuous seventeenth century politics by a distinguished Marxist historian. It contains extensive coverage of the Popish Plot and its impact. There is an index and a list of books for further reading.

Kenyon, J. P. *The Popish Plot*. London: Heineman, 1972. Reprint. London: Phoenix Press, 2000. A carefully researched, scholarly, and highly readable account of the events involving Titus Oates. Emphasizes the impact of the Popish Plot on Catholics in England after 1678. Includes notes, bibliography, and index. Recommended for all readers.

Miller, John L. *Popery and Politics in England, 1660-1688*. Cambridge, England: Cambridge University Press, 1973. Focuses on the development of an anti-Catholic political tradition in England. Miller argues that antipopery was the major political factor in late seventeenth century England. Written for advanced undergraduates and scholars, it contains notes, bibliography, appendices, and index.

Ogg, David. *England in the Reign of Charles II*. 1934. 2d ed. Westport, Conn.: Greenwood Press, 1979. Ogg covers the Titus Oates affair, placing it in the context of Charles II's monarchy. Although somewhat dated, this remains a useful introduction to the king's many

Ogata Kōrin

problems in the 1670's. There are footnotes, a bibliography, and an index.

Pollock, Sir John. *The Popish Plot.* 1903. Rev. ed. Cambridge, England: Cambridge University Press, 1944. Pollock, a lawyer, allows his anti-Catholic bias to seep into his account, which is therefore considered unreliable. His work, however, did inspire others to study Titus Oates and the Popish Plot more closely.

SEE ALSO: Charles II (of England); James II; Mary II; Thomas Pride; First Earl of Shaftesbury; William III.

RELATED ARTICLES in *Great Events from History: The Seventeenth Century, 1601-1700:* August 13, 1678-July 1, 1681: The Popish Plot; 1688-1702: Reign of William and Mary; November, 1688-February, 1689: The Glorious Revolution.

OGATA KŌRIN
Japanese painter

Kōrin worked within traditional Japanese aesthetic forms to produce an art of originality and universality that for many epitomizes Japanese taste. His screen of irises is one of the most widely known of all Japanese paintings.

BORN: 1658; Kyōto, Japan
DIED: 1716; Kyōto
AREA OF ACHIEVEMENT: Art

EARLY LIFE
Ogata Kōrin (oh-gah-tah koh-reen) was the son of Ogata Sōken, a wealthy textile merchant and owner of the shop called Kariganeya (Golden House of the Wild Goose), which specialized in the design and weaving of brocades. Kōrin studied painting first with his father and then with Yamamoto Sōken of the Kyōto branch of the Kanō school of painters. The Kanō school represented aristocratic taste in the era before Kōrin, and the Kariganeya's chief customers were the aristocracy and the feudal lords (daimyo). The daimyo were forced, because of court pressures, to spend enormous sums on clothing, frequently leading to their financial ruin. When the Ogata family's most important customer, the Empress Tofukumon-in, died in 1678, the Kariganeya's fortunes began to decline. The Ogata family had lost money in making loans to the daimyo, loans that proved to be uncollectable. An attempt to attract customers from the lower merchant class failed, and by 1697 family bankruptcy had resulted.

The Ogata family moved in aristocratic circles and the world of learning and the arts, while deriving its livelihood from a business establishment that called for the highest artisan designs and skills. Kōrin continually drew and sketched, studied calligraphy and garden design, and observed the processes and techniques of the textile business. He epitomized the Japanese ideal of a man of learning and refinement, an amateur of the arts, accomplished in painting, poetry, theater, and the tea ceremony. He was a *bunjin*, or man of letters, and the concept of a dilettante was a positive one.

LIFE'S WORK
When Kōrin's father, Sōken, died in 1687, he left an equal share of his still valuable property to each of his sons, Tozaburo, the eldest, who succeeded Sōken as the head of the family and the business, Kōrin, and Kenzan. For a decade, Kōrin lived the life of a wealthy heir, no definite profession being required of him. Yet the lifestyle of Kyōto's upper-middle-class merchants and artisans, intimates of the aristocracy who shared their taste for art and the Nō theater, had ended. The new rising merchant class was less artistic and mostly preoccupied with profit.

In 1697, Tozaburo left the cloth business, moved to Edo (modern Tokyo), and entered the service of a leading feudal lord. The two younger sons realized that they had to earn a living. Kōrin at first designed textiles and lacquerware, while Kenzan, who had studied with the master potter Nonomura Ninsei, began to produce pottery. Kōrin next assisted Kenzan by painting designs on his brother's pottery, a collaboration of great artistic harmony. Kenzan is renowned today as one of the most important potters in the history of Japanese art.

The greatest influence on Kōrin's mature style was the work of another pair of collaborators: Honami Kōetsu, a calligrapher and maker of raku tea bowls, and Sōtatsu, head of the Tawaraya, a decorative painting atelier. It is no exaggeration to say that the Japanese consider this quartet—Kōetsu, Sōtatsu, Kōrin, and Kenzan—as representative of the pinnacle of Japanese painterly and calligraphic achievement. These four were related by family as well, and the Ogata family had a home in Takagamine village, a community of artisans founded by Kōetsu.

In 1701, Kōrin achieved the title of *hokkyo*, an official rank of mastery in painting; by 1704, Kōrin's finances were failing, and he moved to Edo, the seat of the shogunate government, to try his luck there. In 1707, he entered the service of a daimyo, which secured for him a substantial income, but he returned to Kyōto two years later and began working with his brother Kenzan. Kenzan was forced to close his kiln in 1712. After further financial difficulties from 1713 on, Kōrin died a poor man in 1716. Yet these years of his mature style saw the completion of his two masterpieces, the *Irises* and the *Red and White Plum Blossoms*, both folding screens.

Kōrin's small ceramic wares and fan paintings, as well as his large, twelve-panel folding screens, all show the importance of calligraphy to Japanese art. His sure, crisp, swift line, revealing both elegance and energy, is related to his character; in his character, the Japanese see an expression of themselves. In his work, his calligraphic training is evident in a complex interplay of spatial relations, scale and proportion, space intervals, similarities and resemblances, repetitions, sweeping climaxes, abrupt halts, changes of direction, speed, thickness and thinness, accents and silence, and empty spaces. Kōrin used the traditional Japanese themes of "flowers and grasses," poetry, and classic secular literary works as well as Sōtatsu's composition and "wet on wet" technique, Zen "black ink" style, Kanō school drama and power, and the textile techniques of dyeing and stenciling. Continuity with the past, interpreted in a personal style, has long been a Japanese ideal.

The Japanese admire the combination of the powerful and the delicate as an expression of their belief in nonduality, as in Kōrin's *Irises* screen, where a resolution is found of the sharp aggressive leaves in the soft yielding flowers on a gold ground that is both solid and void. Expressions of the unity of humankind and nature, the macrocosm and the microcosm, permeate Kōrin's works and capture the Shinto concept of *kami*, or the inner living energy of all natural phenomena and space.

SIGNIFICANCE

The rise of the style of *ukiyo-e* ("pictures of the floating world"), with its exuberant genre painting and color woodcuts that depict the world of courtesans, Kabuki actors, and the pleasure quarters, caused the momentary eclipse of Ogata Kōrin's reputation. Eventually, however, the innate preference of the Japanese for works that combine traditional Buddhist values of nonduality and traditional Shinto values of the sacredness of all forms of natural life prevailed. It is this preference, more than any

twentieth century appreciation for bold abstract design, that lies behind the Japanese evaluation of Kōrin as central to their concept of a way of life. By the 1820's, a style of painting called Rimpa (a word meaning "school of Kōrin") had arisen largely as the result of the efforts of the painter Sakai Hōitsu, who painted in the manner of Kōrin and published books on Kōrin, making Kōrin once again well known.

—*Karl Lunde*

FURTHER READING

Elisseeff, Danielle, and Vadime Elisseeff. *Art of Japan*. New York: Harry N. Abrams, 1985. A general survey in the Abrams series, very well illustrated, with a section on Kōrin.

Grilli, Elise. *The Art of the Japanese Screen*. New York: John Weatherhill, 1970. A history and analysis of the Japanese screen as well as a study of key artists and examples. The large color details are exceptional, and Grilli's compositional and formal analyses of the works are uniquely perceptive.

Leach, Bernard. *Kenzan and His Tradition: The Lives and Times of Kōetsu, Sōtatsu, Kōrin, and Kenzan*. New York: Transatlantic Arts, 1967. An informative study, with translations of many original documents, by a writer who is himself a master potter. The author's insight gives his remarks on Kenzan special meaning, and his consideration of Kōrin is also acute.

Lillehoj, Elizabeth, ed. *Critical Perspectives on Classicism in Japanese Painting, 1600-1700*. Honolulu: University of Hawaii Press, 2004. Includes an essay on Kōrin and Sōtatsu and their patrons as well as a biographical list of seventeenth century Japanese artists.

Link, Howard, and Toru Shimbo, eds. and comps. *Exquisite Visions: Rimpa Paintings from Japan*. Honolulu: Honolulu Academy of Arts, 1980. A catalog of the exhibition shown at the Honolulu Academy of Arts in the fall of 1980 and at Japan House Gallery in the winter of 1980-1981. An extensive discussion of the Rimpa style and its followers.

Mizuo, Hiroshi. *Edo Painting: Sōtatsu and Kōrin*. New York: John Weatherhill, 1972. A study of the four principal artists of the Rimpa style—Kōetsu, Sōtatsu, Kōrin, and Kenzan—with fine illustrations. Mizuo, however, overemphasizes the dubious concept that the Rimpa style was a kind of quiet artistic rebellion against the crudity of the shogunate and *chōnin* tastes. Instead, the daimyo taste encompassed both *bu* and *bun*, the aggressive and the aesthetic, exemplifying Asian beliefs.

Shimizu, Yoshiaki, ed. *Japan: The Shaping of Daimyo Culture, 1185-1868*. Washington, D.C.: National Gallery of Art, 1988. The catalog of an extraordinary exhibition held at the National Gallery of Art in Washington, D.C. Important for the background of this period and its clear exposition of the coexisting acceptance of warrior traditions (*bu*) and civilian arts, or the arts of peace (*bun*).

Stanley-Baker, Joan. "Azuchi-Muromachi and Edo (1573-1868)." In *Japanese Art*. London: Thames & Hudson, 1984. A brief, well-informed look at Sōtatsu, Kōetsu, and Kōrin within a broad context of three millennia of Japanese art. Especially effective in placing the Rimpa school within broader political and artistic developments of the Hideyoshi and Tokugawa eras. Illustrated.

SEE ALSO: Hishikawa Moronobu; Ihara Saikaku; Matsuo Bashō; Sōtatsu.

RELATED ARTICLE in *Great Events from History: The Seventeenth Century, 1601-1700:* 1688-1704: Genroku Era.

COUNT-DUKE OF OLIVARES
Spanish prime minister

Olivares was one of the great statesmen of seventeenth century Europe, the driving force behind the attempt to unify a Spanish nation and of a final effort in the 1620's and 1630's to maintain Spain's dominant position on the Continent and around the world.

BORN: January 6, 1587; Rome, Papal States (now in Italy)
DIED: July 22, 1645; Toro, Spain
ALSO KNOWN AS: Gaspar de Guzmán y Pimental (given name); Conde-Duque de Olivares
AREAS OF ACHIEVEMENT: Government and politics, diplomacy, patronage of the arts

EARLY LIFE
Born in the Spanish embassy in Rome and named Gaspar de Guzmán y Pimental, Olivares (oh-lee-VAH-rays) was the third son of the Spanish ambassador to Rome, Enrique de Guzmán, and María Pimental Fonseca, who was from a Castilian noble family. María died when Olivares was seven, so he was raised thereafter by his authoritarian father. They remained in Italy until 1600, when Enrique returned to Spain from his ambassadorship to Rome and Naples. With Olivares's eldest brother in line to inherit the family properties, Enrique earmarked Olivares for the Church, sending him to the University of Salamanca, where he studied canon law. His fellow students elected him rector in 1603. Both of his older brothers died unexpectedly, leaving Olivares in 1604 as heir to the family's estates and title. Three years later, in 1607, his father died, and Olivares became a count.

Eager to establish himself at court and hopeful of gaining a grandeeship, the count spent grandiosely and married his own cousin and one of Queen Margaret's ladies-in-waiting, Inés de Zúñiga y Velasco. Inés bore three children, but only daughter María survived to adulthood. Disappointed at his failure to persuade King Philip III or his chief minister, Francisco Gómez de Sandoval y Rojas, the duke of Lerma, to make him a grandee, Olivares moved to Seville, where he remained from 1607 to 1615. He held the largely honorific title of governor of the Alcázar (royal palace/fortress). These were not wasted years, however, as Olivares busied himself building one of the greatest private libraries in Europe and acting as one of Andalusia's chief patrons of the arts. He displayed great energy, and his intellectual curiosity showed in his participation in literary and philosophical circles.

LIFE'S WORK
In 1615, Olivares obtained an appointment as a member of the crown prince's chamber. This made him a figure at court, in the service of the future Philip IV, born in 1605. Olivares assiduously courted the prince, both from personal ambition and out of a desire to improve his education and capacity for government when the time came. Eager to impress the prince with his loyalty, Olivares even kissed Philip's chamber pot in a famous example of obsequiousness. The boy's frivolous father, Philip III, displayed neither ability nor interest in ruling and turned the government over to his venal royal favorite (*valido*), Lerma.

When the king died unexpectedly in 1621 and the sixteen-year-old prince rose to the throne, the count of Olivares found himself ideally placed to wield political power through his influence over Philip IV. Popular sentiment opposed the young king having his own *valido*, and Olivares and others vying for power had to proceed cautiously. Philip IV was too young, inexperienced, and inconstant, however, to govern himself. His need for assistance made Olivares more and more essential.

Olivares and Baltazar (Balthasar) de Zúñiga, his uncle and mentor, outmaneuvered their rivals for influence over Philip and surprised onlookers by their refusal to participate in the corruption that characterized the Lerma period. They saw themselves as the king's tutors and had reform of the monarchy as one of their goals. When Zúñiga died in late 1621, Olivares became Philip's chief mentor. In many ways he was well suited to the task: He was prudent, intelligent, cautious, diligent, and meticulous, characteristics never used to describe the despised Lerma. Olivares, also, was to spend the next two decades, sometimes with the king's active participation and sometimes without it, in a prolonged attempt to reform and strengthen Spain and the monarchy.

The challenges were daunting. Royal revenues from the Americas had begun to decline, and Castile, where royal power was strongest, was increasingly impoverished by the burden of empire. The empire itself was a collection of individual kingdoms rather than a monarchy with unified political and fiscal structures. Among Philip's subjects, the Portuguese and Catalans were especially resentful of their subjection to Madrid. In central Europe, the Thirty Years' War (1618-1648) had erupted, and the Austrian Habsburgs pressed their Spanish cousins for support. Perhaps worst of all, Spain's long, costly war with the Dutch flared up again in 1621.

Olivares hoped to overcome all these problems by radical reform, which he portrayed as a return to the good government of the age of Philip II, when Spain clearly dominated Europe. His plan to unify the empire militarily and fiscally portended a clear break with the Spanish Habsburgs' traditional respect for the laws and taxes of the individual kingdoms. In simple terms, the plan was to relieve Castile of the cost of protecting the other kingdoms by forcing them to supply money and troops for the common defense, but the Catalans, Portuguese, and others saw the plan, which became known as the Union of Arms (1620's), as a violation of their traditional rights. They protested against having to pay with higher taxes and greater military levies for policies devised in Madrid for the benefit of Castilian interests.

Some Spanish ministers urged that Philip IV make peace with the Dutch to stop the war's horrendous drain on Spanish resources, but Olivares was optimistic that with imposition of his reforms, the empire could prevail.

Other factors perhaps heightened his optimism. In 1625, for example, the king made him the duke of Sanlúcar. One of his most cherished dreams was thus satisfied: As the count-duke he was a grandee, in the highest rank of Spanish nobility. The following year, though, the first of a string of disasters hit Olivares. In 1626, his only surviving child, María, died in childbirth, eliminating any hope of passing his titles and estates to a direct heir. With his daughter's death, Olivares seemed morose and fatalistic. In 1628, Olivares intervened in a succession dispute in Mantua, which had the fatal effect of provoking open warfare between Spain and France, a conflict that lasted until the Treaty of the Pyrenees was signed in 1659, recognizing Spanish defeat. Also in 1628, a Dutch squadron commanded by Piet Hein captured the entire treasure fleet returning from the New World and touched off a great fiscal crisis.

Despite his wide-ranging abilities as a statesman, Olivares failed to make Spanish policies conform to the realities of the monarchy's straitened circumstances. The Union of Arms, rather than strengthening imperial defenses and unifying the empire, provoked dangerous rebellion in Catalonia and Portugal. Spain could not subdue the Dutch rebels. Income from the Americas continued to decline. By 1640, Olivares was undoubtedly the most hated man in Spain, even more than Lerma had been. The pressures undermined his physical health, and, in 1642, he displayed growing signs of mental instability. Olivares worried that because of his own weaknesses and sins, God was punishing Philip and Spain. On January 17, 1643, Philip IV removed Olivares from power, and he spent the remainder of his life in exile at Toro. Olivares died there, his mind gone, on July 22, 1645.

SIGNIFICANCE

That Olivares failed, ultimately, was not surprising, in retrospect. Spain's political and military might was illusory, dependent upon outmoded constitutional restraints within the empire and upon a France temporarily weakened by its religious wars. Neither could Castile and Olivares depend permanently on the windfall of silver from the Americas to underwrite a grandiose imperial strategy. For years Olivares carried on with tremendous determination and energy, and he nearly prevailed. As his foremost biographer, J. H. Elliott, concluded, Olivares placed too much faith in Spain's ultimate triumph, that after great struggle time would eventually give him and the monarchy their victory.

—Kendall W. Brown

FURTHER READING

Brown, Jonathan, and J. H. Elliot. *A Palace for a King: The Buen Retiro and the Court of Philip IV*. New Haven, Conn.: Yale University Press, 1993. Built in the 1630's for Philip IV, the Buen Retiro Palace reflected the grandeur of Spanish political and cultural life during the Olivares period.

Darby, Graham. "Lerma Before Olivares." *History Today* 45, no. 7 (1995): 30-36. The author credits Lerma with having a more farsighted foreign policy than Olivares, given Lerma's willingness to negotiate a truce with the Dutch. Olivares wanted to pursue war.

Elliott, J. H. *The Count Duke of Olivares: The Statesman in an Age of Decline*. New Haven, Conn.: Yale University Press, 1986. The monumental biography of Olivares by one of the greatest historians of early modern Europe. An indispensable read for those interested in the Spain of the first half of the seventeenth century.

_____. *Imperial Spain, 1469-1716*. New York: Penguin, 1990. Originally published in 1963, this work has seen many editions and is a still-perceptive survey of the two long centuries that witnessed Spain's rise to dominance in Europe and its subsequent decline. Olivares plays a prominent role.

_____. *Richelieu and Olivares*. New York: Cambridge University Press, 1984. A fascinating comparison of the two great ministers who directed the war efforts of France and Spain as they struggled for supremacy.

Gonzales de Leon, Fernando. "Aristocratic Draft-dodgers in Seventeenth-Century Spain." *History Today* 46, no. 7 (1996): 14-21. The author analyzes the mounting opposition to Olivares's policies within Spain itself, even opposition among the elite.

Lynch, John. *Spain Under the Habsburgs*. 2d ed. 2 vols. New York: Oxford University Press, 1992. The second volume of this text contains considerable information on Olivares, and the second edition is updated with the scholarship of scholar Elliott and others.

SEE ALSO: Baltasar Gracián y Morales; Piet Hein; John IV; Philip III; Philip IV; Diego Velázquez.

RELATED ARTICLES in *Great Events from History: The Seventeenth Century, 1601-1700:* c. 1601-1682: Spanish Golden Age; July, 1620-September, 1639: Struggle for the Valtelline Pass; March 31, 1621-September 17, 1665: Reign of Philip IV; May, 1640-January 23, 1641: Revolt of the Catalans; February 13, 1668: Spain Recognizes Portugal's Independence.

RORY O'MORE
Gaelic Irish rebel leader

O'More's notable accomplishment was fomenting and leading the Irish rebellion that began in 1641 and ended with disastrous consequences in 1651.

BORN: 1592; Ireland

DIED: In or after 1666; probably Ireland

ALSO KNOWN AS: Rory More; Rory Moore; Roger Moore

AREAS OF ACHIEVEMENT: Government and politics, warfare and conquest

EARLY LIFE

Nothing is known with any certainty of Rory O'More's early life, and many popular tales confuse him with Rory Oge O'More, another Irish rebel, who died in 1578. In earlier times, the O'Mores had controlled Leix (Laoighis) County, but English invasions had displaced and dispossessed them. Because the O'Mores were an unreconstructed Catholic and rebellious clan, the plantations carried out under James I scattered them to Connaught, Kerry, and Clare. Rory O'More's father, Calvagh O'More, settled his family in Kildare at Ballina, where they presumably lived as local gentry. Rory was literate and quite accomplished as a speaker in both Gaelic and English, which would indicate some level of education, quite possibly on the Continent. His family's reputation was such that he was able to marry into one of the notable Catholic Old English families of the Pale, the Barnewalls. His father-in-law, Patrick Barnewall, was an outspoken proponent of both the Royalist and the Catholic causes, giving Rory an entrée into these important circles.

LIFE'S WORK

By early 1641, the English king Charles I and Parliament were moving toward open conflict, as Charles's policies in Scotland had led to revolt of the Covenanters and the king's need for money that only Parliament could provide. In February, O'More traveled to the province of Ulster and met with several Ulstermen, including Sir Phelim O'Neill, who led the powerful O'Neill clan while the more notable Owen Roe O'Neill was on the Continent, and the twenty-five-year-old Connor, Lord Maguire, second baron of Enniskillen, a rash, debt-ridden spendthrift from County Fermanagh who was a member of the Irish Parliament and well-connected in Catholic Ulster circles. Together, they sketched out plans for an uprising against the Protestant planter aristocracy in Ulster that would coincide with a rising in Dublin and the Pale.

Ulster Catholics deeply resented the physical dislocations and anti-Catholicism that accompanied the English plantations, and they were crippled by the economic instability and rising debt that resulted from Stuart policies in the province. A rebellion that targeted the planters was a natural outgrowth of the increasingly intolerable conditions in the province and an extension of violence that was already occurring on a small scale. Victory would mean a disruption of England's earlier discriminatory policies against the Irish. O'More and Maguire decided to coordinate the planned Ulster uprising with one in the city of Dublin. The latter attack would target the seat of English military power, Dublin Castle, which was believed to hold arms enough for thirty thousand men.

Organization of manpower in Dublin was accelerated by O'More's plotting with the so-called Colonels—Irish military recruiters in the service of Spain, including Richard Plunkett, James Dillon, and Hugh MacPhelim Byrne—who were allowed by English authorities to travel through Ireland seeking enlistees. In August, 1641, Maguire, O'More, and the Colonels finalized details for a coordinated assault on the castle and Ulster, to take place on October 5. O'More was to lead a hundred men from his home province of Leinster in an assault on the little gate of the castle, while Maguire would command a hundred Ulstermen who would storm the main gate. The event was postponed, however, and the Colonels pulled out.

The remaining rebel leaders, O'More, Maguire, and Phelim O'Neill, met one last time on October 15 to make final arrangements for the rising, now planned for October 23. The 23rd, a Saturday, was a market day, when large crowds would be flooding Dublin's streets. The rising would take advantage of these crowds, partly to provide cover and confusion, partly as a source of additional

manpower in the assault. At the same moment, smaller bands of rebels in the countryside of the Pale were to rise up and attack authorities, providing a diversion for the main castle assault.

On the night of October 22, however, the plot was betrayed when one Owen Connolly appeared at the house of Lord Justice Sir William Parson and outlined the scheme. Word quickly spread, and O'More dashed to Maguire's house to warn him, but the young nobleman was captured and imprisoned by the English and eventually divulged the rebels' plans, including O'More's role as leader. Only eighty of the two hundred rebels appeared in Dublin, and they, along with O'More, aborted their attack and fled to the countryside. Ulster had risen the day before, however, and O'Neill's armies had quickly seized Charlemont and Dungannon. The rebellion had begun in earnest despite the Dublin debacle.

O'More next appeared at the head of a small army that crushed an English column at Julianstown (November 29, 1641). The Catholic Old English rulers of the Pale had balked at participating in the rebellion after the Dublin plot had been foiled, but a large number gathered at Crofty Hill (Knockcrofty) on December 3 to hear O'More's argument for their active participation in the next stages. An eloquent speaker, O'More reminded them of the official anti-Catholic policies that had become increasingly stringent, and he warned them that, with the rising in Ulster and the writ branding the Catholic Ulster leaders rebels against the Crown, the trend was likely to continue.

O'More noted that Parliament had failed to redress any of the grievances raised by the Irish over their poor treatment and that, as Parliament was on the verge of civil war with the king, they were most likely to dispatch an army of Scots Covenanters to crush all Irish Catholics, Gaelic and Old English alike. He stressed that the rebellion was in fact in support of Charles I and against the pernicious and increasingly radical Parliament. The Pale leaders applauded O'More and met together on December 7 at Tara to make their own plans.

The spring of 1642 saw the supposed massacre of tens of thousands of Ulster Protestants by the rebels, which galvanized anti-Catholic sentiment in England, Scotland, and Ireland. In February, thanks to Maguire's testimony, English authorities placed a reward of £400 for O'More's capture, or £300 for clear evidence of his having been slain. At the Battle of Kilrush (April 15), the English routed O'More's army of some six thousand men, who were poorly armed and possessed little powder. O'More and his brother fled to Ballina. He is thought to have escaped to Flanders, where he helped arbitrate Owen Roe O'Neill's return to lead the Ulstermen. If so, he probably arrived with O'Neill in August, 1642.

O'More remained active in O'Neill's service, though details of his activities are sketchy. In the summer of 1648, O'More participated in O'Neill's war on the Confederation of Kilkenny, which resulted in the destruction of that body and set the stage for the campaign of Oliver Cromwell in the spring of the following year. In September, 1648, O'Neill harnessed O'More's eloquence, sending him as a messenger to Murrough O'Brien, sixth Baron Inchiquin (later the first earl of Inchiquin), in what amounted to a last-ditch—and fruitless—attempt at negotiation.

In the last months of the rebellion, O'More served as an infantry colonel in Connaught and finally as rebel commander in Leinster, but he was a commander with practically no army. In early 1652, he and a few followers were driven to one of the rebels' last outposts, Bofin Island (Innisbofin). There, he was finally abandoned both by the governor of the local forces, Colonel George Cusack, and by the bishop of Clonfert, who surrendered his post in February. O'More still had a price on his head and had been specifically exempted from the Cromwellian Act of Settlement (August 12, 1652), which granted pardons to many of the rebellious Irish. His own last years are shrouded in mystery, and there are not-improbable tales of him living as an Ulster fisherman into the 1660's.

SIGNIFICANCE

O'More's personal connections allowed him to coordinate the native, Gaelic leadership in Ulster, best represented by the O'Neills, with the discontented Old English rulers of the Irish Pale centered on Dublin. Though his plan to secure Dublin Castle, and thereby arm a broader uprising, fell through, his efforts did result in a sustained rebellion that lasted for nearly a decade. Capitalizing on the old adage that England's trouble is Ireland's opportunity, O'More timed the rising perfectly, maximizing the Old English fear of Scottish interference and Parliamentarian tyranny. The rebellion ended, however, with Cromwell's disastrous victory and the repression that followed and with O'More's own disappearance into oblivion.

—*Joseph P. Byrne*

FURTHER READING

Bagwell, Richard. *Ireland Under the Stuarts*. Vols. 1 and 2. London: Holland Press, 1963. The rebellion's early phases—especially Maguire's role—are treated in admirable detail.

Bennett, M. *The Civil Wars in Britain and Ireland, 1638-1651*. Cambridge, Mass.: Blackwell, 1997. Standard treatment of the wars and their interconnections.

Casway, J. *Owen Roe O'Neill and the Struggle for Catholic Ireland*. Philadelphia: University of Pennsylvania Press, 1984. An important study of Ulster's roles in the rebellion as background for O'More's contributions.

Fitzpatrick, Brendan. *Seventeenth-Century Ireland: The Wars of Religions*. Totowa, N.J.: Barnes and Noble, 1989. Authors recognize the important mixture of religion and nationalism in the rebellion, and in O'More's motivations.

Kenyon, John, and Jan Ohlmeyer. *The Civil Wars: A Military History of England, Scotland, and Ireland, 1638-1660*. New York: Oxford University Press, 1998. Contains separate chapters on the course of the Irish phases of the struggle, and usefully emphasizes military matters over other considerations.

Perceval-Maxwell, M. *The Outbreak of the Irish Rebellion of 1641*. Dublin: McGill-Queen's University Press, 1994. Well-focused short study of the early phases of the rebellion and O'More's actions.

SEE ALSO: Charles I; Oliver Cromwell; James I.
RELATED ARTICLES in *Great Events from History: The Seventeenth Century, 1601-1700:* March-June, 1639: First Bishops' War; October 23, 1641-1642: Ulster Insurrection; 1642-1651: English Civil Wars; August 17-September 25, 1643: Solemn League and Covenant.

OPECHANCANOUGH

Pamunkey chief (r. before 1607-1644/1646) and head of the Powhatan Confederacy (r. 1618-1644/1646)

An inveterate enemy of the English colonization of Virginia, Pamunkey chief Opechancanough engineered two highly successful attacks during the Powhatan Wars.

BORN: c. 1545; Virginia
DIED: 1644 or 1646; Jamestown, Virginia
ALSO KNOWN AS: Mangopeomen; Massatamohtnock
AREAS OF ACHIEVEMENT: Government and politics, warfare and conquest

EARLY LIFE

Lack of documentation as to the origin and early life of Opechancanough (oh-pehch-uhn-kah-NOH) has brought about a good deal of theorizing, much of it fantastic. It is most likely that he was born during the 1540's, on or near the peninsula between the James and York Rivers. His parentage is unknown: The theory that his actual father was an "unknown Spaniard" has no basis in fact. He has also been speculatively identified as Don Luis de Velasco, a young Native American who was abducted by a Spanish expedition to the present-day Williamsburg-Yorktown area of Virginia in 1561.

Taken to Cuba, to Mexico, and then to Spain, the young man was baptized a Christian and given the name Don Luis de Velasco, after his Spanish patron. He was taken back to his homeland in 1570, when the Spanish Mission of Ajacan was established by seven Jesuit priests led by Juan Bautista de Segura (again, probably in the vicinity of Williamsburg or Yorktown). After a few months, "Don Luis" deserted the mission, returned to his people, and then, in February of 1571, returned to massacre Segura and the others. This story, which is offered as an explanation for the intense hatred later demonstrated by Opechancanough against Europeans, is highly questionable in the sense that it identifies the two Native Americans as being identical individuals, with no conclusive evidence to support this assertion.

The earliest fact that is known with certainty about Opechancanough is that by 1607 he was established as chief of the important Pamunkey tribe and served under his brother Powhatan (also known as Wahunsonacock), who was the high chief (or as the English styled him, emperor) of the Powhatan Confederacy. The confederacy stretched along the coastal plain of the Chesapeake Bay from the Potomac River to near the present site of Nor-

folk, Virginia. It was Opechancanough who actually captured the English adventurer John Smith and turned him over to his brother. Smith later turned the tables on Opechancanough: While pretending to be on a trading mission to the chieftain's village, Smith seized him, placed a gun to his head, and forced him to give a supply of corn to the Jamestown colony. This incident may have intensified Opechancanough's suspicion of and hatred toward the European interlopers.

LIFE'S WORK

Powhatan pursued an erratic policy toward the English Jamestown colony, vacillating between open warfare, toleration, and, especially after Powhatan's daughter Pocahontas married the English planter John Rolfe, peace and coexistence. Opechancanough, in opposition to his brother, consistently favored an aggressive policy aimed at the destruction of the colony. Some believe that he was alarmed over the rapidity with which plantations and settlements were spreading along the James and York River Valleys and that he feared that the English posed a threat to the Powhatan way of life. Certain scholars assert that, as Powhatan himself grew older, Opechancanough steadily advanced in power to the point at which he began to exercise actual leadership.

Pocahontas died at Gravesend, England, in March of 1617, and Powhatan himself passed on in April, 1618. He was at first succeeded by another brother, Opitchapan, but within a few months, Opitchapan was supplanted by Opechancanough. For over three years, Opechancanough feigned friendship with the whites, allowing his people to mingle freely among the settlements. He even accepted the gift of an English log cabin with a specially fashioned lock and key from George Thorpe, who championed a movement to educate and Christianize Powhatan children.

A religious revival, centered around the major Powhatan god Okewas, swept through the villages of the confederacy. When Nenemattanaw ("jack of the feathers"), one of the leaders of this religious movement, was killed in an altercation with English settlers, Opechancanough conspicuously signed a peace agreement with Thorpe, indicating his eventual desire to convert to Christianity. It was a subterfuge, and at 12 noon on March 22, 1622 (Good Friday), Opechancanough launched a meticulously planned and executed attack that virtually annihilated the colonists' outlying settlements and snuffed out one-quarter of the English colony's population (347 individuals) within hours. This so-called Day of Okewas left dead colonists and obliterated towns and homesteads on both banks of the James River, setting off the largest and most viciously fought of the Powhatan Wars.

The strategy of Sir Francis Wyatt, the English governor at Jamestown, was to withdraw the English population within a more easily defensible perimeter around Jamestown and to launch punitive raids on Powhatan villages and cornfields, thus jeopardizing the Indians' food supplies. In May, 1623, while Opechancanough was attending peace talks with the English, they unsuccessfully attempted to poison him with wine and then shot him, leaving the chief for dead. However, he survived and recuperated to continue the fight until 1632, when a semiofficial, uneasy truce was put into place.

Though Opechancanough was generally quiet for some twelve years, he never abandoned the strategy of waiting until the English had been lulled into a false sense of security, and he planned another devastating onslaught. The Second Day of Okewas, on April 18, 1644, was even more bloody than that of 1622: More than five hundred settlers were killed. With a much larger population by this time, however, the English colony was better able to absorb the blow, and countermeasures similar to those initiated by Wyatt twenty-two years earlier were placed in motion by then-governor Sir William Berkeley.

Opechancanough, who may have been close to one hundred years old by this time, was quite feeble. He had to be transported on a litter borne by two warriors. He was ultimately captured, probably in the summer of 1646 (though possibly two years earlier), and taken to Jamestown, where he remained defiant to the end. Berkeley had ordered that the chieftain be kept alive, with the intention of sending him to England to stand trial before King Charles I. However, one of the guards, who may have endured the loss of friends or family members to the Powhatans, violated the orders and slew Opechancanough by shooting him in the back. Opechancanough is known to have had a daughter, Nicketti, who married the Englishman John Rice Hughes. Necotowance, who became high chief in his turn, may have been Opechancanough's son.

SIGNIFICANCE

Opechancanough's death brought an end to serious Native American opposition to English expansion in Tidewater Virginia. His successor, Necotowance, signed a treaty of capitulation in October, 1646. The nations under Necotowance's command became tributaries of the king of England, ceding to the English settlers all land between the York and James Rivers. The Powhatans, notably the Pamunkey and the Mattaponi nations, were eventually shoved onto smaller reservations

Imaginative depiction of the massacre of Jesuit priests by Opechancanough. (Hulton Archive/Getty Images)

or marginalized when they were partially assimilated into the population of Virginia. Opechancanough has variously been depicted as a wily, treacherous warlord and, more recently, as a statesman who was dedicated to preserving his nation's civilization and religious faith against overwhelming odds in the only way available to him.

—*Raymond Pierre Hylton*

FURTHER READING

Bridenbaugh, Carl. *Early America*. New York: Oxford University Press, 1981. Theorizes that Opechanca-nough and Don Luis de Velasco were one and the same and constructs an elaborate—but ultimately un-substantiated—scenario based upon this supposition and circumstantial evidence.

Feest, Christian F. *The Powhatan Tribes*. New York: Chelsea House, 1990. Balanced account that does not demonize the Powhatan chieftain and acknowledges more than other sources the probable impact of reli-gion upon his actions.

Mossiker, Frances. *Pocahontas: The Life and the Leg-end*. New York: Da Capo Press, 1996. Despite the ti-tle, this account also focuses on the political maneu-verings within the Powhatan Confederacy between Powhatan and Opechancanough and the implications of the latter's succession to the leadership position.

Rountree, Helen C. *Pocahontas' People: The Powhatan Indians of Virginia Through Four Centuries*. Nor-man: University of Oklahoma Press, 1990. Includes a scholarly appraisal of Opechancanough's character and motives; offers the controversial opinion that Opechancanough had virtually taken control of the Confederacy during the last two years of Powhatan's reign.

SEE ALSO: Charles I; Pocahontas; Powhatan; John Smith.

RELATED ARTICLES in *Great Events from History: The Seventeenth Century, 1601-1700:* May 14, 1607: Jamestown Is Founded; March 22, 1622-October, 1646: Powhatan Wars.

AXEL OXENSTIERNA
Swedish diplomat and statesman

Combining intellect, courage, humor, and integrity, Oxenstierna mastered every aspect of state service and helped Gustavus II Adolphus to produce Sweden's age of greatness. As chancellor for Queen Christina, he was largely responsible for New Sweden on the Delaware in North America.

BORN: June 16, 1583; Fånö, near Uppsala, Sweden
DIED: August 28, 1654; Stockholm, Sweden
AREAS OF ACHIEVEMENT: Government and politics, diplomacy

EARLY LIFE
Axel Oxenstierna (AK-sehl OOHK-sehn-shehr-nah) was born to Gustavus Oxenstierna and Barbro Bielke, who came from ancient noble families. During his youth, Oxenstierna experienced a Sweden torn by conflict be-tween the monarchy and the aristocracy. His father died early in 1597, and because civil war had broken out, young Axel was sent to Germany to study. He studied history, languages, and practical politics. In 1602, he re-turned to Sweden and swore allegiance to Charles IX. His diplomatic skills were rewarded with a post on the exchequer. He married Anna Boot in 1608 and in the fol-

lowing year became a member of the Swedish Council of State.

LIFE'S WORK
Oxenstierna began his forty-two-year career as chancel-lor in 1612, following the death of Charles IX in 1611. Gustavus II Adolphus, Charles's successor, appointed Oxenstierna, who had confirmed him as king and con-vinced him to issue a charter protecting against royal abuses. Oxenstierna's appointment came at a time of great internal and external unrest. On the domestic front, he represented the aristocracy in its struggle against the monarchy—his success already demonstrated by the king's protective charter. Oxenstierna's skill as a diplo-mat also began to surface in his interactions abroad.

Oxenstierna spent the next several years negotiating war settlements with Denmark, Russia, and Poland. The Peace of Knäred was signed with Denmark in 1613. By 1617, the Treaty of Stolbovo was agreed to by Russia, cutting that country off from the Baltic by extending Swedish control around the Gulf of Finland. Poland's in-terests in using Russia to place Sigismund's heirs on the Swedish throne were effectively delayed at this time, keeping that war in abeyance.

Oxenstierna now turned his attention toward domestic reform. He wrote the *riksdagsordning* (parliamentary law) in 1617. Development of towns to increase the middle class and commerce was the focus of his work in 1619, followed by local government reform in 1623. He was behind the reorganization of the nobility into three classes in 1626.

Meanwhile, diplomatic negotiations continued with Poland and Denmark. In 1626, the king shifted his war against Poland to Prussia and appointed Oxenstierna governor-general of the newly occupied territory. Oxenstierna organized the collection of the tolls from the Baltic ports, which provided much-needed financial support for the Swedish war efforts up to 1635. It was clear that the Swedish dynastic struggles had become deeply involved in the European conflicts of the Thirty Years' War (1618-1648). In 1629, Oxenstierna negotiated peace with Poland, resulting in the Truce of Altmark.

Oxenstierna entered a new phase of his career when he was called to Germany by Gustavus Adolphus in 1631. He organized and led the army that brought relief to the king at Nürnberg in August of 1632. This military success allowed him to add revenues from occupied territory to port tolls and foreign subsidies to finance Sweden's war efforts. The string of victories came to an end with the death of Gustavus Adolphus at the Battle of Lützen in November of 1632. Leadership of Swedish affairs was assumed by Oxenstierna in Germany.

In 1633, he went to Saxony to create the Protestant league that Gustavus Adolphus had planned. The gathering at Heilbronn was led by Oxenstierna, but the Northern German princes never joined. After the military defeat at Nördlingen in 1634, Sweden's allies were disunited and disloyal, and many signed the Peace of Prague in 1635. Sweden was deprived of large parts of German territory, which had largely subsidized the war. Renewal of a truce with Poland meant relinquishing the Prussian port tolls, also in 1635. These revenue losses, along with military reverses as imperialist forces recovered, forced Oxenstierna to overcome severe difficulties. At one time, he was the prisoner of mutinous troops who had not been paid.

When Oxenstierna returned to Sweden in 1636, he was the prime ruler of the country, the major power in the council and the regency. He tutored the young Queen Christina (Gustavus Adolphus had made him her princi-

Axel Oxenstierna. (Library of Congress)

pal guardian before his death), who proved to be an apt pupil. He spent three hours each day discussing foreign and domestic affairs and explaining Sweden's international position and European politics. Christina described him as a tall, proper, straight, handsome man with a sober and fixed countenance and a grave and civil carriage. He is described as being very human in his conversation with Christina. They both derived great pleasure from their study sessions, although their relations were not always harmonious as she grew older.

Conflict between the two first came as a result of Oxenstierna's acceptance of French alliance and support to continue the war after 1638. The opposition of the Holy Roman Emperor, Ferdinand III, and the imperialist forces had forced Oxenstierna into this alliance, but his enemies in Sweden accused him of prolonging the war for personal gain. Christina was also dissatisfied with Oxenstierna's actions and wanted peace. This rift pleased Oxenstierna's opponents in the council. The queen took an active role in all proceedings after this time.

Relations between the queen and Oxenstierna continued to be capricious. Christina, who had begun to rule independently in 1644, made Oxenstierna a count, granting him several estates and high commendation in an assembly of the Estates following his attack of and subsequent peace with Denmark in the Treaty of Brömsebrö in 1645. Friction resurfaced, however, after the Treaty of Westphalia (terminating the war with the emperor and the German princes) was signed on October 24, 1648. This friction was caused in part by Christina's growing fondness for France. Oxenstierna had never trusted Cardinal de Richelieu, nor, after Richelieu's death in 1642, did he trust Jules Mazarin. Swedish aristocrats despised and feared anything, such as French culture, that they considered unnatural and highbrow. Oxenstierna and Mazarin would continue to disagree over foreign policy and over the issue of succession through 1650, when their relations improved.

Oxenstierna's ongoing efforts to improve Sweden and increase its holdings and wealth were exemplified by his negotiations in the New World. Gustavus Adolphus had been presented with the opportunity to take advantage of trade with the New World as early as 1624. Oxenstierna was looking for a way to increase exports of Swedish copper to help finance the war effort, and, with the help of Peter Minuit, a Dutch colonial official, Oxenstierna's attention was riveted on the New World. The New Sweden Company was formed, and two vessels left early in November, 1637, entering the South Bay (Delaware River) early in March, 1638. They moved up the river and established Fort Christina, in honor of the twelve-year-old queen. Thus began the Swedish settlement on the Delaware. Trade supplies were slow in arriving, because Sweden's major attention was focused on the war in Germany. The Dutch in New Netherlands formed a serious threat, finally overcoming the Swedes and Finns in 1655.

Oxenstierna did not live to see the end of New Sweden. He died on August 28, 1654, in Stockholm. The position of chancellor under the new king, Charles X Gustav, who became king upon Christina's abdication, went to Oxenstierna's son, Erik.

SIGNIFICANCE

Oxenstierna was a great statesman of the seventeenth century. He mastered all aspects of state service, from local government reform to finances. He was successful in organizing and executing military campaigns. Known for his courage, intellect, humor, honesty, and devotion to the Vasa family, he, along with Gustavus Adolphus, pushed and pulled Sweden into an age of greatness, mov-

ing it from the edge of European society to center stage in the Thirty Years' War. He continued his work faithfully as Sweden's chancellor for forty-two years. It is possible that his most lasting memorial lies along the Delaware River, spreading throughout the United States: the heirs of the New Sweden Company.

—Mary-Emily Miller

FURTHER READING

Andersson, Ingvar. *A History of Sweden*. Translated by Carolyn Hannay. London: Weidenfeld & Nicolson, 1956. A valuable review of Sweden's place in history and an assessment of Oxenstierna's role in Swedish as well as European history. Chapters 16-19 focus on Oxenstierna's life, with chapter 18 especially valuable on his rule in Sweden during the regency period of Queen Christina.

James, G. P. R. *Lives of the Cardinal de Richelieu, Count Oxenstierna, Count Olivarez, and Cardinal Mazarin.* 2 vols. Philadelphia: Carey, Lea, and Blanchard, 1836. The material on Oxenstierna is in volume 2 and reviews his life with extensive attention to activities during the Thirty Years' War and Oxenstierna's efforts on behalf of Sweden after the death of Gustavus II Adolphus.

Losman, Arne, Agneta Lundström, and Margareta Revera, eds. *The Age of New Sweden*. Translated by Bernard Vowles. Stockholm: Livrustkammaren for the Royal Armoury, 1988. There are five essays in this volume and some excellent illustrations, including one of Oxenstierna's chapel and his residence, Tidö, in Västmanland. The essays are helpful in presenting Sweden's developing culture, learning, and social change in the seventeenth century.

Roberts, Michael. *From Oxenstierna to Charles XII: Four Studies*. New York: Cambridge University Press, 1991. Roberts's four essays examine Swedish history after the death of Gustavus II Adolphus in 1632. The essay on Oxenstierna focuses on the years 1633 to 1636, when he was based in Germany and managing Sweden's affairs.

_____. *Gustavus Adolphus: A History of Sweden, 1611-1632*. 2 vols. London: Longmans, Green, 1953-1958. This definitive biography of Gustavus II Adolphus details his lifelong friendship with Oxenstierna, showing how these two extraordinary men changed the course of Swedish and European history. There are extensive illustrations, maps, bibliography, and a helpful index. Roberts's work is required reading for understanding this period.

Stolpe, Sven. *Christina of Sweden.* Edited by Sir Alec Randall. New York: Macmillan, 1966. Many of the myths about Christina are dispelled, and Oxenstierna's role during the regency period is explained. Contains an excellent review of the literature on Christina. Intended for the general reader.

Weslager, C. A. *New Sweden on the Delaware, 1638-1655.* Wilmington, Del.: Middle Atlantic Press, 1988. Written for the 350th celebration of the founding of New Sweden by an eminent scholar and historian. Very readable, with excellent sketch maps and sketches, a list of place-names, and a selected reading list.

_____. *The Swedes and Dutch at New Castle.* Wilmington, Del.: Middle Atlantic Press, 1987. This study covers the Dutch-Swedish rivalry for control of the Delaware Valley in North America from 1638 to 1664. There is an excellent sketch map of the Delaware River area and eleven other illustrations.

SEE ALSO: Charles X Gustav; Christina; Gustavus II Adolphus; Peter Minuit.

RELATED ARTICLES in *Great Events from History: The Seventeenth Century, 1601-1700:* 1610-1643: Reign of Louis XIII; 1618-1648: Thirty Years' War; 1625: Grotius Establishes the Concept of International Law; November 10, 1630: The Day of Dupes; May 30, 1635: Peace of Prague; 1640-1688: Reign of Frederick William, the Great Elector; July, 1643-October 24, 1648: Peace of Westphalia; July 10, 1655-June 21, 1661: First Northern War.

JOHANN PACHELBEL
German composer

During his life's work as a church musician, Pachelbel developed the Chorale Prelude, an important genre of sacred music used in Lutheran liturgy. He also contributed to the compositional use of the "theme and variations" form. Pachelbel was a teacher and friend of members of the Bach family, and he influenced the work of J. S. Bach.

BORN: September 1, 1653 (baptized); Nuremberg
　　(now in Germany)
DIED: March 3, 1706; Nuremberg
AREAS OF ACHIEVEMENT: Music, religion and
　　theology

EARLY LIFE

As a child, Johann Pachelbel (joh-hahn pahk-EHL-behl) showed talent in music as well as other subjects. Along with his general education in Nuremberg, he was tutored in theory by Heinrich Schwemmer, and in both performance and composition by G. C. Wecker. In 1669, he began studies at the university at Altdorf, and he served as an organist in the town, but he had to curtail his studies for financial reasons. In the following year he was granted a special scholarship to the Gymnasium Poeticum at Regensburg. Continuing a pattern of parallel studies in music and other subjects, he was allowed to undertake advanced study in music with Kaspar Prentz. Prentz was familiar with the international dimensions of musical practice, which at the time was heavily influenced by the Italian masters.

In 1673, Pachelbel left Regensburg for the cosmopolitan environment of Vienna, where he served as the deputy organist at Saint Stephen's cathedral. In this environment, the young musician, who had been immersed in the Protestant liturgical traditions of his hometown and schools, was able to gain valuable knowledge of the Catholic Church composers, as well as the instrumental music of southern Europe.

LIFE'S WORK

After four years, Pachelbel left Vienna for a position as the court organist at Eisenach, under the kapellmeister, or choir/orchestra director, Daniel Eberlin. This job was short lived, however, because Prince Bernhard, the duke of Saxe-Jena, died. Eberlin wrote Pachelbel a letter of reference so that he could find employment elsewhere. His next position, at the Predigerkirche, a Lutheran church in the town of Erfurt, lasted for twelve years and

provided both the opportunity and motivation for Pachelbel to expand and refine his skills as a composer and performer.

Erfurt was an ideal environment for Pachelbel at this time. Its university, where Protestant reformer Martin Luther had studied in the sixteenth century, was internationally known at the time and contributed to the intellectual life of the area. There were several large churches, both Catholic and Protestant, with active musical traditions. The congregation of the Predigerkirche had very high expectations of Pachelbel, and his written job description was quite demanding. Along with the usual duties of accompanying the liturgy, he was required to compose and perform chorale preludes based on the themes of the hymns to be sung that week, had to be reexamined every year, and had to prepare an annual solo recital. Pachelbel was talented and industrious enough, however, to thrive under these terms. In 1679, during his first year at the Predigerkirche, Pachelbel was selected to compose music for the Erbhuldigung (a ceremony of homage) to honor Karl Heinrich von Metternich, taking office as the new prince elector of Mainz.

Pachelbel's musical reputation grew, but he also was struck by tragedy. His wife, to whom he was married just two years earlier, and their infant son perished in an outbreak of plague in 1683. One year later, Pachelbel remarried, and the couple eventually had seven children. Another important relationship developed, one that was musical as well as personal. Pachelbel became a friend of Ambrosius Bach, a musician in Erfurt. Bach was part of a large musical family also associated with the town of Eisenach, where Pachelbel had previously been employed. Pachelbel was godfather to Ambrosius Bach's daughter Johanna Juditha and began teaching music to Ambrosius's son, Johann Christoph Bach. After Pachelbel's friend died in 1695, Johann Christoph in turn became the teacher and guardian of his younger brother Johann Sebastian Bach, extending Pachelbel's influence to subsequent generations of the Bach family.

Throughout his time in Erfurt, Pachelbel continued to compose and perform organ chorales as stipulated in his contract. In these preludes, Pachelbel would take each phrase of a hymn tune as a given theme to be developed by juxtaposing these phrases with contrasting but harmonious countermelodies and repeating them at different pitch levels for elaborate architectural effects. He also composed nonliturgical music for organ and other instruments, often by using the "theme and variations" compositional technique, in which a melody (often in the bass) and its associated chord sequence are repeated, with their metrical proportions preserved in each repetition and while the surface structure changes with each variation. Pachelbel was a master of this compositional practice, which he used in his most famous work, Canon in D, part of a work for strings with continuo, and most likely written during his early years in Erfurt.

Eventually, he was invited to become a musician for the Württemberg court at Stuttgart. This community, which he joined in 1690, gave Pachelbel a wider, more elite audience, and it could have resulted in more secular compositions. The armies of French king Louis XIV, however, were conducting raids in the Rhineland, so Pachelbel left the area in 1692. He declined a position at Oxford University and instead returned east to the Thuringia region, where he worked as an organist in the town of Goth for the next three years.

In 1695, Pachelbel returned with honor to his home town of Nuremberg and accepted an appointment at St. Sebaldus, the most prominent post in Nuremberg at that time. He held this position until he died in 1706. During this period, Pachelbel composed a great deal of religious vocal music, somewhat more dramatic in style than his instrumental music. He also wrote a set of ninety-five Magnificat fugues for Vespers at St. Sebaldus, reflecting an old tradition in which organists would precede the singing of the Magnificat by improvising fugues set in a series of contrasting modes. Some of his organ compositions were written as teaching pieces, which were later copied and modified by his students.

Three of Pachelbel's sons became musicians as well. Wilhelm Hieronymus, the oldest surviving son, took up his father's work at St. Sebaldus after the elder Pachelbel passed away. Charles Theodore moved to the British colonies in North America, where he was an organist, and Johann Michael, well known as an instrument builder in Nuremberg, traveled to Jamaica to perform.

SIGNIFICANCE

Pachelbel had built upon traditions established by generations of composers who had used plainsong melodies as cornerstones for the construction of great polyphonic masses and other works for the Catholic liturgy. In his own work, he used simple Lutheran hymn melodies as the basis for the creation of expanded, sophisticated works known as chorale preludes, a tradition that was continued by J. S. Bach and other composers.

He also contributed to the development of other genres, such as the fantasia, toccata, and fugue, and he made significant contributions to the repertoire for organ, sacred vocal music, and chamber ensemble. His most popular work, Canon in D, is often played at weddings and other ceremonies into the twenty-first century. His teaching influenced many musicians during his time and in subsequent generations.

—*John Myers*

FURTHER READING

Herl, Joseph. *Worship Wars in Early Lutheranism: Choir, Congregation, and Three Centuries of Conflict.* New York: Oxford University Press, 2004. Extensive study that provides comparative and historical context for sacred music by Pachelbel and other organists who performed and composed for the Lutheran liturgy.

Perreault, Jean M., and Donna K. Fitch, eds. *The Thematic Catalogue of the Musical Works of Johann Pachelbel.* Lanham, Md.: Scarecrow Press, 2004. Comprehensive musical identification of Pachelbel's compositions, including an essay on the sources and examinations of authenticity, with extensive notes and comments.

Silbiger, Alexander, ed. *Keyboard Music Before 1700.* Routledge Studies in Musical Genres. New York: Routledge, 2003. A study of composers and their music in England, France, Germany, the Netherlands, Italy, Spain, and Portugal. Bibliographies.

Thompson, Wendy. *Classical Composers: A Guide to the Lives and Works of the Great Composers from the Medieval, Baroque, and Classical Eras.* London: Southwater, 2002. Lavishly illustrated with brief but clearly written biographies, including one of Pachelbel, and overviews of major style periods. Very good introduction for general readers. Chronologically arranged, with many color prints of period paintings, a glossary, and an index.

Welter, Kathryn J. *Johann Pachelbel, Organist, Teacher, Composer: A Critical Reexamination of His Life, Works, and Historical Significance.* Unpublished doctoral dissertation. Harvard University, 1998. A comprehensive study balancing musical analysis and cultural and historical contexts. Illustrations, list of musical works, music examples, bibliography, tables.

Wolff, Christoph. *Johann Sebastian Bach: The Learned Musician.* New York: Norton, 2001. A thorough biography that includes treatment of Pachelbel's influence on Bach's musical style. Illustrations, appendices, music examples, indexes, tables.

SEE ALSO: Francesca Caccini; Arcangelo Corelli; Girolamo Frescobaldi; Orlando Gibbons; Henry Purcell;
Claudio Monteverdi; Heinrich Schütz; Barbara Strozzi.

RELATED ARTICLE in *Great Events from History: The
Seventeenth Century, 1601-1700:* c. 1673: Buxtehude
Begins His Abendmusiken Concerts.

DENIS PAPIN
French physicist and inventor

*Papin, a pioneer in realizing the potential of steam for
the production of power in a piston engine and steam's
ability to move objects, also invented an early type of
pressure cooker. His work was later improved upon by
others, leading to the development of the steam engine
in the mid-eighteenth century.*

BORN: August 22, 1647; near Blois, France
DIED: c. 1712; probably London, England
AREAS OF ACHIEVEMENT: Science and technology,
engineering

EARLY LIFE

Denis Papin (duh-nee paw-pan) was born in a farmhouse
a few miles from Blois, France, into a Huguenot (French
Protestant) family. In 1661 or 1662, he enrolled at the
University of Angers to study medicine, a profession already practiced by several members of his family. He
was graduated with a medical degree in 1669.

Papin also possessed a strong interest in mechanics
and natural philosophy, however, and by 1671 he was in
Paris, working for Christiaan Huygens, the well-known
Dutch mathematician and astronomer. Huygens had
helped Papin get an appointment as the curator of experiments in the laboratory of the French Royal Academy of
Sciences in Paris. The academy had been established in
1666 by King Louis XIV, and Huygens had been a
founding member; thus, he wielded considerable influence. Once installed, Papin began a series of experiments
under Huygens's guidance. Included in this extensive series of examinations were experiments on producing a
vacuum, on determining the weight of air, and on the
force of gunpowder. From his experiments with the vacuum, Papin constructed his own air pump, a feat indicative of his mechanical bent.

In 1674, Papin published a memoir of his work on the
vacuum called *Nouvelles expériences du vuide, avec
les descriptions mechanics qui servent à les faire* (new
experiments in the vacuum, with mechanical descriptions to facilitate them). He also wrote, with Huygens, a
series of five papers about his experiments, which Huygens communicated to the Royal Society of London. In
1675, the papers were published in the Royal Society's
Philosophical Transactions. In that same year, Papin
left Paris in the hope of finding a better position, but possibly to escape religious persecution as well. With the
help of a letter of introduction from Huygens, he obtained employment with Irish chemist Robert Boyle in
London.

LIFE'S WORK

In London, Papin found steady work and a place in which
to continue his studies, especially in pneumatics and hydraulics. Thus settled, he embarked on the most productive period of his life. Boyle quickly capitalized on
Papin's experience by initiating his own series of experiments on pneumatics. A key factor in this research was a
double-barreled air pump of Papin's design. The pistons
in each barrel were connected to stirrups, into which a
person stepped to move the pistons. These experiments
under Boyle continued from July, 1676, to February,
1679.

In May, 1679, Papin demonstrated to the Royal Society of London a new use of steam: his so-called digester,
or what would now be called the pressure cooker. Indicative of his concern for practical ends, the digester occupied Papin's mind sporadically for many years. The
Royal Society published Papin's book on the digester in
December, 1680. In 1682, he even cooked a dinner with
his digester for the Royal Society; it was well received,
according to contemporary accounts.

Following his work with Boyle, Papin worked for the
Royal Society, performing secretarial duties until the society terminated the position in December, 1679. During
1680, he may have returned to Paris to assist Huygens
with work on a gunpowder engine, in which a flash of
gunpowder pushed most of the air out of a cylinder beneath a piston, thereby allowing the weight of the atmosphere to push the piston down. In late 1680, he became a
fellow of the prestigious Royal Society.

In 1681, Papin traveled to Venice at the request of Ambrose Sarotti, whom Papin had met when Sarotti had been in London as the Venetian senate's representative to the English court. Sarotti, a fellow of the Royal Society since 1679, was establishing his own scientific academy in Venice, and he hired Papin as curator of experiments. Papin stayed until 1684, when he once again returned to London, this time as a temporary curator of experiments for the Royal Society. As such, he was required to prepare experiments for each meeting of the society.

Papin was very good at preparing and conducting experiments and demonstrations, and his own work began to reflect the expertise he thus gained. He also continued to publish papers in the society's *Philosophical Transactions*, but he left many others unpublished.

During this stint with the Royal Society, Papin began working on various methods of raising water. By now he had almost fifteen years of experience with pneumatics and hydraulics, and he began applying that knowledge to practical ends. His first scheme, which he presented to the Royal Society in June, 1685, was little more than a toy, in which he used the force of air to raise water. By June, 1686, he published a method for lifting water, which could have been used to drain water from mines or to supply a municipal water system with river water. This second proposal still offered a pneumatic means of lifting water, the power coming from a vertical waterwheel placed in a river.

The next iteration of his pneumatic engine for lifting water used the power of the waterwheel to create a vacuum under large pistons. The weight of the atmosphere then pushed the pistons down, thus doing work. This was the first attempt to use the weight of the atmosphere to provide a continuous effect (in this case the transmission of power). It does not appear that any such machine was ever built.

A few months later, in October, 1687, Papin turned to the use of gunpowder to evacuate a chamber below a piston of air. He was following Huygens's earlier idea, but he claimed to have made important improvements. In this proposal, the explosion of a small charge of gunpowder inside a cylinder (beneath a moving piston) forced much of the air in the cylinder out through one-way valves. The cylinder being thus evacuated, the weight of the atmosphere drove the piston down, doing work in the process. Although this plan had its merits, the gunpowder left a residue inside the cylinder, and Papin's tests showed that the explosion evacuated only about 80 percent of the air.

Shortly after presenting these ideas to the Royal Society in late 1687, Papin moved once again, this time to Germany, where he took the mathematics chair at the University of Marburg. His work suffered little interruption as a result of the move, and in August, 1690, he published a brief memoir of perhaps his most important technological innovation: production of a vacuum under a piston by condensation of steam. Papin built and demonstrated a small model engine working on this principle. He placed a fraction of an inch of water at the bottom of the cylinder, then pushed the piston down the cylinder until it touched the water. He then placed a flame under the cylinder. As the water boiled, the pressure of the steam forced the piston up the cylinder; the steam condensed as the cylinder cooled, leaving a vacuum beneath the piston. As in his earlier engines, the weight of the atmosphere then pushed the piston down, performing work as it went. This scheme solved the major problems of the gunpowder engine, but Papin does not seem to have built a full-size engine of this type.

Denis Papin. (AIP Niels Bohr Library)

Papin moved in 1695 or 1696 from Marburg to Cassel, where his patron, Landgrave Charles of Hesse, employed him as an engineer. Among his many tasks was the job of draining the landgrave's mines. In 1705, still in the landgrave's employ, he received a drawing of Thomas Savery's engine for draining mines. This engine also used a vacuum created by the condensation of steam, but not in conjunction with a piston. Papin attempted to improve upon Savery's engine, but by all accounts the engine he built was inferior to Savery's.

By late 1707, Papin was again in London, but not without mishap. Precipitating his departure from Cassel was the explosion—resulting in fatalities—of an experimental cannon, which was to have used steam rather than gunpowder to propel a projectile. He departed with his family on a small experimental boat propelled by a steam engine, although the exact type of engine remains unclear. Fearing competition from this new mode of transportation, rivermen on the Fulda River pulled the boat ashore and wrecked it. Papin's luck did not change when he reached London. Most of his friends from the Royal Society, especially the influential ones, were dead, and Savery held the patent rights for the steam engine. As a result, he lost his most important means of livelihood. Papin's last years are shrouded in obscurity. He apparently lived for a few years on small payments from the Royal Society for services rendered, but the exact time and place of his death are unknown.

SIGNIFICANCE

Papin was a thinker first and foremost. Although he had a very practical bent, he was not inclined to pursue one line of thought from the original conception to the construction of a working machine. Perhaps he was not capable of following a project from start to finish. Trained as a medical doctor, he had neither business expertise nor an engineering education. Papin also suffered from the lack of a strong supporter and financial backer. Without being able to market and profit from his inventions and without strong financial backing, he had little chance of completing projects that required substantial capital (such as a full-size steam engine).

Finally, it is important to remember that Papin never established a solid reputation. By moving frequently, especially as a younger man, and by failing to publish all but a few of the many papers he wrote, Papin failed to make himself and his ideas widely known.

Clearly, Papin was the first to think of producing a vacuum under a piston by the condensation of steam and letting the weight of the atmosphere perform work. This was the idea behind the early steam engine. It is not so clear what Papin actually contributed to the first engine; it may well be that Thomas Newcomen, whose famous steam engine worked on the same principle, arrived at the idea independently.

—*Brian J. Nichelson*

FURTHER READING

Barr, Scott E. "Denis Papin." *American Journal of Physics* 32 (1964): 290-291. A concise overview of Papin's life and accomplishments. Correctly maintains that Papin devised many original ideas, but because he lacked thoroughness he left many papers unpublished and many inventions unnoticed.

Bernard, Paul P. "How Not to Invent the Steamship." *East European Quarterly* 14 (Spring, 1980): 1-8. Focuses on the claim that Papin invented a steamship, briefly examining the work and obstacles involved in his trip down the Fulda River. Also examines how Papin's reputation has suffered, largely as a result of nationalistic debates between German and French historians.

Dickinson, H. W. *A Short History of the Steam Engine.* Cambridge, England: Cambridge University Press, 1938. Reprint. New York: Augustus M. Kelley, 1965. Dickinson focuses on Papin's contributions to development of the modern steam engine, briefly mentioning his work on the digester, the force of gunpowder, and other inventions. An introduction by A. E. Musson places Dickinson's work in its proper historiographical setting and supplies a few illuminating comments on Papin.

Drucker, Peter. "From Analysis to Perception: The New Worldview." In *The Essential Drucker: The Best Sixty Years of Peter Drucker's Essential Writings on Management.* New York: HarperBusiness, 2001. Management expert Drucker argues that Papin's invention of the steam engine created a new technology and perception of the world.

Galloway, Robert L. *The Steam Engine and Its Inventors: A Historical Sketch.* London: Macmillan, 1881. This work still is perhaps the best English-language account of Papin's work in pneumatics and hydraulics. Galloway briefly treats Papin's early life in chapter 1, while chapters 3 and 4 deal exclusively with Papin and his inventions.

Robinson, H. W. "Denis Papin (1647-1712)." *Notes and Records of the Royal Society of London* 5 (1947): 47-50. Based on the records of the Royal Society, this brief narrative is especially good, as one would expect, on Papin's relationship with the society. Provides a good overview of Papin's inventive life.

SEE ALSO: Robert Boyle; René Descartes; Pierre Gassendi; Otto von Guericke; Christiaan Huygens; Thomas Savery; Evangelista Torricelli.

RELATED ARTICLES in *Great Events from History: The Seventeenth Century, 1601-1700:* 1660-1692: Boyle's Law and the Birth of Modern Chemistry; July 25, 1698: Savery Patents the First Successful Steam Engine.

BLAISE PASCAL
French philosopher, mathematician, and physicist

Pascal was a genius in many areas who made important contributions to mathematics and physics and invented an early form of the calculator. His major contribution, however, is the record of his religious and philosophical struggle to reconcile human experience, God, and the quest for happiness and meaning.

BORN: June 19, 1623; Clermont-Ferrand, France
DIED: August 19, 1662; Paris, France
AREAS OF ACHIEVEMENT: Religion and theology, philosophy, mathematics, physics, science and technology

EARLY LIFE

Blaise Pascal (blehz pahs-kahl) was the third child of Étienne Pascal, a government financial bureaucrat, and Antoinette (Begon), who died when Pascal was about three. After his mother's death, Pascal and his family moved to Paris. Pascal's father decided to educate his children himself, rather than making use of either tutors or schools. Étienne Pascal was associated with the intellectual circles of Paris and thereby exposed Pascal to the best scientific and mathematical thought of his time.

While still a teenager, the precocious Pascal attracted the attention of the court and, in 1640, published his first mathematical treatise. In 1642, he began working on a mechanical calculator to help in his father's work. He continued improving the device for the next ten years and in 1652 sent a version of it to Queen Christina of Sweden. In 1646, Pascal and his two older sisters first came under the influence of Jansenism, a strict, pietistic movement within the Catholic Church that stressed a life of devotion, practical charity, and asceticism. Pascal experienced what is usually called his "first conversion," feeling the need for religious renewal but not wanting to give up his scientific and mathematical endeavors. His scientific work at this time included experiments with vacu-

ums, an important area of exploration in seventeenth century physics.

LIFE'S WORK

By his mid-twenties, Pascal had assumed a pattern of life that he would continue until his death. In 1647, he entered into the first of the public religious controversies that would preoccupy him for the rest of his life. He also continued his scientific work on the vacuum, exchanging information with the great philosopher René Descartes and publishing his own findings. In 1648, he wrote a mathematical essay on conic sections. Throughout this

Blaise Pascal. (Library of Congress)

713

PASCAL ON RECONCILING REASON'S POSSIBILITIES AND LIMITS

Blaise Pascal, a great thinker and innovator, was also deeply religious. The excerpt here shows Pascal "reasoning" the limits of reason, a seeming paradox. Pascal, however, concludes that in the face of overwhelming odds against both knowing absolutely and knowing nothing, one can *still be sure that he or she can know something. It is this unique human ability to think that leads to moral, righteous behavior.*

What is the rank man occupies in Nature? A nonentity, as contrasted with infinity; a universe, contrasted with nonentity; a middle something between every thing and nothing. . . .

Such is our real state; our acquirements are confined within limits which we cannot pass, alike incapable of attaining universal knowledge or of remaining in total ignorance. We are in the middle of a vast expanse, always unfixed, fluctuating between ignorance and knowledge; if we think of advancing further, our object shifts its position and eludes our grasp; it steals away and takes eternal flight that nothing can arrest. This is our natural condition, altogether contrary, however, to our inclinations. We are inflamed with a desire of exploring every thing, and of building a tower that shall rise into infinity, but our edifice is shattered to pieces, and the ground beneath it discloses a profound abyss.

Man is the feeblest reed in existence, but he is a thinking reed. There is no need that the universe be armed for his destruction; a noxious vapour, a drop of water is enough to cause his death. But though the universe were to destroy him, man would be more noble than his destroyer, for he would know that he was dying, while the universe would know nothing of its own achievement. Thus all our dignity consists in the thinking principle. This and not space and duration, is what elevates us. Let us labour then to think aright; here is the foundation of morals.

Source: Pascal, *Pensées* (1670), excerpted in *The Age of Reason: The Culture of the Seventeenth Century*, edited by Leo Weinstein (New York: George Braziller, 1965), pp. 256-257.

the skeptical worldliness of society life and greatly desired something more meaningful. During the middle of the night of November 23, 1654, he had an intense, mystical religious experience that lasted about two hours and changed the direction of his life. During this experience, Pascal felt powerfully and unmistakably the truth of God's existence and the blessing of His love and forgiveness. Pascal had been provided with the kind of experiential certainty for which his scientific mind yearned and, consequently, saw everything thereafter in spiritual terms. In reaction to this experience, he went to Port-Royal, the center of Jansenism, for a two-week retreat in early 1655 to begin the reformation of his life that he now sought. He was particularly concerned with overcoming the willful pride that had marked his life since his spectacular intellectual accomplishments as a boy and the selfishness that showed itself in his resistance to his sister Jacqueline's entrance into the community at Port-Royal.

Jansenism was to dominate his life for the next few years. In 1653, Pope Innocent X had condemned the writings of Cornelius Otto Jansen, bishop of Ypres, upon which the Jansenist movement in the Catholic Church was based. The great enemies of the Jansenists were the rationalistic Jesuits, and in January of 1656, Pascal wrote the first of a series of anonymous letters now titled *Lettres provinciales* (1656-1657; *The Provincial Letters*, 1657). These letters, eighteen in all, came out in May, 1657, and are masterpieces of satire, wit, analytic logic, and French prose style. Especially in the early letters, the fictitious writer adopts a pose of objective, naïve curiosity about the controversy between the Jesuits and Jansenists, which he is purportedly trying to explain to his fellow provincial back home. In reality, the letters are an impassioned defense of the principles and principals of the Jansenist movement and a stinging attack on the Jesuits. The letters were enormously popular, and the local authorities went to great lengths to try to suppress them and discover their author. Pascal's letters have been admired ever since as masterpieces of French prose.

Pascal was not satisfied, however, merely to defend a particular movement within the Catholic Church. He desired to write a great defense of Christianity as a whole at a time when religious faith was increasingly under attack

period, Pascal was afflicted with serious illness, as he would be for the remainder of his life.

Pascal's sister Jacqueline continued to be influenced by Jansenism, and during this time she expressed her desire to enter the Jansenist religious community at Port-Royal. Both Pascal and his father objected, but after her father's death in 1651, Jacqueline entered the convent the following year. Pascal began a brief phase in which he indulged himself in the pleasures and pursuits of French society, finding the experience empty but also finding no other direction for his life at this time.

Pascal experienced a growing disillusionment with

by skepticism, on one hand, and rationalism, on the other. Prompted in part by what he took to be the miraculous cure of his young niece, Pascal began in 1657 to take notes for this work, which he once said would take ten years of steady effort to complete. As it turned out, Pascal never completed the work or even a draft of it. Instead, he produced approximately one thousand notes, some only a few words, others pages long and substantially revised. The majority of these notes were written in 1657 and 1658, after which time he fell into an extremely painful and debilitating illness that would largely incapacitate him until his death. The notes were first published in abbreviated form as *Pensées* (1670; *Monsieur Pascal's Thoughts, Meditations, and Prayers*, 1688; best known as *Pensées*) and have become one of the classic documents of Western culture.

Although Pascal never wrote his great apology for the Christian faith, he did organize many of his notes into groups, from which scholars have speculated as to his ultimate intentions. As enlightening as these speculations sometimes are, the timelessness of *Pensées* comes not from the tantalizing promise of some irrefutable defense of religious faith but from Pascal's compelling, often painful insights into the human condition and from the process of watching one of history's great minds struggle with eternal questions of faith, spirit, and transcendence.

Many of Pascal's most powerful entries poignantly explore the tragedy and folly of the human condition if there were no God. He depicts humankind as lost in an alien and inhospitable world, given over to the empty baubles and distractions of society. Pascal portrays the world as a psychologically frightening place. Men and women are caught between the infinitely large, on one hand, and the infinitely small, on the other. They are torn by a divided nature that is neither angel nor beast, to use one of his images, but is capable of acting like either. Human beings yearn for something sure and permanent but find only illusion and transience. Pascal finds the solution for the human dilemma in the grace of God as manifested in Jesus Christ. Only by knowing who created them, Pascal argues, can humans know who they are and how they can be happy. He does not, however, offer this solution as an effortless one. Part of Pascal's enduring appeal is his very modern awareness of the difficulty of religious faith in a scientific and skeptical world.

Pascal was seriously ill much of the last four years of his life, but that did not prevent him from at least sporadic efforts on a variety of projects. In 1658, he made further mathematical discoveries on the cycloid and publicly challenged the mathematicians of Europe to a contest in solving problems in this area. He was drawn briefly into the Jansenist controversy once again but then withdrew from it altogether. His concern for the poor led him to invent and launch a public transportation system in Paris in March of 1662. Additionally, when health permitted, he worked on his defense of Christianity that became *Pensées*. After much suffering patiently borne, Pascal died on August 19, 1662, at the age of thirty-nine.

SIGNIFICANCE

Pascal is one of those handful of individuals in history whose wide range of accomplishments shows evidence of a fundamental genius that expressed itself wherever it was applied. Proof of his greatness is given by the number of different fields of intellectual effort that claim him. He is considered a mathematician of the first rank, an important physicist at the early stages of that science, an inventor, a literary master of French prose, and, most important, a philosopher and religious thinker who has written brilliantly about fundamental questions of the human condition.

Pascal stood at the beginning of the modern age, one who felt keenly the call of reason and science but who realized the price to be paid if one lost a sense of the spiritual and transcendent. He felt caught between two contrary forces: the rationalism of rising seventeenth century science and the skepticism about all human efforts, reason included, as epitomized by his French predecessor, Michel Eyquem de Montaigne. He sought an approach to life that avoided the arrogance and materialism of the former and the cynicism and moral passivity of the latter. In this sense, Pascal's situation anticipates the modern one. How does one find meaning, values, and faith in a rationalistic, skeptical world where most traditional guidelines are called into question? For more than three hundred years, men and women have found insight and inspiration in Pascal's answers.

—*Daniel Taylor*

FURTHER READING

Adamson, Donald. *Blaise Pascal: Mathematician, Physicist, and Thinker About God*. New York: St. Martin's Press, 1995. A chronological survey of Pascal's work in mathematics, physics, religion, and philosophy.

Coleman, Francis X. J. *Neither Angel nor Beast: The Life and Work of Blaise Pascal*. New York: Routledge & Kegan Paul, 1986. A somewhat poorly organized but still-insightful overview of Pascal's life and work. Good at placing Pascal in the context of seventeenth century thought.

Davidson, Hugh M. *Blaise Pascal*. Boston: Twayne, 1983. A good introduction to Pascal. Short but adequate overview of his life and discussion of all of his major and most of his minor works, including detailed discussion of his mathematical contributions.

Groothius, Douglas. *On Pascal*. Belmont, Calif.: Thomson Learning/Wadsworth, 2003. Concise introduction to Pascal's most important ideas, placing these concepts within a historical context.

Hammond, Nicholas, ed. *The Cambridge Companion to Pascal*. New York: Cambridge University Press, 2003. A collection of essays, including discussions of Pascal's life and times; his work on probability, decision theory, and religion; and the reception of *Pensées* in the seventeenth and eighteenth centuries.

Krailsheimer, Alban. *Pascal*. New York: Hill & Wang, 1980. Brief but helpful summary of Pascal's mathematical and scientific accomplishments. Good on the cultural context and central concerns of the *Pensées*.

Moriarty, Michael. *Early Modern French Thought: The Age of Suspicion*. New York: Oxford University Press, 2003. Examines the philosophy of Pascal, René Descartes, and Nicolas Malebranche.

Nelson, Robert J. *Pascal: Adversary and Advocate*. Cambridge, Mass.: Harvard University Press, 1981. One of the more comprehensive and ambitious studies of Pascal. Takes a psychological approach to Pascal's biography and work, with extensive critical study of individual works.

Pascal, Blaise. *Pensées*. Translated by A. J. Krailsheimer. London: Penguin Books, 1966. One of the better of the many translations of Pascal's great work. Recommended.

SEE ALSO: Pierre Bayle; Christina; René Descartes; Pierre de Fermat; Cornelius Otto Jansen; Marin Mersenne; Jean Racine; Wilhelm Schickard.

RELATED ARTICLES in *Great Events from History: The Seventeenth Century, 1601-1700:* 1601-1672: Rise of Scientific Societies; 1615-1696: Invention and Development of the Calculus; 1623-1674: Earliest Calculators Appear; 1637: Descartes Publishes His *Discourse on Method*; 1638-1669: Spread of Jansenism; 1643: Torricelli Measures Atmospheric Pressure; 1654: Pascal and Fermat Devise the Theory of Probability; March 18, 1662: Public Transportation Begins; 1664: Molière Writes *Tartuffe*; 1673: Huygens Explains the Pendulum.

WILLIAM PATERSON
Scottish businessman and financier

Paterson was cofounder of the Bank of England, an active participant in the so-called Darien scheme to establish a Scottish settlement in Panama, and an innovator in government finance.

BORN: April, 1658; Skipmyre, Tinwald, Dumfriesshire, Scotland
DIED: January 22, 1719; London, England
AREA OF ACHIEVEMENT: Business and economics

EARLY LIFE

William Paterson was born in April, 1658, in Skipmyre in Dumfriesshire, Scotland, the son of John and Elizabeth (Bethia) Paterson. John Paterson was regarded as one of the wealthier tenant farmers in the district. Disagreement about William Paterson's age when he left Scotland to live with a kinswoman in the thriving city of Bristol makes it impossible to determine the extent of his formal education. Whatever formal education Paterson had, if any, his extensive writing primarily on financial and business subjects in later life showed considerable rhetorical adroitness that allowed him to hold up his side in public controversy. Exposure to Bristol's growth as a port left a strong impression on him, and his attention was turned for a time to the West Indian trade. Unable to account for his acquisition of enough capital to begin trading as a merchant, tradition has variously ascribed to him a legacy from the Bristol relative with whom he lived for a while, his having worked for another relative in a London counting house, or, more romantically, an earlier brief career as a missionary followed by a more profitable stint as a buccaneer in the West Indies.

Until after the Glorious Revolution of 1688, Paterson's life is documented only in glimpses that disclose a great variety of early business experiences. Certainly he did go to the West Indies, where he established a reputation for profitable and fair trading. His interest in colonial business expanded to include knowledge of the New England trade. He became a member of the Merchant Taylors' Company in London in 1681 and acquired extensive knowledge about trade with the German states. It may well have been Paterson's politics that took him to Amsterdam, which was a refuge from the religious and political excesses of James II during the late 1680's, but his experience in the most important center of northern European banking and finance must have intensified Paterson's interest in a bank founded on government securities.

LIFE'S WORK

Paterson's various early business ventures made him prosperous. After the Glorious Revolution, he returned to England, where his wealth and broad business experience gave him considerable influence in the business community. The opportunities surrounding government finance offered abundant possibilities for an entrepreneur who could devise a scheme to help the government meet the unprecedented financial needs incurred in the war with France. The fiscal demands of the war, which raised the government's expenditure from less than £2 million a year to between £5 million and £6 million a year, could not be satisfied by traditional methods of raising money on a short-term basis. New procedures for acquiring loans had to be found.

While others proposed stopgap expedients that traded loans for concessions from the government, Paterson, in 1692, suggested to the House of Commons a scheme modeled on existing Dutch practice. Paterson proposed inviting subscriptions for a loan of £1 million. Lenders would receive 6 percent interest. They would receive "bills of property" as security for their loan, the most remarkable feature of which was the negotiability of the "bills" that made them legal currency. This aspect of the proposal was too novel for Parliament, which was moved by complaints that the "bills of property" could be forced on creditors as payment without their consent. Still, Paterson's resourcefulness was recognized, and he received encouragement from Parliament to propose a revised scheme that made only the interest on the loan assignable.

In December, 1692, Paterson offered Parliament a suggestion for another innovative scheme for raising loans; this time, his proposal was accepted, and Paterson thereby came to the attention of Charles Montagu, a treasury commissioner who was later to become first lord of the Treasury and to be elevated to the peerage as the earl of Halifax. With powerful support in the government, Paterson submitted a plan in 1693 that led to the creation of the Bank of England. Paterson proposed that the government borrow £1.2 million from subscribers who would be paid 8 percent interest, but, more important,

William Paterson. (Library of Congress)

would be allowed to incorporate and conduct business as a bank. The proposal excited opposition, and while Montagu attempted to win acceptance for the idea within the government, Paterson set forth his arguments to the public in *A Brief Account of the Intended Bank of England* (1694).

Paterson responded skillfully to his various opponents. Those who objected to a bank for political or constitutional reasons were reassured that Parliament might easily avert a shift in the constitutional balance of power by appropriating money for designated purposes, eliminating the king's freedom to use his new powers to borrow for a political advantage. Adopting a long-range strategy, Paterson argued that the bank would reduce the interest rate by taking money that might otherwise lie in unproductive savings and placing it in circulation. The more money in circulation, the lower the rate of interest. Finally, the landed interests would benefit from the economic effects of the bank because the concentration of money in London caused by the bank would lower interest rates and make money easy to find and cheaper to borrow. Paterson saw clearly that the projected Bank of England would assume a commanding position in the London money market, and that, he considered, would have an entirely beneficial effect.

Paterson's efforts helped allay popular fears about the consequences of establishing the Bank of England to such a considerable extent that when the act was passed and the subscription of the £1.2 million was opened to the public on June 21, 1694, there was astonishing response: £300,000 was subscribed the first day, and except for £18,000, the remainder was subscribed before the end of the month.

Paterson became one of the directors of the new Bank of England in 1694, but he was soon disappointed by the conservative policies of his fellow directors, who wanted the bank to specialize in government finance, thus failing to engage in the broad range of projects Paterson originally envisioned. His enterprising nature and his desire to assist the unfortunate led him early in 1695 to propose consolidating the Orphans Fund of the City of London by raising a public subscription of £400,000.

Perhaps his public association with a subscription for the Orphans Fund caused some of the other directors of the bank to want to put some distance between themselves and Paterson's new venture. Furthermore, some of his fellow trustees in the Orphans Fund were to be drawn from the ranks of recent opponents of the bank, leading the bank's Court of Directors to call Paterson before them on February 20, 1695. Paterson presented arguments defending his recent activities, but his fellow bank directors voted that they were not satisfied with his explanation and requested that Paterson attend no further directors' meetings until he had satisfied their objections. Wounded pride, questioned integrity, and lack of support from his fellow directors induced Paterson to resign his office and sell his stock, thus ending his association with the Bank of England he had been instrumental in creating, less than a year after it was founded.

Paterson's talents were not, however, long unemployed. Shortly after he left the Bank of England, he became involved in the efforts of English and Scottish businessmen to break the profitable monopoly of the East India Company and create an organization that would promote trade with Europe and Scottish colonization of the New World as well. Although Paterson did not found this enterprise, he believed that the grand aspirations of the participants gave him ample scope for the colonial projects he had planned since he was a young man.

Paterson returned to Scotland in 1695 and lent his reputation, capital, knowledge, and boundless enthusiasm to the projects. Indeed, after English merchants encountered opposition from the House of Commons and William III, and most withdrew their capital from the project, Paterson became the most important force behind the venture. When an agent he hired to purchase supplies stole a large part of the £25,000 with which Paterson had entrusted him, however, Paterson was dropped as one of the directors of the company, even though he was cleared of complicity by an investigation. When he sailed on the first expedition to Panama, he went as a private individual. The expedition had to be abandoned; Paterson himself suffered serious illness both in Darien and in the return voyage to New York, and his wife and only son died in Darien. Paterson returned to Edinburgh in December, 1699, hoping to revive the Darien scheme, but his failure to interest the Scots caused him to go back to England.

Paterson did not become involved in the creation of great business institutions during the later years of his life. His fertile imagination designed strategies to improve the administration of government finance. Paterson's subsequent suggestions for government finance were insightful; he proposed a sinking fund to retire the growing government debt as early as 1701, as well as a grand scheme that would consolidate and pay off the national debt in 1717. The proposed union of England and Scotland during Queen Anne's reign was a project he supported with a persuasive pamphlet. The prospective union so excited Paterson that he went to Scotland, where he helped frame the sections of the Treaty of Union that dealt with trade and finance. During his last years, Paterson may have had to live in reduced circumstances, teaching mathematics and navigation to supplement the small return he received on his investments. He died in Queen Square, Westminster, in January, 1719.

SIGNIFICANCE

Paterson was a pioneer in the business world of his day. He drew upon his observations on the Continent and his business experience in England to refine and modify existing borrowing practices. His contribution was greater, however, than simply distilling the best part of previous proposals and foreign experiences. Paterson, together with the activities of supporter Michael Godfrey and the political efforts of Montagu, countered the considerable opposition to the Bank of England. The result of Paterson's vision and labor was the creation of the most important private financial institution in English history.

The Darien scheme was less durable and far less happy than the founding of the Bank of England. The ambitious creation of a large trading company gave Paterson the opportunity to explain the breadth of his vision for the development of trade, including a passionate and persuasive advocacy of the doctrine of free trade. His suggestions for government finance were generally excellent, although their importance was not fully realized in Paterson's lifetime. If his life did not bring him an enormous personal fortune, his work and ideas enriched subsequent generations of Englishmen and Scots.

—*Glenn O. Nichols*

FURTHER READING

Bannister, Saxe. *William Paterson, the Merchant Statesman, and Founder of the Bank of England: His Life and Trials.* Edinburgh: William P. Nimmo, 1858. A traditional, highly partisan biography by the editor of Paterson's writings.

Barbour, James Samuel. *A History of William Paterson and the Darien Company.* Edinburgh: W. Blackwood and Sons, 1907. Barbour explains Paterson's role in the Darien project, but his account is not as readable or as reliable as Insh's study (see below).

Dickson, P. G. M. *The Financial Revolution in England: A Study in the Development of Public Credit, 1688-1756.* London: Macmillan, 1967. Reprint. Brookfield, Vt.: Ashgate, 1993. Dickson gives a splendid account of the financial context of Paterson's achievement.

Forrester, Andrew. *The Man Who Saw the Future: William Paterson's Vision of Free Trade.* New York: Texere, 2004. In the first modern biography, Forrester argues that Paterson's vision of world commerce was far ahead of its time.

Horsefield, J. Keith. *British Monetary Experiments 1650-1710.* London: Garland Publishing, 1983. Horsefield surveys the world of finance and banking. A substantial work that requires an understanding of basic economic terminology.

Insh, George Pratt. *The Company of Scotland Trading to Africa and the Indies.* New York: Charles Scribner's Sons, 1932. Insh gives an admirable history of the Darien scheme.

Paterson, William. *The Writings of William Paterson.* Edited by Saxe Bannister. 3 vols. London: Judd and Glass, 1859. Reprint. New York: A. M. Kelley, 1968. Paterson's own writings are the best source of information about his life and work.

Prebble, John. *Darien: The Scottish Dream of Empire.* Edinburgh, Scotland: Birlinn, 2000. A reprint of *The Darien Disaster,* published in 1968, this book is a popular history of the Darien scheme written by a prolific Scottish historian.

Warburton, Eliot. *Darien: Or, The Merchant Prince, an Historical Romance.* New York: Harper and Brothers, 1852. Paterson is the hero of this work of fiction.

SEE ALSO: James II; Mary II; William III.

RELATED ARTICLES in *Great Events from History: The Seventeenth Century, 1601-1700:* 1688-1702: Reign of William and Mary; November, 1688-February, 1689: The Glorious Revolution.

PAUL V
Italian pope (1605-1621)

A vigorous proponent of papal political supremacy, Paul was a strong governor of his church during the Catholic Counter-Reformation, using excommunication and interdict to compel obedience. Paul canonized saints, completed the building of St. Peter's Basilica, and organized the Vatican archives. His failed political engagements, however, cost the Papacy much influence in affairs of state.

BORN: September 17, 1552; Rome, Papal States (now in Italy)
DIED: January 28, 1621; Rome
ALSO KNOWN AS: Camillo Borghese (given name)
AREAS OF ACHIEVEMENT: Religion and theology, church reform

EARLY LIFE

Pope Paul V (Camillo Borghese) was of Sienese ancestry. His father, Marcantonio Borghese, a lawyer, served Pope Paul III, and his mother, Flaminia Astalli, was of Roman nobility. Paul V studied philosophy at the University of Perugia and received the doctor of laws degree from the University of Padua, after which he served the Vatican and became a distinguished canon lawyer. In 1596, Pope Clement VII made him a cardinal.

During an era of much partisan contention within the papal consistory, Paul joined no faction, a course of behavior that made him an acceptable candidate when, in 1605, the cardinals could not agree about electing a pope. Prior to his elevation to the cardinalate, Paul held the positions of vicar of the Basilica of St. Mary Major and vice-legate of Bologna (1588), general auditor of the Papal Camera (1590), papal ambassador to Spain (1593), and, after receiving a cardinal's red hat, bishop of Iesi (1597-1599), cardinal vicar of Rome (1603), and inquisitor (1603).

Paul's career in papal service and his abstinence from factional disputes among the cardinals made him a likely candidate for the papacy when Clement VIII died in 1605. The College of Cardinals, however, chose Alessandro de' Medici, a former legate to France, as Leo XI, whose pontificate ended twenty-seven days later with his sudden death (1605).

LIFE'S WORK

The demise of Leo XI required a new conclave of cardinals, one in which the French and Spanish members were especially contentious. After failing to agree on the nomination of such distinguished figures as Jesuit theologian and cardinal Robert Bellarmine, a militant enemy of Protestants, and celebrated ecclesiastical historian Caesar Baronius (Cesare Baronio), plus some other cardinals, the college selected Camillo Borghese as a compromise candidate, who assumed the name Paul V.

Once in position, the pontiff pursued the interests of his own family by granting Church offices to his relatives, who consequently enjoyed lucrative incomes from their benefices, in some cases acquiring huge wealth. To his credit, however, Paul required all bishops to reside in their dioceses, as the Council of Trent (1545-1563) had decreed. Absenteeism among prelates had been a scandal for some time, and Paul resolved to eliminate it, so even episcopal cardinals who lived comfortably in Rome had to return to their bishoprics.

Consistent with his conception of papal supremacy, Paul asserted his authority over secular rulers from whom he expected obedience, a policy that brought conflict with Naples, Genoa, and Turin, disputes that did not produce open ruptures. Contention with Venice was, however, serious to the point that it could have led to military combat.

The issue with Venice involved disagreements about the proper boundaries of Ferrara and control over the Venetian clergy. In the manner of his powerful predecessors Gregory VII (1073-1085) and Innocent III (1198-1216), Paul insisted he had a God-given right to depose civil authorities who defied his mandates. In taking this position, the pope received encouragement from the Jesuit polemicist Bellarmine, who argued that clerics were not accountable to secular officials, and from 1605 to 1607 there was a bitter controversy, after Venetian authorities

arrested two priests and accused them of crimes for which they must stand trial in a state court. This decision conflicted with a Tridentine decree that ecclesiastical courts alone had jurisdiction over the clergy. Paul responded to Venetian defiance by excommunicating the doge, the official head of state, and the senate of the Republic. When that did not produce compliance, the pope placed Venice under interdict.

In addition to the controversy about immunity for the clergy from civil prosecution, Paul denounced the action of Venice that required government permission to erect new churches or monasteries and forbade the donation of real estate to the Church. The republic refused to succumb to papal intimidation, and almost all Venetian clerics honored the directive of the state to ignore the interdict. Except for the Jesuits, Theatines, and Capuchins, the priests continued religious services as usual. At points, the government hinted it might adopt Protestantism, and war between the Papacy and the republic seemed likely.

In the struggle to assert his supremacy, the pope had support from Bellarmine and Baronius, the latter a leading scholar who used history as a tool with which to rebut Protestant attacks upon Rome. The Venetian government employed its own historian, Paolo Sarpi, a monk and the leader of the Servite order, who had a reputation for immense learning and disdain for papal authoritarianism. Sarpi's opposition to the veneration of the Virgin Mary aroused the Jesuits, and the Inquisition disputed his orthodoxy. When it became evident that Sarpi could not prevail, Paul accepted a compromise that allowed him to save face while gaining little of substance.

King Henry IV of France arranged negotiations that led to peace. The pope revoked the interdict, and the Republic released the detained priests but did not acknowledge papal authority in matters of state, nor did it revoke the policies about church properties that had angered the pope. Although the banished Capuchins and Theatines were allowed to return to Venice, the Jesuits were not, for authorities there considered them subversive agents of Rome.

Paul V's problems with Venice were compounded by poor relations with Protestant England, where the Gunpowder Plot (1605) had failed to kill King James I and end his parliament. The pope appealed to the king to not punish all Catholics for the crime of a few. When Parliament demanded that Catholics renounce the pope's authority to depose rulers, Paul prohibited them from subscribing the oath, thereby ensuring that English Protestants would continue to regard Catholicism a threat to the kingdom. Even in Catholic France, Paul's policy caused consternation, and the Estates-General declared the king held his authority as a grant from God unrelated to the Papacy. The same body refused to promulgate the decrees of Trent.

The pontificate of Paul V was a dynamic one in that he chartered the Congregation of the Oratory, which Philip Neri founded, and he canonized Neri and several others. Paul promoted missions as far abroad as China, and in the realm of theology he forbade arguments about the efficacy of grace in salvation, a controversy in which the Jesuits had taken a leading role. Paul rejected the heliocentric view of the universe that Copernicus presented, and he censured Galileo for advocating Copernicus's theory. The pontiff contributed to scholarship, nevertheless, by authorizing the cataloging of the Vatican archives. In architecture, he made his mark by completing construction of St. Peter's Basilica.

Paul V died on January 28, 1621, soon after celebrating the victory of Catholic forces over Protestant Bohemians at the Battle of White Mountain near Prague.

SIGNIFICANCE

Paul V led the reform of the Church, reducing the corruption and abuse that had blemished its image and given credence to complaints from Protestants. The pope's patronage of his own relatives, however, displayed an inconsistency in his commitment to wholesome changes, although in most cases he appointed able men. Still, the wealth his favorites acquired encouraged suspicions about his own integrity. His nephew, Cardinal Scipione Borghese (formerly Scipione Caffarelli), for example, gained enormous riches and wielded terrific influence upon papal policy while securing the fortunes of his own family. Paul corrected some abuses in the courts of the Church, promoted public works in Rome—including an aqueduct to improve the water supply—and subsidized the restoration and preservation of ancient structures and monuments. His support of libraries, museums, and charities was substantial.

In contrast with Paul V's achievements is his conspicuous failure in relations with secular rulers. The pontiff insisted upon his temporal supremacy to the point that he had the right to depose disobedient monarchs. His inability to do so made the claim appear ludicrous and thereby impaired the prestige of the Vatican in world affairs. Dynastic politics had become the decisive force in international relations as the nation-state system emerged. The political influence of the Papacy was diminishing, and no pontiff would be able to retrieve it.

—*James Edward McGoldrick*

FURTHER READING

Bouwsma, William J. *Venice and the Defense of Republican Liberty*. Berkeley: University of California Press, 1968. This careful study relates to Renaissance ideas the Venetian resistance to papal political assertions, and it contains perceptive coverage of Paul V.

Grendler, Paul F. *The Roman Inquisition and the Venetian Press, 1540-1605*. Princeton, N.J.: Princeton University Press, 1977. This erudite study of papal policy toward Venice explains tensions that led Paul to impose excommunication and interdict. Includes a large bibliography.

Pastor, Ludwig von. *The History of the Popes from the Close of the Middle Ages*. Translated and edited by Dom Ernest Graf. 1937. Reprint. St. Louis, Mo.: B. Herder, 1952. Despite its age, this Roman Catholic work remains the most comprehensive treatment of Paul's pontificate.

Ranke, Leopold von. *History of the Popes*. Vol. 2. 1901. Reprint. Translated by E. Fowler. New York: Frederick Ungar, 1966. This is a thorough, dispassionate work by the pioneer of modern historiography and is especially useful for its coverage of Paul's relationship with the Jesuit order.

Wright, Anthony D. *The Early Modern Papacy from the Council of Trent to the French Revolution*. London: Longman, 2000. This is a well-documented topical study of the Vatican that is rich in details about Paul V.

SEE ALSO: Alexander VII; Gian Lorenzo Bernini; Santorio Santorio; Urban VIII; Saint Vincent de Paul.

RELATED ARTICLES in *Great Events from History: The Seventeenth Century, 1601-1700:* 1610: Galileo Confirms the Heliocentric Model of the Solar System; 1632: Galileo Publishes *Dialogue Concerning the Two Chief World Systems, Ptolemaic and Copernican*; 1656-1667: Construction of the Piazza San Pietro.

NICOLAS-CLAUDE FABRI DE PEIRESC
French scholar, jurist, and writer

Peiresc was a wealthy judicial official in southern France, a well-known patron of the arts and sciences, a Humanist scholar of encyclopedic interests, and perhaps the most indefatigable letter writer in Europe of the time.

BORN: December 1, 1580; Belgentier, France
DIED: June 24, 1637; Aix-en-Provence, France
AREAS OF ACHIEVEMENT: Scholarship, patronage of the arts, historiography, law, philosophy, science and technology

EARLY LIFE

The son of Raynaud de Fabri, Nicolas-Claude Fabri de Peiresc (nee-koh-law-klowd fah-bree deh peh-rehsk) belonged to a prestigious family of nobles, at once munificent, cultured, and dedicated to the promotion of the French crown, which family members served as judicial officials (*conseillers du roi*) in the provincial court (*parlement*) at Aix-en-Provence.

Having graduated from the Jesuit college at Tournon, Peiresc (the name he took in 1624, after he inherited an alpine estate of that name from his mother) left Aix-en Provence at age nineteen to study law at Padua. Although a serious student, he spent more time in the next three years touring Italian cities, making friends, and seeking out correspondents than he did reading law. Also in Italy, he began collecting ancient books, manuscripts, gems, medallions, coins, mummies, fossils, and objets d'art, each of which he treated as a source for the reconstruction of the fading past. He was particularly enamored with ancient Greece, Rome, Egypt, and the non-European cultures of the Mediterranean and Near East.

He sought out Galileo in Padua, and in Rome, he became friends with Maffeo Barbarini (later Pope Urban VIII), with whom he would intercede in the 1630's on Galileo's behalf. Most important, he met Jean-Vincent Pinelli, a Paduan of encyclopedic humanistic interests, who inspired Peiresc's obsession with all-encompassing scholarship.

Peiresc had been planning a trip to Constantinople and the Levant when his father called him home to study law more seriously and to consider marriage. Although dubbed Prince d'Amour at a royal court celebration held in Aix in 1593, Peiresc's only real love was learning, and his only helpmate was an enormous income sufficient to realize the projects of his clever mind. Turning aside an arranged marriage, the prince of love devoted himself to many passionate interests among the arts and sciences, thereby earning Anatole France's more apt ascription, *prince des bibliophiles* (prince of book lovers). Determined on celibacy, he even contemplated joining the Capuchines, but he reconsidered. Religiously speaking, he remained sincerely Catholic, but he was a voice of toleration, too, in a dogmatic age. He befriended Protestants, Muslims, and Jews.

LIFE'S WORK

At Montpellier in 1604, Peiresc completed his law courses and succeeded to his uncle's position in *parlement*. The following year, however, he again went traveling, this time to Paris as secretary to writer Guillaume du Vair, first president in *parlement*. After two years in Paris, he sailed for England as part of the mission of de La Broderie, the French ambassador. In London, he met King James I and a number of English scholars, William Camden, Robert Bruce Cotton, and John Barclay among them. He returned home through the Netherlands, visiting colleagues of Pinelli and adding new names to his growing address book of international contacts.

At Aix in 1607, Peiresc took up astronomy, and three years later he read Galileo's *Sidereus nuncius* (1610; *The Sidereal Messenger*, 1880). Peiresc became, with Joseph Gautier, one of the first Frenchmen to observe the four moons of Jupiter. Around the same time, he made deep-space observations, discovering the Orion Nebula in 1610. He later investigated the phases of Venus (an important piece of evidence for Earth's rotation) and lunar eclipses, and he used observations of the moons of Jupiter to help determine longitudes.

In 1616, Vair again recruited Peiresc to travel to Paris in his entourage. In the next seven years, Peiresc immersed himself in the intellectual life of the capital, which centered on private, informal academies such as that of the *cabinet* of brothers Pierre Dupuy and Jacques Dupuy, historians and librarians. Surrounded by thousands of books and the brilliance of learned fraternity at the Dupuys', he encountered most of the city's leading thinkers, among them Marin Mersenne, a Minim friar, natural philosopher, and music theorist.

After his return to Provence, Peiresc resumed his position as arbiter of French and Italian culture. He harbored deep affection for the Italian people, from whom he was descended, and for their artistic heritage, which he had studied firsthand as a student. In Italy, he had seen the works of Michelangelo, Raphael, Titian, and Caravaggio. He bought many canvasses, including several by Sir Anthony van Dyck, who painted Peiresc's portrait; by Tintoretto; and by Peter Paul Rubens, the Flemish master he had met during his second trip to Paris. Peiresc helped Rubens choose the subjects for the monumental series of propagandistic tableaux dedicated to the life of Marie de Médicis. Her marriage by proxy to King Henry IV in Florence in October of 1600, represented by the tableaux, was witnessed by Peiresc.

In natural philosophy, or science, Peiresc developed particular affection for geology, archaeology, astronomy, and biology. Between his urban villa in Aix (the Hotel Callas) and his country estate, Belgentier, he kept the third largest garden in France and even had something of a zoo, complete at various times with alligators, antelopes, and tigers. Indoors, he kept smaller felines, Angora cats. He was purportedly the first to have imported them to the kingdom. The cats lounged about in uneasy coexistence with the many vases, statues, and other fragile antiquities he had carefully collected.

He kept his bedroom stocked with songbirds to cheer his days and to lull him to sleep after labors that kept him at work until late in the night; he once wrote forty-two letters in a day. Tireless in the acquisition of scholarly treasures of the Levant and North Africa, he did business with virtually anyone who had something important to sell. He even made deals with pirates—the enterprising middlemen in the commerce of ideas and objects on the Mediterranean—when he believed God had chosen to deliver "learned booty" into his hands through those very pirates.

Unfortunately, his interests were paralyzing in their universality: Wanting to know everything, he published nothing. Most of the more than one hundred volumes of his notes, essays, and letters (totaling more than 100,000 pages) remain unpublished. Peiresc, however, patronized those who did publish (Pierre Gassendi and Mersenne being the most famous examples) with subsidies and sinecures, grants to hire copyists and to defray printing costs, and gifts and loans from his library of more than fifty-four hundred books and more than two hundred manuscripts (a collection his hungry Angoras helped preserve from the ravages of mice and rats).

Peiresc encouraged Hugo Grotius to publish what became groundbreaking reflections on international law, and in the 1630's, he invited Gassendi into his home, where Gassendi produced some of his greatest work. Peiresc also encouraged William Harvey's work on the circulation of blood, and before his death in 1637, he helped to free the utopian writer Tommaso Campanella from the clutches of Spanish authorities in Italy, gave him asylum at Belgentier, and found him refuge in Paris.

Dictated to his secretaries, Peiresc's letters numbered at minimum ten thousand (seven thousand are extant) and were even more voluminous than those of Mersenne, whose correspondence network intersected his own to form a vast international learned journal in manuscript. After Peiresc's death, his brother, Palamede de Fabri de Valence, preserved his letters faithfully. Valence's death in either 1645 or 1646, however, was very nearly catastrophic for these precious records of Peiresc's lifework, for the letters, books, and manuscripts passed to his unsavory nephew, Claude Fabri de Rians, who auctioned them to pay bad debts. Cardinal Jules Mazarin bought many of the ancient manuscripts, and they then passed to the Bibliothèque Nationale in Paris in 1668. Some of the letters eventually found refuge at libraries in Carpentras and Mejanes in Aix. Because of the foolishness of Rians's daughter, Suzanne de Fabri, many letters were destroyed, used as kindling for her hearth or for silkworm nests.

SIGNIFICANCE

Living on the marches between two great periods of intellectual change, Peiresc was a revered scholar and antiquarian. After his death, however, he was soon forgotten, partly because he never published. Although brilliantly supportive of early modern science, he was not in its vanguard. He is more properly regarded as an exemplar of an antiquarian style of scholarship passing from favor in the seventeenth century. Yet his sensitivity to non-Western cultures would echo in the works of eighteenth century Enlightenment philosophes, as would his religious toleration. His esteem for cultural artifacts and sources that are not written continues to resonate with modern historians and anthropologists.

Moreover, his correspondence was so intellectually expansive and geographically far-reaching that it could be compared to the scope and reach of the Internet and World Wide Web of the late twentieth century. Above all, however, Peiresc's Epicurean love of friendship, his extraordinary generosity, and his inexhaustible curiosity to know everything there is to know has inspired in scholars a sense of awe and admiration.

—*David Allen Duncan*

FURTHER READING

Duncan, David Allen. "Campanella in Paris: Or How to Succeed in Society and Fail in the Republic of

Letters." *Cahiers du Dix-Septieme: An Interdisciplinary Journal* 5 (Spring, 1991): 95-110. Examines Peiresc's intellectual and historical "rescue" of Campanella.

Jaffe, David. "The First Owner of the Canberra Rubens, Nicholas-Claude Fabri de Peiresc (1580-1637) and His Picture Collection." *Australian Journal of Art* 5 (1985): 23-45. Explores Peiresc's life as an art collector and art patron.

Miller, Peter. "An Antiquary Between Philology and History: Peiresc and the Samaritans." In *History and the Disciplines: The Reclassification of Knowledge in Early Modern Europe*, edited by Donald R. Kelley. Rochester, N.Y.: University of Rochester Press, 1997. Examines Peirsec's scholarship in the context of how knowledge was defined and classified in seventeenth century Europe.

_____. *Peiresc's Europe: Learning and Virtue in the Seventeenth Century*. New Haven, Conn.: Yale University Press, 2000. The indispensable study of Peiresc as Humanist and antiquarian.

Sarasohn, Lisa. "Nicolas-Claude Fabri de Peiresc and the Patronage of the New Science in the Seventeenth Century." *Isis* 84 (1993): 70-90. Explores Peiresc's support of scholars such as Mersenne and Gassendi.

Tolbert, Jane. "Peiresc and Censorship: The Inquisition and the New Science, 1610-1637." *Catholic Historical Review* 89 (2003): 24-38. Discusses Peiresc's strategy for remaining orthodox while evading censorship.

SEE ALSO: Tommaso Campanella; Sir Anthony van Dyck; Galileo; Pierre Gassendi; Hugo Grotius; Jules Mazarin; Marie de Médicis; Marin Mersenne; Peter Paul Rubens.

RELATED ARTICLE in *Great Events from History: The Seventeenth Century, 1601-1700:* 1625: Grotius Establishes the Concept of International Law.

WILLIAM PENN
English religious leader and American colonist

A leading Quaker, Penn shaped the early development of the religion, conducted a traveling ministry, wrote numerous religious tracts, and was a major advocate of religious toleration in England. He founded Pennsylvania as a refuge for dissenters.

BORN: October 14, 1644; London, England
DIED: July 30, 1718; Ruscombe, England
AREAS OF ACHIEVEMENT: Religion and theology, government and politics

EARLY LIFE

William Penn was born on October 14, 1644, on Tower Hill in London, England. His mother was the widow Margaret Vanderschuren, the daughter of John Jasper, a Rotterdam merchant. His father, Sir William Penn, was an admiral in the British navy who first achieved prominence under Oliver Cromwell and, after the Restoration of the monarchy in 1660, went on to further success under the Stuarts. Despite some ups and downs in his career, the elder Penn accumulated estates in Ireland, rewards for his services, providing sufficient income so that the younger Penn was reared as a gentleman and exposed to the upper echelons of English society.

Penn received his early education at the Chigwell School, followed by a stint at home with a tutor who prepared him for entrance into college. In 1660, he was enrolled at Christ Church, Oxford University, where he remained until March, 1662, when he was expelled for infraction of the rules enforcing religious conformity. He then went on a grand tour of the Continent and spent a year or two at Saumur, France, studying languages and theology at a Huguenot school. After returning to England, he spent a year as a law student at Lincoln's Inn. His legal studies were somewhat sporadic and were never completed, a pattern that was typical for gentlemen of the day. They did, however, influence his subsequent writings and his ability to argue his own cause as well as those of others.

In Ireland, first as a child and later while acting as an agent for his father, Penn was exposed to Quakerism. It was in 1666, while managing the family estates, that he was converted by Thomas Loe, a Quaker preacher. Much to the horror of his father, young Penn took to preaching at Quaker meetings, quickly achieving prominence among the members of the still relatively new nonconforming sect. Parental disapproval continued until a reputedly dramatic reconciliation at the admiral's deathbed.

William Penn, center right, receives the charter of Pennsylvania from Charles II. (Library of Congress)

LIFE'S WORK

It was as a Quaker that Penn found his true calling. In 1668, he was in London preaching at meetings, and he produced his first religious tract, *Truth Exalted* (1668). From that time onward, he spent a good portion of his life traveling, preaching, and writing religious tracts. He made several extended trips to the Continent, speaking at Quaker meetings as well as trying to convert others to the faith. By the end of his life, he had written some 150 works, most of them on religion. Some were descriptions of Quaker doctrines, such as *No Cross, No Crown* (1669); others were defenses of Quaker principles and actions—for example, *Quakerism: A New Nick-Name for Old Christianity* (1672).

There was no toleration in England in the 1660's for those who dissented from the Anglican Church. As a result, Penn, like numerous other Quakers, was arrested for attending Quaker meetings, for preaching, and for publishing a religious tract without a license. Indeed, several of his works were written while he was in prison. As a result of his experiences, as well as of observation of his coreligionists and friends, Penn became an advocate of religious toleration. He wrote several tracts, including *England's Present Interest Discovered* (1675), that pleaded with the government to recognize liberty of conscience for all, not only for Quakers. Penn used his position and friendship with the Stuart kings, Charles II and James II, to aid others.

Support for civil rights also came out of Penn's advocacy of religious toleration. His arrest for preaching at a Friends' meeting in 1670, a violation of England's stringent religious laws, led to two trials that ultimately contributed to the independence of juries. In the first case, Penn and his fellow Quaker William Mead were found not guilty of unlawful assembly by a jury that refused to alter its verdict after being ordered to do so or else "go without food or drink." Members of the jury were then fined; they appealed their case and ultimately were vindicated in their right to establish a verdict free from coercion.

Politically, Penn was caught, in both his beliefs and his friendships, between the liberal dissenting Whig politicians and the conservative followers of the Stuart court. In 1678, he gave his support to Algernon Sidney's bid for a seat in Parliament, while maintaining his friendship with the duke of York. Penn's attempt to keep his balance in the volatile English political scene of that period failed with the Glorious Revolution, when England exchanged the Catholic duke of York, James II, for Mary, his Protestant daughter, and her husband, William III of Orange. Accused of treason and at one point placed under arrest, Penn fled and for several years after 1691 went into hiding. It was not until after the turn of the century, under the rule of Queen Anne, that he again safely participated in the English political scene. Penn's position between the two major camps of the period is also evident in his writings and in the constitutional provisions he made for his colony, Pennsylvania, because they exhibit both liberal and conservative features.

To Americans, Penn is best known for his colonization efforts. His interest in the New World stemmed from his association with the great Quaker leader and preacher George Fox, who traveled through the colonies. Penn's first involvement was in West Jersey, where he acted as an arbitrator in a complex dispute between two Quakers with claims to that colony. He ultimately became one of the proprietors of West Jersey, as well as, after 1682, of East Jersey. Yet because Quaker claims to the government of the Jerseys were under question, he sought a colony of his own, and it was on Pennsylvania that he expended most of his efforts. In 1681, he obtained a charter from Charles II for extensive territories in America, ostensibly as payment owed to his father; the grant gave him rights to the government as well as the land of the colony.

In establishing Pennsylvania, Penn wanted to create both a refuge for Quakers where they would be free to worship without fear of imprisonment and a government with laws based upon their principles. At the same time, as proprietor of the colony, he hoped that the venture would be profitable. He started by preparing a constitution and laws for the colony, consulting numerous friends for their suggestions and comments. The resulting first Frame of Government proved too complex for the colony and was followed by other modified versions.

Penn also worked to obtain both settlers and investors for his project and advertised it in pamphlets such as *A Brief Account of the Province of Pennsylvania* (1681) and *A Further Account of the Province of Pennsylvania and Its Improvements* (1685), which were published in several languages and distributed both in England and on the Continent. Expecting to be the resident proprietor

and governor of the new colony, Penn made plans to move there. He journeyed to America twice, first in 1682 and again in 1699, each time remaining for about two years. Both times he scurried back to England to protect his proprietorship, the first time from a controversy with Lord Baltimore, the proprietor of neighboring Maryland, over boundaries, and the second, to respond to a challenge from English authorities to all proprietary governments.

In the long run, Penn's colony was a success for everyone but him. His anticipated profits never materialized—a serious disappointment because, with advancing age, he was increasingly in financial difficulty. The Quaker settlers also proved to be a disappointment in their failure to get along with one another as well as with Penn. Indeed, they proved to be an exceedingly contentious lot, and the boundary controversy with Maryland was not solved in Penn's lifetime. After 1703, Penn negotiated with English authorities to sell his province back to the Crown, a deal that fell through because he suffered an incapacitating stroke in 1712. Pennsylvania, however, grew rapidly, and Philadelphia, the capital city that he had carefully planned, was an impressive success.

Penn is remembered for more than simply his religious writings and the establishment of Pennsylvania. His *An Essay Towards the Present and Future Peace of Europe* (1693) offered proposals for the establishment of peace between nations. In 1697, he proposed a plan of union for the colonies, suggesting the creation of a congress of representatives from each colony that would meet once a year.

Penn was also a warm, affectionate, and concerned family man. In 1668, he married Gulielma Maria Springett; they had eight children, only three of whom survived childhood. In 1696, two years after his first wife's death, he married Hannah Callowhill, fathering another five children. Unfortunately, his children, like his colony, were a source of disappointment. His oldest son, and favorite, Springett, died at the age of twenty-one. His second son, William Penn, Jr., renounced Quakerism and was something of a rake. The surviving children of his second marriage were, at the time of his death, still young; it was to them that he left his colony of Pennsylvania.

Also contributing to Penn's woes in his later years was a festering problem with his financial agent, Philip Ford. Both were at fault, Ford for making inappropriate charges and Penn for a laxity in supervising his personal affairs. The result was that Ford's wife and children (after his death) pushed for payment—including Pennsylvania—for what they claimed were debts; they had Penn arrested and put in prison. When the dust settled, the Ford claims were taken care of and Pennsylvania had been mortgaged to a group of Penn's Quaker friends.

SIGNIFICANCE

Although Penn was never more than a brief resident in the colonies, his contributions to American history were substantial. He played a prominent role in the proprietorships of both East and West Jersey and was the founder of Pennsylvania. Penn was one of a handful of influential Quaker preachers and authors, and although his ideas were not original, he powerfully expressed and defended the sect's beliefs in numerous pamphlets, as well as in the laws and Frames of Government of Pennsylvania. As a colonizer, his efforts ensured a Quaker presence in America and the sect's role in the political and religious life of the middle colonies.

Penn's advocacy of religious toleration, of protection of the right to trial by jury, and of constitutional government carried across the Atlantic; as a result, provisions for all three were made in the colonies with which his name was associated. Penn thought that settlers would be attracted to America not only for its land but also for the freedoms it could offer, maintaining that Englishmen would leave home only if they could get more, rather than less, of both. He worked to make this happen. Thus, Penn used his connections among Whig and court groups on the English political scene to protect his fellow Quakers, his colony, and his proprietorship.

As the founder of Pennsylvania, he was the most successful of English proprietors and yet personally was a financial failure. He was a gentleman and a Quaker who could be contentious, particularly in religious debates, stubborn in maintaining his position against all opposition, and anything but humble in his lifestyle. In many ways, he was an uncommon and contradictory individual.

Penn's place in American history rests on his success in helping establish one colony and in founding another. The name Pennsylvania, standing for "Penn's woods," continues as a reminder of his significance. Sometimes overlooked, but also important, are his contributions to the fundamental political traditions that Americans have come to take for granted.

—Maxine N. Lurie

FURTHER READING

Beatty, Edward C. O. *William Penn as Social Philosopher.* New York: Columbia University Press, 1939. Reprint. New York: Octagon Books, 1975. Beatty examines Penn's philosophical and social ideas, viewing him as a political theorist, statesman, pacifist, humanitarian, and family man.

Bronner, Edwin B. *William Penn's Holy Experiment: The Founding of Pennsylvania, 1681-1701.* New York: Columbia University Press, 1962. Describes Penn's vision for establishing Pennsylvania, contrasting his plans with the reality of their results.

Dunn, Mary Maples. "The Personality of William Penn." *American Philosophical Society Proceedings* 127 (October, 1983): 316-321. Dunn portrays Penn as a restless rebel, a poor judge of people, and always the aristocrat.

_____. *William Penn: Politics and Conscience.* Princeton, N.J.: Princeton University Press, 1967. Argues that Penn was a creative thinker who, along with others of his age, wrestled with the definition of constitutional government. The key to Penn's political ideas was liberty of conscience; a key to his behavior was his desire to protect his title to Pennsylvania.

Endy, Melvin B., Jr. *William Penn and Early Quakerism.* Princeton, N.J.: Princeton University Press, 1973. Concentrates on Penn's religious thought and its relationship to his political and social life. Evaluates his significance for early Quakerism.

Geiter, Mary K. *William Penn.* New York: Longman, 2000. Assesses Penn's religious and political significance in America and Britain.

Kashatus, William C. *A Virtuous Education: Penn's Vision for Pennsylvania Schools.* Harrisburg, Pa.: Morehouse Group, 1997. Describes how Penn established a community-supported educational system for his state.

Morgan, Edmund S. "The World and William Penn." *American Philosophical Society Proceedings* 127 (October, 1983): 291-315. A good, brief discussion of Penn's life that attempts to place his experiences in the context of English society. Emphasis is on Penn as a Protestant, a gentleman, and an Englishman.

Nash, Gary B. *Quakers and Politics: Pennsylvania, 1681-1726.* Princeton, N.J.: Princeton University Press, 1968. New ed. Boston: Northeastern University Press, 1993. Concentrates on Penn's conflicts with the settlers in Pennsylvania, as well as their problems with one another. Nash emphasizes the religious and economic background of the disagreements. Good source for information on the dynamics of early Pennsylvania politics as well as on Penn.

Peare, Catherine Owens. *William Penn: A Biography.*

Philadelphia: J. P. Lippincott, 1956. The standard modern work on Penn. A readable account with a sometimes excessively flowery style.

Penn, William. *The Papers of William Penn.* Edited by Mary Maples Dunn, Richard S. Dunn, et al. Philadelphia: University of Pennsylvania Press, 1981-1987. An essential collection of primary materials, with informative introductions and bibliography.

SEE ALSO: Charles II (of England); Oliver Cromwell; George Fox; James II; Mary II; William III.

RELATED ARTICLES in *Great Events from History: The Seventeenth Century, 1601-1700:* 1642-1651: English Civil Wars; May, 1659-May, 1660: Restoration of Charles II; March 4, 1681: "Holy Experiment" Establishes Pennsylvania; November, 1688-February, 1689: The Glorious Revolution.

SAMUEL PEPYS
English diarist and bureaucrat

Pepys's diary remains a unique account of the personal and professional life of a man involved in the major historical events of his day. His work for the government, moreover, laid the foundation for a professionally administered British navy.

BORN: February 23, 1633; London, England
DIED: May 26, 1703; Clapham, England
AREAS OF ACHIEVEMENT: Literature, government and politics

EARLY LIFE

Samuel Pepys (SAM-yu-uhl PEEPS) was born February 23, 1633, in a room above his father's tailoring shop, one of eleven children born to John Pepys and Margaret Pepys; four survived to adulthood. Although John Pepys was not wealthy, the family was connected to prominent people, including Sir Sydney Montagu (or Mountagu), a member of one of the nation's most important families. These connections made it possible to remove the young boy from the dirt and disturbances of London.

During Pepys's childhood, King Charles I was overthrown, Oliver Cromwell ruled during the Commonwealth period, and, after Cromwell's death in 1658, social disorder threatened. For much of this period, Pepys studied in the country. Later, he attended Saint Paul's School in London. As a young man, he was a revolutionist and, in 1649, witnessed with approval the execution of Charles I. He won a scholarship to Magdalene College, Cambridge University, entering in 1650, and received a B.A. in 1654. Upon graduation, he went to work for Edward Montagu, the Viscount Hinchingbrooke and future first earl of Sandwich, who was a relation. In 1655, he married fifteen-year-old Elizabeth Marchant de Saint-Michel. On March 26, 1658, he underwent surgery for kidney stones, an extremely hazardous matter in an age

before anesthetics or sterile surgical instruments. Thereafter, he was to celebrate his survival each year on the anniversary of this date.

LIFE'S WORK

Pepys's great literary achievement was his diary, *The Diary of Samuel Pepys* (1825; partial publication, as *Memoirs of Samuel Pepys . . .*, 1848-1849; as *Diary and Cor-*

Samuel Pepys. (Library of Congress)

respondence of Samuel Pepys*, 1875-1879 [6 volumes], 1893-1899 [10 volumes]; as *The Diary of Samuel Pepys: A New and Complete Transcription*, 1970-1983 [11 volumes]). He kept this diary from January 1, 1660, until May 31, 1669, when he was forced by deteriorating eyesight to stop. He used a system of shorthand created by Thomas Shelton (fl. 1612-1620), occasionally punctuating the shorthand with a variety of languages to conceal his sexual exploits. That he intended the diary to be preserved for a later generation is clear from his efforts to save the diary from the 1666 Great Fire of London, as well as his donation of the work to Magdalene College after his death, but he did not want it read during his lifetime.

In his diary, Pepys recorded in unusual detail both his achievements and his faults. His stormy marriage was abusive; he recorded his share of the abuse, his regrets, his pride, and his shame. He pursued other women; these episodes, too, he recorded, along with their consequences. His diary was not intended to impress others, but to record his life as if he were viewing himself under a microscope.

Pepys was involved in the historical and cultural events of his age, and these, too, he recorded. He went to Holland with Edward Montagu on the mission that was to bring back King Charles II to rule over a restored monarchy. His boyhood observations of social chaos had turned him from revolutionist to conservative, and his allegiance to Charles and to the king's brother James, duke of York (the future James II), brought him to the center of power. He became a keen observer of the courts, both attracted by the mistresses of Charles II and appalled by the waste of the monarch's time. The theaters had generally been closed under the Commonwealth. When they reopened, he was a dedicated theatergoer and welcomed the presence of actresses for the first time on the English stage. (Previously, female roles had been played by men.) From his father's family, he gained a love of music. Fascinated by science although not a scientist, he became a member of the scientific Royal Society and was its president from 1684 to 1686.

For later readers, much interest lies in Pepys's eyewitness accounts of two great disasters that swept through London in the 1660's. Plague was common in London, and major outbreaks had occurred in 1592, 1603, 1625, and 1636. Usually, the wealthy left the city; the poor remained and died. The epidemic of 1665, however, was far worse than any previous one. Pepys, dedicated to his work, remained in the city, until more than seventy-four hundred persons died in a single week and the streets

---

PEPYS ATTENDS A COCKFIGHT

Samuel Pepys's diary provides an invaluable record, not merely of the thoughts and experiences of a seventeenth century English subject but also of London culture in the 1660's. At times, as in the excerpt below, Pepys stumbles across a public spectacle, whose inclusion in his diary gives us a crucial glimpse into Restoration urban life.

December 21, 1663: Being directed by sight of bills upon the walls, I did go to Shoe Lane to see a cockfighting at a new pit there, a sport I was never at in my life: but Lord! To see the strange variety of people, from Parliament-man to the poorest 'prentices, bakers, brewers, butchers, and what not; and all these fellows one with another in swearing, cursing, and betting. I soon had enough of it, and yet I would not but have seen it once, it being strange to observe the nature of these poor creatures. . . .

Source: From *The Age of Reason: The Culture of the Seventeenth Century*, edited by Leo Weinstein (New York: George Braziller, 1965), p. 43.

---

were almost empty of living beings. His account of the dead and dying is a vivid one.

Equally vivid is Pepys's account of the Great Fire, which destroyed much of London in 1666. On the morning of September 2, a servant told him that a fire was visible in the distance. Pepys went back to sleep; fires were normal in all cities before the invention of effective firefighting equipment. When the servant returned to tell him that three hundred houses had burned, however, Pepys went to observe the fire. As with his account of the plague, Pepys's eye was for individuals, whether for individual corpses in the streets or individual pigeons flying overhead until, their wings singed, they dropped into the flames. Pepys managed to remove his most treasured possessions, including his diary, and, at the same time, to visit King Charles and the duke of York to warn them of the need to destroy buildings to create a barrier to the passage of the flames.

For military historians, interest lies in Pepys's attempts to create an efficient basis for naval operations, although Pepys's work here continued long after his diary ended. Pepys's rapid ascent to power was largely the result of his laborious attention to detail and his capacity for hard work. He sometimes began work at 4:00 A.M. and ended at midnight. He learned arithmetic, and he learned about ships. He kept detailed records and could justify repeated demands for money from Parliament. Although he shared with his colleagues the habit of taking bribes, especially early in his career, he was increasingly dedicated to his patron, the duke of York, and to the need to curb abuses in fitting out ships, provisioning them, and paying seamen. He laid the groundwork for a formal examination for naval officers, attempting to place ships in the hands of competent leaders, not mere political appointees.

From the position of a simple clerk, Pepys rose to become surveyor-general of the victualing in 1665, and, in 1673, secretary to the Admiralty. In 1684, he was named the king's secretary for naval affairs, and, the following year, was elected to Parliament for the first time. His detailed notes saved him several times when, especially after the Second and Third Anglo-Dutch Wars (1665-1667, 1672-1674), the condition of the navy was questioned in Parliament.

As the life of Charles II drew to a close, the Roman Catholicism of his brother James caused rising anti-Catholic sentiment in England. This rose to hysteria after the king's death in 1685, especially because the Catholic wife of James, now King James II, had borne a son, so there was now a Catholic heir to the throne. James was Pepys's patron, and Pepys himself was threatened by the furor of the time. He was arrested and in danger of his life; again, his eye for detail saved him. Although loyal to James, Pepys sensed that James was jeopardizing his position by forcing his Catholicism upon England.

James was, indeed, forced to leave the country in the Glorious Revolution of 1688. In 1689, William of Orange of the Netherlands and his wife Mary Stuart officially became joint sovereigns as William III and Mary II. Becuase Pepys had sworn allegiance to James, he resigned his position rather than violate his oath. Nonetheless, he was briefly imprisoned again in 1690.

Elizabeth Pepys had died in 1669, and the couple was childless. His health declining, Pepys made his home with Will Hewer, a former servant and clerk who had risen to power with him. After an agonizing recurrence of kidney stones, Pepys died on May 26, 1703.

SIGNIFICANCE

The full significance of Pepys's diary was not apparent until the first publication of the entire diary, *The Diary of Samuel Pepys: A New and Complete Transcription*, an eleven-volume edition, edited by Robert Latham and William Matthews and published between 1970 and 1983. All earlier editions had been abridged, as passages concerning Pepys's sexual activities could not have been published during the nineteenth and much of the twentieth century. Pepys's achievements as a naval administrator had long been praised. Moreover, his diary had already, for more than a century, been considered perhaps the single most important primary source on seventeenth century English history, and its already great importance increased dramatically in the second half of the twentieth century, when social and cultural history arose as major fields of study, equal in stature to traditional military and political history. Nevertheless, it was only with the full publication of the diary that it became possible to recognize Pepys's more intimate achievement, to see the reality of a man's life, laid out with all its flaws, foibles, pains, pleasures, rewards, and achievements. Among published diaries, it is unique.

—Betty Richardson

FURTHER READING

Coote, Stephen. *Samuel Pepys: A Life*. New York: St. Martin's Press, 2000. Shows Pepys's growth from the pleasure-loving man of the diary to the dedicated, severe naval official.

Latham, Robert, ed. *The Shorter Pepys*. Berkeley: University of California Press, 1985. Single-volume abridgment of the eleven-volume Latham and William Matthews edition; 1,096 pages; includes maps, glossary, and chronology.

Latham, Robert, and Linnet Latham, eds. *A Pepys Anthology: Passages from the Diary of Samuel Pepys*. Berkeley: University of California Press, 1999. Extracts published thematically rather than chronologically, under topics such as "The Husband," "The Man of Fashion," "The Theatre-goer," "Christmas," "The Fire of London," "The Plague," and "Street Life."

LeGallienne, Richard, ed. *The Diary of Samuel Pepys*. New York: Modern Library, 2001. Text for general readers first published in Modern Library series (1923) as *Passages from the Diary of Samuel Pepys*; contains an essay about Pepys by Robert Louis Stevenson.

Taylor, Ivan E. *Samuel Pepys*. Updated ed. Boston: Twayne, 1989. First published in 1967 and revised following publication of the Latham and Matthews edition; includes biographical material, chronology, bibliography directed toward general readers.

Tomalin, Claire. *Samuel Pepys: The Unequalled Self*. New York: Random House, 2002. Offers a detailed look at everyday life, a balanced view of the Pepys marriage, and an understanding of connections between historical events and those of modern times.

SEE ALSO: Charles I; Charles II (of England); Oliver Cromwell; James II; Mary II; William III.

RELATED ARTICLES in *Great Events from History: The Seventeenth Century, 1601-1700:* 1601-1672: Rise of Scientific Societies; February 24, 1631: Women First Appear on the English Stage; 1642-1651: English Civil Wars; September 2, 1642: Closing of the Theaters; December 6, 1648-May 19, 1649: Establish-ment of the English Commonwealth; December 16, 1653-September 3, 1658: Cromwell Rules England as Lord Protector; May, 1659-May, 1660: Restoration of Charles II; March 4, 1665-July 31, 1667: Second Anglo-Dutch War; Spring, 1665-Fall, 1666: Great Plague in London; September 2-5, 1666: Great Fire of London; April 6, 1672-August 10, 1678: French-Dutch War.

CHARLES PERRAULT
French writer

Perrault achieved lasting fame with his book Tales of Mother Goose, *which created a new literary genre, the fairy tale. The work has remained timeless and has inspired music, opera, film, and the creation of other fairy tales and moral and ethical works not only for children but also for adults.*

BORN: January 12, 1628; Paris, France

DIED: May 16, 1703; Paris

AREAS OF ACHIEVEMENT: Literature, patronage of the arts, government and politics

EARLY LIFE

Charles Perrault (peh-roh) was born a twin into a prominent and wealthy bourgeois family in Paris. His father was Pierre Perrault, a lawyer at the *parlement* of Paris. Charles's twin brother, François, died at six months of age, but three brothers—Claude, Nicolas, and Pierre—all survived to adulthood and had successful careers.

As a child, Perrault was educated at the best schools, where he was always at the top of his class. In 1637, he enrolled at the College of Beauvais, a private secondary school in the Rue Saint-Jean-de-Beauvais, near the Sorbonne. He excelled in all his classes but stopped attending school at the age of fifteen in 1643. He had quarreled with his teachers, especially in philosophy classes, and preferred to be self-taught. That year, he completed his first literary work, a satirical translation of Vergil's *Aeneid, Book VI.*

In 1651, Perrault earned a law degree from the University of Orleans and was admitted to the Paris bar. In 1653, his first publication appeared. "Les Ruines de Troie: Ou, l'Origine du Burlesque" (walls of Troy, or, the origin of Burlesque) was a short poem cowritten with his brothers. When his brother Pierre became the tax receiver-general of Paris in 1654, Charles gave up his brief law career to become his brother's clerk.

LIFE'S WORK

For almost a decade, Perrault remained in the undemanding occupation of clerk and wrote verse in his leisure time. In 1659, Perrault wrote two allegorical poems: "Portrait d'Iris" (portrait of Iris) and "Portrait de la voix d'Iris" (portrait of the voice of Iris). By 1660, he had developed a literary reputation for his love poetry and light verse. He was also beginning a career as a public poet, glorifying the splendor of King Louis XIV's reign. In 1660, he published "Ode sur le Mariage du roi" (ode on the marriage of the king), "Ode sur la paix," (ode on peace), and "Dialogue de l'Amour et de l'Amitie" (dialogue of love and friendship). In 1661, Perrault published a poem on the birth of the first royal offspring: "Ode au Roi sur la Naissance de Monseigneur le Dauphin" and the allegorical "Le Miroir: Ou, la Metamorphose d'Oronte" (the mirror, or, the metamorphosis of Orante).

In 1663, Perrault was appointed secretary to Jean-Baptiste Colbert, France's powerful minister of finance. Perrault also became secretary-for-life of Colbert's Academy of Inscriptions and Belles-Lettres. When assigned to the department of buildings in 1664, Perrault selected his brother Claude (1613-1688) as an architect for the Louvre. He also persuaded Colbert to establish a fund that would provide pensions to writers and scholars in Europe. In 1671, Perrault was admitted to the French Academy. In 1672, he was elected its chancellor, and he was elected its director in 1681.

On May 1, 1672, the forty-four-year-old Perrault married nineteen-year-old Marie Guichon, and they had a daughter and three sons. In October, 1678, Marie died prematurely, leaving four young children for Perrault to raise. With the death of Colbert in 1683, he left government service and devoted himself to literature.

Perrault's reading of the poem "Le Siècle de Louis le Grand" (the century of Louis the Great) before the Acad-

PERRAULT'S "LITTLE TOM THUMB"

Charles Perrault, with his Tales of Mother Goose *(1697), created a new literary genre: the fairy tale. "Little Tom Thumb" moralizes against despising the downtrodden, in this story a very small boy in a poor family of seven brothers. Perrault writes, in a moral at the end of the piece, that though often "despised, jeered at and scorned! . . . sometimes it is this oddest one who brings good fortune to all the family!" Tom does just that.*

Once upon a time there lived a wood-cutter and his wife, who had seven children, all boys. . . . They were very poor, and their seven children were a great tax on them, for none of them was yet able to earn his own living. And they were troubled also because the youngest was very delicate and could not speak a word. They mistook for stupidity what was in reality a mark of good sense.

The youngest boy was very little. At his birth he was scarcely bigger than a man's thumb, and he was called in consequence "Little Tom Thumb." The poor child was the scapegoat of the family, and got the blame for everything. All the same, he was the sharpest and shrewdest of the brothers, and if he spoke but little he listened much.

There came a very bad year, when the famine was so great that these poor people resolved to get rid of their family. One evening, after the children had gone to bed, the wood-cutter was sitting in the chimney-corner with his wife. His heart was heavy with sorrow as he said to her: "It must be plain enough to you that we can no longer feed our children. I cannot see them die of hunger before my eyes, and I have made up my mind to take them tomorrow to the forest and lose them there. . . ."

After acting as courier for some time, and amassing great wealth thereby, Little Tom Thumb returned to his father's house. . . . He made all his family comfortable . . . not forgetting at the same time to look well after himself.

Source: Perrault's Complete Fairy Tales, translated by A. E. Johnson et al. (New York: Dodd, Mead, 1961), pp. 26-27, 41.

emy in 1687 marked the start of the famous literary controversy *querelle des anciens et des modernes*, or quarrel of the ancients and the moderns. His poem, which compared ancient writers unfavorably with the modern authors from the century of Louis XIV, infuriated the poet and critic Nicolas Boileau-Despréaux and other supporters of the literature of antiquity. As part of the long, heated debate that raged in both France and England, Perrault wrote *Parallele des anciens et des modernes* (parallel between ancients and moderns) from 1688 to 1692.

Perrault published "Peau d'Ane" (donkey skin), his first fairy tale (in verse) in 1694, and "La Belle au bois dormant" (1696; sleeping beauty) first appeared in print in the periodical, *Le Mercure galant*. One year later, Perrault published his most famous and successful literary work, the *Histoires: Ou, Contes du temps passé, avec des moralités* (1697), commonly known in French as *Contes des fées* or *Contes de ma mère l'oye* (1697; *Histories: Or Tales of Past Times*, 1729). It is best known in English as *Tales of Mother Goose*. The book was published under the name of his son Pierre, but it was generally known that Perrault was the author of this instantly popular collection of stories. In *Tales of Mother Goose*, Perrault adapted eight traditional oral folktales into the first major fairy tale collection, which included "Sleeping Beauty," "Little Red Riding Hood," "Blue Beard," "Puss in Boots," "The Fairies," "Cinderella," "Riquet with the Tuft," and "Tom Thumb," sometimes called "Hop o' My Thumb."

During 1699, Perrault worked on his *Memoires de ma vie* (*Memoirs of My Life*, 1989), which was published posthumously in 1755. His son, Pierre, died at the age of twenty-two in 1700. On May 16, 1703, Charles Perrault died at home in Paris.

SIGNIFICANCE

Charles Perrault achieved tremendous, lasting fame with his *Tales of Mother Goose*, which established a new literary genre, the fairy tale. Based on oral folk tradition, his fairy tales became timeless classics that have been popular with children as well as adult audiences.

The book also included the first appearance of the name "Mother Goose" in writing. The frontispiece featured an elderly woman spinning and telling stories to children by firelight. With the first English translation in 1729, "Mother Goose" became a popular term in English. After John Newbery's publication of fifty-two rhymes in *Mother Goose's Melody* in London in 1765, the name became associated with nursery rhymes rather than fairy tales.

Perrault's fairy tales remain in print, and they have influenced the arts and media, inspiring works in opera and music: Béla Bártok's one-act opera, *Duke Bluebeard's Castle* (1918); Jules Massenet's opera, *Cendrillon* (Cinderella); Jacques Offenbach's operetta, *Barbe bleu*; Maurice Ravel's set of five piano pieces titled *Ma Mère l'Oye* (1915); and Gioacchino Rossini's opera, *La ceneren-*

tola (1817; Cinderella). Walt Disney produced animated film versions of *Cinderella* (1950) and *Sleeping Beauty* (1959). Feature films or movies based on Perrault's tales include *The Glass Slipper* (directed by Charles Walters, 1955), *Donkey Skin* (directed by Jacques Demy, 1970), and *Le Petit Poucet* (directed by Olivier Dahan, 2001).

—*Alice Myers*

FURTHER READING

Barchilon, Jacques, and Peter Flinders. *Charles Perrault*. Boston: Twayne, 1981. This standard source on Perrault includes an engraving of him, a chronology, analyses of his literary works and style, and a bibliography of both primary and secondary sources.

Lewis, Philip E. *Seeing Through the Mother Goose Tales: Visual Turns in the Writings of Charles Perrault*. Stanford, Calif.: Stanford University Press, 1996. The author relates Perrault's career as a public intellectual and promoter of the arts with his later-celebrated role as a fiction writer. Appendix, detailed notes, and bibliography.

Perrault, Charles. *Charles Perrault: Memoirs of My Life*. Edited and translated by Jeanne Morgan Zaruchhi. Columbia: University of Missouri Press, 1989. This significant source is Perrault's own record of events in his life. Includes a chronology of his life and principal works, illustrations, and a bibliography.

_____. *Cinderella, Puss in Boots, and Other Favorite Tales*. Translated by A. E. Johnson. New York: Abrams, 2000. A modern translation of Perrault's original eight fairy tales, with color illustrations by a different artist for each story. Bibliography.

_____. *The Complete Fairy Tales of Charles Perrault*. Translated by Neil Philip and Nicoletta Simborowski. New York: Clarion Books, 1993. The complete, unabridged collection of all eleven classic tales, including the three in verse. Includes Perrault's biography and notes on the origin and history of each story.

Tatar, Maria, ed. *The Annotated Classic Fairy Tales*. New York: W. W. Norton, 2002. Tatar, a prominent folklore scholar, examines twenty-six fairy tales from historical, cultural, philosophical, and psychological perspectives. The section on Perrault includes a portrait of him from 1670. Extensive bibliography and beautifully illustrated.

SEE ALSO: Nicolas Boileau-Despréaux; Jean-Baptiste Colbert; Hans Jakob Christoffel von Grimmelshausen; Louis Le Vau; Louis XIV.

RELATED ARTICLE in *Great Events from History: The Seventeenth Century, 1601-1700:* 1673: Renovation of the Louvre.

SIR WILLIAM PETTY
English physician and economist

A distinguished physician and scientist, Petty made demographic and economic surveys of Ireland that constituted the first practical implementation of population studies. He is also credited with introducing the labor theory of value to economics.

BORN: May 26, 1623; Romsey, Hampshire, England
DIED: December 16, 1687; London, England
AREAS OF ACHIEVEMENT: Business and economics, government and politics, mathematics, medicine, science and technology

EARLY LIFE

Even as a young boy, Sir William Petty, the son of a clothier, demonstrated an aptitude for mechanics and mathematics, as well as a penchant for building crafts of various sorts. At the age of thirteen, he joined a merchant ship, where he had the opportunity to learn navigation

skills. Petty's experience as a seaman would serve him in the final years of his life, which he devoted to shipbuilding. Following an injury, Petty was grounded in France after only a year at sea. While there, he studied at the Jesuit college at Caen, where he received a general education.

Although Petty's experience at sea enabled him to support himself in Europe by teaching classes on navigation, his chief aim was to become a physician. After a brief stint in the English navy, he returned to Europe to study medicine, visiting the well-known universities at Utrecht and Leiden. Subsequently, he traveled to Paris, where he met and learned from the philosopher Thomas Hobbes, whose influence on Petty's later political theories would be profound. In 1647, Petty returned to England to continue his medical studies at Oxford. He quickly developed a reputation among other scientists as

Sir William Petty. (Hulton Archive/Getty Images)

an enterprising and innovative thinker, as well as a promising physician, and he received a doctor of physic degree in 1650.

LIFE'S WORK

After he completed his degree at Oxford, Petty's academic and professional successes developed in rapid succession. He was appointed professor of anatomy at Oxford in 1651, in addition to holding an appointment as professor of music at London's Gresham College from 1650 to 1659 (university courses in music at the time were actually more concerned with philosophy and physics than with composition or performance). Petty's most enduring contribution to academic thought during this time was his role as a founding member of the Royal Society. The organization was founded to pursue the "mechanical arts," and it soon became the leading exponent of scientific thought and experimentation in seventeenth century England, including among its members such luminaries as Robert Hooke and Sir Isaac Newton.

It was Petty's reputation as a physician, however, that brought him to the attention of Oliver Cromwell. In 1652, Petty was appointed physician-general to Cromwell's forces during the English invasion of Ireland. Initially, Petty was assigned with reforming medical ser-

vices in the military, but he soon became involved more directly with the surveying and redistribution of Irish lands. The famous Down Survey, which mapped all of Ireland in thirteen months, was the result of this assignment.

Petty's work in Ireland established him for future historians as England's first "econometrician," because he surveyed the country not solely in terms of its geography but also in terms of economic and labor value. The point of Petty's measurements was to partition Ireland under the newly established English governance in such a way as to maximize its financial and military support for the British crown. Petty's *A Treatise on Taxes and Contributions* (1662) drew upon his earlier work in economic theory and made several recommendations for the taxation of Ireland, most notably the reintroduction of the poll (or "head") tax, which levied taxes according to the sheer number of persons in a household, including children. The treatise was praised by the Royal Society as a model of economic theory, and most of its recommendations were adopted by the British government.

Petty's economic assessment of Ireland was deeply grounded in the work on population theory (what we would now call "demographics") that he had begun as an original member of the Royal Society. His *Political Anatomy of Ireland* (1672) was a landmark work in that field, assessing the geographical and economic features of Ireland in terms of its population. The study presented a comprehensive account of the country's population, including the size of families in Ireland and the economic roles played by different segments of the population. It is likely that Petty's expertise in this area had played an important part in securing the favor of Charles II after the Restoration of the monarchy, as Petty was knighted in 1662 despite the evident fact that he had been a staunch supporter of Cromwell.

In addition to his political and economic work in Ireland, which established him as an influential figure in British imperial policy, Petty continued for the rest of his life to engage in the kind of scientific experimentation that had become the hallmark of his tenure in the Royal Society. While in Dublin, Petty designed and built a series of catamarans, a type of sailing vessel composed of two long, narrow hulls connected by a deck. He also produced a large number of economic and scientific treatises through the end of his life, including *Verbum sapienti* (1665), a work that introduced the idea of national income; *Quantulumcunque Concerning Money* (1682); *Discourse on Political Arithmetick* (1690), which attempts to ascertain the population rate of London using statistical methods; *Observations upon the Cities of London and Rome* (1687); and *A Treatise of Ireland* (1687). Despite these impressive publications, most of Petty's recommendations for fiscal reform were not carried out during his lifetime. Petty died in London on December 16, 1687.

SIGNIFICANCE

Petty has become a controversial figure as a result of his great contribution to British imperialist policies, particularly his involvement in England's partitioning and repopulation of Ireland after Cromwell's invasion. Certainly, Petty's treatises on tax collection and population studies became both the practical and the ideological foundation for England's economic exploitation of Ireland in the seventeenth and eighteenth centuries. The harshest critics of Petty, giving him the dubious honor of naming him the creator of modern population theory, have credited him with establishing an ideological and "unscientific" science—demographics—that often still serves as the theoretical cover for acts of genocide and ethnic cleansing in the twenty-first century.

Still, although the negative effects of Petty's work on economic and population theory cannot be ignored, there is little question that he was instrumental in bringing together the study of statistics, economics, and political theory to form a coherent discipline. He is often credited with introducing the labor theory of value, later so central to the thought of Karl Marx, into England's political discourse. His role in establishing the Royal Society, moreover, makes him one of the leading figures in the rise of scientific thought in pre-Enlightenment Europe.

—*Joseph M. Ortiz*

FURTHER READING

Aspromourgos, Tony. *On the Origins of Classical Economics: Distribution and Value from William Petty to Adam Smith.* New York: Routledge, 1996. A study of the development of distribution theory in seventeenth and eighteenth century England, focused primarily on Petty's work. Includes a chapter on Petty's life as it relates to the development of his economic theories. Bibliography, index.

Barnard, T. C. "Sir William Petty: Irish Landowner." In *History and Imagination: Essays in Honour of H. R. Trevor-Roper,* edited by Hugh Lloyd-Jones, Valerie Pearl, and Blair Worden. London: Holmes & Meier, 1981. Contextualizes Petty's economic treatises on Ireland alongside his own interests as one of the newly appointed English landowners.

Gouk, Penelope M. "Performance Practice: Music, Medicine, and Natural Philosophy in Interregnum Oxford." *British Journal for the History of Science* 29 (1996): 257-288. Offers a rich and rare discussion of Petty's significant work on acoustics while he was teaching medicine and music at Oxford and Gresham College in the 1650's.

Hull, Charles H. "Petty's Place in the History of Economic Theory." *Quarterly Journal of Economics* (1900). Although more than a century old, this foundational article on Petty's written work is frequently reproduced, in large part for its concise and useful overview of Petty's biography and theoretical work.

Strauss, Erich. *Sir William Petty: Portrait of a Genius.* London: Bodley Head, 1954. Takes a largely positive view of Petty's work on demographics and economic theory, paying particular attention to Petty's lifelong interests in medicine, mechanics, and education. Illustrations.

SEE ALSO: Charles II (of England); Oliver Cromwell; Thomas Hobbes; Robert Hooke; Sir Isaac Newton.

RELATED ARTICLES in *Great Events from History: The Seventeenth Century, 1601-1700:* 1601-1672: Rise of Scientific Societies; 1642-1651: English Civil Wars; May, 1659-May, 1660: Restoration of Charles II.

PHILIP III
King of Spain (r. 1598-1621)

Philip III has been maligned as a pious but incapable ruler who lacked the will to reverse Spain's accelerating political, socioeconomic, and strategic decline. Overshadowed by a corrupt favorite, Philip nonetheless made peace with Spain's most powerful enemies and kept his Iberian, Italian, and American dominions intact.

BORN: April 14, 1578; Madrid, Spain
DIED: March 31, 1621; Madrid
ALSO KNOWN AS: Felipe III
AREA OF ACHIEVEMENT: Government and politics

EARLY LIFE

Philip III, one of five sons, was the only son to outlive his father, King Philip II (r. 1556-1598). His mother was the king's cousin and fourth wife, Anna of Austria (1549-1580), daughter of Holy Roman Emperor Maximilian II. Reliable information about Philip's personality is lacking, for the prince and future king wrote little. Contemporary, as well as later, descriptions tended to be colored by the political agendas of those who manufactured them. The frail heir's training was entrusted to Philip II's most senior and capable advisers, including García de Loaysa Girón (1534-1599), governor and later archbishop of Toledo, who embraced the Erasmian theory that a just ruler's education must emphasize virtue and self-control.

Influenced by the uncompromising Catholicism of his clerical tutors, the earnest and tractable youth acquired a reputation for piety; even when he was king, Philip favored the company of the clergy and attended mass several times daily.

There had been unflattering rumors that the prince was lazy, immature, and uncomprehending. Philip II was alarmed by these confidences, but incapacitation compelled the aged king to delegate his authority prematurely. By 1595, Philip represented his father at public audiences, and by 1597, the prince signed royal orders. Fearing that his son, as king, would be manipulated by unscrupulous favorites (*privados*), Philip II ordered his informal privy council to meet daily in the prince's chambers. Philip did not embrace his father's choice of advisers, however, and instead placed his trust in an impoverished Castilian grandee—Francisco Gómez de Sandoval y Rojas, the fifth marquis of Denia, fourth count and, under Philip III, first duke of Lerma.

LIFE'S WORK

On September 13, 1598, Philip III became ruler of a "mixed" monarchy, which included the Iberian crowns of Aragon, Castile, and Portugal, each jealous of its constitutional liberties (*fueros*); the duchy of Milan and kingdoms of Naples and Sicily in Italy; the Low Countries, or Flanders (Spanish Netherlands); and a vast empire in the Americas. Few contemporaries doubted that Philip had ascended the throne of the world's greatest economic and military power.

A sense of crisis nonetheless led self-styled *arbitristas* (reformers) to lament that only miracles could save the monarchy. American silver and Castilian resources had sustained Spanish expansion during the sixteenth century, but these twin pillars of Spanish might were crumbling by the year 1600. Average annual silver imports during Philip's reign fell to less than half the imports of the peak years (1584-1587), while onerous taxes, epidemics of bubonic plague, and a declining overseas market for wheat crippled Castilian agriculture and depopulated its countryside.

In foreign affairs, the monarchy had been mired since 1560 in a futile effort to subjugate the United Provinces (now the Netherlands). Spain at this time confronted the steadily growing ambitions of England, France, and Savoy as well. Philip's only reliable allies, his Austrian Habsburg cousins, required constant Spanish financial support.

Philip III also faced Spain's clamoring nobility, which expected to benefit from royal largesse and resented the parsimony of Philip II's later reign. The new king responded with a blizzard of appointments and *mercedes* (royal awards, often financial), leading contemporaries and historians to speak of an "aristocratic reaction" in Spanish government. A fulsome Lerma used this reckless patronage to consolidate his dominance at court. Corruption thereafter became the hallmark of the reign, as Lerma's venal *hechuras* (creatures) obtained posts throughout the royal households and on every governmental council.

The extravagant Philip consistently ignored pleas for fiscal restraint; his annual court expenses far outstripped those incurred by his father or his successors. Lavish patronage gave Spain its first baroque court, but at a crippling cost: Royal debt more than doubled between 1598 and 1621. Although fiscal crises dogged his reign, Philip preferred to leave these and other unpleasantries to Lerma and fourteen regular administrative councils staffed primarily by minor nobles and *letrados* (lawyers). Desperation led to repeated issues of debased copper coinage (*vellón*), which occasioned fitful, damaging bursts of inflation. In 1607, Philip's government was forced to declare bankruptcy (actually, a forced conversion of short-term obligations to long-term state bonds).

Philip could have challenged the *fueros* of subject kingdoms that contributed little to the royal treasury, but he shrank from confronting potentially rebellious regional aristocracies. His monarchy's only recourse was to curtail expenses by reducing its foreign commitments and making peace with its enemies. The loss of an armada sent to support Irish Catholic rebels (1601-1602) cooled Philip's early martial ardor, while the death of Queen Elizabeth II (r. 1558-1603) removed the principal obstacle to rapprochement with his English archenemy. The Treaty of London (1604) brought a welcome end to English piracy against the Spanish treasure fleets and raised expectations for a lengthy detente with King James I (r. 1603-1625). A cease-fire was reached with the Dutch in 1607, and the Twelve Years' Truce followed in 1609. The fortuitous assassination of King Henry IV of France (r. 1598-1610) enabled Philip to engineer a double marriage alliance with Henry's Bourbon successor, which took place on the Pyrenean frontier in 1615. Taken together, these achievements constituted the laudable Pax Hispanica, or Spanish Peace.

Peace with Protestants nonetheless threatened Philip's standing as the pope's anointed Defender of the Faith. To save his reputation and, perhaps, salve his conscience, Philip secretly authorized the expulsion of all Moriscos (descendants of conquered Muslims and dubious Catholics) on the day he ratified the Twelve Years' Truce. Between 1609 and 1614, approximately 300,000 Moriscos were deported to North Africa in an operation that some observers described as organized and peaceful, others as brutal and chaotic. The expulsion of this unassimilated, potentially subversive minority was immensely popular and, despite regional disruptions, did little overall harm to Spain's economy. It also paralleled a reorientation of royal policy toward the Mediterranean, where conflict with the Barbary corsairs and with Islam polished Philip's Catholic credentials while safeguarding Spain's commerce and Italian communications.

Lerma supported disengagement from northern Europe, for the Pax Hispanica lessened fiscal pressures and permitted the monarchy to focus upon its core territories. The duke never monopolized the king's ear, however, for Lerma had to contend with a powerful pro-Austrian Habsburg faction initially centered upon Philip's beloved queen, Margaret of Austria (1584-1611). The *privado* later competed for influence with a bellicose grouping headed by his eldest son, Cristóbal, first duke of Uceda. When the Holy Roman Emperor Matthias (r. 1612-1619) requested Philip's aid to suppress a Bohemian revolt in 1618, the aging duke's objections to yet another costly and hopeless war were overruled. Spain intervened, at first financially and then militarily, in what would become the Thirty Years' War (1618-1648). His influence spent, Lerma was finally ordered to leave the court.

Philip did not delegate his authority to another favorite after Lerma's fall. Spanish domestic policy (or the absence thereof) continued unchanged after 1618. The successes achieved by his earlier foreign policy of retrenchment were squandered, however, as Philip was drawn back into the struggle for European hegemony by his desire to preserve the Habsburgs' position in Germany. Two days before his death, Philip III ordered renewal of the war against the Dutch. The Pax Hispanica died with him.

SIGNIFICANCE

Philip III has been portrayed as a disinterested epicure who immersed himself in the ceremonials and pleasures of courtly life while Spain entered an irreversible political and socioeconomic decline. He has been criticized for delegating too much authority to Lerma, a favorite allegedly fixated upon self-aggrandizement and familial enrichment. Philip pursued no fiscal policy other than expediency, refused to limit royal prodigality, and shrank from challenging the *fueros* of non-Castilian elites.

To be fair, however, Philip inherited a deepening dilemma. Spain's resources no longer matched its commitments or aspirations, yet the feudal conservatism of its government and society presented an insuperable obstacle to recovery or reform. Philip guaranteed his personal authority through unstinting, if biased, patronage, perhaps the one domestic policy available to him that did not threaten his monarchy's aristocratic and clerical bases of support. He was not the first Spanish monarch to govern with the help of favorites, just the first to acknowledge one as de facto chief minister. In foreign policy, Philip's goals were limited and pragmatic. Peace with the English and Dutch gave Spain a needed respite from the struggle against international Protestantism. Catholic militancy was maintained, but redirected against a weaker Islamic opponent.

Philip's reign should therefore be judged not by his failure to reverse Spain's decline, but by his ability to preserve an imperiled monarchy. Philip minimized domestic and international risks without abandoning his underlying commitments to royal supremacy within Spain and universal Catholicism abroad. He thereby managed to pass on his patrimony—as well as Spain's dilemma—to his son and successor, Philip IV (r. 1621-1665).

—*M. Wayne Guillory*

FURTHER READING

Feros, Antonio. *Kingship and Favoritism in the Spain of Philip III, 1598-1621.* New York: Cambridge University Press, 2000. This work discusses the governing partnership of Philip and Lerma within the context of early modern Spanish political theory.

Lynch, John. *The Hispanic World in Crisis and Change, 1598-1700.* Cambridge, Mass.: Blackwell, 1992. Lynch provides masterful analyses of the reigns of Philip III and his successors.

Sánchez, Magdalena S. *The Empress, the Queen, and the Nun: Women and Power at the Court of Philip III of Spain.* Baltimore: Johns Hopkins University Press, 1998. Sánchez discusses the political and personal influence wielded by Philip's queen and other female relations.

SEE ALSO: Anne of Austria; John of Austria; Duke de Lerma; Marie de Médicis; Count-Duke of Olivares; Philip IV; Tirso de Molina.

RELATED ARTICLES in *Great Events from History: The Seventeenth Century, 1601-1700:* c. 1601-1682: Spanish Golden Age; July 5, 1601-April, 1604: Siege of Oostende; 1605 and 1615: Cervantes Publishes *Don Quixote de la Mancha*; November 5, 1605: Gunpowder Plot; November 28, 1607: Martin Begins Draining Lake Texcoco; 1615: Guamán Poma Pleas for Inca Reforms; November 8, 1620: Battle of White Mountain; March 31, 1621-September 17, 1665: Reign of Philip IV; November 10, 1630: The Day of Dupes; May, 1640-January 23, 1641: Revolt of the Catalans; February 13, 1668: Spain Recognizes Portugal's Independence.

PHILIP IV
King of Spain (r. 1621-1665)

As penultimate monarch of a withered Spanish Habsburg Dynasty, Philip IV presided over the end stages of the economic and political decay of the Spanish Empire in Europe and the New World, continuing a stalwart defense of the Catholic Church against Protestantism. At the same time, he was patron of the final, brilliant manifestations of the arts and literature of the Spanish Golden Age.

BORN: April 8, 1605; Valladolid, Spain
DIED: September 17, 1665; Madrid, Spain
ALSO KNOWN AS: Felipe IV
AREAS OF ACHIEVEMENT: Government and politics, religion and theology, patronage of the arts

EARLY LIFE

Philip IV reigned over one of the most politically debilitating yet culturally illustrious periods in Spanish history. His father, Philip III, was king of Spain from 1598 to 1621. Given to suffocating religiosity and bankrupting luxuries, Philip III was indifferent to government, delegating administration to court favorites. His mother was Archduchess Margaret of Austria. Philip III's sister, Anne of Austria, became queen of France and the mother of King Louis XIV. Philip IV's grandfather was Philip II, the most industrious and austere of the Habsburg, or Austrian, kings of Spain. When Philip III died in 1621, Philip IV became, at the age of sixteen, the king of Spain, Portugal, and the vast Spanish and Portuguese colonies in the New World.

During his childhood, Philip IV witnessed some of the most enduring achievements of Spanish culture, the peak of the Golden Age. Miguel de Cervantes (1547-1616) published his classic *Don Quixote de la Mancha* (1605, 1615); Lope de Vega Carpio (1562-1635) staged his masterful plays; and El Greco (Doménikos Theotokópoulos, 1541-1614) painted his greatest masterpieces.

LIFE'S WORK

The glory of Spain and its monarchs in the sixteenth century had been supported by wealth accumulated from the New World. With those sources diminishing, however, Spain's economy dramatically declined by the end of the century and definitively decayed in the following century. Spanish elites were well aware of the economic and international decline their country was experiencing and made efforts for its reverse. Among these elites was Gaspar de Guzmán y Pimental, count-duke of Olivares, whom Philip appointed chief minister, delegating to him almost all authority. The policies of Olivares determined the first half of Philip's reign.

The crisis of Spain in the seventeenth century centered on its core kingdom, Castile. Having been the chief beneficiary of imperial wealth and trade, it could no longer bear the burden of supporting, through troops and taxes, the vast expanse and expense of the Spanish Empire. In Europe, Madrid had to rule the states and provinces of Iberia, the kingdom of Sicily and Naples, and the Habsburg Netherlands. In the Americas, it ruled the Spanish and Portuguese colonies, and in Asia it ruled the Philippine archipelago. This realm was essentially a vast confederation of states allied only by varying degrees of allegiance to the Spanish monarchy.

The financial pressure of imperial administration was so great that in 1627 the Spanish monarchy went bankrupt, unable to pay its creditors or support its currency. Olivares attempted, therefore, to address the problems of Castile and the Spanish monarchy in two ways. To ensure a steady supply of troops that could systematically defend the empire, he formulated around this time a Union of Arms, which would raise and maintain a standard number of reserve troops from each region. To finance this plan and supplement declining colonial revenue, he enacted a series of taxes and fees. Over the decade of the 1630's, the crushing burden of expanded taxes and the enhanced potential for intervention by a larger military prompted elements throughout the Spanish realm to rebel. In 1640, Portugal reasserted its independence. Catalonia then separated from Spain with the support of France. In the face of unprecedented upheaval against a Spanish monarch, Philip IV accepted the resignation of Olivares in 1643.

In the midst of these national crises, Philip IV suffered several personal blows. His first wife, Elizabeth (Isabella), whom he had married in 1621, died in 1644. Her death was followed by the death of his heir two years later. In 1649, he married Mariana de Austria, a niece. Of their two sickly sons, only one survived, the pallid Charles, who would become the final Habsburg monarch of the Spanish throne as Charles II (r. 1665-1700). Philip had twelve legitimate children (four boys, eight girls) and numerous illegitimate ones.

With Olivares banished, Philip IV tried to rule on his own. However, he was soon dependent on the nephew of

Philip IV. (Hulton Archive/Getty Images)

Olivares, Luis de Haro, who acted as a chief minister (until his own death in 1661). Financial crises and military confrontations ensued. In 1647 and 1653, the Spanish monarchy again went bankrupt, definitively ruining the banking and trade system of the country. Moreover, it could no longer defend its treasure ships on the high seas, meaning that the depleted wealth of the colonies, too, was pirated away by other powers. In 1648, Spain was forced to recognize the independence of its possessions in the Netherlands, and, in 1659, Spain surrendered territories to France along their mutual border, territories that almost two centuries previously it had won, on the eve of its ascendance to power.

Nonetheless, the Golden Age of Spain in literature and the arts, begun early in the sixteenth century, continued into the reign of Philip IV. The painter Diego Velázquez (1599-1660) made his first portrait of Philip IV shortly after the young monarch assumed the throne. Recognizing the appeal of the painter's artistry, the king became Velázquez's principal patron. Few monarchs in history have been so thoroughly portrayed throughout their reign by so brilliant an artist. Also, Velázquez was given charge of the royal household and ceremonials of Philip's court. During the closing years of Philip IV's reign, the brilliant dramatist Pedro Calderón de la Barca (1600-1681) was the court playwright. An artist of extraordinary insight into Spanish mores and human psychology, Calderón developed a series of plays at the court focusing on themes of classical mythology.

SIGNIFICANCE

The reign of Philip IV marked the end of Spain's role on the world stage as a major economic and political power. Moreover, it confirmed the position of Spanish monarchs as pawns of their court favorites. Spain was no longer enriched by the vast wealth that had buttressed it a century beforehand from discoveries in the New World. Committed to debilitating wars resulting from the dynastic entanglements of the Habsburgs in Europe, Spain lost its position of paramount continental power to France, but it continued as a bulwark of defense for the Catholic Church against the Protestant Reformation. This commitment, however, eventually fostered paralyzing religious orthodoxy and intellectual stagnation.

Despite political and economic decay, the reign of Philip IV continued to see stellar Spanish accomplishments in the arts and literature. These were sustained by a fertile cultural momentum mounted from the preceding decades. This inheritance was quickened by an acute but waning intellectual consciousness of the tragic decline in which Spanish society and culture were locked.

—*Edward A. Riedinger*

FURTHER READING

Acker, Thomas. *The Baroque Vortex: Velázquez, Calderón, and Gracián Under Philip IV.* New York: P. Lang, 2000. Acker's work examines the visual and literary attempts in classic works of Spanish Baroque culture that attempted to integrate the religious and mythic imagery supporting Habsburg rule in Spain.

Brown, Jonathan, and John H. Elliott. *A Palace for a King: The Buen Retiro and the Court of Philip IV.* New Haven, Conn.: Yale University Press, 2003. Brown analyzes architectural and stylistic details of the palace built by Philip IV on the outskirts of Madrid beginning in the 1630's. Its theater and large salons highlighted the king's interest in drama, painting, and decorative arts. Extensive illustrations.

Darby, Graham. *Spain in the Seventeenth Century.* London: Longman, 1994. Reviews the economic, political, and military conditions of the reign of Philip IV in relation to his Habsburg predecessors and successor.

Elliott, John Huxtable. *The Count-Duke of Olivares: The Statesman in an Age of Decline.* New Haven, Conn.: Yale University Press, 1986. A masterful account of the political strategies and personal flaws of the disastrously failed administration of the most important minister of Philip IV's reign. Black-and-white illustrations and foldout genealogical chart.

_____. *Imperial Spain, 1469-1715.* New York: St. Martin's Press, 1964. A classic work that analyzes the economic conditions and sociopolitical developments in the rise and fall of the Spanish Empire and the Habsburg Dynasty.

Greer, Margaret Rich. *The Play of Power: Mythological Court Dramas of Calderón de la Barca.* Princeton, N.J.: Princeton University Press, 1991. Greer offers a critique of five myth-related court plays of Calderón, examining their political assumptions and insights.

López-Rey, José. *Velázquez: Catalogue Raisonné.* 2 vols. Cologne, Germany: Wildenstein Institute, 1999. This catalog lists and describes all paintings by Velázquez, including portraits of Philip IV, his family, and court officials. Extensive color illustrations.

Orso, Steven N. *Art and Death at the Spanish Habsburg Court: The Royal Exequies for Philip IV.* Columbia: University of Missouri Press, 1989. Orso examines the decorative and symbolic environments of the funerary honors for Philip IV as reflections of aesthetic and sociocultural norms of period. One-third of book is made up of black and white illustrations.

Stradling, R. A. *Philip IV and the Government of Spain, 1621-1665.* New York: Cambridge University Press, 1988. An authoritative analysis of the philosophical and political assumptions, ambitions, policies, and practices of Philip IV and his ministers.

SEE ALSO: Anne of Austria; John of Austria; John IV; Pedro Calderón de la Barca; Charles II (of Spain); Christina; Artemisia Gentileschi; Marie de Médicis; Marie-Thérèse; Jules Mazarin; Count-Duke de Olivares; Philip III; Tirso de Molina; Diego Velázquez; Francisco de Zurbarán.

RELATED ARTICLES in *Great Events from History: The Seventeenth Century, 1601-1700:* 17th century: Europe Endorses Slavery; c. 1601-1620: Emergence of Baroque Art; c. 1601-1682: Spanish Golden Age; 1604-1680: Rise of Criollo Identity in Mexico; 1605 and 1615: Cervantes Publishes *Don Quixote de la Mancha*; 1610-1643: Reign of Louis XIII; July, 1620-September, 1639: Struggle for the Valtelline Pass; March 31, 1621-September 17, 1665: Reign of Philip IV; 1630-1660's: Dutch Wars in Brazil; February 24, 1631: Women First Appear on the English Stage;

May, 1640-January 23, 1641: Revolt of the Catalans; 1644-1671: Ndongo Wars; 1654: Portugal Retakes Control of Brazil; May 10, 1655: English Capture of Jamaica; November 7, 1659: Treaty of the Pyrenees; May 24, 1667-May 2, 1668: War of Devolution; January 23, 1668: Triple Alliance Forms; February 13, 1668: Spain Recognizes Portugal's Independence; February, 1669-January, 1677: John of Austria's Revolts; October 11, 1698, and March 25, 1700: First and Second Treaties of Partition.

KATHERINE PHILIPS

English poet

Philips produced an impressive body of verse and two successful dramatic translations while also founding a circle of literary correspondence called the Society of Friendship.

BORN: January 1, 1631; London, England
DIED: June 22, 1664; London
ALSO KNOWN AS: Orinda (pseudonym); Matchless Orinda (moniker); Katherine Fowler (given name)
AREAS OF ACHIEVEMENT: Literature, theater

EARLY LIFE

Katherine Philips's father, John Fowler, was a Presbyterian merchant. Her mother, Katherine Oxenbridge, also came from Presbyterian roots, being the daughter of Dr. John Oxenbridge, who held a fellowship at the Royal College of Physicians. In her earliest years, Katherine Fowler lived in the vicinity of Saint Mary Woolchurch, in London. Fowler's early education was acquired at a boarding school for girls located in Hackney (a village north of London). The school's headmistress was a Mrs. Salmon. From the very beginning, Fowler distinguished herself as a student at this school, studying languages and biblical writings. It was also at the school at Hackney that Fowler became friends with Mary Aubrey (or Awbrey) and Mary Harvey, both of whom would later figure in the literary circle Katherine was to found.

In 1639, Fowler's father died. In 1646, her mother married Hector Philips, a minor Welsh noble, and the family took up residence for some time in Cardigan, Wales. It was there, in 1647, that Hector Philips arranged the marriage of his stepdaughter Katherine to his son, James Philips. James, who at the age of fifty-four surpassed his young wife in age by some thirty-eight years, was a member of Parliament and a fierce supporter of Oliver Cromwell in the First English Civil War (1642-1646). Although Katherine herself supported the Royalist cause, the husband and wife were not bitterly divided over the subject. Their first child, Hector Philips, was born in 1647 but only lived forty days. Katherine wrote an elegy for Hector in the form of a sonnet, titled "Orinda upon Little Hector Philips" (pb. 1667).

LIFE'S WORK

Although Philips probably began writing poems during her teen years in boarding school (some of her juvenilia survive), she seems to have begun her career as a poet in earnest around the time of her 1647 marriage. As she would do throughout her life, Philips circulated her poems among friends in manuscript form, probably under the pen name Orinda. Her work came to the attention of Henry Vaughan (1621?-1695), who appended Philips's "Elegy for William Cartwright" to his own collection of verse, *Olor Iscanus* (1651). Vaughan referred to Philips as the Matchless Orinda, by which title she is often identified.

In 1651, Philips formed the Society of Friendship for the purpose of literary and philosophical correspondence. The society appears to have been a fairly informal association, composed primarily of women. As few concrete details about the actual nature of the society are known, however, there has been much critical speculation about its exact nature. Members of the society took up pseudonyms derived from classical literature, such as Philips's own moniker, Orinda. It is not clear whether men were allowed membership in the society, although they too were given classical pseudonyms in relevant poems (for example, James Philips was referred to as Antenor). Philips refers in her poetry to a seal for the society, but no evidence for a specific design has surfaced.

Philips's society, which seems to have remained active through at least 1661, focused on a theme that is explored throughout her verse—the topic of friendship. Philips's verse reveals a fascination with the philosophical and spiritual implications of friendship. Her treatment of the theme is often marked by Metaphysical imagery reminiscent of the poetry of John Donne. Philips also inquired about the theological status of friendship, through correspondence with Jeremy Taylor (1613-

1667), whose response to Philips's query is recorded in his *Discourse on the Nature and Offices of Friendship* (1657).

The intensity of Philips's passionate friendships with women has stirred some critics to speculate that she was a lesbian. In particular, critics have focused on Anne Owen (whom Philips refers to by her society pseudonym, Lucasia) as a possible lover, citing the intensity of the emotions Philips revealed in her poetry and the large number of poems that Philips dedicated to Owen. Like-minded critics have also speculated about a lesbian relationship with two other society members, Mary Aubrey ("Rosania") and Elizabeth Boyle ("Celimena"). Whether the powerful expressions of emotion in Philips's verse consist merely of conventional courtly tropes on the theme of Platonic love or are in fact open expressions of lesbianism remains a matter of interpretation.

Philips gave birth in 1656 to a second child, Katherine, who would eventually marry Lewis Wogan and settle in Pembrokeshire. In 1660, with the Restoration of monarchical power to Charles II, pressure was put on Katherine Philips's Parliamentarian husband, who lost his post as M.P. and much of his land. Through the intervention of Charles Cotterell, who was master of ceremonies for Charles II, Philips's husband was spared execution. Cotterell had apparently struck up a lasting friendship with Katherine Philips.

In 1662, Philips traveled to Dublin, Ireland, where she produced, at the request of the dramatist Roger Boyle, first earl of Orrery (1621-1679), a translation of *La Mort de Pompée* (pr. 1642, pb. 1643; *The Death of Pompey*, pr. 1662, pb. 1663), by the French playwright Pierre Corneille. Philips's *Pompey* proved successful in its 1662 production, and several editions were printed, beginning in 1663. Early in 1664, Philips again turned to Corneille, beginning a translation of *Horace* (pr. 1640, pb. 1641; English translation, 1656) that was cut short by her untimely death; her translation was completed by John Denham (1615-1669).

That Philips's poetic compositions generated wide interest is evident from the fact that an unauthorized collection was published, *Poems by the Incomparable, Mrs. K. P.* (1664), which consisted of seventy-four poems. At the request of Philips, however, this edition was taken off the market shortly after its publication. Philips appears to have preferred to circulate her work in manuscript form; indeed, many of her handwritten works survive.

On June 22, 1664, Philips succumbed to smallpox. She was buried in Saint Benet's Church, in London. Her works were printed in a posthumous collection titled

Poems by the Most Deservedly Admired Mrs. Katherine Philips, the Matchless Orinda (1667). The volume also included commendatory verses by the poet Abraham Cowley. Scholars have usually assumed that the collection, which included her *Pompey* and *Horace* translations, was put together by her friend, Charles Cottrell.

SIGNIFICANCE

Although she lived only thirty-three years, Philips stands out as one of the most successful women in the history of seventeenth century poetry, a field largely dominated by males. That there was considerable demand for her plays and the nearly 125 poems she penned is evident from the unauthorized 1664 collection, printed to meet a demand, as well as from the fact that the 1667 edition of her works was reprinted three times (in 1669, 1678, and 1710). Her translations of Corneille were successful both in production and in print, and a number of the songs written for these plays also proved popular in performance, as did many of the poems that later performers set to music.

Philips's verse was admired not only by poets of her own time, such as Vaughan and Cowley, but also by later versifiers, such as John Keats (1795-1821), who was influenced by her poem "To M. A. At Parting" (1664). Though Philips was not very well represented in nineteenth and early twentieth century literary histories and anthologies, there has been a resurgence of interest in her work that has brought her to the foreground of contemporary literary criticism.

—Randy P. Schiff

FURTHER READING

Crawford, Patricia, and Laura Gowing, eds. *Women's Worlds in Seventeenth-Century England: A Sourcebook.* New York: Routledge, 1999. Integrates a variety of primary sources in order to flesh out the cultural contexts in which women of Philips's era were situated.

Cummings, Robert, ed. *Seventeenth-Century Poetry: An Annotated Anthology.* Oxford, England: Blackwell, 2000. Offers a diverse selection of poems by Philips and her contemporaries. Includes notes on cultural and historical contexts, as well as bibliographical data.

Philips, Katherine. *The Collected Works of Katherine Philips: The Matchless Orinda.* Edited by Patrick Thomas. Stump Cross, England: Stump Cross Books, 1990. Well-annotated selection of Philips's verse, offering full notes on historical and literary background, as well as relevant bibliography.

Post, Jonathan F. S. *English Lyric Poetry: The Early Sev-*

enteenth Century. New York: Routledge, 1999. A survey of key authors, with detailed treatment of versification. Includes a chapter on women poets, including Philips, as well as chapters on the canonical poets of the era.

Souers, Philip Webster. *The Matchless Orinda*. Cambridge, Mass.: Harvard University Press, 1931. Highly detailed biography, examining primary evidence and offering interpretation of Philips's place within the canon of English poetry.

Traub, Valerie. *The Renaissance of Lesbianism in Early Modern England*. New York: Cambridge University Press, 2002. Offers very full cultural and historical analysis of female homosexuality relevant to current debate about Philips. Includes detailed criticism about numerous works by Philips.

Williamson, Marilyn L. *Raising Their Voices: British Women Writers, 1650-1750*. Detroit: Wayne State University Press, 1990. Critical analysis of the literary and historical context for Philips and other female writers roughly contemporary with her.

SEE ALSO: Charles II (of England); Abraham Cowley; Oliver Cromwell; John Donne.

RELATED ARTICLES in *Great Events from History: The Seventeenth Century, 1601-1700:* 1642-1651: English Civil Wars; May, 1659-May, 1660: Restoration of Charles II.

ELENA CORNARO PISCOPIA
Italian scholar

Piscopia was known throughout Europe first as a child prodigy. Her intellectual achievements were so astounding and wide-ranging that she became the first woman, anywhere in the world, to be granted a doctorate. Piscopia pioneered the way for women's acceptance into the highest of academic circles.

BORN: June 5, 1646; Venice (now in Italy)
DIED: July 26, 1684; Padua, Republic of Venice (now in Italy)
ALSO KNOWN AS: Elena Lucrezia Piscopia; Elena Lucrezia Scholastica Cornaro Piscopia; Helena Lucretia Scolastica Cornaro Piscopia
AREAS OF ACHIEVEMENT: Scholarship, philosophy, mathematics, religion and theology, education, women's rights

EARLY LIFE

Elena Cornaro Piscopia (EHL-ay-nah cawr-NAHR-oh pihs-COH-pee-ah) was born in the Palazzo Cornaro (now Palazzo Loredano) on the Grand Canal in Venice. She was the third of four surviving children of Giovanni Battista Cornaro, the procurator at St. Mark's Basilica, and Zanetta Givanna Boni, a commoner.

The Cornaro family was one of the richest and most powerful of Venice, tracing its lineage to the ancient Roman Cornelii Scipiones family, and having produced three popes, nine cardinals, four doges (chief magistrates) of Venice, one queen of Cyprus (Caterina), and several ambassadors and military leaders. The Piscopia name was added in the fourteenth century when Peter Lusignan, the king of Cyprus, deeded a castle and estate by that name (now Episkopi) to the Cornaros. Influential in politics and religion, the Cornaros also commissioned works by the greatest artists, sculptors, and architects of the Renaissance.

In this privileged atmosphere, Piscopia's intellectual abilities were recognized early on by Monsignor Gianbattista Fabris, an Aristotelian scholar and tutor to her two older brothers. At age seven, she was tutored in classical Latin and Greek, and, through other tutors, she soon became fluent in Hebrew, Aramaic, Spanish, French, Arabic, and English. Her linguistic success was followed by her mastery of rhetoric, logic, mathematics, astronomy, music, philosophy, and theology. Excelling in every area of study, although philosophy and theology were her favorites, she became famous for her prodigious memory and received visitors from throughout Europe.

In addition to her extraordinary scholarship, Piscopia was dedicated to religious life. From an early age she was drawn to prayer, daily mass, and meditation; despite the important marriage proposals she was offered because of her intelligence, beauty, and virtuous character, she did not wish to marry. In 1665, at the age of nineteen, she renewed her vow of chastity, first made when she was eleven, and became a Benedictine oblate of the Third Order—a person who follows the Benedictine discipline while living "in the world"—and took the name "Scholastica." Committed to living the Benedictine ideal of study and charitable works, she wore her Benedictine habit beneath her lavish gowns throughout her life.

LIFE'S WORK

When Elena Cornaro Piscopia moved to the Palazzo Cornaro (now Palazzo Guistiniana) in Padua in 1672 at the age of twenty-six, she continued her life of scholarship and service to the poor and other marginalized groups. Although she never enrolled formally in classes at the world-renowned University of Padua, she was tutored for six years in the humanities, science, philosophy, and theology by its best professors.

Shunning personal glory, Piscopia did not desire recognition for her accomplishments, but at the insistence of her father an application was made for a doctorate in theology. Gregorio Cardinal Barbarigo, the bishop of Padua and former chancellor of the Theology Faculty, refused the request because that degree led to the priesthood or to teaching theology, both of which were reserved for men. Convinced that his daughter's extraordinary gifts should be officially recognized, Giovanni Cornaro reached a compromise with the cardinal, who accepted an application for a doctorate in philosophy. Professor Carlo Rinaldini, the chair of philosophy department at the University of Padua, helped prepare her for the defense, the public oral examination required for the doctorate.

Piscopia's defense, which took place on Saturday, June 25, 1678, was an international affair, drawing Venetian senators, scholars from universities all over continental Europe and England, and other dignitaries and guests. To accommodate the enormous crowd, the defense was moved from the university to Padua's Cathedral of the Blessed Virgin. As Piscopia spoke in classical Latin for one hour, explaining difficult passages randomly chosen by the examiners from Aristotle's *Physics* (on natural science) and *The Posterior Analytics* (on logic), she was frequently interrupted by spontaneous applause. Her brilliant answers amazed and awed not only the audience but her examiners as well.

Having demonstrated knowledge that far surpassed the requirement for the doctorate, Piscopia, at the age of thirty-two, became the first woman to receive a doctorate in any field. She was granted the degree by unanimous acclamation of all sixty-four examiners, receiving the title Magistra et Doctrix Philosophiae (Master and Doctor of Philosophy). Rinaldini conferred the doctoral insignia on her: the gold doctor's ring, the mozzetta (an ermine cape), and the laurel crown.

Following her unique triumph, she was invited to become a member of many academies in Italy, France, and Germany, which met to debate political, theological, and scientific issues and which were reserved for men. She continued to receive visitors from all over Europe and attracted the attention of such dignitaries as Pope Innocent XI, King John III Sobieski of Poland, and King Louis XIV of France.

In 1684, Piscopia died from multiple system failure at the age of thirty-eight, having suffered over the years from infections, anemia, and kidney and pulmonary problems. Her years of fasting and being exposed to the diseases of the people she served had taken their toll. Her funeral was attended by hundreds of people from all over Europe. People in the streets cried out, "The saint is dead!" Businesses were closed for the day in Venice and Padua, and memorial services were held at universities throughout Europe. Her unusual request to be buried among the Benedictine monks in Padua's Monastery of St. Justina was approved by Cardinal Barbarigo, who had become one of her admirers, and she was buried in St. Luke's Chapel (restored and renamed Cornaro Chapel in 1978).

SIGNIFICANCE

Piscopia continued to receive unique honors posthumously. Shortly after her death, the faculty of the Sacred College of Philosophers and Physicians at the University of Padua had a medal coined in her honor, a prestigious distinction no woman had ever received. Her life-size marble statue, since its donation in 1772, stands at the bottom of the staircase in the Great Hall of the University of Padua. A 22-foot-high stained-glass window, installed in 1906 at the Thompson Memorial Library at Vassar College in New York State, depicts her receiving the doctorate and its insignia. A mural of her surrounded by instruments of learning, painted in 1947 by Giovanni Romagnoli, decorates the Italian Room at the University of Pittsburgh. Perhaps the most famous female intellectual in the world and awarded several honors never given to any woman before, Piscopia left a unique mark on her century and beyond.

Her life and work caused a paradigm shift in higher education. In the seventeenth century, Europe had almost 150 institutions of higher learning, but they had been established exclusively for men. Although it took more than fifty years before the doctorate was conferred upon another woman, Piscopia had pioneered the way for women to be accepted in the highest academic circles.

Her accomplishments outweighed the barriers that accompanied her gender, making her a role model for women everywhere in the pursuit of academic excellence. In 1978, the tercentenary anniversary of her doctorate, an international celebration of her life and achievements, held in 135 locations, brought her prominence once more. Several scholarships and awards in her name have since been established by groups such as the New York Order of the Sons of Italy, the Kappa Gamma Pi Society, and the University of South Africa.

In addition to producing scholarship at its highest level, Piscopia also exemplified the Benedictine lifestyle by her lifelong learning, devotion to spiritual reading and prayer, and ministry to the needy. She remains a unique example of a woman who combined intensive scholarship with a life of compassionate service, and she excelled in both.

—*Marsha Daigle-Williamson*

FURTHER READING

Barcham, William L. *Grand in Design: The Life and Career of Federico Cornaro, Prince of the Church, Patriarch of Venice, and Patron of the Arts.* Padua, Italy: La Garangola, 2001. Lengthy biography of the cardinal, Elena's uncle, describing the Cornaro family's influence in politics, religion, and the arts, and supplying a context for the milieu in which she was raised. Includes illustrations and an index.

Fusco, Nicola. *Elena Lucrezia Cornaro Piscopia.* Pittsburgh, Pa.: U.S. Committee for the Elena Lucrezia Cornaro Piscopia Tercentenary, 1975. A very brief biography with illustrations. Provides an extensive, multilingual bibliography of primary and secondary sources from 1688 to 1975 and a glossary with translations of inscriptions on portraits, statues, and graduation documents.

Guernsey, Jane H. *The Lady Cornaro: Pride and Progeny of Venice.* Clinton Corners, N.Y.: College Avenue Press, 1999. A full-length biography with illustrations, a bibliography of primary and secondary sources, and an index.

Kessler, Ann. "Oblate and Heroine: Elena Lucrezia Scholastica Cornaro Piscopia." In *Benedict in the World: Portraits of Monastic Oblates*, edited by Linda Kulzer and Roberta Bondi. Collegeville, Minn.: Liturgical Press, 2002. A succinct biography with attention to Piscopia's participation in Benedictine spirituality and ministry.

Wills, Gary. *Venice: Lion City.* New York: Simon & Schuster, 2001. Focuses on Renaissance life and art in Venice, including the story of the Cornaro family. Contains more than 130 illustrations, extensive notes, and an index.

SEE ALSO: Marie le Jars de Gournay; Madame Guyon; Innocent XI; John III Sobieski; Louis XIV; Nicolas-Claude Fabri de Peiresc; Anna Maria van Schurman.

POCAHONTAS
Powhatan princess

One of the first women to influence the course of American history and an extremely skilled diplomat, Pocahontas provided aid that was critical to the survival of the first permanent English settlement in the New World.

BORN: c. 1596; Virginia
DIED: March, 1617; Gravesend, Kent, England
ALSO KNOWN AS: Matoaka (given name)
AREA OF ACHIEVEMENT: Diplomacy

EARLY LIFE

According to estimates by early English settlers in Virginia, Pocahontas (poh-kuh-HAHNT-uhs) was born in 1595 or 1596, but her place of birth is unknown. Her father was Powhatan, the head of a confederation of Native American tribes in Tidewater Virginia. Because he had many wives, it is uncertain which of them was Pocahontas's mother. Although Powhatan named her Matoaka, she was more widely known as Pocahontas, a name that the English understood to mean "playful" or "adventuresome."

In the decade prior to the arrival of English settlers in Virginia, Powhatan was busy consolidating one of the most powerful confederations along the East Coast of North America. It is unclear whether he saw the English as potential allies in this effort or simply as intruders. When, in later 1607, his warriors captured and brought the English leader Captain John Smith to him, Powhatan ordered the staging of an elaborate ceremony. After a feast, Smith found himself being dragged to two large rocks where men with clubs appeared to be ready to execute him. At that moment, a girl, who Smith later learned was Pocahontas, raced to his rescue. She placed her head on his and implored her father to spare the white man's life.

The details of this episode, which elevated Smith and Pocahontas into the pantheon of American mythology, come exclusively from John Smith's pen. Yet according to several scholars who have carefully scrutinized the famed adventurer's writings, there is a ring of truth about it. Powhatan probably put Smith through this mock execution as an initiation or adoption ceremony, a ritual similar to those of other tribes in the region. Whatever Powhatan's rationale, John Smith always credited Pocahontas with his rescue, and whether her actions were spontaneous or staged, from that moment, she became a leading figure in the salvation of the Virginia colony.

Powhatan permitted Pocahontas to visit the English settlement at Jamestown several times over the next year and a half. Her presence made it easier for the English to trade with Indians in the confederation. She advised Smith which tribes to avoid and helped the English negotiate for food. The settlers enjoyed this young teen, who lived up to her playful public name. She delighted the boys at Jamestown by turning cartwheels with them in the marketplace. Pocahontas particularly liked John Smith. Smith also seemed genuinely interested in her culture. He eagerly listened as she instructed him in the Powhatan language, and he taught her some English in return.

Pocahontas's diplomatic role was even greater than her role in improving trade relations. Four months after Powhatan freed Smith, she participated in the successful negotiations for the release of native prisoners held by the English. Pocahontas also helped an English messenger boy, Richard Wiffin, escape when her father ordered him killed. In December of 1608, while John Smith and several of his men were in Powhatan's village negotiating for corn, Pocahontas warned them of a plot to kill them. After the men escaped, it was almost eight years before John Smith and Pocahontas saw each other.

LIFE'S WORK

Relations between the English and the natives rapidly deteriorated when Smith had to return to England in 1609 because of a serious wound he suffered in an accident. Prolonged hostility replaced the cautious peace that had previously characterized Indian-English relations. Because of the warfare, Pocahontas had little contact with the settlers. She did not visit Jamestown for four years, and Powhatan sent her north to live with the Potomacs, the most distant of his subject tribes.

In early 1613, Captain Samuel Argall decided to seize Pocahontas and hold her hostage. Argall hoped to obtain

Pocahontas, later known as Rebecca after her marriage to Englishman John Rolfe. (Hall & Travis)

from Powhatan the release of several English prisoners and a substantial supply of corn. On an expedition up the Potomac, Argall persuaded Iapassus, a Potomac chief, to lure Pocahontas aboard his vessel. Argall took his prize to the new settlement of Henrico, about eighty miles upriver from Jamestown, and left her in the care of the Reverend Alexander Whitaker while he awaited Powhatan's response.

Pocahontas now entered the most significant period of her life. Her father, apparently believing that the English would not harm her, released just a few English prisoners and sent only a token amount of corn. Outraged, Deputy-Governor Thomas Dale resolved to hold Pocahontas until Powhatan met his demands. As negotiations continued, the Reverend Whitaker began to instruct his charge in the Christian faith. Joining him in the effort was a widowed planter named John Rolfe.

Rolfe had come to Virginia in the spring of 1610 and had already gained notoriety for introducing a successful variety of tobacco into the colony. Because the native plant was too harsh for European tastes, Rolfe had brought the seeds of milder tobacco from Trinidad in 1611. Through careful cultivation, he was able to send a crop to England the next year. He probably met Pocahontas in the summer of 1613 while experimenting with tobacco plants in the Henrico area.

Rolfe and Whitaker taught Pocahontas the Lord's Prayer, the Ten Commandments, and the ritual of the Church of England. After several months of indoctrination, the young woman accepted the Christian faith, and the Reverend Whitaker baptized her into the Anglican Church, naming her Rebecca.

In the process, Pocahontas gained not only a new faith but also a new suitor. John Rolfe admitted that while instructing the teenager, he had fallen in love with her and wanted to marry her. Acknowledging that he was attempting to bridge an enormous gap between the two very different cultures of Virginia, Rolfe wrote a lengthy letter of explanation to Deputy-Governor Dale. He knew that the church disapproved of marriages with "strange," or heathen, people. Despite Pocahontas's recent instruction in Christianity, Rolfe admitted that he would be marrying a woman "whose education hath been rude, her manners barbarous," and "her generation cursed."

Even as he conceded this problem, however, Rolfe contended that he was presenting Dale with a wonderful opportunity. One of the goals of King James I when he had granted a charter to the Virginia Company of London was the conversion of the peoples they encountered. In the first decade of the colony's existence, it had failed miserably on that score. Now, Rolfe was posing his marriage to Pocahontas as a way to demonstrate to the king that the company could civilize and Christianize natives. This marriage, according to Rolfe, would be for the glory of God, "our Country's good, the benefit of this Plantation, and for the converting [of] an irregenerate to regeneration."

Thomas Dale readily assented to the marriage, but they still needed the permission of Powhatan. Although he likewise agreed, the aging leader decided not to attend the wedding, perhaps wanting to ease the permanent break with his favorite daughter. He sent one of his brothers, Opachisco, to give Pocahontas away at the April 5, 1614, wedding in Jamestown.

The marriage was a momentous event. It inaugurated years of peace between the English and the natives. John Rolfe obviously deserves some of the credit for proposing the match, but Powhatan also played an important role. He may not have wished to jeopardize his daughter with further hostilities, or he may realistically have concluded that the recent warfare had made his confederation too weak to confront the English with superior numbers. Most likely, he was telling the truth when he explained to an English envoy, shortly after the wedding, that he was an old man who wanted to live his remaining days in peace.

Yet it was Pocahontas who was critical in this development. In accepting Christianity and marrying an Englishman, she was renouncing her family and her culture. Given her earlier efforts to ease relations between the Indians and the English, it is not surprising that Pocahontas now would be willing to make such a sacrifice. Since the arrival of white men in her midst, she had always proved willing to act in the interests of peace.

Not wanting to waste the public relations value of the marriage of an Indian princess to an Englishman, the Virginia Company arranged a visit to England for the couple and their infant son, Thomas, in 1616. Accompanied by Deputy-Governor Dale and about a dozen Powhatan Indians, the Rolfes arrived in England in June. Over the next nine months, the Virginia Company worked hard to keep Pocahontas constantly in the public eye. Several appearances at the palace of James I, attendance at a gala staged by the bishop of London, and a sitting for an engraved portrait ensured that all in the city would know of the famous Pocahontas. By year's end, Londoners could purchase a copy of the only likeness of Pocahontas to be painted in her lifetime. In it, the young woman with dark eyes and high cheekbones is dressed in a beaver hat, a cloth coat, a lace collar, and pearl earrings, and she is holding a three-plumed fan.

Perhaps the most difficult part of the trip for Pocahontas was her reunion with John Smith. It was an awkward meeting for her. She had always adored Smith, but everyone in Virginia had told her that he had died. Only upon her arrival at Plymouth had she learned the truth. Shocked to see him again, Pocahontas initially was silent when she saw him, and then she wept, but finally they talked briefly about their experiences in Virginia. When they parted, she told Smith, "you shall call me child, and so I will be for ever and ever your countryman."

The culmination of Pocahontas's visit to England was her attendance with King James and Queen Anne at the Twelfth Night Masque. The gala event at Whitehall on January 6, 1617, held to celebrate the end of the Christmas season, featured a play by Ben Jonson. Pocahontas enjoyed the masque as well as the rest of her stay in England, but her husband was appointed secretary of the Virginia colony, and they had to return. Shortly after their departure from London in mid-March, she became very ill with a fever. Taken ashore at Gravesend, Pocahontas died and was buried in the parish church there.

SIGNIFICANCE

Although Pocahontas's was a short life, it was a truly significant one. Primarily because of John Smith's account of her rescue of him, Pocahontas has been the subject of many novels, biographies, and poems and has become an indelible part of American mythology. More important, she played a role almost always reserved for men in the seventeenth century—that of a diplomat. Undoubtedly, her youth and engaging personality were an advantage. She was her father's favorite, and she captivated the English settlers. Yet Pocahontas demonstrated considerable negotiating skills, which she employed often to improve trade and accomplish prisoner releases for both English and Native American prisoners.

Along with Powhatan, John Smith, and John Rolfe, Pocahontas played a pivotal role in early Virginia's history. She gave the English hope that the Indians could be assimilated into their culture, and she demonstrated that it was possible for English and Indian to coexist. The most authoritative assessment of her role in American history came from Captain John Smith, who concluded that she literally was the savior of the first permanent English settlement in North America. In a letter he wrote to Queen Anne in 1616, Smith explained that Pocahontas had been the instrument that had preserved the colony "from death, famine and utter confusion."

—Larry Gragg

FURTHER READING

Abrams, Ann Uhry. *The Pilgrims and Pocahontas: Rival Myths of American Origin*. Boulder, Colo.: Westview Press, 1999. Abrams explores two myths about America's origins: Virginia's beliefs about Jamestown and Pocahontas, and New England legends about the Pilgrims and Plymouth Rock. She compares and contrasts these mythologies and the messages they convey.

Allen, Paula Gunn. *Pocahontas: Medicine Woman, Spy, Entrepreneur, Diplomat*. San Francisco, Calif.: HarperSanFrancisco, 2003. Allen presents a multifaceted view of Pocahontas's life and historical significance.

Barbour, Philip L. *Pocahontas and Her World*. Boston: Houghton Mifflin, 1970. One of the best accounts of Pocahontas's life and times.

_____. *The Three Worlds of Captain John Smith*. Boston: Houghton Mifflin, 1964. Of the numerous biographies of Smith, this remains the most comprehensive and authoritative.

Davis, Richard Beale. *Intellectual Life in the Colonial South, 1585-1763*. 3 vols. Knoxville: University of Tennessee Press, 1978. Davis provides an excellent analysis of the numerous contemporary writings on Pocahontas and assesses her place in American literature.

Lemay, J. A. Leo. *Did Pocahontas Save Captain John Smith?* Athens: University of Georgia Press, 1992. An interesting study that attempts to discern the truth or falsehood of John Smith's account of his rescue by Pocahontas.

Price, David. *Love and Hate in Jamestown: John Smith, Pocahontas, and the Heart of a New Nation*. New York: Knopf, 2003. Price draws on period letters, chronicles, and documents to relate the founding of the Jamestown colony.

Rountree, Helen C. *Pocahontas, Powhatan, Opechancanough: Three Indian Lives Changed by Jamestown*. Charlottesville: University of Virginia Press, 2005. Rountree examines the impact of colonization upon the lives of Pocahontas, her father, Powhatan, and her uncle, Opechancanough.

Smith, Bradford. *Captain John Smith: His Life and Legend*. Philadelphia: J. B. Lippincott, 1953. Smith's biography is useful because he makes the best case for the veracity of John Smith's writings. In doing so, he draws on the research of Laura Polanyi Striker into John Smith's years in Europe.

Townsend, Camilla. *Pocahontas and the Powhatan Dilemma*. New York: Hill and Wang, 2004. Townsend depicts Pocahontas and her father, Powhatan, not as naïve or innocent, but as people who were able to confront the British with sophistication, diplomacy, and violence.

Tyler, Lyon Gardiner, ed. *Narratives of Early Virginia, 1606-1625*. New York: Charles Scribner's Sons, 1907. This collection of primary sources includes John Rolfe's letter to Thomas Dale, John Smith's letter to Queen Anne, and several selections from Smith's *General Historie of Virginia*.

SEE ALSO: Canonicus; James I; Massasoit; Metacom; Powhatan; John Smith; Squanto.

RELATED ARTICLES in *Great Events from History: The Seventeenth Century, 1601-1700:* May 14, 1607: Jamestown Is Founded; 1617-c. 1700: Smallpox Epidemics Kill Native Americans; December 26, 1620: Pilgrims Arrive in North America; March 22, 1622-October, 1646: Powhatan Wars.

NICOLAS POUSSIN
French painter

Poussin was among the greatest French painters of the seventeenth century and one of the most influential artists of the Baroque era. His work reflects those qualities of rationality and high moral purpose that were so admired by the French classicists, and it profoundly influenced the subsequent development of painting, both in Rome, where he spent most of his life, and in France.

BORN: June, 1594; Villers, near Les Andelys, Normandy, France
DIED: November 19, 1665; Rome, Papal States (now in Italy)
AREA OF ACHIEVEMENT: Art

EARLY LIFE

What little is known of the circumstances of the birth of Nicolas Poussin (puh-sahn), and of his early life, depends almost entirely on the accounts published by his seventeenth century biographers. He was born in 1594, in a hamlet not far from the Norman town of Les Andelys. His father, Jean Poussin, may have originally been a member of the minor nobility, but, after fighting in the Wars of Religion, he went to Normandy, where he supported himself by working the land. His mother was Marie Delaisement, the daughter of a municipal magistrate and the widow of an attorney.

Nothing is known about Poussin's early education. He may have had some instruction in Latin, but he is said to have neglected his studies to devote more time to drawing. In 1612, a mediocre painter named Quentin Varin arrived in Les Andelys, where he executed a number of paintings, some of which are still in place. He is said to have encouraged the young Poussin to try to convince his parents to let him follow an artistic career; when they opposed his plans, Poussin left home. He was eighteen years old.

He went first to Rouen and then to Paris. His activities for the twelve or so years between his arrival in Paris in 1612 or 1613 and his departure for Rome in late 1623 cannot be determined with any certainty, but by the time he left Paris he had acquired some measure of success as an artist, working for the Queen Mother, Marie de Médicis, as well as the archbishop of Paris. He had access to the royal collections, where he had a chance to study the incomparable examples of antique sculpture and Italian Renaissance paintings, from which he drew far more inspiration than he did from the work of his contemporaries.

Poussin also became friendly with the Italian poet Giambattista Marini, who became his patron and for whom he executed a series of drawings illustrating the Roman poet Ovid's *Metamorphoses* (before 8 C.E.). Poussin's goal during those years was to go to Rome, the acknowledged center of the arts, and he made several attempts to reach the city. On one occasion he got as far as Florence before being forced to return to France. A second attempt got him no farther than Lyons. On his third attempt, he finally succeeded, and in March of 1624 he arrived in Rome.

LIFE'S WORK

Except for a brief trip to Paris in 1640-1642, Poussin remained in Rome for the rest of his life. He was thirty years old when he arrived, and although he was almost immediately introduced to important patrons, very few commissions came his way. He spent some time working in the studio of the Bolognese painter Domenico Zampieri, known as Il Domenichino, who was one of the leading classicist painters, but it was not until 1628 that he was given a chance to produce a major altarpiece for an important church. This was an enviable opportunity, for the painting of large-scale altar pictures was the stock-in-trade of Roman artists and the surest way to achieve success and recognition. The painting, *Martyrdom of Saint Erasmus*, was intended for an altar in the church of St. Peter's. Unfortunately, it was not well received. A year or two later, Poussin became very ill, and his illness, coupled with the unpopularity of his *Martyrdom of Saint Erasmus*, seems to have brought on an emotional crisis. He realized that his talents lay elsewhere, and he gave up the attempt to compete with the Roman artists by creating altarpieces or large frescoes. The *Martyrdom of Saint Erasmus* was the only large, public commission he ever completed in Rome.

For the next ten years, Poussin worked almost exclusively for a rather select group of Roman clients who shared his consuming interest in Roman antiquity. He was a friend of Cassiano del Pozzo, the secretary to Cardinal Francesco Barberini, and a man whose great interest was the formation of a collection of drawings recording all aspects of Roman antiquity. Poussin was closely associated with Pozzo in this project, and his paintings of the early 1630's reflect the strong antiquarian interests of Pozzo's circle.

By the middle of the decade, Poussin had begun to

create the works that are among his greatest contributions to Western art. *The Adoration of the Golden Calf* exemplifies these new developments in style and subject matter. The theme is of epic stature, the composition carefully controlled and rigorously organized. Furthermore, Poussin tried to reveal the emotions of the protagonists in his painted drama through their gestures and facial expressions. This rigorously intellectual approach to pictorial problems was henceforth to be one of the major characteristics of his work. At the end of the decade, he painted some of his finest religious works, among them the paintings representing the *Seven Sacraments* which were commissioned from him by Pozzo.

Poussin was much admired in France, and in 1636, Cardinal de Richelieu commissioned him to execute a series of *Bacchanals* for the cardinal's château near Orléans. The cardinal and Louis XIV wanted Poussin to return to France, and he finally agreed. In 1640, he left Rome and went to Paris, but the trip was not a success. He was commissioned to execute several paintings and to plan the decoration of part of the Louvre Palace, but none of the commissions was really suited to his talents and the results were disappointing. Poussin was back in Rome by September of 1642, and the principal result of his trip was that it allowed him to make contact with a number of men who were to become his most important clients during the later part of his life. Most of them were well-educated, middle-class bankers, merchants, and civil servants to whom the seriousness and moral earnestness of Poussin's work had a great appeal. It was for this group that Poussin executed the paintings that are considered to be among the finest examples of French classicism. One of Poussin's most important clients was a civil servant named Paul Fréart de Chantelou, who took care of Poussin while he was in Paris and with whom the artist conducted an extensive correspondence when he returned to Rome. It was for Chantelou that Poussin painted his famous *Self-Portrait*, which is now in the Louvre.

In 1644, Poussin began working on a set of paintings illustrating the *Seven Sacraments* for Chantelou, who had wanted Poussin to make copies of the paintings of the same subject that he had executed earlier for Pozzo. Poussin refused, and the paintings are quite different, revealing Poussin's deepening sense of the tragic in the severity of their composition. The strange and haunting allegory of *The Arcadian Shepherds* of about 1650 is even more moving, as the shepherds remain motionless to hear the message on the sepulchral monument deciphered for them: Even in Arcadia, there is death.

In the late 1640's, Poussin began painting what are in effect pure landscapes. The *Landscape with the Gathering of the Ashes of Phocion* is based on an incident in the ancient Greek historian Plutarch's *Parallel Lives* (105-115), in which the widow of the general whom the Athenians have put to death is allowed to gather up his ashes. It is the lucid arrangement of the landscape, however, that is the principal expressive element. The principles of organization that he had applied to figural compositions he now used to create an image of an ordered and harmonious nature. It is a vision of the natural world in perfect harmony with human concepts of rational order.

The final years of Poussin's life were marred by illness, and he seems to have isolated himself from the art world, seeing only a few friends and devoting himself to his painting. His late paintings, such

Nicolas Poussin. (Library of Congress)

as the *Four Seasons* in the Louvre, are some of his most personal creations, works in which the formal elements of art—light and shadow, color and texture—often seem to be his real subject. Finally, after a long decline, Poussin died in Rome on November 19, 1665.

SIGNIFICANCE

Nicolas Poussin has often been called the Painter-Philosopher. While it is certainly true that in his paintings he tried to give expression to his ethical concepts and religious views, he was certainly not unique in this respect. What is so unusual about Poussin's work is that he was able to evolve a language of artistic forms through which these ideas could be expressed with great clarity. Unlike most seventeenth century artists, he was deeply interested in philosophical concepts, particularly the writings of the Stoic philosophers of antiquity, whose ideal of indifference to feelings or emotion he found particularly appealing and from whom he seems to have learned to interpret classical myths as allegories of eternal truth. His subjects from classical history are often those in which the heroes achieve a moral victory through self-sacrifice, and there are numerous parallels between Poussin's paintings and the work of the French seventeenth century playwright Pierre Corneille. Both try to concentrate the action and eliminate any elements that might distract the spectator from the moral lesson. Both favor the rigidly conventional expression of human emotions and work within a self-imposed set of rigidly conventional forms. Their works form the cornerstones of French seventeenth century classicism.

Poussin has always been considered a master of classical composition, above all in nineteenth century France, where he was equally admired by the classicist Jean-Auguste-Dominique Ingres and the postimpressionist Edgar Degas. Paul Cézanne was also greatly influenced by him and tried to fuse the intensity and clarity of the color of the French Impressionists with the formal order of Poussin. Even the early cubist painters have acknowledged their debt to Poussin, and to artists for whom the expressive implications of pictorial order are major concerns, he will always be an important source of inspiration.

—*Eric Van Schaack*

FURTHER READING

Arikha, Avigdor. *Nicholas Poussin: "The Rape of the Sabines," The Louvre Version.* Houston, Tex.: Museum of Fine Arts, 1983. A catalog of an exhibition focusing on the painting that Poussin executed for Cardinal Aloisio Omodei in the late 1630's. Includes detailed investigations of subject matter and technique, and a discussion of Poussin's art theory.

Blunt, Anthony. *The Drawings of Poussin.* New Haven, Conn.: Yale University Press, 1979. A general introduction to Poussin's graphic work, written by a noted scholar of Baroque art who devoted the greater portion of his life to the study of Poussin.

_____. *Nicholas Poussin.* 2 vols. New York: Pantheon Books, 1967. Another of Blunt's important studies of Poussin.

_____. *The Paintings of Nicholas Poussin: Critical Catalogue.* London: Phaidon Press, 1966. The standard catalog of Poussin's work. Includes a complete survey of literature on the artist.

Friedlaender, Walter. *Nicholas Poussin: A New Approach.* New York: Harry N. Abrams, 1966. A general study providing an excellent introduction to Poussin's work and art theory.

Hibbard, Howard, *Poussin: The Holy Family on the Steps.* London: Allen Lane, 1974. A detailed stylistic and iconographic investigation of a version of the *Madonna on the Steps* held in Washington, D.C. (there is another, and perhaps better, version in the Cleveland Museum of Art). Hibbard's book is also an excellent introduction to a study of the artist.

McTighe, Sheila. *Nicolas Poussin's Landscape Allegories.* New York: Cambridge University Press, 1996. McTighe offers new interpretations of some landscapes Poussin painted late in his career.

Marin, Louis. *Sublime Poussin.* Translated by Catherine Porter. Stanford, Calif.: Stanford University Press, 1999. Collection of essays by Marin, an eminent scholar and art critic whose work was inspired by Poussin. Marin describes how to "read" some of Poussin's paintings, pointing out some of their symbolism.

Olson, Todd P. *Poussin and France: Painting, Humanism, and the Politics of Style.* New Haven, Conn.: Yale University Press, 2002. Although Poussin lived for many years in Rome, Olson maintains the artist remained engaged with the culture and political transformation of France.

Poussin, Nicolas. *Drawings: Catalogue Raisonné.* Edited by Walter Friedlaender and Anthony Blunt. 5 vols. London: Warburg Institute, 1939-1974. The standard catalog of Poussin's drawings.

Scott, Katie, and Genevieve Warwick, eds. *Commemorating Poussin: Reception and Interpretation of the Artist.* New York: Cambridge University Press, 1999.

Collection of essays about Poussin, including a discussion of his thoughts about painting, an examination of how Anthony Blunt interpreted Poussin's work, and an appraisal of Poussin's influence on subsequent artists.

Wright, Christopher. *Poussin Paintings: A Catalogue Raisonné.* New York: Hippocrene Books, 1985. A good, general book by an author who is primarily concerned with the artistic qualities of Poussin's work. Contains excellent illustrations.

SEE ALSO: Claude Lorrain; Pierre Corneille; Louis XIV; Marie de Médicis; Cardinal de Richelieu.

RELATED ARTICLE in *Great Events from History: The Seventeenth Century, 1601-1700:* c. 1601-1620: Emergence of Baroque Art.

POWHATAN
Chief of the Powhatan Confederacy (r. late sixteenth century-1618)

Though better known as the father of the Indian princess Pocahontas, Powhatan made significant contributions to the English settlement in North America. Through his prudent leadership and goodwill, Powhatan provided the basis for a peaceful coexistence between the Indians and the English, which ultimately enabled Jamestown, the first English colony in America, to thrive and expand.

BORN: c. 1550; Powhata, near present-day Richmond, Virginia

DIED: April, 1618; Powhata

ALSO KNOWN AS: Wahunsenacawh (given name); Priest Wahunsenacawh; He Knows How to Crush Them; Ottaniack; Possessor; Mamanatowick; He Who Is Very Superior; Great King

AREAS OF ACHIEVEMENT: Government and politics, diplomacy

EARLY LIFE

Powhatan (pow-HAT-n) was born around the year 1550, but his exact birth date is still in question. It has been documented that Powhatan was of foreign extraction, that his father had come from the West Indies because he had been driven from there by the Spaniards. His given name was Wahunsenacawh, but he came to be called Powhatan for the name of one of the tribes that was later to come under his rule. It is known that Powhatan had at least two brothers: Opechancanough, who later became chief of one of Powhatan's most important tribes, the Pamunkeys, and who was the most formidable enemy of the English after Powhatan's death, and Opitchapan, who succeeded Powhatan.

Unfortunately, virtually nothing has been recorded about Powhatan's early childhood. When he was a young man, he inherited six tribes, thus becoming a chief, or sachem. By force or threat of force, he expanded his reign to include thirty tribes. Powhatan's geographical jurisdiction encompassed most of tidewater Virginia. It began on the south side of the James River, extended northward to the Potomac, and stretched to include two tribes of the lower Eastern Shore of the Chesapeake Bay. In addition to the tribe from which he took his name, he controlled the Pamunkey, the Chickahominy, and the Potomac tribes. He and his people belonged to the Algonquian-speaking family which occupied the coastal areas from upper Carolina to New England and beyond. It has been estimated that Powhatan had a population of between eight thousand and nine thousand under his rule.

Powhatan's portrait, as documented by those with whom he had frequent contact, certainly mirrors his status. Early written records state that he was tall, stately, and well proportioned. Although he was perceived as having a sour look, his overall countenance was described as majestic and grave. Powhatan possessed fabulous robes of costly skins and feather capes. His love for ornamentation was evident from the fact that he was always bejeweled with long chains of pearls and beads. Powhatan has been described as wily and crafty. The English described him as possessing a subtle intelligence, and they had great respect for him.

Powhatan's principal residence was set deep in a thicket of woods in the village of Werowocomoco, on the York River not far from Jamestown. It was approximately fifty to sixty yards in length and was guarded by four decorative sentries: a dragon, a bear, a leopard, and a giant man. In typical kingly fashion, he enjoyed sitting on a throne of mats approximately one foot high. He was flanked on either side by his current favorite women. His chief men sat along each side of the house, and behind them sat many women. All were adorned with jewelry, ornaments, and paint.

Powhatan's status as sachem brought with it many

privileges, one of which was having many wives and, as a result, many children. He selected his favorite women to bear him children and, after they did so, they were free to leave and marry again. One of these women bore him the most loved and most famous of his daughters, Pocahontas. It was through her that Powhatan became personally involved with the first English colony in America in 1607 and ultimately decided its destiny.

LIFE'S WORK

Powhatan's main goal as sachem of such a large number of tribes was to create unity and foster harmony among them. It was under his firm guidance that the largest Algonquian group had been consolidated. Once this was accomplished, their strength and prosperity was evident.

Powhatan's people enjoyed political, economic, and artistic stability and prosperity under his domain. Although Powhatan's tactics may be deemed despotic, his political system offered protection for its people against their numerous and varied foes. The economy was a relatively sophisticated one. Three crops of Indian corn were cultivated each year. Tobacco was also grown. Their foodstuffs were richly supplemented by hunting and fishing, which were carried out in an organized, communal fashion and manifested the tribes' common goals and sense of unity. Together, the Indians hunted wild turkey, beaver, and deer, which not only reinforced their food supply but also provided them with important items for clothing and tools. For fishing, they deftly employed equipment such as the weir, net, fishhook, spear, and arrow. Their canoes were fashioned from a single log and had the capacity to carry approximately forty men. Their implements showed a high level of sophistication and were quite comparable in form and function to those of their English counterparts, except that they were not made of metal. There was also a high degree of sophistication in arts and crafts, especially pottery and basketry. They fashioned their own pipes, in which they smoked the tobacco they grew. They also created musical instruments from reeds, with which they participated in various ceremonial rites.

With the arrival of the English, Powhatan's main goal was to continue the peace, prosperity, and strength of his people. This was based on the naïve assumption that it would be possible for the two groups to coexist peace-

Powhatan. (Library of Congress)

fully and that neither would prosper by the extinction of the other. Hence, Powhatan's wisdom, wiles, and capacity for negotiation were put to the test. In spite of the many trials and tribulations he suffered during this period, Powhatan never wavered from this goal. He was firmly committed to his people and instinctively sought to guard against any disruptive temptations presented by the English. He continued to rule with the same common sense with which he built his empire and to espouse a humane philosophy and sense of statecraft.

Powhatan, however, initially sensed danger from the English. They were on his land, destroying it to build homes, hunting his animals, cultivating his soil, chopping his trees, and eating his fish. Furthermore, they possessed weaponry that was far more sophisticated than that of the Indians. When Powhatan first met the English Captain John Smith, his keen instincts and political acumen told him that he was being deceived. Thus, he decided that Smith should be put to death. At the last minute, however, Pocahontas intervened, and the Englishman's life was spared.

The first tactic that Powhatan used in dealing with Smith and the English was that of trading. He sent a generous quantity of badly needed food to the starving colonists and, in return, demanded cannons, muskets, and a millstone for grinding corn. Although Powhatan's subjects were more numerous and more cohesive than the colonists, he wished to fortify them with sophisticated English weaponry for protection against any surprise attacks. Smith returned to Jamestown a free man, laden with food supplies, only to break his bargain with Powhatan by sending him bells, beads, and mirrors instead of the items he requested.

Powhatan felt deceived and so refused the next request for food. His response was met with a threat from Smith's pistol and the raised muskets of his men. Powhatan became openly angry but knew that bows and arrows were no match for guns. The Indians became resentful and stole tools and weapons, and occasional outbreaks of fighting ensued. The English knew, however, that the success of their colony depended on Powhatan's goodwill, generosity, and humanitarianism, and they tried to appease him and win him over with pardons and gifts.

Powhatan, however, had already been twice deceived, was always on the alert, and adopted a wait-and-see stance. He recognized, resisted, and outwitted all attempts to subjugate him or his people. For example, when Powhatan was asked to participate in a coronation ceremony that would make him a subject of the English king, he became defiant. He did not see the wisdom or the logic of one king serving another king. He did, however, accept all the gifts that were presented to him. These included a huge bed, a red silk cape, and a copper crown. The English, for their part, continued to try to use the Indians while biding their time to build up strength with supplies from England. They never invited Powhatan to visit their colony and, even when they were in desperate need of food, they requested a lesser amount than was actually needed. Powhatan was one step ahead of them, though, and not only decided to charge them more for the corn but also demanded that they build him an English-style house modeled after the largest standing structure of the time. The English had no choice.

When Powhatan realized that Captain Smith was never going to trade his weapons, he made a deal with Captain Christopher Newport, who was not on friendly terms with Smith. They traded twenty wild turkeys for twenty swords. The result was doubly favorable for Powhatan: It created further demoralization and internal strife among the members of the Jamestown community, while at the same time it strengthened and fortified the unity of Powhatan's people. Powhatan's humanitarian side, however, prevailed on most occasions. For example, when a fire destroyed the Jamestown warehouse that contained the colonists' food, Powhatan sent not only food but also his daughter Pocahontas, to serve as ambassador.

When Pocahontas was kidnapped by an English captain and one of the ransom demands was the return of all captured prisoners and pilfered guns, Powhatan again reacted in a shrewd manner. Although Pocahontas was known to be his favorite daughter and he had often said that she was as dear to him as his own life, he knew that the English had always been her friends and would never harm her. He blessed her impending marriage to John Rolfe, promised friendship, sent two of his sons to attend the wedding bearing many gifts, and returned the prisoners—but never the guns.

This act began an era of peace between the Indians and the English known as the Peace of Pocahontas, which lasted until the time of Powhatan's death in 1618. The sachem had achieved his goal without compromising his personal dignity or jeopardizing the strength and peace of his tribes.

SIGNIFICANCE

Powhatan's rule provided his numerous tribes with peace, protection, and prosperity. These vast numbers of people succeeded in forming a binding alliance and uniting against common foes.

Internally, they were prudent and resourceful. They knew their land well and cultivated it with care. Their agricultural system assured them of bountiful harvests, and excess food supplies were always in abundance for emergency use. It was Powhatan himself, in fact, who presented Captain Smith with baskets of corn kernels and even provided him with planting instructions. This act of generosity and goodwill not only prevented famine in the Jamestown colony during its first winter season but also once again attested Powhatan's good faith and humanitarian nature.

There are many theories as to why Powhatan allowed the Jamestown colony to survive. Given the large numbers of people under his rule, it is quite obvious that, had he so wished, he could have easily destroyed the colony in spite of its superior weaponry. He had no apparent reason to do so, however, and perhaps he thought that fair play and a cautious approach in his relations with the English could be mutually advantageous.

The English colony never posed a real threat to Powhatan from the initial landing in the spring of 1607. It was composed of a group of quarrelsome, power-hungry men who were incapable of unifying their small group. Their rate of growth was virtually nil; Powhatan had no forewarning of future events. There were only 350 people in the colony at the time of Powhatan's death. Since its founding, the colonists there had suffered such grave misfortunes that it was only with Powhatan's help that they had survived; he, in turn, reasoned that the English could help him. Their sophisticated weaponry not only would facilitate daily chores such as hunting but also would provide his people with better protection against their foes and further reinforce his own authority. This interdependence would have the potential to lead to an alliance if such a situation presented itself.

The deceit and double-crossing exchanged between the two sides was probably the normal politicking of two very astute leaders. Powhatan's tactic was to outwit the English, punish them at every opportunity, and deny them the opportunity to retaliate. It should be noted, however, that although Powhatan was often a victim of English deceit, he never allowed these discrepancies to interfere with the formation of a long-lasting peace treaty. It is highly doubtful that he allowed sentimental considerations to interfere with his political decisions. Although there is no denying that Powhatan loved Pocahontas, he also knew that her ability to deal with the English could prove fruitful to him; thus, he sent her to negotiate the return of the Indian prisoners in the Jamestown camp. He knew that Smith would yield to Pocahontas what he would yield to no one else. By appointing her as his ambassador, he was able to plant the seeds of friendship between the Old World and the New World.

—*Anne Laura Mattrella*

FURTHER READING

Andrews, Matthew Page. *The Soul of a Nation.* New York: Charles Scribner's Sons, 1943. Concentrates on the founding of Virginia and the projection of New England. Emphasizes the need for a fresh appraisal of American beginnings. Powhatan and his relationships with Captain Smith and Captain Newport are discussed.

Chatterton, E. K. *Captain John Smith.* New York: Harper and Brothers, 1929. Focuses on the early life of Smith, the formation of his character, his spirit of adventure, and his place in history. Details his meetings and dealings with Powhatan and Pocahontas, and provides insight into his respect and sympathy for Powhatan.

Craven, Wesley Frank. *White, Red, and Black: The Seventeenth Century Virginian.* Charlottesville: University Press of Virginia, 1971. Reprint. New York: Norton, 1977. Chronicles the history of the white, Indian, and African black in the early history of Virginia. Emphasizes Powhatan's organizational skills and strong leadership in contrast to the disorganization, lack of leadership, and internal strife of Jamestown.

Fishwick, Marshall W. *Jamestown: First English Colony.* New York: Harper and Row, 1965. The best book on the daily life and customs of the Indians. Discusses all aspects of Powhatan, his tribes, and their dealings with the English.

Gerson, Noel B. *The Glorious Scoundrel: A Biography of Captain John Smith.* New York: Dodd, Mead, 1978. Discusses John Smith's life and ambitions, his role of leadership in the colony, and his diplomatic dealings with Powhatan. It was through his sensitivity that Powhatan was able to be appeased and won over.

Gleach, Frederic W. *Powhatan's World and Colonial Virginia: A Conflict of Cultures.* Lincoln: University of Nebraska Press, 1997. Gleach outlines the cultural differences between the Powhatans and the British colonists.

Rountree, Helen C. *Pocahontas, Powhatan, Opechancanough: Three Indian Lives Changed by Jamestown.* Charlottesville: University of Virginia Press, 2005. Rountree examines the impact of colonization upon Powhatan, his daughter Pocahontas, and his brother Opechancanough.

Rountree, Helen C., and E. Randolph Turner, III. *Before and After Jamestown: Virginia's Powhatans and Their Predecessors.* Gainesville: University Press of Florida, 2002. A comprehensive history of the Powhatans, from their earliest contact with non-Native Americans to the present. Includes a chapter discussing the Jamestown colony from the Powhatan perspective.

Townsend, Camilla. *Pocahontas and the Powhatan Dilemma.* New York: Hill and Wang, 2004. Townsend depicts Pocahontas and her father, Powhatan, not as naïve or innocent, but as people who were able to confront British colonists with sophistication, diplomacy, and violence.

Williamson, Margaret Holmes. *Powhatan Lords of Life and Death: Command and Consent in Seventeenth-Century Virginia.* Lincoln: University of Nebraska

Press, 2003. Anthropologist Williamson focuses on Powhatan's life and the administration of his realm.

Willison, George F. *Behold Virginia: The Fifth Crown.* New York: Harcourt, Brace, 1951. Provides an overview of the early history of Virginia. Powhatan is discussed in terms of his humanitarianism: accepting and aiding the settlers during their times of need. Many of the English plots to subvert him are exposed.

SEE ALSO: Canonicus; James I; Massasoit; Metacom; Pocahontas; John Smith; Squanto.
RELATED ARTICLES in *Great Events from History: The Seventeenth Century, 1601-1700:* May 14, 1607: Jamestown Is Founded; 1617-c. 1700: Smallpox Epidemics Kill Native Americans; December 26, 1620: Pilgrims Arrive in North America; March 22, 1622-October, 1646: Powhatan Wars.

THOMAS PRIDE
English military leader

A member of Parliament's New Model Army during the English Civil Wars, Pride fought in several significant battles. He is best remembered for excluding more than one hundred members of Parliament's House of Commons on December 6, 1648, in Pride's Purge and for serving as a member of the court that condemned Charles I to death.

BORN: c. 1605; probably Ashcott, near Glastonbury, England

DIED: October 23, 1658; Worcester House, Nonsuch, Surrey, England

AREAS OF ACHIEVEMENT: Military, warfare and conquest

EARLY LIFE

Almost nothing is known of Thomas Pride's early life. He may have been born at Ashcott near Glastonbury, and contemporary sources say he was a foundling of Saint Bride's parish who later became a drayman (a hauler of carts) or possibly a brewer. A portrait done during the civil wars shows a handsome man with light hair worn long, a mustache, and a small goatee, which was much in fashion.

During the English Civil Wars, Pride served in Parliament's army against Charles I. Military service offered men of lowly social origins such as Pride the opportunity for adventure and advancement. Pride was a captain, then major, and when the New Model Army was created in 1645, he was promoted to lieutenant colonel in the infantry regiment of Colonel Edward Harley. Pride fought in Cornwall in the west of England as part of the forces of Robert Devereux, earl of Essex, who surrendered to Royalists in 1644. Other military action involved serving with distinction under Lieutenant General Oliver Cromwell at the Parliamentary victory at Naseby (June 14, 1645), and he participated in the captures of Bristol (September 10, 1645) and Dartmouth (January 19, 1646).

During 1646 and 1647, after the king's surrender, Pride supported the right of the common Parliamentary soldiers to petition for back pay and for indemnity for acts committed during the First English Civil War (1642-1646); he was asked to appear before the House of Commons, which did not approve of such actions. Pride supported the army's actions in July, 1647, against eleven members of Parliament who sought to conduct negotiations with the king and disband the army. In 1647, he was promoted to colonel and replaced Harley as commander of his regiment. When Charles I and his allies renewed the civil war in 1648, Pride served under Cromwell in Wales and at the crucial Battle of Preston (August 17-19, 1648) in northwestern England. After the defeat of the king, Pride, as did many in the army, advocated punishing the king for causing the civil wars.

LIFE'S WORK

The army had gained control of Charles I and imprisoned him in Carisbrooke Castle. Attempts by Parliament to reach a negotiated settlement with the king that would accept many of his demands angered the army, which moved the king to Hurst Castle. The commander of the army, the third Baron Fairfax, and Cromwell's son-in-law, Commissary General Henry Ireton, disagreed over the army's course of action. Fairfax ordered the army to occupy London, which it did on December 2, 1648, but he did not support drastic action against Parliament, as did Ireton. On December 5, 1648, the House of Commons voted 129 to 83 to accept terms that would, in effect, have restored Charles I to power. This action led to the hasty formation of a committee of three army officers and three civilian supporters, which decided to remove from the House of Commons members who supported negotiating with the king.

On December 6, 1648, Colonel Pride, assisted by Edmund Ludlow and Lord Grey of Groby, members of the House of Commons, working from a prepared list, turned away more than one hundred members of the House of Commons. About forty-one of the most recalcitrant members were arrested. When challenged to show his authority for this action, Pride pointed to his troops. A number of other members had been forewarned and stayed away, leaving about fifty to sixty members in the House of Commons, who were derisively nicknamed the "Rump." This episode, known as Pride's Purge, set the stage for a series of revolutionary events. Pride's role was that of a soldier following orders—a soldier entrusted with important orders who carried them out as instructed. Such loyalty and his reputation as one of the most radical members of the army led to his selection for this important assignment.

In mid-December, 1648, the army moved the king to Windsor Castle, closer to London. On January 4, 1649, the Rump's attempt to create a special court to try the king was defeated by the House of Lords. Subsequently, the Rump passed resolutions proclaiming that it was the representative of the people and that it alone could make laws. Upon this dubious authority, the House of Commons created the High Court of Justice, made up of 150 men; however, 60 never sat on it. Pride, selected as a member, missed only one session of the king's trial, January 20-27, 1649, and assented to the guilty verdict and sentence of death. His is one of fifty-nine signatures on the warrant for execution, which was carried out on a cold January 30, 1649, after a two-hour delay while the Rump made it illegal for anyone to declare the king's oldest son, Charles, prince of Wales, as king.

Once again, Pride's reputation had caused him to be selected to participate in this unprecedented event—the public trial and execution of a monarch. Although Pride did not play a significant part in the trial, once again, he was present at momentous events that shaped the course of British history. After the execution of the king, the Rump abolished the House of Lords and the monarchy, establishing the Commonwealth (1649-1660) and making England a republic. The army's decision to bring the king to justice precipitated Pride's Purge, which in turn led to regicide and government without a king.

The king's execution touched off the Third English Civil War (1650-1651), as the Scots recognized Prince Charles as Charles II, and Cromwell marched the New Model Army north to assert control over Scotland. Pride was one of the officers who accompanied this force and saw action at the Battle of Dunbar on September 3, 1650, Cromwell's birthday and his most spectacular victory. The difficulty in subduing Scotland and Cromwell's poor health slowed the progress of the army; the Scots regrouped and took advantage of the lack of English forces in southwestern Scotland and western England to launch an invasion of England led by their newly proclaimed Charles II. Cromwell left the military actions in the hands of others in Scotland and wheeled south to catch the invading Scots. At Worcester in western England, the two forces clashed on September 3, 1651, exactly one year after Dunbar. Pride's regiment was part of the English forces that defeated the Scots at Worcester and enabled Prince Charles to escape from the battlefield and flee to renewed exile in France.

Pride's service in the army and to the Commonwealth would pay financial rewards in the form of lands worth five hundred pounds that were confiscated from Scottish rebels, and he, along with several others, in 1654 was given the contract to supply the navy with food. With the wealth he gained, he purchased the Great Park and Worcester House that were part of the Nonsuch royal estate in Surrey, and he became sheriff of Surrey in 1655. He was knighted in 1656 and was known by contemporaries as a vigorous suppressor of bear baiting, part of Cromwell's Puritanical program concerning the national reform of morals, which also involved closing the theater and other forms of popular entertainment.

Pride, who had risen in importance politically, opposed the offer of the crown to Oliver Cromwell, who had been named lord protector of England, Scotland, and Ireland in 1653. Pride's role involved circulating a petition in the army regiments around London against offering kingship to Cromwell. After much soul-searching, Cromwell rejected the offer, largely because so many comrades in arms opposed it and because of his belief that God had destroyed the office of king in the British Isles. Pride's opposition does not appear to have hurt him politically; he was one of the nominees to the "Upper House" of Parliament—a sort of a restored House of Lords—created in 1657.

Pride was also one of the signers of the proclamation that named Cromwell's son Richard Cromwell as lord protector after his father's death on September 3, 1658. Pride did not outlive his former commander very long; he died on October 23, 1658, and was buried on November 2, 1658, at Nonsuch, Surrey. After the Restoration of the monarchy in 1660, vengeance was taken on a number of regicides both alive and dead. Some of the living were executed in brutal fashion. The House of Commons had passed an act of attainder against Pride, which in effect condemned him for treason and confiscated his property, which was given to the Crown. It also ordered that his body be exhumed; hung up at Tyburn, the place for public execution in London; and reburied under the gallows. Apparently this desecration of his remains did not occur, although it did to the bodies of Oliver Cromwell, Henry Ireton, and several others.

Pride had married Elizabeth Monck, the niece of General George Monck, the key figure in the Restoration of monarchy. Their son Robert followed in his father's footsteps, rising to the rank of captain in the military.

SIGNIFICANCE

Although not a decisive figure in any one event, Pride participated in or was present at a number of significant, indeed revolutionary, events in British history. His rise from lowly social origins to officership in the army during the turbulent times was something that irritated many contemporaries. His name is linked to one of the important and controversial episodes of the time: Pride's Purge was the use of naked military force against a legally constituted, if unrepresentative, legislative body. This action indicated the quickening radicalization of the army, which had determined to take drastic measures against the king, leading to an unprecedented public trial of a reigning monarch and an even more extraordinary public execution. Similar actions would be repeated by revolutionaries in France in 1792 and 1793 against Louis XVI.

The fact that Pride was one of the members of the court that condemned Charles I gives evidence of his advanced radical and republican views, which he maintained when he openly opposed the offer of the Crown to Oliver Cromwell. Opposition from trusted, loyal officers such as Pride, with whom Cromwell had served for more than a decade, was a key factor in his rejecting the chance to become king. Pride's service at a number of key battles—Naseby, Preston, Dunbar, and Worcester—was duplicated by many other soldiers who helped defeat the king, Scots, and the prince of Wales and consolidate Cromwell's control over the British Isles. Such control was previously unparalleled in Britain. Pride supported the power of Cromwell as military commander and lord protector, but his scruples would not allow him to serve under Cromwell as monarch.

—*Mark C. Herman*

FURTHER READING

Ashton, Robert. *Counter-Revolution: The Second Civil War and Its Origins*. New Haven, Conn.: Yale University Press, 1994. The origins and events surrounding the renewed English Civil War in 1648, which radicalized the army, are covered in this readable account.

Firth, Charles Harding. "Thomas Pride." In *The Dictionary of National Biography*, edited by Sir Leslie Stephen and Sir Sidney Lee. London: Oxford University Press, 1896. The premier reference source for people in British history gives the fullest treatment of Colonel Pride's life in volume 16.

Gentles, Ian. *The New Model Army in England, Ireland, and Scotland, 1645-1653*. Oxford, England: Blackwell, 1992. The definitive history of the actions of Parliament's military forces in the three civil wars in the British Isles provides extensive coverage of the major battles in which Pride fought.

Hainsworth, Roger. *The Swordsmen in Power: War and Politics Under the English Republic, 1649-1660*. Herndon, Va.: Sutton, 1997. This recent summary of the Commonwealth and Protectorate emphasizes the role of the army in politics, including Cromwell's rejection of the Crown.

Smith, Geoffrey Ridsdill, and Margaret Toynbee. *Leaders of the Civil Wars, 1642-1648*. Kineton, Warwick, England: Roundwood Press, 1977. This series of short biographical sketches accompanied by photographs of portraits and engravings of both royalist and parliamentary military, political, and religious figures contains an engraving of Colonel Pride.

Underdown, David. *Pride's Purge: Politics in the Puritan Revolution*. Oxford, England: Clarendon Press, 1971. Reprint. London: G. Allen & Unwin, 1985. This is the most complete discussion of the background to, and the events and consequences of, Pride's Purge. The author argues that these events amounted to a revolution.

Wedgewood, C. V. *The Trial of Charles I*. New York: Macmillan, 1964. This detailed account of the events that led to the trial and execution of a reigning monarch is written in a vivid, highly readable style.

SEE ALSO: Charles I; Charles II (of England); Oliver Cromwell; Third Baron Fairfax; James II; John Lambert; George Monck.

RELATED ARTICLES in *Great Events from History: The Seventeenth Century, 1601-1700:* November 3, 1640-May 15, 1641: Beginning of England's Long Parliament; 1642-1651: English Civil Wars; July 2, 1644: Battle of Marston Moor; Spring, 1645-1660: Puritan New Model Army; December 6, 1648-May 19, 1649: Establishment of the English Commonwealth; December 16, 1653-September 3, 1658: Cromwell Rules England as Lord Protector; May, 1659-May, 1660: Restoration of Charles II.

SAMUEL VON PUFENDORF
German legal scholar and philosopher

Pufendorf's teachings on jurisprudence, theology, and ethics made possible significant advances in the development of natural law theories in the Western world of the early modern age.

BORN: January 8, 1632; Dorfchemnitz, Saxony (now in Germany)

DIED: October 26, 1694; Berlin, Prussia (now in Germany)

AREAS OF ACHIEVEMENT: Law, philosophy

EARLY LIFE

The family background of Samuel von Pufendorf (PEW-fehn-dohrf) has been described as extending over four generations of Lutheran clergy, who had practiced that calling for about a century. Relatively little has been recorded, however, about Samuel's father, except that he was a pastor of relatively modest means. When Samuel was born, as the third of four children, the family resided in Dorfchemnitz, a village in Saxony. During the next year, they moved to Flöha, about five miles from Chemnitz.

Because of the promise and academic aptitude Samuel and his elder brother Esaias had shown, they received financial support from a wealthy nobleman, which enabled them to attend the well-known Prince's School in Grimma. The education that was received there consisted of lessons in grammar, rhetoric, logic, Bible reading, and Lutheran dogma; although he later complained of excessive rigidity and dullness among his teachers, Pufendorf maintained with some satisfaction that he availed himself of the ample free time that was allowed students to make himself familiar with works of classical Greek and Latin writers.

After attending this secondary school between 1645 and 1650, he was enrolled at the University of Leipzig; though his father had hoped and expected that his son's education there would prepare him for the ministry, Pufendorf, again following the example of his brother, turned away from theology, which both of them regarded as a discipline that was presented in an overly conservative manner. Among the subjects that did interest him were history, jurisprudence, philology, and philosophy; this eclectic bent, bordering sometimes on indiscriminate erudition, may have foreshadowed traits of this sort in his later writings.

In 1656, Pufendorf went on to the University of Jena, where in two years he earned the degree of magister. He read works on mathematics and studied modern philosophy; he devoted special attention to the writings of Hugo Grotius and Thomas Hobbes. Moreover, with the encouragement of Erhard Weigel, a professor of mathematics who was to become known as one of Gottfried Wilhelm Leibniz's early mentors, Pufendorf became impressed with the notion that ethical principles could be adduced with the rigor of mathematical logic. Although schematic conceptions of that sort did not gain Pufendorf's unwavering adherence, a confluence of ideas evidently was taking form by which the conception of natural law guided by natural reason had become foremost.

Shortly after he left Jena, Pufendorf, with the assistance of his brother Esaias, obtained a position as tutor to the family of Peter Julius Coyet, the Swedish minister in Copenhagen. Yet when Sweden, which previously had been at war with Denmark, broke off peace negotiations to reopen hostilities, Danish authorities put the minister's staff and attendants under arrest. During a period of eight months when Pufendorf was imprisoned, he had the opportunity to compose his first work on the principles of law. In 1659, he left for the Netherlands, where Coyet had resumed his diplomatic work in The Hague, and in 1660 Pufendorf's *Elementorum jurisprudentiae universalis* (English translation, 1929) was published. At the University of Leiden, he was able to pursue further studies in classical philology. He also obtained a recommendation from Pieter de Groot, a son of Grotius, who was an agent in the Netherlands for Karl Ludwig, the elector of the Palatinate. Pufendorf had arranged to have his book dedicated to the elector, and in 1661 he was offered a position, the first of its kind in Germany, in philology and international law at the University of Heidelberg.

LIFE'S WORK

Pufendorf's appointment was to the faculty of philosophy, rather than law, and his disenchantment with the place he actually received may have been reflected in a trenchant and polemical, but also bold and insightful, study of the law and constitution of the Holy Roman Empire. His *De statu imperii Germanici* (1667; *The Present State of Germany*, 1690), published abroad under a pseudonym, was banned by the imperial censor. In this work, Pufendorf attacked pretense and empty formality in the imperial constitution. In a famous passage, he contended that the empire, being neither a monarchy nor a democracy nor yet an aristocracy, resembled a monstrosity of irregular proportions; sovereignty on behalf of the state had been compromised, according to Pufendorf, by conflicting forms of authority exercised by its constituent rulers within the empire.

The outcry that attended the circulation of this work, taken with Pufendorf's continuing dissatisfaction with his academic lot, left him open to offers from other patrons of learning. Although he had married Katharina Elisabeth von Palthen, a wealthy widow, in 1665, he felt sufficiently uneasy about his position in Germany that he accepted another appointment, advanced on behalf of King Charles XI of Sweden, to take up a full professorship at the University of Lund. Some of Pufendorf's later publications dealt once more with problems of the German constitution but conceded in effect that easy resolutions were not at hand.

More theoretical, and of greater importance for Pufendorf's subsequent reputation, was the major work *De jure naturae et gentium* (1672; *Of the Law of Nature and Nations*, 1703), of which *De officio hominis et civis juxta legem naturalem* (1673; *The Whole Duty of Man According to the Law of Nature*, 1691) provided a condensed version for the general reading public. Great controversy

Samuel von Pufendorf. (Library of Congress)

arose over his effort to treat natural law at some distance from theological doctrines. According to Pufendorf, although Christianity could be regarded as ordained by the law of God, citizenship was ordered by the law of the state. Although natural law was derived from both rational and religious principles, it imposed obligations of a civic and moral sort, which could not be subsumed with respect to church or state. Pufendorf maintained that every individual, by virtue of intrinsic human dignity, had a right to freedom and equality; although he regarded humans as social beings, he rejected Aristotle's contention that slavery, in distinction to contractual agreements of master and servant, could be upheld on any rational basis.

The impact of Hobbes's thought could be found in many places, for, like Hobbes, Pufendorf took a presumed state of nature as a starting point in his arguments on moral and political relationships; he opposed the notion that by disposition people were hostile to one another, though he seemed to grant that individual self-interest was the wellspring of action in society. He also took issue with the English writer's conception of authority, even as he accorded similar notions an important place in his own works.

Whereas early in his career Pufendorf had endeavored to defend Grotius's views, his interpretation of Hobbes had prompted him as well to counterpose his own positions with respect to Grotius's ideas. Pufendorf had come to oppose any notions of the transfer of natural rights, and instead he contended that self-defense and the preservation of property could be asserted in ways that were not provided for in Grotius's thought. On the international level, where Grotius had maintained that natural law of a special sort was binding upon states, Pufendorf was likely to posit rights and interests of separate sovereigns as principles affecting international relations.

In its outlines, Pufendorf's system of natural law was a vast and, on some counts, imperfectly defined edifice that encompassed ethics, government, jurisprudence, government, and social thought. Whereas some critics have maintained that the very scope of this enterprise may have blunted Pufendorf's purposes, more specific objections have centered on ways by which he sought the reconciliation of opposing postulates by adopting a middle course, which left certain issues murky or incompletely resolved. He upheld the principle of sovereignty as a source of government and argued that self-sufficiency and self-determination were necessary for the existence of any state. His notion of authority led to a justification of actions undertaken for reasons of state; he did not, however, defend the unbridled exercise of power for its own sake, nor did he maintain that encroachments upon the rights of individuals should be permitted at will. Much of the argument he advanced on this front had to do as well with the delimitation of authority between church and state.

In some of his later writings, he set forth positions concerning the authority of the state in civil affairs and the power of the Church over ecclesiastical matters, in ways by which he maintained that freedom of conscience could be observed with respect to individuals. In his own day, Pufendorf was roundly denounced by many theologians for his restrictive views on the province of the Church; in many respects, however, his thought was aimed at the promotion of toleration; indeed, his most notable work on theology also justified the elector of Brandenburg's acceptance of Huguenot refugees after France had revoked the Edict of Nantes in 1685.

After Danish forces, during another war with Sweden, had captured Lund, Pufendorf went to Stockholm. In 1677, he became royal historiographer, with the rank of secretary of state; he was allowed access to government archives. He became concerned particularly with relatively recent historical problems, notably those involving the position of Sweden during and after the Thirty Years' War (1618-1648). Although his voluminous writings in this area have enjoyed relatively little vogue subsequently, his methods—which often consisted in the paraphrasing of, or indeed wholesale quotation from, original documents—occasionally have been cited as suggesting an approach that would allow firsthand materials to elucidate the unfolding of great events. It would appear, however, that he made little effort to allow for any elements of bias that may have arisen in relying upon sources from one side, and his historical writing sometimes exhibited a pronounced moderation in dealing with delicate political matters affecting Sweden or Prussia.

The portraits of Pufendorf that exist show a dignified man of a sober and pensive bearing; to artists, he showed a steady and deliberate gaze. He had a long straight nose and a firm mouth above a relatively small chin; in some representations, he was depicted with somewhat rounded features and thick, fleshy cheeks. Toward the end of his career, Pufendorf was honored by two courts. In 1688, he left Sweden to become historiographer for the elector of Brandenburg, and while he was in Berlin he produced several works, including studies of Hohenzollern rulers. In the last year of his life, Pufendorf received a baronetcy

from the Prussian ruler, thus adding the "von" to his name, and, during a visit to Stockholm, he was similarly ennobled by the Swedish crown. The state of his health had been difficult for some time, and, upon his return to Berlin, he died from an embolism, on October 26, 1694. A work that was published posthumously the following year developed further his ideas on ecclesiastical law and put forward a proposal for Protestant unity.

SIGNIFICANCE

It was the peculiar fate of Pufendorf's thought to be widely discussed and probably more often praised than condemned, for about a century after his death; subsequently, his works were relegated to an obscurity into which few, save scholars and intellectual historians, have ventured. In part this result came about because doctrines of secular law became more widely accepted, while, with the development of modern jurisprudence, natural law theories increasingly were regarded as artifacts of an earlier age.

In any event, while it lasted, interest in Pufendorf's writings involved some public men of note. Although Leibniz disparaged him as "a poor jurist and a worse philosopher," John Locke preferred Pufendorf's works to those of Grotius; important theorists who continued in the natural law tradition included Christian Thomasius and Christian von Wolff. Numerous editions of Pufendorf's works and translations into several languages appeared during the later seventeenth and eighteenth centuries. In one form or another, his influence was cited in works of Sir William Blackstone and of Montesquieu. Jean-Jacques Rousseau and Denis Diderot found Pufendorf's writings admirably suited for instruction and education. At opposite ends of the Western world, Peter the Great of Russia commissioned a translation of one of his famous works, and Pufendorf's writings evidently were consulted in the composition of Catherine the Great's legislative instruction; in the American colonies, clergyman and publicist John Wise referred liberally to the German jurist, and other American leaders paid homage to Pufendorf's thought.

All the while, however, other thinkers, by moving beyond those points where Pufendorf had been most cogent, in effect consigned him to a lesser status over the long term; perhaps because his thought was neither entirely consistent nor strictly innovative, his reputation waned to the point that he has been remembered partly because of the influence he exercised rather than because of the various merits of his original writings.

—J. R. Broadus

FURTHER READING

Gierke, Otto. *Natural Law and the Theory of Society, 1500 to 1800*. 2 vols. Translated by Ernest Barker. Cambridge, England: Cambridge University Press, 1934. This topical study of major themes and concepts deals with Pufendorf's thought, on the whole rather favorably, and suggests comparisons with the ideas of other theorists.

Gross, Hanns. *Empire and Sovereignty: A History of the Public Law Literature in the Holy Roman Empire, 1599-1804*. Chicago: University of Chicago Press, 1973. The author, in providing a chronological survey of pertinent works, discusses Pufendorf's writings on the imperial constitution in a balanced fashion, while also dealing with the broader context of such publications.

Haakonssen, Knud, ed. *Grotius, Pufendorf, and Modern Natural Law*. Brookfield, Vt.: Ashgate, 1999. Includes four essays about various aspects of Pufendorf's philosophy, including his ideas on the modern state and human rights, and an analysis of his place in the history of ethics.

Hunter, Ian. *Rival Enlightenments: Civil and Metaphysical Philosophy in Early Modern Germany*. New York: Cambridge University Press, 2001. Hunter describes the rivalry between civil philosophers, such as Pufendorf, and university metaphysicians, such as Leibniz and Kant, over questions of politics and religion. He maintains that civil philosophers have not received the recognition they deserve, and he aims to reinstate this philosophical tradition.

Krieger, Leonard. *The Politics of Discretion: Pufendorf and the Acceptance of Natural Law*. Chicago: University of Chicago Press, 1965. This study discusses Pufendorf's life and his political and moral thought, legal doctrines, and writings on history and theology. The author critiques the philosophical merits of Pufendorf's teachings, and he concludes that rather little may be found in the way of coherence or logical rigor.

Nutkiewicz, Michael. "Samuel Pufendorf: Obligation as the Basis of the State." *Journal of the History of Philosophy* 21 (1983): 15-30. This study maintains that, by eschewing mechanistic analogies, Pufendorf was able to arrive at ethical theories, utilizing concepts that differed from those employed by Hobbes, Spinoza, and other contemporaries.

Phillipson, Coleman. "Samuel Pufendorf." In *Great Jurists of the World*, edited by John Macdonell and Edward Manson. Boston: Little, Brown, 1914. This sympathetic exposition of Pufendorf's ideas, though partly cast in the context of later controversies over legal positivism, points out how theories of natural law were significant for seventeenth century thought and were of great influence even in areas where later thinkers turned away from such notions.

Tuck, Richard. *Natural Rights Theories: Their Origin and Development*. New York: Cambridge University Press, 1979. In this survey, which considers developments since late medieval times, Pufendorf is discussed in the light of works in which, at various turns, he upheld but subsequently repudiated the ideas of Grotius.

SEE ALSO: René Descartes; Hugo Grotius; Thomas Hobbes; Gottfried Wilhelm Leibniz.

RELATED ARTICLE in *Great Events from History: The Seventeenth Century, 1601-1700:* 1693: Ray Argues for Animal Consciousness.

HENRY PURCELL
English composer

The greatest musical genius of the English Baroque period, Purcell was an extremely prolific composer of consistently high-quality musical works. Among his works are more than seventy anthems for the Anglican service, numerous odes for court and public ceremonies, more than two hundred vocal and instrumental pieces, incidental music for more than forty stage productions, five semioperas, and one opera.

BORN: 1659; London, England
DIED: November 21, 1695; London
AREAS OF ACHIEVEMENT: Music, theater

EARLY LIFE

Henry Purcell (PUR-suhl) was the son of either Henry or Thomas Purcell, brothers and court musicians during the reign of Charles II. He was one of six children born to Elizabeth Purcell; the year of his birth, 1659, is known, but there is no official record of the date. The elder Henry Purcell died when the child was five years old, and Thomas Purcell was responsible for young Henry's education—thus the uncertainty of his parentage. Sometime between the ages of eight and ten, young Henry was chosen as one of twelve boy choristers of the Chapel Royal, the group of court musicians reinstated by Charles II when he came to the throne in 1660. Under the Puritan rule of Oliver Cromwell, music had deteriorated; the Chapel Royal had been disbanded, church organs destroyed, and music manuscripts burned. Charles II, an enthusiastic patron of the arts, restored music to a central role in church and court life.

Young Purcell began his musical studies with Captain Henry Cooke, Master of the Children of the Chapel Royal, by all accounts an excellent musician and teacher. Pelham Humfrey, who succeeded Cooke in 1672, had studied in France and Italy with the Baroque masters and probably influenced Purcell's dramatic style of composition. (The Baroque tradition emphasized the power of music to stir the emotions.)

Purcell's genius was evident at an early age. Several compositions (no longer existing) are attributed to him during his years as a chorister, most notably a birthday piece for King Charles composed when Henry was eleven. Growing up near Westminster Abbey, the child would have witnessed the Great Plague in London in 1664 and 1665 and the Great Fire of 1666, devastating events that, along with the sadness of his family life, may have inspired the mournful quality of his melodies. His voice changed in 1673, ending his services in the boys' choir.

LIFE'S WORK

Even as a student and apprentice, Purcell played a central role in the musical life of the church and court. Like most musicians of his time, he held several appointments simultaneously throughout his life in order to earn a living. Charles II, although a generous patron, was constantly at odds with Parliament over the royal budget. Musicians led a precarious existence, with payments for their services often overdue and difficult to collect.

From 1674 to 1680, Purcell continued his study of composition and keyboard with John Blow, the organist at Westminster Abbey. Purcell was also responsible for maintaining and repairing the king's wind instruments and for tuning the Abbey organ. He was assigned to copy the compositions of the Elizabethan, French, and Italian masters, thus becoming familiar with the best music of the past. In 1677, he was named official Composer to the King's Violins, a post that carried a regular salary. In 1678, he composed his first anthem, or hymn based on Scripture, for solo voices, choir, and orchestra. He had also begun writing incidental music for the theater, a common way for court musicians to supplement their incomes. His appointment as organist for Westminster Abbey in 1680 at the age of twenty-one was evidence of his maturity as an artist.

Purcell married Frances Peters in 1680 or 1681. Three of his children died in infancy, probably of tuberculosis, and three survived him. (Only his son Edward inherited his musical talent, becoming a minor composer and organist.) Little is known about Purcell's personal life, but it was said that he had a pleasant disposition and a sense of humor. Several portraits show him in the elaborately curled Restoration wig and reveal a strong nose, large eyes, and a generous mouth.

Purcell's accomplishments for the next fifteen years (1680-1695), before his early death, established his reputation as the greatest musician of his time. Throughout three monarchies, he retained his official court appointments and performed as a singer (he is listed as a countertenor in court records) and keyboard artist (harpsichord and organ). His compositions, however, were his greatest achievement, evidence of his astonishing range and versatility.

For the Anglican service, Purcell composed both vo-

Henry Purcell. (Library of Congress)

pieces are "Hail, Bright Cecelia" and "Te Deum and Jubilate," tributes to Saint Cecelia, whose feast was celebrated each year with great public ceremony. Purcell's sacred music was composed for the highly trained musicians of the Chapel Royal, in a time notable for excellence in performance. In these years, music was moving from the court and drawing rooms of wealthy patrons to public performances for larger audiences, who paid a shilling for admission. For musicians, this meant another opportunity to supplement their incomes.

Purcell's music for the court included welcome songs for both Charles II and James II, celebrating their return to court after state visits, as well as music for royal birthday celebrations. The inspiration for this music came from Italian and French operas and ballets. Charles II encouraged this style, as he was fond of European music, even adopting Louis XIV's custom of maintaining a band of twenty-four violins to play whenever he appeared at court. Purcell provided the music for the coronation of James II, who succeeded Charles in 1685. The dismal financial straits of musicians of the time are documented in Purcell's request for payment for his services a year after the coronation.

When William and Mary were crowned in 1689, Purcell again composed the music. In the only hint of scandal connected with his life at court, Purcell was ordered to turn over the money collected from spectators who paid to witness the ceremony from the organ loft, an apparent oversight that Purcell corrected. His last two anthems were composed in 1694 for the funeral of Queen Mary.

During these years, Purcell was also writing incidental music for plays at the Dorset Gardens and Drury Lane theaters. Restoration audiences loved spectacles, especially masques with supernatural themes, featuring violent storms, demons, and witches. These elaborately staged scenes (usually irrelevant to the plot) starred great numbers of singers and dancers, accompanied by a full orchestra. So popular was Purcell's reputation with the theatergoing public that his name on the program guaranteed a successful run. Purcell's theater music marked the beginnings of English musical comedy.

Purcell's opera *Dido and Aeneas* (1689), with its theme of tragic love, was performed only once in 1689

cal and instrumental music. For court and public ceremonies, he composed odes (musical settings for dramatic poetry) for such state occasions as official welcomes, royal birthdays, coronations, and funerals. He was also much in demand as a composer of incidental music for the theater. He wrote five semioperas and one true opera (that is, all the words were sung). He also wrote catches, or popular rounds sung on the streets and in taverns, that have been described as indecent—or obscene—depending on the sensibilities of the listener.

His first known publication was a set of trio sonatas for violins, bass, and keyboard in 1683, written in the Italian style. His anthems, performed by the Chapel Royal at Westminster Abbey, were based on Old Testament texts and reveal his greatest gift as a composer: his skill in creating melodies to enhance the words of Scripture. He wrote a number of solos for the Reverend John Gostling, reported to be King Charles's favorite singer, whose powerful bass voice was a wonder of the time. (The low notes are difficult for singers less gifted than Gostling.) Among his most highly regarded sacred and ignored for the next two hundred years. Unlike his other theater music, this work was written for amateurs, commissioned by Josias Priest, a dancing master who headed a school for young ladies. The librettist was Nahum Tate, an undistinguished poet whose words did not match the brilliance of Purcell's music. Performed in a little more than an hour, it was designed to show off the singing and dancing talents of schoolgirls with no professional experience. *Dido and Aeneas* survives in several printed editions. It is Purcell's masterpiece, a work of genius with perfect unity of music and dramatic effect. Apparently, Purcell never attempted to compose another opera.

In the last five years of his life, Purcell devoted his genius to theater music. Possibly he was out of favor with the court; certainly William and Mary showed less enthusiasm for music than their predecessors. In any case, Purcell no doubt welcomed the extra income. *The Prophetess: Or, The History of Diocletian* (pr. 1690; better known as *Dioclesian*) was performed in 1690. With John Dryden, poet laureate, as librettist, Purcell composed the music for *King Arthur* (1691), one of his best works for the stage. Again with Dryden (and Sir Robert Howard), he wrote *The Indian Queen* (1695).

Dryden's complaint that he was forced to alter his words to fit Purcell's music suggests the high regard in which the composer was held. Two badly rewritten versions of texts by William Shakespeare, *The Fairy Queen* (1692), an adaptation of *A Midsummer Night's Dream* (pr. c. 1595-1596), and *The Tempest* (1695), based on the play of the same title (pr. 1611), list Purcell as the composer, although it is doubtful that he completed the last before his death. Many of the songs from these stage productions became popular with the London public.

Purcell died in 1695, on November 21, after a long illness, probably as a result of tuberculosis and overwork. The anthems he had written for Queen Mary were performed at his own funeral, an occasion of great grief for the London public. He was buried in the north aisle of Westminster Abbey, not far from the organ he had played on so many ceremonial occasions.

SIGNIFICANCE

Purcell's life and work provoke controversy among scholars and musicians. Little is known about his personal life; information about him must be reconstructed from public documents of the time. Even the dates of his compositions have been disputed, because most were written for immediate performance and survived (if at all) only in manuscript. Also, musicians who followed

him revised—some say mutilated—his music in an effort to improve it. From 1876 to 1965, the Purcell Society collected and published scholarly editions of his works in order to make authentic copies available to modern musicians.

Purcell composed in the Baroque tradition, in a time when music was dramatic and emotional. Thus, an appreciation of his work depends on individual taste and the style in favor at the moment. Many of his compositions were performed on a grand scale at Westminster Abbey with a full complement of choirs, orchestra, and organ accompaniment, conditions difficult to duplicate. His vocal and instrumental solos, however, are highly regarded by modern musicians. The consistently high quality of his work is remarkable, the more so because of its quantity. Whether writing for the church or for the stage, Purcell devoted the same meticulous technical skill to his compositions.

Purcell was recognized and honored in his own time. He was fortunate in living during the Restoration, when, after years of Puritan austerity, the English people and their monarchs welcomed music back into church and public life with enthusiasm. Unfortunately, however, the poetry of the time was notoriously bad. Therefore, Purcell never found a writer to equal the genius of his music. A performer himself, he understood the requirements of singers and instrumentalists. His greatest gift was the unsurpassed beauty of his melodies, which expressed the meaning of the text. With the words of Scripture for inspiration, his anthems are among his best works.

Scholars disagree on Purcell's role in the development of English music. Some believe his work influenced the music of George Frideric Handel; others believe that the tradition which flourished during Purcell's lifetime died with him, never to be equaled. Like Wolfgang Amadeus Mozart and Franz Schubert, Purcell died young, so it is tempting to speculate what his ultimate contribution might have been had he lived long enough to fulfill the promise of his early genius.

—*Marjorie J. Podolsky*

FURTHER READING

Campbell, Margaret. *Henry Purcell: Glory of His Age.* New York: Oxford University Press, 1995. A popular biography recounting Purcell's life and the political, artistic, and social world in which he lived. Provides a new interpretation of *Dido and Aeneas.*

Cummings, William H. *Henry Purcell: 1658-1695.* London: Samson Low, Marston, 1881. Reprint. New York:

Haskell House, 1969. The author was one of the editors of the Purcell Society (1887), which published corrected versions of the composer's works. Although some of his information may be incorrect (Purcell's date of birth, for example), he provides excerpts from newspapers and court records of interest to readers who want to interpret the evidence themselves.

Holland, Arthur Keith. *Henry Purcell: The English Music Tradition.* Freeport, N.Y.: Books for Libraries Press, 1932. Reprint. 1970. Claims to study Purcell's music for the first time as part of a distinct English tradition, apart from the European Baroque. Takes issue with previous historians and describes Purcell's role in the life of the times, as well as his musical development. Written in a lively style, this is entertaining reading for the nonmusician.

Holman, Peter. *Henry Purcell.* New York: Oxford University Press, 1995. A general survey of Purcell's music, written to coincide with the tercentenary of his death. Depicts Purcell as a musician obsessed with formal counterpoint and well versed in previous English music, yet ready to embrace the new Italian music of the 1680's.

Keates, Jonathan. *Purcell: A Biography.* Boston: Northeastern University Press, 1996. Popular biography offering a detailed explanation of much of Purcell's music. Describes how he absorbed French and Italian influences to create a distinctive English style of music.

Lewis, Anthony, and Nigel Fortune, eds. *Opera and Church Music: 1630-1750.* Vol. 15 in *The New Oxford History of Music.* London: Oxford University Press, 1975. Provides information on the development of English opera and church music with a minimum of technical terminology. Explains Purcell's contribution to the music of his time. Includes musical excerpts of anthems and arias to illustrate the text.

Palisca, Claude V. *Baroque Music.* Englewood Cliffs, N.J.: Prentice-Hall, 1968. Not a complete music history, it selects representative composers from the Baroque period for study. Chapter 10, "Dramatic Music in England," traces the influence of Italian opera on *Dido and Aeneas* and the semioperas.

Sadie, Stanley, and John Tyrell, eds. *The New Grove Dictionary of Music and Musicians.* 2d ed. New York: Grove, 2001. The authoritative, indispensable source for musicians and scholars. The entry for Purcell provides exhaustive detail on his style and development and a critical assessment of his work. Gives a complete listing of Purcell's compositions, including dates of performance or publication and names of authors of the texts.

Zimmerman, Franklin B. *Henry Purcell, 1659-1695: His Life and Times.* 2d rev. ed. Philadelphia: University of Pennsylvania Press, 1983. Claims to correct conjecture about Purcell's life by offering a new interpretation of the slender facts. Using contemporary documents, offers convincing evidence that Purcell was the son of Henry, not Thomas. Probably more quotation than the ordinary reader will tolerate. Still, a controversial revision of previous hypotheses about the composer's life and work, and a fascinating portrayal of Restoration London.

SEE ALSO: Charles I; Charles II (of England); Oliver Cromwell; John Dryden; James II; Mary II; William III.

RELATED ARTICLES in *Great Events from History: The Seventeenth Century, 1601-1700:* c. 1601-1613: Shakespeare Produces His Later Plays; 1642-1651: English Civil Wars; December 6, 1648-May 19, 1649: Establishment of the English Commonwealth; December 16, 1653-September 3, 1658: Cromwell Rules England as Lord Protector; May, 1659-May, 1660: Restoration of Charles II; September 2-5, 1666: Great Fire of London; 1688-1702: Reign of William and Mary.

JOHN PYM
English politician

Pym, a consummately skilled politician, was the leader of the majority in the Long Parliament, which in 1641 outlawed ship money and the other devices by which Charles I had maintained his government without calling a parliament. More than any other single individual, Pym preserved from destruction the institution of Parliament in England.

BORN: May 20, 1584; Brymore, Somerset, England
DIED: December 8, 1643; London, England
AREA OF ACHIEVEMENT: Government and politics

EARLY LIFE

Born on his father's estate at Brymore in the western county of Somerset in 1584, John Pym spent his childhood even farther west, in Cornwall. His father, Alexander Pym, was a landowner who had served as a justice of the peace and member of Parliament. By the time John was four, however, his father had died and his mother had remarried. Pym's stepfather, Sir Anthony Rous of Halton Saint Dominic, Cornwall, was part of a strongly Puritan clan whose views and connections powerfully influenced Pym's life. After study at Oxford and the Middle Temple in London, he was appointed Receiver of Crown Lands for three counties, which meant that rents from the king's lands were paid to him before transmission to the Exchequer in London. Unlike many holders of such offices, who used the money speculatively while it was in their hands, Pym opposed such practices and devoted himself to royal interests.

The date of Pym's marriage to Anne Hooke of Bramshott in Hampshire, a kinswoman of his stepfather, is not certain. They had several children before her death in 1620, and Pym did not remarry. It is difficult even to be certain about Pym's appearance. One portrait miniature that is sometimes said to represent him has not been authenticated. The only other image is a woodcut on the title page of one of his speeches. If it is accurate, he was a portly man with mustache and a Vandyke beard. Those of his letters that have survived concentrate wholly on matters of business. Although information is scanty before his parliamentary career began in 1621, two themes that were to be prominent clearly have roots in his early life: his dislike of those who defrauded the king of his income (likely a result of his work as a receiver) and his concern for protection of English Protestantism against Roman Catholicism (probably a consequence of his upbringing in the Rous family).

LIFE'S WORK

England in the 1620's experienced an unprecedentedly large amount of parliamentary activity. Gaps of five years or more between parliaments had not been unusual under the Tudors, and the 1621 Parliament, Pym's first, was the first in seven years. One reason for the flurry was the international situation. The Thirty Years' War had begun in Germany in 1618, and many were afraid that Roman Catholic victory there would be followed by an attack on Protestant England. In his first speech, Pym demanded punishment of a fellow member who had denounced a bill for being "Puritan." To Pym, such statements tended to create divisions among Protestants and thus to weaken their defense against the enemy, Rome. Accordingly, one reason for his crusade against people who defrauded the king of his revenue was that he believed that the king, who ruled at God's behest, needed money in order to fight against Catholic powers.

In the 1625 Parliament, the first of Charles I's reign, Pym represented a borough controlled by Francis, Lord Russell (who became the earl of Bedford in 1627 and was associated with the Rous family). By 1626, Pym had realized to his horror that the king and his favorite, the first duke of Buckingham, were behind the rise of a group of anti-Calvinist churchmen known as the Arminians. For Pym, the essence of the Protestant faith was the Calvinist doctrine of predestination, and the essence of Arminianism was the rejection of that doctrine in favor of a role for human free will in the process of salvation. To Arminians, all Calvinists were Puritans, and to Calvinists (whether Puritan or not), Arminians were papists. Charles I, by favoring the Arminians, was overthrowing the balance his father had maintained between these factions in the Church of England.

In 1624, Pym had been the first in Parliament to raise the alarm about Arminians, in the conviction that he was helping the king to avoid danger. After 1626, the danger came from the royal court itself, and Pym became a vigorous oppositionist. Encouraged by his patron Bedford, Pym took the lead in the drive to impeach Arminian clerics and even Buckingham. He supported Sir Edward Coke and others in a campaign for the Petition of Right in 1628, but he was more moderate in his tactics and goals than some, hoping that the king could be persuaded to change his advisers and policies. Pym continued to advocate voting the king taxes, understanding that otherwise the king would not continue to call parliaments. Knowing that elsewhere in Europe representative assemblies were disappearing, he was concerned to preserve the traditional English constitution, not least as a means to preserve Protestantism.

During the Personal Rule (the 1630's), Charles I called no parliaments, and he financed his government by a variety of devices of dubious legality such as ship money. His archbishop of Canterbury, William Laud, pursued a policy of liturgical ceremonialism and suppression of Puritan preaching that heightened the identification of Arminianism with Roman Catholicism.

During this period, Pym used his business experience and financial acumen in a series of endeavors, mostly involving Puritan peers and gentlemen, to found colonies in America: the Saybrooke (Connecticut), Providence Island, and Massachusetts Bay Companies. Among their varied goals was certainly the building of colonies that might be at most models of Puritan governance and society and at least places of escape from persecution. When, in 1637, the Scots rebelled against Laud's attempt to impose his liturgical requirements there, Pym and his friends must have been delighted. When the king's efforts to quell the rebellion failed and he was forced to call a parliament in the spring of 1640, they were ready. Pym took the lead in the Short Parliament, speaking forcefully against funding the royal campaign to suppress the Scots.

John Pym. (Library of Congress)

Although Charles quickly dissolved the parliament, he was soon forced to call another.

The Long Parliament, which convened in November, 1640, would outlast both the king and Pym, but it would be the stage on which Pym triumphed. Parliament fully reflected the nation's hatred of Arminianism and the Personal Rule. Archbishop Laud and his friend Thomas Wentworth, first earl of Strafford, were quickly impeached and imprisoned as the advisers most responsible for unpopular royal policies. Strafford's trial, however, tested Pym's political skills to the utmost. Convinced that Strafford had been aiming at making royal authority absolute and destroying Protestantism, his enemies brought about his death by act of attainder. Charles was also pressed into signing a bill that prohibited the dissolution of the Long Parliament without its consent, a constitutional milestone.

Pym's policy throughout this period was not to make Parliament sovereign but to negotiate a settlement in which the king would receive adequate revenues in return for agreeing to oust the Arminians and appoint advisers in whom Parliament had confidence—such as Pym himself and his patron Bedford. Bedford's death in May, 1641, undermined the campaign for a political solution. Pym was no extremist; rather, he garnered support by moderating extreme positions. The king, however, continued to give those fearful of Catholic plotting—meaning most of the members of Parliament—cause for alarm.

Pym, who fully shared those fears, was also a master at manipulating them. When the Irish Rebellion exploded in November, 1641, reawakening the terror of "popery," all were agreed on the need to provide the money for soldiers to suppress it. The difficulty was that Pym and a majority of members suspected that Charles could not be trusted not to use such an army to destroy Parliament before going to Ireland. Pym's Grand Remonstrance, a lengthy list of grievances concerning the Personal Rule and the Arminians/Papists, narrowly passed the House of Commons late in the month. On January 4, 1642, Charles went to the House of Commons in an effort to arrest his opponents, a breach of the Parliament's privileges. The king's effort failed because Pym and his colleagues knew it was coming and escaped to a refuge in the City of London.

On January 10, the king and his family left London, and he soon decided to yield no more powers to Parliament. Civil war, which no one wanted or had expected, became, if not inevitable, increasingly probable. By June, both king and Parliament had asserted authority over the militia, each thinking in terms of self-protection. When the shooting started in the autumn, Pym had only a little more than a year to live. The departure of the king's supporters left his position stronger, yet Pym still had to navigate a tricky course between the extreme factions, one seeking peace at the risk of the gains that had been made and the other wanting victory over the king. By means of patience, hard work, and good judgment, Pym successfully enacted the fiscal measures needed to support parliamentary armies and negotiated an alliance with the Scots; both accomplishments were essential to Parliament's survival.

SIGNIFICANCE

Without the administrative and fiscal structure that Pym created, Parliament would have lost the Civil War, and without Pym's deft management of the Long Parliament in its first two years, there would have been no Civil War. Pym's success owed much to the moderate and nonrevolutionary character of his goals and methods. He led from the center rather than from either end of the political spectrum. He set out not to overthrow monarchy but to make it more powerful—but upon certain terms, especially in religious and foreign policy, to which Charles I was unwilling to agree. Whatever his intentions may have been, Pym preserved Parliament as an effective part of the English system of government.

—J. Sears McGee

FURTHER READING

Fletcher, Anthony. *The Outbreak of the English Civil War.* New York: New York University Press, 1981. A detailed and perceptive narrative of events from the opening of the Long Parliament in November, 1640, to the beginning of the Civil War late in the summer of 1642.

Hexter, J. H. *The Reign of King Pym.* Cambridge, Mass.: Harvard University Press, 1941. Reprint. 1961. A colorfully written analysis of Pym's political strategy and tactics in the Long Parliament. Contains data on Pym's connections with the groups establishing colonies in North America during the 1630's.

Lockyer, Roger. *The Early Stuarts: A Political History of England, 1603-1642.* 2d ed. New York: Longman, 1999. Includes an overview of parliamentary activity from 1603 to 1642, with reference to Pym.

MacDonald, William W. *The Making of an English Rev-*

olutionary: The Early Parliamentary Career of John Pym. Rutherford, N.J.: Fairleigh Dickinson University Press, 1982. A useful biography of Pym.

Russell, Conrad. *The Causes of the English Civil War: The Ford Lectures Delivered in the University of Oxford, 1987-1988.* New York: Oxford University Press, 1990. Pym is prominently featured in these transcripts of lectures delivered by a noted historian.

_____. "The Parliamentary Career of John Pym, 1621-9." In *The English Commonwealth, 1547-1640,* edited by Peter Clark, Alan G. R. Smith, and Nicholas Tyacke. New York: Barnes and Noble Books, 1979. Stresses how Pym was unusual among members of the Stuart House of Commons in his lack of a strong county connection and base and how from the beginning of his public career he was deeply concerned about royal finances and Roman Catholicism.

_____. *Parliaments and English Politics, 1621-1629.* Oxford, England: Clarendon Press, 1979. The definitive study of the parliamentary sessions in which Pym learned his skills. Considers elections, careers of members, patronage, parliamentary procedures, and methods of doing business, and gives a narrative account of each of the sessions.

Somerville, J. P. *Royalists and Patriots: Politics and Ideology in England, 1603-1640.* 2d ed. New York: Wesley Longman, 1999. A concise, well-organized overview of the political ideologies held by Pym and his contemporaries and their role in causing the Civil War.

Watts, Jonathan. "John Pym." In *Statesmen and Politicians of the Stuart Age,* edited by Timothy Eustace. London: Macmillan, 1985. A brief sketch of Pym's career based on recent scholarship. Includes a short bibliographical essay.

SEE ALSO: Charles I; Sir Edward Coke; Oliver Cromwell; William Laud; First Earl of Strafford.

RELATED ARTICLES in *Great Events from History: The Seventeenth Century, 1601-1700:* 1618-1648: Thirty Years' War; May 6-June 7, 1628: Petition of Right; March, 1629-1640: "Personal Rule" of Charles I; March-June, 1639: First Bishops' War; November 3, 1640-May 15, 1641: Beginning of England's Long Parliament; 1642-1651: English Civil Wars; December 6, 1648-May 19, 1649: Establishment of the English Commonwealth.

FRANCISCO GÓMEZ DE QUEVEDO Y VILLEGAS
Spanish poet and writer

Quevedo y Villegas was one of the greatest figures of Spanish letters. He cultivated various genres of poetry and wrote satire, literary criticism, and rich prose that included fictional, philosophical, and political texts. He became the most representative proponent of conceptismo, *a form of witty and satirical literary conceit that played on ideas and was opposed to the style of* culteranismo, *which attempted to ennoble Spanish language through a play on words.*

BORN: September 17, 1580; Madrid, Spain
DIED: September 8, 1645; Villanueva de los Infantes, Ciudad Real, Spain
ALSO KNOWN AS: Francisco de Quevedo y Villegas
AREA OF ACHIEVEMENT: Literature

EARLY LIFE

Francisco Gómez de Quevedo y Villegas (frahn-SEES-koh GOH-mehz day kay-VAY-thoh ee vee-YAY-gahs) was born to a family with close ties to the Spanish court. His father, Pedro Gómez de Quevedo, was the secretary of Princess María (daughter of Charles V) and Queen Anna (wife of Philip II), and his mother, María de Santibáñez (d. 1600), was the queen's chambermaid. His father died in 1586.

Quevedo y Villegas attended the prestigious Jesuit College in Madrid and then in Ocaña. From 1596 to 1600, he studied humanities (including philosophy, Latin, Greek, French, and Italian) at the University of Alcalá. He graduated in 1600 and began his studies in theology, which he finished in Valladolid in 1606. There he came into contact with the literary circles of the time and started to make a name for himself. He befriended the Flemish Humanist and philosopher Joest Lips (Justus Lipsius), with whom he kept an epistolary correspondence. In 1599, he began to write satirical pastiches of Góngora's poetry, rewriting the latter's most serious poems in a mocking vein, thus creating great animosity between the two writers and their followers.

Quevedo y Villegas's poems (eighteen of them) first appeared in poet Pedro de Espinosa's anthology *Flores de poetas ilustres de España* (1605; flowers of illustrious poets of Spain), which earned Quevedo y Villegas respect and popularity among the literary circles of the time. By 1606, he was back in Madrid, seeking the duke of Osuna as protector.

LIFE'S WORK

The years between 1609 and 1613 were marked by intense literary production. Quevedo y Villegas translated and wrote commentaries on classical writers, as well as writing *jacaras* (popular poems) and serious poetry in a neo-Stoic vein. These years coincided with a moment of personal crisis and introspection that inspired the religious and metaphysical poems of *Heráclito cristiano* (wr. 1613, pb. 1670; Christian heraclites).

From 1613 to 1619, Quevedo y Villegas traveled to Italy, where he combined his writing poetry with diplomatic responsibilities and activities as the secretary of the duke of Osuna, who was the viceroy of Sicily and Naples during that period. Around 1621, he wrote a religious and political text based on the Gospels. *Política de Dios, gobierno de Christo, tirania de Satanas* (pb. 1626; *Divine Maxims of Government . . .*, 1715) analyzed the role of the king and his favorite.

Upon the death of King Philip III in 1621, his son Philip IV inherited the throne—at sixteen years of age—and changed the political landscape, while his favorite, the count-duke of Olivares, gained great influence. The political figures of the old reign were persecuted. This included Quevedo y Villegas's protector, the duke of Osuna, who died in prison on September 25, 1624. The writer's proximity to Osuna temporarily tarnished his reputation. In 1620, he was exiled from the court to his estate at La Torre, which did not end his literary career, however. Perhaps to curry favor, he composed *Los grandes anales de quince días* (wr. 1620-1621, pb. 1788), in which he praised the monarch's first fifteen days in power.

Around 1625, Quevedo y Villegas had regained the king's confidence while traveling first to Andalusia with the court and then to Aragón one year later. While Quevedo y Villegas was away, his picaresque novel *La vida del Buscón llamado Pablos, ejemplo de vagabundos y espejo de tacaños* was published in Saragossa in 1626. It is better known as *El Buscón* (wr. 1603-1603) and was translated as *The Life and Adventures of Buscon, the Witty Spaniard* (1657). In this novel, Quevedo y Villegas portrayed the life of a trickster and his marginal world in an indictment of *arrivisme* (aggressive ambition) and moral liberalism. A version of his *Sueños y discursos de verdades encubridoras de engaños* (pb. 1627; *Visions, or Hel's Kingdome and the World's Follies and Abuses,*

1640), which he had begun to write in 1606, was published in Barcelona. Following the concept of classical and medieval visions, the work is a group of six short texts in the form of a dialogue, in which Quevedo y Villegas gives a satiric and moralistic and grotesque depiction of the society of his time.

After involving himself in a polemic defending the candidacy of Saint James (Santiago) as a patron of Spain (he had been a knight of the order since 1618), and not of Saint Teresa as others had proposed, the king confined him to La Torre. Again, this confinement failed to end his literary career.

In 1632, a new period of literary production and political activity started for Quevedo y Villegas, as he became the king's secretary. Two years later, he married Esperanza de Mendoza, but they separated two years later. Coinciding with a second period of personal crisis, he published a philosophical prose text, *La cuna y la sepultura* (pb. 1633; the cradle and the grave), imitating Seneca's stoicism.

After years of conflict, Louis XIII of France declared war against Spain in 1635. This situation moved Quevedo y Villegas to write two texts showing his disapproval of the neighbor country: *Carta al serenísimo Luis XIII* (pb. 1635; letter to the most serene Louis XIII) and *Visita y anatomía de la cabeza del cardenal Richelieu* (wr. 1635; visit and anatomy of the head of Cardinal de Richelieu). Meanwhile, an attack on Quevedo y Villegas, which would tarnish his reputation, appeared in Valencia showing to what extent he had become a controversial figure who was hated by many.

His polemical satire *La hora de todos y la fortuna con seso* (wr. 1635, pb. 1655; *Fortune in Her Wits: Or, The Hour of All Men*, 1697), in which he mixes mythological characters with people of his time, such as Olivares, was published ten years after Quevedo y Villegas's death.

From 1639 to 1643, he was imprisoned in León, this time for unclear reasons, where despite this predicament and his poor health he wrote poetry, satire, and political and religious texts. Aside from a small group of early poems, Quevedo y Villegas did not publish his poetry in his lifetime. It was after his death that his friend Josef Antonio González de Salas published one of the first anthologies with his poems, called *El Parnasso español* (pb. 1648; the Spanish Parnassus). Some of his poetry was translated into English by the poet Philip Ayres (1638-1712) and was published in the anthology *Lyric Poems: Made in Imitation of the Italians* (pb. 1687).

SIGNIFICANCE

Quevedo y Villegas was a prolific man of letters who left a greatly varied legacy. His influence has persisted through the centuries and can be traced in writers such as Miguel de Unamuno y Jugo (1864-1936) and Jorge Luis Borges (1899-1986), among many others.

With the poetry of his rival Góngora, his own work represents a landmark of Spanish poetry. His poetry not only opened a space of experimentation and sharp conceptualization but also offered a way to recover the past by cultivating traditional forms. His at times burlesque poems allowed him to reflect upon religious, metaphysical, existential, and political questions as well as to practice social criticism. In his prose, he depicted and criticized the vices and hypocrisy of his time. The attitudes that he evinced, characterized by both attraction and contempt for the world around him, conveyed, variously, a deep vitality and baroque disillusionment with the vanity of the world.

—Victoria Rivera-Cordero

FURTHER READING

Clamurro, William H. *Language and Ideology in the Prose of Quevedo*. Newark, Del.: Juan de la Cuesta, 1991. This study examines the language and rhetorical strategies used by Quevedo y Villegas in four of his best-known works. Clamurro highlights Quevedo y Villegas's moralistic and satirical flourishes in rhetorical and ideological terms.

Mariscal, George. *Contradictory Subjects: Quevedo, Cervantes, and Seventeenth-Century Spanish Culture*. Ithaca, N.Y.: Cornell University Press, 1991. Mariscal begins his study by asserting the importance of "reconceiving the subject as a product of culture and society." He discusses the notion of subjectivity in seventeenth century Spanish literature. The book includes a chapter on "Individuation and Exclusion" in Quevedo y Villegas.

Martínez, Maricarmen. *The Revolt Against Time: A Philosophical Approach to the Prose and Poetry of Quevedo and Bocángel*. Lanham, Md.: University Press of America, 2003. Martínez examines the concepts of the neo-Stoic "revolt against time" in seventeenth century Spain, specifically the poetry and prose of Quevedo y Villegas and his contemporary, Gabriel Bocángel. She argues that Seneca became a central figure in the neo-Stoic struggle against things and time in the work of both authors.

Schwartz, Lia, and Antonio Carreira, eds. *Quevedo a*

Nueva Luz. Málaga, Spain: Universidad de Málaga, 1997. An edited volume on Quevedo y Villegas's work that includes studies from scholars in Europe and the United States covering Quevedo y Villegas's intellectual formation as a Humanist, his political activities, and the impact of his work on several nineteenth and twentieth century Spanish writers.

SEE ALSO: Pedro Calderón de la Barca; Luis de Góngora y Argote; Count-Duke of Olivares; Philip III; Philip IV; Tirso de Molina; Cardinal de Richelieu.

RELATED ARTICLES in *Great Events from History: The Seventeenth Century, 1601-1700:* c. 1601-1682: Spanish Golden Age; 1605 and 1615: Cervantes Publishes *Don Quixote de la Mancha.*

JEAN RACINE
French playwright

Combining psychological insight, poetic power, and a profoundly pessimistic view of human life, Racine wrote the finest tragedies in French literature.

BORN: December 22, 1639 (baptized); La Ferté-Milon, France
DIED: April 21, 1699; Paris, France
ALSO KNOWN AS: Jean-Baptiste Racine (full name)
AREAS OF ACHIEVEMENT: Literature, theater

EARLY LIFE

Jean Racine (zhahn ra-seen) was born in the village of La Ferté-Milon and was baptized, presumably, shortly after his birth. His mother was Jeanne Sconin Racine, and his father was Jean Racine, a minor local official. When Jean was a year old, his mother died in childbirth. Although his father remarried a year later, he too died, in 1643, leaving Jean and his sister penniless. His grandparents took the two babies; Jean's sister went to his mother's family, and he went to live with his father's parents. When Jean was nine, however, his paternal grandfather died, and his grandmother entered the Convent of Port-Royal des Champs, southwest of Paris, where her sister was a nun and her daughter was a postulant.

Port-Royal was the center of Jansenism, an austere doctrine based on Cornelius Otto Jansen's interpretation of Saint Augustine, arguing that humans were predestined to be saved by grace alone, not by works. After its introduction at the Cistercian convent of Port-Royal in 1634, Jansenism began to spread throughout France, partly because its emphasis on rectitude appealed to those who were disillusioned with the moral corruption around them and partly because its proponents were the outstanding scholars and educators of their day. Realizing the threat that Jansenism posed to their intellectual and educational monopoly, the Jesuits opposed it bitterly and in 1653 obtained the condemnation of its doctrines by Pope Innocent X. Throughout its existence, Port-Royal, its nuns, and its scholars were subject to persecution. The opponents of Jansenism finally succeeded in having the convent abolished in 1708.

Like many other young men of his time, Jean Racine was educated by the Jansenists. Indeed, except for two years in a Jansenist college in Beauvais (1653-1655), he was at the center of Jansenism, Port-Royal des Champs, from 1649 to 1658, reading the literary classics, learning Greek and Latin, studying philosophy and theology, and absorbing the somber view of life that was held by his mentors. For the orphaned boy, Port-Royal was home as well as school. In addition to his aunt, grandaunt, and grandmother in the convent, he had other kinfolk nearby. His grandmother's sister had married M. Vitart, and the Vitarts, too, were ardent Jansenists. Racine's feeling for Port-Royal is evident: Even after his school was closed by royal decree in 1656, he remained at Port-Royal, studying independently. Later, he was to defend the Jansenists as much as he dared; to write a short history of Port-Royal, which was not published even in part until 1742 and not in full until 1767; and to request burial at Port-Royal.

In 1658, Racine went to the Collège d'Harcourt in the University of Paris to study law. The following year, he lived with and was employed by his grandmother's nephew Nicolas Vitart, the steward of the Jansenist duc de Luynes. From his base in the Hôtel de Luynes, Racine ventured into the brilliant, sophisticated world of Louis XIV's France. He became a boon companion of the ecclesiastical amorist, the Abbé le Vasseur, and of Jean de La Fontaine, who was to write the immortal *Fables Written in Verse* (1668). He attended the theater, socialized with actors and actresses, and indulged in a number of love affairs. He also began to write, first light verse, then an ode dedicated to Louis's new queen. This was Racine's first published work.

Because of his association with performers, however, Racine was also developing an interest in writing for the theater. Encouraged by an actress, he wrote his first play, which was never produced and is lost; encouraged by an actress of another troupe, he began a second play that may not have been finished and certainly was never performed.

Although Racine was enjoying himself in Paris, he was sinking deeper and deeper into debt. Furthermore, his family disapproved of his activities. At their insistence, in 1661 he went to Uzès, where a maternal uncle hoped to find the young man a sinecure in the Church. A year later, unsuccessful, Racine was back in Paris. Events had made the decision for him: He was to make his mark not in the Church but in the theater and at court.

LIFE'S WORK

As Racine's letters reveal, the playwright was a complex person. From the Jansenists, he had absorbed the conviction that human beings are at the mercy of emotions over which they have no control and that therefore they have very little control over their lives. As a sensitive human being, he felt compassion for these creatures, yet as an artist he could view their anguish with detachment. Racine liked to think of himself as a scholar-poet, yet he was ambitious, and he planned the political moves that would ensure his success at court. A sketch by his eldest son emphasizes both his confidence and his capacity for detachment. A dark-eyed, dark-wigged man with a prominent nose, rounded features, and an unimpressive chin, Racine looks out at the world with a slight smile, as if he is taking its measure for his plays and for his purposes.

Racine's career as a playwright lasted only thirteen years, from 1664 to 1677. During that time, he produced eleven tragedies and one comedy, rose to social eminence, and, by winning royal favor, gained wealth and a title of nobility. It was the great actor-manager and comic playwright Molière who produced Racine's first tragedy at the Palais Royal on June 20, 1664. Titled *La Thébaïde: Ou, Les Frères ennemis* (1664; *The Theban Brothers*, 1723), it was the account of the struggle between the two sons of Oedipus, Eteocles and Polynices, for the throne of Thebes. Although the play lacks the sureness of touch

Jean Racine. (Library of Congress)

that would later be evident, it does have the typical situation of a Racine tragedy: an emotional obsession, in this case the mutual hatred of two brothers, that cannot be controlled but that results in the destruction of those who are obsessed and of all those who are involved in their lives.

In his second tragedy, *Alexandre le Grand* (1665; *Alexander the Great*, 1714), Racine followed the footsteps of Pierre Corneille, who had for some time been the monarch of French tragic theater. Although it was successful, the play of love, rivalry, and betrayal at the court of Alexander the Great lacks the stature of later plays. Surprisingly, after it had been performed by Molière's troupe, Racine took the play, along with Molière's beautiful leading lady, Marquise Du Parc, to the rival company of the Hôtel de Bourgogne. Biographers have attempted to justify what must be classified as ingratitude by noting that the realistic acting style of Molière's company, so effective in comedy, did not do justice to the raptures and passions of seventeenth century tragedy. At any rate, all of Racine's later plays were presented by the Comédiens du Roy of the Hôtel de Bourgogne.

Racine's success in the theater scandalized his relatives and friends at Port-Royal, who hoped to save him and France from the domination of the theater. When in 1665 the Jansenist Pierre Nicole called novelists and dramatists the poisoners of souls, Racine viciously attacked him in print, thus joining himself to the enemies of Port-Royal. Although Racine has been accused of opportunism at a time when the Jansenists were increasingly unpopular, it may be that he had tired of the Jansenists' unceasing castigation of the art form he loved. In the preface to *Phèdre* (1677; *Phaedra*, 1701), Racine addressed his old teachers in more measured tones, urging them to realize that his tragedies were essentially as didactic as their sermons.

In November, 1667, Du Parc played the lead role in *Andromaque* (*Andromache*, 1674), a superb play about Hector's heroic widow who is doomed by Pyrrhus's obsessive love for her. With this play, Racine had reached the level of tragic grandeur that he was to maintain until the end of his career as a playwright. Although in 1668 he tried his hand at comedy with *Les Plaideurs* (*The Litigants*, 1715), an adaptation of Aristophanes, he soon returned to his own métier and wrote two fine tragedies on subjects from Roman history, *Britannicus* (1669; English translation, 1714) and *Bérénice* (1670; English translation, 1676). With these plays, Racine unseated Corneille from the throne of tragedy and became the recognized monarch.

Racine was never afraid to explore new subject matter. In 1672, he presented *Bajazet* (English translation, 1717), a violent play set in contemporary Turkey; in *Mithridate* (1673; *Mithridates*, 1926), Racine wrote a moving story about an Oriental ruler who could defy Rome but who could not subdue his own passion for a young Greek woman. Of all Racine's plays, this was Louis's favorite.

At this point in his career, Racine's fortunes were at their height. Every play seemed to increase his standing with the king and with the public. The fact that the critics were equally enthusiastic was reflected in his election in 1673 to a seat in the Académie Française, the French society of men of letters. The once-penniless orphan was now well-off. Since his second ode in 1663, he had been awarded pensions from the king, and in 1674 he was given a lucrative post as treasurer of Moulins, which automatically raised him to the ranks of nobility. Ironically, he was only three years away from abandoning the theater, to which he owed everything he had won.

During those three years, however, Racine produced two more masterpieces, this time modeled on those of the Greek playwright Euripides. They were *Iphigénie* (1674; *Iphigenia in Aulis*, 1700), the story of Agamemnon's daughter who was sacrificed for Greek success in the Trojan War, and *Phaedra*, the tale of Theseus's wife, whose desperate desire for her stepson destroyed both him and her.

The year that began with the performance of *Phaedra* marked a turning point in Racine's life. In June, he was married to Cathérine de Romanet, a well-connected, pious young woman in her mid-twenties, who had never read one of his plays but who was to give him seven children. During that year, too, he accepted an extremely profitable post as king's historiographer. Whether ambition dictated that he consolidate his position at court by severing his theatrical connections, or whether, as his son and biographer insists, a religious conversion turned the playwright against his genre, after 1677 Racine wrote no plays for the commercial theater. In 1689, however, at the request of Madame de Maintenon, Louis's wife, he wrote *Esther* (English translation, 1715), a religious tragedy, and he followed it in 1691 with *Athalie* (*Athaliah*, 1722), which was also based on biblical material. Both plays were presented at a girls' school at Saint-Cyr. Racine's final works were the *Cantiques spirituels* (1694), four songs based on biblical texts, and the secretly written history of Port-Royal, published long after his death. During the last two years of his life, Racine seems to have once again embraced Jansenism and as a result to have fallen from the king's favor. Racine died in Paris on April 21, 1699. At his request, he was buried at Port-Royal des Champs. When the king had Port-Royal destroyed in 1710, Racine's remains were moved to a churchyard in Paris.

RACINE'S MAJOR WORKS	
1664	*La Thébaïde: Ou, Les Frères ennemis* (*The Theban Brothers*, 1723)
1665	*Alexandre le Grand* (*Alexander the Great*, 1714)
1667	*Andromaque* (*Andromache*, 1674)
1668	*Les Plaideurs* (*The Litigants*, 1715)
1669	*Britannicus* (English translation, 1714)
1670	*Bérénice* (English translation, 1676)
1672	*Bajazet* (English translation, 1717)
1673	*Mithridate* (*Mithridates*, 1926)
1674	*Iphigénie* (*Iphigenia in Aulis*, 1700)
1677	*Phèdre* (*Phaedra,* 1701)
1685	*Idylle sur la paix* (libretto, with Jean-Baptiste Lully)
1689	*Esther* (English translation, 1715)
1691	*Athalie* (*Athaliah*, 1722)
1694	*Cantiques spirituels*
1742-1767	*Abrégé de l'histoire de Port-Royal*

SIGNIFICANCE

Following Corneille, Jean Racine established French neoclassical tragedy. Like his predecessor, Racine emphasized heroic deeds and heroic language, and like him he elevated the human conflict of love and duty to an almost Olympian level. Yet even their contemporaries realized that Racine had surpassed Corneille. Understanding that the simplicity and the compression of Greek tragedy could produce a maximum effect, Racine mastered the conventions of those earlier plays, producing works in which no character, line, speech, or scene seems superfluous.

Furthermore, writing from his Jansenist background, Racine created a world essentially more tragic than that of Corneille. In Racine's world, divinity created human beings whose passions were uncontrollable and then warned them that they would be destroyed if they did not control them. For three centuries the audiences at Racine's plays have experienced intensely tragic emotions—pity for his trapped creatures and fear that all human beings at some time may be similarly destroyed.

Although new neoclassical plays are seldom written, the seven tragedies of Racine's maturity, from *Andromache* to *Phaedra*, are all frequently presented at the Comédie Française and throughout the world. Along with four of Corneille's tragedies and the comedies of Molière, they are some of the finest plays from France's golden age of drama.

—*Rosemary M. Canfield Reisman*

FURTHER READING

Abraham, Claude. *Jean Racine.* Boston: Twayne, 1977. A survey of Racine's work, especially helpful for its overview of his importance in his genre. Interesting analyses of the major plays.

Barthes, Roland. *On Racine.* Translated by Richard Howard. New York: Hill and Wang, 1964. "Racinian Man" deals with the Racinian hero from a structural and psychoanalytic point of view, and "Racine Spoken," originally a review of *Phaedra*, discusses the problems in acting Racine plays.

Brereton, Geoffrey. *Jean Racine: A Critical Biography.* New York: Harper & Row, 1973. An important biography by a major critic. Brereton realistically assesses Racine's life to ascertain the motives for actions that have been too easily criticized.

Caldicott, Edric E., and Derval Conroy, eds. *Racine: The Power and the Pleasure.* Dublin, Ireland: University College Dublin Press, 2001. Collection of essays that analyze the characterization, use of maxims, and other aspects of Racine's work, and examine the reception of his plays in the eighteenth century.

Clark, A. F. B. *Jean Racine.* Cambridge, Mass.: Harvard University Press, 1939. Reprint. New York: Octagon Books, 1969. A well-written chronological study, with valuable sections on the age of Racine and the development of the French classical tradition up to his time. Contains a full treatment of both biblical plays.

Elmarsafy, Ziad. *Freedom, Slavery, and Absolutism: Corneille, Pascal, Racine.* Lewisburg, Pa.: Bucknell University Press, 2003. Examines the concept of freedom in the work of Racine, Corneille, and Pascal, who shared the belief that freedom could be ensured by absolute authority only. In Racine's view, absolute submission to a most Christian king was the only path toward political and personal salvation.

Mourgues, Odette de. *Racine: Or, The Triumph of Relevance.* Cambridge, England: Cambridge University Press, 1967. A critical work that carefully places Racine within the context of his historical period.

Tobin, Ronald W. *Jean Racine Revisited.* New York: Twayne, 1991. Tobin presents Racine as an icon in French literature. Provides a detailed explication of *Phaedra* and some analysis of the Racine's other works.

_____. *Racine and Seneca.* Lincoln: University of Nebraska Press, 1973. Explores the influence of the Roman tragedian on Racine's plots and themes. An important book because this relationship has been neglected by many critics, who have assumed that Racine followed only Greek models.

Weinberg, Bernard. *The Art of Jean Racine.* Chicago: University of Chicago Press, 1963. An invaluable book on Racine's development as a dramatist, particularly emphasizing structure. Sensibly organized, with one chapter on each of Racine's eleven tragedies.

SEE ALSO: Nicolas Boileau-Despréaux; Pierre Corneille; Cornelius Otto Jansen; Molière; Blaise Pascal.

RELATED ARTICLES in *Great Events from History: The Seventeenth Century, 1601-1700:* 1638-1669: Spread of Jansenism; 1664: Molière Writes *Tartuffe.*

PIERRE ESPRIT RADISSON
French explorer and trader

With his brother-in-law, Pierre Esprit Radisson explored the Canadian wilderness and led the way in organizing trade with the region's indigenous tribes. As a founder of the Hudson's Bay Company, the oldest company in Canada, Radisson helped to promote settlement and commercial development.

BORN: c. 1636; probably Paris, France
DIED: c. June 21, 1710 (day of burial); London, England
ALSO KNOWN AS: Oninga (Mohawk name)
AREAS OF ACHIEVEMENT: Exploration, geography, government and politics, warfare and conquest

EARLY LIFE

Pierre Esprit Radisson (pyehr ehs-pree rah-dee-sohn) was born probably in Paris. Nothing is known about his parentage or his early years, but scholars assume that he would have had a typical middle-class education, which focused primarily on reading and writing. At about fifteen years of age, he would have stopped his formal schooling and begun a kind of apprenticeship, often with a family member. Letters from relatives in New France, the huge French colony that included eastern Canada and the Great Lakes region, apparently stimulated the boy's interest in the region.

In the spring of 1651, he arrived in Trois-Rivières, northeast of what is now Montreal, where his half sister Marguerite Hayet lived with her husband Jean Véron, a fur trader known as Grandmesnil. During his first year there, Radisson learned how the fur-trading business was conducted, and he also picked up two skills that would prove to be critical to his success: He became an excellent hunter, and he learned the Algonquian language.

The following spring, Radisson was captured by a party of Mohawks. Although his two companions were slaughtered, Radisson so impressed the tribe that they decided to take him in, making him a substitute for a young warrior who had been killed. During his two years with the Mohawks, Radisson made two attempts to escape. The first time, he was recaptured, tortured, then welcomed back into the tribe. For a time, he was happy. As a Mohawk warrior of proven courage and skill at hunting, he had a status he had never before enjoyed. However, after a visit to a settlement, he felt compelled to return to his own people. This time he managed to evade his pursuers and reach Fort Orange. Almost immediately, he sailed back to France.

LIFE'S WORK

During the first year of Pierre Esprit Radisson's captivity, a number of French colonists were massacred by the Mohawks, among them his brother-in-law, Jean Véron. His widowed half sister Marguerite married Médard Chouart (1625-1698), who elevated his own social stature by giving himself the title Sieur des Groseilliers. Groseilliers was a highly respected fur trader, about ten years older than Radisson. He had much to teach his younger brother-in-law. However, during the next sixteen years, Groseilliers would find that Radisson, too, had much to contribute to the partnership. Both men were courageous and intelligent, but where Groseilliers was often unbending, Radisson could adapt and compromise.

Radisson was a prolific writer of journal entries, but, one suspects, he had a flair for fiction as well, so scholars have learned to check his statements against outside sources. However, it is certainly true that during the next six years, the men made fur-trading trips to the west and as far south as what is now Minnesota. At first, they remained loyal to New France, but when the authorities in Montreal took most of their profits, using as a pretext that Groseilliers and Radisson had been trading without a license, they decided to transfer their allegiance to the English.

Accordingly, in 1663, Groseilliers and Radisson slipped off to Boston. There they likely made influential friends, for when they arrived in England in December, 1665, they were immediately put into contact with men close to English king Charles II. By 1668, they had persuaded Prince Rupert, the king's cousin, to finance a trading expedition that would take them to Hudson Bay, though Radisson had to turn back. In 1670, they both returned to Hudson Bay, and that same year, the Hudson's Bay Company was chartered. Two years later, John Kirke, who was one of the members of the company's steering committee, agreed to let Radisson marry his daughter Mary, thus ensuring the Frenchman's place in English society.

Nevertheless, because of the growth of anti-French and anti-Catholic sentiment in England, along with drastic changes in the company's steering committee, Radisson and Groseilliers felt they could no longer remain in England. In 1675, they crossed to France, then separated, Groseilliers returning to New France and Radisson investing in and serving in a French expedition against Dutch shipping, which in the end proved disastrous.

While in France, Radisson was told that he could expect no favors unless he proved his loyalty by bringing his wife and children to live with him, but Mary's father adamantly refused to let her go. Inquiries to the company were unsuccessful; they would not have Radisson back. Finally, the French agreed to let a group of merchants in New France send Radisson and Groseilliers to Hudson Bay in order to establish a trading post on the Nelson River. During the winter of 1682-1683, they first made allies of the indigenous peoples and then proceeded to outwit a group of men from New England and another from the company, each of them building a fort and hoping to take over the territory.

Despite their success, Radisson and Groseilliers were still virtually ignored by the French, so they decided once again to try their luck with the company. Returning to the Nelson River, Radisson persuaded Jean-Baptiste des Groseilliers, the son of his old friend, to throw in his lot with the company, and in 1684, Radisson took the Frenchmen and their furs to England. During the next four years, Radisson had considerable authority in the company. However, after the shift of power that came with the Glorious Revolution of 1688, he was never again employed by the company he helped found. In 1700, when he applied for a position as warehouse keeper, he was turned down. He even had to sue the company to keep his pension from being reduced. According to a church record, this "decay'd Gentleman" died—or at least was buried—on June 21, 1710.

SIGNIFICANCE

Pierre Esprit Radisson remains a controversial character, not only because there are so many inconsistencies and actual errors in his journals but also because it is difficult to ascertain the motives for his actions. Thus, although he has been portrayed as an adventurer who did not know the meaning of loyalty, more recently it has been argued that he changed masters only when he was ignored or betrayed. Radisson appeared to prefer absolutism to more democratic forms of government, but he behaved more like a New World revolutionary than a blindly loyal subject of an Old World regime.

Radisson was also a person torn between identities. It has been noted that not only did this Frenchman learn to adapt himself to English society, but during a formative period in his life he also did not merely live as a Mohawk, but, according to his own account, virtually became a Mohawk warrior. However, if the study of Radisson's life leaves one with more questions than answers, there is no doubt he was, at minimum, an important business figure. With Groseilliers, he focused the attention of the Old World on the economic possibilities of the New World and demonstrated how to organize trade so as to maximize benefits for traders, investors, and governments.

—*Rosemary M. Canfield Reisman*

FURTHER READING

Fournier, Martin. *Pierre-Esprit Radisson: Merchant Adventurer, 1636-1710*. Translated by Mary E. Brennan-Ricard. Sillery, Quebec, Canada: Septentrion, 2002. This impressive biography of Radisson explains his changes of allegiance and also argues that the inaccuracies in his writings were necessitated by events beyond his control. Maps and bibliography.

Hudson's Bay Company. *Lords and Proprietors: A Reader's Guide to the Hudson's Bay Company Charter*. Toronto: Quantum Books, 2004. A modern translation of the company's charter. Includes annotations and illustrations.

Laut, Agnes C. *Pathfinders of the West: Being the Thrilling Story of the Adventures of the Men Who Discovered the Great Northwest, Radisson, La Vérendrye, Lewis, and Clark*. Freeport, N.Y.: Books for Libraries Press, 1969. First published in 1904. The first half of this volume is a detailed account of Radisson's life. Illustrated.

Lopez, Barry. *Arctic Dreams*. Reprint. New York: Vintage, 2001. In this now-classic book, Lopez reviews the history of explorers in the far north, including the fur-trading activities of Radisson and Groseillers in the subarctic hinterlands.

MacKay, Douglas. *The Honourable Company: A History of the Hudson's Bay Company*. Freeport, N.Y.: Books for Libraries Press, 1970. First published in 1936, this work contains a wealth of factual, detailed information, such as reports of profits, and a useful chronology. Maps, illustrations, and index.

Newman, Peter C. *An Illustrated History of the Hudson's Bay Company*. Toronto: Penguin Books Canada/Madison Press, 2000. A lively narrative history of the Hudson's Bay Company from its beginnings to the end of the twentieth century.

Nute, Grace Lee. *Caesars of the Wilderness: Médard Chouart, Sieur des Groseilliers, and Pierre Esprit Radisson, 1618-1710*. 1943. Reprint. St. Paul: Minnesota Historical Society Press, 1978. A comprehensive biography of both Groseilliers and Radisson, covering the discovery and exploration of New France and the development of the fur trade. Extensive bibliography.

SEE ALSO: Samuel de Champlain; Charles II (of England); Henry Hudson; Pierre Le Moyne d'Iberville; Saint Isaac Jogues; Sieur de La Salle; Kateri Tekakwitha.

RELATED ARTICLES in *Great Events from History: The Seventeenth Century, 1601-1700:* March 15, 1603-December 25, 1635: Champlain's Voyages; Spring, 1604: First European Settlement in North America; Beginning June, 1610: Hudson Explores Hudson Bay; April 27, 1627: Company of New France Is Chartered; 1642-1684: Beaver Wars; May, 1642: Founding of Montreal; August, 1658-August 24, 1660: Explorations of Radisson and Chouart des Groseilliers; May 2, 1670: Hudson's Bay Company Is Chartered.

MARQUISE DE RAMBOUILLET
French literary patron

Arguably the greatest of the Parisian salonnières, *or salon hostesses, of the seventeenth century, the marquise de Rambouillet contributed greatly to the amelioration of French mores and manners and to the reformation of French language and literature with her salon, the Hôtel de Rambouillet.*

BORN: 1588; Rome, Papal States (now in Italy)
DIED: December 27, 1655; Paris, France
ALSO KNOWN AS: Catherine de Vivonne-Savelli (given name); Catherine d'Angennes
AREAS OF ACHIEVEMENT: Patronage of the arts, social reform

EARLY LIFE

Catherine de Vivonne-Savelli, the marquise de Rambouillet (mawr-keez deh rahm-bew-yay), was the daughter of Jean de Vivonne, the marquis de Pisani and French ambassador to the Holy See, and Giulia Savelli, daughter of Clara Strozzi and Cristofo Savelli and a relative of Catherine de Médicis. Few documents survive relating to the marquise's childhood, but it is said that, while in Rome, the five-year-old Signorina Caterina was often seen in diplomatic circles at the side of her mother, a Roman princess. In Rome, she acquired many of the social skills that were to serve her so well and to make her a cultural icon in her adult life. There, too, she met many of the influential people she would later receive in her salon at the Hôtel de Rambouillet in Paris.

When the marquise was seven years old, the family left Rome for Paris. They first lived on the rue du Plâtre in the Marais; then, her father bought a home on the rue Saint-Thomas-du-Louvre, which would become the Hôtel de Rambouillet after the marquise's marriage. While living in Paris, her father introduced her to the Valois court and to the previous generation of *salonnières*, giving the marquise the chance to hear discussions between her father and such scholarly friends as Jacques-Auguste de Thou, Pierre Pithou, and Étienne Pasquier. She probably knew and was influenced by Claude-Catherine de Clermont, a distant relative and hostess at the Hôtel de Dampierre, and by Marguerite of Valois, wife of King Henry IV of France, whose salon was at the Hôtel du Quai Malaquais.

LIFE'S WORK

The marquise's father died on October 7, 1599, and the following January, she was married at the age of twelve to Charles d'Angennes of Le Mans, who was then twenty-three years old. The couple lived with the marquise's mother until she died in 1606, when the marquise was eighteen. In 1607, Julie-Lucine was born, the marquise and Charles's first child of seven. Julie-Lucine would come to play an integral part in the future life of the Hôtel de Rambouillet.

As a young wife in a noble family, the marquise took her place in the court of King Henry IV, but she soon extricated herself from court life. This may have been as much because of her fragile health, which impelled her to display her vivacious temperament in the comfort of her own home, as to her revulsion at the coarseness of manners and low intrigues at Henry's dissolute court. She established her own minicourt, which reflected the greater refinement of the Roman court circles where her father had been ambassador. Here, in her own world, the emphasis was on sophistication, refinement, courtesy, and propriety, within a setting that balanced intellectual and artistic achievements with lighthearted literary games—such as acrostics, anagrams, and conceits—and the performance of literary and musical works, including the fabled singing of Angélique Paulet. The marquise, known as Arthénice from an anagram that poet François de Malherbe made from her given name, Catherine, created an atmosphere of *féerique*—an enchanted fairyland—far removed from the vulgarities of the royal court.

779

Marquise de Rambouillet. (The Granger Collection, New York)

The marquise de Rambouillet received her "titled" name after her husband inherited the title "marquis de Rambouillet" in 1611, upon the death of his father. From this point on, the house on the rue Saint-Thomas-du-Louvre, formerly the Hôtel de Pisani, became known as the Hôtel de Rambouillet, and was thereafter associated with its gracious and intelligent hostess. It would remain one of the most significant centers of French culture during her lifetime.

The marquise renovated the hotel according to her own architectural design. She enlarged the windows so that they extended from floor to ceiling, allowing as much light as possible to pour in and thus highlight the numerous crystal vases she had filled with elaborate flower arrangements. She moved the central staircase to the side of the grand salon and created a series of reception rooms to facilitate intimate conversation. Most celebrated was her *chambre bleue* (blue room), built so that she could distance herself from the fireplace. The heat from the fire caused her physical distress, but, wanting to participate in the conversations, she had to have the room built. She also used the room to rest and to read for hours on end, for she was a voracious reader. At other times, she would have small gatherings of intimate friends. The

chambre bleue became fashionable and soon was emulated by other *salonnières*, including the French queen Anne of Austria.

Many of the great names of seventeenth century literary France were associated with the Hôtel de Rambouillet, including playwright Pierre Corneille and the poets Paul Scarron, Malherbe, and Vincent Voiture, the hotel's "poet-in-residence." Also visiting the salon were several founding members of the Académie Française, established in 1635 by France's chief minister, Cardinal de Richelieu, including Jean Chapelain, Louis-Guez de Balzac, Voiture, and Claude Favre, seigneur de Vaugelas and author of *Remarques sur la langue françoise* (1647), a book on the French language. The phrase *parler Vaugelas* came to signify the act of speaking elegantly.

The marquise's personality, a model of taste and refinement, informed the life of her salon from its inception. Her salon was a sort of tribunal, where the apposite use of language—*le mot juste*, appropriate vocabulary and usage—and literary merit were evaluated and judged. One of the attributes that differentiated the Hôtel de Rambouillet from other salons before, during, and after its time was that the marquise valued individuals not for their rank in society but for their intelligence and talents and for their ability to engage in polite conversation, which she raised to an art form that would become an enduring element of French culture.

The life of the Hôtel de Rambouillet, like that of the marquise, fell into three distinct phases, the first extending from its inception to the death of Malherbe in 1628. During this first phase, many salon participants were Italian and Spanish guests of her mother, Giulia Savelli, whose interests ranged beyond purely literary topics to the world of politics and diplomacy.

The second period, called the glorious years, ran from 1628 to 1645 and was cohosted by the marquise's daughter Julie-Lucine. There were three kinds of gatherings during this second phase. First were the large crowds in the grand salon, then medium-sized groups, which included Madeleine and Georges de Scudéry, Marshall Bassompierre, Madame de Sablé, Madame de La Fayette, and Madame de Motteville. The third group was the most intimate circle, which the marquise received in the alcove of her *chambre bleue*: Voiture, the princess of Condi; Charles de Montausier (Julie's future husband); Chapelain, le comte de Guiche; Angélique Paulet; Chaudebonne; Conrart; Godeau; and Madame de Clermont and her daughters.

Julie married Montausier on July 4, 1645, after a thirteen-year courtship. Although the match was encouraged by the marquise and most habitués of the hotel, as well as at court by Richelieu and the queen, the marriage changed the character of the hotel, for it took Julie out of its daily life. Julie's marriage inaugurated the third period, in which the hotel was affected by the so-called "sonnet controversy" between Isaac de Benserade's poem "Sonnet sur Job" and Voiture's "L'Amour d'Uranie avec Philis," in which Voiture's supporters gained the upper hand amid vituperative debate. Another event that affected the hotel during this third phase was the bitter faction-fighting of the Wars of the Fronde (1648-1653), setting friends and relatives against each other. By this time, the marquise had experienced many bereavements. She had already lost one son, the vidame of Le Mans, as a seven-year-old, and lost her other son, Léon-Pompée, at the Battle of Nordlingen in 1645. Salon member Voiture died in 1648. In 1652, the marquise lost her husband of more than fifty years.

Arthénice, the legendary hostess, continued maintaining her much-diminished salon until her death in 1665. She had provided an environment that saw the flourishing of conversations among eminent founders of the Académie Française and other habitués regarding the reformation of the French language. She lived long enough, however, to see other salons devolve into *précieuse* affectation, satirized in Moliere's *Les Précieuses ridicules* (pr. 1659, pb. 1660; *The Affected Young Ladies*, 1732), although it is often forgotten that members of the Hôtel de Rambouillet assisted in its first production.

SIGNIFICANCE

Although the marquise de Rambouillet left no literary legacy of her own, she nonetheless played a critical part in the development and success of seventeenth century French letters and culture. Her Hôtel de Rambouillet received and accepted creative people of all backgrounds and social stations. Her salon was a place of gaiety, witnessing the birth of the art of French conversation and the refinement of the French language, letters, and mores. Numerous salons existed after her time, but the marquise de Rambouillet came to be known as the *vraie précieuse* (truly precious), the quintessential embodiment of the French *salonnière*.

—*Donna Berliner*

FURTHER READING

Aronson, Nicole. *Madame de Rambouillet: Ou, La Magicienne de la chambre bleue*. Paris: Librairie Arthème Fayard, 1988. A good modern biography. Little is available in English on the career of the marquise de Rambouillet, but readers of French should consult this work and others listed here.

Cousin, Victor. *Société française au XVIIe siècle d'après le Grand Cyrus de Mlle de Scudéry par M Victor Cousin*. 2 vols. Paris: Didier et Cie, 1858. An important nineteenth century source.

Keating, Louis Clark. *Studies on the Literary Salon in France, 1550-1615*. Cambridge, Mass.: Harvard University Press, 1941. Keating provides background on earlier French salons.

Livet, Charles-Louis. *Précieux et précieuses: Caractères et mœurs littéraires du XVIIe siècle*. Reprint. Coeuvres-et-Valsery, France: Ressouvenances, 2001. A discussion of seventeenth century literary morals.

Lougée, Carolyn C. *Le Paradis de Femmes: Women, Salons, and Social Stratification in Seventeenth-Century France*. Princeton, N.J.: Princeton University Press, 1976. This work provides a social perspective on salons.

Magné, Émile. *Voiture et l'Hôtel Rambouillet*. 2 vols. Paris, 1912, 1929-1930. A rare in-depth discussion of Voiture's involvement with the Hôtel de Rambouillet.

Vincent, Leon H. *Hôtel de Rambouillet and the Précieuses*. Boston: Houghton Mifflin, 1900. A conversational account of the marquise's Paris salon.

Winn, Colette H., and Donna Kuizenga, eds. *Women Writers in Pre-Revolutionary France: Strategies of Emancipation*. New York: Garland, 1997. A 454-page collection that explores how women used writing as a means to gain rights, in the years before the eighteenth century. Includes analysis of women and salon culture.

SEE ALSO: Pierre Corneille; Marie le Jars de Gournay; Jean de La Bruyère; Madame de La Fayette; Jean de La Fontaine; Ninon de Lenclos; François de La Rochefoucauld; Louis XIV; Molière; Duchesse de Montpensier; Cardinal de Richelieu; Madeleine de Scudéry; Madame de Sévigné.

RELATED ARTICLES in *Great Events from History: The Seventeenth Century, 1601-1700:* June, 1648: Wars of the Fronde Begin; 1661: Absolute Monarchy Emerges in France; 1664: Molière Writes *Tartuffe*; 1682: French Court Moves to Versailles; 1689-1694: Famine and Inflation in France.

JOHN RAY
English naturalist and theologian

Devising important early classifications of vertebrate, reptile, and insect species, as well as of all known plants, Ray made significant contributions to the English tradition of natural history. He also published a major, highly successful tract in natural theology.

BORN: November 29, 1627; Black Notley, near Braintree, Essex, England
DIED: January 17, 1705; Black Notley
ALSO KNOWN AS: John Wray
AREAS OF ACHIEVEMENT: Religion and theology, science and technology

EARLY LIFE

John Ray's parents were Roger Ray, a blacksmith, and Elizabeth Ray, whose use of herbal medications in healing may have inspired John's interest in plants. Ray acquired a grammar school education in Braintree, where he received a grounding in Latin. He obtained a scholarship to Catherine Hall, Cambridge University, in 1644 and two years later transferred to Trinity College. He concentrated on languages, mastering Latin and gaining academic distinction in Greek and Hebrew, and he earned a B.A. in 1647 or 1648.

During Ray's time at the university, the Cambridge Platonists were quite prominent on campus, and their theology, as well as scriptural evidence, justified the study of nature, or even made that study a religious duty. Exposure to these ideas had a lifelong effect on Ray's beliefs. In 1649, Ray was elected a fellow at Trinity, soon after which he began to study botany. He earned an M.A. in 1651 and was appointed a lecturer in three disciplines, Greek (1651 and 1656), mathematics (1653), and humanities (1655). During these years, Ray developed a circle of friends who observed dissections in the rooms of John Nidd. In the late 1650's, Ray held several administrative positions at the university, and he was ordained in 1660.

Ray left Cambridge in 1662, because he could not in good conscience take the Oath of Uniformity. During his early years at Cambridge, Ray had met Francis Willughby (1635-1672), with whom he made several trips to collect specimens in the British Isles and on the Continent during the 1660's. A member of a wealthy noble family, Willughby supported Ray financially after he left Cambridge, bequeathing him an annual stipend.

LIFE'S WORK

Ray was a prolific author whose works reveal the synthesis of his talent in languages, his study of plants and later animals, and his religious convictions. The original plan was for him to write botanical works and for Willughby to author zoological works. Ray's first published piece was a catalog of Cambridge plants (1660), which listed the species in alphabetical order. In this catalog, Ray provided summaries of the names given to the plants by previous authors, clarifications and corrections of earlier descriptions, and both English and Latin terminology. At the end of the book, he suggested a scheme of classification, a subject that became increasingly important in his work. Ten years later, he published a catalog of all of the English plant species, followed in 1672 by a catalog of foreign plants.

Ray's skill with languages resulted in several works, including *Collection of English Words* (1673), which listed terms for insects and birds, and *Dictionariolum trilinguae* (1675; little trilingual dictionary), an attempt to clarify the terminology employed to describe plants and animals, by providing terms in Latin, Greek, and English. Clarifying terms helped Ray to create new classifications of species. In his first work on botanical classification, *Methodus plantarum nova* (1682; new method of plants), he departed from custom and based his botanical classifications on several reproductive parts, not just one. Moreover, he divided plants into three major groups—trees, shrubs and herbs—and then subdivided these groups according to characteristics other than their reproductive parts. For example, his classification of herbaceous species consisted of two groups—those with imperfect flowers and those with perfect flowers; the perfect flower group with large seeds contained what were later called monocotyledons and dicotyledons.

The *Methodus plantarum nova* was a prelude to Ray's greatest botanical work, the massive three-volume *Historia plantarum generalis* (1686-1704; history of plants). Contained in this work's first volume was an overview of botany in which Ray described the many parts of plants, provided practical information on the growing of plants and their uses as food and medications, described various habitats, discussed plant diseases and their cures, and even speculated on the possibility of the "transmutation" of plants, accepting it only in plants that were not clearly distinct species. Descriptions of plants arranged according to the classification of the *Methodus plantarum nova* followed. When Ray revised his catalog of English flora in 1690, he dropped the alphabetical listing and arranged the plant families according to his new system of classification.

Unlike his botanical works, Ray's zoological works were not comprehensive, though they remain historically important. Willughby had started works on birds and fish, and after his death, Ray arranged and enlarged the information Willughby had already gathered. As he had done in his books on plants, Ray also collected and critiqued earlier zoological material, clarified its terminology, and reduced the number of distinct species. Again departing from tradition, Ray classified animals not by their habitat or their medical uses but by their external characteristics or morphology. Moreover, as in his botanical studies, Ray took pains with nomenclature and rejected many imaginary beasts such as the unicorn. His goal was a work that enabled its reader to name and identify species.

Ray's works reveal that he investigated the animal kingdom in a rigorous manner. During his continental travels in the 1660's, he attended physiology lectures at Padua, and in 1669, he performed a dissection of a porpoise, published later in the *Philosophical Transactions of the Royal Society of London* in 1672. Ray turned his attention to animals and reptiles in the early 1690's and wrote *Synopsis Animalium Quadrupedum et Serpentini Generis* (1693; synopsis of the types of quadrupedal animals and serpents), which generally followed Aristotle's classification system.

As in his botanical endeavors, Ray searched for a natural basis of animal classification and grouped animals in the first instance based on whether they had lungs or gills. Those with lungs, he divided into groups according to heart structure. He divided live-bearing hairy quadrupeds into ungulates (hoofed animals) and unguiculates (clawed animals), a challenge to the long-standing Aristotelian division into three classes. Ray's final great work on animals was *Historia insectorum* (1710; history of insects), which covered the invertebrates and devoted extensive chapters to butterflies and moths.

Ray wrote many other kinds of works, including travel accounts, sermons, and a late work on geology. Toward the end of his life, he published several tracts on natural or physico-theology. Of note is *The Wisdom of God Manifested in the Works of Creation* (1691), a bestseller that went through four editions. In it, he argued that the nature of living beings can be explained only by attributing design and purpose to them and that the study of nature reveals the hand of God. Ray continued to prepare new editions of previous works and to write until he died in 1705.

SIGNIFICANCE

The life and works of Ray provide an example of an empirical and critical spirit. The goal of all of his works on the classification of plants and animals was to present a natural system, one in which related species were not classified separately and unrelated species were not classified together. In contrast to an artificial system, in which classification rests on one characteristic, a natural system groups species according to the whole. The botanical classification of the *Methodus plantarum nova* contained thirty-seven main groups. When this system of classification gained recognition on the Continent, Ray became embroiled in a controversy with two major continental botanists, Rivinus (Augustus Quirnus Bachman; 1652-1725) and Joseph Pitton de Tournefort (1656-1708), both of whom published much simpler, artificial systems based only on the parts of flowers.

Ray's empiricism, however, seems to have led to a great difficulty in the theory of classification. He accepted John Locke's argument that, because all physical objects were known only through sensations, their essences could not be known. This argument, however, undermines the aim of natural classification, which is to classify species by their essence. In the eighteenth century, artificial classifications prevailed, given authority by the work of Carolus Linnaeus.

—*Kristen L. Zacharias*

FURTHER READING

Cram, David. "Birds, Beasts, and Fishes Versus Bats, Mongrels, and Hybrids: The Publication History of John Ray's *Dictionariolum* (1675)." *Paradigm* 6 (1991). Discusses Ray's contribution to the correction and systematizing of species' names and classification. Includes some illustrations from the work.

Ford, Brian J. "Shining Through the Centuries: John Ray's Life and Legacy—A Report of the Meeting 'John Ray and His Successors.'" *Notes and Records of the Royal Society of London* 54, no. 1 (2000): 5-21. Overview of a conference containing a description of Ray's contributions to natural history tradition and its subsequent history. Also places his natural theology in its contemporary context and outlines its influence in the nineteenth century.

Gillespie, Neal C. "Natural History, Natural Theology, and Social Order: John Ray and the 'Newtonian Ideology.'" *Journal of the History of Biology* 20 (1987):

1-49. Examines how natural theology and natural history were united at the end of the seventeenth century.

Kusukawa, S. "The *Historia Piscium* (1686)." *Notes and Records of the Royal Society of London* 54, no. 2 (2000): 179-197. Discusses how the work on fish departed from earlier approaches to their identification and classification. Also presents details on the difficulties of its publication.

Raven, Charles E. *John Ray, Naturalist: His Life and Works.* Cambridge, England: Cambridge University Press, 1950. Still the only book-length biography of Ray, useful for descriptions of his works, though old-fashioned methodologically.

Sloan, Phillip R. "John Locke, John Ray, and the Problem of the Natural System." *Journal of the History of Biology* 5 (1972): 1-53. Provides details of Ray's dispute with Rivinus in the context of the conflict between natural classification, which Ray supported, and artificial classification, placing the dispute in the context of the seventeenth century debate.

SEE ALSO: John Locke.

RELATED ARTICLES in *Great Events from History: The Seventeenth Century, 1601-1700:* 1601-1672: Rise of Scientific Societies; 1693: Ray Argues for Animal Consciousness.

STENKA RAZIN
Cossack leader

Don Cossack leader Stenka Razin, who led a revolt on behalf of Russian serfs in one of the largest and most brutal rebellions in Russian history, turned his back on traditional military service by leading a large band of pirates on raids in the Caspian Sea and threatening the grand duchy of Muscovy.

BORN: c. 1630; Zimoveyskaya-na-Donu, Russia
DIED: June 16, 1671; Moscow, Russia
ALSO KNOWN AS: Stepan Timofeyvich Razin (full name)
AREAS OF ACHIEVEMENT: Government and politics, military, warfare and conquest, social reform

EARLY LIFE

Stenka Razin (STYEHN-kah RAH-zyihn) was born into a wealthy, landed Cossack family living near one of the Cossack capitals, Cherkassk. The town lies on the lowest reaches of the Don River near its mouth on the Black Sea, and thus Razin's people were known as the Don Host of Cossacks. His godfather was rich and destined to become *ataman*, or leader, of the Don Cossacks.

The Cossacks are believed to be descendants of escaped Russian serfs as well as of Tatars, Turkic-speaking peoples of southeastern Europe and Central Asia. Expert horsemen and fearsome warriors, the Cossacks placed enormous value on their independence, refusing to cultivate their land because they believed that a sedentary life would lead to their subjugation. By the mid-seventeenth century, they had begun to serve as paid mercenaries of the grand duchy of Muscovy, the Russian state lying to

the north, protecting it from the hordes of warlike nomads threatening it from the south and the east.

As befits a future Cossack leader, young Razin visited Moscow, the capital of the grand duchy, in 1652, and made a pilgrimage to the monastery of Solovetsky on an island in the White Sea (northernmost Russia). In 1658, he again visited Moscow, this time as a member of a delegation securing arms and negotiating the Cossacks' wages. In 1661, he concluded an alliance with the nomadic Kalmyks against the Nogai tribe of Tatars, and, in 1663, he led an expedition against a war party of Crimean Tatars—an expedition that resulted in the capture of more than two thousand horses and sheep and the release of 350 slaves into the Cossack fold.

At this stage in his life, Razin seemed poised to join the ranks of his godfather as a Cossack leader, but events were to turn him first into a pirate and then into the instigator of a massive popular revolt against the Russians.

LIFE'S WORK

A number of events seem to have contributed to Razin's turnaround. The first was the death of his brother Ivan, who had served with the Russians but who was hanged by them on charges of desertion in 1665. Other events were less personal in nature.

Increasingly harsh Russian laws were turning free peasants into serfs, virtual slaves who were tied to the land that they worked and who had no hope of bettering their lot. By tradition, fugitives reaching Cossack territory were safe from pursuers, and thus the Cossacks' territory was burgeoning with families and often entire villages of escaped serfs. A ruinous war between Muscovy and the Polish Empire to the west was creating even more refugees. However, the newcomers—known as the "naked ones"—were seldom able to support themselves and frequently turned to piracy and brigandage. In addition to creating internal problems, such actions exacerbated relations between Muscovy and the established Cossacks, or "householders," who depended upon Russian arms and goodwill in fighting the Tatars.

The Cossacks also found themselves at odds with their Turkish neighbors to the south. The Turks had blockaded the mouth of the Don River with towers and heavy chains in 1660 and thus deprived the "new" and impoverished Cossacks of opportunities to prey upon shipping on the Black Sea.

Impelled by these events, Stenka Razin joined the ranks of the newcomers and set out with a raiding party of between six hundred and eight hundred men in the spring of 1667. With access to the Black Sea blocked, he and his men dragged their boats, barges, and supplies the short distance from the Don to the Volga River. Sailing toward the southeast, they then attacked Russian ships on the lower reaches of the Volga and, avoiding the heavily armed city of Astrakhan by sailing down a side channel, entered the Caspian Sea in 1668. Here they raided and pillaged Russian, Turkish, and Persian settlements indiscriminately.

Razin quickly became become a popular hero, attracting thousands of enthusiastic followers from the disaffected peoples of the region and from the ranks of other Cossack hosts. Now, however, his career took another turn, one distinctly political in nature. In the spring of 1670, Razin and his men began an ascent of the Volga toward Muscovy. The Cossacks soon were threatening their traditional masters, but Razin spoke in guarded terms of ridding the Russian state of its noble, landowning class, the boyars, whom he accused of betraying the Russian czar.

The residents of the Volga cities of Astrakhan, Tsaritsyn (now Volgograd), Saratov, and Samara (Kuybyshev) welcomed the rebels, and in no time the lands bordering the middle stretches of the Volga were in open if chaotic revolt. It has been estimated that Razin commanded 250,000 troops at this point, but he proved unable to meld them into an effective army. The garrison at Simbirsk (Ulianovsk), 485 miles (780 kilometers) east of Moscow, had been reinforced by a large contingent of Russian troops, and it refused to capitulate to Razin's ragtag forces. Razin made several unsuccessful assaults and ul-

timately was forced to retreat southward in the fall of 1670, wounded and defeated.

The comfort and security of the settled, landowning Cossacks were now at risk. Upon Razin's return to his Don homeland, he was betrayed by his own godfather and delivered, along with his brother, to the Russians, who executed him on June 16, 1671.

SIGNIFICANCE

Stenka Razin's revolt highlighted the desperate situation of Russian serfs and the growing gap between rich and poor, but it was a terrible disaster for his followers and sympathizers. The Russians tortured and executed tens of thousands of people in the wake of the revolt, and they laid waste to the Volga region that was at the heart of the revolt.

By the time of his death, Razin already had entered Russian and Cossack folklore, and it is here that his impact has been greatest. Razin has been celebrated in legend, art, and song as the legendary outlaw "Robin Hood" has been by the English, as both a swashbuckling hero (particularly for his exploits as a pirate) and as a symbol of the aspirations of the downtrodden. The stirring symphonic poem *Stenka Razin* (1885) by Russian composer Aleksandr Konstantinovich Glazunov (1865-1936) is a musical memorial to his turbulent life.

—*Grove Koger*

FURTHER READING

Avrich, Paul. *Russian Rebels, 1600-1800.* New York: Schocken Books, 1972. A survey of the major peasant revolts of the period, including those led by Razin. Includes illustrations and a short bibliography.

Field, Cecil. *The Great Cossack: The Rebellion of Sten'ka Razin Against Alexis Michaelovitch, Tsar of All the Russias.* London: Herbert Jenkins, 1947. A standard biography, although it lacks documentation and an index. Includes illustrations and a short bibliography.

Longworth, Philip. *The Cossacks.* New York: Holt, Rinehart and Winston, 1970. A popular, well-documented account, with one chapter devoted to Razin. Includes black-and-white illustrations, maps, notes, and a substantial bibliography.

Soloviev, Sergei M. *The Tsar and the Patriarch: Stenka Razin Revolts on the Don, 1662-1675.* Gulf Breeze, Fla.: Academic International, 2000. Volume 21 of Soloviev's *History of Russia*, originally published in Russian (1959-1966). A standard if somewhat romanticized account of the times, supplemented with maps, black-and-white illustrations, an appendix, and substantial notes.

Ure, John. *The Cossacks: An Illustrated History*. Woodstock, N.Y.: Overlook Press, 2002. A comprehensive survey for the general reader, with an entire chapter devoted to Razin. Illustrations (many in color), maps, selected bibliography.

Vernadsky, George. *The Tsardom of Moscow, 1547-1682*. New Haven, Conn.: Yale University Press, 1969. Volume 5 of Vernadsky's *A History of Russia*. A standard history by a Russian-born, American historian, supplemented with maps, an extensive bibliography, and a glossary of Russian terms.

SEE ALSO: Alexis; Nikon; Michael Romanov; Sophia.

RELATED ARTICLES in *Great Events from History: The Seventeenth Century, 1601-1700:* January 29, 1649: Codification of Russian Serfdom; July 10, 1655-June 21, 1661: First Northern War; April, 1667-June, 1671: Razin Leads Peasant Uprising in Russia; Summer, 1672-Fall, 1676: Ottoman-Polish Wars.

REMBRANDT
Dutch painter

Considered by many to be the greatest portrait painter of all time, Rembrandt is also renowned for his etchings and drawings. His works reflect his masterful ability to create realistic images that invite the viewer into his world, composed primarily of working-class and poor subjects living simple lives.

BORN: July 15, 1606; Leiden, United Provinces (now the Netherlands)

DIED: October 4, 1669; Amsterdam, United Provinces (now the Netherlands)

ALSO KNOWN AS: Rembrandt van Rijn

AREA OF ACHIEVEMENT: Art

EARLY LIFE

Rembrandt (REHM-brahnt) was born in Leiden, the son of Harmen van Rijn, a miller, and Neeltgen Willemsdochter van Zuidbroeck, the daughter of a baker. After seven years in Latin school and a very brief period at the University of Leiden, he studied for three years with Jacob van Swanenburch, a pedestrian painter, and for about six months with Pieter Lastman, who influenced his treatment of mythological and religious subjects, particularly with respect to the use of vivid expressions, of lighting, and of the high gloss that appears on many of his earliest works.

Rembrandt's earliest known dated painting, the *Stoning of Saint Stephen* (1625), is a work that brims with action. The saint's face is tilted up toward a central figure, who stands with a large stone raised over his head in both hands, his arms forming a triangle that defines the space around the kneeling saint. Within this space are several men with stones in hand, whose arms and twisted bodies form powerful diagonals in contrast to the saint's own outstretched, diagonally positioned arms. The vividly realized faces and the skillful composition of a large crowd (with numerous faces peering through outstretched arms) suggest Rembrandt's early mastery of both large subjects and individualized figures.

By his early twenties, Rembrandt was working in Leiden as an independent master, making his living by painting portraits but also devoting considerable time to biblical and mythological subjects. He was attracted to the faces of the anonymous poor, often using them to portray philosophers and biblical characters. *Two Scholars Disputing* (1628) is a fair example of his penchant for presenting scenes that seem like a slice of life yet are unconventional and not easily defined. There is nothing particularly symbolic or representative about the scene. It seems rather about an attitude toward life, an intimate observation of two men—one of whom is seen only from the back and side as the other focuses his eyes on him and points to a particular page in the text over which they are evidently arguing. As in much of the artist's later work, there is a sense of something having been left out, of the painting concealing as much as it reveals about its subjects. They share something that is precisely what the viewer is not able to recover from the painting.

The etchings Rembrandt made of himself in 1630 suggest considerable humor and anger. In the 1630's, Rembrandt enjoyed a happy marriage that was otherwise marred by the deaths of his first three children. By the time he had moved to Amsterdam and had wed Saskia van Uylenburgh (who became the model for many of his works), he had already produced great art, such as *The Anatomy Lesson of Dr. Tulp* (1632), a powerfully dramatic painting, with a poised Dr. Tulp able to command the attention and wonder of seven observers, each of whom gazes fixedly on the cadaver's forearm as the doctor proceeds, scissors in hand, to make his demonstration. As in *Two Scholars Disputing*, Rembrandt accomplished the uncanny feat of suggesting that the viewer is witnessing the scene at first hand and not merely observing from the outside.

The Presentation of Jesus in the Temple (1631) is an early, commanding example of Rembrandt's poised skill in representing biblical subjects. As Michael Kitson suggests, this is a picture about looking—the high priest, the rabbis, and the large collection of worshipers are angled in positions that emphasize their excited observation of the Christ child. What is more difficult to see in the reproduction of the painting is the smooth finish of Rembrandt's technique, the way soothing, polished color is applied to this quiet yet epic scene. Although the temple ceiling is very high, the illumination of the central group rivets the viewer's attention.

LIFE'S WORK

There came a tremendous void in Rembrandt's life after Saskia's death in 1642. Yet he managed to paint a masterpiece, *The Company of Captain Frans Banning Cocq and Lieutenant Willem van Ruytenburch*, more popularly known as *The Night Watch* (1642)—an erroneous eighteenth century title that was abandoned when the painting was cleaned, revealing a dramatically lit portrayal of eighteen militiamen. What makes the painting so appealing are Rembrandt's characteristic small touches—the children wandering among the armed men, the dog scampering about, the men in varying stages of readiness, checking their rifles, conferring in small groups, and in general inspecting their equipment. Utterly absent from the scene is any sort of staginess or self-conscious presentation. In its sense of depth, of shadow and light, of strong vertical, horizontal, and diagonal lines, the painting moves the eye just as these figures are moved by their preparations. Somehow Rembrandt puts his viewers in sync with the rhythms of his subjects.

What is extraordinary about such pictures is their lack of subject or theme. On the face of it, such paintings do not have any particular message to convey. They do not commemorate some specific event, and they do not invite viewers to take a specific attitude. Yet such works are authentic and intriguing, as though the figures have just stepped into the artist's frame.

In the 1640's, Rembrandt turned toward religious

Rembrandt. (Library of Congress)

painting, perhaps in response to the death of his wife. *The Holy Family with Angels* (1645) presents an almost homely looking, full-figured Mary bending over the cradle of Jesus as Joseph works on a piece of wood in an interior scene of comforting domesticity. Rembrandt's landscapes and etchings during this period suggest his enormous talent for evoking a place in a few strokes and with great originality, always emphasizing the individuality of scenes.

Toward the end of the 1640's, Rembrandt's servant, Hendrickje Stoffels, became his mistress. A clause in Saskia's will made it impossible for him to marry again, but his depictions of Hendrickje in his art rivaled his deep feelings for Saskia. Hendrickje seems to be the subject of *Woman Bathing* (1654), a lovely illustration of Rembrandt's later manner, where patches of color blend together and human faces have a shaded suggestiveness to them, an expression they seem to have for themselves when they are all alone. Such figures convey the feeling of being seen from the inside out, as though the artist is rendering their feelings and not those of an eavesdropping observer.

Similarly, *An Old Man Seated in an Armchair* (1652) has been described as one of Rembrandt's most poetic paintings, with reds, orange browns, and yellows that blend together and fracture the precise color schemes of earlier paintings. The result is a new fluidity and grace, an artful vigor that is in curious contrast with the aged man's obvious weariness as he rests his right hand against the side of his head and casts his eyes downward.

When Rembrandt reached middle age, he was declared insolvent and his great art collection was sold to satisfy his creditors. He remained a respected figure in Amsterdam but also something of a recluse who did not recover his full powers until the 1660's, when he produced some of his greatest works, including *The Syndics of the Drapers' Guild* (1661), a painting that presents a probing analysis of cloth merchants who seem to have been caught in a moment of business. They have what might be called seasoned faces—eyes, in particular, that gaze out from the painting in various guises of watchfulness and inquiry. The viewer feels the weight of their stares and senses what it must be like to do business with these formidable men.

Although Hendrickje died in 1663 and Titus (Rembrandt's only surviving child by Saskia) in 1668, the artist continued to produce great work—not the least of which were his self-portraits, begun in his youth and continued to the very year of his death. His self-portrait of 1640 presents a handsomely clothed and composed figure—obviously a successful and self-confident artist. His self-portrait of 1650 seems less open, perhaps more reserved, and the one of 1652 offers a man, hands on hips, toughened by experience. Later self-portraits suggest an aging but durable figure, with one (c. 1660) composed of very heavy brush strokes and a roughened texture that indicates the pain and weariness of his later years. There is, however, a majesty in some of these portraits—particularly in the one of 1669, in which old age and experience may have given depth to the eyes but no trace of the weariness Rembrandt painted in the countenances of other old men.

SIGNIFICANCE

In the very year that Rembrandt died, he produced a self-portrait that is massive in its philosophical attitude. No portrait painter has equaled the depth and range of his work or has had the technique to rival his surface polish and attention to detail. Often, Rembrandt's portraits seemed to be grooved with life—a result, in part, of his

---

REMBRANDT'S BANKRUPTCY AND ITS AFTERMATH

On December 15, 1660, to protect against creditors, Rembrandt, his mistress Hendrickje Stoffels, and his son Titus formed an agreement "to carry on a certain company and business, started two years before them, in paintings, pictures on paper, engravings, and woodcuts, the printings of these, curiosities, and all pertaining thereto." The business partnership served as a way for Rembrandt, who became bankrupt around 1656, to keep the money he earned from selling his artwork because he was an employee and not the company's owner. Conditions of the agreement are excerpted here.

• Firstly, that Titus van Rijn and Hendrickje Stoffels will carry on their housekeeping and all pertaining thereto at their joint expense, and having jointly paid for all their chattels, furniture, paintings, works of art, curiosities, tools, and the like, and also the rent and taxes, that they will continue to do so. . . . All that either party earns in the future is to be held in common.

• But as they require some help in their business, and as no one is more capable than the aforementioned Rembrandt van Rijn, the contracting parties agree that he shall live with them and receive free board and lodging and be excused of housekeeping matters and rent on condition that he will, as much as possible, promote their interests and try to make profits for the company; to this he agrees and promises.

• The aforementioned Rembrandt van Rijn will, however, have no share in the business, nor has he any concern with the household effects, furniture, art, curiosities, tools and all that pertains to them, or whatsoever in days and years to come shall be in the house.

• As the aforementioned Rembrandt van Rijn has recently become bankrupt and has had to hand over everything he possessed, it has been necessary to support him, and he acknowledges having received from the said parties the sum of 950 guilders from Titus van Rijn and 800 guilders from Hendrickje Stoffels, both sums to be used for necessities and nourishment. He promises to refund the money as soon as he has earned something again by his painting.

Source: Excerpted in *Michelangelo and the Mannerists: The Baroque and the Eighteenth Century.* Vol. 1 in *A Documentary History of Art*, edited by Elizabeth G. Holt (Garden City, N.Y.: Anchor Books, 1958), pp. 204-206.

using the butt end of the brush to apply paint. His touch was as bold as it was delicate, but in his own time he was faulted for picking working-class subjects and for not staying within the sublime "limits" of great art.

More modern critics, however, have welcomed him as a contemporary, who has shown that it is not the artist's choice of subject but what he or she does with the material that is most important. Rembrandt could make a philosopher of a beggar, and he could turn a painting about businessmen into a work of art that gives the viewer a palpable sense of what it means to transact business with the painter's subjects. Rembrandt's perceptions, in other words, grow out of his subject matter but, in doing so, transcend the subjects of his paintings. In the end, his painting, like his etchings and drawings, exists for its own sake, creating rather than merely reporting its subject matter.

— *Carl Rollyson*

FURTHER READING

Alpers, Svetlana. *The Art of Describing: Dutch Art in the Seventeenth Century*. Chicago: University of Chicago Press, 1983. Essential reading for all students of seventeenth century Dutch art. Alpers relates Dutch painting to the primacy of visual representation, which confirmed seeing and representing over reading and interpretation as the means for a new knowledge of the world. An excellent chapter on the works of Rembrandt and his contemporary Jan Vermeer.

Clark, Kenneth. *Rembrandt and the Italian Renaissance*. New York: New York University Press, 1966. An elegant study by one of the century's great art critics, this volume includes 181 black-and-white plates, a short bibliography, notes, and an excellent index.

Goldscheider, Ludwig. *Rembrandt: Paintings, Drawings, and Etchings*. London: Phaidon Press, 1960. A superb set of 128 plates, 35 in color, with an introduction by Goldscheider and three early biographical accounts reprinted in their entirety. Extensive notes and an index make this a very useful volume.

Haverkamp-Begemann, E. *Rembrandt: The Nightwatch*. Princeton, N.J.: Princeton University Press, 1982. A historical and critical study of one of Rembrandt's most famous paintings. With more than ninety illustrations, including a handsome foldout color plate, this is an excellent example of scholarly thoroughness.

Kitson, Michael. *Rembrandt*. London: Phaidon Press, 1969. A succinct study of Rembrandt's life and art, divided in sections evaluating his art, his "subject pictures," portraits, and landscapes. An "outline biography" gives the most important dates in the artist's life, and forty-eight large color plates provide a handsome and representative sampling of his work.

Rosenberg, Jakob. *Rembrandt: Life and Work*. Rev. ed. Ithaca, N.Y.: Cornell University Press, 1964. A revised edition of the classic 1948 comprehensive study of the artist's life and work, with separate chapters on portraiture, landscape, biblical subjects, Rembrandt in his century, and style and technique. Heavily footnoted and well indexed.

Schama, Simon. *Rembrandt's Eyes*. New York: Alfred A. Knopf, 1999. Schama, a noted art historian who also wrote the now-classic study *The Embarrassment of Riches* (1988), a work examining the seventeenth century Dutch Golden Age, aims to re-create the world in which Rembrandt lived so readers can understand how he thought and conceived his art. Schama intersperses descriptions and interpretations of Rembrandt's artworks with details of his life, creating a well-written and detailed biography. Printed on heavy, high-gloss paper, the book contains numerous full-color illustrations, including double-page color spreads of most of Rembrandt's most memorable paintings.

Wallace, Robert. *The World of Rembrandt, 1606-1669*. New York: Time-Life Books, 1968. A very useful study of the life, the times, and the art of Rembrandt, including chapters on Rembrandt as legend, Rembrandt's Holland, and styles. A rich selection of black-and-white and color plates covers all phases of the artist's career and includes comparisons with the work of his contemporaries and models. A chronology of the artists of Rembrandt's era, an annotated bibliography, and an index make this an essential text.

Westermann, Mariët. *Rembrandt*. London: Phaidon, 2000. One of the publisher's Arts and Ideas titles, a series of books aimed at describing artists' work in nontechnical language. Westermann, a native of the Netherlands and a specialist in Dutch art, recounts the incidents of Rembrandt's life, describes his workshop and business dealings, and explains the unique qualities of his paintings and etchings.

SEE ALSO: Jacques Callot; Frans Hals; Manasseh ben Israel; Jan Vermeer.
RELATED ARTICLES in *Great Events from History: The Seventeenth Century, 1601-1700:* c. 1601-1620: Emergence of Baroque Art; Mid-17th century: Dutch School of Painting Flourishes.

CARDINAL DE RICHELIEU
French diplomat and religious leader

As cardinal, prime minister, and head of the royal council of King Louis XIII, Richelieu was the architect of centralized, absolutist government in France. His brilliant diplomacy helped to end the Habsburg domination of Europe and make France the foremost European power.

BORN: September 9, 1585; Paris, France
DIED: December 4, 1642; Paris
ALSO KNOWN AS: Armand-Jean du Plessis
AREAS OF ACHIEVEMENT: Government and politics, religion and theology, diplomacy, church government

EARLY LIFE

Though he was to rise to be the most powerful person in France, Armand-Jean du Plessis, better known as Cardinal de Richelieu (duh-ree-shuhl-yewh), had relatively humble origins. As a result of a fortunate marriage, his family had risen to upper-middle-class status and had gained the seigneury (title) to the estates of Richelieu in the western province of Poitou. Richelieu's father, François du Plessis, was King Henry III's chief magistrate in Paris, where the future cardinal was born. Richelieu's mother, Suzanne de la Porte, was the daughter of a member of the Parlement de Paris, and it has been said that Richelieu's intelligence, instinct for hard work, and administrative talent derived from these middle-class origins.

The estates of Richelieu's family were devastated during the French Wars of Religion, which raged from 1565 to 1598 between Huguenots (French Calvinist Protestants) and Roman Catholics, and the young Richelieu grew up determined to restore them. When Richelieu was five, his father died and his mother removed her five children from Paris to begin rebuilding the family fortunes. Richelieu, however, was later sent to school in Paris, where he was enrolled in a military academy, despite the fact that he was pale, thin, and sickly.

Among the ruined family possessions was the vacant bishopric of Luçon, near La Rochelle. In 1606, Richelieu journeyed to Rome to obtain a papal dispensation that would allow him to be consecrated as a bishop below the required age of twenty-six. Apparently, his intelligence and charm impressed the pope, and Richelieu was ordained a priest and consecrated as bishop of Luçon on April 17, 1607. As bishop, Richelieu immediately set to work to restore the morale of the parish priests and the obedience of a recalcitrant cathedral chapter. He became the first bishop in France to implement the reforms decreed by the Council of Trent in 1563. The reforms sought to restore strict moral discipline over the clergy and to educate them in church doctrine. Richelieu himself was a brilliant student of theology, and he wrote many papers on this subject, including an influential catechism used throughout the seventeenth century.

In fact, writing was, for Richelieu, the only effective channel for his ambitions and his need to control events around him. Throughout his life, he often suffered ill health, and only immense self-discipline allowed him to accomplish his tasks. Though he could be charming when absolutely necessary, he preferred to avoid emotionally taxing personal confrontations by arguing issues on paper. To many of his contemporaries, therefore, he appeared to be a remote and sinister figure enmeshed in a web of secrecy and intrigue. Actually, he was conscientious, hardworking, and dedicated to the elimination of forces he believed threatened the social and moral order and unity of France.

These forces threatened once again to throw the state into bloody anarchy in 1610, when King Henry IV, who had succeeded to the throne after the murder of Henry III in 1589, also was assassinated. Henry IV, originally a Protestant, had won the crown by converting to Catholicism and ending the Wars of Religion through judicious compromises with both sides. In 1599, he had issued the Edict of Nantes, which guaranteed both religious and political rights to the Huguenots as well as the ability to protect them by maintaining garrisons in all the major cities they controlled. In effect, the Huguenots became a kind of separate republic within the kingdom.

Such an arrangement was bound to create tensions, and religion was used by prominent groups of nobles in their efforts to reduce the authority of the king and reassert the independence they had enjoyed during the Middle Ages. Henry IV's son Louis XIII was only nine years old when his father was killed, so the nobility saw an opportunity to attack the regency of the Queen Mother, Marie de Médicis. Rather than risk an open war, they engaged in threats and protracted negotiations with Marie and her government. At one point in these negotiations, Richelieu was asked to serve as an intermediary, and this led to his being chosen as a delegate to the Estates-General of 1614.

Speaking for the Church, Richelieu offered a brilliant

plea for the reestablishment of strong royal authority, vested in the regent, to prevent the destructive divisions that had previously torn France apart. Though the assembly broke up without reaching any substantial agreements, Richelieu had won the attention and affection of both the young king and his mother. A few months later, he was appointed chaplain to the new queen, Anne of Austria, an office with great political promise. Richelieu's star had begun to rise.

LIFE'S WORK

Cardinal de Richelieu has often been accused of seeking advancement through flattery of the Queen Mother, but this was a universal practice in the seventeenth century; apparently, Richelieu's detractors were simply envious of his superior skills. In fact, it was these skills, used in negotiations with a disobedient faction of nobles, that led to his appointment as secretary of state in 1616. For the next ten years, his fortunes were tied to those of Marie de Médicis. When her Italian lover Concino Concini, who was also the virtual ruler of France, was murdered by a cabal of nobles, Richelieu went into exile to the papal enclave of Avignon. When Louis XIII, who then took over the reins of government, decided to be reconciled with the Queen Mother, Richelieu was again recalled to conduct the negotiations. For his success, in 1622, Richelieu was awarded the cardinal's hat. Two years later, he was appointed to the royal council.

In 1624, Richelieu was called upon to resolve his first foreign policy crisis. For more than a century, France had been intermittently at war with the Habsburg Dynasty, which ruled areas on three sides of France: Spain, the Holy Roman Empire, and the Netherlands. In addition, Spain controlled nearly all of Italy, which was broken into several smaller kingdoms and provinces. The Spanish now moved to capture the Valtelline, an important mountain pass through the northern Italian Alps to Habsburg Austria, from the Protestant Grisons, a Swiss community under a treaty of protection from France. Invoking the treaty, Richelieu astounded and impressed Europe by sending a French army in a lightning strike against the papal troops holding the pass for Spain.

Richelieu's successful action alienated many Catholics within the Queen Mother's faction who had been sympathetic to the Habsburgs. The cardinal had won the confidence of the king, however, and Louis appointed Richelieu head of the royal council, a post that made him essentially the prime minister. From this point onward, Richelieu used all of his talents to weaken the Habsburgs and strengthen the French position in Europe. Because

France was not, at this time, as militarily strong as the Habsburgs, the accomplishment of this goal required a persistent program of small victories in a variety of situations—a chess game on a grand scale.

The board on which Richelieu played included virtually all of Europe, engaged in the Thirty Years' War (1618-1648), the last of the great religious wars between Protestants and Catholics. Richelieu was largely responsible for transforming this long and complex conflict into a political rather than a religious confrontation. He began by giving diplomatic support and subsidies to the enemies of Spain: In 1625, he arranged for Louis XIII's sister to marry Charles I of England; in Italy, he assured that a French duke would inherit the duchy of Mantua to deny Spain a military route to Austria; and perhaps most important, he supported the Dutch Protestant rebels against their Spanish rulers and gave immense subsidies to the Swedish Lutheran king Gustavus II Adolphus, who had gone to war against the Habsburg Holy Roman Emperor.

At the same time, Richelieu reorganized the French army and created a French navy virtually from nothing. After 1640, French armies won consistent victories against the Habsburgs. With the new navy, he sent colonial expeditions to Africa and Canada, chartered royal companies to develop the new colonies, and encouraged

Cardinal de Richelieu. (Library of Congress)

missionaries to convert indigenous peoples to Catholicism. He also attempted to strengthen the French economy by supporting export industries and eliminating the domestic trade barriers. Nevertheless, throughout his career, his primary efforts were centered on diplomacy, and he, or the army of agents he employed, were constantly negotiating alliances and treaties throughout Europe. He even supported the Muslim Turks of the Ottoman Empire against Austria. Ultimately, all these efforts resulted in the end of Habsburg domination and the rise of France as the foremost power on the Continent.

Richelieu sought security and power for France in international affairs; so, also, did he seek stability and order in France itself. He did everything he could, first, to reduce the ability of the nobles to cause civil conflict and, second, to create a royal bureaucracy that would be able to oversee the nobility and provide for consistent administration regardless of who was the head of state. To achieve these ends, Richelieu created a web of spies who ferreted out plots of discontented nobles, several of whom were beheaded. The power of the Parlement de Paris, which had attempted to control royal authority by modifying edicts before it registered them as laws, was forcibly limited. Peasant revolts in the provinces, often encouraged or supported by local nobles, were ruthlessly crushed. Richelieu also persuaded Louis XIII to enforce the laws making dueling—a major source of civil disturbances—punishable by death. Finally, Richelieu expanded the role of officers called intendants, who were sent throughout the kingdom to keep an eye on provincial governments and nobility. Thus, Richelieu was kept constantly informed of conditions throughout France. Eventually, the use of intendants was to evolve, as Richelieu planned, into a system of provincial governors and administrators directly controlled by the Crown. Richelieu's efforts created a principle of centralization that not even the French Revolution could destroy.

Religion continued to be another source of division and disorder in French society. Although Richelieu realized that to end religious toleration could lead to a major civil war, he also believed that the military and political power granted to the Huguenots by the Edict of Nantes was a constant threat to the stability of the state. Richelieu did not attempt to convert the Protestants forcibly; rather, he simply limited their political rights and eliminated their military power.

Toward the end of his life, Richelieu, a profoundly pious man, found himself in conflict both with Pope Urban VIII over French policy in the Thirty Years' War and with the hierarchy of the French church, which disagreed with Richelieu's allocation of church revenues to support the war efforts. Even in his last months, he was not freed from the conspiracies of his enemies, and he was forced to send one of the royal favorites, the marquis de Cinq-Mars, to the block for treason. On his deathbed, Richelieu continued to work on the development of a stable civil government. After nominating his protégé, Jules Mazarin, to succeed him, he died, in the Palais Royal, on December 4, 1642.

SIGNIFICANCE

Cardinal de Richelieu is remembered primarily as the architect of French power in Europe and centralization in royal government. In the area of foreign policy, he was instrumental in destroying the hold of the Habsburgs over European affairs. Through his intricate diplomacy and military successes, he brought France to the brink of leadership of the European powers. In so doing, he also raised the *raison d'état* (reason of state) to primacy as the principle of relations between European states.

Richelieu applied the *raison d'état* as thoroughly in France itself as in his foreign policy. He did not hesitate to use whatever means he believed were necessary to build and maintain the strength of his government and that of France. Yet, respecting history and tradition, he did not seek to overturn completely the accepted structures of administration. A true practical politician, he surprised friends and foes alike with his pragmatism and ability to compromise. He could also be ruthless and seemingly cruel; he justified the state use of force and even the circumvention of the law in matters of national security by insisting that the peace and welfare of the state were simply too important to be confined by the morality applied to personal behavior.

The theoretical vehicle through which Richelieu implemented state power was absolutism, and he is usually given credit for instituting this theory as the principle of authority in France. Louis XIV and other kings would later attempt to transform absolutism into a visible reality. Richelieu's view of royal government was based on his theology, which supported the divine-right concept, in which the monarch was a sacred person who received his crown and powers from God alone. Thus, while bowing to the Papacy in spiritual matters, Richelieu insisted that only the king could be supreme in the secular realm. From this, his devotion to the stability and good order of the state led him logically toward all those measures designed to curb the nobles and the Huguenots, and to increase the power of the central government.

—Thomas C. Schunk

FURTHER READING

Bergin, Joseph. *Cardinal Richelieu: Power and the Pursuit of Wealth*. New Haven, Conn.: Yale University Press, 1985. Scholarly work based on financial records of Richelieu's personal estates. In addition to providing an interesting perspective on Richelieu's use of political office for personal gain—a practice both accepted and very common in his period—it offers fascinating detail on the management of landed estates and the conduct of business in the seventeenth century.

Bergin, Joseph, and Laurence Brockliss, eds. *Richelieu and His Age*. Oxford, England: Clarendon Press, 1992. Collection of essays by eight historians, who reject the depiction of Richelieu as an exponent of *realpolitik* and maintain he was a devout and politically astute diplomat with a genuine desire to establish a more just and peaceful Europe.

Burckhardt, Carl J. *Richelieu and His Age*. 4 vols. Translated by Bernard Hoy. London: Allen & Unwin, 1967-1972. Though somewhat lengthy for the general reader, this is by far both the best biography of Richelieu and the clearest explanation of French politics of the period. Burckhardt's style is highly entertaining yet balanced and scholarly.

Church, William F. *Richelieu and Reason of State*. Princeton, N.J.: Princeton University Press, 1972. A detailed discussion of the conflict between political expediency and moral principles in policy making in seventeenth century France. The author examines the growth of the idea of the reason of state as it evolved in the policies of Richelieu.

Knecht, Robert. *Richelieu*. New York: Longman, 1991. Not a complete biography, but a reassessment of Richelieu focusing on the major features, achievements, and failures of his career.

Levi, Anthony. *Cardinal Richelieu and the Making of France*. New York: Carroll & Graf, 2000. Levi argues that Richelieu sought to create a French national unity as much through cultural symbolism as through political means.

Marvick, Elizabeth Wirth. *The Young Richelieu: A Psychoanalytical Approach to Leadership*. Chicago: University of Chicago Press, 1983. Attempts to psychoanalyze Richelieu's personality to discern how incidents in his youth influenced his approach to policy decisions and administration. Although based on the questionable assumption that it is possible to psychoanalyze a dead historical figure, the book is useful for its detailed information about Richelieu's early years.

O'Connell, D. P. *Richelieu*. Cleveland, Ohio: World, 1968. O'Connell views Richelieu as an intensely religious man who was forced to deal with the tension between policies that were necessary for the good of France and his own religious morality.

Parrott, David. *Richelieu's Army: War, Government, and Society in France, 1624-1642*. New York: Cambridge University Press, 2001. Detailed account of the administration, finances, and activities of the French army. Parrott challenges the conventional wisdom that the army helped create an absolute state, arguing that the expansion of war actually weakened Richelieu's control of France and intensified political and social tensions.

Sturdy, David J. *Richelieu and Mazarin: A Study in Statesmanship*. New York: Palgrave Macmillan, 2004. Concise and comparative analysis of the public and private careers of the two ministers, including an assessment of their historical significance.

Treasure, Geoffrey R. R. *Cardinal Richelieu and the Development of Absolutism*. London: Adam and Charles Black, 1972. A standard work by a well-known expert on seventeenth century France. Treasure views Richelieu not as the cold architect of absolutist monarchy but as a long-suffering minister, fighting for survival in the highly competitive political arena.

SEE ALSO: Anne of Austria; Charles I; The Great Condé; Gustavus II Adolphus; Cornelius Otto Jansen; Louis XIII; Louis XIV; Marie de Médicis; Jules Mazarin; Axel Oxenstierna; Francisco Gómez de Quevedo y Villegas; Urban VIII.

RELATED ARTICLES in *Great Events from History: The Seventeenth Century, 1601-1700:* 1610-1643: Reign of Louis XIII; 1611-1630's: Jesuits Begin Missionary Activities in New France; 1618-1648: Thirty Years' War; May 23, 1618: Defenestration of Prague; 1625-October 28, 1628: Revolt of the Huguenots; April 27, 1627: Company of New France Is Chartered; March 6, 1629: Edict of Restitution; November 10, 1630: The Day of Dupes; May 30, 1635: Peace of Prague; 1638-1669: Spread of Jansenism; 1640-1688: Reign of Frederick William, the Great Elector; May, 1640-January 23, 1641: Revolt of the Catalans; July, 1643-October 24, 1648: Peace of Westphalia; June, 1648: Wars of the Fronde Begin; November 7, 1659: Treaty of the Pyrenees; 1661: Absolute Monarchy Emerges in France; 1661-1672: Colbert Develops Mercantilism; July 13, 1664: Trappist Order Is Founded; 1682: French Court Moves to Versailles; 1685: Louis XIV Revokes the Edict of Nantes.

MICHAEL ROMANOV
Czar of Russia (r. 1613-1645)

Romanov managed to rise to power and stay on the throne of Russia during some of the most difficult years of Russian history. He founded the Romanov Dynasty, which would rule the Russian Empire until the twentieth century.

BORN: July 22, 1596; Moscow, Russia
DIED: July 23, 1645; Moscow
ALSO KNOWN AS: Mikhail Fyodorovich Romanov; Michael
AREA OF ACHIEVEMENT: Government and politics

EARLY LIFE

Michael Romanov (ROH-mahn-ahf) was the youngest of five sons born to Fyodor Nikitich Romanov and Ksenia Romanova. Fyodor Romanov was an influential figure in the politics of late sixteenth century Russia. He was an adviser to Czar Ivan the Terrible (r. 1547-1584) and was close to Boris Godunov, Ivan's chief minister and later czar. Ivan the Terrible began a crisis in Russian history when, in a fit of anger in 1581, he hit his eldest son with an iron-tipped staff. The son soon died of the wound. When Ivan himself died three years later, the only heir to the throne was the weak-minded Fyodor I Ivanovich. Czar Fyodor I had no children. Both Godunov and Fyodor Romanov had ambitions to succeed Czar Fyodor I when the czar died in 1598. Godunov managed to conduct a *zemskii sobor*, or assembly of the land, where Russian nobles proclaimed him ruler.

Godunov accused the family of Fyodor, his former friend and rival, of treason and witchcraft. After a conviction based on evidence planted by agents of Czar Godunov, the entire family, including the five-year-old Michael Romanov, was exiled to the cold northern regions of Russia. Fyodor Romanov was then forced to become a monk with the name Philaret, and Ksenia was forced to become a nun, under the name Marfa. Michael was sent to live in poverty with an aunt in a remote village.

The rule of Boris began a period in Russian history known as the Time of Troubles because of political instability and invasion by Polish forces. After the death of Boris in 1605, Philaret returned to public life and quickly rose to high church office, that of metropolitan of Rostov. However, with Polish support, a pretender to the throne, known as the False Dmitry because he claimed to be the murdered son of Ivan the Terrible, took power in Moscow, but a rebellious crowd killed the pretender in 1606, and the Russian assembly of the land elected a new czar. A second False Dmitry appeared, supported by Polish forces. The Poles took Rostov and then Moscow, and retreated, taking Philaret with them as prisoner.

The young Michael spent several years wandering and hiding with his mother. In 1613, Michael and Marfa had taken refuge in a monastery that was a little more than 200 miles from Moscow. A new assembly of the land met to find a new ruler, and the nobles decided on the sixteen-year-old Michael Romanov. In March, 1613, they met the young man at the monastery and offered him the crown. After some reluctance, he agreed, returning then to Moscow to begin the dynasty that would rule Russia for three hundred years.

LIFE'S WORK

Michael Romanov was crowned czar of Russia in Uspenskii Cathedral in Moscow on July 11, 1613. His first tasks were to obtain his father's release from the Poles and to free Russia from the foreign troops on its ter-

Michael Romanov. (R. S. Peale and J. A. Hill)

ritory. In addition to the Poles, the Russians also had to contend with Swedish forces. Prince Charles Philip, brother of the king of Sweden, claimed to be the rightful czar, and the Swedes occupied the important Russian city of Novgorod. Michael sought the assistance of King James I of England in negotiating with the Swedes. Under the terms of the Treaty of Stolbovo (1617), the Russians paid the Swedes a substantial sum of money and gave up lands along the Baltic Coast that had been taken by Boris Godunov and Ivan the Terrible. In return, Sweden withdrew from Novgorod and Prince Charles Philip gave up his claim to the Russian throne.

Next, Czar Michael turned to making peace with the Poles. By 1619, he obtained a cease-fire with Poland and an agreement for his father's return by handing over several Russian towns and cities to the Poles. After Philaret's return, on June 10, 1619, Michael gave up much of the day-to-day business of running the country. Philaret controlled the government until his death in 1633. In addition, the assembly of the land, which previously had been called to meetings only when needed, remained in session for years to help restore order throughout the country.

One of the most pressing matters for the new Romanov Dynasty was the need for an heir whose clear right to the throne would help Russia avoid the conflicts that had produced the Time of Troubles. At first, Philaret was inclined to find Michael a bride from the European nobility outside Russia, so that the Romanovs would not be allying themselves with any of the factions of Russian families. However, the noble families of Europe were reluctant to tie themselves to the new and unproven dynasty. In 1624, Michael married Marya Dolgorukova, who was related to his mother. Marya died a year later, though, and Michael married Evdokia Streshneva in 1626. Evdokia gave birth to three daughters and three sons, including, in 1629, Alexis, who would become the second Romanov czar.

By the time Philaret died, Russia was once again at war with Poland, and the Polish king Władysław IV Vasa had invaded. Michael was forced to pay the Poles, but he managed to obtain a peace treaty in 1634 (Peace of Polyanov). Poland also recognized his right to be Russian czar, an important step toward political stability. The most serious challenge that remained was to ensure Romanov rule after his own death. His two younger sons had died. The heir, Alexis, was still alive, but in those times of high mortality rates no life was certain. For this reason, Michael attempted to arrange a marriage between his daughter, Irina, and Prince Valdemar of Den-

mark, who could become czar if anything happened to Alexis. However, Valdemar, who had traveled to Moscow, was reluctant to convert from his Lutheran faith to Russian Orthodoxy. Michael kept Valdemar in Moscow until 1645, the year Michael died at the age of forty-nine. Alexis assumed the throne and sent Valdemar back to Denmark.

SIGNIFICANCE

Michael Romanov assumed the throne of Russia as an inexperienced sixteen-year-old, when the country was torn by fighting and by invasions of foreign forces. He had spent much of his childhood in a family that was persecuted and in exile. Still, he managed to achieve relative peace with his country's two greatest foreign enemies, Poland and Sweden.

Michael handed over most of the actual rule of the country to his father during the years from 1619 to 1633. During this time, though, he took care of one of the most essential tasks for establishing order in Russia. By marrying and producing an heir, Michael brought Russia out of the continual political crises that had plagued the country since the death of Czar Fyodor. The Romanov Dynasty that began with Michael was to rule Russia for more than three hundred years, until Czar Nicholas II (r. 1884-1917), the last of the Romanovs, was overthrown during the Russian Revolution of 1917.

After his father's death, Michael achieved a peace treaty with Poland. Although he did not succeed in arranging a marriage between his daughter and the Danish prince, Michael began drawing his country into closer ties with the other nations of Europe. This can be seen as the beginning of the dramatic efforts at Westernization and modernization that reached their highest point during the rule of Michael's grandson, Peter the Great.

—Carl L. Bankston III

FURTHER READING

Dunning, Chester S. L. *Russia's First Civil War: The Time of Troubles and the Founding of the Romanov Dynasty*. University Park: Pennsylvania State University Press, 2001. A massive volume that provides post-Marxist analysis of the civil uprisings, claiming that they were struggles between factions of equal rank, rather than initial attempts by serfs to win their freedom. Includes illustrations, maps, bibliographic references, and index.

Khodarovsky, Michael. *Russia's Steppe Frontier: The Making of a Colonial Empire, 1500-1800*. Bloomington: Indiana University Press, 2003. Looks at the extension of Russian borders, during the Romanov period begun by Michael and by others during the century before his rule.

Kliuchevsky, V. O. *A Course in Russian History: The Seventeenth Century*. Translated by Natalie Dudding-ton. Armonk, N.Y.: M. E. Sharpe, 1994. A translation of a classic work by one of Russia's most eminent historians. Chapter 4, "Political Reconstruction," considers the events of Michael's reign.

Kotilaine, Jarmo, and Marshall Poe, eds. *Modernizing Muscovy: Reform and Social Change in Seventeenth Century Russia*. New York: Routledge Curzon, 2004. A collection of articles that provides an encyclopedic account of politics and society in Russia during the seventeenth century. Includes useful references in footnotes of each article and an index.

Lincoln, W. Bruce. *The Romanovs: Autocrats of All the Russias*. New York: Dial Press, 1981. A comprehensive history of the entire Romanov Dynasty. The first quarter of the book is devoted to the seventeenth century. Enjoyable illustrations, including portraits of Michael and his son Alexis, extensive bibliography, index.

Vernadsky, George. *The Tsardom of Moscow, 1547-1682*. Vol. 5 in *A History of Russia*. New Haven, Conn.: Yale University Press, 1969. Vernadsky is a Russian émigré who has written many books on Russian history, including the multivolume *A History of Russia*. The text has a large bibliography for the entire period.

SEE ALSO: Alexis; Avvakum Petrovich; Charles X Gustav; Christina; Gustavus II Adolphus; James I; Nikon; Boris Morozov; Sigismund III Vasa; Lennart Torstenson.

RELATED ARTICLES in *Great Events from History: The Seventeenth Century, 1601-1700:* c. 1601-1606: Appearance of the False Dmitry; February 7, 1613: Election of Michael Romanov as Czar; 1632-1667: Polish-Russian Wars for the Ukraine; December, 1639: Russians Reach the Pacific Ocean; January 29, 1649: Codification of Russian Serfdom; April, 1667-June, 1671: Razin Leads Peasant Uprising in Russia; Beginning 1689: Reforms of Peter the Great; August 29, 1689: Treaty of Nerchinsk Draws Russian-Chinese Border.

SAINT ROSE OF LIMA
Peruvian saint

The first native-born New World saint, Rose of Lima exhibited an exemplary mysticism and rigorous asceticism that inspired colonial Peruvians, as did her charitable service to Lima's sick and destitute. Her death in 1617 immediately touched off a movement for Rose's canonization, based on her intense spirituality and the miracles attributed to her.

BORN: April 20 or 30, 1586; Lima, Peru
DIED: August 24, 1617; Lima
ALSO KNOWN AS: Isabel Flores de Oliva; Rosa de Santa María; Rosa de Lima; Santa Rosa de Lima
AREA OF ACHIEVEMENT: Religion and theology

EARLY LIFE

Saint Rose of Lima was born Isabel Flores de Oliva, the daughter of Gaspar Flores and María de Oliva. Her father, a Spaniard, probably arrived in Peru from Puerto Rico in 1548, during the tumultous civil wars that followed the conquest of the Inca Empire. For his service to the Crown in helping suppress the rebellion of Gonzalo Pizarro, he was made one of the viceroy's guards. Gaspar

Flores wed María de Oliva, a native of Lima, and they had eleven children. Isabel was born in 1586, when her father was already of an advanced age, perhaps 60.

Isabel displayed characteristics from infancy that afterward seemed to foreshadow her piety and mysticism. Both her childhood and adult life are known chiefly through the documents from the investigation that resulted in her canonization. These portray her in a hagiographic light, seeking to prove her saintliness. According to popular belief, Isabel's future sainthood was foreshadowed by two pink roses that appeared on her cheeks as an infant. Peruvian Catholics associated the rose with the Virgin Mary. The maid who first noticed the symbol and Isabel's mother were both convinced of its miraculous origin and began calling her Rosita, or Little Rose. Soon, other relatives and friends took up the new name. The holdout was her maternal grandmother, Isabel de Herrera, for whom the little girl had been named and who resented the attempt to change it.

Reportedly a lovely young girl, Isabel nonetheless made, as a five-year-old child, a vow of lifelong chastity and butchered her own hair when her brother perhaps jokingly said it was so beautiful that it enticed men. Isabel spent much of her childhood learning skills deemed appropriate to her gender. Her mother taught her to read and write, although Isabel never displayed notable literary or intellectual ability. The girl preferred music, needlework, and gardening. The sale of her embroidery, fruits, and vegetables provided an important supplement to the family income.

Gaspar Flores's salary as a viceregal guard was not enough to make the family financially secure. His occupation did, however, confer social status, as did the fact that Isabel's parents were of Spanish rather than indigenous origin. In 1597, the family moved to the town of Quives, in Canta province, where her father served as mining inspector. While there, Isabel received the sacrament of confirmation from another future Peruvian saint, Archbishop Toribio Alfonso de Mogrovejo. He confirmed her, perhaps at the family's urging, as Rosa de Santa María, thereby giving ecclesiastical sanction to her association with the Virgin. In 1600, the family returned to Lima, where Rose spent the remainder of her life.

LIFE'S WORK
From an early age, Rose showed strong spiritual yearnings and profound mystical abilities. She preferred prayer, meditation, and solitude to social interaction. Her mother had difficulty accepting Rose's childhood vow of virginity, for it frustrated her hopes to improve the family's prospects through her marriage to a wealthy husband (her elderly father rarely appears in her biographies). Rose was determined, however, to reserve herself for a mystical marriage with Jesus Christ. On at least two occasions, she nearly took the vows to become a nun but at the last moment desisted. Instead she remained a *beata*, a single woman who wore monastic robes and committed her life to unceasing religious devotion and acts of charity without ever officially joining a convent. At first, Rose wore a Franciscan habit, but in 1606, she adopted the white Dominican robes that she used until her death.

Hernando, one of Rose's brothers, built a hermitage in the family garden where she could pray and meditate in peace. This hermitage became the setting of many miracles attributed to Rose and soon became the gathering place of important *limeña* ladies, who sought her friendship and religious instruction. Rose dedicated her life to ascetic disciplines: Austere fasts left her body emaciated, and she wore a silver crown of thorns to emulate her savior and bridegroom. Her confessor counseled Rose to sleep more than the two hours per night she allowed herself. At one point she bound a chain tightly about her torso, locked it, and threw the key into the family's well. Fearful that pedestrians might step on the symbol of Christianity, she stopped in the street to separate pieces of straw when she found them crossed.

Rose never received the stigmata, nor did she experience transverberation (piercing of the heart), two of the more extreme signs of saintliness. Through all her austerity, she tried to avoid drawing attention to herself, for public notoriety was not her aim. She humbly sought instead to please God. Thus, she wore a hood to cover her crown of thorns and bloody scalp.

Ecclestiastical officials, including the Inquisition, were wary of mystics, because they sought the divine will via direct communication with God rather than through the authority of the clergy. Thus, as the church hierarchy noticed Rosa's growing fame, it began to investigate her behavior for any signs of heresy. A long interview convinced them that her spirituality was genuine and holy rather than satanic. Rosa devoted much of her time to charitable works, caring for Lima's destitute and sick in her family's home. At first, her mother protested such intrusions, but later she joined in her daughter's efforts. Inspired by Rose's example, other young women became her disciples, whereupon Rose established a Dominican convent in memory of Saint Catherine of Siena, whose pious and mystical example Rose tried to follow. She regularly visited the Lima churches most closely associated with the Virgin Mary (Our Lady of the Rosary, Our Lady of Los Remedios, and Our Lady of Loreto), where the priests allowed her to care for the images of the Mother of God.

One miracle attributed to Rose occurred in 1615, when a Dutch squadron under Joris van Spilbergen attacked Lima. Seeking martyrdom, Rose confronted the raiders as they began to plunder a church. Her appearance allegedly so intimidated the pirates that they sailed away (they continued to plunder the west coast of Spanish America before heading across the Pacific to the Philippines).

Rose's asceticism undermined her health, but her devotions continued. She moved to the home of Doña María de Uzategui, one of her closest friends and wife of the royal accountant. On April 15, 1617, as she prayed before a picture of the Savior, Christ began to perspire. The crowd that gathered to witness soon spread the story, adding to Rose's popular esteem as a holy woman. On Palm Sunday, she had a vision in which the Christ Child invited her to be his bride, satisfying her greatest desire. One of her brothers fashioned a wedding ring for her, and she was secretly married to Christ on Easter Sunday in a ceremony solemnized by clerical friends. Only four months later, on August 24, 1617, Rose died.

SIGNIFICANCE

From a modern, secular perspective, one unsympathetic to miracles and mysticism, the life of Saint Rose of Lima raises questions of psychological abnormality. Rose's own culture, however, gave far greater credence to ascetic mysticism than does ours. Her death touched off a wave of popular mourning in Peru. A tumult erupted at her funeral as worshipers struggling to obtain relics seized pieces of her clothing and her corpse. Officials stopped the rites and buried her secretly. Within a year after her death, church authorities began official inquiries to determine if she qualified for canonization. For the people of Lima, there was no doubt as to Rose's saintliness, and popular devotions to her sprang up throughout Peru. The Inquisition tried to stop them, but it could not block the tide of popular enthusiasm. On April 12, 1671, Rose of Santa Maria became the first American canonized by the Catholic Church. The papacy declared her the spiritual patroness of the New World, the Philippines, and India.

—*Kendall W. Brown*

FURTHER READING

Graziano, Frank. *Wounds of Love: The Mystical Marriage of Saint Rose of Lima*. New York: Oxford University Press, 2004. A profound examination of Rose's mysticism that emphasizes the erotic aspects of her spiritual devotions.

Keyes, Frances Parkinson. *The Rose and the Lily: The Lives of Two South American Saints*. New York: Hawthorn Books, 1961. Contains biographies of both Saint Rose of Lima and Saint Mariana of Jesus in an accessible if not always analytical narrative.

Martín, Luis. *Daughters of the Conquistadores: Women of the Viceroyalty of Peru*. Albuquerque: University of New Mexico Press, 1983. Analyzes the life of Rose of Lima as the chief example of a Peruvian *beata*, while placing her life within the context of women in early colonial Peru.

Morgan, Ronald J. *Spanish American Saints and the Rhetoric of Identity, 1600-1810*. Tucson: University of Arizona Press, 2002. Chapter 4 ("Heretics by Sea, Pagans by Land: St. Rosa de Lima and the Limits of Criollismo in Colonial Peru") presents a biography of Rose of Lima and examines how Andean social and ethnic groups competed to define her spiritual and cultural legacy.

SEE ALSO: Saint Isaac Jogues; Kateri Tekakwitha.

RELATED ARTICLES in *Great Events from History: The Seventeenth Century, 1601-1700:* 1608: Jesuits Found Paraguay; 1615: Guamán Poma Pleas for Inca Reforms; March 31, 1650: Earthquake Destroys Cuzco.

MARY WHITE ROWLANDSON
English-born colonial American writer

Rowlandson's narrative of her captivity by American Indians during Metacom's War became a colonial best-seller. Her book was the first example of the captivity tale literary genre; it remained in print over three hundred years later.

BORN: c. 1637; England
DIED: January 5, 1711; Wethersfield, Connecticut
ALSO KNOWN AS: Mary White (given name); Mary White Rowlandson Talcott
AREA OF ACHIEVEMENT: Literature

EARLY LIFE

In 1639, the parents of Mary White Rowlandson (ROH-luhn-suhn), John and Joan White, joined the Puritan migration to the New World. The family lived in Salem, Massachusetts, prior to moving to the newly established frontier village of Lancaster, where John White was the wealthiest landowner. Mary married Joseph Rowlandson in 1656. He was ordained in 1660, became the first regular minister in Lancaster, and established a reputation as a leading Puritan clergyman. The couple had four children, the first of whom died in infancy.

Until the outbreak of Metacom's War (also known as King Philip's War) in 1675, Rowlandson lived the normal life of a New England housewife, raising her children and running the minister's household. A good Puritan, she read her Bible, attended church services several times a week, and anxiously examined her conscience and behavior for evidence of the state of her soul.

When a coalition of Algonquian Indian tribes, rebelling against English pressure to acquire their land, began to devastate the New England frontier, Lancaster was an obvious target. For protection, the fifty or so families in the village gathered in six garrisons—semifortified houses built with thick timbers, which were pierced with loopholes through which the defenders could safely fire at attackers.

One such garrison was the minister's house. On February 10, 1676, the Rowlandson garrison held thirty-seven people, including Mrs. Rowlandson and her three children (her husband had gone to Boston seeking reinforcements for the endangered town), her two sisters with their families, and several neighbors. The Algonquians attacked. After destroying most of the central village, the Indians attacked the Rowlandson garrison. The house was situated on the side of a hill, down which the Indians rolled combustibles, setting the entire building aflame and forcing the defenders into the open. Of the thirty-seven occupants, only one escaped; twelve were killed, and twenty-four, including Mrs. Rowlandson and her three children, were taken captive.

LIFE'S WORK
For the next eleven weeks and five days, Rowlandson traveled as a captive of the Algonquians, walking as far north as Chesterfield, New Hampshire, before retracing her steps back to Princeton, Massachusetts, where she was ransomed. Rowlandson carefully studied the behavior of her captors as she agonized over the meaning of her captivity. Once she was released, she set about recording her observations in clear, precise prose. She published her story under the title *The Soveraignty and Goodness of God, Together with the Faithfulness of His Promises Displayed: Being a Narrative of the Captivity and Restauration of Mrs. Mary Rowlandson* (1682; commonly known as *The Soveraignty and Goodness of God*).

Rowlandson's only literary work, the book was an immediate and lasting success. Three other editions appeared in England and New England the same year, and her book has been reprinted more than thirty times since then. The first edition was literally read to death: Only four pages of it survived into the twentieth century.

Nineteenth century engraved depiction of Mary White Rowlandson in captivity during Metacom's War. (The Granger Collection, New York)

Rowlandson's account continues to be the most widely anthologized Indian captivity narrative.

Rowlandson's book can be read as a straightforward adventure story, as the publisher of the tenth edition implied when he titled his reprint *A Narrative of the Captivity, Sufferings, and Removes of Mrs. Mary Rowlandson* (1770). Rowlandson began with a brief, graphic description of the successful Indian attack on Lancaster. As she left the burning garrison house, she was shot in the side, and the child she was carrying was wounded in the intestines and hand. Her eldest sister, a brother-in-law, and a nephew were killed, while her son and older daughter were taken away.

Rowlandson structured her captivity narrative into

THE ATTACK ON ROWLANDSON'S HOMESTEAD

Mary White Rowlandson's narrative, excerpted here, describing the attack upon her home by Algonquian Indians and her subsequent captivity, was one of the best-selling books of its time. It significantly influenced the European image of Native Americans, both in the colonies and in the Old World.

Now is the dreadful hour come that I have often heard of, but now mine eyes see it. Some in our house were fighting for their lives, others wallowing in their blood, the house on fire over our heads, and the bloody heathen ready to knock us on the head if we stirred out. Now might we hear mothers and children crying out for themselves and one another, "Lord what shall we do?" Then I took my children (and one of my sisters hers) to go forth and leave the house, but, as soon as we came to the door and appeared, the Indians shot so thick that the bullets rattled against the house as if one had taken a handful of stones and threw them, so that we were forced to give back. We had six stout dogs belonging to our garrison, but none of them would stir, though another time if any Indian had come to the door, they were ready to fly upon him and tear him down. The Lord hereby would make us the more to acknowledge His hand, and to see that our help is always in Him. But out we must go, the fire increasing, and coming along behind us roaring, and the Indians gaping before us with their guns, spears, and hatchets to devour us.

Source: From *The Soveraignty and Goodness of God*, by Mary White Rowlandson, quoted in *Living History America: The History of the United States in Documents, Essays, Letters, Songs, and Poems*, edited by Erik Bruun and Jay Crosby (New York: Tess Press, 1999), p. 65.

twenty sections she called "removes." The first remove took her only a few miles from Lancaster, where the Indians celebrated their victory with roaring and singing that she compared to a scene in hell. Few can read her third remove, in which her six-year-old daughter, unable to eat for nine days, died in her arms, without feeling deep sympathy for Rowlandson. She described the Indians as inhuman, their evil behavior inspired by Satan; her opinion did not change, even when she recorded friendly actions. According to Rowlandson, when the Indians killed a pregnant woman who kept asking to go home, when they laughed at seeing Rowlandson fall down, or when they refused to give her food, they were simply expressing their nature. On the other hand, when an Indian gave her a Bible, or helped her find shelter, or offered her food, as many did, she claimed that it was because God had intervened on her behalf and overruled the Indians' natural state.

As the removes continued, Rowlandson became more effective in managing her relations with the Indians. Although physically weak and fearful of her captors, she learned to use her skills at knitting and sewing clothing to barter for food and shelter. Her descriptions of Indian behavior became more detailed, especially in a striking account of the elaborate ritual performed before attacking Sudbury. Throughout her ordeal, Rowlandson pondered her past life and consulted her Bible, trying to find a meaning for her afflictions. There are more than sixty-five biblical references in the text, mainly from the Old Testament, which was most directly relevant to Rowlandson's experience. She found comfort in God's promises to redeem Israel from captivity and interpreted all favorable events as evidence that God forgave her past transgressions and, through the action of divine providence, used the Indians to prepare her spiritual and physical redemption in this life and the next.

On May 2, 1676, the Indians freed Rowlandson for a ransom of £20 in trade goods raised by her husband and friends. Her children were released soon after. Lancaster had been abandoned, and the Rowlandson family lived for a year in Boston before relocating, in 1677, to Wethersfield, Connecticut, where Joseph Rowlandson was installed as the new minister. He died suddenly on November 24, 1678, aged forty-seven. Rowlandson's manuscript was apparently completed before then, although it was not printed until 1682, for it contains no hint that her husband was no longer alive. On August 6, 1679, Rowlandson married Captain Samuel Talcott. She lived for nineteen years after his death in 1691, before dying herself at the age of about seventy-three.

SIGNIFICANCE

Rowlandson had no model for her book. There were no existing captivity narratives that she might emulate. She therefore created the genre as she wrote. Rowlandson would have been familiar with an existing Puritan literary form, in which the authors examined their relations with God, seeking assurance that they were indeed members of the elect, destined for eternal life in heaven. Such books were read by devout Puritans to inspire their own spiritual reflections. Rowlandson's emotional need to confront her horrifying experience provided the impetus to create the manuscript she wrote for the religious edification of her children and relations. Many early readers would have understood her work as she intended.

Over the centuries, her narrative has had many varying interpretations. Scholars valued the book for its firsthand descriptions of seventeenth century Indian life, ignoring her intensely negative opinion of the natives. Students of religion interpreted it as demonstrating the impact of Puritan theology on everyday life in early New England. Twentieth century feminists hailed her work as the first North American book written by a woman. Secular feminists, repulsed by the deep religiousness in which the book is steeped, have argued that the text was heavily edited, either by her husband or another minister, to stifle Rowlandson's authentically female voice and to force her to conform to Puritan ideology. Some were surprised that a seventeenth century woman could supply such apt biblical references, precisely appropriate to her immediate experiences—a reaction caused by greatly underestimating the biblical fluency and religious intensity of Puritan women.

The variety of these interpretations of *The Sovereignty and Goodness of God* and the passion with which some are advanced testify to the continuing relevance in the twenty-first century of Rowlandson's narrative of the most difficult and doleful twelve weeks of her life.

—*Milton Berman*

FURTHER READING

Breitwieser, Mitchell Robert. *American Puritanism and the Defense of Mourning: Religion, Grief, and Ethnology in Mary White Rowlandson's Captivity Narrative*. Madison: University of Wisconsin Press, 1990. The only full-length study of Rowlandson's narrative. Breitwieser reads her prose as revealing a significant conflict between her acceptance of Puritan cultural ideology and her actual experience of Indian life.

Ebersole, Gary L. *Captured by Texts: Puritan to Postmodern Images of Indian Captivity*. Charlottesville: University Press of Virginia, 1995. Stresses how Rowlandson's understanding of Puritan covenantal theology enabled her to comprehend and survive the reality of her captivity.

Henwood, Dawn. "Mary Rowlandson and the Psalms: The Textuality of Survival." *Early American Literature* 32 (1997): 169-186. Analyzes how Rowlandson's reading of the Psalms during her captivity provided spiritual comfort while also permitting her to express her fury at her situation.

LePore, Jill. *The Name of War: King Philip's War and the Origins of American Identity*. New York: Alfred A. Knopf, 1998. Prize-winning study of the wartime experiences of Indians and Englishmen offers valuable contrasts to Rowlandson's reactions.

Schultz, Eric B., and Michael J. Tougias. *King Philip's War: The History and the Legacy of America's Forgotten Conflict*. Woodstock, Vt.: The Countryman Press, 1999. Detailed examination of the war provides a useful context for Rowlandson's narrative.

SEE ALSO: Metacom.

RELATED ARTICLES in *Great Events from History: The Seventeenth Century, 1601-1700:* May, 1630-1643: Great Puritan Migration; June 20, 1675: Metacom's War Begins.

PETER PAUL RUBENS
Flemish painter and diplomat

One of the most successful artists of his time, with a huge workshop of artists who completed many of his commissions, Rubens is regarded as the most important creator of Baroque art. Also, as a distinguished diplomat, he used his cheerful personality and broad human interests to work for the cause of peace.

BORN: June 28, 1577; Siegen, Westphalia (now in Germany)
DIED: May 30, 1640; Antwerp, Brabant, Spanish Netherlands (now in Belgium)
AREAS OF ACHIEVEMENT: Art, diplomacy

EARLY LIFE

Peter Paul Rubens was the son of a Protestant attorney from Antwerp who moved to Germany to escape religious persecution. Although Rubens was baptized a Calvinist in Germany, he became a devout convert to Catholicism. When his father died in 1587, Rubens and his mother returned to Antwerp, where he apprenticed himself to several local painters. From his last teacher, Otto van Veen (1556-1629), he acquired considerable knowledge of Italian painting. By 1600, Rubens was in Rome, studying and copying the works of the Italian Renaissance and preparing himself to become the first Northern European painter to combine the grandiose and realistic styles of the Italian and Dutch masters.

Very little survives from Rubens's Italian period (1600-1608), but in his *Portrait of the Marchesa Brigida Spinola-Doria* (1606), there is evidence of his early efforts to make his mark in the tradition of international portrait painting. As Jennifer Fletcher notes, the artist's subject came from a family that owned portraits by Titian, who was renowned for his vivid color and expressiveness. The marchesa's exalted social position is suggested by the elegance and amplitude of her luminous dress, the crimson drapery that flows behind her in the center of the frame, and the beautifully sculpted architectural details—all of which convey a richness and harmony of effect. What makes the painting truly remarkable, however, is its liveliness. This is no staid study of a society matron. She looks as though she is about to smile as she moves through the artist's frame. There is energy in her face, in the details of her clothing, and in the setting that makes this scene triumph over the mere reporting of details.

In 1608, Rubens returned to Antwerp but failed to reach his ailing mother in time. He planned to resume residence in Italy, but his success in Antwerp was so immediate and overwhelming (he became court painter to the Spanish viceroys of the Netherlands) and was followed quickly by his marriage in 1609 to Isabella Brant, that he never saw Italy again. His happy marriage is illustrated in a portrait of himself and his wife (1609). They are seated together in a honeysuckle bower, her hand resting gently and comfortably upon his in the center of the frame, his right foot partially underneath her flowing dress. They look out toward the viewer, forming a picture of mutual contentment and intimacy. Most striking is their sense of ease and equality. Although the artist is seated above his wife, he is also leaning toward her—any dominance he might seem to have is mitigated by the fact that his hat is cropped at the top while his wife's is shown in full, making her larger figure command the right side of the frame. When the positioning of their bodies and their clothing is compared, it is clear that Rubens has shown a couple that complement each other in every conceivable way. This dashing portrait reveals a man on the brink of a great career.

LIFE'S WORK

The years immediately following Rubens's return to Antwerp were vigorous and innovative. Two large triptychs, *The Elevation of the Cross* (c. 1610-1611) and *Descent from the Cross* (c. 1611-1614), altarpieces for Antwerp Cathedral, confirmed his great ability to create monumental yet realistic works of art. The fifteen-foot central panels create a sense of deep space and perspective while also conveying great struggle and strain. The cross is raised by heavily muscled men in a powerful diagonal movement that bisects one central panel. Below the cross is a dog in the left corner sticking out its tongue in agitation while the trees in the upper right corner seem to rustle in the wind. This is a painting that concentrates on the dynamism of the event, whereas in the *Descent from the Cross* the limp and ravaged aged body of Christ is carefully taken down by his followers, with each one expressing grief in bodily postures and gestures that concentrate nearly all the emotion of the scene on their reactions. In their bent bodies, outstretched arms and hands, grasping fingers, and intensely focused faces, the coherence of their feelings is evident. They are at one with the event.

Work on such a scale demanded that the artist take on collaborators. Although Rubens would work out the conception of a portrait, a landscape, or a religious or mythical subject, he often left the details or some part of a painting to his pupils and collaborators. Thus, in a letter Rubens notes that the eagle pecking Prometheus's liver was done by Frans Snyders (1579-1657). That these paintings are animated by Rubens's prodigious imagination is proved by his enormously powerful sketches, such as the one of a lioness (c. 1614-1615), which captures its power and grace from the rear—its huge tail sweeping through the center of the drawing and to the left, with its massive head sweeping from the center of the frame to the left, its huge paw lifted in mid-stride.

Rubens was drawn to exotic subjects such as a *Tigers and Lions Hunt* (1617-1618). Although his animals are anatomically correct (he studied them in the menageries of noblemen), this stirring painting is about the enormous courage of the hunters and the natural ferocity of beasts. Such paintings appealed to a Europe that was still discovering foreign lands and were a form of entertainment. As C. V. Wedgwood observes, many of these paintings are still admired today for their composition and restraint, for Rubens tends to emphasize the self-control of his human figures even as they seem about to be torn apart.

Rubens had great energy (often rising at 4:00 A.M. to work), was devoted to his family, was a shrewd businessman, and was an even-tempered artist. Such qualities made him invaluable as a respected emissary in the courts of Europe. Isabella, Regent of the Southern Netherlands, sent him on diplomatic missions to Spain and England, and he worked tirelessly to bring the Netherlands back into the Spanish Catholic company of nations. Having worked as a commissioned artist all of his life, he understood the importance of compromise, of balancing competing interests.

After seventeen years of happy marriage, Rubens's wife died in 1626. Four years later, he married Hélène Fourment, enjoying another happy marriage that is reflected in his mellow, luscious paintings of the 1630's—for example, *The Three Graces*, in which Venus and her handmaidens frolic in a dancelike rhythm, their arms enfolding one another, their flesh visibly showing the imprint of one another's fingers. Rubens paints human flesh that ripples loosely, is firm and yet pliant, and is exquisitely modulated in many different tones of white, red, and brown. No other artist of his time could convey the same quality of a painting ripening into view.

SIGNIFICANCE

In his last years, Rubens returned to landscape painting with renewed vigor. In *Landscape with a Rainbow* (c. 1635), he emphasizes an ordinary country scene—cattle, a pond with ducks, two women walking down a road past a driver and cart—that suggests, in a way, the daily coming and going of a rural scene, of precisely those activities that define a landscape momentarily distinguished by a rainbow. His ploy is the opposite of that of so many of his predecessors, who used rustic settings in a stylized fashion to suggest the sublimity of nature. In *Landscape with a Sunset* (c. 1635), there is a kind of visionary quality, a perfect blending of the land, the trees, the sheep, the building at the far-right edge of the painting, and the individual seated with a dog beside him against a sky turning various shades of gray, purple, and yellow. As in *Landscape with the Château De Steen* (c. 1635), the depiction of nature seems to be an end in itself, an evocation of harmony and balance that expresses the artist's inner nature. Yet the details of these

Peter Paul Rubens. (Library of Congress)

scenes are so sharply realized that they never blur into vague idealizations.

Rubens died in 1640 of a heart attack that was apparently brought on by his gout, a debilitating illness that had crippled him periodically for three years. It did not stop his enormous productivity. If there were days when he could not paint, there were other days when he probably worked faster than any other artist of his time. His lusty spirit was translated into a facility with brushwork that was truly extraordinary. The virility and sensuality of his work have been undiminished by time, though the intensity of his religious devotion may be more difficult to appreciate in a secular world not accustomed to equating the flesh and the spirit as closely as Rubens did in his day.

— Carl Rollyson

FURTHER READING

Belkin, Kristin Lohse. *Rubens*. London: Phaidon Press, 1998. Belkin places Rubens's life and art within the context of the Netherlands in the seventeenth century.

Donovan, Fiona. *Rubens and England*. New Haven, Conn.: Yale University Press, 2004. Donovan explores the political connections between Rubens and the Stuart court of England.

Gritsay, Natalya, et al. *Peter Paul Rubens: A Touch of Brilliance*. New York: Prestel, 2003. A collection of essays about Rubens written by experts in Flemish art, describing the development of some of the artist's works, such as *Descent from the Cross*, the Medici cycle, and the ceiling of the Banqueting House in Whitehall.

Logan, Anne-Marie. *Peter Paul Rubens: The Drawings*. New Haven, Conn.: Yale University Press, 2004. Published to accompany an exhibit of Rubens's drawings at the Metropolitan Museum of Art, the book includes reproductions of more than one hundred of Rubens's finest drawings from public and private collections around the world. Essays provide an overview of Rubens's career as a draftsman and discuss the drawings' functions as preparatory studies for paintings, sculpture, architecture, prints, and book illustrations.

Martin, John R., comp. *Rubens: The Antwerp Altarpieces*. New York: W. W. Norton, 1969. A thorough, copiously illustrated (in black and white) study of Rubens's great triptychs, *The Elevation of the Cross* and *Descent from the Cross*. Martin includes an informative introduction; contemporary documents; important essays by distinguished artists, critics, biographers, and historians; and a bibliography of books and articles.

Oppenheimer, Paul. *Rubens: A Portrait*. New York: Cooper Square Press, 2002. Oppenheimer recounts the life of Rubens, portraying him not only as a talented painted but also as an intellectual with a unique concept of beauty.

Rubens, Peter Paul, and Arnauld Brejon de Lavergnée. *Rubens*. Ghent, Belgium: Snoeck, 2004. A comprehensive biography of the artist, published in conjunction with an exhibition of Rubens's work at the Palais des Beaux Arts in Lille, France. The book contains reproductions of more than 160 paintings, sketches, drawings, and tapestries created by Rubens.

Wedgwood, C. V. *The World of Rubens, 1577-1640*. New York: Time-Life Books, 1967. One of the most comprehensive introductions to Rubens's life and work by one of the most distinguished historians of the seventeenth century. Covers his years in Italy, his diplomatic career, and more, and there is no better volume to consult for a sense of his place in history. A chronology of the artists of the time and an annotated bibliography and index make this an indispensable study.

SEE ALSO: Giovanna Garzoni; Frans Hals; Bartolomé Esteban Murillo; Nicolas-Claude Fabri de Peiresc; Rembrandt; Sir Anthony van Dyck; Diego Velázquez; Jan Vermeer.

RELATED ARTICLES in *Great Events from History: The Seventeenth Century, 1601-1700:* c. 1601-1620: Emergence of Baroque Art; 1610-1643: Reign of Louis XIII; 1619-1622: Jones Introduces Classicism to English Architecture.

PRINCE RUPERT
Bohemian nobleman, soldier, and inventor

From his youth, Rupert chose a military life, fighting in Bohemia and England on behalf of his father, King Frederick V; his uncle Charles I; and his cousin Charles II. Rupert was also a talented inventor and engraver.

BORN: December 17, 1619; Prague, Bohemia (now in Czech Republic)
DIED: November 29, 1682; London, England
ALSO KNOWN AS: Count Palatine of the Rhine; duke of Bavaria; duke of Cumberland; earl of Holderness
AREAS OF ACHIEVEMENT: Warfare and conquest, science and technology

EARLY LIFE
Prince Rupert (RU-purt) was prince Palatine, the third son of Frederick V (the elector Palatine and briefly king of Bohemia) and of Princess Elizabeth Stuart, daughter of King James I of England. His parents, married on Valentine's Day at age sixteen, were a romantic but unfortunate couple. During Rupert's infancy, his father was defeated by supporters of a Catholic claimant to the Bohemian throne, who was a cousin of the Holy Roman Emperor. This defeat occurred at the onset of the Thirty Years' War (1618-1648), which ravaged the German states and in time would involve Denmark and Sweden as well.

In 1621, Rupert's family settled in Holland under the protection of Frederick V's uncle, the prince of Orange. Frederick died of a fever in 1632. Impoverished and with a family of ten children, Elizabeth, nicknamed the Queen of Hearts by her supporters and the Winter Queen by her husband's enemies, contrived to raise her handsome, talented brood as best she could.

In his early teens, Rupert, who was tall and athletic, joined the prince of Orange's bodyguard. In 1636, he visited his English relatives, charming Queen Henrietta Maria and her ladies and sharing the artistic interests of his uncle Charles I, one of the greatest art collectors in Europe. He returned home in 1637 and resumed service in the Dutch army with his younger brother Maurice. The following year, Rupert was taken prisoner by the Austrians and was confined at Linz until 1641. After his release, he briefly visited his mother; then, he and Maurice took ship for England in the summer of 1642 to assist Charles I and the Royalists' cause in the English Civil War.

LIFE'S WORK
On Rupert's arrival in England, Charles I appointed him General of the Horse, a post that suited the young soldier's fiery, independent nature. Rupert was a gifted cavalry leader, and with his experience as a professional soldier, he dominated much of the first phase of the Civil Wars. To Royalists, he was the very embodiment of a Cavalier, but Parliamentarians stigmatized him as ruthless and cruel. His white poodle "Boye," for example, was even reputed by credulous Puritans to be a familiar, that is, Rupert's link with the devil.

In 1642, Rupert distinguished himself at the battles of Powick Bridge (September 21) and Edgehill (October 23), and in 1643, at the captures of Cirencester (February 2) and Bristol (July 25). Although Rupert was popular with the rank and file, his blunt speech and quick temper angered a number of courtiers. His defeat by Oliver Cromwell at Marston Moor (July 2, 1644) and his surrender of Bristol to the Parliamentary forces (September 11, 1645) enraged Charles I, who dismissed both Rupert and Maurice, demanding that they leave the country. When Charles sought refuge with the Scots in May, 1646, Rupert and Maurice remained in Oxford, the Royalist capital; after it surrendered in June, the brothers returned to the Continent.

Still seeking action in 1647, Rupert led a group of English exiles serving with the French army; in 1648, he commanded part of the fleet that revolted against Parliament, but this ragtag Royalist navy was largely ineffective. During this time, Rupert was as rootless and impoverished as his exiled Stuart cousins, Charles, James, and Henry. Ill fortune had stripped them of hope, and on occasion, Rupert and Charles disagreed, usually about funds, or the lack of them. Rupert also quarreled with his elder brother, Elector Palatine Charles Louis, over a grant of land and personal matters and swore that he would never again set foot in the Palatinate. From 1655 to 1660, little is known of his adventures.

The prince's fortunes rose in 1660 with the Restoration of Charles II, who granted him a pension and made him a member of his Privy Council. Rupert's mother at last had the opportunity to return to her homeland, but Elizabeth's long-delayed secure existence was brief. She died on February 13, 1662, in Charles II's arms. Rupert was the chief mourner at her funeral.

Though he had made his reputation as an innovative army commander, Rupert's last military exploits were at sea. In the Second Anglo-Dutch War, the English were initially successful, but by January, 1666, France and Denmark allied with the Dutch. Rupert and George Monck, duke of Albemarle, were appointed joint commanders of the English forces. In the Four Days' Battle (June 1-4), both sides suffered heavy losses. Public blame fell on everyone, including Albemarle and Rupert. They soon defeated the Dutch fleet on July 25 and destroyed many merchant ships and naval stores. However, London's Great Fire (September 2-9, 1666), which devastated the heart of the city, gave the Dutch time to renew the war: In June, 1667, they shattered much of the English fleet and towed away the flagship *Royal Charles*. Suffering from a head wound, Rupert did not take part in the battle. Peace was concluded in July, 1667.

When the Third Anglo-Dutch War broke out in 1672, Rupert felt the navy was still ill prepared. France and England were now allies, a situation he disliked. Rupert's anti-Catholic sentiments created tension with James, duke of York, who had converted to that faith. However, efforts to attach Rupert to the anti-Catholic, anticourt faction (the future Whig party), led by Anthony Ashley Cooper, first earl of Shaftesbury, were not successful. Rupert remained loyal to the king and to James, his heir.

After 1673, Rupert played no major part in public affairs and increasingly immersed himself in science and inventions. Like Charles II, he was a founding member of the Royal Society; both men had laboratories and conducted various experiments. Rupert developed a type of brass called "prince's metal" and created modifications to various types of guns. He was also a notable mezzotint engraver. Rupert never married but had two children. By Francesca Bard, daughter of Irish Royalist Sir Henry Bard, Viscount Bellamont, he had a son named Dudley. With actress Margaret Hughes, he had a daughter, Ruperta. Rupert died of a fever on November 29, 1682, and was buried in Westminster Abbey.

SIGNIFICANCE

Throughout a long life, Prince Rupert held true to the direction he had set for himself as a young man. He was a skillful warrior—on land and sea—and a loyal friend and faithful servant to his mother's family, the Stuarts. He was the epitome of the Cavalier, hot-tempered, plainspoken, and brave, a model of honesty and simplicity in an age of courtiers and wily politicians. Although he remained a person of note at the court of Charles II, he had no real role in the political turbulence of later Restoration England. Perhaps for this reason, as well as his military

prowess, Victorians considered Rupert a romantic hero. However, he is less a subject of interest to contemporary students of the later seventeenth century, due to his noninvolvement in English political and religious life.

—*Dorothy Potter*

FURTHER READING

Bowle, John, ed. *The Diary of John Evelyn.* New York: Oxford University Press, 1985. Evelyn's diary spans 1640 to 1706 and is very detailed. He describes meetings with the prince on numerous occasions.

Chapman, Hester. *The Tragedy of Charles II.* London: Jonathan Cape, 1964. A study of the king's youth and exile. Deals with Rupert as a role model for his cousin Charles. Includes illustrations, notes, and bibliography.

Coote, Stephen. *Royal Survivor: The Life of Charles II.* New York: St. Martin's Press, 2000. A biography that details Charles's survival skills before and after his Restoration. Useful background on court life, various wars, and politics.

Fraser, Antonia. *King Charles II.* London: Phoenix, 2002. A lengthy account, fully describing the politics and personalities related to Charles II. Many illustrations and extensive bibliography.

Latham, Robert, and William Matthews, eds. *The Diary of Samuel Pepys.* 11 vols. London: Bell & Hyman, 1983. After the Restoration, Rupert was active as a naval commander. Pepys worked with him and mentions him frequently in his nine-year (1660-1669) diary.

Macray, W. Dunn, ed. *The History of the Rebellion and Civil Wars in England Begun in the Year 1641: Edward [Hyde] Earl of Clarendon.* Reprint. Oxford, England: Oxford University Press, 1958. Clarendon was Charles II's chief adviser during his exile and most of the first decade of the Restoration. He wrote extensively about Rupert.

Morrah, Patrick. *Prince Rupert of the Rhine.* London: Constable, 1976. This scholarly work of several hundred pages was the first serious biography of Rupert in more than seventy-five years. Its extensive notes and bibliography make it an invaluable work for the serious student.

Powell, J. R., and E. K. Timings, eds. *The Rupert and Monck Letter Book, 1666.* London: Naval Records Society, 1969. A compilation of documents related to Rupert and General George Monck's activities during the First Anglo-Dutch War; most deal with the technicalities of naval warfare. A detailed introduction, maps, and supplementary documents make it more accessible to nonspecialists.

Ross, Josephine. *The Winter Queen: The Story of Elizabeth Stuart*. New York: Dorset Press, 1986. Deals mainly with Elizabeth and her husband Frederick V. Rupert's life and fortunes are part of the latter half of the book. However, it has no bibliography or notes.

Scott, Eva. *Rupert Prince Palatine*. New York: G. P. Putnam's Sons, 1900. Though a significant character in any Restoration study, Rupert has attracted few biographers. Eve Scott's well-written and detailed biography is still the standard work on the prince.

Wedgwood, C. V. *The Great Rebellion*. 2 vols. London: Collins, 1969. One of the standard works on the En-glish Civil Wars, in which Rupert played such an important part.

SEE ALSO: Charles I; Charles II (of England); Oliver Cromwell; Elizabeth Stuart; Frederick V; James I; James II; George Monck.

RELATED ARTICLES in *Great Events from History: The Seventeenth Century, 1601-1700:* 1601-1672: Rise of Scientific Societies; 1618-1648: Thirty Years' War; 1642-1651: English Civil Wars; July 2, 1644: Battle of Marston Moor; October, 1651-May, 1652: Navigation Act Leads to Anglo-Dutch Wars; March 4, 1665-July 31, 1667: Second Anglo-Dutch War; September 2-5, 1666: Great Fire of London.

MICHIEL ADRIAANSZOON DE RUYTER
Dutch admiral

De Ruyter maintained and strengthened the maritime defenses of the United Provinces against a growing number of opponents, especially England in the Anglo-Dutch Wars of 1652 to 1674.

BORN: March 24, 1607; Flushing, Zeeland Province, United Provinces (now the Netherlands)

DIED: April 29, 1676; aboard ship in the Bay of Syracuse, Island of Sicily (now in Italy)

ALSO KNOWN AS: Michiel de Ruyter

AREAS OF ACHIEVEMENT: Warfare and conquest, military

EARLY LIFE

Michiel Adriaanszoon de Ruyter (mih-KEEL aw-dree-AWNS-zohn deh ROY-tehr), the fifth of eleven children born to Adriaan and Aelken Michielsz of Flushing, had little to look forward to in life. His father, a sailor, could scarcely support his growing family, and Michael was a difficult child. The boy found little use in schooling, was several times expelled for insolence and fighting, and was eventually apprenticed to a local ropeyard at the age of ten.

The apprentice, too, failed, and the boy was finally sent to sea in 1618, where he excelled. In the ensuing decades, Michael would visit much of Western Europe, the Baltic, the Mediterranean, and North America selling butter, herring, fats, and hides. Almost devoid of education, he began a program of self-improvement. He studied first with his former teacher before retaining experienced captains and navigators to improve his knowledge of the trade. In time, he would be recognized as one of the best and most respected officers in Zeeland.

As a result of his diligence, he rose in the esteem of his employers and was soon promoted to second-in-command (1633) of one of their smaller ships. He was named master of a ship (1640) at the relatively young age of thirty-three. Although his career in the 1630's and 1640's is hard to document, he held both merchant and whaling commands and captained several privateers. During this time, he began to invest in the firm, owning interest in several ships. Symbolic of his growing affluence, he married, built a comfortable home for his family, and adopted the name of his mother's father, Ruyter, to which he soon added "de," implying nobility.

LIFE'S WORK

His service, his experience, and the support of the Zeeland Admiralty earned him the rank of provincial rear admiralship in 1641. Although not a regular naval officer, de Ruyter, as he was now known, was commissioned third in command of a small fleet in alliance against Spain. He demonstrated conspicuous bravery in saving several ships in battle and was commended by his superiors. More important, he realized the superiority of other nations' ships to those of the Dutch Republic. Spanish, Portuguese, French, and English ships were heavier gunned, were bigger, carried more sail, and were better maintained. Holland's smaller ships, however, were more maneuverable.

The conclusion of hostilities brought an end to his naval command. He returned to Flushing in early 1643, purchased a ship with the assistance of several stockholders, and traded in the North Sea, the Mediterranean, and the West Indies for nearly a decade. By 1652, he was a wealthy man and had planned to retire to his home to manage his investments.

The First Anglo-Dutch War (1651-1652) changed these plans. A clash between the two commercial nations of the United Provinces and England was always possible, but English mercantilism, a belief in trade monopoly, made it inevitable. In particular, the Navigation Act of 1651 forbade the Dutch from carrying English goods. War followed, and England sought to blockade and economically strangle the United Provinces. The Dutch were slow to respond, and it was not until their fleet had sailed that the States-General, the ruling body of the United Provinces, realized the vulnerability of their incoming merchant fleets. They hurriedly assembled a reserve force to warn and cover the incoming convoys. They selected de Ruyter, among others, to command the force, and he kept the English Channel open. The admiral was then transferred to the main fleet and gained the admiration of Maarten Tromp, the leading Dutch admiral. De Ruyter, recognized for his ability to attack, led the way at Dungenes, Portland, Nieuwpoort, and Terheiden. Although Tromp was killed at Terheiden, the blockade was broken and the war brought to a close. The merchant admiral was promoted to vice-admiral of the republic's navy, and a second career, more auspicious than his first, had officially begun.

As an officer of wide experience he was immediately reassigned to areas of need—the Mediterranean (1654-1659 and 1661-1664) and the Baltic (1656 and 1659-1660). He successfully made treaties with the pirates and returned repeatedly to enforce them; he also protected the Danes from the Swedes. He received further assignments to Guinea (1664-1665), the Antilles (1665), and Newfoundland (1665). All of the assignments involved either the recapture of forts owned by the Dutch West India Company or the capture of English posts.

De Ruyter arrived home in 1665 to cheering crowds and a promotion to lieutenant-admiral. He also found the Second Anglo-Dutch War (1665-1667) in progress and that the Dutch had experienced an almost crushing defeat. Seen as the avenging hero and immediately appointed commander of the main battle fleet, he put to sea with what remained of his fleet, not to fight, but to buy time until new ships could be built and old ones refitted. Literally, at his demand, the United Provinces undertook to build bigger, faster, and more heavily armed ships such as those of their enemies.

Fortunately, de Ruyter's maneuvers, a simultaneous blockade of the Thames River, and a severe visitation of plague on the English ships provided the time necessary to reconstruct the fleet. In mid-June, 1666, the two opposing naval forces clashed. The Dutch, for the first time bigger and one-third stronger than their opponent, were victorious. The Four Days' Battle was a major defeat for the English. Two months later, a far stronger English navy beat the Dutch at the Two Days' Battle, only to experience another crushing reverse at Chatham (June, 1667). As de Ruyter's ships followed up the victory by burning English shipping and by landing soldiers along the coast of Britain, peace was quickly arranged.

Now lieutenant-admiral and the supreme chief of the States Fleet, de Ruyter worked out of Amsterdam. It was partly a matter of his health, but it was also a matter of watching England. Sweden, England, and the United Provinces had concluded an arrangement—the Triple Alliance—in 1668 to protect themselves and each other from the rising ambitions of France. Unfortunately, it was soon evident that England was shifting toward France and that the Dutch were to be squeezed between the two nations. As the Third Anglo-Dutch War (1672-1674) approached, de Ruyter and Johan de Witt, the chief official of the States-General, worked long hours to provide forts, soldiers, sailors, and ships from the insufficient resources of the small nation.

The French and English plan was to capture the Dutch frontier fortresses and force the States-General to reinforce the army at the expense of the navy. English and French ships could then crush the reduced Dutch battle fleet, capture their ports, and land an army from the Channel. Fortunately for the Dutch, the plan failed. The States-General rallied behind their hereditary military leader, William III of Orange, found allies, and retained their chief fortresses. The fleet under de Ruyter, even though it was at times badly outnumbered, held its opponents at bay and gained strategic victories at Sole Bay (1672), Schooneveld (1673), and Camperdown (1673). In 1674, England was forced to withdraw from the conflict.

The war with France continued, and de Ruyter was sent to attack French colonies in the West Indies (1674) and to recapture Messina in Sicily (1675-1676) for Spain, the United Provinces' ally. The first expedition achieved little, and the second brought a naval victory at Etna. It was de Ruyter's last victory. He was wounded and died on board his flagship. His remains were embalmed and returned to Zeeland in an iron coffin.

SIGNIFICANCE

De Ruyter was a self-made man. He rose from the working class and obtained wealth through hard work, planning, and frugality, but he was a firm believer in God's will rather than his own abilities alone, and he won the devotion of his men because he always led the way. Yet, his significance should also be viewed in terms of his ability as a naval commander. He took the offense, whenever possible, and on the attack he reduced his opponents' offensive capabilities by isolating one or more parts of their line, either the vanguard or the rear. Then he would concentrate his ships to assault, then split, and then overwhelm the opponent in the center.

—Louis P. Towles

FURTHER READING

Blok, Petrus J. In *The Life of Admiral de Ruyter*. Westport, Conn.: Greenwood, 1975. Still the best study available in English, but it is far from complete.

Cooper, J. P. "Seapower." In *The Decline of Spain and the Thirty Years' War, 1609-1648*. Volume 4 in *The New Cambridge Modern History*. Cambridge, England: Cambridge University Press, 1970. An essential background to the period's naval history.

Hainsworth, Roger, and Christine Churches. *The Anglo-Dutch Naval Wars, 1652-1674*. Stroud, England: Sutton, 1998. The authors maintain the wars were a significant milestone in the development of naval warfare, as they introduced new technologies and strategies.

Kossman, E. H. "The Dutch Republic." In *The Ascendancy of France: 1648-1688*. Volume 5 in *The New Cambridge Modern History*. Cambridge, England: Cambridge University Press, 1961. An elementary discussion of the States-General, John de Witt, and the prince of Orange.

Mahan, Alfred T. *The Influence of Seapower upon History, 1660-1763*. New York: Hill and Wang, 1957. A good discussion of naval strategies, but only those after 1660.

SEE ALSO: Robert Blake; Piet Hein; James II; George Monck; Samuel Pepys; Maarten and Cornelis Tromp; William III.

RELATED ARTICLES in *Great Events from History: The Seventeenth Century, 1601-1700:* 17th century: Age of Mercantilism in Southeast Asia; Beginning Spring, 1605: Dutch Dominate Southeast Asian Trade; 1617-1693: European Powers Vie for Control of Gorée; October, 1625-1637: Dutch and Portuguese Struggle for the Guinea Coast; January 14, 1641: Capture of Malacca; October, 1651-May, 1652: Navigation Act Leads to Anglo-Dutch Wars; March 4, 1665-July 31, 1667: Second Anglo-Dutch War; April 6, 1672-August 10, 1678: French-Dutch War.

SANTORIO SANTORIO
Italian physician, scientist, and scholar

Santorio was an innovator in physiology, applied medicine, and the use of instruments of precision in the practice of medicine. By quantitative experimentation, he encouraged the use of mathematics and experimentation as analytical tools in the study of physiology and pathology. He also is considered the father of scientific metabolism for his studies in "insensible perspiration" and was likely an inventor of the thermometer.

BORN: March 29, 1561; Capodistria, Republic of Venice (now Koper, Slovenia)
DIED: February 22 or March 6, 1636; Venice (now in Italy)
ALSO KNOWN AS: Sanctorius Sanctorius
AREAS OF ACHIEVEMENT: Medicine, science and technology

EARLY LIFE

Santorio Santorio (sahn-TOR-yoh) was born to Antonio, who had settled in Capodistria (now Koper) as the chief steward of ordnance in the Republic of Venice, and Elisabetta Cordonia of Capodistria, a noblewoman. The couple also had another son and two daughters.

Santorio was initially educated at Capodistria and then sent to Venice, where he lived with the high-ranking Morosoni family, friends of the Santorios. The young man, whose first and last names were the same, was given the best of tutors, who were educating the Morosoni sons. As a result, Santorio acquired an unusually firm grounding in classical languages, philosophy, mathematics, and literature.

At fourteen, Santorio entered the Archilyceum of Padua, where he studied philosophy and then medicine, the usual sequence. In the late sixteenth century, the University of Padua was known throughout Europe as one of the best universities, and it had a history of distinguished faculty, including professors Andreas Vesalius, Realdo Colombo, and Gabriello Fallopio. Santorio's professors included physicist Giacomo Zabarella and, in medicine, Bernardino Paterno and Girolamo Fabrici. Having completed his medical degree in 1582, Santorio spent three years in clinical work and then began to practice medicine.

Biographers and commentators have questioned whether or not Santorio was sent to Poland after its king had reportedly asked Paduan administrators to send a brilliant medical doctor there. Santorio might have gone to Poland for as many as fourteen years, but he was consistently appearing in Hungary and Croatia as a medical consultant; he also returned to Venice for months at a time.

It was in 1607, when Santorio happened to be in Venice, that hired killers assaulted Paolo Sarpi, an eminent intellectual and a state counselor in Venice, and left him near death. Sarpi had incurred the wrath of the Papacy when he blocked Pope Paul V's efforts to wrest Venice into papal jurisdiction. Santorio and Fabrici were summoned to treat Sarpi's brutal wounds. When it was known that the assassins escaped to the papal territory, Sarpi is reported to have said, "I recognize the style of the Roman curia" worn by Sarpi. Many biographers of Santorio cite this episode because Sarpi had protected the University of Padua from papal control. The Republic of Venice was kinder than was the Papacy to intellectuals and men of genius. For example, it is well known that Galileo had the misfortune of developing many of his scientific investigations in territory ruled by the Papacy.

LIFE'S WORK

One of Santorio's first important books, *Methodi vitandorum errorum omnium qui in arte medica contingunt* (1602; method of combating all the errors that occur in the art of medicine), a work essentially dealing with differential diagnosis of various diseases, was considered brilliant by contemporaries. The book brought instant fame to Santorio as a clinician and a consultant and with it high respect from the Venetian intellectuals. Although based largely on Santorio's own experiments, it contains references to the work of Hippocrates, Galen, and Avicenna, three illustrious names in the history of medicine. In this treatise, Santorio discusses the pulsilogium, an instrument used to track the motion and rest of the artery, asserting that everything can be measured exactly, observed, and kept in mind for comparison. It is believed by many authorities that the "pulsilogium" was invented by Galileo but that Santorio utilized the instrument and popularized its value. This particular instrument, along with others, forged new standards in observations in physiology and pathology.

Ultimately, this innovative book led to the appointment of Santorio, in 1611, to a professorship of theoretical medicine at the University of Padua for six years, a term that was eventually renewed for another six years. Students came from all over Europe, especially from

Germany, to attend lectures; Santorio's classes were popular and crowded. Galileo, the unrivaled father of experimental science, had taught mathematics at the University of Padua from 1593 to 1610. Both Galileo and the brilliant philosopher Giordano Bruno were Santorio's close friends. The preeminent William Harvey from England, who discovered the theory of the circulation of the blood, had been a student at Padua too, although he never met Santorio. At Padua the professors of the theory of medicine were expected to make commentaries on the aphorisms of Hippocrates, Galen's art of medicine, and Avicenna's first *fen* (an Arabic word meaning part). Santorio's commentaries on these works became the bedrock of his lectures and subsequently his books.

A decade following the appearance of Santorio's first book, he published his *Commentaria in artem medicinalem Galeni* (1612; commentary on the art of medicine of Galen). In addition to following traditional paths, the respected physician made his first mention of the air thermometer. In the history of medicine, it has been discussed at length whether Galileo or Santorio invented the thermometer; evidence points to Galileo as the one who conceptualized a kind of thermometer and to Santorio as the discoverer of a variant and the first physician to utilize the thermometer and discuss it in publications.

With a heavy schedule of medical practice and university lecturing, which also drew prominent physicians, Santorio still found time to publish *Ars de statica medicina sectionibus aphorismorum septem comprehensa* (1614; *Medicina Statica: Or, Rules of Health in Eight Sections of Aphorisms*, 1676), the book that seems to have captured the imagination and attention of more contemporaries and subsequent medical professionals than any other of his publications. This relatively short work discusses weight variation experienced by the body from ingestion to excretion, with weighing procedures after purgation. Experiments that were made over twenty-five years on more than ten thousand subjects were discussed, using scales and other instruments of measurement. The main thesis of the work is that "insensible perspiration" (as opposed to actual perspiration) is capable of systematic recording or weighing, more than all forms of combined sensible body wastes, and is variable according to sleep, cold, fever, and sexual and other activity.

Having caused a sensation, *Medicina Statica* engendered twenty-eight Latin editions and translations into many other languages, along with four Latin editions with commentaries by Martin Lister, the well-known physician to Charles I of England. The book led many to cite Santorio as the father of the science of metabolism.

Many other physicians were inspired to study "insensible perspiration" and to write books on their own experiments. Santorio was now at the apex of his accomplishments and fame. He was deluged with requests for consultations, and in 1616 he was appointed president of the Collegio Veneto in Padua, a new center founded to eliminate abuses in the medical faculty.

When Santorio resigned his academic post at the end of his second term as professor, the Venetian senate, recognizing his enormous contributions to medicine, to the university, and to the republic, granted him a lifetime title of professor and also his full salary for life. Despite invitations by the University of Bologna and those at Messina and Pavia, he rejected them all and returned to Venice.

Now in his mid-sixties, Santorio published *Commentaria in primam fen primi libri canonis Avicennae* (1625; commentaries on the first part of the first book of the Canon of Avicenna), which pleased his contemporaries because of its practicality; it remains a classic medical text. The book emphasized precision instruments in medical practice, a technique that helped physicians to sharpen observations and diagnoses. He discussed the

Santorio Santorio. (Library of Congress)

thermometer and the "pulsilogium," among other instruments. In the commentary on the Avicenna book, Santorio shows the importance of humidity in disease treatment and depicts three types of instruments for humidity measurements. The lack of specific recordings of pulse rates or temperatures of people is conspicuous. Future medical specialists were to work on statistics, whereas Santorio merely explains the instruments.

Another part of the book on the *fen* of Avicenna is given much attention—Santorio's attack on astrology and astrologers. Padua at this time was a virtual nest of astrologists, and there were several astrologers on the faculty of the University of Padua. In fact, their influence throughout the Venetian Republic was powerful, and their attack on medical science and on Santorio was ferocious; still, the venerable doctor survived the counterattacks of the diviners. Santorio's practice flourished along with his reputation, and some of the most important people came to his office.

Santorio was appointed president of the Venetian College of Physicians, and, when Venice was besieged by plague in 1630, he was pressed into service as chief health officer, subsequently making a report to the health officer of the city, a document that still exists and is preserved in the General State Archives in Venice.

Never married, Santorio also was considered to be a misogynist. He was known to be frugal, and biographers agree that he was interested in amassing a fortune and did succeed in becoming wealthy. An engraving by Giacomo Piccini shows the celebrated physician to have had an elongated face, a long goatee, and a furrowed brow. His skeletal remains indicate that he was tall. His style in lectures that were published and in conversations with his brilliant friends indicate that he was archly ironic—contemporary writers agree that he possessed an unusually high level of critical intelligence. All agree on his substantiated contributions to medicine.

Santorio died of a disease of the urinary tract and was buried in the Church dei Servi, which ultimately was destroyed by Napoleon I. A casque containing his bones (together with the bones of others) was given to a professor of anatomy at Padua. He buried the bones but preserved the skull, which today rests in the Museum of Anatomy of Padua. Santorio left a number of bequests to his immediate family and to other relatives. He also granted money to establish a medical college at Padua, to be named "Santorio," and a sum to the Medical College of Venice to have a mass said yearly for his soul on Saint Luke's Day, an annual celebration of the patron saint of medicine.

SIGNIFICANCE

The history of medicine began in the seventeenth century when Galileo, Giordano Bruno, and Santorio Santorio, among others, helped to free science from dogma. Santorio helped to construct the foundation on which modern medicine is based—the necessity to experiment, the measurement of research through observation and instruments, and the need for determination of positive, provable data.

Santorio's contribution in the virtually unknown field of the amelioration of the condition of invalids (the disabled) advanced medicine in a significant area and signaled to future generations of physicians the need to work further on its theory and practice.

Santorio's invention, modification, and employment of instruments provided his profession with measuring devices so that future practitioners could develop resources in recording data for the treatment and the prevention of diseases. Santorio's commentaries on past generations of scholars and his own innovative theories and practice in physiology and pathology significantly advanced medical knowledge. His book on static medicine, apart from William Harvey's theory of blood circulation, was of quintessential importance to medicine. Trained exhaustively in the humanities as well as in the sciences, Santorio developed concepts and techniques of diagnosis well ahead of his time. His research contributed to the advancement of medicine throughout Europe, especially in the first third of the seventeenth century, and have continued to serve medicine in its attempt to treat and to prevent the development of diseases.

—Julia B. Boken

FURTHER READING

Castiglioni, Arturo. *Life and Work of Sanctorius.* Translated by Emilie Recht. New York: Medical Life Press, 1931. A nearly 800-page biographical account of Santorio's life and works, with illustrations and a bibliography.

Drake, Stillman. *Galileo at Work: His Scientific Biography.* Chicago: University of Chicago Press, 1978. An excellent biography of Galileo that also encompasses his relationships with other scientists, including Santorio. There is a discussion of the pulsilogium and the thermoscope, both of which instruments advanced the course of science and which involved studies and practical application by Santorio.

French, Roger. *William Harvey's Natural Philosophy.* New York: Cambridge University Press, 1994. This book, although about Harvey's work, discusses Santorio's theories of blood circulation.

McMullin, Ernan, ed. *Galileo, Man of Science.* New York: Basic Books, 1967. The book is a compilation of essays by worldwide authorities on Galileo, with an evaluation of Santorio in chapter 13. Considerable attention (with illustrations) is paid to medical instruments, including the thermoscope and the pulsilogium, a milestone in the history of medical instruments.

Major, Ralph H. "Santorio Santorio." *Annals of Medical History* 10 (September, 1938): 369-381. A concise treatment of the life and work of Santorio, especially of his books on Herodotus, Galen, and Avicenna. Discusses the medical instruments associated with Santorio, with illustrations and careful descriptions of their design and use.

Middleton, W. E. Knowles. *A History of the Thermometer and Its Use in Meteorology.* Baltimore: Johns Hopkins University Press, 1966. This authoritative history of the thermometer describes Santorio's contribution to its the invention.

Mitchell, S. Weir. *The Early History of Instrumental Precision in Medicine.* New Haven, Conn.: Tuttle, Morehouse, and Taylor, 1892. An overview of the development and use of medical instruments in the seventeenth century, acknowledging Santorio's considerable importance in medicine and the instruments that his innovations utilized.

Sigerist, Henry E. *The Great Doctors.* Translated by Eden Paul and Cedar Paul. New York: W. W. Norton, 1933. Places Santorio in the history of medicine. Sigerist claims that Harvey's theory of blood circulation became more important than Santorio's "insensible perspiration" theory because Harvey was more precise and organized in his use of language.

SEE ALSO: Charles I; Galileo; Jan Baptista van Helmont; Marcello Malpighi; Paul V.

RELATED ARTICLES in *Great Events from History: The Seventeenth Century, 1601-1700:* 17th century: Advances in Medicine; 1612: Sanctorius Invents the Clinical Thermometer; 1676: Sydenham Advocates Clinical Observation.

THOMAS SAVERY
English inventor

Savery invented the first steam engine, patented in England in 1699. Thomas Newcomen, whose steam engine was a modified version of Savery's, worked closely with Savery during the first decade of the eighteenth century.

BORN: c. 1650; Shilstone, Devonshire, England
DIED: May, 1715; London, England
AREAS OF ACHIEVEMENT: Engineering, invention

EARLY LIFE
Little is known about the early life of Thomas Savery (SAYV-ree). His father was a prosperous merchant and landowner in the town of Totnes, Devonshire, and Thomas would have had an upbringing similar to those of others in his class. Thomas Savery first appears in historical documents already bearing either the title or the nickname of Captain Savery. It is therefore likely that he served as a military engineer early in his career. It is possible, however, that Savery managed a lead or tin mine in Cornwall: "Captain" was a common appellation for Cornish mine managers.

Whatever Savery's early occupation may have been,

he spent his spare time doing mechanical experiments. In the 1690's, he invented both a device for polishing glass and a system for rowing ships becalmed by a lack of wind. It consisted of paddle wheels mounted on either side of the vessel, foreshadowing the early steamships of the nineteenth century. The paddle wheels were propelled, however, not by a steam engine but by a capstan turned by the sailors on the vessel. In 1696, Savery received a patent for this invention, but it was never adopted by the British navy.

LIFE'S WORK
Having grown up in Devonshire, close to the tin and lead mines of western England, Savery was no doubt aware of a growing problem in English mining: Water flowed into the mines as the mines went deeper in search of additional material. Savery attempted to address this problem by inventing a steam-driven pump that created a vacuum into which water would be pulled up a pipe. Savery applied for a patent on this device, which was granted on July 25, 1698. At first, the patent ran for just fourteen years, but the following year an act of Parliament extended it for another twenty-one years, until 1733.

The act of Parliament extending Savery's patent suggests that Savery had friends in high places. His naval device had drawn the attention of King William III. In 1705, he became a fellow of the Royal Society, the body of amateur scientists that dominated the world of British science at that time. Sir Isaac Newton was also a fellow of the Royal Society, having been elected in 1672. Newton was president of the Royal Society when Savery was elected a fellow.

Although Savery's patent describes his invention in only very general terms, as a machine "for raising water by the impellent force of fire," he describes the invention in greater detail in his pamphlet "The Miner's Friend" (1701). This pamphlet includes a drawing showing the mechanism mounted within the line of pipes designed to draw the water out of the mine. It was this feature that in fact made the device less useful in mines, because it limited the vacuum pressure of the pump to the atmospheric pressure. As a result, the maximum lift of the pump was 32 feet (10 meters). For best results, the apparatus would have had to be located within the mine shaft itself, which was extremely dangerous. By providing dual pipes, both below the boiler and above it, Savery increased the lift to slightly above 50 feet (15 meters), but this was still well below the depth of many of the mines severely plagued by flooding.

In 1702, Savery created a company to exploit his invention, but it does not seem to have been a financial success, as he dissolved it in 1705. Though the reason is not known, it seems probable that some of the technical difficulties with the pump had become clear over those three years. One of these difficulties was the extreme inefficiency of alternately heating and cooling the boiler to create the vacuum. (It would be James Watt who would solve this problem, almost a century later.) This defect was magnified by the inability of the metalworkers of the time to build boilers that could withstand a higher than atmospheric pressure, which would have increased the lift; some attempts to do so were made, but they almost invariably resulted in explosions.

Given these difficulties, Savery's invention appears not to have solved the problem of water in the mines, and although Savery's reputation lived on, his device was mostly installed in decorative water displays on private estates. Nevertheless, the patent he had secured gave him patent exclusivity on steam engines until 1733. After his death, this exclusivity was transferred to a firm that bought the rights from his widow.

It was Savery's exclusive right to construct and utilize steam engines that led Thomas Newcomen to associate himself with Savery in 1705, and all of Newcomen's early achievements were made under the protection of Savery's patent. Newcomen combined the piston-and-cylinder device of Denis Papin—a Huguenot refugee in England in the 1690's who worked in close association with Robert Boyle of the Royal Society—with Savery's pump, but Newcomen separated the two devices. As a result, the pump in the mine would be powered by Papin's engine, but the engine itself could be located outside the mine, thereby avoiding the inherent risks involved in placing the engine deep within the mine as Savery's device had done. Moreover, the separation of the engine from the pump meant that the engine could be used as a general source of power for many purposes other than pumping.

It is unlikely that Savery could have achieved what he did without the concurrent work of others, including Otto von Guericke in Germany, Robert Boyle in England (both of whom invented air pumps), and Denis Papin, whose marriage of the piston and cylinder was of critical importance in the working of steam engines. Other developments that took place shortly after the work of these pioneers, notably the increases in metallurgical skills that enabled engineers to create pistons and cylinders that were tightly meshed, made possible the further development of the steam engine. The incremental improvements that characterized the early work on steam engines were emblematic of the Industrial Revolution that was to follow.

SIGNIFICANCE

Savery's work, conducted in close association with the scientific amateurs who constituted most of the membership of the Royal Society at the time (Newton excepted), was a first step in a process that has gone on ever since. The members of the Royal Society sponsored and contributed to a growing understanding of the natural world surrounding them. This increased understanding led to the development of new concepts that could in turn be incorporated into the practical construction of the machines that underpinned the Industrial Revolution. Those who have studied these developments closely have come to realize the long-term nature of the process that started with Thomas Savery and his "steam engine." Nevertheless, Savery's was a portentous achievement, as it underlay two centuries of advancement, and the piston-and-cylinder concept used by Savery and intended for industrial purposes is still required for many modern industrial applications.

—Nancy M. Gordon

FURTHER READING

Briggs, Asa. *The Power of Steam: An Illustrated History of the World's Steam Age.* Chicago: University of Chicago Press, 1982. The first chapter of this richly illustrated work discusses the achievements of Savery and Newcomen as predecessors of James Watt, and discusses the problems Savery encountered when he tried to turn his design into an actual industrial pump.

Lynch, William T. *Solomon's Child: Method in the Early Royal Society of London.* Stanford, Calif.: Stanford University Press, 2001. An important contribution to understanding the role the Royal Society played in early scientific development in the seventeenth century. Although Savery is not specifically mentioned, this study provides the background to his accomplishments.

Rolt, L. T. C. *Thomas Newcomen: The Prehistory of the Steam Engine.* London: David & Charles, 1963. A valuable discussion of the work of Savery and Newcomen, complete with illustrations that make the essence of their accomplishments clear. There are occasional factual inaccuracies, however, that make it essential to use this book with care.

Rosenband, Leonard. "Classics Revisited: John U. Nef, *The Conquest of the Material World." Technology and Culture* 44 (2003): 364-370. An evaluation of the work of one of the earliest writers on mining in England in the sixteenth and seventeenth centuries. Important for an understanding of the accuracy of Nef's descriptions.

Sandfort, John F. *Heat Engines.* Garden City, N.Y.: Anchor Books, 1962. Contains a description of the Savery invention, complete with a drawing based on Savery's own drawing in "The Miner's Friend." Is also useful as setting the entire development of "heat engines" in historical perspective.

SEE ALSO: Robert Boyle; Otto von Guericke; Sir Isaac Newton; Denis Papin; William III.

RELATED ARTICLES in *Great Events from History: The Seventeenth Century, 1601-1700:* 1601-1672: Rise of Scientific Societies; July 25, 1698: Savery Patents the First Successful Steam Engine.

SIR GEORGE SAVILE
English politician

Savile, an advocate of moderation in an age of political excess, was one of the architects of the balanced constitution that established Great Britain as the most progressive nation in pre-Revolutionary Europe.

BORN: November 11, 1633; Thornhill, Yorkshire, England

DIED: April 5, 1695; London, England

ALSO KNOWN AS: First marquis of Halifax; the Trimmer (moniker)

AREA OF ACHIEVEMENT: Government and politics

EARLY LIFE

Sir George Savile (SAV-eel), first marquis of Halifax, was the eldest surviving son of Sir William Savile of Thornhill, third Baronet Savile, and Anne, the daughter of Thomas Coventry, Lord Coventry. Sir William was a devoted Royalist who never swerved in his loyalty to King Charles I: Although he was a member of the Short Parliament, Sir William did not hesitate to accept a commission in the Royalist army. He died in 1644, and his eleven-year-old son, George, became the fourth Baronet Savile.

George's mother, Lady Savile, used her considerable influence to protect her son's interests, despite an attempt by her late husband's enemies in the House of Commons to gain control of the youngster and his inheritance. She felt that George would benefit from being educated on the Continent until he achieved his majority, when neither he nor his property would be subject to the restrictions placed upon minors.

George Savile was able to assume control of his inheritance when he returned home without any interference from the government of Oliver Cromwell. On December 29, 1656, he married his first wife, Lady Dorothy Spencer, the daughter of the first earl of Sunderland. In 1660, at the age of twenty-six, he was elected as a member of the Convention Parliament, which restored Charles II. The return of the exiled king marked the real beginning of Savile's public career.

LIFE'S WORK

As a bona fide Royalist, Savile had easy access to the court, with its opportunities for wealth and political influence. Like his father before him, George Savile had commanded a regiment in the county militia, and in 1667, he was made a captain in Prince Rupert's regiment of horse. However, Savile preferred politics to a career in

Sir George Savile. (Hulton Archive/Getty Images)

the military. Through the efforts of his uncle Sir William Coventry and James, duke of York, the heir presumptive, Savile was created Baron Savile of Eland and Viscount Halifax on January 13, 1668. His elevation to the peerage coincided with the removal and disgrace of his uncle's old political adversary, Chancellor Sir Edward Hyde, earl of Clarendon.

As a member of the House of Lords, Halifax had the chance to display his considerable talents as an orator and a wit. Halifax House quickly became the home of one of the most important and powerful political circles in late Stuart England. Unfortunately, Halifax's first wife did not long survive to preside as hostess over that brilliant assembly. Dorothy, Viscountess Halifax, died on December 16, 1670. Halifax was thirty-seven years old and the father of four small children, so in November, 1672, he married Gertrude Pierrepoint, the youngest daughter of an old friend and neighbor, William Pierrepoint.

Halifax also was made a member of the Privy Council early in 1672. Shortly after his appointment, he was entrusted with an embassy to the court of Louis XIV. Unaware of the secret Treaty of Dover between England and France, and wholly devoted to the anti-French policy of the Triple Alliance, Halifax embarked reluctantly on his mission. He was to inform King Louis that England

would not make a separate peace with William III of Orange. Halifax arrived at the French court only to discover that his embassy had been preempted by George Villiers, second duke of Buckingham, and Henry Bennett, earl of Arlington, who were busily imposing a harsh peace upon the Dutch. Halifax openly criticized his fellow envoys' efforts and publicly attacked the government's subservience to France. William of Orange did not forget his support when William took the English throne in the 1688 Glorious Revolution.

Early in 1673, Halifax devoted his considerable talents as an orator to the successful passage of the Test Act, which barred Roman Catholics from holding office in the civilian government or commissions in the armed services. Unfortunately, the act ended Halifax's friendship with the duke of York, a recent convert to Catholicism. Halifax was fast becoming one of the leading spokesmen of the opposition. In 1676, when he turned his sarcasm on Charles II's chief minister, Thomas Osborne, first duke of Leeds, Halifax lost his place on the council, but King Charles enjoyed his company, and he was soon back in favor.

Like many in the autumn of 1678, Halifax initially was convinced of the genuineness the testimony of Titus Oates concerning the so-called Popish Plot to kill King Charles and elevate James, duke of York, to the throne. However, upon careful examination of the evidence, Halifax became convinced that his uncle, Anthony Ashley Cooper, first earl of Shaftesbury, was using the fabrications of Oates and his confederates to advance his own radical political agenda. Halifax used his considerable talents as an orator to thwart his kinsman's plans, but he could not stop the execution of a number of innocent men whose only crime was their Roman Catholic faith. In July, 1679, his efforts on the side of reason and sanity were rewarded with his being made earl of Halifax. His breach with Shaftesbury was permanent.

Having failed in his attempt to establish himself as the power behind the throne through a campaign of terror and hysteria, Shaftesbury tried to exclude the duke of York from the succession and replace him with James Scott, duke of Monmouth, the eldest illegitimate son of Charles II. In November, 1680, Halifax led the opposition to the Exclusion Bill and, in a verbal duel with Shaftesbury that lasted for seven hours, emerged the victor. He then tried to persuade the duke of York to outwardly conform to the Church of England, at the same time attempting to detach the duke of Monmouth from Shaftesbury in the hope of reconciling Monmouth to his father. In both efforts, Halifax failed. In August, 1682, even as Halifax learned that he was to be made marquis and named lord privy seal, Shaftesbury and his confederates were finalizing a plot to assassinate both the king and his brother.

When the details of the Rye House Plot became public and the arrests of the principal conspirators began, Halifax once again cautioned a course of reason and moderation. Unfortunately, the duke of York and his supporters were determined to use the Rye House Plot as an excuse to seek revenge for the earlier, excessive response to the Popish Plot. Disappointed with York's intransigence and Monmouth's fecklessness, Halifax sought to improve relations between King Charles and his nephew, William of Orange. However, on February 6, 1685, Charles II died after suffering a mild stroke. James II became king, and Halifax's influence quickly waned.

On November 5, 1688, just thirty-nine months after his accession, James II was faced with an invasion led by his son-in-law, who was also his nephew. Prince William of Orange had accepted the secret invitation of a number of British peers to deliver the kingdom from its unpopular monarch. Although Halifax had not been part of the plot to remove James, there was no doubt where his sentiments lay. He had opposed every attempt made by the king to subvert the laws and liberties of the English people. During the reign of William III and Mary II, Halifax continued to advocate a course of moderation, and in his speeches and writing he was recognized as the champion of the principles that set England apart from the absolutist monarchies that still dominated continental Europe. The man who placed the defense of habeas corpus above his own political fortunes, the man whom John Dryden immortalized as Jotham in *Absalom and Achitophel* (Part I, 1681, Part II, 1682), died on April 5, 1695, and was buried in Westminster Abbey.

SIGNIFICANCE

The political awakening of Sir George Savile, first marquis of Halifax, began when those who served Charles II exploited his political naïveté during the Second Anglo-Dutch War (1665-1667). Halifax saw French-styled absolutism as the most serious threat to the liberties of England. In his speeches and in his writings, particularly his pamphlet *Character of a Trimmer* (1688), Halifax repeatedly advocated constitutional monarchy as the best form of government for England and as a form of government consistent with the laws and traditions of the kingdom. At first, he hoped that England could be governed without recourse to faction, but in upholding the power of Parliament to alter the succession, Halifax found in the healthy competition of political parties the most reliable safeguard of the constitution.

—Clifton W. Potter, Jr.

FURTHER READING

Coote, Stephen. *Royal Survivor: The Life of Charles II*. New York: St. Martin's Press, 2000. A thorough study of the political sagacity of the "Merry Monarch" and the manner in which he managed and interacted with the politicians who surrounded him.

Foxcroft, Helen Charlotte. *A Character of the Trimmer: Being a Short Life of the First Marquis of Halifax*. Reprint. New York: Cambridge University Press, 1985. The only full-length biography in print; balanced and well written, but the endnotes are far too brief.

Fraser, Antonia. *King Charles II*. London: Phoenix Press, 2002. This is the most balanced biography of the king and places his contemporaries in their proper context.

Halifax, George Savile, Marquis of. *The Works of George Savile, Marquis of Halifax*. Edited by Mark N. Brown. 3 vols. Oxford, England: Clarendon Press, 1989. This most recent edition of Halifax's works replaces an earlier edition by Helen Foxcroft in 1898.

Ogg, David. *England in the Reign of Charles II*. 2d ed. New York: Oxford University Press, 1984. Although somewhat dated in its interpretation of the Restoration, it remains a useful introduction to the period.

_____. *England in the Reigns of James II and William III*. New York: Oxford University Press, 1984. Although the author's sympathies obviously lie with William, it is still perhaps the best survey of the Glorious Revolution and its aftermath.

SEE ALSO: Charles I; Charles II (of England); First Earl of Clarendon; Oliver Cromwell; John Dryden; James II; First Duke of Leeds; Louis XIV; Mary II; Duke of Monmouth; Titus Oates; Prince Rupert; First Earl of Shaftesbury; William III.

RELATED ARTICLES in *Great Events from History: The Seventeenth Century, 1601-1700:* 1642-1651: English Civil Wars; May, 1659-May, 1660: Restoration of Charles II; March 4, 1665-July 31, 1667: Second Anglo-Dutch War; December 19, 1667: Impeachment of Clarendon; January 23, 1668: Triple Alliance Forms; April 6, 1672-August 10, 1678: French-Dutch War; 1673-1678: Test Acts; August 13, 1678-July 1, 1681: The Popish Plot; 1679: Habeas Corpus Act; August, 1682-November, 1683: Rye House Plot; 1688-1702: Reign of William and Mary; November, 1688-February, 1689: The Glorious Revolution.

WILHELM SCHICKARD
German inventor, mathematician, astronomer, and cartographer

Schickard was the first individual to construct an automated calculating, or adding, machine; was one of the first strong advocates of the laws of planetary motion that had been proposed by Johannes Kepler; and employed fundamental principles of cartography to produce some of the seventeenth century's most accurate geographical maps.

BORN: April 22, 1592; Herrenberg, Württemberg (now in Germany)
DIED: October 24, 1635; Tübingen, Württemberg
AREAS OF ACHIEVEMENT: Mathematics, astronomy, geography, science and technology, religion and theology, scholarship

EARLY LIFE

Not much is known about the early life of Wilhelm Schickard (SHEE-kahrd). Born near Tübingen in what is now Germany, Schickard chose to attend the University of Tübingen, graduating in 1609 at age seventeen with a bachelor of arts degree in theology. Continuing his education at the University of Tübingen, Schickard earned in 1611 his master of arts degree in theology and oriental languages. He remained studying at Tübingen until 1613, when he took a position as a pastor in a Lutheran church near the town. From 1613 until 1619, Schickard served as a pastor in various communities around Tübingen.

While serving as a minister, Schickard developed some of his skills working with wood and metals. He became well known in Würrtemberg for his wood carvings, copper-plate designs, and abilities as a mechanic. He also expanded his interests into astronomy, mathematics, and geography.

In 1619, Schickard received an appointment at the University of Tübingen as a professor of Hebrew. Until 1631, he taught biblical languages and Bible studies at the university. During his early years at Tübingen as a student and as a professor, Schickard befriended astronomy professor Michael Mästlin, who was the chair of astronomy at the university. When Mästlin died in 1631, Schickard was appointed as a professor of astronomy and succeeded Mästlin as the chair of astronomy.

LIFE'S WORK

Schickard devoted the major part of his life to teaching, researching, and inventing practical devices. At various times during his career at the University of Tübingen,

Schickard taught Hebrew, Asian languages, mathematics, astronomy, geography, meteorology, and optics. He is most famous for his invention of the first automated calculating machine, although he did not receive credit for the invention until the mid-1900's.

As a young professor at Tübingen, Schickard developed a keen interest in astronomy and mathematics and became a friend and correspondent with astronomer Johannes Kepler and a number of other prominent scientists of the time. Schickard prepared diagrams and illustrations for Kepler's book *Harmonices mundi* (partial translation as *Harmonies of the World*, 1952), which concentrated on Kepler's third law of planetary motion. Some key letters and drawings that Schickard sent to Kepler in 1623 and 1624 were discovered among Kepler's papers and other belongings in 1935, but again were lost, this time during World War II. In 1956, the papers and other artifacts were "discovered" once more, this time in Stuttgart, Germany. The letters and drawings divulge Schickard's invention of the first automated calculating (adding) machine in 1623.

In his letter written to Kepler on September 20, 1623, Schickard described his machine and suggested that it could be used to calculate astronomical tables. He had purportedly built a prototype calculator for his own use and promised Kepler that he would make one for him as well. His letter written to Kepler on February 25, 1624, contained a complete description and drawings of the calculator. He also explained that the calculator he planned for Kepler had been destroyed in a fire at the home of a hired worker. Evidently, the plans for his calculator and the prototype model were lost during the Thirty Years' War, which broke out after Schickard's death.

Schickard apparently became intrigued with the possibility of making a mechanical calculating machine to carry out automated calculations associated with astronomical observations after he read the paper published in 1617 by mathematician John Napier, the inventor of logarithms. Napier's paper discussed using calculating rods to form a calculating device that was referred to as "Napier's Bones." Schickard combined parts of this device with a mechanism that would carry the tens encountered when doing addition and subtraction. Schickard's machine used the device to perform multiplication and division. The lower half of the calculator employed a direct gear drive with rotating wheels to do addition and subtraction of numbers that contained up to six digits. Schickard referred to his invention as the calculating clock because it could calculate the times associated with the locations of planetary bodies.

From Schickard's drawings that were rediscovered in 1956, Bruno Baron Von Freytag Loringhoff, a professor at the University of Tübingen, built in 1960 a working model of Schickard's automated calculating machine. Until that time, credit for the first automated calculating machine had typically been ascribed to Blaise Pascal, who invented the less-versatile Pascaline calculator in 1642. Although Schickard invented his machine first, the Pascaline was the first adding machine to be produced in any quantity and the first to be used by individuals other than the inventor. Neither the machine invented by Schickard nor the one by Pascal was programmable. It would take about two hundred years for Charles Babbage to conceive a programmable calculator, in 1823.

Another significant undertaking of Schickard was the making of accurate geographical maps. His insights into the fundamental principles of cartography led to the production of the most accurate maps possible at that time. In 1629, he explained their construction and advocated their usage, particularly in surveying applications. Using his maps, he surveyed much of Würrtemberg.

Pursuing his astronomical interests in the late 1620's and early 1630's, Schickard invented a handheld planetarium similar to an orrery, a device that shows the relative positions and motions of bodies in the solar system by rotating and revolving a system of balls with respect to each other. He also invented an instrument that calculated astronomical dates. Schickard also saw a lunar ephemeris, observed the comets of 1618, described meteors, and described the transit of Mercury in 1631.

Schickard died of the plague at the relatively young age of forty-three on October 24, 1635. The Wilhelm Schickard Institute of Information at the University of Tübingen, the Wilhelm Schickard Institute for Computer Science at Eberhard Karls University in Tübingen, and the Wilhelm Schickard Museum of Computing History at Concordia University (in Wisconsin) were all named in his honor.

SIGNIFICANCE

Because of his invention of the first automated calculating machine, Schickard rightfully can be referred to as the "father of the modern computing era." His invention had many very important ramifications. Finding a way to automatically carry tens when doing addition or subtraction was a great time saver. During Schickard's time, calculations were done by hand. People who knew how to count and calculate were highly valued. Large numbers of these "human calculators" were employed by small and large businesses. Schickard was aided in his invention by his understanding of how to apply gear technology in practical machines, something known by very few people at that time. His inventions using gears inspired others to develop that technology in other applications.

At the time, Schickard's development of accurate maps was perhaps as important as was his automated calculating machine. Applications included more precise routes of travel and accurate surveying of land for real estate transactions and for boundary disputes. His handheld planetarium was used to clarify and advocate Kepler's laws of planetary motion, providing a much clearer, more understandable explanation of planetary astronomy, and it was incorporated into university instruction.

—*Alvin K. Benson*

FURTHER READING

Asimov, Isaac. *How Did We Find Out About Computers?* New York: Walker, 1984. Asimov tracks the history of the development of the computer, from the abacus through mechanical calculating machines such as that of Schickard to modern electronic technology. Good index.

Aspray, William, ed. *Computing Before Computers.* Ames: Iowa State University Press, 1990. A survey of the concepts, technology, purpose, and impact of

---

SCHICKARD'S EARLY CALCULATOR

In a letter to astronomer Johannes Kepler in 1623, Wilhelm Schickard describes his new calculating machine (an early form of the modern calculator), along with its functions and quickness.

I have conceived a machine consisting of eleven complete and six incomplete sprocket wheels; it calculates instantaneously and automatically from given numbers, as it adds, subtracts, multiplies and divides. You would enjoy to see how the machine accumulates and transports spontaneously a ten or a hundred to the left and, vice-versa, how it does the opposite if it is subtracting.

Source: The Wilhelm Schickard Museum of Computing History, Concordia University Wisconsin. http://www.cs.cuw.edu/museum/. Accessed December, 2004.

computing devices that were developed prior to the electronic digital computer, including the mechanical calculator invented by Schickard. Good bibliography and index.

Grattan-Guinness, Ivor. *Companion Encyclopedia of the History and Philosophy of the Mathematical Sciences.* Vol. 1. Baltimore: Johns Hopkins University Press, 2003. This work examines Schickard's contribution to the development of automation in performing mathematical calculations. Illustrations, bibliography, and an extensive index.

Ifrah, Georges. *The Universal History of Numbers.* Translated by David Bellos, E. F. Harding, Sophie Wood, and Ian Monk. New York: John Wiley & Sons, 2000. This book traces the history of numbers from prehistoric times up to the invention of the computer, noting Schickard and his place in the history of manipulating numbers. Extensive index.

Seck, Friedrich, ed. *Briefwechsel.* Stuttgart, Germany: Frommann-Holzboog, 2002. A compilation of Schickard's writings that reveal his contributions to developments in astronomy, mathematics, and cartography. Extensive bibliography and index, as well as illustrations. In German.

Williams, Michael R. *A History of Computing Technology.* 2d ed. Los Alamitos, Calif.: IEEE Computer Society Press, 1997. An outline of the historical developments in computing technology that focuses on the physical devices that were developed to automate arithmetic operations, including Schickard's calculating clock. Good index and bibliography.

SEE ALSO: René Descartes; David and Johannes Fabricius; Pierre de Fermat; Christiaan Huygens; Johannes Kepler; Gottfried Wilhelm Leibniz; Blaise Pascal.

RELATED ARTICLE in *Great Events from History: The Seventeenth Century, 1601-1700:* 1623-1674: Earliest Calculators Appear.

FRIEDRICH HERMANN SCHOMBERG
German-born military leader

During a fifty-seven-year span, Schomberg steadily gained a reputation as one of the most accomplished soldiers in Europe, holding a career as an officer and commander in several European armies. His life ended while he was in the service of King William III of England, in a battle won by English and Continental troops over Ireland, securing the English crown for William.

BORN: December, 1615, or January, 1616; Heidelberg, the Palatinate (now in Germany)

DIED: July 1, 1690; near Oldbridge, on the Boyne River, Ireland

ALSO KNOWN AS: Friedrich Hermann von Schönberg (given name); Frédéric Armand, duke of Schomberg (von Schönberg)

AREAS OF ACHIEVEMENT: Warfare and conquest, military

EARLY LIFE

Friedrich Hermann Schomberg (SHAWM-behrk) was born the son of Hans Meinhard von Schönberg, a minor Palatine nobleman at the court of Elector Frederick V, and Lady Anne Sutton, who had come to the Palatinate in the entourage of Frederick's wife, Elizabeth Stuart, daughter of King James I of England. Even the beginning of Friedrich's life, like much about him, remains enigmatic: His exact birth date is not known, though some scholars believe it to be December 16, 1615.

He was baptized into the Calvinist faith and trained from the earliest years for a military career, which he embarked upon in 1633, while still in his teens. For the first few months, he was enrolled in the army of the United Provinces of the Netherlands in the service of Stadtholder Frederick Henry. The young soldier, however, was eager to prove himself and to go where actual battles were being fought. So, in 1634, he joined the army of Sweden, which was part of a Protestant Alliance engaged in the Thirty Years' War (1618-1648) against the Catholic League led by Holy Roman Emperor Ferdinand II.

LIFE'S WORK

In 1635, when Cardinal de Richelieu brought France into the war on the side of the Protestants, Schomberg enlisted in the French army, where he would remain for four years. In 1639, he reentered the Dutch military forces, serving once more under Frederick Henry, then under his son, William II.

In 1650, Schomberg's former mentor in the French army, the viscount de Turenne (Henri de La Tour d'Auvergne), appealed to Schomberg to return to France to assist him in quelling the insurgent forces of the prince of Condé (the Great Condé) during the Wars of the Fronde (1648-1653) against King Louis XIV. Schomberg distinguished himself to such an extent that King Louis took pains to keep him on.

Then, in 1659, he accepted a commission from King Charles II of England to journey to Portugal as military adviser. His mission was to prevent the Spanish from reconquering the kingdom of Portugal, which recently had made good on securing its independence. His services earned him an English peerage—Baron Tetford—and the Portuguese title of count of Mertola (1663). On June 17, 1665, he won his first major victory under independent command at the Battle of Montes Claros, turning back Spanish troops under the duke of Parma. In recognition of this victory, he was advanced to the rank of lieutenant-general. Engineering a military coup, Schomberg was responsible for deposing the emotionally unbalanced Afonso VI, king of Portugal (r. 1656-1683), and replacing him with his brother, Peter (Pedro) II (r. 1683-1706).

Schomberg left the Portuguese service in 1668 and returned to France. He participated in the early stages of the Franco-Dutch War of 1672-1678, gaining considerable notice through his capture of the stronghold of Maastricht in 1673. Dispatched to Catalonia in 1674, he suffered a temporary career setback with initial failures, but he redeemed himself in 1675 by capturing the fortress of Bellegarde. Louis XIV then conferred upon him the rank of marshal and title of duke.

Schomberg had by this time secured a reputation as one of Europe's foremost commanders, but he was relatively inactive until the 1680's, when Louis XIV's increasingly vehement campaign against Huguenot Protestantism forced him to make a critical choice. Though he was not, strictly speaking, a Huguenot, and he was granted an exemption from Louis XIV's religious strictures, he was so disturbed by the often brutal treatment of fellow Calvinists, and by the outlawing of Huguenot worship in the Edict of Fontainebleau of 1685, that he decided to go into exile, first to Portugal.

The elector of Brandenburg, who had, through his Edict of Potsdam of 1686, indicated his desire to welcome exiled Huguenots and offer them incentives to settle in his dominions, welcomed Schomberg in 1687 with open arms, conferring upon him the command of all troops in the electorate. Schomberg became, in effect, leader of the Huguenots in Brandenburg. True to form, however, Schomberg did not stay long in one place, par-

ticularly where there was no concerted military action. Stadtholder William III of the Netherlands convinced Elector Frederick III to allow Brandenburger soldiers to enter Holland to help him in his planned military expedition to England against his Catholic father-in-law, James II. It was further agreed that Schomberg be placed in command of the invasion task force, under William himself.

The fleet set sail in November of 1688 and made landfall at Torbay on the southern coast of Britain. The ensuing Glorious Revolution witnessed a brief face-off between James's army and that of William and Schomberg. James's nerve faltered, though, and he fled the country. Parliament instated William and his wife Mary II as joint sovereigns over England. At the height of his fame and success, Schomberg was voted an English dukedom, the marquisate of Harwich, the earldom of Brentford, and the barony of Teyes. Also, he was invested as a Knight of the Garter and granted 100,000 pounds sterling as compensation for the loss of his French estates and revenues.

When Richard Talbot, the duke of Tyrconnel, declared support for King James II, Schomberg was named to command a British expeditionary force to recapture the island for William and Mary. Leading a motley contingent of Huguenots and of Dutch, English, and German levies (troops), Schomberg was at first reasonably successful. His forces landed close to and soon occupied the town of Bangor in County Down in August, 1689. Belfast and Lisburn were taken with little or no resistance, but the Irish Jacobite army, which supported King James, refused to surrender Carrickfergus for five days. A quick advance took Schomberg's forces to the city of Dundalk in September. There, in what was seen in retrospect as a huge miscalculation on his part, he halted, stalled, and, because he erroneously believed that the Jacobite army was much stronger than it actually was, had encamped on the marshy plain just north of the city.

The Encampment of Dundalk, as it became known, proved to be a disaster. A shortage of provisions, poor distribution and planning, and foul weather led to outbreaks of disease and to desertions. Some of the Huguenot troops were discovered to have been French Catholics who had infiltrated the ranks as spies. Morale became so low that some units were close to mutiny. More than seven thousand troops are believed to have died, and, as news of the deteriorating situation at Dundalk leaked out to the Jacobites, King James journeyed to the front to assume command. Caught in a sort of defeatist mind-set, Schomberg gave up the advance and withdrew northward to Lisburn, where most of his army remained from October of 1689 to April of 1690. William's armies had captured all of Ulster, apart from the holdout Jacobite outpost at Charlemont in the County Armagh.

Infuriated at news of the calamity and disappointed at Schomberg's performance, King William reinforced his army in Ireland with Danish, Huguenot, Dutch, English, German, and Scottish levies until it numbered some thirty-seven thousand men. Despite the fact that Marshal Schomberg successfully captured Charlemont in May, 1690, William personally took command the following month, and the duke was in disgrace. William's treatment of Schomberg was noticeably cold, and he rejected out of hand much of his advice, as the armies faced each other in the climactic Battle of the Boyne on July 1, 1690. At a ford near the village of Oldbridge, Schomberg attempted to rally his men for a breakthrough assault, allegedly indicating to his Huguenots that there were French Catholic troops on the other side, and shouted "Forward, my children! Here are your persecutors!" Shortly thereafter, he was killed. Some accounts say he was surrounded and cut down by Jacobite horsemen, others that he was shot in the back of the neck, perhaps by "friendly fire." His body was taken to Dublin, where it was buried in St. Patrick's Cathedral.

SIGNIFICANCE

Schomberg, despite his shortcomings at Dundalk, became, through his heroic death at the Boyne, a legendary Irish-Protestant hero and part of the iconography of Orange Order (a Protestant organization) celebrations in Ulster. His reforms in Brandenburg laid the foundation for the meticulous training and discipline that would later become a hallmark of the Prussian, and then the German, army to 1945.

—*Raymond Pierre Hylton*

FURTHER READING

Bartlett, Thomas, and Keith Jeffrey, eds. *A Military History of Ireland.* New York: Cambridge University Press, 1996. This work provides basic details describing the major military clashes and operations during the period 1689-1690, but there is little new insight into Schomberg's last campaigns.

Maguire, W. A. *Kings in Conflict: The Revolutionary War in Ireland and Its Aftermath, 1689-1750.* Belfast, Ireland: Blackstaff Press, 1990. The author details the failure of Schomberg's Dundalk campaign of 1689 and his subsequent fall from grace but is not totally unsympathetic in the treatment.

Simms, J. G. *War and Politics in Ireland, 1649-1730.* Edited by D. W. Hayton and Gerald O'Brien. London: Hambledon Press, 1986. An entire chapter is devoted to a detailed analysis of the destruction of Schomberg's military reputation as a result of the Dundalk debacle.

Smiles, Samuel. *The Huguenots: Their Settlements, Churches, and Industries in England and Ireland.* Baltimore: Genealogical Publishing, 1972. An old work originally published in 1868, but with still-useful insights on Schomberg's military career and a dramatic account of his death.

SEE ALSO: Charles II (of England); The Great Condé; Ferdinand II; Frederick Henry; Frederick V; James II; Louis XIV; Mary II; Cardinal de Richelieu; Elizabeth Stuart; Viscount de Turenne; William III.

RELATED ARTICLES in *Great Events from History: The Seventeenth Century, 1601-1700:* 1667: Pufendorf Advocates a Unified Germany; February 13, 1668: Spain Recognizes Portugal's Independence; 1685: Louis XIV Revokes the Edict of Nantes; April 18-July 31, 1689: Siege of Londonderry.

ANNA MARIA VAN SCHURMAN
Dutch scholar and artist

Internationally renowned as one of the greatest female scholars of the seventeenth century, van Schurman was skilled in several languages and was a scholar in philosophy and theology. Her influential Latin treatise Dissertatio *(1641) argued that women not only could succeed intellectually in education but also had a right to higher education. She also was an accomplished artist who worked in a variety of media.*

BORN: November 5, 1607; Cologne (now in Germany)
DIED: May 14, 1678; Wieuwerd, Friesland, United Provinces (now in the Netherlands)
AREAS OF ACHIEVEMENT: Scholarship, philosophy, women's rights, education, religion and theology, art

EARLY LIFE

Anna Maria van Schurman (SHUHR-mahn) was one of three children born to the noble family of Frederik van Schurman and Eva von Harff. Although her father's Calvinist family was originally from Antwerp, they moved to Cologne during the late sixteenth century suppression of Protestantism in the Netherlands under King Philip II of Spain and the duke of Alva. Following the Dutch revolt against Spain for independence, the family returned to the Netherlands in 1610 and eventually settled in the city of Utrecht. It was in this university city that van Schurman commenced, with her father's encouragement and support, her pursuit of artistic and scholarly accomplishments.

It is believed that van Schurman initiated her artistic training in 1620 with Magdalena van de Passe, the daughter of a famous family of engravers. Thus, van Schurman began her artistic pursuits engraving and etching portraits and self-portraits. She was also the first woman allowed to study at a Dutch university, where she became interested in philosophy and theology. She mastered an ability to read and write in several languages, which, according to a famous contemporary, Jakob Cats, included Dutch, German, French, English, Latin, Italian, Greek, Hebrew, Ethiopian, Arabic, Syrian, Persian, and Samaritan. In addition to acquiring knowledge of classical philosophy, she studied poetry, rhetoric, dialectics, and mathematics. Although van Schurman had to keep a low profile while attending classes with male colleagues, she eventually obtained the approbation and encouragement of several prominent male scholars, who encouraged her to publish and to pursue her scholarly interests.

LIFE'S WORK

In addition to etching and engraving in copper, van Schurman created artistic works in glass, oil, boxwood, wax, pastels, gouache, embroidery, paper, pencil, and ivory. This demonstration of artistic skill in such a wide variety of media was unusual and reveals her eagerness to experiment with and master several diverse techniques. Her art consists primarily of portraits in miniature, but she also did paper cuttings of coats of arms, as well as decorative texts in glass engravings and calligraphy on parchment.

In 1643, she was admitted to Utrecht's Guild of St. Luke, the painter's guild. Her membership appears to have been primarily honorary, as she essentially stopped producing works after this date. Nevertheless, her artistic accomplishments received so much attention that she continued to be applauded in collections of artist biographies for several decades, including that of Cornelis de Bie and of Arnold Houbraken (1660-1719), who was also a painter. De Bie praised van Schurman particularly for engaging in the traditionally male pursuit of *creating* art. Moreover, he wrote that this "manly" endeavor won her "manly" honor.

Van Schurman's supporters encouraged her to publish her first important text, *Dissertatio* (1641; *The Learned Maid: Or, Whether a Maid May Be a Scholar? A Logick Exercise*, 1659), in which she defended a woman's right to pursue higher education. For its time, the *Dissertatio* was remarkable for its logic and strong insistence that women were equal to men in their ability to think and learn. She makes the scholastic argument that anyone who has a desire for the arts and sciences is suited to such study. Therefore, because women have this desire, they are capable of these pursuits. A French translation of van Schurman's ideas on women's education was published in 1646, and an English translation appeared in 1659. In 1648, van Schurman also published a compilation of her letters and poetry, *Opuscula hebraea, graeca, latina, gallica: Prosaica et metrica* (partial English translation, 1998). As the title suggests, the text demonstrates her facility in Hebrew, Greek, Latin, and French. These texts helped earn her international fame and a number of glorifying epithets including Star of Utrecht, Miracle of Nature, and the Tenth Muse.

Van Schurman had many admirers and correspondents, including the poet and diplomat Constantijn Huygens, the artist Gerard Honthorst, the theologians

Gisbertus Voetius (Gijsbert Voet) and André Rivet, the lawyer-poet Cats, the doctor-author Johann van Beverwijk, the French philosopher René Descartes, the Dutch poet Ann Roemers Visscher, and Princess Elizabeth of the Palatinate. Indeed, van Schurman became an important local attraction for visiting scholars and dignitaries, who had heard of her wisdom and learning. She kept international correspondence with curious and admiring letter writers from around Europe. Eulogies to her knowledge and skills appeared frequently in both texts and images.

One of her self-portraits was used as a frontispiece and dedication page for a popular text by Cats, who introduced the portrait with a verse praising van Schurman's artistic skills and her intelligence. The aggrandizing image is reminiscent of portrayals of her famous male contemporaries. Scholarly texts, the instruments of her fame, are laid out on the table beside her in this image, and a view of the Utrecht church appears out the background window. These elements, combined with her bold pose, declare her prestigious position as the Minerva of Utrecht. Van Beverwijk also dedicated a text to van Schurman dealing with the superiority of women. In his extensive description of van Schurman, he reveals even more of her virtues by extolling her musical abilities and praising her writings and her character.

Increasingly after this early recognition, van Schurman began to withdraw from public attention to care for her elderly aunts. Her fame suffered when she joined the religious community of Jean de Labadie, a Reformed Swiss minister dismissed for heretical beliefs. Although her friends tried to dissuade her from joining, she defended the group in her writings and accompanied the sect in its travels searching for a protected haven. In 1673, she published *Eucleria seu melioris partis electio* (English translation, 1673), which was both an autobiography and an argument for the purer reformation she had found with de Labadie. Van Schurman followed the group to Germany and then to Friesland, where it settled at Walta Castle near Wieuwerd. She died there in 1678.

SIGNIFICANCE

Even during her lifetime, van Schurman achieved a scholarly reputation at the international level, an achievement that was unprecedented for women. The many portraits of her and the eulogizing verses dedicated to her indicate that she was an important role model for girls and women. Her prominence in art and scholarship encouraged other women, particularly Dutch women,

to pursue such "manly" endeavors. The artist and scholar Margarita van Godewyk and the artist Joanna Koerten Blok, for example, were both compared to van Schurman favorably. Women outside the Dutch Republic, however, were also encouraged by her writings and reputation. Indeed, van Schurman's assertions regarding women's intellectual abilities and their rights to an education influenced the arguments of later feminists and others concerned with human rights.

—*Martha Moffitt Peacock*

FURTHER READING

Baar, Mirjam de, et al., eds. *Choosing the Better Part: Anna Maria van Schurman (1607-1678)*. Translated by Lynne Richards. Boston: Kluwer Academic, 1995. A multidisciplinary collection of nine essays on the life, writings, art, and influence of van Schurman.

Dykeman, Therese Boose, ed. *The Neglected Canon: Nine Women Philosophers, First to the Twentieth Century*. Boston: Kluwer Academic, 1999. Provides a 1659 English translation of *Dissertatio* and a brief biography of van Schurman, discussing her philosophical contribution in a contemporary context.

Israel, Jonathan. *The Dutch Republic: Its Rise, Greatness, and Fall, 1477-1806*. Oxford, England: Clarendon Press, 1995. Includes a brief discussion of van Schurman's involvement with de Labadie.

Kersey, Ethel M. *Women Philosophers: A Bio-Critical Source Book*. New York: Greenwood Press, 1989. Gives a brief overview of van Schurman's life and a critical discussion of her writings.

Kloek, Els, Nicole Teeuwen, and Marijke Huisman, eds. *Women of the Golden Age: An International Debate on Women in Seventeenth-Century Holland, England, and Italy*. Hilversum, the Netherlands: Verloren, 1994. Several essays in this anthology discuss the position of van Schurman in Dutch society.

Saxby, Trevor J. *The Quest for the New Jerusalem: Jean de Labadie and the Labadists (1610-1744)*. Hingham, Mass.: Kluwer Academic, 1987. Although focused mainly on Labadie, this work also gives details on the later life of Schurman and provides translations from *Eucleria* unavailable elsewhere.

Schama, Simon. *The Embarrassment of Riches: An Interpretation of Dutch Culture in the Golden Age*. New York: Alfred A. Knopf, 1987. This now-classic cultural history briefly discusses van Schurman in the general context of the position of women in Dutch society and culture.

Schurman, Anna Maria van. *Whether a Christian Woman*

Should Be Educated and Other Writings from Her Intellectual Circle. Translated and edited by Joyce L. Irwin. Chicago: University of Chicago Press, 1998. Centers on English translations of van Schurman's defense of women's education, with excerpts from *Dissertatio*, *Eucleria*, and her letters to other women. Also included are translations of reactions to her work from her male contemporaries.

Waithe, Mary Ellen. *The History of Women Philosophers: Modern Women Philosophers, 1600-1900.* Dordrecht, the Netherlands: Kluwer Academic, 1991. A critical review of van Schurman's writings on the education of women.

Warnke, Frank J., and Katharina M. Wilson, eds. *Women Writers of the Seventeenth Century.* Athens: University of Georgia Press, 1989. Includes English translations of several of van Schurman's letters and excerpts from *Dissertatio* and *Eucleria*.

SEE ALSO: René Descartes; Elizabeth of Bohemia; François de Salignac de La Mothe-Fénelon; Marie le Jars de Gournay; Ninon de Lenclos; Madame de Maintenon; Elena Cornaro Piscopia; Mary Ward.
RELATED ARTICLE in *Great Events from History: The Seventeenth Century, 1601-1700:* 1625: Grotius Establishes the Concept of International Law.

HEINRICH SCHÜTZ
German composer

Schütz was the most important German composer of his era, and his works and pupils had an immense influence on the subsequent development of music in Germany. He is especially noted for combining German church music traditions with the newer Italian styles that had been developed in the early seventeenth century.

BORN: October 9, 1585 (baptized); Köstritz, Reuss (now Bad Köstritz, Germany)
DIED: November 6, 1672; Dresden, Saxony (now in Germany)
ALSO KNOWN AS: Heinricus Sagittarius (Latin name)
AREAS OF ACHIEVEMENT: Music, religion and theology

EARLY LIFE

Heinrich Schütz (HIN-rihk shuhyts) was born into a family of prosperous innkeepers near the capital of the principality of Reuss. The exact day of Schütz's birth is disputed, but he was baptized on October 9. His father, Christoph, had been town clerk in Gera before taking over the Golden Crane Inn in Köstritz. Heinrich was the second of eleven children in a close-knit family.

In the summer before Heinrich turned five, the family moved to Weissenfels, where his father had inherited an inn, the Golden Ring. Christoph provided a good religious and liberal arts education for his children, and Heinrich showed a special talent for music, becoming a fine singer. His voice attracted the attention of Langrave Moritz of Hessen-Kassel when this learned and musical

nobleman stayed at the Schütz family inn. Moritz persuaded Schütz's parents to send Heinrich to his court in Kassel, where the lad served as a choirboy and studied at the Collegium Mauritianum, displaying a special gift for languages—Latin, Greek, and French—as well as music.

It was not the intention of Schütz or his parents that he take up music as a profession; therefore, in the fall of 1608, he entered the University of Marburg to study for a career in law. Once again, however, Moritz intervened in his life by offering to send Schütz to Venice to study music with the renowned Giovanni Gabrieli. This was an exciting prospect for Schütz, and it was not difficult to convince him to postpone his legal studies.

The rich musical life of Venice and the inspiration of Gabrieli and his compositions had a profound influence on Schütz. He acquired a thorough knowledge of contrapuntal writing and published a book of five-voice madrigals as a demonstration of his achievements at the end of his initial two-year stay. He received high praise for his madrigals and for his organ playing, even substituting as organist for Gabrieli on occasion. His study in Venice was extended for a third year and even beyond but was ended by the death of Gabrieli in August of 1612. A close relationship had developed between Schütz and his teacher; Gabrieli gave Schütz one of his rings on his deathbed, and Schütz spoke of Gabrieli only in terms of highest praise.

When Schütz returned to Germany, he assumed a position as second organist at Moritz's court. He also gave serious consideration to his family's urging to return to his legal studies. He probably would have done so but for a request from Johann Georg I, elector of Saxony, for Schütz to come to Dresden to assist with the musical festivities in conjunction with the baptism of the elector's son. Schütz spent several weeks at the elector's court during the fall of 1614, and the next April the elector requested that Moritz lend him Schütz for a two-year period. Although Moritz protested and later tried to regain the services of the musician he had discovered and cultivated, Schütz left Kassel in August, 1615, for what turned out to be a lifetime position in the service of the elector of Saxony.

LIFE'S WORK

Any remaining doubts that Schütz or his family had about his pursuing a musical career were now resolved by his appointment at one of the most important courts in Europe. When he arrived in Dresden in 1615, he took on the duties of Kapellmeister, even though he was not officially given that title until three or four years later.

As music director for the court, Schütz's responsibilities included directing the performances for important

Heinrich Schütz. (Library of Congress)

religious and political ceremonies, composing much of the music that was presented, and hiring and supervising the musicians of the court. Moreover, he instructed the choirboys, taking a special interest in those who showed promise in musical composition. Among his pupils were several who became well-known composers, Heinrich Albert, Christoph Bernhard, Johann Theile, and Matthias Weckmann.

In 1619, Schütz published the *Psalmen Davids* (Psalms of David) a collection of twenty-six psalm settings that, in their use of multiple choirs with eight to twenty voice parts and accompanying instruments, show the influence of Gabrieli and the Venetian style. At about the same time as the publication of the *Psalmen Davids*, Schütz married Magdalena Wildeck, the eighteen-year-old daughter of an electoral court official. Two daughters were born to the couple, but after only six years of an especially happy marriage, Magdalena contracted smallpox and died on September 6, 1625. After his wife's death, Schütz spent more than a year making musical settings of the psalm paraphrases written by a Leipzig theologian, Cornelius Becker. Schütz derived great comfort from his work with these psalms and later (1628) published them as a collection known as the *Becker Psalter*.

In the spring of 1627, Schütz composed *Dafne*, the first opera written in German, set to an adaptation of a libretto by Ottavio Rinuccini. The score for this work, like most of Schütz's secular compositions, has not survived. Toward the end of the 1620's, economic conditions at the Saxon court deteriorated through the increasing financial drain of the Thirty Years' War (1618-1648). Because no elaborate ceremonies requiring music would be likely in such troubled times, and because Schütz wished to learn more about current musical activities in Italy, he requested a leave to travel for a second time to Venice.

Schütz found the prevailing musical style of Venice in the late 1620's to be quite different from that which he had known there twenty years earlier. The famous Claudio Monteverdi was now the leading musical figure, and his perfection of the style of dramatic monody was of great interest to the German composer. Schütz wrote that he learned "how a comedy of diverse voices can be translated into declamatory style and be brought to the stage and enacted in song," a practice that was "still completely unknown in Germany." Schütz's stay was slightly more than a year this time; before he left, he published a collection of Latin church music with instruments, *Symphoniae sacrae* (1629; sacred symphonies), which includes works showing the influence of the new monodic style he encountered during his stay in Venice.

When he returned to Dresden late in 1629, Schütz found conditions unimproved; any hope for betterment of the situation was ended by the official entry of Saxony into the Thirty Years' War in 1631. Over the next two years, musical activity declined to almost nothing, and Schütz spent extended periods of time during the next twelve years serving in other places. He served as director of music for the Danish court in Copenhagen from 1633 to 1635, and again from 1642 to 1644. In 1639 and 1640, he was in a similar position in Hanover and Hildesheim. Schütz continued to compose, whether he was away directing the music for a foreign court or at home in Saxony trying to do the best he could to preserve what was left of the musical establishment there. In 1636 and 1639, he published two books of *Kleine geistliche Concerte* (little sacred concerti), church music written for performance forces appropriate for the times—one to five solo voices and organ.

On May 21, 1645, Schütz wrote a letter to the elector, requesting retirement from active service as Kapellmeister so that he could devote himself to completing various musical compositions; however, Johann Georg did not permit his music director to retire at this time and persistently ignored or rejected similar requests from Schütz over the next eleven years. In 1647, Schütz published the second part of his *Symphoniae sacrae*, consisting of large-scale works that he had written earlier for performance in Copenhagen. In the next year, he published *Geistliche Chormusik* (sacred choral music), a very influential collection of twenty-nine motets in five to seven parts, vocal and instrumental, which emphasized independent polyphonic writing. The third book of *Symphoniae sacrae*, published in 1650, included works written for larger performing forces than Schütz had employed since *Psalmen Davids* of 1619.

Schütz's desire to retire from active direction of musical performances at the court was realized only when Johann Georg died in 1656; his son and successor, Johann Georg II, granted the seventy-one-year-old composer his pension and the retention of the title of Senior Kapellmeister. Even though Schütz retired to Weissenfels and wrote works for the new elector only on special occasions, he remained very active. He visited the Dresden court three or four times a year, traveled and assisted with music at other courts, revised and expanded his *Becker Psalter*, and continued to produce new compositions, including several important works of the oratorio type.

Two authentic portraits of Schütz exist, one a formal court pose, painted by Christoph Spetner when the composer was about sixty-five. The other is an anonymous miniature in oils, dated 1670, which shows the eighty-five-year-old composer with the lines of age clearly visible in his face but with a strong stance and intense gaze giving evidence of a still vital and forceful personality. At about the same time that this portrait was painted, Schütz returned to Dresden to spend his last days. On November 6, 1672, he suffered a fatal stroke. His funeral was held on November 17 at the Frauenkirche, with members of the court chapel performing some of his compositions. He was buried in a place of honor near the chancel of the church.

SIGNIFICANCE

Schütz was both the greatest German composer of the seventeenth century and one of the most important and influential figures in the musical development of the entire Baroque era. He firmly established a musical style that combined German seriousness and sensitive treatment of text with Italian ideas of dramatic monody and the Venetian concerted and polychoral style. By so doing he shaped the direction that German Baroque music would take for the next one hundred years.

Over a long and active career, he composed in all of the genres of music used in his time except independent instrumental music. Unfortunately, many of Schütz's works have not survived; major eighteenth century fires in both Dresden and Copenhagen as well as the usual ravages of time were responsible for the destruction of many of his manuscripts, including the opera and ballet scores he is known to have produced. Despite the evidence of his composition of secular music, it is clear that his greatest interest and contribution was in the field of church music.

Approximately five hundred works by Schütz are extant, most of them included in the fourteen collections that were published during his lifetime. Among these collections, all but the first, his book of madrigals, consist of religious pieces, mainly settings of biblical texts. Although he did set Latin texts, German was the language that Schütz used in the vast majority of his compositions, and scholars credit the skillful utilization of this language for much of the incisive strength and feeling of urgency contained in Schütz's music.

The period from the beginning of the seventeenth century until the middle of the eighteenth century is an important time in German Protestant music, sometimes described as the golden age of Lutheran church music. It is clear that Schütz stands as the dominant figure at the beginning of this major development in Baroque music.

—*Byron A. Wolverton*

FURTHER READING

Moser, Hans Joachim. *Heinrich Schütz: A Short Account of His Life and Works.* Edited and translated by Derek McCulloch. New York: St. Martin's Press, 1967. A concise version of the author's definitive 1959 study. Gives a clear account of Schütz's life and brief discussions of his major works with some musical examples.

_____. *Heinrich Schütz: His Life and Work.* Translated by Carl F. Pfatteicher. St. Louis, Mo.: Concordia, 1959. A monumental biography of the composer that treats both his life and his compositions in great detail. This is the standard work in an excellent English translation. Includes illustrations, lists of works, and extensive musical examples.

Petzoldt, Richard, and D. Berke. *Heinrich Schütz und seine Zeit in Bildern.* Kassel, Germany: Barenreiter, 1972. A most interesting and helpful collection of pictures and reproductions related to Schütz and his time. Arranged chronologically and accompanied by a commentary in both English and German.

Schütz, Heinrich. *The Letters and Documents of Heinrich Schütz, 1656-1672: An Annotated Translation.* Edited by Gina Spagnoli. Ann Arbor, Mich.: UMI Research Press, 1989. Presents letters and documents from the second half of Schütz's life in the original German with English translations and critical commentary.

Skei, Allen B. *Heinrich Schütz: A Guide to Research.* New York: Garland, 1981. A valuable source on Schütz and his time. The main part of this work is a 632-item annotated and classified bibliography that covers not only Schütz's life and works but also the general and musical background of his time, his reputation, and the performance of his works since his death.

Smallman, Basil. *Schütz.* New York: Oxford University Press, 2000. The first comprehensive English-language biography of Schütz to be published in many years. Smallman provides a chronological account of Schütz's life and the creation of his musical compositions.

SEE ALSO: Francesca Caccini; Arcangelo Corelli; Carlo Gesualdo; Jean-Baptiste Lully; Claudio Monteverdi; Johann Pachelbel; Barbara Strozzi.

RELATED ARTICLES in *Great Events from History: The Seventeenth Century, 1601-1700:* c. 1601: Emergence of Baroque Music; February 24, 1607: First Performance of Monteverdi's *La favola d'Orfeo;* c. 1673: Buxtehude Begins His Abendmusiken Concerts.

MADELEINE DE SCUDÉRY
French writer and poet

Scudéry, the preeminent novelist of the seventeenth century, wrote multivolume novels that were famous for their depictions of noted social and political figures and for their elaborate plots; she was a leading member of the précieux *movement. Her other writings, such as letters, conversations, and moral essays, illustrated good manners, worthy conversations, appropriate behaviors, and other mores for schoolchildren as well as adults.*

BORN: November 15, 1607; Le Havre, France
DIED: June 2, 1701; Paris, France
ALSO KNOWN AS: Madame de Scudéry; Sappho (moniker)
AREA OF ACHIEVEMENT: Literature

EARLY LIFE

Madeleine de Scudéry (mahd-lihn deh skew-day-ree), the only surviving daughter of Georges de Scudéry and Madeleine de Martel de Goutemesnil, was born in Le Havre, where her father was captain of the port. She and her elder brother Georges were orphaned in 1613 and then raised by an uncle in Rouen. This uncle had been a courtier to three different kings and was neighbor to a founder of the Académie Française (French Academy), writer Valentin Conrart. Being under their uncle's care broadened the children's cultural exposure.

Madeleine, in particular, benefited from her uncle's attention. He took particular care with her education, ensuring she received the education that was typical for a young woman of the lower gentry. Most young ladies were taught how to write, draw, spell, paint, and dance. However, Madeleine also learned Italian and Spanish, read the ancient histories of figures such as Herodotus, and learned about contemporary art and literature. Conrart has credited her also with knowledge of agriculture, illness, remedies, cooking, gardening, and running a household. Material for her novels came out of these diverse educational achievements; various characters and backgrounds are drawn from her extensive reading.

Scudéry moved to Paris in 1637 to join her brother. He had left the military a few years before, and in 1635, he published a play that earned him some celebrity as a playwright. This celebrity ensured his acceptance into the Parisian salons, and in turn it ensured that his sister would be accepted as well. The most famous of these salons was the Hôtel de Rambouillet, hosted by the marquise de Rambouillet. Shortly after Scudéry's arrival, she became a regular participant there, and its culture proved beneficial for her writings. She developed characters based on the lives of the well-known people who participated in the salons, also praising or deploring the social customs of the time.

LIFE'S WORK

In 1641, Scudéry's first novel, *Ibrahim: Ou, L'Illustre Bassa*, was published in four volumes under her brother's name; it was translated into English in 1652 as *Ibrahim: Or, The Illustrious Bassa*. Publishing under Georges's name, or anonymously, became Scudéry's practice. Her authorship, even though it was not claimed in print, was an open secret, especially among her friends within the salons. Her other novels include *Artamène: Ou, Les Grand Cyrus* (ten volumes, pb. 1649-1653; *Artamenes: Or, The Grand Cyrus*, 1653-1655) and *Clélie: Histoire romaine* (ten volumes, pb. 1654-1661; *Clelia: An Excellent New Romance*, 1678). The last volume of *Artamenes* contains her story "L'Histoire de Sapho" (*The Story of Sapho*, 2003). Her other short stories, or *nouvelles*, include "Célinte, Nouvelle première" (1661, published anonymously), "Mathilde d'Aguilar" (1667, published anonymously), "La Promenade de Versailles" (published 1669), "Les Bains des Thermopyles" (published 1680, in volume 2 of *Conversations sur divers sujets* [*Conversations upon Several Subjects*, 1683], and "L'Histoire du Comte d'Albe" (1684, in *Conversations*).

Scudéry also published essays and is credited with the following: "Les Femmes illustres: Ou, Les Harangues héroiques" (published under the name of Georges, 1642; *Les Femmes illustres: Or, Twenty Heroick Harangues of the Most Illustrious Women of Antiquity*, 1693),

"Discours de la gloire," "Les Conversations morales," *Conversations sur divers sujets* (1680), and *Conversations nouvelle sur divers sujets* (1684). The *Conversations* were used as textbooks of manners and decorum for gently bred girls in seventeenth century schools. The works were influential for more than a century, and as late as the end of the eighteenth century, didactic educator and religious writer Hannah More (1745-1833) criticized their portrayal of *précieux* (refined) culture.

The work of the novels, and then the *nouvelles* and the moral essays, exceeds Scudéry's knack for sensing French literary tastes; they also serve as extraordinary depictions of the principles of salon culture. For her contemporary audience, she provided models of the kinds of behavior that would lead to a pleasant social life and would allow people to approximate *précieux* culture for themselves. For modern readers, she provides a glimpse of the cultural moment of King Louis XIV. In addition, her works are filled with portrayals of well-known contemporaries, such as Madame de Sévigné. These portrayals provided, in the opinion of literary critic Nicolas Boileau-Despréaux, one of the chief reasons for the popularity of Scudéry's works.

Her poetry is not collected in its entirety because much of it no longer exists. She wrote most of her poems extemporaneously, often part of impromptu poetry-writing games at salon gatherings. Her poetry that does exist is available mainly because it was quoted in surviving correspondence or memoirs. Of her two best-known impromptu works, one was dedicated to Louis XIV and the other to the Great Condé, who led the Fronde (Wars of the Fronde) uprising. Her published general writings also contain some poetry; *Clélie* contains an elegy on love, and the *Conversations* include more didactic poems.

Scudéry not only illustrated salon life but also led a salon. Before the Fronde, the best-known salon was the Hôtel de Rambouillet, which continued after the Fronde. Around this time as well, Scudéry began her own salon, known as the Samedi (French for "Saturday"), the day the salon met. She held the gatherings at her home in the Marais section of Paris, where she lived for about fifty years. Like the other salons, her salons gathered for amusement. Guests would participate in extemporaneous poetry contests or arrange trips to interesting places in Paris or pay surprise visits to friends in the country. The Samedi was known to be popular with the bourgeoisie, which gives the impression that it was a gathering of the "mediocre." Rather, at the time, "bourgeoisie" was a term for society's elite.

In 1671, she won the prize for "eloquence" from the French Academy, the first year the prize was offered. At the time, she was sixty-four years old and had been hearing impaired for about a decade. Scudéry died in 1701 in Paris, at the age of ninety-three.

SIGNIFICANCE

Scudéry was the most popular European novelist of the seventeenth century. She supported herself, and her brother while they lived together, with the proceeds from her writings and the patronage that rewarded her writing and conversation. Her works have been translated into Italian, English, German, Spanish, and Arabic.

Contemporary writers across Europe were familiar with her novels and used them as cultural references in their own works, making the works understandable to their readers. Near the end of the 1660's, as literary tastes about the novel, especially, changed, Scudéry's literature was criticized for its lengthiness and immorality and for its futile attempts to portray the spirit of seventeenth century France through characters set in antiquity.

With the acceleration of changes in literary taste, critics of the eighteenth century and later have judged her novels to be unreadable, judgments that had exiled into obscurity Scudéry's life and work. However, in the early twenty-first century, she has been receiving critical attention. Because she was one of the earliest of the female novelists, as well as an early popular novelist, her fiction writing is being reexamined. In addition, her writings reveal a theory of rhetoric based on conversation, placing her among the earliest modern female rhetoricians.

—Clare Callaghan

FURTHER READING

Aronson, Nicole. *Mademoiselle de Scudéry.* Translated by Stuart R. Aronson. Twayne's World Author Series: A Survey of the World's Literature 441. Boston: Twayne-G. K. Hall, 1978. A comprehensive reevaluation of Scudéry's life and work, with synopses of her novels and other writings.

Donawerth, Jane, ed. *Rhetorical Theory by Women Before 1900.* Lanham, Md.: Rowman & Littlefield, 2002. This anthology places Scudéry within the early tradition of women developing rhetorical theory. In particular, Scudéry is placed among other seventeenth century women who published strong arguments in favor of women's voices, such as Margaret Fell and Bathsua Makin.

Donawerth, Jane, and Julie Strongson, trans. and eds. *Madeleine de Scudéry: Selected Letters, Orations, and Rhetorical Dialogues.* Chicago: University of Chicago Press, 2004. This work, part of the Other Voice in Early Modern Europe series, provides four translations of twenty orations from "Les Femmes illustres," analyzing and illuminating Scudéry's rhetorical theory. The selections represent Scudéry's thoughts on conversation across several of her writings, from the speeches through the letters. The annotations help convey both the breadth of her learning and the depth of her wit, especially puns.

Merrick, Jeffrey, and Michael Sibalis, eds. *Homosexuality in French History and Culture.* New York: Harrington Park Press, 2001. The chapter "Female Friendship as the Foundation of Love in Madeleine de Scudéry's 'L'Histoire de Sapho,'" by Leonard Hinds, discusses how the poet Sappho was interpreted in the literature of seventeenth century France and how Scudéry approached the topic of friendship and love in her own work. Includes bibliography and index.

Sainte-Beuve, C. A. *Portraits of the Seventeenth Century: Historic and Literary.* Translated by Katharine P. Wormeley. New York: Frederick Ungar, 1964. The author, Sainte-Beuve, a nineteenth century literary scholar and critic, highlights the lives of literary and historical figures. The essay about Scudéry is notable because it was written at a time when her literary reputation was low. In his portrait, Sainte-Beuve shows Scudéry to be a woman of great learning, but his discussion of her work is charitable only.

Scudéry, Madeleine de. *The Story of Sappho.* Translated and introduced by Karen Newman. Chicago: University of Chicago Press, 2003. Part of the Other Voice in Early Modern Europe Series, a translation of Scudéry's "L'Histoire de Sapho." Includes bibliographical references.

SEE ALSO: Nicolas Boileau-Despréaux; The Great Condé; Madame de La Fayette; François de La Rochefoucauld; Louis XIV; Marquise de Rambouillet; Madame de Sévigné.

RELATED ARTICLE in *Great Events from History: The Seventeenth Century, 1601-1700:* Beginning 1690's: Movement to Reform Manners.

SEKI KŌWA
Japanese mathematician and government official

Seki Kōwa was a key figure in the development of premodern Japanese mathematics. The expansion of commerce under Tokugawa rule created a new need for practical mathematical accounting techniques. Seki and his student Takebe Katahiro were leaders in developing such techniques, and they independently duplicated some major discoveries of leading Western mathematicians, such as Gottfried Wilhelm Leibniz and Sir Isaac Newton.

BORN: March, 1642; Fujioka, Kozuke province, Japan
DIED: October 24, 1708; Edo (now Tokyo), Japan
ALSO KNOWN AS: Seki Takakazu
AREAS OF ACHIEVEMENT: Mathematics, government and politics

EARLY LIFE

Seki Kōwa (sehk-ee koh-wo) was born in 1642, the second son of Uchiyama Shichibei. Uchiyama had been an adviser to a once-powerful domain lord who fell out of favor with the shogun ten years before Seki's birth, and that lord was forced to commit suicide. As a result, Uchiyama's own future prospects were in doubt. Consequently, it may have significantly benefited Seki when he was adopted at an early age by a well-placed samurai named Seki Gorozaemon.

There were a number of retainers in attendance at Gorozaemon's mansion, and they took care of young Seki and kept him company. One day, one of these retainers was reading a book on abacus calculation that happened to attract Seki's attention. The retainer taught Seki the basics of abacus use, and Seki then obtained an abacus and worked through all the exercises in the book on his own. From that point on, he spent most of his waking hours learning as much about mathematics as he could, from every book he could obtain. Seki is known to have studied Yoshida Mitsuyoshi's *Jinkōki* (1627; *Book of Large and Small Numbers*, 2000), working through it page by page on his own.

It was the custom at that time for Japanese mathematicians to write books containing some mathematical problems without solutions, as a challenge for readers. One book Seki read, containing one hundred challenging problems by another brilliant young mathematics prodigy, Isomura Yoshinori, stimulated Seki to work out solutions to all one hundred problems. Throughout his career, Seki worked out original solutions to mathematics

problems by Isomura and others, though he seems not to have created many such problems himself.

Seki obtained a modest official position as an accountant at the Edo mansion of Tokugawa Tsunashige, the domain lord of Kōfu, in modern Yamanashi prefecture. When Tsunashige was made the heir to the reigning shogun, Tokugawa Ietsuna, Seki rose in status along with the rest of Tsunashige's household. In addition to his accounting work, Seki served as the mathematics tutor of the offspring of Tsunashige, his retainers, and other Edo aristocrats.

LIFE'S WORK

The chances of Seki Kōwa's patron Tokugawa Tsunashige becoming shogun were reduced over time as the result of court intrigues by his rivals, and this in turn lowered Seki's own prospects for advancement in Edo. Tsunashige died in 1678, two years before Ietsuna, but this in fact turned out to enhance Seki's prospects. Tokugawa Ienobu, Tsunashige's son, to whom Seki had given lessons and for whom he had subsequently worked as accountant, was in a much better position at the shogun's court than Tsunashige had been. Ienobu succeeded to the position of domain lord of Kōfu in 1678, and he was later adopted as the heir of Shogun Ietsuna's successor, Tokugawa Tsunayoshi, in 1704. Ienobu did not actually become shogun until 1709, a year after Seki's death, but Seki's close relationship with Ienobu assured him a good position as an accountant and tutor at the shogun's court. He enjoyed this position in Edo from 1678 to 1708, providing Seki with both the leisure and the resources he needed to conduct his research.

The early Tokugawa era was an important developmental period for mathematics in Japan. The Tokugawa shogunate had restored order to the country after more than 150 years of civil war. Commerce had once again begun to develop and flourish, and this created a pressing national need for accounting, inventory, and other commercial and financial forms of record-keeping. Practical mathematics had fallen into relative disuse in Japan, so the latest techniques were imported from China. A number of new abacus schools *(soroban-juku)*, using Chinese methods, soon began to appear in Edo, the Kyōto-Ōsaka area, and elsewhere.

One of these abacus schools was run by Mōri Shigeyoshi, a former samurai *(rōnin)* said to have fought on the losing side against the Tokugawas. Mōri was the author of the earliest Japanese mathematics book still extant, the *Warizansho* (1622; writings on division), though it was actually a general abacus calculation manual. Yoshida Mitsuyoshi, who had learned mathematics at Mōri's academy, became the mathematics tutor of the feudal domain lord of Kumamoto and wrote a derivative work of his own, the *Jinkōki*. Because Chinese methods still largely focused on basic abacus calculation methods, however, aspiring Japanese mathematicians began to see a need to move beyond this stage. Building on the familiar Chinese base, these mathematicians created a new set of uniquely Japanese mathematical techniques, known as *wasan*.

Yoshida Mitsuyoshi had established his reputation as a mathematical scholar and tutor to the aristocracy, so it was relatively easier for Seki to achieve the same sort of status a generation later. Most of Seki's posthumous fame, in fact, resulted from accounts of his life and work by his aristocratic students. Unlike most of his contemporaries, Seki did not actively seek to publicize his own mathematical accomplishments. In fact, though he wrote many manuscripts on mathematics, Seki published only one book during his lifetime, *Hatsubi sanpō* (1674), a book of solutions to mathematical problems.

Among Seki's aristocratic students were Takebe Katahiro and Katahiro's older brother Katakira, the sons of an important official at the shogun court in Edo. Together with Seki, they worked on an encyclopedic study of all current Japanese mathematical knowledge, the *Taisei sankei* (1710; collection of classic mathematical texts). It took twenty-eight years to complete this twenty-volume work, which was finally published two years after Seki's death.

Among Seki's other pioneering accomplishments in Japanese mathematics, he developed a workable system of algebraic notation, a theory of determinants, and a formula for calculating the circumference of a circle. Seki also approximated roots of higher-order equations and is believed to have discovered the concept eventually named "Bernoulli numbers" even before Jakob I Bernoulli did. Seki also developed a form of calculus and anticipated important discoveries by Gottfried Wilhelm Leibniz and Sir Isaac Newton.

Takebe Katahiro is considered by historians to be Seki's true intellectual heir, who refined and further developed his teacher's mathematical ideas and methods. Katahiro carefully went through Seki's many manuscripts, systematizing his ideas and preserving his writings for future generations. Katahiro also wrote his own mathematics books and made additional independent

discoveries, succeeding Seki as the court mathematician for several more shoguns until his own death in 1739. The period of more than six decades during which Seki and his students dominated mathematics in Edo assured the continued predominance of Seki's methods and concepts, until Western mathematics replaced traditional Japanese mathematics completely.

SIGNIFICANCE

From the seventeenth century to the second half of the nineteenth century, the field of Japanese mathematics was dominated by *wasan*, as developed by Seki Kōwa, Takebe Katahiro, and others. *Wasan* was also the form of mathematics initially chosen by Japanese modernizers for use in the national school system, until it was officially replaced by European-style mathematics in 1873. A preexisting knowledge of *wasan* methods actually functioned as a bridge to the future, serving as the foundation upon which Meiji-era students were able to learn the new Western style of mathematics. Like Seki and his followers, many nineteenth century *wasan* experts were also from the samurai class, well-placed and well-educated people who often made the transition to become teachers of the new Western-style mathematics.

Kikuchi Dairoku (1855-1917), a pioneer in developing the study of modern mathematics in Japan, began learning Western mathematics at an early age, but later, as a leading mathematics teacher in Japan, he took advantage of his students' basic *wasan* knowledge, using it as a basis on which to teach them equivalent new Western methods. Fujisawa Rikitarō (1861-1933), one of Kikuchi's earliest students who had learned *wasan* as a child, subsequently became a leading figure in modern Japanese mathematics. Far from dismissing the importance of the *wasan* methods developed by Seki Kōwa, Fujisawa gave lectures on those methods in Japan and Europe. When the Tokyo Sugaku Kaisha, the first modern mathematical society in Japan, was established in 1877, more than half of its members had originally been *wasan* mathematicians.

—*Michael McCaskey*

FURTHER READING

Horiuchi, Annick. *Les mathematiques japonaises a l'epoque d'Edo, 1600-1868: Une étude des travaux de Seki Takakazu, ?-1708, et de Takebe Katahiro, 1664-1739*. Paris: Mathesis, 1994. A four-hundred-page study of the work of Seki and Takebe, the only book on this subject so far in a Western language.

Morris-Suzuki, Tessa. *The Technological Transforma-

tion of Japan: From the Seventeenth to the Twenty-first Century. New York: Cambridge University Press, 1994. Contains an essay on Tokugawa technological development.

Nakayama, Shigeru. *Academic and Scientific Traditions in China, Japan, and the West*. Tokyo: University of Tokyo Press, 1984. A standard comparative history of scientific thought and research by a leading Japanese authority.

Smith, David, and Mikami Yoshio. *A History of Japa-nese Mathematics*. Mansfield Center, Conn.: Martino, 2002. The definitive history of Japanese mathematics up to the early twentieth century in English.

SEE ALSO: The Bernoulli Family; Gottfried Wilhelm Leibniz; Sir Isaac Newton; Tokugawa Tsunayoshi.

RELATED ARTICLES in *Great Events from History: The Seventeenth Century, 1601-1700:* 1651-1680: Ietsuna Shogunate; 1680-1709: Reign of Tsunayoshi as Shogun.

MADAME DE SÉVIGNÉ
French writer

Sévigné was a prolific letter writer who corresponded with friends about political and military events, French urban society, and the court at Versailles. She made literary judgments on most of the writers of her time, and she was a keen observer of nature and the arts. Her letters represent an entertaining but still critical introduction to seventeenth century French culture.

BORN: February 5, 1626; Paris, France
DIED: April 17, 1696; Grignan, Provence, France
ALSO KNOWN AS: Marie de Rabutin-Chantal (given name); Marie de Sévigné
AREA OF ACHIEVEMENT: Literature

EARLY LIFE

Madame de Sévigné (mah-dahm deh say-veen-yay), born Marie de Rabutin-Chantal, was left an orphan at age six and brought up by an uncle, the abbé de Coulanges, whose life was devoted to her interests. She was born in the Place Royale in Paris, and much of her young life was spent at the family château at Livry. At the château, she was educated in a manner uncommon for women of that time, being exposed to the arts as well as language (Spanish, Latin, and Italian).

At an early age, Sévigné was introduced to the Hôtel de Rambouillet, a salon hosted by the marquise de Rambouillet, where the elite met to discuss topics of the day, including society life and literature. She readily embraced the salon's intellectual tastes, but at the same time she retained a bold freedom of speech and manner, unlike the refined spirit of the salon. Her special friend was Mademoiselle de la Vergne, later Madame de La Fayette. Her instructors were Jean Chapelain and Gilles Ménage, both frequent visitors to the salon. Chapelain, a poet, scholar, and pedant, taught her language, familiarized her with the poetry of Vergil and Torquato Tasso, and gave her a critical taste for letters. Ménage aspired to be a man of the world and a savant. He reportedly fell in love with Sévigné, and she called him "friend of all friends, the best" in one of her letters.

LIFE'S WORK

On August 4, 1644, at the age of eighteen, she married Henry, marquis de Sévigné, a Breton from a good family. They resided in the Sévigné manor house, Les Rochers.

Madame de Sévigné. (The Granger Collection, New York)

MADAME DE SÉVIGNÉ'S LETTER ON A TRAGIC DINNER AT LOUIS XIV'S COURT

King Louis XIV held a festive dinner to honor his military commander, the Great Condé, upon Louis's declaration of war against the Dutch in 1671. The prince of cooks, Monsieur Vatel, killed himself after the evening did not go as well as planned. The following account of the dinner party and of Vatel's suicide comes—matter-of-factly—from the letters of Madame de Sévigné.

The promenade, the collation [gathering] in a spot carpeted with jonquils [flowering herbs],—all was going to perfection. Supper came; the roast failed at one or two tables on account of a number of unexpected guests. This upset [chef] Vatel. He said several times, "My honor is lost; this is a humiliation that I cannot endure. . . ."

Midnight comes. The fireworks do not succeed on account of a cloud that overspreads them (they cost sixteen thousand francs). At four o'clock in the morning Vatel is wandering about all over the place. Everything is asleep. He meets a small purveyor with two loads of fish and asks him, "Is this all?" "Yes, sir" [Vatel had expected much more for the next day's meal]. . . . Vatel goes up to his own room, puts his sword against the door, and runs it through his heart, but only at the third thrust, for he gave himself two wounds which were not mortal. He falls dead.

Gourville [a court assistant], however, tried to repair the loss of Vatel, and did repair it. The dinner was excellent; so was the luncheon. They supped, they walked, they played, they hunted. The scent of jonquils was everywhere; it was all enchanting.

Source: Madame de Sévigné (letters), excerpted in *Readings in European History*, edited by James Harvey Robinson (Boston: Atheneum Press, 1906), pp. 378-380.

Generally, the letters she originated, especially those to her daughter, are lengthy. She wrote during a time when newspapers were scarce. Gossip of all sorts appears among her subjects, and some of her most famous letters are purely journalistic reporting, whereas others deal with private matters. Her works can be considered "charming" and sometimes show traces of a quaint, affected style with occasionally incorrect phraseology according *to the strict standards of the Académie Française*. Her narration is lively and her expression of domestic and maternal affection is said to be unequaled. She had an eye for minute observation; an appreciation of amusements, pageants, and diversions; and a deep sense of the beauty of nature. She also had a strong inclination toward theology.

Madame de Sévigné portrayed herself clearly and unconsciously, expressing a maternal love filled with joy. Her daughter—more attractive, more learned, and more accomplished than her mother—was nevertheless cold, reserved, haughty, and timid. When Sévigné's daughter moved to Provence with her new husband, the comte de Grignan, Sévigné began the series of letters that made her famous and that shed a direct light on a generation in France. The gossip of the court and the news of her friends were gathered to amuse her daughter, with incidents both insignificant and important. The detail sketched in her letters mirrors the world about her and gives the letters their historical value.

Sévigné's life and nature also are revealed in the letters. She had a taste for society, friendship, and gaiety, as well as for seclusion. She found consolation in books, especially those dealing with morals. Her favorite authors were poet Pierre Corneille and fable writer Jean de La Fontaine Sévigné hosted her own salon, the Hôtel de Carnavalet, which became one of the social centers of the latter part of the seventeenth century.

Among those who were most influential in Sévigné's life was Corbinelli, friend, counselor, and confidant, who devoted his life to letters and the interests of his

A daughter, Françoise Marguerite (the future Madame de Grignan), was born on October 10, 1646, followed by a son, Charles, born in 1648.

After her husband's death in 1651, Madame de Sévigné returned to Paris and spent about ten years in a house in the Place Royale. On January 29, 1669, she married François d'Adhmar, count of Grignan, from one of the noblest families in France.

The letters of Madame de Sévigné, primarily to Madame de Grignan, her daughter, were vivid, allowing the reader to picture life during the seventeenth century. Prior to her frequent correspondence to her daughter, most of her letters were addressed to her cousin Bussy Rabutin, until a misunderstanding about money brought about a quarrel. Sévigné's letters number between sixteen hundred and seventeen hundred, one-third of which are replies of other persons, letters addressed to her, or letters of her family and friends dealing with the subjects of her correspondence.

friends. He compared her letters to those of Cicero. Among her intimate female friends were Madame de La Fayette and later Madame de Coulanges, wife of a cousin of the marquis de Sévigné.

Sévigné's letters were copied and handed out, sometimes under specified titles, as early as 1673. None was published, however, until after her death, when her correspondence with her cousin Bussy was included in his memoirs and correspondence after her death in 1696 and the following year. The remainder did not see publication for thirty years.

SIGNIFICANCE

Madame de Sévigné's copious letters, primarily addressed to her daughter, painted pictures of seventeenth century life, incidents both significant and trivial, grand and mundane, in a style and directness that were admired by her contemporaries as well as modern readers and writers. Virginia Woolf, in an essay on Sévigné, wrote that when we read Sévigné, "we become aware, with some sudden phrase, about spring, about a country neighbour, something struck off in a flash, that we are, of course, being addressed by one of the great mistresses of the art of speech."

—*Marcia J. Weiss*

FURTHER READING

Farrell, Michele Longino. *Performing Motherhood: The Sévigné Correspondence.* Hanover, N.H.: University

Press of New England, 1991. Farrell examines Sévigné's letters to her daughter. The chapter "Sévigné's Apprenticeship," however, discusses the correspondence with her cousin Bussy. Includes detailed notes and Farrell's translations.

Fowlie, Wallace. *French Literature: Its History and Its Meaning.* Englewood Cliffs, N.J.: Prentice-Hall, 1973. A brief but classic survey of French literature.

Ojala, Jeanne A., and William T. Ojala. *Madame de Sévigné: A Seventeenth-Century Life.* New York: St. Martin's Press, 1990. The authors provide a useful biography of Sévigné, a detailed chronology, a genealogical chart, and a bibliography.

Racevskis, Roland. *Time and Ways of Knowing Under Louis XIV: Molière, Sévigné, Lafayette.* Lewisburg, Pa.: Bucknell University Press, 2003. Racevskis discusses how Sévigné's writing style and her way of thinking were often affected by everyday time constraints, including the postal service, social obligations, and even uncertainty in politics.

SEE ALSO: Jean-Baptiste Colbert; Pierre Corneille; Marie le Jars de Gournay; Madame de La Fayette; Jean de La Fontaine; François de La Rochefoucauld; Ninon de Lenclos; Louis XIV; Duchesse de Montpensier; Marquise de Rambouillet.

RELATED ARTICLE in *Great Events from History: The Seventeenth Century, 1601-1700:* 1682: French Court Moves to Versailles.

SHABBETAI TZEVI
Jewish mystic

Shabbetai, considered the most important of Judaism's false messiahs, founded the Shabbetian movement, which had eager followers during an era of renewed persecution of Jews. He taught a Kabbala type of mysticism that emphasized inner union with the divine. Imprisoned by the Turks in 1666, he converted to Islam to save his life.

BORN: August 1, 1626; Smyrna, Ottoman Empire (now İzmir, Turkey)
DIED: September 17, 1676; Dulcigno, Albania (now Ulcinj, Montenegro)
ALSO KNOWN AS: Sabbatai Sevi; Sabbatai Zevi; Sabbatai Zebi; Kapici Bashi; Keeper of the Gate
AREA OF ACHIEVEMENT: Religion and theology

EARLY LIFE

Shabbetai Tzevi (SHAHB-beh-tit-SAY-vee) was born into a family of merchants in İzmir, a prosperous city on the western coast of what is now Turkey. One has to be careful in evaluating details of his life as legendary or authentic. Such is the case with his birth date. It was common for someone born on the Sabbath to receive the name Shabbetai.

It was also common that a bright child in such a well-to-do family be dedicated to the study of the Torah. By the age of eighteen, Shabbetai was ordained a rabbi, though he never had a congregation of his own. Instead, he continued to study the Zohar and other writings of Jewish mysticism known as Kabbalism. He especially focused on the writings of Isaac ben Solomon Luria, who a century earlier had offered messianic interpretations.

Shabbetai was never much of a writer, but he was able to gather a following through his charismatic personality. Many people flocked to the synagogues to hear his melodious voice as he chanted the daily prayers. His dedication and piety were unrivaled. His asceticism was so extreme that two marriages were annulled when he failed to consummate them. He spent long hours in prayer and often took part in midnight ritual baths in the sea.

Also, he gained the reputation of an eccentric. Scholar Gershom Scholem has suggested that he had bipolar disorder (manic-depression). During his higher periods of illumination he had visions of the *shekinah*, the divine presence, and responded by uttering the divine name, an act that was blasphemous for practicing Jews. In response to criticism, he began to speak of a newfound freedom from the law. In 1651, by a decision of local rabbis, he was exiled from İzmir, and he spent the next decade traveling; he continued to gather a following in Salonica and Istanbul.

LIFE'S WORK

The expectation of the coming of the Messiah was high in Shabbetai's day. It was a time of renewed suffering among Jews. A number of Jewish scholars had speculated about the Messiah's appearance in 1648. Instead, 1648-1649 was marked by the Chmielnicki massacres in Poland, where thousands of Polish Jews were killed by the region's Cossacks. Because the Messiah was expected to arrive after a terrible disaster, hopes of his arrival continued to grow, and the date was pushed back to 1666. The date of 1666 also fascinated European Christians, who believed in the possible return of Jesus the Messiah; the number 666 is in the book of Revelation.

In the Gaza region of Palestine, a young Jewish rabbi named Nathan Ghazzati (later called Nathan the Prophet of Gaza) announced in January, 1665, that he had experienced a vision revealing to him the identity of the Messiah. Because of his character as a scholar and as a well-respected preacher of repentance, his word was taken seriously. He reported that the vision was a bright light that continued for twenty-four hours, adding that words came to him from heaven: "Thus says the Lord, behold your savior comes, Shabbetai Tzevi." However, his instructions were not to reveal Shabbetai's name until the following summer.

Shabbetai had come to Jerusalem in 1662, but he and Nathan had never met. Nathan had been engaged in rabbinic study while Shabbetai had devoted himself to the ascetic life and prayer with long trips in the Judean wilderness. When Jerusalem's Jewish community fell upon hard times because of demands to pay the Turkish government exorbitant sums of money, Shabbetai was sent to Egypt to raise funds. He remained there two years, developed a close relationship with members of the Jewish community there, and was apparently successful in his mission. Only after word of Nathan's vision arrived in Cairo was Shabbetai sent to Gaza along with two other delegates to investigate who this newly revealed Messiah might be. Shabbetai was said to have laughed in response to the word that he was the one, but he was soon convinced of its truth.

For many this independent declaration of Shabbetai's messiahship was proof of its authenticity. Others claimed it was an orchestrated event. Shabbetai had earlier reported his own visions. In one vision, the biblical patriarchs appeared anointing him as Messiah. On March 31, 1664, in Cairo, Shabbetai had taken part in a controversial symbolic marriage. His new wife, Sarah, had been a survivor of the Chmielnicki massacre, and as a child also had gained the reputation as a prophet. Moving to Amsterdam in the Netherlands as an orphan, she announced her destiny to marry the Messiah. For some, the marriage in Cairo between Sarah and Shabbetai was a sign. For others, it was another dramatic action by Shabbetai.

At the festival of Pentecost on May 31, 1665, the declaration of Shabbetai as Messiah was made public. During the synagogue worship, Nathan began chanting over and over, "Heed Nathan. Heed Shabbetai Tzevi, my beloved." Shabbetai took for himself the titles Anointed of the God of Jacob and AMIRAH (our lord and king, his majesty be exalted) and signed his named with the symbol of a holy serpent, the numerical equivalent of the word "messiah." His first declaration was that the traditional Jewish fasts should be abolished and that people should instead celebrate. After years of disappointment and rejection, Jews everywhere rejoiced that the Messiah had come. Nathan called for repentance and set a date in June, 1666, for the culmination of Messianic activity.

Initial opposition came primarily from the Jewish rabbis of Jerusalem, who excommunicated him and banned him from the holy city. By the time Shabbetai arrived back in İzmir in December, 1665, reports circulated of prophetic activity in various Jewish communities from Cairo to Aleppo in Syria and from Constantinople to Amsterdam and Hamburg. Women were encouraged to read the Torah in synagogue services. There also were rumors of migration of Jews, including the lost ten tribes of Israel, back to Palestine. Shabbetai showered royal titles on fellow believers and spoke of taking the rule from the Turks. Nathan's own writings, however, emphasized that this was a peaceful movement. There would be no warfare, only the singing of hymns and praying.

After a celebratory Hanukkah in İzmir in which Shabbetai appeared at the synagogue in royal robes, banqueted with forbidden foods, and spoke aloud the name of God, he set sail for Constantinople. However, Shabbetai never arrived. His boat was intercepted by Turkish troops, and he was arrested. For nine months he was imprisoned at Gallipoli, a seaport along the Italian coast, where he continued to issue edicts to a growing mass of followers.

His showdown with the Turkish sultan occurred on September 16, 1666. Some speculated that he would take the crown for himself. Instead, he announced his conversion to Islam, taking the name Kapici Bashi, and accepted a position as a gatekeeper for the sultan. This action has led to continued debate. For his opponents, this was evidence enough that he was a fraud. For some of his followers, their newfound hopes crumbled; some apostatized. Other followers defended his actions, saying that Shabbetai was willing to give himself up rather than to bring further suffering on his people. Others, such as Nathan of Gaza, explained that this was all part of the divine plan, as the now-hidden Messiah worked to bring about the redemption of Gentiles while the Jewish community dedicated itself to repentance and deeper faith.

For the next decade, Shabbetai remained a mysterious character, keeping both Jewish and Muslim prayers—a Muslim for the Turks and a Jew for his followers. The Shabbetian movement continued to flourish. Shabbetai was eventually exiled to Dulcigno in Albania until his death in 1676.

SIGNIFICANCE

Many look at the story of Shabbetai Tzevi as a tragedy. Others see it as an example of the dark side of religion, suggesting his deceptive and self-serving character. Yet the Shabbetian movement continued to thrive even after the demise of its leader.

Shabbetai managed to offer hope in a time of extreme difficulties, while the Jews of Europe continued to experience exile, alienation, and persecution. His focus on faith and inner feeling rather than legal prescriptions and external actions attracted people to his message, a message that superseded his character flaws. For many, his message helped them succeed even in the face of external failure.

—Fred Strickert

FURTHER READING

Freely, John. *The Lost Messiah: In Search of the Mystical Rabbi Sabbatai Sevi.* Woodstock, N.Y.: Overlook Press, 2003. A popular account based primarily on the work of scholar Gershom Scholem. The author, a travel writer, makes the story interesting through his own acquaintance with the cities where Shabbetai flourished.

Schaefer, Peter, and Mark R. Cohen, eds. *Toward the Millennium: Messianic Expectations from the Bible to Waco.* Leiden, the Netherlands: E. J. Brill, 1998. A collection of sixteen scholarly presentations, including several specifically on Shabbetai, from a symposium on messianic movements.

Scholem, Gershom. *Sabbatai Sevi: The Mystical Messiah.* New York: Littman, 1997. Originally written in Hebrew in 1957 and published in English in 1976, this volume remains the standard resource on this topic. The author takes a scholarly approach, evaluating every contemporary letter, document, and liturgical book written in response to Shabbetai and the movement.

SEE ALSO: Manasseh ben Israel; António Vieira.
RELATED ARTICLES in *Great Events from History: The Seventeenth Century, 1601-1700:* 1656-1662: Persecution of Iranian Jews; January, 1665: Shabbetai Tzevi's Messianic Movement Begins.

FIRST EARL OF SHAFTESBURY
English politician

After serving several Interregnum regimes, Shaftesbury played an important role in the Restoration of Charles II and then served in several administrative capacities. In the 1670's, he broke with Charles II over foreign and religious policies and became the opposition leader. He organized an effective political faction, later called the Whigs, that provided the foundation for party politics in England.

BORN: July 22, 1621; Wimborne St. Giles, Dorset, England

DIED: January 21, 1683; Amsterdam, United Provinces (now in the Netherlands)

ALSO KNOWN AS: Anthony Ashley Cooper (given name)

AREA OF ACHIEVEMENT: Government and politics

EARLY LIFE

The first earl of Shaftesbury (SHAFS-bur-ee) was born Anthony Ashley Cooper on July 22, 1621, to a rich, important, and well-connected Dorset family. His father, Sir John Cooper, had been made a baronet, and his mother, Anne, inherited extensive estates from her father, Sir Anthony Ashley. This marriage represented a union between two prominent families, and when he was raised to the peerage himself, Cooper initially chose the title Lord Ashley in honor of his maternal grandfather.

Cooper's mother died in 1628 and Sir John followed in 1631, leaving young Anthony and the family estates to the mercy of the Court of Wards. Cooper later claimed that he lost upward of twenty thousand pounds during his wardship. After receiving his early education from tutors, Cooper entered Exeter College, Oxford. From there he proceeded to the Inns of Court and Lincoln's Inn for some grounding in the law. This was the typical educational pattern for young gentlemen of his day, and in keeping with accepted practices he did not take a degree. Instead, in February, 1639, he married Margaret Coventry, the daughter of Thomas, first Baron Coventry, the lord keeper of England. The match drew young Cooper into the court circle and was, by the standards of the day, highly advantageous. In addition to being wealthy and well connected, Cooper was witty, kind, charming, intelligent, and very ambitious. He appeared to be a young man on the move when Charles I was forced to hold elections for what came to be known as the Short Parliament.

Despite being underage, Cooper was returned to Parliament from Tewkesbury. After the Short Parliament was dissolved, he was elected to the Long Parliament from Downton, Wiltshire. The election was disputed and not settled until 1660, so it is doubtful that he took his seat until just before the Restoration. As England divided between king and Parliament, Cooper first followed his in-laws into the Royalist camp. Present at Nottingham when Charles raised his standard, Cooper served the Royalist cause with both horse and foot regiments, including one raised at his own expense.

Cooper met with Charles I in early 1643 and presented a rather fanciful plan for winning over the Parliamentary garrison in Dorset as a prelude to ending the Civil War. Charles gave qualified approval to the scheme, but Cooper quickly discovered the king's insincerity in his dealing with France. Frustrated and disturbed, he switched sides in early 1644 and became Parliament's commander in his home county.

From the end of the First Civil War until the latter years of the Rump Parliament, Cooper confined himself to his estates and county affairs. After serving on a commission for law reform in 1652, he was made a member of the Barebones Parliament in mid-1653. Given that assembly's sectarian nature, his presence was, to say the least, somewhat unusual, and his role in its dissolution in December, 1653, is clearly in character. Although sympathetic to unorthodox religious opinions, Cooper was first of all a representative of the landed ruling class. It was in that capacity that Cooper came to serve the Protectorate of Oliver Cromwell. He saw Cromwell as the main hope for social and political stability and went so far as to urge him to take the Crown. Cooper was returned to the Protectorate Parliaments from Wiltshire but was denied his seat in 1656 as a result of a disagreement with Cromwell over the proper role of Parliament.

Following Margaret's death, Cooper had concluded another beneficial match with the sister of the earl of Exeter. She died within three years, however, and during the Protectorate Cooper had designs on one of Cromwell's daughters. When that match failed, he turned to another Margaret, the niece of the Royalist earl of Southampton. This favorable match allowed Cooper to hedge his bets against a future Stuart revival. At the same time, Margaret proved to be a devoted spouse even after Cooper's fall and death.

After Cromwell's death, Cooper returned to politics cautiously, developing important ties with General George Monck and being careful not to commit to the

Royalist cause prematurely. With Monck, he had a crucial role in arranging a peaceful Restoration of Charles II and rightfully expected to be rewarded for his troubles. Monck's support was critical in securing his appointment to the Privy Council and the peerage as Baron Ashley. Shortly thereafter, he became chancellor of the Exchequer.

LIFE'S WORK

For several years, Baron Ashley served as an active but junior member of Charles II's government, more a senior bureaucrat than a policymaker. In addition to his responsibilities at the Exchequer, he was a member of the Committee for Plantations. He held a similar post under Cromwell and became quite active in trade and colonization issues. He developed close ties with commercial interests in the City and was one of eight proprietors for the Carolina Colony established in 1663.

When Southampton, the lord treasurer, died in 1667, Ashley was one of five men appointed to the Treasury Commission that replaced him. This appointment brought him close to the power and influence he coveted, but Ashley misread the king and supported the earl of Clarendon too long. Only his ability and his value as a link to former Parliamentarians saved Ashley's position, and he needed several years to recover from this setback.

After Clarendon's fall, Charles's government was dominated by a group of ministers pejoratively known as the Cabal: Thomas, Lord Clifford (first Baron Clifford of Chudleigh); Henry Bennet, first earl of Arlington; George Villiers, second duke of Buckingham; Anthony, Lord Ashley; and John Maitland, duke of Lauderdale. The Cabal was not actually a unified group, and the king did not include all five on every issue. Ashley, for example, knew nothing of the secret Treaty of Dover that Charles arranged with France in 1670. Given his long opposition to Catholicism, Ashley could not have been brought into the king's full confidence. He did, however, support the Third Anglo-Dutch War that grew out of Charles's policy, seeing it as advantageous for English commerce.

In 1672, Charles II made Ashley the earl of Shaftesbury and lord chancellor. The new earl, however, was about to enter the most important phase of his career as the leader of the opposition to the king and his policies. He had expressed for several years concern about the Catholic James, duke of York, succeeding Charles. Now convinced that Charles had deceived him about his policies toward France, Shaftesbury supported the 1673 Test Act, designed to bar Catholics from appointive positions. He also facilitated a resolution by the Commons trying to block James's marriage to the Catholic Mary of Modena. He was ousted as lord chancellor in November, 1673, and lost all other national and local positions by the following May.

Within a year, Shaftesbury was clearly the leader of the opposition, calling for the dissolution of the Cavalier Parliament and for frequent elections in the future. Both measures would reduce the Crown's influence and alter the nature of politics. He proclaimed that he would not accept office unless Charles's policies changed. This was designed to assure supporters that his position was based on principle, not simply ambition.

Parliament met twice in 1675, with Shaftesbury and his supporters successfully frustrating government plans and forcing Charles to prorogue both sessions. A tactical blunder landed the earl in the Tower, courtesy of the House of Lords, when Parliament reconvened in early 1677, but the following year Titus Oates's outlandish tales of a Popish Plot gave Shaftesbury his great opportunity. Although he did not invent the plot, Shaftesbury opportunistically exploited the anti-Catholic hysteria it engendered.

SHAFTESBURY'S MAJOR WORKS

1699	*An Inquiry Concerning Virtue in Two Discourses* (unauthorized edition; also published as *An Inquiry Concerning Virtue or Merit*)
1702	*Paradoxes of State, Relating to the Present Juncture of Affairs in England and the Rest of Europe*
1708	*A Letter Concerning Enthusiasm*
1709	*Sensus Communis: An Essay on the Freedom of Wit and Humour*
1709	*The Moralists: A Philosophical Rhapsody*
1710	*Soliloquy: Or, Advice to an Author*
1711	*Characteristicks of Men, Manners, Opinions, Times* (3 volumes; includes *A Letter Concerning Enthusiasm, Sensus Communis, The Moralists,* and *Soliloquy*)
1713	*A Notion of the Historical Draught or Tablature of the Judgment of Hercules*
1714	*A Letter Concerning the Art or Science of Design*
1716	*Several Letters Written by a Noble Lord to a Young Man at the University*

By early 1679, Charles was forced to dissolve the Cavalier Parliament to save his chief minister, Thomas Osborne, first earl of Danby and later first duke of Leeds, and call new elections. Shaftesbury now concentrated on getting Parliament to pass a bill excluding James from the succession, producing the Exclusion Crisis of 1679-1681 and three general elections.

The key to Shaftesbury's effort was his creation of an extensive political organization in Parliament and among the public. Based on the Green Ribbon Club, this developed into England's first coherent political party, the Whigs. Although the elections for the Parliament that met in March, 1679, were not fought over exclusion, by 1681 the Whigs had built up an effective national network. Supporters of the Crown had, in turn, been forced to adopt similar tactics, bringing the Tory Party into existence.

Shaftesbury made exclusion the Whigs' goal and refused to compromise or allow other issues to distract his followers. He also kept his movement a parliamentary one. Although the Whigs made effective use of petitions to the king in 1680, Shaftesbury did not want the struggle to spill into the countryside, as had happened in the early 1640's.

Shaftesbury believed that Charles would surrender if faced with determined and consistent opposition. With Parliament effectively paralyzed, the king would have to accept exclusion to obtain money. Shaftesbury misjudged the situation badly on several counts. First, the normally indolent king stood firm and refused to cave in. Second, Charles's power to prorogue and dissolve Parliament could deprive the Whigs of their arena when necessary. Third, unbeknown to Shaftesbury, Charles's financial position was secure thanks to administrative reforms, retrenchment, and French subsidies. The Whigs could pass exclusion bills in the Commons, but only the king could bring the Lords to accept such a measure, and he stood firm.

Memories of the Civil War and Interregnum were fresh enough during the Exclusion Crisis that both sides proceeded carefully. Tory propaganda focused on the threat to order that the Whigs posed. In March, 1681, Charles summoned the Third Exclusion Parliament to meet in the Royalist stronghold of Oxford rather than Whiggish London. A number of opposition figures, including Shaftesbury, came to Oxford with armed supporters, making Tory claims appear valid. After another exclusion bill was introduced in the Commons, Charles surprised the Whigs with a sudden dissolution. The session destroyed Shaftesbury's strategy for forcing Charles's hand, killed exclusion, and left the Whigs in shambles. Unable and unwilling to resort to force, Shaftesbury's movement collapsed.

Shaftesbury was sent to the Tower in June and brought before a London Grand Jury on charges of treason in November, 1681. Thanks to a Whig sheriff, the friendly jury refused to indict him. Still, the earl was a marked man, and when Tories got control of the City government in 1682, Shaftesbury was forced to flee. He went to Amsterdam in December and died less than two months later.

SIGNIFICANCE

The first earl of Shaftesbury was an ambitious and at times unscrupulous politician who switched sides several times over the course of his career. Although he sought power and influence, he was by no means devoid of principles and sought to serve the interests of his nation and class as he understood them. He was a sincere supporter of religious toleration and believed in the importance of Parliament. He was unwilling to accept any increase in royal absolutism, just as he opposed republicanism.

Had ambition and personal gain been his primary motive, Shaftesbury would have made his peace with Charles II. The king clearly expected him to mute his dislike of government policies when he granted the earldom. Again in 1679, Charles brought Shaftesbury into the government as Lord President of a reconstituted Privy Council. Shaftesbury refused to be bought off, despite the fact that he could easily have turned the position into that of chief minister.

Shaftesbury's greatest achievement was to introduce party politics and organization into English political life. His Whigs were not a modern party based on mass support, but they did exhibit a coherent system of organization and coordination both in and beyond Parliament. Despite interruptions, English party politics dates from the Exclusion Crisis.

Finally, Shaftesbury served as John Locke's patron from 1666 until his death. Their relationship was sufficiently close that Locke felt compelled to follow the earl into exile. Locke served Shaftesbury as an adviser, secretary, and physician, and the two men influenced each other's thoughts. Many of Locke's works reflect what Shaftesbury sought to accomplish in politics and were written to support Shaftesbury's activities. Locke's loyalty indicates that Shaftesbury did, in fact, seek those ends that Locke and the Whigs of the Glorious Revolution enshrined in 1688.

—Vinton M. Prince, Jr.

FURTHER READING

Clark, Sir George. *The Later Stuarts, 1660-1714*. 2d ed. New York: Oxford University Press, 1955. Reprint. Oxford, England: Clarendon Press, 1961. The basic, if somewhat dated, narrative for the most important parts of Shaftesbury's career.

Haley, K. H. D. *The First Earl of Shaftesbury*. Oxford, England: Clarendon Press, 1968. The definitive account of Shaftesbury's life and works. Very complete and detailed, it replaces W. D. Christie's *A Life of Anthony Ashley Cooper, First Earl of Shaftesbury* (1871) and Louise Fargo Brown's *The First Earl of Shaftesbury* (1931). Brown's work remains useful for commercial and colonial policy.

Hill, Christopher. *The Century of Revolution, 1603-1714*. New York: W. W. Norton, 1966. Reprint. 1982. A livelier and more provocative account of the Stuart years than Clark's, this work combines narrative and topical chapters. Touches all phases of Shaftesbury's career.

Hutton, Ronald. *The Restoration: A Political and Religious History of England and Wales, 1658-1667*. New York: Oxford University Press, 1985. A complete and current account and analysis of the Restoration era, with full coverage of Shaftesbury's role and activities.

Jones, J. R. *Country and Court: England, 1658-1714*. Cambridge, Mass.: Harvard University Press, 1978. An excellent account of England after Oliver Cromwell's death, with a full and enlightening treatment of Shaftesbury. Also useful but far more detailed is Jones's *The First Whigs: The Politics of the Exclusion Crisis, 1673-1683* (1961).

Kenyon, J. P. *Stuart England*. 2d ed. New York: Penguin Books, 1985. An interesting treatment of the seventeenth century that is particularly strong on Shaftesbury in opposition and the Popish Plot. For a detailed treatment of the plot, see Kenyon's *The Popish Plot* (1972).

Lee, Maurice, Jr. *The Cabal*. Urbana: University of Illinois Press, 1965. A good study of the politics and personalities of Charles II's reign from Clarendon's fall to Danby's ascendancy. Provides a useful summary of Shaftesbury's career before 1667 but appeared before Haley's biography and suffers accordingly.

Ogg, David. *England in the Reign of Charles II*. 2d ed. 2 vols. Oxford, England: Oxford University Press, 1956. Reprint. Westport, Conn.: Greenwood Press, 1979. The most complete study of Charles's reign. Remains an important source of information despite its age and Whiggish tone.

Seel, Graham E., and David L. Smith. *Crown and Parliament, 1558-1689*. New York: Cambridge University Press, 2001. Examines the nature and function of Parliament during the Stuart period.

Shotton, Joshua. "The Exclusion Crisis, 1678-81, and the Earl of Shaftesbury." *History* 47 (December, 2003): 33. Shotton defends Shaftesbury, maintaining he is a much-maligned figure who does not deserve his evil reputation.

Smith, David L. *The Stuart Parliaments, 1603-1689*. New York: Arnold, 1999. An account of parliamentary activities and functions during the Stuart monarchy.

SEE ALSO: Charles I; Charles II (of England); First Earl of Clarendon; Oliver Cromwell; James II; First Duke of Leeds; John Locke; Mary of Modena; George Monck; Titus Oates.

RELATED ARTICLES in *Great Events from History: The Seventeenth Century, 1601-1700:* November 3, 1640-May 15, 1641: Beginning of England's Long Parliament; 1642-1651: English Civil Wars; December 6, 1648-May 19, 1649: Establishment of the English Commonwealth; May, 1659-May, 1660: Restoration of Charles II; April 6, 1672-August 10, 1678: French-Dutch War; 1673-1678: Test Acts; August 13, 1678-July 1, 1681: The Popish Plot.

SHAH JAHAN
Emperor of India (r. 1628-1658)

Shah Jahan ruled the Mughal Empire at the culminating phase of its wealth and power, enabling him to act as an unequaled patron of Muslim art and architecture in the Indian subcontinent.

BORN: January 5, 1592; Lahore, India (now in Pakistan)
DIED: January 22, 1666; Āgra, India
ALSO KNOWN AS: Khurram (given name)
AREAS OF ACHIEVEMENT: Government and politics, patronage of the arts, architecture

EARLY LIFE

The future emperor Shah Jahan was the third son of the fourth Mughal Emperor of India, Jahāngīr. The child was given the name Khurram, which he retained until he mounted the throne in 1628. His mother was a Rājput princess, daughter of the maharaja of Jodhpur in western Rajasthan. Thus, Khurram was descended on his father's side from the great Central Asian warlords Genghis Khan and Tamerlane, a lineage that, over time, had been softened by the twin cultural influences of Islam and Persia. On his mother's side, he inherited the warlike traditions of the Hindu Rājputs. His Persian education consisted of penmanship and calligraphy, poetry and belles-lettres, Arabic grammar and rhetoric, and some Chaghatay Turkish, together with the practical skills of the warrior and the hunter.

From an early age, Khurram would have understood that no strict rule of primogeniture stood in the way of a younger brother's usurping an elder brother's place in matters of the succession. Jahāngīr's eldest son and natural heir, Khusru, forfeited his father's trust when, even during his grandfather Akbar the Great's reign, he allowed himself to be put forward as a rival to his father by an unsuccessful court cabal. Thereafter, Jahāngīr never trusted him. After Jahāngīr's accession in 1605, Khusru engaged in further futile conspiracies and was kept under close surveillance. He was eventually placed in Khurram's custody by Jahāngīr in a drunken stupor. Khurram quickly got rid of his prisoner by killing him in cold blood in Burhanpur in 1621, although he ensured that the appropriate public obsequies were observed.

By this time, Khurram had emerged as the obvious successor to Jahāngīr, and with Khusru out of the way, he had little to fear from his elder brother Parviz or his younger, Shahryar, except as pawns in the hands of his enemies. His father, Jahāngīr, was essentially a weak man, vain and capricious, who, early in his reign, had become infatuated with a beautiful Persian woman, Nūr Jahān, whose husband he had murdered so that he could marry her. Nūr Jahān proceeded to advance the interests of her family, especially of her energetic and ambitious brother, Asaf Khan. At first, the Nūr Jahān clique threw their influence behind Khurram, and in 1611 Khurram was betrothed to Asaf Khan's daughter, Arjumand Banu Begum (later to be known as Mumtaz Mahal). The couple had four sons and two daughters who survived infancy. In 1609, Khurram had married a Persian woman descended from the Ṣafavid ruling house, and in 1617, he married a third woman, the granddaughter of a prominent Mughal nobleman.

As Jahāngīr sank into an opium eater's senility, the Nūr Jahān clique realized that Khurram was beyond their control, and they belatedly cast around for an alternative. When Jahāngīr died near Lahore in 1627 (his eldest surviving son, Parviz, had died in the previous year), Khurram himself was far away, campaigning in the Deccan (central India). Nūr Jahān, therefore, attempted to have Khurram's younger brother, Shahryar, who had married her daughter, enthroned, but Asaf Khan, her brother, defeated the forces raised by Nūr Jahān and Shahryar, captured Shahryar, and effectively rendered his sister powerless. Meanwhile, Khurram, by this time hurrying north, sent instructions to Asaf Jah to blind Shahryar and four other rivals. On January 28, 1628, Khurram was proclaimed emperor and assumed the name Shah Jahan (king of the world). Shortly afterward, all five captive princes were executed. Shah Jahan, thirty-six years old, was indubitably master of the Mughal Empire, but he had waded to the throne through his kinsmen's blood.

LIFE'S WORK

Shah Jahan's early years established his reputation as an active soldier, an able administrator, and a wily politician. For the next thirty years, he ruled the Mughal Empire at the apogee of its power, wealth, and splendor, seeking to expand its frontiers in all directions while undertaking a most ambitious program of public works, including a new capital. Seeking to elevate the concept of Mughal kingship, Shah Jahan deliberately harked back to his Central Asian ancestors. Like Tamerlane, he assumed the title of Sahib-i Qiran (lord of the fortunate conjunction of the planets); it was during his reign that Tamerlane's possibly spurious memoirs were translated from Turkish into Persian; and he himself went to great efforts to attempt the reconquest of Tamerlane's ancestral homeland, now in Uzbek hands.

In matters of court ceremony, he set a more formal tone than either Akbar or Jahāngīr, commissioning for himself the construction of the Peacock Throne, which was to become the focal point of the monarchy and which took seven years to fabricate. Even the Taj Mahal, built as a mausoleum for his wife Mumtaz Mahal, who died in 1631, was at once an epitome of dynastic splendor (the entire complex involved vast expenditure and took seventeen years to complete) and a statement of the emperor's Islamic piety. Unlike his father Jahāngīr, a dissolute and lax ruler, or his grandfather, Akbar, heterodox and wayward in matters of religion, Shah Jahan was a strictly orthodox Sunni Muslim who felt no empathy for his Shia Muslim or Hindu subjects.

At the death of Akbar in 1605, the Mughal Empire had consisted of all northern and central India north of the Tapti River, but there remained areas that were only partly integrated into the administrative system and were still controlled by local tribes and lineages. Shah Jahan determined to consolidate this internal frontier. He vigorously harried the tribes of lower Sind and the marches of Baluchistan, and he annexed the Baglana state south of Gujarat and enforced the submission of its Rājput ruler. He mercilessly crushed the ruling line in Bundelkhand, in the course of which his armies penetrated Gondwana to the southeast. On the northern frontiers, Shah Jahan's tenacity enforced, with difficulty, his overlordship of Gahrwal and Baltistan; in the northeast, imperial rule was confirmed in Kuch Bihar and Kamrup on the Brahmaputra, although the emperor was forced to recognize that the Ahom kingdom, formed by Shan tribesmen who had moved from upper Burma down the Brahmaputra, lay beyond his grasp.

In the south, Shah Jahan's gains were more substantial. In the northwestern Deccan, the sultanate of Ahmadnagar, long a thorn in the Mughals' flesh, was the object of vigorous campaigning during 1630 and 1631, leading to the fall of the citadel of Daulatabad in 1632. Thereafter, Ahmadnagar was fully integrated into the imperial

system, with a provincial governor, bureaucracy, and the standard Mughal revenue system. In 1635, Shah Jahan sent embassies to the more distant sultans of Bijapur and Golconda, demanding their submission. Too weak to reject such pressure, they prevaricated, acquiescing in a dependent status while doing everything possible to keep the reality of Mughal authority at arm's length. Shah Jahan's third son, Aurangzeb, as viceroy of the Deccan, fought hard to break their spirit, but Shah Jahan, perhaps fearing his son's ambitions, never permitted him the resources to complete the task. By the end of Shah Jahan's reign, both sultanates were in effect still independent.

Great though the empire's resources were, they were not inexhaustible, and they were severely strained by Shah Jahan's Central Asian ambitions. Qandahār, in southern Afghanistan, marked the border between Mu-

Shah Jahan embraces his dying wife. (Hulton Archive/Getty Images)

ghal India and Ṣafavid Persia and was a bone of contention between these predatory monarchies. Jahāngīr had lost it to Shah ʿAbbās the Great in 1622, but it passed back into Mughal hands in 1638, when its Ṣafavid governor defected to the Mughal side. In 1648, Shah ʿAbbās II (r. 1642-1666) recaptured it. Mughal attempts to regain the stronghold in 1649, 1652, and 1653 all failed ignominiously.

Failure was also the price paid for Shah Jahan's ruinous attempt to reconquer his ancestral lands north of the Hindukush mountains. In 1646, a huge army was dispatched to Balkh in northern Afghanistan, ostensibly to adjudicate an Uzbek dynastic dispute but in fact to annex the city and province. For some months, the Mughals held Balkh, but in 1647, faced with Uzbek intransigence, a harsh terrain, and the logistical difficulties of supplying the army from Kabul, they were forced to withdraw.

In all this campaigning, Shah Jahan's sons served active apprenticeships in the field, vying with each other for commands, revenue, and prestige. Conventional wisdom accepted that the Mughal inheritance would pass to the prince endowed with superior military talent, good fortune, and the blessings of Allah. For years, each brother eyed his siblings with growing hostility. Shah Jahan kept his eldest and favorite son, Dārā, with him in the north, hoping no doubt that he would be well placed to employ the central organs of government to ensure a smooth transition. Of the other sons, Shujah was governor of Bengal, Aurangzeb was governor of the Deccan, and Murad was governor of Gujarat.

Shah Jahan's illness in September, 1657, perhaps marking the onset of senility, was the occasion for the predictably bloodthirsty struggle to break out. In the end, Aurangzeb's superior generalship and cooler head won the day. Dārā was taken and executed, as were his sons; Shujah and his family died as fugitives in Arakan; Murad too was executed; and Aurangzeb proclaimed himself emperor in 1658, with Shah Jahan still alive. Aurangzeb treated him harshly. The old man was incarcerated in the fort at Āgra, in a gorgeous suite of rooms that he himself had constructed in happier times, but he remained a closely confined prisoner. He died there in 1666 and was buried beside Mumtaz Mahal in the Taj Mahal, the great mausoleum he had constructed across the river from the fort.

SIGNIFICANCE

The thirty years of Shah Jahan's reign are regarded as the culmination of the material splendor and artistic achievement of the Mughal Empire. Judged by his patronage of architecture, which draws thousands today to view his monuments, Shah Jahan was the most munificent of builders. Aside from the Taj Mahal, arguably the most famous building in the world, he rebuilt the Āgra palace-fort, with its opulent Pearl Mosque, turning structures of red sandstone into ones of glittering white marble.

Delhi, the capital of the Muslim rulers of northern India since the early thirteenth century, he rebuilt completely on a partly new site, perhaps in emulation of Shah ʿAbbās the Great of Persia, who had laid out a lavish new palace-quarter in Eṣfahān. Shahjahanabad (today referred to as Old Delhi) was designed as the sumptuous capital of an expanding empire, with the Red Fort at its core, while the city's congregational mosque, the Jama Masjid, was to be the largest in India. Other major architectural undertakings included the fort at Lahore, the congregational mosque in Thatta (now in Pakistan), and the garden retreats on the Dal Lake in Kashmir.

In miniature painting and in the sumptuary arts of carpet and textile weaving, and in the fabrication of objets d'art in metal, ivory, jade, and jewelry, the artists of the reign have rarely been equaled, as can be seen in major museum collections, perhaps most particularly that of the Victoria and Albert Museum in London. Vast wealth in precious metals and jewels was accumulated in the Mughal treasury, exemplified by the Peacock Throne, glittering with emeralds, now largely destroyed but preserved in contemporary miniatures. A desiccated version, still encrusted with precious stones and surrounded by other Mughal treasures acquired by the Persian conqueror Nadir Shah during his sack of Delhi in 1737, is preserved in the Bank-i Melli in Tehran, Iran.

The age of Shah Jahan was marked by artistic splendor. However, one should not forget the predatory nature of the Mughal regime and the immense military expenditure authorized by Shah Jahan in unsuccessful attempts to recapture Qandahār and to hold Balkh and in expansive campaigns in the Deccan. These expenditures, together with his building program and the conspicuous waste of an ostentatious court, bled the empire dry. Government revenues were derived mainly from agriculture, and Shah Jahan's three decades of extravagance may well have created the circumstances that made inevitable the empire's impoverishment and gradual decline.

—*Gavin R. G. Hambly*

FURTHER READING

Asher, Catherine. *Architecture of Mughal India.* New York: Cambridge University Press, 1992. The best account of Shah Jahan as a builder and patron of architecture, with accompanying ground plans, diagrams, and photographs.

Beach, M. C., E. Koch, and Wheeler Thackston. *King of the World*. London: Azimuth Editions, 1997. Selected translations from a major chronicle, the *Padshah-nama*, of Abdul Hamid Lahawri, accompanied by sumptuous illustrations of what is perhaps the most splendid surviving Mughal manuscript, now in England's Royal Library at Windsor Castle.

Begley, Wayne E. "The Myth of the Taj Mahal and a New Theory of Its Symbolic Meaning." *Art Bulletin* (March, 1979): 7-37. This important article lays to rest the legend that the Taj Mahal was built as a monument to conjugal love. It was an act of state proclaiming the splendor of the dynasty as well as an act of piety conceived as a symbolic statement affirming the truths of the Muslim faith.

Begley, Wayne E., and Z. A. Desai, eds. *The Shah Jahan Nama of Inayat Khan*. Delhi: Oxford University Press, 1990. An abridged version of one of the most detailed and important chronicles of the reign.

Bernier, François. *Travels in the Mogul Empire, A.D. 1656-1668*. Translated by Archibald Constable. Westminster, England: Archibald Constable, 1891. Reprint of 2d rev. ed. Delhi, India: Low Price Publications, 1989. The observations of the Frenchman Bernier are among the liveliest and most perceptive of European travel writers who visited Mughal India. Essential reading for its portrait of mid-seventeenth century India.

Blake, Stephen. *Shahjahanabad, the Sovereign City in Mughal India, 1639-1739*. New York: Cambridge University Press, 1991. A study of the inception and development of Shah Jahan's new capital, with emphasis on dynastic involvement in urban planning and patronage.

Kozlowski, Gregory C. "Private Lives and Public Piety: Women and the Practice of Islam in Mughal India." In *Women in the Medieval Muslim World: Power, Patronage, and Piety*, edited by Gavin R. G. Hambly. New York: St. Martin's Press, 1998. Establishes the central role of Mughal court women, including Shah Jahan's formidable aunt by marriage, Nūr Jahān, his wives, and his two daughters, as patrons of architecture and urban renewal.

Lal, Muni. *Shah Jahan*. New Delhi, India: Vikas, 1986. A popular biography of the emperor.

Raj Kumar, ed. *India Under Shah Jahan*. New Delhi, India: Anmol, 2000. A collection of articles examining various aspects of Indian life during Shah Jahan's rule.

Saksena, Banarsi Prasad. *History of Shahjahan of Dihli*. Allahabad, India: Central Book Depot, 1962. A complete account of Shah Jahan's life. Packed with information, but somewhat dated in style.

SEE ALSO: ʿAbbās the Great; Aurangzeb; Jahāngīr; Kösem Sultan; Murad IV; Śivājī.

RELATED ARTICLES in *Great Events from History: The Seventeenth Century, 1601-1700:* 17th century: Rise of the Gunpowder Empires; 1602-1639: Ottoman-Ṣafavid Wars; 1605-1627: Mughal Court Culture Flourishes; 1619-1636: Construction of Samarqand's Shirdar Madrasa; 1629: Ṣafavid Dynasty Flourishes Under ʿAbbās the Great; 1632-c. 1650: Shah Jahan Builds the Taj Mahal; 1642-1666: Reign of Shah ʿAbbās II; 1658-1707: Reign of Aurangzeb; c. 1666-1676: Founding of the Marāthā Kingdom; 1679-1709: Rājput Rebellion; March 30, 1699: Singh Founds the Khalsa Brotherhood.

JAMES SHIRLEY
English poet and playwright

A poet and author of grammar texts, Shirley is primarily remembered as a prolific dramatist whose works dominated the London stage between 1625 and 1642. When the theaters reopened in 1660, after the Interregnum, many of his plays were revived and served as templates for the new generation of Restoration dramatists.

BORN: September 7, 1596 (baptized); London, England
DIED: October 29, 1666; London
AREAS OF ACHIEVEMENT: Literature, theater

EARLY LIFE

James Shirley was born in London, probably on September 3, 1596, and baptized four days later at Saint Mary Woolchurch. On October 4, 1608, he enrolled in London's Merchant Taylors' School, where he studied the standard classical curriculum for four years. During the next three years, he may have attended Saint John's College, Oxford, while also apprenticed to Thomas Firth, a scrivener. More certain is his 1715 matriculation at Saint Catherine's College, Cambridge, which awarded him a bachelor of arts degree two years later. Soon after, he was ordained in the Church of England. In the next seven years, Shirley studied for the master of arts degree at Cambridge, married Elizabeth Gilmet, had several children, and accepted a curacy in Hertfordshire. At some time prior to his thirtieth year, he probably converted to Catholicism, resigned his church position, and became headmaster of a Saint Albans grammar school.

Shirley's first published work was *Eccho: Or, The Infortunate Lovers* (1618), a long narrative poem that has not survived, though it could be the same work as *Narcissus: Or, The Self-Lover* (1646). The latter poem, published in *Poems &c. by James Shirley* (1646), is similar in form to William Shakespeare's *Venus and Adonis* (1593). Shirley continued to write poetry, gaining some renown as a Cavalier poet, one of the so-called Sons of Ben (Royalist acolytes of the poet-dramatist Ben Jonson), but in 1624, he went to London to become a playwright. His first play, *The School of Compliment* (pr. 1625, pb. 1631; also known as *Love Tricks: Or, The School of Compliments*), was presented in 1625 at the Phoenix, in Drury Lane; it is a satiric comedy whose pastoral element recalls Shakespeare's *As You Like It* (pr. c. 1599-1600), and it was revived in the 1660's.

LIFE'S WORK

From 1625 to 1635, more than twenty Shirley plays were produced in London, mainly at the Phoenix, whose company enjoyed the patronage of Queen Henrietta Maria. When the plague hit the city in 1636, however, the theaters were closed, so Shirley went to Ireland, where he wrote for John Ogilby's Saint Werburgh Street playhouse, in Dublin. Shirley's comedy *The Royal Master* (pr. 1637, pb. 1638) may have been the first play performed when the new theater, the first outside London, opened in 1637.

Upon returning to London in the spring of 1640, Shirley succeeded Philip Massinger as chief dramatist of the King's Men at the Blackfriars Theatre, but his tenure there was brief: In September of 1642, Oliver Cromwell's Puritan forces closed the theaters. Before the closure, the King's Men had performed three of Shirley's plays; a fourth, *The Court Secret* (wr. 1642, pb. 1653, pr. after 1660), remained in manuscript, though it may have been revised and staged in 1664 as *The Secret*.

With Cromwell's rebellion and the outbreak of the English Civil War, Shirley's career as a playwright came to an end, though he lived to see productions of his works in the early 1660's. During the rebellion, Shirley fought on the Royalist side outside London, and when the Civil War ended in 1645, he returned to the city and resumed his teaching career. He apparently married a second time, and over the next two decades, he published Latin grammars, poetry, and a collection of his plays. When the Great Fire hit London in October, 1666, Shirley and his second wife, Frances, fled to the parish of Saint Giles-in-the-Fields, in Middlesex, where they died—perhaps from effects of the blaze—on October 29, 1666.

The most popular playwright of his time, Shirley wrote in more different dramatic genres than any of his contemporaries. His revenge tragedies recall those of such predecessors as Thomas Kyd and John Webster; his city comedies are in the Thomas Dekker and Thomas Middleton tradition; his humors comedies are indebted to Ben Jonson; and his tragicomedies are in the manner of Francis Beaumont and John Fletcher. In other words, his plays are derivative, for Shirley was not an innovator. Notwithstanding the similarities between his plays and others', however, he was more original than most of his peers, who often borrowed from each other with impunity, and there rarely is a single, direct source for any of his plays. Among the many he wrote, three are most noteworthy: the comedies *Hyde Park* (pr. 1632, pb. 1637) and *The Lady of Pleasure* (pr. 1635, pb. 1637), and the tragedy *The Cardinal* (pr. 1641, pb. 1652); *The Wedding* (pr. 1626?, pb. 1629), an early work, also is of special interest.

An initial success in 1626, occasionally revived and reprinted several times before the closing of the theaters, and popular during the Restoration period, *The Wedding* is a Fletcherian tragicomedy. Typical of its genre, it has multiple plots, serious and comic, that progress relatively independently, albeit with a common focus upon marriage. One subplot functions as a comic contrast to the serious (and potentially tragic) love story of the main plot. In the play are rival suitors, disguise, apparent death, madness, and the bed switch trick—all familiar elements from earlier drama. Tragicomedy is a hybrid form that lacks death but brings people to the brink of it, so it evokes a contradictory mix of responses and lacks the realism and sophistication of comedies of manners; *The Wedding* is a lesser work partly because of its genre.

A much better play, *Hyde Park* is an urbane comedy of manners in which Shirley presents a realistic picture of Cavalier London during the reign of King Charles I. Initially popular, it also was revived in the Restoration. The action—which spans just one day—has three plots that concern a love triangle involving a woman and two men who compete for her affection, and each plot illustrates in turn different types of comedy, including intellectual, sentimental, and situation comedy. Dealing as it does with London's upper classes and their milieu, *Hyde Park* differs from the middle-class city comedies of Dekker and Middleton, and although its love chase intrigues anticipate Restoration comedies of manners, Shirley's rake reforms and Caroline standards of sexual propriety are observed.

Of the same genre is *The Lady of Pleasure*, which presents variations on the honor theme and also may be a commentary upon the Platonic love cult in Queen Henrietta Maria's court. Shirley depicts his characters' movement from folly and libertinism to repentance and reformation, and he celebrates honor, innocence, and moderation, while at the same time presenting the shallowness of upper-class lives. Though less popular than his other comedies, *The Lady of Pleasure* is historically significant, because Richard Brinsley Sheridan borrowed from it the characters and scandal school conceit for his comedy *The School for Scandal* (pr. 1777, pb. 1780).

Only four of Shirley's extant plays are tragedies, of which the best is *The Cardinal*. A direct literary descendant of Kyd's *The Spanish Tragedy* (pr. c. 1585-1589,

pb. 1594?), the prototypical Elizabethan revenge tragedy, *The Cardinal* includes all of the elements that became hallmarks of the genre: murder of a rival by a jealous lover, assistance for the murderer by a Machiavellian villain whose goal is to gain advancement and/or wealth, feigned (or actual) madness presumably caused by grief, a play within a play, and revenge as a controlling motive.

Shirley's prologue to *The Cardinal* is somewhat satiric and teases the audience by speculating whether the play is a comedy or tragedy and suggesting they are about to see the former, which may reflect his uneasiness at offering the sophisticated Blackfriars crowd a new work in the old-fashioned revenge tragedy mode. Popular through the 1630's and revived with considerable success during the Restoration period, the play is one of Shirley's few successes that simply recalls past stage practices and does not concurrently anticipate those of the next age.

SIGNIFICANCE

The length, variety, and productivity of Shirley's career as a dramatist only partly account for his historical significance. Arguably his most important achievement

James Shirley. (Hulton Archive/Getty Images)

was to demonstrate the adaptability and enduring timeliness of the devices, character types, and themes that his predecessors had introduced. Whether writing for public or private theaters, for varied or aristocratic audiences, Shirley fashioned appropriately his themes, plots, and characters—no mean accomplishment for someone who had neither the talent nor the inclination to innovate. Equally important, this major playwright at the end of one era became a leading figure in the next, after an eighteen-year interregnum. Therefore, to Shirley must go a modicum of credit for the continuing vitality of the Caroline stage and the ease with which drama was restored in the 1660's.

—*Gerald H. Strauss*

FURTHER READING

Clark, Ira Granville. *Professional Playwrights: Massinger, Ford, Shirley, and Brome.* Lexington: University Press of Kentucky, 1992. An analysis of how four early seventeenth century playwrights, working within constraints society imposed, produced dramas rife with social criticism.

Forsythe, Robert Stanley. *The Relation of Shirley's Plays to the Elizabethan Drama.* New York: Columbia University Press, 1914. An authoritative study of Shirley's place in the Renaissance drama and of his indebtedness to predecessors.

Lucow, Ben. *James Shirley.* Boston: Twayne, 1981. A concise overview of Shirley's life followed by detailed analyses of the individual works that take into account the range of previous scholarship.

Nason, Arthur Huntington. *James Shirley: Dramatist.* New York: Nason, 1915. The passage of time has not lessened the importance of this comprehensive study of Shirley's life and work, which has not been superseded.

Sanders, Julie. *Caroline Drama: The Plays of Massinger, Ford, Shirley, and Brome.* Plymouth, Mass.: Northcote House, 1999. A brief study of how the plays of four major dramatists reflect the social and political milieu of Caroline London.

Zimmer, Ruth K. *James Shirley: A Reference Guide.* Boston: G. K. Hall, 1980. This comprehensive annotated bibliography of Shirley's works and writings about him also has a useful sketch of his life.

SEE ALSO: Charles I; Oliver Cromwell; Thomas Dekker; John Fletcher; Henrietta Maria; Ben Jonson; Thomas Middleton; John Webster.

RELATED ARTICLES in *Great Events from History: The Seventeenth Century, 1601-1700:* 1642-1651: English Civil Wars; September 2, 1642: Closing of the Theaters; May, 1659-May, 1660: Restoration of Charles II; September 2-5, 1666: Great Fire of London.

SHUNZHI
Emperor of China (r. 1644-1661)

Shunzhi was the first emperor of the Qing Dynasty. The Qing were Manchus, but Shunzhi was attracted to many aspects of Chinese culture and was criticized after his death for abandoning his Manchu heritage. He was the father of Kangxi, one of the greatest rulers in China's long history.

BORN: March 15, 1638; Manchuria (now in China)
DIED: February 5, 1661; Beijing, China
ALSO KNOWN AS: Shun-chih (reign name, Wade-Giles); Fulin (given name, Pinyin), Fu-lin (given name, Wade-Giles)
AREA OF ACHIEVEMENT: Government and politics

EARLY LIFE

Shunzhi (shoon-jih), whose given name was Fulin, was born in 1638. His grandfather, Nurhaci, was a Manchu-

rian of noble birth who had, by 1610, emerged as a leader among the Manchus, descendants of the Jin, who ruled China in the twelfth century. In 1616, Nurhaci declared himself the leader of a second Jin dynasty. By the 1620's, Nurhaci and the Manchus occupied the Shengking region (now Liaoning province), an area claimed by China's Ming Dynasty (1368-1644). Nurhaci died in 1626, and his eighth son, Abahai (Hong Taiji), succeeded him, establishing a new dynasty called the Qing, meaning "pure" or "clear." Much of Ming China was under the control of rebel bands, and several Ming generals deserted to the Manchus. Abahai died in 1643, and Fulin, his ninth son, became his heir, with Abahai's younger brother, Dorgon, as regent.

The following year, the last Ming emperor, Chongzhen, hanged himself, and Dorgon and the Manchus, allied with the Ming general Wu Sangui, occupied Beijing and enthroned Fulin as emperor under the reign name Shunzhi. The Chinese character for *shun* is the same as "obedience," and the character for *zhi* means "to rule." Dorgon and the Manchus thus claimed the traditional "mandate of heaven" and the right to rule China, even though they were only approximately 2 percent of the total population.

LIFE'S WORK

Shunzhi was only six years old when he ascended the throne, and it was his uncle Dorgon, the regent, who ruled China for the next decade and who consolidated Qing control over much of the country. Although Shunzhi was proclaimed emperor, there were many Chinese, including high officials, who refused to accept another foreign dynasty, such as the Mongols or the Yuan Dynasty, who had ruled China before the Ming. In addition to this dissension by legitimate citizens, Dorgon had to face the rebels who had so weakened the Ming as to allow the Manchus to seize power. The two major rebel leaders, Li Zicheng and Zhang Xianzhong, were eliminated, the first in 1645, possibly by suicide, and the second in 1647 by Manchu troops.

Ming princes were also obstacles to Qing rule. The Ming prince of Fu attempted to negotiate with the Manchus, but when negotiations flagged, the prince and his Ming supporters established a military resistance around Nanjing, in central China. After the horrific Manchu sack of nearby Yangzhou, however, the defenders at Nanjing offered little opposition. The prince of Fu was captured and died in 1646 in Beijing. Canton in the south fell to the Manchu armies in 1647. The last major Ming prince, Zhu Youlang, retreated into the interior and finally to Burma. Under threat of a Qing invasion, the Burmese turned Zhu over to the Manchus, and in 1662, after Shunzhi's death, the last major Ming claimant to the imperial throne was strangled.

While regent for Shunzhi, Dorgon initiated one of the most controversial actions of Manchu rule: He ordered that all Chinese adopt Manchu dress and hairstyles. Traditionally, Chinese males wore their hair long as a sign of masculinity. The Manchus shaved their foreheads and braided their hair in the back, the so-called queue. There was considerable opposition to the order, but ultimately the Chinese were left with the choice of keeping their hair and losing their heads or losing their hair and keeping their heads. The queue remained controversial until the fall of the Qing in 1912. Males were also required to wear the Manchu high collar and tight jacket rather than the loose robes of the Ming, and Manchu women were forbidden to practice foot binding, the Chinese custom wherein the feet of young girls were tightly bound and thus deformed, supposedly to make them more attractive to males.

Military reforms implemented even before the Manchu conquest were continued during Shunzhi's reign. Nurhaci had established eight different military units, mostly Manchus, each identified by different colored banners. Under Shunzhi, eight banners were established in areas around Beijing. Hundreds of thousands of acres of agricultural land were confiscated by the new regime, much of it Ming family land, and each bannerman was given six acres to farm, with officers receiving larger allocations. Most Manchus were not farmers, and Chinese worked their lands, often under appalling conditions. By necessity, given the relatively small number of Manchus, the regime used as government officials those Chinese who had proven their loyalty to the new dynasty. It was, particularly during the first decades after the conquest, an uneasy relationship, as the Manchus did not entirely trust the Chinese, even those who seemingly collaborated with the new regime, and many Chinese had little respect for the Qing.

During the early years of Shunzhi's reign, Dorgon not only ruled for the young emperor but also dominated his fellow Manchus, removing the generals of the banners at will, building a fortress-palace outside Beijing, and demanding concubines from Korea. Dorgon died in 1650 while hunting, and after his death the dynasty seemed in danger of disintegrating and disappearing, as the Manchu elite began to war among themselves.

Although he was only twelve or thirteen, with Dorgon's death Shunzhi became emperor in his own right. He pursued the military policy of tracking down and eliminating the Ming claimants to the imperial throne, but he broke with Dorgon and most Manchu nobles in being more willing to adopt many Chinese customs and mores. He studied the Chinese language to enable himself to read court documents, and he was an admirer of Chinese plays and novels. Chinese Buddhist monks were welcomed at his court, as was a Catholic Jesuit missionary, Johann Adam Schall von Bell. Catholic missionaries, especially Jesuits, had been active in China during the latter decades of the Ming dynasty. Because of their knowledge of Western science, they had become advisers and confidants of the emperors, and Shunzhi appointed Schall as director of the Imperial Bureau of Astronomy. The Jesuit also became something of a father figure, as Shunzhi often referred to Schall as "Grandpa."

Shunzhi also gave the palace eunuchs, or castrated males, more authority and responsibility than they had had under Dorgon, to the disgust of the Manchu nobles, who saw this as an act of decadent corruption. The emperor deposed his first empress, Xiao Kang, in 1653. His second empress, Xiao Hui, did not die until 1713, long after Shunzhi. Shunzhi became infatuated with one of his concubines, Xiao Xian, a Mongolian of noble birth, who also admired Chinese culture and Buddhism, and after she died at the age of twenty-two, Shunzhi was inconsolable, threatening to become a Buddhist monk. Toward the end of his life, he possibly suffered from tuberculosis. He died of smallpox in 1661, just four months after the death of his beloved Xiao Xian. His successor, Kangxi, his third son, was only eight years old.

SIGNIFICANCE

After his death, many Manchu nobles harshly criticized Shunzhi. The regents for the young emperor Kangxi produced and publicized a statement, supposedly composed by Shunzhi, confessing that he had abandoned Manchu military values, had become corrupted by Chinese culture, and had favored native Chinese and eunuchs rather than his fellow Manchus. Under the new chief regent, Oboi, the eunuchs were removed from positions of influence, Schall was imprisoned, and Chinese advisers were denigrated.

However, Kangxi removed much of the anti-Chinese discrimination when he became emperor in his own right at the age of fourteen, and over his long reign, he became the paradigm of a traditional Chinese emperor, governing the vast Chinese empire according to the principles of Neo-Confucianism. Kangxi was one of the greatest emperors in China's long history, and his reign and those of his two successors overshadowed that of Shunzhi, but Shunzhi was the first of the Qing emperors, and his admi-

ration of and willingness to adopt Chinese culture prefigured the path followed by his Manchu successors.

—*Eugene Larson*

FURTHER READING

Crossley, Pamela Kyle. *The Manchus.* Cambridge, Mass.: Blackwell, 1997. A volume in the *People of Asia* series, Crossley's work is an exemplary study of the Manchus and includes a discussion of Shunzhi and the origins of the Qing Empire.

Hummel, Arthur, ed. *Eminent Chinese of the Ch'ing Period, 1644-1912.* 2 vols. Washington, D.C.: Government Printing Office, 1943. This classic work contains biographies of the major figures of Qing China, including the emperors.

Paludan, Ann. *Chronicle of the Chinese Emperors.* New York: Thames and Hudson, 1998. This valuable work contains biographies of all of China's many emperors and also includes numerous illustrations.

Spence, Jonathan, and John Wills, eds. *From Ming to Ch'ing: Conquest, Region, and Continuity in Seventeenth-Century China.* New Haven, Conn.: Yale University Press, 1979. An excellent series of essays on seventeenth century China, including the enthronement of Shunzhi.

SEE ALSO: Abahai; Chen Shu; Chongzhen; Dorgon; Kangxi; Liu Yin; Tianqi; Wang Fuzhi; Zheng Chenggong.

RELATED ARTICLES in *Great Events from History: The Seventeenth Century, 1601-1700:* 1616-1643: Rise of the Manchus; 1631-1645: Li Zicheng's Revolt; April 25, 1644: End of the Ming Dynasty; June 6, 1644: Manchus Take Beijing; February 17, 1661-December 20, 1722: Height of Qing Dynasty.

JUSTINE SIEGEMUNDIN
German midwife

Based on her extensive experience assisting in difficult births, Siegemundin published an obstetrics text for midwives that remained an authority through the nineteenth century. One of her birthing techniques, the double handhold, is still used.

BORN: 1636 or 1650; Rohnstock, Silesia (now in Poland)

DIED: 1705; Berlin, Prussia (now in Germany)

ALSO KNOWN AS: Justina Siegmund; Justine Dittrichin Siegmundin (full name)

AREAS OF ACHIEVEMENT: Medicine, science and technology

EARLY LIFE

Little is known about the life of Justine Siegemundin (yoos-TEE-neh seeg-eh-MOON-dihn), who was born Justine Dittrichin Siegmundin, other than what she wrote in the book that was to make her the authority on midwifery during her day. It is known that she was the daughter of Elias Diettrich, a country pastor in Rohnstock, who died before she became an adult. At the age of nineteen, she married a man surnamed Siegemund, and she became known by the feminine form of this surname, Siegemundin.

The next year, at the age of twenty, a midwife believed Justine was pregnant, and at the fortieth week found what she thought was a fetus in the correct position; the midwife insisted that the fetus be delivered. In reality, Siegemundin had experienced a false pregnancy, which was recognized by a soldier's wife from the village, and not by any of the midwives consulted. Instead of being pregnant, Justine had a damming up of blood, a condition cured by a physician.

After this experience, Justine wanted to study midwifery. No midwifery schools existed in Germany at the time, however, so she studied books and outlines of the subject and discussed the material with local midwives. When she was twenty-three years old, one of the midwives called on her to deliver a farm wife's baby, whose elbow had emerged first. She was soon to accompany the midwives in their work and perform difficult deliveries for village women and farm women, including the poor, whom she felt blessed to serve. In particular, people called on her to deliver women whose babies had died. Word of her successful techniques spread, and she was often called to attend women in difficult labor at dis-

tances of 4, 6, and even 8 miles, a great distance then. In addition, well-to-do women, including pastors' wives and noblewomen, sought her help with their difficult labors as well. She spent twelve years delivering babies in her locale.

LIFE'S WORK

Siegemundin's fame and reputation grew, and she gained recognition and influence among the nobility as well as physicians. She published an influential, and what would become authoritative, book on obstetrics for midwives called *Die Chur-Brandenburgische Hoff-Wehe-Mutter* (1690; *The Court Midwife of the Electorate of Brandenburg*, 2005). The book includes her pointed assertion that without her knowledge or her desire, she had received an invitation to travel to Liegnitz (now called Legnica, Poland), where she would receive permission to practice midwifery in 1683. She did go to Liegnitz, and her appointment was somewhat unusual, given that there existed a Prussian regulation stipulating that a midwife had to have given birth herself before she could become a midwife.

While in Liegnitz, a deathly ill noblewoman had suffered with a growth in her uterus, suspected by a physician to be a moon-calf (a mole or monstrous uterine growth) that had begun to decay. Siegemundin removed the growth, and the woman survived, which brought Siegemundin even more fame. The rapid growth of her reputation attracted the attention of the elector of Brandenburg, Frederick William, who invited her to Berlin to be the court midwife. She accepted, and she remained in Berlin until her death in 1705.

Siegemundin's habit of taking notes about her cases came to good use, as she used the notes to form the basis of her textbook. She was further spurred by the recommendations of the princess of Nassau and the queen of England. In 1689, Siegemundin presented her manuscript to the medical faculty at the University of Frankfurt at the Oder River, earning scientific approval of her work. She also acquired assurance from clerics that her book contained nothing heretical. The text appears in nontechnical, accessible German, suitable for reading by the midwives who had no formal education and who could not read Latin, which was the language of the universities. The initial passages of the book present an impassioned defense of her practice of midwifery, despite having borne no children. For example, she asks the reader if it were necessary that a physician experience all the illnesses that he treated before he could practice medicine, and then gives an account of her history of successful deliveries.

The actual text presents a dialogue between Christina, a student of midwifery, and Justina, clearly representing Siegemundin. In the first part of the work, Siegemundin devotes chapters to reproductive anatomy, births with normally positioned fetuses, the means by which the position of the fetus is determined, and the management of obstructed births in which the fetuses lie in positions that prevent birth. Other chapters address prolonged labor, the placenta, and rupturing of the membranes. Following this last chapter are the testimonies of ten women, who attested to Siegemundin's skills. In the second part of the work, the student Christina challenges Justina's teachings "in order," a pedagogical tool used to demonstrate whether or not a student has understood her teacher.

In cases of difficult labors, for example, those lasting more than three days, Siegemundin directed her efforts toward saving the mother's life. She developed techniques to rotate the fetus in utero to lessen the pain of labor, to prevent hemorrhage (by piercing the placenta in the case of a *placenta praevia*, for example), and if need be, to use a hook to perform a craniotomy to extract a dead fetus. She also described techniques of finger palpation and explained when to rupture the membranes artificially. Intervention and the use of instruments formed part of her repertoire, but she rejected their use when they caused unnecessary pain. When, for example, Christina asked why the hook was acceptable, but not the vaginal speculum, Justina replied that the latter produced too much pain. Moreover, Justina also indicated when *not* to intervene in the birthing process. In the case of a fetus who presented an occiput posterior position (back part of the skull or head), the midwife should do nothing, even though the birth would usually be more difficult.

The book contains a number of copper plates, including one based on the anatomy of the female reproductive organs by Dutch physician Regnier de Graaf (1641-1673), as well as a number of instructional illustrations depicting a number of obstetric techniques. Plate 1 of the text illustrates Justine's first case and shows how to push a fetus's arm back into the uterus. A number of the plates depict how to perform a fetal version (that is, a turning of the fetus in the uterus to aid in its delivery), one technique being to hook a looped cord around the feet of the fetus and then rotate it so that the feet are pointed toward the cervix; the birth would most likely take place feet first, then, guided by the midwife's hand. This podalic (feet-first) version was common in the seventeenth century, and Siegemundin devoted more space to it than to the cephalic (head-first) version. However, if the membranes were intact, Siegemundin recommended the cephalic version, a procedure that later came to bear her name. It should be noted that the forceps, invented in the seventeenth century, were unknown in Germany in Siegemundin's time.

SIGNIFICANCE

Siegemundin's text was translated into Dutch in 1691 and appeared in seven German editions between 1690 and 1756; it was translated into English in 2005. The work quickly gained popularity among the private sector as well as acceptance by physicians, and it remained authoritative through the eighteenth century and into the nineteenth century, by which time male physicians had replaced midwives on a fairly wide scale.

Johan van Hoorn, who wrote the first book on midwifery in 1697 (in Swedish), was influenced by Siegemundin's book, which had other imitators. Of significance is the fact that Siegemundin's work did not rely on previously published material, but was the product of years of her own experience as a midwife. By her count, Siegemundin tended to more than five thousand births. The Gedoppelten Handgriff (Siegemundin-Handgriff), or the double handhold, is a still-used technique she developed to turn a fetus that is lying in a transverse position.

Siegemundin's approach to the management of labor and birth differed from many standard practices. She focused on saving the life of the mother and on a successful delivery concluded not only by the version and birth of a baby but also by delivering a woman successfully of a dead fetus. This attitude may have been gendered, as male practitioners seemed to focus on the preservation of an infant, and not on the mother, necessarily. Also of significance is Siegemundin's silence about the character of midwives and about the marital state of the parturient women (the woman giving birth), as well as her omission from the text of superstitious beliefs.

—*Kristen L. Zacharias*

FURTHER READING

Banks, Amanda Carson. *Birth Chairs, Midwives, and Medicine*. Jackson: University of Mississippi Press, 1999. A study of the birthing chair in the context of changing social attitudes toward childbirth and midwives, who were replaced by physicians by the nineteenth century.

Lundgren, Ingela. *Releasing and Relieving Encounters: Experiences of Pregnancy and Childbirth*. Uppsala, Sweden: Acta Universitatis Upsaliensis, 2002. A general account of the experience of childbirth, with a brief section placing the work of Siegemundin in the context of Renaissance developments in midwifery and obstetrics.

O'Dowd, Michael J., and Elliot E. Philipp. *The History of Obstetrics and Gynaecology*. New York: Parthenon, 1994. A massive history, arranged by topics such as "the speculum" and "infertility," and with a chapter on midwifery.

Speert, Harald. *Obstetric and Gynecologic Milestones Illustrated*. New York: Parthenon, 1996. A book focusing on major advances in the practice and understanding of gynecology and obstetrics, with lavish illustrations. Contains a section on older historical works.

Tatlock, Lynn. "Specularum Feminarum: Gendered Perspectives on Obstetrics and Gynecology in Early Modern Germany." *Signs* 17 (1992): 725-760. An analysis contrasting the voices in the writings of Siegemundin and those who were highly critical of female midwives. Places these works within the larger context of German midwifery.

SEE ALSO: Louyse Bourgeois; Frederick William, the Great Elector.

RELATED ARTICLES in *Great Events from History: The Seventeenth Century, 1601-1700:* 17th century: Birth Control in Western Europe; 1640-1688: Reign of Frederick William, the Great Elector.

SIGISMUND III VASA
King of Poland (r. 1587-1632) and King of Sweden (r. 1592-1599)

Sigismund sought unsuccessfully to bring about a union of Poland and Sweden (the latter of which he was briefly king, from 1592 to 1599). Later, he sought to meddle in Muscovite affairs during Russia's Time of Troubles.

BORN: Gripsholm, Sweden; June 20, 1566
DIED: Warsaw, Poland; April 30, 1632
ALSO KNOWN AS: Zygmunt III Waza
AREA OF ACHIEVEMENT: Government and politics

EARLY LIFE

Sigismund III Vasa (ZEE-gihs-moont . . . VAH-sah) must have been one of the few kings in history to have been born in a dungeon. He was born in 1566 in Gripsholm Castle, Sweden, where his parents, the future John III and Katherine, sister of Sigismund II Augustus, last Jagiellonian king of Poland (r. 1548-1572), were held captive by John's mad brother, Eric XIV. When Eric was assassinated in 1568, John became king of Sweden. Sigismund Vasa had a conventional princely upbringing, except in one respect: His mother, being a Catholic, and his father, secretly converting to Catholicism in 1578, resolved to bring up the heir to the throne as a Catholic in what was an overwhelmingly Lutheran country. It may have been this circumstance that led John III and his wife to dream of securing for their son the elective throne of the Polish-Lithuanian Commonwealth, because a Catholic king of Protestant Sweden would be an anomaly.

Sixteenth century Sweden was a difficult country to rule, for the Vasa monarchy was weak, hedged in by constitutional constraints, and confronted by a powerful and freedom-loving nobility, while the Protestant Reformation had made a distinct cultural imprint on society. It was against this background that, in 1587, John III managed to secure the throne of Poland for his son Sigismund, now aged twenty-one. The prince went as a stranger to Poland, where he was regarded as a foreigner, to be crowned in Kraków on December 27, 1587.

LIFE'S WORK

King Sigismund III Vasa was faced with a daunting task. Since the end of the Jagiellonian Dynasty, the Polish monarchy had been elective and was forced to share its authority both with the Sejm, or Diet, and with a turbulent nobility in a country ethnically, culturally, and religiously diverse. The Polish population encompassed Catholics, Lutheran and Calvinist Protestants, Greek Orthodox Christians in the southeast, and a flourishing Jewish community.

For Counter-Reformation Europe, Poland was unusually tolerant in religion and culture, but many Poles regarded Sigismund with suspicion. His predecessor,

Sigismund III Vasa. (Hulton Archive/Getty Images)

Stephen Báthory (r. 1575-1586), formerly prince of Transylvania, had married Anna, another sister of Sigismund II Augustus. Stephen had proved an outstanding ruler, well able to defend Polish-Lithuanian interests in the face of the aggressions of Czar Ivan the Terrible, but his reign was tragically short.

Sigismund's election had been bitterly contested by a rival, the Archduke Maximilian, brother of the Habsburg Holy Roman Emperor Rudolf II, who enjoyed a considerable following among some of the Polish nobility. Stephen Báthory's former chancellor, Jan Zamoyski, secured Sigismund's election in the face of pro-Habsburg dissident opposition, but Sigismund found his power highly circumscribed, because the Sejm at his accession had forced him to accept a diminution of royal authority. He further antagonized his bitterly anti-German subjects by marrying the Habsburg archduchess Anna, sister of Ferdinand of Styria (the future Emperor Ferdinand II), a connection that reinforced his deeply felt Catholicism. Indeed, if Sigismund had one consistent political objective, it was to restore Poland and eventually the Baltic world to the Roman Catholic Church.

In 1592, when John III died, Sigismund sought to obtain his paternal throne, dreaming of a union between Sweden and Poland-Lithuania. Such formal unions were not unknown, but Lutheran Sweden and predominantly Catholic Poland were an ill-matched pair. Surprisingly, though, the Sejm approved the attempt, and Sigismund, accompanied by a bevy of Catholic clerics, reached Stockholm in 1594, where he found a dangerous adversary in his uncle Charles, duke of Södermanland, the effective master of Stockholm and champion of the Protestant nobility.

At Sigismund's coronation in Uppsala (February 18, 1594), he was compelled to assent to an Accession Charter by the Rad (the council of state), upholding Sweden's Protestant constitution. Finding his authority thus diminished, he hurriedly returned to Poland, leaving the Rad and Duke Charles as coregents. Sigismund returned with an army in 1598 but was defeated by Charles's forces at the Battle of Stângebro (September 25, 1598) and was formally deposed the next year, when Charles became the de facto ruler of the country. (He would formally be declared King Charles IX in 1604.) Obstinate and unrealistic, Sigismund refused to recognize the facts on the ground, and decades of intermittent warfare between Sweden and Poland followed, until the Polish Vasas finally abandoned their claim to the Swedish throne in 1660.

In 1601, Sigismund was forced to defend Polish Livonia, into which Duke Charles had advanced and where he had received a warm welcome from the mostly Protestant burghers and landowners. Sigismund responded by sending Polish troops into the province, and in 1605, at Kirkholm, near Riga, one of the greatest Polish soldiers of the age, Jan Chodkiewicz, grand hetman of Lithuania, won a spectacular victory over the Swedes for Sigismund. The victory produced no lasting consequences, however: The Swedes kept up the pressure on Livonia, and it gradually passed out of Polish control. Swedish king Gustavus II Adolphus completed its annexation between 1617 and 1622 with the capture of Riga. When the Treaty of Stummdorf (September 12, 1635) finally brought a temporary peace after Sigismund's death, Sweden was confirmed in possession of Livonia. In retrospect, Sigismund's Swedish adventures had brought disaster to his adopted country. He had done what he had sworn not to do, put Swedish interests before Polish, and his subjects remained in a state of continuous exasperation with him.

Another impractical scheme in which Sigismund became involved occurred when a pretender claiming to be the Czarevich Dmitry (allegedly, the youngest son of Ivan the Terrible, who died mysteriously as a child in 1591), crossed the Lithuanian border from Muscovy in

October, 1603, and was taken under the protection of Jerzy Mniszech, palatine of Sandomiertz. Mniszech was one of a group of Polish-Lithuanian nobles who ardently advocated a renewal of war with Russia. He wrote to Sigismund representing the False Dmitry as a catalyst for the Catholicization of Russia. The Sejm was divided on the scheme to invade Russia, and Chancellor Zamoyski, one of the greatest of Polish statesmen, bitterly opposed it. Meanwhile, Claudio Rangoni, the papal nuncio, and the veteran Jesuit, Antonio Possevino, appealed to Sigismund's conscience to support the cause.

Whatever pressures may have been brought to bear on Sigismund from either side of the debate over the False Dmitry, however, the king had little actual influence on the course of events during the early years of the Russian *smutnoe vremya* (Time of Troubles). On October 13, the False Dmitry crossed the Russian frontier with twenty-five hundred men, half of whom were Ukrainian Cossacks and the rest of whom were raised by Mniszech, who had also betrothed his daughter, Marina, to the pretender. The False Dmitry's advance on Moscow led to the death of Czar Boris Godunov, the coronation of the pretender as czar, and his marriage with Marina Mniszech. However, the unpopularity of his Polish troops and his introduction of Western ways into Russian culture led to an upsurge of xenophobia, which Prince Vasily Shuysky orchestrated into a *coup d'état*. The False Dmitriy was lynched, and Vasily ascended the throne as Czar Vasily IV.

Several years of widespread anarchy followed, with Vasily incapable of coping with Cossack insurrections, uprisings by disenfranchised peasants and disgruntled townsfolk, and a spate of pretenders. In desperation, he sought military assistance from the Swedes in exchange for the cession of Karelia. The czar's offer galvanized Sigismund into action. Hitherto, Polish units had been engaged in the Muscovite civil wars, but only under the leadership of local Polish-Lithuanian nobles. Now, the king intervened in person, leading an army against Smolensk (September, 1609).

Following the Smolensk campaign, a Polish army under Crown Hetman Stanislaw Zolkiewski defeated the Muscovites at the Battle of Klushino (June 24, 1610). On July 17, 1610, Vasily was deposed by the Muscovites and sent to Sigismund, who took him back to Poland as a prisoner. He died there in September, 1612. The Poles now occupied Moscow, but the occupation provoked a national uprising by Muscovites of all classes, and the invaders were expelled from the city in November, 1612. Desultory fighting between Poles and Muscovites con-

tinued until the Treaty of Deulino (1618). Again, through Sigismund's nonchalance, Poland had made great sacrifices of men and resources to no effect.

Finally, Sigismund's pro-Habsburg proclivities brought him into conflict with the Ottomans. In 1620, he rashly provided troops for his brother-in-law, Emperor Ferdinand II, to employ against the Protestant prince of Transylvania, Gabriel Bethlen (r. 1613-1629), despite the fact that the prince was the sultan's vassal. Iskender Paşa, Ottoman governor of Ochakov, swiftly retaliated, defeating Sigismund's Poles at Cecora on the Pruth (September 20, 1620), where Hetman Zolkiewski, the hero of Klushino, was killed. Sigismund remained, impotent, in Warsaw, while Crimean Tatars now penetrated southeastern Poland. A year later, at Choczim on the Dniester, a Polish army under Hetman Chodkiewicz redeemed the nation's reputation by resisting the Ottoman army, which was commanded by Sultan Osman II in person (1618-1622). This led to a negotiatiated settlement (October 9, 1621). Based on the 1617 Treaty of Busza, the antebellum borders were restored, with Poland agreeing not to interfere in Transylvania, Moldavia, or Walachia and to restrain Cossack depredations, as the Ottomans promised to do with the Crimean Tatars.

SIGNIFICANCE

Sigismund III Vasa's military schemes, undertaken on behalf of the Counter-Reformation, proved disastrous for Poland. At the time of his election, a contemporary remarked: "King Stefan was good for the soldiers and this one will be good for the clergy," and it is true that with the help of the Jesuits, Sigismund contributed largely to the re-Catholicization of Poland. It is said that Sigismund's temperament more closely resembled that of the Habsburgs than the Vasas. Stiff and formal, vacillating and diffident, he lacked the personality to appeal to his mercurial Polish subjects. A lover of the arts, Sigismund renovated and enlarged the Wawel Castle in Kraków, traditional residence of Polish kings, and in 1597, he transferred the capital to the more centrally located Warsaw, where he employed Italian architects and craftsmen to beautify the city. Insofar as the Poles regard his reign with any nostalgia, it is as the lavish patron of the Polish Baroque.

—*Gavin R. G. Hambly*

FURTHER READING

Davies, Norman. *God's Playground: A History of Poland.* 2 vols. New York: Columbia University Press, 1982. An excellent general history.

Jasienica, Pawel. *The Commonwealth of Both Nations: The Silver Age*. New York: Hippocrene Books, 1987. A leisurely narrative of Sigismund's reign.

Nowak, F. "Sigismund III, 1587-1632." In *The Cambridge History of Poland, to 1696*, edited by W. F. Reddawa et al. Cambridge, England: Cambridge University Press, 1950. Still the best summary of Sigismund's reign.

Perrie, Maureen. *Pretenders and Popular Monarchism in Early Modern Russia*. New York: Cambridge University Press, 1995. An important account of Poland's involvement in the Time of Troubles.

Roberts, Michael. *The Early Vasas: A History of Sweden, 1523-1611*. Cambridge, England: Cambridge University Press, 1968. A detailed account of Sigismund's Swedish imbroglio by the most authoritative scholar of early modern Sweden writing in English.

SEE ALSO: Ferdinand II; Vasily Shuysky.

RELATED ARTICLES in *Great Events from History: The Seventeenth Century, 1601-1700:* c. 1601-1606: Appearance of the False Dmitry; February 7, 1613: Election of Michael Romanov as Czar; May 19, 1622: Janissary Revolt and Osman II's Assassination; 1632-1667: Polish-Russian Wars for the Ukraine; 1677-1681: Ottoman-Muscovite Wars.

ELISABETTA SIRANI
Italian painter

Among the earliest female artists to receive worldwide recognition, Sirani was also among the first to open a school of art for girls and young women. Remarkably, she was in her teenage years during this time.

BORN: 1638; Bologna, Papal States (now in Italy)
DIED: August, 1665; Bologna
AREAS OF ACHIEVEMENT: Art, patronage of the arts, education

EARLY LIFE

Elisabetta Sirani (sihr-AHN-ee) was the daughter of Giovanni Andrea Sirani (1610-1670), assistant to and follower of Guido Reni, then the leading master of Bologna. At the time, Bologna was a major center of the arts and a city with progressive attitudes toward women. The University of Bologna had admitted female students since the Middle Ages, and the patron saint of Bologna, St. Catherina dei Vigri, was herself an artist and manuscript illuminator. Therefore, women enjoyed greater independence in Bologna than in other Italian cities, and female artists were more readily accepted there and were encouraged to pursue a career. As a result, Bologna produced some of the most respected female painters and sculptors of the period, including Sirani, Lavinia Fontana, and Properzia de' Rossi.

Details on Sirani's training are unknown. In an era when female artists were excluded from guilds and academies, and therefore from formal training, usually the only girls and women who could receive art instruction were the daughters of male masters or noblemen who could afford a private tutor. As the daughter of an artist,

Sirani most likely was trained by her father, though contemporary accounts reveal that, at first, he was against her decision to pursue a career as a painter. Sirani's paintings, which include portraiture as well as complex mythologies, allegories, and religious scenes, show her confidence in rendering the human form, which suggests that she must have worked from the live model in her father's studio. Because her father painted in the classicized style of Guido Reni, Sirani also adopted this mode of painting. Her figures are as pale as Reni's, their anatomical structure purposely de-emphasized to bring out instead their grace and beauty. Sirani's paintings, however, possess a certain degree of sentimentality not found in Reni's work.

Sirani demonstrated early on not only her great talent as a painter, engraver, and draftsperson but also great business sense. Around 1652, when she was about fourteen years old, she established her own workshop, training more than a dozen women, including her two sisters, Anna Maria and Barbara Sirani. Count Carlo Cesare Malvasia, an art critic and family friend, encouraged Sirani's career. He later included a short biography of Sirani in his *Felsina Pittrice* (Bologna, 1675), in which he praised her as an artist of outstanding merit.

LIFE'S WORK

Sirani compiled her own meticulous record of her works, the Nota, which included approximately 190 entries. This diary, which she kept for a decade, has aided in the identification of a considerable number of her paintings. Her prolific output is remarkable, especially considering that her career spanned just a little more than a decade.

She is known to have painted at great speed, which provoked all sorts of gossip about the authorship of her works. To dispel rumors, Sirani invited her accusers to her workshop to watch her paint. Grand Duke Cosimo III de' Medici of Florence was one of the individuals who visited Sirani's studio and observed her at work. He was there in 1664 as she rendered a portrait of his uncle, Prince Leopold. When she had finished, Cosimo asked her to execute a Madonna for his own collection. Sirani rendered the image as quickly as she could to allow the pigments to dry so Cosimo could take the work back with him to Florence.

Sirani's father became ill with gout, which crippled his hands and prevented him from working. It fell on his daughter to run the family workshop to support her parents and her siblings, and she was very successful. Her customers included members of the local nobility, such as Count Annibale Ranuzzi, who commissioned a portrait of his younger sister, Anna Maria Ranuzzi, as *Charity* (1665). Anna Maria was the mother of three children. The children are included in the portrait, which emphasizes not Anna Maria's social standing but her role as mother. Maternity is also the subject of Sirani's *Virgin and Child* (1663), part of the permanent collection of the National Museum of Women in the Arts in Washington, D.C. The two figures in this painting share an intimate moment, smiling lovingly at one another, their heads almost touching. The Virgin wears a turban commonly worn by female Bolognese peasants. In rendering the Madonna in this fashion, rather than as the inaccessible Madonnas of the Renaissance, Sirani emphasized the Virgin's and Christ's humanity.

Among Sirani's favorite subjects were female heroes, including Judith, Lucretia, Saint Catherine, and the penitent Magdalen. Her *Judith with the Head of Holofernes* (1660's) is one such example. Judith was the widow who delivered the Israelites from the clutches of the Assyrians, who had cut off the Israelites' water supply. Judith wined and dined Holofernes, the commander of the Assyrian army, and, when he fell into a drunken stupor, cut off his head. Sirani depicted the moment that Judith showed the severed head of Holofernes to the Israelites to let them know that the threat was over. In the painting, Judith stands heroically in the center of the composition. Abra, her old maidservant, kneels to Judith's right to contrast with Judith's youth and beauty.

In *Portia Wounding Her Thigh* (1664), Sirani depicted a heroine from Roman history. Portia, the wife of Brutus, wounded herself by plunging a dagger into her thigh to demonstrate to her husband her strength of char-

acter. In the painting, Portia is seen in the foreground plunging the knife into her leg to prove that she can be as heroic as a man, while women in the background engage in the feminine task of spinning.

Though most of Sirani's patronage came from private individuals, she also received a few public commissions. In 1656-1657, she painted an *Assumption* for the parish church of Borgo Panigale near Bologna. In 1658, she executed the *Baptism of Christ* for the Certosa di Bologna and a nave painting for the Church of San Girolamo. Among her portraits are her *Self-Portrait* (1660) and that of *Beatrice Cenci* (1662). In the first, Sirani presented herself as the noblewoman who engages in painting. She wears the costume of a lady and wears chandelier pearl earrings, a gold rosette brooch on each shoulder, and another gem in the center of her bodice. Her hair is loose, as fashion for unmarried women dictated. The second portrait is a sympathetic rendition of a woman who was victimized by her father. Beatrice Cenci was a Roman noblewoman, the daughter of the wealthy, powerful, and violent Francesco Cenci. He imprisoned Beatrice and her stepmother in Castel Petrella Salto near Rieti. In 1598, Beatrice, with the blessing of her stepmother and siblings, killed Francesco and was later sentenced to death by Pope Clement VIII. In 1599, she was decapitated in front of a large crowd on the Ponte Sant'Angelo in Rome. Her case aroused great sympathy, captured by Sirani in her painting. Sirani rendered Beatrice the innocent victim. She looks directly at the viewer and smiles, her expression conveying the tragedy of her life story.

Sirani died in 1665 at the age of just twenty-seven. Because she complained of severe stomach pains, her father suspected that she had been poisoned by a jealous maid. The maid was tried and acquitted of the charges, however. Most likely, Sirani died from the perforated ulcers revealed by her autopsy. She was given a grand funeral in the Dominican church in Bologna that included orations, poetry, and music, as well as a large catafalque (ornamental structure) representing the Temple of Fame, adorned with mottoes, emblems, and a life-size figure of the artist engaged in the act of painting. She was buried alongside Guido Reni, which indicates that the Bolognese considered her his heir.

SIGNIFICANCE

Sirani was fortunate to have been born in a city with progressive attitudes toward women, which allowed her to pursue a career as an artist without much obstacle. In an era when female artists were limited to painting mainly portraits and still lifes—genres ranked low on the academic scale—Sirani broke away from such expectations. Though portraiture was one of the subjects she embraced, her main interests were in mythological and religious stories that celebrate the female as hero.

Furthermore, she contributed to girls' and women's empowerment by educating them in the arts, opening the door of opportunity, self-reliance, and self-expression for girls and women in seventeenth century Bologna, and beyond.

—*Lilian H. Zirpolo*

FURTHER READING

Bohn, B. "The Antique Heroines of Elisabetta Sirani." *Renaissance Studies* 16, no. 1 (March, 2002): 52-79. Examines Sirani's portrayals of female historical and biblical figures who performed heroic deeds.

Chadwick, Whitney. *Women, Art, and Society.* 3d ed. New York: Thames and Hudson, 2002. Because a monograph on Sirani does not exist, Chadwick's book remains the principal source on the artist.

Dixon, Annette, ed. *Women Who Ruled: Queens, Goddesses, Amazons in Renaissance and Baroque Art.* London: Merrell, and the University of Michigan Museum of Art, 2002. Catalog of a 2002 exhibition on women in art and women artists of the Renaissance and later periods. Includes works by Sirani.

Heller, Nancy G. *Women Artists: An Illustrated History.* New York: Abbeville Press, 1997. Explores the lives of female artists, from antiquity to the end of the twentieth century, including Sirani's life and career.

Slatkin, Wendy. *Women Artists in History: From Antiquity to the Twentieth Century.* Englewood Cliffs, N.J.: Prentice Hall, 1985. This work includes a section on Sirani's career and works.

SEE ALSO: Giovanna Garzoni; Artemisia Gentileschi.
RELATED ARTICLE in *Great Events from History: The Seventeenth Century, 1601-1700:* c. 1601-1620: Emergence of Baroque Art.

ŚIVĀJĪ
Marāthā emperor of India (r. 1674-1680)

The founder of an independent Marāthā kingdom, Śivājī was a pioneer of guerrilla warfare, a great general, and a fiery Hindu nationalist. He became a symbol of Hindu statesmanship for twentieth century Indians.

BORN: April 6, 1627; Poona, India
DIED: April 3, 1680; Rājgarh, India
ALSO KNOWN AS: Śivājī Bhonsle (given name); Shivaji
AREAS OF ACHIEVEMENT: Government and politics, warfare and conquest, military

EARLY LIFE

Śivājī (dee-VAH-gee) was born in west India, the son of parents from two prominent Marāthā families. His mother, Jija Bai, was the daughter of Lukhji Jadhava of Devagiri, and his father was Shanji Bhonsle. The Marāthās, a resourceful and self-reliant hill people, successfully resisted Muslim rule for three generations and also held the later British invaders at bay. Śivājī's father virtually abandoned him and his mother shortly after Śivājī's birth. Consequently, Śivājī was reared largely by his mother and his guardian Dadaji Kondadev, a clever former official of the neighboring Muslim sultanate of Bijapur.

During the first nine years of his life, Śivājī experienced constant peril. He and his mother were forced to stay on the move, wandering from place to place to escape capture by attacking Mughal armies. Eventually, they settled in Poona in 1636 and lived there for ten years. Then they moved to a newly built mountain fortress, Rājgarh, which in time became the capital of his Marāthā empire.

Three major forces molded Śivājī's character. His mother wielded the paramount influence. This spirited woman was proud of her Kshatriya (warrior caste) heritage and centered her ambition on her son, developing in him traits of defiance and self-assertion. A devout Hindu, she imparted her love of religion to him and provided an education focused on the great epics the *Rāmāyana* and the *Mahābhārata.* He became fond of devotional music and attended the sermons of various Hindu teachers in the Poona vicinity. He never lost his love of Hinduism, later introducing compulsory recitations of the war chapters of the *Rāmāyana* by all his troops.

The second great influence on his character was his guardian, Dadaji. Not merely a clerk or accountant, Dadaji was a strict disciplinarian, a shrewd tactician, and a fierce Hindu nationalist as well. He hated Muslim domination and felt a deep affection for the peasantry. His skill in politics and his passion for justice deeply influenced Śivājī.

The third influence was Mahārāshtra itself. He spent much of his boyhood roaming the secluded hills west of Poona, where he was exposed to nature's demands and learned to cope with deprivation. He developed methods of guerrilla warfare and gained firsthand knowledge of the needs of the common people by constantly moving among them as a youth. Before he reached the age of twenty, Śivājī gained control of several districts west of Poona and began to raise his own army. He repaired and garrisoned forts and improved the local administrative machinery. He thus earned the reputation of an able and upright ruler.

LIFE'S WORK

When Dadaji died in 1647, Śivājī embarked upon a vigorous policy of territorial expansion. Politics of the western Deccan (central India) were dominated by two independent but corrupt Muslim sultanates, Bijapur and Golconda, and languid Mughal armies interested more in personal gain than in imperial conquest. Śivājī took advantage of the absence of aggressive Mughal generals to expand. Intensely pragmatic, he employed any and all means to attain his ends. He had two main objectives in mind as he launched his expansion. First, he wanted to secure the welfare of the Marāthās under his control. Second, he sought to create well-defined frontiers that were easily defended against the Mughals. Between 1648 and 1653, he managed to organize a small, cohesive state encompassing the region around Poona. In addition to forming a formidable army, Śivājī also built naval forts and created a powerful navy backed by shipbuilding yards and arsenals. By the mid-1650's, Śivājī was clearly the outstanding Marāthā statesman and a threat to the surrounding Muslim principalities.

Bijapur reacted to the threat in 1659 by raising a well-equipped army under the control of Afzal Khan to send against Śivājī. Afzal Khan swept into Śivājī's domains in September, 1659, plundering and destroying as he went. Śivājī could not defeat Afzal Khan's forces in open combat and so decided to attack him by deception instead. After complicated negotiations, the two opponents met for a conference on November 10, 1659. Śivājī, a short, wiry adventurer of only five feet in height, seemed to pose no personal danger to the powerfully built Bijapur general. Śivājī, however, took advantage of the situation by wearing an iron vest and a metal skullcap under his turban and by carrying a concealed dagger in one hand

and tiger claws in the other. Although the exact details of the khan's encounter with Śivājī may be lost in legend, the Marāthās claim that when Śivājī came into the conference tent, the khan attempted to kill him with a dagger. Śivājī parried the blow and ripped open the khan's bowels with the tiger claws, killing him nearly instantly. The death of the khan demoralized the Bijapur troops, who left the field without a battle. Bijapur no longer threatened the new Marāthā state.

This success, in addition to Śivājī's general expansion in the western Deccan, alarmed the Mughal emperor, Aurangzeb, who had spent many years in the Deccan as a prince and was intimately familiar with the politics there. Determined to quell the Marāthās, Aurangzeb sent a powerful force against Śivājī in January, 1660, under the direction of Shaista Khan. The khan seized Poona and for three years hunted Śivājī in all directions. Only Śivājī's intimate knowledge of Mahārāshtran geography and guerrilla tactics prevented his capture.

Once again, Śivājī resorted to a stratagem to save himself. Through secret agents, he learned the details of the khan's schedule and the arrangements of his command center. On the evening of April 15, 1663, Śivājī launched a surprise attack on the khan's personal quarters, killing nearly fifty people and wounding the khan. That forced the Mughals to relax the pressure on Śivājī for a time. He took advantage of the lull to plunder the rich port city of Surat, one of the most highly prized Mughal possessions. This direct attack on the Mughal Empire's power and prestige incensed Aurangzeb, who sent a huge new army under the Rājput Jai Singh to deal with the Marāthā "mountain rats."

Jai Singh's powerful force arrived in Poona in March, 1665. Śivājī, unaware of his coming, was campaigning in the south. When he heard of the new danger, he returned immediately to Rājgarh, but Jai Singh established a firm hold on the regions north of Poona, and Śivājī could not hope to defeat him. Accordingly, he signed a treaty with Jai Singh on June 12, 1665, agreeing to hand over twenty-three of his important forts, keeping only twelve minor ones for himself. Śivājī then proceeded to Āgra to attend Aurangzeb's formal accession to the Mughal throne on May 12, 1666.

Aurangzeb then made the single greatest mistake of his life. In return for giving up his forts, Śivājī expected to be made a full ally of the Mughals and to be appointed as a first-class *mansabdar* (commander of horse). Instead, Aurangzeb made him a third-class officer with no title or presents. Śivājī was so insulted that he fussed and fumed and eventually fainted. He was carried from the court and put under house arrest. Instead of making an indispensable ally in the Deccan, Aurangzeb created a bitter enemy. While Aurangzeb debated what to do with him, Śivājī planned a clever escape and fled Āgra on August 19, 1666. Following a circuitous route, he arrived back at Rājgarh on September 12. His daring escape buttressed his already considerable national reputation, and he was welcomed back to the Deccan as a returning monarch.

Thereafter, the persistent Marāthās tried to fight the Mughals to the death. By 1670, Śivājī had recaptured most of the fortresses he had ceded to the Mughals in 1666. He felt strong enough to launch a second, even more successful attack on Surat, plundering it for three full days in October, 1670. In 1674, after thirty years of struggle, Śivājī decided to confirm his conquests by having himself crowned Chatrapati (lord of the universe) in a traditional Hindu coronation in which some eleven thousand Brahmans chanted sacred Vedic mantras and more than fifty thousand of his followers pledged their allegiance to the great Hindu king, the reincarnation of the great god Siva.

This coronation, however, did not confirm Śivājī as ruler of all Mahārāshtra and the surrounding regions. Aurangzeb could not move against the Marāthās because he was occupied with campaigns against the Afghans in the northwest. Within the Deccan, however, Bijapur and Golconda remained unreconciled to Marāthā expansion, and Śivājī waged several campaigns against them over the next four years. Despite his considerable successes, Śivājī never controlled a very sizable domain or incorporated all Marāthās into his empire.

Śivājī died of a fever on April 3, 1680, at his capital of Rājgarh. His death did not bring an end to Mahārāshtra's struggle for independence, however, for he bequeathed to his sons and fellow Marāthās his fierce spirit of Hindu nationalism. They continued his battle against Mughal power, preventing Aurangzeb from ever gaining full control of the Deccan.

SIGNIFICANCE

Śivājī was hailed by his followers as the founding father of the Marāthā nation but was reviled by the Mughals as a "mountain rat." There is little doubt that his exploits made him a savior to the Hindus, a protector of the *tilak*, the ritual paint on Hindu foreheads. Charismatic and shrewd, Śivājī inspired his people to become a nation, rallying Hindus to a sense of their own worth and power. Twentieth century Hindu nationalists have eulogized him as the earliest of the modern Hindus who struggled against foreign oppressors for India's national survival.

Śivājī was a fierce warrior who campaigned relentlessly for Marāthā independence. He sought self-rule and the freedom to practice his own religion. He mastered guerrilla tactics in fighting both Mughal and Bijapur armies. He and his "mountain rats" would wait for the heavily laden armies to enter the hill country and then swoop down to plunder whatever they could use. They employed hit-and-run tactics against numerically superior enemies and chose to fight only when it was to their advantage. He secured mountaintop fortresses to which he could retreat to escape the pursuit of more powerful forces. Using his intimate knowledge of his homeland to the best advantage, he well deserves to be labeled one of the founders of modern guerrilla warfare.

His commitment to Hinduism and religious freedom was genuine. In some respects, he appears to have cared more for religious freedom than for political dominion. At the same time, however, he realized that religious freedom for Hindus could not be achieved without political freedom. In that respect, he articulated a political philosophy in common with the leaders of the twentieth century independence movement. He thus became a symbolic hero to Hindus in the political climate of the early twentieth century.

In their minds, Śivājī began the work that Mohandas Gandhi would complete. Even as he welded the scattered Marāthā people into a political and military unit with a powerful new sense of identity, so did Śivājī create a Hindu national identity. His colorful life and his ruthlessness tinged with fantasy provided the perfect raw material for a legendary hero. Thus, Śivājī was an important historical figure in his own right, as he united the Marāthās as a people and prevented Mughal domination of the Deccan. He is also important as a symbol of the new India, of a people united in a quest for political independence and a new national identity.

—*Loren W. Crabtree*

FURTHER READING

Gascoigne, Bamber. *A Brief History of the Great Moghuls*. New York: Carroll & Graf, 2002. This well-written, general history of the Mughals, originally published in 1971, chronicles the rise and fall of the empire from its founder, Babur, through Aurangzeb. Profusely illustrated, it presents a compelling portrait of Śivājī's struggles against Aurangzeb.

Gordon, Stewart. *The Marathas, 1600-1818*. Vol. 4 in *The New Cambridge History of India*, edited by Gordon Johnson, C. A. Bayly, and John F. Richards. New York: Cambridge University Press, 1993. A comprehensive history of the Marāthās and their kingdom, including a chapter on Śivājī and the Marāthā polity.

Hansen, Waldemar. *The Peacock Throne: The Drama of Mogul India.* New York: Holt, Rinehart and Winston, 1972. A detailed history of the Mughal period, offering many insights into the Deccan problem as it was perceived by Śivājī and Aurangzeb.

Ikram, S. M. *Muslim Civilization in India.* Edited by Ainslie T. Embree. New York: Columbia University Press, 1964. Provides a comprehensive summary of the role of Muslims in India from 712 to 1857. Ikram assesses the role of Śivājī, chronicling from a Muslim perspective his military and political exploits.

Laine, James W. *Shivaji: Hindu King in Islamic India.* New York: Oxford University Press, 2003. Laine traces the origins and development of Śivājī's legend to offer a complex and unconventional view of Hindu-Muslim relationships in India.

Majumdar, R. C., H. C. Raychaudhuri, and Kalikinkar Datta. *An Advanced History of India.* 4th ed. Delhi: Macmillan India, 1978. An especially detailed history of India by Indian scholars. Strikes a balanced view of Śivājī's leadership style, providing a useful appraisal of Śivājī's position in the history of the Indian nationalist movement.

Pearson, M. N. "Shivaji and the Decline of the Mughal Empire." *Journal of Asian Studies* 35 (February, 1976): 221-236. Focuses on the relationship between Śivājī's persistent independence in the Deccan and the decline of Mughal power.

Singh, Mahendra Pratap. *Shivaji, Bhakha Sources and Nationalism.* New Delhi: Books India International, 2001. A history of the Mughals, with special reference to Śivājī, based upon the Braja literature of the time.

Wolpert, Stanley. *A New History of India.* 7th ed. New York: Oxford University Press, 2004. This frequently updated general history of India provides a broad historical context for understanding Śivājī's role during the Mughal period.

SEE ALSO: ʿAbbās the Great; Aurangzeb; Jahāngīr; Kösem Sultan; Murad IV; Shah Jahan.

RELATED ARTICLES in *Great Events from History: The Seventeenth Century, 1601-1700:* 1606-1674: Europeans Settle in India; 1639-1640: British East India Company Establishes Fort Saint George; 1658-1707: Reign of Aurangzeb; June 23, 1661: Portugal Cedes Bombay to the English; c. 1666-1676: Founding of the Marāthā Kingdom; 1679-1709: Rājput Rebellion.

JOHN SMITH
English-born American colonist

Smith's strong leadership in early Virginia and his promotional literature on North America helped ensure the success of England's efforts at colonization.

BORN: January 9, 1580 (baptized); Willoughby, Lincolnshire, England
DIED: June 21, 1631; London, England
AREAS OF ACHIEVEMENT: Government and politics, exploration, literature

EARLY LIFE

John Smith was born in January, 1580, in the small Lincolnshire village of Willoughby. His father, George Smith, a yeoman farmer, and his mother, née Alice Rickard, were from families long linked to the land in northern England. Smith was the eldest of the couple's five sons and one daughter. He attended local schools until age fifteen, primarily studying grammar and mathematics, and then was apprenticed to a merchant in the coastal town of King's Lynn. Though he inherited some land after his father's death in 1596, Smith joined with other English Protestants in their conflict with the Spanish in the Netherlands. After three years of fighting, Smith rambled about France and Scotland, at times as a companion to the sons of his noble patron, Lord Willoughby, and at times as a solitary wanderer.

These episodes prompted the restless young man to seek new adventures. Throughout his life, he was eager to experience the demanding and the dangerous. Motivated in part by the thrill of the challenge, Smith, as a commoner, also sought to prove his worth in an age dominated by gentlemen. Accordingly, Smith decided to take up the seemingly endless Christian crusade against Islam. In 1600, he started across the continent to fight the infidel Turks in Hungary. Over the next four years, Smith engaged in privateering on the Mediterranean Sea as well as in numerous battles in Hungary, suffering serious wounds, capture, and enslavement; after he escaped, Smith trekked through Russia, Poland, Germany, France, and Spain before returning to England. A 1616 portrait of Smith reveals a short and stocky adventurer in military garb. His face features a high forehead, a long, slender nose, and a full beard. The artist captured the confident air that characterized Smith throughout his career.

LIFE'S WORK

In 1606, when Smith learned that the Virginia Company of London intended to settle a colony in North America, he enlisted for what became the most important venture of his life. The approximately 105 men dispatched by the joint stock company in three small ships established a base on the James River in Virginia in the spring of 1607. The company appointed a resident council to supervise affairs in the colony, and Smith was one of the seven selected. During his two and a half years at Jamestown, Smith was instrumental in furthering the survival of the colony. He led numerous exploratory and mapping ventures along the coast and into the interior. He established a vital trade with the leader of the Tidewater natives,

Powhatan. Smith also struck up an important, paternal friendship with the chief's daughter, Pocahontas, a youngster who served as a liaison between the natives and the English. Her role in promoting the trade of food with the colonists led Smith later to claim that she saved them "from death, famine, and utter confusion."

When Smith was elected president of the council in September, 1608, he faced a host of problems. Most of the initial settlers, almost half of whom were gentlemen, were poorly suited to the harsh task of creating a settlement in a hostile environment. Further, several settlers refused to work because they had assumed incorrectly that they, like the Spanish in Mexico and Peru, would be able to compel the natives to do the hard labor. Even those colonists who were willing to work could not contribute because they were often ill (or had died) from malaria or dysentery, a consequence of building Jamestown on swampy ground. Indian attacks, although sporadic, also claimed some lives. The other leaders could provide little guidance because the council suffered from unend-

An 1870 depiction of Pocahontas saving the life of John Smith. (Library of Congress)

ing dissension. Yet, to Smith, the most significant dilemma was gold fever. Hoping to replicate the Spanish success in discovering New York gold, for most, "there was no talk, no hope, no work but dig gold, wash gold, refine gold, [and] load gold," Smith explained.

Smith quickly imposed the discipline necessary to save the colony. He forced the surviving men to build new housing at Jamestown, enlarge the fort, and plant more than thirty acres of grain. In short, he made them work; if they did not, they did not eat. Smith also secured, through cajolery, intimidation, and brutality, a steadier supply of food from the natives and relatively peaceful relations with them. His significance to the fledgling colony was most evident when a serious gunpowder burn forced Smith to return to England in October, 1609. Shortly after his departure, Virginia once again fell into chaos, and almost 90 percent of the settlers died in the winter.

The documentary record permits only occasional glances into Smith's life after he left the troubled colony. He returned to North America in 1614, to explore and map the New England coast. The experience convinced Smith that colonists could prosper there by exploiting the region's fish and fur. He secured financial backing for two more voyages to New England, but French pirates and storms prevented their completion. He was briefly reunited with Pocahontas when she came to England in 1616. She had married planter John Rolfe, and he had changed her name to Rebecca. It was a bittersweet reunion because she died in early 1617. Two years later, Smith offered his expertise and service to a group of religious dissenters, the Pilgrims, when he discovered that they intended to settle in North America, but they turned down his offer. Smith was also snubbed by the Virginia Company of London. They rejected both his plea for compensation and his offer to lead an armed force against the natives to avenge their assault on the colony in 1622.

SMITH'S ACCOUNT OF HIS RESCUE BY POCAHONTAS

In an incident that has become part of American folklore, John Smith was captured by Powhatan Indians and later released. He believed that the Indians intended to kill him, until he was saved through the intervention of the princess Pocahontas, who had fallen in love with him. Some scholars have suggested that Smith merely experienced (and misinterpreted) a ritual killing and rebirth, meant to signal his acceptance into the tribe and his new life as an honorary Powhatan. The following is taken from Smith's own published narrative of the incident, written in the third person.

At his [Smith's] entrance before the king, all the people gave a great shout. The queen of Appamatuck was appointed to bring him water to wash his hands, and another brought him a bunch of feathers, instead of a towel to dry them. Having feasted him after their best barbarous manner they could, a long consultation was held, but the conclusion was, two great stones were brought before Powhatan: then as many as could laid hands on him, dragged him to them, and thereon laids his head, and being ready with their clubs to beat out his brains, Pocahontas, the king's dearest daughter, when no entreaty could prevail, got his head in her arms, and laid her own upon his to save his from death: whereat the emperor was contented he should live to make him hatchets, and her bells, beads, and copper; for they thought him as well as all occupations as themselves. For the king himself will make his own robes, shoes, bows, arrows, pots; plant, hunt, or do anything as well as the rest.

Two days after, Powhatan having disguised himself in the most fearfulest manner he could, caused Captain Smith to be brought forth to a great house in the woods, and there upon a mat by the fire to be left alone. Not long after, from behind a mat that divided the house was made the most dolefulest noise he ever heard; then Powhatan, more like a devil than a man, with some two hundred more as black as himself, came unto him and told him now they were friends, and presently he should go to Jamestown, to send him two great guns, and a grindstone, for which he would give him the county of Capahowosick, and for ever esteem him as his son Nantaquoud.

Source: From *The Generall Historie of Virginia, New-England, and the Summer Isles,* by John Smith, quoted in *Living History America: The History of the United States in Documents, Essays, Letters, Songs, and Poems,* edited by Erik Bruun and Jay Crosby (New York: Tess Press, 1999), p. 43.

SIGNIFICANCE

In the last half of his life, Smith became less a man of action and more a writer and advocate of further colonization. In all, he published ten works. These autobiographical sketches, histories, reprints of other accounts, guides for seamen, and promotional tracts constitute the most important source of information on Smith's life. For generations, historians dismissed them as unreliable because Smith's portrayal of his career was so fantastic. He did include episodes that stretch the limits of credibility. For example, he tended to attribute his escapes from difficult circumstances to the intervention of women. When the

Turks captured him, Smith explained, they sold him as a household slave to a young woman named Charatza Tragabigzanda. She quickly became attracted to the Englishman and worked to ease his enslavement. After he escaped and made his way across Russia, Smith claimed that a noblewoman there aided him as well.

Smith's most famous rescue, however, occurred in Virginia. After his capture by Powhatan's warriors, the eleven-year-old Pocahontas prevented his execution. There were others. As he escaped from the French pirates who had captured his ship headed for New England, Smith wrote that he was helped by a Madame Chanoyes. Finally, when he had difficulty finding a backer for his longest book, *The Generall Historie of Virginia, New-England, and the Summer Isles* (1624), Frances Howard, the duchess of Richmond and Lennox, provided the funds. Smith also included incredible claims of victories over great warriors in single combat. The most prominent example came while he fought in Hungary. He met on successive days three Turkish opponents and not only killed them but also removed their heads for trophies.

Even Smith's most sympathetic biographers have acknowledged his enormous ego and his determination to emphasize his role in the events he chronicled. (In his publications, he referred to himself as captain, or governor of Virginia, or admiral of New England, or all three.) Nevertheless, Smith's writings remain important. Modern research has largely confirmed the accuracy of his histories (although the episodes involving female saviors and single combat have not been substantiated). Indeed, his *A True Relation of Such Occurrences and Accidents of Noate as Hath Hapned in Virginia Since the First Planting of That Collony* (1608) and *A Map of Virginia, with a Description of the Country* (1612) are the most complete accounts of early Virginia and the best sources on the natives of the Tidewater region.

Smith's work, moreover, had significance in his own era. *A Description of New England: Or, Observations and Discoveries of Captain John Smith* (1616), *New Englands Trials* (1620), and *The Generall Historie of Virginia, New-England, and the Summer Isles* served as promotional literature for expanding the English empire. He wrote in glowing terms of the prospects for North America. Yet, to build flourishing colonies, England would have to learn from his experiences in Virginia and New England. Success would come, Smith argued, only from a combination of firm leadership, industrious settlers, and aid from the English crown.

Smith closely followed events in the New World until his death in London in 1631. He lived long enough to learn of Virginia's stability under royal control (King James I revoked the Virginia Company charter in 1624) and of the large Puritan migration to Massachusetts, developments that vindicated his enthusiastic support of empire. The unashamedly ambitious and arrogant Smith had been a crucial figure, both as a leader and as a promoter, in England's efforts to colonize North America.

—Larry Gragg

FURTHER READING

Allen, Paula Gunn. *Pocahontas: Medicine Woman, Spy, Entrepreneur, Diplomat*. San Francisco, Calif.: HarperSanFrancisco, 2003. Allen presents a multifaceted view of Pocahontas's life and historical significance, which includes information about John Smith.

Barbour, Philip L. *The Three Worlds of Captain John Smith*. Boston: Houghton Mifflin, 1964. This is the most complete biography by the leading authority on Smith. Barbour presents the greatest details on Smith's years in Virginia and the most thorough discussion of sources.

Emerson, Everett H. *Captain John Smith*. New York: Twayne, 1971. Rev. ed. New York: Twayne, 1993. Rather than a biography, this is a study that focuses on Smith as a writer. While acknowledging Smith's embellishments, Emerson praises his prose, particularly his ability to draw vivid word pictures.

Hawke, David Freeman, ed. *Captain John Smith's History of Virginia: A Selection*. Indianapolis: Bobbs-Merrill, 1970. Hawke offers an edited reprint of the sections on Virginia in Smith's *The Generall Historie of Virginia, New-England, and the Summer Isles*. Although Hawke has a good, brief introduction, he includes scarcely any footnotes to help the reader.

Lemay, J. A. Leo. *The American Dream of Captain John Smith*. Charlottesville: University Press of Virginia, 1991. Lemay updates Philip L. Barbour's biography, *The Three Worlds of Captain John Smith*, and defends Smith's character and accomplishments.

_____. *Did Pocahontas Save Captain John Smith?* Athens: University of Georgia Press, 1992. An interesting study that attempts to discern the truth or falsehood of John Smith's account of his rescue by Pocahontas.

Morgan, Edmund S. *American Slavery, American Freedom: The Ordeal of Colonial Virginia*. New York: W. W. Norton, 1975. Reprint. New York: W. W. Norton, 2003. Morgan describes the origins of slavery in Virginia and its impact on the colony's economic, social, and political development. The early chapters include an excellent description of the difficulties faced by Smith and the other settlers at Jamestown.

Price, David. *Love and Hate in Jamestown: John Smith, Pocahontas, and the Heart of a New Nation.* New York: Knopf, 2003. Price draws on period letters, chronicles, and documents to relate the founding of the Jamestown colony.

Smith, Bradford. *Captain John Smith: His Life and Legend.* Philadelphia: J. B. Lippincott, 1953. In this well-researched volume, Smith receives his most sympathetic treatment. Particularly valuable on John Smith's early years. The author draws upon the research of Laura Polanyi Striker, which largely substantiates Smith's account of his experiences in Hungary.

Vaughan, Alden T. *American Genesis: Captain John Smith and the Founding of Virginia.* Boston: Little, Brown, 1975. Vaughan does more than present a short, balanced biography of Smith; he also details the history of Virginia from Smith's departure in 1609 until his death in 1631.

SEE ALSO: Canonicus; James I; Massasoit; Metacom; Pocahontas; Powhatan; Squanto; Miles Standish.

RELATED ARTICLES in *Great Events from History: The Seventeenth Century, 1601-1700:* May 14, 1607: Jamestown Is Founded; December 26, 1620: Pilgrims Arrive in North America; March 22, 1622-October, 1646: Powhatan Wars.

SOPHIA
Russian regent (r. 1682-1689)

Sophia acted as regent on behalf of her younger brother, Ivan V, and her half brother, Peter the Great, between 1682 and 1689. She built upon the trickle of reforms initiated by her father, Czar Alexis, accustoming her people to modest innovation, which became a flood under Peter the Great.

BORN: September 27, 1657; Moscow, Russia
DIED: July 14, 1704; Novodevichy convent, Moscow
ALSO KNOWN AS: Sofya Alekseyevna; Susanna
AREAS OF ACHIEVEMENT: Government and politics, diplomacy

EARLY LIFE

Sophia (SAWF-yuh) was the sixth of thirteen children born to Czar Alexis and to his first wife, Maria Miloslavskaya, who belonged to a distinguished Muscovite family. Sophia was one of nine sisters and five brothers, some of whom died prematurely, but two of her brothers became czars, Fyodor II (r. 1676-1682) and Ivan V (r. 1682-1696). Her famous half brother, Czar Peter the Great (r. 1682-1725), was Alexis's son with his second wife, Natalya Kirillovna Naryshkina.

Like all aristocratic Muscovite women prior to Peter the Great's reforms, Sophia was brought up in the Terem (women's quarters) of the Faceted Palace, where women passed their secluded lives in a routine of religious duties, needlework, eating, and drinking. The Terem in many respects resembled the harems of aristocratic Muslim families. Terem women were uneducated, except

for religious instruction, but Sophia was an exception. Somehow (the details remain unknown), she contrived to be present during the instruction given to her brother, Fyodor, and thereby acquired an education far beyond that of other women of the Romanov family.

After her mother's death in 1669 and her father's remarriage, Sophia would soon have become aware of the bitter and relentless rivalry between the families and retainers of the two wives. Alongside these individual intrigues, she would also have observed the deep schism in the Russian Orthodox Church, initiated during the reign of her father. This schism resulted in many conservatives known as Old Believers (*raskolniki*) being savagely persecuted as schismatics. Sophia would also have noticed her father's various attempts to reform the ramshackle Russian state, including military reforms involving the establishment of units under foreign officers. The foreign officers' presence was bitterly resented by the core of the Russian army, the *strelsi*, a reactionary corps of musketeers first established by Ivan the Terrible. For all that, no evidence survives to suggest that Sophia had, or indeed could have expected to have, political aspirations. It was the premature death of Fyodor and the feeble health of Ivan that provided the unique circumstances for her astonishing rise to power.

LIFE'S WORK

The reign of Fyodor II was short and uneventful, with the government firmly in the hands of his Miloslavsky relatives. The czar suffered from poor health and died young.

At her brother's death, Sophia was twenty-five and seems to have enjoyed a following within the court. On the day of Fyodor's death, the patriarch of Moscow summoned a cross-section of the community, drawn mainly from the immediate vicinity of the Kremlin, and offered them the choice of having as ruler one or other of the young princes, Ivan or Peter. The crowd favored Peter, with his mother as regent, thereby empowering the Naryshkins and excluding the Miloslavsky faction from power.

What happened next remains uncertain. At the center of events was Prince Ivan Khovansky, an experienced commander, extremely ambitious and with a reputation as a braggart and a debauché. He enjoyed extensive influence among the restless *streltsi*. His brief political role caused this period to be known as Khovanshchina (Khovansky Mischief, which became the title of Modest Mussorgsky's great opera of 1886). A rumor began, perhaps originating with Prince Khovansky, that Ivan V had been murdered. This caused the *streltsi*, on May 15, 1682, to burst into the Kremlin and riot in front of the Faceted Palace. After further disorders, the young czars, with Peter's mother Natalya, appeared on the Red Staircase. An ally of Natalya and former favorite of Alexis, Artemon Matveev, attempted to soothe the crowd. He was followed by a *streltsi* commander, Prince Mikhail Dolgoruky, son of the head of the Streltsi Prikaz (the *streltsi* bureau), who insulted the men and threatened them. The effect was explosive. The *streltsi* rushed the steps and hacked both Matveev and Dolgoruky to pieces. Then they burst into the palace and murdered any members and supporters of the Naryshkin family they could find.

By the end of May, the triumphant *streltsi* were in control: Ivan and Peter were to reign jointly as co-czars, and Sophia was to be regent, a position that she held from 1682 to 1689. The joint coronation took place on June 25, 1682. Prince Khovansky was appointed head of the Streltsi Prikaz. His son, Prince Andrei, was appointed head of the Sudnyi Prikaz, the bureau of justice. Sophia, while consolidating her position, avoided direct confrontation with Prince Khovansky, the darling of the *streltsi*. Instead, she left Moscow and, during July and August, visited various royal estates and monasteries. She kept apprised of the situation in Moscow, however, and when Prince Khovansky, who was instigating unrest among the Old Believers, failed to appear when summoned, she had him and his son arrested, denounced before the Boyar Duma (council of nobles), and executed (September 17, 1682). Fyodor Shaklovity, Sophia's devoted sup-

porter, who would remain loyal almost to the end, was appointed to replace Khovansky as head of the Streltsi Prikaz.

Sophia, as a woman, could not rule Muscovy in the way later eighteenth century czarinas were to do, and she turned for a mentor and chief minister to the brilliant Prince Vasily Vasilyevich Golitsyn (1643-1714), who had served both czars Alexis and Fyodor in various capacities. Like Alexis and Sophia herself, Golitsyn favored cautious change. The boy-czars, meanwhile, participated in the ceremonial life of the monarchy: Ivan lived in the Kremlin, while Peter lived with his mother in the village of Preobrazhenskoe, where he played war games with his companions and servants and established close ties with various foreign nationals. Sophia, who, despite her willingness to innovate, strictly adhered to the elaborate formality of religious life expected of Muscovite rulers, lived in the Kremlin but regularly visited the famous monastic complexes, such as the Trinity-Saint Sergius monastery at Zagorsk and the Novodevichy, which she built up lavishly in the style known as Muscovite Baroque.

Sophia's six-year regency left a strong imprint upon Russia's foreign relations, replacing the old Muscovite xenophobia with cautious commitment. She negotiated treaties with the Holy Roman Empire, Sweden, Denmark, and Brandenburg. On April 26, 1686, eternal peace with Poland was proclaimed by the Treaty of Moscow, a major triumph for Sophia. In retrospect, it seems clear that it was from this treaty that Russia emerged as a truly great power in eastern Europe, while Poland sank into political decrepitude. Further afield, Cossack penetration of the Amur region had provoked a Manchu counterattack on the fort of Albazin, leading to the Russo-Chinese Treaty of Nerchinsk (August 27, 1689).

The Crimean Khanate, itself a vassal state of the Ottoman Empire, continued to occupy not only the Crimean peninsula but also part of the Ukraine. In February, 1687, Prince Golitsyn led an expedition against the Crimea, while Sophia joined with the Holy Roman Empire, Poland, the Papal States, and the Venetian Republic in the Holy League against the Ottomans, ostensibly out of concern for the welfare of the Orthodox Christians under Muslim rule. Neither the Orthodox patriarch nor his people was comfortable with an alliance with the Catholic powers, however. Moreover, Golitsyn blundered in his campaign on the steppes and turned back in June, 1687. A second expedition between February and July, 1689, fared no better and came at a time when Sophia's regency was already unraveling. She and Golitsyn attempted to present the expedition as a triumph, but the reality of the situation soon became public knowledge.

As Ivan and Peter grew older, Sophia's position was becoming untenable, for there was no precedent for Russian female rule. The seventeen-year-old Peter, eager for power and growing assertive, had publicly clashed with Sophia on July 8, 1689, in Moscow's Kazan Cathedral, even before Golitsyn's return from the Crimea. Peter then withdrew to the Trinity monastery (August 7-8) and summoned the *streltsi* and the service-nobles to join him there. When Sophia attempted to see him, she was turned back (August 29, 1689), and on September 7, she was denied the use of her royal titles ("Great Sovereign Lady, Pious Czarevna and Great Princess Sophia Alekseevna, Autocrat of all the Great and Little and White Russias"). She was confined in the Novodevichy convent. Golitsyn and his family were sent into exile near the White Sea, and the loyal Shaklovity was executed (November, 1689).

Ivan V and Peter I were now indubitably the czars of Russia, with Peter the effective ruler. Ivan died in January, 1696. Peter thereafter departed for his Grand Embassy to Western Europe (1697-1698) but returned prematurely at news of a *streltsi* mutiny. In the course of his brutal interrogation, torture, and execution of the *streltsi*, Peter sought unsuccessfully for proof of Sophia's complicity. In October, 1698, he interrogated her personally at Novodevichy but apparently could not prove her involvement. That same month she was made to take the veil as the nun Susanna. She died in Novodevichy on July 14, 1704.

SIGNIFICANCE

Although conservative in matters of religion, Sophia, with her modest reforms, provided a significant bridge between the reign of her father, Alexis, a cautious and timid innovator, and that of Peter the Great, with his dynamic program of modernization. Her diplomatic career, although short-lived, had lasting effects upon the fate of Eastern Europe. She may also have set a precedent for a series of eighteenth century czarinas—Catherine I, Anna, Elizabeth, and Catherine II—the last of whom raised the Russian state to the pinnacle of its national glory.

—*Gavin R. G. Hambly*

FURTHER READING

Dixon, Simon. *The Modernization of Russia, 1676-1825.* New York: Cambridge University Press, 1999. A good general introduction to early modern Russia.

Hughes, Lindsey. *Russia and the West: The Life of a Seventeenth-Century Westernizer, Prince Vasily Vasil'evich Golitsyn, 1643-1714.* Newtonville, Mass.: Oriental Research Partners, 1984. The biography of Sophia's mentor and prime minister.

_____. *Russia in the Age of Peter the Great.* New Haven, Conn.: Yale University Press, 1998. An essential introduction to Petrine studies.

_____. *Sophia: Regent of Russia, 1657-1704.* New Haven, Conn.: Yale University Press, 1990. The only study of Sophia available in English. A superb biography.

Longworth, Philip. *Alexis: Tsar of All the Russias.* New York: Franklin Watts, 1884. Essential for understanding the world into which Sophia was born.

SEE ALSO: Alexis; Ivan Stepanovich Mazepa.

RELATED ARTICLES in *Great Events from History: The Seventeenth Century, 1601-1700:* 1609-1617: Construction of the Blue Mosque; February 7, 1613: Election of Michael Romanov as Czar; 1632-1667: Polish-Russian Wars for the Ukraine; September 2, 1633: Great Fire of Constantinople and Murad's Reforms; December, 1639: Russians Reach the Pacific Ocean; 1652-1667: Patriarch Nikon's Reforms; April, 1667-June, 1671: Razin Leads Peasant Uprising in Russia; 1672-c. 1691: Self-Immolation of the Old Believers; 1684-1699: Holy League Ends Ottoman Rule of the Danubian Basin; November, 1688-February, 1689: The Glorious Revolution; Beginning 1689: Reforms of Peter the Great; August 29, 1689: Treaty of Nerchinsk Draws Russian-Chinese Border; March 9, 1697-August 25, 1698: Peter the Great Tours Western Europe.

SŌTATSU
Japanese painter

In collaboration with the artist and calligrapher Honami Kōetsu, Sōtatsu founded the Rimpa school of painting. This style, characterized by the use of traditional Japanese themes, bold colors, and innovative paint and ink techniques, would influence Japanese art for nearly two hundred years.

BORN: Unknown; Noto Province, Japan
DIED: c. 1643; Kanagawa, Kaga Province, Japan
ALSO KNOWN AS: Nonomura Sōtatsu; Tawaraya
  Sōtatsu; Kitagawa Sōtatsu
AREA OF ACHIEVEMENT: Art

EARLY LIFE

Sōtatsu's (soh-taht-soo) early life is so cloaked in obscurity that art historians can scarcely agree on such elementary information as the year of his birth, his family name, or formative influences on his art. There is general agreement that he was born in Noto Province, perhaps in the early 1570's. His father is believed to have been a wealthy merchant named Tawaraya, and Sōtatsu is often referred to as Tawaraya Sōtatsu, although his paintings were usually signed with the honorific title *hokkyō* or with the seals *Taiseiken, Taisei,* or *Inen.* His family name is considered to be Kitagawa or possibly Nonomura, and scholars have linked him by marriage to a distinguished line of artisans, including Ogata Dōhaku, the great-grandfather of Rimpa painters Ogata Kōrin and Ogata Kenzan. He is also believed to be related though his wife's sister to Honami Kōetsu.

Little is known of Sōtatsu's formal education, but his painting teacher, Kaihō Yūshō, an artist renowned for his eclectic blend of Chinese and Tosa style influences, appears to have been instrumental in directing Sōtatsu's art toward the native themes of Zen Buddhism and classical literature favored by the imperial court, rather than the Kanō style popular with the shogunate.

Sōtatsu's first official notice seems to have come around 1600, but it was the result of his skill as a craftsperson rather than through an original work. Probably on the recommendation of Yūshō, who visited the Itsukushima shrine in 1598, Sōtatsu was commissioned by the Taira family to restore three medieval Buddhist sutra scrolls there, finishing them in 1602. His talent for matching the highly cultivated style of the Heian period (784-1185) and his love of the Buddhist themes that predominate in much of his early work resulted in his receiving the honorific Buddhist title of *hokkyō* around 1621.

These qualities also provided the bond that joined him to his most important collaborator, Kōetsu.

LIFE'S WORK

Though Sōtatsu's career spanned more than forty years, from 1600 to 1643, his decade of work with Kōetsu, from 1605 to 1615, is often considered to be his most productive period. During this time, the artist developed his mature style and pursued those themes from Japanese classical literature, music, dance, and mythology that were to have a lasting impact on succeeding generations of Rimpa painters. The collaborative aspect of their relationship is considered to have enhanced many of the aspects of their work, as Kōetsu was an acknowledged master of calligraphy as well as a fine painter. The similarity in the styles of both men and the ambiguous nature of their division of labor on many projects have long vexed art scholars in their efforts to establish the authorship of certain works.

Kōetsu had established a workshop at Takagamine, near Kyōto, that attracted artists and craftspeople in such diverse media as painting, pottery, papermaking, landscape gardening, and calligraphy. Sōtatsu undoubtedly frequented the studio but seems to have remained independent of it. He maintained his own establishment, called Tawaraya, in Kyōto, where he did a brisk business selling fans, scrolls, and decorative items. Starting about 1605, the two men began producing hand scrolls with calligraphy by Kōetsu over woodblock prints by Sōtatsu on paper manufactured by the papermaster Sōji. A fine early example of this work is the so-called deer scroll. Here the deceptively simple, cartoonlike deer charm the viewer with their sprightly gait and their sly, haughty smiles.

Far more complex and ambitious were Sōtatsu's screen paintings. It is in these that he was able to bring his skill as a craftsperson to bear on the classical themes favored by Kyōto aesthetes to create works of startling originality. The *yamato-e* style of painting, characterized by the use of themes from Japanese literature and mythology, and represented by the Tosa school, had declined in popularity by the late 1500's. A more vulgar style featuring the use of vivid color and favored by many of the feudal lords increasingly contended with a muted, Chinese inspired, approach (Kanō) favored by the Tokugawa shogunate and the samurai class. The Chinese style, pioneered by Song Dynasty painter Muqi

Fachang, sought to evoke the inner feeling or spirit of the subject rather than to emphasize strictly representational aspects.

Sōtatsu's special genius lay in reviving the particularly Japanese themes of *yamato-e* and combining them with decorative techniques—inkwashes, paint puddling, the use of bright colors, finely executed detail, and grandiose scale—to create art of startling boldness and subtlety. By the later years of Sōtatsu's life, not only the artistocrats of Kyōto but also the court of the shogun at Edo, its attendant daimyo, and large numbers of wealthy merchants eagerly sought his work.

One of the keys to Sōtatsu's skill lies in the enormously varied scope of his works. The Rimpa school is sometimes referred to as the decorative school, and the huge volume of purely decorative work done by Sōtatsu on fans, tea bowls, scrolls, and screens—some are as large as six panels—provided invaluable experience both in the execution of fine detail and in the development of innovative ways of utilizing space.

Both of these elements may be found in Sōtatsu's illustrative works based on the *Ise monogatari* (ninth century; *Tales of Ise*, 1968) and *Genji monogatari* (c. 1004; *The Tale of Genji*, 1925-1933). In the *Sekiya* screen, which illustrates a favorite *yamato-e* theme from *The Tale of Genji*, the scene is fraught with anticipation and tension: Genji encounters his former lover in a closed oxcart stopped at the Sekiya gate. The facial expressions of all the participants betray their relationship to the story, but the focus of the picture is on the unseen and unrequited lover. The details on this large three-panel screen are as finely wrought as those on any of the artist's miniature fans.

The *Bugaku Dancers* reveals a similar love of detail. Additionally, Sōtatsu's simple, almost abstract approach to the use of space in the painting achieves a harmonious balance despite the lack of background. The effect on the viewer is not unlike that of being an eavesdropper on the performance.

Another hallmark of the mature Sōtatsu style is his innovative use of ink and paint, often inverting the standard techniques of both mediums. His painting *The Cormorants*, for example, utilizes a background of heavy ink, added like pigment. Several paintings, notably *The Wind and Thunder Gods* and the *Sekiya* and *Bugaku* screens, feature bold use of gold and silver pigments, reflecting his growing taste for striking color.

Perhaps Sōtatsu's most innovative bending of technical norms was the development of the *tarashikomi*, or boneless method of painting. There is no inked outline of

the subject. Instead, as in the screen painting *The Poppies*, wet colors are applied in successive layers, each before the previous one had dried. The subtle blending of all colors creates the effect of flowers emerging from a mist. A similar effect, this time using gold and silver pigment, can be found in the scroll (done with Kōetsu) *Flowers and Grasses of the Four Seasons*.

So little is known of Sōtatsu's life that it is impossible to give a physical description of him as a mature man. There are no self-portraits, and with the exception of a 1630 copy of a Buddhist scroll, his works have proved tantalizingly difficult to date. His signature seals were often added years after paintings were completed. Indeed, in a number of cases, scholars are not even certain which works are his and which are Kōetsu's and must rely on subtle nuances of style to make their judgments. From the few details that have emerged of Sōtatsu's later life, it is generally accepted that he moved to Kanagawa sometime around 1640. There he spent his last years in the service of the Maeda family of Kaga Province, where he died about 1643.

SIGNIFICANCE

If precious little of Sōtatsu's life is accessible to historians, it is almost impossible to overestimate the impact of the Rimpa school on Japanese art. In a very real sense, Sōtatsu and Kōetsu reflect in art the spirit of the Tokugawa age. Maturing during a period of robust political dynamism and foreign adventure in the 1590's, followed by the concerted effort of the Tokugawas to cultivate Japanese values in an environment free from foreign influences, their art reflects the harmonious synthesis of traditional values and bold, vibrant technique. In the aesthetic hothouse of Edo Japan, the ability of Rimpa painters and artisans continually to develop original personal styles while drawing from centuries of native models ensured their popularity for generations of demanding patrons.

The style of the Sōtatsu-Kōetsu school continued after the passing of both men. Some scholars have argued that it reached its greatest refinement with the Ogata brothers, Kōrin and Kenzan, in the late seventeenth century. Both Sōtatsu's and Kōetsu's sons continued the artistic tradition, and it is probable that the Ogatas received their training from them. Most scholars believe that, following the deaths of the Ogatas in the early eighteenth century, the quality of Rimpa productions declined to a certain extent. The spirit, if not the technical quality, of the school would reappear during the Meiji period (1868-1912), another age of self-conscious Japanese national feeling, in the form of the Nihonga or modernist school of painting.

Sōtatsu's style may be seen as one of the highest expressions of formalism in Japanese art. Although he exhibited considerable skill in the depiction of detail, as well as in evoking emotion, his main emphasis is on bold tonal experiments, eye-pleasing color, and the asymmetrical but harmonious use of space. As Shuichi Kato writes, Sōtatsu "was indeed a perfect visual expression of the traditional Japanese mind and sensitivity, manifest through ages also in other cultural spheres: in architecture, in literature, and, in a sense, even in social and political life."

—Charles A. Desnoyers

FURTHER READING

Grilli, Elise. *Tawaraya Sōtatsu.* Rutland, Vt.: C. E. Tuttle, 1956. Though dated, this work contains the most complete account of Sōtatsu's life and work available to the general reader in English. Grilli provides a well-balanced examination of Rimpa art with an emphasis on the influences of the Tosa, *yamato-e*, and Kanō styles. Illustrated.

Kato, Shuichi. "Notes on Sōtatsu." In *Form, Style, Tradition: Reflections on Japanese Art and Society.* Translated by John Bester. Berkeley: University of California Press, 1971. A capable translation that places Sōtatsu's work in *yamato-e* context. Contains a good analysis of class tastes and their relation to the Rimpa school. The author contends that Sōtatsu represents the best of traditional Japanese eclecticism. Illustrated.

Lillehoj, Elizabeth, ed. *Critical Perspectives on Classicism in Japanese Painting, 1600-1700.* Honolulu: University of Hawaii Press, 2004. Includes an essay on Kōrin and Sōtatsu and their patrons as well as a biographical list of seventeenth century Japanese artists.

Paine, Robert Treat, and Alexander Soper. "The Return to Native Traditions: Edo Period, 1615-1867." In *The Art and Architecture of Japan.* Rev. ed. Baltimore: Penguin Books, 1975. Perhaps the most comprehensive treatment of Japanese art, especially in the Edo period, available in one volume. Provides considerably detailed biographical information on Sōtatsu's early years and his relationship with Kōetsu. The authors see the Rimpa school as a truly original Japanese art tradition. Illustrated.

Rosenfield, John J., and Shūjirō Shimada. "Kōetsu, Sōtatsu, and Their Tradition." In *Traditions of Japanese Art: Selections from the Kimiko and John Powers Collection.* Cambridge, Mass.: Fogg Art Museum, Harvard University, 1970. A large, beautifully executed selection from the Fogg Art Museum's holdings. Each chapter contains a concise overview of the period, and each illustration is highlighted by detailed explanatory text. There is an in-depth examination of Kōetsu's Takagamine salon and perceptive and sensitive explorations of calligraphic technique.

Stanley-Baker, Joan. "Azuchi-Muromachi and Edo (1573-1868)." In *Japanese Art.* London: Thames & Hudson, 1984. A brief, well-informed look at Sōtatsu, Kōetsu, and Kōrin within a broad context of three millennia of Japanese art. Especially effective in placing the Rimpa school within broader political and artistic developments of the Hideyoshi and Tokugawa eras. Illustrated.

SEE ALSO: Hishikawa Moronobu; Ihara Saikaku; Matsuo Bashō; Ogata Kōrin; Tokugawa Ieyasu; Tokugawa Tsunayoshi.

RELATED ARTICLES in *Great Events from History: The Seventeenth Century, 1601-1700:* 1603-1629: Okuni Stages the First Kabuki Dance Dramas; Beginning 1607: Neo-Confucianism Becomes Japan's Official Philosophy; 1617: Edo's Floating World District; 1688-1704: Genroku Era.

BARUCH SPINOZA
Dutch philosopher

The influence of Spinoza, a major figure among seventeenth century philosophers, has reached into the scholarship of the twenty-first century. He helped to lay the groundwork for developments in letters and contributed to the emergence of political and religious tolerance.

BORN: November 24, 1632; Amsterdam, United
    Provinces (now in the Netherlands)
DIED: February 21, 1677; The Hague, United
    Provinces (now in the Netherlands)
ALSO KNOWN AS: Benedict Spinoza
AREAS OF ACHIEVEMENT: Philosophy, government
    and politics, religion and theology

EARLY LIFE

Baruch Spinoza (BAHR-ewk spih-NOH-zah) was born in Amsterdam. His parents, Michael and Hanna Deborah, were Spanish-Portuguese Jews who had emigrated to Holland to escape religious persecution. This persecution was relatively recent in origin. Jews living in Spain during the late Middle Ages had experienced a period of tolerance under the Moors, who were Islamic. The return of Christian rule utterly reversed this trend. Subject to all manner of plunder and murder during the Spanish Inquisition, many Jews decided to convert to Christianity.

A large number of these converts, however, continued to practice Judaism in private. That led to a new round of persecution and finally to the expulsion of Jews from Spain in 1492. Some converted Jews (or Marranos, as they were called) sought refuge in Portugal. Over time, persecution arose there as well. Holland became a logical next step for Jews who desired the freedom to practice their religion and pursue fruitful commerce. Spinoza's parents are believed to have been Marranos who had sought refuge in Jodenburt, the Jewish quarter of Amsterdam. There they could practice Judaism openly, enjoying the fruits of religious tolerance unmatched in all Christendom. They were also free to pursue a broad range of commercial opportunities.

This relatively self-contained community first nurtured Spinoza, providing him with material comforts and an extensive education in Jewish religion and philosophy. Ultimately, however, Spinoza was cast out. How and why that came about is pivotal to an understanding of Spinoza's early life as well as to his subsequent career.

Spinoza's father was in the import-export business and is believed to have been highly successful. Spinoza helped in the family business but at some point became far more interested in his studies than he was in commerce. He wished, moreover, to broaden his studies beyond the usual fare, exploring the less orthodox canons within Jewish thought and acquainting himself with non-Jewish sources of learning. This, in itself, was not unusual. Many members of the Jewish community had opened themselves to the world around them. As a result, Spinoza's father was agreeable, arranging for Spinoza to study Latin outside the Jodenburt in the home of Francis Van den Ende, a freethinker and something of a political radical.

The study of Latin enabled Spinoza to explore the rationalist philosophy of René Descartes. Though Descartes did not openly disparage traditional religion, his philosophy was an attempt to understand the world through reason rather than faith. Spinoza also launched into what was, for a Jew, even more controversial, a study of the New Testament.

The result of these unorthodox studies was that

Baruch Spinoza. (Library of Congress)

Spinoza moved irretrievably beyond the dominant beliefs of the community into which he had been born, rejecting its commercialism as well as the exclusiveness of the Jewish faith. Indeed, it appeared to some that he was rejecting religion altogether. As Spinoza's beliefs became known, the leaders of the Jodenburt responded first by attempting to bribe Spinoza with a generous monetary allowance in return for his outward compliance with orthodox beliefs. Spinoza refused this offer. Shortly thereafter, he was tried and found guilty of what amounted to a charge of heresy. In 1656, Spinoza was excommunicated.

Why Spinoza's accusers acted is not as self-evident as it might seem. The Jewish community in Amsterdam permitted a fair amount of diversity, and Spinoza was outwardly quiet about his dissenting opinions in theological matters. He was not, so far as is known, a gadfly in the image of Socrates. These circumstances have led some scholars to explain Spinoza's excommunication as a response by Jewish leaders to their fear of renewed persecution by Christians flowing either from Spinoza's apparent atheism or from his association with Dutch political radicals. The fact that Spinoza had already begun to divorce himself from the Jewish community (he was no longer living in the Jodenburt at the time of his excommunication) supports such an interpretation. Another theory is that Spinoza was thought dangerous because of his opposition to wealth and privilege within the Jewish community. Whatever the motivation, Spinoza was excommunicated at the age of twenty-four. Shortly afterward, he was forced by Dutch authorities to leave Amsterdam's city boundaries—this, too, at the urging of the Jewish leaders.

LIFE'S WORK

Though Spinoza's excommunication was of great symbolic importance, it did little to change the way he actually conducted his life. Spinoza left behind his Hebrew name, Baruch, substituting for it the Latin equivalent, Benedict (both mean "blessed"). Yet he did not become a Christian. Nor did he marry. He lived quietly, first in Rhijnsburg, later in Voorburg, accumulating only so much money as he needed to pay his bills. A good neighbor and well loved by friends, he devoted the rest of his life to his studies.

What income Spinoza did have may have come from his knowledge of optics and skills as a lens grinder. That, at least, has become part of the Spinoza legend. There is no evidence, however, that Spinoza actually earned a living in this way. It has, therefore, been hypothesized that to sustain himself Spinoza accepted moderate amounts of money from friends, though here, too, the evidence allows for little more than an educated guess. What is known is that Spinoza repeatedly rejected large gifts from wealthy friends and also that he refused a professor's chair at the University of Heidelberg.

Two reasons have been advanced for these actions: Spinoza's humble tastes and, most important, his devotion to writing what he thought was true, regardless of who might be offended. Such candor required thoroughgoing independence. This is not to say that Spinoza led an entirely isolated existence. He exchanged ideas with numerous intellectuals, religious reformers, and political activists until the end of his life. The outcome of this combination of lively discourse and independence of thought was a body of work that drew immediate attention from avid supporters as well as critics and that has stood the test of time.

Spinoza's earliest work of note was his *Renati Des Cartes principiorum philosophiae* (1663; *The Principles of Descartes' Philosophy*, 1905). Though the essay is little more than an exegesis, it demonstrates Spinoza's profound grasp of the system he spent much time criticizing. The appeal of Descartes for Spinoza lies in Descartes's stated goal of explaining the world through the use of reason alone, thus taking a giant step beyond medieval Scholasticism, which, at best, gave reason status nearly equal to that of

---

SPINOZA'S MAJOR WORKS

1663	*Renati des Cartes principia philosophiae* (*Principles of Descartes' Philosophy*, 1905)
1670	*Tractatus theologico-politicus* (*A Theologico-Political Treatise*, 1862)
1677	*Opera posthuma*
1677	*Ethica* (*Ethics*, 1870)
1677	*Tractatus politicus* (*A Political Treatise*, 1883)
1677	*De intellectus emendatione* (*On the Improvement of the Understanding*, 1884)
1677	*Epistolae doctorum quorundam virorum ad B.D.S. et auctoris responsiones* (*Letters to Friend and Foe*, 1966)
1677	*Compendium grammatices linguae hebraeae* (*Hebrew Grammar*, 1962)
1862	*Tractatus de deo et homine eiusque felicitate* (*A Short Treatise on God, Man, and His Well-Being*, 1963)

revelation. Spinoza's central criticism of Descartes was that he continued to take much on faith.

In 1670, Spinoza's *Tractatus theologico-politicus* (*A Theologico-Political Treatise*, 1862) was published anonymously. In this work, Spinoza broke new ground, writing perhaps the most eloquent defense ever of religious freedom. The treatise includes a critical essay on the Bible that points out its rather haphazard assembly of very different works from different eras into a single text. It also distinguishes the role of reason, which is to discern truth, from that of religion, which is to foster piety. Although these points may seem innocent enough to modern readers, the treatise was greeted with a chorus of criticism from a variety of clerics, many of whom branded its author an atheist, and the Catholic Church, which banned it. Spinoza's circle of friends and supporters, on the other hand, deeply appreciated his achievement.

The rancor with which *A Theologico-Political Treatise* was received may well have persuaded Spinoza that it would be neither wise nor prudent to publish again during his lifetime. Although prudence in this matter is easily understood, it is likely that wisdom also played a role in Spinoza's decision. Throughout his life, Spinoza demonstrated a high regard for the atmosphere of tolerance in the United Provinces, which permitted the Jewish people to worship and he himself to think freely. To publish controversial works openly might risk the habits of tolerance that were just then taking root. His other major works remained unpublished until after his death in 1677, and even then remained anonymous (actually, authorship was designated by the use of Spinoza's initials). These include his unfinished *Tractatus politicus* (1677; *A Political Treatise*, 1883), which, beginning from Hobbesian premises about human nature, ends up with a very un-Hobbesian defense of democratic principles, and *Ethica* (1677; *Ethics*, 1870), Spinoza's most substantial and most famous work.

In *Ethics*, Spinoza borrows the language of Descartes (including such notions as "substance"—what might be called matter—and "extension"—what might be called form) to finish the interpretation of the world as it is known through reason. Although God plays a central role in Spinoza's worldview, it is not the role to which one is accustomed by traditional religion. Instead, God is depersonalized and indifferent. For many readers, this translated into atheism; for others, it is a form of pantheism. Whatever one's interpretation, the distinctiveness of *Ethics* lies in the direct connection of this metaphysical framework with a theory of how human beings should seek to do what is right and also achieve happiness in the absence of divine commandments. Ethical

---

SPINOZA ON THE GOOD, THE EVIL, AND INTELLIGENT LIFE

Baruch Spinoza was condemned as an atheist for his idea that it is acceptable for individuals to believe in the rightness of human reason in the light of uncertainties about God and faith. Uncertainty, therefore, is a form of evil, for it keeps humans from obtaining truth and the good, and from living a rational life.

Our actions—that is those desires which are defined by man's power, *or* reason—are always good; but the other [desires] can be both good and evil.

In life, therefore, it is especially useful to perfect, as far as we can, our intellect, *or* reason. In this one thing consists man's highest happiness, *or* blessedness. . . .

No life, then, is rational without understanding, and things are good only insofar as they aid man to enjoy the life of the mind, which is defined by understanding. On the other hand, those [things] which prevent man from being able to perfect his reason and enjoy the rational life, those only we say are evil.

Source: Spinoza, *Ethics*, Part IV, appendix (1677), excerpted in *A Spinoza Reader: The "Ethics" and Other Works*, edited and translated by Edwin Curley (Princeton, N.J.: Princeton University Press, 1994), pp. 239-240.

---

conduct and happiness flow from the proper combination of emotion (or passions) and reason, neither being completely dominant over the other.

Ethics is clearly not designed to be edifying or stylish. It is argued through what Spinoza thought to be the philosophical equivalent of geometric proofs. These, quite frankly, seem tedious at first glance. Yet, for those who were not busy condemning Spinoza's godlessness, the book conveyed (and for many readers still conveys) breathtaking beauty and insight, giving off a special aura that is not strictly intellectual, literary, or spiritual, but that somehow partakes of all three.

In addition to his formal writing, Spinoza left behind a large body of correspondence that is indispensable to an understanding of his life and thought. These letters not only provide a running commentary on Spinoza's philosophical works but also indicate the considerable interest his ideas inspired and the affection in which he was held by many friends. These friends mourned deeply when Spinoza died suddenly and, if reports are correct, peacefully, on February 21, 1677, at the age of forty-four.

SIGNIFICANCE

During his lifetime, Baruch Spinoza established an underground reputation as one of the greatest philosophers of his day. Even those such as Gottfried Wilhelm Leibniz who openly disparaged him could not ignore the forcefulness of his thought.

In addition to his purely intellectual achievements, Spinoza served as an inspirational figure for the circle of freethinkers with whom he was in contact. For them, Spinoza's devotion to truth, defense of tolerance, and humility made him a rallying point in their attempts to bring about further progress. At the same time, however, in the eyes of many observers, Spinoza's name was synonymous with atheism, which was widely held to be nothing less than diabolical.

Over time, the viewpoint of Spinoza's supporters has easily outdistanced that of his critics. It is true that the triumph of analytic philosophy in Anglo-American universities has tended to devalue the broad synthetic enterprise in which Spinoza was engaged, and there is an archaic quality to Spinoza's terminology. Nevertheless, it is well established that Spinoza was one of the three great rationalist philosophers (along with Descartes and Leibniz) and that he had a great influence on later philosophers, such as G. W. F. Hegel.

Yet Spinoza's influence goes beyond the discipline of philosophy. Literary figures such as Gotthold Ephraim Lessing and Johann Wolfgang von Goethe were profoundly influenced by the beauty, if not the logic, of Spinoza's worldview. Psychologists continue to debate Spinoza's treatment of emotion and its relation to knowledge. Libertarians still celebrate his quest for religious freedom and free expression. Intellectual historians look to Spinoza in their search for a bridge between Eastern and Western values or for the roots of modern democracy. There are others who read Spinoza's work or study his life simply for insight into their own lives. In short, Spinoza remains an inspirational figure for those who take the time to learn about him. Paradoxical as it may seem, there is something deeply spiritual about this man who was excommunicated by Jews for heresy and repeatedly condemned by Christians as an atheist.

—*Ira Smolensky*

FURTHER READING

Browne, Lewis. *Blessed Spinoza: A Biography of the Philosopher*. New York: Macmillan, 1932. A lively, well-written account of Spinoza's life by a professional biographer. A good introduction, but the work should be augmented by more current research.

Feuer, Lewis Samuel. *Spinoza and the Rise of Liberalism*. Boston: Beacon Press, 1958. Uses historical, psychological, and philosophical analysis to link Spinoza's excommunication to his political orientation. Feuer portrays Spinoza as the first in a long line of politically radical Jewish intellectuals.

Garrett, Don, ed. *The Cambridge Companion to Spinoza*. New York: Cambridge University Press, 1996. A collection of essays, including a general overview of Spinoza's life and work; more in-depth examinations of his thoughts on metaphysics, knowledge, natural science, ethics, and theology; and an analysis of his biblical scholarship.

Kayser, Rudolf. *Spinoza: Portrait of a Spiritual Hero*. Translated by Amy Allen and Maxim Newmark. New York: Philosophical Library, 1946. As the subtitle suggests, an inspirational and highly sympathetic account of Spinoza's life. Includes a brief introduction by Albert Einstein.

McShea, Robert J. *The Political Philosophy of Spinoza*. New York: Columbia University Press, 1968. Fits Spinoza into the tradition of political philosophy from Plato and Aristotle to the present, offering particularly cogent comparisons of Spinoza's thought to that of Niccolò Machiavelli and Thomas Hobbes. Includes a lengthy bibliography.

Nadler, Steven. *Spinoza: A Life*. New York: Cambridge University Press, 1999. A comprehensive biography of Spinoza, recounting the events of his life, including his Jewish heritage and relationship to the Amsterdam Jewish community that excommunicated him. Describes the emergence of his philosophy, providing a detailed and understandable explanation of his ideas.

Smith, Steven B. *Spinoza's Book of Life: Freedom and Redemption in the "Ethics."* New Haven, Conn.: Yale University Press, 2003. An analysis of *Ethics*, which Smith describes as Spinoza's celebration of human freedom and its attendant joys and responsibilities. Includes chapters on the book's examination of God, thinking, desire, politics, love, and the authority of reason.

Spinoza, Baruch. *The Ethics and Selected Letters*. Edited by Seymour Feldman. Translated by Samuel Shirley. Indianapolis, Ind.: Hackett, 1982. A compact, accessible edition of Spinoza's most extensive philosophical work, together with some of his more philosophically revealing letters.

Steinberg, Diane. *On Spinoza*. Belmont, Calif.: Wadsworth/Thomson Learning, 2002. Overview of Spinoza's life and philosophy intended for a general audience. The introductory chapter provides a brief account of his life, followed by chapters explaining various aspects of his philosophy, including his ideas on metaphysics, mind and body, psychology, ethics, and philosophical methods.

SEE ALSO: Pierre Bayle; Anne Conway; René Descartes; Thomas Hobbes; Gottfried Wilhelm Leibniz; Samuel von Pufendorf.

RELATED ARTICLE in *Great Events from History: The Seventeenth Century, 1601-1700:* 1637: Descartes Publishes His *Discourse on Method.*

SQUANTO
Pawtuxet diplomat, interpreter, and guide

After his initial, unpleasant contact with English settlers, Squanto became a friend and supporter of the Plymouth Colony. The first major Native American interpreter for the colonies, his geographic knowledge of New England was invaluable to the settlers, and his hunting and fishing expertise enabled them to survive the early difficult years in North America.

BORN: c. 1590; Patuxet (near present-day Plymouth Bay, Massachusetts)

DIED: November, 1622; Chatham Harbor, Plymouth Colony (now Chatham, Massachusetts)

ALSO KNOWN AS: Tisquantum (given name)

AREAS OF ACHIEVEMENT: Diplomacy, linguistics, education

EARLY LIFE

The early life of Squanto (SKWAHN-toh), or Tisquantum as he called himself, is mostly unknown. He was a member of the Pawtuxet, a small tribe of about two thousand that was part of the Wampanoag Confederation of tribes along the coast of New England. Squanto's home village was located near the later site of the Plymouth Colony. His date of birth could have been as early as 1580, but since he was apparently very young in 1605, the time of his first contact with the English, he was more likely born about 1590. Nothing is known about his childhood years, but there is some indication that he was a sachem (chief) or at least a potential sachem.

In 1605, more than a century after John Cabot claimed North America for England, English merchants, desiring more information about the natural resources of the area, organized an expedition to explore the coast of Canada and New England. They enlisted the services of Captain George Weymouth to lead the venture. Captain Weymouth sailed down the coast from Maine, eventually stopping in what later became Massachusetts. After trading with Native Americans in the area, the captain decided to take several Native Americans back to England

to show the merchants what the inhabitants were like. Several young men were apparently bribed to go with Weymouth, and two more were forcibly captured. One of these was an especially good representative of the Native American population and was the one Weymouth definitely wanted to take back to England. Based on his apparently early introduction to the English language and on other circumstantial evidence, this young man was most likely Squanto. Weymouth's own account indicates that Squanto willingly agreed to go to England, but that is highly unlikely.

Sir Ferdinando Gorges was the head of the Plymouth Company and was planning to exploit the natural resources of North America. Upon arrival in England, Squanto was taken to live with Gorges. Squanto learned some basics of the English language, which then enabled him to serve as a guide and translator for Weymouth's ship captains, who were sailing the coasts of New England. Despite Squanto's presence on these voyages, however, he was apparently never afforded the opportunity to return to his home on Plymouth Bay.

In 1614, after nine years in the service of Gorges, Squanto's return home was at last made possible when Captain John Smith, earlier of Virginia, agreed to take him on his journey to map the coast of New England. In return for Squanto's assistance in the endeavor, Captain Smith promised in good faith to return the Pawtuxet guide to his native village. Smith had plans for a major trading settlement in New England, and peaceful and friendly tribes were an important part of this plan. When Smith returned to England, he left behind an associate, Thomas Hunt, to trade with the native tribes.

Hunt's plans were far different from Smith's. He soon lured twenty-four trusting Nauset and Pawtuxet men, including Squanto, aboard his ship. He sailed to Málaga, Spain, where he began selling his captives into slavery. Squanto was later rescued by friars at a monastery, converted to Christianity, and somehow made his way to England. For several years he lived in London and became fluent in the English language.

Finally, in 1619, Squanto and Captain Thomas Dermer, with whom Squanto had become friends when both worked for John Smith, led an expedition back to America. Their goal was to re-establish the trade that had ended as a result of the actions of Hunt. After separating from Squanto, Dermer was wounded fighting Native Americans at Martha's Vineyard and later died of his wounds at Jamestown.

LIFE'S WORK

Squanto's return to his home village of Pawtuxet was bittersweet. During the last years of his absence, a plague, most likely smallpox brought to the New World by the Europeans, had broken out among the Nauset and Pawtuxet tribes along Plymouth Bay. Squanto found that his entire village had died. He was the lone survivor. Whatever leadership role Squanto had had before his captivity was now lost, since he had been a leader only within his own village and not in the larger Wampanoag Confederation.

For the next several months, Squanto lived with the Pokanokets and the Namaskets, other tribes of the Wampanoag Confederation. There is some indication that he was actually a captive as a result of the fighting that had wounded Dermer and of Squanto's friendship with the English. Massasoit and his brother Quadequina led these two tribes, and they were the dominant figures in the Wampanoag Confederation as a whole.

The work for which Squanto is best remembered began with the November, 1620, arrival on Plymouth Bay of the *Mayflower* and its cargo of 102 passengers. The Pilgrims, as they were later called, disembarked in December and began building their village of Plymouth. Although the site of the village was on or very near the site of Squanto's old village of Pawtuxet, Squanto did not immediately pay a visit to the settlers. During that first harsh winter, about half the settlers died of disease.

Samoset, a member of the Abenaki tribe in Maine, was visiting the Wampanoag Confederation at this time. On March 16, 1621, he walked into Plymouth, perhaps sent by Massasoit to investigate the conditions of the settlement. Samoset, who had learned a few words of English from fishermen, returned to the village on March 22. With him was Squanto, with his excellent knowledge of the English language, as well as Massasoit and Quadequina. With Squanto as interpreter, the leaders of Plymouth quickly signed a treaty and negotiated a trade agreement with the tribal leaders.

Squanto stayed at Plymouth for the rest of his life, which was about eighteen months. From the first day, he tied his life and fortunes to those of the English settlers. He taught them the basic survival skills needed to be successful in New England. He told them when and how to plant corn. The settlers followed his instructions, planting when the leaves on the trees were the size of squirrel's ears, putting several seeds in a small hill, and including a fish for fertilizer. Squanto even taught the women how to cook the corn. Squanto helped the men build warmer houses and taught them to hunt and fish.

Squanto also greatly assisted the Plymouth Colony in their relationship with the Wampanoag Confederation. A major part of this assistance resulted from his skill as an interpreter. He guided English leaders to various villages, introduced them to the village leaders, and negotiated treaties. However, not all of his work was successful. Although the Pokanokets, led by Massasoit, were pleased with the initial treaty with Plymouth, the Namaskets felt that it gave too much power to the English. At one point, Squanto was captured by the Namaskets and had to be rescued by the settlers. His later negotiations with Massachusett towns north of Plymouth and with other Wampanoag tribes on Cape Cod were more successful. The relationship between the English settlements and the Wampanoag Confederation, which Squanto helped establish, lasted until Metacom's War (also known as King Philip's War) in 1675.

One of Squanto's closest friends at Plymouth was Governor William Bradford. In November, 1622, he accompanied Bradford on a trading expedition to Cape Cod. Bad weather forced them into Manamoyick Bay, where Squanto became ill with Indian fever. As he lay dying, he asked Bradford to pray for him so that he could go to the Englishmen's God in heaven. He bequeathed his few possessions to his English friends.

SIGNIFICANCE

Squanto seems to have, on occasion, tried to use his friendship with the English for his own advantage. On one occasion he tried unsuccessfully to undermine the authority of Massasoit. As a result of this episode and his close friendship with the English, other Wampanoags came to consider him an enemy. This rejection by his own people is indicative of the tense relations between the Wampanoags and the English, even before the settlers made any programmatic attempts to expand their territory.

Squanto's greatest historical significance arguably

lies in his simple, day-to-day value to the Plymouth Colony in teaching the Europeans an American way of life. At the very least, the survival of the colony would have been much more difficult without the aid of their Native American friend, and it might well have failed altogether.

—*Glenn L. Swygart*

FURTHER READING

Brandon, William. *The Rise and Fall of North American Indians*. New York: Taylor Trade, 2003. Chapter 17, "Puritans and Indians," establishes Squanto's role in the complicated and stormy relationships between the English and the Native Americans.

Hoxie, Frederick, ed. *Encyclopedia of North American Indians*. Boston: Houghton Mifflin, 1996. Includes the best-researched and probably the most accurate account of Squanto. Does not include the less documented 1605 capture by George Weymouth. Includes all that is known of his 1614 capture and the next five years.

Salisbury, Neal. *Manitou and Providence: Indians, Europeans, and the Making of New England, 1500-1643*. New York: Oxford University Press, 1982. Full coverage of the relationship between the Native Americans in New England and the European settlements. By one of the best known modern scholars of the period.

_____. "Squanto: Last of the Patuxets." In *Struggle and Survival in Colonial America*, edited by David Sweet and Gary Nash. Berkeley: University of California Press, 1981. An excellent essay on Squanto in the overall context of the colonial confrontations between the Native Americans and the European immigrants.

SEE ALSO: William Bradford; Massasoit; John Smith.
RELATED ARTICLES in *Great Events from History: The Seventeenth Century, 1601-1700:* 1617-c. 1700: Smallpox Epidemics Kill Native Americans; December 26, 1620: Pilgrims Arrive in North America; June 20, 1675: Metacom's War Begins.

MILES STANDISH
English-born American colonist

Standish provided the Pilgrims of Plymouth Colony with basic military training, helped make their settlement defensible, and helped organize a practical system of militia and government for the colony.

BORN: c. 1584; Ellenbane, Isle of Man, England
DIED: October 3, 1656; Duxbury, Massachusetts Bay Colony
AREAS OF ACHIEVEMENT: Exploration, government and politics, military

EARLY LIFE

Although it is typically reported that Miles Standish was born in Chorley, Lancashire, England, modern research indicates that he was born on the Isle of Man. Standish descended from the important Roman Catholic family Standish of Standish, and according to his will, Miles was fraudulently deprived of his inheritance. Although little is known of his early life, he began his military career as a drummer boy in Queen Elizabeth's army. Eventually, he worked his way up in the ranks, and in the early 1600's, he served as a soldier of fortune in the Low Countries (the Netherlands), where English troops under

Horatio Vere had been stationed in Leiden to help the Dutch in their war against Spain.

During the same period when Standish was serving in the Netherlands, members of the English Separatist Church (a sect of the Puritans) fled from England to Leiden in order to escape religious persecution. After struggling for a livelihood in Leiden for more than ten years, the Separatists (Pilgrims) negotiated with a London stock company to finance a pilgrimage to America, where the Pilgrims could seek a more abundant life and freely practice their religion. Standish came to the attention of English Separatist leaders as a skilled, mature professional soldier and was hired by the Pilgrims to go with them to America and serve as their military adviser. Although Standish was not a member of the Leiden congregation, he quickly became a loyal supporter of the Pilgrim venture.

In late 1618, a small ship, the *Speedwell*, carried Standish and thirty-five Leiden Pilgrims to Southampton, England, where they later joined another group of Separatists on the *Mayflower*. Leaving Plymouth, England, on September 16, 1620, the *Mayflower* began its historic voyage to America with 102 passengers aboard.

Miles Standish. (Hulton Archive/Getty Images)

During the voyage, the short, sturdy, reddish-haired Standish demonstrated some of his leadership qualities by encouraging the passengers to maintain a cheerful attitude. Although the ship was initially headed for Virginia, stormy weather and navigational errors forced it five hundred miles farther north to the tip of Cape Cod, near present-day Provincetown, Massachusetts, on November 19, 1620.

LIFE'S WORK

Because Standish was the only man with practical experience in camping, he was given command of three successive expeditions to explore the Cape Cod area; while he was on the third excursion, the small company was attacked by a band of Indians. Standish used his military expertise to rally his amateur soldiers to defend their position, and the Indians gave up the attack and fled. It was also on this expedition that Standish learned about corn, which was later used as seed to save the colony from starvation.

On December 26, 1620, Standish was one of the small

party who made the first landing at the site the Pilgrims called Plymouth. After selecting Plymouth as the Pilgrims' place of settlement, Standish made arrangements for defending the colony. On a hill overlooking the village, Standish supervised the Pilgrims in building platforms where they mounted several pieces of artillery, and then he designed and helped construct a wooden fort on the hill, fence lines extending downward from the fort to protect Plymouth on the most vulnerable sides, and a small wooden fort at the intersection of the two village streets. Standish organized the Pilgrim men into a militia and gave all the adult men compulsory basic training in weaponry and tactics. Thereafter, he was elected as the captain of the Plymouth armed forces and as chief negotiator with the New England Indian tribes, serving in these capacities for thirty-two years.

During the early months of winter in 1621, many of the settlers became sick, and more than half of them, including Standish's wife, Rose, died as a result of poor nutrition and inadequate housing. Only Captain Standish and William Brewster escaped the sickness, and they rendered invaluable service to the others, fetching wood, making fires, preparing meals, washing clothes, making beds, and ministering to the sick. The kindness and fidelity of Standish in attending to the needs of the sick were later documented by Plymouth governor William Bradford in his classic account *History of Plymouth Plantation* (1856). It was probably this kind attentiveness to the Pilgrims' needs that made Standish one of them and not merely their employee.

After spring arrived, Standish interacted with the local Indian tribes, and he and Bradford consummated a treaty with Chief Massasoit of the powerful Wampanoag tribe that guaranteed safety for Plymouth for many decades. Standish proved himself a linguist, quickly learning many Indian dialects and developing expertise in Indian relations. After a good first year's harvest, the Pilgrims held their first Thanksgiving, and the Indians joined with the English settlers in the feasting. Standish impressed the Indians by putting his men through their military exercises.

From time to time, Captain Standish led military expeditions from Plymouth to aid allies or to suppress Indian or non-Puritan enemies. In late 1621, he conquered a minor chief known as Corbitant with very little bloodshed, and on another occasion he led a military party to aid Squanto and a group of friendly Indians. Just as Governor Bradford had befriended Squanto, Standish befriended Hobomok, an Indian warrior of Chief Massasoit, and the two remained very close friends and military consultants for each other for more than thirty years. In 1622, Standish came to the aid of an English village at Wessagussett (now Weymouth, Massachusetts) that was being threatened by an attack from members of the Massachusetts Indian tribe. Standish called for a conference with the uprising Indians and, through deception, led the Indian leaders into a building where he barred the doors shut. Standish and his men then assaulted and killed the Indian leader and several other rebellious members of the tribe.

In the famous poem *The Courtship of Miles Standish* (1858), written by Henry Wadsworth Longfellow, the shy Standish asks his friend John Alden to approach Priscilla Mullins about marriage on behalf of Standish, but there is little historical basis for this story. In 1624, Standish married his second wife, Barbara, who had arrived on the ship *Anne* in 1623. They had six sons and one daughter, with two sons and the daughter dying quite young.

By 1624, Standish had gained enough respect from the Pilgrims that he was chosen as one of the five assistants to the governor of Plymouth Colony. In 1625, the Pilgrims selected Standish to return to England as their agent to represent them in settling some disputes that had arisen with the English merchants who had financed the colony and to negotiate with the Council of New England for rights to land in the New World. With the council he had some success, but very little with the merchants. However, he was successful in securing further loans and purchasing much-needed supplies, which he took back to Plymouth in 1626. The following year, Standish was one of a group of colonists who bought out the English merchant investors, thus allowing the Pilgrims to assume title to their land in New England. Standish and the others who assumed the debts of the colony became known as the Undertakers.

In June of 1628, Captain Standish led a military party to arrest Thomas Morton, the leader of some undisciplined traders, at a settlement at Merrymount (now Quincy, Massachusetts). Morton's emphasis on riotous living, selling firearms to the Indians, and selling and buying furs for exorbitant prices threatened the safety and trading profits of Plymouth. Similar to the way he had confronted the Indians at Wessagussett, Standish barred the doors and made ready to battle Morton. However, Morton and his two associates were so drunk that they could not resist capture, and Standish had Mor-

ton sent back to England. Morton later complained of Standish's hot temper and gave Standish the label of Captain Shrimp.

Desiring to extend their domain, Standish, William Brewster, John Alden, John Howland, Francis Eaton, and Peter Brown founded a new settlement in 1631 in Duxbury, across the harbor from Plymouth. The new colony was named after Duxbury Hall in Lancashire, England, seat of the Standish family, and it became a chartered town in 1637. Since Standish, Brewster, and Alden were deemed too important to be spared for a permanent absence from Plymouth, they returned periodically to Plymouth for political and military councils. In 1637, Standish and his wife, Barbara, established their permanent residence in Duxbury. By that time, Standish was quite wealthy, having accumulated a lot of land and cattle.

The last military confrontation for Standish came in 1645, when he led a forty-man company westward to stand guard at the frontier against a possible attack from the powerful Narragansett tribe of Rhode Island. In addition to his military commission, Captain Standish served as assistant to the governor of the Plymouth Colony from 1624 to 1625, 1633 to 1635, 1637 to 1641, and 1645 to 1656, and as the treasurer of the colony from 1644 to 1649 and from 1652 to 1655. Remaining one of the most influential men in the growing colony of Plymouth until his death, Standish quietly died at his Duxbury estate, known as Captain's Hill, on October 3, 1656, leaving behind considerable wealth for his family and a large library in Plymouth. Standish and John Alden, who were dear friends, are buried near each other in Duxbury, and in 1872, a monument of Standish was erected that overlooks Duxbury.

SIGNIFICANCE

As an explorer, military commander, and political leader, Standish exhibited superior leadership skills and personal courage. During his thirty-two-year tenure as captain of the Plymouth armed forces, he encouraged his men by his own physical endurance and conspicuous bravery. Although an aggressive man with a short temper, he believed in fairness, and he established a policy with the Indians based on just treatment. Standish became a respected, beloved leader of the Plymouth Colony, and he succeeded in establishing peaceful relations with the Indians throughout his lifetime.

Standish was selected as the colony's first agent to return to England, and he also served as an envoy to other New England colonies. In addition, he served as an assistant to the governor of Plymouth for more than eighteen years. However, the greatest contribution of Standish was as the military adviser and commander of the Pilgrims, providing the Pilgrims with military training, a practical system of militia for the colony, and defensive strategies and structures for their settlement. The military and political leadership and dedication of Standish were immeasurably important in the successful establishment and development of Plymouth Colony. Without Standish, it is likely that Plymouth Colony would have failed.

—*Alvin K. Benson*

FURTHER READING

Alden, John. *The Story of a Pilgrim Family from the Mayflower*. Boston: James H. Earle, 1889. The Reverend John Alden, a descendant of Pilgrim John Alden, composes recollections and incidents from his forefather's writings about the *Mayflower* journey, the establishment of the Plymouth Colony, and life in Plymouth.

Bradford, William. *Of Plymouth Plantation*. New York: Alfred A. Knopf, 1959. First published in 1856 under the title *History of Plymouth Plantation*, these writings of Plymouth governor William Bradford give a firsthand account of the trials and successes of the Plymouth Colony as well as many insights into the character and abilities of Miles Standish.

Cheetham, J. Keith. *On the Trail of the Pilgrim Fathers*, Edinburgh: Luath Press, 2001. Cheetham recounts the Pilgrims's origins in England and their journey to the New World.

Deetz, James, and Patricia Scott Deetz. *The Times of Their Lives: Life, Love, and Death in Plymouth Colony*. New York: W. H. Freeman, 2000. Describes daily life in the colony, including how order was maintained, the Pilgrims' relations with Native Americans, gender relations, and the habits of hearth and home.

Langdon, Gregory D. *Pilgrim Colony: A History of New Plymouth, 1620-1691*. New Haven, Conn.: Yale University Press, 1966. An excellent compilation of the history of Massachusetts from 1620 to 1691, citing events in the lives of the Pilgrims and the leadership skills of Miles Standish.

Simmons, C. H. *Plymouth Colony Records*. Camden, Maine: Picton Press, 1996. The genealogies of some of the Pilgrim families are compiled in this work, which contains a chart of the family Miles and Barbara Standish, listing their seven children with birth, death, and marriage information.

Standish, Miles. *The Standishes of America*. Boston: S. Usher, 1895. A publication of the writings of Miles Standish with background about the Standish family, their genealogy and coat of arms, and the history of Plymouth Colony as seen through Standish's eyes.

Stratton, Eugene Aubrey. *Plymouth Colony: Its History and People*. Salt Lake City: Utah Ancestry Publishers, 1986. Stratton's book documents the history of the Pilgrims, Plymouth Colony, and some of the colony leaders, including Miles Standish.

SEE ALSO: William Bradford; Canonicus; James I; Massasoit; Metacom; Pocahontas; Powhatan; John Smith; Squanto.

RELATED ARTICLES in *Great Events from History: The Seventeenth Century, 1601-1700:* May 14, 1607: Jamestown Is Founded; December 26, 1620: Pilgrims Arrive in North America; March 22, 1622-October, 1646: Powhatan Wars.

NICOLAUS STENO
Danish scientist and bishop

Considered by many to be the founder of geology, Steno provided scientific explanations for the existence of fossils, stratification, and the constancy of crystal angles. As an anatomist, he made important discoveries regarding glands, muscles, the heart, and the brain. As a bishop, he was a missionary to Catholics in Protestant lands.

BORN: January 11, 1638; Copenhagen, Denmark
DIED: December 5, 1686; Schwerin (now in Germany)
ALSO KNOWN AS: Niels Stensen (given name); Niels Steensen; Nicolaus Stenon; Niccolò Stenone; Nicholas Stenonis
AREAS OF ACHIEVEMENT: Science and technology, medicine, religion and theology

EARLY LIFE

While the Thirty Years' War (1618-1648) was convulsing Europe, Niels Stensen, who later Latinized his name to Nicolaus Steno (nihk-eh-LAY-uhs STAY-noh), was born on New Year's Day, 1638, according to the Protestant calendar, but on January 11, according to the Catholic Gregorian calendar. His Lutheran father, Sten Pedersen, was a successful goldsmith who counted the king as one of his customers. His mother, Anne Nielsdatter, had, like her husband, been previously married and widowed.

Because of a severe illness, Niels was homebound until he was six years old. His full recovery was followed by the sudden death of his father. His mother remarried, but this husband died within a year. Niels's half sister and her husband took over his care. He attended a Lutheran academy, where he was taught Latin and introduced to chemical experimentation.

Niels pursued his education at a difficult time in Denmark. When he was sixteen, a plague caused the deaths of one-third of Copenhagen's population and, throughout most of his time at the University of Copenhagen, the city was under siege by the Swedes. Nevertheless, the young medical student was able to learn anatomy from Thomas Bartholin and, through his private studies, absorb the new ideas of such scientists as Galileo and René Descartes. Because of the chaotic situation in Copenhagen, Steno was unable to get his degree, and in the fall of 1659, carrying a letter of introduction from Bartholin, he traveled throughout Germany for several months before arriving in Amsterdam in the spring of 1660. Here, and three months later, in Leiden, he continued his medical education and began his first medical research.

LIFE'S WORK

In Amsterdam, while studying with the anatomist Gerhard Blasius, Steno made his first important discovery. While dissecting a sheep's head, he found an oral cavity that proved to be a source of saliva. This duct of the parotid gland became known as Steno's duct (*ductus Stenonianus*). After Steno matriculated into the University of Leiden, he performed other dissections, some of which resulted in new discoveries. One such discovery was the tear-producing glands of the eyes. In 1662, he published a book summarizing his anatomical experiments on glands, called *De musculis et glandulis observationum specimen* (English translation, 1664).

The death of his stepfather in 1663 occasioned his return to Copenhagen, but when he was denied a position at the university, he traveled to Paris. In 1664, still in Paris, he received his medical degree, in absentia, from the University of Leiden. Melchisedec Thévenot, a wealthy government official, supported Steno's work on muscles and the brain. An invitation to become court physician to the grand duke Ferdinand II de' Medici in Florence led him away from France in 1665.

For his first two years in Italy, he worked at the Hospital of Santa Maria Novella on muscles, brain anatomy, and embryology. Using a microscope, he observed muscles as bundles of geometric units, each subdivided into fibrils. In 1667, he published a book called *Elementorum myologiae specimen* (*Specimen of Elements of Myology*, 1994) on his geometric description of muscles, explaining muscle contraction as an aggregation of the tensile forces in each unit. He also recognized that the heart is basically a muscle, which contradicted ancient authorities who saw the heart as the "home of the soul." He published his findings as *Nova musculorum & cordis fabrica* in 1663 (*New Structure of the Muscles and Heart*, 1994). Steno once told friends that his conversion to Roman Catholicism occurred during the evening of All Souls' Day, November 2, 1667, when, through the voice of a woman from whom he was asking directions, he heard God telling him to "cross over" from Lutheranism to Catholicism. His conversion marked a turning point in his life. Steno also believed in the wisdom of the Creator. That is, that God (the Creator) made human beings and made Earth as their home.

In 1669, he published his discourse on the anatomy of the brain, in which he criticized Descartes's writings on the nature of humanity and the soul. For example, Descartes believed that the soul was connected to the body through the pineal gland in the brain, but Steno pointed out that animals other than humans had pineal glands. During the late 1660's, he also conducted embryological research, helping to establish that not only do oviparous creatures produce eggs but also females of viviparous species. His discoveries in embryology were published in the 1670's.

Many scholars consider Steno's work in geology, paleontology, and crystallography to be his most significant. His studies in geology were initiated in the fall of 1667 when he dissected the head of a great white shark that had been clubbed to death on the coast of Leghorn (Livorno). Steno was particularly impressed by the number and structure of the shark's teeth. In his report to Duke Ferdinand, he noted the similarities between the shark's teeth and the "tongue stones" (*glossopetrae*) common in Tuscany and elsewhere. He proposed that these tongue stones were fossilized shark's teeth. The mineralized shark's teeth piqued his curiosity about other fossils, such as seashells found on mountains, and for the next eighteen months he traveled throughout Tuscany, making observations of rock layers, collecting fossils, and visiting quarries, caves, mines, and private geological collections. The result of his studies was his greatest work, *De solido intra solidum naturaliter contento dissertationis prodromus* (1669; *The Prodromus to a Dissertation Concerning Solids Naturally Contained Within Solids*, 1671; better known as the *Prodromus*).

The book was meant to be the prelude to a much larger geological treatise, which he never wrote, but the observations, ideas, and theories that the *Prodromus* contained were important breakthroughs. In this treatise, Steno explained that if seashells were found in any rock layer (stratum), then an ocean must have been there at some time in Earth's history. He then enunciated some of the basic axioms of stratigraphy, including the principle of superposition: In undisturbed stratified rocks, the lowest layers represent the first to be deposited and the top layers represent the most recent. He also believed that the geological history of Tuscany passed through various phases of submersion under the sea and uplift above it. When Tuscany was first submerged, rocks that were not fossiliferous (that is, not containing fossils) were deposited. After uplift, the land was fractured into mountains and valleys. During the second submersion, sedimentation was fossiliferous, and when the land reappeared, cavities in the underlying rock foundation often collapsed, only to be later eroded by flowing water. In this

treatise, Steno also included an interesting section on crystals, in which he stated that crystal faces of a specific mineral have characteristically constant angles (modern crystallographers call this Steno's law).

While Steno was writing the *Prodromus*, he received an invitation from Danish king Frederick to serve in his court, but before reaching Copenhagen, he learned, in February of 1670, that the king had died. He also received word that his patron, Ferdinand, was gravely ill, and by the time he returned to Florence, the grand duke was dead. The new grand duke, Cosimo III de' Medici, was more interested in religion than science, but because he admired Steno's piety, he gave him a villa on the Arno River where he pursued his geological studies. Two years after his return to Florence, Steno's geological research was once again interrupted by another summons to Denmark, which Steno reluctantly accepted. In the winter of 1673 in Copenhagen, Steno gave his final public lecture on science. He had come to feel that as beautiful as science was, what was most beautiful to him was the spiritual world, so he decided to become a priest.

Because of his excellent education, he did not need to attend a seminary, and in April, 1675, four months after his return to Italy from Denmark, he was ordained and said his first Mass on Easter. He served as confessor to Cosimo III and did pastoral work in Florence, but in the spring of 1677, he was called to Rome so that he could be consecrated a bishop by Pope Innocent XI. His titular see was Titiopolis in Asia Minor (now Turkey), but instead, at the request of Duke Johann Friedrich of Hanover, Steno became apostolic vicar for the Nordic Missions. With a base in Hannover, he served as bishop for the small number of Catholics in northern Germany, Denmark, and Norway.

The Catholic duke Friedrich was followed as duke, upon his death, by his Lutheran brother, Ernst August, and Steno moved to Munster, where he instituted many reforms. His high standards, however, created enemies, so he moved to Hamburg, where his extreme asceticism and emphasis on poverty produced critics as well as admirers. He wrote religious works, exhorting clergy and laity to imitate Jesus Christ. After two years in Hamburg, he spent the remainder of his life in Schwerin, about 75 miles east of Hamburg. His harsh ascetic practices weakened his failing health, and, after his final confession, he died on the morning of December 5, 1686. Following Steno's death, Cosimo III had his remains transferred to Florence, where Steno was laid to rest in San Lorenzo Basilica.

SIGNIFICANCE

Historians of medicine have praised Steno's skills as an anatomist, but his most important achievements were in geology. Stephen Jay Gould, a twentieth-century American evolutionary biologist, described Steno as "the founder of geology." Steno's principles of original horizontality and superposition marked the beginning of stratigraphy. His recognition of fossils as remnants of ancient organisms helped elucidate the history of fossil-bearing rocks.

Critics have pointed out that, despite Steno's introduction of the chronological study of Earth's history, he had a weak understanding of the massive length of geological time. Because he was influenced by the prevailing theological analysis of biblical chronology, Steno thought that Earth was only several thousand years old. However, unlike Galileo, he did not suffer persecution for his scientific ideas, and Church censors found nothing problematic with his *Prodromus*. He himself saw no contradiction between his scientific and religious work, since the human body and Earth were both creations of God, just as the Bible was inspired by God.

As a scientist and a bishop, Steno was dedicated to the pursuit of truth. He influenced scientists because of his discoveries in anatomy and geology, and he influenced Christians because of his striving for holiness. In 1988, with twenty thousand scientists, priests, and admirers of Steno in attendance, Pope John Paul II beatified the priest-scientist in St. Peter's Basilica.

—*Robert J. Paradowski*

FURTHER READING

Cutler, Alan. *The Seashell on the Mountaintop: How Nicolaus Steno Solved an Ancient Mystery and Created a Science of the Earth.* New York: Penguin Plume, 2004. This work, intended for general readers, is both a biography of Steno and an analysis of his contributions to geology. Includes illustrations, a section on sources, and an index.

Kermit, Hans. *Niels Stensen, 1638-1686: The Scientist Who Was Beatified.* Leominster, Herefordshire, England: Gracewing, 2003. Although this work might be difficult to obtain, it is nevertheless a worthy biography of Steno as a religious leader. Includes illustrations, a bibliography, and an index.

Moe, Harald. *Nicolaus Steno, An Illustrated Biography: His Tireless Pursuit of Knowledge, His Genius, His Quest for the Absolute.* Translated by David Stoner. Copenhagen, Denmark: Rhodos, 1994. This biography tends to be hagiographical, but the text and illustrations provide general readers with an account of the positive achievements of Steno's life and work as well as the complexities of his character and times.

Oldroyd, David R. *Thinking About the Earth: A History of Ideas in Geology.* Cambridge, Mass.: Harvard University Press, 1996. Considered by many scholars to be the most comprehensive overview of the history of earth sciences. Oldroyd analyzes Steno's work as a significant part of this history. Index.

SEE ALSO: Sir Thomas Browne; Thomas Burnet; René Descartes; Innocent XI; Antoni van Leeuwenhoek; Marcello Malpighi.

RELATED ARTICLES in *Great Events from History: The Seventeenth Century, 1601-1700:* 17th century: Advances in Medicine; 1664: Willis Identifies the Basal Ganglia; 1669: Steno Presents His Theories of Fossils and Dynamic Geology; 1672-1684: Leeuwenhoek Discovers Microscopic Life.

FIRST EARL OF STRAFFORD
English politician

A controversial figure, Strafford was one of the principal advisers of Charles I during the era of personal rule, from 1629 to 1640. As such, he became a focus for the dissatisfaction and resentments of nearly all segments of British society against Charles's arbitrary exercises of royal power and pretensions toward absolutism.

BORN: April 13, 1593; London, England
DIED: May 12, 1641; London
ALSO KNOWN AS: Thomas Wentworth (given name)
AREA OF ACHIEVEMENT: Government and politics

EARLY LIFE

The first earl of Strafford (STRAF-uhrd) was born Thomas Wentworth, the son of William Wentworth of Wentworth Woodhouse, Yorkshire, and his wife, Anne Atkinson of Stowell, Gloucestershire. The Wentworths were an important and wealthy family of southern Yorkshire, with extensive family and political connections among the gentry and peerage of northern England. Thomas Wentworth attended Saint John's College, Cambridge, and studied law at the Inner Temple in London and traveled in France. In 1611 he married Lady Margaret Clifford, daughter of the earl of Cumberland; after Lady Margaret died in 1622, he married Lady Arabella Holles, daughter of the earl of Clare. These marriages allied Wentworth with powerful families, but his relations, at least with the latter, were strained. Even at this early point, Wentworth evinced the harsh and austere personality and the authoritarian tendencies that later made him so useful to the king and so disliked by his contemporaries. His second wife died in 1631, and Wentworth later married Elizabeth Rodes, who long survived him.

LIFE'S WORK

Through his family connections, Wentworth represented Yorkshire in the Parliament of 1614, the Addled Parliament, in which Crown and Parliament fought each other to a stalemate over the growing fiscal and constitutional problems of the country. This was a formative experience for Wentworth, for in this Parliament he first witnessed the intransigence of the Crown and the increasing aggressiveness of the House of Commons and became fully aware of the growing crisis that was to form the background to his adult life.

For a long time Wentworth refused to take sides or accept the possibility that politics might have become hopelessly polarized. Instead, he acted on the assumption that it was possible to reconcile the differences between Crown and Parliament and to restore the balance of the Elizabethan era, which he believed to be the traditional form of governance. He was always clear, however, that the Crown was the supreme authority in the state and that Parliament, in case of conflict, must defer to it, especially during a national emergency. Wentworth was elected to the parliaments of 1621, 1624, and 1625, in each of which he insisted that reconciliation was possible on the major issues of the day and strove to overcome the increasing polarization of public life by means of compromise and negotiation. Wentworth did, however, oppose the Crown's fiscal policies, and he firmly refused to repay a compulsory loan, an offense for which he was briefly imprisoned in 1627.

Wentworth emerged briefly as a leader of the Commons in 1628, largely on the strength of his resistance to forced loans; he also opposed the policies of the first duke of Buckingham, the king's favorite. Wentworth still insisted that it was possible to find a way to preserve the traditional rights and privileges of the subject without injury to the traditional prerogatives of the Crown. The result of this conviction was the Petition of Right, of which he was a principal mover.

Wentworth's position as a parliamentary leader was, however, based not on a general opposition to the royal regime but rather on objections to specific policies, which he believed were weak, corrupt, or ineffective. After the passage of the Petition of Right in 1628, Wentworth began to move rapidly toward the royal camp. Shortly after the prorogation of Parliament, he was created Baron Wentworth, and after the death of the duke of Buckingham he became in rapid succession a viscount, president of the Council of the North, and a member of the Privy Council.

In time, this shift came to be viewed as apostasy to the Parliamentary cause and Wentworth was regularly described as "Black Tom Tyrant" and the "grand apostate"; as late as the nineteenth century he was labeled the "Satan of Apostasy" by Thomas Babington Macaulay. He soon emerged as by far the most able, if also the least popular, of all royal advisers. It is perhaps ironic, in the light of the violent criticism heaped upon him because of his shift to the royal side, that Wentworth appears never really to have enjoyed full royal favor until the last year of his life and that he felt personally aggrieved that the king would not take full advantage of his abilities.

Between 1629 and 1633, Wentworth's principal sphere of activity was northern England, where as lord president of the Council of the North he was a powerful representative of the Crown's interests at all levels and had ample opportunity to demonstrate his harsh, often brutal, manner. He was named lord deputy of Ireland in the summer of 1631 but only took up office in 1633, sailing for Ireland in July of that year. He retained his position in northern England, henceforth exercised through a deputy, and undertook his rule in Ireland with a grant of extraordinary powers from the king.

Once in Ireland, Wentworth immediately undertook to apply his theories of "Thorough" to the country, by which he meant a fiscal, legal, and administrative reorganization carried out to the benefit of the Crown. He was especially interested in the economic development of Ireland, and he had some considerable successes in this line, but the ultimate beneficiaries were intended to be England and especially the king. Land tenure was the most complicated and volatile question in Ireland, and Wentworth was determined to seize every opportunity, and to make opportunities where none clearly existed, to extend the royal interest and to centralize royal power.

Wentworth tried to establish royal control over virtually the entire province of Connaught and sought to continue the practice of supplanting the native population with English settlers. He made no effort whatsoever to comprehend and work within the traditional structure of Anglo-Irish politics but rather, relying on his support from Charles I, rode roughshod over all local interests and created a ferocious hatred of his regime and all of his doings. His famous battles with the first earl of Cork (Richard Boyle), the greatest landlord in Ireland, and with the first Baron Mountnorris were merely the most publicized of his full-dress battles with the Irish establishment. He managed by force and by not-infrequent illegalities to keep the lid on Ireland during his residence there, but the harvest of these years came in the revolt of 1641 and the subsequent collapse of English influence in Ireland for the better part of a decade.

As the crisis in England drifted toward civil war in 1639, Charles I recalled Wentworth to England. He was raised from deputy to lord lieutenant of Ireland and was also raised to the peerage as earl of Strafford. He left Ireland for the king's side in September, 1639, in order to take charge of a situation that, he quickly realized, had been badly misman-

aged. For the next fifteen months, Strafford was the most powerful man in England after the king. He now possessed the supreme authority that he had always wanted, but he needed to act defensively, to try to salvage a situation that he had watched developing for years from his vantage point in Ireland. When he arrived at court, the English armies had already been driven ignominiously from the field by the Covenanting Scots, royal authority had virtually disappeared in Scotland, disaffection was spreading rapidly throughout England, and the royal government, which had few people of any real ability in it, was beginning to disintegrate.

At the beleaguered court, Strafford was the loudest in resisting any compromise or concession and in advocating the fullest use of the king's prerogative power, even if it meant suspending parliamentary statutes. He adamantly opposed all concessions to the Scots, bolstered the king's inclination to resolve his problems by force rather than by negotiation and concession, and undertook to provide the means by which the king might overcome

First Earl of Strafford. (Library of Congress)

his enemies. Strafford returned to Ireland and summoned a thoroughly cowed Irish Parliament to Dublin, where it voted the king taxes, promised him an army of eight thousand infantry and one thousand cavalry, and, for good measure, thanked the king for sending Strafford to govern them. That done, Strafford left Ireland for good on April 3, 1640. As soon as it became clear that he was embroiled in English affairs, Strafford's influence in Ireland rapidly waned and his numerous enemies undermined his regime.

By the time Strafford arrived in London in April of 1640, the Short Parliament was in session and the radical faction had already demonstrated its control over the House of Commons. A crisis soon arose over the king's revenue demands, demands that even Strafford thought unrealistic, and Parliament was peremptorily dissolved. Strafford reluctantly agreed with the king's decision. The afternoon of the dissolution, May 5, the king's closest advisers met to discuss the crisis in affairs and especially the continuing threat of Scottish intervention in northern England. Strafford took a prominent part in the debate and resisted all concessions to the Scots. He urged the king to seek a military solution and alluded to the army that the Irish Parliament had recently promised him. Precisely what Strafford said on this occasion was later the subject of heated debate and was instrumental in destroying his reputation.

Strafford and his policy of force were adopted by King Charles. In August, 1640, Strafford replaced the duke of Northumberland as general commander in the north, and he spent the remainder of that summer and the following autumn attempting to fashion some sort of an army with which to resist the Scots; at the same time, he urged the king to enact strong and authoritarian measures to control the populace. By October, 1640, however, it was clear that no successful resistance could be offered the Scots and a compromise was patched together at Berwick. Charles I agreed to call another parliament, which met on November 3.

When King Charles returned to London, he asked Strafford to join him. Strafford did so, though he must have realized that he was walking into the greatest crisis of his life. He was the most hated man in three kingdoms. Although he was not really responsible for the policies of the era of personal rule during the 1630's (except for those in Ireland), Strafford now became the focus of every complaint. He was also, and more accurately, seen as the most capable man in the royal service by the radical elements in the House of Commons and as the one man who was capable of effecting a dramatic restoration of royal authority by policy or by force. He was marked for destruction by John Pym and his supporters.

Strafford arrived in London on November 10, and the trap was instantly sprung. The attack on him began in the House of Commons the following morning, and by afternoon charges of high treason were lodged against him in the House of Lords. Strafford was in conference with Charles I when word of these proceedings was brought to him and he immediately left to defend himself before the House of Lords. The Lords, however, refused to hear him and had him arrested. In late November, articles of impeachment were presented to the Commons, and Strafford was taken to the Tower.

Impeachment proceedings began in late March of 1641, but Strafford discomfited his enemies by a sustained and brilliant attack on their charges. Eventually, it became clear that Parliament had failed to prove him guilty of the articles of impeachment, and Pym and his associates fell back on a bill of attainder, in which nothing needed to be proved legally and the ordinary safeguards did not apply. The bill of attainder passed easily through the Commons, then through the Lords, but the apparent sticking point was the necessity of obtaining the king's signature. That difficulty was overcome by instigating a crisis over threats of a military plot.

The royal palace at Whitehall was besieged and nearly overrun by rioters; the safety of the royal family was in doubt for a time. Strafford wrote a letter to the king insisting that his life should not stand between possible reconciliation of Crown and people. Though there was little enough reason to expect a reconciliation, Charles I took this opportunity to sign the act of attainder, after which Strafford was promptly and publicly beheaded on Tower Hill. Strafford's behavior throughout the protracted ordeal was nearly sufficient in many eyes to redeem his previous behavior. The king, on the other hand, never ceased to regret his approval of Strafford's attainder. The wisdom of Parliament's strategy was immediately apparent, for with the arrest and then death of Strafford, it became increasingly obvious that the royal cause had no one else of stature significant to sustain it, not even the king himself.

SIGNIFICANCE

The first earl of Strafford has remained a controversial figure down to the present day. He has had the peculiar fate of being most praised and most damned for things he never did. As the most capable and ruthless of King Charles I's servants, he was credited in his own lifetime with a degree of influence that he possessed only in the last, forlorn months of his life. Though in public a firm supporter of royal policies, in private he frequently disagreed with royal policies and deplored the king's reliance on corrupt or incompetent administrators. He had relatively little influence on the broad course of royal policy in England during the 1630's and none whatever on the disastrous Scottish policy of Charles I and William Laud that brought on the Civil War.

It was Strafford's fate to be brought in at the end to try to salvage a crisis for which he was not responsible, and he fell a victim, in large part, to other's mistakes. More recently, he has been seen as a potential man on horseback, a strong, authoritarian ruler who sought to cut through decaying political and administrative forms in order to achieve a more ordered and productive society. In fact, however, he was not a man who somehow transcended his time and anticipated modern methods of strongman rule. There is no evidence of a comprehensive concept of a change or transformation of politics or society. Strafford believed primarily in energy and force and sought to reinvigorate the English government by his own example. In particular, close investigation of his transactions in his native Yorkshire, and most especially in Ireland, reveal a man who failed to transcend contemporary standards of political morality. He was the king's best servant and a man of immense energy and will, but he was not a modern reformer.

—Neal R. Shipley

FURTHER READING

Canny, Nicholas P. *Making Ireland British, 1580-1650.* New York: Oxford University Press, 2001. Argues that Ireland's political allegiance was reshaped by British settlement and cultural assumption, long before the military conquest. Contains a chapter about Wentworth's policy of plantation in Ireland.

Kearney, Hugh F. *Strafford in Ireland, 1633-1641: A Study in Absolutism.* New York: Cambridge University Press, 1989. A revised edition of the standard contemporary work on the subject, offering a detailed examination of a crucial era in Ireland's history.

O'Grady, Hugh. *Strafford and Ireland.* Dublin: Hodges, Figgis, 1923. An older work, largely superseded by Kearney, but still of value.

Pogson, Fiona. "Making and Maintaining Political Alliances During the Rule of Charles I: Wentworth's Associations with Laud and Cottington." *History* 84, no. 273 (January, 1999): 52. Investigates Strafford's associations with key figures at the English court and his relations with Archbishop Laud and Francis, Lord Cottington.

Smith, David L. *Constitutional Royalism and the Search for Settlement, c. 1640-1649.* New York: Cambridge University Press, 1994. Examines Charles I's relationships with Parliament in the 1640's, providing details of Strafford's attainder and execution.

Wedgwood, Cicely V. *The King's Peace, 1637-1641.* London: William Collins Sons, 1960. Reprint. New York: Penguin Books, 1983. Combines scholarship and literary style to produce the most popular survey of the period.

_____. *Thomas Wentworth, First Earl of Strafford, 1593-1641: A Revaluation.* New York: Macmillan, 1962. Reprint. London: Phoenix Press, 2000. The standard life of Strafford. It is, as the full title suggests, a revaluation of Strafford's life in the light of manuscript sources that became available in the 1950's, primarily the Strafford papers in the Sheffield Central Library. A radically different view of Strafford has emerged since the appearance of this material.

SEE ALSO: First Duke of Buckingham; Charles I; William Laud; John Pym.

RELATED ARTICLES in *Great Events from History: The Seventeenth Century, 1601-1700:* May 6-June 7, 1628: Petition of Right; March-June, 1639: First Bishops' War; November 3, 1640-May 15, 1641: Beginning of England's Long Parliament; 1642-1651: English Civil Wars; August 17-September 25, 1643: Solemn League and Covenant.

BARBARA STROZZI
Italian composer and musician

Strozzi was the most prolific composer of printed secular vocal music in Venice. In an era when women composers were uncommon or unwelcome, and when few composers of either gender had their music printed, Strozzi published eight volumes of arias, madrigals, motets, and cantatas between 1644 and 1664.

BORN: 1619; Venice (now in Italy)
DIED: November 11, 1677; Padua (now in Italy)
ALSO KNOWN AS: Barbara Valle (moniker)
AREA OF ACHIEVEMENT: Music

EARLY LIFE

Barbara Strozzi (STRAWT-tsee) was the daughter of Giulio Strozzi, a prominent Italian gentleman who was highly active as a poet, dramatist, and sponsor of literary and musical circles. Strozzi's mother was Isabella Garzoni, known as la Greghetta, a longtime servant of Giulio Strozzi. Barbara Strozzi, who was sometimes referred to by her father as Barbara Valle, was adopted by Giulio probably because she was his illegitimate daughter. Giulio's will of 1628 stipulates that in case of la Greghetta's death, Barbara was to inherit all of his resources. Ultimately, she was her father's sole heir.

Strozzi's primary influence was her father, who, as a writer, was recognized for his orations, plays, and poetry, but most of all for his opera librettos (musical plays). Giulio was active in both the literary and musical life of Venice. He knew most of the leading intellectuals and was a member of groups or academies made of these elite writers and nobles. The groups would meet at the homes of distinguished members to debate artistic, cultural, and philosophical issues and to recite poetry, read plays, or perform music. Giulio founded two such academies in Venice after Barbara was born; one academy met at the home of a group member and the other, the Accademia degli Unisoni (academy of the unisons), founded in 1637, gathered at Giulio's home. This later group, which received some notoriety, had a musical focus.

Barbara had been singing informally at Giulio's home in front of distinguished guests since about 1634, but with the founding of the Unisoni academy, her performances became institutionalized. Through her father, Barbara entered a world that was not, for the most part, open to women, so her entrée into the academy immersed her into a world of famous musicians, with whom she became acquainted. She would eventually play a major role in the Unisoni academy, and so, in her honor, the group's published papers, *Veglie dei Signori Unisoni* (1638), were dedicated to her when she was just nineteen years old.

LIFE'S WORK

Strozzi began her public musical life as a singer. At her father's academy, early on, she served as a type of host or moderator, suggesting to the group topics for discussion. She also would judge debates and award prizes. More important, though, is that she sang at the meetings, singing the songs of others as well as, sometimes, her own compositions. It was apparent that she had a quality voice: In 1636, in book 2 of *Bizzarrie poetiche*, the composer Nicol Fontei refers to her as *la virtuosissima cantatrice*, the "most virtuosic singer." Strozzi did not perform before a large public on a formal stage, but was, instead, a chamber-music singer who would sing in homes at academy meetings and other similar occasions.

Strozzi would eventually learn about music composition from the distinguished musical guests who frequented her father's house. However, her primary music education came from formal study with one of the greatest opera composers of Venice, Franceso Cavalli (1602-1676). It was highly unusually for a woman of the time to receive such training, so there were few professional female composers in Europe. For the most part, women were not welcomed into the music world, but with this exclusion came a reluctance on the part of many women to become professional musicians in the first place. Professional female musicians were often stigmatized as seedy or disreputable in some way. Strozzi's upbringing, by an unconventional and supportive father, influenced her decision to foster a musical career. By the age of twenty-five, she began publishing her music, which was, like composing, a rare accomplishment for women. Eventually, she would publish more cantatas than any of her Italian contemporaries, female *or* male.

Strozzi's first publication (opus 1), *Il primo libro de madrigali; a due, tre, quattore, e cinque voce* (1644), marks the beginning of her career as a professional composer. This volume of madrigals, for two to five voices, has texts (lyrics) by her father, Giulio (she often set his words to music). Her next publication (opus 2), a book of twenty-six cantatas, arias, and duets called *Cantate, ariette, e duetti* (1651), was dedicated to Ferdinand III of

Austria and Leonora II (Eleanora Gonzaga) of Mantua to celebrate their marriage. Only two texts in this volume are by Giulio Strozzi.

Opus 2 was issued seven years after Strozzi's first volume, when Strozzi was thirty-two years old. The lapse in time between the two publications could be attributed to Strozzi having been responsible for caring for many young children during these interim years. Her son Giulio was born around 1641, daughter Isabella around 1642, and Laura (Lodovica) around 1644; the date of her son Massimo is unknown. There is no record of Strozzi ever being married, but three of her four children, at minimum, were fathered by a colleague of Giulio, Giovanni Paolo Vidman, with whom she had a long-term relationship.

Strozzi's only sacred publication, *Sacri musicali affetti* (opus 5), printed in 1655, is made up of fourteen works with Latin texts. All pieces, except one ("Salve regina") are nonliturgical, that is to say, the texts are devotional and not part of a prescribed service such as a Mass.

Strozzi is not known as a composer of operas or large orchestral works; indeed, she wrote no purely instrumental music. She composed primarily intimate, chamber music, meaning songs for solo soprano voice and a continuo instrument—a chord-producing instrument, such as a lute or harpsichord. The texts of her songs include frequent use of puns on her name; therefore, it is believed that she sang most of her music herself and thus composed it to fit her own vocal qualities. Her songs call for a lyric-style voice, not one that is too virtuosic, performing big leaps and trills, nor one with a wide range of low to high notes. Her music is set to carry the poetry of the lyrics in a flowing manner and calls for a clear vocal sound.

Along with a repeated refrain (same words and music that return between sections of new material), her pieces tend to have contrasting sections. Thus, in her cantatas and arias, her style may shift with ease from a duple- to a triple-metered section, or from a passage with a clear beat and pulse to one that is free and unmeasured. She differs from her teacher Cavalli by tending to feature longer melismatic sections (a section where each syllable of a word is set with more than one or several notes), which take some vocal skill to perform. Moreover, she repeats texts more frequently than Cavalli. Her focus on words and repetition is perhaps a consequence of her being raised by a poet and of her own activities as a gifted writer: She may have had a desire to emphasize literary aspects.

SIGNIFICANCE

Strozzi was one of the most significant composers of solo vocal music of mid-seventeenth century Venice. Although women of her time were not afforded the same music education or opportunities as were men, she was able to study with a leading composer, perform her works in public (albeit intimate), and even publish them. Without the support of the Church or noble families, support that was bestowed on male musicians, she was still able to flourish, and indeed, during her lifetime, she had more music in print than the most-famous male musicians in Venice. Such is a testament to the quality of her compositions, which parallel, if not exceed, those of her distinguished male colleagues.

—Lisa Urkevich

FURTHER READING

Glixon, Beth L. "More on the Life and Death of Barbara Strozzi." *Musical Quarterly* 83, no. 1 (1999): 134-141. A continuation of the earlier article cited below. The lives of Strozzi's children are further illuminated, and thus her culture and circumstances.

_____. "New Light on the Musical Career of Barbara Strozzi." *Musical Quarterly* 81, no. 2 (1997): 311-335. Discusses Strozzi's financial situation, her children, her father, and her inner circle.

Jezic, Diane, and Elizabeth Wood. *Women Composers: The Lost Tradition Found.* New York: Feminist Press, 1994. Discusses Strozzi's work as part of a canon of music by female composers lost to history but newly recovered.

Magner, Candace A. "Barbara Strozzi: A Documentary Perspective." *Journal of Singing* 58, no. 5 (2002). Includes a numbered catalog of Strozzi's works, a complete discography, and a classified bibliography of original sources, secondary sources, and analyses.

Rosand, Ellen. "Barbara Strozzi, virtuosissima cantatrice: The Composer's Voice." *Journal of the American Musicological Society* 31, no. 2 (1978): 241-248. An extensive article on the life of Strozzi. Includes discussion of the Venetian academies and reviews Strozzi's musical style and characteristics with examples.

Schulenberg, David. *Music of the Baroque.* New York: Oxford University Press, 2001. Contains a brief section on Strozzi, provides analysis of one of her works and discusses song text.

Wong, Randall. "Barbara Strozzi." *Women Composers:*

Music Through the Ages. Vol. 2. New York: G. K. Hall, 1996. Includes some biographical information, notes on Strozzi's music, and the poetry she used. Includes the following two editions of Strozzi's pieces: "L'Astratto" and "Hor che Apollo," with performance-practice comments. Bibliography.

SEE ALSO: Francesca Caccini; Arcangelo Corelli; Girolamo Frescobaldi; Henry Lawes; Jean-Baptiste Lully; Claudio Monteverdi; Heinrich Schütz.

RELATED ARTICLE in *Great Events from History: The Seventeenth Century, 1601-1700:* c. 1601: Emergence of Baroque Music.

PETER STUYVESANT
Dutch-born colonial American governor

As the last Dutch governor of New Netherland, Stuyvesant brought order and prosperity to the fledgling colony and facilitated the rapprochement between Dutch and English settlers.

BORN: c. 1610; Scherpenzeel, Friesland, United Provinces (now in the Netherlands)
DIED: February, 1672; Manhattan Island, New York
ALSO KNOWN AS: Petrus Stuyvesant (given name)
AREA OF ACHIEVEMENT: Government and politics

EARLY LIFE

Peter Stuyvesant (stewih-vuh-sont) came from a well-to-do family. His father was the Reverend Balthazar Johannes Stuyvesant, a minister in the Dutch Reformed Church, and his mother was Margaretta Hardenstein Stuyvesant. Peter Stuyvesant was born in 1610, or thereabouts, in a Friesland village where his father had a temporary pastorate. For several years, Stuyvesant attended the small theological University of Franeker, in Friesland, but he was expelled, supposedly for having "taken the daughter of his own landlord at Franeker, and was caught at it."

Stuyvesant then became a clerk with the Dutch West India Company. Promoted in 1635, he signed on as a supercargo for the company at Fernando de Noronha, a small island 125 miles east of Brazil. Then he took a company post at Curaçao, where he became director-general in 1643. In 1644, Stuyvesant led an unsuccessful expedition against the Spanish garrison on Saint Martin's Island, where the company once had a trading post. During the siege, Stuyvesant's right leg was crushed below the knee by a cannon ball and part of the leg had to be amputated. For several years Stuyvesant recuperated in the Netherlands, adjusting himself to having a wooden leg.

Stuyvesant, on August 13, 1645, married Judith Bayard, a clergyman's daughter; they had two sons, Nicholas William and Balthazar Lazarus. In July, 1746,

the Dutch States-General commissioned Stuyvesant director-general of "New Netherland and the places thereabouts" and Curaçao and its adjacent islands. In the next year, Stuyvesant, with four vessels, went to Curaçao and then to New Amsterdam, where he arrived on May 11.

At the time of his arrival, Stuyvesant found that New Netherland extended from a few Dutch settlements on the Delaware to Fort Orange (Albany) on the Hudson. The core of this West India Company domain, however, was New Amsterdam, with one thousand inhabitants and about two hundred houses. On the outskirts were fifty "bouweries" (large farms), located along the Hudson (chiefly on Manhattan Island and at "Pavonia," across the river in modern New Jersey) and on Long Island. In 1650, Stuyvesant purchased for six thousand guilders a farm just north of the town, which became known as the "Great Bouwerie" (between modern Fifth and Seventeenth streets, bounded by the East River and Fourth Avenue in New York City).

Stuyvesant found New Amsterdam in chaos. The populace was bitterly divided politically and, having forced the previous governor, William Kieft, to be recalled, was not in the mood to submit to any authority. Drunkenness and riotous behavior were commonplace. Stuyvesant was determined to clean up the city, to promote trade, and to build up the colony. Because he thought the local population consisted of so many undesirables, Stuyvesant believed that the people of New Netherland were incapable of self-rule. He once said: "We derive our authority from God and the West Indian Company, not from the pleasure of a few ignorant subjects."

LIFE'S WORK

Stuyvesant did achieve discipline among his "subjects." Sumptuary regulations were put into effect. Harsh and unusual penalties convinced citizens to abide by the new moral standards. It is notable, however, that there was only one execution during Stuyvesant's tenure. Stuyvesant attempted to deny non-Calvinists the right to worship. He banished Quakers and sought to curtail privileges of citizenship for the Jews. Pressure from the home government, however, forced Stuyvesant to back down from his religious repression. Stuyvesant, who tried to govern entirely by himself, constantly faced opposition from ordinary citizens and prominent leaders alike.

It was difficult to collect taxes. On two occasions, Stuyvesant recalled all loans made to individuals by the West India Company. Adriaen Van der Donck, who was imprisoned for political opposition, spearheaded a drive with the home government to get Stuyvesant removed. The Board of Nine, which Stuyvesant had created as an advisory body, turned against him and charged him with tyrannical conduct and monopolizing the Indian trade. Prodded by the West India Company and the Dutch government, Stuyvesant, in 1653, allowed the establishment of municipal government for New Amsterdam consisting of two burgomasters (mayors), five schepens (aldermen), and a schout (sheriff and prosecuting attorney).

One of Stuyvesant's major achievements was his successful negotiation of peace with the Indians, a task which his predecessor had been unable to accomplish. By a combination of military strength and nonabrasive policies, relations were stabilized between the Dutch and the Mohican, Esopus, Hackensack, and Canarsie tribes. Stuyvesant palisaded the northern end of New Amsterdam and required outlying communities to have blockhouses.

Receiving little support from the West India Company or the Dutch government in populating and defending New Netherland, Stuyvesant realized that his colony was facing a losing situation vis-à-vis the rapidly expanding New England colonies. To spur population growth, Stuyvesant encouraged settlement of refugees and other immigrants from New England. Stuyvesant was, however, able to end the threat posed by the Swedes on the Delaware River. Leading a military expedition himself, Stuyvesant captured the Swedish fort in 1655 and then annexed New Sweden to New Netherland.

The expanding English settlements on the rim of New Netherland posed a difficult problem. Quite aware that belligerence toward New England would lead only to a war that he could not win, Stuyvesant pursued a policy of cordial relations with the Puritan colonies. He rode on horseback to Hartford in 1650 to meet with the commissioners of the United Colonies, who represented the Puritan confederation of four colonies established in 1643, and there negotiated the Treaty of Hartford (the only treaty between foreign powers conducted by American colonies on their own). Both parties agreed to a boundary line ten miles east of the Hudson and a border running north to south through Oyster Bay, Long Island.

Peter Stuyvesant, standing right, destroys the summons to surrender New York. (Library of Congress)

Events at home and abroad over the next fifteen years negated the treaty. Connecticut and New Haven claimed most of Long Island, so that by 1660 one-half of the towns were English. Stuyvesant was able to avert a potential rebellion in 1653-1654 by arresting John Underhill, who had raised the English standard at Hempstead and Flushing. This occurred at the time of the First Anglo-Dutch War; Stuyvesant was fortunate that Massachusetts refused to join the other three colonies of the New England Confederation in making war on New Netherland, in effect preventing an invasion of the Dutch colony.

Stuyvesant's troubles with the English, however, only worsened. In 1662, John Winthrop, Jr., had secured from the king a charter for Connecticut, which included in the colony's borders Long Island and land west to the Hudson—or most all of New Netherland. John Scott, a freebooting Englishman, represented New England settlers on Long Island, who refused to abide by the Connecticut charter. Scott received a commission from the king to take charge of an investigation of the territorial dispute regarding Long Island. He also helped form the "Combination" of local English settlers, who elected him president of Long Island. The king, meanwhile, granted Long Island and all New Netherland to his brother, James, duke of York. A fleet was then sent over to establish the new proprietary and thereby oust Dutch rule.

Colonel Richard Nicolls, with four ships and four hundred soldiers, appeared in the harbor in August, 1664. Stuyvesant could muster only about 150 men; the fort at the Battery was in disrepair, and there was little ammunition and powder. Scott, moreover, was gathering an army on Long Island to march on the Dutch capital. Having no choice but to surrender, Stuyvesant did not make a stand. The terms of the capitulation, signed on September 8, 1664, left everything as it was in New Netherland; about the only visible change was the hoisting of the English flag.

Stuyvesant's New Amsterdam in 1664 had achieved a high degree of prosperity. The population had increased to ten thousand. The Second Anglo-Dutch War ended with the Treaty of Breda (1667), which confirmed English possession of New Amsterdam, which they renamed New York. Stuyvesant, somewhat a recluse, retired to his farm to look after his orchards, cornfields, and livestock, with the aid of several dozen slaves. From 1665 to 1668, Stuyvesant visited the Netherlands to answer charges placed by the West India Company, which sought to make him the scapegoat for the loss of New Netherland. Stuyvesant ably defended himself, but the

company remained convinced of his guilt. The States-General, however, more concerned with the war that was going on, took little note of the charges against him.

Stuyvesant died in February, 1672, at his "Great Bouwerie" and was buried in a vault beneath the chapel which he had built near his house. The chapel was replaced by Saint Mark's Episcopal Church in 1799. Located at Tenth Street and Second Avenue in New York City, it is the oldest church of continuous worship in the city.

SIGNIFICANCE

Stuyvesant brought order and discipline to New Netherland. While faulted for being headstrong, arbitrary, and contemptuous of local democracy, he demonstrated executive ability, military prowess, and foresight in leading the colony to stability and prosperity. With very little bloodshed, Stuyvesant established a lasting peace with the Indians. He conquered New Sweden. Perhaps Stuyvesant's greatest contribution was in furthering intercolonial relations and comity. A man of undisputed personal integrity and a devout member of the Dutch Reformed Church, Stuyvesant served as a deacon and chairman of the consistory. Stuyvesant put the public interest first; he was intolerant of religious and political dissenters because he believed that they tended to subvert authority. Stuyvesant's administration helped to strengthen Dutch identity and solidarity within New Netherland, which in turn left a lasting cultural imprint on English society in New York.

—Harry M. Ward

FURTHER READING

Gehring, Charles T., ed. and trans. *Correspondence, 1654-1658*. Syracuse, N.Y.: Syracuse University Press, 2002. Gehring, a history professor and linguist, has spent 30 years translating thousands of documents from the New Netherland colony from Dutch to English. This book contains translations of Stuyvesant's correspondence.

Jameson, J. Franklin, ed. *Narratives of New Netherland, 1609-1664*. New York: Charles Scribner's Sons, 1909. Provides a miscellany of journals, tracts, notes, and correspondence relating to the whole history of New Netherland. The "Remonstrance of New Netherland," which indicted Stuyvesant's administration, by disaffected leaders of the colony, is included.

Kessler, Henry H., and Eugene Rachlis. *Peter Stuyvesant and His New York*. New York: Random House, 1959. Solid and well-rounded biography, with emphasis on the human side of Stuyvesant. Clarifies several disputed points of Stuyvesant's life, such as his birth date.

O'Callaghan, Edmund B. *History of New Netherland: Or, New York Under the Dutch.* 2 vols. New York: D. Appleton, 1846-1848. Reprint. Spartanburg, S.C.: Reprint Company, 1966. Exhaustive, detailed narrative of New Netherland. While old, the scholarship still stands up. The work remains a classic and is valuable particularly as a reference. Original documents are reproduced in the appendices.

O'Callaghan, Edmund B., and Berthold Fernow, eds. *Documents Relative to the Colonial History of the State of New York.* 15 vols. Albany, N.Y.: Weed, Parsons, Printers, 1853-1857. The documents were collected from archives in England, France, and Holland, as well as the United States. Volumes pertaining particularly to Stuyvesant's administration: 1-3 and 12-15 (contains correspondence between Stuyvesant and the Amsterdam Chamber of the West India Company).

Raesly, Ellis L. *Portrait of New Netherland.* New York: Columbia University Press, 1945. Reprint. Port Washington, N.Y.: Ira J. Friedman, 1965. Emphasizes the social history of New Netherland. Good accounts of Stuyvesant's dealings with various individuals. Full discussion on Indian problems and Stuyvesant's treatment of religious dissenters.

Shorto, Russell. *The Island at the Center of the World: The Epic Story of Dutch Manhattan and the Forgotten Colony That Shaped America.* New York: Doubleday, 2004. Shorto recounts the history of New Netherland and the island's capital, Manhattan, providing information on Stuyvesant and other historical figures. He argues that Dutch Manhattan, where men and women of different races and religions lived together in relative harmony, gave origin to America's eventual belief in tolerance and diversity.

Tuckerman, Bayard. *Peter Stuyvesant.* New York: Dodd, Mead, 1893. This volume in the "Makers of America" series is the best general survey of the life of Stuyvesant and his accomplishments.

Van der Zee, Henri, and Barbara Van der Zee. *A Sweet and Alien Land: The Story of Dutch New York.* New York: Viking Press, 1978. A thorough history, written for the general reader. Detailed coverage of Stuyvesant's Indian and intercolonial relations.

Zwierlein, Frederick J. *Religion in New Netherland, 1623-1664.* New York: Da Capo Press, 1971. Discusses Stuyvesant's persecution of Lutherans, Jews, and Quakers, and the relationship of the Dutch with the Jesuit missions and the Puritans. Evaluates religious life as a whole in Stuyvesant's New Netherland.

SEE ALSO: James I; John Winthrop.

RELATED ARTICLES in *Great Events from History: The Seventeenth Century, 1601-1700:* October, 1651-May, 1652: Navigation Act Leads to Anglo-Dutch Wars; March 4, 1665-July 31, 1667: Second Anglo-Dutch War.

SIR JOHN SUCKLING
English courtier, poet, and playwright

In addition to being a noteworthy playwright and a poet of the Cavalier tradition, Suckling was a staunch supporter of King Charles I. He helped to fund Royalist military ventures and participated directly in the events leading up to the onset of the English Civil War.

BORN: February 10, 1609 (baptized); Whitton, Twickenham, Middlesex, England
DIED: 1642; Paris, France
AREAS OF ACHIEVEMENT: Literature, theater, government and politics

EARLY LIFE
Little is known of the early life of Sir John Suckling. The second of five siblings, he was born into an old, landed Norfolk family that traced its ancestry back to Anglo-Saxon times. His mother, Martha Cranfield, from whom Suckling was said to have inherited his wit, was the daughter of a London merchant and the sister of Lionel Cranfield, first earl of Middlesex, a celebrated lord treasurer to James I. Suckling's father, John Suckling, after whom he was named, was a member of Parliament for Dunwich, and principal secretary of state and comptroller of the household of King James I. In the reign of Charles I, John senior became a privy councillor.

John's mother died at Norwich on October 28, 1613, when he was not yet five years old. Soon thereafter, Suckling was sent to boarding school, possibly at Westminster. His father remarried two years later. John, the son, may have grown up at either the Suckling home, Dorset Court, near Fleet Street, in London, or at Whitton, the place of his birth. There is a tradition that Suckling learned Latin at the precociously early age of five, but this is probably because of an error in determining his birth date.

Suckling went up to Trinity College, Cambridge, in 1623, and he remained there until at least 1627 or 1628, for there is a record of him speaking the prologue in the comedy *Paria* (pr. c. 1628) by Thomas Vincent, which was performed before the king. Suckling was admitted to Grays' Inn in February, 1627, but his stay there may have been short. Little else is known about these early years, except that he maintained a youthful attachment to Mary Cranfield, daughter of Elizabeth Sheppard, the first wife of his uncle Lionel Cranfield. This attachment survived until 1632.

LIFE'S WORK

Suckling's father died on March 27, 1627, leaving behind an estate of between twenty-five thousand and thirty thousand pounds, with most of his properties eventually going to his son John. John, however, was debarred in the will from inheriting anything until he was twenty-six years old, reflecting his father's estimate of his son's profligacy.

Suckling embarked upon the Grand Tour in 1628, proceeding to France and Italy, but he was back in England by September 19, 1630, when he was knighted by the king at Theobald's. In July of 1631, he was part of a force of six thousand men under the marquis of Hamilton who were to reinforce the army of Gustavus II Adolphus, king of Sweden and a Protestant champion in the Thirty Years' War. Suckling is said to have been present at the defeat of Johan Tserclaes, count of Tilly, the imperial general, at Leipzig, in September, 1631, and to have been present at several other sieges as well. Back in England by 1632, he embarked upon a course of extravagance and self-indulgence at court, where he was notorious for his obsession with gambling. John Aubrey (1626-1697) describes the young man sitting up in bed at night, cards strewn on the sheets, working out winning strategies. Aubrey also relates that Suckling's sisters appeared one day at the Piccadilly bowling green, fearful that he was about to gamble away their dowries.

In 1634, Suckling, now approaching the age of twenty-five, entered into his inheritance, which he squandered with such rapidity that he decided he needed to marry an heiress to repair the damage. He became a suitor of Anne Willoughby, daughter of Sir Henry Willoughby.

Sir Henry, however, was determined that Anne should marry Sir John Digby, brother of Sir Kenelm Digby, and not to a man like Suckling, whom he regarded as a wastrel. Charles I, who greatly liked Suckling, supported his pursuit of Anne Willoughby, who was maneuvered into signing a statement promising that she would marry him. The document was later repudiated; Suckling was involved in a brawl with the Digbys, and his prospects for the Willoughby estate vanished. He never married.

The courtier, wit, and poet now embarked upon a career as a playwright with *Aglaura* (pr., pb. 1638), produced at Blackfriars and at the Cockpit Theatre in 1638. Anxious that his new play should be staged well, he paid for all stage expenses, including extravagant costuming. In the same year, Suckling was appointed gentleman of the king's privy chamber extraordinary and possibly wrote his well-known poem, "A Ballad upon a Wedding" (pb. 1646).

By this time, the shadow of the English Civil Wars was beginning to cast gloom over Charles I's court. In 1639, disturbances in Scotland that became the First Bishops' War gave Suckling an opportunity to display his loyalty as well as his extravagance. He raised for the king a troop of one hundred horses and paid all their expenses, including their gear and clothing, which cost about twelve thousand pounds. Suckling's men in scarlet and white rode north with the king's army, but the campaign was a disaster, and the royal army, with Suckling's troop, was soon disbanded.

Suckling was commissioned in February, 1640, as a captain of the Carabineers. Also that year, he wrote the first draft of *Brennoralt* (pr. 1646), then titled *The Discontented Colonel*, and returned to Parliament as a member for Bramber, Sussex. More dangerously, Suckling wrote a letter to the king in the form of a communication to the queen's confidante, Sir Henry Jermyn, urging him to take the initiative against the Parliamentary opposition. By the beginning of March, Suckling was advising the king to undertake a *coup de main* against Parliament. He urged the king to secure control of the army, but the various promoters of this plan, which may not have originated with Suckling, fell out. His friend George Goring revealed the plan to the opposition. A parliamentary committee investigated the plot to take control of the army and was especially irritated with Suckling, who was assumed to have been attempting to enlist mercenaries from Portugal.

On May 2, supporters of the king attempted to break into the Tower of London, supposedly to liberate the king's imprisoned first minister, Thomas Wentworth, first earl of Strafford. On the same day, Suckling had assembled sixty armed men in a tavern for some presumably related illicit purpose, for which he and his companions were charged before the House of Lords. They failed to appear, and on May 8, a proclamation was issued against them. Charles promised Parliament that these unruly courtiers would be detained, but Suckling had already fled abroad, and his friends had gone into hiding. Suckling never returned to England. Penniless and with no prospects, he committed suicide in Paris in 1642, possibly in May or June, and was buried in the Protestant cemetery. What remained of his estates passed to his father's half brother, Charles Suckling, whose great-grandson was the father of Maurice and Catherine Suckling, the patron and mother of Lord Nelson.

SIGNIFICANCE

The life of Sir John Suckling exemplified extremes of both the brilliance and the tragedy of a young courtier who showed immense promise, who inherited a great fortune, who was learned, charming, witty—a favorite of Charles I—but who, through profligacy, ended up alone, without hope, in Paris, taking his own life. Suckling, "the greatest gallant of his time and the greatest gamester for bowling and cards," as Aubrey noted, was also a devoted Stuart loyalist who, in his person and in his wit, may have posthumously served Restoration courtiers as a model. As a writer, Suckling challenged prevailing poetic models of courtliness. With the Caroline order giving way to the approach of civil war, his ironic wit heralded the nervous impulses of a more somber age.

The Cavalier wit, Stuart loyalist, and soldier— "natural, easy Suckling," as he was dubbed by Millamant in William Congreve's *The Way of the World* (pr., pb. 1700)—is remembered today for his small corpus of poems, which combine brilliance in language and a satirical and cynical stance with a seriousness that cuts through the brittle surface, challenging the images of conventional contemporary love poetry. Among his best-known are "The Wits" (1646), "A Ballad upon a Wedding" (1646), "Why So Pale and Wan" (1646), "When, Dearest, I but Think of Thee" (1646), and "Out upon It! I Have Loved" (1646).

Suckling's dramatic works—*Aglaura*, *The Goblins* (pr. 1638), *Brennoralt*, and the unfinished *The Sad One*—were few, and although they were admired in his time, they are scarcely read or performed today. His prose works, read as examples of the purity of seventeenth century diction as well as for their subject matter, include some fifty-four letters and *An Account of Religion by Reason* (wr. 1637, pb. 1646). His collected works first appeared as *Fragmenta Aurea* (1646, revised 1648, 1658, 1661-1662, and 1672); a later collection, *The Last Remains of Sir John Suckling* (1659), collects all of his previously unpublished poems and letters.

—*Donna Berliner*

FURTHER READING

Clayton, Thomas, and L. A. Beaurline, eds. *The Works of Sir John Suckling*. 2 vols. Oxford, England: Clarendon Press, 1971. The definitive edition of Suckling's works.

Gibson, Cheryl M. "'Tis Not the Meat, but 'tis the Appetite': The Destruction of Woman in the Poetry of Sir John Suckling." In *Explorations in Renaissance Culture* 20 (1994): 41-59. An examination of gender and the gendering of desire in Suckling's work.

Henderson, Fletcher Orpin. "Traditions of Précieux and Libertain in Suckling's Poetry." *English Literary History* 4, no. 4 (December, 1937): 274-298. Contextualizes Suckling's work by comparing it to his French influences.

Squier, Charles L. *Sir John Suckling*. Boston: Twayne, 1978. Accessible treatment of Suckling's life and works, with good bibliography.

Summers, Claude J., and Ted-Larry Pebworth, eds. *Renaissance Discourses of Desire*. Columbia: University of Missouri Press, 1993. Contains several useful articles on Suckling.

SEE ALSO: Charles I; Gustavus II Adolphus; James I; First Earl of Strafford.

RELATED ARTICLES in *Great Events from History: The Seventeenth Century, 1601-1700:* 1618-1648: Thirty Years' War; March-June, 1639: First Bishops' War; 1642-1651: English Civil Wars; 1670: Popularization of the Grand Tour.

DUKE DE SULLY
French prime minister

Sully helped to stabilize the French monarchy and the country itself after the disastrous and destructive wars between the Protestant Huguenots and the Catholics. He instituted governmental reforms and promoted infrastructure improvements at the national level.

BORN: December 13, 1559; Rosny-sur-Seine, near Nantes, France

DIED: December 22, 1641; Villebon, near Chartres, France

ALSO KNOWN AS: Maximilien de Béthune (given name); Marquis de Rosny

AREAS OF ACHIEVEMENT: Government and politics, diplomacy, military

EARLY LIFE

The duke de Sully (deh sew-lee) was born in the Seine River valley. His father, François de Béthune, the baron de Rosny, and his mother, Charlotte de Béthune, were part of the French lower nobility as well as members of the Reformed, or Huguenot, faith. As such, in 1562, they joined Louis I de Bourbon (prince of Condé), Admiral Gaspard II de Coligny, and other Calvinists in defense of their religious liberties. The resulting conflict, known as the Wars of Religion (1562-1595), would throw France into civil war and devastate the country. Charlotte died in 1566 and François followed nine years later. Sully, their oldest surviving male child, became baron de Rosny at the age of sixteen.

Even though the young boy's childhood was marred by tragedy, turmoil, and brutal warfare between Catholics and Protestants, his family provided for his future. He was given a gentlemen's education, complete with tutor and social instruction, and while the quality was mediocre, it was enough to permit his introduction at age twelve to Henry of Navarre, the future King Henry IV of France. Henry, six years his senior, took an interest in the young noble and kept him in Paris, where Sully studied mathematics and engineering at the College of Bourgoyne. In 1572, the boy was among a select number of Protestant gentleman who were present at Henry's wedding, and one of the few to escape the ensuing slaughter of Huguenots at the St. Bartholomew's Day Massacre. Like Henry, he saved himself by denying his faith and remained in the city under close surveillance for four years. He was also with the king of Navarre when the two escaped Paris in 1576 to rally the decimated Huguenot party.

LIFE'S WORK

From 1576 to 1594, Sully rose in the esteem of his patron because of his loyalty and efficiency. He learned the trade of war and soon excelled as an engineer, or sapper, and in the use of artillery. He fought at Cazaux (1577), Cahors (1580), Coutras (1587), Arques (1589), d'Ivry (1590), Chartres (1591), Rouen (1592), Dreux (1593), and Laon (1594), and was present at the final capitulation of Paris in 1594 (one year after Henry renounced Protestantism). Although Sully was valuable as a soldier, the young king of France (1589) increasingly used him for other tasks. Sully was sent to raise money for the army, sent on diplomatic missions, and negotiated the surrender of Catholic leaders and strongholds.

Working in the shadow of the king, the young Baron was steadily promoted. In 1578, he became a councilor of Navarre. Twelve years later, he was created a member of the ruling council of state, and in 1596, he was elevated to the council of finance. Three years later, he was named chancellor, and in 1601, named superintendent of finance. Personal rewards also followed: the enlargement of the barony of Rosny (1599), the rank of marquis (1601), count of Moret (1603), duke de Sully (1606), and peer of the realm (also 1606). Governorships, the control of the king's artillery and fortifications, and other offices, each commanding a salary, added to his growing position and wealth.

Henry's favor and support, however, were neither easy to attain nor maintain, because they depended upon results. If Sully failed to produce what the king needed, the young favorite would fall from grace, as other ministers before him had done. In addition, even though Henry understood the needs of the kingdom, he was driven by necessity. Until 1598 the king was obliged to maintain a large army in the field, and its support transcended all other work. The councils of state and finance knew that the peasantry and the clergy were close to bankruptcy, that taxes were insufficient to support the kingdom, and that Henry's personal lands were mortgaged, alienated, or devastated. They also knew that if the army was not paid, all would be lost. In addition, the king was by inclination a generous man. He gave to his friends, like Sully, his mistresses (of which there were many), his children (legitimate and illegitimate), his nobles, and the needy. Some of this was necessary. Likewise, taxes needed to be reduced or rebated for farmers whose lands had been ravaged during the wars and for officials who were unable to collect where there was no profit. Money also was needed for road and bridge repair, for industrial refurbishing, and for reclaiming the lands devastated by years of war.

The solution to France's problems was available. The peasantry needed to be taxed less and the towns more. Furthermore, the crown needed to stop tax farming, the selling of offices, the granting of pensions, and permitting nobles and town councils to preempt royal revenues. Both the king and Sully understood this, but when Henry wrote his minister that "my stew pot is empty" and "for six months I have not received a penny," Sully was compelled to act. He scoured the countryside for untapped sources of money. From two provinces alone he took 72 wheelbarrow loads of money but by questionable means. It came from the church, forced loans from nobles and merchants, and the sale of offices.

Fortunately, the conversion of the king to Catholicism (1593) and a war with Spain (1595-1598) brought the Wars of Religion to an end. Sully supported both policies, even though he remained a Huguenot, convinced that even the most recalcitrant Catholics would rally behind a Catholic king. He also was the minister who negotiated the final peace with Spain. The army was, at last, disbanded and the outward flow of money stemmed.

Sully, with headquarters at the Bastille, soon sought to stabilize the kingdom. The duke worked long hours, waking before sunrise, attending two sessions of the council of finance each day, and spending the rest of his time working either on army accounts or on the king's records. He spent years pouring over old books and recreating missing ones to restore Henry's lost revenues. As before, he pursued old debts and reclaimed mortgaged and sold or granted royal lands if a document was flawed. Taxes were readjusted and nobles as well as towns were brought under stricter control by the Crown. Roads were put back in order, internal security was guaranteed, and trade and travel were promoted. Unfortunately, the selling of offices, tax farming, and internal tolls persisted.

The relationship between the monarch and his minister remained close but difficult. The duke was outspoken and had a low tolerance for bureaucrats and nobles who rendered poor service, calling them buffoons. He also angered Henry when he took positions against the king's generous gifts and building programs. On one occasion, a quarrel reached the point of an open split, in which the king informed the duke that the roads were free and that he could use them at any time. Yet, reflection, especially

upon Henry's part, and the use of individual audiences with Sully, generally kept the peace. The monarch, a good judge of individuals, knew that Sully was devoted to him and would do anything to promote the king's or the kingdom's welfare.

The relationship, unusual as it may have been, came to an end in 1610. Henry, on the verge of war with Spain once again, was assassinated on his way to consult with Sully. The king's Catholic wife became regent for his young son, Louis, and Sully, a Huguenot, was soon excluded from the regency. The duke retired to his favorite residence of Villebon, where he lived until his death more than thirty years later. While there, he wrote a history of the reign of Henry IV, almost as a substitute for the work of state in which he was no longer involved.

SIGNIFICANCE

The duke de Sully rose from obscurity to become the chief minister of Henry IV for nearly fifteen years. He was not a great financier nor a man who was ahead of his time, but he understood the workings of supply and demand and directed the stabilization of France between 1596 and 1610. He brought the return of peace and prosperity, made the life of the peasantry easier, and initiated the reform that prime minister Cardinal de Richelieu and others would continue. In recognition of the former minister's accomplishments, Louis XIII, Henry's son, would make Sully a marshal of France in 1634. The old man, now in his seventies, felt his work validated and was deservedly proud.

—*Louis P. Towles*

FURTHER READING

Barbiche, Bernard. *Sully*. Paris: Albin Michel, 1978. The most complete biography available of the duke de Sully.

Koenigsberger, H. G. "Western Europe and the Power of Spain." *The Counter-Reformation and Price Revolution, 1559-1610*. New Cambridge Modern History. Cambridge, England: Cambridge University Press, 1968. A solid and necessary background for the Huguenot-Catholic conflict.

Lodge, Eleanor C. *Sully, Colbert, and Turgot: A Chapter in French Economic History*. Washington, N.Y.: Kennikat Press, 1931. An excellent economic interpretation of three key financial figures in the *ancien régime*.

Major, J. Russell. *Bellievre, Sully, and the Assembly of Notables of 1596*. Philadelphia: American Philosophical Society, 1974. A fine discussion of the economic woes of the 1590's.

Trevor-Roper, H. R. "Spain and Europe, 1598-1621." In *The Decline of Spain and the Thirty Years' War, 1609-1648*. New Cambridge Modern History. Cambridge, England: Cambridge University Press, 1970. Additional information on Sully and the problems faced by France during the reign of Henry IV.

SEE ALSO: Jean-Baptiste Colbert; Louis XIII; Jules Mazarin; Cardinal de Richelieu.
RELATED ARTICLES in *Great Events from History: The Seventeenth Century, 1601-1700:* 1625-October 28, 1628: Revolt of the Huguenots; November 10, 1630: The Day of Dupes; 1685: Louis XIV Revokes the Edict of Nantes.

JAN SWAMMERDAM
Dutch scientist and naturalist

Swammerdam was among the earliest scientists to apply microscopic techniques to the study of anatomy and physiology in diverse organisms, ranging from insects to human beings. His work marked the beginning of the scientific study of insects, and he is most likely the first to observe red blood cells.

BORN: February 12, 1637; Amsterdam, Holland, United Provinces (now in the Netherlands)
DIED: February 17, 1680; Amsterdam
ALSO KNOWN AS: John Swammerdam
AREAS OF ACHIEVEMENT: Science and technology, medicine

EARLY LIFE

Jan Swammerdam (yahn SVAHM-ehr-dahm) was the son of Jan Jacobszoon Swammerdam, an apothecary and naturalist, and Barentje Corver. Swammerdam's father wanted his son to spend his life in service to the Church, and the younger Jan was tutored in both Latin and Greek with that profession in mind. However, Jan developed a strong interest in the sciences, and he was able to convince his father that a career in medicine was closer to his interests.

As a youth, Jan learned science by arranging and cataloging his father's collections of natural specimens brought from throughout the world, eventually producing a museum-quality selection considered one of the finest in the country. Jan's interests, which included the catching and study of insects, led him to discoveries of insect life cycles, studies that were considered among the most complete of the time. It has been suggested that during these early years, Jan might have met Antoni van Leeuwenhoek, the Dutch lensmaker credited with developing the first "modern" microscope, when Leeuwenhoek visited Jan's father. No mention of this is made in any original sources, and the story cannot be otherwise confirmed.

Swammerdam's life as a student of medicine began in 1661, as he studied both in Amsterdam and Leiden under the tutelage of distinguished professors such as Gerard Blaes; Johannes van Horne, the anatomist who discovered the role of the thoracic duct; and Regnier de Graaf, a fellow student later known for his studies of female reproductive organs. Swammerdam became known in the school for his abilities at dissection. In 1664, while still a student, Swammerdam discovered the presence of valves in lymphatic vessels (now called Swammerdam valves). His study of respiration became the basis for his doctoral thesis, in which he concluded that inhaled air passed through the windpipe into the lungs, and from there traveled through vessels into the heart. He also suggested that air contains a volatile element of some sort that passes into the lungs and, eventually, into the heart. In February, 1667, Swammerdam was awarded his doctoral degree.

LIFE'S WORK

Though his father had hoped he would develop a medical practice, the younger Swammerdam's interests were primarily in research. Consequently, he devoted all of his time to that endeavor and created a rift with his father, which resulted in the loss of his financial support. Though Swammerdam's father died in 1675, the years of deprivation, coupled with long hours at work, eventually eroded the younger Swammerdam's health. In his later years, he became a hypochondriac and a follower of mysticism.

Swammerdam's studies extended through a large number of scientific fields. While visiting Paris in 1665, he met and developed a friendship with Melchisedec Thévenot, a French patron of the arts and a diplomat, who encouraged Swammerdam to specialize in areas of reproduction and development. Much of his research time was spent in the study of insects, and it involved extensive use of the newly developed microscopes. His inspiration was found in a 1669 monograph on silkworms published by the Italian anatomist and botanist Marcello Malpighi and sent to Swammerdam by Thévenot. Swammerdam's publication of this work, *Historia insectorum generalis* (1669; general treatise on insects), marked the beginning of the scientific study of insects. Swammerdam classified insects into four "orders," based primarily on their processes of development. He noted the various stages in their life cycles, a process known as metamorphosis. He also determined that what had been called a "king" bee was actually a female bee. Though his classification scheme has since been modified, three of his orders are still in use today.

Swammerdam is frequently credited with the discovery of red blood cells. William Harvey had proposed a role for the circulatory system earlier in the century but had not actually *observed* blood capillaries; contemporaries such as Malpighi reported capillaries in mesenteric tissue and had even observed blood corpuscles, mistaking them for fat globules. In his dissections of the frog, probably in the period between 1658 and 1665 (the precise date is unknown), Swammerdam noted the presence of "orbicular particles," describing them as regular flattened ovals that slowly moved through the capillaries. He also reported blood that appeared "like cow's milk" in his dissection of the louse, most likely an observation of white blood cells; they were not identified as such, however.

Even while carrying out investigations on insects, Swammerdam continued his study of anatomy, including the dissection of fish. Also, he noted the presence of ducts in humans that passed from the pancreas into its intestine. He collected pancreatic juice and sent it to colleagues for subsequent study.

Swammerdam never practiced medicine, but he did participate in dissections and medical examinations of patients at Amsterdam Hospital. In conjunction with his colleague Justus Schrader, a physician at the hospital, Swammerdam described the anatomy of a hernia as a blind sac originating in the peritoneum and extending into the scrotum (c. 1674). By inflating the sac with a tube, Swammerdam demonstrated it was closed on one end. His work and subsequent depictions through illustrations became important facets in understanding the nature of hernias. The significance of this work in part was its refutation of the belief that hernias were the result

of the rupture, rather than an extension, of the peritoneum.

Swammerdam's work also extended into the area of human reproduction. While still a student, he studied the anatomy of uterine vessels and illustrated the vessels of the uterus and the ovaries. He isolated human eggs, describing them as being analogous to those from birds, and also described sperm tubes found within the male testis, noting that penile erection is the result of the movement of blood into the organ.

Swammerdam spent a portion of his last years in the study of religious mysticism. Returning to science about 1676, he attempted to compile his studies into one massive work. The loss of support from his father and the subsequent death of the elder, however, left Swammerdam without funds. He was forced to sell his father's museum collections. Weakened by malaria, Swammerdam died in February, 1680.

Much of Swammerdam's scientific work was published posthumously as the *Bybel der naturre* (1737-1738) by the Dutch physician Hermann Boerhaave. In 1758, it was published in English as the *Book of Nature: Or, The History of Insects*. The two-volume manuscript includes more than five hundred illustrations from Swammerdam's work.

SIGNIFICANCE

Considering the diverse range of organisms he studied, Swammerdam could arguably be called the first scientist to develop the field of comparative anatomy as well as entomology. While Leeuwenhoek had invented the first modern microscope, Swammerdam was able to apply the technology in the study of a variety of subjects as diverse as blood flow, the lymphatic system, and the life cycles of insects.

When Swammerdam began his work, science was dominated by the teachings of the Greek philosopher Aristotle, whose philosophy was based on deductive reasoning and speculation; the structure of an organism was determined in part by its functions, and organisms were placed on a continuum that led to increasing perfection (for example, humans). Swammerdam preferred to base his conclusions on his own research. He also believed that the transmission of knowledge transcended politics, as illustrated by his submission of work on the human ovary to the Royal Society of London, despite the ongoing war that had been raging between the Dutch and British.

One could also argue that his study of insect metamorphosis, the change from one form to another during the life cycle of the organism, provided refutation of the idea that creatures can change from one type into another. Eventually, he applied this information into the earliest classification scheme for these organisms, while at the same time provided ammunition for those opposing the notion of spontaneous generation. Swammerdam's contributions to biology thus encompassed a range far broader than that developed by contemporaries of the period.

—*Richard Adler*

FURTHER READING

Boorstin, Daniel. *The Discoverers*. New York: H. N. Abrams, 1991. A classic history of science from the perspective of scientific researchers, first published in 1983. Passing reference is made to the work of Swammerdam, and emphasis is placed on new scientific thought that often opposes prevailing ideas in the sciences.

Fournier, Marian. *The Fabric of Life: Microscopy in the Seventeenth Century*. Baltimore, Md.: Johns Hopkins University Press, 1996. Examines the reasons for the microscope's appearance and eventual eclipse in the seventeenth century.

Huerta, Robert D. *Giants of Delft: Johannes Vermeer and the Natural Philosophers, the Parallel Search for Knowledge During the Age of Discovery*. Lewisburg, Pa.: Bucknell University Press, 2003. Although this book focuses on Dutch artist Vermeer's perception of the world, it describes how that perception was influenced by the microscope and other discoveries in the science of optics. Several chapters describe how scientists created a "more optical" way of viewing the world.

McClellan, James, and Harold Dorn. *Science and Technology in World History: An Introduction*. Baltimore, Md.: Johns Hopkins University Press, 1999. The authors present a history of science and technology and explore the development of the microscope and Swammerdam's application of the instrument.

Oster, Malcolm. *Science in Europe, 1500-1800: A Secondary Source Reader*. New York: Palgrave, 2002. A relatively brief account of scientific endeavors as carried out during this era. Swammerdam's work is placed in historical context.

Ruestow, Edward G. *The Microscope in the Dutch Republic: The Shaping of Discovery*. New York: Cambridge University Press, 1996. The author traces the development of microscopy from its origins in the seventeenth century, as well as its early applications. One chapter is devoted to the work of Swammerdam. Extensively illustrated.

Schierbeek, Abraham. *Jan Swammerdam: His Life and Works*. Amsterdam: Swets & Zeitlinger, 1967. In addition to a brief biography of Swammerdam, the author provides a systematic summary of Swammerdam's work, including excerpts from notable books and manuscripts. Also included is a bibliography of Swammerdam's known and assumed works.

Swammerdam, John. *The Book of Nature*. Translated by Thomas Flloyd. 1758. Reprint. New York: Arno Press, 1978. A modern reprint of Swammerdam's influential work. Includes illustrations and an index.

_____. *The Letters of Jan Swammerdam to Melchisedec Thévenot*. Translated by G. A. Lindeboom. Amsterdam: Swets & Zeitlinger, 1975. A collection of correspondence between Swammerdam and arts patron Thévenot, with letters in English, Dutch, French, and Latin. Includes illustrations and indexes.

SEE ALSO: William Harvey; Jan Baptista van Helmont; Robert Hooke; Antoni van Leeuwenhoek; Marcello Malpighi; Nicolaus Steno.

RELATED ARTICLES in *Great Events from History: The Seventeenth Century, 1601-1700:* 17th century: Advances in Medicine; 1637: Descartes Publishes His *Discourse on Method*; 1660's-1700: First Microscopic Observations; 1672-1684: Leeuwenhoek Discovers Microscopic Life.

THOMAS SYDENHAM
English physician

Sydenham laid the foundations for modern clinical, scientific, and public-health medicine, and he has been credited with the invention of the modern conception of disease, understood as a morbid entity in nature with its own history. This conception replaced the earlier model of disease as a set of peculiar events in people's lives with only particular case histories.

BORN: September 10, 1624 (baptized); Wynford Eagle, Dorset, England
DIED: December 29, 1689; London, England
AREA OF ACHIEVEMENT: Medicine

EARLY LIFE

Thomas Sydenham (SIHD-nuhm) was born at Wynford Eagle, Dorset, early in September of 1624. The date September 10, which is conventionally given for his birthday, is in fact his baptismal day, which suggests that his birthday was a few days earlier. The Sydenham family were West Country Puritan gentry powerful in the county. Sydenham's father was William Sydenham; his mother, Mary Jeffrey Sydenham. They were the parents of ten children, of which Thomas was the fifth son of seven, five of whom survived infancy. The eldest son became Colonel William Sydenham (1615-1661), a parliamentary commander in the English Civil War and prominent politician of the Commonwealth and Protectorate. Thomas had the conventional upbringing of a younger son of the gentry, and later, despite his international reputation and success in medicine, he would never completely outgrow his Puritan and provincial origins.

The Sydenhams were conspicuous on the Parliamentary side in the English Civil Wars, leading the Parliamentary forces in Dorset; serving in campaigns in England, Scotland, and Ireland; and shedding their blood for the cause. Father and sons held commissions: Thomas was a captain in the cavalry. His mother and three of her sons were killed in battle by the Royalists or died afterward of war wounds. Sydenham was so seriously wounded at the Battle of Worcester on September 3, 1651, that he was left for a while among the slain on the battlefield.

Sydenham had gone to Oxford and matriculated at Magdalen Hall in 1642, but almost immediately he had left Oxford to join the Parliamentary army at the outbreak of the Civil War. He fought bravely but was captured by the Royalists and imprisoned at Exeter. He was released and saw action again. He returned to Oxford in 1647 and entered Wadham College to resume study, which he now concentrated in medicine. In 1648, Sydenham was elected as a fellow of All Souls, but he left Oxford a second time for military service in 1651. He returned again, before resigning his fellowship in 1655.

Sydenham's studies were desultory, his medical degrees nominal, and his formal academic medical education quite irregular. He received his bachelor of medicine degree in 1648 after only a few months of study and his master of medicine degree a year or so later. He would not receive his doctor of medicine degree from Cambridge until 1676, by which time he had been for a decade the leading English physician. This irregularity is explained not only by the disruption of academic life during the Civil War but also by Sydenham's own scorn for mere book learning in medicine. He did read the classic medical texts of Hippocrates, and he was influenced by the works of the English philosopher Francis Bacon and especially by Bacon's emphasis on experience, observation, inductive reasoning, and experimentation. At Oxford, too, Sydenham met and became lifelong friends with the scientist Robert Boyle. Sydenham later befriended the philosopher John Locke, who was also a physician.

Sydenham's decision to enter the medical profession was made in 1646, on the advice of Thomas Coxe, an eminent physician who had served in the parliamentary army. Sydenham's motives were altruistic: He sought, as he admitted to his colleagues, not to acquire riches but to find happiness in the greater felicity of reducing the sufferings of humankind. The cure of even one of the slightest of the diseases affecting humankind, as he put it, was worth much more than the fabled riches of Croesus. Sydenham was generous, tireless in his work, and open and unselfish in sharing his medical discoveries.

In 1655, Sydenham resigned his fellowship of All Souls, married Mary Gee of Wynford Eagle, and moved to Westminster, where he tentatively began to set up his practice. He was much involved with his brother William in the politics of the Protectorate and could not devote all of his efforts to medicine until his brother slipped from power around 1659. The Restoration in 1660 closed all political doors to the Sydenhams.

LIFE'S WORK

Sydenham practiced medicine at Westminster part-time from 1655 and full-time from about 1659 until his death

Thomas Sydenham. (Library of Congress)

there in 1689. There, too, he wrote in English numerous medical treatises, some of which his friends translated into Latin and published for the international medical fraternity. Sydenham's greatest published works include *Methodus Curandi Febres* (1666; the method of treating fevers), *Observationes Medicae* (1676; medical observations), *Tractatus de Podagra et Hydrope* (1683; treatise of gout and dropsy), and the last work published during his lifetime, *Schedula Monitoria de Novae Febris Ingressu* (1686; the warning of the appearance of a new fever).

Sydenham published other works in his lifetime, works were published posthumously, and he left unpublished manuscripts and correspondence. His practice and publications earned for Sydenham a large reputation and international distinction, and he treated patients from the wealthy London merchant class, gentry, nobility, and even royalty, when in the 1660's he attended the infant duke of Cambridge, son of James, duke of York, who would later succeed to the throne as James II.

It is significant that Sydenham was never knighted or made a fellow of the Royal College of Physicians or of the Royal Society. He never won acceptance at court and in high society, although the royalty, nobility, and socialites availed themselves of his medical skills when they needed to do so. His past as a parliamentary soldier, his Puritan and provincial background, his somewhat rustic manner, and his independent opinions about medicine were all held against him in society. Enemies, who were less knowledgeable and skillful physicians than he, mocked him as a "rebel," a "Western bumpkin," the Roundhead "trooper turned physician," and the "ploughman doctor." Sydenham did not resent his ostracism; his circle of close friends included Boyle and Locke, and his own clinical apprentices who lived in his household and assisted in his practice included some of the greatest physicians of the next generation, such as Hans Sloane, Thomas Dover, Richard Blackmore, and Charles Goodall.

Sydenham the physician was a plain, stocky man whose broad, frank face was framed by long, uncoiffed hair severely parted in the middle. Even after the Restoration he dressed in simple and somber Puritan garb. His character was that of a rebel, both in youth and in maturity. He refused to defer to authority unless that authority could prove and justify itself. His approach to medicine was pragmatic and empirical rather than dogmatic and theoretical. He said plainly that his medical writings were based on "downright matter-of-fact."

Like Hippocrates, Sydenham trusted in *vis medicatrix naturæ*, the healing power of nature, and he often opined that doctors killed more people than diseases did. Consequently, he advocated noninvasive therapies such as proper diet, bed rest, travel, and exercise, and was suspicious of medications and surgery except as a last resort. Still, it was Sydenham who pioneered such medications as quinine in the treatment of intermittent fevers and iron in the treatment of chlorosis or anemia. Sydenham also, perhaps because of his personal imperative to relieve suffering, prescribed analgesic medications generously and even developed a palatable, potable form of opium in wine, which is still called Sydenham's laudanum. More controversial and subject to misinterpretation was his advocacy of accubitus, the revitalization of sick and especially elderly patients by having them cuddle a pet or a child. Accubitus often worked, so the pragmatic Sydenham recommended it.

Sydenham's most significant contributions were made in the field of clinical medicine, but he also laid the foundations of modern public-health medicine and epidemiology and modern scientific medicine. His observations of epidemics in London from 1661 to 1675 were so acute that it remained only for modern microbiology and the germ theory of disease, the definitive work of the later German scientist Robert Koch to complete his pioneer work. Even without the germ theory, Sydenham's work still has value for epidemiology in its emphasis on periodic, cosmic, telluric, and meteorological factors in epidemic disease.

From the mid-1650's onward, Sydenham suffered from gout, renal colic, and calculus or stone, and on December 29, 1689, these diseases would kill him. It is characteristic of this great physician that he translated his own suffering into what remains the classic medical description of gout. His works abound in classic disease descriptions too numerous to relate. To give one more example, in his last published work during his lifetime in 1685, Sydenham wrote the classic medical description of Saint Vitus's dance, the neurological complication of rheumatic fever that in medical nomenclature is still known as Sydenham's chorea.

When his clinical apprentice Blackmore asked Sydenham for the titles of the most authoritative medical textbooks to read to qualify him for practice, Sydenham replied, "Read *Don Quixote*, it is a very good book, I read it still." His reply expressed not only his scorn for abstract medical theorizing and his questioning of authority but also his knowledge of Miguel de Cervantes' powers of observation. The sound advice concealed in this quip unhappily was lost on the apprentice, who merely wanted an easy answer.

SIGNIFICANCE

Sydenham's medical practice and writings mark the divide between ancient and medieval medicine on the one hand and modern medicine on the other. His empiricism, natural histories of diseases, and pragmatism led medicine out of the cul-de-sac of abstract theorizing into the thoroughfare of modern clinical, public-health, and scientific medicine. A brave young rebel captain of the parliamentary cavalry in the English Civil War became the "English Hippocrates" and father of modern medicine.

—*Terence R. Murphy*

FURTHER READING

Debus, Allen G., ed. *Medicine in Seventeenth Century England: A Symposium Held at UCLA in Honor of C. D. O'Malley*. Berkeley: University of California Press, 1974. A collection of many specialized revisionist scholarly papers that all contribute to the understanding of Sydenham's milieu. One by L. J. Rather tendentiously argues the superiority of Thomas Willis over Sydenham.

Dewhurst, Kenneth. *Dr. Thomas Sydenham (1624-1689): His Life and Original Writings*. Berkeley: University of California Press, 1966. Scholarly biography with an edition of some selected works and correspondence of Sydenham, but badly organized and somewhat flawed; for example, there is no discussion of Sydenham's death, and the author proceeds erratically over topics.

Healy, Margaret. *Fictions of Disease in Early Modern England: Bodies, Plagues and Politics*. New York: Palgrave, 2001. Describes how people imagined their bodies and how the cultural imagery of human disease had political consequences in the seventeenth century.

Hunter, Richard, and Ida Macalpine, eds. *Three Hundred Years of Psychiatry, 1535-1860: A History Presented in Selected English Texts*. New York: Oxford University Press, 1963. Reprint. Hartsdale, N.Y.: Carlisle, 1982. Reprints Sydenham's short but important piece on hysteria and an illuminating anecdote about his treatment of depression.

Lambert, Samuel W., and George M. Goodwin. *Medical Leaders from Hippocrates to Osler*. Indianapolis: Bobbs-Merrill, 1929. Brief essay that adds new details and regards Sydenham in the context of the history of medicine.

Martí-Ibáñez, Felix. *Centaur: Essays on the History of Medical Ideas*. New York: MD Publications, 1958. Contains several relevant essays, including "Books in the Physician's Life," which persuasively explains Sydenham's recommendation of *Don Quixote* as the most instructive book on medicine. Other medical history essay collections by Martí-Ibáñez and Henry E. Sigerist contain pertinent material as well.

Power, Sir D'Arcy, ed. *British Masters of Medicine*. Baltimore, Md.: William Wood, 1936. Reprint. Freeport, N.Y.: Books for Libraries Press, 1969. Contains Sir Humphry Davy Rolleston's brief but insightful essay on Sydenham and much background material.

Singer, Charles, and E. Ashworth Underwood. *A Short History of Medicine*. 2d ed. New York: Oxford University Press, 1962. A standard work, very useful for Sydenham's place in the history of medicine.

Sloan, A. W. *English Medicine in the Seventeenth Century*. Durham, Scotland: Durham Academic Press, 2002. Sloan provides an overview of English medical, surgical, pharmaceutical, and obstetric practice during Sydenham's lifetime.

Wear, Andrew. *Knowledge and Practice in English Medicine, 1550-1680*. New York: Cambridge University Press, 2000. Although Sydenham is not mentioned, the book explains medical practice within the social and cultural context of his time, describing remedies, notions of disease, and notions of preventive medicine. Provides a detailed examination of the pox and plague, the major medical problems of the period.

SEE ALSO: Robert Boyle; James II; John Locke.

RELATED ARTICLE in *Great Events from History: The Seventeenth Century, 1601-1700:* 1642-1651: English Civil Wars; May, 1659-May, 1660: Restoration of Charles II.

ABEL JANSZOON TASMAN
Dutch explorer

Tasman was a navigator who discovered for the Dutch the countries now known as New Zealand, Australia, Tonga, and the Fiji Islands. The Australian island-state of Tasmania bears his name.

BORN: c. 1603; Lutjegast, Groningen, United
  Provinces (now in the Netherlands)
DIED: 1659; place unknown
AREAS OF ACHIEVEMENT: Exploration, geography

EARLY LIFE

Abel Janszoon Tasman (AHB-ehl YAHNTS-sohn TAHS-mahn) was born around 1603. Little is known about his early life except that in 1632 he entered the services of the Dutch East India Company. In the early 1600's, the Dutch were replacing the Portuguese as the most powerful European influence in Asia. The East India Company was established as a monopoly that would control the enormously successful spice trade, mainly in pepper, from the East. The center of the company's operations was in the city of Jakarta, which the Dutch called Batavia, on the island of Java.

During his first ten years as a company employee, Tasman became familiar with the trade routes from Holland to India and then to the islands that make up modern Indonesia. He had led one expedition a thousand miles beyond the limits reached by any previous navigator in the cold and stormy northern parts of the Pacific Ocean. In 1642, he was chosen to lead a voyage in search of the "Great Unknown Southern Continent," or the Terra Australia Incognita. Many mapmakers and geographers of the time had proposed the existence of a huge, undiscovered continent in the South Pacific, the existence of which they considered necessary to balance the large continents in the Northern Hemisphere. Tasman was instructed to find and map this missing continent.

Ferdinand Magellan, the Portuguese explorer, had been the first European to enter the Pacific in 1519. The Portuguese were the first to build a colonial empire in southeast Asia and the Pacific, but they were quickly challenged by Spanish expeditions coming from Mexico and Peru. Spanish explorers sighted New Guinea in 1528 and began colonizing the Philippines in the 1560's. These expeditions were looking for gold and silver to add to the wealth Spain had already found in its South American colonies, but in this search they were disappointed. The trade in spices, however, was lucrative. Various other European powers soon became involved in a contest to see who would control the spice trade.

LIFE'S WORK

The Dutch established themselves in Jakarta in 1602 and three years later made their first attempt to explore the Pacific. Dutch merchant ships made their way to the Indies by following the old Portuguese route around the Cape of Good Hope at the tip of South Africa to the island of Madagascar. From there they would sail either to India or to Java. This route, though, was difficult and dangerous. There were numerous rocks and islands along the way, and the winds were not always blowing in a favorable direction. It was not uncommon for a voyage from Holland to Jakarta to last at least thirteen months. The difficulty of navigation was not the only problem; the longer the voyage, the more likely the possibility of scurvy, a deadly disease linked to the shortages of fresh food and water. Perhaps, company managers suggested, a faster route could be found by sailing across the Pacific to the tip of South America and then up the Atlantic to home. Directors of the East India Company wanted to test this possibility, and they also wanted to know if the Unknown South Land really existed.

The East India Company had been given the sole right to trade in East Asia by the Dutch king. The company made huge profits from this enterprise, and the directors decided to find out whether the Pacific contained any huge continent with even larger quantities of spices—and, perhaps, even deposits of gold and silver. Several expeditions were sent out between 1605 and 1628. The results of these voyages indicated that the eastern and southern coasts of Australia had been traced and mapped. The Dutch called this coastline the "Known South Land" to distinguish it from the unexplored regions farther north and west, which they still called the "Unknown South Land."

Such was the state of knowledge when Antony van Diemen became governor-general of the Dutch East Indies in 1636. His goal was to increase the wealth and power of the East India Company by sending expeditions to complete the geographical knowledge of the Pacific. One of his immediate objects was to determine whether New Guinea and the Known South Land made up one continent or whether there was a strait between them by which access could be gained to the Pacific. (Unknown to the Dutch was that the Spanish had already discov-

Abel Janszoon Tasman. (Hulton Archive/Getty Images)

minded Tasman of the enormous wealth the early Spanish and Portuguese explorers had found in the West Indies and South America, and he expressed his hope that the Dutch expedition would yield a similar return. Moreover, the Spanish and Portuguese had made many converts to Christianity during their conquest of the New World; perhaps, the governor said, Tasman's explorers could likewise bring "uncounted blind heathen" to the "wholesome light of Christianity."

The governor's instructions described the course the ships were to follow. Directions were also given for the survey and description of any lands discovered. Tasman was to make an accurate record of winds, currents, and weather. The native peoples were to be treated well, and no harm was to be done to them. Information was to be obtained concerning the natural resources of the lands visited and the possibilities of trade. The ships would bring with them a wide variety of trade goods, including tools, mirrors, and cotton cloth. The explorers were to be especially vigilant in their search for gold and silver, but they were cautioned to be careful in showing how important these metals were to the Dutch.

The expedition left Batavia on August 14, 1642. After twenty-two days, they reached the Dutch-controlled Indian Ocean island of Mauritius. The ships arrived in very poor condition. The wooden hull of the *Zeehan* had partly rotted and was in need of extensive repair. Both ships were leaky, and the rigging for their sails was old and weak. It took more than a month to repair the vessels. During that time, the sailors took in supplies of water and firewood and hunted on the island for wild hogs, goats, and other animals. The Dutch governor of Mauritius gave Tasman maps of the previously surveyed Solomon Islands and the coastline of New Guinea.

The ships were set to sail on October 4, but because of a storm and excessively high winds, they could not get out of the harbor until four days later. By late November, the ships sighted an island Tasman called Van Diemen's Land, after the Batavian governor (later, the island would be known as Tasmania). Violent weather made exploration of the coast of Van Diemen's Land very difficult. Not until December 1 was the crew able to land and explore the east coast of the island. A crew member hoisted the Dutch flag and claimed possession of the whole island in the name of the king. Tasman left the island after a week because he could not find good water. As his ships

ered, in 1606, that such a strait did indeed exist.) Governor van Diemen hoped to discover a new Peru, rich in gold and silver, in the Unknown South Land; if that did not happen, he hoped at least to find a new land with unknown spices, or fruits and vegetables, that would make his company even richer.

In 1642, Van Diemen gathered an expedition to search for the Unknown South Land. The governor expected the exploration to open up important new areas for trade while also finding a more convenient route across the Pacific to South America. The pilot for the voyage was Frans Jacobsz Visscher, one of the most respected pilots in Holland. Two ships were outfitted for the voyage, the *Heemskerck*, with a crew of sixty, and the smaller *Zeehan*, with a crew of fifty. The expedition was commanded by Tasman, who said he was eager to make the journey. The ships were made ready for the voyage and were instructed to explore the Unknown and the Known South Land, the southeastern coast of New Guinea, and all the islands "lying round about." Van Diemen recontinued east, they saw land again, having reached the shore of the south island of New Zealand.

While anchored in a bay, one of Tasman's small boats was rammed by a native Maori canoe, and three Dutchmen were killed. Tasman ordered his ships to sail east again, and the bay he left was labeled "Murderer's Bay" on his maps in memory of the incident.

He passed the north island of New Zealand and, continuing north, encountered the Tonga Islands, where he picked up a fresh supply of water. In February, he found himself in the midst of many islands that the native peoples called the Fiji. These islands did not appear on any of his maps, so he was unsure of his location.

Tasman decided to return to Batavia, but for two weeks bad weather made it impossible for him to determine his position by celestial navigation. At the end of March, conditions brightened, and he was able to head for Batavia. By the end of May, he reached the western edge of New Guinea, and on June 14 he was back in his home port, ending his ten-month journey.

Though his voyage had discovered the existence of previously unknown lands, the Dutch East India Company considered it a failure. No new trading partnerships had been opened, and no gold, silver, or other major resource had been found. Moreover, Tasman had not found a passage through the south ocean to Chile or Peru. Nevertheless, Tasman's sailing skills impressed the directors, so he was hired to lead another trip in the search for a route to South America. The second voyage was also aimed at finding a route from the East Indies to Chile; in the last months of 1644, however, the Dutch became involved in a war with Portugal, and the voyage to find that route was never undertaken.

Tasman was given three ships and told to determine whether Van Diemen's Land was the southern part of New Guinea or was a separate island. He was also supposed to determine the geography and nature of any islands he came across that lay between the coast of what is now Australia and New Zealand. One such island investigated on this second voyage was Timor. Little is known of the actual voyage, except that the northern coast of Australia was mapped; the Dutch called it New Holland. On his return to Batavia in August, 1644, Tasman reported that the indigenous peoples he encountered along the coast were miserable and seemed to offer little in trade possibilities. The East India investors were told that Tasman's explorations had cost much money but returned nothing of value to their investment. Despite his discoveries and navigational achievements, his efforts were not regarded highly by the company.

SIGNIFICANCE

Tasman's discoveries expanded knowledge of the islands in the southwest Pacific and added to the size of the Dutch East Indian colony. He was the first European to reach the island now called Tasmania and the first to sight New Zealand. On his first voyage, he sailed completely around Australia but never saw it. As a result, the question of whether Australia or New Zealand were parts of a great southern continent, the Unknown South Land, was not answered until the voyages of the English explorer James Cook in the 1760's. The Dutch would eventually lose control of many of Tasman's land claims during wars with England.

Despite his many accomplishments, Tasman was considered something of a failure during his lifetime because he added no gold or silver to the wealth of the Dutch Republic. He was also unable to find a passage through the islands to South America. His major contributions to geography were the maps he made of the islands he came across.

—Leslie V. Tischauser

FURTHER READING

Allen, Oliver E. *The Pacific Navigators.* Alexandria, Va.: Time-Life Books, 1980. This volume in Time-Life's Seafarers series contains text and illustrations about the voyages of Tasman and others who explored the Pacific Ocean.

Anderson, Grahame. *The Merchant of the Zeehan: Isaac Gilsemans and the Voyages of Abel Tasman.* Wellington, New Zealand: Te Papa Press, 2001. Anderson, a yachtsman, recounts Tasman's life and the voyage that brought him to New Zealand. He also describes the role of Gilsemans, an illustrator who sailed with Tasman and drew coastal profiles of the islands they visited. These profiles have traditionally been thought to be rudimentary sketches, but Anderson argues they are accurate and precise cartographic renderings.

Beaglehole, John C. *The Discovery of New Zealand.* 2d ed. Wellington, New Zealand: Oxford University Press, 1961. Describes Tasman's first journey in great detail. Includes a bibliography and index.

_____. *The Exploration of the Pacific.* 2d ed. London: Black, 1947. Contains selections from Tasman's journal and includes a detailed description of the two expeditions led by the Dutch explorer. The brief account of his life presented here is still the most reliable source.

Buck, Peter H. *Explorers of the Pacific: European and American Discoveries in Polynesia.* Honolulu, Hawaii: Bishop Museum Publications, 1953. A great book by a Maori historian and anthropologist. Covers all the explorers from the earliest Portuguese to the pioneers of the mid-nineteenth century.

Grattan, C. Hartley. *The Southwest Pacific to 1900: A Modern History*. Ann Arbor: University of Michigan Press, 1963. An older but still useful account of the region. Includes an interesting chapter on the European discoveries of Australia, New Zealand, the South Pacific islands, and Antarctica. Includes an especially detailed account of the creation of the Dutch East India Company.

Tasman, Abel Janszoon. *Abel Janszoon Tasman and the Discovery of New Zealand*. Wellington, New Zealand: Department of Internal Affairs, 1942. Contains the complete text of Tasman's journal. Useful for the observations on Maori living conditions and Tasman's difficulties with navigation. Also has some descriptions of animal and plant life.

SEE ALSO: Piet Hein; Michiel Adriaanszoon de Ruyter; Maarten and Cornelis Tromp.

RELATED ARTICLES in *Great Events from History: The Seventeenth Century, 1601-1700:* 17th century: Age of Mercantilism in Southeast Asia; 17th century: The Pepper Trade; December, 1601: Dutch Defeat the Portuguese in Bantam Harbor; March 20, 1602: Dutch East India Company Is Founded; Beginning Spring, 1605: Dutch Dominate Southeast Asian Trade; April 29, 1606: First European Contact with Australia; January 14, 1641: Capture of Malacca; 1642 and 1644: Tasman Proves Australia Is a Separate Continent; April, 1652: Dutch Begin to Colonize Southern Africa; Late 17th century: Sulawesi Traders Make Contact with Australian Aborigines; Early 1690's: Brazilian Gold Rush.

KATERI TEKAKWITHA
Iroquois beatified saint

Because of her heroic practice of prayer, chastity, mortification, and Christian virtue, Tekakwitha became the first Native American to be beatified by the Roman Catholic Church. Devotion to Kateri Tekakwitha is responsible for establishing Native American ministries in Catholic churches throughout the United States and Canada.

BORN: 1656; Ossernenon, Mohawk Valley (near present-day Auriesville, New York)

DIED: April 17, 1680; Sault St. Louis, New France (near present-day Montreal, Canada)

ALSO KNOWN AS: Tekakwitha (given name); Catherine Tagaskouita; Tegakwith; She Pushes with Her Hands

AREA OF ACHIEVEMENT: Religion and theology

EARLY LIFE

Kateri Tekakwitha (KAHT-uh-ree tehk-uh-KWIHTH-uh) was born in Ossernenon in the Mohawk Valley in 1656, near what is today Auriesville, New York. Her Indian name, Tekakwitha, means "putting things in order," and her Christian surname Kateri (Catherine) was given to her at her baptism at age twenty-one in Fonda, New York. Her mother, Kahenta, was a Christian Algonquian who had been captured by the Iroquois and saved from torture and death by the Mohawk warrior Kenhoronkwa,

to whom she also bore a son. Kenhoronkwa was a member of the Tortoise clan of the Iroquois Nation, one of the designated groups listed by the Great Council at the beginning of the Five Nations Confederacy.

When Tekakwitha was four, her parents and brother died in a smallpox epidemic that swept through the Mohawk Valley. The arrival of the Jesuits coincided with the beginning of a series of epidemics that wiped out at least half the population of eastern Canada and adjacent parts of the United States. These epidemics began in the period 1634-1640 and recurred periodically for the next half century. Tekakwitha survived, but the disease left her partially blind, with a pocked face and weakened legs. She was adopted by her aunts and an uncle who had become chief of the Turtle clan and hated the "Black Robes," as the Jesuit priests were called among the tribes because of their distinctive dress. Despite her disfigured face and reserved and shrinking nature, her aunts began to form marriage plans for her when she was still very young.

After about five years of the sickness, the survivors of the village moved to the north bank of the Mohawk River. Tekakwitha and her relatives moved into the Turtle Clan village called Gandaouaue, today the Caughnawaga/Kahnawahe Reserve near what is now the town of Fonda, New York. In 1667, the Jesuit missionaries Jacques

Fremin, Jacques Bruyas, and Jean Pierron, who were part of a peace mission between the Mohawks and the French, spent three days in the lodge of her uncle.

Tekakwitha's mother had given her early instruction in the faith. However, this was the first time she had an opportunity to receive knowledge of Christianity from the "Black Robes." For the next eight years, Tekakwitha secretly practiced and remained true to the Christian religion, even though she was not yet baptized and adherence to the new religion caused great risk to her reputation and acceptance by the tribe. She refused to work on Sunday, would not hear of marriage, and refused to fulfill other tribal obligations that interfered with her Christian way of life. When her uncle punished her with beatings, increased her workload, and withheld food from her, she would not succumb. Continual sarcasm, criticism, and mockery were her constant lot.

LIFE'S WORK

In 1674, Jacques de Lamberville took charge of the mission that included the Turtle clan. One year later, Tekakwitha finally managed to meet with the priest when he visited her home and told him about her desire to be baptized. She began to take religious instruction, and on Easter Sunday, April 5, 1676, she was baptized and was given the Mohawk name Kateri, in honor of Saint Catherine of Siena. She was only twenty years of age. Her great fervor after the reception of this sacrament induced her to increase her penances and prayers. This further incited the anger of many of the tribe. Children and drunken men used to chase her and pelt her with stones, calling her "the Christian." To punish her for abandoning tribal beliefs and customs, her own relatives treated her like a slave, and her uncle even threatened to kill her if she refused to marry.

In July, 1677, Tekakwitha was assisted by Christian Indians to escape her village to go to live at the mission town of Saint Francis Xavier du Sault St. Louis near Montreal, called Caughnawaga by the native people. After a two-month and two-hundred-mile journey through woods, rivers, and swamps, Tekakwitha finally arrived at the mission. Mission towns provided converts with new identities and allegiances by isolating them from their unconverted kinsmen, thus preventing the kind of reversion to traditional belief all missionaries feared.

Tekakwitha lived in the cabin of Anastasia Tegonhatsihonga, another Christian Indian woman, who became her close friend and companion in the practice of Christian virtue. The two women devoted all of their extra time to helping the aged and sick and teaching the children

catechism. To go to Mass, Tekakwitha had to arise at four in the morning and walk barefoot even in the snow. Both young women performed extraordinary penances, and the two asked permission to start a religious community. This request was denied, although Tekakwitha was enrolled in the pious association called the Brotherhood of the Holy Family in 1678 because of her extraordinary practices of all the virtues.

Two features stand out in the life of Kateri Tekakwitha: her resolute determination to live a life of virginity as a spouse of Jesus Christ and her persevering spirit of penance and prayer. Even before her baptism when she lived among the Mohawks, Tekakwitha felt drawn to the idea of celibate life, although she had never seen or heard anything concerning the voluntary state of virginity such as the Catholic sisters observed it. The Mohawks knew that the Black Robes lived without marriage but did not know women also practiced this ideal. Even in Caughnawaga, to which she had fled so that she might better practice her faith, the normally obedient Mohawk maiden persisted in her resolve not to marry.

Finally, Tekakwitha approached a Black Robe with her desire to dedicate herself to a life of virginity. Responding to his protests about her material welfare, she insisted with such firmness and clear understanding of the celibate life as practiced in the Catholic Church that he was forced to accede to her request. On the feast of the Annunciation of the Blessed Virgin, March 25, 1679, Kateri Tekakwitha privately made the vow of perpetual virginity, placing herself in her new state of life under the special protection of the Virgin Mary. She thus became the first recorded Iroquois woman to bind herself by a religious vow to the observance of the evangelical counsels.

After this, Tekakwitha's desire for prayer and penance for her sins and the wrongdoings of her people was insatiable. Even though she suffered repeated attacks of heavy fever and had to spend most of the time on her cot, when she could walk, she staggered barefoot over the ice of the river while saying the rosary for the conversion of her people. In imitation of how the Iroquois branded the right foot of their slave girls above the ankle as a lasting mark of their servitude, she pressed a burning faggot from the fire to the flesh of her own foot, indicating that she belonged to Christ, body and soul. Despite the advice of her spiritual director, Tekakwitha persisted in performing many acts of penance until she became so weak that she was confined to bed. As she steadily declined, she continued to catechize the children of the village from her sickbed, a cot on the ground.

Kateri Tekakwitha, age twenty-four, died in Holy Week of 1689 on April 17. Immediately after her death, a mysterious event allegedly occurred. According to the accounts of the priests and others present, after her death, her face changed completely within the space of a few minutes. The smallpox marks that had disfigured her countenance from childhood disappeared, and her flesh took on a healthy hue.

The *Jesuit Relations and Allied Documents* (1896-1901), one of the most important primary sources for insights into Indian government, law, and religion, notes that a young Indian woman "who lived like nuns" died with the reputation of sanctity and that journeys were being made to her tomb by many Native Americans; it also remarks on miracles and favors reportedly worked through her intercession.

SIGNIFICANCE

Kateri Tekakwitha was declared Venerable by the Catholic Church in 1943, and in June, 1980, in the presence of hundreds of North American Indians, she became the first Native American to be beatified. Her feast day in the Calendar of Saints was designated as July 14. In his homily address, Pope John Paul II praised her "solid faith, straightforward humility, calm resignation and radiant joy, even in the midst of terrible sufferings."

Devotion to Kateri Tekakwitha, who has been named the patron saint of the environment and ecology, is responsible for establishing Native American ministries in Catholic churches across the United States and Canada. Thousands of pilgrims have visited shrines to Kateri erected at both Saint Francis Xavier in Caughnawaga and at her birthplace in Auriesville, New York.

—*Marian T. Horvat*

FURTHER READING

Brown, Evelyn M. *Kateri Tekakwitha, Mohawk Maiden.* San Francisco: Ignatius, 1991. The first five chapters relate events of her life; the remainder closely follow written records and source documents in old French. For high school students and young adults. Illustrated.

Bunson, Margaret R. *Kateri Tekakwitha: Mystic of the Wilderness.* Preface by Paul A. Lenz. Huntington, Ind.: Our Sunday Visitor, 1992. Emphasis on Native Americans as a link to the vital past of North America. The first chapter gives a detailed description of the customs and culture of Native Americans. Illustrated biography.

Fisher, Lillian M. *Kateri Tekakwitha: The Lily of the Mohawks.* Boston: Pauline Books & Media, 1996. A brief illustrated biography of Tekakwitha.

Greer, Allen. *Mohawk Saint: Catherine Tekakwitha and the Jesuits.* New York: Oxford University Press, 2004. A more recent biography written by a professor of history at the University of Toronto.

Markowitz, Harvey, ed. *American Indians.* 3 vols. Pasadena, Calif.: Salem Press, 1995. A biography of Tekakwitha is included in this three-volume set.

Petrash, Antonia. *More than Petticoats: Remarkable New York Women.* Guilford, Conn.: TwoDot, 2002. Tekakwitha is one of women profiled in this collection of brief biographies.

SharkeyLemire, PaulaAnne, comp. *Blessed Kateri Tekakwitha Prayers and Devotions.* New Hope, Ky.: New Hope, 2003. The book contains a brief biography of Tekakwitha and a series of prayers and devotions in her honor.

Walworth, Ellen H. *The Life and Times of Kateri Tekakwitha, the Lily of the Mohawks, 1656-1680.* Buffalo, N.Y.: P. Paul and Bro., 1893. Classic biography with information gathered from primary sources and multiple documents. Full account of her life and times. Includes photographs, maps, and appendices with Mohawk vocabularies, maps of trails, and other documents.

SEE ALSO: Pocahontas; Pierre Esprit Radisson; Saint Rose of Lima.

RELATED ARTICLE in *Great Events from History: The Seventeenth Century, 1601-1700:* 1617-c. 1700: Smallpox Epidemics Kill Native Americans.

TIANQI
Emperor of China (r. 1621-1627)

Tianqi was a weak emperor, uninterested in politics on either a grand or a small scale. During his seven-year reign, he became little more than a figurehead for his eunuch, Wei Zhongxian, who actually made most of the decisions carried out in Tianqui's name.

BORN: December 23, 1605; Beijing, China
DIED: September 30, 1627; Beijing
ALSO KNOWN AS: T'ien-ch'i (reign name, Wade-Giles); Zhu Youjiao (given name, Pinyin), Chu Yu-chiao (given name, Wade-Giles); Xizong (temple name, Pinyin), Hsi-tsung (temple name, Wade-Giles); Yizong (temple name, Pinyin), I-tsung (temple name, Wade-Giles)
AREA OF ACHIEVEMENT: Government and politics

EARLY LIFE

Tianqi (tyan-chee), whose given name was Zhu Youjiao, came to the throne in the wake of the death of his father, Emperor Taichang (T'ai-Ch'ang, r. August to September, 1620), who died unexpectedly only one month after his ascension. The fifteen-year-old new emperor chose a reign name meaning "the opening (of a ruler's way) by heaven." Emperor Tianqi was the oldest son of the late emperor and Empress Wang (d. 1619). Soon after emperor Taichang's death, however, the emperor-to-be was forced into captivity by his father's ambitious consort Li, who had once tried unsuccessfully to persuade the late emperor to make her empress. Li wanted to be the guardian to the motherless Tianqi so as to effectively seize power. Only after the intervention of the high ministers was the new emperor released, and Li agreed to leave the principal palace.

The sudden death of his father remained an enigma throughout Tianqi's reign. Historians named it the Red Pill Case, because the sick emperor was given red pills by his eunuch and his concubine, Zheng (c. 1568-1630), whose son was a rival to Zhu Youjiao. After two doses of the red pills, Taichang died on September 26, 1620, after suffering from a serious case of diarrhea. In the midst of shock and confusion, Tianqi succeeded his father, never having expected to rule at such a young age.

LIFE'S WORK

The young emperor had no formal education or training in political science. In view of this deficiency, the ministers at court suggested that private tutoring be carried out in the palace. However, Tianqi was not eager to learn, and he used pretexts to cancel classes that were held only briefly. He spent most of his time in the back palace, working at his favorite hobby, carpentry. With his dexterous hands, Tianqi created wood models of the palace. Chinese opera was also a great source of pleasure to the emperor. In 1621, his ministers arranged his marriage, which they hoped would help him mature and become responsible. The marriage proved to have no effect on Tianqi, however, who continued with his usual ways. He left court business to his most trusted eunuch, Wei Zhongxian (Wei Chong-hsien, 1568-1628). Another important person in Tianqi's life was his wet nurse, Madame Ke, with whom he was enamored. There were even rumors that the emperor had an illicit relationship with this thirty-eight-year-old woman.

Wei began his career at court by serving as a butler for Tianqi's mother, Empress Wang. Through her, he earned the trust of the Taichang emperor and of Madam Ke, who became a conspiratorial partner with Wei after Tianqi's ascension. Often, Wei would give out disguised imperial orders bearing Tianqi's seal. Although he was only entitled grand eunuch, Wei had the authority of the emperor behind him, enforcing all of his decisions regarding the placement of officials and military command. Loyal ministers at court, such as the Donglin faction, declared war openly with Wei, who used the emperor's power to overcome his enemies.

To make matters worse, in 1623, Tianqi promoted Wei to be the director of the Eastern Depot, the imperial secret service. This directorship provided Wei with a perfect opportunity to eliminate his political opponents. A blacklist of the Donglin party and its associates was made up, and one by one, Wei chopped them down. Between 1624 and 1627, Wei effectively acted as a dictator, raising taxes as he pleased and executing Donglin members with equal ease. All over the country, temples were built in Wei's honor. Publically, he was respected and treated on a par with Confucius, the sage of China. Everywhere he went, his entourage numbered as many as that of the emperor. Wei's downfall did not come until the emperor's death in 1627.

Tianqi's administration faced other political issues as well. In 1622, the Manchus, led by Nurhaci, invaded Liaodong in the northeast, and the Chinese army was unable to repel them. At the same time, in southwestern China, the aboriginal Miao people also created unrest. As if this were not enough, in the same year, another rebellion under the banner of the White Lotus Society broke out in Shandong province. This 100,000-man rebel group severed the Grand Canal and blocked all transport between the north and the south. Fortunately, the rebellion was suppressed at the end of the year. On the other hand, on the southwestern coast of China, the Dutch and the Portuguese were fighting for the rights to trade in China. Although China was not directly involved in the conflict, it had to send troops to pacify the Dutch.

The greatest damage to the Ming administration at this time, however, came from natural disasters. There were earthquakes in Beijing in 1623, 1624, and 1626 and in Nanking in 1624 and 1626. In 1620, 1621, and 1626, fires broke out in the imperial palace that called for extensive and expensive repairs. During Tianqi's reign, the people of China were plagued by floods, droughts, and locust attacks, followed by famines and epidemic diseases. These disasters drained the nation's economy as well as the life of the commoners. Looking for the means to survive, the starved population turned into bandits who roamed from one province to another, stealing the means of subsistence. In order to help the poor and fight the rebels, the Ming administration decided to raise taxes on land, salt, and imports. This decision placed the middle class in jeopardy, however, while the poor were still not necessarily fed. Inflation skyrocketed, and even rice became too expensive for the poor to afford.

All this was happening while Tianqi carried on with his lifelong pastime of carpentry. He punished his critics and arbitrarily promoted officials. For his wedding, he spent an extravagant sum. Afterward, when an official sought to persuade him to reduce the amount of his clothing allowance, he had the man beaten and dismissed. Others came to the poor man's rescue, and Tianqi at last decided merely to suspend his salary for one year. All in all, Tianqi was not an effective ruler.

In the summer of 1627, Tianqi went to row in the river adorned in winter clothing. He fell into the water and was rescued. For some time afterward, however, he was sick, and the medical care he received did not help. A remedy called "the magic potion" was offered to him from the court. Tianqi liked the taste of the potion and continued to use it for a number of days, until he became edematous. On August 24, 1627, he knew his end was near. Calling his brother Zhu Youjian to his bedside, he asked him to succeed the throne. Tianqi was twenty-two.

SIGNIFICANCE

For all his seven-year reign, Tianqui was never part of the political scene in the Ming government. Another man, the eunuch Wei Zhongxian, ruled in his place and caused one of the most infamous political scandals in Chinese history. During his short rule, Tianqi created a nearly irredeemable political regime, which his brother inherited when he assumed the imperial throne as Emperor Chongzhen. It would not be unduly harsh to say that Tianqi's negligent rule hastened the demise of the Ming Dynasty. Chongzhen worked hard to repair the damage done by his brother's administration, but ultimately, he could only watch as China fell into the hands of the Manchus in 1644.

—*Fatima Wu*

FURTHER READING

Dardess, John W. *Blood and History in China: The Donglin Faction and Its Repression, 1620-1627*. Honolulu: University of Hawaii Press, 2002. On the political intrigues during the Tianqi reign. Has details on the battle between the Donglin faction and the emperor's favorite eunuch Wei Zhongxian.

Hucker, Charles O. *The Censorial System of Ming China*. Stanford, Calif.: Stanford University Press, 1966. The chapter on "Censorial Impeachments and Counsel in a Chaotic Era, 1620-1627" gives insight into the political situation during Tianqi's reign.

Mote, Frederick W. *Imperial China 900-1800*. Cambridge, Mass.: Harvard University Press, 1999. Part 4 on the Ming Dynasty gives comprehensive information on the course of failure of the Ming Dynasty.

Paludan, Ann. *Chronicles of the Chinese Emperors*. London: Thames and Hudson, 2001. A comprehensive chronicle on Chinese emperors beginning with Qin Shihuangdi, the first emperor of China, up to the last emperor, Puyi of the Qing. Besides biographical details for each emperor, Paludan also presents cultural and political highlights for each dynastic era. Portraits, illustrations, and maps are helpful.

Tsai, Shih-shan, Henry. *The Eunuchs in the Ming Dynasty*. New York: State University of New York Press, 1996. Has comprehensive discussions on the havoc wreaked by the Grand Eunuch Wei Zhongxian who was responsible for the chaotic politics during Tianqi's reign.

SEE ALSO: Abahai; Chen Shu; Chongzhen; Dorgon; Kangxi; Liu Yin; Shunzhi; Wang Fuzhi; Zheng Chenggong.

RELATED ARTICLES in *Great Events from History: The Seventeenth Century, 1601-1700:* 1616-1643: Rise of the Manchus; April 25, 1644: End of the Ming Dynasty; June 6, 1644: Manchus Take Beijing.

TIRSO DE MOLINA
Spanish dramatist and playwright

Tirso de Molina, who introduced the figure of Don Juan into world literature, was one of the most influential dramatists of the Spanish Golden Age. Both a man of letters and a clergyman, he cultivated a wide variety of dramatic genres, poetry, narrative fiction, and historical works. He was one of numerous disciples of Lope de Vega Carpio. In his comedias, *he followed the guidelines of Lope de Vega's comedia nueva.*

BORN: 1580?; Madrid, Spain
DIED: February, 1648; Almazán, Soria, Spain
ALSO KNOWN AS: Gabriel Téllez (given name)
AREAS OF ACHIEVEMENT: Literature, theater, religion and theology

EARLY LIFE

Tirso de Molina (TEER-soh day-moh-LEE-nah) was the pseudonym of Gabriel Téllez. He was born in Madrid though his date of birth, early years, and family origins have always been a source of debate and controversy. In the 1920's, a prominent Tirso critic, Blanca de los Ríos, stated that Tirso was born in 1584, based upon a birth certificate dated March 9 of that year for a "Fray Gabriel," whose mother was Gracia Juliana. Ríos also believed that Tirso's father might have been the duke of Osuna. One scholar has argued that on January 25, 1638, Tirso had stated at the court of the Inquisition in Toledo that he was fifty-seven years old, suggesting that his year of birth was 1580 or 1581. More recently, research suggests that Tirso may have been the son of the count of Molina Herrera, Andrés López, and Juana Téllez. Vázquez fixed the writer's date of birth in 1579, probably on March 24.

Tirso entered into the Mercedarian order in 1600 as a novice after studying the humanities in Madrid. After professing in 1601, he pursued the study of theology and the arts in Toledo and Guadalajara. It was not until Tirso completed his studies, in 1609, that he began his career as a playwright.

LIFE'S WORK

Between 1610 and 1616, Tirso lived in Toledo, where he wrote his first plays under his pseudonym, Tirso de Molina. His early works include *El vergonzoso en palacio* (wr. 1611?; *The Bashful Man at Court*, 1991); *La villana de La Sagra* (wr. c. 1611; the village woman of *La Sagra*), a play of love and intrigue; and *Don Gil de las calzas verdes* (wr. 1615?, pb. 1635; *Don Gil of the Green Breeches*, 1991). His *comedias* share the same themes of humor, intrigue, love, deceit, and disguise (often a woman dressed as a man). From the beginning of his career, he gained the reputation, among some members of the Church, of a frivolous and profane writer, in spite of his religious and devotional plays such as the hagiographical trilogy *La Santa Juana* (wr. 1613-1614). Despite the reaction of the Church, Tirso's popularity reached the highest levels of society, gaining the approval of King Philip III's prime minister, Francisco Gómez de Sandoval y Rojas, the duke de Lerma, and that of the monarch himself, whom Tirso admired.

After spending two years in the Americas, in Santo Domingo, where he obtained the title of *definidor*, or member of the Mercedarian order's government, he returned to Spain in 1618 to attend the general chapter in Guadalajara, and then he taught theology in Segovia and Toledo until 1620. For his lectures, he earned the title of teacher, *presentado*, of theology.

By about 1622, he was back in Madrid, writing profusely and participating in poetry contests, among other activities, which were organized by the literary academies. This was the time when his literary production and political activities relating to his order reached their height. Two of his most famous plays were written during this period, although some critics question his authorship of them. *El condenado por desconfiado* (wr. 1615?, pb. 1634; *The Saint and the Sinner*, 1952; also known as *Damned for Despair*, 1986) explores questions of salvation and free will, and in *El burlador de Sevilla* (pb. 1630; *The Love Rogue*, 1924), he forged the universal figure of Don Juan. Also of this period is *Los cigarrales de Toledo* (wr. 1621, pb. 1624; the country houses of Toledo), a prose miscellany including several stories told by different narrators following the model of Giovanni Boccaccio's *Decameron: O, Prencipe Galetto* (1349-1351; *The Decameron*, 1620). Other works of this period include *El amor médico* (wr. 1621?; love medicine) and a play of intrigue, *La fingida Arcadia* (wr. 1622?; the feigned arcady), which is not only a commentary on Lope de Vega Carpio's pastoral novel *La Arcadia* (1598) but also a political satire. Also, Tirso wrote the historical play *La prudencia en la mujer* (wr. 1627-1633; *Prudence in Woman*, 1964), inspired by the medieval Spanish queen, María de Molina.

When Philip III died in 1621, his sixteen-year-old son, Prince Philip, inherited the throne, becoming Philip IV.

This was unfortunate for Tirso and the many others who opposed the new monarch and his prime minister, the count-duke of Olivares, a quite unpopular figure. A period of repression and persecution began for many intellectuals and members of the previous reign. While Tirso praised Philip III in plays such as *La villana de Vallecas* (wr. 1620?; the village woman of Vallecas), he harshly criticized his son Philip IV's reign in several other plays. For example, in *Prudence in Women*, Tirso used a historical play to criticize his own time. As a result of Tirso's open enmity for the government, in 1625, he was condemned by the committee for reform of the Council of Castile (Junta de Reformación) to stop writing. Tirso un-

Statue of Spanish dramatist Tirso de Molina. (The Granger Collection, New York)

successfully attempted to have this sentence revoked. Subsequently, he was expulsed from the court to the convent of Trujillo, where he was named *comendador* (commander).

Despite the condemnation and sentence, Tirso was able to publish a group of plays in five parts. The first was written in Seville (1627) and the third in Tortosa (1634), while the second and fourth (1635), and fifth (1636) were published in Madrid. He wrote a second miscellany text, *Deleytar aprovechando* (pb. 1635; teaching while entertaining), which included the narrative *El bandolero* (the bandit) and some *autos sacramentales* (religious plays in one act celebrating the Eucharist).

Tirso was named general chronicler of the Mercedarian order in 1632, where he was tasked with writing the order's history. It was in this capacity that he wrote the *Historia general de la orden de Nuestra Señora de las Mercedes* (wr. 1639; general history of the order of our lady of mercy). He was transferred to Cuenca, possibly because of conflicts with the ecclesiastic authorities, and was deprived of his position of chronicler.

In 1645, Tirso was named *comendador* of the monastery of Soria, where he had been sent to live, and in 1647, he gained the title of *definidor* of Castile. He died one year later, in February of 1648, in Almazán, Soria.

SIGNIFICANCE

Tirso is considered, with Lope de Vega Carpio and Pedro Calderón de la Barca, one of the most important and prolific playwrights of the Spanish Baroque in a period where the *nueva comedia* was at its peak. Critics believe that he wrote about four hundred *comedias*, although only eighty-four of them actually exist and only fifty-four are his without doubt. In his plays, he followed Lope de Vega's style, while conferring on his work a personal touch of wit, humor, and erudition, and creating characters with deep psychological traits (particularly strong women) as well as universal passions.

However, like many other figures of his period, Tirso's popularity decreased in the eighteenth century, almost falling into oblivion, only to be recovered one century later. His texts were studied and edited by Spanish playwright Juan Eugenio Hartzenbusch (1806-1880), and later by Emilio Cotarelo y Mori (1857-1936). Subsequently, other editions of his works were produced, notably those of scholars Blanca de los Ríos Lampérez (1862-1956) and María del Pilar Palomo Vázquez.

It is perhaps Tirso's character, Don Juan, that most assured his international fame, since it inspired Molière, Corneille, Lord Byron, George Bernard Shaw, Alexandre Dumas, and Wolfgang Amadeus Mozart (*Don Giovanni*, 1787), among others. One of the most-performed plays in Spain is *Don Juan Tenorio* (pr., pb. 1844), by the nineteenth century writer, José Zorrilla y Moral.

— *Victoria Rivera-Cordero*

FURTHER READING

Levin, Leslie. *Metaphors of Conversion in Seventeenth-Century Spanish Drama*. London: Tamesis Books, 1998. Explores the metaphor of "conversion" in seventeenth century Spanish poetry, preaching, and painting. Levin argues that the three media made use of the same body of sources and symbols, while they concentrated on the use of metaphors to communicate the experience of conversion. Includes analysis of Tirso's *The Saint and the Sinner*.

Stoll, Anita K., and Dawn L. Smith, eds. *Gender, Identity, and Representation in Spain's Golden Age*. Lewisburg, Pa.: Bucknell University Press, 2000. This volume examines issues of gender, identity, and representation in Golden Age Spanish theater and prose. Includes a chapter on cross-dressing in Tirso's *El*

amor médico and *El Aquiles* by Anita K. Stoll, who argues that cross-dressing female characters reveal the "illusiveness of sexual categories" and drew audiences for precisely this reason.

Thacker, Jonathan. *Role Play and the World as Stage in the Comedia*. Liverpool, England: Liverpool University Press, 2002. Analyzes the concept of "reinventing the self" in Spanish Golden Age theater, using role theory. Thacker argues that playwrights such as Lope de Vega, Tirso, and Calderon used role-playing to criticize their societies more than has been previously asserted.

SEE ALSO: Pedro Calderón de la Barca; Pierre Corneille; Luis de Góngora y Argote; Baltasar Gracián y Morales; Count-Duke of Olivares; Philip III; Philip IV; Francisco Gómez de Quevedo y Villegas; Lope de Vega Carpio.

RELATED ARTICLES in *Great Events from History: The Seventeenth Century, 1601-1700:* c. 1601-1682: Spanish Golden Age; 1605 and 1615: Cervantes Publishes *Don Quixote de la Mancha*.

TOKUGAWA IEYASU
Japanese shogun (r. 1603-1605)

Ieyasu united Japan under a feudal administration and brought it to the height of its cultural tradition in a closed society that lasted for more than two centuries.

BORN: January 31, 1543; Okazaki, Mikawa Province (now in Aichi Prefecture), Japan
DIED: June 1, 1616; Sumpu, Suruga Province (now Shizuoka, Shizuoka Prefecture), Japan
ALSO KNOWN AS: Matsudaira Takechiyo (given name)
AREAS OF ACHIEVEMENT: Government and politics, warfare and conquest

EARLY LIFE

Tokugawa Ieyasu (toh-koo-gah-wah ee-eh-yo-soo) was born Matsudaira Takechiyo in Okazaki Castle, the son of a minor warrior chieftain, Matsudaira Hirotada, whose lands lay between the domains of the Imagawa and the Oda families on the Pacific Ocean. To cement an alliance with Imagawa Yoshimoto, Hirotada dispatched Ieyasu as a hostage in 1547. Ieyasu, however, was seized by Oda Nobuhide, who held him hostage for two years. A truce between Yoshimoto and Nobuhide allowed Ieyasu, whose father had died in the meantime, to be taken as

hostage to Sumpu, the castle town of Yoshimoto. His grandmother, Keyoin, a nun in Sumpu, started Ieyasu's education by teaching him calligraphy and arranging for a Zen monk, Tagen Sufu, adviser and kin of Yoshimoto, to educate him further. Sufu, an expert in the principles and practice of warfare and well versed in tactics and strategy, taught Ieyasu the relationship of warfare to government and administration. Ieyasu's education in both military and civil affairs, continually internalized through practical application, eventually refined him into the greatest political and military figure in the history of Japan.

As early as the age of ten, Ieyasu began to participate in military duties, initially in noncombatant positions, such as commander of the castle guard. At age twelve, he became an adult and took the name Motonobu. The following year, in 1556, he returned to Okazaki as head of the family to find his Matsudaira retainers awaiting him, although the Imagawa family continued to garrison the castle. In 1558, at the age of fifteen, he made his first sortie, an assault on a peripheral fortress of Oda Nobunaga, who had succeeded his father, Nobuhide. Ieyasu de-

Tokugawa Ieyasu. (Library of Congress)

Ieyasu made an alliance with Hōjō Ujimasa in Odawara and split the eastern Takeda domains, taking the Kai and Southern Shinano Provinces. When Hideyoshi became *kampaku* (regent to the emperor) in 1585, some Tokugawa allies went over to his side, and Ieyasu, to maintain peace on his western borders, struck a deal with Hideyoshi in 1586 and swore loyalty to him in 1588. Thus, when Ujimasa refused to submit to Hideyoshi, Hideyoshi attacked, using Ieyasu as his point man.

When Odawara fell in 1590, the Hōjō leaders were ordered to disembowel themselves, and the Kanto Plain, with its six provinces of Izu, Sagami, Musashi, Kozuke, Kazusa, and Shimosa, was given to Ieyasu along with 110,000 *koku* (one *koku* is equivalent to an area that would harvest five bushels of rice) of land in the Omi and Ise Provinces not far from Kyōto in exchange for Ieyasu's lands in the Mikawa, Totomi, and Suruga Provinces. It provided Ieyasu with a one-million-*koku* increase in land, separated him further from Hideyoshi, and made him point man for further expansion of Hideyoshi's control to the east. Ieyasu now established his castle in Edo, which is the modern Imperial Palace in Tokyo, and began a promising future.

LIFE'S WORK

The 1590's was a decade of preparation. The policies Ieyasu followed in consolidating his control in the Kanto Plain were later successfully pursued to unify and administer Japan for two and a half centuries of peace following the Battle of Sekigahara in 1600 and the subsequent subordination of all the feudal lords under Ieyasu's control.

Ieyasu believed that good government consisted of keeping the goodwill of the governed. Consequently, he immediately lightened taxation, punished or got rid of administrators who exploited or abused the collection of taxes, tightened administrative regulations to restrict the authority of district administrators, and established mechanisms of inspection to audit their performance. It is not surprising that peasants from other domains began filtering into Tokugawa holdings to escape high taxes and harsh rule.

stroyed the fort, raided the area, and before withdrawing smashed a pursuit force dispatched by Nobunaga. When Yoshimoto refused to recall the Imagawa garrison at Okazaki, Ieyasu changed his name to Motoyasu. For two more years, he served Yoshimoto until Yoshimoto was killed in battle by Nobunaga forces at Okehazama in 1560. Although Ieyasu had successfully overrun a Nobunaga frontier fortress, he realized that Nobunaga had been victorious and that Yoshimoto's heir was incompetent. Ieyasu thus returned to Okazaki, reclaimed the domain for his family, forced the Imagawa garrison out, and established himself as an independent lord at the age of seventeen.

In 1561, Matsudaira Takechiyo joined hands with Nobunaga and took the name Ieyasu. Little by little, he encroached on Imagawa holdings until he controlled both Mikawa and Totomi provinces. In 1567, an imperial order pronounced him Lord Tokugawa Ieyasu, and, as an ally of Nobunaga, he extended his holdings eastward along the seacoast. Fighting much of the time against the Takeda family, he added Suruga Province to his holdings.

When Nobunaga was murdered in 1582, his chief general, Toyotomi Hideyoshi, began taking over his domains and alliances. In 1583, to offset Hideyoshi's power,

Ieyasu regarded religion as one of the instruments of government and guaranteed the lands of temples and shrines that accepted his leadership. He issued sets of regulations to guide abbots in administering the temples and priestly behavior and made religious controversy against the law. Eventually, everyone had to carry an identification card that stipulated to which Shinto shrine and Buddhist temple he belonged. Ieyasu adroitly used nuptial services in politics, marrying his daughters and granddaughters to important feudal lords. These marriages eventually related Ieyasu to almost every major feudal lord in the country, thus consolidating his relations with the strategic feudal houses. Moreover, he soon began arranging marriages among feudal houses, thus strengthening his political infrastructure.

Ieyasu was the perfect specimen of a type that Japanese nationality and training tends to produce. With a powerful physique, he ensured his own physical health with a frugal diet, the avoidance of any excess, a fondness for all kinds of exercise, and an outdoor, active life. Hawking was his real interest, although he was skilled in archery, fencing, and horsemanship and excelled at shooting.

A disciplined man with great self-control, Ieyasu kept his powder dry during Hideyoshi's two Korean campaigns between 1592 and 1598 and after Hideyoshi's death was in a position to consolidate his strength and establish an administration that covered all Japan. Ieyasu was appointed shogun by the imperial court in 1603 and reconstituted the *bakufu* (shogunate), which both Nobunaga and Hideyoshi had ignored.

In patterning his shogunate on the previous Kamakura and Ashikaga shogunates, Ieyasu studied the basic codes of those regimes in the *Azuma Kagami* (mirror of the east) and *Kenmoku Shikimoku* (code of the Kenmu year period), respectively. The *Azuma Kagami* particularly provided historical justification for his regime. As a history of the founding of the Kamakura shogunate, its lessons are clear. A shogun rules through his vassal bands. He rules justly, punishing insurgents and rewarding loyal followers. He keeps the peace and, through the action of a grateful and cooperative court, receives and at the same time passes on to his heir and descendants the title of shogun. Consequently, Ieyasu took care to ensure that no person or institution should be able to interfere with Tokugawa rule and that the military class under his family should be the ruling power. To protect his family position, he retired in 1605 and had his son Tokugawa Hidetada appointed shogun, although he continued to rule. He also saw to it that his grandson

Iemitsu would succeed his father, Hidetada, when Ieyasu died.

In a strategic distribution of fiefs following the Battle of Sekigahara, Ieyasu placed *fudai* lords (hereditary lieges) in key domains throughout Japan to keep an eye on the *tozama* (outside lords) with whom he had no hereditary ties. In order to reduce their wealth and thus limit their military strength, Ieyasu imposed upon the feudal lords obligations such as rebuilding castles, expanding the Imperial Palace in 1611, and building roads.

Ieyasu was devoted to the accumulation of wealth, but he did not spend it. Instead, he repeatedly advised vassals to live frugally and in his own daily habits tried to serve as a model. This is one of the reasons why the pursuit of profitable foreign trade was inimicable to his interests. Ieyasu had taken the English captain Will Adams into his service in 1601, sanctioned the visits of the Dutch in 1606 and the English in 1613, and approved Japanese trading ventures to Southeast Asia. Profits on a six-month round-trip voyage to Southeast Asia, for example, ranged from 35 percent to 110 percent, averaging 50 percent per voyage. Once Toyotomi power had been eliminated by the capture of Ōsaka Castle in 1616, however, two other factors came into play discouraging foreign trade. One was the persecution of Christians, who were regarded as the advance guard of foreign invasion. The other and most important was the domestic policy of Ieyasu, which brought all the feudal lords under his control. Foreign trade could only help the western *tozama* lords become wealthy, and that caused gradual foreign restrictions until the country was closed off completely in 1640 under Iemitsu.

SIGNIFICANCE

In his early years and all through his life, Tokugawa Ieyasu was a good fighter and a born strategist. He fought more than forty-five battles. He did not win them all, but at Mikatagahara he defeated a force led by Takeda Shingen twice as great as his own. Later, he defeated Hideyoshi twice at Komakiyama and Nagakute before submitting himself as a vassal. The Battle of Sekigahara showed his true mettle as a general. He smashed a combined force larger than his own and settled once and for all his military supremacy over all the other feudal lords.

In his later years after 1590, when he took over the Kanto Plain, he showed his genius as an administrator. Ieyasu made no effort to create a systematic government. He gave direct orders rather than governing by legislation. What legislation there was was neither bulky nor particularly original. It carried on the codes of the Kamakura and Ashikaga shogunates with the purpose of keeping the Tokugawa family in a position of complete and unassailable domination. It included terms of the oath to be taken by all daimyos (feudal lords) and laws to be observed by the imperial house and court nobles and by the feudal lords and their samurai retainers. Ieyasu exacted unconditional obedience of the whole military class. Moreover, the court could do nothing without the consent of the shogunate, restricting itself to ceremony and aesthetics.

—Edwin L. Neville, Jr.

FURTHER READING

Boxer, C. R. *The Christian Century in Japan, 1549-1650.* Berkeley: University of California Press, 1951. A classic examination of the century of foreign trade prior to the closing of the country in 1640. Examines Ieyasu's changing attitude toward Christians.

Gordon, Andrew. *A Modern History of Japan: From Tokugawa Times to the Present.* New York: Oxford University Press, 2003. Gordon, a professor of history at Harvard University, devotes several chapters to the establishment of the Tokugawa regime, discussing the country's social, economic, and intellectual transformation during the Tokugawa period.

Jansen, Marius B. *The Making of Modern Japan.* Cambridge, Mass.: Harvard University Press, 2000. Includes chapters on Tokugawa Ieyasu's rise to power, the creation of his government and shogunate, and foreign relations, culture, education, and religion during the Tokugawa period.

Menton, Linda K., Noren W. Lush, Eileen H. Tamura, and Chance I. Gusukuma. *The Rise of Modern Japan.* Honolulu: University of Hawaii Press, 2003. The first chapter, "Building the Early Modern State, 1600-1912," devotes a section to the Tokugawa shogunate. Extensively illustrated with photographs, graphs, charts, maps and time lines.

Sadler, A. L. *The Maker of Modern Japan: The Life of Tokugawa Ieyasu.* London: Allen & Unwin, 1937. The first major effort to capture the life and times of Ieyasu and the meaning of his life.

Sansom, George. *A History of Japan, 1334-1615.* Stanford, Calif.: Stanford University Press, 1961. Contains two excellent chapters on Ieyasu's life and the early years of the Tokugawa shogunate, as well as a chapter on the Tokugawa government.

Totman, Conrad. *Tokugawa Ieyasu: Shogun.* San Francisco: Heian International, 1983. A well-written, in-depth biography of Ieyasu that employs flashbacks to heighten interest.

SEE ALSO: Tokugawa Tsunayoshi.

RELATED ARTICLES in *Great Events from History: The Seventeenth Century, 1601-1700:* 17th century: The Pepper Trade; 1602-1613: Japan Admits Western Traders; 1603: Tokugawa Shogunate Begins; 1603-1629: Okuni Stages the First Kabuki Dance Dramas; Beginning 1607: Neo-Confucianism Becomes Japan's Official Philosophy; 1614-1615: Siege of Ōsaka Castle; January 27, 1614: Japanese Ban Christian Missionaries; 1615: Promulgation of the *Buke shohatto* and *Kinchū narabini kuge shohatto*; 1617: Edo's Floating World District; 1624-1640's: Japan's Seclusion Policy; October, 1637-April 15, 1638: Shimabara Revolt; 1651-1652: Edo Rebellions; 1651-1680: Ietsuna Shogunate; 1657: Work Begins on Japan's National History; January 18-20, 1657: Meireki Fire Ravages Edo; 1680-1709: Reign of Tsunayoshi as Shogun; 1688-1704: Genroku Era.

TOKUGAWA TSUNAYOSHI
Japanese shogun (r. 1680-1709)

Tokugawa Tsunayoshi was the fifth Tokugawa shogun. His reign coincides roughly with the Genroku period of Japanese history, a period of flowering for literature, the arts, and urban culture. Despite this fact, however, Tsunayoshi is remembered mostly for his eccentric policies, including the laws protecting animals that earned him the nickname The Dog Shogun.

BORN: February 23, 1646; Edo (now Tokyo), Japan
DIED: February 19, 1709; Edo
ALSO KNOWN AS: The Dog Shogun (moniker)
AREAS OF ACHIEVEMENT: Government and politics, law, philosophy

EARLY LIFE

Tokugawa Tsunayoshi (toh-koo-gah-wah tsoo-nah-yoh-shee) was the fourth son of Tokugawa Iemitsu, the shogun who presided over what is considered by many scholars to have been the height of power of the Tokugawa shogunate. Iemitsu is famous for his ruthless persecution of Christians and for enacting a policy of national seclusion—two acts designed to enforce Tokugawa rule. Iemitsu was initially succeeded by his eldest son, Tokugawa Ietsuna, who governed between 1651 and 1680. Tsunayoshi was five years old when his brother came to power. He was well cared for as a member of the shogun's household, and upon coming of age, Tsunayoshi was given control of the fief of Tatebayashi, in central Japan. His experience as a daimyo gave him confidence, and when Ietsuna died without an heir in 1680, Tsunayoshi became shogun.

LIFE'S WORK

Unlike his father Iemitsu, Tokugawa Ietsuna was a weak and indecisive ruler who relied mostly on his councilors for decision making. After Ietsuna's death, Tsunayoshi also relied on councilors' advice, particularly that of the *tairo* (great elder) Hotta Masatoshi, in deciding matters of government. Unlike Ietsuna, however, Tsunayoshi did not allow himself to be dominated and instead showed considerable energy as an administrator during the first part of his time in power. His relationship with Hotta was more of a partnership, but it is clear that Tsunayoshi relied on the old man for advice.

When Hotta died in 1684, just four years into Tsunayoshi's reign, the shogun's policies and administrative initiatives began to become more erratic. Tsunayoshi devoted less and less time to the business of government and what major administrative decisions he did make in the years following 1684 were mostly reactionary. For example, in response to a financial crisis facing the shogunate as a result of overspending, Tsunayoshi ordered the debasement of gold and silver coinage as a solution to the central government's financial woes. This debasement caused massive inflation and general instability in prices, trade, and commerce. The period of Tsunayoshi's rule is generally considered by scholars to be a period of prosperity, but economic hardship existed as well, and the decisions of the central administration, often designed as a quick fix, did little to lead Japan toward economic prosperity. Tsunayoshi also increased land taxes, a move that increased hardship in the countryside and caused general discontent.

Tsunayoshi's relative apathy for matters of government can be contrasted with his strong interest in philosophy, education, and learning. Since the early Tokugawa period, the shoguns had demonstrated an interest in using the philosophical system of the Chinese Neo-Confucian thinker Zhu Xi (Chu Hsi; 1130-1200) as a guiding principal of government. The Neo-Confucian system of thought supported the hierarchical class system that the Tokugawa rulers put into place. Tsunayoshi, though, was sincerely interested in Neo-Confucian philosophy on a personal level, not just as a means of justifying the form of social organization promoted by Tokugawa law.

The first of Tsunayoshi's Neo-Confician-inspired moral precepts was promulgated in 1685, just one year after the death of his adviser, Hotta. Tsunayoshi issued the first of his Edicts on Compassion for Living Things. The main focus of these edicts was to prevent cruelty to animals, particularly dogs. Tsunayoshi was born in the year of the dog, and as a result, he felt that he had a karmic duty to care for the animals. His affinity for them led him to make killing a dog a capital offence. Not surprisingly, these edicts were widely unpopular because of the extreme penalties prescribed for offences that were considered trivial by the majority of the population. Coupled with the economic turmoil brought about by Tsunayoshi's policy of currency debasement and his increase in land taxes, his edicts protecting dogs made him a very unpopular ruler.

From the perspective of the common people, Tsunayoshi's moral precepts became even more ridiculous. Applying leashes to cats and dogs was prohibited. Hawking, a favorite pastime of the warrior class, was banned, and hawkers were forced into other occupations. Hunting was severely limited, which adversely affected the livelihoods of many. Eventually, Tsunayoshi devised a complex system of prohibitions of the eating of animals and fish and the use of certain animal parts; leather, too, was banned by his decree. In 1695, Tsunayoshi went even further, when he used the funds of the shogunate—which were already low because of irresponsible spending—to build tremendous kennels to house stray dogs at several sites in Edo. The largest of these buildings was eventually expanded to house more than 100,000 animals. The climate in Edo degenerated to the point where some peasants began to address dogs as *oinu-sama* or "honorable lord dog" out of fear of the authorities.

These moral regulations continued to be maintained until Tsunayoshi's death in 1709. He failed to produce a son and was succeeded by his nephew, Tokugawa Ienobu. Ienobu immediately repealed most of Tsunayoshi's widely unpopular legislation. Ienobu's reign was short: He came to power in 1709 and died in 1712, and he is most well known for incorporating the ideas of Confucian scholar Arai Hakuseki into government. As a result, Tsunayoshi's legacy of moral precepts is generally considered to have been completely undone shortly after his death.

SIGNIFICANCE

When assessing Tokugawa Tsunayoshi's significance, scholars have typically considered the negative aspects of his reign. His erratic moral legislation increased popular discontent but did not foment rebellion. He weakened central government in other ways, however. The currency debasement that he sponsored, despite the fact that it caused runaway inflation and chaotic prices through the Genroku era and beyond, did little to settle the Tokugawa government's financial problems. Overspending, particularly on luxury and ceremony, were to blame for the excesses of the shogunate, and these problems only became worse during Tsunayoshi's reign. The more extravagant side of his moral reforms, such as feeding more than 100,000 dogs with white rice and fish, a luxurious diet that the majority of the Japanese peasantry could never hope to enjoy, did nothing to help government finances.

While Tsunayoshi's fiscal irresponsibility did not bring the shogunate to ruin, undoing the economic damage he caused through both extravagance and neglect proved to be a challenge for his successors. Both Tokugawa Ienobu and Tokugawa Yoshimune would struggle with the finanacial legacy of Tsunayoshi. In short, the excessive spending and currency debasement carried out by Tsunayoshi's regime, coupled with the fact that toward the end of the seventeenth century there was a shortage of new cultivatable land in the more populous regions of Japan, led to significant economic stagnation in the eighteenth century. While Tsunayoshi's policies were not solely to blame for this stagnation, they did much to exasperate an already declining situation.

—*Matthew Penney*

FURTHER READING

Nishiyama, Matsunosuke. *Edo Culture: Daily Life and Diversions in Urban Japan, 1600-1868*. Honolulu: University of Hawaii Press, 1997. A history of urban culture with a strong focus on the Genroku period, which coincided roughly with Tsunayoshi's time in power.

Sansom, George. *A History of Japan, 1615-1867*. Stanford, Calif.: Stanford University Press, 1963. Sansom's three-volume history of premodern Japan is still the most authoritative coverage of the subject in English. Includes detailed coverage of Tsunayoshi's time in power.

Totman, Conrad. *Early Modern Japan*. Berkeley: University of California, 1993. The most comprehensive single-volume treatment of the Edo period of Japanese history in English. Includes a comprehensive discussion of Tsunayoshi's time in power and the lasting effects of his reign.

Tsukamoto, Manabu. *Tokugawa Tsunayoshi*. Tokyo: Yoshikawa Kobunkan, 1997. A biography of Tsunayoshi focusing on his philosophical interests and moral reforms.

SEE ALSO: Tokugawa Ieyasu; John Ray.

RELATED ARTICLE in *Great Events from History: The Seventeenth Century, 1601-1700:* 1693: Ray Argues for Animal Consciousness.

EVANGELISTA TORRICELLI
Italian mathematician and physicist

Torricelli extended Galileo's system of mechanics to fluids, invented the barometer, theorized the origin of winds on Earth, influenced the development of the science of hydrodynamics, and made improvements to the telescope. He also stands among the founders of modern integral and differential calculus.

BORN: October 15, 1608; Faenza, Romagna (now in Italy)

DIED: October 25, 1647; Florence, Tuscany (now in Italy)

AREAS OF ACHIEVEMENT: Physics, mathematics, science and technology

EARLY LIFE

Evangelista Torricelli (ay-vahn-jay-LIHS-tah tohr-ree-CHEHL-lee) was the eldest of three children born to Gaspare Torricelli, a textile artisan, and Caterina Angetti. Possessing only moderate income, Torricelli sent his talented young son to his uncle, who directed his education. After covering the humanities, the young Torricelli studied mathematics and philosophy with the Jesuits in Faenza from 1625 to 1626, displaying remarkable talent. Consequently, in 1626, Torricelli's uncle sent him to study with mathematician and hydraulic engineer Benedetto Castelli in Rome. Castelli recognized his student's outstanding scientific ability and soon appointed Torricelli his secretary.

While serving in this capacity in September, 1632, Torricelli replied for Castelli to a letter from Castelli's former teacher, the great Italian astronomer and physicist Galileo. Torricelli introduced himself to Galileo as a mathematician who had studied classical Greek geometry. In astronomy, Torricelli declared that he had studied both traditional Aristotelian astronomy and the new astronomy but was convinced of the superiority of the Copernican system. Noting that he had studied Galileo's book, *Dialogo sopra i due massimi sistemi del mondo, tolemaico e copernicano* (1632; *Dialogue Concerning the Two Chief World Systems, Ptolemaic and Copernican,* 1661), Torricelli proclaimed himself a member of the "Galilean sect."

Historians today are unsure of Torricelli's whereabouts, activities, or studies between late 1632 and 1640. It is likely, however, that during those years Torricelli was secretary to Galileo's friend Giovanni Ciampoli, governor of various cities in the Marches and Umbria.

LIFE'S WORK

During these years, Torricelli's interest in mathematics and physics grew, and many of the propositions published in *Opera geometrica* (1644; geometric works) were formulated around 1640 or 1641. For example, about 1640, Torricelli rectified a section of the logarithmic spiral and thus completed the first mathematical rectification of a curved line other than the circle. Before returning to Rome in 1641, Torricelli presented Castelli a treatise he had written extending Galileo's theory of the parabolic motion of projectiles. Castelli praised the paper, and in April of 1641 delivered it to Galileo. During his visit, Castelli recommended Torricelli to help Galileo with his scientific work.

On October 10, 1641, Torricelli joined Galileo and physicist Vincenzo Viviani in Galileo's home at Arcetri. There he was Galileo's assistant and secretary until Galileo's death in January, 1642. Torricelli then succeeded Galileo as mathematician and philosopher to Ferdinand II de' Medici, the grand duke of Tuscany. For the remaining five years of his life, Torricelli flourished at the ducal court. Charming, witty, and well liked, Torricelli wrote comedies, lectured (sometimes on scientific topics), and continued his scientific work.

In 1644, Torricelli published *Opera geometrica*. The first of its three sections, entitled *De sphaera et solidis sphaeralibus libri duo* (two books concerning the sphere and spherical solids), has two parts. The first, written around 1641, concerns figures produced by the rotation of a regular polygon inscribed in or circumscribed around a circle on one of its axes of symmetry. In the second part, Torricelli considered the motion of projectiles.

The second section of Torricelli's *Opera geometrica* contains his 1641 treatise *De motu gravium naturaliter descendentium et proiectorum libri duo* (two books concerning falling bodies and projectiles). In it, Torricelli continued Galileo's mathematical study of falling bodies and the motion of projectiles, broached topics in differential calculus, and extended Galileo's mechanics to fluid flow. Torricelli sought a dynamic explanation, which Galileo had not, and, although he employed medieval impetus theory, Torricelli obtained mathematical conclusions still accepted in the twentieth century.

It was also in this treatise that Torricelli first formally stated Torricelli's principle, that a rigid system of bodies can move spontaneously on Earth's surface only if its center of gravity descends. Examination of the tangents of the trajectories of projectiles led him to the fundamental problem of differential calculus, to determine the tangent of a given curve at a given point. His unpublished notes contain an implicit recognition of the inverse character of differentiation and integration, the fundamental theorem of the calculus. In another historic passage, Torricelli treated jets of liquids as falling bodies and projectiles and arrived at Torricelli's theorem. This theorem, formulated in 1643, states that the speed v of a liquid at the point of efflux from an orifice in a container is equal to that which a single drop of the liquid would have if it were falling freely in a vacuum the vertical distance h, from the top of the liquid to the orifice, that is, $v = \sqrt{2gh}$, where g is the acceleration caused by gravity. He furthermore demonstrated that liquid issuing from an orifice in the side of a vessel assumes a parabolic trajectory.

Line drawing of Evangelista Torricelli, from an 1877 edition of Harper's Monthly *magazine.* (Library of Congress)

The third section of Torricelli's *Opera geometrica* contains his *De dimensione parabolae, solidique hyperbolici problemata duo* (two problems concerning the dimension of the parabola and the hyperbolic solid). Among its most notable features is Torricelli's quadrature of the cycloid, the first publication of a mathematical determination of the area of this important new curve. The treatise also includes the first publication of a method to determine the tangent of any point of the cycloid.

In *Opera geometrica*, Torricelli employed and extended the newly developed "method of indivisibles" of Bonaventura Cavalieri. Viewing the area of plane figures and the volume of solid figures as the sum of infinitely small chords or planes, respectively, Cavalieri formulated the basic principle of integration. By 1641, Torricelli had developed a method of indivisibles utilizing curved chords and planes, and numerous theorems derived by it appear in *Opera geometrica*. The most notable one calculates the finite volume of a solid generated by the rotation of an infinite section of an equilateral hyperbola.

Opera geometrica spread Torricelli's fame as a geometer and physicist across Europe. It was the only work Torricelli published in his lifetime; the remainder of his scientific achievements were communicated through letters in which he penned noteworthy contributions to analytic geometry, the development of integral and differential calculus, and physics. For example, in 1646 he proposed his universal theorem for determining the center of gravity of any geometrical figure through the relation between two integrals. His correspondence also contains arguments on priority of discovery, particularly with Gilles Personne de Roberval. In 1646, Roberval accused Torricelli of plagiarizing his discoveries, made in 1634-1638, of the quadrature of the cycloid and the measurement of the solid generated by the rotation of the cycloid around its base.

In addition to his mathematical research, Torricelli contributed to the field of meteorology. Abandoning the accepted theory that wind is generated by the evaporation of exhalations from the earth, Torricelli posed the modern theory that winds occur because of differences in the temperature and density of atmospheric air. Observation of the temperature and density of atmospheric air thus interested Torricelli, and he developed new devices for this task. Some historians claim that Torricelli transformed an air thermoscope (an air-filled, uncalibrated glass bulb with its open end submerged in water) developed by Galileo into a thermoscope or thermometer containing water and later alcohol, but this seems dubious.

There is little doubt, however, that Torricelli invented the mercury barometer while attempting to determine why water rose to only approximately thirty-four feet in pumps and why siphons would not draw water over hills greater in height. To find an answer, in 1644, Torricelli devised an experiment involving a four-foot-long, mercury-filled glass tube, sealed at the top and inverted in a dish, which it appears Viviani first executed. Observing that the weight of the air was able to push mercury (fourteen times heavier than water) to a height of only twenty-nine inches in the tube (one-fourteenth the height it could push water), Torricelli concluded in a June 11 letter that the force maintaining the mercury was not an internal suctional "force of vacuum" in the tube but was the weight of the external air pressing on the mercury in the bowl. (The letters on atmospheric pressure—translated into English—are included in an appendix of a 1937 book on the treatises of Torricelli's contemporary Blaise Pascal.) Torricelli also remarked that he was striving to construct an instrument to show changes in atmospheric pressure—the first barometer. Torricelli's work was praised by Ferdinand II, and after October, 1644, news of Torricelli's barometric experiments traveled quickly across Europe.

In astronomy, Torricelli developed exceptional technical ability in manufacturing telescope lenses. By 1643, he was selecting high-quality glass, accurately grinding the lenses, and following Hieronymus Sirturi's suggestion to avoid pitch and fire in fastening the lenses to produce lenses equaling or surpassing those of the best contemporary Italian telescope maker. In 1644, the duke presented Torricelli a gold collar and medallion in recognition of his expertise.

In October, 1647, Torricelli contracted a brief and violent fever, probably typhoid. After dictating his memoirs, he died on October 25, at age thirty-nine. He was buried in Florence in the Church of San Lorenzo.

SIGNIFICANCE

Torricelli was one of the most prominent mathematicians of the seventeenth century. His quadrature of the cycloid, development of curved indivisibles, and work on solids of rotation moved mathematics toward modern integral calculus. Torricelli's *Opera geometrica* possesses added historical significance because it clearly presented Cavalieri's methods, thus paving the way for the diffusion of the geometry of indivisibles, from which integral calculus stemmed, throughout Europe. Torricelli's successful attempts to determine the tangents of curves and his work on maxima and minima assisted in the foundation of differential calculus. In his treatment of the parabolic motion of projectiles, Torricelli implicitly recognized the inverse character of differentiation and integration, which forms the fundamental theorem of the calculus. Consequently, when Isaac Barrow published that theorem in 1670, he recognized Torricelli's contribution to its development.

Torricelli's work in hydrodynamics was considered so fundamentally important that the twentieth century physicist Ernst Mach awarded Torricelli the title of "the founder of hydrodynamics."

The seventeenth century saw the development of radically new optical and physical instruments that greatly affected scientific research, among them the thermometer and Torricelli's barometer (called the "Torricelli tube" until Robert Boyle gave it the name barometer in 1667). Even today, the space above the liquid is known as the "Torricelli vacuum." Although the barometer was not widely used until long afterward, Torricelli's invention and his barometric experiments provoked a rash of experimental work and theoretical speculation. More important, these experiments discredited the ancient Aristotelian idea that "nature abhors a vacuum," forced scientists to reevaluate their worldview in the light of the existence of a vacuum, and assisted in the establishment of the mechanical philosophy in the scientific revolution.

—*Martha Ellen Webb*

FURTHER READING

Boyer, Carl B. *A History of Mathematics*. 2d ed., revised by Uta C. Merzbach. New York: John Wiley & Sons, 1991. In the best treatment of Torricelli in any English-language history of mathematics, Boyer presents a thorough and illuminating discussion of Torricelli's mathematical contributions, relates him to the seventeenth century mathematical community, and places his work within the general context of the development of mathematics. Includes a foreword by Isaac Asimov.

Burke, James. "A Few Notes." *Scientific American* 281, no. 1 (July, 1999). Describes Torricelli's experiments with a mercury tube, which led to his invention of a barometer.

Driver, R. D. "Torricelli's Law—An Ideal Example of an Elementary ODE." *American Mathematical Monthly* 105, no. 5 (May, 1998). Uses Torricelli's law for a leaking water container to illustrate ordinary differential equations.

Haven, Kendall. *Great Moments in Science: Experiments and Readers Theatre*. Englewood, Colo.:

Teacher Ideas Press, 1996. Includes the chapter "A Weighty Matter: Evangelista Torricelli's Discovery of Air Pressure in 1642."

Middleton, W. E. Knowles. *The History of the Barometer*. Baltimore, Md.: Johns Hopkins University Press, 1964. Chapter 2 of this excellently researched book discusses Torricelli's barometer and barometric experiments and includes translations of Torricelli's letters describing them.

_____. *A History of the Thermometer and Its Use in Meteorology*. Baltimore, Md.: Johns Hopkins University Press, 1966. This authoritative history of the thermometer does not support the view that Torricelli made major improvements in that instrument.

Nemenyi, Paul F. "The Main Concepts and Ideas of Fluid Dynamics in Their Historical Development." *Archive for History of Exact Sciences* 2 (1962): 52-86. One of the few works available on pre-Eulerian fluid dynamics, this article describes Torricelli's work in hydrodynamics and places it within the historical development of ideas in the field.

Simmons, George Finlay. *Calculus Gems: Brief Lives and Memorable Mathematics*. New York: McGraw-Hill, 1992. This collection of biographies includes a chapter on Torricelli and his calculus problems, his invention of the barometer, and his law of fluid dynamics.

Westfall, Richard S. *The Construction of Modern Science: Mechanisms and Mechanics*. 1971. Reprint.

New York: Cambridge University Press, 1977. Part of the Cambridge History of Science series, this work contains a concise discussion of Torricelli's barometric experiments and his theories of free fall and impact, placing them within the context of the scientific revolution.

Williams, James Thaxter. *The History of Weather*. Commack, N.Y.: Nova Science, 1999. An exploration of the history of weather and its impact and study from the beginnings of human history through the end of the twentieth century. Includes a discussion of the theory of meteorology, of which Torricelli played a large and significant part. Bibliography, index.

Woods, Robert O. "Harnessing the Void." *Mechanical Engineering* 125, no. 12 (December, 2003). Traces Torricelli's contribution toward the invention of a practical steam engine.

SEE ALSO: Giovanni Alfonso Borelli; René Descartes; Galileo; Pierre Gassendi; James Gregory; Otto von Guericke; Hans Lippershey; Marin Mersenne; Sir Isaac Newton; Denis Papin; Blaise Pascal.

RELATED ARTICLES in *Great Events from History: The Seventeenth Century, 1601-1700:* 1601-1672: Rise of Scientific Societies; 1612: Sanctorius Invents the Clinical Thermometer; 1643: Torricelli Measures Atmospheric Pressure; 1660-1692: Boyle's Law and the Birth of Modern Chemistry; 1686: Halley Develops the First Weather Map.

LENNART TORSTENSON
Swedish military leader

Torstenson has been called the "father of field artillery." He ably advanced the reforms in artillery introduced by King Gustavus II Adolphus and made standardized, mobile, rapid-firing field artillery the decisive factor in several Swedish victories of the Thirty Years' War, thereby introducing these reforms to the rest of Europe.

BORN: August 17, 1603; Forstena, Västergötland, Sweden
DIED: April 7, 1651, Stockholm, Sweden
AREAS OF ACHIEVEMENT: Military, invention, warfare and conquest

EARLY LIFE
Lennart Torstenson (LEHN-nahrt TOHR-stehn-sohn) began his service to the Swedish crown as a page in 1618.

From 1621 to 1623, he accompanied the king on the Livonian Campaign. During that service, he impressed the king sufficiently to be sent to study for two years in the Netherlands under Maurice of Nassau, prince of Orange. Maurice was one of the first to recognize fully the potential of artillery, and he was a pioneer in developing professional, regularly paid, and rigidly trained and disciplined armies. He developed a dependable supply system for the army, which provided well-stocked commissariats wherever the army moved. He introduced the concept of well-coordinated, combined use of infantry and cavalry, to which he now added artillery. He also began to standardize artillery calibers. Maurice, however, still envisioned a rather static role for artillery in siege work as well as on the battlefield. Students from all over

Europe, especially from the Protestant countries, were introduced by him to these military reforms, and nowhere were these reforms more effectively adopted and advanced than in Sweden.

Following this training, the young Torstenson served in the campaign against Prussia during the early part of the Thirty Years' War, a war that raged from 1618 to 1648. Gustavus II Adolphus, himself a pioneer in the modernization and standardization of field artillery, put Torstenson, age twenty-seven, in command of the first field artillery regiment organized in Europe. By that time, Gustavus had carried out impressive modifications of the formerly unwieldy and unreliable artillery. He had reduced the former sixteen types of guns to three—the 3-, 12-, and 24-pounders. The latter was now the heaviest gun, replacing the former 48-pounder. Only the 3-pounders (in British sources frequently referred to as 4-pounders) and 12-pounders, however, were classed as field artillery. The comparatively light 3-pounder (weighing five hundred pounds) could be moved and operated in the field by one or two horses and two or three men, thus making it possible to employ artillery in fluid battlefield situations.

For the first time, artillery was an effective antipersonnel weapon, usually firing canister or grapeshot, having almost the effect of an automatic weapon. These new guns could also provide more rapid fire than older guns, since the shot was attached by straps to the bag holding the powder charge, enabling rapid loading. Newer technology also made possible the construction of lighter and shorter gun barrels. The development of a more standard and safer gunpowder helped to maintain and even improve consistency in range and accuracy, despite the lighter weight and the shorter barrels. Science and technology were rapidly becoming integral elements of modern warfare. Another aspect of these reforms was the substantial increase in the number of artillery pieces in the Swedish army, made possible in part by Sweden's ample supply of copper, until the ratio between guns and men was an unprecedented 9.4 guns for every one thousand men. Gustavus attached two of the light and mobile 3-pounder field guns to every infantry and cavalry regiment. Torstenson inherited these reforms and continued to build on them.

LIFE'S WORK

Torstenson's first major achievement came during the Swedish phase of the Thirty Years' War, in the Battle of

Lennart Torstenson. (Library of Congress)

Breitenfeld near Leipzig (September, 1631), when his gunners were able to deliver a rate of fire three times that of their German imperial opponents. (The 3-pounders could also fire eight rounds for every six fired by the musketeers.) He was also able to exploit his artillery's greater mobility and move the guns up with the advancing infantry during the decisive counterattack, thus cinching a clear Swedish victory, the Protestants' first major success. While the Swedes lost 4,000 of the 40,000 men engaged, the imperial forces lost a total of 21,600 of the 32,000 men involved. Swedish artillery, which outnumbered imperial artillery fifty-four to twenty-six, played a major role in achieving this uneven casualty ratio.

This battle also marked the victory of Sweden's new linear formations (originally introduced by Maurice of Nassau) over the old massive formations (the "Spanish square"), which, in one form or another, had dominated European military tactics for centuries. The Swedish linear formation was usually five men deep, thus putting every man in direct contact with the enemy during the melee. Mobility had won over mass. The best commentary on these new tactics is the fact that the imperial forces now attempted to imitate these methods, though they were initially not very successful. As a result of the Breitenfeld victory, Sweden was recognized as a major European military power, and northern Germany remained Protestant. Torstenson's reward was a promotion to general in 1632. If Breitenfeld pointed to the end of the old "Spanish square," the Battle of Rocroi in northeastern France in 1643 (won by the dynamic French commander the Great Condé over the Spanish) sealed its fate.

In April, 1632, Torstenson's artillery again provided the decisive difference in the Battle of Lech, in which his artillery covered the Swedish army's crossing of that river and enabled the Swedish forces to penetrate into Bavarian territory. Torstenson, however, was captured by imperial forces in the Battle of the Alte Feste later that year. Significantly, this battle, which turned into a Swedish defeat, was primarily lost because the terrain was so rough that the Swedes were unable to maneuver their field guns during the engagement. As a result of his capture, Torstenson was not present at the fateful Battle of Lützen (November 16, 1632), a victory that was diminished by the death of Gustavus. Torstenson was exchanged a year later.

After serving as chief of staff to Johan Banér in 1635 in eastern and central Germany, and after Banér's death, he was put in command of the Swedish army in Germany, having been promoted to field marshal. Torstenson was still in Sweden at the time of his appointment and arrived in Germany to assume command in time to prevent a mutiny against the temporary commander, General Karl Gustav Wrangel. The troops had not been paid for some time and threatened to quit, leaving Sweden without an army in Germany. Torstenson proved his worth in this command position as well, turning an undisciplined rabble (to which most armies had deteriorated during the latter stage of the Thirty Years' War) again into an effective field force, soon winning a series of victories. Torstenson regained control over the mutinous rabble by legalizing and formalizing the practice of looting occupied territory by which soldiers compensated themselves for their service. At the same time, Torstenson enforced a rigid and brutal discipline against all who went against his orders—against his own soldiers and the civilian population alike. Hangings of disobedient soldiers and uncooperative civilians were the order of the day. His men hated him, but he brought them victories and hence plunder. The unspeakable brutality of the soldiers during this final phase of the Thirty Years' War, and especially of the Swedish troops, still haunts German folklore.

In 1642, Torstenson advanced the Swedish forces to within twenty-five miles of Vienna and later that year won another decisive victory in the Second Battle of Breitenfeld, which effectively eliminated the imperial army as a viable military force in Germany. In the 1645 campaign, Torstenson again drove deep into Habsburg territory and, in the Battle of Jankow (March 15, 1645), about forty miles south of Prague, won yet another brilliant Swedish victory. This victory was an outstanding and decisive example of Torstenson's artillery's mobility, which was shifted from sector to sector as needed, making Jankow the hitherto most dramatic example of artillery's flexibility. Following this battle, the Swedes conquered all Moravia and again threatened Vienna.

Early in 1646, following repeated pleas by Torstenson, he was permitted to retire from military service because of ill health. Wrangel succeeded him. A year later, Torstenson was made count of Ortala. Torstenson had suffered from gout for some time, being restricted to a bed or a litter during much of the last campaign, his hands so gnarled that he was at times unable even to sign orders. His last service was that of general-governor of Sweden's western border province of Westgotland.

SIGNIFICANCE

Though the "military revolution" was already under way when Torstenson appeared on the scene, he can properly be called the father of field artillery. Building on the work of Maurice of Nassau and Gustavus, Torstenson converted the reforms of those two men to full reality on the battlefield.

Under the military reforms, the musketeers (firing ordered volleys, introduced by Gustavus, rather than scattered individual fire) had the task of opening a path for the pikemen, who were still the force to clinch the victory in the melee, or hand-to-hand combat. The light, mobile regimental artillery, able to move with the advancing infantry, assisted the musketeers in providing a breach in the enemy formation in a more massive and decisive fashion through its rapid, coordinated, and concentrated fire. That is also true of cavalry charges, which increased their shock effect through the use of their own regimental guns.

Though these reforms gradually spread to other countries, most armies during the Thirty Years' War still employed artillery in a static role, even on the battlefield. In fact, during the period of pre-French revolutionary "neoclassical" warfare, European armies experienced regressive developments in artillery employment as well as in other reforms introduced during the early seventeenth century. In the French army, artillery officers did not hold military rank until 1732, and drivers in many armies continued to be civilians. The use of contract artillery with privately owned horses substantially reduced the potential of mobility on the battlefield, since the contractors removed their valuable horses from harm's way during the battle, restricting the ability to move the guns to the limits of human muscle power. King Frederick the Great introduced the use of army horses in the Prussian army during the middle of the century.

The Battles of Breitenfeld and Jankow demonstrate Torstenson's innovations most dramatically and completed the conversion of field artillery from a purely static function on the battlefield to its modern role as part of the combined arms of infantry, cavalry, and artillery. At least some of the credit that is frequently attributed to Gustavus has to be shared with Torstenson.

—Frederick Dumin

FURTHER READING

Bonney, Richard. *The Thirty Years' War, 1618-1648.* Oxford, England: Osprey, 2002. A modern account of the war, containing information on Torstenson's role in the conflict. Provides a concise summary, including discussion of the warring parties, battles, and portraits of soldiers and civilians.

Brzenski, Richard. *The Army of Gustavus Adolphus: Cavalry.* Men-at-Arms 262. Oxford, England: Osprey, 1993. This book is a history of Gustavus's calvary, and includes information on its organization, arms, armor, tactics, and uniforms, as well as color illustrations.

_____. *The Army of Gustavus Adolphus: Infantry.* Men-at-Arms 235. Oxford, England: Osprey, 1991. The first of two books about Gustavus's army, this book focuses on the history of the infantry. Includes information on the infantry's organization, arms, armor, and uniforms, as well as color illustrations.

Montgomery of Alamein, Viscount. *A History of Warfare.* Cleveland, Ohio: World, 1968. A general history of warfare that places the Thirty Years' War and Sweden's role in a broader perspective.

Ogg, David. *Europe in the Seventeenth Century.* 6th ed. London: Adam and Charles Black, 1952. A general history that is still of great value. Has an extensive section on the Thirty Years' War and Sweden's role in the conflict.

Roberts, Michael. *Essays in Swedish History.* Minneapolis: University of Minnesota Press, 1967. The essay "Gustav Adolf and the Art of War" is excellent on the overall and extensive military reforms of the early seventeenth century, with an emphasis on Gustavus's contributions. Includes six pages of footnotes that provide excellent bibliographical information.

Scott, Franklin D. *Sweden: The Nation's History.* Minneapolis: University of Minnesota Press, 1977. A general history of Sweden, with Chapter 7, "Sweden's Age of Greatness," devoted to the period from 1611 to 1654.

Wedgwood, C. V. *The Thirty Years' War.* New Haven, Conn.: Yale University Press, 1939. A standard work of the war with excellent overall discussions of Sweden's role. Includes maps, illustrations, an index, and an extensive bibliography.

SEE ALSO: The Great Condé; Gustavus II Adolphus; Maurice of Nassau.

RELATED ARTICLES in *Great Events from History: The Seventeenth Century, 1601-1700:* 1618-1648: Thirty Years' War; November 8, 1620: Battle of White Mountain; 1630-1648: Destruction of Bavaria; July, 1643-October 24, 1648: Peace of Westphalia; July 10, 1655-June 21, 1661: First Northern War.

CYRIL TOURNEUR
English playwright

As the author of one or two powerful revenge tragedies who emphasized the perversity of his characters and the corruption of the society in which they lived, Tourneur was influential in establishing conventions of subject matter and tone in later Jacobean drama.

BORN: c. 1575; place unknown
DIED: February 28, 1626; Kinsale, Ireland
AREAS OF ACHIEVEMENT: Literature, theater

EARLY LIFE

Very little is known about the life of Cyril Tourneur (SUHR-ul TUHR-nur). Since his poem *The Transformed Metamorphosis* (1600) was obviously the work of an immature writer, it seems reasonable to assume that at the time it was published, Tourneur was no more than fifteen or twenty. That would place his birth date about 1575 or perhaps 1580. Nothing is known about his parentage. However, Tourneur would later be closely associated with the influential Cecil family, and in his definitive study of Tourneur, Samuel Schuman points out that also serving the Cecils was a Captain Richard Turner, whose father, Edward, was a resident of Canons, Essex. Edward Turner had a number of children, several of whom were given unusual Christian names that, like "Cyril," were of Greek derivation. Since in Elizabethan times "Tourneur," "Turner," and "Turnor" were all variants of the same name, Cyril might have been one of Edward's children, born in Essex.

Tourneur must have been reasonably well educated, for he is mentioned in a letter as having been the secretary of Sir Francis Vere, the diplomat and military leader who commanded the English forces in the Netherlands during England's war with Spain (1587-1604). Tourneur would probably have begun his military service as a foot soldier. His vivid description of the Siege of Ostend (1601-1604) in his play *The Atheist's Tragedy: Or, The Honest Man's Revenge* (pr. c. 1607, pb. 1611) has been taken to mean that he was present at that particular action. Tourneur later expressed high regard for his commanding officer in *A Funerall Poem: Upon the Death of Sir Francis Vere* (1609).

LIFE'S WORK

At some point between 1600 and 1604, Tourneur evidently left military service for London and a literary career. His first works were obviously experimental. *The Transformed Metamorphosis* was an allegorical and satirical poem in which a world dominated by evil is finally redeemed. Unfortunately, the work is so confusing that critics cannot agree either as to its references or its meaning. There followed a prose pamphlet, *Laugh and Lie Down: Or, The World's Folly* (1605), which has been ascribed to Tourneur, for it was signed by "C. T." and, moreover, though it is much simpler than the earlier work, the two have notable similarities. Like *The Transformed Metamorphosis*, *Laugh and Lie Down* is a satirical allegory, and it deals with corrupt characters in a chaotic world. The pamphlet is significant in that it is the first work in which Tourneur ventures into dialogue. Upon its completion, he was evidently ready to try his hand at drama.

There is now significant doubt as to whether or not Tourneur was in fact the author of the play once generally agreed to be his masterpiece. *The Revenger's Tragedy* (pr. 1606-1607, pb. 1607) was probably first performed at the Globe Theatre. In 1607, it appeared in print as an anonymous work. In 1656, the dramatist Edward Archer attributed the play to Tourneur. Late in the nineteenth century, however, some scholars began to voice their doubts, and many now argue that the author was a better-known playwright, Thomas Middleton. Others, however, note how closely *The Revenger's Tragedy* resembles *The Atheist's Tragedy*, which was published as Tourneur's work in 1611.

The Revenger's Tragedy is set in an Italian dukedom, ruled by a corrupt and lustful duke, whose wife, bastard son, and three stepchildren are all as lecherous and murderous as he. Vindice, the protagonist, is bent on revenge, because his beloved Gloriana was poisoned by the duke when she resisted his advances. The action of the play includes deception, seduction, procuring, attempted rape, incest, and murder. At the end, Vindice has obtained his revenge but feels compelled to boast of it, with the result that he is sentenced to death. Interpretations of *The Revenger's Tragedy* vary. Certainly it presents a dark vision of the world and of the human beings who inhabit it, but it may also be seen as a play with a moral, that anyone who takes revenge risks losing his soul in the process.

The latter interpretation links *The Revenger's Tragedy* to *The Atheist's Tragedy*. Although the title page of the latter play indicates that it had often been acted, there is no known evidence of specific performances. From internal evidence, however, scholars have been able to deduce that it postdates *The Revenger's Tragedy*.

Like its predecessor, *The Atheist's Tragedy* explores the issue of revenge. The title character in this play, however, is not the revenger. Because he is an atheist, D'Amville has no moral values whatsoever but is motivated solely by avarice and pride. In order to acquire the estate of his older brother, Baron Montferrers, he has the baron's son and heir, Charlemont, sent off to war, has Montferrers murdered, and seizes the baron's property. Again, the evil characters in the play are both treacherous and lecherous; they do not shrink from incest, rape, or homosexual necrophilia. However, unlike Vindice, Charlemont renounces revenge. At the end of the play, Charlemont has a providential deliverance from death, and D'Amville is punished, presumably by the God he has denied. Just when D'Amville is about to execute Charlemont, the axe in his hands turns upon its owner, knocking out his brains. Thus, *The Atheist's Tragedy* may be read as completing the message of *The Revenger's Tragedy* that revenge is best left to God.

Another play by Tourneur, *The Nobleman* (pr. 1612), was performed at court, but it has not survived. Tourneur was also asked by the playwright Robert Daborne to write an act of *The Arraignment of London* (pr. 1613), which has also been lost. Tourneur may well have been financially desperate enough at that point to do hack work.

Tourneur's final literary works were a prose character written in 1612 as a tribute to the late Robert Cecil, earl of Salisbury, and "A Griefe on the Death of Prince Henrie" (1613), an elegy on the death of the prince of Wales. Only a little more is known about Tourneur's life. In 1613, he was serving as a diplomatic courier. In 1617, he was arrested on unknown charges but was released to Sir Edward Cecil. In October, 1625, while serving as Cecil's secretary, Tourneur participated in an unsuccessful expedition against Cádiz, Spain. On December 11, wounded or gravely ill, Tourneur was put ashore at Kinsale, Ireland, where he died on February 28, 1626. The fact that he was married is known only because in 1632 his widow, Mary Tourneur, who claimed to be destitute, petitioned the council of war for her husband's back pay.

SIGNIFICANCE

Since Cyril Tourneur spent only about a fourth of his life pursuing a literary career, it is perhaps surprising that he is ranked as one of the most important dramatists of the Jacobean period. Ironically, that assessment rests primarily on a play that he may not have written. However, though no student of Jacobean drama can ignore the con-

troversy over the authorship of *The Revenger's Tragedy*, it is so closely linked to Tourneur's *The Atheist's Tragedy* that the two dramas should be considered together.

Both *The Revenger's Tragedy* and *The Atheist's Tragedy* are rooted in earlier dramatic traditions. Ultimately, they both derive from the medieval morality play, and the revenge tragedy genre dates back to Thomas Kyd's prototype play, *The Spanish Tragedy* (pr. c. 1585-1589, pb. 1594?). Critics have suggested that some of Tourneur's characters resemble the superhuman figures in the plays of Christopher Marlowe, and that others, notably his obsessed, tormented souls, are like the heroes of tragedies by William Shakespeare. However, Tourneur is primarily remembered as an innovator, as the playwright who recreated the revenge tragedy, transforming it into both a psychological study of the revenger and a warning against vengeance. Tourneur's place in literary history is also ensured by the fact that his plays so influenced the other dramatists of the period that his dark vision of the world came to define Jacobean tragedy.

—*Rosemary M. Canfield Reisman*

FURTHER READING

Auchincloss, Louis. "Cyril Tourneur." In *The Man Behind the Book: Literary Profiles*. Boston: Houghton Mifflin, 1996. The author speculates as to what Tourneur may have been like and why he became so disenchanted with life.

Champion, Larry S. "Tourneur." In *Tragic Patterns in Jacobean and Caroline Drama*. Knoxville: University of Tennessee Press, 1977. Discusses each of the plays at length.

Eliot, T. S. "Cyril Tourneur." In *Essays on Elizabethan Drama*. New York: Harcourt, Brace, 1956. Sees the playwright's defining quality as his preoccupation with death. On the basis of style and content, Eliot is certain that Tourneur was the author of *The Revenger's Tragedy*.

Murray, Peter B. *A Study of Cyril Tourneur*. Philadelphia: University of Pennsylvania Press, 1965. Tourneur's plays reflect Christian, and specifically Anglican, theology, emphasizing the doctrine that grace is essential for salvation.

Neill, Michael. *Issues of Death: Mortality and Identity in English Renaissance Tragedy*. Oxford, England: Clarendon Press, 1997. Argues that Tourneur's works reflect his times, when Christian certainties were being eroded, causing death to be redefined. Illustrated. Extensive bibliography and index.

Schuman, Samuel. *Cyril Tourneur*. Boston: Twayne,

1977. The standard critical work. Contains sections on Tourneur's life and times, his plays, and his minor works. Includes chronology, notes, annotated bibliography, and index.

White, Martin. *Middleton and Tourneur*. New York: St. Martin's Press, 1992. Includes analysis of both plays attributed to Tourneur. The writers also presents his reasons for believing that *The Revenger's Tragedy* was written by Middleton.

SEE ALSO: Thomas Middleton.

RELATED ARTICLE in *Great Events from History: The Seventeenth Century, 1601-1700:* July 5, 1601-April, 1604: Siege of Oostende.

MAARTEN AND CORNELIS TROMP
Dutch admirals

While the Tromps and other Dutch naval heroes such as Michiel Adriaanszoon de Ruyter were in command, the Netherlands came close to being the chief naval power in Europe. The competition between the elder Tromp and the English commanders resulted in a revolution in naval tactics.

MAARTEN TROMP

BORN: April 23, 1598; Brielle, South Holland, United Provinces (now in the Netherlands)

DIED: August 10, 1653; at sea, near Scheveningen, Holland, United Provinces (now in the Netherlands)

ALSO KNOWN AS: Maarten Harpertszoon Tromp (full name)

CORNELIS TROMP

BORN: September 9, 1629; Rotterdam, Holland (now in the Netherlands)

DIED: May 29, 1691; Amsterdam, Holland (now in the Netherlands)

ALSO KNOWN AS: Cornelis Maartenszoon Tromp (full name)

AREAS OF ACHIEVEMENT: Military, warfare and conquest

EARLY LIVES

Though both Maarten Tromp (MAHR-tehn TROHMP) and Cornelis Tromp (kohr-NAY-lis TROHMP), father and son, had distinguished careers and rose to the position of lieutenant-admiral, their lives show some interesting contrasts. The early life of Maarten Tromp contained enough experience to last an ordinary mortal a lifetime. He first went to sea in a warship commanded by his father and took part in the Battle of Gibraltar (April 25, 1607), when Jacob van Heemskerck crushed a superior Spanish fleet under the guns of their own fortress. Several years later, he accompanied his father on a merchant voyage. The ship was attacked by an English pirate, Maarten's father was slain, and Maarten himself was compelled to endure a life of "the utmost abandonment and cruelty" as cabin boy to his father's slayer. Released or escaped, he made other voyages and was captured by the Barbary pirates; he was released either on the payment of a heavy ransom or by impressing the Bey of Tunis with his skill in gunnery and navigation.

In 1627, he entered the Dutch navy. For some years, he was occupied either in reforming the Dutch marine establishment or in fighting the privateers of Dunkerque, then under Spanish rule and a menace to Dutch commerce. Maarten was, then, a "tarpaulin" officer, one who had lived his life at sea and made his way up through the ranks, in contrast to the English commanders, who were likely to be either gentlemen volunteers or converted army officers. Throughout life, he lived plainly, contenting himself with a pickled herring for breakfast.

Cornelis Tromp, Maarten's second son, was far less austere in his habits; in later life, he married into a family with money and was able to afford a country estate, De Trompenburgh. His portrait shows a handsome man, but one inclined to stoutness, while his father's portrait shows the elder Tromp as lean and sharp featured. Cornelis went to sea early, however, and at the age of nineteen commanded a squadron against the Barbary pirates.

LIVES' WORK

Maarten's first and possibly greatest deed as lieutenant-admiral of the Dutch fleet was to counter a Spanish invasion. In September of 1639, he fought a series of engagements near the Straits of Dover in which the Spanish fleet was all but destroyed. The victory caused immense rejoicing in the Netherlands; the battle had been fought, however, on seas over which England claimed jurisdiction and against the express order of Charles I, king of England.

There were other potential sources of friction with England: the herring fisheries; the navigation acts, limiting the right of Dutch ships to trade in English ports; England's claim to have her ships saluted in the "Narrow Seas"; and, after the outbreak of civil war in England, apparent Dutch sympathy with the Royalists (Maarten himself had escorted Queen Henrietta Maria of England when she returned from the Continent with supplies for Charles). Still, there was no open breach until 1652. On May 29, English Admiral Robert Blake was in the Channel with an English fleet and Maarten was there with a Dutch one; somehow—the guilt was never established—the accumulated irritations erupted into a full-scale naval battle, at the end of which Maarten retired with the loss of two small ships. Though there was as yet no formal declaration of war, it was obvious that the English would strike at Dutch commerce, and Maarten had the job of protecting it (July and August). In the North Sea, he encountered terrible storms, which scattered his fleet; he was unable to save the herring fishermen but did see some Indiamen safely to port with their valuable cargoes. Though most of his scattered fleet eventually made port, Maarten was disgraced and forced to resign. Another officer, Witte de With, was appointed to the vacant command but was so unpopular with the fleet that he too was dismissed.

Maarten was now reinstated, and again his task was to protect commerce and specifically to see a convoy of three hundred outbound merchant ships through the Channel (December). This he performed with ease. Blake, with a much smaller fleet than that of Maarten, attacked but was beaten off with the loss of five ships. Legend has it that Maarten sailed up the Channel with a broom at his masthead as proof that he could sweep the seas.

The next action (February, 1653) was again a convoying operation, this time inbound. Maarten was bringing some 150 merchantmen up the Channel when Blake attacked with a force nearly equal to that of Maarten. The fight lasted three days, with heavy losses on both sides. In the end, Maarten brought most of the convoy and his warships to port. He did not do so well in the Battle of the Gabbard Shoal in June. The reorganized English fleet had much the advantage, and Maarten, with his lighter ships, had to take refuge among the sandbanks of his own coast.

The English now set up a blockade, with devastating effects on the Dutch economy. Maarten was ordered to break the blockade. By a masterful maneuver, he brought the scattered Dutch fleet together, and, on August 10, he confronted the English fleet, now commanded by General George Monck, who would later engineer the Restoration of Charles II of England and become the first duke of Albemarle. The battle began at seven in the morning, and by eleven Maarten was dead, struck down by a musket ball. After his death, many of the Dutch captains deserted, and the battle ended in disaster. The Dutch had to make their peace with Oliver Cromwell. Maarten was buried at Delft, where a lavish monument recalls his services.

Meanwhile, Cornelis Tromp was serving in the Mediterranean, rising to the rank of rear admiral (1653). It was in the Second Anglo-Dutch War that he came into prominence, though in a rather controversial way. On June 13, 1665, an English fleet commanded by the duke of York (later James II) encountered a Dutch fleet led by Jacob van Wassenaer, lord of Obdam. Obdam was killed early in the action; Cornelis attempted to assume command, but another admiral had a better claim, and in the confusion the Dutch fleet was routed. In 1666, Cornelis had to serve under Michiel Adriaanszoon de Ruyter, a brilliant leader of whom he was intensely jealous. In the action of July 25, when the Dutch were again at a disadvantage, Cornelis disgraced himself by breaking the line of battle to fight an independent action against the English rear and lost his command.

In the complications of Dutch politics, Cornelis was wise enough, or lucky enough, to support the stadtholder William, prince of Orange (later King William III of England), who reinstated him in the navy. He took part in the Third Anglo-Dutch War, in which the Netherlands was forced to fight France as well as England and to neglect its fleet in favor of the army. Nevertheless, de Ruyter, with a depleted fleet and forced on the defensive, more than held his own. In August, 1673, there was a general action in which Cornelis again found himself fighting a detached action against the English rear. Apparently there was no disobedience of de Ruyter's orders, for he remained in favor; the battle, moreover, had a part in the decision of Charles II to make peace (1674). The naval war was nearly over, though the land war continued until 1678. Cornelis was sent with a squadron to help the Danes against the Swedes and won a great victory (1676). In the same year, Cornelis attained his father's rank of lieutenant-admiral. He died on May 29, 1691, and was buried at Delft.

SIGNIFICANCE

During Maarten Tromp's and Cornelis Tromp's lifetimes and those of other Dutch heroes such as de Ruyter, the Netherlands came close to being the chief naval power in Europe. The Dutch completely defeated Spain and Portugal; they built warships for France; and they fought the English as equals and were sometimes the victors. Their naval operations extended from Denmark to Sicily. This was a brief glory, for later in the century they were forced to divert their resources to defend themselves on land against the French and had to accept an unequal alliance with England.

Some historians would see the Anglo-Dutch Wars as chiefly important for producing a revolution in naval tactics and discipline. Prior to these wars, fleets had gone into battle in no particular order and had fought in a confused mass; the commander could exercise little control once the fighting started. Individual captains could do almost as they pleased, even to the point of deserting the fight. The new tactics, which remained standard for more than one hundred years, required the ships to go into action in a line so that all the guns could be brought to bear; a system of signals was devised, so that the commander could exercise some control.

This system was first put into effect by Blake, Monck, and Richard Deane, all of whom were former officers in Cromwell's army; Blake was also responsible for the fearsome Articles of War, which defined the duties of seamen and, even more important, those of their officers. Maarten's relationship to these reforms is uncertain. He is said to have been responsible for the idea of dividing a large fleet into squadrons, and he is supposed to have invented the line earlier but to have been unable to put it into practice; he did respond to the English line by putting his ships into a parallel formation. The Dutch indiscipline continued, however, and Maarten's own son was not innocent in this respect.

—John C. Sherwood

FURTHER READING

Boxer, C. R. *The Dutch Seaborne Empire, 1600-1800.* New York: Alfred A. Knopf, 1965. This book is chiefly useful for what it relates about the political atmosphere in the Tromps' time and the social condition of seafaring folk. Contains a chronology and a bibliography.

Geyl, Pieter. *History of the Low Countries: Episodes and Problems.* London: Macmillan, 1964. A series of lectures rather than a connected narrative. Useful for what it relates of the tangled diplomatic relations with England and the Tromps' part in them.

Hainsworth, Roger, and Christine Churches. *The Anglo-Dutch Naval Wars, 1652-1674.* Stroud, England: Sutton, 1998. The Tromps' role in the battles is included in this history of the wars. The authors maintain the wars were significant milestones in the development of naval warfare, introducing new technologies and strategies.

Haley, K. H. *The Dutch in the Seventeenth Century.* New York: Harcourt Brace Jovanovich, 1972. Chiefly useful for an account of the social and cultural life of the period in which the Tromps lived. Among the numerous illustrations are an eyewitness sketch of one of Maarten's victories and a photograph of his monument.

Howarth, David. *The Men-of-War.* Alexandria, Va.: Time-Life Books, 1978. A popular, well-illustrated, and carefully researched account of the first two Anglo-Dutch Wars. Very thorough on technical matters as well as on the characters and careers of the chief commanders, including Maarten.

Jones, J. R. *The Anglo-Dutch Wars of the Seventeenth Century.* London: Longman, 1996. Contains a great deal of information and insight about the wars, but provides little explanation of the historical context of the battles. Intended for a reader who has some knowledge of seventeenth century history.

Landström, Björn. *The Ship: An Illustrated History.* Garden City, N.Y.: Doubleday, 1961. A well-illustrated work, useful for its comments on Dutch and English ship types of the period.

Mahan, Alfred Thayer. *The Influence of Sea Power upon History, 1660-1783.* New York: Sagamore Press, 1957. Mahan analyzes the Second and Third Anglo-Dutch Wars to develop his thesis about the influence of sea power. Contains some material on Cornelis.

Mets, J. A. *Naval Heroes of Holland.* New York: Abbey Press, 1902. This laudatory work contains much that one suspects is fiction, but it nevertheless is useful as a counterbalance to other sources available in English, which generally take an English point of view.

SEE ALSO: Charles II (of England); Frederick Henry; Piet Hein; Maurice of Nassau; Michiel Adriaanszoon de Ruyter; Abel Janszoon Tasman.

RELATED ARTICLES in *Great Events from History: The Seventeenth Century, 1601-1700:* 17th century: Age of Mercantilism in Southeast Asia; Beginning Spring, 1605: Dutch Dominate Southeast Asian Trade; 1609: Bank of Amsterdam Invents Checks; 1617-1693: European Powers Vie for Control of Gorée; January 14, 1641: Capture of Malacca; October, 1651-May, 1652: Navigation Act Leads to Anglo-Dutch Wars; March 4, 1665-July 31, 1667: Second Anglo-Dutch War.

VISCOUNT DE TURENNE
French military leader

The Viscount de Turenne, a French Protestant noble who converted to Catholicism, was considered one of the greatest military minds of the seventeenth century. He played a crucial role in the Thirty Years' War, the Wars of the Fronde, the War of Devolution, and the Franco-Dutch Wars, and the Rhineland Campaign.

BORN: September 11, 1611; Sedan, France
DIED: July 27, 1675; Sasbach, Baden (now in Germany)
ALSO KNOWN AS: Henri de La Tour d'Auvergne (given name)
AREAS OF ACHIEVEMENT: Warfare and conquest, military

EARLY LIFE

The Viscount de Turenne (tyuh-rehn), who was given the name Henri de La Tour d'Auvergne at birth, was born into the Huguenot (French Protestant) elite. His father was the duke de Bouillon and his mother was Elizabeth of Nassau, a princess of the House of Orange and the daughter of Prince William the Silent of the Netherlands (reigned as stadtholder, 1572-1584).

Steeped in the French Protestant-Dutch Calvinist military tradition, he entered into an army career almost on the basis of birthright. Through the efforts of his mother, he was apprenticed in the service of his uncle, Prince Maurice of Nassau, who had succeeded his father William the Silent as stadtholder of the United Provinces of the Netherlands (1585-1625). Turenne was kept on by another uncle, Stadtholder Frederick Henry. By the age of nineteen, Turenne had become an officer, with command responsibilities. For the next five years, he drifted between the French and the Dutch services.

When France entered the Thirty Years' War (1618-1648) in 1635, Turenne had attained the rank of general and served in eastern and northern France before being sent into the Rhineland. He particularly distinguished himself by coordinating and leading the assault on Breisach on December 17, 1638, taking the city by storm and firmly establishing a reputation as a first-rate commander.

LIFE'S WORK

During the remainder of the Thirty Years' War, Turenne was dispatched from one battlefront to another: taking the city of Turin, Italy, in 1640; assisting in the Siege of Perpignan in southern France in 1642; and being sud-

denly transferred to Germany in 1643 to forestall an imminent invasion of France by the Bavarian army. Turenne's German campaign of 1643-1648 was a masterpiece of maneuver and audacity, and it ended in the decisive victory in 1648 at Sommershausen over Austrian and Bavarian troops. Shortly thereafter, hostilities were suspended and the Thirty Years' War came to an end. It was during this campaign that Turenne began his long, sometimes adversarial relationship with another notable military leader, Louis de Bourbon, duke of Enghien, and later Louis II, prince de Condé (later known as the Great Condé). On this occasion, though, Turenne and Condé worked very well in tandem.

The most controversial years of Turenne's career occurred during the Wars of the Fronde (1648-1653), when dissident nobles sided with bourgeois and artisan elements in Paris against the royal government of the youthful monarch, Louis XIV, the Queen Mother Anne of Austria, and the first minister, Cardinal Jules Mazarin. During the initial phase, Turenne was on the side of the rebels, aligning himself closely with the duchesse de Longueville, Condé's sister (with whom he was very likely carrying on an affair). Defeated at the Battle of Champ Blanc in Champagne on October 15, 1650, Turenne nevertheless benefited from a pardon and ceasefire in 1651. That year, he married Charlotte de Caumont and was free from the duchesse de Longueville's influence.

Renewed fighting began in 1652, with Turenne on the royalist side. He defeated Condé at the Battle of Bléneau and then again at the Faubourg St.-Antoine on July 5, 1652. The Fronde would thereafter peter out.

Condé, however, escaped to join the service of Spain, with which France had been engaged in warfare since 1635. In August, 1654, Turenne lifted the Siege of Arras and went on to best Condé at the Battle of the Dunes (June 14, 1658). This battle was Turenne's most innovative victory: He had used the ebb and flow of the oceanic tides to surprise and outflank his adversaries. His forces pushed as far as Ypres before the Spanish sued for peace, and the long Franco-Spanish Wars of 1635-1659 ended with the Treaty of the Pyrenees.

The early 1660's was a time of relative peace for France. For Turenne, it was a time of change and bereavement; his wife, Charlotte died in 1666. Two years later, probably for career advancement reasons, he abjured the Huguenot faith and became a Catholic. The outbreak of the War of Devolution in 1667 marked a new beginning for Turenne: He had been appointed general marshal of France, holding the highest French army command next to that of the king himself. He was assigned to the invasion of the Spanish Netherlands. The invasion was marked by a generally smooth campaign for Turenne, climaxed by the investment and capture of the fortress at Lille on September 26, 1667.

In 1672, when King Louis XIV launched a massive surprise attack deep into the Dutch Netherlands, marking the start of the French-Dutch Wars (1672-1678), Turenne, despite his parental link with the House of Orange, led the most crucial wave. However, when the Dutch opened the dikes in desperation and the French advance bogged down as a result of the flooding, it was deemed necessary to dispatch Turenne to Germany to counter a threatened invasion by the German States, which was aimed at eastern France.

The Rhineland Campaign of 1674-1675 is considered to be Turenne's most consummate tour de force. Invariably outnumbered, he threw superior enemy forces off balance, played the game of maneuver and bluff virtually to perfection, and generally bided his time to set up and act on the opportunity to divide and then individually

pounce on the isolated units of his foes. Denied reinforcements, Turenne played a deadly game of bluff, deception, march, and counter-march with his brilliant adversary, imperialist Marshal Raimundo Montecuccoli; but Turenne was steadily forced across the Rhine and deep into eastern France. Having seemingly lost Alsace, and with the door perhaps open for imperial troops to march on Paris, Turenne won back the province in spectacular fashion. He executed his march across the Vosges, using the mountain range to shield his forces and deceive the imperials as to his true intentions and whereabouts. In the dead of winter, he parceled out his units, split them as they went through the mountains, and reassembled them at Belfort. He then rapidly pressed northward and overwhelmed the German army at Mulhouse.

His greatest triumph came at Turkheim on January 5, 1675. A well-planned and energetic surprise flank attack sent imperial forces back across the Rhine, thereupon Turenne secured the city of Strasbourg, put eastern France out of danger, and was in position to resume the offensive into German territory. During the summer of 1675, Turenne's army was pushing eastward against that of Marshal Montecuccoli. At Sasbach on July 27, there was a clash, and while reconnoitering, Turenne was felled by an artillery shell, dying immediately.

SIGNIFICANCE

As the most accomplished and celebrated French commander of the seventeenth century, Turenne often paid the price for his ability by being assigned to the most difficult tasks and being allocated provisions and manpower that were often barely adequate to sustain his efforts. His generalship is credited as being the crucial factor on three occasions: The final phases of the Thirty Years' War, the defeat of the Frondists, and the turning away of the imperialist invasion of France during the winter of 1674-1675. He was interred at the abbey church at Saint-Denis, the burial place of many French monarchs, until Napoleon moved his body to the Church of the Invalides in Paris.

—Raymond Pierre Hylton

FURTHER READING

Cronin, Vincent. *Louis XIV*. London: Harvill Press, 1996. Turenne is credited with serving as King Louis XIV's primary mentor in the intricacies of warfare.

Goubert, Pierre. *Louis XIV and Twenty Million Frenchmen*. Translated by Anne Carter. New York: Vintage Books, 1972. The author celebrates Turenne as Louis XIV's greatest soldier and implies that his demise

Viscount de Turenne. (Library of Congress)

played a role in the first downturn in French military and diplomatic fortunes, which he believes occurred during the late 1670's.

Jones, Archer. *The Art of War in the Western World*. New York: Oxford University Press, 1987. This work includes a detailed analysis of the 1673-1674 war in Germany between Turenne and Montecuccoli.

Lynn, John A. *Giant of the Grand Siècle: The French Army, 1610-1715*. New York: Cambridge University Press, 1997. A comprehensive overview of army administration and tactics, including the direction of military officials.

_____. *The Wars of Louis XIV*. New York: Longman, 1999. An excellent analysis of the Louis's record in military matters, largely confirming Turenne's high place among the great commanders of the age.

Ranum, Orest. *The Fronde: A French Revolution, 1648-1652*. New York: W. W. Norton, 1993. The author puts into perspective Turenne's enigmatic role in the Fronde and attempts to explain his turnaround in terms of family interests.

SEE ALSO: Anne of Austria; Duchesse de Chevreuse; The Great Condé; Frederick Henry; John of Austria; François de La Rochefoucauld; Duchesse de Longueville; Louis XIV; Marquis de Louvois; Maurice of Nassau; Jules Mazarin; Philip IV; Friedrich Hermann Schomberg; Sébastien Le Prestre de Vauban.

RELATED ARTICLES in *Great Events from History: The Seventeenth Century, 1601-1700:* 1617-1693: European Powers Vie for Control of Gorée; 1618-1648: Thirty Years' War; November 8, 1620: Battle of White Mountain; May 24, 1667-May 2, 1668: War of Devolution; April 6, 1672-August 10, 1678: French-Dutch War; August 10, 1678-September 26, 1679: Treaties of Nijmegen.

URBAN VIII
Italian pope (1623-1644)

Urban guided the Catholic Church through most of the Thirty Years' War by aligning it with France, continued the advance of the Catholic Reformation, saw his old friend Galileo be punished, combated Jansenism, and patronized the great sculptor and architect Gian Lorenzo Bernini, the architect Francesco Borromini, and the painter Pietro da Cortona.

BORN: April 5, 1568 (baptized); Florence (now in Italy)
DIED: July 29, 1644; Rome, Papal States (now in Italy)
ALSO KNOWN AS: Maffeo Vincenzo Barberini (given name)
AREAS OF ACHIEVEMENT: Religion and theology, government and politics, patronage of the arts

EARLY LIFE

The Barberinis were a prosperous Florentine cloth merchant family whose coat of arms sported three golden horseflies. Maffeo, the future Pope Urban (uhr-bahn) VIII, was the fifth son of Antonio and was groomed for a life in the Church. He was educated by Jesuits in Florence and then attended the Collegio Romano with the support of his uncle, Francesco Barberini, a well-placed papal bureaucrat. Maffeo obtained his doctorate in civil and canon law from the University of Pisa and then returned to Rome to work in the Papal Curia in a position purchased for him by Francesco for 8,000 crowns. He rose in the Curia and, in 1592, was named governor of the papal territory of Fånö.

Maffeo was affable and well-liked, noted for his horsemanship but also his temper. Pope Clement VIII sent him to Paris to congratulate King Henry IV on the birth of his heir. In 1604, Maffeo was ordained to the priesthood and became the papal nuncio to Paris. At Henry's urging, Pope Paul V named Maffeo cardinal in 1606.

Two years later, Maffeo returned to Italy where he served as bishop of Spoleto, and from 1611 to 1614, he served as papal legate to the city of Bologna. When residing in Rome he occupied the large house (*casa grande*) of his uncle, who had died in 1600 and left it to Maffeo. He expanded and redecorated it and soon it became Palazzo Barberini, and the family's coat of arms, the golden horseflies, was changed to golden bees, the most recognizable symbol of the Barberini pope. The palace served as an art gallery, library of rare books, and academy for an elite circle of writers and artists with whom he discussed his interests in poetry and astrology.

In the summer of 1623, the College of Cardinals met in conclave to elect the successor to Gregory XV, using a secret ballot for the first time. On August 6, with many suffering from malaria, Maffeo was elected the compromise candidate and assumed the name Urban VIII.

LIFE'S WORK

Upon assuming the papal throne, Urban began a campaign of nepotism that was notorious even in an age notorious for nepotism. He linked familial control of key positions at the curia and in Rome with a keen desire to oversee personally every aspect of papal governance. In the face of militant Protestantism, Urban sought to posit a unified and powerful Catholic Church that acted under one will and spoke with a single voice. It was in this context that the Inquisition silenced Galileo in 1633, despite Urban's earlier support of his ideas.

The court condemned Galileo's *Dialogo sopra i due massimi sistemi del mondo, tolemaico e copernicano* (1632; *Dialogue Concerning the Two Chief World Systems, Ptolemaic and Copernican*, 1661) as a violation of the 1616 ban on the teaching of Copernican ideas. The aging scientist denounced his ideas under threat of torture and was placed under house arrest at his residence in Tuscany until his death in 1642. The Catholic Church, in the late twentieth century, formally acknowledged its mistake when it admitted that Galileo's tribunal overstepped its bounds when it pronounced on a scientific and not strictly theological matter. Also, the Church recognized that Urban's opposition to the ideas of the French bishop of Ypres, Cornelius Otto Jansen, was based on the same foundation as his opposition—as pope—to Galileo: Both men had challenged Church authority.

Jansen died in 1638, but in 1642, Urban condemned his major theological work, *Augustinus* (1640), which was gaining a powerful following in France. The work expounded an Augustinian/Calvinistic doctrine of grace that challenged the traditional Catholic teaching on the role of human free will, a position whose teaching had been banned in 1611 and 1625. French Jansenists organized themselves despite both political and papal opposition and defended Jansen's teaching. Their defiance of papal opposition would continue late into the century.

Urban had always been pro-French, a position that would become less and less tenable as the great conflict of the Thirty Years' War (1618-1648) dragged on. Fearful of Habsburg power in Spain and the Holy Roman Empire, Urban hampered Habsburg political interests in northern Italy and supported the French. When Cardinal de Richelieu allied France with the Swedish and German Protestant forces in 1635, however, the pope was incredulous. He certainly could not promote Protestant interests, even if France threatened to split from Rome along the lines of the English Reformation. Having long snubbed the imperial cause, Urban could not suddenly become a trusted ally of the Habsburgs. He accelerated his program of fortifying papal territorial possessions in Italy, including his own Roman fortress, the Castel Sant'Angelo, and managed to keep not only the Papal States but also most of Italy free from the ravaging that Germany was undergoing in the 1630's and 1640's. With France supporting the enemies of the Catholic Church, Urban became a weak arbitrator, though his efforts to broker a peace did lead to peace talks at Münster, Germany, in the year of his death (1644). In the end, peace was made in the face of papal opposition in 1648, and political Protestantism was vindicated.

Urban's desire to magnify the prestige of the Papacy and his own family resulted in a program of outstanding architectural and artistic contributions to Rome's heritage. Barberini support for the architects Gian Lorenzo Bernini, whom Urban made architect of St. Peter's Basilica, and Francesco Borromini, who was entrusted with enlarging the University of Rome (the Sapienza), and the painter Pietro da Cortona began the High Baroque transformation of the city and its artistic patrimony. In honor of early Catholic victories in the Thirty Years' War, Urban pushed completion of the interior of St. Peter's, which he formally consecrated in 1626. He had Bernini build the great baldachin over the main altar, a bronze canopy atop four twisted columns. Bernini also decorated the huge piers that held up the church's dome and contained important relics from the life of Jesus, and he executed Urban's enormous tomb sculpture in St. Peter's. The Palazzo Barberini on the Quirinal Hill in Rome underwent expansion at the hands of Bernini and Borromini, being transformed into a villa complete with a theater for lavish productions. On the ceiling of the Palazzo's Great Hall, Pietro painted one of the century's masterpieces.

SIGNIFICANCE

When Urban died, the people of Rome rejoiced. They viewed him as a shameless nepotist ruled by his ambitious family and as a tyrant with an insatiable hunger for their tax money. History has softened this judgment,

tempering and contextualizing the criticisms while admitting their validity. While Urban was profligate in granting his brothers and nephews high Church offices, they held sway over the pope in his waning years only. High taxes in the papal territories were necessary in part for military defense during perilous times. Large expenditures on churches and his palace added magnificence to the city that remains to this day. Both nepotism and architectural magnificence were aspects of political absolutism in the seventeenth century, and Urban, despite his affability, ruled the Church and its states as an absolutist monarch. By supporting the independent French position early in the Thirty Years' War, Urban undermined the Catholic cause of the Habsburgs and their allies, and contributed to the ultimate collapse of militant Catholicism.

—*Joseph P. Byrne*

FURTHER READING

Hammond, Frederick. *Music and Spectacle in Baroque Rome: Barberini Patronage Under Urban VIII*. New Haven, Conn.: Yale University Press, 1994. A cultural study of the role of music and theatrics in Urban's Rome and under his patronage.

Kerwin, William C., and Philipp P. Fehl. *Powers Matchless: The Pontificate of Urban VIII, the Baldachin, and Gian Lorenzo Bernini*. New York: P. Lang, 1997. The first study of the baldachin over the high altar in St. Peters, Urban's patronage, and Bernini's early development.

Magnuson, Torgil. *Rome in the Age of Bernini*. Vol. 1. New Jersey: Humanities Press, 1982. Chapter 3 of volume 1 contains an extended essay on Urban's pontificate, "The Barberini Era," which goes well beyond artistic considerations.

Nussdorfer, Laurie. *Civic Politics in the Rome of Urban VIII*. Princeton, N.J.: Princeton University Press, 1992. Study of the relations between Urban and his *famiglia* and the civic government of Rome as the Papacy became ever more absolutist in theory and action.

Pastor, Ludwig. *History of the Popes from the Close of the Middle Ages*. Vols. 28, 29, 30. Translated by Ernest Graff. St. Louis, Mo.: Herder, 1923-1969. The fullest discussion in English of Urban by the foremost historian of the post-medieval Papacy.

Prodi, Paolo. *The Papal Prince, One Body and Two Souls: The Papal Monarchy in Early Modern Europe*. Translated by Susan Haskins. New York: Cambridge University Press, 1988. A scholarly study of the pontificate of Urban in the larger context of seventeenth century popes.

Scott, John Beldon. *Images of Nepotism: The Painted Ceiling of Palazzo Barberini.* Princeton, N.J.: Princeton University Press, 1991. A study of the palace and the familial iconography of the ceiling painting that was commissioned by Urban.

SEE ALSO: Gian Lorenzo Bernini; Francesco Borromini; Galileo; Cornelius Otto Jansen; Paul V; Cardinal de Richelieu.

RELATED ARTICLES in *Great Events from History: The Seventeenth Century, 1601-1700:* 17th century: Europe Endorses Slavery; 1610: Galileo Confirms the Heliocentric Model of the Solar System; 1610-1643: Reign of Louis XIII; November 10, 1630: The Day of Dupes; 1632: Galileo Publishes *Dialogue Concerning the Two Chief World Systems, Ptolemaic and Copernican*; 1638-1669: Spread of Jansenism; 1656-1667: Construction of the Piazza San Pietro; July 13, 1664: Trappist Order Is Founded.

JAMES USSHER
Irish archbishop

As archbishop of Armagh, Ireland, shortly after the English Reformation, Ussher opposed Roman Catholicism and encouraged an authentic Irish Protestant movement. Writing a master history of the world, he promulgated the notion that the Creation occurred in 4004 B.C.E.

BORN: January 4, 1581; Dublin, Ireland
DIED: March 21, 1656; Reigate, Surrey, England
AREA OF ACHIEVEMENT: Religion and theology

EARLY LIFE

James Ussher (UHSH-uhr) was born into an Anglo-Irish family that had participated in government for four centuries. His grandfather James Stanihurst had been speaker of the Irish Parliament, and his uncle Henry Ussher had been archbishop of Armagh from 1595 to 1613. In order to promote the education of Irish Protestants, Queen Elizabeth I authorized the establishment of Trinity College, the University of Dublin, in 1592. With a reputation for having a bright mind and a gift for language, James was invited to enroll in one of the first classes at Trinity at the age of twelve. By the age of twenty, he had earned a masters degree.

Ussher was ordained as a clergyman of the Anglican Church and soon gained a reputation as a defender of Protestantism in opposition to those continuing in the Catholic Church in Ireland. By 1605, he was chancellor at Saint Patrick's Cathedral in Dublin. His scholarly work led him, in 1607, to a position as professor of theology at Trinity College. By 1620, he was appointed bishop of Meath and, in 1625, archbishop of Armagh.

LIFE'S WORK

As the one hundredth archbishop of Armagh, an archbishopric first established by Saint Patrick himself, Ussher focused his scholarship on the history of Irish Christianity. This scholarly focus took a polemical tone, since he concluded that Protestantism was consistent with the historical Irish church: It was Roman Catholicism that had strayed. Soon after taking up the office of archbishop, Ussher summoned other bishops to join him in the 1626 document, *Judgment of the Archbishops and Bishops of Ireland*, which referred to Catholics as "superstitious and idolatrous" and their faith as "heretical." He argued that it was a "grievous sin" to tolerate them and to allow them to worship freely.

At the same time, Ireland's version of Protestantism was complex. Ussher was a clergyman of the Church of England, but the early decades of his career saw a large influx of settlers in Ireland from Scotland, where the Presbyterian Church flourished. For most of his life Ussher found himself in a moderating position between disparate religious beliefs and traditions. This position was itself complicated as the leadership in England also went through changes, including the influence of William Laud, who as archbishop of Canterbury promoted high church ritualism and theology at odds with the beliefs of Presbyterian Calvinists.

When it came to church organization, Ussher leaned toward episcopalianism, defending the role of archbishops, bishops, and deacons. On other issues, Ussher was willing to compromise. Already in 1615, he was called upon to draft a document, known as the Irish Articles. Episcopalians had suggested that the Thirty-nine Articles adopted by the Anglican Church in 1562 were sufficient to define church doctrine. Others, such as the Calvinist cleric John Whitgift (c. 1530-1604), argued for a distinctive Irish statement. However, his 1604 Lambeth articles were rejected by King James I. Ussher's solution to this impasse was to draft a document that was distinctively Irish, but that still emphasized unity with the Church of England. Among the 104 Irish articles, most of the 39 Anglican articles were included verbatim. Likewise, many of the Lambeth articles were also included. Both sides were satisfied with the compromise, because it helped to distinguish Irish Protestants from the majority Roman Catholic Church, thereby strengthening the Anglican Church's position in Ireland.

For the most part, Ussher turned to scholarship to underscore the historic foundation of the Irish church. He translated into Irish Bede the Venerable's *Ecclesiastical History of the English People* (731; English translation, 1723). His research led to the discovery of the *Book of Kells* (ninth century), the historic illuminated manuscript of the Gospels. He later published *A Discourse of the Religion Anciently Professed by the Irish and the British* (1631). On one point, Ussher was surprisingly inconsistent. In the Irish Articles, he had written about the importance of translating the Bible into the Irish language. His contemporary at Trinity College, William Bedell, supervised the Irish translation of the Bible and proposed an Irish language liturgy. Ussher, however, opposed such a liturgy, pointing to an act of Parliament that forbade preaching in Irish.

Ussher was a scholar at heart, spending many summers at London or Oxford doing research. He valued the study of Scripture in the original languages, collecting ancient manuscripts, including a valuable copy of the Samaritan Pentateuch. He made use of critical reasoning and was the first scholar to determine the seven authentic letters of the early Bishop Ignatius.

In 1641, when the Great Rebellion broke out in Ulster and Dublin, Ussher chose to remain in London, dedicating the rest of his life to scholarship. He disappointed the Irish Puritans when he defended the monarchy. It was during the Commonwealth that Ussher published his best known work, *The Annals of the Old and New Testament* (1650, 1654). His intention in this book was to integrate biblical and secular history.

Ussher is best known for his detailed chronology of

James Ussher. (Hulton Archive/Getty Images)

Old Testament history, which places Creation at 12:00 noon on October 23, 4004 B.C.E. His starting point in determining this date was his placement of the death of the Babylonian king Nebuchadnezzar in 562 B.C.E., Ussher considered the latter date to be reliably verifiable through nonbiblical documents, which made it an objective starting point. He then worked backward from Nebuchadnezzar's death, using a literal reading of the various genealogies within the Bible to come up with precise dates for biblical events.

As a critical scholar, Ussher realized that his conclusions must be considered tentative because of the nature of the oldest genealogical lists. He noted discrepancies in length the period from Creation to the Flood: The Septuagint computation was 2,242 years, the Ethiopic text indicated a duration of 2,262 years, and the Samaritan Pentateuch only placed it at 1,307 years. Ussher decided to rely upon the Hebrew text computation of 1,656 years, and using this number as his basis, he adopted the 4004 B.C.E. date, realizing its provisional character.

Ussher's specific date of October 23 may seem odd, but it is based on the Jewish New Year occurring in the fall. The Gregorian calendar, made official at the Roman Catholic Council of Trent, would not be adopted in England until 1752. Ussher still employed the Julian calendar and noted his assumption that Creation would have occurred on the first Sunday following the autumnal equinox.

Ussher's conclusion was not in fact particularly original. In 1644, Bishop James Lightfoot of Cambridge had published his own chronology with similar conclusions. Ussher was also very much aware that Bede the Venerable had suggested 3952 B.C.E. as the date of creation, and the French scholar Joseph Scalinger (1540-1609) had come up with 3950 B.C.E. This view of the general age of the world, with variations of only a few hundred years, simply was the popular view in the prescientific era.

What differed about Ussher's chronology, however, is that it was circulated, not just among scholars, but also among the general public. A new, authorized version of the Bible in English, commonly known as the King James Bible, had been published in 1611 under the rule of King James I. Archbishop Ussher's reputation was such that subsequent editions of the King James Bible included his chronology in the marginal notes. Thus, the date 4004 B.C.E. is found in the margin for the Creation in Genesis 1; 2348 B.C.E. is the date provided for the Flood; 1921 B.C.E. is the date of the call of Abraham, 1491 B.C.E. that of the Exodus from Egypt, 1012 B.C.E. that of the foundation of the Jerusalem Temple, and 586 B.C.E. that of the Babylonian destruction of Jerusalem.

In 1656, Ussher died in Reigate, England. Oliver Cromwell ordered a magnificent funeral and burial in London's Westminster Abbey.

SIGNIFICANCE

A recent opinion poll of the American public found that 40 percent of responders accept a recent date for the creation of the earth, with 19 percent giving the date 4004 B.C.E. Ussher's name is remembered for his contribution to this interpretation of the Bible. For some, Ussher is a bulwark against evolutionary theory and billion-year estimates of the age of the universe.

Another large segment of the public, however, rejects Ussher's estimated age of the earth as incompatible with modern science. For the most part, the assumption of this latter group is that Ussher was naive and narrow-minded. His methodology led him to base his chronology entirely on biblical data. A comparison with Egyptian archaeological data, for example, shows that his dating of the exodus was off by 240 years. If current scientific methods are taken seriously, Ussher's dating of the age of the earth is off by an order of magnitude.

Yet other people stress that Ussher was a contemporary of Galileo and Johannes Kepler. The Scientific Revolution was just dawning. It is impossible to know how Ussher would have responded to later geological findings and the contributions of Darwin. Some argue that Ussher's passion for learning developed the climate for continued research and enlightenment concerning the cosmos, helping to make possible the very advances that seem to prove him wrong.

— *Fred Strickert*

FURTHER READING

Gould, Stephen Jay. *Eight Little Piggies: More Reflections in Natural History*. New York: W. W. Norton, 1994. Harvard geopaleontologist examines a number of issues regarding time, including an analysis of Ussher's chronology.

Gribbon, Crawford. *The Irish Puritans: James Ussher and the Reformation of the Church*. Darlington, England: Evangelical Press, 2003. A study of James Ussher as church leader during Puritan era.

Knox, Robert B. *James Ussher, Archbishop of Armagh, 1581-1656*. Leiden, the Netherlands: E. J. Brill, 1968. A dissertation discussing contributions to church and scholarship.

Pierce, Larry, and Marion Pierce, eds. *Annals of the World: James Ussher's Classic Survey of World History*. Green Forest, Ark.: Master Books, 2003. This is a recent republication of James Ussher's classic work written in Latin in 1658, a history of the world from creation to 70 C.E. when the Jerusalem Temple was destroyed.

Steel, Duncan. *Marking Time: The Epic Quest to Invent the Perfect Calendar*. New York: John Wiley and Sons, 2000. A thorough discussion of various issues concerning calendar calculations.

SEE ALSO: Oliver Cromwell; James I; William Laud.

RELATED ARTICLES in *Great Events from History: The Seventeenth Century, 1601-1700:* 1611: Publication of the King James Bible; October 23, 1641-1642: Ulster Insurrection; 1642-1651: English Civil Wars; December 6, 1648-May 19, 1649: Establishment of the English Commonwealth.

SIR HENRY VANE THE YOUNGER
English politician, statesman, and colonial American governor

An English Puritan, Vane served as governor of Massachusetts, and after his return to England, he served as an administrator for the navy and a member of Parliament, where he was a staunch opponent of King Charles I during the English Civil Wars. He was instrumental in drafting important legislation and negotiating the Solemn League and Covenant with Scotland.

BORN: May 26, 1613 (baptized); Debden, Essex, England
DIED: June 14, 1662; London, England
AREA OF ACHIEVEMENT: Government and politics

EARLY LIFE
Sir Henry Vane the Younger was born and baptized in May, 1613. His father, Sir Henry Vane the Elder, was secretary of state under Charles I. The younger Vane was educated at Westminster School, which was noted for producing a number of prominent Puritans. Later, Vane studied at Oxford University, after having undergone a profound religious experience at about age fifteen in 1628, an experience that left him with decidedly Puritan views and a strong interest in religious issues. He left Oxford and spent some time on the European continent at Geneva and Vienna from 1631 to 1632.

During the decade of the 1630's, many Puritans migrated to Massachusetts; Vane was one of them and arrived in Massachusetts in October, 1635. At age twenty-three, Vane had become a strong opponent of state interference in religion, and his support for Anne Hutchinson in her struggle with Massachusetts's authorities cost him reelection as governor of Massachusetts in March, 1637. He returned to England, where he wrote "A Brief Answer to a Certain Declaration" (1637), defending his support for Hutchinson and decrying persecution in the name of religion.

In 1639, the First Bishops' War broke out when the Scots rebelled as a result of an attempt by Charles I to impose changes in liturgy in the Church of Scotland. It was in this volatile situation that Vane the Younger became joint treasurer of the navy, a position purchased for him by his father. Because of the Scottish problems, Charles I called Parliament into session in 1640, after an eleven-year hiatus. Vane returned as a member of the House of Commons from Hull. He was knighted in June, 1640, and married Frances Wray on July 1, 1640. It was as a member of Parliament that Vane became a prominent political figure.

LIFE'S WORK
In the House of Commons, Vane was appointed to important committees and supported John Pym, Oliver St. John, Oliver Cromwell, John Hampden, and other strong opponents of Charles I. In the spring of 1641, Vane played a vital role in the condemnation of Thomas Wentworth, first earl of Strafford, by an act of attainder: Vane produced his father's notes of a Privy Council meeting during which Strafford had supported using Irish troops in England. Vane supported the Root and Branch Bill, which called for the abolition of the episcopacy in the Church of England. These actions moved Charles I in 1641 to strip Vane of his position as joint treasurer of the navy, but Parliament reappointed him in August, 1642.

With the outbreak of the First Civil War (1642-1646), Vane became one of the leaders of Parliamentary actions against the Royalists because of his wealth, connections, intelligence, and assiduousness. In August, 1643, he played a major role in negotiating the Solemn League and Covenant, which provided for Scottish military assistance to Parliament in the war against the king and also for changes in the Anglican Church. Vane's insertion of the phrase "according to the Word of God" in the covenant was a way of preventing imposition of a Scottish style Presbyterian system in England. His forward, radical thinking in support of religious toleration and his fear of government interference in private religious matters had not been completely compromised.

Vane, one of the leaders of the Independents, maneuvered adroitly within the shifting factions in Parliament and was influential in preparing the 1644 Self-Denying Ordinance, which called upon members of Parliament to give up any military or civil positions that they held. He was also instrumental in helping his old friend Roger Williams obtain a charter for Rhode Island (or Providence Plantation), and Vane attempted to convince John Winthrop, governor of Massachusetts, to be more tolerant of religious dissenters in the colony. With the surrender of Charles I in 1646, Parliamentary leaders attempted to work out a post-Civil War solution to the problems of the relationship between king and Parliament. Vane supported the Treaty of Newport (1648), which proposed a negotiated settlement with the king on the basis of a modified system of Episcopal governance in the Church of

England, but he felt that the king's concessions were not adequate.

As he was wont to do when his view was in the minority, Vane did not attend Parliament during Pride's Purge (December, 1648) or during the Trial and Execution (January, 1649) of Charles I. He resumed attendance and duties at the navy only in February, 1649, and was a leading figure in many important undertakings during the Commonwealth (1649-1660). Vane was a member of the Council of State, he helped negotiate the union of England and Scotland in March, 1652, after Cromwell's conquest of Scotland, he worked to strengthen the English fleet, and, although he opposed the First Anglo-Dutch War (1651-1652) because he believed the Dutch and English should cooperate with each other, his administrative skills helped ensure English victory.

Vane also influenced England's foreign policies and worked closely with England's Latin secretary, the poet John Milton, who honored Vane with a sonnet in 1652 praising his "sage counsel." Although Vane had had a slight falling out with Cromwell over the First Anglo-Dutch War, Vane was at the peak of his influence and power by April, 1653, when Cromwell, angered by the attempt by members of Parliament to remain members in the new Parliament then being organized, forcibly dissolved the Rump Parliament and created a permanent breach between himself and Vane. After this episode, Vane retired from politics and wrote his most significant work, "A Healing Question" (1656), which maintained that Cromwell had abandoned the principles they had fought for. Vane in "A Healing Question" renewed his call for liberty of conscience and proposed that a written constitution be prepared for England. Vane was imprisoned from September-December, 1656, for espousing such views.

After Cromwell's death in September, 1658, and the coming to power of Cromwell's son Richard as lord protector, Vane reemerged as an active participant in Parliament representing, Whitchurch in Hampshire. He was appointed to the Council of State and other important committees. When General John Lambert overthrew Parliament in October, 1659, Vane refused to serve Lambert's government but continued his naval duties. When General George Monck restored the Long Parliament, Vane was expelled and ordered to return home. After the Restoration of Charles II, Vane was excluded from the special Act of Indemnity of June, 1660 , and imprisoned in the Tower of London. He was later transferred to the Scilly Islands. Vane was charged with treason, tried, and found guilty in London in June, 1662. At his execution

on June 14, 1662, his attempt to address the assembled crowd was drowned out by the beat of drums and blasts of trumpets. Although not a regicide, he had been too dangerous for the king of allow him to live.

SIGNIFICANCE

Vane combined the rare qualities of active politician, statesman, and political theorist. His guiding principles, to which he held steadfastly save for a couple of strategic compromises, were for liberty of conscience, or religious toleration, which would allow the individual believer the greatest possible freedom from state interference, as well as for a government based on the consent of its citizenry. More than a century later, these principles were in large measure incorporated into fabric of the fledgling government of the United States. Although his governorship of Massachusetts was short and troubled, it was under his tenure that Harvard College (later Harvard University) was established. Vane developed friendships with Roger Williams and Anne Hutchinson, key figures in American colonial history and the New World struggle for religious toleration.

In England, Vane was an influential figure throughout the English Civil Wars and Interregnum period. He was regarded by his contemporaries as an extremely able and hard-working public servant; his supporters valued those traits, and his opponents feared him. He was at times unscrupulous and Machiavellian, which led some to regard his efforts as based on personal aggrandizement rather than principle. Modern scholars perhaps have not paid the attention to Vane that is merited.

—*Mark C. Herman*

FURTHER READING

Adamson, J. H., and H. F. Folland. *Sir Harry Vane: His Life and Times, 1613-1662.* Boston: Gambit, 1973. A major biography that adequately covers his political and administrative career while also analyzing his political and religious views.

Hirst, Derek. *England in Conflict, 1603-1660: Kingdom, Community, Commonwealth.* New York: Oxford University Press, 1999. A survey that is especially strong on explaining and analyzing the maneuvering among the parliamentary supporters in the 1640's.

Judson, Margaret A. *The Political Thought of Sir Henry Vane the Younger.* Philadelphia: University of Pennsylvania Press, 1969. This short monograph analyzes Vane's thought and places it within the context of the great political thinkers of the seventeenth century.

Rowe, Violet A. *Sir Henry Vane the Younger: A Study in*

Political and Administrative History. London: The Athlone Press, University of London, 1970. An analytical study of Vane's political career from 1640 until his execution in 1662.

Woolrych, Austin. *Britain in Revolution, 1625-1660.* New York: Oxford University Press, 2002. An analytical survey that covers the period when Vane was an influential political figure.

SEE ALSO: Charles I; Charles II (of England); Oliver Cromwell; Anne Hutchinson; John Lambert; John Milton; George Monck; John Pym; First Earl of Strafford; Roger Williams; John Winthrop.

RELATED ARTICLES in *Great Events from History: The Seventeenth Century, 1601-1700:* May, 1630-1643: Great Puritan Migration; June, 1636: Rhode Island Is Founded; March-June, 1639: First Bishops' War; November 3, 1640-May 15, 1641: Beginning of England's Long Parliament; 1642-1651: English Civil Wars; August 17-September 25, 1643: Solemn League and Covenant; December 6, 1648-May 19, 1649: Establishment of the English Commonwealth; October, 1651-May, 1652: Navigation Act Leads to Anglo-Dutch Wars; December 16, 1653-September 3, 1658: Cromwell Rules England as Lord Protector; May, 1659-May, 1660: Restoration of Charles II.

VASILY SHUYSKY
Czar of Russia (r. 1606-1610)

As Czar Vasily IV, Shuysky was the ineffectual ruler of Russia for much of the period known in Russian history as Smutnoe Vremya, or the Time of Troubles.

BORN: 1552; Moscow, Russia
DIED: September 12, 1612; Gostynin, near Warsaw, Poland
ALSO KNOWN AS: Vasily Ivanovich; Vasily Shuisky; Vasily IV; Prince Shuysky
AREA OF ACHIEVEMENT: Government and politics

EARLY LIFE

Prince Vasily Shuysky (vuhs-YEEL-yuhih SHEW-ihs-kuhih) was born in Moscow in 1552, in the family residence of the Shuyskys, one of the most distinguished of Muscovite boyars and a cadet line of the Rurik Dynasty (the legendary ruling family that reigned in Novgorod and Muscovy from 862 until the death of Fyodor I in 1598). Nothing is known of Vasily's upbringing except that he received the education and military training suitable to the scion of a boyar family. The Shuyskys had come into prominence during the reign of Vasily III (r. 1505-1533), and during the minority of his son, Ivan the Terrible (r. 1547-1584), they had displayed unfettered ambition. The family was suspected of poisoning Ivan's mother, and they exiled or killed their rivals at court. The young Ivan feared and hated them.

In September, 1543, Prince Andrei Shuysky physically assaulted a favorite of the thirteen-year-old Ivan right in front of him. Ivan subsequently ordered Andrei's seizure by the kennel-keepers, who either beat him to death or fed him to the dogs. Vasily Shuysky was the grandson of this Prince Andrei.

In the light of these events, it is surprising that Vasily survived Ivan's bloodletting of the boyars and seemingly even enjoyed the favor of the tyrant. Vasily was to be found, as a teenager, in Ivan's Oprichnika, the pseudo-Tatar "knightly order" that also constituted Russia's first secret police. There, between 1564 an 1572, along with such notorious figures as Alexander Basmanov, Matvei Skuratov, and Boris Godunov (the future czar), he participated in Ivan's exaggerated religious ceremonials, insane cruelties, and orgies at Aleksandrova Sloboda.

During the reign of Fyodor I (r. 1584-1598), Vasily was a prominent member of the boyar council, and in 1591, he led a commission of inquiry to Uglich to investigate the mysterious death of Prince Dmitry Ivanovich, the youngest son of Ivan the Terrible. Contrary to rumor, Shuysky's commission reported that there had been no foul play and that Dmitry, a mere six-year-old, had stabbed himself during an epileptic fit.

LIFE'S WORK

At Czar Fyodor's death, his able brother-in-law Boris Godunov had himself elected czar. Vasily considered himself a more appropriate candidate, but Godunov's position was unassailable, despite Vasily's best efforts: When Vasily several times intrigued against Godunov in the Boyar Duma (council of nobles), he found himself repeatedly sent into exile. His hopes were raised, however, during the last years of Godunov's reign, when northern Russia, in particular, was swept by famine. Popular discontent mounted, and it was unclear whether Godunov could ride out the storm. Then, toward the end of 1604, an incredible rumor reached Moscow: the supposedly dead Prince Dmitry Ivanovich was marching on the capital from the west, supported by a Polish army.

Godunov prepared to repel the invaders and sent an army commanded by Vasily, which the pretender defeated near Kromy, forcing Vasily to fall back to Moscow. Events now moved quickly: The czar died in 1605, and Vasily instigated the murder of Godunov's young son, Fyodor II, and the rape of his sister Xenia, who was relegated to a nunnery, accompanied by her mother. As the False Dmitry (as he became known) approached Moscow, Vasily, reversing his earlier position, declared that the pretender was in fact the true czar and participated in his coronation on July 21, 1605. Ironically, when the False Dmitry displayed signs of great energy and shrewdness, Vasily's jealousy was aroused, and he began to intrigue against the pretender. When his intrigues were found out, Vasily was arrested for treason and sentenced to death, but he was granted a last-minute reprieve. Sent into exile yet again, he was soon brought back and restored to his estates.

Vasily had not abandoned his resolve to get rid of the False Dmitry. For all the latter's intelligence and vigor, he made a fatal mistake: In 1606, Marina Mniszech, the daughter of the new czar's Polish patron, arrived in Moscow with a large force of Poles, whose entry into the city unleashed Muscovite xenophobia, always simmering below the surface of events. On May 8, the False Dmitry and Marina were married in the Kremlin, but they were married in a Catholic ceremony that made no concessions to Russian Orthodox tradition. Unwittingly, the new czar had signed his own death warrant. Vasily organized a mob, which broke into the Kremlin on May 17 and lynched the False Dmitry, after which his body was burnt and his ashes scattered.

Vasily now put himself forward as a candidate for the throne and was accepted by a consensus of boyar families. He was crowned Czar Vasily IV on June 1, 1606. Apart from his inner clique, however, his rule lacked solid support. He was seen as a "boyar-czar," the agent of an oppressive aristocracy, and among the population at large (especially the Cossacks), he was detested. Among his foremost opponents were members of the Romanov family, whom the False Dmitry had restored to favor after their disgrace at the hands of Boris Godunov. More serious than these court opponents of Vasily, however,

was the Cossack rebel Ivan Bolotnikov, who would seriously threaten Vasily IV's rule. Formerly a boyar slave, Bolotnikov had fled to join the Cossacks but was captured by Crimean Tatars, who sold him into the Ottoman navy as a galley-slave. Rescued by a German vessel, he made his way via Venice and Poland back to Russia, where he raised the Cossacks against the government. Bolotnikov's force now marched on Moscow, and laid it under partial siege during 1606.

Vasily appointed his able nephew, Prince Mikhail Skopin-Shuysky, to defend the capital, and the latter decisively defeated Bolotnikov in December, 1606, forcing him to withdraw his forces to Kaluga, where he remained for the next six months. Vasily remained the master of Moscow during this time, but Bolotnokov's fortunes improved when the Cossacks advanced a new pretender, the so-called Czar Peter, claiming he was the son of Fyodor and Godunov's sister Irina. Czar Peter, however, soon abandoned Bolotnikov and established himself at Tula. Throughout this period, Vasily remained holed up in the Kremlin, beleaguered and essentially passive. He did, however, seek to win support from the *pomeshchiki* (middle-ranking service cavalry) by issuing a decree in March, 1607, allowing landowners a fifteen-year limit for recovering runaway serfs, a further stage on the inexorable road to serfdom.

In May, 1607, Bolotnikov broke out of Kaluga and joined Czar Peter at Tula. Here, the rebels were attacked and dispersed by Prince Mikhail Skopin-Shuysky (June, 1607). In October, 1607, both Czar Peter and Bolotnikov were captured. Czar Peter was hanged (January, 1608), and Bolotnikov was blinded and drowned (March, 1608). At Vasily's instigation, the rebellious nobles were sent into exile, and the rank and file were massacred or handed over to loyalists as slaves. Meanwhile, a Second False Dmitry had appeared, with renewed assistance from the Poles (June, 1607).

Failing to take Moscow, the Second False Dmitry established himself at Tushino. Meanwhile, Philaret (Fyodor Nikitich Romanov), a Romanov who had been forced by Godunov to take monastic vows, had become the metropolitan of Rostov. He was now captured by the troops of the Second False Dmitry, brought to Tushino, and proclaimed patriarch of Moscow. The Tushino regime proceeded to consolidate its position, reinforced by further Cossack contingents. A degree of legitimacy was conferred upon the pretender when Marina Mniszech fell into the rebels' hands (September, 1608). Presumably under duress, she formally recognized the pretender as her former murdered husband and married him. In effect, there were now two governments, that of the Second False Dmitry at Tushino and that of Vasily IV in Moscow.

In the preceding months, Vasily had accomplished little except the elimination of Bolotnikov. Desperate now, he looked abroad for assistance. In February, 1609, he made an agreement with Charles IX of Sweden (r. 1604-1611), who promised fifteen thousand Swedish troops to join Skopin-Shuysky in expelling the Second False Dmitry's forces from northwestern Russia. In return, Vasily was to cede Karelia to Sweden. News of this agreement galvanized the Poles. In September, 1609, Sigismund III Vasa besieged and took Smolensk. Dmitry, exposed to attack by Vasily's troops and now abandoned by his Polish allies, who preferred to join their king at Smolensk, fled from Tushino to Kaluga. Now a fugitive, he was murdered on December 11, 1610.

Meanwhile, however, many Muscovite boyars, unable to stomach Vasily's rule, joined with Sigismund instead. On reaching the Polish camp, they offered the throne to Sigismund's son, Władysław (the future King Władysław IV Vasa), if he would convert to Orthodoxy. In April, 1610, the one man who had kept the Moscow regime afloat, Prince Skopin-Shuysky, died—murdered, it was said, by Vasily himself, who was jealous of the prince's popularity. In June, 1610, came the final disaster for Vasily when his troops were defeated by the Poles at Klushino (June 24, 1610). Thereafter, the boyars, still in Moscow, engineered a riot on July 17, 1610, which led to the seizure of Vasily and his forced abdication, his reign ending as it had begun, in mob violence. He, with his brothers, was now removed to Smolensk and handed over to Sigismund, who took him to Warsaw, where he died two years later. The Time of Troubles dragged on, but in November of 1612, a patriotic army took Moscow and expelled the Poles. In February, 1613, the election of Michael Romanov as czar inaugurated a new dynasty.

SIGNIFICANCE

Vasily Shuysky reigned during four of the most turbulent years in Russian history. Ambitious and unscrupulous but devoid of talent, vision, and any qualities of leadership, he was a despised figurehead in a Russian regime that encapsulated all the problems that had been festering since the time of Ivan the Terrible. He left no significant mark on his troubled times, surviving only as a sinister vignette in Alexander Pushkin's tragedy, *Boris Godunov* (wr. 1824-1825, pb. 1831, pr. 1870; English translation, 1918).

—*Gavin R. G. Hambly*

FURTHER READING

Bussow, Conrad. *The Disturbed State of the Russian Realm*. Translated by G. Edward Orchard. Montreal: McGill-Queen's University Press, 1994. A German mercenary, Bussow's account is that of an astute, informed eyewitness.

Dunning, Chester S. L. *Russia's First Civil War*. University Park: Pennsylvania State University Press, 2001. A magisterial narrative of this complicated phase of Russian history.

Kollmann, N. S. *Kinship and Politics: The Making of the Muscovite Political System, 1345-1547*. Stanford, Calif.: Stanford University Press, 1987. Essential for the origins of the Shuysky family.

Margeret, Jacques. *The Russian Empire and Grand Duchy of Muscovy: A Seventeenth-Century French Account*. Translated by Chester S. L. Dunning. Pittsburgh, Pa.: University of Pittsburgh Press, 1983. The eyewitness account of Margaret, a French mercenary, is invaluable.

Massa, Isaac. *A Short History of the Muscovite Wars*. Translated by G. Edward Orchard. Toronto: University of Toronto Press, 1982. Massa, a Dutch merchant, wrote a detailed eyewitness account of the period.

Perrie, Maureen. *Pretenders and Popular Monarchism in Early Modern Russia*. New York: Cambridge University Press, 1995. A penetrating and detailed analysis.

SEE ALSO: Michael Romanov; Sigismund III Vasa.
RELATED ARTICLES in *Great Events from History: The Seventeenth Century, 1601-1700*: c. 1601-1606: Appearance of the False Dmitry; February 7, 1613: Election of Michael Romanov as Czar; January 29, 1649: Codification of Russian Serfdom.

SÉBASTIEN LE PRESTRE DE VAUBAN
Spanish military leader

Vauban is chiefly remembered as Europe's best and most prolific military engineer at a time when siege works and fortifications were crucial to the art of military affairs.

BORN: May 15, 1633; Saint-Léger-de-Foucherest, France
DIED: March 30, 1707; Paris, France
AREAS OF ACHIEVEMENT: Military, engineering, science and technology

EARLY LIFE

Sébastien Le Prestre de Vauban (say-bahs-tyahn leh prehtr deh voh-bahn) was born to a family whose position in society lay between the lower nobility and the bourgeoisie. His education, completed at Semuren-Auxois, consisted of drawing, mathematics, and history. In 1651, while still seventeen, Vauban enlisted as a cadet in a regiment that elected to fight on the side of the Fronde rebels (during the Wars of the Fronde, 1648-1653) against the very young King Louis XIV. Because of his education, Vauban was put to work as a military engineer, fortifying the town of Clermont-en-Argonne. Later, he participated in the Siege of Sainte-Menehould. Both experiences were solid preparation for his life's work.

Captured by the Royalists, Vauban was pardoned, converted to the cause of the king, and sent back to Sainte-Menehould, this time to lay siege to his former friends. At the end of the Fronde wars in 1653, Vauban was returned to Sainte-Menehould to repair much of what he had previously helped destroy. Vauban had been fortunate in 1653 to have entered the royal service under the chevalier de Clerville, by reputation, if perhaps not in practice, France's best military engineer. The advent of gunpowder had ushered in the age of artillery and with it the decline of the castle in favor of less vulnerable, lower, bastioned fortifications. Transitional work had already begun, but the times were right for someone of meticulous genius such as Vauban. After conducting sieges on behalf of Louis XIV, Vauban was commissioned *ingénieur ordinaire du roi* within de Clerville's department, a position from which he could gain the increasing affection of the king.

LIFE'S WORK

Vauban traveled on the king's behalf from 1659 to 1667, repairing old or developing new frontier fortifications. It

was a long peace in Louis's very long reign, a reign filled with wars of aggrandizement and expansion. In 1667, Louis attacked Spanish troops in Flanders, and the dedicated Vauban excelled in siege craft in the king's royal service. Vauban fortified the key strategic towns of Lille and Tournai. Vauban's work had by this time so surpassed de Clerville that Louis promoted him over de Clerville. Vauban became *commissaire général*, or virtual director of France's fortifications and siege works.

Louis's schedule of wars was formidable. From 1667 to 1668, France fought in the War of Devolution, from 1672 to 1678 in the Franco-Dutch Wars, from 1688 to 1697 in the Wars of the League of Augsburg, and from 1701 to 1714 in the War of the Spanish Succession. The average-looking, rugged Vauban worked diligently at his post, shunning the splendors of the Sun King's fabulous court at Versailles. His world was the dusty trail and the supervision of field work while staying at modest frontier inns. Even after 1675, when Louis granted him an estate, Vauban spent little time there or with his wife. In his old age, Vauban carried out his work from the back of his sedan chair, borne by horses. In 1706, Vauban was elevated to marshal of France before dying a year later of pneumonia. Throughout, Vauban was one of Louis's longest-serving and most-trusted servants, compiling to his credit the construction of at least thirty-three new fortresses, the restoration of more than one hundred older fortresses, and the execution of fifty-three successful sieges.

Vauban's contributions were in his offensive siege craft and defensive fortifications. After the horrors of the Thirty Years' War (1618-1648), nations wanted to regulate the military art with certain established, recognized rules. Military operations were carried out along the lines of chessboard moves. The capture of fortifications became the chesslike pieces and the actions that determined the winner in the wider military and diplomatic context.

Good fortifications were situated to offer a high degree of enfilading fire and mutually supporting positions, and they were layered for defense in depth. Walls and bastions were thickened and lowered to cushion against the effect of artillery. Vauban was recognized as a master at overcoming defenses as well as of creating them. He was a legend in his own time; indeed, it was noted that "a town besieged by Vauban was a town taken." Vauban's method of siege was first to blockade a fortified town, then to determine the best single point in the defenses where he could effect a decisive breach. Earthworks would be built to provide protective cover for the artillery and engineers. Vauban would then build three trench systems progressively toward and parallel to the particular point to be breached. These trenches, which were connected by zig-zag communications trenches, were referred to as the first parallel, second parallel, and third parallel. Offensive artillery was divided into three functions: mortar batteries and ricocheting batteries, which would suppress defensive musketry and artillery, and the heavy or main breaching batteries. The entire system was geometrically calculated with Vauban's mathematical precision. Often, days in advance, Vauban could predict the exact hour of a defense's fall. Once a breach had been made and assuming no relieving force was in sight, the conventions of the day permitted a garrison to surrender honorably. In fact, a town that refused and had to be taken by storm could rightfully, by the same rules, be sacked.

Vauban was equally skilled in defensive fortification. His methods were based not only on mathematics but also on common sense and his experience in analyzing the advantages of terrain. Vauban looked upon his talent as the art of being able to build to suit a given location rather than as a systematic adventure into applied science. Nevertheless, his emulators categorized his methods into three systems. His first system represented little more than adaptations from previous French and Italian engineers. His early development also borrowed from Blaise François Comte de Pagan, who had retired from active French service in 1642. Greatly simplified, Vauban's fortifications were polygonal, with bastions at strategic points.

As a starting point for calculations, a standard length of fortifications front was set at 360 yards. This measure could be reduced or extended depending on the size of area to be protected and the intervening terrain. The other architectural components of the fortification, the ditches, lunettes, ravelins, bonettes, curtain walls, crown work, and horn work, were constructed as fractional expressions of the basic measure. The overall geometrical designs took the effects of contemporary musketry and artillery into consideration to provide for the best possible defense.

Vauban reintroduced the tenaille and orillon, or ear, onto the bastion. Vauban's second system detached the bastions from the main works and created tower bastions, both feats intended to improve the realities of defense during a siege. His third system was used only once, at Neuf-Brisach. The defense was again extended in depth and the tower bastions were modified. Completed in 1706, one year before his death, it was arguably his finest work.

SIGNIFICANCE

During his lifetime, Vauban was appreciated as Europe's leading military engineer. He was, however, more than that, for he wrote on a wide and complex series of issues in his twelve volumes of unpublished memoirs. In 1699, he was elected to the Académie des Sciences for accomplishments in applied science and mathematics.

Throughout his travels in the four corners of France, Vauban amassed volumes of economic and social details, and he espoused a concern for humanitarian ideals. In the arena of military affairs, he invented, among others, the ricochet firing technique for artillery and the first good bayonet. Voltaire was inspired to pronounce Vauban to be "the finest of citizens." Yet this well-rounded individual will be forever remembered primarily for

Sébastien Le Prestre de Vauban. (Library of Congress)

his fortifications and siege craft, at which he enjoyed unparalleled success in the seventeenth century and unrivaled adulation in the eighteenth. Vauban's reputation has come to the twenty-first century intact.

Controversy still shrouds the originality of his work, but that is hardly surprising, for he labored under financial constraints, diplomatic restraints, and the whims of his monarch, and quite often he simply had to work from preexisting structures. The original elements of his second and third system, however, seem beyond dispute, as is the sheer proliferation and essence of his construction. The fortified town of Neuf-Brisach is usually considered his masterpiece. As late as 1870, this 164-year-old fort stood against modern Prussian artillery and siege craft for thirty-six days, so long did Vauban's skill outlive the man.

—David L. Bullock

FURTHER READING

Britt, Albert Sidney, III, et al. *The Dawn of Modern Warfare.* Wayne, N.J.: Avery, 1984. Provides information about Vauban's place within Louis XIV's government and the wars occurring during Louis's regime.

Chandler, David G. *Atlas of Military Strategy, 1618-1878.* London: Arms and Armour Press, 1980. Vauban is profiled in two oversize pages. Includes a timetable of sieges created by Vauban.

De La Croix, Horst. *Military Considerations in City Planning: Fortifications.* New York: George Braziller, 1972. The author traces his subject from the primitive world to the seventeenth century, concluding with Vauban. More attention is devoted to Vauban's defensive rather than his offensive techniques.

Duffy, Christopher. *Fire and Stone: The Science of Fortress Warfare, 1660-1860.* Newton Abbot, England: David and Charles, 1975. Duffy uses a topical approach to describe Vauban's methods of military engineering, explaining them methodically in simplified but comprehensive detail. Well-chosen illustrations illuminate the text.

_____. *Siege Warfare: The Fortress in the Early Modern World, 1494-1660.* London: Routledge & Kegan Paul, 1979. An indispensable book for creating the overall setting in which Vauban began his early work. The milieu of siege and fortification work is excellently portrayed from the close of the medieval period through Blaise François Comte de Pagan and the Chevalier de Ville, both of whom influenced Vauban.

Hebbert, F. J., and G. A. Rothrock. *Soldier of France: Sébastien Le Prestre de Vauban, 1633-1707.* New York: P. Lang, 1990. A modern English-language biography.

Hogg, Ian V. *Fortress: A History of Military Defence.* London: Macdonald and Jane's, 1975. Devotes two chapters to Vauban's era. The text and accompanying illustrations are the best available for demonstrating the geometrical angles in Vauban's work.

_____. *The History of Fortification.* London: Orbis, 1981. A chapter on classical fortification sets the stage for the succeeding chapter, "The Age of Vauban." Contains illustrations of Vauban's military architecture, including Neuf-Brisach, considered his crowning structural achievement.

Lynn, John A. *Giant of the Grand Siècle: The French Army, 1610-1715.* New York: Cambridge University Press, 1997. Vauban is prominently featured in this examination of the French army, with information about his life and contributions to siege craft.

Paret, Peter, ed., with Gordon A. Craig and Felix Gilbert. *Makers of Modern Strategy: From Machiavelli to the Nuclear Age.* Princeton, N.J.: Princeton University Press, 1986. Henry Geurlac's article is probably the best single treatment of Vauban as a well-rounded individual. The article explores Vauban's contributions in mathematics and applied science while recognizing his most significant contributions as siege craft and the science of fortifications. Vauban's writings are examined, as are controversies over his originality.

SEE ALSO: Louis XIV; Viscount de Turenne.

RELATED ARTICLE in *Great Events from History: The Seventeenth Century, 1601-1700:* April 6, 1672-August 10, 1678: French-Dutch War.

LOPE DE VEGA CARPIO
Spanish playwright

Lope de Vega was the creator of the Spanish national theater of the Golden Age. He established the norms that would characterize Spanish theater until the late seventeenth century.

BORN: November 25, 1562; Madrid, Spain
DIED: August 27, 1635; Madrid
ALSO KNOWN AS: Lope Félix de Vega Carpio (full name)
AREAS OF ACHIEVEMENT: Theater, literature

EARLY LIFE

Lope de Vega Carpio (LOH-pay day BAY-ghah KAHR-pyoh) was of humble origins. His father, an embroiderer, died when Lope de Vega was still a boy. At an early age, Lope de Vega was taken to Seville for a brief period, but he spent most of his life in Madrid, at that time a highly stimulating city and cultural center. Juan Pérez de Montalbán, Lope de Vega's disciple and first biographer, relates that at five years of age, Lope de Vega could read in Spanish and in Latin. At seven, he was writing his first compositions, and at ten, his first plays. Lope de Vega continued his studies at the Colegio de la Compañía de Jesús. About 1576, he entered into the service of Jerónimo Manrique de Lara, Bishop of Ávila. He probably later attended the University of Alcalá. In 1580, he left for Salamanca, where he was a student at the university.

Lope de Vega was involved in many amorous relationships and participated in several military campaigns. In 1579, when he had just turned seventeen, he fell in love with María de Aragón, then fifteen. In 1583, he accompanied Alvaro de Bazán on a military campaign to Terceira Island. It was upon his return that he met Elena Osorio, then unhappily married to a comic actor, and became her lover. By this time, Lope de Vega's reputation as a writer was starting to grow, and Elena's father, who recognized the young man's potential, did not oppose the relationship, but Lope de Vega, fiercely jealous of Elena's husband, wrote some provocative verses that caused a scandal. Elena reacted violently to his behavior, and the playwright then responded by attacking Elena and her family, once more in verse. In 1587, Lope de Vega was detained by the authorities for libel, and the following year he was condemned to exile. He then ran away with Isabel de Urbina, whom he married before embarking on the ill-fated Spanish Armada.

After Isabel's death in 1595, Lope de Vega was permitted to return to Madrid. During the following years,

he developed into the leading Spanish playwright. It was during this period that he became embroiled in a heated literary polemic with the poet Luis de Góngora y Argote, whose ornate style Lope de Vega disliked intensely. In 1598, Lope de Vega married Juana de Guardo, while continuing his amorous relationship with Micaela de Luján, called Camila Lucinda in his verses. During the fifteen years he was married to Juana, he engaged in numerous affairs. In 1605, he entered into the service of the duke of Sessa, who became his patron. When Juana died in 1613, Lope de Vega took holy orders without diminishing either his involvement in love intrigues or his literary production. By this point in his life, he had become the model for all the playwrights of his generation.

LIFE'S WORK

Lope de Vega's active love life did not distract him from writing. He was one of the most prolific literary figures in Spanish history. He claimed to have written about fifteen hundred plays, although modern critics maintain that this figure is certainly an exaggeration. About 470 of his full-length plays survive. In addition, he wrote short, one-act religious plays known as *autos sacramentales*, as well as poetry and novels. Because of his almost superhuman talents and energy, he was called the "Phoenix of Geniuses" and the "Monster of Nature."

Following the lead of Lope de Rueda, Lope de Vega began early in his career to write for the masses. He chose themes that would interest the common man, often dramatizing well-known and popular legends or historical events. Many of his plays were based on episodes from chronicles or on folk songs. By selecting subjects that were familiar and popular, Lope de Vega created a theater that would hold the interest of his audience, and one that was distinctly Spanish in nature.

In *El arte nuevo de hacer comedias en este tiempo* (*The New Art of Writing Plays*, 1914), published in 1609, Lope de Vega explained his dramatic theory. He recommended that playwrights choose subjects, such as love and honor, that would elicit strong reactions from the audience. He abandoned many of the conventions that characterized earlier Spanish theater. For example, classical tradition dictated that dramatists respect the unities of time, place, and action, according to which a plot must take place within the period of a day, must occur in one specific location, and must not include subplots. Lope de Vega found these rules artificial and restrictive. He preferred a more natural approach that would allow events to take place wherever and whenever appropriate. In one of his most popular plays, *Fuenteovejuna* (wr. 1611-1618, pb. 1619; *The Sheep-Well*, 1936), written between 1611 and 1618, the first act begins in the palace of the Calatrava order, in Almagro; moves to the plaza of the town of Fuenteovejuna; skips to the palace of the Catholic monarchs Ferdinand and Isabella; and ends in the countryside surrounding Fuenteovejuna.

Lope de Vega wrote tragedy and comedy and also developed the *tragicomedia*, a play that mixes elements of both. His purpose was to imitate nature, in which tragedy and comedy exist side by side. He defined the structure of the Spanish drama, fixing the number of acts at three. He wrote all of his plays in verse and fixed the function of each metric form. For example, the romance, a traditional ballad form, was to be used for narrations, while the *décima*, a ten-line stanza, was to be used for laments. Lope de Vega explored other dramatic genres as well: He

wrote historical, mythological, religious, pastoral, and novelistic plays. He also wrote *comedias de capa y espada* (cape-and-sword plays), so called because they depicted contemporary situations, and the actors therefore wore street clothes, which included a cape and sword. These plays usually revolved around love and intrigues, misunderstandings, and tricks. The most famous are *El perro del hortelano* (wr. 1613-1615, pb. 1618; *The Gardener's Dog*, 1903), based on one of Aesop's fables about a dog that neither eats nor allows others to do so, and *La dama boba* (1617; *The Lady Nit-Wit*, 1958), based on the commonplace that love makes fools wise. Lope de Vega's best-known works deal with events in Spanish history; others are based on legends.

Throughout his career, Lope de Vega argued for simplicity and naturalness on stage. When, in the seventeenth century, complex productions with special effects and complicated stage devices came into fashion, he opposed them. He also resisted the trend toward ornate language that characterized baroque literature. Nevertheless, his later plays reflect the new tendencies. *El castigo sin venganza* (1635; *Justice Without Revenge*, 1936) contains many erudite passages that include allusions to history and mythology.

Although Lope de Vega is known primarily as a dramatist, he began his career as a poet and wrote much religious and secular poetry in his later years. He also wrote one of Spain's greatest pastoral novels, *La Arcadia* (1598). Lope de Vega received many honors, among them membership in the Order of Saint John of Jerusalem, which was conferred upon him in 1627. His funeral was a national event and is said to have lasted nine days.

SIGNIFICANCE

Prior to Lope de Vega Carpio, Spanish theater was highly dependent on Italian themes and forms. Lope de Vega created a theater that was an authentic expression of the Spanish personality. Even when he depicted foreigners, his characters were always Spanish in essence. His objective was to entertain his audience rather than to instruct or edify. Unlike his best-known follower, Pedro Calderón de la Barca, who was a court dramatist, Lope de Vega wrote for an audience that was often rowdy. To please these undisciplined theatergoers, he wrote plays imbued with humor, wit, and action. Even his trag-

Lope de Vega Carpio. (Library of Congress)

VEGA CARPIO'S MAJOR WORKS

1596-1598	*Los comendadores de Córdoba*
1596-1603	*El nuevo mundo descubierto por Cristóbal Colón* (*The Discovery of the New World by Christopher Columbus*, 1950)
1598	*La Arcadia*
1598	*La Dragontea*
1599	*El Isidro*
1599-1606	*El mayordomo de la duquesa de Amalfi* (*The Majordomo of the Duchess of Amalfi*, 1951)
1602	*La hermosura de Angélica*
1602	*Rimas*
1602-1608	*El anzuelo de Fenisa*
1603	*La corona merecida*
1604	*El peregrino en su patria* (*The Pilgrim: Or, The Stranger in His Own Country*, 1621)
1605	*La noche toledana*
1606-1608	*Los melindres de Belisa*
1606-1612	*El acero de Madrid* (*Madrid Steel*, 1935)
1606-1612	*Castelvines y Monteses* (English translation, 1869)
1607-1612	*La niña de plata*
1609	*El arte nuevo de hacer comedias en este tiempo* (*The New Art of Writing Plays*, 1914)
1609	*Jerusalén conquistada*
1609-1612	*Peribáñez y el comendador de Ocaña* (*Peribáñez*, 1936)
1610	*La buena guarda*
1610-1615	*Las flores de don Juan, y rico y pobre trocados*
1611	*El villano en su rincón* (*The King and the Farmer*, 1940)
1611-1618	*Fuenteovejuna* (*The Sheep-Well*, 1936)
1612	*Los pastores de Belén*
1612-1624	*Lo cierto por lo dudoso* (*A Certainty for a Doubt*, 1936)
1613-1615	*El perro del hortelano* (*The Gardener's Dog*, 1903)
1614	*Rimas sacras*
1615-1626	*El caballero de Olmedo* (*The Knight from Olmedo*, 1961)
1617	*La dama boba* (*The Lady Nit-Wit*, 1958)
1620-1622	*Amar sin saber a quién*
1620-1623	*El mejor alcalde, el rey* (*The King, the Greatest Alcalde*, 1918)
1620-1628	*Los Tellos de Meneses I*
1621	*La Circe*
1621	*La filomena*
1621	*Novelas a Marcia Leonarda*
1624-1625	*El premio del bien hablar*
1625	*Triunfos divinos*
1625-1626	*La moza de cántaro*
1627	*La corona trágica*
1627-1635	*El guante de doña Blanca*
1630	*Laurel de Apolo*
1632	*La Dorotea*
1633	*Amarilis*
1634	*La gatomaquia* (*Gatomachia*, 1843)
1634	*Rimas humanas y divinas del licenciado Tomé de Burguillos*
1635	*Filis*
1635	*El castigo sin venganza*, pb. 1635 (based on Matteo Bandello's novella; *Justice Without Revenge*, 1936)
1637	*Las bizarrías de Belisa*
1637	*La Vega del Parnaso*
1637	*Égloga a Claudio*

edies contain humor, usually introduced by the servants or *graciosos*.

Although his plays are not particularly philosophical, they reveal a deep understanding of human nature. Lope de Vega introduced a psychological element into the theater of his time, which was later developed by dramatists such as Tirso de Molina and Calderón. It is perhaps surprising to what degree Lope de Vega's followers respected the norms he established. The Spanish play maintained its three-act format until the end of the seventeenth century and beyond. The basic character types, themes, and devices that Lope de Vega introduced were used by all the major Spanish playwrights of the Golden Age.

—*Barbara Mujica*

FURTHER READING

Fitzmaurice-Kelly, James. *Lope de Vega and the Spanish Drama*. London: R. B. Johnson, 1902. Reprint. Brooklyn, N.Y.: Haskell House, 1970. An overview of the state of the Spanish theater at the time of Lope de Vega and of his innovations.

Fox, Dian. *Refiguring the Hero: From Peasant to Noble in Lope de Vega and Calderón*. University Park: University of Pennsylvania Press, 1991. Fox reevaluates nine plays by Lope de Vega and Calderón within the larger context of European literary heroism.

Hayes, Francis C. *Lope de Vega*. Boston: Twayne, 1967. Contains historical and biographical information and an examination of the elements of Lope de Vega's comedy. Analyzes genre, style, and technique for the beginning student.

Larson, Donald R. *The Honor Plays of Lope de Vega*. Cambridge, Mass.: Harvard University Press, 1977. An in-depth study of the evolution of Lope de Vega's treatment of honor, starting with early plays, in which the characters adopt unconventional solutions, through the plays of the middle period, which include some of the most brutal scenes ever to appear on the Spanish stage, to the late plays, in which he tempers his approach.

Moir, Duncan, and Edward M. Wilson. *The Golden Age Drama, 1492-1700*. Vol. 3 in *A Literary History of Spain*. London: Ernest Benn, 1971. An overview of the development of Spanish theater from early Spanish masterpieces until the decline of baroque drama at the end of the seventeenth century. Special attention is paid to Lope de Vega, his innovations, his genius, and his influence.

Rennert, Hugo Albert. *The Spanish Stage in the Time of Lope de Vega*. Reprint. Mineola, N.Y.: Dover, 1963. An overview of the growth of Spanish theater, the development of the *corrales*, and Lope de Vega's contributions.

Shergold, N. D. *A History of the Spanish Stage from Medieval Times Until the End of the Seventeenth Century*. Oxford, England: Clarendon Press, 1967. Special attention is given to the *corrales* and Lope de Vega's contribution to the development of a national theater. Contains essential information about the physical facilities in which his plays were performed.

Smith, Marlene K. *The Beautiful Woman in the Theater of Lope de Vega: Ideology and Mythology of Female Beauty in Seventeenth Century Spain*. New York: Peter Lang, 1998. Analyzes the dramatic function of beautiful women in Lope de Vega's plays, placing these characters within a framework of medieval, Renaissance, and baroque and contemporary feminist concepts of beauty. One of several books about Lope de Vega published by Peter Lang, including *Lope de Vega and the Comedia de Santos* by Robert R. Morrison (2000) and *The Recreation of History in the Fernando and Isabel Plays of Lope de Vega* by Delys Ostlund (1997).

Wilson, Margaret. *Spanish Drama of the Golden Age*. Oxford, England: Pergamon Press, 1969. Describes the development and characteristics of the *corrales* and of Lope de Vega's craftsmanship. Discusses his themes and techniques as well as his influence on subsequent writers.

Zuckerman-Ingber, Alix. *El bien más alto: A Reconsideration of Lope de Vega's Honor Plays*. Gainesville: University Presses of Florida, 1984. Argues that critics have misjudged Lope de Vega's attitude toward honor. Contends he does not condone the honor code but rather attacks it by showing the violent extremes to which the obsession with honor can lead. Explores Lope de Vega's use of irony and his techniques of characterization in the honor plays, and how these convey his true attitude toward honor.

SEE ALSO: Pierre Corneille; Molière; Tirso de Molina.
RELATED ARTICLES in *Great Events from History: The Seventeenth Century, 1601-1700:* c. 1601-1682: Spanish Golden Age; 1605 and 1615: Cervantes Publishes *Don Quixote de la Mancha*; March 31, 1621-September 17, 1665: Reign of Philip IV.

DIEGO VELÁZQUEZ
Spanish painter

In his role as court painter to King Philip IV, Velázquez produced a series of masterly works that made him the preeminent artist in his native Spain and one of the greatest painters of the entire Baroque era in Europe.

BORN: June 6, 1599 (baptized); Seville, Spain
DIED: August 6, 1660; Madrid, Spain
AREA OF ACHIEVEMENT: Art

EARLY LIFE

Diego Velázquez (DYAY-goh vay-LAHZ-kayz) was born the eldest of the seven children of Juan Rodriguez de Silva and Jerónima Velázquez. The exact date of his birth is unknown, but he was baptized on June 6, undoubtedly shortly after his birth. As was commonplace among many Spaniards, Diego adopted his mother's surname. His family belonged to the hidalgo class, the lowest order of Spanish nobility.

A bright boy and an excellent student, Velázquez received the Humanistic education typical for boys of his class; yet he early demonstrated a proclivity for a career in painting, considered a respectable vocation for the scion of a hidalgo family. Seville had a flourishing community of painters, and his parents encouraged their son's aspirations. In 1611, they apprenticed him to Francisco Pacheco, one of Seville's leading artists, although his training had possibly begun a year earlier under Francisco de Herrera, the Elder. Pacheco agreed to provide his charge with room, board, and clothing and to train him as both a painter and a gentleman. Pacheco's workshop provided a fertile atmosphere for the development of Velázquez's talents. Pacheco had a strong interest in the humanities, and poets, scholars, and public officials often gathered at his workshop to discuss the arts. Pacheco provided rigorous instruction in drawing for all of his students, but he allowed the young Velázquez considerable freedom to develop his own unique style.

Having passed the qualifying examination, Velázquez gained admission to the local painters' guild on March 14, 1617. This authorized him to have his own studio and accept commissions. The following year, on April 23, 1618, he married Pacheco's daughter Juana. Within three years, the young couple had two daughters, but only the elder, Francisca, survived infancy.

Of the approximately twenty paintings by Velázquez that have survived from his early period (1617-1621), the most distinctive are *bodegones*, a unique form of Spanish still life depicting ordinary people engaged in mundane activities involving food and drink. These works demonstrated Velázquez's concern for careful attention to composition and detail and utilized dramatic lighting reminiscent of the Italian baroque master Caravaggio.

Had Velázquez chosen to remain in Seville, he could undoubtedly have become the city's preeminent painter and enjoyed a lucrative career accepting commissions from local churches. Yet he already clearly preferred secular art to religious art and had ambitions for advancement that could be achieved only at the royal court in Madrid. In April, 1622, he left Seville for the capital, ostensibly to view the famous collection of art at El Escorial Palace; yet he also had aspirations to paint Spain's new sovereign, Philip IV.

LIFE'S WORK

The dominant figure at Philip's court for the first two decades of his reign was Gaspar de Guzmán y Pimental, the count-duke of Olivares, who had many close friends in Seville, including Pacheco. During his initial visit, Velázquez failed to win a commission to paint Philip, but he won favorable attention with his portrait of the poet Luis de Góngora y Argote. In the spring of 1623, following the death of the king's favorite painter, Olivares summoned Velázquez to Madrid. The young artist's subsequent portrait of the king's chaplain, Juan de Fonseca, won for him widespread praise at court and gained for him the opportunity to paint Philip. This royal portrait, now lost, was so favorably received that Olivares immediately invited Velázquez to move to Madrid permanently. He also decreed that in the future no one else would be permitted to paint the king. Velázquez formally entered royal service on October 6, 1623. For the remaining thirty-seven years of his life, his fortunes were closely tied to Philip and his court.

Velázquez's sudden rise aroused the jealousy of more established court painters, but he firmly entrenched his position by defeating three of his elder rivals in a 1627 competition for a painting based on the theme of the expulsion of the Moors from Spain. The king rewarded Velázquez with the post of Usher of the Chamber, the first of many such favors he bestowed on his favorite painter over the years.

In 1627, Philip permitted Velázquez to travel to Italy, still the paramount place for artistic education during the

Diego Velázquez. (Library of Congress)

to hang in its rooms, Velázquez also painted six major works for the lodge, including life-size hunting portraits of Philip, Baltasar Carlos, and the king's brother Ferdinand.

Velázquez's works for the Buen Retiro and Torre de la Parada cemented his position as the nation's leading artist and resulted in his continued advancement at court. Throughout these years, he retained the king's favor and carefully avoided becoming entangled in the complex world of court politics. Philip expressed his confidence in his favorite artist by naming him a Gentleman of the Wardrobe in 1634 and promoting him to Gentleman of the Bedchamber in 1643. Later in the same year, he appointed Velázquez Assistant Superintendent of Works, which empowered Velázquez to oversee Philip's numerous building projects. Despite his royal offices and commissions, Velázquez's salary was frequently in arrears; yet throughout this period the king allowed him to supplement his wages by accepting commissions from private individuals.

In 1649, the king permitted Velázquez to make a second trip to Italy, principally to purchase paintings and sculptures for a new gallery in the Alcázar Palace. Velázquez arrived in Genoa in March, 1649, and remained in Italy for more than two years, stimulated by the artistic company and the freedom to paint whom he pleased. He again spent the majority of his time in Rome, where he was an honored guest at the papal court. His most famous painting from this period was a portrait of Pope Innocent X. In gratitude for this work, the pontiff presented Velázquez with a gold medallion bearing Innocent's portrait. Velázquez's fellow artists in Rome also honored him in January, 1650, by electing him to membership in the Academy of Saint Luke.

After returning to Madrid, Velázquez soon achieved a more exalted position at court when Philip chose him over several rivals in 1652 for the post of royal chamberlain. This office brought Velázquez a greatly augmented salary and rent-free apartments in the treasury house adjoining the Alcázar Palace. The post also entailed time-consuming responsibilities that decreased his opportunities to paint. He found himself in charge of the decoration of all royal palaces, the upkeep of their furnishings, and the supervision of all arrangements for the king's visits around the country.

During this final decade of his life, Velázquez continued to paint numerous portraits of the royal family, in-

seventeenth century. After initial visits to Genoa, Milan, Venice, and certain other cities, Velázquez settled for nearly a year in Rome. While there, he eagerly studied and sketched many works of the great masters and also painted several canvases of his own, including *The Bloody Cloak of Joseph* (1630), his only known work on an Old Testament theme. This initial Italian sojourn influenced Velázquez's style by inducing him to use freer brush strokes and lighter colors.

Upon his return to Madrid in January, 1631, Velázquez found many commissions awaiting him. Among the earliest was a portrait of the new heir to the throne, Prince Baltasar Carlos, born during Velázquez's absence in Italy. Among the major projects that occupied his time in the 1630's was his role in the decoration of the Buen Retiro, the newly built royal palace in Madrid. By late 1635, he had completed three masterful paintings for its Hall of Realms—equestrian portraits of Philip and Baltasar Carlos and *The Surrender of Breda* (1634-1635), a grand, life-size canvas that celebrated a Spanish military victory against the Dutch in 1625. Soon afterward, Velázquez became preoccupied with the redecoration of Philip's hunting lodge known as the Torre de la Parada. In addition to selecting paintings by other artists cluding the innovative *Las Meninas* (1656), considered by many to be his masterpiece. In 1658, the king nominated him for the Order of Santiago, one of the nation's three great orders of knighthood. After securing a papal brief waiving the necessity of proving noble ancestry on both sides, Velázquez was formally admitted to the order on November 28, 1659.

Velázquez's last known works were portraits of the aging monarch's two children by his second marriage, the Infanta Margarita and her sickly younger brother, Prince Philip Prospero. He devoted his last months to the time-consuming preparations for the marriage of the king's elder daughter Maria Teresa to Louis XIV of France, which occurred in April, 1660, on the Franco-Spanish border. Only three months after returning to Madrid from these festivities, Velázquez fell ill from a fever while attending his sovereign at court. Despite the efforts of royal physicians, he died within a week, on August 6, 1660. Clad in the costume of the Order of Santiago, the king's favorite painter was buried the following night at services attended by numerous nobles and court officials. His wife of forty-two years died a mere week after her husband.

SIGNIFICANCE

During an active career spanning more than four decades, Velázquez established himself as the premier artist of the Golden Age of Spanish painting, as well as one of the most significant painters of the baroque era. Unlike contemporaries such as Rembrandt in the Netherlands, Velázquez very early in his life secured a generous lifelong patron who provided him with financial security and creative opportunities to demonstrate his genius. With the exception of Peter Paul Rubens, no other artist better personified the genre of aristocratic baroque painting.

For such a long career, Velázquez's known output was relatively meager. Only some 120 of his 162 known paintings have survived. His output declined as his duties as a courtier increased. One of the great ironies of Velázquez's career is that the royal patronage that afforded him the opportunities to achieve lasting fame also demanded great amounts of his time for pursuits other than painting. Although best known for his penetrating royal portraits, Velázquez dealt with a wide variety of subjects in his paintings, including *bodegones*, religious works, mythological studies, and a moving series of works depicting royal dwarfs and jesters. He was the only significant Spanish painter of his era to devote himself mainly to secular subject matter.

Velázquez founded no great school of painters. His closest follower was his son-in-law, Juan Bautista del Mazo, who succeeded him as court painter but failed to achieve his greatness. Velázquez's works did have a significant impact on artists of subsequent centuries, especially the Romantic painter Francisco de Goya, the realist Gustave Courbet, and the Impressionist Édouard Manet.

—Tom L. Auffenberg

FURTHER READING

Brown, Dale. *The World of Velázquez, 1599-1660.* New York: Time-Life Books, 1969. Emphasizes Velázquez's life and career in relation to the Spain of Philip IV. Includes lavish color illustrations and a brief bibliography.

Brown, Jonathan, and Carmen Garrido. *Velázquez: The Technique of Genius.* New Haven, Conn.: Yale University Press, 1998. An introduction to Velázquez's paintings, primarily the works housed at Museo del Prado in Madrid. Garrido, head of technical services at the Prado, includes in this work photographed details of the paintings to accompany Brown's text.

Harris, Enriqueta. *Velázquez.* Ithaca, N.Y.: Cornell University Press, 1982. Contains a well-written survey of Velázquez's life and works, and two valuable appendices. The first appendix is a translation of Pacheco's study of his son-in-law's early career, found in his 1649 *Arte de la pintura; the* second appendix is an eighteenth century biography by court painter Antonio Palomino de Castro y Velasco.

Kahr, Madlyn Millner. *Velázquez: The Art of Painting.* New York: Harper & Row, 1976. Discusses Velázquez's life with a particular emphasis on his masterpiece, *Las Meninas.* Includes nearly one hundred black-and-white illustrations and a useful bibliography.

López-Rey, José. *Velázquez: A Catalogue Raisonné of His Oeuvre, with an Introductory Study.* London: Faber & Faber, 1963. After initially surveying the artist's life, this lavishly illustrated book devotes chapters to the various types of paintings he produced during his lengthy career. Also useful for its illustrated chronological catalog of more than one hundred extant Velázquez works.

Sérullaz, Maurice. *Velázquez.* New York: Harry N. Abrams, 1985. A volume from the Library of Great Painters series, this study includes an interpretative introductory essay and a chapter on Velázquez's drawings. Particularly useful are the forty-eight color plates with accompanying explanations and a chronological survey of the major events in Velázquez's life.

Stratton-Pruitt, Suzanne L. *The Cambridge Companion to Velázquez*. New York: Cambridge University Press, 2002. Collection of essays on various aspects of seventeenth century life and art, including a review of critical literature about Velázquez, becoming a seventeenth century artist, Velázquez and Italy, and the relation of painting, theater, and the visual arts at the Spanish court.

Wolf, Norbert. *Diego Velázquez, 1599-1660: The Face*

of Spain. Cologne, Germany: Taschen, 1999. Intersperses commentary by Wolf, an art historian, with numerous illustrations of Velázquez's work.

SEE ALSO: Baltasar Gracián y Morales; Bartolomé Esteban Murillo; Count-Duke of Olivares; Philip IV; Peter Paul Rubens; Francisco de Zurbarán.

RELATED ARTICLES in *Great Events from History: The Seventeenth Century, 1601-1700:* c. 1601-1620: Emergence of Baroque Art; c. 1601-1682: Spanish Golden Age; March 31, 1621-September 17, 1665: Reign of Philip IV.

JAN VERMEER
Dutch painter

Although most scholars firmly attribute fewer than thirty-five paintings to the hand of Vermeer, he is considered a master of seventeenth century Dutch painting and a major artist of the Western world.

BORN: October 31, 1632 (baptized); Delft, Holland, United Provinces (now in the Netherlands)

DIED: December, 1675; Delft

ALSO KNOWN AS: Jan van der Meer; Johannes Vermeer; Jan van Delft; Vermeer van Haarlem

AREA OF ACHIEVEMENT: Art

EARLY LIFE

The city of Delft was both a commercial center and a provincial place at the time Jan Vermeer (yahn vehr-MAYR) was born. The city's artistic traditions reflected the court of the House of Orange in The Hague, since the court had once been in Delft and city-court ties remained strong. Little is known of Vermeer's early life. His father was a silk weaver who was also an art dealer and a member of the Guild of St. Luke, to which artists, dealers, and artisans belonged. He owned a large house, known as the "Mechelen," which contained an inn in the market square of Delft.

The young Vermeer may not have inherited his father's role as innkeeper, but he apparently took over the art dealership in 1652 and continued to buy and trade paintings until his death. Since Vermeer painted very few works annually, he would have needed the dealership to support his wife and the eight children who survived infancy. In April, 1653, he married Catharina Bolnes and reared all of their children in her faith, al-

though Catholicism was not in favor in the United Provinces. A master in the Delft Guild of St. Luke, Vermeer was elected to its governing board and twice was elevated to the highest office as dean.

Few documents remain to testify to Vermeer's training as an artist. Certainly, he would have been influenced by the paintings that his father—and later he himself—bought and traded. He would have visited the studios of other artists in Delft. He may have studied with the Delft painter Leonaert Bramer. Bramer served on the guild's governing board and was a witness for Vermeer at the time of his betrothal to Catharina Bolnes. Bramer had traveled and knew the work of Michelangelo and his followers, the Haarlem Classicists, and Flemish artists. Vermeer's appreciation of these works is known by the type of paintings he owned and also by his own paintings. Vermeer was also influenced by one of Rembrandt's students, Carel Fabritius, who settled in Delft around 1650. Both Vermeer and Fabritius shared a common interest in perspective and optics, the close interaction of figure and environment, and light and shadow effects.

Vermeer's early work consisted of biblical and mythological subjects, such as *Christ in the House of Martha and Mary* (c. 1654-1655) and *Diana and Her Companions* (c. 1655-1656). *The Procuress* (1656), Vermeer's earliest dated painting, probably was intended to suggest an episode from the story of the prodigal son, a common theme in Dutch art. Indeed, many of his subjects in both early and mature works correspond to well-established iconographic tradition. His unique talents did not depend on the types of scenes he portrayed but rather the way in which he depicted them.

LIFE'S WORK

Vermeer is known as a poetic painter whose mature work consists almost entirely of quiet, intimate interior scenes that contain one or, at most, two persons. The viewer almost has a sense of intruding on someone's privacy when studying the carefully composed scene, for example, a picture of a young woman going about her daily tasks. The subject matter is restricted and the environment consists of the same or similar rooms. The entire scene is captured in such a luminous, pearl-like atmosphere that even the most commonplace task seems to take on extraordinary significance. A cool light envelops the forms, flowing smoothly over a soft patterned tablecloth, enhancing the crisp white linen of a woman's headdress, picking out three-dimensional highlights on a metallic bowl, and finally dissolving itself in the velvety darkness of a heavy curtain fold.

In many ways, Vermeer's approach to painting was not unlike that of other Dutch painters in the second half of the seventeenth century. They were interested in realism, in light and texture, and in an accurate depiction of three-dimensional space. Some were quite interested in their subjects' psychological response to the environment. These artists recorded in great detail the ordinary objects of daily life—the ever-popular maps and paintings with which they decorated their interior walls, the textures of clothing and curtains, the polished gleam of a chandelier, the cool black-and-white checkerboard patterning of floors, and the way sunlight spread across a room from an open window. Like them, Vermeer's apparent realism sometimes carries overtones of symbolism and reference with which viewers of the time could identify.

Earlier Flemish artists, such as Robert Campin and Jan van Eyck, had used extensive symbolism in their religious paintings. A taste for allegorical content continued in seventeenth century Dutch art. Sometimes the symbolism was obvious. In *The Allegory of Painting* (1666-1667), for example, Vermeer depicts an artist, seated on a stool and with his back to the viewer, painting his young model who wears a crown of laurel and holds both a trumpet and a heavy volume of Thucydides. She represents Clio, the muse of history, and Vermeer seems to suggest that she should be the artist's inspiration and source of fame, since history painting was considered the highest category of art. The large map prominently displayed on the back wall implies that the country's fame will be enhanced by the artist's work. Vermeer's clientele probably was limited to the more intellectual and refined person who would immediately have recognized and appreciated the implications of the painting.

Emblem books, popular throughout Europe in the sixteenth and seventeenth centuries, contained a moral that often was abstrusely presented. Thus, a letter or a musical instrument in a painting could often be identified with the emotion of love. In the same manner, Vermeer often included in his work a "painting within a painting"—a map or landscape or seascape on the wall that carried some reference to the main subject. Unlike many of his contemporaries, however, who delighted in lively narrative carrying a didactic theme, Vermeer seldom indulged in storytelling and his references are much more subtle. In Vermeer's famous *The Love Letter* (1669-1670), for example, in which the mistress has just received a letter given to her by a servant, the seascape on the back wall, showing a calm sea, was understood as an omen of good luck in love. This emotion is reinforced by the musical instrument held by the mistress.

Vermeer shared with others of his time a keen interest in the mirror and lens and optical devices, such as the camera obscura. By using this, an image could be focused on a surface opposite the light source. Thus, the artist could experiment with heightened contrasts of light and dark, enhancement of color, variations of perspective, and halation of highlights. It would appear from his paintings that Vermeer did not trace directly from the image but instead used the camera obscura as another means to explore expressive possibilities.

Realist that he was, Vermeer was nevertheless far from being merely an imitator of nature. More than his contemporaries, he is noted for his success in bringing a mood of intimacy to a scene, while at the same time setting up a psychological tension that compels the viewer to continued investigation of the canvas. Relatively recent theories of perspective fascinated Dutch artists of the time, but Vermeer utilized its expressive potential rather than a rigid formula. He also changed the scale of the same maps and wall paintings to fit a particular work. Sometimes his background is dark and sometimes quite light to fit a special artistic vision. No one is more successful than Vermeer in creating a psychological mood between subject and environment.

Scholars have often remarked on Vermeer's special quality of pearly light. It does not startle with sudden contrasts, as is seen in some of the great Italian masters. It is nevertheless equally dramatic in the subtle way in which it envelops and defines each form, sparkles in highlights, and creates an interlocking perfection within the composition. This quality of light is beautifully demonstrated in *View of Delft* (c. 1660-1661). Larger than most of Vermeer's works, the painting seems to draw the viewer into a crystal-clear atmosphere of a huge, cloud-filled sky and shimmering water against a background cluster of buildings. Although Vermeer adjusted perspective and scale in this scene, he followed a long Dutch tradition of topographic views of cities.

The Astronomer (1668) is one of the only two dated paintings by the artist and offers a good example of his mature style. It probably is a companion piece to *The Geographer*, and both show the rare male figure in Vermeer's work, engaged in scholarly pursuits. The facile handling of lights and darks and the typical air of preoccupation in the subject matter represent Vermeer at his best. The gloves and maps so carefully represented reflect the intense scientific interests of the period.

The exact chronology of Vermeer's works continues to cause lively debate among scholars, since only two paintings are dated. Generally, it can be ascertained that in the early works brushstrokes are not as free and expressive, planes of color are less sharply defined, there is a greater concentration on specific texture, and the focus of the composition is more centered. *The Guitar Player*, usually dated in the early 1670's, indicates Vermeer's greater freedom of technique in his later years.

SIGNIFICANCE

The works of Vermeer are extremely popular. Museums fortunate enough to hold works by this artist treasure them immensely, and it is rare for a Vermeer painting to come on the art market. Despite these facts, the artist's name was not widely known until the middle to late nineteenth century. Even though he was an official of St. Luke's Guild twice, little is known about commissioned work by Vermeer and no certain record of possible students he may have had has been located. The earliest principal source of information on seventeenth century Dutch artists was a book written by Arnold Houbraken, published around 1720. It only mentions Vermeer's name and birth date. Since the number of Vermeer paintings is so small and probably those who owned them were a select and sophisticated group of collectors, very little information about the artist and his contributions was widely disseminated.

In 1866, the French critic Théophile Thoré (the pseudonym of W. Bürger) wrote a series of articles praising Vermeer's work with much enthusiasm. Within a short while, Vermeer's popularity was such that his name was often mentioned in art-historical writing and many of his works that had heretofore been attributed to more fash-

ionable artists were returned to him. His popularity also presented a fertile field for forgers; the famous trial, in 1945, of Hans van Meegeren on charges of forging Vermeer's work spotlighted the avid interest of both scholars and the public in this artist.

The Impressionists of the late nineteenth century were greatly affected by Vermeer's sensitivity to his subject and his handling of light and color. Several of the French Impressionists, including Pierre-Auguste Renoir, considered Vermeer one of the greatest artists. There is little doubt that art historians will continue to probe the enigma that is Vermeer. It is even more certain that an increasing number of art lovers will discover and respond favorably to the works of the great master of Delft.

—*Mary Sweeney Ellett*

FURTHER READING

Alpers, Svetlana. *The Art of Describing: Dutch Art in the Seventeenth Century.* Chicago: University of Chicago Press, 1983. Essential reading for all students of seventeenth century Dutch art. Alpers relates Dutch painting to the primacy of visual representation, which confirmed seeing and representing over reading and interpretation as the means for a new knowledge of the world. Includes an excellent chapter on the works of Rembrandt and Vermeer.

Huerta, Robert D. *Giants of Delft: Johannes Vermeer and the Natural Philosophers, the Parallel Search for Knowledge During the Age of Discovery.* Lewisburg, Pa.: Bucknell University Press, 2003. An examination of the thirst for scientific and artistic knowledge during the Dutch golden age among Vermeer and his contemporaries, including scientist Antoni van Leeuwenhoek. Describes how perception was influenced by the microscope and other discoveries in the science of optics. Includes illustrations, a bibliography, and an index.

Koningsberger, Hans. *The World of Vermeer, 1632-1675.* Rev. ed. New York: Time-Life Books, 1973. An excellent overview of Vermeer within the context of his time, especially useful as an introduction to the artist. Discusses works of earlier Dutch artists who pioneered in developing the Dutch golden age in art. Artistic tastes, influences of the time, and the contemporary art market are addressed in clear terms. Includes color plates.

Liedtke, Walter, Michael C. Plomp, and Axel Rüger. *Vermeer and the Delft School.* New York: Metropolitan Museum of Art, 2001. A catalog from a highly acclaimed exhibition presented in 2001 at New York's

Metropolitan Museum of Art and London's National Gallery. Contains reproductions of sixteen Vermeer canvases accompanied by analyses of these works. Discusses the artistic life in Delft from 1200 to 1700, describing the work of Vermeer and other area artists and assessing these artists' influence on Dutch culture.

Slatkes, Leonard J. *Vermeer and His Contemporaries.* New York: Abbeville Press, 1981. Slatkes, a recognized scholar in seventeenth century Dutch art, provides solid discussion to accompany the numerous full-color reproductions. Describes many artists of the 1650's and 1660's who were influenced by Vermeer. Includes a comprehensive summary of iconography and Dutch art in general. Useful for the undergraduate and the general reader.

Steadman, Philip. *Vermeer's Camera: Uncovering the Truth Behind the Masterpieces.* New York: Oxford University Press, 2001. Some art historians have speculated that Vermeer used an optical devise to help him capture intricate and precise details in his paintings. In an effort to resolve this question, Steadman offers recent evidence to prove that Vermeer used a camera obscura. Steadman provides detailed descriptions of Vermeer's artistic techniques and of the studio in which he created his paintings.

Vermeer, Johannes. *The Paintings: Complete Edition.* Introduction, catalog, and attribution by Ludwig Gold-scheider. 2d ed. London: Phaidon Press, 1967. The notes to the plates are outstanding, referring to important iconological interpretations and suppositions on Vermeer's use of optical means to enhance reality. Summarizes almost all significant earlier publications.

Wheelock, Arthur K., Jr. *Jan Vermeer.* New York: Abrams, 1988. Full-page color reproductions of Vermeer's paintings enhance this book greatly. Each full-page plate has a facing page of interpretative text. An introductory section places Vermeer within the context of his time.

Wolf, Bryan Jay. *Vermeer and the Invention of Seeing.* Chicago: University of Chicago Press, 2001. Examines Vermeer's work in light of newly discovered and employed methods of observeration, including the camera obscura. Also explores Dutch genre painting. Includes illustrations, some in color, a bibliography, and an index.

SEE ALSO: Frans Hals; Antoni van Leeuwenhoek; Rembrandt; Peter Paul Rubens; Sir Anthony van Dyck.

RELATED ARTICLES in *Great Events from History: The Seventeenth Century, 1601-1700:* c. 1601-1620: Emergence of Baroque Art; Mid-17th century: Dutch School of Painting Flourishes; 1660's-1700: First Microscopic Observations; 1672-1684: Leeuwenhoek Discovers Microscopic Life.

ANTÓNIO VIEIRA
Portuguese missionary, diplomat, and writer

The Jesuit Vieira opposed his nation's enslavement of the Brazilian Indians but condoned enslaving Africans, so long as they were treated well and were encouraged to become Christians. His twelve-volume compilation of his sermons represents some of the finest literature and oratory of the Portuguese baroque, but his writings also caused him to be censured by the Portuguese Inquisition.

BORN: February 6, 1608; Lisbon, Portugal
DIED: July 18, 1697; Salvador, Brazil
AREAS OF ACHIEVEMENT: Government and politics, literature, religion and theology

EARLY LIFE
António Vieira (ahn-TAWN-yew VYAY-ee-ruh) was born in Lisbon at a time when Portugal and Spain shared the same monarch, King Philip III of Spain (also known as Philip II of Portugal). Although a Spanish king and Spanish laws ruled the Portuguese world, however, much of the everyday work in the national and colonial bureaucracies continued to be carried out by Portuguese functionaries. Vieira's father was one such official, sent from Lisbon to occupy an administrative post in Brazil in 1614. At the age of six, then, António left Portugal with his family and sailed to the Brazilian capital city of Salvador.

Against his parents' wishes, Vieira decided when still an adolescent to follow a religious vocation: He entered the Jesuit college in Bahia when he was fifteen years old. While he was preparing for the priesthood, a Dutch fleet attacked Salvador in 1624, hoping to wrest the rich sugar lands of Brazil from Spanish and Portuguese control.

The fleet was repulsed the following year. (The Dutch would return in 1630, however, to seize the captaincy of Pernambuco, to the north of Bahia, where they would remain until 1654.) The Brazilian military struggle between the Portuguese and the Dutch became early fodder for Vieira's extraordinary writing skills, when, in 1626, the 18-year-old initiate was chosen by his superiors to write the annual letter from the Jesuits in Brazil to their superiors in Rome.

In the 1630's, Vieira established a reputation as a passionate and compelling preacher. He exercised this talent not only in the churches frequented by the Portuguese, but also in missions among the Brazilian Indians of Bahia and in services attended by African slaves. The earliest of the sermons he later published was preached to the slave members of a black brotherhood whose patron was Our Lady of the Rosary. Throughout his life, Vieira remained committed to the missionary charge to evangelize all people, including Europeans, Brazilian Indians, and Africans. Because he believed that all Christians were equal before God, he urged Portuguese masters not to mistreat their African slaves, and although he never condemned the practice of enslaving Africans, he warned masters on several occasions that God would punish them for abuses against their slaves.

LIFE'S WORK

When the Braganza Dynasty came to power in Portugal in 1640, ending sixty years of rule by Spain, Vieira was sent to Lisbon to assure King John IV that he had the support of his Brazilian subjects. Vieira quickly became a favorite of the new king and a frequent preacher in the royal chapel. He was also chosen to conduct diplomatic missions for the king, and in that capacity he traveled throughout Europe. Vieira's efforts to negotiate a marriage for the Portuguese prince that would bring Portugal an alliance with France or Spain failed. He was more successful, though, in gaining the financial backing of Portuguese New Christians (Jews who had converted to Christianity) to establish a trading company that would strengthen the Brazilian sugar trade and provide the revenue necessary to expel the Dutch from Pernambuco.

Vieira reciprocated King John's admiration. He became convinced that God had great things planned for the new Portuguese king; in fact, he believed John would usher in the Millennium, the one thousand years of peace prophesied in Scriptures. Even when John died in 1656 without accomplishing this mission, Vieira did not lose hope. Instead, he claimed that God would miraculously raise up the king to unite and rule the world in peace.

In the 1650's, Vieira was appointed head of the Jesuit mission to convert the Indians of Maranhão, in Brazil's Amazon region. Many of the Portuguese settlers in the New World saw the Indians as nothing more than a source of slave labor, and they tenaciously resisted the efforts of missionaries who tried to keep them from enslaving the indigenous Americans. Vieira became a staunch ally of the Indians, boldly preaching against the avarice and sin of the settlers who continued to enslave them. He successfully petitioned the king to grant the Jesuits custody of the Amazonian Indians. His efforts to protect the roughly 200,000 Indians evangelized by the Jesuits in Maranhão so angered the Portuguese settlers that they drove all members of the Society of Jesus from the region. Upon his return to Europe in 1661, with his patron and protector John IV now dead, Vieira came under attack by the Portuguese Inquisition.

In his diplomatic missions during the 1640's, Vieira had developed friendships with Jews and New Christians in Amsterdam. Many of them had fled Portugal, fearing the persecution of the Inquisition. He lobbied the king to lift restrictions on New Christians, and to seek their help in funding a company that would make Brazil more profitable for the Portuguese. These sympathies toward New Christians probably helped to bring Vieira under the scrutiny of the Inquisition. The official reason for Vieira's trial by the Inquisition, however, had to do with his prophetic writings. While in Maranhão, he had begun writing a *History of the Future*, in which he proclaimed that King John would be resurrected and, with the support of the people who would convert in large numbers to Christianity, would usher in the Fifth Reign, God's kingdom of peace on earth. After a series of thirty interrogations, Vieira was found guilty of ideas that bordered on heresy.

In 1669, Vieira decided to leave Lisbon and travel to Rome, where he hoped to convince the pope to grant him protection against future attacks by the Portuguese Inquisition. There he became a favorite of Queen Christina of Sweden, who had abdicated her throne and moved to Rome when she converted from Protestantism to Catholicism. Although Cristina urged him to become her private confessor and remain in Rome, Vieira returned to Portugal and from there sailed back to Brazil in 1681. He spent the remaining sixteen years of his very long life in Bahia, organizing his sermons for publication and continuing to minister to Brazilians of a variety of ethnic and social class backgrounds.

SIGNIFICANCE

For centuries, the sermons of Vieira served as models of Portuguese baroque rhetoric. His work interested primarily theologians and students of Portuguese literature. More recently, however, Vieira has come to the attention of historians for his strong defense of Brazilian Indians. He saw in Portugal's global missionary enterprise, which included efforts to evangelize the indigenous people of the New World, a clear sign of the special mission God had for his countrymen. This bolstered his belief that a Portuguese king would usher in the Millennium. He also asserted that African slaves in Brazil who accepted Christianity were full members of the Christian community, equal in every way to their masters. Moreover, in an age when Jews and New Christians were being persecuted and even forced to leave Portugal, Vieira spoke out in favor of including them in national life. Thus, one of the greatest Portuguese orators of his time has come to symbolize the quest for equality and toleration in the pre-Enlightenment world.

—Joan E. Meznar

FURTHER READING

Alden, Dauril. "Some Reflections on António Vieira: Seventeenth-Century Troubleshooter and Troublemaker." *Luso-Brazilian Review* 40, no. 1 (Summer, 2003): 7-16. An excellent overview of Vieira's political contributions in Brazil and in Europe.

Boxer, Charles R. *A Great Luso-Brazilian Figure: Padre António Vieira, S.J., 1608-1697.* London: The Hispanic & Luso-Brazilian Councils, 1957. Short account, first delivered as a lecture, of the life of António Vieira.

Cohen, Thomas M. *The Fire of Tongues: António Vieira and the Missionary Church in Brazil and Portugal.* Stanford, Calif.: Stanford University Press, 1998. Focuses on the centrality of the missionary experience for understanding Vieira's vision of Portugal's unique role in history.

Jordán, María V. "The Empire of the Future and the Chosen People: Father António Vieira and the Prophetic Tradition in the Hispanic World." *Luso-Brazilian Review* 40, no. 1 (Summer, 2003): 67-78. Provides good background on the millenarian tradition in late medieval Europe and thus situates Vieira's prophetic writings in their broader historical context.

Schwartz, Stuart B. "The Contexts of Vieira's Toleration of Jews and New Christians." *Luso-Brazilian Review* 40, no. 1 (Summer, 2003): 33-44. Demonstrates how others in the seventeenth century shared Vieira's more tolerant views of New Christians. Thus, the author argues that Vieira was not unique; he was of his times.

Vieira, António. *António Vieira's Sermon Against the Dutch Arms.* New York: Peter Lang, 1996. One of the few of Vieira's sermons translated into English, it provides an excellent example of both his oratorical skills and his conviction that God must take the side of Portuguese Catholics against Dutch Protestants.

SEE ALSO: Christina; John IV; Philip III.

RELATED ARTICLES in *Great Events from History: The Seventeenth Century, 1601-1700:* 1619-c. 1700: The Middle Passage to American Slavery; 1630's-1694: Slaves Resist Europeans at Palmares; 1630-1660's: Dutch Wars in Brazil; June-August, 1640: *Bandeirantes* Expel the Jesuits; 1654: Portugal Retakes Control of Brazil; January, 1665: Shabbetai Tzevi's Messianic Movement Begins; Beginning 1680's: Guerra dos Bárbaros.

SAINT VINCENT DE PAUL
French religious leader and social reformer

Most renowned for his charitable and educational work, Saint Vincent de Paul founded the Congregation of the Mission, the Confraternities of Charity, and, with Saint Louise de Marillac, the Daughters of Charity. He also helped in the revival of French Catholicism, and the Roman Catholic Church has named him the universal patron of its charitable institutions.

BORN: April 24, 1581; Pouy (now Saint-Vincent-de-Paul), France
DIED: September 27, 1660; Paris, France
AREAS OF ACHIEVEMENT: Education, religion and theology, social reform

EARLY LIFE

Saint Vincent de Paul was born the third of six children in a peasant family and spent his childhood in poverty. His education, financed through the sacrifices of his parents and his own work as a teacher, included studies in the humanities under Franciscan teachers at Dax, France, from 1595 to 1597, and in theology at the University of Toulouse, where he earned a baccalaureate degree in 1604. He was ordained a Roman Catholic priest in 1600. There are unconfirmed stories about his having been captured by Barbary pirates at sea in 1605 and enslaved in Tunis for two years before escaping by ship in 1607.

From 1607 to 1608, Vincent was at Avignon and Rome, and at this time his aspirations were not particularly saintly: He hoped to obtain an ecclesiastical benefice that would enable him to retire to his home and support his mother. While in Rome, he attracted the attention of Pope Paul V, who sent him on a mission to the French court of Henry IV. Arriving in Paris in 1608, Vincent met Pierre de Bérulle, an eminent and otherworldly priest who became Vincent's confessor and spiritual guide and who influenced him profoundly. Between 1609 and 1620, Vincent gradually reoriented his life goals from the material to the spiritual. Beginning in 1610, he served as almoner to Queen Marguerite of Valois, the former wife of Henry IV, and in 1612 he became pastor of the parish of Clichy, near Paris. He served in this position until 1626, working, according to what he regarded as his special vocation, among the poor peasantry of the countryside.

During this period, Vincent also served as chaplain (from 1613 to around 1625) to the family of Philippe-Emmanuel de Gondi, general of the French galleys. This position afforded Vincent the opportunity to work among the peasants on the Gondi estates, to begin organizing the charitable efforts of women of means, and to alleviate the sufferings of galley slaves. He directed the charitable works of Madam Gondi, who persuaded him to deliver, on January 25, 1617, the sermon on general confession that he considered the first sermon of his mission. For five months in 1617, Vincent ran the parish of Chatillon-les-Dombes near Lyons, where he found his first Confraternity of Charity, an organization of pious laywomen who ministered to the sick and the poor. He returned to the Gondi estates late in 1617 with plans to evangelize all of their lands, preaching many missions and organizing charitable confraternities. He also worked to bring spiritual and physical comfort to convicts condemned to forced labor on galleys, and his work was so successful that King Louis XIII made him royal chaplain of the galleys, in charge of all other fleet chaplains, on February 8, 1619.

Vincent was frail in physique; he has been described as sunny, smiling, and humble in facial expression; accounts of his personality reveal patience, kindness, prudence, energy, and courage. His friend and first biographer, Louis Abelly, reports that Vincent was deeply devoted to the divine presence and that each time he heard a clock strike he would make the sign of the cross and renew his awareness of God's presence.

LIFE'S WORK

Vincent's success on the Gondi territories led to his founding, on April 17, 1625, of the Congregation of the Mission (also known as Vincentians and Lazarists), with the help of a gift of forty-five thousand livres from the Gondi family. The purpose of the congregation was to preach missions to poor peasants. It was approved by the archbishop of Paris in April, 1626, given legal existence by the king of France in May, 1627, and finally approved by the Holy See in Rome in 1633. On January 8, 1632, Vincent took over the priory of Saint-Lazare in Paris, and it was there that the congregation's activities were centered until the time of the French Revolution. From Saint-Lazare, 550 missions to the rural poor were organized before Vincent died in 1660. The congregation grew in size and influence; in 1642, a permanent house was opened in Rome, and soon thereafter the pope ordered that all those to be ordained in Rome must make a retreat with the Vincentians.

While he pursued his work among the poor, Vincent also began to make significant contributions as a clerical reformer. Realizing that such reform was necessary for the revitalization of religious life in France, he began giving ten-day retreats in Beauvais in 1626 for men about to be ordained into the priesthood.

In 1633, Vincent worked with Louise de Marillac, whom he had met in 1625, to found the religious congregation of the Daughters of Charity. It was an innovative undertaking: The Daughters of Charity was the first noncloistered religious institute of women devoted to active charitable works. It developed from the Confraternities of Charity, which Vincent had established in Paris and other towns. Vincent composed a rule of life for the daughters, gave them conferences, and governed as superior general of their order. At first, they nursed the poor at home but went on quickly to teach poor children, care for foundlings, and establish hospitals.

Vincent's work as a clerical reformer led him into the field of formal education. In 1636, at Bons-Enfants, he established a seminary for young boys. In 1642, he expanded it to include the first of eighteen seminaries of ordinands conducted by the Vincentians during his lifetime.

Beginning in the late 1630's, Vincent's work carried him more and more into high official circles of the French government. At the request of King Louis XIII, he sent fifteen priests to serve as chaplains with the French army in 1636 and drew up a rule of life and procedures for them. He organized a mission that was preached at court in 1638 and resulted in the formation of a Confraternity of Charity, composed of ladies of the court. He made appeals for peace in war-stricken Lorraine and organized charitable relief there and in other provinces during the Wars of Religion. In 1643, Vincent was called to assist at the bedside of Louis XIII, who was dying. After the king's death, Queen Anne asked Vincent to become her confessor. He also became a member of the Council of Conscience, the body in charge of ecclesiastical matters in France. The council was headed by Cardinal Jules Mazarin, the powerful chief minister who succeeded Cardinal de Richelieu during the regency of Queen Anne. Mazarin, an aggressive and worldly politician, opposed and thwarted many of Vincent's efforts and ultimately forced him to quit the council in 1653.

One of Vincent's constant concerns during these years was the morals both of the members of the French court and of the public in general. He helped to secure the suppression of indecent plays and books, worked to curb licentious behavior during the Carnival and other festivals, and promoted bans on blasphemy and dueling. He warned the queen against the indecency of the comedies being produced at court.

As a member of the council, Vincent worked, not always successfully, to ensure that only the best candidates would be chosen for the bishopric, and he opposed appointments motivated by nepotism or hopes for political gain. Here again he ran into difficulties with Mazarin; nevertheless, his practical and spiritual guidance was frequently sought by new bishops. It was also sought by reformers within the monastic orders, and Vincent was active in promoting reforms among the Benedictines, Augustinians, and Dominicans.

Saint Vincent de Paul. (Hulton Archive/Getty Images)

An orthodox believer, Vincent actively opposed teachings that ran counter to traditional Roman Catholic dogma. He waged a lengthy struggle against Jansenism, a heterodox reform movement that asserted that human nature is essentially evil and that only a small number of humans are predestined to obtain grace and win eternal salvation. He also worked to prevent Jansenist doctrine from being taught at the Sorbonne and rallied the bishops of France to petition the pope to condemn Jansenist errors. Pope Innocent X did so in 1655, as did his successor, Pope Alexander VII, in 1657. Vincent completed writing the rules of his congregation in 1658, falling ill that same year. He died peacefully, his mental faculties intact, on September 27, 1660.

SIGNIFICANCE

Vincent's contemporaries regarded him as a saint; the Roman Catholic Church formally beatified him in 1729 and later canonized him on June 13, 1737, proclaiming July 19 as his feast day in the liturgical calendar. His missionary, educational, and charitable works were recognized throughout France and on the Continent during his lifetime, and these works continued to bear fruit after his death. He was one of the most influential social workers in world history; Vincent's own organizations have survived into the twentieth century.

Through his life and works, Vincent has come to epitomize Christian social action for succeeding generations. His example inspired Frédéric Ozanam, a French historian, lawyer, and scholar, to found the Society of Saint Vincent de Paul in the 1830's. This celebrated charitable organization had about two thousand centers in the twenty-nine countries by the time of Ozanam's death in 1853 and continues to serve the poor throughout the world. In 1885, Pope Leo XIII declared Saint Vincent de Paul the universal Patron of Charity. He has been honored with the titles of "Father of the Poor" and "The Inspiration of the Clergy."

—*Eileen Tess Tyler*

FURTHER READING

Coste, Pierre. *The Life and Works of Saint Vincent de Paul*. Translated by Joseph Leonard. 3 vols. Westminster, Md.: Newman Press, 1952. This 1932 study, which received the French Academy's prestigious Grand Prix Gobert, is the standard biography of Vincent. Complete, methodical, and scholarly, it offers the fullest available account of Vincent's life and achievements.

Dodin, André. *Vincent de Paul and Charity: A Con-temporary Portrait of His Life and Apostolic Spirituality*. Translated by Jean Marie Smith and Dennis Saunders, edited by Hugh O'Donnell and Marjorie Gale Hornstein. New Rochelle, N.Y.: New City Press, 1993. Dodin's book is divided into three sections: information about Vincent's life, an analysis of his spirituality, and excerpts from his writings. Includes sixteen pages of photographs and an annotated bibliography.

Kovacs, Arpad F., ed. *St. Vincent de Paul*. Jamaica, N.Y.: St. John's University Press, 1961. Seven essays addressing Vincent's background, life, and influence. They cover the spiritual climate of his century, the social work of Vincent, his relationship to Jansenism, and other topics.

Marynard, Abbé. *Virtues and Spiritual Doctrine of Saint Vincent de Paul*. Revised by Carlton A. Princeville. St. Louis, Mo.: Vincentian Foreign Mission Press, 1961. Draws from the conferences, correspondence, and personal lives of Vincent and Louise de Marillac to present their ideas about Christian virtues and doctrine. The majority of this volume is devoted to Vincent.

Pujo, Bernard. *Vincent de Paul, Trailblazer*. Translated by Gertrud Graubart Champe. Notre Dame, Ind.: University of Notre Dame Press, 2003. In this English translation of his French biography, Pujo describes how Vincent was able to attain spiritual goals within the secular world of political, economic, and religious upheaval.

Purcell, Mary. *The World of Monsieur Vincent*. New York: Charles Scribner's Sons, 1963. Reprint. Chicago: Loyola University Press, 1989. A sensible, clear, and lively narrative of Vincent's life and times. Purcell focuses on Vincent's social and historical milieus, drawing vivid portraits of persons and places important in his life. An excellent introduction for the general reader.

Saint Vincent de Paul: A Tercentenary Commemoration of His Death, 1600-1960. Jamaica, N.Y.: St. John's University Press, 1960. Includes twelve Saint Vincent de Paul Annual Lectures delivered at St. John's University between 1948 and 1959. The lectures address Vincent's personality, spiritual and social views, educational and charitable endeavors, relations with other social reformers and political figures, and the process of his canonization to sainthood.

Vincent de Paul, Saint. *The Conferences of St. Vincent de Paul to the Sisters of Charity*. Edited and translated by Joseph Leonard. 4 vols. London: Burns, Oates and

Washbourne, 1938. Texts of 120 conferences delivered by Vincent to the Daughters of Charity between 1634 and 1660. The conferences address the practical and spiritual lives of the sisters. Leonard includes an introduction, explanatory narrative, and footnotes.

_____. *Letters of St. Vincent de Paul*. Edited and translated by Joseph Leonard. London: Burns, Oates and Washbourne, 1937. Vincent reportedly wrote about thirty thousand letters, the majority of which were lost over the centuries. The nearly 250 letters in this book, written between 1607 and 1659, cover all aspects of Vincent's life and work. Includes a biographical introduction by Henri Bremond, as well as copious notes, an index, and illustrations.

SEE ALSO: Alexander VII; Cornelius Otto Jansen; Paul V.
RELATED ARTICLE in *Great Events from History: The Seventeenth Century, 1601-1700:* 1638-1669: Spread of Jansenism.

ALBRECHT WENZEL VON WALLENSTEIN
Bohemian military leader

A master of recruiting and logistics, Wallenstein raised and commanded the armies that saved the Catholic Habsburgs from losing the Thirty Years' War to their Protestant opponents. He was able to amass great wealth and power and may even have aspired to an independent crown of his own.

BORN: September 24, 1583; Heřmanice, Bohemia (now in the Czech Republic)

DIED: February 25, 1634; Eger, Bohemia (now in the Czech Republic)

ALSO KNOWN AS: Albrecht Wenzel Eusebius von Wallenstein (full name)

AREAS OF ACHIEVEMENT: Military, warfare and conquest, government and politics

EARLY LIFE

The son of Wilhelm Wallenstein and his wife, Margarethe, Albrecht Wenzel von Wallenstein (VAHL-ehn-shtin) was one of seven children. His mother died when he was not quite ten years old, and his father died within two years of her death. Albrecht was sent to live with his mother's brother-in-law, Heinrich Slawata von Chlum. The Wallenstein family, although not wealthy, was fairly well connected among the Bohemian aristocracy. While he was later to convert and become an outstanding commander of the Catholic forces, Wallenstein was reared as a Protestant.

At age fifteen, Albrecht went to the Lutheran school at Goldberg, Silesia, remained there for two years, and then attended the academy at Altdorf, near Nuremberg. It was a stay of only six months, Wallenstein being noted primarily for his violent behavior: The records indicate a number of brawls in which he was involved, and he spent at least some time in the student prison at the academy.

When Wallenstein left Nuremberg, he traveled through Europe, spending the greatest amount of time at Padua, where he studied under the unusual combination of Jesuits and astrologers. By 1606, he had converted to Roman Catholicism and would remain a dutiful son of the Church for the rest of his life. At the same time, however, he developed a firm belief in astrology, especially as it controlled his destiny. He believed his life to be under the influence of Saturn, which promised great accomplishments. In 1607, he had his horoscope cast by the famed astronomer Johannes Kepler and often referred to the predictions that had been fulfilled in later years.

Holding such contradictory beliefs was only one facet of Wallenstein's enigmatic personality.

In 1604, Wallenstein embarked on his first military campaign, serving as an ensign, then a captain, with the artillery of the Holy Roman Empire in a campaign in what is now Romania. In command was Johan Tserclaes, count of Tilly; along with Wallenstein, Tilly would later be one of the two outstanding imperial generals of the Thirty Years' War (1618-1648).

Wallenstein married in 1609. His wife, Lucretia von Landek, was a much older and very wealthy widow. According to some unconfirmed but often-repeated stories, Wallenstein nearly died from a love potion given him by his new wife, but he survived. Lucretia died on March 23, 1614, leaving her vast wealth, including many Moravian estates, to Wallenstein.

Wallenstein's appearance aptly fits the description "saturnine," for he was somber, even austere, with a long face, sallow complexion, and dark eyes and hair. He wore the neatly trimmed beard characteristic of the period. He had irregular features and high cheekbones, and he rarely displayed his emotions; when he did, he could break into sudden, deadly fury. Throughout his life, Wallenstein inspired a number of emotions, but fear, respect, and envy were inspired more often than love or affection.

LIFE'S WORK

In May, 1618, the Defenestration of Prague marked the beginning of the Thirty Years' War. Seldom has so trivial, even ludicrous, an incident been the spark for such a long and destructive conflict. The true causes for the war were more profound than Bohemian Protestant rebels throwing Catholic imperial councillors out a window. Indeed, there was a mesh of religion (Protestant Reformation against Catholic Counter-Reformation), politics (the various smaller German states against the Holy Roman Empire), and dynastic struggle (the Habsburgs of Spain and Austria against most of Europe).

The war was Wallenstein's springboard to greatness. When the Bohemian Protestants rose in revolt against the Habsburg Emperor Matthias, Wallenstein moved swiftly, removing the contents of the Moravian treasury to the safety of imperial coffers in Vienna. Welcomed into imperial service, Wallenstein began well: At the Battle of Tein, in southern Bohemia, he smashed through the lines of a rebel army that was moving to threaten Vienna. Although he was often successful in battle, it was as an organizer and recruiter that Wallenstein proved most capable and effective.

Although his Moravian estates had been seized in the uprising, Wallenstein still retained considerable wealth, and he freely loaned this to the emperor and to his successor, Ferdinand II, who was elected to the throne in 1619. On June 9, 1623, Wallenstein remarried, taking Isabella Katharina von Harrach as his bride. Isabella came from one of the wealthiest and most influential families of the empire; Emperor Ferdinand attended the wedding, and the match further swelled Wallenstein's treasury. Much of this, too, he loaned to Ferdinand.

As the imperial forces regained Bohemia and Moravia, Ferdinand repaid his debts by granting Wallenstein lands that had been confiscated from his rebellious subjects. The Wallenstein domains steadily increased, and in 1624 the emperor created him duke of Friedland; eventually the duchy included hundreds of thousands of acres in what is modern northern Czechoslovakia. From Friedland, Wallenstein drew grain, cattle, cloth, weapons, and other supplies needed by the imperial army. These necessities returned a flow of riches to Friedland, which remained prosperous and at peace in the midst of war.

Wallenstein became increasingly important in the imperial army, rising in 1623 to the position of "Major over all infantry," but he remained basically an organizer and staff officer. In 1624, Wallenstein made a dramatic offer: He would provide an army of fifty thousand men, and put this force into the field at no cost to the emperor. Asked how the troops could be supplied and maintained, Wallenstein gave the grim but truthful answer, "War must feed war." The troops were raised, and in 1625 Wallenstein was named imperial commander. Moving northward, he swept a powerful Danish army from Silesia, and rolled it back to the Baltic Sea. In honor of Wallenstein's victories, the emperor granted him the duchies of Mecklenburg and Pomerania on the Baltic coast. This added to the discontent and mistrust that was already felt for Wallenstein among court circles in Vienna.

In 1629, peace came briefly to Europe, and Ferdinand maneuvered Wallenstein into resigning his command. Apparently the emperor had doubts about his powerful subject as well. In July, 1630, a Swedish army under King Gustavus II Adolphus landed on the German coast and marched southward; volunteers soon swelled its ranks to forty thousand troops. Still, Ferdinand kept Wallenstein in retirement, hoping to avoid a cause for disunity in the empire, for many of the nobility and courtiers disliked Wallenstein. Wallenstein used this time well, improving and enlarging Friedland; his duchy seems to have been the sole passion of his life. In 1632, Ferdinand, hard pressed by Swedish victories, was forced to recall Wallenstein to command. He granted Wallenstein terms that made him more a viceroy than a general: Wallenstein was given virtual independence in the territories he reconquered, with no political or religious interference in his operations. Wallenstein recognized that renewed religious persecutions would only prolong the war and increase its destruction.

Wallenstein and Gustavus sparred through the spring and summer of 1632, and the imperial general gradually forced the Swedish king northward and out of Bavaria. On November 16, 1632, the two met at the Battle of Lützen. Only the death of Gustavus at the head of his troops and the timely arrival of imperial reinforcements

Albrecht Wenzel von Wallenstein. (Library of Congress)

saved Wallenstein from defeat. Although left in possession of the field, the Swedish army was forced to retreat, and the most dangerous threat to the imperial cause had been repulsed.

In the fall of 1633, Wallenstein began secret negotiations with members of the Protestant Party. His motives in these talks are unclear: He might have aspired to the crown of Bohemia, or perhaps he sought a general peace for Europe. Emperor Ferdinand assumed the worst, and officers were sent to arrest Wallenstein; if he resisted, force was to be used. Wallenstein attempted to flee but was caught at the fortress of Eger, in Bohemia. There, on the night of February 25, 1634, he was killed by a blow from a halberd. His body was removed in a blood-soaked rug.

SIGNIFICANCE

As duke of Friedland, Wallenstein issued his own coinage, and the motto he chose for it was Invita Invida: "I invite envy." Seldom have fewer words been more aptly chosen, for Wallenstein's career excited jealousy and fear among his contemporaries, even those he served. His aims and motives were a mystery to his time and have remained so long after his death. Was he merely a grasping opportunist intent upon personal aggrandizement, or did he have some far-reaching goal for all Europe?

On one hand, Wallenstein seized every opportunity to enlarge his lands, increase his wealth, and consolidate his power. His position rested upon two pillars: one, the army, nominally that of the emperor but raised, equipped, and led by Wallenstein; the second, his duchy of Friedland. Add to this Wallenstein's thirst for land and titles, and it would seem that his vision was limited strictly to personal gain.

On the other hand, Wallenstein's policies seem to have been calculated to increase the power of the emperor and the empire by reuniting central Europe as a religiously tolerant state no longer divided by sectarian conflict. His actions in his own territories and in those conquered by his armies show a man less interested in religious disputes than in productive farms and prosperous merchants. Some historians, notably C. V. Wedgwood, contend that he aimed at a realignment of the Holy Roman Empire into one centered on Bohemia, the valley of the Elbe River, and the Baltic Sea—a sort of Slavic-Germanic empire. In another theory, Francis Watson, Wallenstein's premier English-writing biographer, believes that Wallenstein's long-range goal was the expulsion of the Turks from Europe.

As a soldier, he was a master of raising, organizing, and supplying an army, but he was less skilled at commanding it in battle. Although successful in his campaigns, Wallenstein inspired no new tactics; his strategy was traditional, if skillfully implemented. His major contribution to warfare was to demonstrate that an enormous force could be maintained in the field for prolonged periods of time.

Wallenstein's undoubted accomplishments are considerable: From 1625 to 1629, he regained northern Germany for the empire and gave the Catholic Church the opportunity to retrieve lands that had been lost to the Protestants. Forced into retirement, he returned to defeat the formidable invasion by Gustavus II Adolphus and restore imperial power in central Europe. In the meantime, he established a secure and prosperous duchy in the midst of a Europe torn by war. This is the work of one with considerable powers and abilities—perhaps even one whose destiny was secured by the stars.

—*Michael Witkoski*

FURTHER READING

Bonney, Richard. *The Thirty Years' War, 1618-1648.* Essential Histories 29. Oxford, England: Osprey, 2002. A short but detailed and insightful account of the reasons for the conflict and a description of the battles.

Guthrie, William P. *Battles of the Thirty Years' War: From White Mountain to Nordlingen, 1618-1635.* Contributions in Military Studies 213. Westport, Conn.: Greenwood Press, 2003. This first of two books describes the battles fought during Wallenstein's lifetime.

Liddel Hart, B. H. "Wallenstein-The Enigma of History." In *Great Captains Unveiled.* Reprint. New York: De Capo Press, 1996. The outstanding and individual British military thinker, historian, and soldier provides his own unique insight into Wallenstein's career and accomplishments. Provides an excellent thumbnail biography as well.

Mann, Golo. *Wallenstein: His Life Narrated.* Translated by Charles Kessler. New York: Holt, Rinehart and Winston, 1976. A thorough, massive, and imaginative rendering of Wallenstein's life and career. An excellent, sometimes poetic, study of Wallenstein's psychology as well as his actions.

Parker, Geoffrey, ed. *The Thirty Years' War.* 2d rev. ed. New York: Routledge, 1997. Several historians collaborated to provide this account of the war. It is the best single work for providing the reader with an overview of the conflict and with pertinent bibliographical information.

Watson, Francis. *Wallenstein: Soldier Under Saturn.* New York: D. Appleton-Century, 1938. An essential English-language biography of Wallenstein, this work provides considerable background on the times and milieu of its subject. A comprehensive study, written in an engaging style.

Wedgwood, C. V. *The Thirty Years' War.* New Haven, Conn.: Yale University Press, 1949. Reprint. New York: Methuen, 1981. This classic work remains the best single-volume introduction to the Thirty Years' War. It contains much material on Wallenstein and

his part in the struggle and is very helpful for understanding the complex military and political events of the period.

SEE ALSO: Ferdinand II; Frederick William, the Great Elector; Gustavus II Adolphus.

RELATED ARTICLES in *Great Events from History: The Seventeenth Century, 1601-1700:* 1618-1648: Thirty Years' War; May 23, 1618: Defenestration of Prague; November 8, 1620: Battle of White Mountain; March 6, 1629: Edict of Restitution; 1630-1648: Destruction of Bavaria; May 30, 1635: Peace of Prague; 1640-1688: Reign of Frederick William, the Great Elector.

JOHN WALLIS
English mathematician

Wallis made advances in mathematical notation and created new methods for making mathematical discoveries. He paved the way for the work of Sir Isaac Newton and consequently for the invention of the calculus.

BORN: December 3, 1616; Ashford, Kent, England
DIED: November 8, 1703; Oxford, England
AREAS OF ACHIEVEMENT: Mathematics, science and technology

EARLY LIFE

John Wallis (WAHL-uhs) was born in the village of Ashford, Kent, the son of the village rector, John Wallis, senior, and his second wife, Joanna Wallis, née Chapman. Wallis's father died in 1622. He was left with sufficient resources to obtain a good elementary education and enrolled at an Essex school run by Martin Holbech in 1630. There, he was told by the master that he was the best prepared student in mathematics he had encountered. Wallis was, in addition to his mathematical learning, something of a calculating prodigy. From Holbech's school, he proceeded to Emanuel College, Cambridge, where he studied medicine and took courses in physics as well as moral philosophy.

After receiving a bachelor's degree in 1637 and a master's degree in 1640, Wallis became a fellow at Queen's College. As was typical for the period, such fellowships were limited to unmarried scholars, so when he married Susanna Glyde in 1645, he was deprived of his fellowship. The marriage lasted forty-two years, until his

wife's death in 1687. They had one son and two daughters. In the early years of his marriage, Wallis was able to make a living as a private chaplain in Yorkshire and Essex, where he had connections.

The English Civil War soon intervened in Wallis's life, however. Wallis was active on behalf of the Parliamentary side, and, in particular, he put his code-breaking talents to use to help with deciphering intercepted Royalist messages. When the Parliamentary forces triumphed, this put Wallis in an enviable position, and he became Savilian Professor of Geometry at Oxford, thanks to the previous occupant's having had the bad fortune to support the Royalist cause. Since Wallis's mathematical skills at the time (1649) had scarcely even been tested, the political nature of the appointment is evident.

There were many political appointments made at the time that were reversed with the Restoration of the monarchy in 1660. Wallis, however, was not evicted from his chair under Charles II, and the explanation for his retention is usually found in Wallis's having signed the remonstrance against the execution of Charles I. Charles II, Charles I's son, remembered those who had not acquiesced in the death of his father. It was also true that by the time of the Restoration, Wallis had made a name for himself in mathematics worthy of the position he held.

LIFE'S WORK

The first work of Wallis to achieve notice was his *Arithmetica Infinitorum* (1655; the arithmetic of infinitesimals). In this book, he sought to combine the ideas of the Italian mathematician Bonaventura Cavalieri with the style of argument made famous by the French mathematician and philosopher René Descartes. Cavalieri had tried to break down geometrical objects in a given dimension into slices of one dimension lower. Thus, Cavalieri's principle argued that two solids would have the same volume if the areas of all the corresponding cross-sections were equal. Descartes's use of analytical methods helped to make the ideas of Cavalieri more palatable.

In 1659, Wallis published a treatise on conic sections, a subject familiar since the days of the Greeks. What was distinctive about Wallis's approach, though, was that he provided an alternative to the traditional approach of deriving the properties of the conic sections (like the circle and the ellipse) from their geometric origin. Wallis, instead, showed that certain quadratic equations would generate the points that made up the conic section and that the properties of the curves could be derived from the equations without having to go back to cones.

One general subject upon which Wallis was employed was trying to find the areas under certain curves. In order to go beyond the work done previously in the area by mathematicians like Pierre de Fermat, he worked out some of the values for the areas for curves that were already known and then showed how other curves could be obtained as the complements of those curves. In general, Wallis made progress by the use of two assumptions, induction and interpolation. Wallis would establish a result for the first few positive whole number values of the variable and would then claim that it must hold for the rest of the whole numbers. Having done that, he would then claim that some principle of continuity would also guarantee that the result would hold for the rest of the real numbers as well.

Wallis's, then, was scarcely a rigorous procedure, but it had a great influence on Sir Isaac Newton, whose early calculations of areas were quite similar to those of Wallis. If Newton made any progress beyond Wallis in these early years, it was by virtue of recognizing the advantages of taking variable limits for the regions whose area he was trying to find. This enabled him to recognize patterns where Wallis had only obtained numerical values.

One of Wallis's most celebrated results was an infinite product for the number 4/π. Again, this was not the first arithmetic expression that involved π, but Wallis's approach served as the basis for further work in the subject. In addition to his work on areas, Wallis also looked at the volumes of three-dimensional solids of rotation. He was the first to use the symbol ∞ for infinity and provided the notation subsequently used for logarithms as well.

Typical of Wallis's later years was his volume on algebra published in 1685. It included the use of notation to represent complex numbers well before what became the standard representation was devised. In addition, the book also included a good deal of questionable history, in which Wallis took potshots at the work of Descartes and held up the work of Thomas Harriot, an English mathematician, as superior. Subsequent historians have seen Wallis as going well beyond the evidence both in his praise of Harriot and in his disregard for Descartes. On the other hand, it was indicative of Wallis's nationalism and his willingness to ignore generally accepted valuations.

Among Wallis's most notorious quarrels were those with Thomas Hobbes and the defenders of the German mathematician Gottfried Wilhelm Leibniz as an inventor of the calculus. Hobbes was nowhere near the mathematical level that Wallis achieved, but he was a careful reader and pointed out some of the shortcomings in

John Wallis. (Library of Congress)

Wallis's attempts to explain the foundations of calculus, shortcomings he shared with the other mathematicians of the time. Wallis kept the argument with Hobbes going for many years, as he found repugnant Hobbes's attempt to found his philosophical materialism on mathematics. With regard to the creation of the calculus, Wallis was determined to keep Newton and Leibniz at odds for the sake of the glory of English mathematics. He also opposed the Gregorian calendar.

After the Glorious Revolution of 1688, Wallis was once more confirmed in his academic positions, possibly because of his continued willingness to put his code-breaking talents to use for the state. During much of his later years, he devoted time to the preparation of editions of other authors' works, as well as his own collected works. While his quarrels with contemporaries were many, it is worth mentioning that Samuel Pepys, the diarist, ordered a portrait of Wallis painted by the Sir Godfrey Kneller. Since Pepys did not get along with everyone, this is something of a contrast to Wallis's feuds.

SIGNIFICANCE

Wallis was arguably the most important precursor of Newton in England. His willingness to go out on a limb in pursuit of a mathematical discovery served as a model for Newton's efforts and led to the latter's discovery of the proof for the binomial theorem for general exponents. Wallis was one of the first to make a serious effort to provide an arithmetic form for geometry, especially for the heavily geometric parts of Euclid's *Stoicheia* (c. 300 B.C.E.; *The Elements of Geometrie of the Most Auncient Philosopher Euclide of Megara*, 1570, commonly known as the *Elements*), such as Books II and V. His innovations in notation helped to make mathematics easier to communicate, even across international boundaries.

—*Thomas Drucker*

FURTHER READING

Fauvel, John, et al., eds. *Oxford Figures: 800 Years of the Mathematical Sciences*. New York: Oxford University Press, 2000. The sixth chapter is devoted to Wallis and traces his contributions to the teaching of mathematics at Oxford and the growth of the university's mathematical reputation.

Mahoney, Michael Sean. *The Mathematical Career of Pierre de Fermat, 1601-1665*. Princeton, N.J.: Princeton University Press, 1973. The last chapter of the book takes up Fermat's arguments and relations with British mathematicians toward the end of his life and points to Wallis's disappointing reaction to questions proposed by Fermat.

Merton, Robert K. *On the Shoulders of Giants: A Shandean Postscript*. Chicago: University of Chicago Press, 1993. Looks at the impression Wallis created among his contemporaries of being greedy for glory and taking credit for the work of others.

Pears, Iain. *An Instance of the Fingerpost*. London: Jonathan Cape, 1997. This historical novel is a mystery in four parts, the third of which is narrated by Wallis, who has the reader's sympathy by the end of the narrative.

Scott, J. F. *The Mathematical Work of John Wallis, D.D., F.R.S., 1616-1703*. 1938. Reprint. New York: Chelsea, 1981. Seeks to restore Wallis's reputation among historians of science. While defending Wallis's mathematics, much of his history is treated as falsification.

Scriba, Christoph J. "John Wallis." In *Dictionary of Scientific Biography*, edited by Charles C. Gillispie. Vol. 14. New York: Charles Scribner's Sons, 1971. Much briefer than Scott's survey of Wallis's mathematics but clearer to the modern reader.

Stillwell, John. *Mathematics and Its History*. New York: Springer-Verlag, 1989. Looks at Wallis primarily as a precursor to Newton.

Westfall, Richard S. *Never at Rest: A Biography of Isaac Newton*. New York: Cambridge University Press, 1980. The best explanation of how Newton imitated Wallis's manipulations.

SEE ALSO: Charles I; Charles II (of England); René Descartes; Pierre de Fermat; Thomas Hobbes; Gottfried Wilhelm Leibniz; Sir Isaac Newton; Samuel Pepys.

RELATED ARTICLES in *Great Events from History: The Seventeenth Century, 1601-1700*: 1615-1696: Invention and Development of the Calculus; 1642-1651: English Civil Wars; May, 1659-May, 1660: Restoration of Charles II; November, 1688-February, 1689: The Glorious Revolution.

WANG FUZHI
Chinese philosopher and scholar

Ontologically, Wang stressed the materiality and objectivity of the universe; epistemologically, he insisted that human knowledge is a representation of the objective world and that practical experimentation is necessary to acquire such knowledge. He placed a high value on human effort and initiative, asserting the philosophical legitimacy of humans' material and sensual desires.

BORN: October 7, 1619; Hengyang, Hunan province, China
DIED: February 18, 1692; Hengyang
ALSO KNOWN AS: Wang Fu-chih (Wade-Giles)
AREA OF ACHIEVEMENT: Philosophy

EARLY LIFE

Wang Fuzhi (wahng foo-jih) was born into an intellectual family, his father, uncle, and elder brother all being distinguished scholars. Under their guidance, Wang started, at the age of four, to study Confucian classics, especially the *Si shu* (1190; Four Books) and *Wujing* (500-400 B.C.E.; Five Classics), as well as history and poetry composition. At the age of fourteen, he passed the county-level civil service examination and obtained the "budding-talent" degree (*xiucai*, equivalent of the bachelor's degree). At the age of twenty, he went to pursue his education at the famous Yuelu Academy in Shangsha.

In 1642, Wang successfully passed the prefectural or provincial-level civil service examination and obtained the "lifted-person" degree (*juren*, equivalent of the master's degree). Wang was unable to progress further and take the metropolitan (national-level) examination in Beijing, however, because of the interruption of transportation during Li Zicheng's Revolt. During these formative years of his life, besides studying, Wang also demonstrated keen interest in social and political activities; he became actively involved in organizing various intellectual societies and in discussing or commenting on social and political issues.

In 1644, the Ming Dynasty was brought down by the Manchus and replaced by a Manchu dynasty, the Qing. Refusing to accept Qing rule and still considering himself a Ming subject, Wang participated in the Ming loyalists' anti-Qing movement, which aimed at restoring Ming rule. He was frustrated, however, with the ineffectiveness of the resistance movement, which was plagued by endless factionalist bickering within its leadership. In 1650, Wang returned to his hometown, presumably at the news of his mother's illness. During the next ten years, he lived as a refugee, moving from one locality to another to escape pursuit and capture by the Qing regime.

LIFE'S WORK

Wang eventually settled down in a solitary rural area in Hongyang. He remained there for the rest of his lifetime, from 1660 to 1692. Still a staunch Ming loyalist, Wang refused to cooperate with or to serve the Qing regime, despite the dynasty's proclamation of a nationwide amnesty, which alleviated his fears of political persecution. Instead of joining the civil service, Wang preoccupied himself with teaching, scholarly research, and writing, and most of his works were written during this Hongyang period.

One of the most prolific writers in Chinese history, Wang is believed to have produced about one hundred works, comprising five million Chinese characters. Seventy of these works are extant. Wang's writings are extensive in scope, covering a great variety of subjects and issues, including history, poetry, economics, politics, and, above all, philosophy. It was in the field of philosophy that Wang made his most remarkable contributions to Chinese scholarship. Wang's philosophical works primarily take the form of commentaries or annotations on Confucian classics. Most prominent of these works are *Inner Commentary to the Book of Changes, Outer Commentary to the Book of Changes, Minor Commentary to the Book of Changes, Elaboration on the Meaning of the Book of Documents,* and *Investigation of the Meaning of the Four Books.*

Wang's philosophy emphasizes the material nature of all existence, including human society. Wang believed that the universe is composed of *qi*, a general and ubiquitous material force or substance or energy. *Qi* is self-contained and self-sufficient, free from the control of any transcendental force or Creator. (As a matter of fact, Wang did not acknowledge the existence of such a transcendental force.) *Qi* has two opposite but mutually complementary aspects, *yin* (negativity, femininity, and so forth) and *yang* (positivity, masculinity, and so forth); the interaction (both conflict and cooperation) between *yin* and *yang* gives birth to the myriad things in the universe. *Qi* permeates or fills the whole universe, and the various concrete physical things, including humans, are only embodiments or forms of *qi*. Since the universe is material in Wang's philosophy, it is fundamentally a "real (or substantial) existence" (*shi you*) rather than "empty" and "void," as Daoist and Buddhist philosophy assert.

Wang further enunciated the relations between *qi* and *li* (that is, principle, theory, law, or abstraction). He insisted that *li*, also a real existence, is inherent in *qi* and that *li* is the function of *qi*. In other words, *li* derives from *qi* rather than vice versa. There is no *li* that is independent of *qi*. *Li* manifests itself in the process of the change of material things. This understanding of the *qi-li* relationship represents a rejection of the philosophy of Zhu Xi (1130-1200), the leading Neo-Confucian philosopher in the Song Dynasty, whose view was that *li* exists prior to *qi* and *qi* derives from *li*. Given Wang's insistence on the materiality of the universe and on the precedence of the material world of *qi* over the spiritual world of *li*, Wang's philosophy is identified by many modern scholars, especially those in China, as (embryonic or nascent) materialism, in contrast to idealism.

In Wang Fuzhi's view, the material world, instead of being still, is in flux and subject to ceaseless changes and transformations, the dynamic of which lies in the interaction of the two opposite but unified forces, *yin* and *yang*. Applying this approach to human society, Wang asserted that there was a natural evolution of human society from lower stages to higher ones and justified many political changes, such as the replacement of the feudal system by the bureaucratic system, as evolutionary progress.

Epistemologically, Wang held that cognition is a process in which a person's subjective consciousness or mind reflects the objective material world, and knowledge is based on or comes from the observation or experience of objective things. However, Wang did not believe that the mind is a mere passive reflector. Instead, people can take the initiative to use their minds to "investigate things" in order to "extend knowledge" and to "exhaust principles." Wang stressed the importance of "doing," or practice, for "knowing," or knowledge. Accepting but going beyond the Neo-Confucian doctrine of "integration of knowing with doing," he put forth the theory that "doing takes precedence over knowing." According to this theory, the best way to learn is through practice—by participating in daily the activities of human society. This pragmatic or empirical perspective was a straightforward denial of Zhu Xi's idealistic approach, which asserted that "knowing takes precedence over doing."

In elucidating both his ontological and epistemo-logical theories, Wang treated human beings with high regard. For him, like the human body, human feelings and desires (be they for sex or for material wealth) are among the most basic concrete realities and are both natural and legitimate. This position, too, was a repudiation of orthodox Neo-Confucian asceticism, which identified human desires as evil. For Wang, purposeful, thoughtful, effortful, and creative humans are capable of understanding and changing the objective world, both natural and social. This view on the value of humankind and its abilities has, for some modern scholars, the flavor of humanism.

SIGNIFICANCE

Wang's philosophy represented a new stage in the development of Chinese philosophy. Wang put forward many new and distinctively modern ideas, including those on the role of practice and experiment in knowledge acquisition, those on change and the evolution of societies, and, above all, those on humanity's inherent value and ability. Wang broke with more than two thousand years of Eastern philosophy when he asserted that human desire was a foundation to build on, rather than an impediment to overcome. Not surprisingly, then, he has been praised by some Chinese scholars as an Enlightenment thinker.

Wang's philosophy has had far-reaching influence on both Chinese scholarship and politics. His brand of materialism has been embraced by Chinese Marxists, who have persistently upheld Marx's dialectical materialism. In the late Qing and early republican era, reformers and revolutionaries, including Tang Sitong, Sun Yatsen, and Yang Changji, used Wang's theory of social change to justify their reformist and revolutionary activities. Some of these people found inspiration in what they deemed to Wang's nationalism, embodied in his condemnation of and resistance to the foreign, Manchurian rule of China.

— *Yunqiu Zhang*

FURTHER READING

Black, Alison Harley. *Man and Nature in the Philosophical Thought of Wang Fu-Chih.* Seattle: University of Washington Press, 1989. A critical study of Wang Fuzhi's ideas about the role of humans in the universe.

Chen Yusen, and Chen Xianyou. *Illumination of "The Commentary to the Book of Changes."* Beijing: Chinese Press, 2000. A detailed annotation on one of Wang Fuzhi's major philosophical works.

Lu Fuchu. *Wang Fuzhi's Scholarship.* Wuhan, China: Hubei People's Press, 1987. A collection of quotations from various works of Wang Fuzhi, which are categorized according to different philosophical topics. The author offers an inspiring introduction to each section.

Meng, Peiyuan. *The Evolution of Neo-Confucianism: From Zhu Xi to Wang Fuzhi and Dai Zhen.* Taibei, China: Wenjin Press, 1990. Contains an important chapter on Wang Fuzhi's philosophy.

Wang, Fuzhi. *Surviving Works of Wang Fuzhi.* Beijing: Beijing Press, 1999. A collection of most of Wang Fuzhi's major works.

Zhang Liwen. *Orthodoxy Learning and Intellectual Creativity: Wang Fuzhi's Philosophy.* Beijing: People's Press, 2001. An insightful exploration of how Wang Fuzhi creatively reinterpreted the Confucian classics.

SEE ALSO: Abahai; Chen Shu; Chongzhen; Dorgon; Kangxi; Liu Yin; Shunzhi; Tianqi; Zheng Chenggong.

RELATED ARTICLES in *Great Events from History: The Seventeenth Century, 1601-1700:* 1631-1645: Li Zicheng's Revolt; June 6, 1644: Manchus Take Beijing.

MARY WARD

English religious leader and educator

The founder of the Institute of Blessed Virgin Mary, Ward overcame hostility and resistance to establish schools and houses for Catholic women across Europe.

BORN: January 23, 1585; Mulwith, Yorkshire, England
DIED: January 30, 1645; Heworth, near York, Yorkshire
AREA OF ACHIEVEMENT: Religion and theology

EARLY LIFE

In 1585, Mary Ward was born to Marmaduke Ward and Ursula Ward, wealthy landowners from Yorkshire. The eldest of six children, Ward was influenced by the stringent anti-Catholic restrictions in Protestant England. Known as recusants, Ward's family harbored fugitive priests, fed Catholics in hiding, and served time in jail. Ward spent much of her childhood apart from her parents, including five years with her grandmother and several with other relatives. At the age of fifteen, she decided to pursue a religious life, yet her father required Mary to wait until she turned twenty-one. She finally gained her spiritual director's permission when he overturned a chalice during mass, interpreting this event as an act of divine providence. Ward thwarted four arranged marriages.

LIFE'S WORK

In 1606, Ward crossed the English Channel to pursue her religious vocation in Flanders. Arriving at Saint-Omer and learning that the Poor Clares (an order of nuns descended from the Second Order of Saint Francis of Assisi, founded by Saint Clare of Assisi in 1212) were not accepting "foreign" women, Ward was advised by a

local Jesuit to enter the Poor Clares as a lay-sister. Unhappy with her primary responsibility of begging for food and living outside the convent, Ward resumed secular dress after five months and set out to establish an English foundation of Poor Clare sisters in nearby Gravelines.

Ward remained at Gravelines until May, 1609, when she returned to England, still uncertain about how to fulfill God's mission and having renounced a nun's habit twice. Ward resided in London, where she helped persecuted Catholics and continued her apostolic mission while remaining true to her vow of celibacy. By the fall of 1609, she had returned to Saint-Omer, invigorated by her desire to establish a boarding school for English girls and a day school for local children. As this School of the Blessed Mary developed, it gradually took on the nature of a religious order, and today scholars credit Mary Ward with the establishment of the Institute of the Blessed Virgin Mary (IBVM).

Between 1609 and 1615, Ward began to define her apostolic mission. The women active in Ward's circle lived and worked among the people of the community while wearing modest black clothing. Known sometimes as English Ladies or English Virgins, these women were educated and had strong financial resources, even servants; women who wished to join and were uneducated could enter as lay-sisters. Jesuits served as the circle's spiritual advisers initially, and Ward relied on their institutional structure and mission to envision her society of active women.

A 1611 vision revealed to Ward that she was to "take the same of the Society," meaning that she should model her community after the Jesuits, although she wished to remain independent. Houses were established in Bavaria, the Rhineland, Austria, Italy, and Flanders with the support of local bishops and even Duke Maximilian I Wittelsbach of Bavaria. When told that women's religious vocation frequently lapsed because women were weaker than men, Ward responded by arguing that there was no difference between men and women. Women lost their fervor, she countered, because they were as capable of imperfection as men were. After walking from Brussels to Rome in 1621, Ward released the new guidelines for her society, reaffirming her commitment to contemplative and spiritual activity without the need for strict enclosure or habits, her desire to instruct young girls in Christian doctrine, and her subjection to the pope.

Ward and her mission were clearly subjected to scrutiny. In its reform of the Church, the Council of Trent had proclaimed that strict enclosure, or seclusion from the material world, was necessary for all nuns. Many members of the Catholic Church came to question a religious woman's desire to remain uncloistered, and visits to local homes were sometimes taken to indicate scandalous behavior. The first attack in print against Ward came in 1614. Later, she was investigated in London for causing "more hurt than six to seven Jesuits." A 1621 complaint lodged by English clergymen reveals concern over the order's close association with the Jesuits, its lack of strict enclosure, and its "speaking with authority about spiritual things."

The Jesuits themselves were ordered no longer to support Ward's group, which had at times been called the "Jesuitesses," "wandering gossips," and the "galloping nuns." By 1624, enclosure was adopted by all the houses; by 1625, the papacy had ordered all Italian houses to be closed, except in Rome. In 1628, papal nuncios called for additional suppression of houses, although these calls seem to have been widely ignored. Meanwhile, Ward continued her work, writing letters and even appointing someone to visit the houses in Trier, Cologne, and Liège. One such letter asked the Liège sisters to "ignore unauthorized attempts to close the house." This letter received scrutiny by the papal nuncio, and he advised Ward's imprisonment immediately.

In 1631, Ward was charged with heresy, and a papal bull announced the suppression of the institute. The document expressed hostility toward women who "wandered about at will," and who lived together without approval. The burden was "too heavy a task for weak women" and thus the "poisonous growths" (the houses) were declared null and void. Imprisoned for nine weeks in München, Ward decried her situation in a letter to the pope, revealing anger at being labeled a heretic and begging for help. Other letters, written in lemon juice and requiring heat to be read, indicate her precarious situation.

Brought to Rome after her arrest and then exonerated of heresy, Ward lived under papal watch in Rome with female companions from 1632 to 1637. She apparently maintained a close relationship with the pope, visiting him several times. Ward traveled to Viterbo when she fell ill and spent the winter of 1637-1638 in Paris. She then went to Liège and Saint-Omer, finally reaching London in 1639, where she received the patronage of Queen Henrietta Maria. Caught in the English Civil War and Oliver Cromwell's governmental strife, Ward moved to Hewarth in Yorkshire in April, 1642, with her female companions and loaded ox wagons, then took refuge in York in September. She died January 30, 1645, and was buried in the village church of Osbaldwick.

SIGNIFICANCE

Ward left behind two brief autobiographies, narrating a series of events that shaped her identity. As early as 1621, Ward's portrait was painted, revealing her black pilgrim's clothing. Her letters and prayers, often written in prose verse, provide useful accounts of her life. Sometimes relying on code words, her letters demonstrate that she was aware of the controversial nature of her work. Ward's followers continued her religious vocation in Paris after her death, and by 1703, the IBVM had been granted canonical status as a religious order once again. Within fifty years of her death, an anonymous artist depicted her life in *The Painted Life*, a series of fifty large oil paintings located in the IBVM house in Augsburg, Germany.

In 1909, Ward was officially declared the founder of the Institute of the Blessed Virgin Mary, a religious order still in existence today (Mother Theresa served in the Loreto branch of the order for twenty years). Ward's determination provided a new path for religious women, one that emphasized education and active missionary work. Her actions both demonstrated and attempt to ameliorate the limitations of the Church in addressing women's spiritual needs. Ward can be seen as a strong female leader in an increasingly conservative and patriarchal era.

—Shelley Amiste Wolbrink

FURTHER READING

Cameron, Jennifer. *A Dangerous Innovator: Mary Ward, 1585-1645.* Strathfield, N.S.W.: St. Paul's, 2000. One of the more useful biographies on Ward with some translated primary sources including papal bulls and Ward's prison declaration. Timeline, map, and bibliography.

Cover, Jeanne. *Love—the Driving Force: Mary Ward's Spirituality, Its Significance for Moral Theology.* Milwaukee, Wis.: Marquette University Press, 1997. Examination of Ward's spirituality with bibliography and citations.

Littlehales, Margaret Mary. *Mary Ward: Pilgrim and Mystic.* Tunbridge Wells, Kent, England: Burns & Oates, 2001. Although lacking footnotes, a thorough biography and a few translated primary sources. Photograph of tombstone, and visuals from *The Painted Life.*

Orchard, M. Emmanuel, ed. *Till God Will: Mary Ward Through Her Writings.* London: Darton, Longman, and Todd, 1985. An edited collection of primary sources. Provides a useful introduction, and then divides Ward's writings thematically into reflections on

her childhood, her conflicts, and the growth of the institute. Map.

Peters, Henriette. *Mary Ward: A World in Contemplation.* Translated by Helen Butterworth. Leominster, Herefordshire, England: Gracewing Books, 1994. Detailed and authoritative biography that relies on archival manuscripts and unpublished sources. Illustrations and extensive bibliography.

Wright, Mary. *Mary Ward's Institute: The Struggle for Identity.* Sydney: Crossing Press, 1997. A useful text for understanding Mary Ward's contribution to the institute. Provides detailed information on the contemporary institute. Index and bibliography.

SEE ALSO: Oliver Cromwell; Henrietta Maria.
RELATED ARTICLE in *Great Events from History: The Seventeenth Century, 1601-1700:* 1642-1651: English Civil Wars.

JOHN WEBSTER
English playwright

Webster, in his two major tragedies, captured what many consider to be the quintessence of Jacobean drama. His work is characterized by depictions of evil, torture, murder, and the struggles of complex individuals against corruption, portrayed through lyric, poetic language.

BORN: c. 1577-1580; London, England
DIED: before 1634; London
AREAS OF ACHIEVEMENT: Literature, theater

EARLY LIFE

John Webster's parents were John Webster, senior, and Elizabeth Coates Webster, who had married in 1577. His father was registered in the Merchant Taylors' Company, one of the main trade guilds in London. However, the elder John Webster was actually a coach maker, a trade that had no separate guild. His son John the younger most likely attended the Merchant Taylors' School, known for its good academic program and its famous graduates, including dramatists Thomas Lodge and Thomas Kyd.

There is a 1598 record of a John Webster being admitted to the Middle Temple, one of the London Inns of Court, places of both training and practice for lawyers. While it is not certain if this John Webster was in fact the future playwright, most researchers believe that he was;

the many references to the law in Webster's plays support the possibility of his legal studies. It is supposed that Webster began his studies at New Inn before moving on to more advanced training at the Middle Temple. Webster probably did not complete a law degree; he may have attended the inns in order to help with his father's business. In addition to his studies, Webster would have viewed the dramatic works of his contemporaries, as students often wrote and performed plays at the Inns of Court. His classmates would have included fellow playwrights John Marston and John Ford.

Webster left the inns to begin writing for professional theater, both in collaboration with other playwrights and on his own. He married Sara Peniall, then seven months pregnant, in 1606; the couple had at least five children.

LIFE'S WORK

Webster's works chiefly fall within the Jacobean era, that is, during the reign of James I (r. 1603-1625). This period is known for city comedies and gruesome tragedies, the latter often associated with a prevailing pessimism that marked much public sentiment during James's rule. Webster's tragedies in particular feature almost unbearable cruelty. Critics often cite political overtones in Webster's plays, which may be meant to critique problems of the Jacobean court. Webster's plays were staged at a variety of theaters, particularly more intimate, enclosed ones. His style was strongly influenced by the Roman playwright Seneca the Younger (c. 4 B.C.E.-65 C.E.), as well as by his contemporary playwrights.

Theater owner Philip Henslowe paid Webster for collaborative script work on *Caesar's Fall* (pr. 1602), *Lady Jane* (pr. 1602, pb. 1607), and *Christmas Comes but Once a Year* (pr. c. 1602-1603?) in 1602. Only *Lady Jane* survives, as part of *Sir Thomas Wyatt*, a tragedy published in 1607. Webster's important collaboration with playwright Thomas Dekker produced two early city comedies, *Westward Ho!* (pr. 1604, pb. 1607) and *Northward Ho!* (pr. 1605, pb. 1607), both performed by the Children of Paul's troupe. He was also hired in 1604 to write the Induction to John Marston's important tragedy *The Malcontent* (pr., pb. 1604) for the King's Men, the prestigious acting company, named for King James, for which William Shakespeare wrote.

Webster's independent writing period probably began with his work on *The White Devil* (pr. c. 1609-1612, pb. 1612), which was performed by the Red Bull Company. The first of his important tragedies, the play is loosely based upon actual events of 1580 in Italy and portrays Vittoria Corombona, a woman involved in an adulterous affair with a duke through the assistance of her social-climbing brother Flamineo. Both Vittoria's and Duke Brachiano's spouses die; Vittoria is placed on trial for the murder, and sentenced; she escapes and marries Brachiano. Her brother and Duke Francisco de Medici, the brother of Brachiano's dead wife, kill Brachiano under the direction of Count Lodovico, an enemy of Brachiano. Lodovico and his friend Gasparo then kill Flamineo, Vittoria, and her servant Zanche. At the play's conclusion, the English ambassador passes sentence on Lodovico, and Giavonni, Brachiano's son by his first wife, Isabella, is left to rule.

Webster next wrote *The Duchess of Malfi* (pr. 1614, pb. 1623), featuring a young widow who remarries despite her two brothers' prohibitions. This play is also based upon actual events in sixteenth century Italian history. Duke Ferdinand and the cardinal, the brothers, are corrupt representatives of state and church, respectively, in clear contrast to the virtuous duchess and her household treasurer and secret new husband, Antonio. Ferdinand hires the opportunistic ex-soldier Bosola to spy on and then murder his sister; after her death, Bosola retaliates by taking revenge upon the brothers, but he acciden-

WEBSTER'S MAJOR WORKS

1604	*Westward Ho!* (with Thomas Dekker)
1605	*Northward Ho!* (with Dekker)
c. 1609-1612	*The White Devil*
1614	*The Duchess of Malfi*
c. 1619-1622	*The Devil's Law-Case*
1624	*Monuments of Honour*
c. 1624-1625	*A Cure for a Cuckold* (with William Rowley)
1634?	*Appius and Virginia* (with Thomas Heywood)

tally kills Antonio and is in turn killed by Ferdinand. Order is restored when Antonio and the duchess's eldest son is brought to power. The play, performed by the King's Men at Blackfriars and the Globe, was published in 1623 with *The Devil's Law-Case* (pr. c. 1619-1622, pb. 1623).

The Devil's Law-Case was Webster's solo tragicomedy. It centers on an unusual trial in which a widow tries to declare her son illegitimate, in order to remove him as an impediment to her remarriage and to deed his estate to her daughter. The work has two important elements that reverberate throughout Webster's dramas: an unconventional, independent female lead and a courtroom setting, replete with legal banter. The Queen Anne's Men first performed the play sometime between 1619 and 1622.

After *The Devil's Law-Case*, Webster again worked on plays in collaboration with other playwrights. He wrote *Anything for a Quiet Life* (pr. c. 1621, pb. 1662) with Thomas Middleton, the now-lost *The Late Murder of the Son upon the Mother: Or, Keep the Widow Waking* (pr. 1624) with Thomas Dekker, John Ford, and William Rowley, and *A Cure for a Cuckold* (pr. c. 1624-1625, pb. 1661) with Rowley. He began *The Fair Maid of the Inn* (pr. 1626, pb. 1647) in 1625 with John Fletcher, who died of the plague in the course of writing, and he finished the play with Ford and Philip Massinger. His last work is believed to be *Appius and Virginia* (pr. 1634?, pb. 1654), a Roman play about a virgin trying to protect her chastity from a corrupt official; it is generally thought to have been written jointly with Thomas Heywood.

Webster also wrote several nondramatic works, including his elegy "The Monumental Column" (1612), on the death of James I's son Henry, prince of Wales. He composed prose descriptions of character types as a part of Sir Thomas Overbury's *Characters* (1615). Two of Webster's contributions to this collection were "The Virtuous Widow" and "The Common Widow," the former remaining true to her husband's memory by not remarrying, the latter a loose woman marrying as soon as she could after her first husband's death. These portrayals paralleled the brothers' views toward their sister in *The Duchess of Malfi*. In 1624, Webster was hired by the Merchant Taylors' Company to write a pageant celebrating the election of the lord mayor's of London.

SIGNIFICANCE

Webster is most remembered for his remarkable tragedies, *The White Devil* and *The Duchess of Malfi*, and less so for the entire body of his work. He developed his female characters into multidimensional people, who arguably supercede William Shakespeare's tragic heroines in their complexity and depth. His dark worldview and special attention to brilliant dialogue has continued to intrigue and provoke audiences and readers, resonating with such early modernist playwrights as Bertolt Brecht and Antonin Artaud, and with modernist poets, especially T. S. Eliot. Contemporary critics, readers, and audiences are drawn to these two principle plays, still often performed, which feature power struggles, court intrigue, family conflicts, and independent women.

—Carol Blessing

FURTHER READING

Aughterson, Kate. *Webster: The Tragedies*. New York: Palgrave, 2001. This introduction to Webster provides a biography of Webster and a look at the Jacobean background to his writing integrated with studies of *The White Devil* and *The Duchess of Malfi*.

Bradbrook, M. C. *John Webster: Citizen and Dramatist*. New York: Columbia University Press, 1980. Bradbrook attempts a reconstruction of Webster's life, including a family tree and discussion of his works.

Edmond, Mary. "In Search of John Webster." *Times Literary Supplement*, December 24, 1976, pp. 1621-1622. Edmond's research sheds some light on Webster's life, especially his father's trade, and Webster's connection to the Merchant Taylors' Guild.

Forker, Charles R. *Skull Beneath the Skin: The Achievement of John Webster*. Carbondale: Southern Illinois University Press, 1986. Exhaustively researched, this is the most comprehensive study of Webster and his works available; an invaluable resource. Forker particularly explores the paired themes of love and death in the plays.

Gunby, David, David Carnegie, and Antony Hammond, eds. *The Works of John Webster*. 1 volume to date. New York: Cambridge University Press, 1995-   . A projected multivolume work that aims at replacing the older standard edition by F. L. Lucas. Contains a good biography of Webster, as well as carefully edited texts of *The White Devil* and *The Duchess of Malfi*, including excellent introductions to the plays, commentary, and reproductions of important primary sources.

Lucas, F. L., ed. *The Complete Works of John Webster*. 4 vols. Reprint. New York: Gordian, 1966. Since its original publication in 1927, this has been the standard edition. Beside inclusion of all plays, prose characters, and occasional verse of Webster, it includes extensive textual, source, and critical information, although limited by its lack of current information. Still the only edition of Webster's lesser-known works.

Ranald, Margaret Loftus. *John Webster*. Boston: Twayne, 1989. A good starting place for a study of Webster, this non-specialist-friendly volume includes an overview of Webster's life and works.

Wymer, Rowland. *Webster and Ford*. New York: St. Martin's Press, 1995. In this helpful contemporary reassessment of Webster, Wymer discusses *The White Devil*, *The Duchess of Malfi*, and *The Devil's Law-Case*, overviews the works' critical reception, and covers Webster's Jacobean background and influences.

SEE ALSO: Thomas Dekker; John Fletcher; James I; Thomas Middleton.

RELATED ARTICLES in *Great Events from History: The Seventeenth Century, 1601-1700:* c. 1601-1613: Shakespeare Produces His Later Plays; March 24, 1603: James I Becomes King of England.

WILLIAM III
Stadtholder of the United Provinces (r. 1672-1702) and king of England (r. 1689-1702)

As stadtholder of the United Provinces of the Netherlands and as joint sovereign, with Mary II, of England, Scotland, and Ireland, William III organized the Grand Alliance of European powers, which eventually defeated Louis XIV and prevented French domination of Europe.

BORN: November 14, 1650; The Hague, United Provinces (now in the Netherlands)
DIED: March 19, 1702; Kensington Palace, London, England
ALSO KNOWN AS: William of Orange
AREAS OF ACHIEVEMENT: Government and politics, diplomacy

EARLY LIFE
William III of Orange was born November 14, 1650, in The Hague, the only son of William II, stadtholder of the Netherlands, and Mary Stuart, eldest daughter of Charles I of England. William's childhood was harsh and loveless. His birth came eight days after the sudden death of his father, who was snatched away by smallpox at the conclusion of a failed attempt to overturn the federal structure of the United Provinces and to establish sovereignty in the House of Orange.

The years that followed were dominated by a bitter quarrel over William's guardianship between his mother; his grandmother, Countess Amalia of Solms-Braunsfeld; and his uncle, Frederick William of Brandenburg. In addition, it was the public policy of the province of Holland, led by Johan de Witt, to strengthen its political position during William's minority by depriving the House of Orange of its traditional offices and powers. As a child and an adult, William was also plagued by ill health. He was slight of stature, hunchbacked, hooknosed, and asthmatic. Thus, while his formal education provided him with a professional's understanding of the art of war, a connoisseur's appreciation for fine painting and architecture, and the language skills to express himself in Dutch, French, German, Latin, Spanish, and English, the normal lessons of his youth left him with a cold, cynical, and ruthless personality.

William's recovery of his political influence was probably inevitable, although the process was hastened when de Witt's policy of excluding him from his family's traditional offices came to an abrupt end in 1672. De Witt preferred friendship and alliance with France; thus his foreign policy was fatally undermined when Louis

XIV invaded the United Provinces in April. Public opinion demanded and received William's appointment to all of his ancestral offices. Unable to stop the French by any other means, the new stadtholder opened the dikes and flooded a wide belt of the Netherlands. His desperate strategy worked; Louis withdrew his army, the war settled down to a stalemate, and a compromise peace was signed at Nijmegen in 1678. Supported by his deep Calvinist faith, William had now begun his life's work of defeating Louis XIV and preserving the liberties of Europe.

LIFE'S WORK
Although the ten years following the Treaty of Nijmegen were nominally a time of peace, Louis XIV used the threat offered by his large standing army to carry out a series of pseudolegal annexations along his eastern border. In 1686, William constructed the League of Augsburg, a coalition of Sweden, Spain, Austria, and various German states, to resist French aggression. Even more significant, however, was his intervention in England. In 1677, he had strengthened his dynastic ties to that country by his marriage to Mary, the eldest daughter of James, duke of York and future King James II of England.

William's main concern was to contain French ambition, however, and not to gain a crown, and from 1687 on, he became increasingly anxious to secure English resources for the struggle against Louis XIV. At the same time, the English were growing disenchanted with their Roman Catholic king, whose policies appeared designed to overthrow the ancient constitution, destroy the Protestant religion, and establish absolutism on the French model. Worried by the threatened success of James II's plan to pack a subservient Parliament and by the birth of a son who would supplant his Protestant sister Mary in the succession, a group of eminent Englishmen invited the Dutch prince to invade the island to preserve English liberties. In November, 1688, William landed on the south coast at Tor Bay. Deserted by his realm, James II, his queen, and his infant son fled to France.

It was a bloodless invasion. In January and February, 1689, the Convention Parliament legalized the Glorious Revolution and offered the throne jointly to William and Mary. It was William, however, who directed the government; though a captivating personality, Mary deferred to her husband in every respect and played only the slightest role in affairs of state. The newly crowned king now added the might of England to the League of

William III. (Library of Congress)

Augsburg. Although the Nine Years' War, which raged from 1688 to 1697, ended in the exhaustion of all the major combatants, the Treaty of Rijswijk was a defeat for France. The French king was compelled to restore most of his conquests since 1679 and to recognize William III as king of England. For the first time in Louis XIV's reign, France had lost a war.

William's last years were spent seeking a solution to the crisis of the Spanish succession. Charles II of Spain lacked direct heirs, and the grant of the Spanish empire to a foreign prince threatened to destroy the balance of power in Europe. William negotiated the First and Second Treaties of Partition with Louis XIV to divide the Spanish inheritance among various European nations. Unfortunately, William's labors were undone by the will of Spanish king Charles II, which left all of his possessions to Louis XIV's grandson.

William was appalled, but public opinion in England and the Netherlands preferred this solution to either war or the second partition treaty. Only Louis XIV's blunders—his assertion that his grandson had a right to both

the Spanish and French thrones, his occupation of the barrier fortresses in the Spanish Netherlands, his economic discrimination against English and Dutch merchants in France and Spain, and his recognition of James III as rightful king of England—brought English and Dutch public opinion to support war and allowed William to create the Grand Alliance of European powers that decisively defeated Louis XIV. William, however, was not to direct the War of the Spanish Succession himself. In February, 1702, his horse stumbled on a molehill, causing him to fall and break his collarbone. Complications developed, and on March 19, William died, worn out by his labors.

SIGNIFICANCE

Despite poor health and an ill-shaped body, William III was one of the great men of his age, an international figure with a sincere concern for the security of all Europe. Perhaps nowhere was his impact greater, however, than in England. Cosovereign in name only, his reign is one of the most significant periods in English history. William did not invade England in 1688 out of personal ambition to acquire a royal title. He journeyed to London because he hoped that it would prove to be the shortest path to Paris.

Thus, virtually William's first act as king was to revolutionize English foreign policy. Both of his Stuart predecessors had ignored the rise of France and had turned away from Europe. The cosmopolitan Dutchman, however, was determined that England should no longer evade its international responsibilities but should become involved in Continental affairs. Although his policies eventually encountered resistance and at one point made him so unpopular that he considered withdrawing from the conduct of the government, William's impact on English foreign policy was both profound and enduring. Despite occasional lapses into isolationism, England remained committed to active intervention in European affairs in defense of the balance of power.

It was not enough that England have the will to intervene in foreign affairs; it must also have the power to do so. Throughout the seventeenth century, Stuart England had proved remarkably incapable of waging successful war, largely as a consequence of an obsolete and ineffective system of government. In place of the old machinery of the state, William substituted a more powerful, professional, and effective financial and administrative structure, with an enlarged bureaucracy and a completely new system of public credit. Without these changes, England's emergence as a great power and its numerous military and naval exploits in the Nine Years' War and the War of the Spanish Succession would have been impossible.

The impact of William's reign also extended to the English constitution, though this charge was unintentional on his part. It is certain that he had no wish to be a constitutional monarch; his temperament was autocratic, and he fully intended to rule as well as reign. Nor had the Glorious Revolution and the events of 1689 seriously curtailed the powers and prerogatives of the monarchy. Nevertheless, the unprecedented financial demands of the Nine Years' War made annual sessions of Parliament essential and gave the political nation the unexpected leverage to put additional limits on the Crown not even contemplated in 1689. Because William valued his throne chiefly as a means of bringing English resources into the war against France, he was forced to compromise and to make concessions that altered significantly the balance of power between king and Parliament and which contributed to the development of limited monarchy in England.

Little respected and less than loved by his English subjects, William deserved a better fate. His reign had profound consequences for both England and Europe, not the least of which was to demonstrate that parliamentary government could be as effective as the government in the much admired Continental states without resorting to their methods of centralization and absolutism.

—*William R. Stacy*

FURTHER READING

Baxter, Stephen B. *William III and the Defense of European Liberty, 1650-1702.* New York: Harcourt, Brace and World, 1966. The best biography of William III, though weak in its understanding of Dutch politics and foreign affairs.

Bevan, Bryan. *King William III: Prince of Orange, the First European.* London: Rubicon Press, 1997. In his brief but extensive biography, Bevan argues that William III was a true defender of liberty throughout Europe.

Burnet, Gilbert. *Bishop Burnet's History of His Own Time.* Edited by J. Routh. 2d enlarged ed. Oxford, England: Oxford University Press, 1833. One of the best contemporary accounts of the period. Burnet, a staunch Whig, was in exile in the Netherlands during much of the 1680's, sailed with William to invade England in 1688, and was appointed bishop of Salisbury.

Carswell, John. *The Descent on England: A Study of the English Revolution of 1688 and Its European Background.* London: Cresset Press, 1969. Valuable chiefly for establishing the Glorious Revolution in its European context instead of treating it solely as an English event.

Claydon, Tony. *William III and the Godly Revolution.* New York: Cambridge University Press, 1996. Describes how royal propaganda sought to legitimize William's regime by depicting him as a godly magistrate who would restore piety and virtue to England after the Glorious Revolution.

Geyl, Pieter. *The Netherlands in the Seventeenth Century.* London: E. Benn, 1961-1964. A well-documented study that offers critical insights into the decline of the Netherlands and the puzzling character of William III.

Grimblot, Paul, ed. *The Letters of William III and Louis XIV.* London: Longman, Brown, and Green, 1848. A valuable collection of the correspondence between the two monarchs in the years 1697-1700. Essential for understanding the foreign policy of this period.

Holmes, Geoffrey, ed. *Britain After the Glorious Revolution, 1689-1714.* London: Macmillan, 1969. A collection of ten concise and informative essays that examine the impact of the Glorious Revolution on English government and society. The essays on the transformation of English foreign policy and the impact of the Nine Years' War on constitutional developments in the 1690's are particularly valuable.

Horwitz, Henry. *Parliament, Policy, and Politics in the Reign of William III.* Newark: University of Delaware Press, 1977. A detailed narrative of English politics in the reign of William III. Indispensable, but not easy to read.

Jones, J. R. *The Revolution of 1688 in England.* New York: W. W. Norton, 1972. The best study of the Glorious Revolution. Particularly useful for explaining the motivation for and the timing of William's involvement in English affairs.

Macaulay, Thomas Babington. *The History of England, from the Accession of James II.* Edited by C. H. Firth. London: Macmillan, 1913-1915. Although dated and marred by the author's Whig bias, this remains a classic survey of late seventeenth century England.

Troost, Wouter. *William III the Stadholder-King: A Political Biography.* Translated by J. C. Grayson. Burlington, Vt.: Ashgate, 2004. Translated from the Dutch, the book offers a thorough recounting of William's life, including detailed information about the position of the House of Orange before and after his birth.

Van der Kiste, John. *William and Mary*. Stroud, England: Sutton, 2003. Examines the life and relationship of the cousins who wed and became joint monarchs of England.

SEE ALSO: Charles I; Charles II (of Spain); James II; Louis XIV; Mary II.

RELATED ARTICLES in *Great Events from History: The Seventeenth Century, 1601-1700:* 1688-1702: Reign of William and Mary; November, 1688-February, 1689: The Glorious Revolution.

ROGER WILLIAMS
English-born colonial American religious leader

A dissenter within the New England colonies, Williams argued for the separation of church and state, freedom of conscience in religious matters, and the possibility of social order in the absence of state regulation of religion. He founded Rhode Island as a haven for those oppressed by the American Puritans.

BORN: c. 1603; London, England

DIED: between January 16 and March 15, 1683; Providence, Rhode Island

AREAS OF ACHIEVEMENT: Government and politics, religion and theology

EARLY LIFE

Roger Williams was born in London, England, in Saint Sepulchre parish, sometime around 1603. His parents were James Williams, a shopkeeper in Cow Lane and a member of the Merchant Taylors' Company, and Alice Pemberton Williams, whose family owned land in Hertfordshire and held public office there and in London. In 1617, Williams worked as a stenographer for the famous common-law theorist and practitioner, Sir Edward Coke, whose patronage enabled Williams to enroll at Charterhouse, a London grammar school, in June, 1621. Williams was admitted to Pembroke Hall, Cambridge, as a scholarship student in 1623, where he gained a B.A. with honors in January, 1627.

At commencement, Williams signed a statement required of all university graduates to uphold the Thirty-nine Articles of the Church of England, the religious validity of the Book of Common Prayer, and royal supremacy in ecclesiastical affairs. In October, 1627, he began a three-year theology course leading to an M.A., certainly in anticipation of a career in the Church, but he became alienated from the religious establishment over its liturgy. He may, by this time, have also decided that the Church was unacceptably corrupt. He left the university about a year and a half later, in 1629, roughly twenty-six years old, and never finished the degree.

By February, 1629, Williams had become chaplain to the household of Sir William Masham of Otes, in Essex, about ten miles east of London in an area deeply influenced by Puritanism and quite sympathetic to Parliament in its struggles with the Crown. While in residence, he married Mary Barnard in December, 1629. They sailed to New England in December, 1630, to escape punitive measures leveled by Archbishop William Laud against religious Dissenters and Puritan clergy.

LIFE'S WORK

From February, 1631, to January, 1636, Williams searched throughout New England, to the dismay of Massachusetts Bay officials, for a religious community that had completely disowned the Church of England. His charges, in 1633, that the civil state could not on religious grounds grant a royal patent allowing the Bay Colony to claim Indian lands; his opposition to the administration of loyalty oaths, which were religious acts, to the unregenerate; and his resistance to Bay Colony authorities enforcing religious uniformity provoked the General Court of Massachusetts Bay to vote to deport Roger Williams to England in January, 1636. Before the decision could be carried out, he fled south to Narragansett Bay, where in May, on land purchased from the Indians, he founded the town of Providence as a haven for religious refugees and dissenters.

He spent much time from 1636 to 1643 corresponding with officials in Massachusetts Bay, particularly Governor John Winthrop. He was also in contact with John Cotton, a prominent Bay Colony minister, with whom Williams engaged in serious and bitter theological polemics. In this period, Williams came to believe that the medieval Papacy had abandoned the true principles of Christianity and destroyed Christ's visible church. It would not recover its "primitive" or apostolic purity until the millennium, or Christ's thousand-year rule upon earth. In anticipation of this restoration of the Church's pristine condition. Christ's prophets or witnesses, among whom Williams counted himself, were to denounce the errors of false Christendom. Accordingly, he determined that there were at present no true churches, no legitimate exercise of Christian sacraments, and no means apart from divinely appointed, apostolic messengers to found new churches.

While Williams was in England in 1643-1644 to obtain a colonial charter for Rhode Island, this perspective undergirded three of his London publications, *Mr. Cottons Letter Lately Printed, Examined, and Answered* (1644), *Queries of Highest Consideration* (1644), and *The Bloudy Tenent of Persecution, for Cause of Conscience, Discussed* (1644). In these tracts, Williams disagreed with Presbyterian and Congregational pronouncements in England that prevailing authorities and institutions were legitimate agents and forerunners of a godly commonwealth and a millennial age that would culminate in the reestablishment of the organization and holiness of the apostolic Church.

Williams, instead, emphasized the disjunction between existing institutions and the millennium. He argued that the restoration of Christ's true, visible church would come only after the prophetic activity of divinely ordained witnesses described in the Book of Revelation. Their denunciations of ecclesiastical corruption anticipated Christ's apocalyptic intervention in behalf of his church. Williams complained that the Massachusetts Bay officials, with the approval of John Cotton, had driven him into the wilderness because he had undertaken such a task in New England.

Finally, Williams urged that in the Christian era the nation of Israel was no longer a valid model for church and state relationships. The two now had separate realms of authority, reinforcing his contention that public peace, contrary to conventional wisdom, did not require civil regulation of religious beliefs and church order. Mixing the two realms had brought civil unrest, religious strife, war, and suffering. This situation could be resolved and true religious reform inaugurated, Williams claimed, if the church were strictly separated from the unregenerate state. Furthermore, this would grant to eschatological

Roger Williams finds refuge among the Narragansett Indians of Rhode Island. (Library of Congress)

witnesses such as himself the liberty to speak out against religious error in preparation for Christ's millennial restoration of the primitive, apostolic church.

In this same vein, Williams issued additional pamphlets in England during a 1651-1654 trip made to gain reconfirmation of Rhode Island's colonial charter. In a rejoinder to John Cotton, *The Bloody Tenent Yet More Bloody* (1652), two replies to proposals before the Rump Parliament for regulation of religion, *The Fourth Paper Presented by Major Butler* (1652) and *The Hireling Ministry None of Christs* (1652) and a summation of the issues entitled *The Examiner Defended* (1652), Williams's eschatological and restorationist assessment of the true church was a common thread.

He repeated his contention that the church should allow ungodly men to live unmolested in the sphere of the civil state, while Christ's martyrs and witnesses were to offer incessant testimony against decline and error in continued anticipation of the coming of the millennium and the restoration of the church. The state, similarly, should reject proposals before Parliament to punish heretics, to maintain ministers through tithes, or to certify university-trained candidates for preaching, since it was an incompetent judge of spiritual affairs.

Williams worked, from his expulsion from Massachusetts Bay in 1636 to his death in Providence in 1683, to unite the townships and settlements of Narragansett Bay under an orderly and effective government. He did so despite opposition from factious rivals, such as William Coddington and Samuel Gorton, predatory threats from Massachusetts Bay to swallow up contested land, and changing political conditions in England. It was after a lifetime of such struggles that, in 1672, he debated several itinerant Quaker missionaries, an account of which appeared with supplementary material in 1676 with the sarcastic title *George Fox Digg'd Out of His Burrows*.

Quakers interpreted religious experiences through an inner light, which they presumed to be the Holy Spirit. They also believed that such an indwelling was the mark of perfectibility and the threshold to a millennial age. Their piety was contrary to Williams's firm conviction, expressed in 1652 in *Experiments of Spiritual Life and Health*, that Scripture was the sole objective standard by which one evaluated religious experiences. Quaker sentiments were also in conflict with his unchanged conviction that this was an age of imperfection for both saints and the outward, visible Church. His millenarian and restorationist hopes, strained but never lost in his late seventies, remained the framework in which he interpreted Colonial religious and political issues.

SIGNIFICANCE

Williams contributed a rigorous and systematic apology for three important ideals long celebrated in American culture. He argued for separation of Church and State. His case, however, did not rest upon humanitarian concerns or a theory of natural rights. Instead, he based his claims upon theological and religious grounds—the radical discontinuity between the political and social powers of Old Testament Israel and the exclusively religious and spiritual responsibilities of the New Testament Church. Correspondingly, Williams advanced the cause of liberty of conscience, not because he regarded all human opinions as tentative and worthy of equal consideration, but to expedite attacks against false state religions and so to hasten the restoration of the primitive purity of the Church. He vigorously insisted upon the possibility of social order in the absence of state regulation of religion. His colonial experiment in Rhode Island was a lifelong test of the validity of this audacious assertion.

While the theological backdrop of these concepts has little in common with the Whig republican ideology and Oppositionist rhetoric employed so effectively by eighteenth century revolutionaries in North America and offers no confirmation for or support of nineteenth century American platitudes about desirable and inevitable progress, Williams's ideals have provided a curious and ironic comfort to twenty-first century pluralists, who advocate similar concerns but on the basis of utterly secular premises, far removed from the worldview of Williams. Nevertheless, the course of events in North America has confirmed Williams's fundamental contention that releasing man from the constraints of government-imposed religious uniformity and leaving the state to maintain order and to protect property is a practical and efficacious means to maintain social order and individual freedom.

—*James B. McSwain*

FURTHER READING

Byrd, James P., Jr. *The Challenges of Roger Williams: Religious Liberty, Violent Persecution, and the Bible.* Macon, Ga.: Mercer University Press, 2002. Describes how Williams paid the price of banishment for advocating religious liberty amid the often violent and fatal persecution of religion im the American colonies.

Gaustad, Edwin S. *Liberty of Conscience: Roger Williams in America.* Valley Forge, Pa.: Judson Press, 1999. A biography of Williams that traces his reputation and influence from the seventeenth to the twentieth centuries.

Gilpin, W. Clark. *The Millenarian Piety of Roger Williams*. Chicago: University of Chicago Press, 1979. Thoughtful monograph that makes clear that millenarian speculation shaped Williams's ideas, piety, and historical perspective.

Hall, Timothy. *Separating Church and State: Roger Williams and Religious Liberty*. Urbana: University of Illinois Press, 1998. The author explores how Williams's ideas of religious freedom were among the theoretical underpinnings of the First Amendment to the U.S. Constitution.

James, Sidney V. *Colonial Rhode Island: A History*. New York: Charles Scribner's Sons, 1975. Excellent survey that takes sympathetic note of Williams's patient and persistent efforts to unify the antecedent settlements of colonial Rhode Island, to make self-government effective, and to maintain goodwill between Indians and Englishmen.

Keary, Anne. "Retelling the History of the Settlement of Providence: Speech, Writing, and Cultural Interaction on Narragansett Bay." *New England Quarterly: A Historical Review of New England Life and Letters* 69, no. 2 (June, 1996): 250-286. Discusses Williams's book, *A Key Into the Language of America*, an account of the language and customs of the Native Americans in Rhode Island.

Morgan, Edmund S. *Roger Williams: The Church and the State*. New York: Harcourt Brace and World, 1967. Readable, lucid investigation of important themes developed by Williams's undoubtedly theological cast of mind within a Puritan context. Celebrates Williams's individualism to a degree incommensurate with his pietistic orientation. Clear explanation of Williams's political contributions but weak with regard to his millenarian and restorationist frame of mind.

Skaggs, Donald. *Roger Williams's Dream for America*. New York: P. Lang, 1993. Examines how Williams's concepts of religious liberty have influenced America's ideas of religious freedom.

Williams, Roger. *The Complete Writings of Roger Williams*. Edited by Perry Miller. 6 vols. Providence, R.I.: Providence Printing, 1866-1874. Reprint. 7 vols. New York: Russell and Russell, 1963. Volume 7 contains an original essay by Miller plus five tracts that did not appear in the original six-volume edition.

SEE ALSO: Canonicus; Sir Edward Coke; John Cotton; Anne Hutchinson; William Laud; Massasoit; John Winthrop.

RELATED ARTICLES in *Great Events from History: The Seventeenth Century, 1601-1700:* May, 1630-1643: Great Puritan Migration; June, 1636: Rhode Island Is Founded; July 20, 1636-July 28, 1637: Pequot War; September 8, 1643: Confederation of the United Colonies of New England; April 21, 1649: Maryland Act of Toleration.

THOMAS WILLIS
English physician, anatomist, physiologist, and chemist

Willis discovered several important anatomical and physiological features of the human body, coined the term "neurology," and improved the understanding of brain function, the circulatory system, diabetes, bubonic plague, and stroke. He is best known for discovering the physiological purpose of the cerebral arterial circle (circulus arteriosus cerebri), *commonly called the "circle of Willis."*

BORN: January 27, 1621; Great Bedwyn, Wiltshire, England

DIED: November 11, 1675; London, England

AREAS OF ACHIEVEMENT: Medicine, science and technology

EARLY LIFE

Thomas Willis was born on his father's farm, the eldest child in the large family of Thomas Willis, Sr., and Rachel Howell. When he was about ten, his family moved to North Hinksey, a village about a mile and a half from Oxford. After attending Edward Sylvester's private school in Oxford and becoming, in 1636, a servant to the Reverend Dr. Thomas Iles, canon of the local Anglican community, Willis entered Christ Church College, Oxford University, in 1637 as Iles's "batteler," or indebted student. He received a B.A. in 1639, an M.A. in 1642, and a B.Med. in December, 1646. In the 1640's, Willis became the leader of the "Oxford physiologists," an informal group of biomedical researchers working in the tradition of William Harvey. Willis's students at Oxford included Richard Lower and Robert Hooke.

Willis was a fervent Royalist and a conservative Anglican. Oxford was a Royalist town. Thus, for most of the English Civil War and throughout the era of Oliver Cromwell's Commonwealth and Protectorship, he had to be careful to avoid arrest, especially after the Parliamentary army of the third Baron Fairfax occupied Oxford on June 24, 1646. Yet Willis remained true to his faith, hiding Royalist fugitives, providing secret places for outlawed Anglican services to be held, and generally putting himself in political danger despite the threat to his career and liberty. In 1657, he married Mary Fell, daughter of Samuel Fell (dean of Christ Church College), and sister of John Fell, bishop of Oxford. His close connections to prominent Anglican clergy extended also to his patient Gilbert Sheldon, who was imprisoned during the Commonwealth but elevated to archbishop of Canterbury after the Restoration of Charles II. Sheldon's influence proved important in gaining key appointments for Willis in Oxford and London after 1660.

Thomas Willis. (Library of Congress)

LIFE'S WORK

Willis was an iatrochemist, that is, a follower of the medical theories of Paracelsus, Johannes Baptista van Helmont, and Franz Deleboe, which asserted that either chemistry or alchemy was the key to medical mysteries. The terms iatrochemistry, iatrochemism, or chemiatry, by which this group of theories was variously known, derive from the Greek words *iatros*, meaning "physician," and *chymeia*, whose meaning is obscure but refers to flowing juices and the transmutation of metals. The agenda of the iatrochemists was at odds with that of iatromechanists, such as René Descartes and Giovanni Alfonso Borelli, who claimed that physiology is best understood through physics and mathematics. Both approaches advanced physiology, but iatrochemistry was more flexible and more empirical and thus probably more useful than iatromechanics.

A prolific writer, Willis published many scientific papers and seven books. He achieved instant fame with his first book, *Diatribae duae medico-philosophicae* (1659; *Of Fermentation* and *Of Feavours*, 1681), which concerned fermentation, urine, fevers, and other physiological phenomena. Turning then toward anatomy and enlisting the help of Lower as dissector, Sir Christopher Wren as illustrator, and Thomas Millington as general collabo-

rator, Willis created his masterpiece, *Cerebri anatome* (1664; *The Anatomy of the Brain*, 1681), which added physiological explanations to accurate and detailed anatomical descriptions. Among the discoveries included in this book is the function of the cerebral arterial circle to protect the brain from interruption of blood flow. This insight of Willis into brain function was so important that, since the mid-eighteenth century, the cerebral arterial circle has commonly been called the "circle of Willis."

Willis reported further research into the physiology, anatomy, and pathology of the nervous system in *Pathologiae cerebri et nervosi generis specimen* (1667; *An Essay of the Pathology of the Brain and Nervous Stock*, 1681). His *Affectionum quae dicuntur hystericae et hypochondriacae* (1670; of the affections called hysteria and hypochrondia) defended his theories of psychosis and neurosis against the recent attacks of Nathaniel Highmore, challenged the prevailing view that hysteria was caused by uterine rather than nervous disorders, and argued that hypochrondria was a form of epilepsy.

Willis considered comparative anatomy in his *De anima brutorum* (1672; *Two Discourses Concerning the Soul of Brutes Which Is That of the Vital and Sensitive of Man*, 1683). His final work was a pharmacological casebook, *Pharmaceutice rationalis* (part 1, 1674, part 2, 1675; English translation, 1679). Posthumously and in the vernacular appeared *Dr. Willis's Practice of Physick* (1681, expanded ed., 1684), Samuel Pordage's translation of all his Latin books except the *Affectionum*, and *A Plain and Easie Method of Preserving (by God's Blessing) Those That Are Well from the Infection of the Plague, or Any Contagious Distemper in City, Camp, Fleet &c.* (1691).

Although most famous for his research, Willis was equally adept as a clinician. In 1650, he revived Ann Green, who had been hanged for infanticide, was presumed dead, and had been delivered to Willis in her coffin for dissection. His positive outcomes with patients suffering from diabetes, stroke, and several diseases of the nervous system enhanced his understanding of these afflictions and spurred him toward further investigations of their therapeutics. He depended mostly on Lower for raw anatomical knowledge, but he was uniquely able to interpret Lower's data to understand the physiology and function of the various body parts Lower cataloged, especially the cerebral cortex.

Willis was already the most prosperous physician in Oxford when the Stuart monarchy was restored in 1660, but immediately his fortunes got even better. That year, the university awarded him a D.Med. and named him Sedleian Professor of Natural Philosophy, a post that he held until his death, even though he relocated permanently to London in 1666. Also in 1660, in order to promote scientific investigation in general, Willis and several colleagues cofounded the Royal Society. As physician to the king, he was able to bequeath the most lucrative medical practice in England to his devoted assistant, Lower. He died on November 11, 1675, and was buried in Westminster Abbey.

SIGNIFICANCE

As the leading physiologist of the seventeenth century, Willis made important progress in understanding the nervous and circulatory systems and the interaction between them. He essentially invented the concept of the nervous system as a unified structure and has been praised as standing to neurology and the nervous system as Harvey stands to cardiology and the circulatory system. Keenly aware of the relationship between anatomy and physiology and their joint clinical significance, he helped to pave the way for the study of pathological anatomy that would emerge in the eighteenth and early nineteenth centuries through Giovanni Battista Morgagni, Matthew Baillie, Xavier Bichat, and Jean Cruveilhier.

In addition to the circle of Willis, many other eponyms arose from Willis's research. These include "Willis's centrum nervosum," the solar or celiac ganglia, a system of nerve roots near the abdominal aorta that innervate most of the abdominal organs; "Willis's cords," fibrous bodies traversing the superior sagittal sinus, a venous duct of the dura mater inside the cranium; "Willis's gland," the corpus luteum, an endocrine structure in the ovary; "Willis's nerve," the ophthalmic branch of the fifth cranial nerve; "Willis's pancreas," the processus uncinatus pancreatis, a part of the head of the pancreas; "Willis's paracusis," an improvement in hearing either because of or despite a noisy environment; and "Willis's pouch," the omentum minus, a fold in the peritoneum near the stomach and liver.

—Eric v.d. Luft

FURTHER READING

Coulter, Harris L. *The Origins of Modern Western Medicine: J. B. van Helmont to Claude Bernard.* Vol. 2 in *Divided Legacy: A History of the Schism in Medical Thought.* Berkeley, Calif.: North Atlantic Books, 2000. The second chapter, "Seventeenth-Century Rationalism," explores the rivalry between iatrochemistry and iatromechanics.

Debus, Allen G., ed. *Medicine in Seventeenth-Century England: A Symposium Held at UCLA in Honor of C. D. O'Malley.* Berkeley: University of California Press, 1974. Includes Lelland J. Rather's "Pathology at Mid-Century: A Reassessment of Thomas Willis and Thomas Sydenham," a well documented article, but biased in favor of Willis.

Eadie, M. J. "A Pathology of the Animal Spirits—The Clinical Neurology of Thomas Willis, 1621-1675, Part I: Background and Disorders of Intrinsically Normal Animal Spirits." *Journal of Clinical Neuroscience* 10, no. 1 (January, 2003): 14-29. Analysis of Willis's *Pathologiae cerebri et nervosi generis specimen* and *De anima brutorum* to show his influence on the contemporary understanding of nervous system diseases.

Hughes, J. Trevor. *Thomas Willis, 1621-1675: His Life and Work.* London: Royal Society of Medicine Services, 1991. A solid biography in the "Eponymists in Medicine" series.

Isler, Hansruedi. *Thomas Willis, 1621-1675: Doctor and Scientist.* New York: Hafner, 1968. The standard biography.

O'Connor, J. P. "Thomas Willis and the Background to *Cerebri Anatome.*" *Journal of the Royal Society of*

Medicine 96, no. 3 (March, 2003): 139-143. A philosophical interpretation of *Cerebri anatome* that discusses how Willis used his research on the brain to understand the soul and to bolster the design argument for the existence of God.

Williams, A. N. "Thomas Willis's Practice of Paediatric Neurology and Neurodisability. *Journal of the History of the Neurosciences* 12, no. 4 (December, 2003): 350-367. An interesting sidelight on Willis's career.

SEE ALSO: Giovanni Alfonso Borelli; Charles II (of England); Oliver Cromwell; René Descartes; Third Baron Fairfax; William Harvey; Johannes Baptista van Helmont; Robert Hooke; Richard Lower; Sir Christopher Wren.

RELATED ARTICLES in *Great Events from History: The Seventeenth Century, 1601-1700:* 1601-1672: Rise of Scientific Societies; 1642-1651: English Civil Wars; December 6, 1648-May 19, 1649: Establishment of the English Commonwealth; December 16, 1653-September 3, 1658: Cromwell Rules England as Lord Protector; May, 1659-May, 1660: Restoration of Charles II.

GERRARD WINSTANLEY
English political activist

An English radical and one of the first modern theorists of communism, Winstanley published pamphlets during the English Civil Wars advocating communal ownership of property; he and a group of followers who called themselves Diggers or True Levellers established several agricultural communes in 1649-1650.

BORN: October 10, 1609 (baptized); Wigan, Lancashire, England
DIED: c. September 10, 1676; London, England
AREAS OF ACHIEVEMENT: Government and politics, social reform

EARLY LIFE
The details of Gerrard Winstanley's (JUHR-ahrd WIN-stuhn-lee) life outside the years 1648-1652 are scant, and some are in dispute among scholars attempting to identify the origins of his extremely radical ideas. Born at Wigan, Lancashire, in northern England, to Edward Winstanley, a mercer, and his wife, Gerrard Winstanley was raised in a Protestant religious environment, and it has been speculated by scholars that he received some formal education because of his use of Latin in his writings, although he may also have learned Latin during his term as an apprentice. Nothing more is known of his life until March 25, 1630, when he became an apprentice to Sarah Gater of the Merchant Taylor's Company. Sarah, a young widow, ran a small retail business at St. Michael, Cornhill, in London, and Winstanley remained an apprentice there until February 20, 1638.

After finishing his apprenticeship, Winstanley became a shopkeeper in London, and in September, 1640, he married Susan King. Several actions he took in London in the early 1640's indicate that he was a supporter of Parliament during the First Civil War (1642-1646). On January 4, 1642, Winstanley and two other men lodged a dissenting opinion against the traditional method of selecting London Common Councilmen, and on October 8, 1643, he joined in the Solemn League and Covenant.

Because the radical changes brought on by the rebellions and wars within the British Isles disrupted commerce, Winstanley experienced severe financial problems and was forced to liquidate his business by making partial payment to creditors. He left London and moved to Cobham, Surrey, close to his wife's family in December, 1643. In his later pamphlets, he condemned commerce and trade; obviously this was a bitter experience for him. In Cobham, he became a cattle grazier—one who purchased, raised, and sold cattle. Records indicate that by April, 1646, he had a residence in the village of Street Cobham, and by 1648, he had become a Baptist, having undergone baptism by immersion.

LIFE'S WORK
Climatic problems and disruption caused by the First Civil War and Second Civil War (1647-1649) created extreme hardship in England's rural areas. Drought had created poor harvests and shortages of hay and grain, which became extremely expensive, causing a subsequent shortage of livestock. Taxes to support Parliament's army were heavy. Such was the background against which Winstanley began to write pamphlets and attempted to put his radical ideas into practice. Winstanley had come into contact with radicals such as William Everard, a former member of Parliament's army who

would collaborate with him in the Digger movement. Historians have raised questions about the influence of these contacts upon Winstanley's ideas, since he claimed that the ideas expressed in his pamphlets came to him during a mystic trance in late 1648. Highly significant political and military events had occurred in late 1648 and early 1649, culminating in the execution of King Charles I and the abolition of monarchy.

Winstanley's first major pamphlet, *The New Law of Righteousness* (1649), appeared on January 26, 1649, and presented the views that the concept of private property was evil and that God's will was that the poor would set things right through communal property ownership. Winstanley was very vague as to how the advent of communal property was to come about, although he believed it would occur soon and peacefully spread throughout England. On April 1, 1649, Winstanley, Everard, and perhaps a dozen others began "digging" and planting crops on the common or waste lands on Saint George's Hill in Surrey. Eventually, more than ten of these so-called Digger communes were attempted in Buckinghamshire, Northamptonshire, and Kent. At first the Diggers were regarded as harmless, but local opposition developed, and the Diggers were harassed, physically assaulted, and charged with trespass. Their crops and animals were damaged.

These events were chronicled by Winstanley in a series of pamphlets written throughout 1649 and 1650, especially in *A New Yeers Gift for the Parliament and Armie* (1650), published January 1, 1650. The Saint George's Hill Commune, which peaked at about fifty participants, was abandoned in July or August, 1649, as Winstanley and his followers moved to nearby Cobham Heath, where they maintained their settlement until abandoning it altogether in April, 1650, because of legal charges against them, unrelenting opposition, and financial hardship. Several local men guarded the site to prevent the Diggers' return.

Scholarly work done on both the Diggers and their opponents reveals that the Diggers were local men from the lower rungs of the socio-economic ladder, while opponents were wealthy landowners, who encouraged their renters and laborers to attack the Diggers. The landowners also had greater access to the local legal machinery, through which they brought legal charges against the Diggers. After Winstanley's Cobham experiment was disbanded, he and some of his followers worked for Lady Eleanor Davies in Hertfordshire. This arrangement apparently ended on bad terms in December, 1650.

After the publication of Winstanley's last work, *The Law of Freedom on a Platform* (1652), details of his life become sketchy. He lived in the Cobham area and held some minor local offices, including waywarden, overseer of the poor, churchwarden, and constable. It is ironic that the man who had offered revolutionary ideas challenging established authority should end up holding public office.

Winstanley apparently engaged in trade again, and from 1660 to 1662, he was the defendant in a lawsuit brought by a creditor seeking to recover debt from Winstanley's 1643 bankruptcy. His wife Susan died sometime before 1664, and he remarried Elizabeth Stanley (or Standley), with whom he had three children, Gerrard, Clement, and Elizabeth. In 1675, he was resident in Saint Giles in the Fields, Middlesex. Most scholars accept that the Gerrard Winstanley, "corn chandler," whose death was recorded in September, 1676, in the Westminster Quaker burial records was Winstanley the Digger. Apparently, he ended his days as a Quaker.

SIGNIFICANCE

The radical, revolutionary ideas Winstanley expressed in his pamphlets are worthy of serious analysis. The most radical of these ideas was his rejection of private ownership of land in favor of communal property ownership and communal labor. He used biblical, theological language to express his views, but he used them in a metaphorical vein, which has caused great debate among scholars over Winstanley's religion, with some questioning if he should even be considered Christian. He rejected the concept of a literal heaven and hell and referred to the "great Creator Reason." In his early pamphlets and in his Digger experiments, Winstanley rejected local and national government and a state church and adopted pacifism in the face of opposition.

In his final published work, *The Law of Freedom on a Platform*, Winstanley addressed Parliament's General Oliver Cromwell directly, asking him to impose Winstanley's model of utopia upon the Commonwealth. In this society, there would be no use for money transactions, and Parliament would make laws supporting freedom, oversee foreign policy, and raise troops. Winstanley believed that office holders became corrupt if in office too long, so there was to be a rotation of office holders. Retirement from manual labor would come at age forty, when a man would become a supervisor. Education, which would focus primarily on vocational skills, would be free and mandatory. "Postmasters" would exchange information and news with other towns. Sunday was to be a day of rest, and church attendance was to be voluntary; the clergy would not deliver sermons so much as present learned papers.

The government in Winstanley's utopian plan would retain punitive power; the death penalty would be in place for murder, rape, attempting to earn a living at law or religion, or claiming ownership of land. Although he shifted to a system in which society had this compulsory power, Winstanley remained consistent in his vision of the earth as a "common treasury" that should be worked through a communal effort. His views are rich and original, and he stands as an important precursor to later socialist and communist thinkers.

—Mark C. Herman

FURTHER READING

Bradstock, Andrew, ed. *Winstanley and the Diggers, 1649-1999*. London: Frank Cass, 2000. This collection of eleven essays provides an overview of the historical context in which the Diggers operated and Winstanley's life and ideas, as well as the investigation of specialized topics. Especially valuable are the pieces by Gerald Aylmer, James D. Alsop, and John Gurney.

Hill, Christopher. *The Religion of Gerrard Winstanley*. Past and Present Supplement 5. Oxford, England: The Past and Present Society, 1978. The Marxist historian Hill has written extensively on radicals such as Winstanley, and in this fifty-seven-page essay he analyzes the origin, evolution and impact of Winstanley's theological views.

_____. *The World Turned Upside Down: Radical Ideas During the English Revolution*. New York: Viking, 1972. This study, which many consider Hill's masterpiece, provides the context for the radical groups that developed in England in the 1640's and 1650's. It contains extensive material on Winstanley.

Sabine, George H., ed. *The Works of Gerrard Winstanley*. Ithaca, N.Y.: Cornell University Press, 1941. Reprint. New York: Russell and Russell, 1965. This collection of Winstanley's pamphlets along with the editor's introduction is an essential starting point for studying Winstanley's thought.

Webb, Darren. "The Bitter Product of Defeat? Reflections on Winstanley's *Law of Freedom*." *Political Studies* 52 (2004): 199-215. This revisionist essay challenges the generally held view that Winstanley's final pamphlet, *The Law of Freedom in a Platform*, was a major departure from his previous works by arguing that it is consistent with earlier expositions of his ideas.

SEE ALSO: Charles I; Oliver Cromwell; Lady Eleanor Davies.

RELATED ARTICLES in *Great Events from History: The Seventeenth Century, 1601-1700:* 1642-1651: English Civil Wars; August 17-September 25, 1643: Solemn League and Covenant; December 6, 1648-May 19, 1649: Establishment of the English Commonwealth.

JOHN WINTHROP
English-born American colonist

Winthrop served as the first governor of the Massachusetts Bay Colony. He was committed to the ideal of creating a Christian commonwealth, and his determined leadership was crucial to the establishment and success of the colony.

BORN: January 22, 1588; Edwardstone, Suffolk, England

DIED: April 5, 1649; Boston, Massachusetts Bay Colony (now in Massachusetts)

AREA OF ACHIEVEMENT: Government and politics

EARLY LIFE

John Winthrop (WIHN-thruhp) was the son of Anne Browne and Adam Winthrop, who lived at Groton Manor in Suffolk. Winthrop's grandfather, a successful London cloth merchant also named Adam, had purchased the manor from Henry VIII in 1544. It had been part of a monastery confiscated by the monarch. Winthrop received an extensive education beginning at age seven with instruction from a local vicar. At fifteen, he entered Trinity College, Cambridge. Winthrop remained there less than two years but later studied law at Gray's Inn, one of the London Inns of Court.

Winthrop started a family at a tender age; his father arranged a marriage to Mary Forth when he was only seventeen, and he became a father at eighteen. Over the next twelve years, Winthrop moved from his dowry lands at Great Stambridge back to Groton, presided over the manorial court, served as a justice of the peace, and assumed control of the family lands on the manor. In the 1620's, he widened his horizons by developing a lucrative London law practice. It enabled Winthrop to make contacts in the government and led to his selection in 1627 as an attorney in the King's Court of Wards and Liveries, a court which administered the estates of minor heirs to lands held from the king.

As he matured, Winthrop became ever more committed to the faith of the Puritan reformers in the Church of England. Advocates of the teaching of John Calvin, Puritans believed that God had predestined salvation for only a few. From his early teens, Winthrop had followed a rigorous regimen of prayer and study in search of signs that God had selected him. While he struggled for assurance of that elect status, Winthrop also sought to place his relationship with God ahead of all else—his family, his work, and his love of hunting, food, and drink. He never became an ascetic; he believed God's creations should be enjoyed but always with proper moderation. His faith made Winthrop a stern and determined man; this was clearly evident in a painting of the mature Winthrop. His serious countenance, graced by a Vandyke beard and ruffled collar, befits a man with a sense of purpose.

Engraving of John Winthrop by O. Pelton. (Library of Congress)

LIFE'S WORK

Winthrop probably would have been known only as one of the lesser English gentry had not a series of economic, religious, and personal crises in the late 1620's caused him to leave England. Inflation, smaller returns from the fixed rents he could charge the tenants on his land, and a depression in the Suffolk textile trade all dearly cost the squire of Groton. His disappointing financial situation worsened in 1629 when Winthrop lost his attorneyship in the Court of Wards and Liveries. He was only one of numerous casualties in the campaign of Charles I to remove Puritans from secular and religious positions. The king's Catholic wife, the appointment of William Laud (a resolute anti-Puritan) as bishop of London, and the dissolution in 1629 of a Parliament heavily influenced by Puritans all caused Dissenters to despair about their future in England. They did not see much hope for their faith under a monarch who opposed their advocacy of simpler services and a Calvinist theology in the Church of England.

Winthrop had a more immediate reason for feeling that he was living in an evil and declining nation. Long concerned by what he considered a lax moral climate in the nation, Winthrop was appalled by the behavior of his son Henry. The nineteen-year-old had gone to the West

Indian island of Barbados in 1627. Upon his return two years later, Henry did little more than carouse with boisterous friends in London. Winthrop believed that it was imperative that he act to save his family and preserve his faith. He worried that migration meant abandoning his homeland, but he hoped that the creation of a model Christian community in North America would show England the way to reform.

Winthrop worked with the members of the Massachusetts Bay Company to achieve his goal. Made up of substantial landowners, merchants, and clergymen, the company selected Winthrop as its governor. He organized the ships, settlers, and provisions for the expedition and then led more than one thousand people to Massachusetts in 1630. In the next nineteen years, Winthrop retained an important role in the colony's government; twelve times he was elected governor. Throughout those years, he struggled to keep the settlers committed to building a cooperative, godly commonwealth.

Challenges to Winthrop's vision emerged quickly. Few were willing to settle in a single, compact town as Winthrop had hoped; in addition to Boston, six towns were formed in the first year alone. The cheap land, the high wages paid to scarce skilled workers, and the profits to be made in commerce led many to a greater concern over the material benefits of Winthrop's colony than its spiritual. Price and wage controls mitigated the impact of the more acquisitive settlers but could not completely suppress the growing economic individualism. More troubling to Winthrop than the greed of some colonists and the dispersal of settlement, however, was religious dissent. Winthrop and his supporters did not migrate to Massachusetts to create a utopia of toleration; rather they moved to worship in a singular fashion—in self-governing congregations of God's elect. Consequently, Winthrop fought all attempts to undermine that effort.

The first significant trouble came from Roger Williams, a minister who arrived in the colony in 1631. Among other things, Williams demanded that the colonists repudiate all ties to the Church of England, a position contrary to Winthrop's resolve to reform, not break from, the established church. Williams also argued that the elect should not worship with the unregenerate, an idea repugnant to Winthrop, whose hope for a unified colony dictated that persons of all conditions worship together.

A brilliant woman, Anne Hutchinson, presented an even greater threat. Not long after her arrival in 1634, she began to hold mid-week meetings in her home. Hutchinson used these popular gatherings to criticize ministers whom she believed erred in their sermons. All but two, she charged, taught a Covenant of Works—that good conduct could lead to salvation—rather than a Covenant of Grace—that salvation was obtained only through God's grace. Her attacks on the clergy made Hutchinson a danger to the established order. When she later claimed that she received divine revelation, Hutchinson became a pariah to Winthrop.

When persuasion failed to convince the two dissenters to retreat from their positions, Winthrop supported the decision to banish them, Williams in 1636 and Hutchinson two years later. Other dissenters also suffered banishment or were forced to migrate to other regions. The departure of these people ensured a religious orthodoxy that prevailed throughout the colony's first two decades.

In addition to these religious conflicts, Massachusetts faced other vexing problems. Disputes over who could participate in the government were resolved by permitting male church members to vote. Complaints from outlying settlements that their interests were not being served by Boston lawmakers were handled by allowing each town to have representation in the colony's General Court.

The outbreak of civil war in England in the early 1640's dramatically reduced the immigration to Massachusetts. Immigrants had been the chief consumers of the colony's produce, and with the decline in their numbers, the economy slumped badly. Prices fell until the Puritans found new markets in the Canaries and the Caribbean Islands. Winthrop figured prominently in the resolution of these difficulties; he helped work out the political problems, and he maintained contacts and promoted trade in the West Indies.

Winthrop usually avoided the extremes in both secular and religious matters. He deplored the ideas of separatist dissenters such as Williams, for example, because he believed that they would lead to the chaos of dozens of little utopias. Yet other leaders in the colony, notably Thomas Dudley, criticized Winthrop for being too lenient with dissenters. His general commitment to moderate positions offended many, but it helped preserve the Puritan experiment in the New World, one with more than fifteen thousand inhabitants at his death in 1649. Besides a grateful colony, Winthrop was survived by six of his sixteen children and his fourth wife.

SIGNIFICANCE

As he led the Puritan expedition across the Atlantic in early 1630, Winthrop had time to think about the meaning of their collective effort. He drafted a lay sermon containing those reflections, and he delivered it to the passengers prior to their arrival in Massachusetts. Entitled "A Modell of Christian Charity," it remains one of the most eloquent statements of Christian brotherhood. He explained to his followers,

> wee must be knitt together in this worke as one man, wee must entertaine each other in brotherly Affeccion . . . wee must delight in eache other, make others Condicions our owne rejoyce together, mourne together, labour, and suffer together, allwayes haveing before our eyes . . . our Community as members of the same body. . . .

His effort to convince settlers to subordinate their self-interest to the good of the community was far from successful. Yet through his example and his support of laws governing economic behavior, Winthrop helped keep in check the individualism he believed would destroy the colony.

Perhaps Winthrop's greatest impact on American life was his evocation of a sense of mission. He thought that the tired generations of the Old World were eagerly observing the Puritan effort to build a model religious society. "For wee must Consider," he claimed, "that wee shall be as a Citty upon a Hill, the eies of all people are uppon us." Winthrop and fellow Puritans believed that they were God's new chosen people, a new Israel. Succeeding generations have shared this sense that America had a special destiny to be a light to other nations. They have revealed their debt to the great Puritan leader each time they borrowed his metaphor and claimed that America must be as a city upon a hill.

—Larry Gragg

FURTHER READING

Bercovitch, Sacvan. "Puritan Origins Revisited: The 'City upon a Hill' as a Model of Tradition and Innovation." In *Early America Re-explored: New Readings in Colonial, Early National, and Antebellum Culture*, edited by Klaus H. Schmidt and Fritz Fleischman. New York: Peter Lang, 2000. Examines Winthrop's sermon, "A Modell of Christian Charity."

Bremer, Francis J. *John Winthrop: America's Forgotten Founding Father*. New York: Oxford University Press, 2003. Bremer, editor of the Winthrop papers for the Massachusetts Historical Society, draws upon those papers to produce this exhaustively detailed biography.

Crilly, Mark. "John Winthrop: Magistrate, Minister, Merchant." *Midwest Quarterly: A Journal of Contemporary Thought* 40, no. 2 (Winter, 1999): 187-196. Discusses the many roles Winthrop played in the life of the Massachusetts Bay Colony.

Miller, Perry. "Errand into the Wilderness." In *Errand into the Wilderness*. Cambridge, Mass.: Harvard University Press, 1956. This is an essay by the leading historian on the Puritan mind. He describes both the exhilarating sense of mission Winthrop shared with other leaders in the 1630's and the disappointment of a later generation when it realized that England had paid scant attention to the errand of reform they had run for God.

Morgan, Edmund S. *The Puritan Dilemma: The Story of John Winthrop*. Boston: Little, Brown, 1958. 2d ed. New York: Longman, 1999. Morgan's book is not only the best available biography of Winthrop, but also one of the clearest presentations of Puritan thought. He discusses Winthrop's life in England and America and in the process details the struggle faced by a pious man in a corrupt world.

_____, ed. *The Founding of Massachusetts: Historians and the Sources*. Indianapolis: Bobbs-Merrill, 1964. This is a helpful collection of primary sources from the first five years of the Massachusetts Bay Colony. Notably, Morgan includes more than one hundred pages from Winthrop's letters, journal, and miscellaneous other papers. There are also excerpts from the works of four historians' accounts of the colony.

Morison, Samuel Eliot. *Builders of the Bay Colony*. Boston: Houghton Mifflin, 1930. Reprint. Boston: Northeastern University Press, 1981. Morison profiles more than a dozen individuals in these lively essays originally published in 1930. The profiles attempt to rehabilitate the long-tarnished image of Puritans, they serve as an excellent introduction to the leading personalities in seventeenth century Massachusetts. The longest is on Winthrop, and in it Morison portrays him as a pious yet practical leader.

Moseley, James G. *John Winthrop's World: History as a Story, The Story as History*. Madison: University of Wisconsin Press, 1992. This book is composed of two parts. The first is a short biography of Winthrop; the second examines how subsequent historians have perceived Winthrop and the Puritan experiment.

Rutman, Darrett B. *Winthrop's Boston: A Portrait of a Puritan Town, 1630-1649*. Chapel Hill: University of North Carolina Press, 1965. A well-researched and well-written work on the Puritan capital during Winthrop's life. A study of the town's government, church policies, population trends, and economic development, it reveals how far Bostonians strayed from Winthrop's goal of a cooperative godly community.

Vaughan, Alden T., and Francis J. Bremer, eds. *Puritan New England: Essays on Religion, Society and Culture*. New York: St. Martin's Press, 1977. This collection of essays, written by leading scholars, covers many areas of Puritan life—religion, witchcraft, government, economics, family, and race relations. Several include references to Winthrop.

Wall, Robert E. *Massachusetts Bay: The Crucial Decade, 1640-1650*. New Haven, Conn.: Yale University Press, 1972. A detailed account of the political events of the 1640's. Wall describes the growing conflict between leaders from Boston and those in other towns jealous of their power.

SEE ALSO: Charles I; Anne Hutchinson; William Laud; Roger Williams.

RELATED ARTICLES in *Great Events from History: The Seventeenth Century, 1601-1700:* March, 1629-1640: "Personal Rule" of Charles I; 1642-1651: English Civil Wars.

SIR CHRISTOPHER WREN
English architect, inventor, and scientist

Combining his skill as an engineer with a thorough knowledge of the classical principles of art, Wren became one of the greatest architects of all time, influencing not only the designers and builders of his own era but also those of successive generations.

BORN: October 20, 1632; East Knoyle, Wiltshire, England

DIED: February 25, 1723; London, England

AREAS OF ACHIEVEMENT: Architecture, invention, science and technology

EARLY LIFE

Sir Christopher Wren was the son of the well-known clergyman Christopher Wren, who was at one time chaplain to Charles I, and the nephew of Matthew Wren, bishop of Hereford, Norwich, and Ely. He was very young when his mother, Mary Cox Wren, died, and his elder sister, Susan, assumed the task of rearing the sickly child. His brother-in-law, the Reverend William Holder, a noted mathematician, later introduced young Wren to one of the academic interests of his life.

His health improved, Wren was sent to Westminster School in London, which, under Richard Busby, was quickly becoming one of the great public schools. Wren thrived in the school's rigorous atmosphere, and while he excelled in all of his subjects, he did particularly well in mathematics and the natural sciences. When his studies were finished at Westminster in 1646, he was selected to assist Charles Scarburgh, who was a regular lecturer at Surgeons' Hall in London; for a brief period, Wren built the models that Scarburgh used in his lectures in anatomy. Wren matriculated at Wadham College, Oxford, in 1649 as a "fellow commoner." Although he was only in residence at Wadham for two years during the four and a half years he was a member of the college, Wren nevertheless became a part of the group of scholars that formed the nucleus of the future Royal Society. He took his bachelor of arts degree in 1651 and his master of arts degree two years later.

At the age of twenty-one, Wren was elected a fellow of All Souls College. His time during the next four years was devoted to his many scientific interests, until the chair of astronomy at Gresham College, London, became vacant and he was appointed to fill it in 1657. Many of Wren's friends from his college days gathered around him again in London and continued their scientific stud-

ies and philosophical inquiries, while the political situation in England began to disintegrate following the death of Oliver Cromwell in 1658. Then in May, 1660, the return of Charles II restored stability to the kingdom. In December, Wren and his associates petitioned the king, who was also an amateur scientist, to grant them a charter for a permanent scientific society. Wren proved to be one of the most faithful members of the Royal Society, and from 1680 to 1682 he served as its president.

Wren resigned his professorship in February of 1661, shortly after the founding of the Royal Society, to become Savilian Professor of Astronomy at Oxford. He also received two honorary degrees that same year—a doctor of civil laws from Oxford and a doctor of laws from Cambridge—but his life in the academic cloister was about to end. Although he retained his professorship in astronomy until 1673, Wren had been seduced by the real passion of his life, architecture. After Sir Isaac Newton, he was probably the most gifted scientist of his day, and his inventions were numerous and useful. His experiments with the barometer established its use as a device for predicting changes in the weather. An interest in medicine born of his student days provided a constant source of experiments, but these accomplishments are all but forgotten when compared to the vast legacy of architectural treasures left by Wren.

LIFE'S WORK

Charles II was obviously impressed by Wren, for in 1661 the king offered the young professor the position of assistant to Sir John Denham, surveyor general to His Majesty's Works. This post was not a frivolous appointment; Wren was a well-known mathematician, and he had some knowledge of both architectural design and building techniques, thanks to his father, who had been an amateur architect. For two years, Wren devoted himself to mastering his new profession, and then, in 1663, his first two original designs appeared.

Chronologically, the chapel at Pembroke College, Cambridge, is the first work by Wren to be completed. Built with funds supplied by Bishop Matthew Wren, his uncle, it was finished by 1665 when Wren made a journey to Paris to broaden his knowledge of classical architectural forms. The second structure, the Sheldonian Theater at Oxford, was not completed until 1669 and clearly shows a number of refinements obviously gleaned from his travels and his encounter with the great Italian master of the baroque style, Gian Lorenzo Bernini. After six months on the Continent, Wren returned home overflowing with ideas but with limited opportunities to apply his newly acquired knowledge. Then in September, 1666, most of London was destroyed in the Great Fire, which raged for six days. This tragedy gave Wren the chance for which he longed, and he fully realized the opportunity.

Denham, more poet than builder, willingly surrendered most of his authority to his assistant; before the embers were cold, Wren presented a plan for the rebuilding of London to Charles II, who enthusiastically endorsed it. Unfortunately, the private landowners refused to pool their property in the interest of the city's future. They insisted on rebuilding on streets and plots that dated from the Middle Ages, reproducing the maze of twisting streets and narrow lanes that were familiar to their great-grandparents. Wren's magnificent plan, which would have created the most beautiful capital in Europe, was shelved. Luckily, some of its components were salvaged to adorn the city of red bricks that arose from the ashes of an earlier London.

Wren was not one who allowed disappointment to discourage him. Instead of brooding over his lost plan for London, he devoted his energies and talents to the overwhelming task of rebuilding Saint Paul's Cathedral, more than fifty parish churches, and a number of public buildings and private homes. In recognition of his efforts, Charles II created a special title for him, but Wren was less concerned with honors than with the resistance to his dream for a new and better London.

Despite the damage done to the fabric of Saint Paul's, a number of the members of the chapter wanted to repair the decayed medieval structure. As early as 1662, Wren had made a thorough study of the building and submitted a report calling for drastic changes. While the dean and the chapter argued over his findings, the Great Fire essentially ended their debate. The dean, William Sancroft, agreed with Wren that a new cathedral was both more practical and more desirable, but the collapse of another part of the building was necessary before those who still resisted Wren's planned reconstruction were persuaded. It took two years to pull

down the cathedral's remains, and Wren devoted those months to developing his first plan for the new Saint Paul's.

In 1669, Denham died, and Wren was finally named surveyor general, an office he held until 1718. He also married Faith Coghill in December of that year. Their first son was born in 1672, the year that Wren was knighted and finished his first design for the cathedral. Charles II approved the plan, finding it innovative and exciting, but many opposed it, especially among the clergy. Even James, duke of York, voiced his objections to it.

Disappointed but undaunted, Wren began to prepare a series of new designs reflecting a number of ideas. Finally, in 1675, one of them was approved, but the death of his wife robbed Wren of his satisfaction at finally succeeding in pleasing most of the factions. If the cathedral had been built according to his original specifications, it would not have been an exceptional building, but luckily,

Sir Christopher Wren. (Library of Congress)

995

as Saint Paul's was being built, the architect was able to make a number of important changes. He was fortunate to secure the talents of a number of exceptional artists and craftspeople to adorn his masterpiece, such as the superb woodcarver Grinling Gibbons, whom his friend John Evelyn had discovered.

The cornerstone was laid on June 2, 1675, the choir was opened for use on December 2, 1697, and the final stone was placed in 1711. Wren was able to oversee the entire project, and almost every detail reflects his genius. In the early stages of the cathedral's construction, Wren had the complete support as well as the advice of Charles II.

Wren literally devoted the rest of his life to rebuilding the parish churches of London. Each year saw a plan completed or a cornerstone laid. Each decade saw the skyline of London change, as new and elegant spires rose heavenward. No two churches were alike, and each one had its particular feature that made it unique. Like the floor plans, these special features were chosen to harmonize with their surroundings.

While he was designing churches by the score, Wren was also busily engaged in carrying out a number of commissions, both royal and private. Despite political upheavals and a revolution, Wren continued to adorn England with buildings of exceptional beauty, such as the original Ashmolean Museum and Tom Tower at Oxford, Chelsea Hospital, and Greenwich Hospital, as well as additions to Kensington Palace and Hampton Court. The only building actually designed by Wren for construction in America was the main academic building at the College of William and Mary in Virginia, but the Colonies were filled with structures that reflected the ideas of design and construction that he had made distinctly his own.

Despite the loss of his second wife and two of his four children, Wren never lost his creative abilities or his desire to master new fields of endeavor. In 1685, he entered politics as a Member of Parliament. He remained active until he was forced out of office in 1718 by his rivals, who had the support of the first Hanoverian monarch, George I. Wren died, after a short illness, on February 25, 1723, and was buried in Saint Paul's. The last words of his epitaph are a fitting summation of his career: "Si monumentum requiris, circumspice" (If you seek a monument, look around you).

SIGNIFICANCE

Trained in mathematics and the natural sciences, Wren left a successful career as a professor to pursue his partic-

ular passion for architecture. Charles II recognized his genius, and when the city of London was ravaged by fire in 1666, he commissioned Wren to develop a plan for the rebuilding of the capital. Unfortunately, it was not adopted, but Wren was able to adorn the rebuilt city with a number of beautiful churches, including the new Saint Paul's Cathedral, and countless public buildings. He was the English master of the baroque style, and his ideas were widely copied by his contemporaries in England and America. No English architect has had so profound an influence as Wren had on public taste in his own time as well as in future generations.

—*Clifton W. Potter, Jr.*

FURTHER READING

Briggs, Martin S. *Wren the Incomparable*. London: Allen and Unwin, 1953. The treatment of Wren's early life is brief, since this work concentrates on his achievements in the field of architecture. The book is rich in photographs and drawings.

Dutton, Ralph. *The Age of Wren*. London: B. T. Batsford, 1951. A profusely illustrated work containing an interesting treatment of "the lesser company," the architects, artists, and artisans who were Wren's contemporaries and copied his style.

Edwards, Ralph, and L. G. G. Ramsey, eds. *The Stuart Period, 1603-1714*. London: Connoisseur, 1957. Within this survey of the arts in the seventeenth century, Margaret Whinney's essay on architecture places Wren in the context of his time by examining what preceded and followed him in his field.

Fürst, Viktor. *The Architecture of Sir Christopher Wren*. London: Lund Humphries, 1956. Exhausting as well as exhaustive, this work is sometimes turgid, but it never lacks detail. Many of the drawings are remarkable, and the notes give insight into the character of Wren the artist.

Gilbert, Adrian. *The New Jerusalem*. New York: Bantam, 2002. Discusses Wren and the other architects who rebuilt London as the site of the New Jerusalem after the Great Fire of 1666.

Jardine, Lisa. *On a Grander Scale: The Outstanding Life of Christopher Wren*. New York: HarperCollins, 2002. A recent biography describing the tumultuous nature of Wren's life and the versatility and genius of his career.

Sekler, Eduard F. *Wren and His Place in European Architecture*. New York: Macmillan, 1956. Sekler takes a novel approach to Wren and his work, making the great architect's accomplishments even more outstanding. Includes an exceptionally good bibliography.

Summerson, John. *Architecture in Britain, 1530-1830.* Rev. ed. London: Penguin Books, 1969. The third part of this survey, "Wren and the Baroque," contains seven well-written and comprehensive chapters.

_____. *Sir Christopher Wren.* New York: Macmillan, 1953. Brief, compact, and well balanced, this is an excellent biography.

Tinniswood, Adrian. *His Invention So Fertile: A Life of Christopher Wren.* New York: Oxford University Press, 2001. A scholarly yet entertaining biography by a British architectural historian, providing a detailed study of Wren's personality, life, and work.

Webb, Geoffrey. *Wren.* London: Duckworth, 1937. This slim volume is well written and provides a good introduction to Wren and the major events of his life and career.

SEE ALSO: Gian Lorenzo Bernini; Charles I; Charles II (of England); Oliver Cromwell; John Evelyn; James II; Sir Isaac Newton.

RELATED ARTICLES in *Great Events from History: The Seventeenth Century, 1601-1700:* 1601-1672: Rise of Scientific Societies; 1642-1651: English Civil Wars; December 16, 1653-September 3, 1658: Cromwell Rules England as Lord Protector; May, 1659-May, 1660: Restoration of Charles II; September 2-5, 1666: Great Fire of London; 1675-1707: Wren Supervises the Rebuilding of St. Paul's Cathedral.

YUI SHŌSETSU
Japanese rebel and military teacher

A noted teacher of military science beloved by his samurai students, Yui Shōsetsu staged an unsuccessful assault on the Tokugawa shogunate known as the Keian Incident. The rebellion was meant to highlight the plight of the rōnin, *or masterless samurai, who had been robbed of their livelihood by the Tokugawa reorganization of Japan's nobility.*

BORN: 1605; Suruga Province (now Shizuoka Prefecture), Japan
DIED: September, 1651; Sumpu, Suruga Province
AREAS OF ACHIEVEMENT: Military, education

EARLY LIFE

Yui Shōsetsu (yoo-ee shoh-seh-tsoo) was born to a samurai family in 1605 in Suruga province, which was situated on the southern coast of Honshu island, facing the Pacific Ocean. Suruga province was almost halfway between the old imperial capital of Kyōto to the west and Edo (now Tokyo), the new capital of the Tokugawa shoguns, to the east. Yui's life would come to exemplify the conflict between medieval and Edo Japan.

Since 1603, Tokugawa Ieyasu had ruled Japan as shogun, officially in the name of the emperor, whom he reduced to a figurehead. In the year when Yui was born, Ieyasu officially resigned in favor of his third son, Tokugawa Hidetada, and moved his own court out of Edo to Sumpu, the capital of Suruga province. Until his death in 1616, Ieyasu kept residence in Sumpu, giving the town where Yui grew up an important position.

Because Yui was born in the samurai class, under the rules of feudal Japan he was destined to remain a samurai for life and to abide by the codes of conduct for his class. Since 1588, samurai had been the only men allowed to bear arms in Japan. Yui was educated in the *bushidō* code, a mixture of Zen Buddhism and Zhu Xi Confucianism imported from the Chinese in the twelfth century. *Bushidō* stressed a samurai's absolute loyalty to his lord, the highest moral standards, and the necessity to live an exceptional life. When Yui was ten, the shogun promulgated the *buke shohatto*, or laws governing military (samurai) houses, and Yui received instruction in their precepts. His education included rigorous training in martial arts, archery, swordsmanship, and equestrian combat. As a teenager, Yui was given spiritual training, subjected to strict discipline, and taught to accept the inevitability of death with equanimity.

LIFE'S WORK

Unable or unwilling to follow the traditional path and become a samurai in the service of a daimyo, or feudal lord, Yui was faced with limited choices as he entered adulthood. One option was to become a teacher. Education, especially in subjects considered related to the warrior's life, was not considered work and was thus allowed to samurai. Yui became a student of Kusunoki Fuden, studying military arts with great success. After graduating, Yui opened his own school in Edo and taught military science.

Military science as understood in the Edo period of feudal Japan encompassed more than warfare. Traditional modes of fighting were part of the curriculum, which ironically excluded the modern European weapons such as muskets and cannons that had won the Tokugawa their position as shoguns. Besides strategy and tactics, Yui's teaching included philosophy, religion, literature, and the arts. These subjects were considered essential for the comprehensive education of a samurai.

The teachings of Yui Shōsetsu soon became famous among the cultural and military elite of Edo. Even daimyo and senior vassals of the Tokugawa shogun, the *hatamoto*, became his students. As the third ruler of the dynasty, Tokugawa Iemitsu, consolidated the power of the shogunate, Yui taught in the capital and witnessed these developments firsthand. His students also provided him with topical information.

As shoguns, one of the greatest powers of the Tokugawa was the power to allocate the land to be ruled by the approximately 270 daimyos of feudal Japan. Immediately upon taking control of the shogunate, the Tokugawa used this power to reward their followers and to punish their opponents. From 1600 to 1650, the first three Tokugawa shoguns created 172 new daimyos, enlarged the domains of 206 others, and transferred 281 daimyos from one domain to another. However, 213 daimyos lost their domains or saw them significantly reduced.

In order to retain samurai under his command, a daimyo was required to possess a domain of at least 2,500 acres (1,012 hectares). When a daimyo lost his land, or lost enough to fall below this 2,500-acre minimum, he had to discharge all of his samurai. These discharged warriors became masterless samurai, or *rōnin*. With so much turbulence created by the Tokugawa redistribution of lands, increasing numbers of *rōnin* moved to Edo and roamed the streets of the capital. Often very poor because they neither were allowed to work nor had land or possessions of their own, the *rōnin* became desperate and sometimes molested the other citizens. *Rōnin* had high social status and prestige but very little material income or capital.

Many *rōnin* flocked to military schools, including Yui's, and Yui considered ways to help these displaced samurai. One plan of Yui's was to make his *rōnin* the samurai of daimyo Tokugawa Yorinobu of Kii province (now Wakayama prefecture). The *rōnin* ardently admired their teacher for this proposal, but the plan failed to materialize.

In 1651, shogun Tokugawa Iemitsu died and was succeeded by his ten-year-old son, Tokugawa Ietsuna. By this time, Yui Shōsetsu had become a close friend with a fellow teacher, Marubashi Chūya, himself a *rōnin*. To support himself, this expert with the samurai lance had opened a martial arts school and taught in Edo as well. The two teachers plotted a major public disturbance against the Tokugawa shogunate. Because their planned plot fell into the last year of the Keian era of the traditional Japanese calendar, the ensuing event is often called the Keian Incident in Japanese history.

Yui and Marubashi resolved to launch a massive attack. Whether their goal was actually to overthrow the Tokugawa regime or merely to demonstrate against the shogunate politics that had disenfranchised so many warriors is a question that has been debated among historians. Whatever the case, the conspirators were able to enlist the secret aid of the traitorous deputy commander of the shogun's military arsenal, Kawara Jūrōbei. They planned to explode the facility, set fire to the city of Edo, kill senior ministers, and take over Edo Castle, where the boy shogun resided with his adult advisers. Close to the planned date of the attack, Yui moved back to Sumpu with ten handpicked *rōnin*. His plan was to launch a simultaneous attack, burning Sumpu and seizing the shogun's shrine at Kunōzan, outside the city gates.

Most likely because Marubashi began talking about their plan in increasingly boastful terms, government informants learned of the attack in advance. They told senior councilor Matsudaira Nobutsuna, a loyal adviser to the late shogun. Matsudaira was nicknamed Chie Izu (clever Izu), a play on his noble title of Izu no Kami. Clever Izu acted immediately and decisively, bringing the Keian Incident to a quick end. He arrested Marubashi and thirty-three of his fellow plotters, including some of

their male family members. The conspirators were interrogated and then executed on September 24, 1651.

Learning of the arrest and execution of the Edo rebels, Yui Shōsetsu committed suicide in Sumpu. Adding flames to the later controversy over the true goals of the rebels, Yui left behind a suicide note. In it, he claimed that the goal of his rebellion had not been to overthrow the Tokugawa shogunate. Instead, he said, his intention had merely been to call attention to the dire position of the *rōnin*.

SIGNIFICANCE

As a teacher of military science, Yui Shōsetsu insisted that the proper place of the samurai was with a daimyo. He considered it an injustice to deprive samurai of this relationship. Whether his attempted rebellion, including the burning of two cities, was ethical remains debatable, especially from the point of view of modern standards. Yui, however, chose to act on his beliefs, and this endeared him to the populace.

Yui Shōsetsu almost immediately became a folk hero. Astonishingly, later Tokugawa shoguns did not object when he and his fellow conspirator Marubashi Chūya became the heroes of popular historical fiction in the late seventeenth and eighteenth centuries. His fate was turned into a famous Kabuki play as well, and his support for the roaming *rōnin* was represented favorably.

Rōnin launched another rebellion one year after Yui's death in 1652, but Matsudaira "Clever Izu" quickly crushed it as well. Nevertheless, Yui's planned plot and the later incident seem to have changed Tokugawa politics towards the daimyo. While the first three shoguns had taken away from disfavored daimyos a total of 2,700,000 acres (1,093,000 hectares) in fifty years, that figure dropped for the fourth shogun. Under Tokugawa Ietsuna, from 1651 to 1680, only 182,000 acres (74,000 hectares) were confiscated and reassigned. The figures crept up again under the next shogun (425,000 acres; 172,000 hectares), but the total number of Japan's *rōnin* dropped significantly.

—*R. C. Lutz*

FURTHER READING

De Benneville, James. *The Haunted House: More Samurai Tales of the Tokugawa.* 2d ed. London: Kegan Paul, 2001. Historical fiction based on contemporary Japanese chronicles of the era that also features Yui Shōsetsu as a character. Illustrated.

Ikegami, Eiko. *The Taming of the Samurai.* Cambridge, Mass.: Harvard University Press, 1995. Academic study of development of samurai culture. Chapter 4 deals with samurai in the Tokugawa shogunate and sheds light on the forces leading to Yui's rebellion. Illustrated, notes, index.

Jansen, Marius. *The Making of Modern Japan*. Cambridge, Mass.: Belknap Press of Harvard University Press, 2000. Useful description of the Tokugawa state that reveals what Yui rebelled against; also provides background on the time in which he lived and his society, culture, lifestyle, and beliefs. Illustrated, notes, index, bibliography.

McClain, James. *Japan: A Modern History*. New York: Norton, 2001. First three chapters deal with the Tokugawa period and illuminate the lifestyle shared by men like Yui and his adherents; the work shows what drove *rōnin* to rebel and why the shogunate remained successful. Illustrated, maps, index.

Turnbull, Stephen. *Samurai: The World of the Warrior*. Oxford, England: Osprey, 2003. Richly illustrated book, brings to life the subjects of Yui's military studies and his planned revolt.

SEE ALSO: Tokugawa Ieyasu.

RELATED ARTICLES in *Great Events from History: The Seventeenth Century, 1601-1700:* 1603: Tokugawa Shogunate Begins; 1615: Promulgation of the *Buke shohatto* and *Kinchū narabini kuge shohatto*; 1651-1652: Edo Rebellions; 1651-1680: Ietsuna Shogunate.

ZHENG CHENGGONG
Chinese pirate leader

Zheng was a sea lord who fought for the failing Ming Dynasty against the conquering Manchus. Seeking a secure base of operations, he seized Taiwan from the Dutch and established traditional Chinese political and cultural institutions on the island.

BORN: August 28, 1624; Hirado, near Nagasaki, Japan
DIED: June 23, 1662; Taiwan
ALSO KNOWN AS: Cheng Ch'eng-kung (Wade-Giles); Koxinga; Guo Xingye (Pinyin), Kuo Hsing-yeh (Wade-Giles)
AREAS OF ACHIEVEMENT: Government and politics, warfare and conquest

EARLY LIFE

Zheng Chenggong (juhng juhng-goong) was born in the declining years of the Ming Dynasty (1368-1644). The Ming were steadily losing ground against the expanding Manchus, who would soon take control of China, establishing the Qing Dynasty (1644-1911). Zheng Chenggong's father, Zheng Zhilong (Cheng Chih-lung), was born in 1601 in the coastal province of Fujian (Fukien). Like many Fujianese, Zheng Zhilong took to the sea; he lived in the Portuguese colony of Macao, where he was baptized and known to the Europeans as Nicholas Iquan. Asian waters were dangerous, and there was a thin line between commerce and piracy. Zheng Zhilong controlled a pirate fleet of Chinese and Japanese adventurers and built a trading empire.

Zheng Chenggong was born August 28, 1624, in Hirado, Japan, where his father had a Japanese wife of the Tagawa family. He lived with his mother until he was seven, learning Japanese culture to such an extent that the Japanese would later adopt him as a cultural hero, describing him as "a Japanese with a Chinese father." Meanwhile, his father was becoming an important political figure at the Ming court. Initially attacked as a pirate, he was so powerful that the court had no option but to grant him office. In return, he agreed to defend the southern coast against other pirates.

Now more secure, Zheng Zhilong brought the seven-year-old Zheng Chenggong to live with him in China. The boy studied the classical writings that were the focus of Confucian education. Zheng Chenggong was a talented, diligent student, who took his first degree at fifteen, entering the Imperial Academy in 1644. Had he lived at another time, he might have become a major Confucian scholar or a holder of high office within the civil bureaucracy, the ultimate goal of many Confucian students. The Ming Dynasty was collapsing before the Manchus, however, who were expanding southward from their ancestral home in Manchuria.

The Manchus were a vigorous, seminomadic warrior race who had learned Confucian ways through long-standing ties to China. Even many Chinese saw their rule as preferable to that of the Ming, who had grown corrupt and oppressive. The Ming lost their capital, Beijing, and their last formally recognized emperor to the Manchus in April, 1644. The Ming successor to the throne founded a second capital at Nanjing (Nanking), which fell in June, 1645; a third successor founded another capital at Fuzhou (Foochow), Fujian.

LIFE'S WORK

Fujian was virtually controlled by Zheng Zhilong, a fact that made his eldest son and heir, the young Zheng Chenggong, even more important. Zheng Chenggong was presented to the Ming emperor, who made him a member of the imperial clan. He was known at court as Guo Xingye (Kuo Hsing-yeh), or "lord of the imperial surname," from which Europeans would derive his Latinized name, Koxinga. Zheng Chenggong's father was ordered to guard the main pass into Fujian against the Manchus. Zheng Chenggong himself was drawn into the military defense of the failing regime and given the court rank of earl and the military title of field marshal in 1645.

His father foresaw the fate of the Ming Dynasty, which had little legitimacy after losing two capitals and two emperors. The Manchus, presenting themselves as reformers rather than conquerors, offered office and rewards to any Chinese who joined them; Zheng Zhilong came to terms with the invaders and abandoned the pass. The conflict between family ties and loyalty to the state has traditionally been quite strong for the Chinese, and Zheng Chenggong must have felt torn between his father and the Ming court. The traditional version of his life has it that he remonstrated with his father, calling him a traitor. Certainly, the young man came to a decision that marked a turning point in his life: He decided to stay with the Ming. With the critical pass unguarded, Fuzhou fell to the Manchus, and the third refugee emperor killed himself in 1646. Zheng Chenggong left Fujian with a small band of followers (legend says ninety men) and sailed for the southern province of Guangdong (Kwang-tung), centered upon the great international port Guang-zhou (Canton).

Within a year, Zheng Chenggong commanded a major fleet, whose forces, when operating on land, formed a formidable army. Considering that he was only twenty-two years old, this was a remarkable achievement. Part of the explanation for this achievement lies in Zheng's personal abilities and magnetism. As a successful scholar and court figure, he was much admired, but he was also a man of action. He was physically impressive and inspired awe in even the prejudiced Europeans who would meet him later. Many of his father's forces also saw the elder Zheng's defection as immoral, deserted Zheng Zhilong, and rallied to Zheng Chenggong.

Zheng understood well the importance of traditional cultural models to the historically minded Chinese and always presented himself within the established tradition of loyalty in the face of adversity. This adversity heightened when his mother, who had come to China some time earlier, died at the fall of Xiamen (Amoy) in Fujian. With his new fleet and army, Zheng now operated against the Manchus in Fujian, retaking lost territory. There was now yet another refugee Ming court, in Guangdong, and Zheng pledged loyalty to this fourth refugee emperor.

In Zheng's later life, there is often confusion between his commitment to the Ming and his commitment to self-interest. One event that highlights this ambiguity is Zheng's murder of his cousin, Zheng Lian (Cheng Lien), while retaking Xiamen. Later, he also executed an uncle. Removing these potential competitors gave him control of the Zheng family's land and sea empire, including southern Fujian and islands off Guangdong.

With this base, Zheng began to operate in the key Chang (Yangtze) River Valley of central China, even trying but failing to retake Nanjing in September, 1659. After mopping up other Ming loyalist forces, the Manchus turned their entire attention to Zheng and began to take his mainland bases. He decided that it was necessary to relocate to continue the fight. He turned to the island of Taiwan, across a narrow strait from Fujian. Taiwan had been largely ignored by the Chinese. Its small population was split about equally between aboriginal tribal peoples of Malayan descent and Chinese immigrants from Fujian, attracted to the island's rich agricultural resources. The Portuguese had been the first to recognize the island's importance as a base for trade and had given it its European name, Formosa. The Dutch saw it as an important adjunct to their base at Batavia in the Indonesian islands and had seized it in 1624.

The Dutch had occupied the island easily, suppressing several local uprisings, and as a result, they had grown contemptuous of the abilities of Chinese warriors. The Dutch holdings on the island were therefore only lightly defended when Zheng's fleet of about one thousand ships appeared out of the morning mists on April 3, 1661. Several hundred Dutch infantrymen marched out to meet the battle-hardened veterans of the Manchu wars. Zheng's men "discharged so great a storm of arrows that they darkened the sky," in the words of a Dutch observer. The Dutch stubbornly defended their fortifications, which fell months later. The siege was savage, and many Dutch civilians died, including missionaries, women, and children. This siege made Zheng, or as he was now known, Koxinga, an exemplar to the Europeans of the ruthless Asian warlord, in the tradition of Attila and Genghis Khan.

The Zheng family's control of Taiwan was a positive one, as Zheng and his descendants encouraged Chinese immigration and founded a Chinese educational and administrative system. Zheng did not live to see these successes, however; he died, probably of malaria, in June, 1662, at the age of thirty-seven. When the Manchus finally took the island from his heirs in 1683, it was indisputably Chinese, and it became a Chinese province. In 1949, Taiwan became the bastion of another refugee regime, the Nationalist Chinese, who had been defeated by Mao Zedong's Communist forces. Under their administration, Taiwan grew to become the second strongest economy in Asia after Japan.

SIGNIFICANCE

Zheng was at the center of the events of the seventeenth century, which saw a major realignment in power relations in East Asia, affecting China and the Western powers. These were violent times, and Zheng had the necessary qualities to thrive in them, including ruthlessness, martial talents, and immense self-confidence. As he told the Dutch negotiators when they surrendered to him in Taiwan: "If I wish to set my forces to work then I am able to move Heaven and Earth; wherever I go, I am destined to win." Although he was one of the few Chinese to be known by a Latinized name, showing his stature in Europe, his reputation was to remain a dreadful one until the more accurate historical portrayals of the twentieth century. To the Japanese, he became a model samurai, adventuring in romantic China. To the Chinese, however, Zheng was always to exemplify loyalty and perseverance in the face of certain defeat. Eventually, he was made a protective deity of popular religion in Taiwan, the island that he was the first to incorporate into China.

—*Jeffrey G. Barlow*

FURTHER READING

Coyett, Fredric. *Neglected Formosa*. Translated by Inez de Beauclair. San Francisco: Chinese Materials Center, 1975. These are the memoirs of the last Dutch governor of Taiwan. They are a key source for the battle of Taiwan and were the primary influence upon European attitudes toward Zheng.

Croizier, Ralph C. *Koxinga and Chinese Nationalism: History, Myth, and the Hero*. Cambridge, Mass.: Harvard University Press, 1977. Considered the standard analysis of Zheng's life and its meaning for later Chinese, both Communist and anti-Communist, as well as for the Japanese and Europeans. An analytical bibliography of sources in Chinese, Japanese, and English is included. Well written and balanced in its interpretations.

Davidson, James W. *The Island of Formosa, Past and Present: History, People, Resources and Commercial Prospects, Tea, Camphor, Sugar, Gold, Coal, Sulphur, Economical Plants, and Other Products*. London: Macmillan, 1903. Reprint. New York: Oxford University Press, 1988. This work is not only a useful history of Taiwan but also the first positive Western account of Zheng.

Hummel, Arthur W., ed. *Eminent Chinese of the Ch'ing Period, 1644-1912*. Washington, D.C.: Government Printing Office, 1943-1944. The standard reference for the lives of Zheng Chenggong and for his father, Zheng Zhilong.

Hung, Chien-chao. *A History of Taiwan*. Rimini, Italy: Il Cerchio, 2000. Includes information about Zheng's takeover and administration of Taiwan.

Keliher, Macabe. *Out of China: Or, Yu Yonghe's Tales of Formosa—A History of Seventeenth-Century China*. Taipei, Taiwan: SMC Books, 2003. In 1696, the Chinese empire's gunpowder supply was depleted by an explosion at Fuzhou. Chinese officials asked Yu Yonghe to travel to Taiwan and obtain the sulphur needed to replenish their gunpowder stores. Keliher uses Yonghe's diaries to create this account of the trip and describe life in seventeenth century Taiwan.

Willis, John E., Jr. "Seventeeth Century Transformation: Taiwan Under the Dutch and the Cheng Regime." In *Taiwan: A New History*, edited by Murray Rubinstein. Armonk, N.Y.: M. E. Sharpe, 1999. This book of essays includes Willis's historical account of Taiwan during the seventeenth century.

SEE ALSO: Abahai; Chen Shu; Chongzhen; Dorgon; Kangxi; Liu Yin; Shunzhi; Tianqi; Wang Fuzhi.

RELATED ARTICLES in *Great Events from History: The Seventeenth Century, 1601-1700:* 1616-1643: Rise of the Manchus; April 25, 1644: End of the Ming Dynasty; June 6, 1644: Manchus Take Beijing; 1645-1683: Zheng Pirates Raid the Chinese Coast.

FRANCISCO DE ZURBARÁN
Spanish painter

Zurbarán was a leading painter of baroque Seville and painter to the king of Spain. He is famed for his intense naturalism, inspiring religious paintings, and probing portrayals of monastic life.

BORN: November 7, 1598 (baptized); Fuente de Cantos, Spain
DIED: August 27, 1664; Madrid, Spain
AREA OF ACHIEVEMENT: Art

EARLY LIFE
The son of a small-town shopkeeper, Francisco de Zurbarán (fran-SEES-koh day-zuhr-bah-RAHN) left his Extremadura mountain home of Fuente de Cantos in 1614 to pursue his fortune in the prosperous and vibrant city of Seville, then the third largest in Europe. Several of Spain's greatest baroque painters began their careers in Seville, including Diego Velázquez (1599-1660) and Alonso Cano (1601-1667), who were students in the workshop of art theorist and painter Francisco Pacheco (1564-1654) while Zurbarán was apprenticed to the obscure painter Pedro Díaz de Villanueva.

Though little is known about his teacher, Zurbarán's work shows knowledge of Seville's leading naturalistic painters, including Pacheco, Velázquez, Juan de Roelas, and Francisco de Herrera, the Elder. Villanueva's shop may have exposed Zurbarán to the art of polychrome sculpture, and a document of 1624 suggests that Zurbarán worked as a sculptor, which helps to explain the physicality and rich tactility of his figures and surfaces. Unfortunately, no works from his student years or early solo career survive.

Heading homeward in 1617, Zurbarán settled in the Extremadura mountain-town of Llerena, where he married María Páez by early 1618. She gave birth to two daughters and a son, Juan, but died in September of 1623. Soon thereafter, Zurbarán married the daughter of a prominent local family, Beatriz de Morales, whose status brought the artist prestige. Widowed again in 1639, Zurbarán was married for the third and final time in 1644 to Leonor de Tordera, with whom he had six children, most of whom died young. His son Juan would be the only of his offspring to become a painter, though he, too, died before his father, of plague in 1649.

LIFE'S WORK

On January 16, 1626, Zurbarán was commissioned to paint twenty-one canvases for the Dominican convent of San Pablo el Real in Seville. The young artist accepted quite modest remuneration, for he received about three to four times less than his Sevillian counterparts for similar work. However, this

Seventeenth century portrait of Francisco de Zurbarán. (The Granger Collection, New York)

project earned him important recognition in Seville, and he quickly began to win more lucrative commissions from patrons attracted to his powerfully naturalistic religious works.

Following Pacheco's theory that religious images should "perfect our understanding, move our will, [and] refresh our memory of divine things," Zurbarán aimed to stir viewers' emotions with riveting naturalism and intense immediacy, as seen in his *Christ on the Cross* (or *Crucifixion*), commissioned in 1627 by the Dominicans at San Pablo to hang in their sacristy. Zurbarán did not portray the historical event of the Crucifixion but only the lifeless body of Christ, which hangs on the cross before an empty, dark background. Without any competing narrative detail, Zurbarán directs the spectator's attention to the pain, suffering, and ultimate gift of Christ's sacrifice. Greatly admired, this painting earned Zurbarán an invitation from Seville's city council to reside there permanently despite protests from local painters who demanded that he take Seville's official guild entrance

exam, which he had avoided at the end of his apprenticeship. Zurbarán refused the exam, and the city council dismissed the guild's complaint. Unimpeded by his rivals' challenge, Zurbarán became Seville's preeminent painter in the 1630's.

Zurbarán's next major commission came in August of 1628 from the Sevillian monastery of Nuestra Señora de la Merced for twenty-two biographical narratives portraying their Order's founder, Saint Peter Nolasco. The high sum earned for these works—almost four times the amount received two years earlier from the Dominicans—demonstrates Zurbarán's improved reputation. His workshop, by this time quite busy with numerous projects, received a commission in 1629 to complete a series of canvases for the Franciscan College of San Buenaventura, left unfinished by Francisco de Herrera, the Elder. While this change of artists most likely resulted from Herrera's inability to fulfill his contract on schedule, it also signals Zurbarán's increasing status in Seville.

Like his Italian predecessor Caravaggio (1571-1610), Zurbarán recognized the expressive possibilities of honest naturalism and dramatic lighting, adapting these elements to create a powerful and personal artistic style, seen in his compelling portrayal of *St. Serapion* (1628) or his subdued image of *St Francis in Meditation*. The impressive image of *St. Serapion* was a second commission from the Mercedarians, painted in 1628 for their Sala de Profundis, a room where deceased monks were placed for viewing before burial. Zurbarán's *St. Francis in Meditation*, most likely painted between 1635 and 1640, was probably also for monastic patrons. In both paintings, surface details of simple clothing and individualized physiognomy emerge from deep shadows. Each saint's figure fills its canvas, as Zurbarán pushes his subjects toward the spectator to invite close inspection and deep contemplation, offering a solemnity and quiet drama that appealed to his monastic patrons. Zurbarán's dark backgrounds are typical of early seventeenth century Sevillian painting. His innovation lies in his intense lighting, which enhances the sculptural quality of his figures and furthers their sense of immediacy and presence.

Zurbarán excelled not only as a painter of sacred images but also of hauntingly beautiful still lifes. Like his countrymen Juan Sánchez Cotán (1561-1627) and Juan van der Hamen y León (1596-1631), Zurbarán depicted carefully arranged objects with great attention to texture, color, and optical effects. Zurbarán's strong contrasts of light and dark give humble objects a power that belies their real-world values, creating mystical compositions that invite viewers to contemplate nature and divinity through simple forms. Typical of these works is his 1633 *Still-Life with Oranges*, in which a plate of lemons, a basket of oranges, and a cup of water are brought vividly to life through exquisite attention to surface detail.

In 1634, Zurbarán traveled to Madrid to join Velázquez in the decoration of the Hall of Realms at the Buen Retiro Palace with royal portraits, contemporary battles, and mythological scenes. Zurbarán painted two military victories of King Philip IV as well as ten Labors of Hercules. This trip allowed Zurbarán to explore the royal collections, where he studied canvases by Titian, Peter Paul Rubens, and Velázquez. After his service, Zurbarán received the esteemed title of painter to the king, demonstrating his continuing success.

Upon his return to Seville in 1635, Zurbarán continued to receive monastic commissions and worked for more than ten different religious orders, including the Jesuits, Dominicans, and Franciscans. He also made numerous altarpieces for local churches, and devotional works for private meditation. One of his most important commissions was for the Hieronymite monastery of San Jerónimo in Guadalupe. Canvases from this series show Zurbarán's debt to his fellow countryman Jusepe de Ribera (1588-1652), whose work was well known and loved in Seville. The emaciated figure who dominates *Life of St. Jerome* (1638-1639) shares Ribera's brutal naturalism, and Zurbarán ably captures the essence of ascetic life, providing his Hieronymite patrons an excellent exemplar for their meditations.

Seville experienced serious economic decline in the 1640's, which required Zurbarán to look elsewhere for patrons. He found eager clients in the Americas and exported several hundred canvases to Lima (now in Peru) and Buenos Aires (now in Argentina). Zurbarán's participation in the New World art market may also have been driven by competition from Bartolomé Esteban Murillo (1618-1682), a younger "rising star" in Seville whose idealism began to attract local audiences more than the severe austerity of Zurbarán.

Though his motivation remains unclear, Zurbarán left Seville in May, 1658, for Madrid, where he painted at least three large canvases for the Franciscan monastery of Alcalá de Henares and twelve small works for private devotional use before his death in 1664 at the age of sixty-five.

SIGNIFICANCE

Despite his waning popularity toward the end of his career, Zurbarán is heralded as one of Spain's greatest painters. Throughout his career, Zurbarán remained interested in simple forms and clear compositions, always attentive to the details of optical experience. His devotional images instill their subjects with a power and significance highly conducive to thoughtful religious meditation. Whether through mundane objects or characters from monastic history, Zurbarán imbued his paintings with a respect for texture and form that maintains his appeal.

In addition to training his son Juan as a still life painter, Zurbarán had profound influence on modern European artists, such as Édouard Manet (1832-1883) and Pablo Picasso (1881-1973), who were attracted to Zurbarán's bold forms and restrictive palette.

—*Anne Leader*

FURTHER READING

Baticle, Jeannine. *Zurbarán*. New York: Metropolitan Museum of Art, 1987. A catalog from the only comprehensive American exhibition of Zurbarán's works.

Brown, Jonathan. *Francisco de Zurbarán.* 1974. Rev. ed. New York: Abrams, 1991. The standard monographic study of Zurbarán's works in English.

_____. *Painting in Spain, 1500-1700.* New Haven, Conn.: Yale University Press, 1998. This work places Zurbarán within the context of Spain's Golden Age.

Delenda, Odile, and Luis Garraín Villa. "Zurbarán sculpteur: aspects inédits de sa carrière et de sa biographie." *Gazette des Beaux-Arts* 131 (1998): 125-138. This article fleshes out the artist's early life and suggests that Zurbarán worked as a sculptor. In French with English summary.

Jordan, William B., and Peter Cherry. *Spanish Still Life from Velázquez to Goya.* London: National Gallery Publications, 1995. The authors provide historical context for Zurbarán's still life paintings.

Navarrete Prieto, Benito. *Zurbarán y su Obrador: Pinturas Para el Nuevo Mundo.* New York: Spanish Institute, 1999. An exhibition of Zurbarán's works created for the Americas. Includes English translation.

Tomlinson, Janis. *From El Greco to Goya: Painting in Spain, 1561-1828.* New York: Abrams, 1997. An insightful overview of Spanish painting.

SEE ALSO: Bartolomé Esteban Murillo; Philip IV; Peter Paul Rubens; Diego Velázquez.

RELATED ARTICLES in *Great Events from History: The Seventeenth Century, 1601-1700:* c. 1601-1620: Emergence of Baroque Art; c. 1601-1682: Spanish Golden Age; 1605 and 1615: Cervantes Publishes *Don Quixote de la Mancha.*

Appendices

Rulers and Dynasties

Major world leaders during and beyond the period covered in *Great Lives from History: The Seventeenth Century, 1601-1700* are listed below, beginning with the Roman Catholic popes and followed by rulers of major nations or dynasties, alphabetically by country. Within each country section, rulers are listed chronologically. It is important to note that name spellings and regnal dates vary among sources, and that variations do not necessarily suggest inaccuracy. For example, dates when leaders took power may not match dates of coronation, and the names by which leaders have been recorded in history may represent given names, epithets, or regnal names. Date ranges and geographical borders of nations and dynasties vary, given the complexities of politics and warfare, and the mere fact that "nations" (a concept just beginning to be defined during the early modern era) evolved over time from competing and allied principalities. Hence, not every civilization, dynasty, principality, or region can be covered here; we have, however, attempted to provide lists of rulers for those countries most likely to be addressed in general history courses and area studies.

Contents

Popes and Antipopes	1009	Islamic Caliphs	1031
Africa	1012	Italy	1032
Americas	1014	Japan	1036
Bohemia	1015	Kingdom of Jerusalem	1038
Bulgaria	1016	Korea	1038
Byzantine Empire	1017	Mongols	1039
China	1018	Netherlands	1042
Denmark	1019	Norway	1042
Egypt	1020	Ottoman Empire	1043
England	1021	Poland	1043
Frankish Kingdom and France	1022	Portugal	1044
Germanic Tribes	1024	Russia	1044
Holy Roman Empire	1026	Scotland	1045
Hungary	1027	Seljuk Empire	1046
India	1028	Spain	1047
Iran (Persia)	1030	Sweden	1049
Ireland	1031	Vietnam	1050

Popes and Antipopes

Asterisked (*) names indicate popes who have been sainted by the Church. Names appearing in square brackets [ ] are antipopes.

Term	Pope
440-461	*Leo I the Great
461-468	*Hilarius
468-483	*Simplicius
483-492	*Felix III
492-496	*Gelasius I
496-498	Anastasius II
498-514	*Symmachus
498-505	[Laurentius]
514-523	*Hormisdas

Term	Pope
523-526	*John I
526-530	*Felix IV
530-532	Boniface II
530	[Dioscursus]
533-535	John II
535-536	*Agapetus I
536-537	*Silverius
537-555	Vigilius
556-561	Pelagius I
561-574	John III
575-579	Benedict I
579-590	Pelagius II
590-604	*Gregory I the Great

Term	Pope	Term	Pope
604-606	Sabinian	885-891	Stephen V
607	Boniface III	891-896	Formosus
608-615	*Boniface IV (Adeodatus I)	896	Boniface VI
615-618	*Deusdedit	896-897	Stephen VI
619-625	Boniface V	897	Romanus
625-638	Honorius I	897	Theodore II
638-640	Vacant	898-900	John IX
640	Severinus	900-903	Benedict IV
640-642	John IV	903	Leo V
642-649	Theodore I	903-904	Christopher
649-655	*Martin I	904-911	Sergius III
655-657	*Eugene I	911-913	Anastasius III
657-672	*Vitalian	913-914	Lando
672-676	Adeodatus II	914-928	John X
676-678	Donus	928	Leo VI
678-681	*Agatho	929-931	Stephen VII
682-683	*Leo II	931-935	John XI
684-685	*Benedict II	936-939	Leo VII
685-686	John V	939-942	Stephen IX (VIII)
686-687	Conon	942-946	Marinus II
687	[Theodore II]	946-955	Agapetus II
687-692	[Paschal I]	955-963	John XII
687-701	*Saint Sergius I	963-964	Leo VIII
701-705	John VI	964	Benedict V
705-707	John VII	965-972	John XIII
708	Sisinnius	973-974	Benedict VI
708-715	Constantine	974-983	Benedict VII
715-731	*Gregory II	983-984	John XIV
731-741	*Gregory III	983-984	Boniface VII
741-752	*Zachary	985-996	John XV
752-757	Stephen II	996-999	Gregory V
757-767	*Paul I	996-998	[John XVI]
767	[Constantine]	999-1003	Sylvester II
767	[Philip]	1003	John XVII
767-772	Stephen III	1003-1009	John XVIII
772-795	Adrian I	1009-1012	Sergius IV
795-816	*Leo III	1012-1024	Benedict VIII
816-817	Stephen IV	1012	[Gregory VI]
817-824	*Paschal I	1024-1033	John XIX
824-827	Eugene II	1033-1045	Benedict IX
827	Valentine	1045	Sylvester III
827-844	Gregory IV	1045-1046	Gregory VI (John Gratian Pierleoni)
844	[John VIII]	1046-1047	Clement II (Suitgar, count of Morslegen)
844-847	Sergius II	1048	Damasus II (Count Poppo)
847-855	*Leo IV	1049-1054	*Leo IX (Bruno of Egisheim)
855-858	Benedict III	1055-1057	Victor II (Gebhard, count of Hirschberg)
855	[Anastasius III]	1057-1058	Stephen IX (Frederick of Lorraine)
858-867	*Nicholas I the Great	1058	Benedict X (John, count of Tusculum)
867-872	Adrian II	1058-1061	Nicholas II (Gerhard of Burgundy)
872-882	John VIII	1061-1073	Alexander II (Anselmo da Baggio)
882-884	Marinus I	1061-1064	[Honorius II]
884-885	*Adrian III	1073-1085	*Gregory VII (Hildebrand)

Term	Pope	Term	Pope
1080-1100	[Clement III]	1328-1330	[Nicholas V (Pietro di Corbara)]
1086-1087	Victor III (Desiderius, prince of Beneventum)	1334-1342	Benedict XII (Jacques Fournier)
1088-1099	Urban II (Odo of Lagery)	1342-1352	Clement VI (Pierre Roger de Beaufort)
1099-1118	Paschal II (Ranieri da Bieda)	1352-1362	Innocent VI (Étienne Aubert)
1100-1102	[Theodoric]	1362-1370	Urban V (Guillaume de Grimord)
1102	[Albert]	1370-1378	Gregory XI (Pierre Roger de Beaufort, the Younger)
1105	[Sylvester IV]		
1118-1119	Gelasius II (John Coniolo)	1378-1389	Urban VI (Bartolomeo Prignano)
1118-1121	[Gregory VIII]	1378-1394	[Clement VII (Robert of Geneva)]
1119-1124	Callixtus II (Guido, count of Burgundy)	1389-1404	Boniface IX (Pietro Tomacelli)
1124-1130	Honorius II (Lamberto dei Fagnani)	1394-1423	[Benedict XIII (Pedro de Luna)]
1124-1130	[Celestine II]	1404-1406	Innocent VII (Cosmto de' Migliorati)
1130-1143	Innocent II (Gregorio Papareschi)	1406-1415	Gregory XII (Angelo Correr)
1130-1138	[Anacletus II (Cardinal Pierleone)]	1409-1410	[Alexander V (Petros Philargi)]
1138	[Victor IV]	1410-1415	[John XXIII (Baldassare Cossa)]
1143-1144	Celestine II (Guido di Castello)	1415-1417	Vacant
1144-1145	Lucius II (Gherardo Caccianemici)	1417-1431	Martin V (Ottone Colonna)
1145-1153	Eugene III (Bernardo Paganelli)	1423-1429	[Clement VIII]
1153-1154	Anastasius IV (Corrado della Subarra)	1424	[Benedict XIV]
1154-1159	Adrian IV (Nicolas Breakspear)	1431-1447	Eugene IV (Gabriele Condulmero)
1159-1181	Alexander III (Roland Bandinelli)	1439-1449	[Felix V (Amadeus of Savoy)]
1159-1164	[Victor IV]	1447-1455	Nicholas V (Tommaso Parentucelli)
1164-1168	[Paschal III]	1455-1458	Calixtus III (Alfonso de Borgia)
1168-1178	[Calixtus III]	1458-1464	Pius II (Enea Silvio Piccolomini)
1179-1180	[Innocent III (Lando da Sessa)]	1464-1471	Paul II (Pietro Barbo)
1181-1185	Lucius III (Ubaldo Allucingoli)	1471-1484	Sixtus IV (Francesco della Rovere)
1185-1187	Urban III (Uberto Crivelli)	1484-1492	Innocent VIII (Giovanni Battista Cibò)
1187	Gregory VIII (Alberto del Morra)	1492-1503	Alexander VI (Rodrigo Borgia)
1187-1191	Clement III (Paolo Scolari)	1503	Pius III (Francesco Todeschini Piccolomini)
1191-1198	Celestine III (Giacinto Boboni-Orsini)	1503-1513	Julius II (Giuliano della Rovere)
1198-1216	Innocent III (Lothario of Segni)	1513-1521	Leo X (Giovanni de' Medici)
1216-1227	Honorius III (Cencio Savelli)	1522-1523	Adrian VI (Adrian Florensz Boeyens)
1227-1241	Gregory IX (Ugo of Segni)	1523-1534	Clement VII (Giulio de' Medici)
1241	Celestine IV (Goffredo Castiglione)	1534-1549	Paul III (Alessandro Farnese)
1243-1254	Innocent IV (Sinibaldo Fieschi)	1550-1555	Julius III (Giovanni Maria Ciocchi del Monte)
1254-1261	Alexander IV (Rinaldo di Segni)	1555	Marcellus II (Marcello Cervini)
1261-1264	Urban IV (Jacques Pantaléon)	1555-1559	Paul IV (Gian Pietro Carafa)
1265-1268	Clement IV (Guy le Gros Foulques)	1559-1565	Pius IV (Giovanni Angelo de' Medici)
1268-1271	Vacant	1566-1572	Pius V (Antonio Ghislieri)
1271-1276	Gregory X (Tebaldo Visconti)	1572-1585	Gregory XIII (Ugo Buoncompagni)
1276	Innocent V (Pierre de Champagni)	1585-1590	Sixtus V (Felice Peretti)
1276	Adrian V (Ottobono Fieschi)	1590	Urban VII (Giambattista Castagna)
1276-1277	John XXI (Pietro Rebuli-Giuliani)	1590-1591	Gregory XIV (Niccolò Sfondrato)
1277-1280	Nicholas III (Giovanni Gaetano Orsini)	1591	Innocent IX (Giovanni Antonio Facchinetti)
1281-1285	Martin IV (Simon Mompitie)	1592-1605	Clement VIII (Ippolito Aldobrandini)
1285-1287	Honorius IV (Giacomo Savelli)	1605	Leo XI (Alessandro de' Medici)
1288-1292	Nicholas IV (Girolamo Masci)	1605-1621	Paul V (Camillo Borghese)
1294	*Celestine V (Pietro Angelari da Murrone)	1621-1623	Gregory XV (Alessandro Ludovisi)
1294-1303	Boniface VIII (Benedict Caetani)	1623-1644	Urban VIII (Maffeo Barberini)
1303-1304	Benedict XI (Niccolò Boccasini)	1644-1655	Innocent X (Giovanni Battista Pamphili)
1305-1314	Clement V (Raimond Bertrand de Got)	1655-1667	Alexander VII (Fabio Chigi)
1316-1334	John XXII (Jacques Duèse)	1667-1669	Clement IX (Giulio Rospigliosi)

Term	Pope
1670-1676	Clement X (Emilio Altieri)
1676-1689	Innocent XI (Benedetto Odescalchi)
1689-1691	Alexander VIII (Pietro Ottoboni)
1691-1700	Innocent XII (Antonio Pignatelli)
1700-1721	Clement XI (Giovanni Francesco Albani)
1721-1724	Innocent XIII (Michelangelo Conti)
1724-1730	Benedict XIII (Pierfrancesco Orsini)
1730-1740	Clement XII (Lorenzo Corsini)
1740-1758	Benedict XIV (Prospero Lambertini)
1758-1769	Clement XIII (Carlo Rezzonico)
1769-1774	Clement XIV (Giovanni Ganganelli)
1775-1799	Pius VI (Giovanni Angelo Braschi)
1800-1823	Pius VII (Barnaba Gregorio Chiaramonti)
1823-1829	Leo XII (Annibale della Genga)
1829-1830	Pius VIII (Francesco Saverio Castiglioni)
1831-1846	Gregory XVI (Bartolomeo Cappellari)
1846-1878	Pius IX (Giovanni Mastai-Ferretti)
1878-1903	Leo XIII (Gioacchino Pecci)
1903-1914	Pius X (Giuseppe Sarto)
1914-1922	Benedict XV (Giacomo della Chiesa)
1922-1939	Pius XI (Achille Ratti)
1939-1958	Pius XII (Eugenio Pacelli)
1958-1963	John XXIII (Angelo Roncalli)
1963-1978	Paul VI (Giovanni Battista Montini)
1978	John Paul I (Albino Luciani)
1978-2005	John Paul II (Karol Wojtyla)
2005-	Benedict XVI (Joseph Ratzinger)

AFRICA. *See also* EGYPT

BENIN

Reign	Ruler
1200-1235	Eweke I
1235-1243	Uwakhuanhen
1243-1255	Ehenmihen
1255-1280	Ewedo
1280-1295	Oguola
1295-1299	Edoni
1299-1334	Udagbedo
1334-1370	Ohen
1370-1400	Egbeka
1400-1430	Orobiru
1430-1440	Uwaifiokun
c. 1440-1473	Ewuare the Great
1473	Ezoti (14 days)
1473-1480	Olua
1481-1504	Ozolua
c. 1504-1550	Esigie
1550-1578	Orhogbua
1578-1606	Ehengbuda
1606-1641	Ohuan

Reign	Ruler
1641-1661	Ahenzae
1661-1669	Ahenzae
1669-1675	Akengboi
1675-1684	Akenkpaye
1684-1689	Akengbedo
1689-1700	Oroghene
1700-1712	Ewuakpe
1712-1713	Ozuaere
1713-1735	Akenzua I
1735-1750	Eresonyen
1750-1804	Akengbuda
1804-1816	Obanosa

ETHIOPIA

The evidence for the succession of Ethiopian rulers is debated by scholars; here, the regnal dates reflect primarily the order of succession and vary widely among sources.

Early Kings

Reign	Ruler
c. 320-350	Ezana
c. 328-370	Shizana
c. 356	Ella Abreha
?	Ella Asfeha
?	Ella Shahel
474-475	Agabe
474-475	Levi
475-486	Ella Amida (IV?)
486-489	Jacob I
486-489	David
489-504	Armah I
504-505	Zitana
505-514	Jacob II
c. 500-542	Ella Asbeha (Caled)
542-c. 550	Beta Israel
c. 550-564	Gabra Masqal
?	Anaeb
?	Alamiris
?	Joel
?	Israel
?	Gersem I
?	Ella Gabaz
?	Ella Saham
c. 625	Armah II
?	Iathlia
?	Hataz I
?	Wazena
?	Za Ya'abiyo
?	Armah III
?	Hataz II
?	Gersem II
?	Hataz III

Zagwe Dynasty

Reign	Ruler
c. 1137-1152	Mara Tekle Haimanot
c. 1152-1181	Yimrehane-Kristos
c. 1181-1221	Lalibela
c. 1221-1260	Na ʿakuto La ʿab
c. 1260-1270	Yitbarek (Yetbarek)
1270	Solomonid Dynasty begins; reign of Yekuno Amlak

Solomonid Dynasty

Reign	Ruler
1270-1285	Yekuno Amlak
1285-1294	Solomon I
1294-1297	Bahr Asgad
1294-1297	Senfa Asgad
1297-1299	Qedma Asgad
1297-1299	Jin Asgad
1297-1299	Saba Asgad
1299-1314	Wedem Arad
1314-1344	Amade Tseyon I
1344-1372	Newaya Krestos
1372-1382	Newaya Maryam
1382-1411	Dawit (David) I
1411-1414	Tewodros (Theodore) I
1414-1429	Isaac
1429-1430	Andrew
1430-1433	Takla Maryam
1433	Sarwe Iyasus
1433-1434	Amda Iyasus
1434-1468	Zara Yacob (Constantine I)
1468-1478	Baeda Mariam I
1478-1484	Constantine II
1494	Amade Tseyon II
1494-1508	Naod
1508-1540	Lebna Dengel (David II)
1529	Battle of Shimbre-Kune
1540-1559	Galawedos (Claudius)
1543	Battle of Lake Tana (defeat of Muslims)

Later Rulers

Reign	Ruler
1560-1564	Menas
1564-1597	Sarsa Dengel
1597-1603	Jacob
1603-1604	Za Dengel
1604-1607	Jacob
1607-1632	Susneyos (Sissinios)
1632-1667	Fasilidas (Basilides)
1667-1682	Yohannes (John) I
1682-1706	Iyasu (Jesus) I the Great
1706-1708	Tekle Haimanot I
1708-1711	Tewoflos (Theophilus)
1711-1716	Yostos (Justus)

Reign	Ruler
1716-1721	Dawit (David) III
1721-1730	Bekaffa
1730-1755	Iyasu II
1755-1769	Iyoas (Joas) I
1769	Yohannes II
1769-1777	Tekle Haimanot II
1777-1779	Salomon (Solomon) II
1779-1784	Tekle Giorgis I (first)
1784-1788	Jesus III
1788	Ba'eda Maryam I
1788-1789	Tekle Giorgis I (second)
1789-1794	Hezekiah
1794-1795	Tekle Giorgis I (third)
1795	Ba'eda Maryam II
1795-1796	Tekle Giorgis I (fourth)
1796-1797	Solomon III
1797-1799	Tekle Giorgis I (fifth)
1799	Solomon III
1799-1800	Demetrius
1800	Tekle Giorgis I (sixth)
1800-1801	Demetrius

KONGO

Reign	Ruler
Before 1482-1506	João I (Nzinga Nkuwu)
1506-1543	Afonso I (Nzinga Mbemba)
1543-1545	Peter I
1545-1545	Francis I
1545-1561	Diogo I
1561-1561	Affonso II
1561-1566	Bernard I
1566-1567	Henry I
1568-1587	Alvare I
1587-1614	Alvare II
1614-1615	Bernard II
1615-1622	Alvare III
1622-1624	Peter II
1624-1626	Garcia I
1626-1631	Ambrosio
1631-1636	Alvaro IV
1636-1636	Alvaro V
1636-1642	Alvaro VI
1642-1661	Garcia II
1661-1665	Antonio I
1665	Battle of Mbwila, decline of independent Kingdom of Kongo

MOROCCO

Almoravids

Reign	Ruler
1061-1106	Yūsuf ibn Tāshufīn
1107-1142	ʿAlī ibn Yūsuf

Reign	Ruler
1142-1146	Tāshufīn ibn ʿAlī
1146	Ibrāhīm ibn Tāshufīn
1146-1147	Isḥāq ibn ʿAlī

Almohads

Reign	Ruler
To 1130	Ibn Tūmart
1130-1163	ʿAbd al-Muʾmin
1163-1184	Yūsuf I Abū Yaʿqūb
1184-1199	Yaʿqūb Yūsuf al-Manṣūr
1199-1213	Muḥammad ibn Yaʿqūb
1213-1224	Yūsuf II Abū Yaʿqūb
1224	ʿAbdul Wāḥid I
1224-1227	ʿAbdallah Abū Muḥammad
1227-1235	Yaḥyā Abū Zakariyyāʾ
1227-1232	Idrīs I ibn Yaʿqūb
1232-1242	ʿAbd al-Wāḥid ibn Idrīs I
1242-1248	ʿAlī ibn Idrīs I
1248-1266	ʿUmar ibn Isḥāq
1266-1269	Idrīs II ibn Muḥammad
After 1269	Dissolution; power divided among Marīnids, Ḥafṣids, and Zayyānids

Marīnids

Reign	Ruler
1269-1286	Abū Yūsuf Yaʿqūb
1286-1307	Abū Yaʿqūb Yūsuf al-Nasīr
1307-1308	Abū Tabit
1308-1310	Abū Rabia
1310-1331	Abū Said Othman (Osman ibn Yaʿqūb)
1331-1348	Abū al-Hasan
1348-1358	Abū Inan Faris
1358-1361	Vacant
1361-1366	Moḥammad ibn Yaʿqūb
1366-1372	ʿAbd al-Aziz I
1372-1384	Vacant
1384-1387	Mūsā ibn al-Fers
1387-1393	ʿAbu al-ʿAbbās
1393-1396	ʿAbd al-Aziz II
1396-1398	Abdallah
1398-1421	Osman III
1421-1465	ʿAbd al-Haqq

Wattasides

Reign	Ruler
1472-1504	Moḥammad al-Saih al-Mahdi
1505-1524	Abū Abdallah Moḥammad
1524-1550	Abul ʿAbbās Aḥmad

Saʿdīs (Cherifians)

Reign	Ruler
1510-1517	Muḥammad al-Qāʿim
1517-1544	Aḥmad al-Aʿraj
1544-1557	Muḥammad I al-Shaykh

Reign	Ruler
1557-1574	Abdallah al-Ghālib
1574-1576	Muḥammad al-Mutawakkil
1576-1578	ʿAbd al-Malik
1578	Battle of the Three Kings
1578-1603	Aḥmad al-Manṣūr
1603-1607	ʿAbd al ʿAbd Allah Moḥammad III
1607-1628	Zaidan al-Nāṣir
1628-1631	Abū Marwan ʿAbd al-Malik II
1631-1636	al-Walīd
1636-1654	Moḥammad IV
1654-1659	Aḥmad II
1659-1665	War

Alawis

Reign	Ruler
1666-1672	Rashid ben Ali Cherif (founder)
1672-1727	Ismael ben Ali Cherif
1727-1729	Civil war
1729-1757	Abdallah
1757-1790	Mohamed III
1790-1792	Yazid
1792-1822	Suleiman
1822-1859	Abdelrahman
1859-1873	Mohamed IV
1873-1894	Hassan I
1894-1908	Aziz
1908-1912	Hafid

SONGHAI

Reign	Ruler
c. 1464-1492	Sonni ʿAlī
1493	Sonni Baru
1493-1528	Mohammed I Askia (Mohammed Ture)
1528-1531	Askia Mūsā
1549-1582	Askia Daud
1588-1591	Askia Ishak II

AMERICAS

MAYA KINGS OF TIKAL

The Maya, who occupied the region of Central America from the Yucatán to Guatemala, maintained several centers in the region, but one, Tikal, recorded in Mayan glyphs a line of kings for nearly eight hundred years, roughly corresponding to the Classic Period now considered by scholars to be the height of Mayan civilization. The list below is from Chronicle of the Maya Kings and Queens, *by Simon Martin and Nikolai Grube (New York: Thames and Hudson, 2000).*

Reign	Ruler
c. 90-150	Yax Ehb Xook (First Step Shark)
c. 307	Siyaj Chan K'awiil I

Reign	Ruler
d. 317	Ix Une Balam (Baby Jaguar)
d. 359	K'inich Muwaan Jol
360-378	Chak Tok Ichaak I (Great Jaguar Paw)
378-404	Nuun Yax Ayiin I (Curl Snout)
411-456	Siyaj Chan K'awiil II (Stormy Sky)
458-c. 486	K'an Chitam
c. 486-508	Chak Tok Ich'aak II
c. 511-527	Kaloomte' B'alam
537-562	Wak Chan Ka'awiil
c. 593-628	Animal Skull
c. 657-679	Nuun Ujol Chaak
682-734	Jasaw Chan K'awiil I
734-746	Yik'in Chan K'awiil
768-794	Yax Nuun Ayiin II
c. 800	Nuun Ujol K'inich
c. 810	Dark Sun
c. 849	Jewel K'awiil
c. 869	Jasaw Chan K'awiil II
c. 900	End of Mayan Classic Period

AZTEC KINGS OF TENOCHTITLÁN (MEXICO)

Reign	Ruler
Legendary	Ténoch (founder)
1375-1395	Acamapichtili
1395-1417	Huitzilíhuitl
1417-1427	Chimalpopoca
1427-1440	Itzcóatl
1440-1469	Montezuma (Moctezuma) I
1469-1481	Axayacatl
1481-1486	Tízoc
1486-1502	Ahuitzotl (Auítzotl)
1502-1520	Montezuma (Moctezuma) II
1520	Cuitláhuac
1520-1521	Cuauhtémoc

INCAS (PERU)

Reign	Ruler
c. 1200	Manco Capac I
?	Sinchi Roca
?	Lloque Yupanqui
?	Mayta Capac
?	Capac Yupanqui
?	Inca Roca
?	Yahuar Huacac
?	Viracocha
1438-1471	Pachacuti
1471-1493	Topa
1493-1525	Huayna Capac
1525-1532	Huáscar
1525-1533	Atahualpa
1532-1533	Spanish conquest (Pizzaro)
1533	Manco Capac II

Reign	Ruler
1544-1561	Sayri Tupac
1561-1571	Titu Cusi
1571	Tupac Amaru I

AUSTRIA. *See* HOLY ROMAN EMPIRE

BOHEMIA. *See also* HUNGARY, POLAND

PŘEMYSLIDS

Reign	Ruler
c. 870-888/889	Borivoj I
894/895-915	Spytihnev I
915-921	Vratislav I
921-935	Duke Wenceslaus I
935-972	Boleslaus I the Cruel
972-999	Boleslaus II the Pious
999-1002	Boleslaus III
1002-1003	Vladivoj
1003	Boleslaus III
1003	Jaromir
1003	Boleslaus III
1003-1004	Boleslaus I (nondynastic Piast)
1004-1012	Jaromir
1012-1033	Oldrich
1033-1034	Jaromir
1034	Oldrich
1035-1055	Bretislav I
1055-1061	Spytihnev II
1061-1092	Vratislav II
1092	Konrad I
1092-1100	Bretislav II
1101-1107	Borivoj II
1107-1109	Svatopluk
1109-1117	Vladislav I
1117-1120	Borivoj II
1120-1125	Vladislav I
1125-1140	Sobeslav I
1140-1172	Vladislav II
1172-1173	Bedrich
1173-1178	Sobeslav II
1178-1189	Bedrich
1189-1191	Konrad II Ota
1191-1192	Duke Wenceslaus II
1192-1193	Ottokar I
1193-1197	Jindrich Bretislav
1197	Vladislav Jindrich
1197-1230	Ottokar I
1230-1253	King Wenceslaus I
1253-1278	Ottokar II
1278-1305	King Wenceslaus II

Reign	Ruler
1305-1306	King Wenceslaus III
1306	Henry of Carinthia (nondynastic)
1306-1307	Rudolph I of Habsburg (nondynastic)
1307-1310	Henry of Carinthia (nondynastic)

LUXEMBOURGS

Reign	Ruler
1310-1346	John of Luxembourg
1346-1378	Charles I
1378-1419	Wenceslaus IV
1419-1420	Sigismund
1420-1436	Hussite wars
1436-1437	Sigismund

HABSBURGS

Reign	Ruler
1437-1439	Albert of Habsburg
1439-1457	Ladislas I (V of Hungary)
1458-1471	George of Podebrady (nondynastic)
1469-1490	Matthias Corvinus (antiking)

JAGIEŁŁOS

Reign	Ruler
1471-1516	Vladislav (Ladislaus) II
1516-1526	Louis

HABSBURGS

Reign	Ruler
1526-1564	Ferdinand I
1564-1575	Maximilian
1575-1611	Rudolf II
1612-1619	Matthias
1619	Ferdinand II
1619-1620	Frederick, Elector Palatine (Wittelsbach)
1620-1637	Ferdinand II
1627-1657	Ferdinand III
1646-1654	Ferdinand IV
1656-1705	Leopold I
1705-1711	Joseph I
1711-1740	Charles II
1740-1780	Maria Theresa

HABSBURG-LOTHRINGENS

Reign	Ruler
1780-1790	Joseph II
1790-1792	Leopold II
1792-1835	Francis
1835-1848	Ferdinand V
1848-1916	Francis Joseph
1916-1918	Charles III

BULGARIA

EARLY BULGARIA

Reign	Czar
c. 681-701	Asparukh
c. 701-c. 718	Tervel
c. 718-750	Sevar
750-762	Kormesios
762-763	Vinekh
762-763	Teletz
763	Umar
763-765	Baian
765	Tokt
c. 765-777	Telerig
c. 777-c. 803	Kardam
c. 803-814	Krum
814-815	Dukum
814-816	Ditzveg
814-831	Omurtag
831-836	Malamir (Malomir)
836-852	Presijan
852-889	Boris I
865	Boris converts to Christianity
889-893	Vladimir
893-927	Simeon I the Great
927-969	Peter I
969-972	Boris II
971	Bulgaria conquered by John I Tzimisces
971-1018	Dissolution, instability
1018	Basil II annexes Bulgaria to Macedonia

ASEN LINE

Reign	Czar
1186	Bulgarian Independence
1186-1196	John I Asen
1196-1197	Peter II Asen
1197-1207	Kalojan Asen
1207-1218	Boril
1218-1241	John II Asen
1242	Mongol invasion
1242-1246	Kaloman I
1246-1257	Michael II Asen
1257-1258	Kaloman II
1257-1277	Constantine Tich
1277-1279	Ivalio
1278-c. 1264	Ivan Mytzes
1279-1284?	John III Asen
c. 1280	Terter takeover

TERTER LINE

Reign	Czar
1280-1292	George I Terter
1285	Mongol vassal

Reign	Czar
1292-1295/8	Smilech
1295/8-1298/9	Caka (Tshaka)
1298/9-1322	Theodore Svetoslav
1322-1323	George II

SHISHMANS

Reign	Czar
1323-1330	Michael III Shishman
1330-1331	John IV Stephan
1331-1371	John V Alexander
1355-1371	John Sracimir
1360-1393	John VI Shishman
1385-1396	Decline
1396-1879	Ottoman rule

BYZANTINE EMPIRE

Reign	Emperor or Empress
330-337	Constantine I the Great
337-361	Constantius
361-363	Julian the Apostate
363-364	Jovian
364-378	Valens
379-395	Theodosius I the Great
395-408	Arcadius
408-450	Theodosius II
450-457	Marcian
457-474	Leo I the Great
474	Leo II
474-475	Zeno
475-476	Basiliscus
476-491	Zeno (restored)
491-518	Anastasius I
518-527	Justin I
527-548	Theodora
527-565	Justinian I the Great
565-578	Justin II
578-582	Tiberius II Constantinus
582-602	Maurice
602-610	Phocas
610-641	Heraclius
641	Constantine III and Heracleonas
641-668	Constans II Pogonatus
668-685	Constantine IV
685-695	Justinian II Rhinotmetus
695-698	Leontius
698-705	Tiberius III
705-711	Justinian II (restored)
711-713	Philippicus Bardanes
713-715	Anastasius II
716-717	Theodosius III
717-741	Leo III the Isaurian (the Syrian)

Reign	Emperor or Empress
741-775	Constantine V Copronymus
775-780	Leo IV the Khazar
780-797	Constantine VI
797-802	Saint Irene
802-811	Nicephorus I
811	Stauracius
811-813	Michael I
813-820	Leo V the Armenian
820-829	Michael II the Stammerer
829-842	Theophilus
842-867	Michael III the Drunkard
867-886	Basil I the Macedonian
886-912	Leo VI the Wise (the Philosopher)
912-913	Alexander
913-919	Constantine VII Porphyrogenitus (Macedonian)
919-944	Romanus I Lecapenus (Macedonian)
944-959	Constantine VII (restored)
959-963	Romanus II (Macedonian)
963	Basil II Bulgaroktonos (Macedonian)
963-969	Nicephorus II Phocas (Macedonian)
969-976	John I Tzimisces
976-1025	Basil II (restored)
1025-1028	Constantine VIII (Macedonian)
1028-1034	Zoë and Romanus III Argyrus (Macedonian)
1034-1041	Zoë and Michael IV the Paphlagonian (Macedonian)
1041-1042	Zoë and Michael V Calaphates (Macedonian)
1042	Zoë and Theodora (Macedonian)
1042-1050	Zoë, Theodora, and Constantine IX Monomachus (Macedonian)
1050-1055	Theodora and Constantine IX (Macedonian)
1055-1056	Theodora (Macedonian)
1056-1057	Michael VI Stratioticus
1057-1059	Isaac I Comnenus
1059-1067	Constantine X Ducas
1067-1068	Michael VII Ducas (Parapinaces)
1068-1071	Romanus IV Diogenes
1071-1078	Michael VII Ducas (restored)
1078-1081	Nicephorus III Botaniates
1081-1118	Alexius I Comnenus
1118-1143	John II Comnenus
1143-1180	Manuel I Comnenus
1180-1183	Alexius II Comnenus
1183-1185	Andronicus I Comnenus
1185-1195	Isaac II Angelus
1195-1203	Alexius III Angelus
1203-1204	Isaac II (restored) and Alexius IV Angelus
1204	Alexius V Ducas
1204-1205	Baldwin I
1206-1222	Theodore I Lascaris

Reign	Emperor or Empress
1222-1254	John III Vatatzes or Ducas
1254-1258	Theodore II Lascaris
1258-1261	John IV Lascaris
1259-1282	Michael VIII Palaeologus
1282-1328	Andronicus II Palaeologus
1328-1341	Andronicus III Palaeologus
1341-1376	John V Palaeologus
1347-1355	John VI Cantacuzenus (usurper)
1376-1379	Andronicus IV Palaeologus
1379-1391	John V Palaeologus (restored)
1390	John VII Palaeologus (usurper)
1391-1425	Manuel II Palaeologus
1399-1412	John VII Palaeologus (restored as coemperor)
1425-1448	John VIII Palaeologus
1449-1453	Constantine XI Palaeologus
1453	Fall of Constantinople to the Ottomans

CHINA

SUI DYNASTY

Reign	Ruler
581-604	Wendi
604-617	Yangdi
618	Gongdi

TANG DYNASTY

Reign	Ruler
618-626	Gaozu (Li Yuan)
627-649	Taizong
650-683	Gaozong
684	Zhonggong
684-690	Ruizong
690-705	Wu Hou
705-710	Zhongzong
710-712	Ruizong
712-756	Xuanzong
756-762	Suzong
762-779	Daizong
779-805	Dezong
805	Shunzong
805-820	Xianzong
820-824	Muzong
824-827	Jingzong
827-840	Wenzong
840-846	Wuzong
846-859	Xuanzong
859-873	Yizong
873-888	Xizong
888-904	Zhaozong
904-907	Aizong

LIAO DYNASTY

Reign	Ruler
907-926	Abaoji (Taizu)
926-947	Deguang (Taizong)
947-951	Shizong
951-969	Muzong
969-982	Jingzong
982-1031	Shengzong
1031-1055	Xingzong
1055-1101	Daozong
1101-1125	Tianzuodi

WESTERN LIAO DYNASTY

Reign	Ruler
1125-1144	Dezong
1144-1151	Empress Gantian
1151-1164	Renzong
1164-1178	Empress Chengtian
1178-1211	The Last Ruler

JIN DYNASTY

Reign	Ruler
1115-1123	Aguda (Wanyan Min; Taizu)
1123-1135	Taizong (Wanyan Sheng)
1135-1149	Xizong
1150-1161	Wanyan Liang, king of Hailing
1161-1190	Shizong
1190-1209	Zhangzong
1209-1213	Wanyan Yongji, king of Weishao
1213-1224	Xuanzong
1224-1234	Aizong
1234	The Last Emperor

NORTHERN SONG DYNASTY

Reign	Ruler
960-976	Taizu (Zhao Kuangyin)
976-997	Taizong
998-1022	Zhenzong
1022-1063	Renzong
1064-1067	Yingzong
1068-1085	Shenzong
1086-1101	Zhezong
1101-1125	Huizong
1125-1126	Qinzong

SOUTHERN SONG DYNASTY

Reign	Ruler
1127-1162	Gaozong
1163-1190	Xiaozong
1190-1194	Guangzong
1195-1224	Ningzong
1225-1264	Lizong
1265-1274	Duzong

Reign	Ruler
1275-1275	Gongdi
1276-1278	Duanzong
1279	Bing Di

YUAN DYNASTY. *See also* MONGOL EMPIRE

Reign	Ruler
1279-1294	Kublai Khan (Shizu)
1294-1307	Temür Oljeitu (Chengzong)
1308-1311	Khaishan (Wuzong)
1311-1320	Ayurbarwada (Renzong)
1321-1323	Shidelbala (Yingzong)
1323-1328	Yesun Temür (Taiding)
1328-1329	Tugh Temür (Wenzong Tianshundi)
1329	Tugh Khoshila (Mingzong)
1329-1332	Tugh Temür (Wenzong)
1333-1368	Toghon Temür (Shundi)
1368	Ming Dynasty begins: Hongwu

MING DYNASTY

Reign	Ruler
1368-1398	Hongwu (Zhu Yuanzhang)
1399-1402	Jianwen (Zhu Yunwen)
1402-1424	Yonglo (Zhu Di)
1424-1425	Hongxi
1426-1435	Xuande
1436-1449	Zhengtong
1449-1457	Jingtai
1457-1464	Tianshun
1465-1487	Chenghua (Xianzong)
1488-1505	Hongzhi (Xiaozong)
1505-1521	Zhengde
1522-1567	Jiajing
1567-1572	Longqing
1573-1620	Wanli
1620	Taichang
1621-1627	Tianqi
1628-1644	Chongzhen

SOUTHERN MING DYNASTY

Reign	Ruler
1644-1645	Fu (Hongguang)
1645-1646	Tang (Longwu)
1645	Lu (Luh)
1645-1653	Lu (Lou)
1646	Tang (Shaowu)
1646-1662	Gui (Yongli)

QING (MANCHU) DYNASTY

Reign	Ruler
1616-1626	Nurhachi
1626-1643	Hong Taiji
1643-1661	Shunzi

Reign	Ruler
1644	Occupation of China; defeat of the Ming
1661-1722	Kangxi
1722-1735	Yongzheng
1735-1796	Qianlong
1796-1820	Jiaqing
1820-1850	Daoguang
1850-1861	Xianfeng
1861-1875	Tongzhi
1875-1908	Guangxu
1908-1924	Puyi

DENMARK. *See also* NORWAY, SWEDEN

Reign	Ruler
588-647	Ivar Vidfamne
647-735?	Harald I Hildetand
735-750?	Sigurd I Ring (poss. 770-812)
c. 750	Randver
850-854	Horik I
c. 854-?	Horik II
c. 860-865	Ragnar Lobrok
865-873	Sigurd II Snogoje
873-884	Hardeknut I
884-885	Frodo
885-889	Harald II
c. 900-950	Gorm
c. 950-985	Harald III Bluetooth
985-1014	Sweyn I Forkbeard
1014-1019	Harald IV
1019-1035	Canute I (III) the Great
1035-1042	Hardeknut
1042-1047	Magnus the Good
1047-1074	Sweyn II
1074-1080	Harald V Hen
1080-1086	Canute II (IV) the Holy
1086-1095	Olaf IV the Hungry
1095-1103	Eric I the Evergood
1103-1134	Niels Elder
1134-1137	Eric II
1137-1146	Eric III
1146-1157	Sweyn III
1147-1157	Canute III (V) Magnussen
1157-1182	Valdemar I the Great
1182-1202	Canute IV (VI) the Pious
1202-1241	Valdemar II the Victorious
1241-1250	Eric IV
1250-1252	Abel
1252-1259	Christopher I
1259-1286	Eric V
1286-1319	Eric VI
1320-1326	Christopher II
1326-1330	Instability

Reign	Ruler
1330-1332	Christopher II (restored)
1332-1340	Instability
1340-1375	Valdemar III
1376-1387	Olaf V (or II; IV of Norway)
1380	Unification of Denmark and Norway
1376-1412	Margaret I of Denmark, Norway, and Sweden
1397	Unification of Norway, Denmark, and Sweden
1412-1439	Eric VII (III of Norway, XIII of Sweden)
1439-1448	Christopher III

HOUSE OF OLDENBURG

Reign	Ruler
1448-1481	Christian I
1481-1513	John (Hans)
1523	Sweden leaves Kalmar Union
1523-1533	Frederick I
1523-1536	Union with Norway
1534-1559	Christian III
1559-1588	Frederick II
1588-1648	Christian IV
1648-1670	Frederick III
1670-1699	Christian V
1699-1730	Frederick IV
1730-1746	Christian VI
1746-1766	Frederick V
1766-1808	Christian VII
1808-1839	Frederick VI
1839-1848	Christian VIII
1848-1863	Frederick VII

EGYPT

After the rise of Islam in the seventh century, Egypt was Islamicized and came under the control of a succession of emirs and caliphs.

ṬULUNID EMIRS

Reign	Ruler
868-884	Aḥmad ibn Ṭūlūn
884-896	Khumārawayh
896	Jaysh
896-904	Hārūn
904-905	Shaybān
905	Recovered by Abbasids

IKHSHIDID EMIRS

Reign	Ruler
935-946	Muḥammad ibn Ṭughj al-Ikhshīd
946-961	Unūjūr
961-966	ʿAlī
966-968	Kāfūr al-Lābī (regent)

Reign	Ruler
968-969	Aḥmad
969	Fāṭimid conquest

FĀṬIMID CALIPHS IN EGYPT

Reign	Ruler
975-996	al-ʿAzīz
996-1021	al-Ḥākim
1021-1036	al-Zahīr
1036-1094	al-Mustanṣir
1094-1101	al-Mustadī
1101-1130	al-Amīr
1130-1149	al-Ḥāfiz
1149-1154	al-Zafīr
1154-1160	al-Fāʾiz
1160-1171	al-ʿAdīd

AYYŪBID SULTANS

Reign	Ruler
1169-1193	Saladin
1193-1198	al-ʿAzīz Imad al-Dīn
1198-1200	al-Manṣūr Naṣīr al-Dīn
1200-1218	al-ʿAdil I Sayf al-Dīn
1202-1204	Fourth Crusade
1217-1221	Fifth Crusade
1218-1238	al-Kāmil I Nāṣir al-Dīn
1227-1230	Sixth Crusade
1238-1240	al-ʿAdil II Sayf al-Dīn
1240-1249	al-Ṣāliḥ II Najm al-Dīn
1249-1250	al-Muʿaẓẓam Tūrān-Shāh Ghiyāt al-Dīn
1248-1254	Seventh (or Eighth) Crusade
1252	Cairo seized by Mamlūks

MAMLŪK SULTANS

Baḥrī Line (Mongol, then Turkish)

Reign	Ruler
1252-1257	Aybak al-Turkumānī
1257-1259	ʿAlī I
1259-1260	Quṭuz al-Muʿizzī
1260-1277	Baybars I (defeats Mongols 1260)
1277-1279	Baraka (Berke) Khān
1279	Salāmish (Süleymish)
1279-1290	Qalāʾūn al-Alfī
1290-1293	Khalīl
1291	Fall of Acre
1293	Baydarā (?)
1293-1294	Muḥammad I
1294-1296	Kitbughā
1296-1299	Lāchīn (Lājīn) al-Ashqar
1299-1309	Muḥammad I
1303	Earthquake destroys Pharos lighthouse
1309-1310	Baybars II al-Jāshnakīr (Burjī)
1310-1341	Muḥammad I

Reign	Ruler
1341	Abū Bakr
1341-1342	Kūjūk (Küchük)
1342	Aḥmad I
1342-1345	Ismāʿīl
1345-1346	Shaʿbān I
1346-1347	Ḥājjī I
1347-1351	al-Ḥasan
1351-1354	Ṣāliḥ
1354-1361	al-Ḥasan
1361-1363	Muḥammad II
1363-1377	Shaʿbān II
1377-1382	ʿAlī II
1382	Ḥājjī II
1389-1390	Ḥājjī II

Burjī (Circassian) line

Reign	Ruler
1382-1398	Barqūq al-Yalburghāwī
1399-1405	Faraj
1405	ʿAbd al-ʿAzīz
1405-1412	Faraj (second rule)
1412	al-Mustaʿīn
1412-1421	Shaykh al-Maḥmūdī al-Ẓāhirī
1421	Aḥmad II
1421	Ṭāṭār
1421-1422	Muḥammad III
1422-1438	Barsbay
1438	Yūsuf
1438-1453	Chaqmaq (Jaqmaq)
1453	ʿUthmān
1453-1461	Ināl al-ʿAlāʾī al-Ẓāhirī
1461	Aḥmad III
1461-1467	Khushqadam
1467	Yalbay
1467-1468	Timurbughā
1468-1496	Qāyit Bay (Qāytbāy) al-Ẓāhirī
1496-1498	Muḥammad IV
1498-1500	Qānṣawh I
1500-1501	Jānbulāṭ
1501	Tūmān Bay I
1501-1516	Qānṣawh II al-Ghawrī
1516-1517	Tūmān Bay II
1517	Ottoman conquest

ʿABBĀSID CALIPHS OF EGYPT

Unlike the earlier ʿAbbāsid line (see Islamic Caliphs, below), these were ʿAbbāsid figureheads in place under the Mamlūks.

Reign	Ruler
1261	Aḥmad al-Mustanṣir
1261-1302	Aḥmad al-Ḥākim I (Aleppo 1261-1262, Cairo, 1262-1302)
1302-1340	Sulaymān al-Mustakfī I
1340-1341	Ibrāhīm al-Wāthiq I

Reign	Ruler
1341-1352	Aḥmad al-Ḥakīm II
1352-1362	Abū Bakr al-Muʿtaḍid I
1362-1377	Muḥammad al-Mutawakkil I
1377	Zakariyyāʿal-Muʿtaṣim
1377-1383	Muḥammad al-Mutawakkil I
1383-1386	ʿUmar al-Wāthiq II
1386-1389	Zakariyyāʿal-Muʿtaṣim
1389-1406	Muḥammad al-Mutawakkil I
1406-1414	Sulṭān
1412	ʿAbbās or Yaʿqūb al-Mustaʿīn
1414-1441	Dāwūd al-Muʿtaḍid II
1441-1451	Sulaymān al-Mustakfī II
1451-1455	Ḥamza al-Qāʾim
1455-1479	Yūsuf al-Mustanjid
1479-1497	ʿAbd al-ʿAzīz al-Mutawakkil II
1497-1508	Yaʿqūb al-Mustamsik
1508-1516	al-Mutawakkil III
1516-1517	Yaʿqūb al-Mustamsik
1517	Ottoman conquest

ENGLAND

ANGLO-SAXONS (HOUSE OF WESSEX)

Reign	Ruler
802-839	Egbert
839-856	Æthelwulf
856-860	Æthelbald
860-866	Æthelbert
866-871	Ethelred (Æthelred) I
871-899	Alfred the Great
899-924	Edward the Elder (with sister Æthelflæd)
924-939	Æthelstan
939-946	Edmund the Magnificent
946-955	Eadred
955-959	Eadwig (Edwy) All-Fair
959-975	Edgar the Peaceable
975-978	Edward the Martyr
978-1016	Ethelred (Æthelred) II the Unready
1016	Edmund II Ironside

DANES

Reign	Ruler
1016-1035	Canute (Knud) the Great
1035-1040	Harold I Harefoot
1040-1042	Harthacnut

WESSEX (RESTORED)

Reign	Ruler
1043-1066	Edward the Confessor
1066	Harold II

NORMANS

Reign	Ruler
1066-1087	William I the Conqueror
1087-1100	William II Rufus
1100-1135	Henry I Beauclerc
1135-1154	Stephen

PLANTAGENETS: ANGEVINS

Reign	Ruler
1154-1189	Henry II (with Eleanor of Aquitaine, r. 1154-1189)
1189-1199	Richard I the Lion-Hearted
1199-1216	John I Lackland
1216-1272	Henry III
1272-1307	Edward I Longshanks
1307-1327	Edward II (with Isabella of France, r. 1308-1330)
1327-1377	Edward III (with Philippa of Hainaut, r. 1327-1369)
1377-1399	Richard II

PLANTAGENETS: LANCASTRIANS

Reign	Ruler
1399-1413	Henry IV
1413-1422	Henry V
1422-1461	Henry VI

PLANTAGENETS: YORKISTS

Reign	Ruler
1461-1470	Edward IV
1470-1471	Henry VI (Lancaster)
1471-1483	Edward IV (York, restored)
1483	Edward V (York)
1483-1485	Richard III Hunchback (York)

TUDORS

Reign	Ruler
1485-1509	Henry VII
1509-1547	Henry VIII
1547-1553	Edward VI
1553	Lady Jane Grey
1553-1558	Mary I
1558-1603	Elizabeth I

STUARTS

Reign	Ruler
1603-1625	James I (VI of Scotland)
1625-1649	Charles I

COMMONWEALTH (LORD PROTECTORS)

Reign	Ruler
1653-1658	Oliver Cromwell
1658-1659	Richard Cromwell

STUARTS (RESTORED)

Reign	Ruler
1660-1685	Charles II
1685-1689	James II (VII of Scotland)
1689-1702	William of Orange (III of England, II of Scotland) and Mary II
1702-1707	Anne
1707	Act of Union (Great Britain and Ireland)
1707-1714	Anne

HANOVERS

Reign	Ruler
1714-1727	George I
1727-1760	George II
1760-1801	George III
1801	Act of Union creates United Kingdom
1801-1820	George III
1820-1830	George IV
1830-1837	William IV

FRANKISH KINGDOM AND FRANCE

The Merovingians and Carolingians ruled different parts of the Frankish kingdom, which accounts for overlapping regnal dates in these tables. The term "emperor" refers to rule over what eventually came to be known as the Holy Roman Empire.

THE MEROVINGIANS

Reign	Ruler (Principality)
447-458	Merovech
458-481	Childeric I
481-511	Clovis I (with Clotilda, r. 493-511)
511	Kingdom split among Clovis's sons
511-524	Chlodomer (Orléans)
511-534	Theodoric I (Metz)
511-558	Childebert I (Paris)
511-561	Lothair I (Soissons 511-561, all Franks 558-561)
534-548	Theudebert I (Metz)
548-555	Theudebald (Metz)
561	Kingdom split among Lothair's sons
561-567	Charibert I (Paris)
561-575	Sigebert I (Austrasia)
561-584	Chilperic I (Soissons)
561-592	Guntram (Burgundy)
575-595	Childebert II (Austrasia 575-595, Burgundy 593-595)
584-629	Lothair II (Neustria 584, all Franks 613-629)
595-612	Theudebert II (Austrasia)
595-613	Theodoric II (Burgundy 595-612, Austrasia 612-613)
613	Sigebert II (Austrasia, Burgundy)

Reign	Ruler (Principality)
623-639	Dagobert I (Austrasia 623-628, all Franks 629-639)
629-632	Charibert II (Aquitaine)
632-656	Sigebert III (Austrasia)
639-657	Clovis II (Neustria and Burgundy)
656-673	Lothair III (Neustria 657-673, all Franks 656-660)
662-675	Childeric (Austrasia 662-675, all Franks 673-675)
673-698	Theodoric III (Neustria 673-698, all Franks 678-691)
674-678	Dagobert II (Austrasia)
691-695	Clovis III (all Franks)
695-711	Childebert III (all Franks)
711-716	Dagobert III (all Franks)
715-721	Chilperic II (Neustria 715-721, all Franks 719-720)
717-719	Lothair IV (Austrasia)
721-737	Theodoric IV (all Franks)
743-751	Childeric III (all Franks)

THE CAROLINGIANS

Reign	Ruler
687-714	Pépin II of Heristal (mayor of Austrasia/Neustria)
714-719	Plectrude (regent for Theudoald)
719-741	Charles Martel (the Hammer; mayor of Austrasia/Neustria)
747-768	Pépin III the Short (mayor of Neustria 741, king of all Franks 747)
768-814	Charlemagne (king of Franks 768, emperor 800)
814-840	Louis the Pious (king of Aquitaine, emperor)
840-855	Lothair I (emperor)
843	Treaty of Verdun divides Carolingian Empire into East Franks (Germany), West Franks (essentially France), and a Middle Kingdom (roughly corresponding to Provence, Burgundy, and Lorraine)
843-876	Louis II the German (king of Germany)
843-877	Charles II the Bald (king of Neustria 843, emperor 875)
855-875	Louis II (emperor)
877-879	Louis II (king of France)
879-882	Louis III (king of France)
879-884	Carloman (king of France)
884-887	Charles III the Fat (king of France, emperor 881)
887-898	Odo (Eudes; king of France)
887-899	Arnulf (king of Germany 887, emperor 896)
891-894	Guy of Spoleto (Wido, Guido; emperor)
892-898	Lambert of Spoleto (emperor)
893-923	Charles III the Simple (king of France)
915-923	Berengar I of Friuli (emperor)
923-929?	Robert I (king of France)

Reign	Ruler
929-936	Rudolf (king of France)
936-954	Louis IV (king of France; Hugh the Great in power)
954-986	Lothair (king of France; Hugh Capet in power 956)
986-987	Louis V (king of France)

THE CAPETIANS

Reign	Ruler
987-996	Hugh Capet
996-1031	Robert II the Pious
1031-1060	Henry I
1060-1108	Philip I the Fair
1108-1137	Louis VI the Fat
1137-1179	Louis VII the Younger (with Eleanor of Aquitaine, r. 1137-1180)
1179-1223	Philip II Augustus
1223-1226	Louis VIII the Lion
1223-1252	Blanche of Castile (both queen and regent)
1226-1270	Louis IX (Saint Louis)
1271-1285	Philip III the Bold
1285-1314	Philip IV the Fair
1314-1316	Louis X the Stubborn
1316	Philip, brother of Louis X (regent before birth of John I and during his short life)
1316	John I the Posthumous
1316-1322	Philip V the Tall
1322-1328	Charles IV the Fair

Valois Dynasty, Main Branch

Reign	Ruler
1328-1350	Philip VI the Fortunate
1350-1364	John II the Good
1364-1380	Charles V the Wise
1380-1382	Louis I of Anjou (regent for Charles VI)
1380-1422	Charles VI the Well-Beloved
1422-1461	Charles VII the Victorious
1461-1483	Louis XI
1483-1484	Anne de Beaujeu (regent for Charles VIII)
1483-1498	Charles VIII the Affable

Valois-Orléans Branch

Reign	Ruler
1498-1515	Louis XII, the Father of His People

Valois-Angoulême Branch

Reign	Ruler
1515-1547	Francis I
1547-1559	Henry II (with Catherine de Médicis)
1559-1560	Francis II
1560-1563	Catherine de Médicis (regent for Charles IX)
1560-1574	Charles IX
1574-1589	Henry III (King of Poland, 1573-1574)

BOURBON DYNASTY

Reign	Ruler
1589-1610	Henry IV (Henry III of Navarre, 1572-1610)
1610-1614	Marie de Médici (regent for Louis XIII)
1610-1643	Louis XIII the Well-Beloved
1643-1651	Anne of Austria (regent for Louis XIV)
1643-1715	Louis XIV the Sun King
1715-1723	Philip II of Orléans (regent for Louis XV)
1715-1774	Louis XV the Well-Beloved
1774-1792	Louis XVI the Beloved
1792-1804	First Republic
1804-1814	First Empire (Napoleon I Bonaparte)
1814-1824	Louis XVIII
1824-1830	Charles X
1830-1848	Louis-Philippe of Orléans

GERMANIC TRIBES. *See also* HOLY ROMAN EMPIRE

In the fifth and sixth centuries, Europe was invaded from the east by several "barbarian" tribes from eastern Europe and Central Asia, including the Visigoths, who inflicted the earliest damage on Rome in the late fourth and early fifth centuries; the Burgundians, from central and northeastern Europe; the Vandals, who eventually settled in Spain and North Africa; the Suevi, who made their way to the north of Spain and finally fell to the Visigoths; the Alans, a non-Germanic steppe tribe from Iran who, along with the Suevi and the Visigoths, overran Gaul (France) and the Iberian Peninsula; and the Franks (see Frankish Kingdom and France, above), who occupied most of Gaul during the later Roman Empire and were the only of these early tribes to survive. The Franks would evolve into the Merovingian and Carolingian lines, and by the ninth century they dominated Europe. Below is a list of some of the Germanic tribes and tribal leaders before and during the Frankish period. The region known today as Germany was initially occupied by these tribes and then came under the subjugation of the Frankish Merovingians and Carolingians. In 962, the Holy Roman Empire came into existence and held sway over Germany for nearly a millennium (see Holy Roman Empire, below). Not until the late nineteenth century did the nation-state of Germany come into existence.

ALEMANNI (OR ALAMANNI)

The Alemanni occupied Swabia.

Reign	Ruler
c. 536-554	Leuthari
c. 536-554	Butilin
d. c. 539	Haming

Reign	Ruler
c. 570-587	Leutfred I
588-613	Uncilen
d. 613	Gunzo
c. 615-639	Chrodebert
c. 640-673/95	Leutfred II
c. 700-709	Godefred
d. c. 712	Huocin
d. c. 712	Willehari
c. 720-730	Lanfred I
c. 737-744	Theodobald
d. 746	Nebi
746-749	Lanfred II
791-799	Gerold
799-806	Isenbard
After 806	Annexed by the Franks

BAVARIANS

The Bavarians occupied a region approximating present-day Bavaria.

Reign	Ruler
508-512	Theodo I
512-537	Theodo II
537-565	Theodo III
537-567	Theodobald I
550-590	Garibald I
590-595	Grimwald I
591-609	Tassilo I
609-630	Agilulf
609-640	Garibald II
640-680	Theodo IV
680-702	Theodo V
702-715	Theodobald II
702-723	Grimwald II
702-725	Theodobert
702-730	Tassilo II
725-737	Hubert
737-748	Odilo
748-788	Tassilo III
After 788	Annexed by Franks

BURGUNDIANS

The Burgundians occupied central and southeastern France.

Reign	Ruler
c. 407	Gebicca
407-434	Gundahar/Gondikar/Gunther
434-473	Gundioc/Gunderic
443-c. 480	Chilperic I
473-486	Gundomar I
473-493	Chilperic II
473-501	Godegisel
473-516	Gundobad
516-524	Sigismund

Reign	Ruler
524-532	Gudomar II
532	Frankish conquest

FRANKS

The Franks initially occupied the area now known as the Netherlands and northern France, and they eventually dominated Europe. See Frankish Kingdom and France, above.

LOMBARDS

The Lombards occupied northern Italy.

Reign	Ruler
565-572	Alboin
573-575	Celph
575-584	Unstable
584-590	Authari
590-591	Theodelinda
591-615	Agilulf
615-625	Adaloald
625-636	Arioald
636-652	Rotharis
652-661	Aribert I
661-662	Godipert
662-671	Grimoald
671-674	Garibald
674-688	Bertharit
688-700	Cunibert
700-701	Liutpert
701	Raginpert
701-712	Aribert II
712-744	Liutprand
744-749	Rachis of Friuli
749-756	Aistulf of Friuli
756-774	Desiderius
774	Frankish conquest

OSTROGOTHS

The Ostrogoths migrated from the east into the Balkans and Italian peninsula.

Reign	Ruler
474-526	Theodoric the Great
526-534	Athalaric
534-536	Theodahad (with Amalasuntha)
536-540	Vitiges (Witiges)
540	Theodobald (Heldebadus)
541	Eraric
541-552	Totila (Baduila)
552-553	Teias
553-568	Roman domination (Byzantine emperor Justinian I)
568-774	Lombard domination
774	Frankish conquest

SUEVI

The Suevi migrated from the east into northern Spain.

Reign	Ruler
409-438	Hermeric
428-448	Rechila
439	Mérida
441	Seville
448-456	Rechiar
452	Peace with Romans
456	Visigoths defeat Rechiar
456-457	Aioulf
457-460	Maldras
460-c. 463	Richimund
460-c. 465	Frumar
c. 463-?	Remisund
c. 500-550	Unknown kings
c. 550-559	Carriaric
559-570	Theodemar
561	Catholic
570-582	Miro
582-584	Eboric
584-585	Andeca
After 585	Visigoth conquest

VANDALS

The Vandals migrated west into southern Spain and northern Africa.

Reign	Ruler
c. 406-428	Gunderic
428-477	Gaiseric
477-484	Huneric
484-496	Gunthamund
496-523	Thrasamund
523-530	Hilderic
530-534	Gelimer
After 534	Roman overthrow

VISIGOTHS

The Visigoths migrated west into southwestern France.

Reign	Ruler
395-410	Alaric I
410-415	Athaulf (Ataulfo)
415	Sigeric
415-417	Wallia
417-451	Theodoric I
451-453	Thorismund
453-466	Theodoric II
466-484	Euric I
484-507	Alaric II
508-511	Amalaric
511-526	Theodoric the Great
526-531	Amalaric
531-548	Theudes

Reign	Ruler
548-549	Theudegisel
549-554	Agila
554-567	Athanagild
567-571	Theodomir
571-572	Leuva (Leova) I
572-586	Leuvigild
586-601	Reccared I
601-603	Leova II
603-610	Witterich
610-612	Gundemar
612-621	Sisebut (Sisebur)
621	Reccared II
621-631	Swintilla (Suinthila)
631-636	Sisenand
636-640	Chintila
640-642	Tulga
642-653	Chindaswind
653-672	Recdeswinth
672-680	Wamba
680-687	Euric (Erwig) II
687-702	Egica (Ergica)
702-709	Witiza
709-711	Roderic (Rodrigo)
711	Overthrown by Umayyads
718	Christian Kingdom of Asturias

GERMANY: FIRST REICH. SEE HOLY ROMAN EMPIRE

HOLY ROMAN EMPIRE

Although some sources consider the Holy Roman Empire to have begun with Otto I's coronation in 962, others date the Empire's beginning as early as Charlemagne's consolidation of the Franks and his coronation as emperor of the Frankish Empire in 800. The term "Sacrum Romanum Imperium" (Holy Roman Empire) dates to 1254, the use of the term "Holy Empire" to 1157, and the term "Roman Empire" to 1034 (reign of Conrad II). "Roman emperor" was applied to Otto I during his reign; however, Charlemagne also used the term to refer to his own reign. The concept of a "Holy" Roman Empire goes back to the beginning of the Byzantine Empire and the reign of the first Christian Roman emperor, Constantine the Great. Hence, the concept of this political entity can be considered to have evolved incrementally over time. The practice of papal coronation to legitimate the emperor began with Otto I. Regnal dates are therefore often listed as beginning with the date of coronation. However, the

German kings who became Holy Roman Emperors frequently asserted their de facto power earlier as rulers of West Frankia (France), East Frankia (essentially Germany), and/or Italy (roughly the northern portion of modern Italy). In the table below, where a date of ascension to the West Frankish (French), East Frankish (German), Middle Frankish (Lorraine south to Italy), or other throne is different from that to Emperor, the former date is set before a slash and the date of assuming the rule of the Empire falls after the slash. Asterisks indicate that the monarch was not formally crowned at Rome by the pope, a practice that officially ended with Frederick II, although Charles V was last to be crowned outside Rome.

Reign	Emperor (House)
768/800-814	Charlemagne (Carolingian)
814/813-840	Louis I the Pious (Carolingian)
840/817-855	Lothair I (Carolingian)
840-876	Louis II the German (Carolingian; first king of East Franks only)
840/875-877	Charles II the Bald (Carolingian)
855/850-875	Louis II of Italy (Carolingian)
877-881	Empire unstable
876/881-888	Charles III the Fat (Carolingian)
888-891	Viking and Arab incursions
891	Italian line begins
888/891-894	Guy (Guido, Wido) of Spoleto (Italian)
894/892-898	Lambert of Spoleto (Italian, co-emperor)
888/896-899	Arnulf (East Frankish)
899/901-905	Louis III of Provence (Carolingian, deposed)
905/915-924	Berengar I of Friuli (Italian)
911-918	*Conrad
919	Saxon line begins
919-936	*Henry I the Fowler (Saxon)
936/962-973	Otto I (Saxon): crowned in 962 by Pope John XII; the Empire no longer lays claim to West Frankish lands (essentially France), but now is basically a union of Germany and northern Italy.
973/967-983	Otto II (Saxon)
983/996-1002	Otto III (Saxon)
1002/14-1024	Henry II the Saint (Saxon)
1024	Franconian/Salian line begins
1024/27-1039	Conrad II (Franconian/Salian)
1039/46-1056	Henry III (Franconian/Salian)
1056/84-1106	Henry IV (Franconian/Salian)
1077-1080	*Rudolf of Swabia
1081-1093	*Hermann (of Luxemburg)
1093-1101	*Conrad (of Franconia)
1106/11-1125	Henry V (Franconian/Salian)
1125	Franconian/Salian line ends

Reign	Emperor (House)
1125/33-1137	Lothair II (duke of Saxony)
1138	Hohenstaufen line begins
1138-1152	*Conrad III (Hohenstaufen)
1152/55-1190	Frederick I Barbarossa (Hohenstaufen)
1190/91-1197	Henry VI (Hohenstaufen)
1198-1208	*Philip of Swabia (Hohenstaufen)
1208/09-1215	Otto IV (married into Hohenstaufens)
1215/20-1250	Frederick II (Hohenstaufen): Last emperor crowned at Rome.
1246-1247	*Henry Raspe
1247-1256	*William of Holland
1250-1254	*Conrad IV
1254-1273	Great Interregnum
1257-1272	*Richard of Cornwall (rival, Plantagenet)
1257-1273	*Alfonso X of Castile (rival)
1273-1291	*Rudolf I (Habsburg)
1292-1298	*Adolf of Nassau
1298-1308	*Albert (Albrecht) I (Habsburg)
1308/11-1313	Henry VII (Luxembourg)
1314/28-1347	Louis IV of Bavaria (Wittelsbach)
1314-1325	*Frederick of Habsburg (co-regent)
1346/55-1378	Charles IV (Luxembourg): Changes the name to the Holy Roman Empire of the German Nation as France begins to assert power; Charles abandons the Empire's French and Italian claims, and the history of the Holy Roman Empire and Germany are now basically the same.
1349	*Günther of Schwarzburg
1378-1400	*Wenceslaus (Luxembourg; deposed)
1400	*Frederick III (of Brunswick)
1400-1410	*Rupert of the Palatinate (Wittelsbach)
1410-1411	*John (of Moravia)
1410/33-1437	Sigismund (Luxembourg)
1438-1439	*Albert II (Habsburg)
1440/52-1493	Frederick III (Habsburg)
1486/93-1519	*Maximilian I (Habsburg)
1499	Peace of Basle; Swiss independence
1513	Swiss Confederation of the Thirteen Cantons
1519-1558	*Charles V (Habsburg, last emperor crowned)
1555	Peace of Augsburg
1558-1564	*Ferdinand I (Habsburg)
1559	Peace of Cateau-Cambrésis
1564-1576	*Maximilian II (Habsburg)
1576-1612	*Rudolf II (Habsburg)
1612-1619	*Matthias (Habsburg)
1619-1637	*Ferdinand II (Habsburg)
1637-1657	*Ferdinand III (Habsburg)
1648	Peace of Westphalia
1658-1705	*Leopold I (Habsburg)

Reign	Emperor (House)
1686-1697	War of the League of Augsburg, conquest of Hungary, Nine Years' War (1688-1697)
1705-1711	*Joseph I (Habsburg)
1711-1740	*Charles VI (Habsburg)
1713	Peace of Utrecht
1740-1742	Interregnum
1742-1745	*Charles VII (Wittelsbach-Habsburg)
1745-1765	*Francis I (Lorraine)
1745-1780	*Maria Theresa (empress consort; queen of Hungary, 1740; empress dowager, 1765)
1756-1763	Seven Years' War
1765-1790	*Joseph II (Habsburg-Lorraine)
1790-1792	*Leopold II (Habsburg-Lorraine)
1792-1806	*Francis II (Habsburg-Lorraine; abdicated)
1806	Holy Roman Empire falls to Napoleon I of France

HUNGARY. *See also* BOHEMIA, POLAND

Reign	Ruler
c. 896-907	Árpád
d. 947	Zsolt
d. 972	Taksony
997	Géza
997-1038	Saint Stephen (István) I
1038-1041	Peter Orseleo
1041-1044	Samuel
1044-1046	Peter (second rule)
1047-1060	Andrew I
1060-1063	Béla I
1063-1074	Salamon
1074-1077	Géza I
1077-1095	Saint László (Ladislas) I
1095-1116	Kalman
1116-1131	Stephen II
1131-1141	Béla II
1141-1162	Géza II
1162-1163	László II
1163-1172	Stephen III
1163-1165	Stephen IV
1172-1196	Béla III
1196-1204	Imre
1204-1205	László III
1205-1235	Andrew II
1235-1270	Béla IV
1270-1272	Stephen V
1272-1290	László IV
1290-1301	Andrew III (end of the Árpád line)
1301-1304	Wenceslaus (Václav) II
1304-1308	Otto I of Bavaria
1305-1306	Wenceslaus (Václav) III
1306	End of the Přemlysid line

Reign	Ruler
1306-1310	Instability
1310-1342	Károly (Charles Robert) I
1342-1382	Lajos (Louis) I
1382-1395	Maria
1387-1437	Sigismund
1438-1439	Albert II of Habsburg
1440-1444	Ulászló I (Władysław III, Poland)
1444-1457	László (Ladislas) V
1458-1490	Matthias (Matyas) I Corvinus
1490-1516	Ulászló II (Vladislav or Władisław Jagiełło)
1516-1526	Louis II
1526-1564	Ferdinand I (Habsburg claims suzerainty)
1526-1540	John I Zápolya (simultaneous claimant)
1540-1571	John II Sigismund
1556-1559	Isabel
1562	Split between Habsburgs, Ottomans, and Ottoman principality Transylvania
1563-1576	Maximilian II (Holy Roman Emperor)
1571-1575	Stephen Báthory
1572-1608	Rudolf II (Holy Roman Emperor)
1575-1581	Christopher (Kristóf) Báthory
1581-1599	Sigismund Báthory
1599	Andrew Cardinal Báthory
1599-1602	Sigismund Báthory
1604-1606	Stephen Bocskay
1607-1608	Sigismund Rákóczy
1608-1619	Matthias (Holy Roman Emperor)
1608-1613	Gabriel (Gábor) Báthory
1613-1629	Gábor Bethlen
1618-1637	Ferdinand II
1625-1657	Ferdinand III
1630-1648	George (György) I Rákóczy
1647-1654	Ferdinand IV
1648-1657	George II Rákóczy
1655-1705	Leopold I
1660-1682	Emeric Thököly (Tökölli)
1687-1711	Joseph I
1703-1711	Francis II Rákóczy leads liberation movement
1711-1740	Charles III
1740-1780	Maria Theresa
1780-1790	Joseph II
1790-1792	Leopold II
1792-1835	Francis
1835-1848	Ferdinand V
1848	Revolutions of 1848

INDIA

FIRST CĀLUKYA DYNASTY

Reign	Ruler
543-566	Pulakeśin I
c. 566-597	Kīrtivarman I

Reign	Ruler
598-610	Maṇgaleśa
610-642	Pulakeśin II
655-680	Vikramāditya I
680-696	Vinayāditya
696-733	Vijayāditya
733-746	Vikramāditya II
747-757	Kīrtivarman II

PALLAVAS

Reign	Ruler
c. 550-575	Simhavarman (some sources give c. 436)
c. 575-600	Simhavishnu
c. 600-630	Mahendravarman I
c. 630-668	Narasiṃhavarman I Mahāmalla
c. 668-670	Mahendravarman II
c. 670-700	Paramesvaravarman I
c. 695-728	Narasiṃhavarman II
c. 728-731	Paramesvaravarman II
c. 731-796	Nandivarman
750-770	Gopāla
770-810	Dharmapāla
810-850	Devapāla
854-908	Narayanpāla
c. 988-1038	Māhipāla I
c. 1077-1120	Rāmapāla
1143-1161	Madanpāla

SECOND WESTERN CĀLUKYA DYNASTY

Reign	Ruler
973-997	Taila II
997-1008	Satyaśraya
1008-1014	Vikramāditya I
1014-1015	Ayyana
1015-1042	Jayasimha I
1043-1068	Someśvara I
1068-1076	Someśvara II
1076-1126	Vikramāditya VI
1127-1135	Someśvara III
1135-1151	Jagadhekamalla II
1151-1154	Taila III
1155-1168	Bijjala
1168-1177	Someśvara IV
1177-1180	Saṇkama II
1180-1183	Āhavamalla
1183-1184	Singhana
1184-1189/90	Someśvara IV

GURJARA-PRATIHĀRA DYNASTY

Reign	Ruler
c. 730-c. 756	Nāgabhaṭa I
n.d.	Devaraja
c. 778-c. 794	Vatsarāja

Reign	Ruler
c. 794-c. 833	Nāgabhaṭa II
c. 836-c. 885	Mihira Bhoja I
c. 890-c. 910	Mahendrapāla I
c. 914-?	Mahipāla
n.d.	Mihira Bhoja II
n.d.	Vinayakapāla
c. 946-c. 948	Mahendrapāla II
c. 948-c. 960	Devapāla
c. 960-?	Vijayapāla
n.d.	Rājyapāla
c. 1018-c. 1027	Trilocanapāla

THE CŌLAS

Reign	Ruler
c. 850-c. 870	Vijayālaya
871-907	Āditya I
907-955	Parāntaka I
956	Arinjayā
956	Parāntaka II
956-969	Āditya II
969-985	Madhurantaka Uttama
985-1014	Rājarāja I
1014-1044	Rājendracōla Deva I
1044-1052	Rājadhirāja I
1052-1060	Rājendracōla Deva II
1060-1063	Ramamahendra
1063-1067	Virarājendra
1067-1070	Adhirājendra
1070-1122	Rājendra III
1122-1135	Vikrama Cōla
1135-1150	Kulottuṅga II Cōla
1150-1173	Rājarāja II
1173-1179	Rājadhirāja II
1179-1218	Kulottuṅga III
1218-1246	Rājarāja III
1246-1279	Rājendra IV

DELHI SULTANATE

Muʿizzī Slave Sultans

Reign	Ruler
1206-1210	Quṭ al-Dīn Aybak
1210-1211	Ārām Shāh
1211-1236	Iltutmish
1236	Ruknuddin Firūz Shāh
1236-1240	Raziya
1240-1242	Bahrām Shāh
1242-1246	Masʿūd Shāh
1246-1266	Maḥmūd Shāh
1266-1287	Balban Ulugh Khān
1287-1290	Kay Qubādh
1290	Kayūmarth

Khaljī Dynasty

Reign	Ruler
1290-1296	Jalāl-ud-Dīn Fīrūz Khaljī
1296-1316	ʿAlāʾ-ud-Dīn Muḥammad Khaljī
1316	ʿUmar Shāh
1316-1320	Mubārak Shāh
1320	Khusraw Khān Barwārī

Tughluq Dynasty

Reign	Ruler
1320-1325	Tughluq I (Ghiyās-ud-Dīn)
1325-1351	Muḥammad ibn Tughluq
1351-1388	Fīrūz III
1388-1389	Tughluq II (Ghiyās-ud-Dīn)
1389-1390	Abū Bakr
1390-1394	Nāṣir-ud-Dīn
1394	Sikandar I (Humayun Khān)
1394-1395	Maḥmūd II
1395-1399	Nuṣrat
1401-1412	Maḥmūd II (second rule)
1412-1414	Dawlat Khān Lōdī

Sayyid Dynasty

Reign	Ruler
1414-1421	Khiḍr
1421-1434	Mubārak II
1434-1443	Muḥammad IV
1443-1451	ʿĀlām

Lodī Dynasty

Reign	Ruler
1451-1489	Bahlūl
1489-1517	Sikandar II
1517-1526	Ibrāhīm II

MUGHAL EMPERORS

Reign	Ruler
1526-1530	Bābur
1530-1540	Humāyūn
1540-1545	Shīr Shāh Sūr
1545-1553	Islām Shāh Sūr
1554	Muḥammad V Mubāriz Khān
1554-1555	Ibrāhām III Khān
1555	Aḥmad Khān Sikandar Shāh III
1555-1556	Humāyūn (second rule)
1556-1605	Akbar I
1605-1627	Jahāngīr
1627-1628	Dāwar Bakhsh
1628-1657	Jahān I Khusraw
1658-1707	Aurangzeb (Awrangzīb ʿĀlamgīr I)
1707-1712	ʿĀlam I Bahādur
1712-1713	Jahāndār Muʿizz al-Dīn
1713-1719	Farrukh-siyar
1719	Shams al-Dīn Rāfʿ al-Darajāt

Reign	Ruler
1719	Jahān II Rāfiʿ al-Dawla
1719	Nīkūsiyar Muḥammad
1719-1720	Muḥammad Shāh Nāṣir al-Dīn
1720	Mohammed Ibrahim
1720-1748	Muḥammad Shāh Nāṣir al-Dīn
1739	Nādir Shāh sacks Delhi
1748-1754	Aḥmad Shāh Bahadur
1754-1779	Alamgir II
1760?	Shāh Jahān III
1779-1806	Shāh Alam II
1806-1837	Akbar Shāh II
1837-1857	Bahadur Shāh II (Bahadur Shāh Zafar)

IRAN (PERSIA). *See also* ISLAMIC CALIPHS, OTTOMAN EMPIRE, SELJUK EMPIRE

LATER SĀSĀNIAN EMPIRE

Reign	Ruler
309-379	Shāpūr II
379-383	Ardashīr II
383-388	Shāpūr III
388-399	Barham (Varahran) IV
399-421	Yazdegerd (Yazdgard) I
421-439	Barham (Varahran) V
439-457	Yazdegerd (Yazdgard) II
457-459	Hormizd III
459-484	Peroz
484-488	Valash
488-496	Kavadh I
496-498	Zamasp
499-531	Kavadh I (restored)
531-579	Khosrow (Khusro or Chosroes) I
579-590	Hormizd IV
590-628	Khosrow (Khusro or Chosroes) II
628	Kavadh II
628-629	Ardashīr III
629-630	Boran
630-632	Hormizd V and Khosrow III
633-651	Yazdegerd (Yazdgard) III
651	Islamic conquest
651-656	ʿUthmān ibn ʿAffān
656-661	Alī ibn Abī Ṭālib
661-750	Umayyad caliphs (*see* Islamic Caliphs)
750-821	ʿAbbāsid caliphs (*see* Islamic Caliphs)

LATER IRANIAN DYNASTIES

Dates	Dynasty
821-873	Ṭāhirid Dynasty (in Khorāsān, northeastern Persia)
c. 866-c. 900	Ṣafārrid Dynasty
c. 940-1000	Sīmjūrid Dynasty (in Khorāsān)

Dates	Dynasty
945-1055	Būyid Dynasty (western Iran)
977-1186	Ghaznavid Dynasty (in Khorāsān, Afghanistan, northern India)
999-1211	Qarakhanid Dynasty (Transoxania)
c. 1038	Seljuks take power (*see* Seljuk Empire)
1153-1231	Khwārezm-Shāh Dynasty (in Khwārezm, northeastern Iran)
c. 1231	Mongol invasion
1256-1353	Il-Khanid (Mongol) Dynasty
1353-1393	Mozaffarid Dynasty
1393-c. 1467	Timurid Dynasty
c. 1467-1500	Turkmen/Ottoman incursions

ṢAFAVID DYNASTY

Reign	Ruler
1501-1524	Ismāʿīl I
1524-1576	Ṭahmāsp I
1576-1578	Ismāʿīl II
1578-1587	Muḥammad Khudabanda
1587-1629	ʿAbbās I
1629-1642	Safi
1642-1667	ʿAbbās II
1667-1694	Süleyman I
1694-1722	Ḥoseyn I
1722-1732	Ṭahmāsp II
1732-1736	ʿAbbās III
1736-1750	Afshāid shahs
1750	Süleyman II in Mashad
1750-1765	Ismāʿīl III (Karim Khān, regent 1751-1765)

AFSHĀR DYNASTY

Reign	Ruler
1736-1747	Nāder Shāh (regent)
1747	ʿĀdel Shāh
1748	Ibrāhim
1748-1750	Shāh Rukh
1755-1796	Shāh Rukh in Khorāsān
1796-1803	Nāder Mīrza in Mashad

ZAND DYNASTY (WESTERN IRAN)

Reign	Ruler
1750-1779	Karim Khān
1779	Abu'l Fath (Shirāz)
1779	Moḥammad ʿAlī (Shirāz)
1779-1781	Moḥammad Ṣādiq (Shirāz)
1781-1785	ʿAlī Morād (Eṣfahān)
1785-1789	Ja'far (Eṣfahān, later Shirāz)
1789-1794	Luṭf ʿAlī (Shirāz)
1796	Qajar Dynasty begins

IRELAND

THE HIGH-KINGS

Reign	Ruler
379-405	Niall Noígillach of the Nine Hostages
405-428	Dathi (Nath) I
429-463	Lóeguire MacNéill
456-493	Saint Patrick converts Irish
463-483	Ailill Motl MacNath I
483-507	Lugaid MacLóeguiri O'Néill
507-534	Muirchertach MacErcae O'Néill (Muiredach)
534-544	Tuathal Máelgarb MacCorpri Cáech O'Néill
544-565	Diarmait MacCerbaill O'Néill
565-566	Domnall MacMuirchertaig O'Néill and Forggus MacMuirchertaig O'Néill
566-569	Ainmere MacSátnai O'Néill
569-572	Báetán MacMuirchertaig O'Néill and Eochaid MacDomnaill O'Néill
572-581	Báetán MacNinnedo O'Néill
581-598	Aed MacAinmerech O'Néill
598-604	Aed Sláine MacDiarmato O'Néill
598-604	Colmán Rímid MacBáetáin O'Néill (rival)
604-612	Aed Uaridnach MacDomnaill O'Néill
612-615	Máel Cobo MacAedo O'Néill
615-628	Suibne Menn MacFiachnai O'Néill
628-642	Domnall MacAedo O'Néill
642-658	Conall Cóel MacMáele Cobo O'Néill and Cellach MacMáele Cobo O'Néill
656-665	Diarmait MacAedo Sláine O'Néill and Blathmac MacAedo Sláine O'Néill
665-671	Sechnussach MacBlathmaic O'Néill
671-675	Cenn Fáelad MacBlathmaic O'Néill
675-695	Finsnechtae Fledach MacDúnchada O'Néill
695-704	Loingsech MacOengus O'Néill
704-710	Congal Cinn Magir MacFergus Fánat O'Néill
710-722	Fergal MacMáele Dúin O'Néill
722-724	Fogartach MacNéill O'Néill
724-728	Cináed MacIrgalaig
724-734	Flaithbbertach MacLoingsig O'Néill
734-743	Aed Allán MacFergal O'Néill
743-763	Domnall Midi O'Néill
763-770	Niall Frossach MacFergal O'Néill
770-797	Donnchad Midi MacDomnaill Midi O'Néill
797-819	Aed Oirdnide MacNéill Frossach O'Néill
819-833	Conchobar MacDonnchado Midi O'Néill
833-846	Niall Caille MacAedo Oirdnide O'Néill
846-862	Máel Sechnaill MacMáele Ruanaid O'Néill
862-879	Aed Findliath MacNéill Caille O'Néill
879-916	Flann Sionna MacMáele Sechnaill O'Néill
916-919	Niall Glúndubh MacAedo Findliath O'Néill
919-944	Donnchad Donn MacFlann O'Néill
944-950	Ruaidrí ua Canannáin (rival)
944-956	Congalach Cnogba MacMáel Mithig O'Néill

Reign	Ruler
956-980	Domnall MacMuirchertaig O'Néill
980-1002	Máel Sechnaill MacDomnaill O'Néill
1002-1014	Brian Bóruma MacCennétig and Brian Boru
1014-1022	Máel Sechnaill MacDomnaill O'Néill (restored)
1022-1064	Donnchad MacBrian
1064-1072	Diarmait MacMáil na mBó
1072-1086	Toirdelbach O'Brien
1090-1121	Domnall MacArdgar O'Lochlainn O'Néill
1121-1135	Toirrdelbach MacRuaidrí na Saide Buide ua Conchobair (Turlogh)
1141-1150	Toirrdelbach MacRuaidrí na Saide Buide ua Conchobair (Turlogh)
1150-1166	Muirchertach MacNéill MacLochlainn (Murtagh)
1166-1175	Ruaidrí MacToirrdelbaig (Rory O'Connor)
1175-1258	Henry II of England claims title Lord of Ireland
1258-1260	Brian Catha an Duin
1260-1316	English rule restored
1316-1318	Edward de Bruce
1318	English rule restored
1801	Act of Union: Ireland is joined with Britain

KINGDOM OF IRELAND (WITH ENGLAND/GREAT BRITAIN)

Reign	Ruler
1509-1547	Henry VIII
1547-1553	Edward VI
1553-1558	Mary I
1558-1603	Elizabeth I
1603-1625	James (I of England, VI of Scotland)
1625-1649	Charles I
1649-1660	Commonwealth and Restoration
1660-1685	Charles II
1685-1689	James (II of England, VII of Scotland)
1689-1702	William and Mary
1702-1707	Anne
1707	Act of Union (Great Britain and Ireland)
1707-1714	Anne
1714-1727	George I
1727-1760	George II
1760-1801	George III
1801	Act of Union creates United Kingdom

ISLAMIC CALIPHS. *See also* IRAN, OTTOMAN EMPIRE, SELJUK EMPIRE, SPAIN

ORTHODOX (SUNNI) CALIPHS, 632-661

Reign	Caliph
632-634	Abū Bakr
634-644	ʿUmar I

Reign	Caliph
644-656	ʿUthmān ibn ʿAffān
656-661	Alī ibn Abī Ṭālib

UMAYYAD CALIPHS, 661-750

Reign	Caliph
661-680	Muʾāwiyah I (Muʾāwiyah ibn Abī Sufyna)
680-683	Yazīd I
683	Muʾāwiyah II
684-685	Marwān I
685-705	ʿAbd al-Malik
705-715	al-Walīd I
715-717	Sulaimān
717-720	ʿUmar II
720-724	Yazīd II
724-743	Hishām
743-744	al-Walīd II
744	Yazīd III
744	Ibrāhīm
744-750	Marwān II

ʿABBĀSID CALIPHS, 750-1256

Reign	Caliph
750-754	Abū al-ʿAbbās al-Saffāḥ
754-775	al-Manṣūr
775-785	al-Mahdī
785-786	al-Hādī
786-809	Hārūn al-Rashīd
809-813	al-Amīn
813-833	al-Maʾmūn (Maʾmūn the Great)
833-842	al-Muʿtaṣim
842-847	al-Wathīq
847-861	al-Mutawakkil
861-862	al-Muntaṣir
862-866	al-Mustaʿin
866-869	al-Muʿtazz
869-870	al-Muqtadī
870-892	al-Muʿtamid
892-902	al-Muʿtaḍid
902-908	al-Muktafī
908-932	al-Muqtadir
932-934	al-Qāhir
934-940	al-Rāḍī
940-944	al-Mustaqfī
946-974	al-Mutī
974-991	al-Ṭāʾiʿ
991-1031	al-Qadir
1031-1075	al-Qāʾim
1075-1094	al-Muqtadī
1094-1118	al-Mustazhir
1118-1135	al-Mustarshid
1135-1136	al-Rashīd
1136-1160	al-Muqtafī

Reign	Caliph
1160-1170	al-Mustanjid
1170-1180	al-Mustadī
1180-1225	al-Nāṣir
1225-1226	al-Ẓāhir
1226-1242	al-Mustanṣir
1242-1256	al-Mustaʿṣim

FĀṬIMID CALIPHS, 909-1171

Reign	Caliph
909-934	al-Mahdī
934-945	al-Qāʾim
945-952	al-Manṣūr
952-975	al-Muʿizz
975-996	al-ʿAzīz
996-1021	al-Ḥākim
1021-1036	al-Zahīr
1036-1094	al-Mustanṣir
1094-1101	al-Mustadī
1101-1130	al-Amīr
1130-1149	al-Ḥāfiz
1149-1154	al-Zafīr
1154-1160	al-Fāʾiz
1160-1171	al-ʿAdīd

ITALY

The Italian peninsula was occupied by a number of fiefs and principalities during the better part of the millennium that made up the Middle Ages. These included Lombardy in the north, the Papal States in the center, and various duchies, margavates, and republics, including Sardinia, Benevento, Spoleto, Modena, Milan, Tuscany, Parma, Montferrat, and independent centers of trade such as Venice and Genoa. Only those early rulers who dominated the area are listed below; thereafter, the northern part of the peninsula was primarily under the power of the Carolingians (see Frankish Kingdom and France), the Holy Roman Emperors (see Holy Roman Empire, above), and the Papacy (see Popes and Antipopes, above). In the south, Naples and Sicily dominated. Thus, during the millennium 476-1453, the Italian Peninsula was a complex of ever-shifting jurisdictions, of which only the more prominent rulers are listed below.

BARBARIAN RULERS

Reign	Ruler
476-493	Odoacer
493-526	Theodoric
526-534	Athalaric
534-536	Theodatus (Theodahad)
536-540	Vitiges (Witiges)

Reign	Ruler
540-541	Theodobald (Heldebadus)
541	Eraric
541-552	Totila
552-553	Teias

BYZANTINE (EAST ROMAN) RULE

Reign	Ruler
518-527	Justin I
527-565	Justinian I

LOMBARDS (NORTHERN ITALY)

Reign	Ruler
565-572	Alboin
573-575	Celph
575-584	Unstable
584-590	Authari
590-591	Theodelinda
591-615	Agilulf
615-625	Adaloald
625-636	Arioald
636-652	Rotharis
652-661	Aribert I
661-662	Godipert
662-671	Grimoald
671-674	Garibald
674-688	Bertharit
688-700	Cunibert
700-701	Liutpert
701	Raginpert
701-712	Aribert II
712-744	Liutprand
744-749	Rachis of Friuli
749-756	Aistulf of Friuli
756-774	Desiderius
774-888	Frankish conquest, subsumed under Carolingian Empire

KINGDOM OF ITALY

Reign	Ruler
888-891	Berengar I of Friuli
891-894	Guy of Spoleto (Guido, Wido)
894-896	Lambert of Spoleto
896-899	Arnulf, King of Germany
899-905	Louis III
905-922	Berengar I of Friuli (restored)
922-933	Rudolf II
933-947	Hugh of Arles
947-950	Lothair II of Arles
950-961	Berengar II of Ivrea
961	Conquest by Otto I; Italian peninsula divided among Holy Roman Empire, Papacy, and other principalities until unification in 1861

NAPLES AND SICILY

Reign	Ruler (Line)
1042-1046	William Iron Arm (Norman)
1046-1051	Drogo (Norman)
1051-1057	Humphrey (Norman)
1057-1085	Robert Guiscard (Norman)
1071-1101	Roger I (Norman)
1101-1154	Roger II of Sicily (Norman; king in 1130)
1154-1166	William I (Norman)
1166-1189	William II the Good (Norman)
1190-1194	Tancred of Lecce (Norman)
1194	William III (Norman)
1194-1197	Henry VI (Hohenstaufen)
1197-1250	Frederick II (Hohenstaufen)
1250-1254	Conrad IV (Hohenstaufen)
1250-1266	Manfred (Hohenstaufen)
1267-1268	Conradin (rival)
1266-1285	Charles I of Anjou (Angevin)
1282	Sicily and Naples split

SICILY

Reign	Ruler
1282-1285	Pedro III of Aragón
1285-1296	James II of Aragón
1296-1337	Frederick II (or I)
1337-1342	Peter II
1342-1355	Louis
1355-1377	Frederick III (or II) the Simple
1377-1401	Mary
1390-1409	Martin the Younger
1395-1410	Martin (I) the Older Aragón
1412-1416	Ferdinand I Sicily & Aragón
1416-1458	Alfonso (V of Aragón)
1458-1468	John II
1468-1516	Ferdinand II (III of Naples)
1516-1713	United with Spain
1713-1720	Victor Amadeus II (duke of Savoy)
1720	Returned to Spain as part of Kingdom of the Two Sicilies
1720-1735	Austrian rule
1735-1759	Charles (Bourbon king of Spain)
1759-1825	Ferdinand I/IV
1825-1830	Francis I
1830-1859	Ferdinand II/V
1859-1860	Francis II
1861	Annexed to Italy

NAPLES

Reign	Ruler
1285-1309	Charles II (Angevin)
1309-1343	Robert Ladislas (Angevin)
1343-1382	Joanna I (Angevin)
1382-1386	Charles III (Angevin)

Reign	Ruler
1386-1414	Ladislas (Angevin)
1414-1435	Joanna II (Angevin)
1435-1442	René of Anjou
1442-1458	Alfonso I (V of Aragón)
1458-1494	Ferdinand I
1494-1495	Alfonso II (Naples only)
1495-1496	Ferdinand II (Ferrandino)
1496-1501	Frederick IV (III)
1501-1503	French occupation
1504-1516	Ferdinand III (II of Sicily)
1516-1713	United with Spain
1713	Ceded to Austria
1720	Returned to Spain as part of Kingdom of the Two Sicilies
1799	Parthenopean Republic
1805	Bourbons deposed
1806-1808	Joseph Bonaparte
1808-1815	Joachim Murat
1815	Bourbon restoration
1825-1830	Francis I
1830-1859	Ferdinand II/V
1859-1860	Francis II
1861	Annexed to Italy

VISCONTIS (GENOA)

Reign	Ruler
1310-1322	Matteo Visconti
1322-1328	Galeazzo I
1328-1339	Azzo
1339-1349	Lucchino
1349-1354	Giovanni
1354-1355	Matteo II and Bernabò
1354-1378	Galeazzo II
1378-1402	Gian Galeazzo II
1402-1447	Filippo Maria

SFORZAS (GENOA)

Reign	Ruler
1450-1466	Francesco Sforza
1466-1476	Galeazzo Maria
1476-1481	Gian Galeazzo
1481-1499	Ludovico
1500-1512	[Louis XII of France]
1512-1515	Massimiliano
1521-1535	Francesco Maria

DOGES OF VENICE

Reign	Doge
727-738	Orso (Ursus) Ipato
742, 744-736	Teodato (Deusdedit) Ipato
756	Galla Gaulo
756-765	Domenico Monegaurio

Reign	Doge
765-787	Maurizio I Galbaio
787-802	Giovanni and Maurizio II Galbaio
802-811	Obelerio Antenorio
808-811	Beato
811-827	Angello Partecipazio
827-829	Giustiniano Partecipazio
829-836	Giovanni I Partecipazio
836-864	Pietro Tradonico
864-881	Orso I Badoer (I Partecipazio)
881-888	Giovanni Badoer (II Partecipazio)
887	Pietro I Candiano
888-912	Pietro Tribuno
912-932	Orso II Badoer (II Partecipazio)
932-939	Pietro II Candiano
939-942	Pietro Badoer (Partecipazio)
942-959	Pietro III Candiano
959-976	Pietro IV Candiano
976-978	Pietro I Orseolo
978-979	Vitale Candiano
979-991	Tribuno Menio (Memmo)
991-1009	Pietro II Orseolo
1009-1026	Ottone Orseolo
1026-1030	Pietro Centranico (Barbolano)
1030-1032	Ottone Orseolo (second rule)
1032-1043	Domenico Flabianico
1043-1070	Domenico Contarini
1070-1084	Domenico Silvio (Selvo)
1084-1096	Vitale Falier
1096-1101	Vitale I Michiel (Michel)
1101-1118	Ordelafo Falier
1118-1129	Domenico Michiel
1129-1148	Pietro Polani
1148-1155	Domenico Morosini
1155-1172	Vitale II Michiel
1172-1178	Sebastiano Ziani
1178-1192	Orio Mastropiero (Malipiero)
1192-1205	Enrico Dandolo
1205-1229	Pietro Ziani
1229-1249	Giacomo Tiepolo
1249-1253	Marino Morosini
1253-1268	Reniero Zeno
1268-1275	Lorenzo Tiepolo
1275-1280	Jacopo Contarini
1280-1289	Giovanni Dandolo
1289-1311	Pietro Gradenigo
1311-1312	Marino Zorzi
1312-1328	Giovanni Soranzo
1328-1339	Francesco Dandolo
1339-1342	Bartolomeo Gradenigo
1343-1354	Andrea Dandolo
1354-1355	Marino Falier
1355-1356	Giovanni Gradenigo

Reign	Doge
1356-1361	Giovanni Dolfin
1361-1365	Lorenzo Celsi
1365-1368	Marco Corner
1368-1382	Andrea Contarini
1382	Michele Morosini
1382-1400	Antonio Venier
1400-1413	Michele Steno
1414-1423	Tommaso Mocenigo
1423-1457	Francesco Foscari
1462-1471	Cristoforo Moro
1471-1473	Nicolò Tron
1473-1474	Nicolò Marcello
1474-1476	Pietro Mocenigo
1476-1478	Andrea Vendramin
1478-1485	Giovanni Mocenigo
1485-1486	Marco Barbarigo
1486-1501	Agostino Barbarigo
1501-1521	Leonardo Loredan
1521-1523	Antonio Grimani
1523-1538	Andrea Gritti
1539-1545	Pietro Lando
1545-1553	Francesco Donato
1553-1554	Marcantonio Trevisan
1554-1556	Francesco Venier
1556-1559	Lorenzo Priuli
1559-1567	Girolamo Priuli
1567-1570	Pietro Loredan
1570-1577	Alvise I Mocenigo
1577-1578	Sebastiano Venier
1578-1585	Nicolò da Ponte
1585-1595	Pasquale Cicogna
1595-1605	Marino Grimani
1606-1612	Leonardo Donato
1612-1615	Marcantonio Memmo
1615-1618	Giovanni Bembo
1618	Nicolò Donato
1618-1623	Antonio Priuli
1623-1624	Francesco Contarini
1625-1629	Giovanni Corner
1630-1631	Nicolò Contarini
1631-1646	Francesco Erizzo
1646-1655	Francesco Molin
1655-1656	Carlo Contarini
1656	Francesco Corner
1656-1658	Bertucci (Albertuccio) Valier
1658-1659	Giovanni Pesaro
1659-1675	Domenico Contarini
1675-1676	Nicolò Sagredo
1676-1684	Luigi Contarini
1684-1688	Marcantonio Giustinian
1688-1694	Francesco Morosini
1694-1700	Silvestro Valier

Reign	Doge
1700-1709	Alvise II Mocenigo
1709-1722	Giovanni II Corner
1722-1732	Alvise III Mocenigo
1732-1735	Carlo Ruzzini
1735-1741	Alvise Pisani
1741-1752	Pietro Grimani
1752-1762	Francesco Loredan
1762-1763	Marco Foscarini
1763-1778	Alvise IV Mocenigo
1779-1789	Paolo Renier
1789-1797	Lodovico Manin
1797	Venice Falls to Napoleon Bonaparte

FLORENCE (MEDICIS)

Reign	Ruler
1434-1464	Cosimo the Elder
1464-1469	Piero I
1469-1478	Giuliano
1469-1492	Lorenzo I the Magnificent
1492-1494	Piero II
1494-1512	Charles VIII expels the Medici
1512-1519	Lorenzo II
1519-1527	Giulio (Pope Clement VII)
1527	Sack of Rome
1527-1530	Second expulsion
1530-1537	Alessandro
1537-1574	Cosimo I
1574-1587	Francesco I
1587-1609	Ferdinand I
1609-1621	Cosimo II
1621-1670	Ferdinand II
1670-1723	Cosimo III
1723-1737	Gian Gastone

TUSCANY (AFTER THE MEDICIS)

Reign	Ruler
1738-1745	Francis
1745-1790	Leopold I
1790-1801	Ferdinand III
1801-1803	Louis of Parma (king of Etruria)
1803-1807	Charles Louis of Parma
1803-1807	Maria Louisa of Parma (regent)
1807-1814	Annexed to France
1824-1859	Leopold II
1859-1860	Ferdinand IV
1860	Annexed to Italy

PARMA

Farneses

Reign	Ruler
1545-1547	Pier Luigi
1547-1586	Ottavio

Reign	Ruler
1586-1592	Alessandro
1592-1622	Ranuccio I
1622-1646	Odoardo I
1646-1694	Ranuccio II
1694-1727	Francesco
1727-1731	Antonio

Bourbons

Reign	Ruler
1731-1736	Charles
1738-1748	Habsburg rule
1748-1765	Philip
1765-1802	Ferdinand
1805-1814	French rule
1814-1847	Marie Louise (Habsburg)
1848-1849	Charles II Louis
1849-1854	Charles III
1854-1859	Robert
1859	Annexed to Italy

SARDINIA

Reign	Ruler
1720-1730	Victor Amadeus II (duke of Savoy)
1730-1773	Charles Emanuel III
1773-1796	Victor Amadeus III
1796-1802	Charles Emanuel IV
1802-1821	Victor Emanuel I
1821-1831	Charles Felix
1831-1849	Charles Albert
1849-1861	Victor Emanuel II
1861	Annexed to Italy

JAPAN

ASUKA PERIOD

Reign	Ruler
539-571	Kimmei
572-585	Bidatsu
585-587	Yōmei
587-592	Sushun
593-628	Suiko (empress)
629-641	Jomei
642-645	Kōgyoku (empress)
645-654	Kōtoku
655-661	Saimei (empress)
661-672	Tenji
672	Kōbun
673-686	Temmu
686-697	Jitō (empress)
697-707	Mommu
707-715	Gemmei (empress)

NARA PERIOD

Reign	Ruler
707-715	Gemmei (empress)
715-724	Genshō (empress)
724-749	Shōmu
749-758	Kōken (empress)
758-764	Junnin
764-770	Shōtoku (Kōken, empress)
770-781	Kōnin

HEIAN PERIOD

Reign	Ruler
781-806	Kammu
806-809	Heizei
809-823	Saga
823-833	Junna
833-850	Nimmyō
850-858	Montoku
858-876	Seiwa
876-884	Yōzei
884-887	Kōkō
887-897	Uda
897-930	Daigo
930-946	Suzaku
946-967	Murakami
967-969	Reizei
969-984	En'yu
984-986	Kazan
986-1011	Ichijō
1011-1016	Sanjō
1016-1036	Go-Ichijō
1036-1045	Go-Suzaku
1045-1068	Go-Reizei
1068-1073	Go-Sanjō
1073-1087	Shirakawa (cloistered, 1086-1129)
1087-1107	Horikawa
1107-1123	Toba (cloistered, 1129-1156)
1123-1142	Sutoku
1142-1155	Konoe
1155-1158	Go-Shirakawa (cloistered, 1158-1192)
1158-1165	Nijō
1165-1168	Rokujō
1168-1180	Takakura
1180-1185	Antoku

KAMAKURA PERIOD AND KEMMU RESTORATION

Reign	Ruler
1183-1198	Go-Toba
1198-1210	Tsuchimikado
1210-1221	Jintoku
1221	Chukyo
1221-1232	Go-Horikawa
1232-1242	Shijō

Reign	Ruler
1242-1246	Go-Saga
1246-1260	Go-Fukakusa
1260-1274	Kameyama
1274-1287	Go-Uda
1287-1298	Fushimi
1298-1301	Go-Fushimi
1301-1308	Go-Nijō
1308-1318	Hanazonō
1318-1339	Go-Daigo

KAMAKURA SHOGUNATE

Reign	Shogun
1192-1199	Minamoto Yoritomo
1202-1203	Minamoto Yoriie
1203-1219	Minamoto Sanetomo
1226-1244	Kujo Yoritsune
1244-1252	Kujo Yoritsugu
1252-1266	Prince Munetaka
1266-1289	Prince Koreyasu
1289-1308	Prince Hisaaki
1308-1333	Prince Morikuni

HŌJŌ REGENTS

Reign	Regent
1203-1205	Hōjō Tokimasa
1205-1224	Hōjō Yoshitoki
1224-1242	Hōjō Yasutoki
1242-1246	Hōjō Tsunetoki
1246-1256	Hōjō Tokiyori
1256-1264	Hōjō Nagatoki
1264-1268	Hōjō Masamura
1268-1284	Hōjō Tokimune
1284-1301	Hōjō Sadatoki
1301-1311	Hōjō Morotoki
1311-1312	Hōjō Munenobu
1312-1315	Hōjō Hirotoki
1315	Hōjō Mototoki
1316-1326	Hōjō Takatoki
1326	Hōjō Sadaaki
1327-1333	Hōjō Moritoki

NAMBOKUCHŌ PERIOD

Emperors: Southern Court

Reign	Ruler
1318-1339	Go-Daigo
1339-1368	Go-Murakami
1368-1383	Chōkei
1383-1392	Go-Kameyama

Ashikaga Pretenders: Northern Court

Reign	Ruler
1336-1348	Komyō
1348-1351	Sukō
1351-1371	Go-Kogon
1371-1382	Go-En'yu

MUROMACHI PERIOD

Reign	Ruler
1382-1412	Go-Komatsu
1412-1428	Shōkō
1428-1464	Go-Hanazono
1464-1500	Go-Tsuchimikado
1500-1526	Go-Kashiwabara
1526-1557	Go-Nara
1557-1586	Ōgimachi

ASHIKAGA SHOGUNATE

Reign	Shogun
1338-1358	Ashikaga Takauji
1359-1368	Ashikaga Yoshiakira
1368-1394	Ashikaga Yoshimitsu
1395-1423	Ashikaga Yoshimochi
1423-1425	Ashikaga Yoshikazu
1429-1441	Ashikaga Yoshinori
1442-1443	Ashikaga Yoshikatsu
1449-1473	Ashikaga Yoshimasa
1474-1489	Ashikaga Yoshihisa
1490-1493	Ashikaga Yoshitane
1495-1508	Ashikaga Yoshizumi
1508-1521	Ashikaga Yoshitane (second rule)
1522-1547	Ashikaga Yoshiharu
1547-1565	Ashikaga Yoshiteru
1568	Ashikaga Yoshihide
1568-1573	Ashikaga Yoshiaki

AZUCHI-MOMOYAMA PERIOD

Reign	Ruler
1573-1582	Oda Nobunaga (dictator)
1586-1611	Go-Yōzei (emperor)

EDO PERIOD

Emperors

Reign	Emperor
1612-1629	Go-Mi-no-o
1630-1643	Meishō (Myōshō)
1644-1654	Go-Kōmyō
1655-1662	Go-Saiin
1663-1686	Reigen
1687-1709	Higashiyama
1710-1735	Nakamikado
1736-1746	Sakuramachi
1746-1762	Momozono

Reign	Emperor
1763-1770	Go-Sakuramachi
1771-1779	Go-Momozono
1780-1816	Kōkaku
1817-1846	Ninkō
1847-1866	Kōmei

Tokugawa Shogunate

Reign	Shogun
1603-1605	Tokugawa Ieyasu
1605-1623	Tokugawa Hidetada
1623-1651	Tokugawa Iemitsu
1651-1680	Tokugawa Ietsuna
1680-1709	Tokugawa Tsunayoshi
1709-1712	Tokugawa Ienobu
1713-1716	Tokugawa Ietsugu
1716-1745	Tokugawa Yoshimune
1745-1760	Tokugawa Ieshige
1760-1786	Tokugawa Ieharu
1787-1837	Tokugawa Ienari
1837-1853	Tokugawa Ieyoshi
1853-1858	Tokugawa Iesada
1858-1866	Tokugawa Iemochi
1867-1868	Tokugawa Yoshinobu

KINGDOM OF JERUSALEM

The Christian rulers of Jerusalem were ushered in by the First Crusade and essentially were ushered out after the last Crusade.

Reign	King
1095-1099	First Crusade
1099-1100	Godfrey of Boulogne (or Bouillon)
1100-1118	Baldwin I of Boulogne
1118-1131	Baldwin II of Le Bourg
1131-1153	Melisende
1131-1143	Fulk V of Anjou
1143-1162	Baldwin III
1147-1149	Second Crusade
1162-1174	Amalric I
1174-1183	Baldwin IV the Leper
1183-1186	Baldwin V
1185-1190	Sibylla
1186-1192	Guy of Lusignan
1189-1192	Third Crusade
1190-1192	Conrad of Montferrat
1192-1197	Henry of Champagne
1192-1205	Isabella I
1197-1205	Amalric II
1202-1204	Fourth Crusade
1205-1210	Maria of Montferrat (regent)
1210-1225	John of Brienne
1210-1228	Isabella (Yolanda) II

Reign	King
1217-1221	Fifth Crusade
1225-1228	Frederick II
1227-1230	Sixth Crusade
1228-1254	Conrad IV Hohenstaufen
1244	Fall of Jerusalem
1248-1254	Seventh (or Sixth) Crusade
1254-1268	Conradin Hohenstaufen
1268-1284	Hugh III
1268-1284	Charles of Anjou (rival)
1270	Eighth (or Seventh) Crusade
1284-1285	John I
1285-1306	Henry I of Jerusalem (II of Cyprus)
1291	Fall of Acre to the Mamluks

KOREA

UNIFIED SILLA DYNASTY

Reign	Ruler
661-681	Munmu Wang
681-692	Sinmun Wang
692-702	Hyoso Wang
702-737	Sŏngdŏk Wang
737-742	Hyosŏng Wang
742-765	Kyŏngdŏk Wang
765-780	Hyesong Wang
780-785	Sŏndŏk Wang
785-798	Wŏnsŏng Wang
798-800	Sosŏng Wang
800-809	Aejang Wang
809-826	Hŏndŏk Wang
826-836	Hŭngdŏk Wang
836-838	Hŭigang Wang
838-839	Minae Wang
839	Sinmu Wang
839-857	Munsŏng Wang
857-861	Hŏnan Wang
861-875	Kyŏngmun Wang
875-886	Hŏn'gang Wang
886-887	Chŏnggang Wang
887-896	Queen Chinsŏng
897-912	Hyogong Wang
912-917	Pak Sindŏ Wang
917-924	Kyŏngmyŏng Wang
924-927	Kyŏngae Wang
927-935	Kyŏngsun Wang

KORYŎ DYNASTY

Reign	Ruler
918-943	T'aejo (Wang Kŏn)
944-945	Hyejong
946-949	Chŏngjong

Reign	Ruler
949-975	Kwangjong (Wang So)
975-981	Kyŏngjong (Wang Yu)
981-997	Sŏngjong (Wang Ch'i)
997-1009	Mokshong
1009-1031	Hyŏnjong
1031-1034	Tokjong
1034-1046	Chŏngjong
1046-1083	Munjong (Wang Hwi)
1083	Sunjong
1083-1094	Sŏnjong
1094-1095	Hŏnjong
1095-1105	Sukjong
1105-1122	Yejong I
1122-1146	Injong I (Wang Hae)
1146-1170	Ŭijong
1170-1197	Myŏngjong
1197-1204	Sinjong
1204-1211	Hŭijong
1211-1213	Kangjong
1214-1259	Kojong I
1260-1274	Wŏnjong
1274-1308	Ch'unguyŏl Wang
1308-1313	Ch'ungsŏn Wang
1313-1330	Ch'ungsuk Wang
1330-1332	Ch'unghye Wang
1332-1339	Ch'angsuk Wang
1339-1344	Ch'unghye Wang
1344-1348	Ch'ungmok Wang
1348-1351	Ch'ungjŏng Wang
1351-1374	Kongmin Wang
1374-1388	U (Sin-u)
1389	Sinch'ang
1389-1392	Kongyang Wang

YI DYNASTY

Reign	Ruler
1392-1398	Yi T'aejo
1398-1400	Chŏngjong
1400-1418	T'aejong
1418-1450	Sejong
1450-1452	Munjong
1452-1455	Tanjong
1455-1468	Sejo
1468-1469	Yejong
1469-1494	Sŏngjong
1494-1506	Yŏnsan Gun
1506-1544	Chungjong
1544-1545	Injong
1546-1567	Myŏngjong
1567-1608	Sŏnjo
1608-1623	Kwanghae-gun
1623-1649	Injo

Reign	Ruler
1649-1659	Hyojong
1659-1674	Hyŏnjong
1674-1720	Sukchong
1720-1724	Kyŏngjong
1724-1776	Yŏngjo
1776-1800	Chŏngjo
1800-1834	Sonjo

MONGOLS. SEE ALSO CHINA: YUAN DYNASTY

From his base in Mongolia, founder Genghis Khan conquered a large and diverse region covering much of Asia from the Far East to the steppes of Russia, Turkey and the Middle East, Central Asia, and even parts of Southeast Asia. Although the individual leaders of those who inherited this empire remain unfamiliar to most, Genghis's heirs, among whom are the "great khans" of the immediate generations to follow, would indelibly change and shape the world from Russia to China, the Mideast to India. Genghis divided his empire among four sons. Jochi, the eldest, received the northwestern quadrant of this expanse, and his sons would found the "hordes" (armies) the would become known as the Blue, White, and eventually Golden Hordes; the latter would not meet its match until Russia's founder, Ivan the Great, refused to pay tribute in 1476 and thereafter would dissolve into the various khanates of Kazan, Astrakhan, and the Crimea. Genghis's second son, Chaghatai, would receive the area of Central Asia lying north of India and east of the Caspian and Aral seas, sometimes called Moghulistan or Mughulistan. Genghis's third son, Ogatai, oversaw the southeastern and far east coastal "quadrant" or swathe, which would eventually become part of the huge realm of his nephew Kublai Khan, who in turn was the son of Genghis's youngest, Tolui, heir to the Mongolian homeland. It was Tolui's sons, beginning with Kublai, who would spawn the Chinese emperors of the Yuan Dynasty in the east and, beginning with Hulegu, the great Ilkhans who conquered the Middle East. The Ilkhans' successors, the Jalāyirids, Black Sheep Turks, White Sheep Turks, and ultimately the Timurids (founded by the part-Mongol Timur or Tamerlane), would dominate the Mideast and also give rise to the Mughal Dynasty in India.

GREAT KHANS

Reign	Ruler
1206-1227	Genghis Khan (founder)
1227-1229	Tolui
1229-1241	Ogatai Khan

Reign	Ruler
1241-1246	Toregene (regent, wife of Ogatai)
1246-1248	Güyük
1248-1251	Oghul Qaimish (regent, wife of Güyük)
1251-1259	Mongu
1259-1260	Arigböge (regent, brother of Mongu and Kublai)
1260-1294	Kublai Khan

KHANS OF CHINA'S YUAN DYNASTY

Reign	Ruler
1267-1279	Mongols conquer Southern Song
1294-1307	Temür Öljeitü (Chengzong)
1307-1311	Kaishan (Wuzong)
1311-1320	Ayurbarwada (Renzong)
1321-1323	Shidebala (Yingzong)
1323-1328	Yesün Temür (Taiding)
1328	Arigaba (Aragibag)
1328-1329	Tugh Temür (Wenzong)1
1329	Tugh Koshila (Mingzong)
1329-1332	Tugh Temür (restored)
1333-1368	Toghon Temür (Shundi)
1368	Chinese expel Mongols

LATER MONGOLIAN KHANS

Reign	Ruler
1370-1388	Togus-Temür
1370-1379	Biliktu
1379-1389	Usaqal
1389-1393	Engke Soriktu
1393-1400	Elbek
1400-1403	Gun Timur
1403-1411	Oljei Timur
1411-1415	Delbeg
1415-1425	Eseku
1425-1438	Adai Qa'an
1438-1440	Esen Toghan Tayisi
1440-1452	Tayisung Qa'an
1452-1455	Esen Tayisi
1452-1454	Molon Khan Togus
1454-1463?	Maqa Kurkis
1463?-1467	Mandughuli
1467-1470	Bayan Mongke
1470-c.1485	Civil war
1479-1543	Dayan Khan
1543-1582	Altan Khan
1547-1557	Kudeng Darayisun
1557-1592	Tumen Jasaghtu
1592-1604	Sechen Khan
1604-1634	Ligdan Khan
1628-1759	Manchurian conquest

MIDDLE EAST (IRAQ, IRAN, EASTERN TURKEY, ARABIA)

Il Khāns

Reign	Ruler
1256-1265	Hülegü (Hülägü)
1255-1260	Invasion of Middle East
1260	Battle of 'Ain Jalut (defeat by Mamlūks)
1265-1282	Abaqa
1282-1284	Aḥmad Tegüder
1284-1291	Arghūn
1291-1295	Gaykhatu
1295	Baydu
1295-1304	Maḥmūd Ghāzān
1304-1316	Muḥammad Khudābanda Öljeytü
1316-1335	Abū Saʿīd ʿAlāʾ ad-Dunyā wa ad-Dīn
1335-1336	Arpa Ke'ün
1336-1337	Mūsā
1337-1338	Muḥammad
1338-1353	Conflict among successor states

Jalāyirids

Reign	Ruler
1340-1356	Shaykh Ḥasan-i Buzurg Tāj ad-Dīn
1356-1374	Shaykh Uways
1374-1382	Ḥusayn I Jalāl ad-Dīn
1382-1410	Sulṭān Aḥmad Ghiyāth ad-Dīn
1410-1411	Shāh Walad
1411	Maḥmūd
1411-1421	Uways II
1421-1425	Maḥmūd
1421	Muḥammad
1425-1532	Ḥusayn II
1432	Conquest by Kara Koyunlu

Kara Koyunlu (Black Sheep Turks)

Reign	Ruler
1351-1380	Bayram Khōja (Jalāyirid vassal)
1380-1389	Kara Muḥammad
1382	Independent
c. 1390-1400	Kara Yūsuf
1400-1406	Occupation by Tamerlane
1406-1420	Kara Yūsuf
1420-1438	Iskandar
1439-1467	Jahān Shāh
1467-1469	Ḥasan ʿAlī
1469	Abū Yūsuf
1469	Conquest by Ak Koyunlu

Ak Koyunlu (White Sheep Turks)

Reign	Ruler
1403-1435	Kara Osman (Qara Yoluq ʿUthmān Fakhr ad-Dīn)
1435-1438	ʿAlī Jalāl ad-Dīn
1438-1444	Ḥamza Nūr ad-Dīn
1444-1453	Jahāngīr Muʾizz ad-Dīn
1453-1478	Uzun Ḥasan

Reign	Ruler
1478	Sulṭān Khalīl
1478-1490	Yaʿqūb
1490-1493	Baysonqur
1493-1497	Rustam
1497	Aḥmad Gövde
1497-1502	Alwand (Diyār Bakr and Azerbaijan)
1497-1500	Muḥammad (Iraq and Persia)
1500-1508	Sulṭān Murād (Persia)
1504-1508	Zayn al-ʿAbidīn (Diyār Bakr)
1508	Ṣafawid conquest

SOUTH CENTRAL ASIA

Chaghatayid or Jagataiid (Turkistan and the Tarim Basin)

Reign	Ruler
1227-1244	Chaghatay (Jagatai)
1244-1246	Kara Hülegü
1246-1251	Yesü Möngke
1251-1252	Kara Hülegü
1252-1260	Orqina Khātūn
1260-1266	Alughu
1266	Mubārak Shāh
c. 1266-1271	Baraq Ghiyāth ad-Dīn
1271-1272	Negübey
1272-1282	Buqa/Toqa Temür
c. 1282-1306	Duʾa
1306-1308	Könchek
1308-1309	Taliqu
1309	Kebek
1309-1320	Esen Buqa
c. 1320-1326	Kebek
1326	Eljigedey
1326	Duʾa Temür
1326-1334	Tarmashīrīn ʿAlāʾ ad-Dīn
1334	Buzan
1334-1338	Changshi
c. 1338-1342	Yesün Temür
c. 1342-1343	Muḥammad
1343-1346	Kazan
1346-1358	Danishmendji
1358	Buyan Kuli
1359	Shāh Temür
1359-1363	Tughluq Temür
c. 1363	Timurids rule Mughulistan

Timurids

Reign	Ruler
1370-1405	Tamerlane (Timur)
1402	Capture of Bayezid, Battle of Ankara
1405-1407	Pīr Muḥammad (Kandahar)
1405-1409	Khalīl Sulṭān (Samarqand)
1405-1409	Shāh Rukh (Khorāsān)
1409-1447	Shāh Rukh (Transoxania, Iran)

Reign	Ruler
1447-1449	Ulugh Beg (Transoxania, Khorāsān)
1449-1450	ʿAbd al-Laṭīf (Transoxania)
1450-1451	ʿAbdallāh
1451-1469	Abū Saʿīd (Transoxania, Iran)
1469-1494	Sulṭān Aḥmad (Transoxania)
1494-1495	Maḥmūd
1495-1500	Baysonqur, Masʾūd, ʿAlī (Transoxania)
1500	Özbeg conquest of Transoxania

WESTERN ASIA, RUSSIA, NORTH CENTRAL ASIA

Blue Horde

Reign	Ruler
1227-1256	Batu
1236-1239	Russia conquered
1239-1242	Europe invaded
1256-1257	Sartaq
1257	Ulaghchi
1257-1267	Berke
1267-1280	Möngke Temür
1280-1287	Töde Möngke
1287-1291	Töle Buqa
1291-1313	Toqta
1313-1341	Muḥammad Özbeg
1341-1342	Tīnī Beg
1342-1357	Jānī Beg
1357-1359	Berdi Beg
1357-1380	Period of anarchy
1378	Union with White Horde

White Horde

Reign	Ruler
1226-1280	Orda
1280-1302	Köchü
1302-1309	Buyan
1309-1315	Sāsibuqa?
c. 1315-1320	Ilbasan
1320-1344	Mubārak Khwāja
1344-1374	Chimtay
1374-1376	Urus
1376-1377	Toqtaqiya
1377	Temür Malik
1377-1395	Toqtamïsh
1378	White and Blue Hordes form Golden Horde

Golden Horde

Reign	Ruler
1378-1395	Toqtamïsh
1395-1419	Edigü (vizir)
1395-1401	Temür Qutlugh
1401-1407	Shādī Beg
1407-1410	Pūlād Khān
1410-1412	Temür

Reign	Ruler
1412	Jalāl ad-Dīn
1412-1414	Karīm Berdi
1414-1417	Kebek
1417-1419	Yeremferden?
1419-1422	Ulugh Muḥammad/Dawlat Berdi (rivals)
1422-1433	Baraq
c. 1433-1435	Sayyid Aḥmad I
c. 1435-1465	Küchük Muḥammad
c. 1465-1481	Aḥmad
1476	Ivan refuses to pay tribute
1480	Russian independence
1481-1498	Shaykh Aḥmad
1481-1499	Murtaḍā
1499-1502	Shaykh Aḥmad
1502	Annexed to Crimean khanate

Remnants of the Golden Horde

Reign	Rulers
1437-1552	Kazan khans
1449-1783	Crimean khans
1466-1554	Astrakhan khans

THE NETHERLANDS

Date	Ruler/Government/Event
1559-1567	William I, the Silent, Prince of Orange, Count of Nassau (stadtholder)
1568	Dutch Revolt
1568-1648	Eighty Years' War
1572-1584	William the Silent
1579	Union of Utrecht
1581	Dutch independence declared
1585-1625	Maurice (Maurits)
1609-1621	Twelve Years' Truce
1618-1648	Thirty Years' War
1625-1647	Frederik Hendrik
1647-1650	William II
1648	Peace of Westphalia, Spanish recognition of Dutch independence
1652-1654	First Anglo-Dutch War
1664-1667	Second Anglo-Dutch War
1672-1702	William III
1672-1678	Dutch War with France
1672-1674	Third Anglo-Dutch War
1688-1697	War of the League of Augsburg
1689-1702	England rules
1701-1713	War of the Spanish Succession
1702-1747	Republic
1747-1751	William IV Friso
1751-1795	William V
1780-1784	Fourth Anglo-Dutch War
1795-1806	Batavian Republic

NORWAY. *See also* DENMARK, SWEDEN

Reign	Ruler
680-710	Olaf the Tree Hewer
710-750	Halfdan I
750-780	Oystein (Eystein) I
780-800	Halfdan II White Legs
800-810	Gudrod the Magnificent
810-840	Olaf Geirstade
840-863	Halfdan III the Black
863-872	Civil war
872-930/33	Harald I Fairhair
933-934	Erik I Bloodaxe
934-961	Hákon I the Good
961-970	Harald II Grayfell
970-995	Earl (Jarl) Hákon
995-1000	Olaf I Tryggvason
1000-1015	Erik I
1016-1028	Saint Olaf II Haraldsson
1028-1035	Canute the Great
1035-1047	Magnus I the Good
1047-1066	Harald III Hardrada
1066-1069	Magnus II
1069-1093	Olaf III the Peaceful
1093-1103	Magnus III the Barefoot
1103-1122	Oystein (Eystein) II
1103-1130	Sigurd I the Crusader
1130-1135	Magnus IV the Blinded
1130-1136	Harald IV Gillechrist
1136-1155	Sigurd II
1136-1161	Inge I
1142-1157	Oystein (Eystein) III
1161-1162	Hákon II
1163-1184	Magnus V
1184-1202	Sverre Sigurdsson
1202-1204	Hákon III
1204-1217	Inge II
1217-1263	Hákon IV
1263-1281	Magnus VI
1281-1299	Erik II Magnusson
1299-1319	Hákon V
1320-1343	Magnus VII (II of Sweden)
1343-1380	Hákon VI
1376-1387	Olaf IV (V of Denmark)
1380	Unification of Norway and Denmark
1380-1410	Margaret I of Denmark, Norway, and Sweden
1397	Unification of Norway, Denmark, and Sweden
1412-1439	Erik III (VII of Denmark, XIII of Sweden)
1439-1448	Christopher (III of Denmark)
1448-1481	Christian I of Oldenburg
1481-1513	Hans/John (II of Sweden)
1513-1523	Christian II
1523-1533	Frederick I

Reign	Ruler
1536-1814	Union with Denmark
1534-1559	Christian III
1559-1588	Frederick II
1588-1648	Christian IV
1648-1670	Frederick III
1670-1699	Christian V
1699-1730	Frederick IV
1730-1746	Christian VI
1746-1766	Frederick V
1766-1808	Christian VII
1808-1814	Frederick VI
1814	Christian Frederik
1814-1818	Carl II
1814-1905	Union with Sweden

OTTOMAN EMPIRE. *See also* IRAN, ISLAMIC CALIPHS, SELJUK EMPIRE, SPAIN

Reign	Sultan
1281/88-1326	Osman I
1326-1360	Orhan I
1360-1389	Murad I
1389-1402	Bayezid I
1402-1421	Mehmed I
1421-1444	Murad II
1444-1446	Mehmed II
1446-1451	Murad II (second rule)
1451-1481	Mehmed II (second rule)
1453	Ottomans take Constantinople
1481	Djem I
1481-1512	Bayezid II
1512-1520	Selim I
1520-1566	Süleyman I the Magnificent
1566-1574	Selim II
1574-1595	Murad III
1595-1603	Mehmed III
1603-1617	Ahmed I
1617-1618	Mustafa I
1618-1622	Osman II
1622-1623	Mustafa I
1623-1640	Murad IV
1640-1648	Ibrahim I
1648-1687	Mehmed IV
1687-1691	Süleyman II
1691-1695	Ahmed II
1695-1703	Mustafa II
1703-1730	Ahmed III
1730-1754	Mahmud I
1754-1757	Osman III
1757-1774	Mustafa III
1774-1789	Abd-ul-Hamid I
1789-1807	Selim III

Reign	Sultan
1807-1808	Mustafa IV
1808-1839	Mahmud II
1839-1861	Abd-ul-Mejid
1861-1876	Abd-ul-Aziz
1876	Murad V
1876-1909	Abd-ul-Hamid II
1909-1918	Mehmed V
1918-1922	Mehmed VI

POLAND

Reign	Ruler
962-992	Mieszko I
992-1025	Bolesław I the Brave
1025-1034	Mieszko II
1034-1037	Instability
1037-1058	Casimir I the Restorer
	Instability
1058-1079	Bolesław II
1079-1102	Władysław (Vladislav or Ladislas) I
1102-1106	Zbigniev (rival to brother Bolesław III)
1102-1138	Bolesław III
1138-1146	Instability following Bolesław III's division of Poland into five principalities
1146-1173	Bolesław IV
1173-1177	Mieszko III
1177-1194	Casimir II
1194-1227	Leszek I
1227-1279	Bolesław V
1228-1288	Instability: arrival of Teutonic Knights followed by Mongol incursions
1288-1290	Henry Probus
1290-1296	Przemyslav II (crowned 1295)
1297-1300	Instability
1300-1305	Wenceslaus (Vacław) I
1306-1333	Władysław I (Vladislav IV, Lokietek)
1333-1370	Casimir III the Great
1370	End of the Piast Dynasty
1370-1382	Ludvik I the Great (Louis of Anjou)
1382-1384	Confederation of Radom and civil war
1384-1399	Queen Jadwiga
1386-1434	Władysław II Jagiełło
1410-1411	Battle of Tannenberg and Peace of Thorn
1434-1444	Władysław (Vladislav) III
1444-1447	Instability; Poland united with Lithuania
1447-1492	Casimir IV
1454-1466	Poles defeat Teutonic Order, gain access to the Baltic in the Second Peace of Thorn
1471-1516	Vladislav Jagiełło (son of Casimir IV) king of Bohemia and then Hungary
1492-1501	John I Albert
1496	Statute of Piotrkow (Poland's Magna Carta)

Reign	Ruler
1501-1506	Alexander Jagiełło
1506-1548	Sigismund I, the Old
1548-1572	Sigismund II Augustus
1573-1574	Henry Valois (Henry III)
1575-1586	Stephen Báthory

VASA KINGS OF SWEDEN AND POLAND

Reign	Ruler
1587-1632	Sigismund III Vasa
1632-1648	Vladislaus IV Vasa
1648-1668	Jan Kazimierz Vasa
1669-1673	Michael Korybut Wisniowiecki
1674-1696	John III Sobieski

WETTIN ELECTORS OF SAXONY OF HOLY ROMAN EMPIRE

Reign	Ruler
1697-1706	Augustus II, the Strong (Wettin)
1706-1709	Stanisław Leszczynski
1709-1733	Augustus II, the Strong (Wettin)
1733-1736	Stanisław Leszczynski
1733-1763	August III Wettin
1764-1795	Stanisław August Poniatowski

DUCHY OF WARSAW

Reign	Ruler
1807-1815	Ksiestwo Warszawskie (dependent from France)
1807-1815	Frederick Augustus I of Saxony Wettin

PORTUGAL

Reign	Ruler
1093-1112	Henry of Burgundy, count of Portugal
1112-1185	Afonso I (count of Portugal 1112-1139, king 1139-1185)
1185-1211	Sancho I
1211-1223	Afonso II
1223-1245	Sancho II
1245-1279	Afonso III
1279-1325	Diniz (Denis)
1325-1357	Afonso IV
1357-1367	Peter I
1367-1383	Ferdinand I
1385-1433	John I of Avis
1433-1438	Edward I
1438-1481	Afonso V
1481-1495	John II
1495-1521	Manuel I
1521-1557	John III
1557-1578	Sebastian I
1578-1580	Cardinal Henry

Reign	Ruler
1580-1598	Philip I of Portugal (Philip II of Spain)
1598-1621	Philip II of Portugal (Philip III of Spain)
1621-1640	Philip III of Portugal (Philip IV of Spain)
1640	Revolt of Portugal
1640-1656	John IV (duke of Braganza)
1656-1667	Afonso VI
1667-1706	Pedro II
1706-1750	John V
1750-1777	José I
1777-1786	Pedro III
1777-1816	Maria I Francisca
1799-1816	John VI (regent)
1816-1826	John VI
1826	Pedro IV (I of Brazil)
1826-1828	Maria II da Glória
1828-1834	Miguel I (exiled)
1834-1853	Maria II da Glória
1853-1861	Pedro V
1861-1889	Luis I
1889-1908	Carlos I
1908	Manuel II
Oct. 5, 1910	Republic declared

RUSSIA

PRINCES OF KIEVAN RUS

Reign	Ruler
c. 862-879	Rurik
879-912	Oleg
912-945	Igor
945-964	Saint Olga (regent)
964-972	Svyatoslav I
972-980	Yaropolk
980-1015	Vladimir I (with Anna, Princess of the Byzantine Empire)
1015-1019	Sviatopolk I
1019-1054	Yaroslav
1054-1073	Iziaslav
1073-1076	Svyatoslav II
1076-1078	Iziaslav (restored)
1078-1093	Vsevolod
1093-1113	Sviatopolk II
1113-1125	Vladimir II Monomakh
1125-1132	Mstislav
1132-1139	Yaropolk
1139-1146	Vyacheslav
1146-1154	Iziaslav
1149-1157	Yuri I Dolgoruky
1154-1167	Rostislav

PRINCES OF VLADIMIR

Reign	Ruler
1169-1174	Andrei I Bogolyubsky
1175-1176	Michael
1176-1212	Vsevolod III
1212-1217	Yuri II
1217-1218	Constantin
1218-1238	Yuri II (restored)
1238-1246	Yaroslav II
1240	Mongol conquest
1246-1247	Svyatoslav III
1248-1249	Michael
1249-1252	Andrei II
1252-1263	Saint Alexander Nevsky
1264-1271	Yaroslav III of Tver
1272-1276	Vasily
1276-1281	Dmitry
1281-1283	Andrei III
1283-1294	Dmitry (restored)
1294-1304	Andrei III (restored)
1304-1319	Saint Michael of Tver
1319-1326	Yuri III of Moscow
1326-1327	Alexander II of Tver
1328-1331	Alexander III

PRINCES OF MOSCOW

Reign	Ruler
1263-1303	Daniel
1303-1325	Yuri III
1328-1341	Ivan I
1341-1353	Simeon
1353-1359	Ivan II
1359-1389	Dmitry Donskoy
1389-1425	Vasily I
1425-1462	Vasily II
1462-1505	Ivan III the Great
1480	Fall of the Golden Horde
1505-1533	Vasily III

CZARS OF ALL RUSSIA

Reign	Ruler
1547-1584	Ivan IV the Terrible
1584-1613	Time of Troubles
1584-1598	Fyodor I
1598-1605	Boris Godunov
1605	Fyodor II
1605-1606	False Dmitri I
1606-1610	Vasily IV Shuysky
1610-1613	Ladislaus IV of Poland
1613-1645	Michael I (first Romanov)
1645-1676	Aleksey I
1676-1682	Fyodor III
1682-1696	Ivan V (with Peter I)
1682-1721	Peter I (with Ivan V)

EMPERORS OF ALL RUSSIA

Reign	Ruler
1721-1725	Peter I
1725-1727	Catherine I the Great
1727-1730	Peter II
1730-1740	Anne
1740-1741	Ivan VI
1741-1762	Elizabeth
1762	Peter III
1762-1796	Catherine II
1796-1801	Paul
1801-1825	Alexander I
1825-1855	Nicholas I
1855-1881	Alexander II
1881-1894	Alexander III
1894-1917	Nicholas II
1917	Michael II (exiled)
1918	Execution of Romanovs
1917-1921	Revolution

SCOTLAND

Reign	Ruler
404-420	Fergus
420-451	Eugenius II
451-457	Dongardus
457-479	Constantine I
479-501	Congallus
569-606	Aldan
606-621	Eugenius III
646-664	Ferchard II
664-684	Mulduinns
684-688	Eugenius V
688-699	Eugenius VI
699-715	Eugenius VII
715-730	Mordachus
730-761	Etfinus
761-767	Interregnum
767-787	Solvatius
787-819	Achaius
819-824	Dongallus III
824-831	Dongal
831-834	Alpine
834-854	Kenneth
854-858	Donald V
858-874	Constantine II
874-893	Gregory
893-904	Donald VI
904-944	Constantine III
944-953	Malcolm I
953-961	Gondulph
961-965	Duff
965-970	Cullen

Reign	Ruler
970-995	Kenneth II
995-1005	Grimus
1005-1034	Malcolm II
1034-1040	Duncan I
1040-1057	Macbeth
1057-1058	Lulach
1058-1093	Malcolm III
1093-1094	Donaldbane
1094	Duncan II
1094-1097	Donaldbane (second rule)
1097-1107	Edgar
1107-1124	Alexander I
1124-1153	David I
1153-1165	Malcolm IV
1165-1214	William I the Lion
1214-1249	Alexander II
1249-1286	Alexander III
1286-1290	Margaret
1290-1292	Interregnum
1292-1296	John Baliol
1296-1306	Interregnum
1306-1329	Robert I the Bruce
1329-1371	David II
1371	Ascendancy of Robert II, House of Stuart
1371-1390	Robert II
1390-1406	Robert III
1406-1437	James I
1437-1460	James II
1460-1488	James III
1488-1513	James IV
1513-1542	James V
1542-1567	Mary
1567-1625	James VI
1625	Joined with England

SELJUK EMPIRE. *See also* **IRAN, ISLAMIC CALIPHS, OTTOMAN EMPIRE, SELJUK EMPIRE**

GREAT SULTANS

Reign	Sultan
1037-1063	Toghrïl Beg
1063-1072/73	Alp Arslan
1073-1092	Malik Shāh I
1092-1093	Maḥmūd I
1093-1104	Berk Yaruq (Barkyaruk, Barkiyarok)
1104-1105	Malik Shāh II
1105-1117	Muḥammad Tapar
1117-1157	Aḥmad Sanjar (Sinjar)

SULTANS OF IRAQ

Reign	Sultan
1105-1118	Maḥmūd Tapar
1118-1131	Maḥmūd
1131-1132	Dāʿūd (Dawd)
1132-1135	Toghrïl I
1135-1152	Masʿūd
1152-1153	Malik Shāh
1153-1159	Muḥammad
1159-1161	Sulaimān Shāh
1161-1177	Arslan Shāh
1177-1194	Toghrïl II

SELJUK SULTANS OF ANATOLIA/RUM

Reign	Sultan
1077-1066	Sulaimān Shāh
1092-1107?	Qïlïch (Kilij) Arslan I
1107?-1116	Malik Shāh I
1116-1156	Masʿūd I
1156-1192	Qïlïch (Kilij) Arslan II
1192	Malik Shāh II
1192-1196	Kai Khusrau (Khosrow, Khosru, Khusraw) I
1196-1204	Suleiman II
1203-1204	Qïlïch (Kilij) Arslan III
1204-1210	Kai Khusrau I (second rule)
1210-1219	Kai Kāʾūs I
1219-1236	Kai Qubād (Kobadh) I
1236-1246	Kai Khusrau II
1246-1259	Kai Kāʾūs II
1248-1264	Qïlïch (Kilij) Arslan IV
1249-1257	Kai Qubād (Kobadh) II
1264-1283	Kai Khusrau III
1283-1298	Masʿūd II
1298-1301?	Kai Qubād (Kobadh) III
1303-1308	Masʿūd II (second rule)

SELJUK SULTANS OF SYRIA

Reign	Sultan
1078-1094	Tutush
1095-1113	Riḍwān (Damascus)
1098-1113	Duqaq (Aleppo)
1113-1114	Alp Arslan
1114-1117	Sultan Shāh

SULTANS OF KIRMĀN (KERMAN)

Reign	Sultan
1041-1073	Qāvurt (Qawurd)
1073-1074	Kirmān (Kerman) Shāh

Reign	Sultan
1074-1085	Sultan Shāh
1085-1097	Turān Shāh I
1097-1101	Īrān Shāh
1101-1142	Arslan Shāh I
1142-1156	Muḥammad I
1156-1170	Toghrïl Shāh
1170-1175	Bahrām Shāh
1170-1177	Arslan Shāh II
1175-1186	Muḥammad Shāh II
1177-1183	Turān Shāh II

SPAIN. *See also* PORTUGAL

The Iberian Peninsula now occupied by Spain and Portugal was a turbulent region during the Middle Ages, a place where numerous cultures clashed, notably Christianity and Islam but also a broad and ethnically diverse group of peoples, from the Suevi and Visigoths of the seventh century through the Berbers and Islamic peoples in the south. Through most of the Middle Ages the region saw a succession of fluctuating principalities in the north—primarily Asturias, Galicia, Aragón, Navarre, León, and Castile, while in the south Islam held sway from the eighth century to the time of Columbus's voyage to the Americas in 1492. In that year the Reconquista concluded with the Fall of Granada, and Christianity claimed the peninsula. In 1516, the Kingdom of Spain united all former kingdoms, with the exception of Portugal, into one Kingdom of Spain.

MAJOR ISLAMIC RULERS

Córdoba's Umayyad Caliphs (emirs until 929)

Reign	Ruler
756-788	'Abd al-Raḥmān I (emir)
788-796	Hishām I (emir)
796-822	al-Hakam I (emir)
822-852	'Abd al-Raḥmān II (emir)
852-886	Muḥammad I (emir)
886-888	al-Mundhir (emir)
888-912	'Abd Allāh (emir)
912-961	'Abd al-Raḥmān III al-Nāṣir
961-976	al-Hakam II al-Mustanṣir
976-1008	Hishām II al-Muayyad
1008-1009	Muḥammad II al-Mahdī
1009	Sulaimān al-Mustaʿīn
1010-1013	Hishām II (restored)
1013-1016	Sulaimān (restored)
1016-1018	Alī ben Hammud
1018	'Abd al-Raḥmān IV
1018-1021	al-Qasim

Reign	Ruler
1021-1022	Yaḥyā
1022-1023	al-Qasim (restored)
1023-1024	'Abd al-Raḥmān V
1024-1025	Muḥammad III
1025-1027	Yaḥyā (restored)
1027-1031	Hishām III
1031	End of Umayyads; dissolution of Umayyad Spain into small states

After the Umayyads, Turbulence: Some Major Rulers

Reign	Ruler
1031-1043	Jahwar ibn Muḥammad ibn Jahwar
1043-1058	Muḥammad ar-Rashīd
1058-1069	'Abd al-Malik Dhu's-Siyādat al-Manṣur
1069	'Abbādid conquest
1085	Toledo falls to León and Castile; Christian Reconquista begins

Almoravid Sultans (Spain and North Africa)

Reign	Ruler
1061-1107	Yūsuf ibn Tāshufīn
1086	Entry into Spain; Alfonso VI defeated at Zallāqa
1107-1142	'Alīx ibn Yūsuf
1142-1146	Tāshufīn ibn 'Alī
1146	Ibrāhīm ibn Tāshufīn
1146-1147	Isḥāq ibn 'Alī
1147	Almohad conquest

Almohad Caliphs (Spain and North Africa)

Reign	Ruler
1130-1163	'Abd al-Muʾmin
1163-1184	Abū Yaʿqūb Yūsuf
1184-1199	Abū Yūsuf Yaʿqūb al-Manṣur
1199-1213	Muḥammad ibn Yaʿqūb
1212	Christians defeat Almohads at Las Navas de Tolosa
1213-1224	Yūsuf II Abū Yaqūb
1224	'Abd al-Wāḥid Abū Muḥammad
1224-1227	'Abd Allāh Abū Muḥammad
1227-1232	Idrīs I ibn Yaʿqūb
1227-1235	Yaḥyā Abū Zakariyyāʿ
1228-1229	Retreat from Spain
1232-1242	'Abdul-Wāḥid ibn Idrīs I
1242-1248	'Alī ibn Idrīs I
1248-1266	'Umar ibn Isḥāq
1266-1269	Idrīs II ibn Muḥammad
1269	End of Almohad domination in North Africa

Naṣrid Sultans of Granada

Reign	Ruler
1232-1273	Muḥammad I al-Ghālib (Ibn al-Aḥmar)
1273-1302	Muḥammad II al-Faqīh
1302-1309	Muḥammad III al-Makhlūʿ

Reign	Ruler
1309-1314	Naṣr
1314-1325	Ismāʿīl I
1325-1333	Muḥammad IV
1333-1354	Yūsuf I al-Muʾayyad
1354-1359	Muḥammad V al-Ghani
1359-1360	Ismāʿīl II
1360-1362	Muḥammad VI al-Ghālib (El Bermejo)
1362-1391	Muḥammad V al-Ghani (restored)
1391-1392	Yūsuf II al-Mustahgnī
1392-1408	Muḥammad VII al-Mustaʿin
1408-1417	Yūsuf III an-Nāṣir
1417-1419	Muḥammad VIII al-Mustamassik (al-Ṣaghīr, El Pequeño)
1419-1427	Muḥammad IX al-Ghālib (al-Aysar, El Zurdo)
1427-1429	Muḥammad VIII al-Mustamassik
1429-1432	Muḥammad IX al-Ghālib
1432	Yūsuf IV, Abenalmao
1432-1445	Muḥammad IX al-Ghālib
1445	Muḥammad X al-Aḥnaf (El Cojo)
1445-1446	Yūsuf V (Aben Ismael)
1446-1447	Muḥammad X al-Aḥnaf
1447-1453	Muḥammad IX al-Ghālib
1451-1455	Muḥammad XI (El Chiquito)
1454-1464	Saʿd al-Mustaʿīn (Ciriza, Muley Zad)
1462	Yūsuf V (Aben Ismael)
1464-1482	ʿAlī (Muley Hácen)
1482-1483	Muḥammad XII al-Zughūbī (Boabdil, El Chico)
1483-1485	ʿAlī (Muley Hácen)
1485-1490	Muḥammad ibn Saʿd al-Zaghal
1482-1492	Muḥammad XII al-Zughūbī (Boabdil, El Chico)
1492	Conquest by Castile and Aragón, end of Islamic Spain

NON-ISLAMIC AND CHRISTIAN RULERS

Asturias and Galicia

Reign	Ruler
718-737	Pelayo
737-739	Favila
739-757	Alfonso I the Catholic
757-768	Fruela I
768-774	Aurelio
774-783	Silo
783-788	Mauregato
788-791	Vermundo I
791-842	Alfonso II the Chaste
842-850	Ramiro I
850-866	Ordoño I
866-910	Alfonso III the Great
910	Subsumed by León

Navarre

Reign	Ruler
840-851	Inigo Arista
905-925	Sancho Garces
925-970	Garcia Sanchez I
970-994	Sancho Abarca
994-1000	Garcia Sanchez II
1000-1035	Sancho III the Great
1035-1054	Garcia IV
1054-1076	Sancho IV
1076-1094	Sancho Ramirez
1094-1134	Subsumed under Aragón, Castile, León; reemerges with reduced territory
1134-1150	Garcia V Ramirez
1150-1194	Sancho VI
1194-1234	Sancho VII
1234-1253	Teobaldo I of Champagne
1253-1270	Teobaldo II
1270-1274	Henry I
1274-1305	Juana I
1305-1316	Luis (Louis)
1316-1322	Philip V the Tall
1322-1328	Charles I
1328-1349	Juana II
1349-1387	Charles II the Bad
1387-1425	Charles III the Noble
1425-1479	Blanca & John
1479	Leonora
1479-1483	Francis Febo
1483-1517	Catalina
1516	Part of Navarre annexed to Spain
1517-1555	Henry II
1555-1572	Jeanne d'Albret
1572-1589	Henry III (IV of France); French rule

León

Reign	Ruler
910-914	Garcia
914-924	Ordoño II
924-925	Fruela II
925-930	Alfonso IV the Monk
930-950	Ramiro II
950-956	Ordoño III
956-967	Sancho I the Fat
967-982	Ramiro III
982-999	Vermundo II
999-1028	Alfonso V the Noble
1028-1037	Vermundo III
1038-1065	Fernando
1065-1070	Sancho II
1070-1072	Sancho III
1072-1109	Alfonso VI (king of Castile)
1109-1126	Urraca (married to Alfonso I of Aragón)
1126-1157	Alfonso VII

Reign	Ruler
1157-1188	Ferdinand II
1188-1230	Alfonso IX
1230-1252	Saint Fernando III
1252	Subsumed under Castile

Castile

Reign	Ruler
1035-1065	Ferdinand I
1065-1072	Sancho II
1072-1109	Alfonso VI
1109-1157	Castile joins with León
1157	Castile restored as separate principality
1157-1158	Sancho III
1158-1214	Alfonso VIII
1214-1217	Henry I
1217-1252	Saint Ferdinand III
1252	Castile rejoins with León
1252-1284	Alfonso X (emperor)
1284-1295	Sancho IV
1295-1312	Ferdinand IV
1312-1350	Alfonso XI
1350-1369	Peter the Cruel
1369-1379	Henry II
1379-1390	John I
1390-1406	Henry III
1406-1454	John II
1454-1474	Henry IV
1474-1504	Ferdinand V (II of Aragon) and Isabella I
1492	Fall of Granada, end of Reconquista
1504-1516	Joan (Juana) the Mad and Philip I of Habsburg
1516	Formation of Kingdom of Spain

Aragon

Reign	Ruler
1035-1063	Ramiro I
1063-1094	Sancho Ramirez
1094-1104	Pedro I
1104-1134	Alfonso I (co-ruled León and Castile, 1109-1126)
1134-1137	Ramiro II
1137	Union with County of Barcelona
1137-1162	Petronilla
1162-1196	Alfonso II
1196-1213	Pedro II
1213-1276	James I the Conqueror (under regency to 1217)
1276-1285	Pedro III
1285-1291	Alfonso III
1291-1327	James II
1327-1336	Alfonso IV
1336-1387	Peter IV
1387-1395	John I
1395-1410	Martin I
1412-1416	Ferdinand I

Reign	Ruler
1416-1458	Alfonso V
1458-1479	John II
1479-1516	Ferdinand II and Isabella I (d. 1504)

KINGDOM OF SPAIN

Reign	Ruler
1516-1556	Carlos (Charles) I (V as Holy Roman Emperor)
1556-1598	Philip (Felipe) II
1598-1621	Philip III
1621-1665	Philip IV
1665-1700	Carlos II

BOURBONS

Reign	Ruler
1700-1724	Philip V
1724	Luis I
1724-1746	Philip V (restored)
1746-1759	Fernando VI
1759-1788	Carlos III
1788-1808	Carlos IV
1808	Fernando VII
1808	Carlos IV (restored)

BONAPARTES

Reign	Ruler
1808-1813	José I Napoleón

SWEDEN. *See also* DENMARK, NORWAY

Reign	Ruler
647-735?	Harald Hildetand
735-750?	Sigurd Ring
750-794?	Ragnar Lodbrok
?	Eystein Beli
794-804	Björn Järnsida
804-808	Erik II (to 870?)
808-820	Erik III
820-859	Edmund I
860?-870	Erik I (poss. Erik II)
870-920	Björn
920-930	Olaf I Ring
?	Erik IV
930-950	Erik V
950-965	Edmund II
965-970	Olaf II
970-995	Erik VI the Victorious
995-1022	Olaf III Skötkonung
1022-1050	Anund Jakob Kolbrenner
1050-1060	Edmund III
1066-1067	Erik VII (VIII)

Reign	Ruler
1066-1070	Halsten
1066-1080	Inge I Elder
1080-1083	Blot-Sven
1083-1110	Inge I Elder
1110-1118	Filip Halstensson
1118-1125	Inge II Younger
1125-1130	Magnus Nielsson
1130-1156	Sverker I Elder
1156-1160	Sain Erik IX
1161-1167	Charles VII
1167-1196	Knut I
1196-1208	Sverker II Younger
1208-1216	Erik X
1216-1222	John I
1222-1229	Erik XI
1229-1234	Knut II the Long
1234-1250	Erik XI
1250-1275	Valdemar
1275-1290	Magnus I
1290-1320	Berger
1320-1365	Magnus II (VII of Norway)
1356-1359	Erik XII
1364-1389	Albert
1389-1412	Margaret I of Denmark, Norway, and Sweden
1397	Unification of Norway, Denmark, and Sweden
1412-1439	Erik XIII (VII of Denmark, III of Norway)
1439-1448	Christopher (III of Denmark)
1448-1481	Christian I of Oldenburg
1481-1513	Hans/John II
1513-1523	Christian II
1523-1560	Gustav I Vasa
1560-1568	Erik XIV
1568-1592	Johan/John III
1592-1604	Sigismund
1604-1611	Carl/Charles IX
1611-1632	Gustav II Adolf
1632-1654	Christina
1654-1660	Charles X
1660-1697	Charles XI
1697-1718	Charles XII (Madman of the North)
1718-1720	Ulrika
1730-1751	Frederick (landgrave of Hesse)
1751-1771	Adolphus Frederick
1771-1792	Gustav III
1792-1809	Gustav IV Adolf
1809-1818	Charles XIII
1814	Sweden and Norway joined
1818-1844	Charles XIV
1844-1859	Oscar I
1859-1872	Charles XI
1872-1907	Oscar II
1905	Norway separates

Reign	Ruler
1907-1950	Gustav V
1950-1973	Gustav VI Adolf
1973-	Karl/Charles XVI Gustaf

VIETNAM

NGO DYNASTY

Reign	Ruler
939-945	Kuyen
945-951	Duong Tam Kha
951-954	Suong Ngap
951-965	Suong Van

DINH DYNASTY

Reign	Ruler
968-979	Dinh Tien
979-981	Dinh De Toan

EARLY LE DYNASTY

Reign	Ruler
981-1005	Hoan
1005-1009	Trung Tong

LATER LI (LY) DYNASTY

Reign	Ruler
1010-1028	Thai To
1028-1054	Thai Tong
1054-1072	Thanh Tong

LATER LE DYNASTY

Reign	Ruler
1072-1127	Nan Ton
1127-1138	Than Tong
1138-1175	Anh Tong
1175-1210	Kao Tong
1210-1224	Hue Tong
1224-1225	Tieu Hoang

EARLY TRAN DYNASTY

Reign	Ruler
1225-1258	Thai Tong
1258-1277	Thanh Tong
1278-1293	Nan Tong
1293-1314	Anh Tong
1314-1329	Minh Tong
1329-1341	Hien Tong
1341-1369	Du Tong
1370-1372	Nghe Tong
1372-1377	Due Tong
1377-1388	De Hien

Reign	Ruler
1388-1398	Tran Thuan Tong
1398-1400	Tran Thieu De

HO DYNASTY

Reign	Ruler
1400	Kui Li
1400-1407	Han Thuong
1407-1428	Ming Chinese occupation

LATER TRAN DYNASTY

Reign	Ruler
1407-1409	Hau Tran Jian Dinh De
1409-1413	Hau Tran
1413-1428	vacant

CHAMPA

Reign	Ruler
1390-1400	Ko Cheng
1400-1441	Jaya Sinhavarman v
1441-1446	Maija Vijaya
1446-1449	Qui Lai
1449-1458	Qui Do (Bi Do)
1458-1460	Ban La Tra Nguyet (Tra Duyet)
1460-1471	Ban La Tra Toan
1471-1478	Bo Tri Tri

LATER LE DYNASTY

Reign	Ruler
1428-1433	Thai To
1433-1442	Thai Tong

Reign	Ruler
1442-1459	Nan Tong
1460-1497	Thanh Tong
1497-1504	Hien Tong
1504-1509	Vi Muc De
1509-1516	Tuong Duc De
1516-1522	Tieu Tong
1522-1527	Kung Hoang
1533-1548	Le Trang Tong (restored)

MAC DYNASTY

Reign	Ruler
1527-1530	Dang Dung
1530-1540	Dang Doanh
1533	Kingdom divides

NGUYEN DYNASTY

Reign	Ruler
1533-1545	Kim
1545-1558	Civil war
1558-1613	Hoang
1613-1635	Phuc Nguyen
1635-1648	Phuc Lan
1648-1687	Phuc Tan
1687-1691	Phuc Tran
1691-1725	Phuc Chu I
1725-1738	Phuc Chu II
1738-1765	Phuc Khoat
1765-1778	Phuc Thuan
1778-1802	Anh
1802	Absorbs other Vietnamese kingdoms

CHRONOLOGICAL LIST OF ENTRIES

The arrangement of personages in this list is chronological on the basis of birth years. All personages appearing in this list are the subjects of articles in *Great Lives from History: The Seventeenth Century, 1601-1700*. Subjects of multi-person essays include Jakob I Bernoulli, Johann I Bernoulli, and Daniel Bernoulli ("The Bernoulli Family"); David and Johannes Fabricius; Johannes Hevelius and Elisabetha Hevelius; Laura Mancini, Olympia Mancini, Hortense Mancini, Marie-Anne Mancini ("The Mancini Sisters"); and Maarten and Cornelis Tromp.

1540-1550

Tokugawa Ieyasu (January 31, 1543-June 1, 1616)
Opechancanough (c. 1545-1644 or 1646)

Powhatan (c. 1550-April, 1618)

1551-1560

Vasily Shuysky (1552-September 12, 1612)
Sir Edward Coke (February 1, 1552-September 3, 1634)
Paul V (September 17, 1552-January 28, 1621)
Duke de Lerma (1553-May 17, 1625)

Lancelot Andrewes (1555-September 26, 1626)
François de Malherbe (1555-October 6, 1628)
Duke de Sully (December 13, 1559-December 22, 1641)

1561-1570

Henry Hudson (1560's?-1611)
Santorio Santorio (March 29, 1561-February 22 or March 6, 1636)
Luis de Góngora y Argote (July 11, 1561-May 23, 1627)
Lope de Vega Carpio (November 25, 1562-August 27, 1635)
Louyse Bourgeois (c. 1563-December, 1636)
Michael Drayton (1563-December 23, 1631)
Galileo (February 15, 1564-January 8, 1642)
David Fabricius (March 9, 1564-May 7, 1617)
Canonicus (c. 1565-June 4, 1647)
Marie le Jars de Gournay (October 6, 1565-July 13, 1645)
James I (June 19, 1566-March 27, 1625)

Sigismund III Vasa (June 20, 1566-April 30, 1632)
Richard Burbage (c. 1567-March 13, 1619)
Thomas Campion (February 12, 1567-March 1, 1620)
Claudio Monteverdi (May 15, 1567-November 29, 1643)
Maurice of Nassau (November 14, 1567-April 23, 1625)
Samuel de Champlain (c. 1567/1570-December 25, 1635)
Urban VIII (Baptized April 5, 1568-July 29, 1644)
Tommaso Campanella (September 5, 1568-May 21, 1639)
Jahāngīr (August 31, 1569-October 28, 1627)
Hans Lippershey (c. 1570-c. 1619)

1571-1580

Izumo no Okuni (1571-1658)
ʿAbbās the Great (January 27, 1571-January 19, 1629)
Johannes Kepler (December 27, 1571-November 15, 1630)

Thomas Dekker (c. 1572-August, 1632)
John Donne (Between January 24 and June 19, 1572-March 31, 1631)
Thomas Heywood (c. 1573-August, 1641)

Marie de Médicis (April 26, 1573-July 3, 1642)
Ben Jonson (June 11, 1573-August 6, 1637)
Inigo Jones (July 15, 1573-June 21, 1652)
William Laud (October 7, 1573-January 10, 1645)
Robert Fludd (Baptized January 17, 1574-
    September 8, 1637)
Cyril Tourneur (c. 1575-February 28, 1626)
Jakob Böhme (April 24, 1575-November 17, 1624)
John Webster (c. 1577/1580-before 1634)
Robert Burton (February 8, 1577-January 25,
    1640)
Peter Paul Rubens (June 28, 1577-May 30, 1640)
Piet Hein (November 15, 1577-June 18, 1629)
William Harvey (April 1, 1578-June 3, 1657)
Philip III (April 14, 1578-March 31, 1621)
Ferdinand II (July 9, 1578-February 15, 1637)

John Fletcher (Baptized December 20, 1579-August,
    1625)
George Calvert (1579 or 1580-April 15, 1632)
Sōtatsu (Unknown-c. 1643)
Tirso de Molina (1580?-February, 1648)
Peter Minuit (c. 1580-June, 1638)
Massasoit (c. 1580-1661)
John Smith (Baptized January 9, 1580-June 21, 1631)
Jan Baptista van Helmont (January 12, 1580-
    December 30, 1644)
Thomas Middleton (Baptized April 18, 1580-July 4,
    1627)
Francisco Gómez de Quevedo y Villegas
    (September 17, 1580-September 8, 1645)
Nicolas-Claude Fabri de Peiresc (December 1, 1580-
    June 24, 1637)

1581-1590

James Ussher (January 4, 1581-March 21, 1656)
Saint Vincent de Paul (April 24, 1581-September 27,
    1660)
Njinga (1582-December 17, 1663)
Orlando Gibbons (1583-June 5, 1625)
Frans Hals (c. 1583-September 1, 1666)
Hugo Grotius (April 10, 1583-August 28, 1645)
Axel Oxenstierna (June 16, 1583-August 28, 1654)
Girolamo Frescobaldi (September, 1583-March 1, 1643)
Albrecht Wenzel von Wallenstein (September 24,
    1583-February 25, 1634)
Miles Standish (c. 1584-October 3, 1656)
Frederick Henry (January 29, 1584-March 14, 1647)
John Pym (May 20, 1584-December 8, 1643)
John Cotton (December 4, 1584-December 23, 1652)
Kösem Sultan (1585-September 2, 1651)
Mary Ward (January 23, 1585-January 30, 1645)
Cardinal de Richelieu (September 9, 1585-
    December 4, 1642)
Heinrich Schütz (Baptized October 9, 1585-
    November 6, 1672)

Cornelius Otto Jansen (October 28, 1585-May 6, 1638)
Saint Rose of Lima (April 20 or 30, 1586-August 24,
    1617)
Thomas Hooker (probably July 7, 1586-July 7, 1647)
Robert Carr (c. 1587-July 17, 1645)
Count-Duke f Olivares (January 6, 1587-July 22, 1645)
Johannes Fabricius (January 8, 1587-March 19, 1616)
Francesca Caccini (September 18, 1587-After June,
    1641)
Marquise de Rambouillet (1588-December 27, 1655)
John Winthrop (January 22, 1588-April 5, 1649)
Thomas Hobbes (April 5, 1588-December 4, 1679)
Marin Mersenne (September 8, 1588-September 1,
    1648)
Lady Eleanor Davies (1590-July 5, 1652)
Boris Ivanovich Morozov (1590-November 11, 1661)
Squanto (c. 1590-November, 1622)
William Bradford (March, 1590-May 9, 1657)
Roger Ludlow (Baptized March 7, 1590-June, 1666)
Cosimo II de' Medici (May 12, 1590-February 28,
    1621)

1591-1600

Mustafa I (1591-January 20, 1639)
Angélique Arnauld (1591-August 6, 1661)
Anne Hutchinson (Baptized July 20, 1591-August 20,
    1643)

Robert Herrick (Baptized August 24, 1591-October,
    1674)
Jacques Callot (1592-March 25, 1635)
Rory O'More (c. 1592-in or after 1666)

Shah Jahan (January 5, 1592-January 22, 1666)

Pierre Gassendi (January 22, 1592-October 24, 1655)

Nicholas Ferrar (February 22, 1592-December 4, 1637)

Jan Komenský (March 28, 1592-November 15, 1670)

Wilhelm Schickard (April 22, 1592-October 24, 1635)

First Duke of Buckingham (August 28, 1592-August 23, 1628)

Abahai (November 28, 1592-September 21, 1643)

Georges de La Tour (March 13, 1593-January 30, 1652)

George Herbert (April 3, 1593-March 1, 1633)

First Earl of Strafford (April 13, 1593-May 12, 1641)

Artemisia Gentileschi (July 8, 1593-1652 or 1653)

Nicolas Poussin (June, 1594-November 19, 1665)

Gustavus II Adolphus (December 9, 1594-November 6, 1632)

Bohdan Khmelnytsky (c. 1595-August 16, 1657)

Pocahontas (c. 1596-March, 1617)

Henry Lawes (Baptized January, 5, 1596-October 21, 1662)

René Descartes (March 31, 1596-February 11, 1650)

Michael Romanov (July 22, 1596-July 23, 1645)

Elizabeth Stuart (August 19, 1596-February 13, 1662)

Frederick V (August 26, 1596-November 29, 1632)

James Shirley (Baptized September 7, 1596-October 29, 1666)

John Davenport (April, 1597-March 15, 1670)

François Mansart (January 23, 1598-September 23, 1666)

Maarten Tromp (April 23, 1598-August 10, 1653)

Francisco de Zurbarán (Baptized November 7, 1598-August 27, 1664)

Gian Lorenzo Bernini (December 7, 1598-November 28, 1680)

John Alden (c. 1599-September 12, 1687)

Alexander VII (February 13, 1599-May 22, 1667)

Sir Anthony van Dyck (March 22, 1599-December 9, 1641)

Oliver Cromwell (April 25, 1599-September 3, 1658)

Diego Velázquez (Baptized June 6, 1599-August 6, 1660)

Robert Blake (Late August?, 1599-August 7, 1657)

Francesco Borromini (September 25, 1599-August 2, 1667)

Marie de l'Incarnation (October 28, 1599-April 30, 1672)

Giovanna Garzoni (1600-February, 1670)

Margaret Brent (c. 1600-c. 1671)

Claude Lorrain (1600-November 23, 1682)

Pedro Calderón de la Barca (January 17, 1600-May 25, 1681)

Maria Celeste (August 12, 1600-April 2, 1634)

Charles I (November 19, 1600-January 30, 1649)

Duchesse de Chevreuse (December, 1600-August 12, 1679)

1601-1610

Baltasar Gracián y Morales (January 8, 1601-December 6, 1658)

Pierre de Fermat (August 17, 1601-January 12, 1665)

Anne of Austria (September 22, 1601-January 20, 1666)

Louis XIII (September 27, 1601-May 14, 1643)

Jules Mazarin (July 14, 1602-March 9, 1661)

Otto von Guericke (November 20, 1602-May 11, 1686)

Abel Janszoon Tasman (c. 1603-1659)

Roger Williams (c. 1603-between January 16 and March 15, 1683)

Lennart Torstenson (August 17, 1603-April 7, 1651, Stockholm, Sweden

Manasseh ben Israel (c. 1604-November 20, 1657)

John IV (March 18, 1604-November 6, 1656)

John Eliot (Baptized August 5, 1604-May 21, 1690)

Yui Shōsetsu (1605-September, 1651)

Thomas Pride (c. 1605-October 23, 1658)

Nikon (1605-August 27, 1681)

Philip IV (April 8, 1605-September 17, 1665)

Sir Thomas Browne (October 19, 1605-October 19, 1682)

Tianqi (December 23, 1605-September 30, 1627)

Pierre Corneille (June 6, 1606-October 1, 1684)

Rembrandt (July 15, 1606-October 4, 1669)

Saint Isaac Jogues (January 10, 1607-October 18, 1646)

Michiel Adriaanszoon de Ruyter (March 24, 1607-April 29, 1676)

Anna Maria van Schurman (November 5, 1607-
May 14, 1678)

Madeleine de Scudéry (November 15, 1607-June 2,
1701)

Giovanni Alfonso Borelli (January 28, 1608-
December 31, 1679)

António Vieira (February 6, 1608-July 18, 1697)

Evangelista Torricelli (October 15, 1608-October 25,
1647)

George Monck (December 6, 1608-January 3,
1670)

John Milton (December 9, 1608-November 8, 1674)

Kâtib Çelebî (February, 1609-September 24, 1657)

Sir John Suckling (Baptized February 10, 1609-1642)

First Earl of Clarendon (February 18, 1609-
December 9, 1674)

Lodowick Muggleton (July, 1609-March 14, 1698)

Gerrard Winstanley (Baptized October 10, 1609-
c. September 10, 1676)

Matthew Hale (November 1, 1609-December 25,
1676)

Henrietta Maria (November 25 or 26, 1609-
September 10, 1669)

Peter Stuyvesant (c. 1610-February, 1672)

1611-1620

Johannes Hevelius (January 28, 1611-January 28,
1687)

Chongzhen (February 6, 1611-April 25, 1644)

Innocent XI (May 16, 1611-August 12, 1689)

Viscount de Turenne (September 11, 1611-July 27,
1675)

Richard Crashaw (c. 1612-August 21, 1649)

Louis Le Vau (1612-October 11, 1670)

Anne Bradstreet (1612?-September 16, 1672)

Third Baron Fairfax (January 17, 1612-November 12,
1671)

Sieur de Maisonneuve (Baptized February 15, 1612-
September 9, 1676)

Murad IV (July 27, 1612-February 9, 1640)

Dorgon (November 17, 1612-December 31, 1650)

André Le Nôtre (March 12, 1613-September 15,
1700)

Sir Henry Vane the Younger (Baptized May 26, 1613-
June 14, 1662)

François de La Rochefoucauld (September 15, 1613-
March 16 or 17, 1680)

John Lilburne (c. 1615-August 29, 1657)

John Biddle (Baptized January 14, 1615-
September 22, 1662)

Richard Baxter (November 12, 1615-December 8,
1691)

Friedrich Hermann Schomberg (December, 1615, or
January, 1616-July 1, 1690)

John Wallis (December 3, 1616-November 8, 1703)

Richard Lovelace (1618-1656 or 1657)

Liu Yin (1618-July 21, 1664)

Abraham Cowley (1618-July 28, 1667)

Hishikawa Moronobu (1618-1694)

Bartolomé Esteban Murillo (Baptized January 1, 1618-
March 28, 1682)

Francesco Maria Grimaldi (April 2, 1618-December
28, 1663)

Aurangzeb (November 3, 1618-March 3, 1707)

Elizabeth of Bohemia (December 26, 1618-February 8,
1680)

Jeremiah Horrocks (c. 1619-January 3, 1641)

Barbara Strozzi (1619-November 11, 1677)

Charles Le Brun (Baptized February 24, 1619-
February 12, 1690)

Cyrano de Bergerac (March 6, 1619-July 28, 1655)

Duchesse de Longueville (August 28, 1619-April 15,
1679)

Jean-Baptiste Colbert (August 29, 1619-September 6,
1683)

John Lambert (Baptized September 7, 1619-March,
1684)

Wang Fuzhi (October 7, 1619-February 18, 1692)

Prince Rupert (December 17, 1619-November 29,
1682)

Frederick William, the Great Elector (February 16,
1620-May 9, 1688)

Saint Marguerite Bourgeoys (April 17, 1620-
January 12, 1700)

John Evelyn (October 31, 1620-February 27, 1706)

Ninon de Lenclos (November 10, 1620-October 17,
1705)

Avvakum Petrovich (1620 or 1621-April 14, 1682)

1621-1630

Thomas Willis (January 27, 1621-November 11, 1675)

Rebecca Nurse (Baptized February 21, 1621-July 19, 1692)

Hans Jakob Christoffel von Grimmelshausen (March 17, 1621?-August 17, 1676)

Andrew Marvell (March 31, 1621-August 16, 1678)

Jean de La Fontaine (July 8, 1621-April 13, 1695)

First Earl of Shaftesbury (July 22, 1621-January 21, 1683)

The Great Condé (September 8, 1621-December 11, 1686)

Molière (Baptized January 15, 1622-February 17, 1673)

Charles X Gustav (November 8, 1622-February 13, 1660)

Duchess of Newcastle (1623-December 15, 1673)

François Laval (April 30, 1623-May 6, 1708)

Sir William Petty (May 26, 1623-December 16, 1687)

Blaise Pascal (June 19, 1623-August 19, 1662)

Guarino Guarini (January 17, 1624-March 6, 1683)

George Fox (July, 1624-January 13, 1691)

Zheng Chenggong (August 28, 1624-June 23, 1662)

Thomas Sydenham (Baptized September 10, 1624-December 29, 1689)

Gian Domenico Cassini (June 8, 1625-September 14, 1712)

Madame de Sévigné (February 5, 1626-April 17, 1696)

Shabbetai Tzevi (August 1, 1626-September 17, 1676)

Christina (December 8, 1626-April 19, 1689)

Robert Boyle (January 25, 1627-December 31, 1691)

Śivājī (April 6, 1627-April 3, 1680)

Duchesse de Montpensier (May 29, 1627-April 5, 1693)

Jacques-Bénigne Bossuet (September 27, 1627-April 12, 1704)

John Ray (November 29, 1627-January 17, 1705)

Charles Perrault (January 12, 1628-May 16, 1703)

Marcello Malpighi (March 10, 1628-November 29, 1694)

John Bunyan (Baptized November 30, 1628-August 31, 1688)

Alexis (March 19, 1629-February 8, 1676)

John of Austria (April 7, 1629-September 17, 1679)

Christiaan Huygens (April 14, 1629-July 8, 1695)

John III Sobieski (August 17, 1629-June 17, 1696)

Cornelis Tromp (September 9, 1629-May 29, 1691)

Stenka Razin (c. 1630-June 16, 1671)

Charles II of England (May 29, 1630-February 6, 1685)

1631-1640

Katherine Philips (January 1, 1631-June 22, 1664)

Richard Lower (Baptized January 29, 1631-January 17, 1691)

John Dryden (August 19, 1631-May 12, 1700)

Anne Conway (December 14, 1631-February 18, 1679)

Samuel von Pufendorf (January 8, 1632-October 26, 1694)

First Duke of Leeds (February 20, 1632-July 26, 1712)

John Locke (August 29, 1632-October 28, 1704)

Sir Christopher Wren (October 20, 1632-February 25, 1723)

Antoni van Leeuwenhoek (October 24, 1632-August 26, 1723)

Jan Vermeer (Baptized October 31, 1632-December, 1675)

Baruch Spinoza (November 24, 1632-February 21, 1677)

Jean-Baptiste Lully (November 29, 1632-March 22, 1687)

Samuel Pepys (February 23, 1633-May 26, 1703)

Sébastien Le Prestre de Vauban (May 15, 1633-March 30, 1707)

James II (October 14, 1633-September 16, 1701)

Sir George Savile (November 11, 1633-April 5, 1695)

Merzifonlu Kara Mustafa Paşa (1634 or 1635-December 25, 1683)

Madame de La Fayette (Baptized March 18, 1634-May 25, 1693)

Thomas Betterton (c. 1635-April 28, 1710)

Thomas Burnet (c. 1635-September 27, 1715)

Johann Joachim Becher (May 6, 1635-October, 1682)

Robert Hooke (July 18, 1635-March 3, 1703)

Madame de Maintenon (November 27, 1635-April 15, 1719)

Laura Mancini (1636-February 8, 1657, Paris, France

Pierre Esprit Radisson (c. 1636-buried c. June 21, 1710)
Justine Siegemundin (1636 or 1650-1705)
Nicolas Boileau-Despréaux (November 1, 1636-March 13, 1711)
Mary White Rowlandson (c. 1637-January 5, 1711)
Jan Swammerdam (February 12, 1637-February 17, 1680)
Jacques Marquette (June 1, 1637-May 18, 1675)
Elisabetta Sirani (1638-August, 1665)
Nicolaus Steno (January 11, 1638-December 5, 1686)
Shunzhi (March 15, 1638-February 5, 1661)
Louis XIV (September 5, 1638-September 1, 1715)
Marie-Thérèse (September 10, 1638-July 30, 1683)

James Gregory (November, 1638-October, 1675)
Catherine of Braganza (November 25, 1638-December 31, 1705)
Metacom (c. 1639-August 12, 1676)
Olympia Mancini (1639-1708)
Marquis de Louvois (January 18, 1639-July 16, 1691)
Ivan Stepanovich Mazepa (March 20, 1639-October 2, 1709)
Jean Racine (Baptized December 22, 1639-April 21, 1699)
Jacob Leisler (Baptized March 31, 1640-May 16, 1691)
Leopold I (June 9, 1640-May 5, 1705)
Aphra Behn (July?, 1640-April 16, 1689)

1641-1650

Ihara Saikaku (1642-September 9, 1693)
Seki Kōwa (March, 1642-October 24, 1708)
Sir Isaac Newton (December 25, 1642-March 20, 1727)
Sieur de La Salle (November 22, 1643-March 19, 1687)
Matsuo Bashō (1644-October 12, 1694)
William Penn (October 14, 1644-July 30, 1718)
William Kidd (c. 1645-May 23, 1701)
Eusebio Francisco Kino (August 10, 1645-March 15, 1711)
Jean de La Bruyère (August 16, 1645-May 10, 1696)
Louis Jolliet (Baptized September 21, 1645-May, 1700)
Tokugawa Tsunayoshi (February 23, 1646-February 19, 1709)
Jules Hardouin-Mansart (c. April 16, 1646-May 11, 1708)

Elena Cornaro Piscopia (June 5, 1646-July 26, 1684)
Hortense Mancini (June 6, 1646-July 16, 1699)
Gottfried Wilhelm Leibniz (July 1, 1646-November 14, 1716)
Elisabetha Hevelius (c. 1647-1693)
Nathaniel Bacon (January 2, 1647-October 26, 1676)
Denis Papin (August 22, 1647-c. 1712)
Pierre Bayle (November 18, 1647-December 28, 1706)
Richard Cameron (c. 1648-July 22, 1680)
Madame Guyon (April 13, 1648-June 9, 1717)
Sor Juana Inés de la Cruz (November, 1648-April 17, 1695)
Marie-Anne Mancini (1649-June 20, 1714)
Duke of Monmouth (April 9, 1649-July 15, 1685)
Titus Oates (September 15, 1649-July 12 or 13, 1705)
Thomas Savery (c. 1650-May, 1715)
Nell Gwyn (February 2, 1650-November 14, 1687)
William III (November 14, 1650-March 19, 1702)

1651-1660

William Dampier (August?, 1651-March, 1715)
François de Salignac de La Mothe-Fénelon (August 6, 1651-January 7, 1715)
Engelbert Kämpfer (September 16, 1651-November 2, 1716)
Arcangelo Corelli (February 17, 1653-January 8, 1713)
Johann Pachelbel (Baptized September 1, 1653-March 3, 1706)
Kangxi (May 4, 1654-December 20, 1722)

Jakob I Bernoulli (January 6, 1655-August 16, 1705)
Kateri Tekakwitha (1656-April 17, 1680)
Edmond Halley (November 8, 1656-June 14, 1742)
Sophia (September 27, 1657-July 14, 1704)
Ogata Kōrin (1658-1716)
William Paterson (April, 1658-January 22, 1719)
Mary of Modena (October 5, 1658-May 7, 1718)
Henry Purcell (1659-November 21, 1695)
Chen Shu (March 13, 1660-April 17, 1735)

1661-1670

Pierre Le Moyne d'Iberville (Baptized July 20, 1661-
    July 9, 1706)
Charles II of Spain (November 6, 1661-November 1,
    1700)

Mary II (April 30, 1662-December 28, 1694)
Mrs. Anne Bracegirdle (c. 1663-September 12, 1748)
Johann I Bernoulli (August 6, 1667-January 1, 1748)

Category Index

List of Categories

Architecture 1059
Art 1059
Astronomy 1059
Business and economics 1059
Chemistry 1059
Church government 1059
Church reform 1059
Diplomacy 1060
Education 1060
Engineering 1060
Exploration 1060
Geography 1060
Government and politics 1060
Historiography 1061
Invention 1061
Law 1061
Linguistics 1061
Literature 1061
Mathematics 1062
Medicine 1062
Military 1062
Music 1062
Patronage of the arts 1062
Philosophy 1062
Physics 1063
Religion and theology 1063
Scholarship 1063
Science and technology 1063
Social reform 1064
Theater 1064
Warfare and conquest 1064
Women's rights 1064

ARCHITECTURE
Alexander VII, 9
Gian Lorenzo Bernini, 45
Francesco Borromini, 67
Guarino Guarini, 330
Robert Hooke, 383
Inigo Jones, 436
Charles Le Brun, 504
André Le Nôtre, 523
Louis Le Vau, 532
François Mansart, 587
Jules Hardouin-Mansart, 590
Shah Jahan, 842
Sir Christopher Wren, 994

ART
Alexander VII, 9
Gian Lorenzo Bernini, 45
Jacques Callot, 116
Chen Shu, 156
Claude Lorrain, 171
Sir Anthony van Dyck, 244
Giovanna Garzoni, 302
Artemisia Gentileschi, 307
Baltasar Gracián y Morales, 316
Frans Hals, 352

Hishikawa Moronobu, 375
Georges de La Tour, 493
Charles Le Brun, 504
André Le Nôtre, 523
Liu Yin, 540
Marie de Médicis, 598
Bartolomé Esteban Murillo, 670
Ogata Kōrin, 695
Nicolas Poussin, 749
Rembrandt, 786
Peter Paul Rubens, 802
Anna Maria van Schurman, 823
Elisabetta Sirani, 856
Sōtatsu, 868
Diego Velázquez, 953
Jan Vermeer, 956
Francisco de Zurbarán, 1003

ASTRONOMY
The Bernoulli Family, 48
Giovanni Alfonso Borelli, 65
Robert Burton, 108
Gian Domenico Cassini, 134
David and Johannes Fabricius, 259
Galileo, 298
James Gregory, 319

Francesco Maria Grimaldi, 321
Edmond Halley, 348
Johannes and Elisabetha Hevelius, 371
Jeremiah Horrocks, 388
Christiaan Huygens, 397
Johannes Kepler, 457
Wilhelm Schickard, 818

BUSINESS AND ECONOMICS
Mrs. Anne Bracegirdle, 82
Jean-Baptiste Colbert, 180
William Paterson, 716
Sir William Petty, 733

CHEMISTRY
Johann Joachim Becher, 39
Robert Boyle, 78

CHURCH GOVERNMENT
Cardinal de Richelieu, 790

CHURCH REFORM
Innocent XI, 405
Cornelius Otto Jansen, 419
Paul V, 719

DIPLOMACY
John Alden, 7
Aurangzeb, 23
Canonicus, 129
Frederick Henry, 286
Piet Hein, 359
Marquis de Louvois, 558
Jacques Marquette, 603
Massasoit, 612
Jules Mazarin, 620
Metacom, 633
Peter Minuit, 643
Count-Duke of Olivares, 697
Axel Oxenstierna, 704
Pocahontas, 745
Powhatan, 752
Cardinal de Richelieu, 790
Peter Paul Rubens, 802
Sophia, 865
Squanto, 875
Duke de Sully, 896
William III, 979

EDUCATION
Saint Marguerite Bourgeoys, 75
François de Salignac de La
    Mothe-Fénelon, 265
Baltasar Gracián y Morales, 316
Jan Komenský, 469
Madame de Maintenon, 572
Jules Hardouin-Mansart, 590
Marie de l'Incarnation, 595
Boris Ivanovich Morozov, 663
Elena Cornaro Piscopia, 743
Anna Maria van Schurman, 823
Elisabetta Sirani, 856
Squanto, 875
Saint Vincent de Paul, 962
Yui Shōsetsu, 998

ENGINEERING
Johann Joachim Becher, 39
Otto von Guericke, 333
Denis Papin, 710
Thomas Savery, 813
Sébastien Le Prestre de Vauban,
    946

EXPLORATION
Samuel de Champlain, 139

William Dampier, 215
Henry Hudson, 390
Louis Jolliet, 433
Eusebio Francisco Kino, 467
Sieur de La Salle, 490
Jacques Marquette, 603
Peter Minuit, 643
Pierre Esprit Radisson, 777
John Smith, 861
Miles Standish, 877
Abel Janszoon Tasman, 905

GEOGRAPHY
David and Johannes Fabricius,
    259
Kâtib Çelebî, 454
Eusebio Francisco Kino, 467
Pierre Esprit Radisson, 777
Wilhelm Schickard, 818
Abel Janszoon Tasman, 905

GOVERNMENT AND POLITICS
Abahai, 1
'Abbās the Great, 4
John Alden, 7
Alexander VII, 9
Alexis, 11
Anne of Austria, 18
Aurangzeb, 23
Nathaniel Bacon, 29
Richard Baxter, 32
Johann Joachim Becher, 39
Robert Blake, 55
William Bradford, 84
Margaret Brent, 92
First Duke of Buckingham, 96
George Calvert, 119
Canonicus, 129
Robert Carr, 131
Catherine of Braganza, 137
Samuel de Champlain, 139
Charles I, 143
Charles II (of England), 147
Charles II (of Spain), 151
Charles X Gustav, 153
Duchesse de Chevreuse, 158
Chongzhen, 160
Christina, 163
First Earl of Clarendon, 166
Sir Edward Coke, 174

Jean-Baptiste Colbert, 180
Oliver Cromwell, 204
John Davenport, 218
Dorgon, 234
Elizabeth Stuart, 253
Third Baron Fairfax, 261
Ferdinand II, 267
Frederick V, 293
Frederick Henry, 286
Frederick William, the Great
    Elector, 290
Hugo Grotius, 326
Gustavus II Adolphus, 336
Nell Gwyn, 342
Matthew Hale, 345
Henrietta Maria, 364
Thomas Hooker, 386
Anne Hutchinson, 394
Pierre Le Moyne d'Iberville, 401
Innocent XI, 405
Jahāngīr, 410
James I, 413
James II, 416
John III Sobieski, 427
John IV, 430
John of Austria, 425
Kangxi, 448
Merzifonlu Kara Mustafa Paşa,
    451
Kâtib Çelebî, 454
Bohdan Khmelnytsky, 461
William Kidd, 464
Kösem Sultan, 472
John Lambert, 483
William Laud, 495
First Duke of Leeds, 506
Jacob Leisler, 518
Leopold I, 526
Duke de Lerma, 530
John Lilburne, 534
Duchesse de Longueville, 548
Louis XIII, 551
Louis XIV, 554
Marquis de Louvois, 558
Roger Ludlow, 567
Sieur de Maisonneuve, 574
Manasseh ben Israel, 582
The Mancini Sisters, 585
Marie de Médicis, 598
Marie-Thérèse, 600

Andrew Marvell, 605
Mary II, 610
Mary of Modena, 607
Massasoit, 612
Maurice of Nassau, 618
Jules Mazarin, 620
Ivan Stepanovich Mazepa, 624
Cosimo II de' Medici, 626
Metacom, 633
Peter Minuit, 643
George Monck, 650
Duke of Monmouth, 653
Duchesse de Montpensier, 660
Boris Ivanovich Morozov, 663
Murad IV, 668
Mustafa I, 673
Nikon, 683
Njinga, 687
Titus Oates, 692
Count-Duke of Olivares, 697
Rory O'More, 699
Opechancanough, 702
Axel Oxenstierna, 704
William Penn, 724
Samuel Pepys, 728
Charles Perrault, 731
Sir William Petty, 733
Philip III, 736
Philip IV, 738
Powhatan, 752
John Pym, 767
Pierre Esprit Radisson, 777
Razin, Stenka, 784
Cardinal de Richelieu, 790
Michael Romanov, 794
Sir George Savile, 815
Seki Kōwa, 831
First Earl of Shaftesbury, 838
Shah Jahan, 842
Shunzhi, 848
Sigismund III Vasa, 853
Śivājī, 858
John Smith, 861
Sophia, 865
Baruch Spinoza, 871
Miles Standish, 877
First Earl of Strafford, 884
Peter Stuyvesant, 890
Sir John Suckling, 893
Duke de Sully, 896

Tianqi, 911
Tokugawa Ieyasu, 915
Tokugawa Tsunayoshi, 919
Urban VIII, 936
Sir Henry Vane the Younger, 941
Vasily Shuysky, 943
António Vieira, 959
Albrecht Wenzel von Wallenstein, 966
William III, 979
Roger Williams, 982
Gerrard Winstanley, 988
John Winthrop, 990
Zheng Chenggong, 1001

HISTORIOGRAPHY
Pierre Bayle, 36
Jacques-Bénigne Bossuet, 70
Kâtib Çelebî, 454
Nicolas-Claude Fabri de Peiresc, 722

INVENTION
Johann Joachim Becher, 39
Christiaan Huygens, 397
Thomas Savery, 813
Lennart Torstenson, 924
Sir Christopher Wren, 994

LAW
Alexis, 11
Margaret Brent, 92
Sir Edward Coke, 174
Hugo Grotius, 326
Matthew Hale, 345
Roger Ludlow, 567
Boris Ivanovich Morozov, 663
Rebecca Nurse, 689
Nicolas-Claude Fabri de Peiresc, 722
Samuel von Pufendorf, 759
Tokugawa Tsunayoshi, 919

LINGUISTICS
John Eliot, 247
Squanto, 875

LITERATURE
Avvakum Petrovich, 26
Aphra Behn, 42

Nicolas Boileau-Despréaux, 63
Jacques-Bénigne Bossuet, 70
William Bradford, 84
Anne Bradstreet, 88
John Bunyan, 100
Robert Burton, 108
Tommaso Campanella, 124
Thomas Campion, 127
First Earl of Clarendon, 166
Abraham Cowley, 199
Richard Crashaw, 202
Sor Juana Inés de la Cruz, 208
Cyrano de Bergerac, 211
Lady Eleanor Davies, 220
Thomas Dekker, 223
John Donne, 230
Michael Drayton, 237
John Dryden, 239
François de Salignac de La Mothe-Fénelon, 265
John Fletcher, 277
Luis de Góngora y Argote, 312
Marie le Jars de Gournay, 314
Baltasar Gracián y Morales, 316
Hans Jakob Christoffel von Grimmelshausen, 324
Madame Guyon, 339
George Herbert, 366
Robert Herrick, 368
Thomas Heywood, 373
Ihara Saikaku, 403
Ben Jonson, 439
Engelbert Kämpfer, 445
Kâtib Çelebî, 454
Jean de La Bruyère, 475
Madame de La Fayette, 477
Jean de La Fontaine, 480
François de La Rochefoucauld, 487
Ninon de Lenclos, 520
Liu Yin, 540
Richard Lovelace, 562
François de Malherbe, 577
Andrew Marvell, 605
Matsuo Bashō, 615
Thomas Middleton, 636
John Milton, 639
Molière, 646
Duchesse de Montpensier, 660
Lodowick Muggleton, 665

Duchess of Newcastle, 676
Samuel Pepys, 728
Charles Perrault, 731
Katherine Philips, 741
Francisco Gómez de Quevedo y
    Villegas, 770
Jean Racine, 773
Mary White Rowlandson, 798
Madeleine de Scudéry, 828
Madame de Sévigné, 833
James Shirley, 846
John Smith, 861
Sir John Suckling, 893
Tirso de Molina, 913
Cyril Tourneur, 928
Lope de Vega Carpio, 949
António Vieira, 959
John Webster, 976

MATHEMATICS
The Bernoulli Family, 48
Giovanni Alfonso Borelli, 65
Gian Domenico Cassini, 134
René Descartes, 226
Pierre de Fermat, 271
Galileo, 298
Pierre Gassendi, 304
James Gregory, 319
Christiaan Huygens, 397
Johannes Kepler, 457
Gottfried Wilhelm Leibniz, 513
Marin Mersenne, 628
Blaise Pascal, 713
Sir William Petty, 733
Elena Cornaro Piscopia, 743
Wilhelm Schickard, 818
Seki Kōwa, 831
Evangelista Torricelli, 921
John Wallis, 969

MEDICINE
Johann Joachim Becher, 39
The Bernoulli Family, 48
Giovanni Alfonso Borelli, 65
Louyse Bourgeois, 73
Sir Thomas Browne, 94
Robert Burton, 108
Robert Fludd, 280
William Harvey, 355
Jan Baptista van Helmont, 361

Engelbert Kämpfer, 445
Richard Lower, 564
Marcello Malpighi, 579
Sir William Petty, 733
Santorio Santorio, 810
Justine Siegemundin, 851
Nicolaus Steno, 881
Jan Swammerdam, 898
Thomas Sydenham, 901
Thomas Willis, 985

MILITARY
ʿAbbās the Great, 4
Alexis, 11
Robert Blake, 55
The Great Condé, 184
Cyrano de Bergerac, 211
Third Baron Fairfax, 261
Frederick Henry, 286
Frederick William, the Great
    Elector, 290
Gustavus II Adolphus, 336
Piet Hein, 359
John of Austria, 425
John III Sobieski, 427
Merzifonlu Kara Mustafa Paşa,
    451
William Kidd, 464
Leopold I, 526
Louis XIII, 551
Marquis de Louvois, 558
Maurice of Nassau, 618
George Monck, 650
Duke of Monmouth, 653
Murad IV, 668
Thomas Pride, 756
Razin, Stenka, 784
Michiel Adriaanszoon de Ruyter,
    807
Friedrich Hermann Schomberg,
    820
Śivājī, 858
Miles Standish, 877
Duke de Sully, 896
Lennart Torstenson, 924
Maarten and Cornelis Tromp,
    930
Viscount de Turenne, 933
Sébastien Le Prestre de Vauban,
    946

Albrecht Wenzel von Wallenstein,
    966
Yui Shōsetsu, 998

MUSIC
Francesca Caccini, 111
Thomas Campion, 127
Arcangelo Corelli, 190
Girolamo Frescobaldi, 295
Orlando Gibbons, 309
Izumo no Okuni, 408
John IV, 430
Henry Lawes, 502
Jean-Baptiste Lully, 569
Marin Mersenne, 628
Claudio Monteverdi, 656
Johann Pachelbel, 708
Henry Purcell, 763
Heinrich Schütz, 825
Barbara Strozzi, 888

PATRONAGE OF THE ARTS
ʿAbbās the Great, 4
Alexander VII, 9
Thomas Betterton, 51
Jacques Callot, 116
Christina, 163
Jean-Baptiste Colbert, 180
Marie le Jars de Gournay, 314
Jahāngīr, 410
John IV, 430
Charles Le Brun, 504
Ninon de Lenclos, 520
Marie de Médicis, 598
Jules Mazarin, 620
Cosimo II de' Medici, 626
Count-Duke of Olivares, 697
Nicolas-Claude Fabri de Peiresc,
    722
Charles Perrault, 731
Philip IV, 738
Marquise de Rambouillet, 779
Shah Jahan, 842
Elisabetta Sirani, 856
Urban VIII, 936

PHILOSOPHY
Pierre Bayle, 36
Jakob Böhme, 59
Sir Thomas Browne, 94

Robert Burton, 108
Tommaso Campanella, 124
Anne Conway, 187
René Descartes, 226
Elizabeth of Bohemia, 250
Robert Fludd, 280
Pierre Gassendi, 304
Baltasar Gracián y Morales, 316
Thomas Hobbes, 378
Jan Komenský, 469
Gottfried Wilhelm Leibniz, 513
Ninon de Lenclos, 520
John Locke, 542
Marin Mersenne, 628
Duchess of Newcastle, 676
Blaise Pascal, 713
Nicolas-Claude Fabri de Peiresc, 722
Elena Cornaro Piscopia, 743
Samuel von Pufendorf, 759
Anna Maria van Schurman, 823
Baruch Spinoza, 871
Tokugawa Tsunayoshi, 919
Wang Fuzhi, 972

PHYSICS

Johann Joachim Becher, 39
The Bernoulli Family, 48
Giovanni Alfonso Borelli, 65
Robert Boyle, 78
René Descartes, 226
Galileo, 298
Francesco Maria Grimaldi, 321
Otto von Guericke, 333
Christiaan Huygens, 397
Johannes Kepler, 457
Marin Mersenne, 628
Sir Isaac Newton, 679
Blaise Pascal, 713
Evangelista Torricelli, 921

RELIGION AND THEOLOGY

'Abbās the Great, 4
Alexander VII, 9
Alexis, 11
Lancelot Andrewes, 14
Angélique Arnauld, 20
Avvakum Petrovich, 26
Richard Baxter, 32
Pierre Bayle, 36

John Biddle, 53
Jakob Böhme, 59
Jacques-Bénigne Bossuet, 70
Saint Marguerite Bourgeoys, 75
John Bunyan, 100
Thomas Burnet, 106
Robert Burton, 108
Richard Cameron, 121
Tommaso Campanella, 124
John Cotton, 196
John Davenport, 218
Lady Eleanor Davies, 220
John Eliot, 247
David and Johannes Fabricius, 259
François de Salignac de La Mothe-Fénelon, 265
Nicholas Ferrar, 274
Robert Fludd, 280
George Fox, 283
Frederick V, 293
Orlando Gibbons, 309
Baltasar Gracián y Morales, 316
Madame Guyon, 339
George Herbert, 366
Thomas Hooker, 386
Anne Hutchinson, 394
Innocent XI, 405
Cornelius Otto Jansen, 419
Saint Isaac Jogues, 423
Eusebio Francisco Kino, 467
Jan Komenský, 469
William Laud, 495
François Laval, 498
Madame de Maintenon, 572
Sieur de Maisonneuve, 574
Manasseh ben Israel, 582
Maria Celeste, 593
Marie de l'Incarnation, 595
Jacques Marquette, 603
Jules Mazarin, 620
Marin Mersenne, 628
Lodowick Muggleton, 665
Nikon, 683
Johann Pachelbel, 708
Blaise Pascal, 713
Paul V, 719
William Penn, 724
Philip IV, 738
Elena Cornaro Piscopia, 743

John Ray, 782
Cardinal de Richelieu, 790
Saint Rose of Lima, 796
Wilhelm Schickard, 818
Anna Maria van Schurman, 823
Heinrich Schütz, 825
Shabbetai Tzevi, 835
Baruch Spinoza, 871
Nicolaus Steno, 881
Kateri Tekakwitha, 908
Tirso de Molina, 913
Urban VIII, 936
James Ussher, 938
António Vieira, 959
Saint Vincent de Paul, 962
Mary Ward, 974
Roger Williams, 982

SCHOLARSHIP

Angélique Arnauld, 20
Johann Joachim Becher, 39
Nicolas Boileau-Despréaux, 63
Sir Thomas Browne, 94
David and Johannes Fabricius, 259
Pierre Gassendi, 304
Johannes and Elisabetha Hevelius, 371
Engelbert Kämpfer, 445
Kâtib Çelebî, 454
Manasseh ben Israel, 582
Nicolas-Claude Fabri de Peiresc, 722
Elena Cornaro Piscopia, 743
Wilhelm Schickard, 818
Anna Maria van Schurman, 823

SCIENCE AND TECHNOLOGY

Johann Joachim Becher, 39
Jakob Böhme, 59
Giovanni Alfonso Borelli, 65
Robert Boyle, 78
Thomas Burnet, 106
Robert Burton, 108
Jacques Callot, 116
William Dampier, 215
René Descartes, 226
John Evelyn, 256
David and Johannes Fabricius, 259

Robert Fludd, 280
Galileo, 298
Pierre Gassendi, 304
James Gregory, 319
Francesco Maria Grimaldi, 321
Otto von Guericke, 333
Edmond Halley, 348
William Harvey, 355
Jan Baptista van Helmont, 361
Johannes and Elisabetha Hevelius, 371
Robert Hooke, 383
Jeremiah Horrocks, 388
Christiaan Huygens, 397
Engelbert Kämpfer, 445
Johannes Kepler, 457
Antoni van Leeuwenhoek, 509
Hans Lippershey, 537
Richard Lower, 564
Marcello Malpighi, 579
Manasseh ben Israel, 582
Maria Celeste, 593
Duchess of Newcastle, 676
Sir Isaac Newton, 679
Denis Papin, 710
Blaise Pascal, 713
Nicolas-Claude Fabri de Peiresc, 722
Sir William Petty, 733
John Ray, 782
Prince Rupert, 805
Santorio Santorio, 810
Wilhelm Schickard, 818
Justine Siegemundin, 851
Nicolaus Steno, 881
Jan Swammerdam, 898
Evangelista Torricelli, 921
Sébastien Le Prestre de Vauban, 946
John Wallis, 969
Thomas Willis, 985
Sir Christopher Wren, 994

SOCIAL REFORM
Richard Baxter, 32
John Lilburne, 534
Manasseh ben Israel, 582
Marquise de Rambouillet, 779
Razin, Stenka, 784
Saint Vincent de Paul, 962
Gerrard Winstanley, 988

THEATER
Aphra Behn, 42
Thomas Betterton, 51
Mrs. Anne Bracegirdle, 82
Richard Burbage, 104
Pedro Calderón de la Barca, 113
Pierre Corneille, 193
Thomas Dekker, 223
John Dryden, 239
John Fletcher, 277
Nell Gwyn, 342
Thomas Heywood, 373
Ihara Saikaku, 403
Izumo no Okuni, 408
Inigo Jones, 436
Ben Jonson, 439
Jean de La Fontaine, 480
Jean-Baptiste Lully, 569
Thomas Middleton, 636
Molière, 646
Katherine Philips, 741
Henry Purcell, 763
Jean Racine, 773
James Shirley, 846
Sir John Suckling, 893
Tirso de Molina, 913
Cyril Tourneur, 928
Lope de Vega Carpio, 949
John Webster, 976

WARFARE AND CONQUEST
Abahai, 1
'Abbās the Great, 4
Aurangzeb, 23
Robert Blake, 55
Canonicus, 129
Charles X Gustav, 153
The Great Condé, 184
Oliver Cromwell, 204
Dorgon, 234
Third Baron Fairfax, 261
Gustavus II Adolphus, 336

Piet Hein, 359
Pierre Le Moyne d'Iberville, 401
Jahāngīr, 410
John III Sobieski, 427
Merzifonlu Kara Mustafa Paşa, 451
Bohdan Khmelnytsky, 461
John Lambert, 483
Leopold I, 526
Maurice of Nassau, 618
Ivan Stepanovich Mazepa, 624
Metacom, 633
George Monck, 650
Duke of Monmouth, 653
Duchesse de Montpensier, 660
Murad IV, 668
Rory O'More, 699
Opechancanough, 702
Thomas Pride, 756
Pierre Esprit Radisson, 777
Razin, Stenka, 784
Prince Rupert, 805
Michiel Adriaanszoon de Ruyter, 807
Friedrich Hermann Schomberg, 820
Śivājī, 858
Tokugawa Ieyasu, 915
Lennart Torstenson, 924
Maarten and Cornelis Tromp, 930
Viscount de Turenne, 933
Albrecht Wenzel von Wallenstein, 966
Zheng Chenggong, 1001

WOMEN'S RIGHTS
Mrs. Anne Bracegirdle, 82
John III Sobieski, 427
Ninon de Lenclos, 520
Madame de Maintenon, 572
Marie de l'Incarnation, 595
Duchesse de Montpensier, 660
Rebecca Nurse, 689
Elena Cornaro Piscopia, 743
Anna Maria van Schurman, 823

GEOGRAPHICAL INDEX

AFRICA
Njinga, 687

ALBANIA
Shabbetai Tzevi, 835

AMERICAN COLONIES
John Alden, 7
Nathaniel Bacon, 29
William Bradford, 84
Anne Bradstreet, 88
Margaret Brent, 92
Canonicus, 129
John Cotton, 196
John Davenport, 218
John Eliot, 247
Thomas Hooker, 386
Anne Hutchinson, 394
Pierre Le Moyne d'Iberville, 401
Eusebio Francisco Kino, 467
Sieur de La Salle, 490
Jacob Leisler, 518
Roger Ludlow, 567
Massasoit, 612
Metacom, 633
Rebecca Nurse, 689
Opechancanough, 702
William Penn, 724
Pocahontas, 745
Mary White Rowlandson, 798
John Smith, 861
Squanto, 875
Miles Standish, 877
Peter Stuyvesant, 890
Sir Henry Vane the Younger, 941
Roger Williams, 982
John Winthrop, 990

AUSTRALIA
Abel Janszoon Tasman, 905

AUSTRIA
Ferdinand II, 267
Frederick V, 293
Merzifonlu Kara Mustafa Paşa,
    451
Leopold I, 526

BAVARIA
Frederick V, 293

BELGIUM
Frans Hals, 352
Jan Baptista van Helmont, 361
Cornelius Otto Jansen, 419
Peter Paul Rubens, 802

BOHEMIA
Elizabeth Stuart, 253
Frederick V, 293
Prince Rupert, 805
Albrecht Wenzel von Wallenstein,
    966

BRAZIL
António Vieira, 959

CANADA
Saint Marguerite Bourgeoys, 75
Samuel de Champlain, 139
Saint Isaac Jogues, 423
Sieur de La Salle, 490
François Laval, 498
Sieur de Maisonneuve, 574
Marie de l'Incarnation, 595
Pierre Esprit Radisson, 777

CHINA
Abahai, 1
Chen Shu, 156
Chongzhen, 160
Dorgon, 234
Kangxi, 448
Liu Yin, 540
Shunzhi, 848
Tianqi, 911
Wang Fuzhi, 972
Zheng Chenggong, 1001

DENMARK
Charles X Gustav, 153
Nicolaus Steno, 881

EGYPT
Shabbetai Tzevi, 835

ENGLAND
Lancelot Andrewes, 14
Richard Baxter, 32
Johann Joachim Becher, 39
Aphra Behn, 42
Thomas Betterton, 51
John Biddle, 53
Robert Blake, 55
Robert Boyle, 78
Mrs. Anne Bracegirdle, 82
Margaret Brent, 92
Sir Thomas Browne, 94
First Duke of Buckingham, 96
John Bunyan, 100
Richard Burbage, 104
Thomas Burnet, 106
Robert Burton, 108
George Calvert, 119
Thomas Campion, 127
Robert Carr, 131
Catherine of Braganza, 137
Charles I, 143
Charles II (of England), 147
First Earl of Clarendon, 166
Sir Edward Coke, 174
Anne Conway, 187
John Cotton, 196
Abraham Cowley, 199
Richard Crashaw, 202
Oliver Cromwell, 204
William Dampier, 215
John Davenport, 218
Lady Eleanor Davies, 220
Thomas Dekker, 223
John Donne, 230
Michael Drayton, 237
John Dryden, 239
Sir Anthony van Dyck, 244
John Eliot, 247
Elizabeth of Bohemia, 250
Elizabeth Stuart, 253
John Evelyn, 256
Third Baron Fairfax, 261
Nicholas Ferrar, 274
John Fletcher, 277
Robert Fludd, 280
George Fox, 283

Frederick V, 293
Orlando Gibbons, 309
James Gregory, 319
Nell Gwyn, 342
Matthew Hale, 345
Edmond Halley, 348
William Harvey, 355
Henrietta Maria, 364
George Herbert, 366
Robert Herrick, 368
Thomas Heywood, 373
Thomas Hobbes, 378
Robert Hooke, 383
Thomas Hooker, 386
Jeremiah Horrocks, 388
Henry Hudson, 390
Anne Hutchinson, 394
James I, 413
James II, 416
Inigo Jones, 436
Ben Jonson, 439
William Kidd, 464
John Lambert, 483
William Laud, 495
Henry Lawes, 502
First Duke of Leeds, 506
Antoni van Leeuwenhoek, 509
John Lilburne, 534
John Locke, 542
Richard Lovelace, 562
Richard Lower, 564
Roger Ludlow, 567
Manasseh ben Israel, 582
Marie de Médicis, 598
Andrew Marvell, 605
Mary II, 610
Mary of Modena, 607
Thomas Middleton, 636
John Milton, 639
George Monck, 650
Duke of Monmouth, 653
Lodowick Muggleton, 665
Duchess of Newcastle, 676
Sir Isaac Newton, 679
Titus Oates, 692
Johann Pachelbel, 708
Denis Papin, 710
William Paterson, 716
William Penn, 724
Samuel Pepys, 728

Sir William Petty, 733
Katherine Philips, 741
Thomas Pride, 756
Henry Purcell, 763
John Pym, 767
Pierre Esprit Radisson, 777
John Ray, 782
Prince Rupert, 805
Thomas Savery, 813
Sir George Savile, 815
Friedrich Hermann Schomberg, 820
First Earl of Shaftesbury, 838
James Shirley, 846
John Smith, 861
Miles Standish, 877
First Earl of Strafford, 884
Sir John Suckling, 893
Thomas Sydenham, 901
Cyril Tourneur, 928
James Ussher, 938
Sir Henry Vane the Younger, 941
John Wallis, 969
Mary Ward, 974
John Webster, 976
William III, 979
Roger Williams, 982
Thomas Willis, 985
Gerrard Winstanley, 988
John Winthrop, 990
Sir Christopher Wren, 994

FLANDERS
Sir Anthony van Dyck, 244

FRANCE
Anne of Austria, 18
Angélique Arnauld, 20
Pierre Bayle, 36
Nicolas Boileau-Despréaux, 63
Jacques-Bénigne Bossuet, 70
Louyse Bourgeois, 73
Saint Marguerite Bourgeoys, 75
Jacques Callot, 116
Gian Domenico Cassini, 134
Samuel de Champlain, 139
Duchesse de Chevreuse, 158
Christina, 163
Claude Lorrain, 171
Jean-Baptiste Colbert, 180
The Great Condé, 184

Pierre Corneille, 193
Cyrano de Bergerac, 211
René Descartes, 226
François de Salignac de La
    Mothe-Fénelon, 265
Pierre de Fermat, 271
Pierre Gassendi, 304
Marie le Jars de Gournay, 314
Madame Guyon, 339
Henrietta Maria, 364
Christiaan Huygens, 397
Innocent XI, 405
Saint Isaac Jogues, 423
John of Austria, 425
Jean de La Bruyère, 475
Madame de La Fayette, 477
Jean de La Fontaine, 480
François de La Rochefoucauld, 487
Sieur de La Salle, 490
Georges de La Tour, 493
François Laval, 498
Charles Le Brun, 504
Ninon de Lenclos, 520
André Le Nôtre, 523
Louis Le Vau, 532
Marie de l'Incarnation, 595
Duchesse de Longueville, 548
Louis XIII, 551
Louis XIV, 554
Marquis de Louvois, 558
Jean-Baptiste Lully, 569
Madame de Maintenon, 572
Sieur de Maisonneuve, 574
François de Malherbe, 577
The Mancini Sisters, 585
François Mansart, 587
Jules Hardouin-Mansart, 590
Marie de Médicis, 598
Marie-Thérèse, 600
Jacques Marquette, 603
Mary of Modena, 607
Jules Mazarin, 620
Marin Mersenne, 628
Molière, 646
Duchesse de Montpensier, 660
Count-Duke of Olivares, 697
Denis Papin, 710
Blaise Pascal, 713
Nicolas-Claude Fabri de Peiresc, 722
Charles Perrault, 731

Nicolas Poussin, 749
Jean Racine, 773
Pierre Esprit Radisson, 777
Marquise de Rambouillet, 779
Cardinal de Richelieu, 790
Friedrich Hermann Schomberg,
    820
Madeleine de Scudéry, 828
Madame de Sévigné, 833
Nicolaus Steno, 881
Duke de Sully, 896
Viscount de Turenne, 933
Sébastien Le Prestre de Vauban,
    946
Saint Vincent de Paul, 962
Mary Ward, 974

GERMANY
Johann Joachim Becher, 39
Jakob Böhme, 59
Elizabeth of Bohemia, 250
David and Johannes Fabricius,
    259
Frederick V, 293
Frederick William, the Great
    Elector, 290
Hans Jakob Christoffel von
    Grimmelshausen, 324
Hugo Grotius, 326
Otto von Guericke, 333
Gustavus II Adolphus, 336
Johannes and Elisabetha Hevelius,
    371
Engelbert Kämpfer, 445
Johannes Kepler, 457
Gottfried Wilhelm Leibniz, 513
Jacob Leisler, 518
Leopold I, 526
Hans Lippershey, 537
Marie de Médicis, 598
Johann Pachelbel, 708
Samuel von Pufendorf, 759
Peter Paul Rubens, 802
Wilhelm Schickard, 818
Friedrich Hermann Schomberg,
    820
Heinrich Schütz, 825
Justine Siegemundin, 851
Nicolaus Steno, 881
Viscount de Turenne, 933

HUNGARY
Merzifonlu Kara Mustafa Paşa, 451

INDIA
Aurangzeb, 23
Jahāngīr, 410
Shah Jahan, 842
Śivājī, 858

INDONESIA
Abel Janszoon Tasman, 905

IRAN
ʿAbbās the Great, 4

IRELAND
George Calvert, 119
Rory O'More, 699
Sir William Petty, 733
Friedrich Hermann Schomberg,
    820
James Ussher, 938

ITALY
Alexander VII, 9
Gian Lorenzo Bernini, 45
Giovanni Alfonso Borelli, 65
Francesco Borromini, 67
Francesca Caccini, 111
Tommaso Campanella, 124
Gian Domenico Cassini, 134
Claude Lorrain, 171
Arcangelo Corelli, 190
Girolamo Frescobaldi, 295
Galileo, 298
Giovanna Garzoni, 302
Artemisia Gentileschi, 307
Francesco Maria Grimaldi, 321
Guarino Guarini, 330
Innocent XI, 405
Eusebio Francisco Kino, 467
Jean-Baptiste Lully, 569
Marcello Malpighi, 579
The Mancini Sisters, 585
Maria Celeste, 593
Marie de Médicis, 598
Jules Mazarin, 620
Cosimo II de' Medici, 626
Claudio Monteverdi, 656
Count-Duke of Olivares, 697

Paul V, 719
Nicolas-Claude Fabri de Peiresc,
    722
Elena Cornaro Piscopia, 743
Nicolas Poussin, 749
Santorio Santorio, 810
Elisabetta Sirani, 856
Nicolaus Steno, 881
Barbara Strozzi, 888
Evangelista Torricelli, 921
Urban VIII, 936

JAPAN
Hishikawa Moronobu, 375
Ihara Saikaku, 403
Izumo no Okuni, 408
Engelbert Kämpfer, 445
Matsuo Bashō, 615
Ogata Kōrin, 695
Seki Kōwa, 831
Sōtatsu, 868
Tokugawa Ieyasu, 915
Tokugawa Tsunayoshi, 919
Yui Shōsetsu, 998
Zheng Chenggong, 1001

MANCHURIA
Abahai, 1
Dorgon, 234
Shunzhi, 848

MEXICO
Sor Juana Inés de la Cruz, 208
Eusebio Francisco Kino, 467

MORAVIA
Jan Komenský, 469

NATIVE AMERICA
Canonicus, 129
Massasoit, 612
Opechancanough, 702
Pocahontas, 745
Powhatan, 752
Squanto, 875
Kateri Tekakwitha, 908

NETHERLANDS
Pierre Bayle, 36
Johann Joachim Becher, 39

The Bernoulli Family, 48
René Descartes, 226
Sir Anthony van Dyck, 244
Elizabeth of Bohemia, 250
Frederick Henry, 286
Hugo Grotius, 326
Frans Hals, 352
Piet Hein, 359
Jan Baptista van Helmont, 361
Christiaan Huygens, 397
Cornelius Otto Jansen, 419
Jan Komenský, 469
Antoni van Leeuwenhoek, 509
Hans Lippershey, 537
Manasseh ben Israel, 582
Maurice of Nassau, 618
Peter Minuit, 643
Rembrandt, 786
Peter Paul Rubens, 802
Michiel Adriaanszoon de Ruyter, 807
Friedrich Hermann Schomberg, 820
Anna Maria van Schurman, 823
Baruch Spinoza, 871
Peter Stuyvesant, 890
Jan Swammerdam, 898
Abel Janszoon Tasman, 905
Maarten and Cornelis Tromp, 930
Viscount de Turenne, 933
Jan Vermeer, 956
William III, 979

NEW ZEALAND
Abel Janszoon Tasman, 905

NORWAY
Charles X Gustav, 153

OTTOMAN EMPIRE
Merzifonlu Kara Mustafa Paşa, 451
Kâtib Çelebî, 454
Kösem Sultan, 472
Murad IV, 668
Mustafa I, 673
Shabbetai Tzevi, 835

PAKISTAN
Shah Jahan, 842

PERU
Saint Rose of Lima, 796

POLAND
Charles X Gustav, 153
Johannes and Elisabetha Hevelius, 371
John III Sobieski, 427
Merzifonlu Kara Mustafa Paşa, 451
Bohdan Khmelnytsky, 461
Justine Siegemundin, 851
Sigismund III Vasa, 853

PORTUGAL
Catherine of Braganza, 137
John IV, 430
John of Austria, 425
António Vieira, 959

PRUSSIA
Frederick William, the Great Elector, 290
Samuel von Pufendorf, 759
Justine Siegemundin, 851

RUSSIA
Alexis, 11
Avvakum Petrovich, 26
Charles X Gustav, 153
Engelbert Kämpfer, 445
Boris Ivanovich Morozov, 663
Nikon, 683
Razin, Stenka, 784
Michael Romanov, 794
Sophia, 865
Vasily Shuysky, 943

SCOTLAND
Richard Cameron, 121
Robert Carr, 131
Charles I, 143
Charles II (of England), 147
Elizabeth Stuart, 253
James Gregory, 319
James I, 413
William Kidd, 464
William Paterson, 716

SLOVENIA
Santorio Santorio, 810

SPAIN
Anne of Austria, 18
Pedro Calderón de la Barca, 113
Charles II (of Spain), 151
Duchesse de Chevreuse, 158
Luis de Góngora y Argote, 312
Baltasar Gracián y Morales, 316
John IV, 430
John of Austria, 425
Duke de Lerma, 530
Duchesse de Longueville, 548
Manasseh ben Israel, 582
Marie-Thérèse, 600
Maurice of Nassau, 618
Bartolomé Esteban Murillo, 670
Count-Duke of Olivares, 697
Philip III, 736
Philip IV, 738
Francisco Gómez de Quevedo y Villegas, 770
Tirso de Molina, 913
Lope de Vega Carpio, 949
Diego Velázquez, 953
Francisco de Zurbarán, 1003

SWEDEN
Charles X Gustav, 153
Christina, 163
René Descartes, 226
Gustavus II Adolphus, 336
Jan Komenský, 469
Peter Minuit, 643
Axel Oxenstierna, 704
Friedrich Hermann Schomberg, 820
Sigismund III Vasa, 853
Lennart Torstenson, 924

SWITZERLAND
The Bernoulli Family, 48

UKRAINE
John III Sobieski, 427
Bohdan Khmelnytsky, 461
Ivan Stepanovich Mazepa, 624

WALES
George Herbert, 366

Great Lives from History

Indexes

PERSONAGES INDEX

Abahai, 1-3, 234, 848

ʿAbbās I. *See* ʿAbbās the Great

ʿAbbās II, 844

ʿAbbās the Great, 4-7, 411, 627, 668, 844

Adams, Will, 917

Adolphus, Gustavus II. *See* Gustavus II Adolphus

Adriaanszoon de Ruyter, Michiel. *See* Ruyter, Michiel Adriaanszoon de

Afonso VI, 821

Afzal Khan, 859

Ahmed I, 472, 673

Ahmed Paşa, Fazıl, 452

Akbar, 25, 410

ʿĀlamgīr I. *See* Aurangzeb

Albemarle, first duke of. *See* Monck, George

Alden, John, 7-9, 879

Alderman (killed Metacom), 634

Alexander VII, 9-11, 46, 165, 406, 964

Alexis, 11-14, 28, 428, 463, 663, 683, 795, 865

Alfonso Borelli, Giovanni. *See* Borelli, Giovanni Alfonso

Allouez, Claude-Jean, 433, 603

Alonso, Giovanni Francesco Antonio. *See* Borelli, Giovanni Alfonso

Amin (Jin prince), 1

Amis, Aphara. *See* Behn, Aphra

Ana de Souza. *See* Njinga

Ana Nzinga Mbande, Ngola. *See* Njinga

Anastasia. *See* Kösem Sultan

Andrei Shuysky, 943

Andrewes, Lancelot, 14-17, 202, 247, 366, 496

Andros, Sir Edmond, 518

Angélique, Mother. *See* Arnauld, Angélique

Aniello, Tommaso. *See* Masaniello

Anne of Austria, 18-20; and the Great Condé, 185; and Cosimo II de' Medici, 627; and Saint Isaac Jogues, 424; and Madame de La

Fayette, 477; and François de La Rochefoucauld, 487; and the duchesse de Longueville, 549; and Louis XIII, 551; and Louis XIV, 554; and Madame de Maintenon, 572; and the Mancini Sisters, 585; and François Mansart, 589; and Marie de Médicis, 598; and Marie-Thérèse, 601; and Jules Mazarin, 621; and the duchesse de Montpensier, 660; and Philip IV, 738; and Cardinal de Richelieu, 791; and Hercule Rohan, 158; and Viscount de Turenne, 933

Antoine Lefebre. *See* La Barre, sieur de

Argall, Samuel, 746

Argyll, earl of. *See* Campbell, Archibald

Arjumand Banu Begum. *See* Mumtaz Mahal

Arlington, first earl of, 507, 839

Arnauld, Angélique, 20-23

Asaf Khan, 842

Asbaje y Ramírez de Santillana, Juana Inéz. *See* Cruz, Sor Juana Inés de la

Ashley, Lord. *See* Shaftesbury, first earl of

Aston, Sir Walter, 238

Aubigné, Françoise d'. *See* Maintenon, Madame de

Aurangzeb, 23-26, 843, 859

Austria, Anne of. *See* Anne of Austria

Austria, John of. *See* John of Austria

Avvakum Petrovich, 26-28, 685; *Life of the Archpriest Avvakum, by Himself, The*, 27

Awashonks, 634

Azzolino, Decio, 165

Bach, Ambrosius, 708

Bach, Johann Christoph, 708

Bach, Johann Sebastian, 708

Bachmann, Augustus Quirnus. *See* Rivinus

Bacon, Francis, 175, 227, 357, 378; influence on Robert Boyle, 78

Bacon, Nathaniel, 29-32

Bahādur Shāh, 25

Baltimore, first Lord. *See* Calvert, George

Barberini, Maffeo Vincenzo. *See* Urban VIII

Barca, Pedro Calderón de la. *See* Calderón de la Barca, Pedro

Baronius, Caesar, 720

Barrow, Isaac, 923

Barry, Elizabeth, 83

Bartholin, Thomas, 881

Bashō. *See* Matsuo Bashō

Bavaria, duke of. *See* Rupert, Prince

Baxter, Richard, 32-36, 347

Bayard, Nicholas, 519

Bayle, Pierre, 36-39; list of works, 37

Bayn, Aphra. *See* Behn, Aphra

Beauclerk, Charles, 343

Beaujeu, sieur de, 491

Beaumont, Francis, 105, 278, 636, 846

Becher, Johann Joachim, 39-41

Bedell, William, 939

Bedford, countess of. *See* Harington, Lucy

Bedford, earl of. *See* Francis, Lord Russell

Behn, Aphra, 42-44, 82; list of works, 43

Béjart, Armande, 648

Béjart, Madeleine, 646

Bellamont, earl of. *See* Coote, Richard

Bellarmine, Robert, 16, 720

Bellasis, John, 484

Ben Israel, Manasseh. *See* Manasseh ben Israel

Bénigne Bossuet, Jacques. *See* Bossuet, Jacques-Bénigne

Bennet, Henry. *See* Arlington, first earl of

Benserade, Isaac de, 781

Bentivoglio, Enzo, 295

Bentivoglio, Guido, 295

Bergerac, Cyrano de. *See* Cyrano de Bergerac

Berkeley, Sir William, 29, 703

Bernières de Louvigny, Jean de, 499

Bernini, Gian Lorenzo, 10, 45-47, 68, 303, 330, 532, 937, 995

Bernini, Giovanni Lorenzo. *See* Bernini, Gian Lorenzo

Bernoulli family; Daniel, 48-50; Jakob I, 48-50, 832; Johann I, 48-50

Bérulle, Pierre de, 962

Bethlen, Gabriel, 855

Béthune, Maximilien de. *See* Sully, duke de

Betterton, Thomas, 51-53, 82

Beverwijk, Johann van, 824

Bhonsle, Śivājī. *See* Śivājī

Biddle, John, 53-55

Bishop, Nicholas, 104

Blaes, Gerard, 898

Blake, Robert, 55-59, 651, 931

Boerhaave, Hermann, 511

Bogot, 498

Böhme, Jakob, 59-62; "Of the Mixed Tree of Evil and Good," 61

Boileau-Despréaux, Nicolas, 63-65, 482, 578, 732, 829

Bolotnikov, Ivan, 944

Bonham, Thomas, 176

Booth, George, 485

Borelli, Giovanni Alfonso, 65-67, 362, 579, 986

Borghese, Camillo. *See* Paul V

Borghese, Scipione, 45

Borromini, Francesco, 67-70, 330, 532, 937

Bossuet, Jacques-Bénigne, 70-73, 186, 265, 339, 488

Boteler, Sir William, 562

Bouillon, duchesse de. *See* Mancini, Marie-Anne

Bourbon-Condé, Anne-Geneviève de. *See* Longueville, duchesse de

Bourgeois, Louyse, 73-75

Bourgeoys, Saint Marguerite, 75-77, 576

Boursier, Louyse. *See* Bourgeois, Louyse

Bouvier de La Motte, Jeanne-Marie. *See* Guyon, Madame

Boyle, Richard, 885

Boyle, Robert, 37, 48, 78-81, 257, 306, 335, 383, 514, 544, 564, 814, 901, 923

Bracegirdle, Mrs. Anne, 51, 82-83

Bradford, William, 84-87, 130, 613, 876, 878; list of works, 86

Bradstreet, Anne, 88-91

Braganza, duke of. *See* John IV (king of Portugal)

Brahe, Tycho, 259, 372, 458

Bramer, Leonaert, 956

Brent, Margaret, 92-93

Brewster, William, 84, 878

Brome, Richard, 374, 443

Browne, Sir Richard, 676

Browne, Sir Thomas, 94-96

Bruno, Giordano, 630, 811

Bruyas, Jacques, 909

Buade, Louis de. *See* Frontenac, comte de

Buckingham, first duke of, 18, 96-99, 132, 143, 158, 166, 177, 364, 368, 414, 496, 552, 650, 767, 884

Buckingham, second duke of, 149, 241, 506, 816, 839

Bulkeley, Peter, 386

Bull, John, 310

Bunyan, John, 100-103; list of works, 101

Burbage, Cuthbert, 104

Burbage, James, 104

Burbage, Richard, 104-106, 279, 441

Burnet, Thomas, 106-108

Burton, Robert, 108-110

Butler, James. *See* Ormond, first duke of

Byrd, William, 310

Caccini, Francesca, 111-112

Calderón de la Barca, Pedro, 113-116, 210, 740, 914, 950; list of works, 114

Callot, Jacques, 116-119

Calvert, Cecilius, 92, 120

Calvert, George, 92, 119-121

Cameron, Richard, 121-124

Campanella, Giovanni. *See* Campanella, Tommaso

Campanella, Tommaso, 65, 124-126, 629, 723

Campbell, Archibald, 147, 655

Campini, Giuseppe, 134

Campion, Thomas, 127-129; list of works, 128

Cano, Alonso, 1003

Canonchet, 634

Canonicus, 129-131, 613

Carew, Thomas, 503

Cargill, Donald, 122

Carlos II. *See* Charles II (king of Spain)

Carmarthen, marquis of. *See* Leeds, first duke of

Carpio, Lope de Vega. *See* Vega Carpio, Lope de

Carr, George, 221

Carr, Robert, 16, 131-133, 414

Cartwright, William, 443, 503

Casaubon, Isaac, 281

Cassiano del Pozzo, 302, 307

Cassini, Gian Domenico, 134-136, 348

Castelli, Benedetto, 65, 921

Castelli, Francesco. *See* Borromini, Francesco

Castiglione, Giovanni, 330

Castlemaine, countess of, 137

Catherine d'Angennes. *See* Rambouillet, Marquise de

Catherine of Braganza, 137-139, 148, 343, 654

Cats, Jakob, 824

Cavalieri, Bonaventura, 922, 969

Cavalli, Francesco, 888

Cavelier, René-Robert. *See* La Salle, sieur de

Cavendish, Sir Charles, 676

Cavendish, Margaret. *See* Newcastle, duchess of

Cavendish, William, 262, 676

Cecchina, La. *See* Caccini, Francesca

Cecil, Robert. *See* Salisbury, first earl of

Cecil, William, 175

Çelebî, Kâtib. *See* Kâtib Çelebî

Celeste, Maria. *See* Maria Celeste

Cervantes, Miguel de, 738

Champlain, Samuel de, 139-143, 433

Chantelou, Paul Fréart de, 750

Chapelain, Jean, 833

Charles I (king of England), 143-146; and Richard Baxter, 33; and Aphra Behn, 42; and Thomas Betterton, 51; and Robert Blake, 55; and Jacques-Bénigne Bossuet, 72; and Anne Bradstreet, 89; and the first duke of Buckingham, 98; and George Calvert, 120; and Richard Cameron, 121; and Canonicus, 130; and Robert Carr, 133; and Catherine of Braganza, 137; and Charles II of England, 149; and the first earl of Clarendon, 166; and Sir Edward Coke, 177; and John Cotton, 198; and Abraham Cowley, 199; and Richard Crashaw, 202; and Oliver Cromwell, 204; and Lady Eleanor Davies, 221; and John Dryden, 240; and Sir Anthony van Dyck, 245; and John Eliot, 247; and Elizabeth of Bohemia, 252; and Elizabeth Stuart, 254; and John Evelyn, 256; and Third Baron Fairfax, 262; and Nicholas Ferrar, 275; and Frederick Henry, 288; and Artemisia Gentileschi, 308; and Orlando Gibbons, 311; and Nell Gwyn, 343; and Matthew Hale, 345; and William Harvey, 357; and Henrietta Maria, 364; and Robert Herrick, 369; and James I, 415; and James II, 416; and Inigo Jones, 436; and Ben Jonson, 443; and John Lambert, 483; and William Laud, 496; and Henry Lawes, 503; and John Lilburne, 535; and Louis XIII, 552; and Richard Lovelace, 562; and Roger Ludlow, 567; and Marie de Médicis, 599; and Andrew Marvell, 605; and Mary II, 610; and Thomas Middleton, 638; and John Milton, 640; and George Monck, 650; and Rory O'More, 699; and Opechancanough, 703; and Samuel Pepys, 728; and Thomas Pride, 756; and John Pym, 767; and Cardinal de Richelieu, 791; and Prince Rupert, 805; and Santorio Santorio, 811; and Sir George Savile, 815; and the first earl of Shaftesbury, 838; and James Shirley, 847; and the first earl of Strafford, 885; and Sir John Suckling, 893; and Maarten and Cornelis Tromp, 930; and Sir Henry Vane the Younger, 941; and John Wallis, 969; and William III, 979; and Gerrard Winstanley, 989; and John Winthrop, 991; and Sir Christopher Wren, 994

Charles II (king of England), 147-150; and Nathaniel Bacon, 29; and Richard Baxter, 34; and Aphra Behn, 42; and John Biddle, 54; and Robert Blake, 58; and Robert Boyle, 80; and Sir Thomas Browne, 94; and John Bunyan, 101; and Richard Cameron, 121; and Catherine of Braganza, 137; and the first earl of Clarendon, 168; and Abraham Cowley, 200; and Oliver Cromwell, 205; and John Davenport, 219; and John Dryden, 240; and Elizabeth Stuart, 254; and John Evelyn, 256; and the third Baron Fairfax, 264; and George Fox, 284; and James Gregory, 319; and Nell Gwyn, 342; and Matthew Hale, 346; and Edmond Halley, 348; and Henrietta Maria, 364; and Robert Herrick, 369; and Thomas Hobbes, 380; and James II, 416; and John IV, 431; and John Lambert, 485; and Henry Lawes, 503; and the first duke of Leeds, 506; and John Locke, 544; and Roger Ludlow, 568; and the Mancini sisters, 586; and Andrew Marvell, 606; and Mary II, 610; and Mary of Modena, 607; and John Milton, 640; and George Monck, 650; and the duke of Monmouth, 653; and the duchesse de Montpensier, 661; and the duchess of Newcastle, 677; and Titus Oates, 692; and William Penn, 725; and Samuel Pepys, 729; and Sir William Petty, 734; and Katherine Philips, 742; and Thomas Pride, 757; and Henry Purcell, 763; and Prince Rupert, 805; and Sir George Savile, 815; and Friedrich Hermann Schomberg, 821; and the first earl of Shaftesbury, 839; and Maarten and Maarten and Cornelis Tromp, 931; and Sir Henry Vane the Younger, 942; and John Wallis, 969; and Thomas Willis, 986; and Sir Christopher Wren, 994

Charles II (king of Spain), 151-153, 426, 528, 555, 602, 739, 980

Charles III (king of Spain). See Charles VI (Holy Roman Emperor)

Charles IV (duke of Lorraine), 493, 528

Charles VI (Holy Roman Emperor), 152

Charles IX (king of Sweden), 336, 854, 945

Charles X Gustav, 153-155, 164, 527, 706

Charles XI (king of Sweden), 155

Charles XII (king of Sweden), 625

Charles the Mad. See Charles II (king of Spain)

Charleton, Walter, 240

Chen Shu, 156-158

Cheng Ch'eng-kung. See Zheng Chenggong

Cheng Chih-lung. See Zheng Zhilong

Chesnoy, Madame de Guyon du. See Guyon, Madame

Chevreuse, duchesse de, 18, 158-160, 487

Chigi, Fabio. See Alexander VII

Ch'ing T'ai-tsung. See Abahai

Chini, Eusebio Francesco. See Kino, Eusebio Francisco

Chmielnicki, Bohdan. See Khmelnytsky, Bohdan

Chodkiewicz, Jan, 854

Chomedey, Paul de. See Maisonneuve, sieur de

Chongde. *See* Abahai

Chongzhen, 160-162, 235, 848, 912

Chouart, Médard. *See* Groseilliers,
sieur des

Christina (queen of Sweden), 163-
166; and Giovanni Alfonso
Borelli, 66; and René Descartes,
164, 228; and Frederick William,
290; and Ninon de Lenclos, 521;
and the duchesse de
Montpensier, 661; music
patronage, 190; and Blaise
Pascal, 713; and António Vieira,
960

Christoffel von Grimmelshausen,
Hans Jakob. *See*
Grimmelshausen, Hans Jakob
Christoffel von

Chu Yu-chiao. *See* Tianqi

Chu Yu-chien. *See* Chongzhen

Chuang Lieh-ti. *See* Chongzhen

Ch'ung-chen. *See* Chongzhen

Ch'ung-te. *See* Abahai

Church, Benjamin, 634

Cicognini, Jacopo, 111

Clarendon, first earl of, 147, 166-
170, 240, 507, 816, 839

Clarke, Samuel, 516

Clarkson, Laurence, 666

Claude Lorrain, 171-173

Clement VIII, 720

Clement IX, 406, 422

Clement X, 406

Clerville, chevalier de, 946

Clifford, Thomas. *See* Clifford of
Chudleigh, first Baron

Clifford of Chudleigh, first Baron,
507, 839

Clyfton, Richard, 84

Coddington, William, 130

Coke, Sir Edward, 132, 174-179,
414, 767, 982

Colbert, Jean-Baptiste, 135, 180-
183, 398, 505, 554, 558, 570,
588, 590, 622, 731

Coligny, Gaspard II de, 896

Colle, Giovanni, 565

Colonna, princess of. *See* Mancini,
Marie

Comenius, Jan (Johann, John)
Amos. *See* Komenský, Jan

Concini, Concino, 551, 598, 791

Condé, The Great, 159, 184-187,
549, 559, 621, 661, 821, 829,
896, 926, 933

Condé, third prince of, 548, 551

Congreve, William, 52, 82

Connolly, Owen, 700

Conway, Anne, 187-189, 252

Cooper, Anthony Ashley. *See*
Shaftesbury, first earl of

Coote, Richard, 464

Corbett, Richard, 443

Corelli, Arcangelo, 190-192

Cork, first earl of. *See* Boyle,
Richard

Cornaro Piscopia, Elena. *See*
Piscopia, Elena Cornaro

Corneille, Pierre, 193-196; and Jean
de La Fontaine, 482; list of
works, 194; and the duchesse de
Longueville, 550; and Jean-
Baptiste Lully, 570; and Molière,
647; and Katherine Philips, 742;
and Nicolas Poussin, 751; and
Jean Racine, 774; and the French
salons, 780; and Madame de
Sévigné, 834

Cortlandt, Stephanus van, 519

Cortona, Pietro da, 937

Cosimo II. *See* Medici, Cosimo II
de'

Cosin, John, 202

Cotán, Juan Sánchez, 1005

Cotterell, Charles, 742

Cotton, John, 196-199, 218, 386,
394, 982

Coûture, Guillaume, 423

Cowley, Abraham, 199-201, 203,
232, 742

Coxe, Thomas, 901

Cranfield, Lionel, 275

Crashaw, Richard, 202-204, 232,
276, 562

Cromwell, Oliver, 204-207; and
Richard Baxter, 33; and John
Biddle, 54; and Robert Blake, 56;
and John Bunyan, 100; and
Richard Cameron, 121; and
Catherine of Braganza, 137; and
Charles I, 145; and Charles II of
England, 147; and the first earl of
Clarendon, 168; and the Great
Condé, 186; and John Cotton,

198; and Abraham Cowley, 199;
and John Dryden, 239; and the
third Baron Fairfax, 262; and
George Fox, 284; and Frederick
Henry, 288; and Matthew Hale,
346; and Thomas Hobbes, 380;
and Inigo Jones, 437; and John
Lambert, 483; and Henry Lawes,
502; and Roger Ludlow, 568;
and Manasseh ben Israel, 583;
and Andrew Marvell, 606; and
George Monck, 651; and Rory
O'More, 701; and William Penn,
724; and Samuel Pepys, 728; and
Sir William Petty, 734; and
Katherine Philips, 741; and
Thomas Pride, 756; and Henry
Purcell, 763; and Prince Rupert,
805; and Sir George Savile, 815;
and the first earl of Shaftesbury,
838; and James Shirley, 846; and
Maarten and Cornelis Tromp,
931; and James Ussher, 940; and
Sir Henry Vane the Younger,
941; and Mary Ward, 975; and
Thomas Willis, 986; and Gerrard
Winstanley, 989; and Sir
Christopher Wren, 994

Cromwell, Richard, 485, 757, 942

Crooke, Andrew, 94

Cruz, Sor Juana Inés de la, 208-210;
list of works, 209

Cumberland, duke of. *See* Rupert,
Prince

Cuyen, 1

Cyrano de Bergerac, 211-214

Dablon, Claude, 433, 603

Daisan (Jin prince), 1

Dampier, William, 215-218

Danby, first earl of. *See* Leeds, first
duke of

Daniel, Samuel, 128

Dārā, 23, 844

Daumont, Simon François. *See* Saint
Lusson, sieur de

Davenant, Sir William, 51, 502

Davenport, John, 218-220

Davies, Lady Eleanor, 220-222,
989

Davies, Sir John, 221

Davison, Francis, 127

Day, Thomas, 311

Deane, Richard, 56, 651, 932

Defoe, Daniel, 216

Deimier, Pierre de, 578

Dekker, Thomas, 132, 223-225, 441, 636, 846, 977; list of works, 224

De la Gardie, Magnus Gabriel, 153, 164

Deleboe, Franz, 361

Delorme, Marion, 521

Denham, Sir John, 994

Denis, Jean Baptiste, 565

Dermer, Thomas, 876

Desargues, Girard, 630

Descartes, René, 226-229; and Jakob Bernoulli, 48; and Giovanni Alfonso Borelli, 67; and Queen Christina, 164; and Anne Conway, 188; on doubt, 228; and Elizabeth of Bohemia, 251; and Pierre de Fermat, 271; and Pierre Gassendi, 305; and William Harvey, 357; and Christiaan Huygens, 398; iatromechanism, 362; and Jean de La Fontaine, 482; and Gottfried Wilhelm Leibniz, 514; list of works, 227; and Marin Mersenne, 628; and the duchess of Newcastle, 677; and Blaise Pascal, 713; and Anna Maria van Schurman, 824; on space and matter, 333; and Baruch Spinoza, 871; and Nicolaus Steno, 881; on thinking, 228; and John Wallis, 970; and Thomas Willis, 986

Deshayes, Catherine. See Monvoisin, Madame

Desportes, Philippe, 577

Despréaux, Nicolas Boileau-. See Boileau-Despréaux, Nicolas

Devereux, Robert (1566-1601). See Essex, second earl of

Devereux, Robert (1591-1646). See Essex, third earl of

Diemen, Antony van, 905

Divini, Eustachio, 134

Dmitry, False, 794, 854, 944

Dmitry, Second False, 794, 944

Dmitry Ivanovich, 943

Dodo (Dorgon's brother), 234

Dog Shogun. See Tokugawa Tsunayoshi

Dolgoruky, Vasily Vladimirovich, 12

Domenichino, Il, 749

Domenico Cassini, Gian. See Cassini, Gian Domenico

Donne, John, 16, 132, 200, 202, 230-234, 253, 366, 741; list of works, 231

Dorgon, 1, 234-237, 848

Doroshenko, Petro, 452, 624

Douglas, Sir Archibald, 221

Douglas, Thomas, 122

Dowland, John, 127, 502

Drayton, Michael, 237-239

Druilletes, Gabriel, 603

Drummond, William, 443

Dryden, John, 43, 52, 64, 201, 233, 239-243, 342, 394, 442, 765, 817; list of works, 242

Dudley, Anne. See Bradstreet, Anne

Dudley, Robert. See Leicester, first earl of

Dudley, Thomas, 992

Dyck, Sir Anthony van, 244-246, 302, 671, 723

Eaton, Theophilus, 218

Egerton, Sir Thomas, 231

Eliot, John, 247-250

Elizabeth I (queen of England), 15, 104

Elizabeth of Bohemia (1596-1662). See Elizabeth Stuart

Elizabeth of Bohemia (1618-1680), 250-253, 254; correspondence with Descartes, 251

Elizabeth Stuart, 250, 253-255, 275, 293, 310, 805, 820

Elwes, Sir Gervase, 132

Endicott, John, 386

Enghien, duke of. See Condé, The Great

Épernon, duc d'. See Nogaret de La Valette

Espinosa, Pedro de, 770

Essex, second earl of, 175, 230

Essex, third earl of, 132, 756

Este, Marie Beatrice Eleanor Anne Margaret Isabella d'. See Mary of Modena (queen of England)

Eugene (prince of Savoy), 528

Evelyn, John, 95, 256-258, 677, 996

Everard, William, 988

Faber, David. See Fabricius, David

Fabri de Peiresc, Nicolas-Claude. See Peiresc, Nicolas-Claude Fabri de

Fabricius, David, 259-261; solar gazing, 260; telescopes, 260

Fabricius, Johannes, 259-261; solar gazing, 260; telescopes, 260

Fabricius ab Aquapendente, Hieronumus, 355

Fabritius, Carel, 956

Fairfax, third Baron, 205, 261-265, 483, 605, 756, 986

Fairfax, Thomas. See Fairfax, third Baron

Fawkes, Guy, 16, 442

Fayette, Madame de La. See La Fayette, Madame de

Felipe III. See Philip III (king of Spain)

Felipe IV. See Philip IV (king of Spain)

Fénelon, François de Salignac de La Mothe-, 265-267, 339, 573

Ferdinand II (Holy Roman Emperor), 267-270, 293, 317, 627, 820, 854-855, 967

Ferdinand II de' Medici, 297, 881, 921

Ferdinand III (Holy Roman Emperor), 269, 526, 661, 705

Fermat, Pierre de, 271-274, 630, 970

Ferrar, Nicholas, 202, 274-277, 367

Filmer, Robert, 546

Finch, Anne. See Conway, Anne

Finch, Daniel. See Nottingham, second earl of

Flamsteed, John, 348, 371

Fletcher, Giles, the Younger, 278

Fletcher, John, 105, 277-280, 636, 846, 977; list of works, 278

Fletcher, Phineas, 278

Flores de Oliva, Isabel. See Rose of Lima, Saint

Fludd, Robert, 280-282, 629

Fontaine, Jean de La. See La Fontaine, Jean de

Fontana, Domenico, 67
Fontei, Nicol, 888
Ford, John, 279, 976
Ford, Philip, 726
Forman, Simon, 132
Fouquet, Nicolas, 180, 481, 523, 532, 622
Fowler, Katherine. *See* Philips, Katherine
Fox, George, 283-286, 726
Francis, Lord Russell, 767
Frederick I of Bohemia. *See* Frederick V
Frederick II, 415
Frederick V, 97, 143, 250, 253, 268, 275, 293-295, 310, 805, 820
Frederick Henry, 286-290, 619, 820, 933
Frederick William, the Great Elector, 154, 290-293, 851
Fremin, Jacques, 909
Frescobaldi, Girolamo, 295-297
Friedrich Wilhelm von Hohenzollern, Kurfürst von Brandenburg. *See* Frederick William, the Great Elector
Fritzius, Joachim, 281
Frontenac, comte de, 433, 490, 500, 603
Fulin. *See* Shunzhi
Furetière, Antoine, 480
Fyodor I Ivanovich, 683, 794, 943
Fyodor II, 865

Gabrieli, Giovanni, 825
Gagliano, Marco da, 297
Galigai, Leonora, 598
Galilei, Maria Celeste. *See* Maria Celeste
Galilei, Virginia. *See* Maria Celeste
Galileo, 298-301; and Giovanni Alfonso Borelli, 66; influence on Robert Boyle, 78; and Tommaso Campanella, 125; and René Descartes, 227; *Dialogue Concerning the Two Chief World Systems, Ptolemaic and Copernican*, 299; and Pierre Gassendi, 305; and Artemisia Gentileschi, 307; and William Harvey, 356; and Thomas Hobbes, 379; and Christiaan

Huygens, 397; and Johannes Kepler, 459; and daughter Maria Celeste, 593; tutor to Cosimo II de' Medici, 626; and Marin Mersenne, 630; and John Milton, 640; and Sir Isaac Newton, 680; censured by Pope Paul V, 721; and Nicolas-Claude Fabri de Peiresc, 722; and observations of planetary motion, 349; and Santorio Santorio, 811; and Nicolaus Steno, 881; observations of sunspots, 260; and telescopes, 539; and Evangelista Torricelli, 921; and Pope Urban VIII, 936
Garzoni, Giovanna, 302-304
Gassendi, Pierre, 211, 304-306, 389, 630, 723
Gaston (brother of Louis XIII), 551
Gellée, Claude. *See* Claude Lorrain
Gendret, Father Antoine de, 76
Gentileschi, Artemisia, 307-309
George I (king of England), 255
Ghazzati, Nathan, 836
Gibbons, Grinling, 996
Gibbons, Orlando, 309-311
Gifford, John, 100
Gilbert, William, 335
Godfrey, Sir Edmund Berry, 692
Godunov, Boris, 794, 855, 943
Goldsmid, Johann. *See* Fabricius, Johannes
Golitsyn, Vasily Vasilyevich, 624, 866
Gondi, Philippe-Emmanuel de, 962
Góngora y Argote, Luis de, 312-314, 949, 953
Good, Sarah, 690
Goodwin, Thomas, 198
Gorges, Sir Ferdinando, 875
Goring, George, 894
Gosson, Stephen, 374
Goupil, René, 423
Gournay, Marie le Jars de, 314-316
Graaf, Regnier de, 852, 898
Gracián, Baltasar. *See* Gracián y Morales, Baltasar
Gracián, Lorenzo. *See* Gracián y Morales, Baltasar
Gracián y Morales, Baltasar, 316-318

Grand Mademoiselle, La. *See* Montpensier, duchesse de
Great Condé. *See* Condé, The Great
Great Elector. *See* Frederick William, the Great Elector
Greco, El, 738
Green, Thomas, 92
Gregory, James, 319-321
Griffin, John, 54
Griggs, William, 690
Grimaldi, Francesco Maria, 134, 321-323
Grimmelshausen, Hans Jakob Christoffel von, 324-326; *Simplicissimus*, 324
Groot, Huig de. *See* Grotius, Hugo
Groseilliers, sieur des, 777
Grotius, Hugo, 17, 326-329, 723, 759; list of works, 328
Guarini, Guarino, 330-332
Guericke, Otto von, 79, 333-336, 814
Guillemeau, Charles, 74
Guo Xingye. *See* Zheng Chenggong
Gustav, Charles X. *See* Charles X Gustav
Gustavus II Adolphus, 163, 184, 254, 262, 269, 294, 336-339, 527, 704, 791, 854, 894, 925, 967
Guyart, Marie. *See* Marie de l'Incarnation
Guyon, Madame, 265, 339-341
Guzmán y Pimental, Gaspar de. *See* Olivares, count-duke of
Gwyn, Nell, 138, 240, 342-344

Haçi Halife. *See* Kâtib Çelebî
Hackston, David, 122
Hājī Khalīfa. *See* Kâtib Çelebî
Hale, Matthew, 345-348
Halifax, first marquis of. *See* Savile, Sir George
Halley, Edmond, 348-351, 371, 680
Hals, Frans, 352-354
Hamen y León, Juan van der, 1005
Hamilton, duke of, 345
Hampden, John, 144
Haoge, 234
Hardouin, Jules. *See* Mansart, Jules Hardouin-

Hardouin-Mansart, Jules. *See* Mansart, Jules Hardouin-

Harington, Lucy, 238

Haro, Luis de, 739

Harriot, Thomas, 970

Harrison, Thomas, 484

Harvey, William, 66, 280, 355-358, 543, 564, 579, 723, 811, 899, 986

Hechizado, El. *See* Charles II (king of Spain)

Hedong, Madame. *See* Liu Yin

Heemskerck, Jacob van, 930

Hein, Piet, 288, 359-361, 698

Heinricus Sagittarius. *See* Schütz, Heinrich

Helmont, Franciscus Mercurius van, 188, 251, 362

Helmont, Jan Baptista van, 361-363

Henrietta Anne, 72

Henrietta Maria, 364-366; Catholicism of, 496; and King Charles I of England, 144; and son King Charles II of England, 147; and the first earl of Clarendon, 168; and Abraham Cowley, 199; and Richard Crashaw, 202; and Lady Eleanor Davies, 221; and Sir Anthony van Dyck, 246; and son King James II of England, 416; and Richard Lovelace, 562; daughter of Marie de Médicis, 598; and naming of Maryland, 120; and the duke of Monmouth, 653; and the duchesse de Montpensier, 661; and the Netherlands, 288; and the duchess of Newcastle, 676; patronage, 846, 975; and Prince Rupert, 805; and the theater, 374; and Maarten Tromp, 931

Henry II de Bourbon. *See* Condé, third prince of

Henry IV (king of France), 111, 141, 315, 364, 551, 577, 587, 598, 737, 779, 790, 896

Henry, Frederick. *See* Frederick Henry

Henslowe, Philip, 223, 440, 977

Herbert, George, 17, 203, 232, 276, 366-368; list of works, 367

Herrera, Francisco, the Younger, 671

Herrera, Francisco de, the Elder, 1004

Herrick, Robert, 368-371, 443

Hevelius, Elisabetha, 371-373

Hevelius, Johannes, 348, 371-373

Hewel, Johann. *See* Hevelius, Johannes

Heywood, Thomas, 373-375, 977

Hinchingbrooke, Viscount. *See* Sandwich, first earl of

Hirayama Tōgo. *See* Ihara Saikaku

Hishikawa Moronobu, 375-377

Hobbes, Thomas, 147, 188, 300, 306, 357, 378-382, 543, 630, 676, 733, 759, 970; list of works, 380

Hobomok, 879

Hohenzollern, Friedrich Wilhelm von. *See* Frederick William, the Great Elector

Hōjō Ujimasa, 916

Holderness, earl of. *See* Rupert, Prince

Honami Kōetsu, 695, 868

Hong Taiji. *See* Abahai

Honthorst, Gerard, 823

Hooke, Robert, 48, 79, 349, 372, 383-385, 509, 564, 677, 680, 734, 986

Hooker, Richard, 15

Hooker, Thomas, 196, 247, 386-388, 567

Hoorn, Johan van, 852

Horne, Johannes van, 898

Horrocks, Jeremiah, 388-390

Horrox, Jeremiah. *See* Horrocks, Jeremiah

Hotta Masatoshi, 919

Ho-tung, Madame. *See* Liu Yin

Howard, Lady Frances, 16, 132

Howard, Sir Robert, 240, 765

Howe, Elizabeth, 690

Howelcke, Jan. *See* Hevelius, Johannes

Hsi-tsung. *See* Tianqi

Huai-tsung. *See* Chongzhen

Huaizong. *See* Chongzhen

Huang Yuan Jie, 541

Hudson, Henry, 390-393

Huet, Pierre-Daniel, 477, 661

Hung Taiji. *See* Abahai

Hunt, Thomas, 875

Hutchinson, Anne, 196-197, 247, 386, 394-396, 941, 992

Huygens, Christiaan, 135, 320, 323, 335, 371, 385, 397-400, 510, 514, 710; *Cosmotheoros*, 398

Huygens, Constantijn, 250, 397, 823

Hyde, Edward. *See* Clarendon, first earl of

Iberville, Pierre Le Moyne d', 401-403

İbrahim, 472, 670

Ihara Saikaku, 403-405; list of works, 404

Imagawa Yoshimoto, 915

Inés de la Cruz, Sor Juana. *See* Cruz, Sor Juana Inés de la

Ingle, Richard, 92

Ingoldsby, Richard, 519

Innocent X, 9, 68, 422, 773

Innocent XI, 405-407, 744, 882

Innocent XIII, 265

Ireton, Henry, 484, 756

Iskender Paşa, 855

Islam Giray III, 462

Isomura Yoshinori, 831

Israel, Manasseh ben. *See* Manasseh ben Israel

I-tsung. *See* Tianqi

Ivan V, 865

Ivan the Terrible, 943

Iwasa Matabe, 375

Izumo no Okuni, 408-409

Jahan, Shah. *See* Shah Jahan

Jahāngīr, 410-412, 842

Jai Singh, 859

James I (king of England), 413-416; and Lancelot Andrewes, 15; and William Bradford, 84; and the first duke of Buckingham, 96; and Richard Burbage, 105; and Robert Burton, 109; and George Calvert, 119; and Richard Cameron, 121; and Robert Carr, 131; and Charles I, 143; and Sir Edward Coke, 175; and Thomas Dekker, 223; and Sir Anthony van Dyck, 244; and John Eliot,

247; and Elizabeth of Bohemia, 250; and Elizabeth Stuart, 253; and Nicholas Ferrar, 274; and Frederick V, 293; and Orlando Gibbons, 309; and William Harvey, 355; and Jahāngīr, 412; and Inigo Jones, 436; and Ben Jonson, 442; and William Laud, 496; and Richard Lower, 565; and Thomas Middleton, 636; and Rory O'More, 699; and Paul V, 720; and Nicolas-Claude Fabri de Peiresc, 722; and Philip III, 737; and Pocahontas, 747; and Michael Romanov, 795; and Prince Rupert, 805; and Friedrich Hermann Schomberg, 820; and John Smith, 864; and Sir John Suckling, 893; and James Ussher, 939; and John Webster, 976

James II (king of England), 416-419; and Richard Baxter, 34; and John Bunyan, 102; and Thomas Burnet, 106; and Richard Cameron, 123; and Catherine of Braganza, 138; and John Dryden, 241; and George Fox, 285; and Nell Gwyn, 343; and Henrietta Maria, 364; and Innocent XI, 407; and the first duke of Leeds, 508; and Jacob Leisler, 518; and Leopold I, 528; and Mary II, 610; and Mary of Modena, 607; and the duke of Monmouth, 655; and Sir Isaac Newton, 681; and Titus Oates, 692; and William Paterson, 717; and William Penn, 725; and Samuel Pepys, 729; and Henry Purcell, 764; and Sir George Savile, 817; and Thomas Sydenham, 902; and Maarten and Cornelis Tromp, 931; and William III, 979

James VI (king of Scotland). See James I (king of England)

Jansen, Cornelius Otto, 419-422, 714, 773, 936

Janssen, Zacharias, 537

Jehangir. See Jahāngīr

Jinga. See Njinga

Jirgalang, 234

João IV. See John IV (king of Portugal)

Jogues, Saint Isaac, 423-424

Johann Georg I (elector of Saxony), 826

Johann Georg II (elector of Saxony), 827

John II Casimir Vasa, 154, 186, 428, 462, 624

John III Sobieski, 406, 427-430, 453, 528, 744

John IV (king of Portugal), 137, 425, 430-432, 960

John of Austria, 151, 425-427

John of Spain, the Younger, Don. See John of Austria

John the Fortunate. See John IV (king of Portugal)

John the Restorer. See John IV (king of Portugal)

Johnson, Aphra. See Behn, Aphra

Jolliet, Louis, 433-435, 490, 603

Jones, Inigo, 436-438, 442

Jonson, Ben, 52, 105, 167, 223, 232, 278-279, 368, 373, 436, 439-444, 649, 747, 846; list of works, 441

Juan de Austria, Don. See John of Austria

Jurieu, Pierre, 36

Kaihō Yūshō, 868

Kalckstein, Christian Ludwig von, 292

Kambun Kyōshi, 375

Kämpfer, Engelbert, 445-448; The History of Japan, 446

K'ang-hsi. See Kangxi

Kangxi, 448-451, 850

Kapici Bashi. See Shabbetai Tzevi

Kara Mustafa Paşa, Merzifonlu, 451-454, 528

Kâtib Çelebî, 454-456

Kawara Jūrōbei, 999

Ke, Madame, 161, 911

Keeper of the Gate. See Shabbetai Tzevi

Kempe, Will, 104

Kenzan. See Ogata Kenzan

Kepler, Johannes, 259, 281, 299, 305, 349, 357, 388, 457-461, 680, 818, 966

Ker (Kerr), Robert. See Carr, Robert

Khatib Chelebi. See Kâtib Çelebî

Khatib Shalabî. See Kâtib Çelebî

Khayronnesa Begum, 4

Khmelnytsky, Bohdan, 452, 461-463, 624

Khmelnytsky, Yurii, 452

Khovansky, Ivan, 866

Khurram. See Shah Jahan

Khusru, 410, 842

Kichibē. See Hishikawa Moronobu

Kidd, William, 464-467

Kilajua, 687

Killigrew, Thomas, 240, 342

King, Edmund, 565

Kino, Eusebio Francisco, 467-469

Kirkby, Christopher, 692

Kitagawa Sōtatsu. See Sōtatsu

Kober, Tobias, 60

Kōetsu. See Honami Kōetsu

Komenský, Jan, 469-471

Köprülü Mehmed Paşa, 451

Kōrin, Ogata. See Ogata Kōrin

Kösem Mahpeyker. See Kösem Sultan

Kösem Sultan, 472-474, 668

Kōwa, Seki. See Seki Kōwa

Koxinga. See Zheng Chenggong

Kōwa, Seki. See Seki Kōwa

Kühn, Eusebio Francesco. See Kino, Eusebio Francisco

Kuo Hsing-yeh. See Zheng Chenggong

Kusunoki Fuden, 998

Labadie, Jean de, 824

La Barre, sieur de, 491

La Bruyère, Jean de, 475-476; list of works, 476

Lacombe, François, 339

La Fayette, Comtesse de. See La Fayette, Madame de

La Fayette, Madame de, 72, 477-479, 487, 662, 833; The Princess of Clèves, 478

La Ferté-Sénectère, Henri, maréchal de, 494

La Fontaine, Jean de, 186, 480-483, 586, 773, 834; list of works, 481

Lalande, John, 424

Lalemant, Jerôme, 596

Lambert, John, 483-486, 651, 942

Lamberville, Jacques de, 909

La Motte, Jeanne-Marie Bouvier de. *See* Guyon, Madame

La Rochefoucauld, François de, 477, 487-489, 548, 662; *Maximes*, 488

La Sablière, Madame de, 482

La Salle, sieur de, 401, 435, 490-493

La Tour, Georges de, 493-495

La Tour d'Auvergne, Henri de. *See* Turenne, Viscount de

Laud, William, 145, 167, 197, 218, 247, 275, 345, 386, 495-498, 768, 887, 938, 982, 991

Lauderdale, first duke of, 507, 839

Lauzun, Antonin-Nompar de Caumont de, 662

Laval, François, 76, 498-501, 576

Laval-Montmorency, François-Xavier de. *See* Laval, François

La Valette, Nogaret de. *See* Nogaret de La Valette

La Vallière, Françoise-Louise de la Baume Le Blanc de, 586, 601

La Voisin, Madame. *See* Monvoisin, Madame

Lawes, Henry, 370, 502-503

Le Brun, Charles, 504-506, 523, 532

Le Brun, Nicolas, 504

Leeds, first duke of, 149, 506-508, 693, 816, 840

Leeuwenhoek, Antoni van, 399, 509-513, 898, 958; "Containing Some Microbial Observations, About Animals in the Scurf of the Teeth . . .", 511

Legate, Bartholomew, 16

Leibniz, Gottfried Wilhelm, 513-517; and Pierre Bayle, 37; dispute over invention of calculus, 49, 681; and Anne Conway, 188; and Elizabeth of Bohemia, 252; and Pierre de Fermat, 271; list of works, 514; and John Locke, 545; and Sir Isaac Newton, 681; and Seki Kōwa, 832; and Baruch Spinoza, 874; and John Wallis, 970; and Erhard Weigel, 759

Leicester, first earl of, 618

Leisler, Jacob, 518-520

Lemercier, Jacques, 523, 532, 589

Le Moyne, Pierre. *See* Iberville, Pierre Le Moyne d'

Lenclos, Anne de. *See* Lenclos, Ninon de

Lenclos, Ninon de, 520-522

Le Nôtre, André, 523-526, 532, 590

Leo XI, 720

León, Alonso de, 491

Leopold I, 40, 151, 406, 453, 526-529, 555

Leopold Ignatius. *See* Leopold I

Lerma, duke de, 530-532, 697, 736, 913

Le Tellier, François-Michel. *See* Louvois, marquis de

Le Tellier, Michel, 72, 180, 266, 558

Le Vau, Louis, 523, 532-534, 590

LeVeau, Louis. *See* Le Vau, Louis

Li Tzu-Ch'eng. *See* Li Zicheng

Li Zicheng, 161, 235, 849

Libavius, Andreas, 565

Lightfoot, James, 940

Lilburne, John, 534-536

Lionne, Hugues de, 622

Lippershey, Hans, 537-540

Lipsius, Justus, 314

Liu Shi. *See* Liu Yin

Liu Yin, 540-542

Locke, John, 37, 107, 306, 381, 516, 542-548, 564, 642, 761, 783, 840, 901; list of works, 546

Lodewijk, Willem, 618

Longueil, René de, 588

Longueville, duchesse de, 487, 548-550, 933

Lorrain, Claude. *See* Claude Lorrain

Louis II de Bourbon. *See* Condé, The Great

Louis XIII, 18, 126, 141, 144, 158, 184, 193, 211, 493, 532, 551-553, 585, 627, 660, 897; and architecture, 587; arts patronage, 118, 523; and Louyse Bourgeois, 74; and Catalonia, 425; support of exiled Hugo Grotius, 327; and Henrietta Maria, 364; and the duchesse de Longueville, 548; and Louis XIV, 554; and François de Malherbe, 578; and mother Marie de Médicis, 598; and Jules Mazarin, 621; and

Francisco Gómez de Quevedo y Villegas, 771; and Cardinal de Richelieu, 790; and Saint Vincent de Paul, 962

Louis XIV, 158, 487, 554-557; Anne of Austria as regent for, 19, 660; and architecture, 533, 590; arts patronage, 46, 750; ascension, 425, 585; and Nicolas Boileau-Despréaux, 63; and Jacques-Bénigne Bossuet, 70; and Saint Marguerite Bourgeoys, 77; Canadian settlement, 499; and Catherine of Braganza, 137; and Queen Christina, 165; and Jean-Baptiste Colbert, 180; and the Great Condé, 185; and Cyrano de Bergerac, 212; and England, 149; financial crises, 475; France as world power, 464; and Frederick William, the Great Elector, 291; French Royal Academy of Sciences, 710; and the Fronde, 549; vs. the Huguenots, 518; support of Christiaan Huygens, 398; opposition to Pope Innocent XI, 406; opposition to Jansenism, 22, 422; and John III Sobieski, 429; and Jean de La Fontaine, 481; and François Laval, 499; and the first duke of Leeds, 507; and Gottfried Wilhelm Leibniz, 514; and Ninon de Lenclos, 521; and André Le Nôtre, 523; and Leopold I, 527; and Louis XIII, 551; Louisiana colony, 402; and the marquis de Louvois, 558; marriage to Marie-Thérèse, 601; and Mary of Modena, 608; and Jules Mazarin, 621; and Molière, 647; and music at court, 764; opposition to mysticism, 340; attack on the Spanish Netherlands, 151; and the Papacy, 10; Partition Treaties, 547; and Charles Perrault, 731; and Philip IV, 738; and Elena Cornaro Piscopia, 744; and Jean Racine, 773; and Cardinal de Richelieu, 792; and Sir George Savile, 816; and Friedrich

Hermann Schomberg, 821; and Madeleine de Scudéry, 829; and Spain, 151; Treaty of Dover (1670), 693; and Viscount de Turenne, 933; and Sébastien Le Prestre de Vauban, 946; and Diego Velázquez, 955; and William III, 979

Louis the Great. *See* Louis XIV

Louis the Just. *See* Louis XIII

Louvois, marquis de, 182, 186, 555, 558-561, 622

Love, Christopher, 345

Lovelace, Richard, 443, 503, 562-564

Lower, Richard, 564-566, 986

Lucas, Margaret. *See* Newcastle, duchess of

Ludlow, Roger, 567-569

Lulli, Giovanni Battista. *See* Lully, Jean-Baptiste

Lully, Jean-Baptiste, 482, 554, 569-571

Madeleine de Scudéry. *See* Scudéry, Madeleine de

Maderno, Carlo, 67

Maguire, Connor, Lord, 700

Mahabat Khan, 411

Maintenon, Madame de, 266, 340, 572-574, 602, 775

Maisonneuve, sieur de, 76, 574-576

Maitland, John. *See* Lauderdale, first duke of

Malebranche, Nicolas de, 252, 514

Malherbe, François de, 315, 480, 577-579, 779

Malpighi, Marcello, 66, 510, 579-582, 899

Malvasia, Carlo Cesare, 856

Mamanatowick. *See* Powhatan

Manasseh ben Israel, 582-584

Mance, Jeanne, 76, 575

Mancini, Victoria. *See* Mancini, Laura

Mancini sisters, 585-587; Hortense, 585; Laura, 585; Marie, 19, 585; Marie-Anne, 585; Olympia, 585

Mander, Karel van, 352

Manggultai (Jin prince), 1

Mangopeomen. *See* Opechancanough

Manoel Dias Soeiro. *See* Manasseh ben Israel

Mansart, François, 523, 573, 587-590

Mansart, Jules Hardouin-, 533, 589-593

Mansfeld, Peter Ernst, 98

Marbury, Anne. *See* Hutchinson, Anne

Margaret of Austria, 18, 737

Margaret Theresa. *See* Marie-Thérèse

Maria Anna of Bavaria-Neuburg, 152

Maria Celeste, 593-595

Maria Magdalena of Austria, 627

María Teresa de Austria. *See* Marie-Thérèse

Maria Theresa of Spain. *See* Marie-Thérèse

Mariana de Austria, 151, 426

Marie Casimire de la Grange d'Arquien. *See* Marysieńka

Marie de l'Incarnation, 595-597

Marie de Médicis, 598-600; and Anne of Austria, 18; and Louyse Bourgeois, 74; and Francesca Caccini, 111; and daughter Henrietta Maria, 364; marriage to Henry IV, 551; and François de Malherbe, 578; and Nicolas Poussin, 749; and Cardinal de Richelieu, 790

Marie Louise (queen of Poland), 428

Marie Louise (queen of Spain), 151

Marie-Thérèse, 19, 151, 572, 585, 600-602, 622, 662

Marillac, Louise de, 963

Marini, Giambattista, 202, 749

Marlones, García de. *See* Gracián y Morales, Baltasar

Marquette, Jacques, 433, 603-605

Marsillac, Prince de. *See* La Rochefoucauld, François de

Marston, John, 105, 223, 441, 976

Martin, Susannah, 690

Marubashi Chūya, 999

Marvell, Andrew, 232, 563, 605-607; list of works, 605

Mary II (queen of England), 138, 169, 284, 508, 608, 610-612,

817, 821, 979; American colonists reaction to her enthronement, 518

Mary of Modena (queen of England), 138, 417, 607-610, 839

Mary of the Incarnation. *See* Marie de l'Incarnation

Marysieńka, 429

Masaniello, 425

Massasoit, 86, 129, 249, 612-614, 633, 876, 878

Massatamohtnock. *See* Opechancanough

Massinger, Philip, 279, 846

Matoaka. *See* Pocahontas

Matsudaira Hirotada, 915

Matsudaira Nobutsuna, 999

Matsudaira Takechiyo. *See* Tokugawa Ieyasu

Matsuo Bashō, 403, 615-617; list of works, 616

Matsuo Kinsaku. *See* Matsuo Bashō

Matsuo Munefusa. *See* Matsuo Bashō

Matthiae, John, 163

Matthias (Holy Roman Emperor), 737, 966

Matveyev, Artamon Sergeyevich, 13

Maucroix, François, 480

Maurice of Nassau, 286, 326, 337, 538, 618-620, 924, 933

Maurits van Nassau. *See* Maurice of Nassau

Maximilian I (elector of Bavaria), 268, 293

Maynard, François, 578

Maypeyker Sultan. *See* Kösem Sultan

Mazarin, duchesse de. *See* Mancini, Hortense

Mazarin, Jules, 9, 620-624; and Anne of Austria, 19; architecture, 532; arts patronage, 504; and the duchesse de Chevreuse, 158; and Queen Christina, 165; and Jean-Baptiste Colbert, 180; and the Great Condé, 185; Council of Conscience, 963; and Cyrano de Bergerac, 212; and the Fronde, 549; and Guarino Guarini, 331;

opposition to Jansenism, 421; and François de La Rochefoucauld, 487; and the duchesse de Longueville, 549; and Louis XIV, 554; uncle of the Mancini sisters, 585; and Marie-Thérèse, 601; and the duchesse de Montpensier, 660; and music, 570; and Peiresc's letters, 723; and Cardinal de Richelieu, 792; and Sweden, 706; and Viscount de Turenne, 933

Mazarini, Giulio. *See* Mazarin, Jules

Mazepa, Ivan Stepanovich, 624-626

Mbande, 687

Mead, William, 725

Meara, Edmund, 564

Medici, Cosimo II de', 112, 118, 307, 593, 626-628

Medici, Cosimo III de', 857, 882

Médicis, Marie de. *See* Marie de Médicis

Mehmed IV, 451, 472

Ménage, Gilles, 833

Menshikov, Aleksander, 625

Mercoeur, duchesse de. *See* Mancini, Laura

Mersenne, Marin, 281, 305, 628-632, 722

Mertola, count of. *See* Schomberg, Friedrich Hermann

Metacom, 249, 612, 633-635, 876

Mézy, chevalier de, 500

Miantonomo, 129

Michael. *See* Romanov, Michael

Michal Wiśniowiecki, 429

Middlesex, first earl of. *See* Cranfield, Lionel

Middleton, Thomas, 224, 279, 636-638, 846, 928, 977; list of works, 637

Mignard, Pierre, 505

Mikhail Skopin-Shuysky, 944

Mikhailovich, Aleksei. *See* Alexis

Milborne, Jacob, 519

Miloslavsky, Ilya, 664

Milton, John, 109, 201, 300, 502, 605, 639-643, 942; list of works, 641

Minin, Nikita. *See* Nikon

Minnewit, Peter. *See* Minuit, Peter

Minuit, Peter, 643-646, 706

Mniszech, Jerzy, 855

Molière, 19, 186, 212, 305, 482, 487, 521, 524, 554, 570, 646-649, 662, 774; list of works, 648

Molina, Tirso de. *See* Tirso de Molina

Molinos, Miguel de, 340, 406

Moller, Martin, 59

Monaldeschi, Gian Rinaldo, 165

Monck, George, 57, 137, 148, 206, 485, 650-653, 758, 806, 838, 931, 942

Monk, George. *See* Monck, George

Monmouth, duke of, 122, 149, 241, 417, 545, 653-656, 693, 816

Montagu, Charles, 717

Montagu, Edward. *See* Sandwich, first earl of

Montecuccoli, Raimundo, 527, 934

Montespan, Madame de, 572, 590, 601

Monteverdi, Claudio, 296, 656-660, 826

Montpensier, Anne-Marie-Louise d'Orléans, duchesse de. *See* Montpensier, duchesse de

Montpensier, duchesse de, 477, 569, 660-663

Montrose, James Graham, marquess of, 147

Monvoisin, Madame, 586

Moore, Roger. *See* O'More, Rory

Moore, Rory. *See* O'More, Rory

Morales, Baltasar Gracián y. *See* Gracián y Morales, Baltasar

More, Henry, 187, 252

More, Rory. *See* O'More, Rory

Mōri Shigeyoshi, 831

Moritz of Hessen-Kassel, 825

Moronobu, Hishikawa. *See* Hishikawa Moronobu

Morozov, Boris Ivanovich, 11, 663-665

Mortemart, Françoise-Athénaïs, Rochechouart de. *See* Montespan, Madame de

Morton, Thomas, 232, 879

Mothe-Fénelon, François de La. *See* Fénelon, François de Salignac de La Mothe-

Motteville, Françoise Bertaut de, 662

Mountfort, William, 82

Muggleton, Lodowick, 665-667

Muhī-ud-Dīn Muhammad Aurangzeb. *See* Aurangzeb

Mukai Kyorai, 616

Mullins, Priscilla, 7

Mumtaz Mahal, 842

Murad (governor of Gujarat), 844

Murad (Mughal prince), 24

Murad IV, 451, 454, 472, 668-670, 674

Murad Oglu Ahmed I. *See* Murad IV

Murillo, Bartolomé Esteban, 670-672, 1005

Muse's Hannibal, The. *See* Cowley, Abraham

Mustafa I, 472, 668, 673-675

Mustafa ibn 'abd Allāh. *See* Kâtib Çelebî

Nāder Shāh, 4

Napier, John, 818

Naryshkina, Natalya Kirillovna, 13

Nashe, Thomas, 440

Nassau, count of. *See* Frederick Henry

Nassau, Maurice of. *See* Maurice of Nassau

Necotawance, 703

Nenemattanaw, 702

Neri, Philip, 721

Newcastle, duchess of, 676-678

Newcomen, Thomas, 814

Newport, Christopher, 754

Newton, Sir Isaac, 37, 49, 66, 79, 107, 271, 306, 319, 323, 349, 385, 390, 398, 459, 515, 547, 679-682, 734, 832, 970, 994; list of works, 681

Nicholson, Francis, 518

Nicole, Pierre, 774

Nicolet, Jean, 433

Nicolls, Richard, 892

Nikon, 13, 27, 683-686

Njinga, 687-689

Nogaret de La Valette, 598

Nonomura Sōtatsu. *See* Sōtatsu

Nord, Le. *See* Colbert, Jean-Baptiste

Nôtre, André Le. *See* Le Nôtre, André

Nottingham, second earl of, 508

Noy, William, 345
Nozawa Bonchō, 616
Nūr Jahān, 411, 842
Nurhaci, 1, 234, 848, 911
Nurse, Rebecca, 689-691
Nye, Philip, 198
Nzinga. *See* Njinga

Oates, Titus, 138, 149, 692-695,
816, 839
Oboi, 448
Oda Nobuhide, 915
Oda Nobunaga, 915
Odescalchi, Benedetto. *See*
Innocent XI
Ogata Kenzan, 377, 695, 868
Ogata Kōrin, 377, 695-697, 868
Ogilby, John, 846
Okuni. *See* Izumo no Okuni
Oldcastle, Sir John, 238
Oldenbarnevelt, Johan van, 288,
326, 618
Oldham, John, 130
Olivares, count-duke of, 317, 431,
697-699, 739, 770, 914, 953
O'More, Rory, 699-701
O'Neill, Owen Roe, 700
O'Neill, Sir Phelim, 700
Oninga. *See* Radisson, Pierre Esprit
Opachisco, 747
Opechancanough, 702-704, 752
Opitchapan, 702, 752
Oquendo, Antonio de, 288
Orange, prince of. *See* Frederick
Henry; Maurice of Nassau
Orange, William of. *See* William III
(king of England)
Orinda. *See* Philips, Katherine
Orléans, Anne-Marie-Louise d'. *See*
Montpensier, duchesse de
Orléans, Gaston d', 598, 660
Ormond, first duke of, 507
Osborne, Thomas. *See* Leeds, first
duke of
Osburn, Sarah, 690
Osman II, 472, 674, 855
Osuna, duke of, 770
Ottaniack. *See* Powhatan
Ottoboni, Pietro, 190
Ousamequin. *See* Massasoit
Overbury, Sir Thomas, 132
Overton, Richard, 535

Owen, Anne, 742
Oxenstierna, Axel, 153, 163, 328,
337, 704-707

Pacheco, Francisco, 953, 1003
Pachelbel, Johann, 708-710
Palatine of the Rhine, count. *See*
Rupert, Prince
Palmer, Barbara Villiers. *See*
Castlemaine, countess of
Papin, Denis, 710-713, 814
Parigi, Giulio, 627
Parr, Thomas, 357
Parris, Elizabeth, 690
Parris, Samuel, 689
Parviz, 842
Paşa, Merzifonlu Kara Mustafa. *See*
Kara Mustafa Paşa, Merzifonlu
Pascal, Blaise, 37, 271, 422, 487,
514, 632, 713-716, 819, 923
Paterson, William, 716-719
Paul, Saint Vincent de. *See* Vincent
de Paul, Saint
Paul IV, 330
Paul V, 45, 67, 719-721, 810, 936,
962
Peacham, Edmund, 176
Peiresc, Nicolas-Claude Fabri de,
304, 577, 722-724
Pellisson, Paul, 480
Peltrie, Madame de la, 575, 596
Penn, William, 57, 252, 724-728
Pepys, Samuel, 51, 342, 349, 677,
728-731, 971
Peri, Jacopo, 658
Perrault, Charles, 64, 533, 731-733;
"Little Tom Thumb," 732
Perrier, François, 504
Peter, Czar (pretender), 944
Peter II (king of Portugal), 821
Peter the Great, 13, 445, 625, 685,
795, 865
Petrovich, Avvakum. *See* Avvakum
Petrovich
Petty, Sir William, 564, 733-735
Philaret, 663, 794, 944
Philip, King. *See* Metacom
Philip I (king of Portugal). *See*
Philip II (king of Spain)
Philip II (king of Spain), 431
Philip III (king of Spain), 736-738,
959; and daughter Anne of

Austria, 18; decline of Habsburg
Spain, 425; and the duke de
Lerma, 530; and Count-Duke of
Olivares, 697; and son Philip IV,
738, 770; and Tirso de Molina,
913
Philip IV (king of Spain), 138, 551,
738-741; and Anne of Austria,
19; arts patronage, 307;
ascension, 770; and Pedro
Calderón de la Barca, 113; and
son Charles II (of Spain), 151;
Queen Christina's conversion to
Catholicism, 165; and Elizabeth
de Médicis, 598; and John IV,
431; and son John of Austria,
425; and Marie-Thérèse, 585,
600; and Jules Mazarin, 622; and
Cosimo II de' Medici, 627; and
the duchesse de Montpensier,
661; and the count-duke of
Olivares, 697; opposition to
intellectuals, 913; and father
Philip III, 738; and Diego
Velázquez, 953; and Francisco
de Zurbarán, 1005
Philip V (king of Spain), 152
Philip of Anjou. *See* Philip V (king
of Spain)
Philip of Poakanoket. *See* Metacom
Philip the Pious. *See* Philip III (king
of Spain)
Philips, Frederick, 519
Philips, Katherine, 741-743
Pierron, Jean, 909
Pinelli, Jean-Vincent, 722
Pioche de la Vergne, Marie-
Madeleine. *See* La Fayette,
Madame de
Piscopia, Elena Cornaro, 743-745
Plessis, Armand-Jean du. *See*
Richelieu, Cardinal de
Pocahontas, 702, 745-748, 753, 862-
863
Popham, Edward, 56
Poquelin, Jean-Baptiste. *See*
Molière
Porter, Endymion, 563
Possevino, Antonio, 855
Poussin, Nicolas, 171, 303, 749-752
Powhatan, 702, 745, 752-756, 862-
863

Pozzo, Cassiano del, 749
Pride, Thomas, 205, 651, 692, 756-758
Prynne, William, 497
Pufendorf, Samuel von, 545, 759-762
Purcell, Henry, 311, 763-766
Putnam, Ann, 690
Pym, John, 167, 767-769, 886, 941

Qian Chen Qun, 156
Qian Feng, 156
Qian Jie, 156
Qian Long Guang, 156
Qian Qian Yi, 540
Qian Rui Cheng, 156
Qian Zeng, 541
Qianlong, 236
Qing Taizong. See Abahai
Quadequina, 876
Quevedo y Villegas, Francisco Gómez de, 312, 770-772
Quinault, Philippe, 570

Rabutin-Chantal, Marie de. See Sévigné, Madame de
Racine, Jean, 64, 72, 186, 194-195, 482, 554, 573, 773-776; list of works, 775
Radisson, Pierre Esprit, 777-779
Raffaelli, Francesca. See Caccini, Francesca
Raffaelli, Tomaso, 112
Ralegh, Sir Walter, 132, 175, 230, 414
Rambouillet, Julie-Lucine de, 780
Rambouillet, Marquise de, 779-781
Ramírez de Santillana, Juana Inés de Asbaje y. See Cruz, Sor Juana Inés de la
Randolph, Thomas, 443
Rangoni, Claudio, 855
Ranuzzi, Annibale, 857
Ravaillac, François, 598
Ray, John, 29, 782-784
Raymbault, Charles, 423
Razin, Stenka, 12, 784-786
Reeve, John, 666
Reeve, William, 665
Rembrandt, 117, 353, 583, 786-789, 956
Rensselaer, Nicholas van, 518

Rhodes, John, 51
Rians, Claude Fabri de, 723
Ribera, Jusepe, 1005
Riccioli, Giambattista, 322
Rich, Christopher, 52, 83
Richelieu, Cardinal de, 141, 184, 315, 470, 487, 521, 660, 780, 790-793; and regency of Anne of Austria, 18; arts patronage, 193, 750; and Tommaso Campanella, 126; and the duchesse de Chevreuse, 158; and Frederick Henry, 287; and Cornelius Otto Jansen, 420; and reign of Louis XIII, 552; and Marie de Médicis, 599; and Jules Mazarin, 620; and alliance with Protestant forces, 937; and Friedrich Hermann Schomberg, 820; science patronage, 305; and reforms of the duke de Sully, 897; and Sweden, 706
Richter, Gregorius, 60
Rijn, Rembrandt van. See Rembrandt
Rinuccini, Ottavio, 111, 658
Riva, Giovanni Guglielmo, 565
Rivet, André, 824
Rivinus, 783
Roberval, Gilles Personne de, 922
Robins, John, 666
Robinson, John, 84
Rochester, Viscount. See Carr, Robert
Roestraten, Pieter, 352
Rogni, Giacomo, 302
Rohan, Marie de. See Chevreuse, duchesse de
Rolfe, John, 702, 746, 754, 863
Romanov, Aleksei Mikhailovich. See Alexis
Romanov, Fyodor Nikitich, 794. See also Philaret
Romanov, Michael, 11, 337, 663, 794-796, 945
Rømer, Olaus, 135
Rosa de Santa Maria. See Rose of Lima, Saint
Rose of Lima, Saint, 796-798
Rosny, marquis de. See Sully, duke de
Rosseter, Philip, 127

Rostand, Edmond, 211
Roth, Hieronymus, 292
Rowlandson, Mary White, 798-801
Rowley, William, 636, 977
Rubens, Peter Paul, 244, 302, 352, 438, 599, 657, 671, 723, 802-804, 955, 1005
Rudbeck, Olaf, 445
Rudolf II (Holy Roman Emperor), 459
Rupert, Prince, 56, 255, 262, 777, 805-807, 815
Russell, Lucy. See Harington, Lucy
Ruyter, Michiel Adriaanszoon de, 57, 807-809, 931

Sabbatai Sevi. See Shabbetai Tzevi
Sabbetai Zevi. See Shabbetai Tzevi
Sablé, marquise de, 487
Saffray, Augustin de. See Mézy, chevalier de
Saikaku, Ihara. See Ihara Saikaku
Saint-Denis, Charles de Marguetel de, 521
Saint-Étienne, sieur de, 520
Saint-Evremond. See Saint-Denis, Charles de Marguetel de
Saint Lusson, sieur de, 433
Saint-Vallier, Jean-Baptiste de, 77
Salignac de La Mothe-Fénelon, François de. See Fénelon, François de Salignac de La Mothe-
Salīm. See Jahāngīr
Salisbury, first earl of, 132, 414
Sam Mīrzā. See Shāh Safi I
Sambhājī, 25
Samoilovych, Ivan, 624
Samoset, 86, 612, 876
Sanctorius, Sanctorius. See Santorio, Santorio
Sandoval y Rojas, Francisco Gómez de. See Lerma, duke de
Sandwich, first earl of, 57, 728
Santillana, Juana Inés de Asbaje y Ramírez de. See Cruz, Sor Juana Inés de la
Santorio, Santorio, 810-813
Sarotti, Ambrose, 711
Sarpi, Paolo, 720, 810
Sassamon, John, 634
Saunderson, Mary, 51, 82

Savelli, Giulia, 780
Savery, Thomas, 712, 813-815
Savile, Sir George, 815-817
Scarron, Françoise. *See* Maintenon, Madame de
Scarron, Paul, 521, 780
Schall, Adam, 448
Schall von Bell, Johann Adam, 849
Scheiner, Christoph, 260
Schickard, Wilhelm, 818-820; on calculators, 819
Schomberg, Friedrich Hermann, 426, 820-822
Schrader, Justus, 899
Schurman, Anna Maria van, 823-825
Schütz, Heinrich, 825-828
Schwarzenberg, Adam von, 290
Scott, James. *See* Monmouth, duke of
Scudéry, Madame de. *See* Scudéry, Madeleine de
Scudéry, Madeleine de, 477, 487, 662, 828-830
Scultetus, Johannes, 566
Segrais. *See* La Fayette, Madame de
Segrais, Jean Regnault de, 477, 661
Séguie, Pierre, 504
Segura, Juan Bautista de, 702
Seki Kōwa, 831-833
Seki Takakazu. *See* Seki Kōwa
Selim Giray I, 452
Selkirk, Alexander, 216
Sévigné, Madame de, 183, 477, 487, 521, 661-662, 829, 833-835
Sévigné, Marie de. *See* Sévigné, Madame de
Shabbetai Tzevi, 835-837
Shadwell, Thomas, 384
Shaftesbury, first earl of, 149, 507, 544, 654, 693, 806, 816, 838-841; list of works, 839
Shah Jahan, 23, 411, 842-845
Shāh Safi I, 5
Shahryar, 411, 842
Shaista Khan, 859
Shakespeare, William, 104, 278, 440, 637, 639
Shaklovity, Fyodor, 866
Sharp, James, 122
Sheldon, Gilbert, 986
Shelton, Thomas, 729

Shepard, Thomas, 395
Shirley, James, 279, 846-848
Shivaji. *See* Śivājī
Shōsetsu, Yui. *See* Yui Shōsetsu
Shujah, 23, 844
Shun-chih. *See* Shunzhi
Shunzhi, 3, 234, 448, 848-850
Shuysky, Prince Vasily. *See* Vasily Shuysky
Siegemundin, Justine, 851-853
Sigismund III Vasa, 336, 853-856, 945
Signorini, Francesca. *See* Caccini, Francesca
Signorini, Giovanni Battista, 112
Signorini-Malaspina, Francesca. *See* Caccini, Francesca
Sirani, Elisabetta, 856-858
Sirtori, Girolamo, 537
Sirturus, Hieronymus. *See* Sirtori, Girolamo
Śivājī, 25, 858-861
Sloane, Sir Hans, 447
Sloughter, Henry, 519
Smith, John, 391, 702, 745, 753, 861-865, 875
Sobieski, Jan. *See* John III Sobieski
Socinus, Faustus, 54
Sofya Alekseyevna. *See* Sophia
Soissons, comtesse de. *See* Mancini, Olympia
Soltān Moḥammad Shāh, 4
Somerset, earl of. *See* Carr, Robert
Sophia, 445, 624, 865-867
Sor Juana. *See* Cruz, Sor Juana Inés de la
Sōtatsu, 695, 868-870
Souvré, Madeleine de. *See* Sablé, marquise de
Sozzini, Fausto Paolo. *See* Socinus, Faustus
Sparre, Ebba, 164
Spilbergen, Joris van, 797
Spínola, Ambrosio de, 294, 619
Spinoza, Baruch, 37, 188, 515, 871-875; list of works, 872
Squanto, 86, 612, 875-877, 879
Ssu-tsung. *See* Chongzhen
Standish, Miles, 7, 86, 614, 877-880
Stayner, Sir Richard, 57
Steensen, Niels. *See* Steno, Nicolaus
Steno, Nicolaus, 881-883

Stevin, Simon, 619
Stone, Samuel, 386
Strafford, first earl of, 145, 167, 345, 768, 884-887, 895, 941
Striggio, Alexander, the Younger, 658
Strozzi, Barbara, 888-890
Strozzi, Giulio, 888
Stuart, Elizabeth. *See* Elizabeth Stuart
Stuart, James. *See* James I (king of England)
Stuart, Mary. *See* Mary II (queen of England)
Stuyvesant, Peter, 518, 645, 890-893
Suckling, Sir John, 503, 893-895
Süleyman II, 472
Sully, duke de, 896-898
Sultan, Kösem. *See* Kösem Sultan
Sun King. *See* Louis XIV
Susanna. *See* Sophia
Swammerdam, Jan, 362, 510, 898-900
Sydenham, Thomas, 901-904
Sylvius, Franciscus. *See* Deleboe, Franz

Tagaskouita, Catherine. *See* Tekakwitha, Kateri
Tagen Sufu, 915
T'ai Ch'iang. *See* Taichang
Taichang, 911
Takebe Katahiro, 832
Takebe Katakira, 832
Talbot, Richard, 821
Talcott, Mary White Rowlandson. *See* Rowlandson, Mary White
Talon, Jean-Baptiste, 433
Tasman, Abel Janszoon, 905-908
Tawaraya Sōtatsu. *See* Sōtatsu
Taylor, Jeremy, 741
Tegakwith. *See* Tekakwitha, Kateri
Tekakwitha, Kateri, 908-910
Téllez, Gabriel. *See* Tirso de Molina
Tempesta, Antonio, 116
Temple, Sir William, 507
Theotokópoulos, Doménikos. *See* Greco, El
Thérèse, Marie-. *See* Marie-Thérèse
Thévenot, Melchisedec, 898
Thököly, Imre, 453

Thomassin, Philippe, 116
Thorpe, George, 702
Tiancong. *See* Abahai
Tianqi, 160, 911-912
T'ien-ch'i. *See* Tianqi
T'ien-ts'ung. *See* Abahai
Tilly, count of (Johan Tserclaes), 294, 333, 337, 894, 966
Tirso de Molina, 114, 913-915, 952
Tisquantum. *See* Squanto
Tituba, 690
Tofukumon-in, 695
Tokugawa Hidetada, 917, 998
Tokugawa Iemitsu, 917, 919, 998
Tokugawa Ienobu, 831, 920
Tokugawa Ietsuna, 831, 919, 999
Tokugawa Ieyasu, 408, 915-918, 998
Tokugawa Tsunashige, 831
Tokugawa Tsunayoshi, 831, 919-920
Tokugawa Yorinobu, 999
Tokugawa Yoshimune, 920
Tonge, Israel, 692
Tonty, Henry de, 490
Torricelli, Evangelista, 65, 333, 921-924
Torrington, earl of. *See* Monck, George
Torstenson, Lennart, 153, 924-927
Touchet, Eleanor. *See* Davies, Lady Eleanor
Tour, Georges de La. *See* La Tour, Georges de
Tournefort, Joseph Pitton de, 783
Tourneur, Cyril, 928-930
Towne, Rebecca. *See* Nurse, Rebecca
Toyotomi Hideyoshi, 916
Tromp, Cornelis, 930-932
Tromp, Maarten, 57, 288, 619, 808, 930-932
Tserclaes, Johan. *See* Tilly, count of (Johan Tserclaes)
Tsunayoshi, Tokugawa. *See* Tokugawa Tsunayoshi
Turenne, Viscount de, 184, 416, 425, 549, 558, 820, 933-935
Turhan, 472
Turner, Anne, 132
Tymish, 463

Tyrconnel, duke of. *See* Talbot, Richard
Tzevi, Shabbetai. *See* Shabbetai Tzevi

Uncas, 130
Underhill, John, 892
Urban VIII, 9, 45, 68, 126, 405, 421, 424, 620, 722, 792, 936-938
Ussher, James, 35, 53, 938-940

Vair, Guillaume du, 577
Valence, Palamede de Fabri de, 723
Valle, Barbara. *See* Strozzi, Barbara
Van Delft, Jan. *See* Vermeer, Jan
Van der Meer, Jan. *See* Vermeer, Jan
Van Dijck, Anthonie (Anton, Antonie, Antoon). *See* Dyck, Sir Anthony van
Van Rijn, Rembrandt. *See* Rembrandt
Van Schurman, Anna Maria. *See* Schurman, Anna Maria van
Vanbrugh, Sir John, 52
Vane, Sir Henry, the Younger, 57, 395, 941-943
Vasile, 463
Vasily Ivanovich. *See* Vasily Shuysky
Vasily Shuysky, 855, 943-945
Vauban, Sébastien Le Prestre de, 559, 946-948
Vaugelas, seigneur de, 780
Vaughan, Henry, 741
Veen, Otto van, 802
Vega Carpio, Lope de, 113, 279, 312, 738, 914, 949-952; list of works, 951
Velázquez, Diego, 160, 671, 739, 953-956, 1003
Vere, Sir Francis, 928
Vere, Sir Horace, 261
Vergne, Mademoiselle de la. *See* La Fayette, Madame de
Vergne, Marie Madeleine Pioche de la, 487
Vermeer, Jan, 353, 511, 956-959
Vieira, António, 959-961
Villamena, Francesco, 116
Villanueva, Pedro Díaz de, 1003

Villegas, Francisco Gómez de Quevedo y. *See* Quevedo y Villegas, Francisco Gómez de
Villiers, George. *See* Buckingham, duke of (first and second)
Vincent, Thomas, 894
Vincent de Paul, Saint, 962-965
Visscher, Ann Roemers, 824
Visscher, Frans Jacobsz, 906
Viviani, Vicenzo, 921
Vivonne-Savelli, Catherine de. *See* Rambouillet, Marquise de
Voet, Gijsbert. *See* Voetius, Gisbertus
Voetius, Gisbertus, 824
Voiture, Vincent, 780
Voltaire, 521
Vonifatiev, Stephen, 27, 683
Vouet, Simon, 523

Waban, 248
Wahunsenacawh. *See* Powhatan
Wallenstein, Albrecht Wenzel von, 269, 290, 337, 460, 966-969
Wallis, John, 564, 969-971
Walther, Bathasar, 60
Walwyn, William, 535
Wamsutta, 614, 633
Wang Fu-chih. *See* Wang Fuzhi
Wang Fuzhi, 972-974
Ward, Mary, 974-976
Waters, Frank, 614
Webster, John, 132, 279, 636, 846, 976-978; list of works, 977
Wei Chong-hsien. *See* Wei Zhongxian
Wei Zhongxian, 161, 911
Wentworth, Thomas. *See* Strafford, first earl of
Wenzel von Wallenstein, Albrecht. *See* Wallenstein, Albrecht Wenzel von
Weymouth, George, 875
Wheelwright, John, 386, 395
Whitaker, Alexander, 746
White, Mary. *See* Rowlandson, Mary White
Whitgift, John, 939
Wildes, Sarah, 690
William I (stadtholder of the Netherlands). *See* William the Silent

William III (king of England), 138, 149, 608, 610, 718, 808, 816, 979-982; aided against James II by Brandenburg, 821; American colonists reaction to his enthronement, 518; and chaplain Thomas Burnet, 106; and English theater, 83; and Holy Roman Empire, 526; and James II, 418; and the first duke of Leeds, 507; First Treaty of Partition (1698), 152; and Quakers, 284; support of Pope Innocent XI against France, 407

William of Orange. *See* William III (king of England)

William the Silent, 286, 618, 933

Williams, Abigail, 690

Williams, John, 275

Williams, Roger, 130, 197, 612, 941, 982-985, 992

Willis, Thomas, 362, 564, 985-988

Willoughby, Anne, 894

Willughby, Francis, 782

Winslow, Edward, 86

Winstanley, Gerrard, 988-990

Winter King. *See* Frederick V

Winthrop, John (1588-1649), 386, 395, 470, 941, 982, 990-993

Winthrop, John, Jr. (1606-1676), 219, 892

Witt, Johan de, 57, 808, 979

Wittelsbach, Friedrich. *See* Frederick V

Władysław IV Vasa, 111, 250, 290, 462, 795, 945

Wrangel, Karl Gustav, 154, 926

Wray, John. *See* Ray, John

Wren, Sir Christopher, 80, 349, 383, 547, 564, 589, 986, 994-997

Wu Sangui, 235

Wyatt, Sir Francis, 703

Xizong. *See* Chongzhen; Tianqi

Yang Ai. *See* Liu Yin

Yang Ying. *See* Liu Yin

Yellow Feather. *See* Massasoit

Yizong. *See* Tianqi

Yoshida Mitsuyoshi, 831

Yuan Chung Huan, 2

Yui Shōsetsu, 998-1000

Zamoyski, Jan, 854

Zampieri, Domenico. *See* Domenichino, Il

Zhang Geng, 157

Zhang Xianzhong, 849

Zheng Chenggong, 449, 1001-1003

Zheng Jing, 449

Zheng Zhilong, 161, 1001

Zhinga, N'. *See* Njinga

Zhu Youjian. *See* Chongzhen

Zhu Youjiao. *See* Tianqi

Zhu Youlang, 849

Zhuang Liedi. *See* Chongzhen

Zolkiewski, Stanislaw, 461, 855

Zrínyi, Peter, 528

Zúñiga, Baltazar de, 698

Zurbarán, Francisco de, 671, 1003-1006

Zygmunt III Waza. *See* Sigismund III Vasa

SUBJECT INDEX

All personages appearing in **boldface type** in this index are the subjects of articles in *Great Lives from History: The Seventeenth Century, 1601-1700*. Subjects of multi-person essays include Jakob I Bernoulli, Johann I Bernoulli, and Daniel Bernoulli ("The Bernoulli Family"); David and Johannes Fabricius; Johannes Hevelius and Elisabetha Hevelius; Laura Mancini, Olympia Mancini, Hortense Mancini, Marie-Anne Mancini ("The Mancini Sisters"); and Maarten and Cornelis Tromp.

A secreto agravio, secreta venganza. See *Secret Vengeance for Secret Insult* (Calderón)

Abahai, 1-3, 234, 848

ʿAbbās I. *See* ʿAbbās the Great

ʿAbbās II, 844

ʿAbbās the Great, 4-7, 411, 627, 668, 844

Abdelazer (Behn), 43

Abenakis, 612

Abentheuerliche Simplicissimus, Der. See *Simplicissimus* (Grimmelshausen)

Absalom and Achitophel (Dryden), 241, 817

Académie de France de Rome, 182

Académie de l'art poétique (Deimier), 578

Académie d'Opéra, 570

Académie Française, 482, 775, 780

Académie Royale de Musique, 570

Académie Royale des Sciences, 182, 398

Academy of Architecture, 182

Academy of Inscriptions, 182

Acadians, 142

Accademia degli Unisoni, 888

Accademia Reale, 165

Account of Religion by Reason, An (Suckling), 895

Account of the Growth of Popery and Arbitrary Government in England, An (Marvell), 606

Acetaria (Evelyn), 257

Acis et Galaté (Lully), 570

Act of _____. *See* _____, Act of

Actorum laboratorii chymici monacensis, seu, physicae subterranae libri duo. See *Physica subterranea* (Becher)

Acts of the Witnesses, The (Muggleton), 667

Ad Vitellionem paralipomena, quibus astronomiae pars optica traditur. See *Optics* (Kepler)

Adams, Will, 917

Adamus Exul, The (Grotius), 327

Addled Parliament (1614), 884

Admiral's Men, 440, 636

Adolphus, Gustavus II. *See* Gustavus II Adolphus

Adonis (La Fontaine), 481

Adoration of the Golden Calf, The (Poussin), 750

Adoration of the Shepherds (La Tour), 494

Adriaanszoon de Ruyter, Michiel. *See* Ruyter, Michiel Adriaanszoon de

Adventures of Telemachus, the Son of Ulysses, The (Fénelon), 265

Adventurous Simplicissimus, The. See *Simplicissimus* (Grimmelshausen)

Advis, Les (Gournay), 315

Aeneas, Anchises, and Ascanius Fleeing Troy (Bernini), 45

Aeneid (Claude Lorrain), 172

Affairs of the Poisons (1680), 586

Affected Young Ladies, The (Molière), 521, 647, 781

Affectionum quae dicuntur hystericae et hypochondriacae (Willis), 986

Afonso VI, 821

Africa; *maps*, xxvii, li. *See also* Geographical Index

African colonization, 687

Afzal Khan, 859

Agitators, 535

Aglaura (Suckling), 894

Agreement of the Free People (Lilburne, Walwyn, and Overton), 535

Agreement of the People, 535

Agudeza y Arte de ingenio. See *Mind's Wit and Art, The* (Gracián)

Ahmadnagar, 843

Ahmed I, 472, 673

Ahmed Paşa, Fazıl, 452

Airds Moss, Battle of (1680), 123

Akbar, 25, 410

ʿĀlamgīr I. *See* Aurangzeb

Albania. *See* Geographical Index

Albemarle, first duke of. *See* Monck, George

Alcalde de Zalamea, El. See *Mayor of Zalamea, The* (Calderón)

Alceste (Lully and Quinault), 570

Alchemist, The (Jonson), 442

Alden, John, 7-9, 879

Alderman (killed Metacom), 634

Alexander VII, 9-11, 46, 165, 406, 964

Alexander the Great (Racine), 774

Alexandre le Grand. See *Alexander the Great* (Racine)

Alexis, 11-14, 28, 428, 463, 663, 683, 795, 865

Alfonso Borelli, Giovanni. *See* Borelli, Giovanni Alfonso

Algonquians, 141, 423, 499, 634, 799

All for Love (Dryden), 241

Allegory of Inclination (Artemisia), 307

Allegory of Painting (Artemisia), 308

Allegory of Painting, The (Vermeer), 957

Allouez, Claude-Jean, 433, 603

Almagestum novum (Riccioli), 322

Alonso, Giovanni Francesco Antonio. *See* Borelli, Giovanni Alfonso

Alte Feste, Battle of the (1632), 338, 926

Altmark, Truce of (1629), 337, 705

Ameixal, Battle of (1663), 426

American colonies. *See* Geographical Index

Amin (Jin prince), 1

Amis, Aphara. *See* Behn, Aphra

Amoenitatum exoticarum (Kämpfer), 446

Amor, honor y poder (Calderón), 113

Amor médico, El (Tirso), 913

Amorous Prince, The (Behn), 43

Amours de Psyché et de Cupidon, Les. See *Loves of Cupid and Psyche, The* (La Fontaine)

Amphitryon (Molière), 648

Ana de Souza. *See* Njinga

Ana Nzinga Mbande, Ngola. *See* Njinga

Anastasia. *See* Kösem Sultan

Anatome plantarum (Malpighi), 581

Anatomical Exercises of Dr. William Harvey . . . Concerning the Motion of the Heart and Blood, The (Harvey), 356

Anatomical Exercitations, Concerning the Generation of Living Creatures (Harvey), 357

Anatomical studies; England, 355, 564, 986; Germany, 852; Italy, 580; Netherlands, 881, 899

Anatomy Lesson of Dr. Tulp, The (Rembrandt), 786

Anatomy of Melancholy, The (Burton), 109

Anatomy of the Brain, The (Willis), 564, 986

Anatomy of the World, An (Donne), 232

Ancients and the Moderns, Quarrel of the, 194, 732

Andrei Shuysky, 943

Andrewes, Lancelot, 14-17, 202, 247, 366, 496

Andromache (Racine), 774

Andros, Sir Edmond, 518

Andrusovo, Treaty of (1667), 452

Angélique, Mother. *See* Arnauld, Angélique

Angels (Bernini), 46

Anglo-Dutch War, First (1651-1652), 57, 808, 931, 942

Anglo-Dutch War, Second (1665-1667), 148, 169, 417, 650, 806, 808, 817, 892, 931

Anglo-Dutch War, Third (1672-1674), 215, 417, 806, 808, 839, 931

Aniello, Tommaso. *See* Masaniello

Animadversions on the First Part of the Machina coelestis of the Honourable, Learned, and Deservedly Famous Astronomer Johannes Hevelius (Hooke), 372

Annals of the Old and New Testament, The (Ussher), 939

Anne of Austria, 18-20; and the Great Condé, 185; and Cosimo II de' Medici, 627; and Saint Isaac Jogues, 424; and Madame de La Fayette, 477; and François de La Rochefoucauld, 487; and the duchesse de Longueville, 549; and Louis XIII, 551; and Louis XIV, 554; and Madame de Maintenon, 572; and the Mancini Sisters, 585; and François Mansart, 589; and Marie de Médicis, 598; and Marie-Thérèse, 601; and Jules Mazarin, 621; and the duchesse de Montpensier, 660; and Philip IV, 738; and Cardinal de Richelieu, 791; and Hercule Rohan, 158; and Viscount de Turenne, 933

Annus Mirabilis (Dryden), 240

Another Essay for Investigation of the Truth (Davenport), 219

Answer of the Elders of the Severall Churches in New England, An (Davenport), 219

Antinomianism, 395

Antoine Lefebre. *See* La Barre, sieur de

Anything for a Quiet Life (Middleton and Webster), 636, 977

Apaches, 468

Apollo and Daphne (Bernini), 45

Apologia Roberti S.R.E. Cardinalis Bellarmini, pro responsione sua ad librum Jacobi. See *Apology for the Responsio* (Bellarmine)

Apologie for the Oath of Allegiance, An. See *Triplicinodo triplex cuneus* (King James)

"Apologie pour celle qui escrit." See *Apology for the Woman Writing and Other Works* (Gournay)

Apology for Actors, An (Heywood), 374

Apology for the Responsio (Bellarmine), 16

Apology for the Royal Party, An (Evelyn), 256

Apology for the Woman Writing and Other Works (Gournay), 315

Apotheosis of Henry IV and the Proclamation of the Regency of Marie de Médicis, The (Rubens), 599

Appearance or Presence of the Son of Man, The (Davies), 220

Appius and Virginia (Webster and Heywood), 977

Arcadia, La (Lope de Vega), 950

Arcadian Academy, 191

Arcadian Shepherds, The (Poussin), 750

Archaeologiae philosophicae (Burnet), 107

Architecture; Baroque, 995; England, 436, 994; France, 523, 532, 587, 590; Italy, 10, 68, 330, 937; Mughal Empire, 843-844; Poland, 855; Russia, 866. *See also* Category Index

Architettura civile (Guarini), 331

Areopagitica (Milton), 640

Argall, Samuel, 746

Argyll, earl of. *See* Campbell, Archibald

Arianna, L' (Monteverdi), 658

Arie musicali per cantarsi (Frescobaldi), 297

Arithmetica Infinitorum (Wallis), 969

Arjumand Banu Begum. *See* Mumtaz Mahal

Arlington, first earl of, 507, 839

Armamentarium chirurgicum (Scultetus), 566

Arminianism, 327, 767

Arms, Union of (1620's), 698, 739

Army; Brandenburg-Prussia, 291; England, 205, 262; France, 184, 554; Netherlands, 619, 924; Sweden, 338

Army Council, 263

Arnauld, Angélique, 20-23

Arras, Siege of (1654), 933

Arrêt burlesque, L' (Boileau-Despréaux), 63

Ars conjectandi (Jakob I Bernoulli), 49

Ars de statica medicina sectionibus aphorismorum septem comprehensa. See *Medicina Statica* (Santorio)

Art. *See* Category Index

Art of Poetry, The (Boileau-Despréaux), 63

Art patronage; China, 450; England, 244; France, 182, 599, 723; Italy, 627, 937; Russia, 625; Ṣafavid Dynasty, 5; Spain, 739. *See also* Category Index under Patronage of the arts

Art poétique, L'. See *Art of Poetry, The* (Boileau-Despréaux)

Artamenes (Scudéry), 662, 829

Arte de ingenio (Gracián), 317

Arte nuevo de hacer comedias en este tiempo, El. See *New Art of Writing Plays, The* (Lope de Vega)

Artillery; China, 2; England, 651; France, 184, 946; Sweden, 925

Asaf Khan, 842

Asbaje y Ramírez de Santillana, Juana Inéz. *See* Cruz, Sor Juana Inés de la

Ascanius and the Stag (Claude Lorrain), 172

Ashley, Lord. *See* Shaftesbury, first earl of

Asia; *maps*, xxviii, lii

Assumption (Sirani), 857

Aston, Sir Walter, 238

Astraea Redux (Dryden), 240

Astronomer, The (Vermeer), 958

Astronomia nova. See *New Astronomy* (Kepler)

Astronomia reformata (Riccioli), 322

Astronomie cometicae synopsis (Halley), 350

Astronomy; England, 348, 388; France, 135, 304, 722; Germany, 259, 458, 818; Italy, 66, 134,

299, 921; Netherlands, 397; Poland, 371; Scotland, 319. *See also* Category Index

Athaliah (Racine), 775

Atheist's Tragedy, The (Tourneur), 928

Aubigné, Françoise d'. *See* Maintenon, Madame de

Augsburg, League of, 407, 560, 979

Augsburg, War of the League of (1689-1697), 401, 407, 528, 555, 560, 611, 946, 979

Augustinus (Jansen), 420, 936

Aurangzeb, 23-26, 843, 859

Aurora, The (Böhme), 60

Australia, 905; European exploration of, 216. *See also* Geographical Index

Austria. *See* Geographical Index

Austria, Anne of. *See* Anne of Austria

Austria, John of. *See* John of Austria

Autos sacramentales, 115, 949

Autre Monde, L' (Cyrano), 211

Avare, L'. See *Miser, The* (Molière)

Aventures de Télémaque, Les. See *Adventures of Telemachus, the Son of Ulysses, The* (Fénelon)

Avvakum Petrovich, 26-28, 685; *Life of the Archpriest Avvakum, by Himself, The*, 27

Awashonks, 634

Ayres and Dialogues (Lawes), 503

Azzolino, Decio, 165

Bach, Ambrosius, 708

Bach, Johann Christoph, 708

Bach, Johann Sebastian, 708

Bachmann, Augustus Quirnus. *See* Rivinus

Bacon, Francis, 175, 227, 357, 378; influence on Robert Boyle, 78

Bacon, Nathaniel, 29-32

Bacon's Laws, 30

Bacon's Rebellion (1676), 30

Baghchesaray Treaty of. *See* Bakchisaray, Treaty of (1681)

Bahādur Shāh, 25

Bahia, 288

Bajazet (Racine), 775

Bakchisaray, Treaty of (1681), 453

Balance of Truth, The (Kâtib Çelebî), 455

Balkh, 844

Balli di Sfessania (Callot), 118

Ballo delle ingrate, Il (Monteverdi), 658

Baltimore, first Lord. *See* Calvert, George

Bandolero, El (Tirso), 914

Bank of England, 717

Baptism of Christ (Sirani), 857

Barberini, Maffeo Vincenzo. *See* Urban VIII

Barca, Pedro Calderón de la. *See* Calderón de la Barca, Pedro

Barebones Parliament (1653), 484, 838

Baronius, Caesar, 720

Baroque style; Africa, 688; architecture, 69, 330, 468, 532, 588, 591, 599, 625, 855, 866, 995; drama, 914; England, 202, 310, 763, 995; fashion, 688; female artists, 303, 308; female writers, 315; France, 212, 478, 493, 504, 532, 569, 578, 588, 591, 599, 749; Germany, 827; Italy, 10, 45, 69, 192, 295, 302, 308, 330, 528, 656, 937; literature, 212, 315, 317, 325, 478, 577, 640, 950, 961; music, 192, 296, 310, 571, 658, 763, 827; Netherlands, 802; North America, 468; origins, 802; painting, 303, 308, 493, 504, 671, 749, 802, 937, 955, 1003; poetry, 202, 209, 313; Poland, 855; Russia, 625, 866; Spain, 312, 317, 671, 914, 955, 1003

Barrow, Isaac, 923

Barry, Elizabeth, 83

Bartholin, Thomas, 881

Bartholomew Fair (Jonson), 442

Bashful Man at Court, The (Tirso), 913

Bashō. *See* Matsuo Bashō

Basilikon Doron (James I), 413

Batavia. *See* Jakarta

Batih, Battle of (1652), 463

Battaile of Agincourt, The (Drayton), 238

Battle of _____. *See* _____,
  Battle of
Bavaria. *See* Geographical Index
Bavaria, duke of. *See* Rupert, Prince
Baxter, Richard, 32-36, 347
Bay Psalm Book, 247
Bayard, Nicholas, 519
Bayle, Pierre, 36-39; list of works,
  37
Bayn, Aphra. *See* Behn, Aphra
Beata Lodovica Albertoni (Bernini),
  46
Beatrice Cenci (Sirani), 857
Beauclerk, Charles, 343
Beaujeu, sieur de, 491
Beaumont, Francis, 105, 278, 636,
  846
Becher, Johann Joachim, 39-41
Becker Psalter (Schütz), 826
Bedell, William, 939
Bedford, countess of. *See*
  Harington, Lucy
Bedford, earl of. *See* Francis, Lord
  Russell
Beggar's Bush, The (Fletcher and
  Massinger), 279
Behemoth (Hobbes), 381
Behn, Aphra, 42-44, 82; list of
  works, 43
Béjart, Armande, 648
Béjart, Madeleine, 646
Belgium. *See* Geographical Index
Bellamont, earl of. *See* Coote,
  Richard
Bellarmine, Robert, 16, 720
Bellasis, John, 484
Bellérophon (Lully and Corneille),
  570
Ben Israel, Manasseh. *See* Manasseh
  ben Israel
Bénigne Bossuet, Jacques. *See*
  Bossuet, Jacques-Bénigne
Bennet, Henry. *See* Arlington, first
  earl of
Benserade, Isaac de, 781
Bentivoglio, Enzo, 295
Bentivoglio, Guido, 295
Bérénice (Racine), 774
Berestechno, Battle of (1651), 463
Bergerac, Cyrano de. *See* Cyrano de
  Bergerac
Berkeley, Sir William, 29, 703

Berlin Society of Sciences, 516
Bernières de Louvigny, Jean de,
  499
Bernini, Gian Lorenzo, 10, 45-47,
  68, 303, 330, 532, 937, 995
Bernini, Giovanni Lorenzo. *See*
  Bernini, Gian Lorenzo
Bernoulli family; Daniel, 48-50;
  Jakob I, 48-50, 832; Johann I,
  48-50
Bérulle, Pierre de, 962
Bethlen, Gabriel, 855
Béthune, Maximilien de. *See* Sully,
  duke de
Betterton, Thomas, 51-53, 82
Beverwijk, Johann van, 824
Bhonsle, Śivājī. *See* Śivājī
Biathanatos (Donne), 232
Bible; Algonquian, 248; Hebrew,
  583; Irish, 939; King James, 15,
  247, 940
Biddellians. *See* Unitarianism
Biddle, John, 53-55
Bijapur, 859
Bila Tserkva, Battle of (1651), 463
Bill of Rights, English (1689), 34
Biology; England, 564, 783, 903,
  987; Italy, 66, 356, 580;
  Netherlands, 510, 899
Bishop, Nicholas, 104
Bishops' War, First (1639), 262,
  562, 894, 941
Bishops' War, Second (1640), 562
Bizzarrie poetiche (Fontei), 888
Blackfriars Theatre, 51, 104, 279,
  442, 846, 977
Blaes, Gerard, 898
Blake, Robert, 55-59, 651, 931
Bléneau, Battle of (1652), 933
Bloody Cloak of Joseph, The
  (Velázquez), 954
Bloody Tenent Yet More Bloody,
  The (Williams), 984
Bloudy Tenent of Persecution, for
  Cause of Conscience, Discussed,
  The (Williams), 983
Blunderer, The (Molière), 647
Boerhaave, Hermann, 511
Bogot, 498
Bohemia, 97, 250, 254, 268, 293,
  415, 495, 526, 737, 805, 966. *See*
  also Geographical Index

Böhme, Jakob, 59-62; "Of the
  Mixed Tree of Evil and Good,"
  61
Boileau-Despréaux, Nicolas, 63-
  65, 482, 578, 732, 829
Bois-le-Duc, Siege of (1629), 261
Bolotnikov, Ivan, 944
Bonham, Thomas, 176
Book of Large and Small Numbers
  (Yoshida), 831
Book of Nature (Swammerdam), 899
Booke of Ayres, A (Campion and
  Rosseter), 127
Booth, George, 485
Borelli, Giovanni Alfonso, 65-67,
  362, 579, 986
Borghese, Camillo. *See* Paul V
Borghese, Scipione, 45
Borromini, Francesco, 67-70, 330,
  532, 937
Bossuet, Jacques-Bénigne, 70-73,
  186, 265, 339, 488
Botany; England, 200, 257, 782;
  Germany, 445; Italy, 581;
  Netherlands, 510, 899
Boteler, Sir William, 562
Bothwell Bridge, Battle of (1679),
  122, 654
Bouillon, duchesse de. *See* Mancini,
  Marie-Anne
Bourbon-Condé, Anne-Geneviève
  de. *See* Longueville, duchesse de
Bourbon Dynasty, 152, 184, 269,
  426, 431, 527, 548, 622
Bourgeois, Louyse, 73-75
Bourgeois gentilhomme, Le. See
  Would-Be Gentleman, The
  (Molière)
Bourgeoys, Saint Marguerite, 75-
  77, 576
Boursier, Louyse. *See* Bourgeois,
  Louyse
Bouvier de La Motte, Jeanne-Marie.
  See Guyon, Madame
Boyars, 785
Boyle, Richard, 885
Boyle, Robert, 37, 48, 78-81, 257,
  306, 335, 383, 514, 544, 564,
  814, 901, 923
Boyle's law, 79
Boyne, Battle of the (1690), 418,
  611, 822

Bracegirdle, Mrs. Anne, 51, 82-83
Bradford, William, 84-87, 130, 613, 876, 878; list of works, 86
Bradstreet, Anne, 88-91
Bragança Dynasty. *See* Braganza Dynasty
Braganza, duke of. *See* John IV (king of Portugal)
Braganza Dynasty, 425, 430, 960
Brahe, Tycho, 259, 372, 458
Bramer, Leonaert, 956
Brave Are My People (Waters), 614
Brazen Age, The (Heywood), 374
Brazil. *See* Geographical Index
Breda, Declaration of (1660), 137, 148, 168, 651
Breda, Treaty of (1667), 148, 892
Breitenfeld, First Battle of (1631), 338, 925
Breitenfeld, Second Battle of (1642), 926
Brennoralt (Suckling), 894
Brent, Margaret, 92-93
Brewster, William, 84, 878
Brief Account of the Intended Bank of England, A (Paterson), 717
Brief Account of the Province of Pennsylvania, A (Penn), 726
Bristol, Battle of (1645), 756, 805
Britannicus (Racine), 774
British East India Company, 137, 412, 465, 718
Brome, Richard, 374, 443
Brömsebrö, Treaty of (1645), 706
Browne, Sir Richard, 676
Browne, Sir Thomas, 94-96
Browne's Vulgar Errors (Browne), 95
Bruno, Giordano, 630, 811
Bruyas, Jacques, 909
Buade, Louis de. *See* Frontenac, comte de
Buckingham, first duke of, 18, 96-99, 132, 143, 158, 166, 177, 364, 368, 414, 496, 552, 650, 767, 884
Buckingham, second duke of, 149, 241, 506, 816, 839
Buczacz, Peace of (1672), 429
Buddhism; Lamaism, 2; Zen, 868, 998

Buen Retiro, 954
Bugaku Dancers (Sōtatsu), 869
Buke hyakunin isshu (Moronobu), 376
Bulkeley, Peter, 386
Bull, John, 310
Bunyan, John, 100-103; list of works, 101
Burbage, Cuthbert, 104
Burbage, James, 104
Burbage, Richard, 104-106, 279, 441
Burlador de Sevilla, El. See *Love Rogue, The* (Tirso)
Burnet, Thomas, 106-108
Burton, Robert, 108-110
Buscón, El. See *Life and Adventures of Buscon, the Witty Spaniard, The* (Quevedo y Villegas)
Bushidō, 998
Business. *See* Category Index
Busza, Treaty of (1617), 855
Butler, James. *See* Ormond, first duke of
Bye Plot, 253
Byrd, William, 310

Cabal, 507, 839
Caccini, Francesca, 111-112
Cadmus et Hermione (Lully and Quinault), 570
Calculating machine; France, 713; Germany, 514, 818; Japan, 832
Calculator, invention of, 819
Calculus; England, 679, 970; France, 271; Germany, 515; Italy, 922; Japan, 832; Scotland, 319; Switzerland, 48
Calderón de la Barca, Pedro, 113-116, 210, 740, 914, 950; list of works, 114
Calligraphy, Japanese, 696, 868
Callot, Jacques, 116-119
Calvert, Cecilius, 92, 120
Calvert, George, 92, 119-121
Calvinism, 327, 495
Cameron, Richard, 121-124
Cameron's Covenant, 123
Campanella, Giovanni. *See* Campanella, Tommaso
Campanella, Tommaso, 65, 124-126, 629, 723

Campbell, Archibald, 147, 655
Campini, Giuseppe, 134
Campion, Thomas, 127-129; list of works, 128
Canada; colonization, 141, 499; education, 500. *See also* Geographical Index
Cano, Alonso, 1003
Canon in D (Pachelbel), 709
Canonchet, 634
Canonicus, 129-131, 613
"Canonization, The" (Donne), 231
Cantate, ariette, e duetti (Strozzi), 888
Cantique des cantiques de Salomon, Le. See *Song of Songs of Solomon, The* (Guyon)
Cantiques spirituels (Racine), 775
Cape-and-sword plays, 950
Caprices, The (Callot), 117
Captain Dampier's Vindication of His Voyage to the South Seas in the Ship St. George (Campier), 216
Capuchins, 720
Caractères, Les (La Bruyère), 475
Cardinal, The (Shirley), 847
Cardinal Guido Bentivoglio (van Dyck), 244
Carew, Thomas, 503
Cargill, Donald, 122
Carlos II. *See* Charles II (king of Spain)
Carlowitz, Treaty of. *See* Karlowitz, Treaty of
Carmarthen, marquis of. *See* Leeds, first duke of
Carmen Deo Nostro (Crashaw), 203
Carpio, Lope de Vega. *See* Vega Carpio, Lope de
Carr, George, 221
Carr, Robert, 16, 131-133, 414
Carta al serenísimo Luis XIII (Quevedo y Villegas), 771
Carta atenagórica (Cruz), 209
Cartwright, William, 443, 503
Casaubon, Isaac, 281
Case Is Altered, The (Jonson), 440
Cassiano del Pozzo, 302, 307
Cassini, Gian Domenico, 134-136, 348
Castelli, Benedetto, 65, 921

Castelli, Francesco. *See* Borromini, Francesco

Castiglione, Giovanni, 330

Castigo sin venganza, El. See *Justice Without Revenge* (Lope de Vega)

Castlemaine, countess of, 137

Catalan uprising, 425

Catalogus Stellarum Australium (Halley), 348

Cathedra Petri (Bernini), 46

Catherine d'Angennes. *See* Rambouillet, Marquise de

Catherine of Braganza, 137-139, 148, 343, 654

Catholic League, 268, 293

Catholicism; Austria, 268; Bohemia, 966; England, 120, 132, 417, 608, 692, 721, 974, 979; France, 265, 573, 593, 598, 629, 962; Germany, 882; Ireland, 700, 938; Italy, 406, 720, 936; North America, 909; Peru, 797; Sweden, 165

Catiline (Jonson), 442

Cats, Jakob, 824

Cavalier poets, 443, 563

Cavalieri, Bonaventura, 922, 969

Cavalli, Francesco, 888

Cavelier, René-Robert. *See* La Salle, sieur de

Cavendish, Sir Charles, 676

Cavendish, Margaret. *See* Newcastle, duchess of

Cavendish, William, 262, 676

Caversham Entertainment, The (Campion), 128

Cecchina, La. *See* Caccini, Francesca

Cecil, Robert. *See* Salisbury, first earl of

Cecil, William, 175

Cecora on the Pruth, Battle of (1620), 855

Çelebî, Kâtib. *See* Kâtib Çelebî

Celeste, Maria. *See* Maria Celeste

Cerebri anatome. See *Anatomy of the Brain, The* (Willis)

Cervantes, Miguel de, 738

Champ Blanc, Battle of (1650), 933

Champlain, Samuel de, 139-143, 433

Changeling, The (Middleton and Rowley), 637

Chantelou, Paul Fréart de, 750

Chapel of the Holy Shroud, 331

Chapel Royal, 502

Chapelain, Jean, 833

Character of a Trimmer (Savile), 817

Character of England, A (Evelyn), 256

Characters or Pourtaicts of the Present Court of France, The (Montpensier), 662

Charity (Sirani), 857

Charles I (king of England), 143-146; and Richard Baxter, 33; and Aphra Behn, 42; and Thomas Betterton, 51; and Robert Blake, 55; and Jacques-Bénigne Bossuet, 72; and Anne Bradstreet, 89; and the first duke of Buckingham, 98; and George Calvert, 120; and Richard Cameron, 121; and Canonicus, 130; and Robert Carr, 133; and Catherine of Braganza, 137; and Charles II of England, 149; and the first earl of Clarendon, 166; and Sir Edward Coke, 177; and John Cotton, 198; and Abraham Cowley, 199; and Richard Crashaw, 202; and Oliver Cromwell, 204; and Lady Eleanor Davies, 221; and John Dryden, 240; and Sir Anthony van Dyck, 245; and John Eliot, 247; and Elizabeth of Bohemia, 252; and Elizabeth Stuart, 254; and John Evelyn, 256; and Third Baron Fairfax, 262; and Nicholas Ferrar, 275; and Frederick Henry, 288; and Artemisia Gentileschi, 308; and Orlando Gibbons, 311; and Nell Gwyn, 343; and Matthew Hale, 345; and William Harvey, 357; and Henrietta Maria, 364; and Robert Herrick, 369; and James I, 415; and James II, 416; and Inigo Jones, 436; and Ben Jonson, 443; and John Lambert, 483; and William Laud, 496; and Henry

Lawes, 503; and John Lilburne, 535; and Louis XIII, 552; and Richard Lovelace, 562; and Roger Ludlow, 567; and Marie de Médicis, 599; and Andrew Marvell, 605; and Mary II, 610; and Thomas Middleton, 638; and John Milton, 640; and George Monck, 650; and Rory O'More, 699; and Opechancanough, 703; and Samuel Pepys, 728; and Thomas Pride, 756; and John Pym, 767; and Cardinal de Richelieu, 791; and Prince Rupert, 805; and Santorio Santorio, 811; and Sir George Savile, 815; and the first earl of Shaftesbury, 838; and James Shirley, 847; and the first earl of Strafford, 885; and Sir John Suckling, 893; and Maarten and Cornelis Tromp, 930; and Sir Henry Vane the Younger, 941; and John Wallis, 969; and William III, 979; and Gerrard Winstanley, 989; and John Winthrop, 991; and Sir Christopher Wren, 994

Charles I at the Hunt (van Dyck), 246

Charles I on Horseback (van Dyck), 246

Charles II (king of England), 147-150; and Nathaniel Bacon, 29; and Richard Baxter, 34; and Aphra Behn, 42; and John Biddle, 54; and Robert Blake, 58; and Robert Boyle, 80; and Sir Thomas Browne, 94; and John Bunyan, 101; and Richard Cameron, 121; and Catherine of Braganza, 137; and the first earl of Clarendon, 168; and Abraham Cowley, 200; and Oliver Cromwell, 205; and John Davenport, 219; and John Dryden, 240; and Elizabeth Stuart, 254; and John Evelyn, 256; and the third Baron Fairfax, 264; and George Fox, 284; and James Gregory, 319; and Nell Gwyn, 342; and Matthew Hale,

346; and Edmond Halley, 348; and Henrietta Maria, 364; and Robert Herrick, 369; and Thomas Hobbes, 380; and James II, 416; and John IV, 431; and John Lambert, 485; and Henry Lawes, 503; and the first duke of Leeds, 506; and John Locke, 544; and Roger Ludlow, 568; and the Mancini sisters, 586; and Andrew Marvell, 606; and Mary II, 610; and Mary of Modena, 607; and John Milton, 640; and George Monck, 650; and the duke of Monmouth, 653; and the duchesse de Montpensier, 661; and the duchess of Newcastle, 677; and Titus Oates, 692; and William Penn, 725; and Samuel Pepys, 729; and Sir William Petty, 734; and Katherine Philips, 742; and Thomas Pride, 757; and Henry Purcell, 763; and Prince Rupert, 805; and Sir George Savile, 815; and Friedrich Hermann Schomberg, 821; and the first earl of Shaftesbury, 839; and Maarten and Maarten and Cornelis Tromp, 931; and Sir Henry Vane the Younger, 942; and John Wallis, 969; and Thomas Willis, 986; and Sir Christopher Wren, 994

Charles II (king of Spain), 151-153, 426, 528, 555, 602, 739, 980

Charles III (king of Spain). *See* Charles VI (Holy Roman Emperor)

Charles IV (duke of Lorraine), 493, 528

Charles VI (Holy Roman Emperor), 152

Charles IX (king of Sweden), 336, 854, 945

Charles X Gustav, 153-155, 164, 527, 706

Charles XI (king of Sweden), 155

Charles XII (king of Sweden), 625

Charles the Mad. *See* Charles II (king of Spain)

Charleton, Walter, 240

Chaste Maid in Cheapside, A (Middleton), 636

Château de Balleroy, 588

Château de Berny, 588

Château de Clagny, 590

Château de Maisons, 588

Château de Vaux-le-Vícomte, 532

Chatham, Battle of (1667), 808

Cheat with the Ace of Clubs (La Tour), 494

Cheat with the Ace of Diamonds (La Tour), 494

Chemistry; Belgium, 362; England, 79; Germany, 40. *See also* Category Index

Chen Shu, 156-158

Cheng Ch'eng-kung. *See* Zheng Chenggong

Cheng Chih-lung. *See* Zheng Zhilong

Chesnoy, Madame de Guyon du. *See* Guyon, Madame

Chevreuse, duchesse de, 18, 158-160, 487

Chickahominys, 752

Chickasaws, 402

Chigi, Fabio. *See* Alexander VII

China. *See* Geographical Index

Ch'ing Dynasty. *See* Qing Dynasty

Ch'ing T'ai-tsung. *See* Abahai

Chini, Eusebio Francesco. *See* Kino, Eusebio Francesco

Chippawas, 433, 603

Chmielnicki, Bohdan. *See* Khmelnytsky, Bohdan

Chmielnicki massacres (1648-1649), 836

Chodkiewicz, Jan, 854

Choice Psalms Put into Music (Lawes), 503

Chomedey, Paul de. *See* Maisonneuve, sieur de

Chongde. *See* Abahai

Chongzhen, 160-162, 235, 848, 912

Chouart, Médard. *See* Groseilliers, sieur des

Christ in the House of Martha and Mary (Vermeer), 956

Christ on the Cross (Zurbarán), 1004

Christ with Saint Joseph in the Carpenter's Shop (La Tour), 494

Christian Morals (Browne), 95

Christianity; England, 94, 545; France, 71, 715; Germany, 60; Italy, 125; Russia, 27; science and, 106; Scotland, 121

Christina (queen of Sweden), 163-166; and Giovanni Alfonso Borelli, 66; and René Descartes, 164, 228; and Frederick William, 290; and Ninon de Lenclos, 521; and the duchesse de Montpensier, 661; music patronage, 190; and Blaise Pascal, 713; and António Vieira, 960

Christoffel von Grimmelshausen, Hans Jakob. *See* Grimmelshausen, Hans Jakob Christoffel von

Christ's Passion (Grotius), 327

Christus patiens. See Christ's Passion (Grotius)

Chu Yu-chiao. *See* Tianqi

Chu Yu-chien. *See* Chongzhen

Chuang Lieh-ti. *See* Chongzhen

Ch'ung-chen. *See* Chongzhen

Ch'ung-te. *See* Abahai

Chur-Brandenburgische Hoff-Wehe-Mutter, Die. See Court Midwife of the Electorate of Brandenburg, The (Siegemundin)

Church, Benjamin, 634

Church and state, separation of, 984

Church government and reform. *See* Category Index

Church of England, 15, 939

Church of Scotland, 941

Church of the Feillants, 588

Church of the Val-de-Grâce, 589

Cicognini, Jacopo, 111

Cid, The (Corneille), 193

Cigarrales de Toledo, Los (Tirso), 913

Cinna (Corneille), 194

Circulation of the Blood, The (Harvey), 357

Cirencester, Battle of (1642), 805

Città del sole, La. See City of the Sun (Campanella)

City of the Sun (Campanella), 126

Clarendon, first earl of, 147, 166-170, 240, 507, 816, 839

Clarendon Code (1661-1665), 121, 148, 169, 347

Clarke, Samuel, 516

Clarkson, Laurence, 666

Claude Lorrain, 171-173

Clelia (Scudéry), 829

Clement VIII, 720

Clement IX, 406, 422

Clement X, 406

Clerks Regular, 330

Clerville, chevalier de, 946

Clifford, Thomas. *See* Clifford of Chudleigh, first Baron

Clifford of Chudleigh, first Baron, 507, 839

Clyfton, Richard, 84

Cockpit (theater). *See* Phoenix (theater)

Coddington, William, 130

Code of 1650 (Connecticut), 568

Coke, Sir Edward, 132, 174-179, 414, 767, 982

Colbert, Jean-Baptiste, 135, 180-183, 398, 505, 554, 558, 570, 588, 590, 622, 731

Colchester, Siege of (1648), 263

Coligny, Gaspard II de, 896

Coliseo del Buen Retiro, El, 113

Colle, Giovanni, 565

Collection of English Words (Ray), 782

Collection of Private Devotions, A (Cosin), 202

Collège des Quatre-Nations, 533

Colonels (Irish military recruiters), 700

Colonization; Dutch of New Amsterdam, 393; Dutch of New England, 890; Dutch of New York, 644; England of New England, 768, 875, 878; England of North America, 864; England of Pennsylvania, 726; England of the Jerseys, 726; France of Canada, 141, 499; France of Louisiana, 402, 491; *maps*, xxvii, xxx, xxxi, xxxii, li, liv, lv, lvi; Portugal of Africa, 687; Sweden of North America, 645. *See also* Exploration

Colonna, princess of. *See* Mancini, Marie

Comedias de capa y espada. See *Cape-and-sword plays*

Comédiens du Roy, 774

Comédies-ballets, 570

Comenius, Jan (Johann, John) Amos. *See* Komenský, Jan

Cometographia (J. Hevelius), 372

Commentaire philosophique sur ces paroles de Jésus-Christ "Contrain-les d'entrer." See *Philosophical Commentary on These Words in the Gospel, Luke XIV, 23, A* (Bayle)

Commentaire sur Desportes (Malherbe), 577

Commentaria in artem medicinalem Galeni (Santorio), 811

Commentaria in primam fen primi libri canonis Avicennae (Santorio), 811

Commentary on the Law of Prize and Booty (Grotius), 327

Commonwealth (English, 1649-1660), 33, 51, 54, 56, 137, 168, 256, 263, 345, 640, 757, 942, 989

Company of Captain Frans Banning Cocq and Lieutenant Willem van Ruytenburch, The. See *Night Watch, The* (Rembrandt)

Compleat Gentleman, The (Gracián), 317

Comtesse de Tende, The (La Fayette), 478

Comulgatorio, El. See *Sanctuary Meditations* (Gracián)

Comus (Milton), 502, 640

Concerning the Election of Grace (Böhme), 61

Concerning the Three Principles of the Divine Essence (Böhme), 61

Conciliator of R. Manasseh ben Israel, The (Manesseh), 583

Concini, Concino, 551, 598, 791

Condé, The Great, 159, 184-187, 549, 559, 621, 661, 821, 829, 896, 926, 933

Condé, third prince of, 548, 551

Condenado por desconfiado, El. See *Saint and the Sinner, The* (Tirso)

Confession of Faith Touching the Holy Trinity, According to Scripture, A (Biddle), 53

Confirming and Restoring of Ministers, Act for (1660), 34

Confraternity of Charity, 962

Congrégation de Nôtre-Dame, 75

Congregation of the Mission, 962

Congregation of the Oratory, 721

Congregationalism, 197, 205

Congregazione dei Virtuosi di Santa Cecilia, 190

Congreve, William, 52, 82

Connecticut, 567, 892

Connolly, Owen, 700

Conquest of Granada by the Spaniards, The (Dryden), 241, 343

Conscience, Council of, 963

Consolation à Monsieur du Périer sur la mort de sa fille (Malherbe), 577

Constant Prince, The (Calderón), 114

Constantia and Philetus (Cowley), 199

"Containing Some Microbial Observations, About Animals in the Scurf of the Teeth . . ." (Leeuwenhoek), 511

"Contemplations" (Bradstreet), 90

Contes de ma mère l'oye. See *Tales of Mother Goose* (Perrault)

Contes des fées. See *Tales of Mother Goose* (Perrault)

Contes et nouvelles en vers. See *Tales and Short Stories in Verse* (La Fontaine)

Conventicle Act (1664), 34, 101, 122

Conventicle of God's Real Servants, 59

Conversations nouvelle sur divers sujets (Scudéry), 829

Conversations sur divers sujets. See *Conversations upon Several Subjects* (Scudéry)

Conversations upon Several Subjects (Scudéry), 829

Conway, Anne, 187-189, 252

Cooper, Anthony Ashley. *See* Shaftesbury, first earl of

Coote, Richard, 464

Copenhagen, Treaty of (1660), 155

Coquette vangée, La (Lenclos), 521

Corbett, Richard, 443

Corelli, Arcangelo, 190-192

Cork, first earl of. *See* Boyle, Richard

Cormorants, The (Sōtatsu), 869

Cornaro Chapel, 46

Cornaro Piscopia, Elena. *See* Piscopia, Elena Cornaro

Corneille, Pierre, 193-196; and Jean de La Fontaine, 482; list of works, 194; and the duchesse de Longueville, 550; and Jean-Baptiste Lully, 570; and Molière, 647; and Katherine Philips, 742; and Nicolas Poussin, 751; and Jean Racine, 774; and the French salons, 780; and Madame de Sévigné, 834

Corpuscular philosophy, 80

Correntes, 296

Cortlandt, Stephanus van, 519

Cortona, Pietro da, 937

Cosimo II. *See* Medici, Cosimo II de'

Cosin, John, 202

Cosmotheoros (Huygens), 398

Cossacks, 12, 428, 452, 461, 624, 668, 784, 836, 855, 944

Cotán, Juan Sánchez, 1005

Cotterell, Charles, 742

Cotton, John, 196-199, 218, 386, 394, 982

Counter-Remonstrants, 288

Courage, the Adventuress (Grimmelshausen), 325

Court Midwife of the Electorate of Brandenburg, The (Siegemundin), 851

Court Secret, The (Shirley), 846

Courtiers Manual Oracle, The (Gracián), 317

Coûture, Guillaume, 423

Covenant of Grace Opened, The (Hooker), 387

Covenanters, 147, 700, 885

Cowley, Abraham, 199-201, 203, 232, 742

Coxe, Thomas, 901

Cranfield, Lionel, 275

Crashaw, Richard, 202-204, 232, 276, 562

Crimean Khanate, 866

Crimson Cloud Mansion, 541

Critick, The (Gracián), 317

Criticón, El. See *Critick, The* (Gracián)

Critique générale de l'histoire du calvinisme de M. Maimbourg (Bayle), 36

Cromwell, Oliver, 204-207; and Richard Baxter, 33; and John Biddle, 54; and Robert Blake, 56; and John Bunyan, 100; and Richard Cameron, 121; and Catherine of Braganza, 137; and Charles I, 145; and Charles II of England, 147; and the first earl of Clarendon, 168; and the Great Condé, 186; and John Cotton, 198; and Abraham Cowley, 199; and John Dryden, 239; and the third Baron Fairfax, 262; and George Fox, 284; and Frederick Henry, 288; and Matthew Hale, 346; and Thomas Hobbes, 380; and Inigo Jones, 437; and John Lambert, 483; and Henry Lawes, 502; and Roger Ludlow, 568; and Manasseh ben Israel, 583; and Andrew Marvell, 606; and George Monck, 651; and Rory O'More, 701; and William Penn, 724; and Samuel Pepys, 728; and Sir William Petty, 734; and Katherine Philips, 741; and Thomas Pride, 756; and Henry Purcell, 763; and Prince Rupert, 805; and Sir George Savile, 815; and the first earl of Shaftesbury, 838; and James Shirley, 846; and Maarten and Cornelis Tromp, 931; and James Ussher, 940; and Sir Henry Vane the Younger, 941; and Mary Ward, 975; and Thomas Willis, 986; and Gerrard Winstanley, 989; and Sir Christopher Wren, 994

Cromwell, Richard, 485, 757, 942

Crooke, Andrew, 94

Crucified Christ with Saint Dominic and Saint Catherine of Siena, The (van Dyck), 245

Crucifixion (Zurbarán). See *Christ on the Cross* (Zurbarán)

Crucifixion with Angels (Le Brun, C.), 504

Cruz, Sor Juana Inés de la, 208-210; list of works, 209

Cumberland, duke of. *See* Rupert, Prince

Cuna y la sepultura, La (Quevedo y Villegas), 771

Cupid and Psyche (van Dyck), 246

Cure for a Cuckold, A (Webster and Rowley), 977

Custom of the Country, The (Fletcher and Massinger), 279

Cutter of Coleman Street, The (Cowley), 200

Cuyen, 1

Cynthia's Revels (Jonson), 441

Cyrano de Bergerac, 211-214

Cyrano de Bergerac (Rostand), 211

Dablon, Claude, 433, 603

Daemonologie (James I), 413

Dafne (Schütz), 826

Daisan (Jin prince), 1

Dakotas, 603

Daling He, Siege of (1631), 2

Dama boba, La. See *Lady Nit-Wit, The* (Lope de Vega)

Dama duende, La. See *Phantom Lady, The* (Calderón)

Damned for Despair. See *Saint and the Sinner, The* (Tirso)

Dampier, William, 215-218

Danby, first earl of. *See* Leeds, first duke of

Daniel, Samuel, 128

Dārā, 23, 844

Darien scheme, 718

Dartmouth, Battle of (1646), 756

Daughters of Charity, 963

Daumont, Simon François. *See* Saint Lusson, sieur de

Dauversière, Jérôme Le Royer de la, 575

Davenant, Sir William, 51, 502

Davenport, John, 218-220

David (Bernini), 45

Davideis (Cowley), 200

Davies, Lady Eleanor, 220-222, 989

Davies, Sir John, 221

Davison, Francis, 127

Day, Thomas, 311

Day of the Dupes. *See* Dupes, Day of the (1630)

De anima brutorum. See Two Discourses Concerning the Soul of Brutes Which Is That of the Vital and Sensitive of Man (Willis)

De bombyce (Malpighi), 580

De cerebro (Malpighi), 580

De circulatione sanguinis. See Circulation of the Blood, The (Harvey)

De Cive. See Philosophical Rudiments Concerning Government and Society (Hobbes)

De Corpore Politico (Hobbes), 379

De creatione problmata XXX (Manasseh), 583

De dimensione parabolae, solidique hyperbolici problemata duo. See Opera geometrica (Torricelli)

De doctrina Christiana (Milton), 641

De fide et officiis Christianorum liber. See Faith and Duties of Christians, The (Burnet)

De fundamentis astrologiae certioribus (Kepler), 458

De iure belli ac pacis libri tres. See On the Law of War and Peace (Grotius)

De jure naturae et gentium libri octo. See Of the Law of Nature and Nations (Pufendorf)

De jure praede commentarius. See Commentary on the Law of Prize and Booty (Grotius)

De la fragilidad humana (Manasseh), 583

De l'Éloquence française (Vair), 577

De maculis in sole observatis (Johannes Fabricius), 260

De magnetica vulnerum curatione (Helmont), 362

De motu animalium. See On the Movement of Animals (Borelli)

De motu corporum in gyrum (Newton), 349

De motu gravium naturaliter descendentium et proiectorum libri duo. See Opera geometrica (Torricelli)

De musculis et glandulis observationum specimen (Steno), 881

De officio hominis et civis juxta legem naturalem libri duo. See Whole Duty of Man According to the Law of Nature, The (Pufendorf)

De ovo incubato. See Marcello Malpighi and the Evolution of Embryology (Malpighi)

De pulmonibus observationes anatomicae (Borelli), 580

De revolutionibus (Galileo), 300

De sensu rerum et magia (Campanella), 125

De solido intra solidum naturaliter contento dissertationis prodromus. See Prodromus (Steno)

De sphaera et solidis sphaeralibus libri duo. See Opera geometrica (Torricelli)

De statu imperii Germanici, ad Laelium fratrem, dominum Trezolani, liber unus. See Present State of Germany, The (Pufendorf)

De statu mortuorum et resurgentium liber. See Treatise Concerning the State of Departed Souls, Before, and at, and After the Resurrection, A (Burnet)

De stella nova in pede serpentarii (Kepler), 458

De termino vitae (Manasseh), 583

De venarum ostiolis (Fabricius), 355

De vi percussionis (Borelli), 66

De viscerum structura exercitatio anatomica (Malpighi), 580

De vita et rebus gentis Guillielmi Duicis Novo-castrensis. See Life of William Cavendish, Duke of Newcastle, The (Newcastle)

Deane, Richard, 56, 651, 932

Death of Agrippina, The (Cyrano), 211

Debauchee, The (Behn), 43

Deccan, 25

Declaration of Rights (1689), 611

Defenestration of Prague (1618), 293, 470, 966

Defense of Rhyme, A (Daniel), 128

Defoe, Daniel, 216

Deimier, Pierre de, 578

Dekker, Thomas, 132, 223-225, 441, 636, 846, 977; list of works, 224

De la Gardie, Magnus Gabriel, 153, 164

Deleboe, Franz, 361

Deleytar aprovechando (Tirso), 914

Délices de la poésie française (Malherbe), 578

Delle cagioni de le febbri maligna (Borelli), 65

Delorme, Marion, 521

Denham, Sir John, 994

Denis, Jean Baptiste, 565

Denmark. *See* Geographical Index

Dépit amoureux, Le. See Love-Tiff, The (Molière)

Dermer, Thomas, 876

Dernier recueil (Malherbe), 578

Desargues, Girard, 630

Descartes, René, 226-229; and Jakob Bernoulli, 48; and Giovanni Alfonso Borelli, 67; and Queen Christina, 164; and Anne Conway, 188; on doubt, 228; and Elizabeth of Bohemia, 251; and Pierre de Fermat, 271; and Pierre Gassendi, 305; and William Harvey, 357; and Christiaan Huygens, 398; iatromechanism, 362; and Jean de La Fontaine, 482; and Gottfried Wilhelm Leibniz, 514; list of works, 227; and Marin Mersenne, 628; and the duchess of Newcastle, 677; and Blaise Pascal, 713; and Anna Maria van Schurman, 824; on space and matter, 333; and Baruch Spinoza, 871; and Nicolaus Steno, 881; on thinking, 228; and John Wallis, 970; and Thomas Willis, 986

Descent from the Cross (Rubens), 802

Description of a New Blazing World, The (Newcastle), 677

Description of New England, A (Smith), 864

Desegni d'architettura civile e ecclesiastica (Guarini), 331

Deshayes, Catherine. *See* Monvoisin, Madame

Desportes, Philippe, 577

Despréaux, Nicolas Boileau-. *See* Boileau-Despréaux, Nicolas

Deulino, Treaty of (1618), 855

Devereux, Robert (1566-1601). *See* Essex, second earl of

Devereux, Robert (1591-1646). *See* Essex, third earl of

Devil Is an Ass, The (Jonson), 442

Devil's Law-Case, The (Webster), 977

Devolution, War of (1667-1668), 151, 186, 555, 558, 602, 934, 946

Devotions upon Emergent Occasions (Donne), 232

Dialogue Between Some Young Men Born in New England and Sundry Ancient Men That Came Out of Holland (Bradford), 86

Dialogue Concerning the Two Chief World Systems, Ptolemaic and Copernican (Galileo), 300, 594, 631, 936

Dialogues Concerning Eloquence in General, and Particularly That Kind Which Is Fit for the Pulpit (Fénelon), 266

Diana and Her Companions (Vermeer), 956

Diary of Samuel Pepys, The (Pepys), 728

Diatribae duae medico-philosophicae. See Of Fermentation (Willis)

Diatribae Thomae Willisii de febribus vindicatio (Lower), 564

Dictionariolum trilinguae (Ray), 782

Dictionnaire historique et critique. See Historical and Critical Dictionary, An (Bayle)

Dido and Aeneas (Purcell), 764

Diemen, Antony van, 905

Dietwald und Amelinde (Grimmelshausen), 325

Diggers, 989

Dioclesian (Purcell), 765

Dioptrice (Kepler), 458

Diplomacy. *See* Category Index

"Disappointment, The" (Behn), 44

Discontented Colonel, The. See Brennoralt (Suckling)

Discours à Mme de La Sablière (La Fontaine), 482

Discours de la cause de la pesanteur (Huygens), 399

Discours de la méthode. See Discourse on Method (Descartes)

Discours sur l'histoire universelle. See Discourse on the History of the Whole World, A (Bossuet)

Discourse of the Religion Anciently Professed by the Irish and the British, A (Ussher), 939

Discourse on Method (Descartes), 227

Discourse on Political Arithmetick (Petty), 734

Discourse on the History of the Whole World, A (Bossuet), 70

Discourse on the Nature and Offices of Friendship (Taylor), 742

Discreto, El. See Compleat Gentleman, The (Gracián)

Dissertatio. See Learned Maid, The (Schurman)

Dissertatio epistolica de formatione pulli in ovo. See Marcello Malpighi and the Evolution of Embryology (Malpighi)

Dissertatiocum nuncio sidereo. See Kepler's Conversation with Galileo's Sidereal Messenger (Kepler)

Divers portraits (La Fayette), 477

Divers portraits (Montpensier). *See Characters or Pourtaicts of the Present Court of France, The* (Montpensier)

Divine Looking-Glass, A (Muggleton and Reeve), 667

Divine Maxims of Government . . . (Quevedo y Villegas), 770

Divine Narcissus, The (Cruz), 209

Divini, Eustachio, 134

Divino Narciso, El. See Divine Narcissus, The (Cruz)

Dmitry, False, 794, 854, 944

Dmitry, Second False, 794, 944

Dmitry Ivanovich, 943

Doctor Fludd's Answer (Fludd), 282

Doctor in Spite of Himself, The (Molière), 648

Dr. Willis's Practice of Physick (Willis), 987

Doctrine and Discipline of Divorce, The (Milton), 640

Dodo (Dorgon's brother), 234

Dog Shogun. *See* Tokugawa Tsunayoshi

Dolgoruky, Vasily Vladimirovich, 12

Domenichino, Il, 749

Domenico Cassini, Gian. *See* Cassini, Gian Domenico

Don Gil of the Green Breeches (Tirso), 913

Don Juan (Molière), 648

Don Quixote de la Mancha (Cervantes), 738

Dong shan chou he ji (Liu and Qian), 541

Donglin faction, 911

Donne, John, 16, 132, 200, 202, 230-234, 253, 366, 741; list of works, 231

Dorgon, 1, 234-237, 848

Doroshenko, Petro, 452, 624

Dort, Synod of (1618), 619

Douglas, Sir Archibald, 221

Douglas, Thomas, 122

Dover, Treaty of (1670), 149, 693, 816, 839

Dowland, John, 127, 502

Down Survey, 734

Downs, Battle of the (1638), 288

Drayton, Michael, 237-239

Druilletes, Gabriel, 603

Drummond, William, 443

Drury Lane Theatre, 51

Dryden, John, 43, 52, 64, 201, 233, 239-243, 342, 394, 442, 765, 817; list of works, 242

Duchess of Malfi, The (Webster), 977

Dudley, Anne. *See* Bradstreet, Anne

Dudley, Robert. *See* Leicester, first earl of

Dudley, Thomas, 992

Duke's Company, 51

Dunbar, Battle of (1650), 205, 757

Dundalk, Encampment of (1689), 821

Dunes, Battle of the (1658), 206, 417, 425, 933

Dungeness, Battle of (1652), 57

Dunkirk, Siege of (1646), 562

Dupes, Day of the (1630), 19, 552, 599

Dustūr al-amal li islah al-khalal (Kâtib Çelebî), 455

Dutch East India Company, 288, 445, 618, 905

Dutch Wars of Independence (1568-1648), 287, 289, 618

Dutch West India Company, 359, 518, 618, 643, 890

Duxborough. *See* Duxbury

Duxbury, 8, 879

Dyck, Sir Anthony van, 244-246, 302, 671, 723

Earl Marshal's Court, 167

East India Company. *See* British East India Company; Dutch East India Company

Eastward Ho! (Marston, Chapman, and Jonson), 442

Eaton, Theophilus, 218

École des femmes, L'. See School for Wives, The (Molière)

École des maris, L'. See School for Husbands, The (Molière)

Economics. *See* Category Index under Business and economics

Economy; China, 912; England, 717; France, 182, 554, 897; Ireland, 734; Massachusetts Bay Colony, 992; Powhatans, 753. *See also* Mercantilism

Ecstasy of Saint Teresa (Bernini), 46

Edgehill, Battle of (1642), 204, 416, 805

Edicts on Compassion for Living Things, 919

Education; Canada, 500; China, 1002; England, 640; France, 266, 573, 622, 963; Japan, 998; medical, 355; Ottoman Empire, 456; Persian, 842; Sweden, 337; universal, 470; women, 265, 314, 364, 744, 823, 828, 865. *See also* Category Index

Edward IV, Parts I and II (Heywood), 373

Egerton, Sir Thomas, 231

Egypt. *See* Geographical Index

Eighty Years' War (1568-1648), 618, 698, 739

Eikonoklastes (Milton), 640

Elaboration on the Meaning of the Book of Documents (Wang), 972

Elegy on the Death of Dudley, Lord Carlton (Cowley), 199

Elementorum jurisprudentiae universalis (Pufendorf), 759

Elementorum myologiae specimen. See *Specimen of Elements of Myology* (Steno)

Elements of Law, Natural and Politic, The (Hobbes), 379

Elevation of the Cross, The (Rubens), 802

Eliot, John, 247-250

Elizabeth I (queen of England), 15, 104

Elizabeth of Bohemia (1596-1662). *See* Elizabeth Stuart

Elizabeth of Bohemia (1618-1680), 250-253, 254; correspondence with Descartes, 251

Elizabeth Stuart, 250, 253-255, 275, 293, 310, 805, 820

Elwes, Sir Gervase, 132

Elysium Britannicum (Evelyn), 257

Emperor of the Moon, The (Behn), 43

Emperor Theodosius Is Forbidden by Saint Ambrose to Enter Milan Cathedral, The (van Dyck), 244

Endicott, John, 386

Endimion and Phoebe (Drayton), 237

Enghien, duke of. *See* Condé, The Great

Engineering; England, 814; France, 135, 712; Italy, 49; Switzerland, 49. *See also* Category Index

England. *See* Geographical Index

England's Birth-Right (Lilburne), 535

Englands Heroicall Epistles (Drayton), 238

England's New Chains Discovered (Lilburne), 535

England's Present Interest Discovered (Penn), 725

English Civil Wars (1642-1651), 650, 756, 769, 805, 901, 988; First (1642-1646), 32, 55, 121, 137, 145, 147, 199, 205, 262, 379, 416, 483, 535, 838, 846, 941; Second (1647-1649), 205, 263, 484; Third (1650-1651), 757

English East India Company. *See* British East India Company

English Traveler, The (Heywood), 374

Entomology; England, 783; Italy, 581; Netherlands, 510, 898

Épernon, duc d'. *See* Nogaret de La Valette

Epicoene (Jonson), 442

Epictetus Junior: Or, Maximes of Modern Morality. See *Maximes* (La Rochefoucauld)

Epidemiology; Belgium, 362; England, 903, 987; Italy, 810; Netherlands, 511

Epigrammatum Sacrorum Liber (Crashaw), 202

Episcopacy, 15, 33, 122, 496, 938

Epistola de Tolerantia. See *Letter Concerning Toleration, A* (Locke)

Epitome astronomiae Copernicanae (Kepler), 459

Épître à Huet (La Fontaine), 482

Épîtres (Boileau-Despréaux), 63

"Equality of Men and Women, The" (Gournay), 315

Erklärung über das erste Buch Mosis. See *Mysterium Magnum* (Böhme)

Eşfahan, 5

Esperança de Israel. See *Hope of Israel, The* (Manasseh)

Espinosa, Pedro de, 770

Essais de théodicée sur la bonté de Dieu . . . See *Theodicy* (Leibniz)

Essay Concerning Human Understanding, An (Locke), 545

Essay of the Pathology of the Brain and Nervous Stock, An (Willis), 986

Essay Towards the Present and Future Peace of Europe, An (Penn), 726

Essayes of a Prentise in the Divine Art of Poesie, The (James I), 413

Essex, second earl of, 175, 230

Essex, third earl of, 132, 756

Essex divorce case (1613), 16

Este, Marie Beatrice Eleanor Anne Margaret Isabella d'. *See* Mary of Modena (queen of England)

Esther (Racine), 775

Estilo culto, 312

Estilo llano, 312

Etching, Italy, 117

Ethics (Spinoza), 873

Étourdi, L'. See Blunderer, The (Molière)

Eucleria seu melioris partis electio (Schurman), 824

Euclides adauctus et methodicus (Guarini), 331

Eugene (prince of Savoy), 528

Europe; *maps*, xxix, liii

Evelyn, John, 95, 256-258, 677, 996

Everard, William, 988

Every Man in His Humour (Jonson), 440

Every Man Out of His Humour (Jonson), 440

Examen diatribae Thomae Willisii de febribus (Meara), 564

Examiner Defended, The (Williams), 984

Exclusion Crisis (1679-1681), 608, 840

Exercitatio anatomica de motu cordis et sanguinis in animalibus. See Anatomical Exercises of Dr. William Harvey . . . Concerning the Motion of the Heart and Blood, The (Harvey)

Exercitationes de generatione animalium. See Anatomical Exercitations, Concerning the Generation of Living Creatures (Harvey)

Exercitationes geometricae (Gregory), 320

Exercitationes paradoxicæ adversus Aristoteleos (Gassendi), 304

Experiments and Considerations Touching Colours (Boyle), 79

Experiments of Spiritual Life and Health (Williams), 984

Explication des maximes des saints sur la vie intérieure, L'. *See Maxims of the Saints Explained, Concerning the Interiour Life, The* (Fénelon)

Exploration; Americas, 140; England of Australia, 216; England of New England, 875, 878; England of North America, 391; England of the South Seas, 215; Europeans of Japan, 446; France of North America, 433, 491; France of the Mississippi, 603; Netherlands of Australia, 905; Netherlands of New Guinea, 906; Netherlands of New Zealand, 907; Netherlands of Tasmania, 907; Netherlands of the Fiji Islands, 907; Netherlands of the Pacific Ocean, 905. *See also* Category Index

Faber, David. *See* Fabricius, David

Fable of Polyphemus and Galatea (Góngora), 312

Fables choisies, mises en vers. See Fables Written in Verse (La Fontaine)

Fables Written in Verse (La Fontaine), 481

Fabri de Peiresc, Nicolas-Claude. *See* Peiresc, Nicolas-Claude Fabri de

Fabricius, David, 259-261; solar gazing, 260; telescopes, 260

Fabricius, Johannes, 259-261; solar gazing, 260; telescopes, 260

Fabricius ab Aquapendente, Hieronumus, 355

Fabritius, Carel, 956

Fábula de Polifemo y Galatea. See Fable of Polyphemus and Galatea (Góngora)

Fair Maid of the Exchange, The (Heywood), 374

Fairfax, third Baron, 205, 261-265, 483, 605, 756, 986

Fairfax, Thomas. *See* Fairfax, third Baron

Fairy tale (genre), 732

Faith and Duties of Christians, The (Burnet), 107

Faithful Shepherdess, The (Fletcher), 279

False Messiah, The (Grimmelshausen), 325

Fame and Confession of the Fraternity of R:C:, The (Fludd), 282

Fantasies of Three Parts (Gibbons), 309

Fatal Galantry (La Fayette), 478

Faubourg St.-Antoine, Battle of (1652), 933

Favola d'Orfeo, La (Monteverdi), 658

Fawkes, Guy, 16, 442

Fayette, Madame de La. *See* La Fayette, Madame de

Fehrbellin, Battle of (1675), 291

Felipe III. *See* Philip III (king of Spain)

Felipe IV. *See* Philip IV (king of Spain)

Felsina Pittrice (Malvasia), 856

Femmes illustres, Les (Scudéry), 829

Fénelon, François de Salignac de La Mothe-, 265-267, 339, 573

Feoffees for Impropriations (Puritan organization), 497

Ferdinand II (Holy Roman Emperor), 267-270, 293, 317, 627, 820, 854-855, 967

Ferdinand II de' Medici, 297, 881, 921

Ferdinand III (Holy Roman Emperor), 269, 526, 661, 705

Fermat, Pierre de, 271-274, 630, 970

Ferrar, Nicholas, 202, 274-277, 367

Fiji Islands, 907

Filmer, Robert, 546

Finch, Anne. *See* Conway, Anne

Finch, Daniel. *See* Nottingham, second earl of
Fingida Arcadia, La (Tirso), 913
Finta pazza Licori, La (Monteverdi), 659
Fiori musicali di diverse compositioni (Frescobaldi), 297
First Anniversary of the Government Under His Highness the Lord Protector, The (Marvell), 606
First Church (Boston), 219
First Dream (Cruz), 209
First Part of the True and Honorable Historie of the Life of Sir John Old-Castle the Good Lord Cobham, The (Drayton), 238
First Set of Madrigals and Mottets, The (Gibbons), 310
Five Women Who Loved Love (Saikaku), 404
Flamsteed, John, 348, 371
Flanders. *See* Geographical Index
Flea Catcher, The (La Tour), 494
Fletcher, Giles, the Younger, 278
Fletcher, John, 105, 277-280, 636, 846, 977; list of works, 278
Fletcher, Phineas, 278
Flores de Oliva, Isabel. *See* Rose of Lima, Saint
Flores de poetas ilustres de España (Espinosa), 770
Flowers and Grasses of the Four Seasons (Sōtatsu and Kōetsu), 869
Fludd, Robert, 280-282, 629
Folles-Avoines, 433, 603
Fontaine, Jean de La. *See* La Fontaine, Jean de
Fontainebleau, Edict of (1685), 821
Fontainebleau, Treaty of (1612), 598
Fontana, Domenico, 67
Fontei, Nicol, 888
Forced Marriage, The (Behn), 42
Ford, John, 279, 976
Ford, Philip, 726
Forman, Simon, 132
Fort Orange, 643
Fort St. Louis, 491
Fortune in Her Wits (Quevedo y Villegas), 771

Fortune Teller (La Tour), 494
Forty Questions of the Soul (Böhme), 61
Fouquet, Nicolas, 180, 481, 523, 532, 622
Four Days' Battle (1666), 806, 808
Four Monarchies, The (Bradstreet), 89
Four Prentices of London, The (Heywood), 373
Four Rivers Fountain, 46
Four Seasons (Poussin), 751
Fourth Paper Presented by Major Butler, The (Williams), 984
Fowler, Katherine. *See* Philips, Katherine
Fox, George, 283-286, 726
Fragmenta Aurea (Suckling), 895
Frames of Government of Pennsylvania, 727
France. *See* Geographical Index
Francis, Lord Russell, 767
Franco-Dutch Wars (1672-1678), 291, 507, 559, 654, 821, 934, 946
Franco-Spanish War of 1595-1598, 897
Franco-Spanish Wars of 1635-1659, 417, 425, 554, 933
Frederick I of Bohemia. *See* Frederick V
Frederick II, 415
Frederick V, 97, 143, 250, 253, 268, 275, 293-295, 310, 805, 820
Frederick Henry, 286-290, 619, 820, 933
Frederick William, the Great Elector, 154, 290-293, 851
Freedom of the Seas, The (Grotius), 327
Fremin, Jacques, 909
French Academy (Rome), 504. *See also* Académie Française
French-Canadians, 76
Frescobaldi, Girolamo, 295-297
Friedrich Wilhelm von Hohenzollern, Kurfürst von Brandenburg. *See* Frederick William, the Great Elector
Fritzius, Joachim, 281
Fronde, Wars of the (1648-1653), 19, 22, 159, 180, 185, 212, 477,

487, 521, 549, 554, 622, 661, 781, 821, 829, 933, 946
Frontenac, comte de, 433, 490, 500, 603
Fuenteovejuna. See *Sheep-Well, The* (Lope de Vega)
Fujian, 1001
Fukien. *See* Fujian
Fulin. *See* Shunzhi
Fumifugium (Evelyn), 257
Fundamental Orders of Connecticut, 387, 568
Funeral Oration for Henrietta of England (Bossuet), 71
Funerall Poem, A (Tourneur), 928
Furetière, Antoine, 480
Further Account of the Province of Pennsylvania and Its Improvements, A (Penn), 726
Fyodor I Ivanovich, 683, 794, 943
Fyodor II, 865

Gabbard Shoal, Battle of the (1653), 57, 931
Gabrieli, Giovanni, 825
Gagliano, Marco da, 297
Galigai, Leonora, 598
Galilei, Maria Celeste. *See* Maria Celeste
Galilei, Virginia. *See* Maria Celeste
Galileo, 298-301; and Giovanni Alfonso Borelli, 66; influence on Robert Boyle, 78; and Tommaso Campanella, 125; and René Descartes, 227; *Dialogue Concerning the Two Chief World Systems, Ptolemaic and Copernican*, 299; and Pierre Gassendi, 305; and Artemisia Gentileschi, 307; and William Harvey, 356; and Thomas Hobbes, 379; and Christiaan Huygens, 397; and Johannes Kepler, 459; and daughter Maria Celeste, 593; tutor to Cosimo II de' Medici, 626; and Marin Mersenne, 630; and John Milton, 640; and Sir Isaac Newton, 680; censured by Pope Paul V, 721; and Nicolas-Claude Fabri de Peiresc, 722; and observations of planetary motion, 349; and

Santorio Santorio, 811; and Nicolaus Steno, 881; observations of sunspots, 260; and telescopes, 539; and Evangelista Torricelli, 921; and Pope Urban VIII, 936

Gallican Liberties, Declaration of (1682), 406

Game at Chess, A (Middleton), 638

Garden of Cyrus, The (Browne), 95

Gardener's Dog, The (Lope de Vega), 950

Garzoni, Giovanna, 302-304

Gassendi, Pierre, 211, 304-306, 389, 630, 723

Gaston (brother of Louis XIII), 551

Geistliche Chormusik (Schütz), 827

Gellée, Claude. *See* Claude Lorrain

Gendret, Father Antoine de, 76

Generall Historie of Virginia, New-England, and the Summer Isles, The (Smith), 863-864

Genroku Era (1688-1704), 376

Gentileschi, Artemisia, 307-309

Geographer, The (Vermeer), 958

Geography; Japan, 447; Netherlands, 907; Ottoman Empire, 455. *See also* Category Index

Geology; England, 106; Italy, 882

Geometriae Pars Universalis (Gregory), 319

Geometry; England, 970; France, 227, 272; Italy, 330, 921; Scotland, 319; Switzerland, 48

George I (king of England), 255

George Fox Digg'd Out of His Burrows (Williams), 984

Germany. *See* Geographical Index

Ghazzati, Nathan, 836

Ghost of Lucrece, The (Middleton), 636

Gibbons, Grinling, 996

Gibbons, Orlando, 309-311

Gibraltar, Battle of (1607), 930

Gifford, John, 100

Gilbert, William, 335

Globe Theatre, 105, 279, 441-442, 928

Glorious Revolution (1688), 123, 418, 464, 508, 518, 546, 609, 611, 694, 726, 730, 816, 821, 979

Goat Amalthea with the Infant Jupiter and a Faun, The (Bernini), 45

Gobbi and Other Bizarre Figures (Callot), 118

Gobelin Manufactory, 505

Goblins, The (Suckling), 895

Godfrey, Sir Edmund Berry, 692

Godunov, Boris, 794, 855, 943

Golconda, 859

Golden Age, The (Heywood), 374

Golden Age, Spain, 113, 312, 317, 739, 913, 950, 953

Goldsmid, Johann. *See* Fabricius, Johannes

Golitsyn, Vasily Vasilyevich, 624, 866

Gomarists, 619

Gondi, Philippe-Emmanuel de, 962

Góngora y Argote, Luis de, 312-314, 949, 953

Gongorismo, 313

Good, Sarah, 690

Goodwin, Thomas, 198

Gorges, Sir Ferdinando, 875

Goring, George, 894

Gosson, Stephen, 374

Goupil, René, 423

Gournay, Marie le Jars de, 314-316

Government. *See* Category Index

Governor Bradford's Letter Book (Bradford), 86

Graaf, Regnier de, 852, 898

Grace Abounding to the Chief of Sinners (Bunyan), 101

Gracián, Baltasar. *See* Gracián y Morales, Baltasar

Gracián, Lorenzo. *See* Gracián y Morales, Baltasar

Gracián y Morales, Baltasar, 316-318

Gran teatro del mundo, El. See *Great Theater of the World* (Calderón)

Grand Alliance, 980

Grand Alliance, War of the. *See* Augsburg, War of the League of (1689-1697)

Grand Mademoiselle, La. *See* Montpensier, duchesse de

Grand Remonstrance (1641), 167, 204, 768

Grande Opéra. *See* Académie Royale de Musique

Grandes anales de quince días, Los (Quevedo y Villegas), 770

Great Condé. *See* Condé, The Great

Great Elector. *See* Frederick William, the Great Elector

Great Fire of London (1666), 148, 346, 384, 729, 806, 995

Great Mirror of Male Love, The (Saikaku), 404

Great Northern War (1700-1721), 625

Great Plague (1665), 148, 342, 729

Great Protestation (1621), 177

Great Swamp Battle (1675), 634

Great Swamp Fight (1637), 567

Great Theater of the World (Calderón), 115

Greco, El, 738

Green, Thomas, 92

Green Spring Faction, 29

Gregory, James, 319-321

Griffin, John, 54

Griggs, William, 690

Grimaldi, Francesco Maria, 134, 321-323

Grimmelshausen, Hans Jakob Christoffel von, 324-326; *Simplicissimus*, 324

Groot, Huig de. *See* Grotius, Hugo

Groseilliers, sieur des, 777

Grotius, Hugo, 17, 326-329, 723, 759; list of works, 328

Grounds of Natural Philosophy (Newcastle), 677

Guarini, Guarino, 330-332

Guericke, Otto von, 79, 333-336, 814

Guild of St. Luke, 352

Guillemeau, Charles, 74

Guitar Player, The (Vermeer), 958

Gunpowder Plot (1605), 16, 175, 224, 414, 442, 720

Guo Xingye. *See* Zheng Chenggong

Gustav, Charles X. *See* Charles X Gustav

Gustavus II Adolphus, 163, 184, 254, 262, 269, 294, 336-339, 527, 704, 791, 854, 894, 925, 967

Guyart, Marie. *See* Marie de l'Incarnation
Guyon, Madame, 265, 339-341
Guzmán y Pimental, Gaspar de. *See* Olivares, count-duke of
Gwyn, Nell, 138, 240, 342-344

Haarlem Academy, 352
Habitants, 575
Habsburg Dynasty, 526, 966; and Pope Alexander VII, 10; and King Charles II of Spain, 151, 739; financial burdens, 739; vs. France, 431, 493, 554; and Frederick V, 293; and Frederick Henry, 286; and Gustavus II Adolphus, 337; conflict with Holy Roman Empire, 267; and John of Austria, 425; and Jan Komenský, 469; military, 337; in the Netherlands, 286, 618; and Philip III of Spain, 737; and Cardinal de Richelieu, 791; and Sigismund III Vasa, 854; Thirty Years' War, 621; and Pope Urban VIII, 937
Haçi Halife. *See* Kâtib Çelebî
Hackston, David, 122
Haikai, 617
Haiku, 615
Ḥāji Khalīfa. *See* Kâtib Çelebî
Hale, Matthew, 345-348
Hale Commission, 346
Halifax, first marquis of. *See* Savile, Sir George
Halley, Edmond, 348-351, 371, 680
Halley's comet, 350
Hals, Frans, 352-354
Hamen y León, Juan van der, 1005
Hamilton, duke of, 345
Hampden, John, 144
Hampton Court Conference, 15
Haoge, 234
Harbor Scene, The (Claude Lorrain), 172
Hardouin, Jules. *See* Mansart, Jules Hardouin-
Hardouin-Mansart, Jules. *See* Mansart, Jules Hardouin-
Harington, Lucy, 238

Harmonices mundi. See *Harmonies of the World* (Kepler)
Harmonie universelle (Mersenne), 631
Harmonies of the World (Kepler), 459, 818
Haro, Luis de, 739
Harriot, Thomas, 970
Harrison, Thomas, 484
Hartford, Treaty of (1643), 891
Harvey, William, 66, 280, 355-358, 543, 564, 579, 723, 811, 899, 986
Hatsubi sanpō (Seki), 832
"Healing Question, A" (Vane), 942
Hechizado, El. *See* Charles II (king of Spain)
Hedong, Madame. *See* Liu Yin
Heemskerck, Jacob van, 930
Hein, Piet, 288, 359-361, 698
Heinricus Sagittarius. *See* Schütz, Heinrich
Helmont, Franciscus Mercurius van, 188, 251, 362
Helmont, Jan Baptista van, 361-363
Henge ga maki (Moronobu), 376
Henrietta Anne, 72
Henrietta Maria, 364-366; Catholicism of, 496; and King Charles I of England, 144; and son King Charles II of England, 147; and the first earl of Clarendon, 168; and Abraham Cowley, 199; and Richard Crashaw, 202; and Lady Eleanor Davies, 221; and Sir Anthony van Dyck, 246; and son King James II of England, 416; and Richard Lovelace, 562; daughter of Marie de Médicis, 598; and naming of Maryland, 120; and the duke of Monmouth, 653; and the duchesse de Montpensier, 661; and the Netherlands, 288; and the duchess of Newcastle, 676; patronage, 846, 975; and Prince Rupert, 805; and the theater, 374; and Maarten Tromp, 931
Henry, Frederick. *See* Frederick Henry

Henry II de Bourbon. *See* Condé, third prince of
Henry IV (king of France), 111, 141, 315, 364, 551, 577, 587, 598, 737, 779, 790, 896
Henslowe, Philip, 223, 440, 977
Heráclito cristiano (Quevedo y Villegas), 770
Herbert, George, 17, 203, 232, 276, 366-368; list of works, 367
Hercules and Omphale (Artemisia), 308
Hermeticists, 629
Hermitage, 499
Hero, The (Gracián), 317
Heroic Stanzas (Dryden), 240
Herrera, Francisco, the Younger, 671
Herrera, Francisco de, the Elder, 1004
Herrick, Robert, 368-371, 443
Hesperides (Herrick), 369
Hetman state, 461
Hevelius, Elisabetha, 371-373
Hevelius, Johannes, 348, 371-373
Hewel, Johann. *See* Hevelius, Johannes
Heywood, Thomas, 373-375, 977
High and Deep Searching Out of the Threefold Life of Man, The (Böhme), 61
Hinchingbrooke, Viscount. *See* Sandwich, first earl of
Hind and the Panther, The (Dryden), 241
Hinduism; Mughal Empire, 24; Śivājī, 858
Hirayama Tōgo. *See* Ihara Saikaku
Hireling Ministry None of Christs, The (Williams), 984
His Maiesties Poeticall Exercises at Vacant Houres (James I), 413
Hishikawa Moronobu, 375-377
Histoire comique des états et empires de la lune, L'. See *Other World, The* (Cyrano)
Histoire comique des états et empires du soleil, L'. See *States and Empires of the Sun, The* (Cyrano)
Histoire de la princesse de Paphlagonie (Montpensier), 662

Histoire de Madame Henriette d'Angleterre. See *Fatal Galantry* (La Fayette)
Histoires. See *Tales of Mother Goose* (Perrault)
Historia general de la orden de Nuestra Señora de las Mercedes (Tirso), 914
Historia insectorum (Ray), 783
Historia insectorum generalis (Swammerdam), 899
Historia plantarum generalis (Ray), 782
Historical and Critical Dictionary, An (Bayle), 37
Historiography. *See* Category Index
History of Japan, The (Kämpfer), 446-447
History of Plymouth Plantation (Bradford), 86, 130, 878
History of the Common Law (Hale), 347
History of the Future (Vieira), 960
History of the Pleas of the Crown (Hale), 347
History of the Rebellion and Civil Wars in England, The (Clarendon), 167
Histriomastix (Marston), 223
Hobbes, Thomas, 147, 188, 300, 306, 357, 378-382, 543, 630, 676, 733, 759, 970; list of works, 380
Hobomok, 879
Hohenzollern, Friedrich Wilhelm von. *See* Frederick William, the Great Elector
Hōjō Ujimasa, 916
Holderness, earl of. *See* Rupert, Prince
Holy Family (Garzoni), 302
Holy Family of the Little Bird (Murillo), 671
Holy Family with Angels, The (Rembrandt), 787
Holy Roman Empire; *maps,* xxix, liii
Holy War, The (Bunyan), 102
Honami Kōetsu, 695, 868
Honest Whore, The (Dekker and Middleton), 224, 636
Hong Taiji. *See* Abahai

Honthorst, Gerard, 823
Hooke, Robert, 48, 79, 349, 372, 383-385, 509, 564, 677, 680, 734, 986
Hooker, Richard, 15
Hooker, Thomas, 196, 247, 386-388, 567
Hooke's law, 384
Hoorn, Johan van, 852
Hope of Israel, The (Manasseh), 583
Hora de todos y la fortuna con seso, La. See *Fortune in Her Wits* (Quevedo y Villegas)
Horace (Corneille), 194
Horne, Johannes van, 898
Horologium (Huygens), 398
Horologium oscillatorium (Huygens), 398
Horrocks, Jeremiah, 388-390
Horrox, Jeremiah. *See* Horrocks, Jeremiah
Hôtel de Bourgogne, 774
Hôtel de Carnavalet, 834
Hôtel de Noailles, 591
Hôtel de Rambouillet, 780, 829, 833
Hôtel des Invalides, 590
Hotta Masatoshi, 919
Ho-tung, Madame. *See* Liu Yin
House of Savoy, 331
Householders (Cossacks), 785
Howard, Lady Frances, 16, 132
Howard, Sir Robert, 240, 765
Howe, Elizabeth, 690
Howelcke, Jan. *See* Hevelius, Johannes
Hsi-tsung. *See* Tianqi
Huai-tsung. *See* Chongzhen
Huaizong. *See* Chongzhen
Huang Yuan Jie, 541
Hudson, Henry, 390-393
Hudson's Bay Company, 401, 777
Huet, Pierre-Daniel, 477, 661
Huguenots, 98, 552, 598, 790, 821, 896; New York, 518; persecution of, 407, 555, 560
Hull, Siege of (1643), 262
Human Nature (Hobbes), 379
Humble Petition and Advice (1657), 206, 485
Hundred Associates, 141
Hung Taiji. *See* Abahai

Hungary, 453, 528, 861. *See also* Geographical Index
Hunt, Thomas, 875
Hurons, 141, 423, 499, 575, 603
Hutchinson, Anne, 196-197, 247, 386, 394-396, 941, 992
Huygens, Christiaan, 135, 320, 323, 335, 371, 385, 397-400, 510, 514, 710; *Cosmotheoros,* 398
Huygens, Constantijn, 250, 397, 823
Hyde, Edward. *See* Clarendon, first earl of
Hyde Park (Shirley), 847
Hydriotaphia Urne-Buriall (Browne), 95
Hydrodynamica. See *Hydrodynamics* (Daniel Bernoulli)
Hydrodynamics (Daniel Bernoulli), 49

Iatrochemistry, 361, 986
Iatromechanism, 362
Iberville, Pierre Le Moyne d', 401-403
İbrahim, 472, 670
Ibrahim (Scudéry), 829
Icones principum vivorum doctorum pictorum . . . See *Iconography, The* (van Dyck)
Iconography, The (van Dyck), 245
Idea, the Shepheards Garland (Drayton), 237
Ideas Mirrour (Drayton), 237
If You Know Not Me, You Know Nobody (Heywood), 374
Ignatius His Conclave (Donne), 232
Ihara Saikaku, 403-405; list of works, 404
Illinois (tribe), 434
Illusion comique, L' (Corneille), 193
Illustrated Account Given by Hevelius in His "Machina celestis" of the Method of Mounting His Telescopes and Erecting an Observatory, The. See *Machina coelestis* (J. Hevelius)
Imagawa Yoshimoto, 915
Imaginary Invalid, The (Molière), 648

Imbangala, 687

Imitating Tang Yin's "Dwelling in the Summer Mountains" (Chen), 157

Immaculate Conception of the Escorial, The (Murillo), 671

Impiété des déistes, athées, et libertins de ce temps, L' (Mersenne), 629

Importants, Les, 159

Incoronazione di Poppea, L' (Monteverdi), 659

Indemnity, Act of (1660), 169, 942

Index of Forbidden Books, 300

India. *See* Geographical Index

Indian Emperor, The (Dryden), 240

Indian Grammar, The (Eliot), 248

Indian Queen, The (Dryden, Purcell, and Howard), 240, 765

Indonesia. *See* Geographical Index

Indulgence, Act of (1667), 122

Indulgence, Declaration of (1672), 101

Indulgence, Declaration of (1687), 417

Inés de la Cruz, Sor Juana. *See* Cruz, Sor Juana Inés de la

Ingle, Richard, 92

Ingle's Rebellion (1644), 92

Ingoldsby, Richard, 519

Inleidinge tot de Hollandsche Rechts-geleerdheyd. See *Introduction to Dutch Jurisprudence* (Grotius)

Inner Commentary to the Book of Changes (Wang), 972

Innocent X, 9, 68, 422, 773

Innocent XI, 405-407, 744, 882

Innocent XIII, 265

Inquisition; Bologna, 581; Campanella, 125; Ferdinand II's use of, 269; Galileo, 227, 300, 594, 936; Helmont, 362; Jewish conversions, 871; Netherlands, 288; Rose of Lima, 797; Sarpi, 720; Vieira, 960

Institut de France. *See* Collège des Quatre-Nations

Institute of the Blessed Virgin Mary, 974

Institutes (Coke), 178

Instructions for the Education of a Daughter (Fénelon), 265

Instrument of Government (1653), 54, 206, 485

Introduction to Dutch Jurisprudence (Grotius), 327

Invention. *See* Category Index

Investigation of the Meaning of the Four Books (Wang), 972

Invisible College, 79

Iphigenia in Aulis (Racine), 775

Iran. *See* Geographical Index

Ireland. *See* Geographical Index

Ireton, Henry, 484, 756

Iris and Roses (Chen), 157

Irises (Kōrin), 696

Irish Articles (1615), 938

Irish Rebellion (1641-1650), 700, 768, 885, 939

Iron Age, The (Heywood), 374

Ironsides (English regiment), 205

Iroquois, 423, 499, 644, 908; in Quebec, 575

Isabella Brandt (van Dyck), 244

Iskender Paşa, 855

Islam; India, 859; Mughal Empire, 23, 843; Ottoman Empire, 454; Safavid Dynasty, 4; Twelver Shia, 6

Islam Giray III, 462

Island Princess, The (Fletcher), 279

Isle of Dogs, The (Nashe and Jonson), 440

Isomura Yoshinori, 831

Israel, Manasseh ben. *See* Manasseh ben Israel

Istanbul, Treaty of (1590), 4

Italy. *See* Geographical Index

I-tsung. *See* Tianqi

Ivan V, 865

Ivan the Terrible, 943

Iwasa Matabe, 375

Izumo no Okuni, 408-409

Jacobites, 821

Jahan, Shah. *See* Shah Jahan

Jahāngīr, 410-412, 842

Jai Singh, 859

Jakarta, 905

Jama Masjid, 844

James I (king of England), 413-416; and Lancelot Andrewes, 15; and William Bradford, 84; and the first duke of Buckingham, 96; and Richard Burbage, 105; and Robert Burton, 109; and George Calvert, 119; and Richard Cameron, 121; and Robert Carr, 131; and Charles I, 143; and Sir Edward Coke, 175; and Thomas Dekker, 223; and Sir Anthony van Dyck, 244; and John Eliot, 247; and Elizabeth of Bohemia, 250; and Elizabeth Stuart, 253; and Nicholas Ferrar, 274; and Frederick V, 293; and Orlando Gibbons, 309; and William Harvey, 355; and Jahāngīr, 412; and Inigo Jones, 436; and Ben Jonson, 442; and William Laud, 496; and Richard Lower, 565; and Thomas Middleton, 636; and Rory O'More, 699; and Paul V, 720; and Nicolas-Claude Fabri de Peiresc, 722; and Philip III, 737; and Pocahontas, 747; and Michael Romanov, 795; and Prince Rupert, 805; and Friedrich Hermann Schomberg, 820; and John Smith, 864; and Sir John Suckling, 893; and James Ussher, 939; and John Webster, 976

James II (king of England), 416-419; and Richard Baxter, 34; and John Bunyan, 102; and Thomas Burnet, 106; and Richard Cameron, 123; and Catherine of Braganza, 138; and John Dryden, 241; and George Fox, 285; and Nell Gwyn, 343; and Henrietta Maria, 364; and Innocent XI, 407; and the first duke of Leeds, 508; and Jacob Leisler, 518; and Leopold I, 528; and Mary II, 610; and Mary of Modena, 607; and the duke of Monmouth, 655; and Sir Isaac Newton, 681; and Titus Oates, 692; and William Paterson, 717; and William Penn, 725; and Samuel Pepys, 729; and Henry Purcell, 764; and Sir George Savile, 817; and Thomas

Sydenham, 902; and Maarten and Cornelis Tromp, 931; and William III, 979

James VI (king of Scotland). *See* James I (king of England)

Jamestown, 30, 702, 746, 752, 862

Janissaries, 668, 674

Jankow, Battle of (1645), 926

Jansen, Cornelius Otto, 419-422, 714, 773, 936

Jansenism, 22, 265, 406, 421, 713, 773, 936, 964

Janssen, Zacharias, 537

Japan. *See* Geographical Index

Japanese Family Storehouse, The (Saikaku), 404

Jaworów, Treaty of (1675), 429

Jehangir. *See* Jahāngīr

Jerseys, colonization of, 726

Jesuit Relations, 575, 596, 910

Jesuits, 420, 714, 720, 773, 974; American Southwest, 467; Brazil, 960; Canada, 77, 423, 499, 575, 596, 603, 908; China, 161, 449, 849

Jews; England, 206; Netherlands, 582; persecution of, 871; Poland, 462; Portugal, 961; return to England, 583; Turkey, 837

Jihannuma (Kâtib Çelebî), 455

Jin Dynasty, Later, 1

Jinga. *See* Njinga

Jinkōki. See Book of Large and Small Numbers (Yoshida)

Jirgalang, 234

João IV. *See* John IV (king of Portugal)

Jogues, Saint Isaac, 423-424

Johann Georg I (elector of Saxony), 826

Johann Georg II (elector of Saxony), 827

John II Casimir Vasa, 154, 186, 428, 462, 624

John III Sobieski, 406, 427-430, 453, 528, 744

John IV (king of Portugal), 137, 425, 430-432, 960

John of Austria, 151, 425-427

John of Spain, the Younger, Don. *See* John of Austria

John the Fortunate. *See* John IV (king of Portugal)

John the Restorer. *See* John IV (king of Portugal)

Johnson, Aphra. *See* Behn, Aphra

Jolliet, Louis, 433-435, 490, 603

Jones, Inigo, 436-438, 442

Jonson, Ben, 52, 105, 167, 223, 232, 278-279, 368, 373, 436, 439-444, 649, 747, 846; list of works, 441

Journal of George Fox, The (Fox), 283

Juan de Austria, Don. *See* John of Austria

Judaism. *See* Jews

Judas Macabeo (Calderón), 113

Judgment of the Archbishops and Bishops of Ireland (Ussher et al.), 938

Judith and Her Maidservant (Artemisia), 307

Judith Slaying Holofernes (Artemisia), 307

Judith with the Head of Holofernes (Sirani), 857

Julianstown, Battle of (1641), 700

Jurieu, Pierre, 36

Justice Without Revenge (Lope de Vega), 950

Kabbalism, 835

Kabuki, 408

Kahlenberg, Battle of (1683), 429, 528

Kaihō Yūshō, 868

Kalckstein, Christian Ludwig von, 292

Kalendarium Hortense (Evelyn), 257

Kambun Kyōshi, 375

Kämpfer, Engelbert, 445-448; *The History of Japan*, 446

K'ang-hsi. *See* Kangxi

Kangxi, 448-451, 850

Kanō school, 695

Kapici Bashi. *See* Shabbetai Tzevi

Kara Mustafa Paşa, Merzifonlu, 451-454, 528

Kardis, Treaty of (1660), 155

Karlowitz, Treaty of (1699), 453, 528

Kashf al-ẓunūnʿan asāmī al-kutub wa al-funūn (Kâtib Çelebî), 455

Kashima kikō. See Visit to the Kashima Shrine, A (Bashō)

Kâtib Çelebî, 454-456

Kawara Jūrōbei, 999

Ke, Madame, 161, 911

Keeper of the Gate. *See* Shabbetai Tzevi

Keian incident (1651), 999

Kempe, Will, 104

Kentish Knock, Battle of (1652), 57

Kentish Petition, 562

Kenzan. *See* Ogata Kenzan

Kepler, Johannes, 259, 281, 299, 305, 349, 357, 388, 457-461, 680, 818, 966

Kepler's Conversation with Galileo's Sidereal Messenger (Kepler), 459

Ker (Kerr), Robert. *See* Carr, Robert

Keusche Joseph, Der (Grimmelshausen), 325

Khatib Chelebi. *See* Kâtib Çelebî

Khatib Shalabî. *See* Kâtib Çelebî

Khayronnesa Begum, 4

Khmelnytsky, Bohdan, 452, 461-463, 624

Khmelnytsky, Yurii, 452

Khotin, Battle of (1673), 429

Khovanshchina, 866

Khovansky, Ivan, 866

Khovansky Mischief. *See* Khovanshchina

Khurram. *See* Shah Jahan

Khusru, 410, 842

Kichibē. *See* Hishikawa Moronobu

Kidd, William, 464-467

Kilajua, 687

Kilkenny, Confederation of, 701

Killiecrankie, Battle of (1689), 611

Killigrew, Thomas, 240, 342

Kilrush, Battle of (1642), 700

King, Edmund, 565

King and No King, A (Fletcher and Beaumont), 279

King Arthur (Dryden and Purcell), 765

King Philip's War. *See* Metacom's War (1675-1676)

King William's War. *See* Augsburg, War of the League of (1689-1697)

King's Men, 105, 279, 342, 442, 636, 846, 977. *See also* Lord Chamberlain's Men

King's Private Musick, 502

Kino, Eusebio Francisco, 467-469

Kirkby, Christopher, 692

Kirkholm, Battle of (1605), 854

Kitagawa Sōtatsu. *See* Sōtatsu

Kleine geistliche Concerte (Schütz), 827

Klushino, Battle of (1610), 855, 945

Knäred, Treaty of (1613), 336, 704

Kober, Tobias, 60

Kōetsu. *See* Honami Kōetsu

Komenský, Jan, 469-471

Königsberg, Treaty of (1656), 154

Köprülü Mehmed Paşa, 451

Kōrin, Ogata. *See* Ogata Kōrin

Kormchaia Kniga, 684

Kösem Mahpeyker. *See* Kösem Sultan

Kösem Sultan, 472-474, 668

Kōshoku gonin onna. See *Five Women Who Loved Love* (Saikaku)

Kōshoku ichidai onna. See *Life of an Amorous Woman, The* (Saikaku)

Kōshoku ichidai otoko. See *Life of an Amorous Man, The* (Saikaku)

Kōwa, Seki. *See* Seki Kōwa

Koxinga. *See* Zheng Chenggong

Kühn, Eusebio Francesco. *See* Kino, Eusebio Francisco

Kuo Hsing-yeh. *See* Zheng Chenggong

Kusunoki Fuden, 998

La Hogue, Battle of (1692), 609

Labadie, Jean de, 824

La Barre, sieur de, 491

La Bruyère, Jean de, 475-476; list of works, 476

Labyrint světa a Ráj srdce. See *Labyrinth of the World and the Paradise of the Heart* (Komenský)

Labyrinth of the World and the Paradise of the Heart (Komenský), 470

Lacombe, François, 339

Lady Eleanor Her Appeal, The (Davies), 221

Lady Jane (Webster and Henslowe), 977

Lady Nit-Wit, The (Lope de Vega), 950

Lady of Pleasure, The (Shirley), 847

La Fayette, Comtesse de. *See* La Fayette, Madame de

La Fayette, Madame de, 72, 477-479, 487, 662, 833; *The Princess of Clèves*, 478

La Ferté-Sénectère, Henri, maréchal de, 494

La Fontaine, Jean de, 186, 480-483, 586, 773, 834; list of works, 481

Lalande, John, 424

Lalemant, Jerôme, 596

Lalement, Charles, 575

Lambert, John, 483-486, 651, 942

Lamberville, Jacques de, 909

Lambeth articles (1604), 939

La Motte, Jeanne-Marie Bouvier de. *See* Guyon, Madame

Landscape After Wang Meng (Zhang), 157

Landscape with a Rainbow (Rubens), 803

Landscape with a Sunset (Rubens), 803

Landscape with the Château De Steen (Rubens), 803

Landscape with the Gathering of the Ashes of Phocion (Poussin), 750

Larmes de Saint Pierre, Les (Malherbe), 577

La Rochefoucauld, François de, 477, 487-489, 548, 662; *Maximes*, 488

La Rochelle, siege of (1627-1628), 552

La Rochelle Assembly, 552

La Sablière, Madame de, 482

La Salle, sieur de, 401, 435, 490-493

Last Remains of Sir John Suckling, The (Suckling), 895

Late Lancashire Witches, The (Heywood and Brome), 374

Later Jin Dynasty. *See* Jin Dynasty, Later

La Tour, Georges de, 493-495

La Tour d'Auvergne, Henri de. *See* Turenne, Viscount de

Laud, William, 145, 167, 197, 218, 247, 275, 345, 386, 495-498, 768, 887, 938, 982, 991

Lauderdale, first duke of, 507, 839

Laugh and Lie Down (Tourneur), 928

Laughing Cavalier, The (Hals), 353

Lauzun, Antonin-Nompar de Caumont de, 662

Laval, François, 76, 498-501, 576

Laval-Montmorency, François-Xavier de. *See* Laval, François

La Valette, Nogaret de. *See* Nogaret de La Valette

La Vallière, Françoise-Louise de la Baume Le Blanc de, 586, 601

La Voisin, Madame. *See* Monvoisin, Madame

Law; Americas, 93; England, 174; natural, 543, 759; Netherlands, 327; Russia, 12. *See also* Category Index

Law of Freedom on a Platform, The (Winstanley), 989

Lawes, Henry, 370, 502-503

Laws and Ordinances of the Sea (1652), 57

Laxism, 406

Lazarists. *See* Congregation of the Mission

League of _____. *See* _____, League of

League of Augsburg, War of the. *See* Augsburg, War of the League of

Learned Maid, The (Schurman), 823

Lebensbeschreibung der Ertzbetrügerin und Landstörtzerin Courasche. See *Courage, the Adventuress* (Grimmelshausen)

Le Brun, Charles, 504-506, 523, 532

Le Brun, Nicolas, 504

Lech, Battle of (1632), 926

Leeds, first duke of, 149, 506-508, 693, 816, 840

Leeuwenhoek, Antoni van, 399, 509-513, 898, 958; "Containing

Some Microbial Observations, About Animals in the Scurf of the Teeth . . . ," 511
Legate, Bartholomew, 16
Leibniz, Gottfried Wilhelm, 513-517; and Pierre Bayle, 37; dispute over invention of calculus, 49, 681; and Anne Conway, 188; and Elizabeth of Bohemia, 252; and Pierre de Fermat, 271; list of works, 514; and John Locke, 545; and Sir Isaac Newton, 681; and Seki Kōwa, 832; and Baruch Spinoza, 874; and John Wallis, 970; and Erhard Weigel, 759
Leicester, first earl of, 618
Leipzig, Battle of (1631), 894
Leisler, Jacob, 518-520
Lemercier, Jacques, 523, 532, 589
Le Moyne, Pierre. *See* Iberville, Pierre Le Moyne d'
Lenclos, Anne de. *See* Lenclos, Ninon de
Lenclos, Ninon de, 520-522
Le Nôtre, André, 523-526, 532, 590
Lens, Battle of (1648), 549, 621
Leo XI, 720
León, Alonso de, 491
Leopold I, 40, 151, 406, 453, 526-529, 555
Leopold Ignatius. *See* Leopold I
Lerma, duke de, 530-532, 697, 736, 913
Le Tellier, François-Michel. *See* Louvois, marquis de
Le Tellier, Michel, 72, 180, 266, 558
Letter Concerning Toleration, A (Locke), 545
Letter to a Friend, upon Occasion of the Death of His Intimate Friend, A (Browne), 95
Letters to Father (Maria Celeste), 594
Lettre sur la comète. See Miscellaneous Reflections Occasion'd by the Comet Which Appear'd in December, 1680 (Bayle)
Lettres (Cyrano), 212

Lettres provinciales. See Provincial Letters, The (Pascal)
Le Vau, Louis, 523, 532-534, 590
LeVeau, Louis. *See* Le Vau, Louis
Levellers, 205, 263, 535
Levellers' Large Petition, 535
Leviathan (Hobbes), 379, 543
Li Fan Yuan, 2
Li Tzu-Ch'eng. *See* Li Zicheng
Li Zicheng, 161, 235, 849
Li Zicheng's Revolt (1642), 161, 235, 972
Libavius, Andreas, 565
Liber veritatis (Claude Lorrain), 171
Liberazione di Ruggiero dall'isola d'Alcina, La (Caccini), 111
Libri Plantarum (Cowley), 200
Liechao shiji, 541
Life and Adventures of Buscon, the Witty Spaniard, The (Quevedo y Villegas), 770
Life and Death of Mr. Badman, The (Bunyan), 102
Life and Strange Surprizing Adventures of Robinson Crusoe, of York, Mariner, Written by Himself, The. See Robinson Crusoe (Defoe)
Life Is a Dream (Calderón), 114
Life of an Amorous Man, The (Saikaku), 403
Life of an Amorous Woman, The (Saikaku), 403
Life of Courage, The. See Courage, the Adventuress (Grimmelshausen)
Life of Edward, Earl of Clarendon, The (Clarendon), 167
Life of Ferdinand de' Medici, The (Callot), 117
Life of St. Jerome (Zurbarán), 1005
Life of the Archpriest Avvakum, by Himself, The (Avvakum), 26
Life of William Cavendish, Duke of Newcastle, The (Newcastle), 677
Lightfoot, James, 940
Lilburne, John, 534-536
Lille, Battle of (1667), 934
Lincoln's Inn Fields Theatre, 51
Lionne, Hugues de, 622
Lippershey, Hans, 537-540

Lipsius, Justus, 314
Lisbon, Treaty of (1668), 426, 432
Literary criticism; England, 128; France, 63
Literature; England, 729; France, 63, 475, 477, 481, 487, 732, 829; Germany, 325; Japan, 403; Spain, 317, 771, 913, 950. *See also* Category Index; specific genre
Litigants, The (Racine), 774
Little Gidding, 202, 275, 367
"Little Tom Thumb" (Perrault), 732
Liu Shi. *See* Liu Yin
Liu Yin, 540-542
Livonia, 854
Locke, John, 37, 107, 306, 381, 516, 542-548, 564, 642, 761, 783, 840, 901; list of works, 546
Lodewijk, Willem, 618
Lomellini Family, The (van Dyck), 245
London, Treaty of (1604), 737
Londonderry, Siege of (1689), 609
Long Parliament (1640-1648), 55, 145, 148, 497, 562, 651, 768, 838, 942
Longueil, René de, 588
Longueville, duchesse de, 487, 548-550, 933
Lord Admiral's Men, 104, 373
Lord Chamberlain's Men, 104, 440. *See also* King's Men
Lord Hay's Masque (Campion), 128
Lord's Masque, The (Campion), 128
Lorrain, Claude. *See* Claude Lorrain
Louis II de Bourbon. *See* Condé, The Great
Louis XIII, 18, 126, 141, 144, 158, 184, 193, 211, 493, 532, 551-553, 585, 627, 660, 897; and architecture, 587; arts patronage, 118, 523; and Louyse Bourgeois, 74; and Catalonia, 425; support of exiled Hugo Grotius, 327; and Henrietta Maria, 364; and the duchesse de Longueville, 548; and Louis XIV, 554; and François de Malherbe, 578; and mother Marie de Médicis, 598; and Jules Mazarin, 621; and Francisco Gómez de Quevedo y

Villegas, 771; and Cardinal de Richelieu, 790; and Saint Vincent de Paul, 962

Louis XIV, 158, 487, 554-557; Anne of Austria as regent for, 19, 660; and architecture, 533, 590; arts patronage, 46, 750; ascension, 425, 585; and Nicolas Boileau-Despréaux, 63; and Jacques-Bénigne Bossuet, 70; and Saint Marguerite Bourgeoys, 77; Canadian settlement, 499; and Catherine of Braganza, 137; and Queen Christina, 165; and Jean-Baptiste Colbert, 180; and the Great Condé, 185; and Cyrano de Bergerac, 212; and England, 149; financial crises, 475; France as world power, 464; and Frederick William, the Great Elector, 291; French Royal Academy of Sciences, 710; and the Fronde, 549; vs. the Huguenots, 518; support of Christiaan Huygens, 398; opposition to Pope Innocent XI, 406; opposition to Jansenism, 22, 422; and John III Sobieski, 429; and Jean de La Fontaine, 481; and François Laval, 499; and the first duke of Leeds, 507; and Gottfried Wilhelm Leibniz, 514; and Ninon de Lenclos, 521; and André Le Nôtre, 523; and Leopold I, 527; and Louis XIII, 551; Louisiana colony, 402; and the marquis de Louvois, 558; marriage to Marie-Thérèse, 601; and Mary of Modena, 608; and Jules Mazarin, 621; and Molière, 647; and music at court, 764; opposition to mysticism, 340; attack on the Spanish Netherlands, 151; and the Papacy, 10; Partition Treaties, 547; and Charles Perrault, 731; and Philip IV, 738; and Elena Cornaro Piscopia, 744; and Jean Racine, 773; and Cardinal de Richelieu, 792; and Sir George Savile, 816; and Friedrich Hermann Schomberg, 821; and

Madeleine de Scudéry, 829; and Spain, 151; Treaty of Dover (1670), 693; and Viscount de Turenne, 933; and Sébastien Le Prestre de Vauban, 946; and Diego Velázquez, 955; and William III, 979

Louis the Great. *See* Louis XIV

Louis the Just. *See* Louis XIII

Louisiana, colonization of, 402, 491

Louvois, marquis de, 182, 186, 555, 558-561, 622

Louvre, Palais de, 533

Love, Christopher, 345

Love Letter, The (Vermeer), 957

Love Letters Between a Nobleman and His Sister (Behn), 44

Love Rogue, The (Tirso), 913

Love-Tiff, The (Molière), 647

Love Tricks. See *School of Compliment, The* (Shirley)

Love, the Greatest Enchantment (Calderón), 114

Lovelace, Richard, 443, 503, 562-564

Loves of Cupid and Psyche, The (La Fontaine), 482

Loves Riddle (Cowley), 199

Lower, Richard, 564-566, 986

Lowestoft, Battle of (1665), 417

Lucas, Margaret. *See* Newcastle, duchess of

Lucasta: Epodes, Odes, Sonnets, Songs, &c. to Which Is Added Aramantha, a Pastorall (Lovelace), 563

Lucasta: Posthume Poems of Richard Lovelace, Esq. (Lovelace), 562

Lucky Chance, The (Behn), 43

Ludlow, Roger, 567-569

Lulli, Giovanni Battista. *See* Lully, Jean-Baptiste

Lully, Jean-Baptiste, 482, 554, 569-571

Lute Player, The (Hals), 354

Lutheranism, 267

Lützen, Battle of (1632), 163, 338, 705, 926, 967

Luxembourg Palace, 599

Lyric Poems (Quevedo y Villegas), 771

Maastricht, Battle of (1673), 821

Mac Flecknoe (Dryden), 241

Machina coelestis (J. Hevelius), 372

Mad Lover, The (Fletcher), 279

Mad World, My Masters, A (Middleton), 636

Madeleine de Scudéry. *See* Scudéry, Madeleine de

Maderno, Carlo, 67

Madonna of the Rosary (van Dyck), 244

Madrigals, 656

Mágico prodigioso, El. See *Wonder-Working Magician, The* (Calderón)

Magnalia Naturæ (Becher), 40

Magnetic Lady, The (Jonson), 443

Magnificent Entertainment Given to King James, The (Dekker), 224

Maguire, Connor, Lord, 700

Magyars, 528

Mahabat Khan, 411

Maharashtra, 25

Mahicans, 643

Maid's Tragedy, The (Fletcher and Beaumont), 279

Main Plot, 253

Maintenon, Madame de, 266, 340, 572-574, 602, 775

Maisonneuve, sieur de, 76, 574-576

Maitland, John. *See* Lauderdale, first duke of

Malade imaginaire, La. See *Imaginary Invalid, The* (Molière)

Malebranche, Nicolas de, 252, 514

Malherbe, François de, 315, 480, 577-579, 779

Malpighi, Marcello, 66, 510, 579-582, 899

Malvasia, Carlo Cesare, 856

Mamanatowick. *See* Powhatan

Manasseh ben Israel, 582-584

Mance, Jeanne, 76, 575

Manchuria. *See* Geographical Index

Manchus, 1, 160, 234, 448, 848, 911, 1001

Mancini, Victoria. *See* Mancini, Laura

Mancini sisters, 585-587; Hortense, 585; Laura, 585; Marie, 19, 585; Marie-Anne, 585; Olympia, 585

Mander, Karel van, 352

Manggultai (Jin prince), 1

Mangopeomen. *See* Opechancanough

Mannerism, 504

Manoel Dias Soeiro. *See* Manasseh ben Israel

Mansart, François, 523, 573, 587-590

Mansart, Jules Hardouin-, 533, 589-593

Mansfeld, Peter Ernst, 98

Mantua, succession of (1629), 552

Manual of Private Devotions, The (Andrewes), 16

Maoris, 907

Map of Virginia, with a Description of the Country, A (Smith), 864

Marāthā Empire, 25, 858

Marbury, Anne. *See* Hutchinson, Anne

Marcello Malpighi and the Evolution of Embryology (Malpighi), 580

March Commission, 567

Mare liberum. See Freedom of the Seas, The (Grotius)

Margaret of Austria, 18, 737

Margaret Theresa. *See* Marie-Thérèse

Maria Anna of Bavaria-Neuburg, 152

Maria Celeste, 593-595

Maria Louisa de Tassis (van Dyck), 245

Maria Magdalena of Austria, 627

María Teresa de Austria. *See* Marie-Thérèse

Maria Theresa of Spain. *See* Marie-Thérèse

Mariana de Austria, 151, 426

Marie Casimire de la Grange d'Arquien. *See* Marysieńka

Marie de l'Incarnation, 595-597

Marie de Médicis, 598-600; and Anne of Austria, 18; and Louyse Bourgeois, 74; and Francesca Caccini, 111; and daughter Henrietta Maria, 364; marriage to Henry IV, 551; and François de Malherbe, 578; and Nicolas Poussin, 749; and Cardinal de Richelieu, 790

Marie Louise (queen of Poland), 428

Marie Louise (queen of Spain), 151

Marie-Thérèse, 19, 72, 151, 572, 585, 600-602, 622, 662

Marillac, Louise de, 963

Marini, Giambattista, 202, 749

Marinism, 202

Marlones, García de. *See* Gracián y Morales, Baltasar

Marquette, Jacques, 433, 603-605

Marranos, 582. *See also* Moriscos' expulsion from Spain

Marriage of Isaac and Rebecca, The (Claude Lorrain), 172

Mars gallicus (Jansen), 420

Marsillac, Prince de. *See* La Rochefoucauld, François de

Marston, John, 105, 223, 441, 976

Marston Moor, Battle of (1644), 199, 205, 262, 484, 805

Martin, Susannah, 690

Martiro di S Agata, Il (Cicognini), 111

Martyrdom of Saint Erasmus (Poussin), 749

Martyrs; French in North America, 424; Quakers, 284

Marubashi Chūya, 999

Marvell, Andrew, 232, 563, 605-607; list of works, 605

Mary II (queen of England), 138, 169, 284, 508, 608, 610-612, 817, 821, 979; American colonists reaction to her enthronement, 518

Mary of Modena (queen of England), 138, 417, 607-610, 839

Mary of the Incarnation. *See* Marie de l'Incarnation

Maryland Colony, 92, 120

Marysieńka, 429

Masaniello, 425

Mascherata delle ninfe di Senna, La (Rinuccini), 111

Mascoutens, 433, 603

Maske Presented at Ludlow Castle, A (Milton and Lawes), 502

Masque of Blackness, The (Jonson), 436, 442

Masque of Proteus and the Adamantine Rock, The (Campion and Davison), 127

Masque Presented at Ludlow Castle 1634 on Michaelmas Night, A (Milton), 640

Masques, 436, 442, 502, 764

Massachusetts Bay Colony, 8, 88, 130, 197, 218, 247, 386, 394, 567, 982, 991

Massachusetts Indians, 248, 879

Massasoit, 86, 129, 249, 612-614, 633, 876, 878

Massatamohtnock. *See* Opechancanough

Massinger, Philip, 279, 846

Mathematical Principles of Natural Philosophy. See Principia (Newton)

Mathematics; England, 679, 969; France, 226, 271, 631; Germany, 514; Italy, 66, 921; Japan, 831; Netherlands, 397; Scotland, 319; Switzerland, 48. *See also* Category Index

Matilda (Drayton), 237

Matoaka. *See* Pocahontas

Matsudaira Hirotada, 915

Matsudaira Nobutsuna, 999

Matsudaira Takechiyo. *See* Tokugawa Ieyasu

Matsuo Bashō, 403, 615-617; list of works, 616

Matsuo Kinsaku. *See* Matsuo Bashō

Matsuo Munefusa. *See* Matsuo Bashō

Matthiae, John, 163

Matthias (Holy Roman Emperor), 737, 966

Matveyev, Artamon Sergeyevich, 13

Maucroix, François, 480

Maurice of Nassau, 286, 326, 337, 538, 618-620, 924, 933

Maurits van Nassau. *See* Maurice of Nassau

Maximes (La Rochefoucauld), 487, 488

Maximilian I (elector of Bavaria), 268, 293

Maxims as a genre, 487

Maxims of the Saints Explained, Concerning the Interior Life, The (Fénelon), 265, 340

Mayflower (ship), 7

Mayflower Compact, 7, 85

Maynard, François, 578

Mayor encanto, amor, El. See Love, the Greatest Enchantment (Calderón)

Mayor of Zalamea, The (Calderón), 114

Maypeyker Sultan. *See* Kösem Sultan

Mazarin, duchesse de. *See* Mancini, Hortense

Mazarin, Jules, 9, 620-624; and Anne of Austria, 19; architecture, 532; arts patronage, 504; and the duchesse de Chevreuse, 158; and Queen Christina, 165; and Jean-Baptiste Colbert, 180; and the Great Condé, 185; Council of Conscience, 963; and Cyrano de Bergerac, 212; and the Fronde, 549; and Guarino Guarini, 331; opposition to Jansenism, 421; and François de La Rochefoucauld, 487; and the duchesse de Longueville, 549; and Louis XIV, 554; uncle of the Mancini sisters, 585; and Marie-Thérèse, 601; and the duchesse de Montpensier, 660; and music, 570; and Peiresc's letters, 723; and Cardinal de Richelieu, 792; and Sweden, 706; and Viscount de Turenne, 933

Mazarini, Giulio. *See* Mazarin, Jules

Mazepa, Ivan Stepanovich, 624-626

Mbamba, 687

Mbande, 687

Mbundus, 687

Mead, William, 725

Meara, Edmund, 564

Médecin malgré lui, Le. See Doctor in Spite of Himself, The (Molière)

Medici, Cosimo II de', 112, 118, 307, 593, 626-628

Medici, Cosimo III de', 857, 882

Medicina Catholica (Fludd), 281

Medicina Statica (Santorio), 811

Medicine; Amsterdam, 898; England, 902, 987; France, 74; Germany, 851; Italy, 66, 355, 810. *See also* Category Index

Médicis, Marie de. *See* Marie de Médicis

Médico de su honra, El. See Surgeon of His Honor, The (Calderón)

Meditationes de prima philosophia. See Meditations on First Philosophy (Descartes)

Meditations Divine and Moral (Bradstreet), 90

Meditations on First Philosophy (Descartes), 227, 251, 305

Mehmed IV, 451, 472

Mélite (Corneille), 193

Mémoires de la cour de France pour les années 1688 et 1689. See Memoirs of the Court of France for the Years 1688-1689 (La Fayette)

Memoires de ma vie. See Memoirs of My Life (Perrault)

Mémoires de mademoiselle de Montpensier (Montpensier), 661

Mémoires sur la régence d'Anne d'Autriche. See Memoirs of the Duke de La Rochefoucault, The (La Rochefoucauld)

Memoirs of My Life (Perrault), 732

Memoirs of the Court of France for the Years 1688-1689 (La Fayette), 478

Memoirs of the Duke de La Rochefoucault, The (La Rochefoucauld), 487

Memoriae Matris Sacrum (Herbert), 367

Ménage, Gilles, 833

Meninas, Las (Velázquez), 955

Menshikov, Aleksander, 625

Mercantilism; England, 808; France, 181, 554

Mercoeur, duchesse de. *See* Mancini, Laura

Mercurius in sole visus (Gassendi), 305

Mermaid Tavern, 278

Merrymount, 879

Mersenne, Marin, 281, 305, 628-632, 722

Mertola, count of. *See* Schomberg, Friedrich Hermann

Metacom, 249, 612, 633-635, 876

Metacom's War (1675-1676), 249, 614, 635, 798, 876

Meteorology; England, 384; Italy, 922

Methodi vitandorum errorum omnium qui in arte medica contingunt (Santorio), 810

Methodus Curandi Febres (Sydenham), 902

Methodus plantarum nova (Ray), 782

Metius, Jacob, 537

Mexico. *See* Geographical Index

Mézy, chevalier de, 500

Miantonomo, 129

Miaos, 911

Michael. *See* Romanov, Michael

Michaelmas Term (Middleton), 636

Michal Wiśniowiecki, 429

Micro-cynicon (Middleton), 636

Micrographia (Hooke), 383, 509, 677

Middlesex, first earl of. *See* Cranfield, Lionel

Middleton, Thomas, 224, 279, 636-638, 846, 928, 977; list of works, 637

Midwifery, 74

Mignard, Pierre, 505

Mikhail Skopin-Shuysky, 944

Mikhailovich, Aleksei. *See* Alexis

Milborne, Jacob, 519

Military; England, 205; France, 184, 559, 946; Japan, 998; Netherlands, 619; Russia, 12; Sweden, 925. *See also* Army, Artillery, Navy

Mill, The (Claude Lorrain), 171

Miloslavsky, Ilya, 664

Milton, John, 109, 201, 300, 502, 605, 639-643, 942; list of works, 641

Mind's Wit and Art, The (Gracián), 317

Ming Dynasty (1368-1644), 1, 160, 448, 848, 912, 972, 1001

Minin, Nikita. *See* Nikon

Minnewit, Peter. *See* Minuit, Peter
Minor Commentary to the Book of Changes (Wang), 972
Minuit, Peter, 643-646, 706
Misanthrope, The (Molière), 648
Miscellaneous Poems (Marvell), 606
Miscellaneous Reflections Occasion'd by the Comet Which Appear'd in December, 1680 (Bayle), 36
Miscellany Tracts (Browne), 95
Miser, The (Molière), 648
Miseries of War (Callot), 118
Missionaries; French in North America, 433; Jesuits in Brazil, 960; Jesuits in Canada, 499; Jesuits in China, 161, 449, 849; Jesuits in North America, 423, 603, 908; Jesuits in the American Southwest, 467; Massachusetts, 247
Mississippi River exploration, 433, 491, 603
Mistress, The (Cowley), 199
Mithridates (Racine), 775
Mizan al-ḥaqq fi lkhtijārī al-ahaqq. See *Balance of Truth, The* (Kâtib Çelebî)
Mniszech, Jerzy, 855
Model of Moses His Judicials (Cotton), 219
Mohawks, 141, 424, 634, 643, 777, 909
Mohegans, 130
Moldavia, 463
Molière, 19, 186, 212, 305, 482, 487, 521, 524, 554, 570, 646-649, 662, 774; list of works, 648
Molina, Tirso de. *See* Tirso de Molina
Molinos, Miguel de, 340, 406
Moller, Martin, 59
Monaldeschi, Gian Rinaldo, 165
Monck, George, 57, 137, 148, 206, 485, 650-653, 758, 806, 838, 931, 942
Monde, Le (Descartes), 227
Monism, 188
Monk, George. *See* Monck, George
Monkey's Raincoat, 616

Monmouth, duke of, 122, 149, 241, 417, 545, 653-656, 693, 816
Monody, 112
Monsieur Pascal's Thoughts, Meditations, and Prayers. See *Pensées* (Pascal)
Montagnais, 141
Montagu, Charles, 717
Montagu, Edward. *See* Sandwich, first earl of
Montecuccoli, Raimundo, 527, 934
Montes Claros, Battle of (1665), 426, 821
Montespan, Madame de, 572, 590, 601
Monteverdi, Claudio, 296, 656-660, 826
Montijo, Battle of (1644), 432
Montpensier, Anne-Marie-Louise d'Orléans, duchesse de. *See* Montpensier, duchesse de
Montpensier, duchesse de, 477, 569, 660-663
Montreal, Canada, 574
Montrose, James Graham, marquess of, 147
Monvoisin, Madame, 586
Moore, Roger. *See* O'More, Rory
Moore, Rory. *See* O'More, Rory
Moors' expulsion from Spain (1603), 530. *See also* Islam
Morales, Baltasar Gracián y. *See* Gracián y Morales, Baltasar
Moravia. *See* Geographical Index
More, Henry, 187, 252
More, Rory. *See* O'More, Rory
More Reasons for the Christian Religion (Baxter), 35
Mōri Shigeyoshi, 831
Moriscos' expulsion from Spain, 737. *See also* Marranos
Moritz of Hessen-Kassel, 825
Moronobu, Hishikawa. *See* Hishikawa Moronobu
Morozov, Boris Ivanovich, 11, 663-665
Mort d'Agrippine, La. See *Death of Agrippina, The* (Cyrano)
Mortemart, Françoise-Athénaïs, Rochechouart de. *See* Montespan, Madame de
Mortimeriados (Drayton), 237

Morton, Thomas, 232, 879
Mosaicall Philosophy (Fludd), 281
Moscow, Treaty of (1686), 429, 866
Mothe-Fénelon, François de La. *See* Fénelon, François de Salignac de La Mothe-
Motteville, Françoise Bertaut de, 662
Mountfort, William, 82
Mourt's Relation (Bradford and Winslow), 86
Moyen court et très facile de faire oraison. See *Worship of God in Spirit and in Truth, The* (Guyon)
Mr. Cottons Letter Lately Printed, Examined, and Answered (Williams), 983
Muggleton, Lodowick, 665-667
Muggletonians, 666
Mughal Empire, 23, 410, 842, 859
Muhī-ud-Dīn Muḥammad Aurangzeb. *See* Aurangzeb
Mukai Kyorai, 616
Mullins, Priscilla, 7
Mumtaz Mahal, 842
Münster, Treaty of (1648), 619
Murad (governor of Gujarat), 844
Murad (Mughal prince), 24
Murad IV, 451, 454, 472, 668-670, 674
Murad Oglu Ahmed I. *See* Murad IV
Murillo, Bartolomé Esteban, 670-672, 1005
Muscovy, 784
Muses Elizium, The (Drayton), 238
Muse's Hannibal, The. *See* Cowley, Abraham
Music; England, 127, 309, 502, 763; France, 569, 630; Germany, 708, 826; Italy, 111, 190, 295, 656, 825, 888. *See also* Category Index
Muslims; expulsion from Spain (1603), 530
Mustafa I, 472, 668, 673-675
Muṣṭafa ibn ʿabd Allāh. *See* Kâtib Çelebî
Mysterium cosmographicum. See *Secret of the Universe, The* (Kepler)
Mysterium Magnum (Böhme), 61

Mystical Marriage of Saint Catherine, The (Murillo), 672

Mysticism; Belgium, 362; England, 284; France, 339-340, 499; Germany, 62; Peru, 797; Spain, 265

Nāder Shāh, 4

Namaskets, 876

Nanshoku ōkagami. See Great Mirror of Male Love, The (Saikaku)

Napier, John, 818

Narcissus (Shirley), 846

Narragansetts, 129, 612, 633, 879

Narrow Road to the Deep North, The (Bashō), 616

Naryshkina, Natalya Kirillovna, 13

Naseby, Battle of (1645), 205, 263, 756

Nashe, Thomas, 440

Nassau, count of. *See* Frederick Henry

Nassau, Maurice of. *See* Maurice of Nassau

Native American-European treaties, 8, 130, 567, 613, 644, 876, 878, 891

Native Americans. *See* Geographical Index under Native America; Native American-European treaties; Smallpox and Native Americans; specific tribes

Nature's Pictures (Newcastle), 676

Naufragium Joculare (Cowley), 199

Navigation Act (1651), 57, 808

Navy; England, 57-58; Netherlands, 932

Ndongo, 687

Neck of the Quakers Broken, The (Muggleton), 667

Necotawance, 703

Nenemattanaw, 702

Neo-Confucianism, 919, 973

Neptuno alegórico, El (Cruz), 209

Nerchinsk, Treaty of (1689), 449, 866

Neri, Philip, 721

Netherlands. *See* United Provinces of the Netherlands, Geographical Index

Neuf-Brisach, 947

New Amsterdam, 393, 518, 644, 892. *See also* New York

New Art of Writing Plays, The (Lope de Vega), 949

New Astronomy (Kepler), 459

New Christians, 960

New England colonization, 768, 875, 878, 890

New England Confederation, 568

New Englands Trials (Smith), 864

New Essays Concerning Human Understanding (Leibniz), 516

New Experiments and Observations Touching Cold (Boyle), 79

New Experiments Physio-Mechanicall, Touching the Spring of the Air and Its Effects (Boyle), 79

New France, 141, 500, 603

New Guinea, 906

New Haven Colony, 219

New Haven's Case Stated (Davenport), 219

New Holland, 907

New Inn, The (Jonson), 443

New Law of Righteousness, The (Winstanley), 989

New Model Army, 205, 262, 756

New Netherland, 643, 890

New Structure of the Muscles and Heart (Steno), 881

New Sweden, 706, 891; colonization of, 645

New Voyage Round the World, A (Dampier), 215

New Way of Making Fowre Parts in Counter-point, A (Campion), 128

New Yeers Gift for the Parliament and Armie, A (Winstanley), 989

New York, 518, 892; colonization of, 644. *See also* New Amsterdam

New Zealand, 907. *See also* Geographical Index

New-born, The (La Tour), 494

Newcastle, duchess of, 676-678

Newcomen, Thomas, 814

Newcomers (Russia), 785

Newfoundland, 120

Newport, Christopher, 754

Newport, Treaty of (1648), 941

Newton, Sir Isaac, 37, 49, 66, 79, 107, 271, 306, 319, 323, 349, 385, 390, 398, 459, 515, 547, 679-682, 734, 832, 970, 994; list of works, 681

Nicholson, Francis, 518

Nicole, Pierre, 774

Nicolet, Jean, 433

Nicolls, Richard, 892

Nicomède (Corneille), 195

Night Watch, The (Rembrandt), 787

Nijmegen, Treaty of (1678), 426, 507, 560, 979

Nikon, 13, 27, 683-686

Nine Years' War (1688-1697). *See* Augsburg, War of the League of (1689-1697)

Nippon eitaigura. See Japanese Family Storehouse, The (Saikaku)

Njinga, 687-689

No Cross, No Crown (Penn), 725

Nobleman, The (Tourneur), 929

Nogaret de La Valette, 598

Nonconformists, 34, 54, 100, 122, 386, 414

Nonomura Sōtatsu. *See* Sōtatsu

Nord, Le. *See* Colbert, Jean-Baptiste

Nördlingen, Battle of (1634), 705

North America; *maps,* xxxi, lv

Northern War, First (1655-1660), 12, 154, 290, 428, 527

Northward Ho! (Webster and Dekker), 977

Northwest Passage, 391

Norway. *See* Geographical Index

Nôtre, André Le. *See* Le Nôtre, André

Nôtre-Dame de Recouvrance, 596

Nottingham, second earl of, 508

Nouveaux essais sur l'entendement humain. See New Essays Concerning Human Understanding (Leibniz)

Nouvelles, 477, 829

Nouvelles Catholiques, 265

Nouvelles françaises, Les (Segrais), 477

Nova musculorum et cordis fabrica. See New Structure of the Muscles and Heart (Steno)

Novels; England, 42, 102; France, 266, 314, 477, 662, 829; Germany, 325; Japan, 403; Spain, 317, 770, 913, 949

Novgorod, uprising in (1650), 684

Noy, William, 345

Nozarashi kikō. See *Records of a Weather-Exposed Skeleton, The* (Bashō)

Nozawa Bonchō, 616

Nueva comedia, 914

Nūr Jahān, 411, 842

Nurhaci, 1, 234, 848, 911

Nurse, Rebecca, 689-691

Nye, Philip, 198

Nzinga. See Njinga

Oates, Titus, 138, 149, 692-695, 816, 839

Oblivion, Act of (1652), 54

Oboi, 448

Observationes Medicae (Sydenham), 902

Observations diverses (Bourgeois), 74

Observations in the Art of English Poesie (Campion), 128

Observations upon Experimental Philosophy (Newcastle), 677

Observations upon the Cities of London and Rome (Petty), 735

Oda Nobuhide, 915

Oda Nobunaga, 915

Odescalchi, Benedetto. See Innocent XI

Œuvres diverses (Boileau-Despréaux), 63

Of Dramatic Poesie (Dryden), 241

Of Education (Milton), 640

Of Feavours (Willis), 986

Of Fermentation (Willis), 986

Of Myself (Cowley), 200

"Of Poets and Poesie" (Drayton), 238

Of Reformation Touching Church Discipline in England (Milton), 640

Of the Law of Nature and Nations (Pufendorf), 760

"Of the Mixed Tree of Evil and Good" (Böhme), 61

Of the Progress of the Soule (Donne), 232

Ogata Kenzan, 377, 695, 868

Ogata Kōrin, 377, 695-697, 868

Ogilby, John, 846

Oi no kobumi. See *Records of a Travel Worn Satchel, The* (Bashō)

Ojibways, 423

Okewas, First Day of (1622), 703

Okewas, Second Day of (1644), 703

Oku no hosomichi. See *Narrow Road to the Deep North, The* (Bashō)

Okuni. *See* Izumo no Okuni

Old Believers, 13, 27, 685, 865

Old Man Seated in an Armchair, An (Rembrandt), 788

Old Ritualists. *See* Old Believers

Oldcastle, Sir John, 238

Oldenbarnevelt, Johan van, 288, 326, 618

Oldham, John, 130

Oliva, Treaty of (1660), 155, 290, 428, 527

Olivares, count-duke of, 317, 431, 697-699, 739, 770, 914, 953

Olod Mongols, 449

Olor Iscanus (Vaughan), 741

O'More, Rory, 699-701

"On Desire" (Behn), 43

On the Circulation of the Blood (Leeuwenhoek), 510

On the Death of Mr. Crashaw (Cowley), 199

On the Death of Mr. William Hervey (Cowley), 199

On the Law of War and Peace (Grotius), 328

On the Movement of Animals (Borelli), 66

On the Revolutions of the Heavenly Spheres. See *De revolutionibus* (Galileo)

O'Neill, Owen Roe, 700

O'Neill, Sir Phelim, 700

Oninga. *See* Radisson, Pierre Esprit

O'odhams, 467

Opachisco, 747

Opechancanough, 702-704, 752

Opera; England, 52, 764; France, 570; Italy, 111, 658, 888

Opera geometrica (Torricelli), 921

Opera posthuma (Horrocks), 389

Opitchapan, 702, 752

Optica Promota (Gregory), 319

Optics; England, 679; France, 272; Germany, 458; Italy, 322, 923; Netherlands, 399, 509, 537; Poland, 372; Scotland, 319

Optics (Kepler), 458

Opuscula hebraea, graeca, latina, gallica (Schurman), 823

Opuscula medica inaudita. See *Unheard of Little Works on Medicine* (Helmont)

Oquendo, Antonio de, 288

Oráculo manual y arte de prudencia. See *Courtiers Manual Oracle, The* (Gracián)

Oraison funèbre d'Henriette Anne d'Angleterre. See *Funeral Oration for Henrietta of England* (Bossuet)

Orange, prince of. *See* Frederick Henry; Maurice of Nassau

Orange, William of. *See* William III (king of England)

Orangist faction, 519

Orations of Divers Sorts (Newcastle), 677

Oratory, 71

Orbis sensualium pictus. See *Visible World* (Komenský)

Orinda. *See* Philips, Katherine

Orléans, Anne-Marie-Louise d'. *See* Montpensier, duchesse de

Orléans, Gaston d', 598, 660

Ormond, first duke of, 507

Oroonoko (Behn), 44

Orphans Fund of the City of London, 718

Ortus medicinae. See *Ternary of Paradoxes, A* (Helmont)

Osborne, Thomas. *See* Leeds, first duke of

Osburn, Sarah, 690

Osman II, 472, 674, 855

Ostend, Siege of (1601-1604), 928

Osuna, duke of, 770

Other World, The (Cyrano), 211

Ottaniack. *See* Powhatan

Ottawas, 603

Ottoboni, Pietro, 190

Ottoman Empire, 4, 406, 668, 866. *See also* Geographical Index

Ottoman-Polish Wars (1672-1676), 429

Our Lady of the Immaculate Conception (Murillo), 672

Ousamequin. *See* Massasoit

Outer Commentary to the Book of Changes (Wang), 972

Overbury, Sir Thomas, 132

Overton, Richard, 535

Owen, Anne, 742

Oxenstierna, Axel, 153, 163, 328, 337, 704-707

Pacheco, Francisco, 953, 1003

Pachelbel, Johann, 708-710

Painting; Baroque, 955; Belgium, 244; China, 156, 540; France, 171, 493; Italy, 45, 171, 302, 307, 749, 856; Japan, 695, 868; Netherlands, 352, 786, 802, 956; Spain, 953, 1003

Pakistan. *See* Geographical Index

Palace of Luxembourg, 587

Palatinate, 293

Palatine of the Rhine, count. *See* Rupert, Prince

Palazzo Carignano, 331

Paleontology, 882

Palmer, Barbara Villiers. *See* Castlemaine, countess of

Pamunkeys, 702, 752

Pan-sensism, 125

Pansophy, 470

Papin, Denis, 710-713, 814

Paradise Lost (Milton), 640

Paradise Regained (Milton), 642

Parallele des anciens et des modernes (Perrault), 732

Paria (Vincent), 894

Parigi, Giulio, 627

Parliamentarians, 484, 535, 805

Parnasso español, El (Quevedo y Villegas), 771

Parr, Thomas, 357

Parris, Elizabeth, 690

Parris, Samuel, 689

Part of King James, His Royall and Magnificent Entertainment (Jonson), 442

Parthenia, 310

Particular Open Communion Baptist, 100

Partition, First Treaty of (1698), 152, 547, 980

Partition, Second Treaty of (1700), 152, 547, 980

Parviz, 842

Paşa, Merzifonlu Kara Mustafa. *See* Kara Mustafa Paşa, Merzifonlu

Pascal, Blaise, 37, 271, 422, 487, 514, 632, 713-716, 819, 923

Passions de l'âme, Les. See *Passions of the Soul, The* (Descartes)

Passions of the Soul, The (Descartes), 228

Paterson, William, 716-719

Pathologiae cerebri et nervosi generis specimen. See *Essay of the Pathology of the Brain and Nervous Stock, An* (Willis)

Patriarcha (Filmer), 546

Patronage of the arts. *See* Category Index

Paul, Saint Vincent de. *See* Vincent de Paul, Saint

Paul IV, 330

Paul V, 45, 67, 719-721, 810, 936, 962

Pawtuxets, 86, 612, 875

Pax Hispanica, 737

Payment of Dues (La Tour), 494

Peace of _____. *See* _____, Peace of

Peacham, Edmund, 176

Peacock Throne, 843

Pedant Imitated, The. See *Ridiculous Pedant, The* (Cyrano)

Pédant joué, Le. See *Ridiculous Pedant, The* (Cyrano)

Peiresc, Nicolas-Claude Fabri de, 304, 577, 722-724

Pellisson, Paul, 480

Peltrie, Madame de la, 575, 596

Penei rabbah (Manasseh), 583

Penitent Magdalene (Artemisia), 307

Penn, William, 57, 252, 724-728

Pennsylvania colony, 726

Penruddock's Uprising (1655), 206

Pensées (Pascal), 715

Pepys, Samuel, 51, 342, 349, 677, 728-731, 971

Pequots, 130, 567

Pereyaslavl, Treaty of (1654), 463, 624

Peri, Jacopo, 658

Perpignan, Siege of (1642), 933

Perrault, Charles, 64, 533, 731-733; "Little Tom Thumb," 732

Perrier, François, 504

Perro del hortelano, El. See *Gardener's Dog, The* (Lope de Vega)

Persecution, religious; England, 34, 84, 92, 101, 218, 284, 877, 982; France, 36, 182, 407, 555, 560; Germany, 61; Jansenists, 422, 773; Japan, 917, 919; Jews, 582, 837, 871, 960-961; New Amsterdam, 891; Quakers, 284, 725; Scotland, 122; Virginia, 120

Persia. *See* Geographical Index under Iran

Personal Rule (the 1630's), 768

Pertharite, roi des Lombards (Corneille), 195

Peru. *See* Geographical Index

Peter, Czar (pretender), 944

Peter II (king of Portugal), 821

Peter the Great, 13, 445, 625, 685, 795, 865

Petition of Right (1628), 98, 144, 178, 767, 884

Petrovich, Avvakum. *See* Avvakum Petrovich

Petty, Sir William, 564, 733-735

Phaedra (Racine), 774

Phaethon (Dekker), 223

Phantom Lady, The (Calderón), 114

Pharmaceutice rationalis (Willis), 987

Phèdre. See *Phaedra* (Racine)

Philaret, 663, 794, 944

Philaster (Fletcher and Beaumont), 279

Philip, King. *See* Metacom

Philip I (king of Portugal). *See* Philip II (king of Spain)

Philip II (king of Spain), 431

Philip III (king of Spain), 736-738, 959; and daughter Anne of Austria, 18; decline of Habsburg Spain, 425; and the duke de Lerma, 530; and Count-Duke of Olivares, 697; and son Philip IV,

738, 770; and Tirso de Molina, 913

Philip IV (king of Spain), 138, 551, 738-741; and Anne of Austria, 19; arts patronage, 307; ascension, 770; and Pedro Calderón de la Barca, 113; and son Charles II (of Spain), 151; Queen Christina's conversion to Catholicism, 165; and Elizabeth de Médicis, 598; and John IV, 431; and son John of Austria, 425; and Marie-Thérèse, 585, 600; and Jules Mazarin, 622; and Cosimo II de' Medici, 627; and the duchesse de Montpensier, 661; and the count-duke of Olivares, 697; opposition to intellectuals, 913; and father Philip III, 738; and Diego Velázquez, 953; and Francisco de Zurbarán, 1005

Philip V (king of Spain), 152

Philip of Anjou. *See* Philip V (king of Spain)

Philip of Poakanoket. *See* Metacom

Philip the Pious. *See* Philip III (king of Spain)

Philippe le Roy (van Dyck), 245

Philips, Frederick, 519

Philips, Katherine, 741-743

Philosophaster (Burton), 109

Philosophia Moysaica. See Mosaicall Philosophy (Fludd)

Philosophia sensibus demonstrata (Campanella), 125

Philosophiae Naturalis Principia Mathematica. See Principia (Newton)

Philosophical and Physical Opinions (Newcastle), 676

Philosophical Commentary on These Words in the Gospel, Luke XIV, 23, A (Bayle), 37

Philosophical Letters (Newcastle), 677

Philosophical Rudiments Concerning Government and Society (Hobbes), 379

Philosophicall Fancies. See Philosophical and Physical Opinions (Newcastle)

Philosophy; China, 972; England, 95, 188, 379, 543, 677; France, 227, 252, 305, 630, 715; Germany, 60, 514, 760; Italy, 125; Netherlands, 872. *See also* Category Index

Phoenix (theater), 51

Phoenix, The (Middleton), 636

Physica subterranea (Becher), 40

Physico-mathesis de lumine, coloribus, et iride (Grimaldi), 322

Physics; England, 710; Germany, 333, 458; Italy, 322, 922; Netherlands, 399. *See also* Category Index

Piedra gloriosa, o de la Estatua de Nebuchadnessar (Manasseh), 583

Pierron, Jean, 909

Pilgrim, The (Fletcher), 279

Pilgrims, 84-85, 613, 876-877

Pilgrim's Progress from This World to That Which Is to Come, The (Bunyan), 101

Pima Uprising. *See* Tubutama Revolt (1695)

Pimas. *See* O'odhams

Pimería Alta, 467

Pindaric Odes (Cowley), 200

Pinelli, Jean-Vincent, 722

Pioche de la Vergne, Marie-Madeleine. *See* La Fayette, Madame de

Piracy; China, 1001; England, 464; South Seas, 215

Piscopia, Elena Cornaro, 743-745

Pitti Palace, 627

Place royale, La (Corneille), 193

Place Vendôme, 591

Placita philosophica (Guarini), 331

Plaideurs, Les. See Litigants, The (Racine)

Platonists, Cambridge, 782

Plays (Newcastle), 677

Plessis, Armand-Jean du. *See* Richelieu, Cardinal de

Pluto and Persephone (Bernini), 45

Plymouth Colony, 7, 85, 129, 876, 878

Pocahontas, 702, 745-748, 753, 862-863

Pocahontas, Peace of, 754

Podhajce, Battle of (1667), 429

Poemata (Campion), 127

Poemata Latina (Cowley), 200

Poems (Cowley), 200

Poems (Drayton), 238

Poems &c. by James Shirley (Shirley), 846

Poems and Fancies (Newcastle), 676

Poems by the Incomparable, Mrs. K. P. (Philips), 742

Poems by the Most Deservedly Admired Mrs. Katherine Philips, the Matchless Orinda (Philips), 742

Poet laureate, England, 240, 442

Poetaster (Jonson), 223, 441

Poeticall Blossomes (Cowley), 199

Poetry; Americas, 88; China, 157, 540; England, 43, 127, 199, 202, 232, 237, 240, 366, 368, 443, 503, 562, 606, 639, 676, 731, 741, 846, 894, 928; France, 315, 481, 577, 829; Góngora, 312; Japan, 403, 615; Metaphysical, 202-203, 231, 367; Mexico, 209; Netherlands, 327; Spain, 770

Pokanokets, 876

Poland. *See* Geographical Index

Polish-Lithuanian Commonwealth, 462

Polish-Ottoman War (1618-1621), 461

Política de Dios, gobierno de Christo, tirania de Satanas. See Divine Maxims of Government . . . (Quevedo y Villegas)

Political Anatomy of Ireland (Petty), 734

Political Treatise, A (Spinoza), 873

Político Don Fernando el Católico, El (Gracián), 317

Politics. *See* Category Index under Government and politics

Poltava, Battle of (1709), 625

Polyanov, Peace of (1634), 795

Polyeucte (Corneille), 194

Poly-Olbion (Drayton), 238

Popham, Edward, 56

Popish Plot (1678), 138, 149, 417, 508, 692, 816, 839

Poppies, The (Sōtatsu), 869

Poquelin, Jean-Baptiste. *See* Molière

Port-Royal abbey, 21

Port Royal colony, 141

Port-Royal des Champs, Convent of, 773

Porter, Endymion, 563

Portia Wounding Her Thigh (Sirani), 857

Portrait of the Marchesa Brigida Spinola-Doria (Rubens), 802

Portugal, 821. *See also* Geographical Index

Possevino, Antonio, 855

Potawatomis, 433

Potomacs, 746, 752

Potsdam, Edict of (1686), 821

Pottery, Japan, 695

Poussin, Nicolas, 171, 303, 749-752

Powhatan, 702, 745, 752-756, 862-863

Powhatan Confederacy, 702, 752

Powhatan Wars (1622-1646), 703

Powick Bridge, Battle of (1642), 805

Pozzo, Cassiano del, 749

Prague, Peace of (1635), 269, 705

Précieuses ridicules, Les. See Affected Young Ladies, The (Molière)

Presbyterianism, 122, 145, 206, 941

Presbytery, 15, 33

Present State of Germany, The (Pufendorf), 759

Presentation of Jesus in the Temple, The (Rembrandt), 787

Preston, Battle of (1648), 205, 484, 756

Pride, Thomas, 205, 651, 692, 756-758

Pride's Purge (1648), 263, 651, 757, 942

Primero sueño. See First Dream (Cruz)

Primo libro de' madrigali, Il (Frescobaldi), 295

Primo libro de madrigali, Il (Strozzi), 888

Primo libro delle canzoni, accomodate per sonare con ogni sorte di stromenti, Il (Frescobaldi), 297

Primo libro delle fantasie, Il (Frescobaldi), 296

Primo libro delle musiche, Il (Caccini), 112

Primo libro di capricci, Il (Frescobaldi), 296

Princess of Clèves, The (La Fayette), 478

Princess of Monpensier, The (La Fayette), 477

Princesse de Clèves, La. See Princess of Cleves, The (La Fayette)

Princesse de Monpensier, La. See Princess of Monpensier, The (La Fayette)

Príncipe constante, El. See Constant Prince, The (Calderón)

Principia (Newton), 349, 385, 390, 680

Principia philosophiae. See Principles of Philosophy (Descartes)

Principia philosophiae antiquissima et recentissimae. See Principles of the Most Ancient and Modern Philosophy, The (Conway)

Principles de la nature et de la grâce, fondés en raison. See Principles of Nature and of Grace, The (Leibniz)

Principles of Descartes' Philosophy, The (Spinoza), 872

Principles of Nature and of Grace, The (Leibniz), 516

Principles of Philosophy (Descartes), 251

Principles of the Most Ancient and Modern Philosophy, The (Conway), 188

Pro Populo Anglicano Defensio (Milton), 640

Procuress, The (Vermeer), 956

Prodromus (Steno), 882

Prodromus astronomiae. See Star Atlas, The (E. Hevelius)

Prodromus to a Dissertation Concerning Solids Naturally Contained Within Solids, The. See Prodromus (Steno)

Promenade, The (Gournay), 314

Prophesie of the Last Day to Be Revealed in the Last Times, and Then of the Cutting Off the Church and of the Redemption Out of Hell, A (Davies), 221

Prophetess, The (Fletcher and Massinger), 279

Prophetess, The (Purcell). See *Dioclesian* (Purcell)

Prophetia de die Novissimo novissimis hisce temporibus manifestando. See Prophesie of the Last Day to Be Revealed in the Last Times . . . (Davies)

Proposition for the Advancement of Experimental Philosophy, A (Cowley), 200

Protectorate of England, 168, 346, 417, 485, 838

Protestant Union, 268, 293, 338

Protestantism; Bohemia, 966; England, 33, 145, 275, 507, 767; France, 36, 265; Germany, 338; Ireland, 938

Proumenoir de Monsieur de Montaigne, Le. See Promenade, The (Gournay)

Providence, 982

Provincial Letters, The (Pascal), 714

Proximus und Lympida (Grimmelshausen), 325

Prudence in Woman (Tirso), 913

Prudencia en la mujer, La. See Prudence in Woman (Tirso)

Prussia. *See* Geographical Index

Prynne, William, 497

Psalmen Davids (Schütz), 826

Pseudodoxia Epidemica. See Browne's Vulgar Errors (Browne)

Pseudo-Martyr (Donne), 232

Psyché (Lully and Corneille), 570

Pueblo Revolt (1680), 467

Pufendorf, Samuel von, 545, 759-762

Purcell, Henry, 311, 763-766

Puritan and the Papist, The (Cowley), 199

Puritan Revolution, 256

Puritan Widow, The (Middleton), 636

Puritanism, 386, 768, 798;
  Americas, 196; conversion of
  Native Americans, 633; England,
  101, 145, 202, 218, 247, 414,
  496, 534, 991; Massachusetts,
  941; New England, 387, 394
Puritan's Lecture (Cowley), 199
Putnam, Ann, 690
Pyliavtsi, Battle of (1648), 462
Pym, John, 167, 767-769, 886, 941
Pyrenees, Treaty of the (1659), 10,
  186, 425, 549, 586, 600, 622,
  698, 933

Qandahār, 843
Qi, 972
Qian Chen Qun, 156
Qian Feng, 156
Qian Jie, 156
Qian Long Guang, 156
Qian Qian Yi, 540
Qian Rui Cheng, 156
Qian Zeng, 541
Qianlong, 236
Qing Dynasty (1644-1911), 1, 162,
  234, 448, 848, 972, 1001
Qing Taizong. *See* Abahai
Quadėquina, 876
*Quaestiones celeberrimæ in
  Genesim* (Mersenne), 629
Quakerism; American colonies, 984;
  Anne Conway, 188; England,
  206, 284; William Penn, 724
Quakerism (Penn), 725
Quakerism A-la-mode (Bossuet),
  341
*Quantulumcunque Concerning
  Money* (Petty), 734
Quapaw, 434, 604
Queen Anne's War. *See* Spanish
  Succession, War of the (1701-
  1714)
*Queens of Persia at the Feet of
  Alexander* (Le Brun, C.), 505
Queen's Theatre, 52
Queensferry Paper. *See* Cameron's
  Covenant
Queries of Highest Consideration
  (Williams), 983
**Quevedo y Villegas, Francisco
  Gómez de**, 312, 770-772
Quietism, 265, 339, 406

Quinault, Philippe, 570
Quincy, Massachusetts. *See*
  Merrymount

Rabutin-Chantal, Marie de. *See*
  Sévigné, Madame de
Racine, Jean, 64, 72, 186, 194-195,
  482, 554, 573, 773-776; list of
  works, 775
Radisson, Pierre Esprit, 777-779
Raffaelli, Francesca. *See* Caccini,
  Francesca
Raffaelli, Tomaso, 112
Ralegh, Sir Walter, 132, 175, 230,
  414
Rambouillet, Julie-Lucine de, 780
Rambouillet, Marquise de, 779-
  781
Ramírez de Santillana, Juana Inés de
  Asbaje y. *See* Cruz, Sor Juana
  Inés de la
Randolph, Thomas, 443
Rangoni, Claudio, 855
Ranters, 666
Ranuzzi, Annibale, 857
Raskol, 13
Rathstübel Plutonis
  (Grimmelshausen), 325
Ratisbon, Diet of (1630), 552
Ravaillac, François, 598
Ray, John, 29, 782-784
Raymbault, Charles, 423
Razin, Stenka, 12, 784-786
*Ready and Easy Way to Establish a
  Free Commonwealth, The*
  (Milton), 640
*Reason of Church-Government
  Urg'd Against Prelaty, The*
  (Milton), 640
*Reasonableness of Christianity as
  Delivered in the Scriptures, The*
  (Locke), 546
*Reasons of the Christian Religion,
  The* (Baxter), 35
*Records of a Travel-Worn Satchel,
  The* (Bashō), 616
*Records of a Weather-Exposed
  Skeleton, The* (Bashō), 615
*Recueil des pieces nouveles et
  galantes* (Montpensier), 662
Recueil des plus beaux vers
  (Malherbe), 578

Recueil des secrets (Bourgeois), 74
Recusants, 414
Red and White Plum Blossoms
  (Kōrin), 696
Red Pill Case, 911
Reeve, John, 666
Reeve, William, 665
Réflexions critiques sur Longin
  (Boileau-Despréaux), 64
*Réflexions: Ou, Sentences et
  maximes morales. See Maximes*
  (La Rochefoucauld)
Regent faction, 519
*Regulae ad directionem ingenii. See
  Rules for the Direction of the
  Mind* (Descartes)
Rehearsal, The (Buckingham), 241
Rehearsal Transpros'd, The
  (Marvell), 606
Relation d'un voyage en Limousin
  (La Fontaine), 481
*Relation écrite par la Mère
  Angélique sur Port-Royal*
  (Arnauld), 22
*Relation sur le quiétisme. See
  Quakerism A-la-mode* (Bossuet)
Religio Laici (Dryden), 241
Religio Medici (Browne), 94
Religion; England, 221; France,
  211; Japan, 917. *See also*
  Antinomianism; Arminianism;
  Buddhism; Calvinism;
  Catholicism; Christianity;
  Congregationalism; Episcopacy;
  Hinduism; Huguenots; Islam;
  Jansenism; Jews; Laxism;
  Lutheranism; Mysticism;
  Presbyterianism; Presbytery;
  Protestantism; Quakerism;
  Quietism; Unitarianism
Religion, Wars of (1562-1595), 896
Religious orders and churches. *See*
  Capuchins; Church of England;
  Church of Scotland;
  Confraternity of Charity;
  Congregation of the Mission;
  Congregation of the Oratory;
  Daughters of Charity; Gomarists;
  Jesuits; Pilgrims; Recusants;
  Remonstrants; Separatists
Religious persecution. *See*
  Persecution, religious

Religious Society of Friends. *See* Quakerism

Rembrandt, 117, 353, 583, 786-789, 956

Remonstrants, 288, 619

Renati Des Cartes principiorum philosophiae. See *Principles of Descartes' Philosophy, The* (Spinoza)

Rengae, 403

Rensselaer, Nicholas van, 518

Repentance of Mary Magdalene (La Tour), 494

Repertorium (Browne), 95

Reply to Sor Filotea de la Cruz (Cruz), 209

Reports (Coke), 174

Responsio Matthaei Torti (Bellarmine), 16

Respuesta de la poetisa a la muy ilustre Sor Filotea de la Cruz. See *Reply to Sor Filotea de la Cruz* (Cruz)

Restitution, Edict of (1629), 269

Restoration, War of (1641-1668), 432

Restoration of Charles II, 506, 677; and Anglo-Catholicism, 497; and Robert Blake, 58; and John Bunyan, 101; and the first earl of Clarendon, 169; and Elizabeth Stuart, 254; execution of regicides, 757; and the third Baron Fairfax, 264; Fundamental Orders of Connecticut, 568; and Matthew Hale, 346; and Henrietta Maria, 365; and Thomas Hobbes, 381; and John Lambert, 485; and John Milton, 641; and George Monck, 652; Nonconformists, 54, 101; and William Penn, 724; and Sir William Petty, 734; Presbyterians, 121; and the Quakers, 284; and Prince Rupert, 805

Revenger's Tragedy, The (Middleton), 637

Revenger's Tragedy, The (Tourneur), 928

Rhineland Campaign (1674-1675), 934

Rhode Island, 941, 983

Rhodes, John, 51

Rians, Claude Fabri de, 723

Ribera, Jusepe, 1005

Riccioli, Giambattista, 322

Rich, Christopher, 52, 83

Richelieu, Cardinal de, 141, 184, 315, 470, 487, 521, 660, 780, 790-793; and regency of Anne of Austria, 18; arts patronage, 193, 750; and Tommaso Campanella, 126; and the duchesse de Chevreuse, 158; and Frederick Henry, 287; and Cornelius Otto Jansen, 420; and reign of Louis XIII, 552; and Marie de Médicis, 599; and Jules Mazarin, 620; and alliance with Protestant forces, 937; and Friedrich Hermann Schomberg, 820; science patronage, 305; and reforms of the duke de Sully, 897; and Sweden, 706

Richter, Gregorius, 60

Ridiculous Pedant, The (Cyrano), 211

Right, Petition of (1628). *See* Petition of Right (1628)

Rijn, Rembrandt van. *See* Rembrandt

Rijswijk, Treaty of (1697), 152, 980

Rimpa (school of painting), 696, 868

Rinuccini, Ottavio, 111, 658

Ritorno d'Ulisse in patria, Il (Monteverdi), 659

Riva, Giovanni Guglielmo, 565

River Slaak, Battle of the (1631), 287

Rivet, André, 824

Rivinus, 783

Roaring Girl, The (Middleton and Dekker), 637

Roberval, Gilles Personne de, 922

Robins, John, 666

Robinson, John, 84

Robinson Crusoe (Defoe), 216

Rochester, Viscount. *See* Carr, Robert

Rocroi, Battle of (1643), 184, 553, 926

Roestraten, Pieter, 352

Rogni, Giacomo, 302

Rohan, Marie de. *See* Chevreuse, duchesse de

Rolfe, John, 702, 746, 754, 863

Romanov, Aleksei Mikhailovich. *See* Alexis

Romanov, Fyodor Nikitich, 794. *See also* Philaret

Romanov, Michael, 11, 337, 663, 794-796, 945

Romanov Dynasty, 11, 663, 794

Rømer, Olaus, 135

Root and Branch Bill (1641), 167, 204

Rosa de Santa Maria. *See* Rose of Lima, Saint

Rose of Lima, Saint, 796-798

Rosicrucians, 281

Roskilde, Treaty of (1658), 154

Rosny, marquis de. *See* Sully, duke de

Rosseter, Philip, 127

Rostand, Edmond, 211

Roth, Hieronymus, 292

Rover, The (Behn), 43

Rowlandson, Mary White, 798-801

Rowley, William, 636, 977

Royal Academy of Painting and Sculpture (France), 504

Royal Academy of Sciences, 710

Royal King and the Loyal Subject, The (Heywood), 374

Royal Master, The (Shirley), 846

Royal Society of England, 80, 256, 348, 383, 470, 510, 514, 681, 734, 806, 814, 987, 994

Royal Society of Physicians, 280

Royalists; England, 345, 484; support from Henrietta Maria, 365; and Prince Rupert, 805; and the first earl of Shaftesbury, 838

Rubens, Peter Paul, 244, 302, 352, 438, 599, 657, 671, 723, 802-804, 955, 1005

Rudbeck, Olaf, 445

Rudolf II (Holy Roman Emperor), 459

Rueil, Treaty of (1649), 549

Rules for the Direction of the Mind (Descartes), 227

Rump Parliament (1648-1653), 484, 651, 757, 838

Rupert, Prince, 56, 255, 262, 777, 805-807, 815

Rurik Dynasty, 943

Russell, Lucy. *See* Harington, Lucy

Russia. *See* Geographical Index

Russian Orthodox Church, 13, 27, 684, 865; and Old Believers, 27; schism in, 13

Rutherglen Declaration (1679), 122

Ruyter, Michiel Adriaanszoon de, 57, 807-809, 931

Rye House Plot (1683), 149, 609, 655, 817

Ryswick, Treaty of (1697), 401

Sabbatai Sevi. *See* Shabbetai Tzevi

Sabbetai Ẓevi. *See* Shabbetai Tzevi

Sablé, marquise de, 487

Sacred Theory of the Earth, The (Burnet), 106

Sacri musicali affetti (Strozzi), 889

Ṣafavid Dynasty, 4, 411, 844

Saffray, Augustin de. *See* Mézy, chevalier de

Saga nikki (Bashō), 616

Saggiatore (Galileo), 300

Saikaku, Ihara. *See* Ihara Saikaku

Saint and the Sinner, The (Tirso), 913

Saint Andrew (Garzoni), 302

St. Anne-la-Royale, 331

Saint Augustine in Ecstasy (van Dyck), 245

Saint-Denis, Charles de Marguetel de, 521

Saint-Étienne, sieur de, 520

Saint-Evremond. *See* Saint-Denis, Charles de Marguetel de

St. Francis in Meditation (Zurbarán), 1005

Saint Francis Xavier, Mission of, 433

Saint-Germain-en-Laye, Treaty of (1632), 142

Saint Jerome (van Dyck), 244

Saint Lusson, sieur de, 433

St. Paul's Cathedral, 995

St. Peter's Basilica, 45, 68, 721

St. Peter's Square, 10

Saint Sebastian Tended by Saint Irene (La Tour), 494

St. Serapion (Zurbarán), 1005

Saint Theresa in Ecstasy (Bernini), 330

Saint-Vallier, Jean-Baptiste de, 77

Saint Werburgh Street, 846

Sakonnets, 634

Salem witch trials, 689

Salignac de La Mothe-Fénelon, François de. *See* Fénelon, François de Salignac de La Mothe-

Salīm. *See* Jahāngīr

Salisbury, first earl of, 132, 414

Salons (French), 487, 521, 779, 829, 833

Sam Mīrzā. *See* Shāh Safi I

Sambhājī, 25

Samedi, 829

Samoilovych, Ivan, 624

Samoset, 86, 612, 876

Samugarh, Battle of (1658), 24

San Andrea al Quirinale, 46

San Carlo alle Quattro Fontane, 68

San Ivo della Sapienza, 68

San Lorenzo, 331

San Stefano, Order of, 627

Sanctorius, Sanctorius. *See* Santorio, Santorio

Sanctuary Meditations (Gracián), 317

Sandoval y Rojas, Francisco Gómez de. *See* Lerma, duke de

Sandwich, first earl of, 57, 728

Sanquhar Declaration (1680), 123

Santa, Battle of (1697), 528

Santa Juana, La (Tirso), 913

Santillana, Juana Inés de Asbaje y Ramírez de. *See* Cruz, Sor Juana Inés de la

Santorio, Santorio, 810-813

Sarachina Kikō. See *Visit to Sarashina Village, A* (Bashō)

Sarotti, Ambrose, 711

Sarpi, Paolo, 720, 810

Sarumino. See *Monkey's Raincoat*

Sassamon, John, 634

Satire, 63

Satires, Les (Boileau-Despréaux), 63

Satiromastix (Dekker), 223, 441

Satyrische Pilgram, Der (Grimmelshausen), 325

Saunderson, Mary, 51, 82

Savelli, Giulia, 780

Savery, Thomas, 712, 813-815

Savile, Sir George, 815-817

Scarron, Françoise. *See* Maintenon, Madame de

Scarron, Paul, 521, 780

Sceptical Chymist, The (Boyle), 79

Schall, Adam, 448

Schall von Bell, Johann Adam, 849

Schedula Monitoria de Novae Febris Ingressu (Sydenham), 902

Scheiner, Christoph, 260

Schickard, Wilhelm, 818-820; on calculators, 819

Scholar(s), The (Lovelace), 562

Scholarship; China, 972; England, 80, 939; France, 722; Italy, 743; Jewish, 583; Netherlands, 824; Ottoman Empire, 455. *See also* Category Index

Schomberg, Friedrich Hermann, 426, 820-822

School for Husbands, The (Molière), 647

School for Wives, The (Molière), 648

School of Compliment, The (Shirley), 846

Schoole of Abuse, The (Gosson), 374

Schrader, Justus, 899

Schurman, Anna Maria van, 823-825

Schütz, Heinrich, 825-828

Schwarzenberg, Adam von, 290

Science; England, 200, 280, 357, 383, 734; France, 227, 306, 630; Italy, 322. *See also* Astronomy; Biology; Calculus; Category Index; Chemistry; Entomology; Epidemiology; Geography; Geology; Geometry; Iatrochemistry; Mathematics; Medicine; Meteorology; Optics; Paleontology; Physics; Zoology

Scotland. *See* Geographical Index

Scott, James. *See* Monmouth, duke of

Scudéry, Madame de. *See* Scudéry, Madeleine de

Scudéry, Madeleine de, 477, 487, 662, 828-830

Scultetus, Johannes, 566

Seated Man Holding a Branch (Hals), 354

Seconda pratica (musical style), 296

Secondo libro di toccate . . . , Il (Frescobaldi), 297

Secret Love (Dryden), 343

Secret of the Universe, The (Kepler), 458

Secret Vengeance for Secret Insult (Calderón), 114

Sedgemoor, Battle of (1685), 655

Segrais. *See* La Fayette, Madame de

Segrais, Jean Regnault de, 477, 661

Séguie, Pierre, 504

Segura, Juan Bautista de, 702

Sejanus (Jonson), 441

Seki Kōwa, 831-833

Seki Takakazu. *See* Seki Kōwa

Sekigahara, Battle of (1600), 916

Selenographia (J. Hevelius), 372

Self-Denying Ordinance (1644), 205, 941

Self-Portrait (van Dyck), 244

Self-Portrait (Murillo), 670

Self-Portrait (Poussin), 750

Self-Portrait (Sirani), 857

Selim Giray I, 452

Selkirk, Alexander, 216

Seltsame Springinsfeld, Der. See Singular Life Story of Heedless Hopalong, The (Grimmelshausen)

Selva confusa, La (Calderón), 113

Separatists; England, 84; Holland, 122

Serfdom; Russia, 12, 664, 784, 944

Sermon on Death (Bossuet), 71

Sermon on Providence (Bossuet), 71

Sermon sur la mort. See Sermon on Death (Bossuet)

Sermon sur la providence. See Sermon on Providence (Bossuet)

Settlement, Act of (1652), 701

Settlement, Act of (1701), 694

Seven Sacraments (Poussin), 750

Sévigné, Madame de, 183, 477, 487, 521, 661-662, 829, 833-835

Sévigné, Marie de. *See* Sévigné, Madame de

Sganarelle (Molière), 647

Shabbetai Tzevi, 835-837

Shabbetian movement, 837

Shadwell, Thomas, 384

Shaftesbury, first earl of, 149, 507, 544, 654, 693, 806, 816, 838-841; list of works, 839

Shah Jahan, 23, 411, 842-845

Shāh Safi I, 5

Shahryar, 411, 842

Shaista Khan, 859

Shakespeare, William, 104, 278, 440, 637, 639

Shaklovity, Fyodor, 866

Sharp, James, 122

Sheep-Well, The (Lope de Vega), 950

Sheldon, Gilbert, 986

Sheldonian Theater, 994

Shelton, Thomas, 729

Shepard, Thomas, 395

Ship Money Case, 144

Shirley, James, 279, 846-848

Shivaji. *See* Śivājī

Shoemaker's Holiday, The (Dekker), 223

Shokunin zukushi emaki (Moronobu), 376

Short Parliament (1640), 55, 145, 768, 838, 886

Shōsetsu, Yui. *See* Yui Shōsetsu

Shujah, 23, 844

Shun-chih. *See* Shunzhi

Shunzhi, 3, 234, 448, 848-850

Shuysky, Prince Vasily. *See* Vasily Shuysky

Sidereal Messenger, The (Galileo), 299, 627

Sidereus nuncius. See Sidereal Messenger, The (Galileo)

Siege of _____. *See* _____, Siege of

Siegemundin, Justine, 851-853

Sigismund III Vasa, 336, 853-856, 945

Signatura Rerum (Böhme), 61

Signorini, Francesca. *See* Caccini, Francesca

Signorini, Giovanni Battista, 112

Signorini-Malaspina, Francesca. *See* Caccini, Francesca

Silver Age, The (Heywood), 374

Simplicianischer zweyköpffiger Ratio Status (Grimmelshausen), 325

Simplicissimus (Grimmelshausen), 324

Singular Life Story of Heedless Hopalong, The (Grimmelshausen), 325

Sirani, Elisabetta, 856-858

Sirtori, Girolamo, 537

Sirturus, Hieronymus. *See* Sirtori, Girolamo

Sitio de Breda, El (Calderón), 113

Śivājī, 25, 858-861

Sketches from Life (Chen), 156

Slaughter of the Innocents, The (Marini), 202

Slavery; Native Americans, 468, 635; Portugal, 687, 960; Spanish colonies, 152; Ukraine, 428; Virginia, 31

Sloane, Sir Hans, 447

Sloughter, Henry, 519

Slovenia. *See* Geographical Index

Smallpox and Native Americans, 130, 423, 876, 908

Smith, John, 391, 702, 745, 753, 861-865, 875

Smutnoe Vremya. See Time of Troubles

Sobieski, Jan. *See* John III Sobieski

Sobornoye Ulozheniye (1649), 12, 664

Social reform. *See* Category Index

Society for the Propagation of the Gospel in New England and Parts Adjacent in North America, 248

Society of Friendship, 741

Society of Gentlemen and Ladies of Nôtre-Dame of Montreal, 575

Socinus, Faustus, 54

Sofya Alekseyevna. *See* Sophia

Soissons, comtesse de. *See* Mancini, Olympia

Soledades. See Solitudes of Don Luis de Góngora, The (Góngora)

Solemn League and Covenant (1643), 205, 941, 988

Solitudes of Don Luis de Góngora, The (Góngora), 312

Soltān Moḥammad Shāh, 4

Some Considerations of the Consequences of Lowering of Interest, and Raising the Value of Money (Locke), 546

Some Thoughts Concerning Education (Locke), 546

Somerset, earl of. *See* Carr, Robert

Somerset Masque, The (Campion), 128

Sommershausen, Battle of (1648), 933

Song of Songs of Solomon, The (Guyon), 340

Songe de Vaux, Le (La Fontaine), 481

Songs and Sonnets in *Poems, by J. D.* (Donne), 231

Sons of Ben, 846. *See also* Tribe of Ben

Sophia, 445, 624, 865-867

Sor Juana. *See* Cruz, Sor Juana Inés de la

Sospetto d'Herode. See Suspicion of Herod, The (Marini)

Sōtatsu, 695, 868-870;), 869

Soules Humiliation, The (Hooker), 387

Soules Possession of Christ, The (Hooker), 387

Soules Preparation for Christ, The (Hooker), 386

South America; *maps,* xxxii, lvi

Southwold Bay, Battle of (1672), 417

Souvré, Madeleine de. *See* Sablé, marquise de

Sovereignty and Goodness of God, The (Rowlandson), 799-800

Sozzini, Fausto Paolo. *See* Socinus, Faustus

Spain. *See* Geographical Index

Spanish Succession, War of the (1701-1714), 152, 265, 402, 555, 602, 946, 980

Sparre, Ebba, 164

Specimen of Elements of Myology (Steno), 881

Specimen of Some Observations Made by a Microscope, A (Leeuwenhoek), 510

Spilbergen, Joris van, 797

Spínola, Ambrosio de, 294, 619

Spinoza, Baruch, 37, 188, 515, 871-875; list of works, 872

Spiritual Torrents (Guyon), 340

Squanto, 86, 612, 875-877, 879

Ssu-tsung. *See* Chongzhen

Stadtholder, 618

Standish, Miles, 7, 86, 614, 877-880

Stângebro, Battle of (1598), 854

Staple of News, The (Jonson), 443

Star Atlas, The (J. and E. Hevelius), 372

Staroobriadtsy. See Old Believers

Starovery. See Old Believers

State of France, The (Evelyn), 256

States and Empires of the Sun, The (Cyrano), 211

Stayner, Sir Richard, 57

Steam engine, 711, 814

Steensen, Niels. *See* Steno, Nicolaus

Steno, Nicolaus, 881-883

Steno's law, 882

Steps to the Temple (Crashaw), 203

Stevin, Simon, 619

Stiava, La (Caccini), 111

Stile antico, 296

Still-Life with Oranges (Zurbarán), 1005

Stolbovo, Treaty of (1617), 337, 704, 795

Stone, Samuel, 386

Stoning of Saint Stephen (Rembrandt), 786

Story of Sapho, The (Scudéry), 829

Strafford, first earl of, 145, 167, 345, 768, 884-887, 895, 941

Strage degli innocenti, La. See Slaughter of the Innocents, The (Marini)

Striggio, Alexander, the Younger, 658

Strozzi, Barbara, 888-890

Strozzi, Giulio, 888

Stuart, Elizabeth. *See* Elizabeth Stuart

Stuart, James. *See* James I (king of England)

Stuart, Mary. *See* Mary II (queen of England)

Stummdorf, Treaty of (1635), 854

Stuyvesant, Peter, 518, 645, 890-893

Suceava, Battle of (1653), 463

Suckling, Sir John, 503, 893-895

Sueños y discursos de verdades encubridoras de engaños. See Visions: Or, Hel's Kingdome and the World's Follies and Abuses (Quevedo y Villegas)

Suivante, La (Corneille), 193

Süleyman II, 472

Sully, duke de, 896-898

Sulpicians, 76, 265, 401, 490, 499, 576, 596

Sultan, Kösem. *See* Kösem Sultan

Summum Bonum, quod est verum magiae, cabalae, alchymae verae, Fratrum Roseae Crucis verorum subjectum (Fritzius), 281

Sun King. *See* Louis XIV

Suréna (Corneille), 195

Surgeon of His Honor, The (Calderón), 114

Surrender of Breda, The (Velázquez), 954

Survey of the Summe of Church-Discipline, A (Hooker), 387

Survivance, Acte of (1631), 289

Susanna. *See* Sophia

Susanna and the Elders (Artemisia), 307

Suspicion of Herod, The (Marini), 202

Susquehannocks, 30

Swammerdam, Jan, 362, 510, 898-900

Sweden. *See* Geographical Index

Switzerland. *See* Geographical Index

Sydenham, Thomas, 901-904

Sylva (Evelyn), 257

Sylvius, Franciscus. *See* Deleboe, Franz

Symphoniae sacrae (Schütz), 827

Syndics of the Drapers' Guild, The (Rembrandt), 788

Synopsis Animalium Quadrupedum et Serpentini Generis (Ray), 783

Syntagma philosophicum (Gassendi), 305

Szentgotthárd, Battle of (1664), 527

Tabulae Rudolphinae (Kepler), 460

Tagaskouita, Catherine. *See* Tekakwitha, Kateri

Tagen Sufu, 915

T'ai Ch'iang. *See* Taichang

Taichang, 911

Taisei sankei, 832

Taiwan, 1002

Taj Mahal, 843

Takebe Katahiro, 832

Takebe Katakira, 832

Talbot, Richard, 821

Talcott, Mary White Rowlandson. *See* Rowlandson, Mary White

Tales and Short Stories in Verse (La Fontaine), 481

Tales of Mother Goose (Perrault), 732

Ta-ling Ho, Siege of (1631). *See* Daling He, Siege of (1631)

Talon, Jean-Baptiste, 433

Tarashikomi, 869

Tartuffe (Molière), 19, 521, 648

Tasman, Abel Janszoon, 905-908

Tasmania, 907

Tatars, 428, 624, 784

Taunton, Siege of (1644), 56

Tawaraya Sōtatsu. *See* Sōtatsu

Taxation; Americas, 568; China, 449, 912; Ireland, 734; Japan, 916, 919; Russia, 12; Virginia, 29

Taylor, Jeremy, 741

Technology. *See* Category Index under Science and technology

Tegakwith. *See* Tekakwitha, Kateri

Tein, Battle of (1618), 966

Tekakwitha, Kateri, 908-910

Telescopes, 135, 259, 299, 319, 372, 388, 397, 537

Telescopium (Sirtori), 537

Téllez, Gabriel. *See* Tirso de Molina

Telluris theoria sacra. See Sacred Theory of the Earth, The (Burnet)

Tempesta, Antonio, 116

Temple, The (Herbert), 203, 367

Temple, Sir William, 507

Temptation of Saint Anthony, The (Callot), 117

Tenth Muse Lately Sprung up in America, The (Bradstreet), 89

Tenure of Kings and Magistrates, The (Milton), 640

Ternary of Paradoxes, A (Helmont), 362

Test Act (1673), 148, 507, 693, 816, 839

Testimonies Concerning That One God, and the Persons of the Holy Trinity, The (Biddle), 53

Teustsche Michel, Der (Grimmelshausen), 325

Texel, Battle of the (1653), 57

Theater; England, 42, 51, 82, 104, 109, 223, 238, 240, 373, 436, 440, 502, 636, 729, 765, 846, 894, 928; France, 193, 212, 646, 774; Japan, 408; Spain, 113, 740, 913, 949. *See also* Category Index

Theaters, War of the, 223

Theatines, 330, 720

Theatre, The (playhouse), 104

Thébaïde, La. See Theban Brothers, The (Racine)

Theban Brothers, The (Racine), 774

Theodicy (Leibniz), 516

Theologico-Political Treatise, A (Spinoza), 873

Theology. *See* Category Index under Religion and theology

Theoricae Mediceorum planetarum ex causis physicis deductae (Borelli), 66

Théorie de la maneuvre des vaisseaux (Johann I Bernoulli), 49

Theosophic Questions (Böhme), 61

Theotokópoulos, Doménikos. *See* Greco, El

Thérèse, Marie-. *See* Marie-Thérèse

Thévenot, Melchisedec, 898

Third and Fourth Booke of Ayres, The (Campion), 127

Third Letter for Toleration, A (Locke), 37, 546

Thirty Years' War (1618-1648), 250, 268, 470, 705, 805, 820; and Pope Alexander VII, 9; and Charles X Gustav, 153; and the Great Condé, 184; Dutch participation, 619; English participation, 97, 261, 415, 495, 767; English refugees to North America, 218; and Frederick William, the Great Elector, 290; French participation, 554, 933; generals, 966; Grimmelshausen on, 324; in literature, 325; peace talks, 621; political writings, 761; and Portugal, 431; and Cardinal de Richelieu, 791; in Spanish literature, 115; Spanish participation, 737; Swedish participation, 163, 337, 925; and high taxes in France, 549; and Pope Urban VIII, 936

Thököly, Imre, 453

Thomas Howard, Second Earl of Arundel (van Dyck), 244

Thomassin, Philippe, 116

Thorpe, George, 702

Three Days' Battle (1653), 57

Three Feudatories, 449

Three Graces, The (Rubens), 803

Tiancong. *See* Abahai

Tianqi, 160, 911-912

Tibet, 2

T'ien-ch'i. *See* Tianqi

T'ien-ts'ung. *See* Abahai

Tigers and Lions Hunt (Rubens), 803

Tilly, count of (Johan Tserclaes), 294, 333, 337, 894, 966

Time of Troubles, 11, 683, 794, 855, 945

Timon of Athens (Middleton and Shakespeare), 637

Tirso de Molina, 114, 913-915, 952

Tisquantum. *See* Squanto

Tituba, 690

"To My Dear and Loving Husband" (Bradstreet), 88

Toccate e partite d'intavolatura di cimbalo (Frescobaldi), 296

Tofukumon-in, 695

Tokugawa Hidetada, 917, 998

Tokugawa Iemitsu, 917, 919, 998

Tokugawa Ienobu, 831, 920

Tokugawa Ietsuna, 831, 919, 999

Tokugawa Ieyasu, 408, 915-918, 998

Tokugawa Tsunashige, 831

Tokugawa Tsunayoshi, 831, 919-920

Tokugawa Yorinobu, 999
Tokugawa Yoshimune, 920
Toleration Act (1649), 93
Toleration Act (1689), 34, 284
Tonge, Israel, 692
Tonty, Henry de, 490
Tories, 149, 464, 840
Torre de la Parada (King Philip IV's hunting lodge), 954
Torrents spirituels, Les. See *Spiritual Torrents* (Guyon)
Torricelli, Evangelista, 65, 333, 921-924
Torricelli's principle, 921
Torricelli's theorem, 922
Torrington, earl of. *See* Monck, George
Torstenson, Lennart, 153, 924-927
Tortura Torti (Andrewes), 16
Touchet, Eleanor. *See* Davies, Lady Eleanor
Tour, Georges de La. *See* La Tour, Georges de
Tournefort, Joseph Pitton de, 783
Tourneur, Cyril, 928-930
Town Fop, The (Behn), 43
Towne, Rebecca. *See* Nurse, Rebecca
Toyotomi Hideyoshi, 916
Tractatus apologeticus integritatem societatis de Rosea Cruce defendens (Fludd), 281
Tractatus de corde. See *Treatise on the Heart, A* (Lower)
Tractatus de Podagra et Hydrope (Sydenham), 902
Tractatus politicus. See *Political Treatise, A* (Spinoza)
Tractatus theologico-politicus. See *Theologico-Political Treatise, A* (Spinoza)
Trade; Brazil, 960; China, 912; Dutch and Native Americans, 644; England and Native Americans, 633, 746, 754; France and North America, 401, 490, 644; French and Native Americans, 499; Japan and China, 161; Japan and Europe, 917; Portugal and Africa, 687; spices, 905; Sweden and Native Americans, 645

Tragédies lyriques, 570
Tragicall History of Piramus and Thisbe, The (Cowley), 199
Tragicomedia, 950
Tragicomedy, 279
Traité de l'education des filles. See *Instructions for the Education of a Daughter* (Fénelon)
Transcendent Spiritual Treatise, A (Reeve and Muggleton), 666
Transformed Metamorphosis, The (Tourneur), 928
Transit of Venus over the Sun, The (Horrocks), 389
Transylvania, 463
Travel diaries; Germany, 445; Japan, 615
Treatise Concerning the State of Departed Souls, Before, and at, and After the Resurrection, A (Burnet), 107
Treatise of Ireland, A (Petty), 735
Treatise on Taxes and Contributions, A (Petty), 734
Treatise on the Heart, A (Lower), 566
Treaty of _____. See _____, Treaty of
Tribe of Ben, 368, 443. *See also* Sons of Ben
Trick to Catch the Old One, A (Middleton), 636
Trinity, denial of, 53
Triple Alliance of 1668, 559
Triplicinodo triplex cuneus (King James), 16
Triumph of Health and Prosperity, The (Middleton), 637
Triumphs of the Prince d'Amour, The (Davenant), 502
Troia Britannica (Heywood), 374
Tromp, Cornelis, 930-932
Tromp, Maarten, 57, 288, 619, 808, 930-932
True Constitution of a Particular Visible Church, The (Cotton), 197
True Interpretation of the Eleventh Chapter of the Revelations of Saint John, A (Muggleton), 667
True Law of Free Monarchies, The (James I), 413

True Levellers. *See* Diggers
True Relation of Such Occurrences and Accidents of Noate as Hath Hapned in Virginia Since the First Planting of That Collony, A (Smith), 864
Truth Exalted (Penn), 725
Tserclaes, Johan. *See* Tilly, count of (Johan Tserclaes)
Tsunayoshi, Tokugawa. *See* Tokugawa Tsunayoshi
Tubutama Revolt (1695), 468
Tuhfat al-Kibar fi Asfar il-Bihar (Kâtib Çelebî), 455
Tuileries, 523, 533
Turenne, Viscount de, 184, 416, 425, 549, 558, 820, 933-935
Turhan, 472
Turkheim, Battle of (1675), 934
Turner, Anne, 132
Twelve Arguments Drawn Out of Scripture (Biddle), 53
Twelve Years' Truce (1609-1621), 359, 530, 619, 737
Two Bookes of Ayres (Campion), 127
Two Days' Battle (1666), 808
Two Discourses Concerning the Soul of Brutes Which Is That of the Vital and Sensitive of Man (Willis), 986
CCXI Sociable Letters (Newcastle), 677
Two Kings, War of the (1689-1691), 609
Two Sacred Songs for Voice and Piano (Frescobaldi), 297
Two Scholars Disputing (Rembrandt), 786
Two Treatises of Government (Locke), 381, 544, 546
Twofold Catechism, A (Biddle), 54
Tymish, 463
Tyrannic Love (Dryden), 343
Tyrconnel, duke of. *See* Talbot, Richard
Tzevi, Shabbetai. *See* Shabbetai Tzevi

Ueno hanami zu oshiebari byōbu (Moronobu), 376
Uighurs, 2

Ukiyo-e, 375
Ukiyozoshi, 403
Ukraine. *See* Geographical Index
Ulozheniye. *See* Sobornoye Ulozheniye (1649)
Ulster Protestants, massacre of (1642), 700
Uncas, 130
Underhill, John, 892
Undertakers, 879
Unheard of Little Works on Medicine (Helmont), 362
Uniformity, Act of (1661), 34, 121
Union of _____. *See* _____, Union of
Unitarianism, 54
United Colonies of New England, 86
United Company, 51
United Provinces of the Netherlands, 618
Unreasonableness of Infidelity, The (Baxter), 35
Uranographia (E. Hevelius), 372
Urban VIII, 9, 45, 68, 126, 405, 421, 424, 620, 722, 792, 936-938
Ursuline order, 77, 595
Ussher, James, 35, 53, 938-940
Utriusque cosmi maioris scilicet et minoris metaphysica, phsycica atque technica historia (Fludd), 281
Uzbeks, 4

Vair, Guillaume du, 577
"Valediction" (Donne), 231
Valence, Palamede de Fabri de, 723
Válido (Spanish royal minister), 530
Valle, Barbara. *See* Strozzi, Barbara
Vanbrugh, Sir John, 52
Van Delft, Jan. *See* Vermeer, Jan
Van der Meer, Jan. *See* Vermeer, Jan
Van Dijck, Anthonie (Anton, Antonie, Antoon). *See* Dyck, Sir Anthony van
Vane, Sir Henry, the Younger, 57, 395, 941-943
Van Rijn, Rembrandt. *See* Rembrandt
Van Schurman, Anna Maria. *See* Schurman, Anna Maria van

Vasile, 463
Vasily Ivanovich. *See* Vasily Shuysky
Vasily Shuysky, 855, 943-945
Vasvár, Treaty of (1664), 527
Vatican Virgil (Claude Lorrain), 172
Vauban, Sébastien Le Prestre de, 559, 946-948
Vaugelas, seigneur de, 780
Vaughan, Henry, 741
Vaux-le-Vicomte, 523
Veen, Otto van, 802
Vega Carpio, Lope de, 113, 279, 312, 738, 914, 949-952; list of works, 951
Vegetables, Fruit, and Asters (Chen), 157
Veglie dei Signori Unisoni, 888
Velázquez, Diego, 160, 671, 739, 953-956, 1003
Venice, 720
Venus in sole visa. See *Transit of Venus over the Sun, The* (Horrocks)
Vera Circuli et Hyperbolae Quadratura (Gregory), 319
Verbum sapienti (Petty), 734
Vere, Sir Francis, 928
Vere, Sir Horace, 261
Vergne, Mademoiselle de la. *See* La Fayette, Madame de
Vergne, Marie Madeleine Pioche de la, 487
Vergonzoso en palacio, El. See *Bashful Man at Court, The* (Tirso)
Vérité des sciences, contre les sceptiques ou Pyrrhoniens, La (Mersenne), 630
Vermeer, Jan, 353, 511, 956-959
Versailles, 505, 524, 533, 554, 590
Verses Lately Written upon Several Occasions (Cowley), 200
Versions de quelques pièces de Virgile, Tacite et Saluste . . . (Gournay), 315
Vespers of 1610 (Monteverdi), 658
Veuve, La (Corneille), 193
Vida del Buscón llamado Pablos . . . , La. See *Life and Adventures of Buscon, the Witty Spaniard, The* (Quevedo y Villegas)

Vida es sueño, La. See *Life Is a Dream* (Calderón)
Vieira, António, 959-961
Vienna, Siege of (1683), 453, 528
Viertzig Fragen von der Seele. See *Forty Questions of the Soul* (Böhme)
View of Delft (Vermeer), 958
Villamena, Francesco, 116
Villana de la sagra, La (Tirso), 913
Villana de Vallecas, La (Tirso), 914
Villanueva, Pedro Díaz de, 1003
Ville-Marie de Montreal, 575
Villegas, Francisco Gómez de Quevedo y. *See* Quevedo y Villegas, Francisco Gómez de
Villiers, George. *See* Buckingham, duke of (first and second)
Vincent, Thomas, 894
Vincent de Paul, Saint, 962-965
Vincentians. *See* Congregation of the Mission
Vindiciae judaeorum (Manasseh), 583
Virgin and Child (Sirani), 857
Virginia, 29, 120, 275
Virtuoso, The (Shadwell), 384
Visible World (Komenský), 470
Vision of the Blessed Herman Joseph (van Dyck), 245
Visions, or Hel's Kingdome and the World's Follies and Abuses (Quevedo y Villegas), 770
Visit to Sarashina Village, A (Bashō), 616
Visit to the Kashima Shrine, A (Bashō), 616
Visita y anatomía de la cabeza del cardenal Richelieu (Quevedo y Villegas), 771
Visscher, Ann Roemers, 824
Visscher, Frans Jacobsz, 906
Vitalism, 188
Vittoria d'amore, La (Monteverdi), 659
Viviani, Vicenzo, 921
Vivonne-Savelli, Catherine de. *See* Rambouillet, Marquise de
Voet, Gijsbert. *See* Voetius, Gisbertus
Voetius, Gisbertus, 824
Voiture, Vincent, 780

Volpone (Jonson), 442
Voltaire, 521
Vom dreyfachen Leben des Menschen. See *High and Deep Searching Out of the Threefold Life of Man, The* (Böhme)
Von den drei Principien göttlichen Wesens. See *Concerning the Three Principles of the Divine Essence* (Böhme)
Von der Gerburt und Bezeichnung aller Wesen. See *Signatura Rerum* (Böhme)
Von der Gnadenwahl. See *Concerning the Election of Grace* (Böhme)
Von 177 theosophischen Fragen. See *Theosophic Questions* (Böhme)
Vonifatiev, Stephen, 27, 683
Vouet, Simon, 523
"Voyage to the Island of Love" (Behn), 43
Voyages and Descriptions (Dampier), 215

Waban, 248
Wahunsenacawh. *See* Powhatan
Walachia, 463
Wales. *See* Geographical Index
Wallenstein, Albrecht Wenzel von, 269, 290, 337, 460, 966-969
Wallis, John, 564, 969-971
Walloons, 643
Walther, Bathasar, 60
Walwyn, William, 535
Wampanoags, 86, 130, 612, 633, 876, 878
Wamsutta, 614, 633
Wang Fu-chih. *See* Wang Fuzhi
Wang Fuzhi, 972-974
War of Beauty, The (Callot), 117
War of Love, The (Callot), 117
War(s) of _____. *See* _____, War(s) of
Ward, Mary, 974-976
Warfare. *See* Category Index
Warizansho (Mōri), 832
Warning to the Dragon and All His Angels (Davies), 221
Warsaw, Battle of (1656), 154
Wasan, 832

Waters, Frank, 614
Way of the Churches of Christ in New England, The (Cotton), 198
Way of the Congregational Churches Cleared, The (Cotton), 198
Way to Christ, The (Böhme), 61
Webster, John, 132, 279, 636, 846, 976-978; list of works, 977
Wedding, The (Shirley), 847
Weg zu Christo, Der. See *Way to Christ, The* (Böhme)
Wei Chong-hsien. *See* Wei Zhongxian
Wei Zhongxian, 161, 911
Wentworth, Thomas. *See* Strafford, first earl of
Wenzel von Wallenstein, Albrecht. *See* Wallenstein, Albrecht Wenzel von
Westminster Confession, 33
Westmorland Seekers, 284
Westphalia, Treaty of (1648), 9, 153, 164, 185, 254, 290, 359, 470, 555, 619, 621, 706
Westward Ho! (Webster and Dekker), 977
Weymouth, George, 875
What You Will (Marston), 441
Wheelwright, John, 386, 395
Whigs, 149, 464, 507, 693, 840
Whitaker, Alexander, 746
White, Mary. *See* Rowlandson, Mary White
White Devil, The (Webster), 977
White Lotus Society, 911
White Mountain, Battle of (1620), 254, 294, 470, 721
Whitgift, John, 939
Whole Duty of Man According to the Law of Nature, The (Pufendorf), 760
Whore of Babylon, The (Dekker), 224
Widow Ranter, The (Behn), 43
Wife, The (Overbury), 132
Wild Gallant, The (Dryden), 240
Wild Goose Chase, The (Fletcher), 279
Wildes, Sarah, 690
William I (stadtholder of the Netherlands). *See* William the Silent

William III (king of England), 138, 149, 608, 610, 718, 808, 816, 979-982; aided against James II by Brandenburg, 821; American colonists reaction to his enthronement, 518; and chaplain Thomas Burnet, 106; and English theater, 83; and Holy Roman Empire, 526; and James II, 418; and the first duke of Leeds, 507; First Treaty of Partition (1698), 152; and Quakers, 284; support of Pope Innocent XI against France, 407
William of Orange. *See* William III (king of England)
William the Silent, 286, 618, 933
Williams, Abigail, 690
Williams, John, 275
Williams, Roger, 130, 197, 612, 941, 982-985, 992
Willis, Thomas, 362, 564, 985-988
Willoughby, Anne, 894
Willughby, Francis, 782
Winceby, Battle of (1643), 262
Wind and Thunder Gods, The (Sōtatsu), 869
Winnebagos, 433
Winslow, Edward, 86
Winstanley, Gerrard, 988-990
Winter King. *See* Frederick V
Winthrop, John (1588-1649), 386, 395, 470, 941, 982, 990-993
Winthrop, John, Jr. (1606-1676), 219, 892
Wisdom of God Manifested in the Works of Creation, The (Ray), 783
Wisdom of Solomon, Paraphrased, The (Middleton), 636
Wise Woman of Hogsdon, The (Heywood), 374
Wit at Several Weapons (Middleton and Rowley), 636
Witt, Johan de, 57, 808, 979
Wittelsbach, Friedrich. *See* Frederick V
Władysław IV Vasa, 111, 250, 290, 462, 795, 945
Woman Bathing (Rembrandt), 787
Woman Killed with Kindness, A (Heywood), 374

Women; childbirth, 851; education, 265, 314, 364, 744, 823, 828, 865; England, 677; France, 662; Mexico, 209

Women Beware Women (Middleton), 637

Women's rights. *See* Category Index

Wonder-Working Magician, The (Calderón), 114

Worcester, Battle of (1651), 168, 757, 901

Works of Monsieur Boileau, Made English by Several Hands, The (Boileau-Despréaux), 64

World's Olio, The (Newcastle), 676

Worship of God in Spirit and in Truth, The (Guyon), 340

Would-Be Gentleman, The (Molière), 570, 648

Wrangel, Karl Gustav, 154, 926

Wray, John. *See* Ray, John

Wren, Sir Christopher, 80, 349, 383, 547, 564, 589, 986, 994-997

Wu Sangui, 235

Wu School, 156

Wunderbarliche Vogelsnest, Das. See False Messiah, The (Grimmelshausen)

Wyatt, Sir Francis, 703

Xizong. *See* Chongzhen; Tianqi

Yamato-e, 868

Yang Ai. *See* Liu Yin

Yang Ying. *See* Liu Yin

Yellow Feather. *See* Massasoit

Yizong. *See* Tianqi

Yorkshire Tragedy, A (Middleton), 637

Yorozu no fumihōgu (Saikaku), 404

Yoshida Mitsuyoshi, 831

Young King, The (Behn), 42

Yuan Chung Huan, 2

Yue di yanliu tu (Liu), 541

Yui Shōsetsu, 998-1000

Zaïde, une histoire espagnole. See Zayde, a Spanish History (La Fayette)

Zamoyski, Jan, 854

Zampieri, Domenico. *See* Domenichino, Il

Zaporozhian Cossacks. *See* Cossacks

Zayde, a Spanish History (La Fayette), 478

Zboriv, Treaty of (1649), 462

Zhang Geng, 157

Zhang Xianzhong, 849

Zheng Chenggong, 449, 1001-1003

Zheng Jing, 449

Zheng Zhilong, 161, 1001

Zhinga, N'. *See* Njinga

Zhitiye protopopa Avvakuma. See Life of the Archpriest Avvakum, by Himself, The (Avvakum)

Zhu Youjian. *See* Chongzhen

Zhu Youjiao. *See* Tianqi

Zhu Youlang, 849

Zhuang Liedi. *See* Chongzhen

Zolkiewski, Stanislaw, 461, 855

Zoology; England, 783; Italy, 581

Żórawno, Treaty of (1676), 429, 452

Zrínyi, Peter, 528

Zúñiga, Baltazar de, 698

Zurbarán, Francisco de, 671, 1003-1006

Zygmunt III Waza. *See* Sigismund III Vasa